Lucy — 25-27 Wed
28-32 — Fri.

Black is the eye of an eagle
Black is the eye of a rook,
But blacker still
Will be the eye
Of the one who steals this book!

3
1.

This book is dedicated to any poor
suffering soul and student
of European history.

May you have a long life!
(P.S. Don't forget your history.)

A Survey of

EUROPEAN CIVILIZATION

Editor · First Edition
CARL L. BECKER
Late John Stambaugh Professor of History
Cornell University

Editor · Second Edition
WILLIAM L. LANGER
Coolidge Professor of History
Harvard University

A Survey of

SINCE 1500

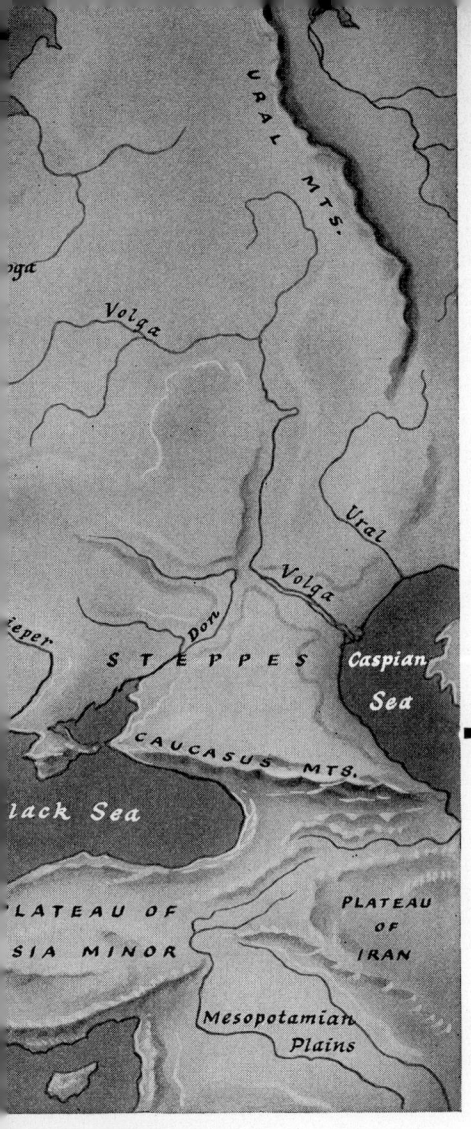

SECOND EDITION

UROPEAN CIVILIZATION

WALLACE K. FERGUSON, Professor of History, New York University

GEOFFREY BRUUN, Visiting Lecturer in History, Columbia University

Houghton Mifflin Company

BOSTON · NEW YORK · CHICAGO · DALLAS · ATLANTA · SAN FRANCISCO

The Riverside Press Cambridge

COPYRIGHT, 1947, BY WALLACE K. FERGUSON
AND GEOFFREY BRUUN. COPYRIGHT, 1936, 1939,
1942, BY WALLACE K. FERGUSON AND GEOFFREY
BRUUN. ALL RIGHTS RESERVED INCLUDING
THE RIGHT TO REPRODUCE THIS BOOK OR PARTS
THEREOF IN ANY FORM The Riverside Press
CAMBRIDGE · MASSACHUSETTS
PRINTED IN THE U.S.A.

TO

*John and Grace
Musser*

WITH ADMIRATION
AND AFFECTION

Editor's Introduction ★ SECOND EDITION

IN THE ORIGINAL EDITOR'S INTRODUCTION the late Professor Carl Becker set forth in his own inimitable way various ideas about the teaching of history and about the function of the present textbook in an introductory survey course. I have no desire to load the book further with front matter, and indeed have had so little to do with the plan and structure of the work that it would be presumptuous on my part to discuss it in detail.

I would like to say, however, that I have always considered this Survey of Civilization one of the best-balanced and most interestingly written books of its kind. The authors have succeeded in striking a happy balance between factual narrative and interpretative comment, and the wide use of the first edition is undoubtedly the most eloquent testimony of their success in filling a real need. They have now gone over the entire text with great care, making many corrections and emendations. Beyond that they have written additional chapters to cover the crowded events of the war period.

I am proud to be associated with this enterprise even in a slight supervisory way, and I am sure that the new edition of this Survey will be even more warmly received than the old.

WILLIAM L. LANGER

Chapter

30 THE CATHOLIC OR COUNTER-REFORMATION ... 432

1. The Early Catholic Reformation 433   2. Loyola and the Society of Jesus 436
3. The Council of Trent (1545–63) 438   4. The Counter-Reformation in Action 442

31 THE STATES OF EUROPE IN THE AGE OF PHILIP II (1556–98) ... 444

1. Spain Under Philip II 444   2. The Revolt in the Netherlands 447   3. The Wars of Religion in France 450   4. England under Elizabeth and the Scottish Reformation 454

32 THE ECONOMIC REVOLUTION ... 460

1. The Accumulation of Capital 460   2. Capital Revolutionizes Commerce and Industry 464   3. Capital and the State 470   4. Capital and Society 474

33 THE RECONSTRUCTION OF FRANCE AND THE ESTABLISHMENT OF ABSOLUTE MONARCHY (1598–1660) ... 476

1. Henry IV Reconstructs France (1598–1610) 476   2. Richelieu and Mazarin Establish Absolute Monarchy (1624–61) 480   3. Growth of French Literature and Culture 484

34 THE DECLINE OF THE MONARCHY IN ENGLAND (1603–60) ... 489

1. The Legacy of the Tudors 489   2. Decline of the Monarchy — James I and Charles I (1603–40) 491   3. The Civil War, the Commonwealth, and the Protectorate (1640–60) 496

35 THE THIRTY YEARS' WAR ... 501

1. The Background of the Thirty Years' War 501   2. The Thirty Years' War (1618–48) 503   3. Results of the War — The Peace of Westphalia and the Peace of the Pyrenees 508

SECTION G · Europe in the Age of Louis XIV · 1660–1715

36 EUROPE IN THE MIDDLE OF THE SEVENTEENTH CENTURY ... 513

1. The System of Centralized Territorial States 514   2. The European States in 1660 518   3. Life in the Seventeenth Century 522

37 LOUIS XIV DOMINATES FRANCE AND ASPIRES TO DOMINATE EUROPE ... 526

1. France at the Accession of Louis XIV 526   2. How Louis XIV Conducted His Government 529   3. The Court of the Sun King 532   4. The "Great Age" in Literature and Art 534   5. Why Louis XIV Persecuted the Jansenists and Huguenots 535   6. The Wars of Louis XIV 537

Chapter

38 THE TRIUMPH OF PARLIAMENTARY GOVERNMENT IN ENGLAND ... 542

1. Charles II: A Despot in Disguise 543   2. James II: A Despot in Difficulties 546   3. The Glorious Revolution of 1688 547   4. England and Scotland Become Great Britain 548   5. Significance of the Seventeenth Century in English History 549

39 THE DECLINING EMPIRE OF THE HAPSBURGS ... 553

1. The Austrian Hapsburgs 553   2. The Turkish Menace 554   3. Spain in Decline 556   4. The Italian States 559   5. Summary of the Period, 1660 to 1715 560

SECTION H · The Eighteenth Century · 1715–89

40 THE EMERGENCE OF RUSSIA ... 565

1. The Rise of Muscovy 566   2. Peter the Great of Russia 568   3. The Great Northern War (1700–21) 569   4. The Successors of Peter the Great 570   5. Catherine the Great (1762–96) 570   6. The Dismemberment of Poland 572

41 THE RISE OF PRUSSIA ... 575

1. The Electorate of Brandenburg 575   2. Frederick the Great (1740–86) 576   3. The War of the Austrian Succession (1740–48) 578   4. The Diplomatic Revolution 578   5. The Seven Years' War (1756–63) 580   6. Frederick the Great in Time of Peace 580

42 OVERSEAS EXPANSION AND THE STRUGGLE FOR COMMERCE AND COLONIES ... 585

1. A World to Win 585   2. The Sixteenth Century: Spain and Portugal Exploit the Wealth of the Two Indies 588   3. The Seventeenth Century: Competition of the Dutch, the French, and the English for Colonies and Trade (1588–1688) 590   4. The Eighteenth Century: The Duel of France and Britain for Colonial Supremacy (1689–1763) 592   5. The British Colonies in America Win Their Independence 594   6. The Abatement of Colonial Rivalry after 1783 598

43 THE INTELLECTUAL REVOLUTION ... 600

1. The Beginnings of the Scientific Revolution 600   2. The Progress of Mathematics 603   3. The Experimental Method 604   4. The Scientific Academies 605   5. The Intellectual Revolution 608

44 GOVERNMENT AND SOCIETY UNDER THE OLD RÉGIME ... 612

1. Divine-Right Monarchy in Theory and Practice 612   2. The Privileged and Unprivileged Classes 613   3. Legal and Financial Abuses 616   4. The Criticism of the Philosophers 617   5. The Enlightened Despots 619   6. Rousseau and the Doctrine of Popular Sovereignty 624

SECTION I · The French Revolution and Napoleon · 1789–1815

Chapter

45 THE FRENCH PEOPLE DESTROY THE RELICS OF FEUDALISM AND OVERTURN THE MONARCHY — 629

1. The States General Is Summoned 629   2. The States General Meets 632   3. The Capture of the Bastille 634   4. The Destruction of Feudalism and the Declaration of the Rights of Man 634   5. The March to Versailles 637   6. The Civil Constitution of the Clergy 638   7. The Constitution of 1791 638   8. The Legislative Assembly (1791–92) 641

46 THE FIRST FRENCH REPUBLIC AND ITS STRUGGLE TO SURVIVE — 643

1. The National Convention (1792–95) 643   2. The Organization of Victory 644   3. The Jacobin Dictatorship 646   4. The Thermidorian Reaction 648   5. The Directory (1795–99) 649   6. The Achievements of the Revolution (1789–99) 650

47 NAPOLEON AND FRANCE — 652

1. The Advent of Bonaparte 652   2. Collapse of the Second Coalition 655   3. Napoleon Reconstructs France 656   4. The Imperial Adventure 659   5. Results of Napoleon's Rule in France 661

48 NAPOLEON AND EUROPE — 663

1. The Revolution Spreads 663   2. The Reconstruction of Italy 664   3. The Reorganization of the Germanies 664   4. Napoleon and England 668   5. The Russian Disaster and the War of Liberation 670   6. The Hundred Days 672

49 THE VIENNA CONGRESS — 674

1. The Congress Assembles 674   2. The Political Settlements 677   3. The Concert of Europe 681

SECTION J · The Growth of Nationalism and Liberalism · 1815–71

50 THE ERA OF RESTORATION AND REACTION — 685

1. The Reaction from the Age of Rationalism 685   2. The Romantic Movement 687   3. The Triumph of Conservatism: Austria and Russia 688   4. The Bourbon Restoration in France 692   5. Temporary Reaction in Great Britain 695   6. The First Rifts in the Conservative System 695

51 THE BOURGEOISIE SECURE CONTROL IN GREAT BRITAIN AND FRANCE — 698

1. The Industrial Revolution 698   2. The Factory System 699   3. The English Reform Bill of 1832 700   4. The Chartist Movement 704   5. The French Revolution of 1830 706

Chapter

52 THE REVOLUTIONARY MOVEMENT OF 1848–49 AND ITS COLLAPSE ... 711

1. Discontent in France under the July Monarchy 711 2. The February Revolution in France (1848) and Its Sequel 712 3. The German People Fail to Achieve Political Unity (1848–49) 715 4. Austria Restores Her House to Order 718 5. Italy Remains in Bondage 720 6. The Lessons of 1848–49 721

53 THE ESTABLISHMENT OF THE SECOND FRENCH EMPIRE: NAPOLEON III ... 723

1. "The Empire Is Peace" 723 2. All Things to All Men 724 3. The Liberal Nemesis 728 4. The Second Empire at War: The Crimean Conflict (1854–56) 728

54 THE POLITICAL UNIFICATION OF ITALY ... 732

1. The National Spirit Stirs (1815–48) 732 2. Three Conflicting Projects for Unification 734 3. The Defeated Hopes of 1848–49 735 4. Cavour Contrives 736 5. Garibaldi Marches 739 6. The Winning of Venice and Rome 740 7. The Roman Catholic Church in the Nineteenth Century 740

55 THE FORMATION OF THE GERMAN EMPIRE ... 744

1. The Decade of Repression after 1848 744 2. The Expansion of German Industry 746 3. The Prussian System 747 4. Otto von Bismarck (1815–98) 748 5. The Austro-Prussian War 748 6. The North German Confederation 749 7. Opposition of France to German Unification 751 8. The Franco-Prussian War 752

56 RUSSIA IN THE NINETEENTH CENTURY ... 755

1. The Aftermath of the Crimean War 755 2. The Emancipation of the Serfs 756 3. Other Reforms of Alexander II 756 4. The Reaction in the Later Years of Alexander II 758 5. The Spread of Anarchism, Nihilism, and Terrorism 759 6. Alexander III and the Policy of Russification 760 7. Nicholas II and the Revolution of 1905 763

57 THE LESSER STATES OF EUROPE IN THE NINETEENTH CENTURY ... 765

1. The Scandinavian Countries 765 2. Holland, Belgium, and Switzerland 768 3. Spain and Portugal 769 4. The Crumbling Empire of the Sultan (1815–78) 772

SECTION K · The New Industrialism and Imperialism · 1871–1914

58 THE NEW WORLD WHICH SCIENCE AND INDUSTRY CREATED ... 779

1. The March of Science 779 2. New Conceptions of Man's Place in Nature 782 3. The New Environment Which Science and Industry have Provided: The "Civilization of City Dwellers" 785 4. The Industrialized Society: The Conflict Between Capital and Labor and the Riddle of Social Justice 787 5. The Industrialized State: The Competition among the Great Powers for Colonies and Markets 790

Chapter

59 THE SOCIAL CONFLICT WITHIN THREE INDUSTRIAL STATES: GREAT BRITAIN, FRANCE, AND GERMANY (1871–1914) — 795

1. The March of Democracy in Great Britain (1867–1914) 795 2. Great Britain (1871–1914): The Quest for Social Justice 798 3. France (1871–1914): Consolidating the Bourgeois Republic 801 4. France (1871–1914): The Spread of Syndicalism and Socialism 803 5. The German Empire (1871–1914): Foundation and Expansion 806 6. The German Empire (1871–1914): Economic and Social Problems 808

60 THE COMPETITION AMONG THE INDUSTRIALIZED STATES: THE RACE FOR COLONIES AND MARKETS (1871–1914) — 811

1. The New Imperialism After 1871 811 2. The British Empire in 1871 812 3. British Acquisitions (1871–1914) 814 4. French Colonial Enterprise 816 5. Italy Entertains Imperialistic Dreams 816 6. Germany Enters the Race for Colonies 818 7. The Rivalries of the Powers in Africa 820 8. The Rivalries of the Great Powers in Asia 822

61 THE GROWTH OF ALLIANCES: INTERNATIONAL TENSION AND THE ARMED PEACE (1871–1914) — 826

1. The German Hegemony After 1871 826 2. The Triple Alliance 827 3. France Searches for Allies 828 4. Anglo-German Rivalry 829 5. The Triple Entente 830 6. International Crises: Morocco 831 7. International Crises: The Balkans 833 8. The Growth of Armaments 835

SECTION L · Two World Wars and the Years Between · 1914–47

62 THE FIRST WORLD WAR — 841

1. The Coming of the War 841 2. The War on Land (1914–17) 843 3. The War on the Sea 846 4. The War on Land (1917–18) 848 5. The Cost of the War 852

63 THE PEACE SETTLEMENT OF 1919 — 855

1. Ideals and Realities 855 2. The Treaty of Versailles 857 3. The Settlement with Austria-Hungary, Bulgaria, and Turkey 861 4. The Fate of the Fourteen Points 862 5. The League of Nations 864

64 THE IMPACT OF EUROPEAN CIVILIZATION ON ASIA — 868

1. Modern India 868 2. Indian Nationalism and the Demand for Autonomy 870 3. The Remaking of China 873 4. The Rise of Japan 874 5. Japan over Asia 878

65 THE RÔLE OF AMERICA — 883

1. The "Miracle of America" 883   2. Social Welfare and Natural Resources 886   3. Political Liberty 887   4. Foreign Relations 891   5. Latin America 893

66 RUSSIA UNDER THE RULE OF THE SOVIETS — 896

1. The March Revolution 896   2. The Bolsheviki in Power 898   3. The Philosophy and Program of the Russian Communists 900   4. The Structure of the Soviet Government 902   5. Economic Progress and the Five-Year Plan 903   6. Foreign Relations of Russia after 1917 905

67 FASCIST ITALY — 907

1. Post-War Confusion in Italy 907   2. Benito Mussolini 908   3. The Corporate State 910   4. Effects of the Fascist Administration 912   5. The Fascist State and the Papacy 914

68 THE UNITED KINGDOM AND THE BRITISH EMPIRE COMMONWEALTH — 915

1. The British Economic Dilemma 915   2. British Political Parties After 1919 917   3. The Irish Free State 918   4. Egypt, Iraq, and Palestine 920   5. The Self-Governing Dominions 922

69 FRANCE SEEKS SECURITY — 925

1. The Work of Reclamation 925   2. The Reparations Tangle 926   3. The Search for Security 927   4. The Peace Pacts 932

70 GERMANY SEEKS EQUALITY — 934

1. The Organization of the German Republic 934   2. Economic Chaos and Recovery 935   3. Stresemann and the Spirit of Conciliation 937   4. Hitler and the Spirit of Recalcitrance 938   5. The Totalitarian State 940   6. German Foreign Policy After 1932 942

71 TWO DECADES OF INTERNATIONAL TENSION (1919–39) — 945

1. Economic Imperialism 945   2. The "Haves" and the "Have-Nots" 948   3. Collective Security 949   4. The Great Depression (1929–33) 951   5. Recovery and Rearmament 952   6. The Failure of Collective Security (1933–39) 956   7. Aggression and Appeasement 958

72 THE SECOND WORLD WAR (1939–45) — 963

1. From the Fall of Poland to the Fall of France (September, 1939–June, 1940) 963   2. The Battle of Britain 965   3. The Battle of Russia 967   4. Global Strategy: Gibraltar to Singapore 970   5. The American Achievement 972   6. The Liberation of Europe 974   7. The War in the Pacific 975   8. The Cost of World War II 978

Chapter

73 THE POST-WAR WORLD 981

1. The United Nations 981   2. The Reconstruction of Europe 982   3. The Balance of Power in Asia 986   4. Policing the Post-War World 987   5. Conclusion 988

Appendixes

Chronological Outlines	ii
The Preparation of History Reports	xviii
Genealogical Tables	xxi
A List of European Rulers to the Middle of the Seventeenth Century	xxv
A List of European Rulers since the Middle of the Seventeenth Century	xxvii
Suggestions for Further Reading	xxix

Indexes

Persistent Factors in European Civilization	lii
List of Maps	liii
Index of Charts and Illustrations	liv
General Index	lviii

Picture Acknowledgments

Page	Source	Page	Source
355. *top left*	University Prints	485. *bottom*	Ewing Galloway
355. *top right*	Brown Brothers	493. *top (both pictures)*	Brown Brothers
355. *bottom*	Brown Brothers	493. *bottom left*	Bettmann Archive
361. *top left*	University Prints	498. *top*	Brown Brothers
361. *center right*	Courtesy of Phaidon Press, London	505. *(all pictures)*	Brown Brothers
361. *bottom right*	Brown Brothers	517. *(both pictures)*	Metropolitan Museum of Art
365. *top left*	Brown Brothers	521. *bottom*	From Ducros: *French Society in the Eighteenth Century* (G. P. Putnam's Sons)
365. *top right and bottom*	Courtesy of Phaidon Press, London	523. *top*	Metropolitan Museum of Art
368. *top left*	Bettmann Archive	523. *bottom*	Bettmann Archive
368. *bottom*	University Prints	530. *top*	Ewing Galloway
369. *(all pictures)*	University Prints	530. *bottom left*	Brown Brothers
374. *top right*	Ewing Galloway	530. *center right*	Bettmann Archive
378. *(all pictures)*	University Prints	530. *bottom right*	Bettmann Archive
379. *top left*	University Prints	533. *top left*	Boston Museum of Fine Arts
379. *top right*	Sawders	545. *top left*	Ewing Galloway
379. *bottom*	Ewing Galloway	545. *top right*	Bettmann Archive
390. *top left*	Bettmann Archive	545. *bottom (both pictures)*	Brown Brothers
390. *top right*	Keystone View Co.		
390. *bottom (both pictures)*	Courtesy of Phaidon Press, London	551. *top left*	Brown Brothers
		551. *top right*	Metropolitan Museum of Art
397. *top (three pictures)*	Brown Brothers	555. *bottom*	Keystone View Co.
406. *top right*	University Prints	557. *top left*	Brown Brothers
406. *bottom left*	University Prints	557. *top right*	New York Public Library
409. *top left*	Brown Brothers	557. *bottom left*	Brown Brothers
409. *top right*	Bettmann Archive	557. *bottom right*	Keystone View Co.
414. *top (both pictures)*	Brown Brothers	561. *top*	Bettmann Archive
422. *top left*	University Prints	561. *bottom*	University Prints
422. *top right*	Brown Brothers	567. *top (both pictures)*	Brown Brothers
425. *top*	University Prints	571. *top left*	Brown Brothers
425. *bottom*	Courtesy of Phaidon Press, London	577. *top left*	Culver Service
		577. *bottom*	Metropolitan Museum of Art
429. *top left*	Brown Brothers	581. *bottom*	Ewing Galloway
429. *top right*	University Prints	589. *top*	New York Public Library
429. *bottom*	Brown Brothers	589. *bottom*	Metropolitan Museum of Art
435. *top left*	Bettmann Archive	595. *top left*	Metropolitan Museum of Art
435. *bottom left*	Brown Brothers	595. *top right*	Keystone View Co.
435. *top right*	Metropolitan Museum of Art	595. *bottom (both pictures)*	Bettmann Archive
439. *top left*	Brown Brothers		
439. *top right*	Hispanic Society of America, N.Y.	597. *top left*	Brown Brothers
		597. *top right*	New York Historical Society
439. *bottom left*	National Gallery of Canada, Ottawa	597. *bottom*	Ewing Galloway
		599.	Bettmann Archive
441. *top left*	Brown Brothers	601. *bottom left*	Science Service
446. *top (both pictures)*	Brown Brothers	601. *bottom right*	Keystone View Co.
451. *bottom*	University Prints	606. *top right*	Bettmann Archive
457. *top right*	Keystone View Co.	606. *bottom*	Bettmann Archive
462. *top right*	Brown Brothers	607. *bottom*	Bettmann Archive
462. *bottom*	Bettmann Archive	615. *top (both pictures)*	Bettmann Archive
465. *top*	University Prints	618. *top left*	Keystone View Co.
473. *(both pictures)*	Bettmann Archive	618. *top right*	Science Service
478. *top right*	University Prints	618. *bottom left*	Bettmann Archive
478. *bottom*	Ewing Galloway	618. *bottom right*	Brown Brothers
481. *top left*	Bettmann Archive	622. *top (both pictures)*	Metropolitan Museum of Art
485. *top left*	Bettmann Archive	622. *bottom*	Bettmann Archive
485. *top right*	Brown Brothers	623. *top*	New York Public Library

PICTURE ACKNOWLEDGMENTS

Page	Source	Page	Source
623. bottom	Bettmann Archive	767. top	American-Swedish News Exchange
631. top left	Brown Brothers		
631. top right	Bettmann Archive	767. center	Ewing Galloway
636. top left	Brown Brothers	770. top	Ewing Galloway
636. top right	Bettmann Archive	770. bottom	Brown Brothers
640. top	Bettmann Archive	781. top right	Keystone View Co.
640. bottom	Chase National Bank Collection	783. top right	Keystone View Co.
		783. bottom	British Combine
647. top left	Bettmann Archive	789. top	Science Service
647. top center	Keystone View Co.	789. bottom	Bettmann Archive
647. top right	Bettmann Archive	791. bottom right	New York Edison Company
654. bottom	Bettmann Archive	793. top	Bettmann Archive
657. bottom (both pictures)	Metropolitan Museum of Art	793. center	Keystone View Co.
		793. bottom	Smithsonian Institution
660. top left	Keystone View Co.	796. top left	Ewing Galloway
660. top right	New York Public Library	796. bottom	Bettmann Archive
660. bottom	Bettmann Archive	800.	British Information Services
665. bottom	New York Public Library	805. top right	French Press and Information Services
669.	New York Public Library		
670. top left	Keystone View Co.	805. bottom left	Bettmann Archive
670. top right	Bettmann Archive	807. (both pictures)	Ewing Galloway
675. top (both pictures)	Bettmann Archive	817. top left	Keystone View Co.
675. bottom	Brown Brothers	817. top right	Bettmann Archive
678. top left	Keystone View Co.	817. bottom	Ewing Galloway
678. top right	New York Public Library	823. bottom	Bettmann Archive
678. bottom	New York Public Library	834. top left	Reproduced by permission of the Proprietors of Punch
684.	Ewing Galloway		
689. top	Metropolitan Museum of Art	834. top right	Bettmann Archive
689. bottom	Metropolitan Museum of Art	834. bottom	Reproduced by permission of the Proprietors of Punch
691. top left	Bettmann Archive		
691. top center	Brown Brothers	837. (all pictures)	Brown Brothers
691. top right	Bettmann Archive	845. top	Ewing Galloway
691. bottom	Ewing Galloway	845. bottom	British Combine
694. top left	From a Painting by Goya	849. top left	Ewing Galloway
694. top right	Keystone View Co.	849. top right	Brown Brothers
694. bottom (both pictures)	Brown Brothers	849. bottom	U.S. Signal Corps
		851. top	U.S. Signal Corps
701. center left	Bettmann Archive	851. bottom	National Archives
701. center right	New York Public Library	858. top left	Ewing Galloway
701. bottom	Bettmann Archive	858. top right	Brown Brothers
703. top left	Brown Brothers	858. bottom	National Archives
703. top right	Bettmann Archive	863. top	Sawders
703. bottom left	Keystone View Co.	863. bottom	National Archives
703. bottom right	Bettmann Archive	865. top	Ewing Galloway
705. (both pictures)	Bettmann Archive	865. bottom	British Combine
709. top left	Brown Brothers	871. top	Joseph K. Abeles, Talbot Studio
713. top (both pictures)	Keystone View Co.		
716. top left	Bettmann Archive	871. bottom	New York Times Magazine
716. bottom left	Bettmann Archive	876. (all pictures)	Acme
725. top right	Bettmann Archive	877. top	Boston Museum of Fine Arts
725. bottom	Bettmann Archive	877. bottom	Sawders
727. (both pictures)	Bettmann Archive	879. (all pictures)	Metropolitan Museum of Art
737. left	Bettmann Archive	885. top	Bettmann Archive
737. right	Brown Brothers	885. bottom	Caterpillar Tractor Company
741. top (both pictures)	Brown Brothers	888. top	Ewing Galloway
741. bottom	Ewing Galloway	888. bottom	Acme
750. (both pictures)	Bettmann Archive	889. top	Keystone View Co.
753. (both pictures)	Brown Brothers	889. bottom	Brown Brothers
757. bottom	Bettmann Archive	897. top	Authenticated News
761. top right	Chase National Bank Collection	897. bottom	Sovfoto
		901. (all pictures)	Sovfoto
761. bottom	Brown Brothers	905.	Ewing Galloway

PICTURE ACKNOWLEDGMENTS

Page	Source	Page	Source
909. (*both pictures*)	Keystone View Co.	939. *bottom*	British Combine
913. *top*	International News	941. *bottom*	British Combine
913. *bottom*	Ewing Galloway	944.	National Archives
916.	British Information Services	953. *top*	Ewing Galloway
919. (*both pictures*)	British Combine	953. *center*	Courtesy of the *New York Herald Tribune*
923. *top*	Ewing Galloway		
923. *center*	Brown Brothers	953. *bottom*	Associated Press
923. *bottom*	Brown Brothers	961. *top*	Museum of Modern Art, New York
929. *top*	Ewing Galloway		
929. *bottom* (*both pictures*)	Brown Brothers	961. *bottom*	Press Association, Inc.
		965. *top*	*Life Magazine*
931. *top left*	Gendreau	965. *bottom*	British Official Photograph
931. *top right*	Ewing Galloway	971. (*both pictures*)	British Combine
931. *bottom*	Pierre Matisse Gallery, New York	977. *top*	Sovfoto
		977. *bottom*	International News
936. *top left*	National Archives	979. (*both pictures*)	Acme
936. *top right*	Keystone View Co.	985. *top*	Courtesy of *The Christian Science Monitor*
936. *bottom*	Chase National Bank Collection, New York		
		985. *bottom*	Acme
939. *top*	European		

SECTION E

The Later Middle Ages and the Renaissance

There is no date of which it may definitely be said: here the Middle Ages ended or here modern history began. The year 1500 has been affixed to the title of this volume because 1500 is a good round number and easy to remember. There are other histories of modern Europe which commence before or after this date, in 1453, 1492, 1517, or 1543. It seems logical to pick a year near the center of this cluster.

The really significant fact, of course, is that European people who lived around 1500 might have noted half a dozen trends which (the historian now sees) made their age a watershed between medieval and modern times. They knew the Italian Renaissance in that golden hour when Raphael, Michelangelo, and Leonardo da Vinci were producing their immortal works. They were contemporaries of a Genoese captain named Columbus who crossed the western ocean (1492) and of a Portuguese navigator, Vasco da Gama, who sailed around Africa to India (1498). In their lifetime a German friar, Martin Luther, started a controversy (1517) which disrupted the Church Universal, a naval expedition (Magellan's) first circumnavigated the Earth (1519–22), and a Polish astronomer, Copernicus, propounded a theory (1543) which dissolved the firmament.

An age in which Renaissance man discovered, or rediscovered, himself; in which Protestant reformers dismembered the universal church; in which explorers revealed a new world and astronomers a new heaven, was obviously an age of extraordinary vitality and versatility. The contemporary economic quickening, which fortified the national states and fostered the rise of the commercial classes, was an historical development which proved even more momentous and irresistible than the intellectual awakening. Any year in such an epoch would seem an auspicious moment at which to enter the unfolding drama. But before the student steps onto that crowded Renaissance stage he may wish to orient himself by a swift backward glance across the preceding centuries. For this the brief introduction which follows may be of aid.

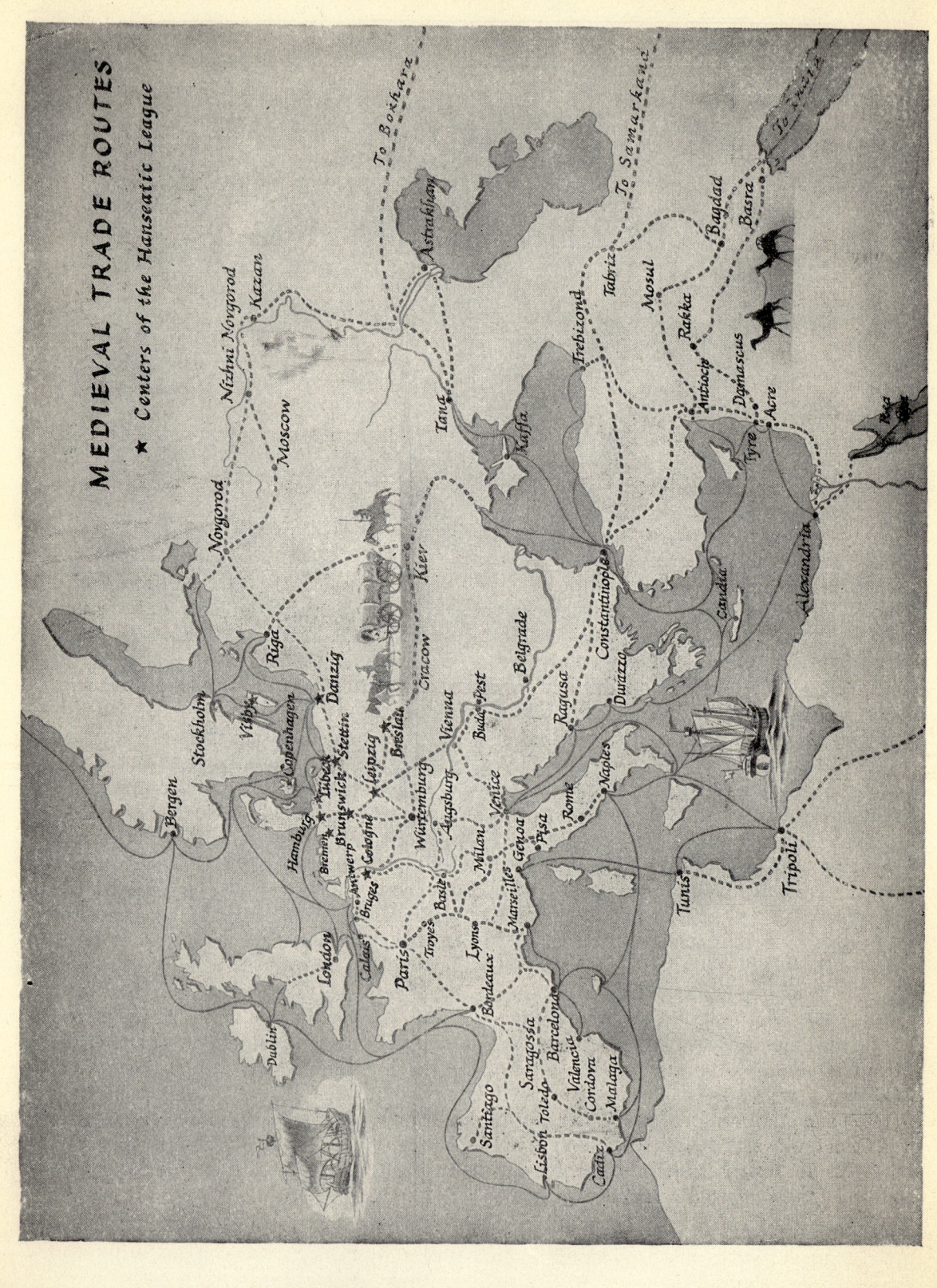

Introduction: Europe in the Middle Ages

1. MEDIEVAL AGRARIAN SOCIETY

WHEN the Roman Empire declined and its western half disintegrated in the third and fourth centuries A.D., Europe was plunged into disorder and misery. The decline was not arrested until the eighth century, and was then followed by five centuries of gradual but increasing recovery. Thus for nearly a thousand years, roughly from the fifth to the fifteenth century, the peoples of Europe lived under a slowly disintegrating and then slowly reintegrating pattern of culture which we call Medieval Civilization.

The economic foundations of this culture were agrarian: the great majority of the people toiled on the land and wrung a frugal living from agricultural pursuits. The distinctive political organization which emerged in these centuries was feudalism, which was less a system than a complicated, decentralized method of land tenure. Local military leaders came to exercise hereditary administrative functions and to extend, in return for tribute, a measure of protection to the serfs who tilled their estates.

Within the limits of his narrow domain each lord exercised what amounted to sovereign rights. Economically and politically Europe was thus broken into thousands of uncorrelated fragments. While this tendency toward administrative disjunction remained dominant, no effective centralized government could arise to unify the laws and customs, exploit the resources, discipline and co-ordinate the energies of the people over an extensive territorial area: to organize, in short, what today we know as a sovereign territorial state. The only real unity among all Christian peoples of Europe in the Middle Ages was a common religion. Christendom was a community of faith. It is the purpose of this introduction to analyze very briefly the culture of Medieval Christendom, and to seek the latent forces developing within that culture. For after the thirteenth century those latent forces were to transmute and expand European civilization into the civilization which has dominated Europe and has come to dominate a great part of the world in the last five hundred years.

Christendom

With the decline of the Roman Empire, and the destructive inroads of the barbarian tribes in the fifth century, European society disintegrated, lost cohesion, broke down gradually into small semi-isolated agrarian settlements where people labored selfishly and doggedly to keep alive. The population of the Roman Empire in Europe, which may have exceeded forty million in the great days of the second century A.D., was reduced by war, disease, and famine until by the seventh century it is doubtful if there were twenty-five million people in all Europe. Once populous cities had become heaps of plundered ruins where wolves roamed unmolested through the deserted streets. The flow of trade within Europe, the life-blood of cities, dwindled to an insignificant trickle, especially after the Mohammedan conquests in the seventh century interrupted communication between Europe and the eastern Mediterranean lands. Roads and bridges fell into disrepair, coins and currency all but ceased to circulate. Western Europe, from the Rhine to the Atlantic, from Britain to the Mediterranean, which Roman leadership and genius for organization had raised to a level of civilization hitherto unknown, seemed destined to relapse once more into barbarism.

Society decentralized

To survive through those dark centuries, from the fifth to the eleventh, which form the early Middle Ages, each community had to learn the arduous lesson of self-sufficiency. Denied other means of livelihood, cut off from other sources of supply, men turned of necessity to those sources which had not failed them — to the fields and orchards which, if cultivated, would still produce their yield; to the raising of poultry, sheep, cows, and pigs, for eggs, meat, wool,

Agrarian economy

leather, and tallow; to the lakes or the sea for fish; to the forests for timber and firewood. Medieval economy became inevitably a decentralized and largely an agrarian economy, and its unit was the village with its surrounding fields, the feudal manor, or, at its simplest, the household in a clearing, ringed by the threatening forest. Here, at the price of unremitting and self-centered toil, life could go on, though dynasties crumbled and empires decayed.

Unfortunately, these isolated medieval communities were weak and helpless: they were open to attack by marauding bands from the forest, or to the murderous forays of the Northmen from Scandinavia, who pushed up the rivers in their swift ships. Peasants and laborers, living on the margin of subsistence, could not well maintain the horses and weapons nor spare the time needed to master the warrior's art. Hence, since protection, like food, was a necessity of existence, they bought it where they could and paid the price demanded. The elements of a bargain were already present. Land had become the major, almost the exclusive, source of income, but the land would not yield unless cultivated. The peasants had their worth, therefore, their indispensable function as producers, and they could offer a part of their produce for protection, offer it to any local leader, even to a robber chief, with the understanding, that, in return for a regular tribute, he would respect their lands and keep marauders at bay. From such bargains emerged the elements of the peculiarly medieval institution known as feudalism. Such a brief account of its origin is, of course, oversimplified, but it serves to suggest the manner in which the social and economic realities of the early Middle Ages dictated a new organization of society, the feudal order.

Feudalism

Thus it came about that the great majority of the people, certainly over nine tenths of them, lived severely restricted lives in the Middle Ages, for they were restricted in their activities, in their communication with others, and even in their thoughts. Men who live in small groups, on the margin of want if not of actual starvation, and divide

Initiative stifled

their duties so that there is an intimate dependence upon one another's efforts, are not friendly toward innovations. This becomes especially true after centuries of hard experience have deepened the conviction that most changes are changes for the worse. Necessity is not always the mother of invention, nor privation the mother of initiative. When severe conditions prevail so long that the memory of man runneth not to the contrary, they are likely to induce a spirit of dogged and unenlightened conservatism. To the dweller in a medieval hamlet the hamlet was his world, and if echoes of distant events reached him, or rumors of new devices, he paid scant heed and attended to his business.

This inevitable parochialism is probably the outstanding quality about medieval European people which would most provoke and astonish us if we could leap the interim with our twentieth-century minds and spend a day in a typical medieval hamlet. The European child born eight or nine hundred years ago accepted his destiny without much question, imbibed the lore and prejudices of his neighbors, learned the use of spade and yoke, distaff and spindle, sang the songs and believed the legends of his locality, inherited the loyalties, the habits, and the hates of his kinsfolk, and was buried a few yards from the cottage in which he was born. Throughout his short span of years he remained relentlessly preoccupied with local affairs and almost as oblivious to the world beyond the horizon, to the happenings in distant countries and to alien ways of life, as a domestic animal confined to its pasture.

Limited horizon

It is not easy to understand how a love of learning could persist and a precious heritage of classical culture survive in such a straitened society. That the love of learning did not entirely die out in Western Europe after the Fall of Rome was to be credited to the clergy, especially to the monks in the Benedictine monasteries, and to the Church schools. These medieval centuries brought and wrought a slow synthesis of diverse elements which conditioned the spirit and character of later European civilization. This preparatory period of a thousand years, full

Culture and learning

of outward confusion and vicissitudes, was the period in which modern European culture was germinating and taking form, the period when the Classical, Christian, and Germanic elements were fusing in the European mind. Like all formative eras it is difficult to evaluate because its contributions were cumulative.

Yet it is clear, from the literature and art of the twelfth and thirteenth centuries, that the Greek passion for truth, the Roman genius for law, and the Christian search for good, had fused into a philosophy of Christian humanism. Though life in medieval times was subject to many physical restrictions, the impulses of the mind, the heart, and the spirit were free to flower. Even in the midst of the gloomy tenth and eleventh centuries a love of life, a thirst for knowledge, an aspiration toward the ideal were not lacking.

Christian humanism

2. PREMISES OF MEDIEVAL THOUGHT

Since the dawn of civilization men with a philosophical disposition of mind have sought to discover an implicit order, an ordained pattern, in the universe about them. Leading thinkers of the twelfth and thirteenth centuries, wrestling with this age-old problem, succeeded in weaving the historical, scientific, and religious beliefs of their time into a system of thought which has, perhaps, never been surpassed in its coherence and grandeur. It was the crowning expression of a thousand and more years of evolving thought on the destiny of man and the meaning of things, a mansion built with devout intention for the intellectual security of mankind. To comprehend the debt which modern culture owes to medieval thought, and to form some impression of the systematized faith in divine authority which then found expression, the modern reader can turn to the great poem of Dante, the *Divina Commedia*.

Medieval philosophy

The universe, as conceived by Dante the poet, was a universe laid out according to a pre-established pattern, an order ordained for it by the Creator. Dante's cosmology was geocentric; the earth was accepted as the center of the universe, and about it the sun, moon, planets, and stars, set in invisible crystalline spheres, revolved in their appointed rounds. Beyond the ninth sphere was the empyrean, the abode of blessed spirits. This closed and orderly cosmology, based upon ideas enunciated by the Alexandrian astronomer, Claudius Ptolemaeus, in the second century after Christ, seemed a reasonable theory in an age without telescopes or other instruments for precise observation.

Cosmology

The first principle to note, therefore, in Dante's thought, is this concept of order. The second is the concept of hierarchy. Not alone for the heavenly bodies, but for the earth and all the creatures thereon a definite and orderly existence had been ordained. All things inanimate or animate had been ranged in categories according to a scale of ascending values. Each object had an appointed place and an appointed function; if it failed to perform its function or strayed from its place, the divine order would be disturbed. Such opposition to the divine order, when indulged by a rational being, constituted what was termed sin. The discord, the confusion, and the suffering which inevitably beset the sinner were the necessary penalties of his transgression.

Concept of hierarchy

To the Apostles, Christ had confided the power to forgive sins, and this power had been transmitted to later generations through the Apostolic Succession. Thus the clergy not only guided the consciences of the faithful; they administered to them, through the ritual of the Church, the sacraments which maintained them in a state of grace and opened the way to redemption and to eternal salvation. Secular rulers had power over the perishable bodies of men and their earthly fortunes, but churchmen had the cure for their souls. Furthermore, as the spiritual world was superior to the physical world, the power of pope and bishop was regarded as superior to the power of prince or baron. If lay rulers adopted policies in opposition to the decrees of the Church, they endangered their own souls.

The way to salvation

Upon those who accepted it (and all medieval Christians professed obedience to the Church) such a religion brought the sense of belonging to a universal society. It also brought a sense of shared responsibility, of duty toward one's fellow men, of obligation and interdependence. It was the duty of all to serve faithfully in that station in which it had pleased God to place them. To nourish the desire to rise above one's class, to better one's profession, to seize authority, was to yield to the temptation of pride, of ambition, of envy. The constrictions of medieval society, imposed upon men by their limited opportunities, and intensified for the great majority by the rigidity of a simple agrarian economy, were thus dignified and perpetuated by a religion which assured them that to rebel against their lot or to resist established authority was to defy God's will.

Social stratification

The initiative required to experiment with new methods, to push forth on voyages of discovery, to introduce novel tools or alien techniques does not come easily to men whose habits of life are thus frozen by custom. Compared to the flood of inventions in modern times, few important discoveries or inventions in chemistry, in physics, in mechanics, or medicine were made during the Middle Ages. Curiosity was stifled by the lack of means to satisfy it, and to probe Nature for her secrets came to be regarded as irrelevant if not actually irreverent. God had revealed to man what it was necessary for him to know. To seek to press beyond the bounds of the known was to be seduced by the pride of knowledge.

Inventiveness checked

This medieval disposition to respect authority, to refrain from audacious and irreverent speculation, to seek in Nature only such proofs and evidences as would confirm the truths of revealed religion, helps to explain the neglect of scientific experiment. But the limitations imposed were more physical than mental. There was no dearth, throughout the Middle Ages, of restless, turbulent individuals. Men broke with the monotony of custom whenever a legitimate chance arose: the popularity of pilgrimages and the extraordinary response to the crusading movement are proofs of this. It is clear that, latent in medieval society, there was a driving energy, repressed for the time, but ready to press outward with irresistible pertinacity when the release came and new channels opened.

Latent energy

The real limitations, therefore, which curbed scientific experimentation, curiosity, and progress in medieval times seem to have been obstacles which have checked such progress in all ages. The lack of leisure, of wealth, of opportunity to conduct experiments and compare conclusions hindered the acquisition of knowledge and improvement of technique. The segregation of social groups, already noted, was an almost insurmountable barrier to the sharing of knowledge and diffusion of ideas. Where improved methods or new crops or remedies for disease did circulate, the diffusion seems to have been almost exclusively the work of the monkish orders.

Barriers to progress

The population of that segment of Europe which had once formed part of the Roman Empire has been estimated at thirty-five million for A.D. 1000, or something less than fifty people to the square mile. It was necessary for men to congregate more closely, to experience the stimulus of town life, to promote the exchange of goods and ideas through expanding trade, to acquire wealth and justify the pursuit of secular knowledge for its own sake, before they could respond to the spirit of secular enterprise and escape from the conservative habits which bound their thoughts and actions.

3. THE INTEGRATION OF MEDIEVAL SOCIETY

The transition from medieval to modern civilization in Europe has been, in its political aspect, a transition from a decentralized and amorphous society, immobilized by incohesion, divided by a thousand inherited feuds and local loyalties, to a society of aggressive, unified, territorial states. Each century since the close of the Middle Ages has seen European society grow increasingly complex and dynamic. With each generation new techniques were improvised, new methods of production and integration devel-

Rise of a secular society

oped, until the Europeans, organized, enriched, and armed by these secular crafts, sailed forth to subdue the other continents and exploit them for tribute. There was still, as in medieval times, an element of crusading zeal behind this imperial expansion, and many backward peoples acquired the benefits of a superior civilization from their European teachers. But in the process European society was itself transformed, and became more secular and materialistic as the products of the world flooded its markets. Western man, in extending his influence over alien continents, was impelled by dual motives, a greed for material gain which drove him to exploit conquered peoples, and a worthier, humanitarian desire to elevate and educate his brothers. The drama of European expansion was a complex pattern woven by soldiers and slaves, merchants and missionaries, pirates and martyrs.

Imperialism in embryo
Such a spirit was not, of course, entirely lacking in the Middle Ages. The crusades themselves, especially the later efforts, were in part the essays of an embryo imperialism, and the conquest and colonization of Prussia after 1231 under the leadership of the Teutonic Knights provided a rehearsal for the drama of European expansion. These outward thrusts were a preliminary expression of the transforming forces which were slowly generating within Christendom. Of these forces the most powerful, probably, was the steady increase in population which affected almost all parts of Europe in the later Middle Ages.

Rise in population
There is good reason to believe that by the thirteenth century the population of Europe had risen to over fifty million souls, and must, in the more thickly settled areas of France and Italy, have exceeded one hundred people to the square mile. Under the relatively static economy of the times the pressure of the rising birth-rate would thus provide a motive for improvements in farming methods and for emigration to unexploited regions. This increase in numbers was further accelerated in the fourteenth century, and the overflow from the hamlets helped to augment the rising towns. It also helped to infuse a new and more restless spirit into what had been so long a declining or almost stationary population. Thus the first dynamic factor which disturbed the relative equilibrium and immobility of medieval society was itself a product of the equilibrium achieved. The increase in population was made possible through the coalescence of the feudal order and the decline of the murderous forays of Northmen, Saracens, and Slavs. For such marauders were no longer so free, after the tenth century, to make inroads upon a society which had become more consolidated, and had entrusted its defense to a professional military caste. Whatever defects may be urged against feudalism as a system of administration, it bred a warrior class and fortified Europe against invasion and domination by Mohammedans or Mongols.

Expansion of farming
The revival and reintegration of European society, which had already begun by the eleventh century, proceeded slowly at first and then with notable acceleration. If we could imagine ourselves flying over Europe at fifty-year intervals from A.D. 1000 to 1500, the changes taking place would have been apparent to even the most casual observer. The thick forests which covered much of the continent were receding, cut down to provide additional cultivable land. Where once the sunlight had been reflected back from mottled pools and swamps, a later trip might reveal lush, well-drained pasture land with cattle grazing. In Eastern Europe the expanding rim of Christendom could be traced by the advance of the monasteries, the formal pattern of the buildings making them easily recognizable, with their widening area of vineyards, orchards, and plowlands surrounding each. As feudalism entrenched itself, the gray, crenellated walls of baronial castles dotted defensible hilltops in increasing numbers. Even more unmistakable to an aerial observer would have been the multiplication of church spires, climbing slowly heavenward from a hundred, then a thousand, devout settlements, fingers of faith visible leagues away through the luminous country air, as yet untarnished by the smoke from blast furnaces and factories.

...uous of all, by river ford or ...round a bishop's seat, or at the foot of a mountain pass, the voyager might have noted ...owns emerging, with tall houses over-...ng the narrow streets, towns which ...flowed their walls into the countryside ... the years passed, linked themselves together with highways, piled their merchandise upon the jetties for the puny-looking ships, scarcely larger than a modern lifeboat, which began to crowd their wharves. These towns, with their busy, curious-minded, aggressive citizens, were the visible heralds of the future, for in their market squares and their guildhalls, their workshops and their counting-houses, a new age was coming to birth.

New ages come to birth but slowly. The medieval framework of society and the medieval system of values, which had reached a maximum integration by the thirteenth century, proved elastic enough to survive the growing internal tensions for some three centuries longer without manifest disruption. Medieval society fought to defend and perpetuate itself, almost like a living organism, against the changing conditions. It curbed, contained, and incorporated within itself, so far as it could, the new and alien forces which threatened to transform or destroy it. In the outcome a new social and political framework was to be constructed, indebted deeply in its customs, character, and spirit to medieval precedents, but amplified by new political and economic institutions.

New institutions necessary

4. MEDIEVAL SOCIETY IN TRANSITION

To the political theorists of the Middle Ages, Christendom was not merely one in faith and culture; it was also, in theory at least, a single political body. From A.D. 800, when Charlemagne was crowned emperor at Rome, the tradition lived that the whole of Christian Europe, the *Respublica Christiana*, was, or ought to be, subject to a single temporal head, an emperor. Despite interregna, despite the disputes of rival claimants to the imperial title, this ideal of unity persisted until long after the rise of sovereign territorial states had rendered it unreal and anomalous.

It is not possible to trace here, but only to note briefly, some of the reasons for "the medieval empire's brilliant failure." The long struggle between emperors and popes for supremacy in Europe culminated in the thirteenth century with the empire definitely in second place. The weakened imperial power proved inadequate thereafter to control the arrogant Italian city-states; the rising North-German cities banded together in the Hanseatic League for the promotion of their own interests; and the Swiss defied the emperors and successfully maintained their independence. By the fifteenth century, when the Turks captured Constantinople and invaded southeastern Europe, the emperors found themselves scarcely able to defend their own hereditary possessions in the Germanies. Their claims to universal suzerainty had become little more than a vain traditional pretension, and they failed, even in their German domains, to curb the forces of feudalism sufficiently to knit these domains into a centralized national state as the Spanish, French, and English monarchs were doing. Yet so strong was the tincture of tradition, so indelible was the memory of the ancient Roman world imperium, that the European peoples continued for centuries to pay lip-service to its shadowy successor, the medieval empire.

Decline of the empire

The Papacy, which had proved itself the stronger in its long struggle with the medieval empire, underwent external transformations as it continued its historic mission. The authority of the popes was challenged by the monarchs of the rising territorial states and a series of sharp controversies resulted. Had the papal government remained as strong, efficient, and united after 1300 as it had been under Innocent III a century earlier, it might have mastered the new opposition, but it was crippled by internal difficulties which ended in a disastrous schism. At the same time new tides of thought and speculation, products of the changing age, assailed the metaphysical foundations of medieval philosophy. The great theologians of the thirteenth century,

The Papacy

the "Realists," had offered logical proofs for the articles of faith, basing these proofs upon abstractions for which they claimed universal validity. The fourteenth century produced a conflicting school of thinkers, the Nominalists, who argued that reality is to be found in individual things rather than in abstract ideas or categories. At Rome a solution was approved which was not Platonic realism nor rigid Nominalism, but might be termed a moderate Realism. But the Nominalists, by emphasizing the particular and concrete as worthy of attention, rather than the impalpable and the abstract, prefigured that shift in thought which inspired their successors to a more critical study of the world around them, and thus prepared in one way the rise of natural science.

By the fourteenth century feudalism was also undergoing a transformation, though its decline was not yet advanced. **Feudalism outgrown** The distinctive symbols of the feudal order were the armored knight and the fortified castle. Knighthood was still in flower in 1500, but there were signs that it might soon run to seed. At the battle of Courtrai in 1302, an army of Flemish burghers routed the military aristocracy of France and gathered seven hundred gold spurs from the bodies of the vanquished. At Crécy, forty-four years later, English archers mowed down the ranks of heavily armed French knights as they charged in vain against the lances of the dismounted men-at-arms. These events were omens of a changing order, and the fifteenth century was to bring further humiliations to the knightly class. So long as there was no appeal from the lawless rule of the feudal nobles, their subjects had perforce to endure their exactions and depredations. But with the emergence of national monarchies, townsmen in particular learned the advantage of supporting the king in his struggle to curb the barons, for one tyrant was preferable to many. Feudal nobles, with their motley array of retainers, began to lose ground before the regular forces equipped from the royal treasury, and this triumph of gold over steel was a further omen of a new age. A final factor in the decline of the knightly order was the rising cost of living. With the revival of a money economy at the close of the Middle Ages, feudal landlords, whose income was fixed by custom, grew relatively poorer as prices rose. The final subjugation of the barons was to be completed when they became pensionaries of the royal purse.

From this brief introductory survey it should be evident that by 1500 medieval civilization was in transition. "Each age," a poet has said, **Europe in transition** "is a dream that is dying or one that is coming to birth." The new European civilization which was coming to birth owed its spirit and character to the classical and Christian culture upon which it was to be reared. But it was to acquire social and political institutions, scientific techniques, and a heritage of wealth and power unequaled by any previous culture. To trace the triumphant progress of the European peoples during the past five hundred years is to relive the most extraordinary epic of expansion in recorded history, the "Europeanization" of the world.

xxi

25

The Age of the Renaissance in Italy

IN THE TWO AND A HALF CENTURIES between the last of the crusades and the beginning of the Lutheran Reformation, there occurred a profound, if gradual, transformation in the character of European civilization. It was an age of transition in which medieval institutions were slowly crumbling and characteristically medieval ways of thinking were losing their force, while at the same time evidences of modern society and modern culture began to make their appearance, at first in partial form, but as time passed with ever-increasing completeness. In Italy, the land of wealth and cities, this change began earlier and progressed with greater rapidity than in the more thoroughly feudalized lands north of the Alps. Moreover, in that land of golden opportunities, of political unrest and swiftly shifting fortunes, the break-up of medieval civilization seemed to give a new and stimulating freedom to the human spirit, so that the age of transition became also an age of great intellectual activity. New vistas opened up before the eager curiosity and limitless ambition of men who were shaking themselves free from the bondage of ecclesiastical authority and corporate society. They awoke to a new appreciation of the glories of the mortal world they lived in, with its unbounded possibilities for wealth, power, artistic pleasure, and intellectual satisfaction for those who had the will to seize them. Finally, on this rich soil, provided by the awakened genius of the Italian people, fell the seeds of antique culture, to bring forth such plentiful fruit that for centuries men thought of that age as a *renaissance* or rebirth of the civilization of ancient Rome and Greece. But the culture of the Italian Renaissance (we may as well keep the word, since it has been hallowed by centuries of use) did not owe its existence primarily to the revival of antiquity, though it was influenced by it. Its roots were fixed firmly in the Middle Ages, but the conditions of its growth were changing and the fruit was not always the same. So far as it can be defined, the age of the Renaissance was an age of chaotic change, in which there was much that was still medieval, much that was recognizably modern, and much also that was peculiar to itself. It bridged the gap between the High Middle Ages and modern times, but it was also an age to itself, filled with a great political, social, and intellectual ferment.

1. RENAISSANCE SOCIETY

If we would seek one fundamental cause for the transformation of Europe during this age, we will find it in the great increase in wealth, which came earlier and in more concentrated form in Italy than elsewhere. It was wealth that made the luxury and brilliance of the Italian Renaissance possible, and it was wealth that made a new type of society necessary. This growth of material prosperity was no new thing. It had been an increasingly potent factor in the shaping of

Increase in wealth

European civilization since the beginning of the High Middle Ages. The revival of commerce, spreading north from Italy, had gradually built up city life with a vigorous and independent middle class, and had introduced the general use of money economy. For a time these forces had adjusted themselves, though uneasily, to the scheme of medieval society. The burghers had formed corporate societies in the communes and guilds which gave them a secure place in the midst of feudalism. But as wealth continued to increase and the volume of business to expand, the new economic force grew too great to be contained within the structure of a social system that had not been designed for it. Its explosive energy brought medieval institutions crumbling to the ground. In time it destroyed feudalism and also its own corporate organization, which gave place to the modern individualistic methods of capitalism.[1] The effects of its action were not contemporaneous or exactly similar in all parts of Europe. In Italy, the result was the rise of a society that was distinctly urban, secular, i.e., worldly, in its interests, and highly individualistic.

Italy was a land of cities. It was perfectly situated to become the center of commerce for the western world, halfway between the fabulous East, where Venetian and Genoese merchants bought luxuries that could not be produced in Europe, and the market provided by the less advanced people of the West. Stimulated by these unique opportunities for commerce and the industry that rose from it, cities sprang up thickly during the Middle Ages in Lombardy, Tuscany, and the States of the Church. They enjoyed unique opportunities in other respects. The long quarrel between the emperors and the popes in the twelfth and thirteenth centuries, followed by the temporary collapse of the empire and the absence of the papacy from Italy, enabled the Italian cities to win freedom from outside control. By the beginning of the Renaissance, most of the cities of Italy, except in the Neapolitan Kingdom to the south, were practically independent states, dominating the country districts

Urban society

[1] See Chapter 32.

about them. They thus became the centers of political and social as well as economic life for the whole land. The feudal nobles could not resist their attraction. Leaving their isolated rural castles, they moved into the cities and became the neighbors of the non-noble burghers. In this urban society, in which all classes were represented, medieval class distinctions inevitably became less pronounced. Birth still meant a great deal, but wealth or political power might mean more, and where these were lacking, literary, artistic, or any other outstanding ability was sufficient to gain an entry into the homes of the noble or the rich.

The changes in society brought about by wealth and city life were reflected by equally significant changes in the interests and mental attitude of at least the wealthy and leisured classes. The busy life of the cities, the new possibilities for the enjoyment of life and for the satisfaction of esthetic tastes or intellectual curiosity, provided by luxury, wealth, and leisure, all tended to thrust thoughts of religion and of the future world farther into the background of men's minds. The growing disrespect for the papacy and the organized church, due to the scandals of the Babylonian Captivity and the schism, and the influence of the pagan philosophy inherent in the classic literature that was becoming so popular, did something to heighten this tendency. But more important than these in breaking the dominating force of religion were the manifold distractions and worldly interests inseparable from the society of the age. This may be easily exaggerated. Men of the Renaissance were seldom really irreligious. Few if any were atheists or even unorthodox. They were merely less vitally interested in the things of the spirit and more in the things of this world than their ancestors of the days when the life of the ascetic monk had represented the highest ideal, though seldom realized, of thinking men. Perhaps they had fallen into that "forgetfulness of God in time of prosperity" against which medieval preachers were wont to warn their flocks. Certainly the world and the flesh had no terrors for this generation, even though they might still fear the

The secular spirit

FEDERIGO DA MONTELFELTRO, DUKE OF URBINO

This portrait of one of the outstanding personalities of the Renaissance is by Piero della Francesca.

BALDASSARE CASTIGLIONE

The author of the "Book of the Courtier" is shown here in a portrait by Raphael.

FLORENTINE INTERIOR ABOUT 1490

This room in a Florentine house, from Ghirlandaio's fresco of "The Nativity of the Virgin," suggests the wealth and luxury of upper-class Renaissance society.

devil. This is what is meant by the "secular spirit" of the Renaissance men who threw themselves heart and soul into the full enjoyment and eager exploration of the world about them.

In this vital urban society, with its strong secular spirit, men awoke to a new consciousness of themselves as individuals. Of the modern characteristics that were making their appearance in this chaotic age of transition, few are more significant or more difficult to define than the individualism that so many historians have noted as a contrast to the corporate or class consciousness of medieval society. Men, of course, have always known that they were individuals. But in the perilous world of the Middle Ages, where security in this world depended on membership in a close corporation, whether guild, monastery, church, manor, or rank in the feudal system, and hope of salvation depended on strict obedience to the corporate church, men were inevitably more conscious of their ordained place in the scheme of things than of the potentialities of their own individual personality. As the medieval social structure began to crumble, however, careers were thrown open to talent. In the rapidly shifting politics of the Italian cities, nobility of birth was not essential to power; the new capitalistic methods of business enabled individuals to accumulate wealth far beyond their fellows; and the generous patronage of art raised lowborn artists high above the level of the ordinary artisan. There seemed no limit to what any man might accomplish, aided only by his own ability and fortune. In the new secular spirit, too, men found a double incentive for the full development of their individual powers. Immortal fame in this world came to seem more important than immortal life in the next; and the eager enjoyment of all that this world had to offer stimulated men to the development of all sides of their personalities, so as to wring the maximum of experience or pleasure out of life.

This new realization of individual potentialities brought to life a new social ideal — that of the well-rounded personality — to take the place of the medieval ideal of the man who perfectly represented the qualities of his class or group. It was an ideal that found practical expression in the amazing versatility that characterized so many Italians in the fifteenth century. Statesmen like Cosimo and Lorenzo de' Medici, the bankers who ruled Florence, soldier-despots like Duke Federigo of Urbino, and business men like the Florentine Palla Strozzi were also scholars and cultivated patrons of the arts, while innumerable examples might be cited of artists who practiced painting, sculpture, and architecture with equal facility and still found time for the pursuit of scholarship and philosophy. And this versatility of interest was not limited to men of unusual genius. The average man of culture now sought consciously to acquire at least an adequate familiarity with all branches of human activity so as to develop his personality to its fullest extent. In the schools conducted by Guarino (1374–1460) at Ferrara and Vittorino da Feltre (1378–1446) at Mantua, the practice of arms and all forms of athletics, music and courtly manners, as well as a thorough training in the arts and classical literature, were included among the things that a gentleman should know. The Renaissance, indeed, produced a new standard for the gentleman or courtier. As Baldassare Castiglione (1478–1529), himself a paragon of courtiers, tells us in his charming *Book of the Courtier*, the man who would make his way successfully into the highest ranks of society must now be not merely, or necessarily, nobly born, though that is an advantage, nor a great warrior, though he should be skilled in arms, but a fully developed personality, an amateur of all arts and all branches of learning and a master of some, possessing, above all, grace, tact, good manners, and personal charm. The contrast between the boisterous and often brutal manners of a Richard the Lion-hearted and the wide education and sensitive *finesse* of a Castiglione marks the development from the medieval to the modern ideal of a gentleman.

So far, as seems inevitable in dealing with the Renaissance, we have dwelt chiefly on the high lights of the age, the signs of progress and the evidences of modern tendencies. But there were also deep shadows, and the evolution away from medieval conditions was not always a progress toward higher standards. The age of the Renaissance in Italy was above all an age of confusion and contrast in politics, in religion, in morality, and in individual characters. Medieval and modern characteristics existed side by side in the same society or the same person, producing violent contradictions and startling incongruities. As the fifteenth century drew to a close, the people of Florence, who for years had followed the leadership of Lorenzo de' Medici, most cultured and worldly of statesmen, fell suddenly under the spell of the thoroughly medieval ascetic monk, Savonarola (1452–98), only to react again in a short time and burn their former idol. The despots, who ruled by force and cunning, recognized the binding power of no law, human or divine. The eager development of all man's faculties meant only too often the development of the baser as well as the higher instincts. Princes like the Visconti of Milan might combine inhuman cruelty with the most delicate appreciation of art, and artists like Benvenuto Cellini (1500–70) might be little better than thugs in their private life. The most enlightened and rational of Italian statesmen guided their policies by the auguries of charlatan astrologers. In every court in Italy the veneer of refined and learned society covered dark stains of immorality, and lavish magnificence paraded the streets of every city in glaring contrast to the most wretched poverty.

Violent contrasts

All that has been said about the Renaissance did not, of course, occur at once, nor would it all be true of any one time. The age of the Renaissance evolved slowly and was constantly changing. In the remainder of this chapter, we shall trace the historical developments of the age in politics, literature, and art in an attempt to place the whole in its proper historical perspective.

2. EVOLUTION OF THE ITALIAN STATES TO 1494

The Italian Renaissance was born in the midst of political chaos. The history of Italy in the fourteenth century is the history of confusion thrice confounded. In that century, Italian merchants and bankers were heaping up unprecedented fortunes; Italian industry was growing to vast proportions; the greatest of Italian poets were laying the foundations of a national literature; but as a nation in the political sense, Italy did not yet exist. Only in the southern kingdom of Naples was there any political unity. The rest of the peninsula was divided into a host of petty city-states, which had acquired almost complete independence from the overlordship of emperor and pope. Each of these states was torn by hostile factions and was frequently at war with its neighbors. The traditional feud between the Guelf and Ghibelline parties gives some slight coherence to Italian politics in this century, but that ancient quarrel had lost almost all of its original meaning in the tangle of local interests and antagonisms. Cities fought each other for control of trade routes or merely to destroy commercial rivals; country districts rebelled against domination by the cities; and within the cities the wealthy merchants and industrialists strove to control the laboring classes, who rose in revolt whenever possible, while the nobles sided with one party or the other and mercenary soldiers fished happily in the troubled waters.

Italy in the fourteenth century

In the midst of this confusion, two general tendencies may be observed; first, the destruction of democratic republican governments at the hands of despots or merchant oligarchies, and second, the expansion of the larger city-states at the expense of the less powerful ones. The first of these, indeed, was well under way at the beginning of the fourteenth century. Nearly all the cities of northern and central Italy had begun their independent career as more or less democratic communes, but this form of government proved neither strong enough to protect the city from its enemies nor sufficiently stable to provide the internal peace and order that were essential to the prosperity of business. The only possible solution of the problem seemed to be the government of the city by a

Rise of the despots

dictator or despot, who would be strong enough to keep order and who would impose peace on the warring factions by taking political liberty from all. Some few states, like Venice and Florence, escaped actual despotism, but they were scarcely more democratic, since their republican government was controlled by a small group of wealthy families. The manner in which the despots acquired their absolute power differed, of course, from place to place according to local conditions. Some turned a temporary authority, legally delegated to them as officers of the state, into an extra-legal power; others were mercenary soldiers or local feudal lords who seized the government by force of arms; while still others used their wealth to gain control of the republican governmental machine.

The despots, like men of any other class, differed widely in character, but certain characteristics were common to almost all. They were mostly men of unusual ability and force of character, for only so could they have risen to power without the support of legal or constitutional claims. They were often ruthless, cruel, and treacherous, because they had to rule by force and through fear. Nevertheless, they frequently gave their cities a wiser and more stable government than they had enjoyed under the old republican communes. As Machiavelli pointed out in his justly celebrated handbook for despots, *The Prince* (1513), it was to the interest of the despot himself to maintain the prosperity of the city he ruled, and no despot could rule for long unless he did so. Most of the despots were intelligent enough to realize that they must win the respect, and, in some measure, the gratitude, of their people. It was this desire, as well as genuine love of culture, that caused so many of them to gather poets, scholars, and artists to their courts by the promise of generous rewards. No small part of the artistic and literary glory of the Renaissance was due to their liberal and remarkably discriminating patronage.

Character of the despots

Still the despots could neither have won nor held their power had not the people of Italy generally lost the ability or desire to fight in defense of their liberties. Even under the old republican governments the citizens seldom took an active part in the army. The responsible citizens were too busy with profitable business to waste time in military training, and no republican party government, nor for that matter any despot, could afford to take the risk of revolution involved in arming the lesser populace. The best recruiting ground for a citizen militia should have been the *contado*, the rural territory and villages surrounding the city. But since all the growing city-states had spread their territory by conquest and steadily refused to grant citizenship to the conquered population, they could not trust the latter to fight for the state. The Italian states, therefore, were forced to depend on mercenary soldiers from outside for defense against foreign enemies and to keep down rebellion among discontented citizens or the disaffected subjects of the conquered towns and country. These mercenary soldiers were organized in large bands under their own leaders, called *condottieri*, who sold the services of the whole band to the highest bidder. They did not care for whom they fought or why, so long as they were paid. Their chief interest was to keep the war going as long as possible, for peace meant unemployment. In the main they seem to have been fairly good soldiers, though Machiavelli criticized them severely, but their methods were behind the times. The temporary nature of their employment made it impossible for the *condottieri* to train large bands of infantry, at a time when Swiss and Spanish pikemen were proving the superiority of infantry as the English archers had a century before. They had to depend on cavalry though the terrain of Italy is for the most part unsuited to cavalry tactics. They resorted, therefore, to endless marches and countermarches, maneuvering for position, and they were always more dangerous to noncombatants than to each other. It was a vicious system, and not the least of its evils was that it left Italy without any really adequate defense against foreign invaders from the great territorial states of Europe.

Condottieri

The second general tendency in the history

ITALY IN THE 15th CENTURY

of Italy during this period, the expansion of the greater states at the expense of the less powerful ones, began later than the rise of the despots and was not completed till the fifteenth century. But by 1494, the year in which the first French invasion opened a new era in Italian history, it had progressed so far that only five great states and some three or four lesser ones remained of the scores that had dotted the map of Italy at the beginning of the Renaissance. The five great states were respectively, the duchy of Milan, the republics of Venice and Florence, the States of the Church, and the kingdom of Naples. Of the lesser states, the republic of Siena still maintained its independence in southern Tuscany, as did the marquisate of Mantua and the duchy of Ferrara on the upper borders of the Romagna, though the latter was in theory subject to the papacy. In the States of the Church, too, there were still some practically independent, little, despotic city-states; but they were soon to be suppressed by the popes, Alexander VI and Julius II.

Expansion of states

An attempt to trace the history of each of the original Italian states would be neither possible in the space at our command nor particularly profitable. We will limit our attention, therefore, to the development of those great states which survived.

All through the Middle Ages, Milan had been the wealthiest and most powerful of the numerous cities in the rich Lombard plain which commands the Alpine passes to northern Europe. In the twelfth century it led the Lombard League in the struggle for independence from imperial control. Like its neighbors, however, Milan lost its freedom to a despotic ruler at the dawn of the Renaissance. In 1311, Matteo Visconti, head of a Ghibelline family already powerful in the city, established a lasting dictatorship with the approval of the Emperor Henry VII, who gave him the title of Imperial Vicar. He also began the expansion of the city-state by the conquest of several neighboring towns. The great period of Milanese expansion, however, did not begin till the reign of Gian Galeazzo Visconti (1378–1402). This cun-

Milan

ning and unscrupulous despot succeeded in conquering nearly the whole of Lombardy and seriously threatened Tuscany and the States of the Church. He also won international recognition for his family by purchasing from the Emperor Wenceslas the title of Duke of Milan (1395) and by marrying his daughter Valentina to Louis of Orléans, the son of Charles V of France. During the next half-century, the sons of the great Visconti, Giovanni Maria (1402–12) and Filippo Maria (1412–47), had to wage an almost constant war against Venice and its allies to defend their heritage. When Filippo Maria died, his duchy included only the western half of Lombardy. He was the last Visconti duke, having left no heirs except an illegitimate daughter who had married the vigorous, common-born *condottiere*, Francesco Sforza. The citizens of Milan took advantage of the situation to re-establish republican government, but they had lost the ability to rule themselves and within three years Sforza had made himself Duke of Milan (1450–66). Four years later he made peace with Venice, and from then on almost to the last year of the century the house of Sforza ruled Milan in comparative peace, making it one of the richest states in Italy, as well as a center of art and learning to which men of genius resorted gladly.

Venice

To the east of Lombardy the great merchant city of Venice, built out over her lagoons, commanded the Adriatic Sea. Since the first revival of medieval commerce, Venice had been one of the richest cities in Europe. Her geographical position made her the natural middleman in the trade between the eastern Mediterranean and western Europe, while the lagoons which cut her off from the mainland gave her a security that enabled her to stand aloof from the tangled feuds of Italian politics. Moreover, unlike the other Italian republics, Venice had evolved a stable system of government that prevented revolutions and party strife. Since the thirteenth century, the mass of the people had been excluded entirely from the government, which was monopolized by an oligarchy of wealthy families. From these the doge (a life president) was elected, as were also the grand council, the senate, and the powerful Council of Ten, who, after 1310, kept check on the doge and senate. This political stability enabled Venice to recover from a desperate struggle with her trade rival, Genoa, in the fourteenth century, whereas Genoa was left so badly shaken that it fell under the domination, first of France, then of Milan. The beginning of the fifteenth century marks a decided turning point in the history of the republic. Alarmed by the Visconti conquest of Lombardy, the Venetians determined to abandon their aloof position among their lagoons and to acquire a landward state that would protect the city from its too powerful neighbor and would keep open the routes to the Alpine passes, which were so necessary to Venetian commerce. After conquering Padua, famous for its ancient university, in 1405, the republic's forces moved on into Visconti territory. The long war which followed was fought chiefly by mercenaries and the superior wealth of the merchant city was the deciding factor. When the final peace treaty was signed with the new Sforza Duke of Milan in 1454, Venice ruled a mainland state in eastern Lombardy and around the head of the Adriatic as large or larger than that of its rival Milan.

Florence

On the western coast of Italy, to the south of Lombardy, lies the district of Tuscany, bounded on the east and south by the States of the Church. All this territory, except Siena, was gradually brought under the rule of the expanding republic of Florence, which conquered even the great mercantile city of Pisa in 1406. Florence had grown tremendously rich from its woolen and other industries. It was also one of the greatest banking centers of Europe and was, besides, the recognized leader of Italy in all branches of culture. But despite their unusually high level of intelligence and the amazingly large number of men of genius to be found among them, the people of Florence had never succeeded in working out a sound republican constitution. All through the fourteenth century and the first part of the fifteenth, the city was a prey to frequent revolutions or party feuds and was dominated most of the time by a small group of wealthy families. This system caused so

COSIMO DE' MEDICI

Above: This painting by Pontormo suggests the tight-lipped competence of the banker who became the real ruler of Florence.

LORENZO DE' MEDICI

Top right: Lorenzo "the Magnificent" had apparently **more grace** of mind than of feature. Portrait by Ghirlandaio.

FRANCESCO SFORZA

Center right: The condottiere who became Duke of Milan was **a** forceful and strong-willed man. Portrait relief by Gian Cristoforo Romano.

CESARE BORGIA

Bottom right: The painter, Palmesano, has caught something of the cruelty, intelligence, and ruthless will that characterized the ill-reputed son of Alexander VI.

FOUR FIFTEENTH-CENTURY RULERS

much disturbance and injustice that in 1434 the majority of the Florentine people accepted without protest the control of their government by Cosimo de' Medici, the head of a great banking family which was to rule the city for the next sixty years. Florence remained a republic in form, but Cosimo and his successors were in reality its despotic rulers, though they held no official title and merely controlled the republican machinery from behind the scenes, rather after the fashion of a modern American municipal boss. On the death of Cosimo after thirty years of wise government that won him the title of *Pater Patriae* (father of his country), he was followed by his son Piero (1464–69). Under Piero's rather uncertain guidance the power of the Medici seemed to be slipping, but it was fully restored by his brilliant son Lorenzo "the Magnificent" (1469–92). With Lorenzo the prestige of the Medici name reached its highest point. He was a man of complex character and versatile genius, at once poet, patron of art and learning, statesman and diplomat. It was in no small measure due to his diplomatic skill that Italy was kept in a state of relative peace during his lifetime. His son Piero, however, proved unfit to carry on the family tradition. His weakness in dealing with the French invasion of 1494 roused the Florentine people to drive the Medici out of the city, though they were to return later.

The States of the Church stretched clear across central Italy and included the Romagna, which extended up the eastern coast almost to the borders of Venetia. This large territory was in theory ruled by the pope, but during the Babylonian Captivity and the schism petty despots had set up practically independent governments in nearly every city except Rome, and even there the popes were none too secure. After the schism was ended by the Council of Constance (1417), the fifteenth-century popes had to face the problem of bringing these independent lords to obedience, no easy task since most of them were professional *condottieri*. Greater progress might have been made had not some of the popes been more eager to replace these despots by members of their own families than to subject them to papal rule. Engrossed in these family and political interests, the Renaissance popes became more worldly until there was little to distinguish them from the other Italian princes. They formed diplomatic alliances, made and broke treaties, and hired armies of *condottieri* for wars of conquest or defense. Like the other princes, too, they kept up a luxurious court and spent huge sums of money on magnificent buildings and in the patronage of artists and scholars. Nicholas V (1447–55), who originated the Vatican Library, and Pius II (1458–64) were enthusiastic devotees of the revived classical literature. The latter, indeed, had gained an international reputation as a classical scholar under his own name of Aeneas Silvius before he became pope, though afterward he did rather repent his devotion to pagan letters. His successor, Paul II (1464–71), had reasonably sound ideals, though he was unable to put them very successfully into practice, but the three following pontificates showed a steady decline in papal morality. Sixtus IV (1471–84) and Innocent VIII (1484–92) had no interest beyond the advancement of their numerous nephews and children, and at the end of the century the infamous Borgia pope, Alexander VI (1492–1503), reduced the papacy to the lowest depths of degradation. The reign of the Borgia, however, did much to strengthen the States of the Church politically. Alexander's vigorous son Cesare Borgia at last succeeded in reducing the greater part of the States to obedience, thus enabling the warlike Julius II (1503–13) to complete the task and build up a strong secular state. Under the latter pope and his successor, the Medicean Leo X (1513–21), the golden age of the artistic Renaissance cast over Rome a sunset light shortly to be followed by gathering shadows.

All of Italy south of the States of the Church was included in the kingdom of Naples, to which at times the kingdom of Sicily was united. Its history during the age of the Renaissance consists almost entirely of dynastic struggles between the different branches of the French family of Anjou and the Spanish family of

Aragon. Here feudalism still survived as an active force, and the intellectual movements of the time made little impression save as importations at the royal court. The Angevin rule in Naples dated back to the conquest of Naples and Sicily from the last Hohenstaufen by Charles of Anjou in 1266. The Sicilian part of the kingdom, however, soon broke away. In 1282, the people of the island rebelled and gave the crown of Sicily to Peter III, King of Aragon, who had married a daughter of the Hohenstaufen Manfred. From that date till the death of Queen Giovanna II of Naples in 1435, the Angevin house ruled in Naples and the Aragonese in Sicily. As Giovanna had died without heirs, the crown of Naples was claimed and won, despite the opposition of the French branch of the family of Anjou, by Alfonso of Aragon and Sicily (1435–58), thus reuniting the two kingdoms during his lifetime. It was divided between his sons, but an Aragonese king was still ruling in Naples when Charles VIII of France revived the old Angevin claim and invaded Italy in 1494.

For a full generation before the beginning of the foreign invasions in 1494, Italy was kept in a more or less peaceful condition by the establishment of a balance of power among the five great states. Diplomatic relations shifted from time to time, but for the most part Milan, Florence, and Naples formed a loose alliance to hold the balance against Venice and the papacy. This alliance was cemented by a series of marriages between the Sforza family and the Aragonese house of Naples, and depended also on the friendship of both with the diplomatic Lorenzo de' Medici. Even the small, though warlike, states of Ferrara, ruled by the family of Este, and Mantua, ruled by the Gonzagas, were drawn into the circle of family marriages. This system, however, could do no more than keep a temporary and uneasy peace within Italy. It offered no basis for union against a foreign enemy. The way for the invasion of Italy by France and the other great European powers was paved by the suspicion and antagonism with which the Italian states regarded one another and by their complete lack of Italian patriotism. But the story of the invasions, which involved all the countries of Europe in one way or another, must be left to a later chapter devoted to the states of Europe as a whole.

Italy on the eve of the invasion

3. THE LITERARY RENAISSANCE

We have already noted in passing that the age of the Renaissance was characterized not only by economic, social, and political changes — increasing wealth, the development of urban society, individualism and the secular spirit, and the rise of despotic states — but also by a great intellectual and artistic activity along new lines, which expressed or resulted from the other changes in Italian society. It is this latter characteristic of the age that is often referred to exclusively when men speak of the Italian Renaissance. Like the former it marks a transition from medieval to modern times, with much that was typically its own.

One of the earliest developments of the new age was the creation of an Italian literature, which gave to Italy a national language that served as a bond of cultural unity never realized in the political field. Some signs of this development may be observed in the last years of the High Middle Ages, in the adaptation to Italian uses of forms taken from the lyric poetry of southern France, and in the synthetic "court language" fostered by Frederick II in Sicily. But the close relation between spoken Italian and the Latin that was the general literary medium, as well as the great variety of dialects represented in the numerous Italian states, had prevented the growth of a universal Italian literary tongue. Literary Italian was largely the creation of three fourteenth-century men, who were at least sufficiently typical of their age to abandon old traditions and, confident in their own creative genius, to strike out new paths for themselves.

Beginnings of Italian literature

Dante, Petrarch, and Boccaccio, these three were the triumvirate who first formed the literary language of modern Italy. All three were Florentine by descent, and they used the Tuscan dialect as the basis of their literary language. In other respects, however, they

The Tuscan triumvirate

were very dissimilar, and the differences in their character are typical of the gradual drift away from medieval modes of thought. The first and greatest of the three, Dante Alighieri (1265–1321), seems to belong more to the Middle Ages than to the Renaissance. The idealized love poetry of his *Vita Nuova* is nearer to the troubadour tradition of medieval Provence than to the worldly and almost pagan loves of the Renaissance poets. Above all, his greatest work, the magnificent *Divine Comedy*, presents, in its breath-taking voyage through Hell, Purgatory, and Paradise, a panoramic survey of all medieval thought. Yet he is not purely medieval. In his confident individualism he foreshadows the coming age, and, despite his interest in religion and philosophy, he was a layman, a member of that secular, urban society that was to fashion the new world.

The second of the triumvirate, Francesco Petrarca or Petrarch (1304–74) was considerably less medieval. His introspective absorption in his own personality, his longing for immortal fame and the intensely human quality of his lyric poems addressed to Laura, together with his passionate interest in pagan antiquity, mark him as a true man of the Renaissance, though his occasional religious reactions and ascetic impulses show that he is not entirely removed from the Middle Ages. His influence on the shaping of Italian poetry, especially on the sonnet and brief *canzonieri*, is second only to Dante's, whose use of the Tuscan dialect he reinforced and purified.

The chief contribution of Giovanni Boccaccio (1313–75) was the shaping of an Italian prose style. Lacking the depth of character and spiritual insight of his two great fellow citizens, this amiable and worldly Florentine burgher was perhaps more typical of his city and his age than either of them. He observed the surface of life with keen enjoyment and described it with a clarity that made the stories of his *Decameron* models for later novelists.

The revival of antiquity The rapid development of Italian literature was cut short with the death of Petrarch and Boccaccio and it was not revived again till the second half of the fifteenth century. The new language could not compete with the amazing revival of interest in the classic literature of ancient Rome. Even Petrarch and Boccaccio were far more interested in this than in their Italian writings, and for two full generations after their death it thrust the "vulgar" tongue completely into the background. The relation between the "revival of antiquity" and the Renaissance has not always been clearly understood. It seems certain, however, that the former was the result rather than the cause of the economic, social, and psychological changes that we have already noted as characteristic of this age, though in turn it influenced and altered their development. The Latin classics were not a discovery of the Renaissance. Many of them were in common use, though chiefly as models of grammatical construction, throughout the Middle Ages. But the deep chasm which separated medieval life and medieval ideals and modes of thought from those of pagan antiquity made any real understanding of the ancient writers almost impossible. In the fourteenth and fifteenth centuries, however, there was growing up in Italy a state of society, essentially urban, secular, and based on wealth, which was not so far removed from the civilization of ancient times, though it was not yet nearly so perfectly formed. It is not surprising, then, that Italians of this age should discover a new meaning in the classics. In these pre-Christian writings they found a culture that seemed to embody everything for which they were blindly groping. They applied themselves, therefore, with devout enthusiasm to the study and imitation of antiquity, inspired by the conviction that the road to progress lay in a return to the glorious past that lay beyond what they considered the Gothic barbarism of the Middle Ages.

The men who devoted their lives to the study of the classics were called humanists, i.e., those who sought to acquire *humanitas*. This word was used **Humanists** in the sense made familiar by Cicero of the mental cultivation which befits a man, particularly as expressed in refined literary form. To the men of the Renaissance it inevitably meant, by implication, a philosophy

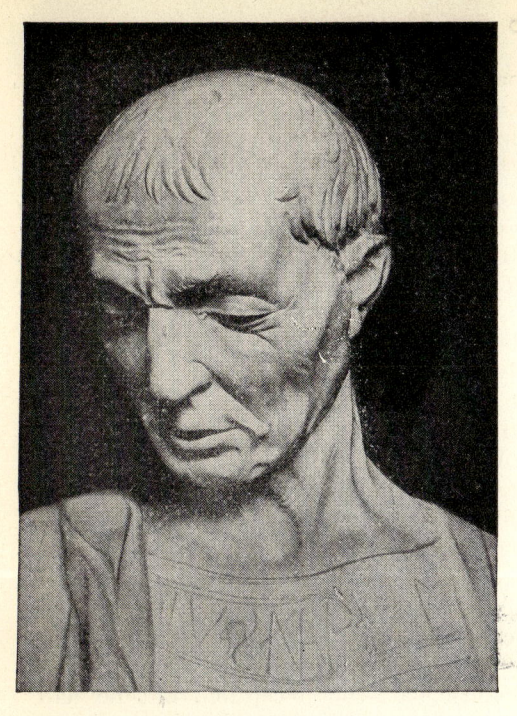

POGGIO BRACCIOLINI

Poggio was a witty and polished writer, a distinguished classical scholar, and collector of manuscripts.

POLIZIANO AND GIULIANO DE' MEDICI

The humanist, Angelo Poliziano, is painted here by Ghirlandaio with one of the sons of Lorenzo de' Medici.

A RENAISSANCE SCHOLAR IN HIS STUDY

The subject of the above painting by Carpaccio is supposed to be Saint Jerome, the humanist among the Church Fathers; but the scene is obviously contemporary.

of life and one in strong contrast to the preoccupation with the things of the spirit and the future world that had played so large a part in the learned writings of the Middle Ages. It both expressed and strengthened the secular tendencies of the new age. The humanists remained Christian in faith, some of them devoutly so; but few of them escaped the influence for better or for worse of pagan philosophy and morals.

The humanists were indefatigable workers. They were driven by their reverence for antiquity to undertake the double task of restoring the works of classical authors to their original form, while at the same time perfecting their own knowledge of classical Latin style, including the details of spelling, inflection, syntax, scansion, and so forth, which had been almost forgotten during the Middle Ages. The only copies of the ancient authors they could find were the work of medieval scribes who were often careless and ignorant of the niceties of style. Every manuscript was filled with errors. The humanists had, therefore, to learn the rules of classic style from the study of imperfect manuscripts and then to apply that knowledge as they acquired it to the correction of the errors. This could be accomplished only by constant and painstaking comparison of all the manuscripts available.

Restoration of classical Latin

This necessity led to a frantic search for old manuscripts. Petrarch led the hunt and inspired his friend Boccaccio and others to take it up. Monastery libraries were ransacked and every new fragment was hailed with delirious enthusiasm. Often the searchers found that they were too late, for many old monastic foundations had degenerated and their libraries had been allowed to moulder from neglect. Boccaccio tells us how he sat down and wept amidst the wreckage of priceless manuscripts in Saint Benedict's old monastery at Monte Cassino. For three generations and more the search continued. Fortunes were spent and emissaries sent to the farthest corners of Europe. One of the most fortunate of the discoverers was the Florentine humanist Poggio (1380–1459), who for forty years was attached to the

Search for manuscripts

papal court and made good use of the embassies on which he was sent to hunt manuscripts in the countries north of the Alps. Merchants, princes, and popes shared the scholar's enthusiasm and spent vast sums in the collection of libraries. It was they, too, who rewarded with generous patronage the humanists who wrote in the newly recovered classical style.

The revival of ancient Greek literature in Italy came later than that of classical Latin. The knowledge of Greek had died out almost completely in the West and it was hard to find instructors who could teach even the rudiments of the language. The beginning of the revival may be dated from 1397, when a competent Greek scholar from Constantinople, Manuel Chrysoloras, was persuaded to come to Florence to teach. He stayed only three years, though he had been given the most flattering reception, but he had done enough to give the Italian humanists a start. After that they studied Greek almost as enthusiastically as the ancient Latin. The ecumenical council of Florence in 1438–39, which brought a host of Greek scholars to that city, gave a further impetus to Greek studies. A few years later, in 1453, the conquest of Constantinople by the Turks drove great numbers of Byzantine refugees to seek a living in Italy by teaching or copying and translating Greek manuscripts. The humanists of Italy eagerly absorbed all the Greek classics, but they reserved their greatest enthusiasm for the philosophy of Plato, now made available for the first time in its original form. Cosimo de' Medici found time in the midst of his manifold duties to found a Platonic Academy in Florence. There, in the later years of the fifteenth century, the learned Ficino (1433–99) and the brilliant Pico della Mirandola (1463–94) taught a synthesis of Platonic philosophy and Christian theology that was to have a profound influence on the humanists of northern Europe.

The revival of Greek

A new era in Italian humanism and literature opened with the generation who were the contemporaries of that most liberal and understanding of patrons, the magnificent Lorenzo de' Medici (1449–92). Having

The age of Lorenzo de' Medici

learned good classical Latin and Greek in childhood, the men of this generation enjoyed a wider horizon and displayed greater originality than their predecessors who had had to struggle with the task of learning and restoring the two ancient languages. They were prepared to use the classic tongues to express the thought garnered from the ancient treasury and adapted to the uses of their own age, and they were free to turn their attention to the revival of their own native language which had been allowed to lapse since the days of the triumvirate. Lorenzo himself set the example by writing verses of first-rate quality in Italian, and under his influence the scholar-poet Poliziano (1454–94) produced highly polished poems in all three languages. Thereafter, Italian was used more and more widely, until the generation after Lorenzo raised it to full equality with Latin and Greek, dignifying it with the epic poetry of Ariosto (1474–1533) and the clean-cut prose of the Florentine historians Machiavelli (1469–1527) and Guicciardini (1482–1540).

The critical spirit

We cannot leave the humanists without mentioning one important by-product of their intense interest in antiquity — namely, the development of an independent critical spirit. They were often as prone to accept without question the validity of anything found in the ancient writers as their medieval predecessors had been to accept the authority of the Bible, the Fathers, and Aristotle. But the change from one authority to another had given them a new point of view, and the training they received in comparing, correcting, and restoring the manuscript copies of the classics had furnished them with a sound critical method. This method of literary and historical criticism, detached from reverence for religious authority, was used by the Roman humanist Lorenzo Valla (1405?–57) to good effect in proving that the "Donation of Constantine," on which the papacy had based a large part of its claims to secular power, was a ninth- or tenth-century forgery. The Christian humanists of the north were later to use the same critical spirit in a much more far-reaching attack on medieval religious institutions.

4. THE ARTISTIC RENAISSANCE

As in literature, so in art. The social and intellectual changes that were taking place in Italy during the age of the Renaissance were reflected by changes in spirit and form in all the arts, and these were accompanied by a change in the character and status of the artist.

Individualism and the secular spirit in art

The medieval artist had been typical of his age. He was a member of a corporation — nearly all medieval artists were guildsmen — and he worked within the traditions and rules of his craft. He was regarded, and regarded himself, as an artisan. He no doubt took an honest pride in his work, but he was scarcely more likely to attach his name to it than a carpenter or an armorer would be. Being practically anonymous, he had little incentive to break away from the traditional methods used by his fellows, nor, probably, was he free to do so. Moreover, the purpose of his art was most often religious, not so much because religion played such a large part in his life that it was bound to inspire his work as because the church was the wealthiest and most frequent patron of his services. Here, too, he was limited by tradition, for the character of religious art had become highly conventionalized and he was not encouraged to make innovations or to copy too closely natural beauty, which was always suspected by the medieval church. Now, in the Late Middle Ages and the Renaissance, the development of a wealthy educated secular society, with a keen interest in art as it portrayed the beauties of this world, gradually changed the status of the artist and the conditions affecting his art. The artist of outstanding genius was in great demand. He might receive from princes, merchants, and bankers rewards far beyond those of the ordinary artisan. His name and the individual character of his work became assets to be highly valued. Working for men who were losing their respect for tradition and who were more interested in this world than the next, the artist was free to strike out along new lines

GIOTTO: THE KISS OF JUDAS

Above: Giotto is generally considered the earliest of the great Renaissance painters. This is a detail from a fresco in Padua.

LEONARDO DA VINCI: MONA LISA

Above: Leonardo was one of the great masters of the high point of Renaissance art. The Mona Lisa, one of his most famous works, now hangs in the Louvre.

BOTTICELLI: PRIMAVERA

Below: Few painters have possessed the grace and delicate charm of Botticelli, here shown at its best in his imaginative conception of Spring.

MICHELANGELO: GIULIANO DE' MEDICI

The marble figure above shows Renaissance sculpture at its height.

GHIBERTI: THE SACRIFICE OF ABRAHAM

This scene from the bronze doors of the Florentine cathedral demonstrates Ghiberti's ability to get the effects of painting in sculptured relief.

DONATELLO: GATTAMELATA

In this great bronze equestrian statue, the first of its kind, Donatello portrayed one of the condottieri with vivid realism.

and to develop his individual genius to its fullest extent in the reproduction of beauty for its own sake. Even when he was employed by the church, this was becoming increasingly true, for the ecclesiastical princes of Renaissance Italy shared the growing secular spirit of their age.

Of the major arts, painting was the most characteristic of the Renaissance and was developed to the highest degree of perfection. Here the Italian love of color and natural beauty found its fullest expression. Until almost the end of the period, Florence was the greatest center of painting, as of literature and the other arts. There, in the opening years of the fourteenth century, Giotto (1276–1336) took a long stride away from the stiffly formalized technique of earlier religious painting toward a greater naturalism. Throughout the rest of the century his successors were moving steadily in the direction he had indicated, though their work was still mostly religious and they had not yet acquired the technical knowledge or skill required to accomplish their full objective. The fifteenth century was a period of adventurous experimentation and rapid progress in technique. Driven by the desire to copy natural beauty or the outward appearance of their fellow men as accurately as possible, the fifteenth-century artists mastered the laws of perspective and shadow, discovered how to give their figures the appearance of roundness and depth, and greatly improved the methods of blending colors. The art of this period was almost entirely secular, even when the subject was religious. Portrait painting, the result of that desire to be remembered by posterity which all the great or wealthy men of the Renaissance felt strongly, became for the first time a fashionable form of art. We have not space to mention all the fifteenth-century painters, but it would be unforgivable to ignore entirely the names of the three Florentine painters, Masaccio (1402–29?), who in his brief life at the beginning of the century set a standard of technical perfection far ahead of his generation, the worldly-minded friar, Fra Lippo Lippi (1406–69), whose love of realism led him to paint portraits of his fellow citizens in scenes of the Holy Family, and Botticelli (1447–1510), whose graceful paintings show most clearly the influence of classical paganism on the thought and art of the age.

After the artists of this age of experimentation and naturalism had worked out the necessary rules of technique came the golden age of Renaissance painting with the work of the great masters who were able to use that technical knowledge and skill as a means for the expression of their artistic conceptions rather than to seek it as an end in itself. The first of these was the Florentine Leonardo da Vinci (1452–1519), the most versatile man of his age. He was a master of all the arts, a poet and musician as well as a practical engineer and an experimental scientist of the first rank. In this enigmatic genius there was a driving curiosity that impelled him to discover what lay beneath the surface of things. His Mona Lisa, whose mysterious smile has puzzled and fascinated generations of critics, and the disciples grouped about Christ in the Last Supper are studies in character as well as works of impelling beauty. The work of Raphael (1483–1520) is not so profound, but no one surpassed him in the perfection of his coloring or the serene harmony that pervades all his paintings. Though he died in early middle age, he produced an amazingly large number of finished works, many of them under the patronage of the popes Julius II and Leo X, including the marvelous Madonna for the Sistine Chapel and the School of Athens. It was Julius II, too, who patronized some of the best work of Michelangelo (1475–1564), having persuaded him to turn from sculpture to painting for the decoration of the Sistine Chapel. The result was a magnificent fresco, covering the whole roof of the chapel, which secures the place of Michelangelo for all time among the master painters. In it, as in everything he did, one can see the tragic driving force, the grandeur of design, and the deep religious emotion that make Michelangelo unique among the artists of the Renaissance.

The development of sculpture followed in most respects the same general lines as did that of painting. In the Middle Ages it had

Sculpture

shared the religious and corporate character of the other arts, having been used mainly for the decoration of churches and cathedrals. Beginning with Niccolo Pisano before the end of the thirteenth century, Renaissance sculptors gradually worked away from Gothic conventions toward a more realistic copying of nature. As in painting, the fifteenth century was a period of experiment and technical progress, influenced to a greater extent than was true of painting by imitation of classical models, for many ancient statues were now being disinterred and studied with keen interest. Sculpture was rapidly securing recognition as an independent art devoted to secular uses and freed from its subordination to religious architecture, though many artists, like Ghiberti (1378–1455), whose bronze gates in bas-relief for the doors of the cathedral baptistery were the wonder of all Florence, still worked on the decoration of churches. The masterly equestrian statue of the *condottiere* Gattamelata by the Florentine Donatello (1386?–1466) is one of the best examples of the new independent and secular type of sculpture. The golden age of sculpture coincides with that of painting, and here again the powerful figure of Michelangelo towers above the other masters. In this, his most natural medium, his best work, including the noble David, the deeply religious Pietà, and the magnificent tombs of the Medici, were done in his native Florence before and after the years with Julius in Rome.

The changing conditions and ideals of the Renaissance inevitably brought changes in architectural style, often resulting in buildings of great beauty. Yet it is doubtful if the changes mark a clear improvement.

Architecture

Though perhaps better suited to the spirit and needs of their own age, the Renaissance buildings lack the harmony and grandeur of the medieval Gothic cathedrals. In the experimental period of the fifteenth century, individualism ran riot as each architect strove to adapt the antique Roman and medieval Gothic types to contemporary needs, while at the same time expressing his own originality. Of these, Brunelleschi (1377–1446), who built the churches of San Lorenzo and Santo Spirito in Florence, was perhaps the most successful, but it remained for the Lombard architect, Bramante (1444–1514), who drew the original plans for Saint Peter's Church in Rome, later altered by Michelangelo, to evolve out of the old traditions a really harmonious style suitable to his own age.

Having reached its golden age, the artistic and intellectual Renaissance did not last long. It faded with the passing of the peculiar social and economic conditions that had produced it. The loss of political liberty through conquest by foreign powers, the loss of intellectual freedom through the action of the Counter-Reformation, and the decline of economic prosperity due to the shifting of trade routes to the west sapped the energy of Italy. But meanwhile the spirit of the Renaissance had crossed the Alps to exert a great influence on the culture of the North.

26

The Waning of the Middle Ages and the Renaissance in the North

THE PERIOD OF TRANSITION from medieval to modern civilization began later in northern Europe than it did in Italy and once begun, it developed more slowly and along somewhat different lines. For in the north, feudalism was more firmly entrenched behind its moats and castle walls; religion lay closer to the hearts of men far removed from the pagan beauty of the sun-drenched Italian land; and in the quadrangles of Oxford and the dusty halls of the Sorbonne, the ghosts of Thomas Aquinas and Duns Scotus walked undisturbed, long after Italian scholars had deserted them to follow after the still older ghosts of ancient Greece and Rome. But throughout the whole of northern Europe, the same leaven was at work as had transformed society in the more prosperous south. Here, too, commerce and industry were bringing wealth and with it thriving urban centers and an aggressive, self-confident new middle class, whose energy was to disrupt medieval society. Yet the product of the transformation would not be altogether the same as in Italy, for in the north cities were fewer and farther between, and the new society would find its focus in the centralized territorial state rather than in the city.

The fifteenth century and the early sixteenth witnessed the gradual disappearance of many medieval characteristics in society, religion, and culture, and the contemporary growth of much that we recognize as modern. The old and the new existed side by side or inextricably interwoven, and the old gave place to the new so slowly that major changes are discernible only through the lengthened perspective of the years. Men of the fifteenth century did not know that the Middle Ages were dying. They knew only that times were not what they had been; that graybearded men bewailed the passing of the good old days, while aggressive youngsters who had studied in Florence or Bologna spoke slightingly of Gothic barbarism; and that there was now something very like contempt mixed with the envy on the face of the stolid burgher as he watched the gaily dressed knights passing the windows of his countinghouse.

1. DECAY OF MEDIEVAL INSTITUTIONS

In the fifteenth century, feudalism was fading fast. Its economic and social forms might survive for three centuries and more, but of its independent political power there remained only a shadow by the beginning of the sixteenth century. As in Italy, it was the power of money, steadily increasing with the growth of commerce and industry, that wrecked the older forms of society. But in the great territorial states of the north, the influence of money was less direct, for there

Decay of feudalism

it worked through the growing power of the rulers of the states, and it was the state that absorbed feudalism into itself.

All through the Middle Ages, the political independence of the nobles and their privileged position in society had depended in large part on their exclusive monopoly of the arts of warfare. So long as their castle walls remained a sure defense against all enemies, so long as their expensive weapons and armor, their great war-horses and the skill that comes only from long years of training gave them an indisputable superiority over common men in battle, so long as prince and people must depend on them for the defense of the state, for so long was the position of the nobles at the apex of society secure. But in the fifteenth century, the introduction of gunpowder as an effective instrument of war and siege placed a weapon in the hands of common men which enabled them to meet the heavy armed knights on relatively even terms. At the same time, the increase in the amount of money available through taxation or loans gave to the rulers of the states a tremendous advantage over the less wealthy nobles in the use of this new weapon. The kings of great states like England, France, and Spain, and even the princes of smaller territorial states like those of Germany, could now raise and maintain armies, composed largely of common soldiers, against which the nobles were helpless. As early as the fourteenth century, the English kings had used the plebeian long bow to good effect and had demonstrated the superiority of a disciplined army over a feudal levy on the fields of Crécy and Poitiers. The use of gunpowder made the state army a universal institution. Unable to ignore or oppose their king, the nobles enlisted in the royal army and took the king's pay. They still fought, such being their nature, but they fought at the bidding of the twin powers of monarchy and money.

Nobles lose monopoly of fighting

In yet another way, money — or the lack of it — was working to deprive the nobles of their cherished independence. While the business men, who were beginning to discover the profitable uses of capital, and the monarchs, who were acquiring greater powers of taxation, were growing wealthier, the nobles as a general rule were becoming poorer, for the feudal system had never been designed to produce fluid wealth. The increase in the amount of money in circulation was having the inevitable effect of raising prices, while the income of the nobles, based on hereditary rights and immemorial custom, remained relatively the same. To make matters worse, their pride forced them to maintain their social position by an ostentatious display of luxury and pomp that would have been ruinous to men of much larger incomes. Confronted by failing resources and rising expenses, the nobles were forced to seek aid from the royal purse. And the kings were well content to aid them by the gift of pensions, sinecure offices at court, or positions in the army and church, thereby establishing a system of patronage that made the nobles more than ever dependent upon them.

Economic decline of the nobles

Meanwhile, the same forces that were bringing about the ruin of political feudalism were also causing the break-up of medieval institutions in the non-feudal society of the towns and cities. There the corporate society which centered about the guilds and the city government was slowly going to pieces, to give way to a new individualistic social order. The social and economic structure of the towns in the Middle Ages had been designed to meet the needs of a still primitive system of commerce and industry, maintaining a precarious existence in the midst of a disorganized state and a hostile society. The men of each trade and the burghers of each city had been forced to adopt a strong corporate solidarity for mutual protection. That necessity was now less evident. The growing power of the central governments offered adequate protection, while at the same time the expanding volume of business and new opportunities for the accumulation of wealth tempted men to break away from the restrictions which the guild or the city government had placed upon individual enterprise in the interests of the whole community. Within and without the guilds, the modern methods of capitalism were slowly

Decay of the guild system

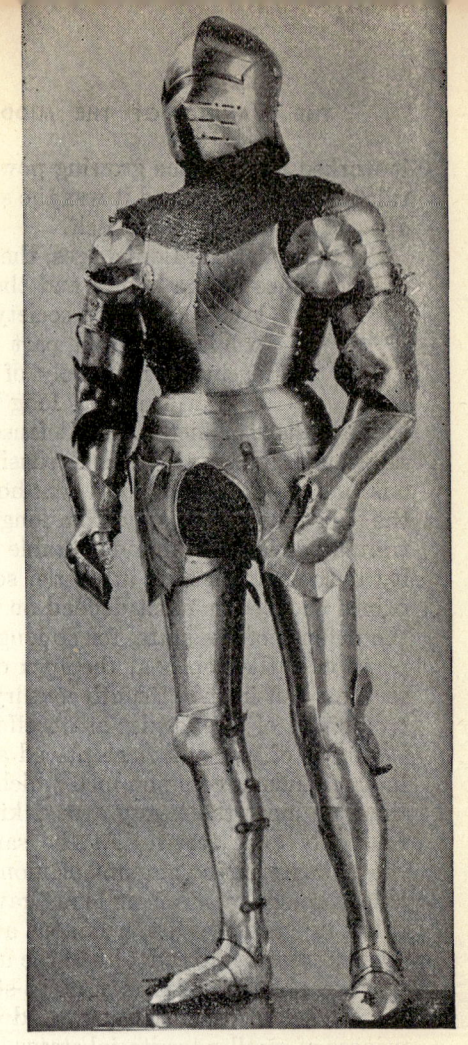

A HUNTING PARTY IN THE FIFTEENTH CENTURY

Upper left: As the nobles lost power and became courtiers, they also spent money more recklessly to maintain their social pretensions.

A KNIGHT'S ARMOR, ABOUT 1480

Upper right: Full plate armor, the product of highly skilled workmanship, was the knight's ineffective answer to the invention of gunpowder.

THE JOUST

Left: The tournament became an expensive and highly artificial game in the period when chivalry was ceasing to be an effective part of actual warfare.

THE DECLINE OF FEUDALISM AND CHIVALRY

but surely triumphing over the corporate methods of the Middle Ages. The economic and social revolution which this change brought about, dividing the commercial and industrial class into two widely separated classes of proletarian laborers and capitalist employers, was not completed during the period we are discussing, but its effects were already visible. In the most influential, because most wealthy, class of city dwellers in northern Europe, something like the same shift from corporate consciousness to self-confident individualism that we have noted in a more extreme form in Italy was already taking place.

Among the other medieval institutions whose strength was decaying during the Later Middle Ages, the universal church which for centuries had held sway over a united Christendom was rapidly declining in power and prestige. In a great many ways the fourteenth and fifteenth centuries were disastrous ones for the Catholic Church. The papacy, with its wide claims to supremacy over all Catholic Christians, had come into violent conflict with the growing power of the centralized territorial states and had been defeated. National interests had combined with moral disapproval to break the vast authority that the church had wielded during the High Middle Ages. The fourteenth century witnessed the tragedy of Boniface VIII, the Babylonian Captivity, the scandal of the Great Schism, the growth of a strong anti-clerical sentiment, the destructive criticisms of William of Occam and Marsiglio of Padua and the still more telling attacks on the sacramental system brought forward by John Wyclif and John Huss. The fifteenth century, in turn, opened with the menace to papal authority of the conciliar movement, and when that had passed, the popes were left in an anomalous position as Italian princes, whose power over secular governments had vanished and whose control of the church itself was limited by the rulers of the great states.

Decay of the universal church

2. RISE OF THE CENTRALIZED TERRITORIAL STATES

From the foregoing summary of the decay of medieval institutions, social, economic, and religious, during the Later Middle Ages and the beginning of modern times, one fact emerges clearly. While other and older institutions were crumbling, the centralized territorial states — in some cases one may almost call them national states — were rising to ever-greater power and importance, aided by the power of money and supported by the moneyed burgher class whose business interests demanded order and strong government. This is a fact that deserves a little further consideration in a general way. We shall see more clearly how its final steps were worked out in detail in the following chapter.

The decline of political feudalism left the rulers of the territorial states without serious rivals. Economic and social factors had contributed to this result, but from the constitutional point of view it was accomplished by a double process of consolidation of territory and centralization of governmental authority in the hands of more or less absolute princes. The growth of France as a united monarchical state is the most perfect example of this dual process. There one can see clearly how the kings used both means to transform an indirect feudal lordship into a direct royal government over the whole state. Generation after generation, they consolidated the territory under their direct rule until every fief in the kingdom had been incorporated into the royal domain. Meanwhile, by constantly enforcing their royal rights so far as they were able, they had gradually acquired the power to deal directly with all the people of the state, not merely with their immediate vassals. During the Hundred Years' War they won the right to tax all their subjects directly, going over the heads of the feudal lords. For a time the States General had seemed a possible rival to royal power, but when feudalism collapsed, the estates proved too weak to exercise an effective check on the authority of the king. With variations due to differences in their past history, most of the other states of Europe were undergoing a similar development as the Later Middle Ages drew to a close.

Centralization and consolidation

The consolidation of the territorial states

carried with it the centralization of economic as well as political control. During the Middle Ages commerce and industry had been controlled by the individual cities, because the city government was the only power to which the burghers could look for adequate protection. Each city was an isolated economic unit, presenting a united front to all outsiders. However, as the central government of the state grew strong enough to preserve order, this dependence on the city ceased to be necessary. And because the state government was stronger than any city government and covered a much larger territory, the burghers found that it could be of far greater service to them, especially to those whose new individual interests ran counter to the traditional restrictions that were a part of the old city system. The central government, on the other hand, needed the support of the wealthy business men on whom the prosperity of the state so largely depended. They must be taught to depend on the state for aid and guidance. It was therefore to the mutual advantage of both to transfer the control of commerce and industry from the city to the state, thereby ending the economic isolation of the cities and concentrating the interests of the most powerful economic class on the state as a whole.

Economic control

This tendency toward centralization and the resulting unification of the interests of the people could not but have an effect, quite as important if less tangible, on the culture and sentiments of the people. As the concept of the united state loomed larger before their vision, local traditions and local interests waned. Differences in speech and custom in different parts of the state gradually became less pronounced. In short, the strengthening of the centralized state was accompanied by the growth of a common culture that was national in scope rather than local. The invention of printing in the middle of the fifteenth century by facilitating the circulation of books in the national tongue gave a great impetus to the movement, but more time than the period we are now considering would be needed to establish it completely.

National culture

Still the beginnings of the tendency can already be seen. Cause and effect, however, are not always too clear and there was probably more involved in the growth of national cultures than the mere development of centralized states. The appearance of a certain amount of national culture in Italy and Germany, where the whole country was not included in a strong centralized state, are exceptions worth noting.

We are on a little firmer ground when we turn to the consideration of the growth of national sentiment or, at least, of a growing feeling of loyalty to the state. Here Italy is no exception to the rule, for the Italian's loyalty was more strongly attached to his state than to Italy, and what national consciousness there was in Germany, over and above the immediate loyalty to the individual state, may be accounted for by the tradition of a united German state in the past. In the other countries, where cultural and political boundaries more or less coincided, the incipient growth of national consciousness or sentiment clearly followed the development of a strong state. In part, no doubt, it was the natural result of the established fact that the state was now the all-important unit and its ruler the power to whom all men turned for protection and government. That one was a Norman became less important than that one was a Frenchman in proportion as the feudal government of Normandy was merged with the royal government of France. The great international wars of the fourteenth and fifteenth centuries and the early sixteenth also played their part in building up national sentiment, for war is always a powerful stimulus to patriotism. Whereas wars in the Middle Ages had been mostly feudal and had tended to strengthen local loyalties, these later wars developed a national character. The Hundred Years' War, with its memories of Crécy, Agincourt, and Joan of Arc, made Frenchmen conscious that they were Frenchmen and Englishmen conscious that they were not Frenchmen, and therein lay the seeds at least of modern nationalism.

National sentiment

So far we have emphasized the triumph of the territorial state over local interests and the resulting expansion of the people's horizon from the narrow confines of the fief or city to the larger circle of the state. But that is only part of the story. Equally important is the contraction of common interest from the larger unity of Catholic Christendom to the smaller one of the individual state. For in the Middle Ages, localism had existed side by side with an internationalism unparalleled in modern times. The two are not mutually exclusive. To the man of narrow local loyalties, all people from outside his little circle are foreigners. It matters little whether they come from his own state or another. Feudalism had recognized no national frontiers. A Norman lord would do homage as cheerfully to an English as to a French king. Trade, too, was as much international as local. Merchants wandered freely from one country to another, attending the open fairs and being judged by the common merchant law. The only exclusive monopoly they encountered was that of the city governments or guilds, and that operated equally against natives of the country. Finally, the church was a great international institution that held all men of Catholic Europe together in the common brotherhood of the Christian faith and in common obedience to its laws. It gave to Europe a common culture and in the Latin tongue a common language for education and learning. This international unity was broken up by the rise of the centralized states. In so far as the political, economic and cultural interests of the people were concentrated on the state, they ceased to be international. Even the church was falling under the control of state governments. The state was too powerful to tolerate particular interests within itself or to admit the interference within its borders of any outside power. It is this fact that goes far to explain the breaking away from the ancient church of so many of the northern states during the Protestant Reformation.

Break-up of the unity of Christendom

3. THE NEW PIETY IN THE NORTH

Despite the waning power of the universal church, however, the people of northern Europe were not lacking in piety. Corruption in the church and the failure of its authority were not necessarily accompanied by a decline in popular religion, though that was doubtless often the case. On the contrary, much of the criticism of the clergy, the opposition to the papacy, and the attacks on the sacramental system which we have noted in the fourteenth and fifteenth centuries were inspired by a genuine piety that engendered a sincere moral indignation against manifest abuses, and only incidentally served the interests of the state governments. At the same time there was a powerful movement of awakening piety in Germany and the Netherlands which was to have a strong influence on both the Renaissance and the Reformation in the north. But it was not piety of a kind to strengthen the loyalty of the people to the organized church of their day. This movement originated with a group of religious mystics who, though orthodox sons of the church, cherished ideals that were not altogether in keeping with its contemporary practices, and who strove to transcend without breaking away from its mechanical organization.

Germany and the Netherlands

To describe or analyze pure mysticism is almost impossible. There have always been mystics and probably there always will be, but they themselves have never been able to describe their emotions in a way fully understandable to the practical mind. Perhaps it will be sufficient to say that, to the mystic, religion is a purely personal aspiration of the individual soul seeking unity and harmony with the divine power. In that ecstatic feeling of unity with God and harmony with His universe the mystic finds his supreme happiness. For our purposes, the important effects of a revival of mysticism at this time are, first, the increase in fervid piety in an age that had begun to take religion for granted, and second, a growing indifference to the sacramental system in an age when that system, though of vital importance to the authority of the church, was becoming formal and mechanical in its operation. The mystics did not doubt the necessity of the sacraments as had the Lollards and other heretics of the age. But they did place less

The mystics

**HOLBEIN: THE MADONNA OF BURGO-
MASTER MEYER**

*The portrait of the donor and his family
add a secular note to a religious subject.*

DURER: ADORATION OF THE MAGI

*Style and technique suggest the influence of
the Italian upon the northern Renaissance.*

LUCAS VAN LEYDEN: THE CHESS PLAYERS

*The genre scene above is an early example of
a type much practiced in the Netherlands.*

DURER: PORTRAIT OF A LADY

*Durer's portraits have a timeless quality. One
might expect to meet this lady anywhere.*

ART OF THE NORTHERN RENAISSANCE

SIR THOMAS MORE, HUMANIST AND CHANCELLOR OF HENRY VIII

This portrait by Holbein suggests the firm will that made him a martyr, if not the wit and amiability that made him Erasmus's dearest friend.

DESIDERIUS ERASMUS OF ROTTERDAM

This Holbein portrait of the Prince of the Humanists shows him in a very characteristic pose. Note the keen, fine-cut features, the nose as sharp as its owner's wit, and the general suggestion of a strong intelligence.

THE GUTENBERG BIBLE

The invention of printing was an immense aid to the spread of lay learning in the North. Above are pages from the first printed book. Note the exquisite workmanship.

THE LITERARY RENAISSANCE IN THE NORTH

emphasis upon their importance. Their aims were too personal, too immediate, for them to place much reliance on formalized observances, or to feel the need of having a priest to act as an intermediary between the individual soul and God.

The new mysticism began in Germany. Its creator was a German Dominican friar, Master Eckhart (1260–1327), and to him the movement owed its philosophy. Its influence on popular piety, however, came through the work of one of his disciples, John Tauler (c. 1300–61), who preached to the common people and gained a wide hearing. Unlike most preachers of the time, he did not represent salvation as the aim and end of religion, but emphasized the love of God as an end in itself. To this end any man, no matter how poor or ignorant, might aspire through simple faith, prayer, and purity of life. This was a practical mysticism within the comprehension of the masses. He was the leader of an organization or society, fittingly known as the Friends of God, which did a great deal to raise the standards of German morality and piety. The essence of the mystics' teaching was gathered together toward the end of the fourteenth century in a little anonymous volume which Luther, who admitted its great influence on his thought, named *The German Theology*.

Mysticism in Germany

In the Netherlands, mysticism flowered later and exercised a more direct influence on the thought of the new age. Here as in Germany it produced one great book, the immortal *Imitation of Christ* of Thomas à Kempis, written in the first quarter of the fifteenth century and still popular after more than five hundred years. The doctrine of this most widely read expression of the new piety, or *devotio moderna* as it was called, was very simple: he who would be a true Christian must live as Christ lived, think as he thought, and imitate him in every possible way. It was an ideal with which the church could not quarrel, yet it ignored the elaborate system, whereby the clergy were made responsible for the salvation of men. In the Netherlands, too, the mystics formed a society, devoted to public service, known as the

The Dutch mystics

Brethren of the Common Life. Its founders, Gerard Groote (1340–84) and Florentius Radewyn (1350–1400), had great faith in enlightened education as an aid to true religion, and under their guidance the Brethren devoted themselves to the education of boys. Throughout the fifteenth century, the schools of the Brethren, especially the large school at Deventer in Holland, were important instruments in spreading the new learning of the northern Renaissance, and did much to shape the ideals of many of the most influential humanists.

4. THE RENAISSANCE CROSSES THE ALPS

In northern Europe the Middle Ages died more slowly than in Italy. The new economic and social developments appeared later and in less concentrated form than in the crowded urban society of the south. It is not surprising, then, that the intellectual Renaissance, which was inspired by the revival of the classics to meet the intellectual needs of the new society, did not cross the Alps until a century after Petrarch and Boccaccio had begun to spread the gospel of antiquity in Italy. And when the Renaissance did cross the Alps, it changed its character to fit the character and interests of a different people with a different past. The Latin spirit had not survived in the Germanic north as it had in Italy; and in these last years of the transitional age, there was a deeper piety and a more profound preoccupation with religion than was common among the more secularly minded Italians. Hence, when the north turned to the classics with new zeal, under the influence of the Italian Renaissance, it was more indifferent to the pagan spirit of the ancient writers. Humanists of the north might revolt against the restrictions and abuses of the medieval church, but they remained Christian, and that not merely in form, but with a deep moral and religious interest as well. They sought in the Latin and Greek classics a more humane morality and philosophy than the scholasticism of the Middle Ages had provided, but they did not ignore the Christian past. Like the Italian humanists, they turned for guidance to antiquity, but it was to Christian as well as to classical antiquity, to the Bible and the Fathers of the church, to Jerome and Augustine, not less than to Cicero and Virgil.

The first generation of northern humanists, whose activity falls within the second half of the fifteenth century, were teachers. They were far-wandering men, who had been to Italy to study and who returned to their own people to share the intellectual treasure they had discovered there. Few of them wrote anything of note, for their acquisition of the new learning was too recent to be thoroughly digested. They were pioneers, breaking the ground and sowing the seed against the time of harvest. Rudolph Agricola (c. 1444–85), aptly named "the educator of Germany," was characteristic of this generation both in his eager teaching of the ancient tongues and in his deep piety. It was from him that Alexander Hegius (1433–98), the influential head master of the school of the Brethren of the Common Life at Deventer, first learned Greek. At first the old universities, with their long-established curricula, would have nothing to do with these wandering innovators. The new learning spread much more easily in the cities, among the wealthy burghers who had leisure for the pursuit of culture and the financial resources to support and encourage scholars. They had no vested interest in the old type of education as had the university faculties. Eventually, however, even the universities were forced to recognize the new learning. By the end of the century, the humanists had gained a foothold in the faculties of arts and were waging a bitter fight against the champions of medieval tradition.

The early teachers

The spread of the new classical learning in the north was greatly aided by the rapidly increasing use of printed books during the second half of the fifteenth century, which followed the invention of printing, generally attributed to John Gutenberg of Mayence about the year 1447. Part of the technique of printing was known and used before the time of Gutenberg's epoch-making invention. A few short pamphlets or books had been printed by means of wood-cut blocks, the whole contents of a page, usually a picture and a few lines of text, being cut on a single wooden block. But this method was expensive, awkward, and wasteful. The blocks were difficult to make, could be used for only one work, and were soon worn out. The important part of Gutenberg's innovation, which made printing really practicable, was the use of movable metal type. Each letter was cast in a matrix or model. Any number could be cast from the same matrix, thus making the production of type inexpensive and guaranteeing uniformity. The type could then be assembled in a case in any desired order, and after the book was printed could be taken apart or "distributed" and used again and again for other books.

Invention of printing

The effects of the printing press on the general intellectual development of Europe can scarcely be overestimated. Its immediate result for the spread of humanism in the north was to place the classics and the writings of Christian antiquity at the disposal of all who could read them, at a moderate price, and to afford the humanists themselves a far wider audience than would have been possible before. Hitherto all books had been written by hand and were often inaccurate as well as expensive. Even in Italy manuscripts were scarce and dear. In the north, where there were proportionately fewer wealthy bibliophiles and the distance between libraries was greater, the study of the ancient writings would have presented enormous difficulties. Within a few years after the invention of printing, however, the number of books in existence had increased tremendously and the cost of each would average less than an eighth of that of a manuscript copy. The new technique spread with amazing rapidity to all parts of Europe. Before the end of the fifteenth century, there were more than a thousand printers whose names are still known, and more than thirty thousand editions had been published.

Its effects

The last decade of the fifteenth century and the first two of the sixteenth marked the high tide of northern humanism. These years witnessed the mature labors of the second generation of humanists, who in their youth had entered into the full inheritance

Second generation of humanists

of classical and Christian antiquity. Under its inspiration they strove to reform contemporary education and religious thought and practice. They prepared the way for the Protestant Reformation, only to find many of the reforms, for which they had been working, overwhelmed in a sea of dogmatic argument and partisan passions.

These northern humanists had all the reverence for antiquity, and all the scorn for the Middle Ages, that was characteristic of their Italian brethren. Indeed, reaction against medievalism may be taken as the keynote of their thought. The charm and purity of the ancient Latin style made them look with contempt upon the crabbed Latin of the medieval theologians, whose spiritual descendants still ruled in most of the schools and universities. The sane and well-balanced attitude toward life in this world, which they found in the classics, appealed to them more strongly than the one-sided, other-worldly philosophy of the medieval scholastic doctors. But above all, and this was their unique contribution, they found in the Scriptures and the writings of Christian antiquity a simple, vivid religion, which they felt had been distorted by long centuries of involved theological argument and buried beneath the accumulated mass of medieval church tradition. It was their task to restore this early "evangelical" faith in all its purity. To do this they believed that they must first restore and study all the Christian sources, the Bible and the early Fathers of the church, in their original form and in their original language. This necessitated a full scholarly knowledge of Greek and Hebrew as well as of good Latin. All this brought them into violent conflict with the conservative teachers and theologians, who still clung to the medieval traditions in education and theology, who preferred the medieval commentaries to the original texts, and who were ignorant and therefore suspicious of Greek and Hebrew.

Christian humanism

In Germany, the outstanding leader of the new movement was John Reuchlin (1455–1522). He had studied in Italy, and after his return to Germany devoted his life to the study of Hebrew as an aid to the understanding of the Old Testament. As a preliminary step he published the first Hebrew grammar north of the Alps in 1506, a work of great service to the new scholarship. His open opposition to a scheme for the suppression of Hebrew books caused him to be charged with heresy by the inquisitor of Cologne, backed by the Dominican teachers in the university there. The resulting trial, which lasted six years, roused a storm of controversy. It was one of the first cases in which both sides appealed to public opinion through the medium of the printing press. On Reuchlin's side were the humanists, on the other the monks and conservative theologians. In this literary debate, the humanists, equipped with a far superior Latin style, had all the best of it. When argument failed, they resorted to ridicule with devastating effect. One work in particular remains an immortal monument to the wit of the humanists. The *Letters of Obscure Men,* written anonymously by one of the young humanists at the University of Erfurt, is still good reading for its hilarious humor and biting satire. It is composed of a series of letters addressed to one of Reuchlin's principal opponents, presumably from his humble admirers. Written in comically barbarous Latin, the letters exposed the ignorance, superstition, and naïve gullibility of the obscure monks and priests who rallied to the defense of tradition. A supplement, even more bitter, appeared shortly after from the pen of the bellicose German knight and poet, Ulrich von Hutten.

Reuchlin

In France, James Lefèvre d'Étaples (c. 1455–1536) did for the New Testament what Reuchlin was doing for the Old. He, too, had studied in Italy, returning to teach at Paris. The aim of his work was to discover the real meaning of the New Testament text, treating it as a human document, though divinely inspired. His study of the Greek originals brought new light to bear on the teaching of Christ and the apostles, and had a considerable influence on the thought of Luther and other reformers.

Lefèvre d'Étaples

The principal figure among the Christian humanists in England was John Colet (d. 1519), the dean of Saint Paul's Cathedral in London and founder of Saint Paul's School. Though not a great scholar, despite his years of study in Italy, he was a man of high character and deeply interested in reforming the thought and practice of the church. His influence directed the activity of a number of writers more learned than himself. Among his friends was Sir Thomas More (c. 1478–1535), whose famous *Utopia*, published in 1516, presented the humanist's picture of an ideal society, one that has given inspiration to social reformers ever since.

Colet and More

By far the most influential of all the Christian humanists, however, was Desiderius Erasmus of Rotterdam (c. 1469–1536). It was he more than anyone else who formulated and popularized the reform program of Christian humanism. He was born in Holland, educated by the Brethren of the Common Life in their school at Deventer, and entered a monastery at an early age. However, he soon escaped from that narrow environment and thereafter led a wandering existence, living for years in France, England, Italy, Germany, and Switzerland, equally at home wherever there were learned men who could converse with him in the classical Latin that was almost his mother tongue. Until Erasmus was about thirty years of age, the study of the classics absorbed his attention to the exclusion of almost everything else. During these years he acquired a thorough knowledge of classical literature and the easy, graceful Latin style that was to secure him universal recognition as "the Prince of the Humanists." It was not till about the time of his first visit to England in 1499, during which he met John Colet and Thomas More who became his lifelong friends, that he turned seriously to the religious studies that were to occupy the largest share of his attention for the rest of his life.

Erasmus

The chief aim of Erasmus's work in the field of religious thought was the restoration of Christianity to its early simplicity as taught by Christ himself and by his disciples. He thought of Christianity as a guiding philosophy for the direction of daily life, rather than as a system of dogmatic beliefs or ecclesiastical practices as the medieval church had all too often made it appear. He described his religious ideal in a significant phrase, "the philosophy of Christ," in which, perhaps, we can trace the influence of the Brethren of the Common Life and the *Imitation of Christ*. This conception of religion made a thorough understanding of the original meaning of the Scriptures vitally necessary. He felt that the Vulgate, as the Latin version of the Bible accepted by the church was called, could not be entirely trusted, since it was a translation to start with and had been recopied with possible errors for centuries. Erasmus, therefore, undertook the task of editing the Greek text of the New Testament from the earliest available manuscripts. After years of labor he finally published it, with extensive annotations, in 1516. It was the first time that the New Testament had been printed in its original language. The conservative theologians, who had been accustomed to following the Vulgate as the final authority and many of whom were ignorant of Greek, were profoundly suspicious of the new edition and attacked Erasmus bitterly.

Greek New Testament

Meanwhile, Erasmus was also working busily for the reform of those doctrines and practices in the church that to him seemed out of harmony with the Christian spirit. This he hoped would be accomplished by the growth of enlightened education and a clearer understanding of the philosophy of Christ, aided in the meantime by common-sense criticism of existing abuses. The best known of his numerous works in this field were the *Praise of Folly* and the *Familiar Colloquies*, wherein he ridiculed the wealth and self-seeking power of the clergy, the worship of saints, the monastic orders, indulgences, pilgrimages, and fasts. Erasmus had a devastatingly satirical wit and had early discovered that ridicule can sometimes be a more effective weapon than heavy argument. Because of his masterly command of Latin style and his clear intelligence and humor, everything he wrote was widely read. He helped to prepare the way for the Reformation, though he himself refused to be drawn into the conflict that followed it and remained within the church.

Erasmian reform

27

The States of Europe at the Dawn of the Modern Age

(c. 1450–1519)

IN THE LAST HALF of the fifteenth century and the first two decades of the sixteenth, the period of transition from the High Middle Ages to the early modern era was drawing to its close. The general characteristics of that change we have already noted. The purpose of this chapter is to pass in brief review the history of the principal European states during these years, so as to show the general structure of Europe at the beginning of modern times, and also to describe the work of those early explorers who were then opening up new opportunities for European trade and expansion, before we pass on to the new era that began with the Protestant Reformation, the foundation of the vast Hapsburg empire of Charles V, and the long struggle between the rival dynasties of Hapsburg and Valois. In all parts of Europe we shall find somewhat similar developments taking place. Under strong and more or less absolute rulers, aided by the support of the rising middle class, the territory of the various states was being consolidated and the authority of the central government was triumphing over the last remnants of feudal independence. At the same time, the territorial princes were transferring control of industry and commerce from the cities, which had been the focal centers of economic life under the medieval guild system, to the state government, thus laying the foundations of modern economic nationalism. Strengthened by this newly won control of the political and economic forces of their states, the monarchs of Europe also began in these years to seek additions to their territory by conquest, from which sprang those dynastic wars, alliances and counter-alliances, so characteristic of European history in the first centuries of the modern era. Finally, this period witnessed a significant shift in the center of gravity of European trade from the east to the west, due to the discovery of new lands and new trade routes in the Atlantic.

1. SPAIN AND PORTUGAL

Nowhere can the developments listed above be more clearly observed than in the history of Spain, which rose during this period to the first rank among European states. *The Spanish peninsula* Hitherto the various kingdoms of the Spanish peninsula had played a relatively insignificant rôle in the general history of Europe. They were cut off from the remainder of the continent by the high barrier of the Pyrenees and had not yet learned to use the Atlantic as a highway of commerce to the Far East and West. Moreover, the Christian states had had to wage a long war of conquest to win their land from the Moslems, and they had since wasted much energy in fighting among themselves. In the middle of the fifteenth century, the peninsula was still divided into five separate kingdoms. Of these Castile, with which Leon had been incorporated, was much the largest. It occupied the whole central plateau and included more than sixty per cent of the entire peninsula. The smaller kingdoms of Aragon and Portugal lay along the coast to east and west respectively. Far to the north, the little kingdom of Navarre straddled the Pyrenees, and in the extreme south the Moslem kingdom of Granada still remained as a reminder that Spain had once belonged to Islam.[1]

The long period of warfare with the Moslems and the gradual expansion by conquest had left a permanent impress on the character of Castile. The Castilian people had grown up a fighting race, rigidly orthodox. Moreover, Castile had acquired its territory bit by bit, and each new acquisition formed a separate unit in the state under the control of half-independent feudal nobles or the orders of crusading knights. As a result, the condition of feudal anarchy common to most countries in the Middle Ages had lasted in Castile till after the middle of the fifteenth century. The power of the crown was also limited to some extent by the Cortes, an assembly representing the upper and middle classes something like the French States General. Castile was mostly an agricultural and pastoral country, none too rich, though its industry and commerce were soon to be stimulated by the opening-up of exclusive markets in the New World, and the importation of gold and silver from Mexico and Peru would bring it for a time a false prosperity. Aragon had a stronger central government, though there, too, the king was hampered by feudal nobles and the Cortes. Thanks to its position on the eastern coast, it had a more highly developed commerce than had Castile. The acquisition of Sicily in the thirteenth century and the islands of Majorca and Sardinia in the fourteenth by the ruling family of Aragon gave it a considerable share of the Mediterranean trade.

Castile and Aragon

[1] See map, page 386.

The foundations of the future greatness of Spain were laid by the union of all the peninsula except Portugal under the rule of Ferdinand of Aragon (1479–1516) and Isabella of Castile (1474–1504), who were married in 1469. When they inherited their respective kingdoms a few years later, the two greatest states in Spain were brought under a common government, though for another generation they remained separate in theory. The combined power of the two monarchs made further conquest possible. In 1492, the year in which Columbus carried the flag of Castile to the New World, they conquered the kingdom of Granada, thus wiping out the last independent Moslem state. Thereafter, Ferdinand launched an ambitious and very astute foreign policy, designed to make Spain a power to be reckoned with in European affairs and to add territory to the possessions of his family. As a result of his part in the Italian wars, of which more later, he acquired the kingdom of Naples from the lesser branch of the Aragonese dynasty in 1503, and in 1512 he conquered all of Navarre south of the Pyrenees.

Union of Spain

The reign of Ferdinand and Isabella accomplished not only the territorial consolidation of Spain, but also the centralization of authority in the hands of a strong royal government. This was especially necessary in Castile, where the independence of the feudal nobles had sadly weakened the government and had produced a frightful amount of lawlessness and disorder. The monarchs began by restoring order and security for life and property through the foundation of a mounted police system recruited from the populace, called the Hermandad or Holy Brotherhood. This popular police force dispensed summary justice to all offenders and was remarkably effective. The next step was to strip the feudal nobles and the great crusading orders of their independent powers and to reduce them to subjection to the crown. In this task, Ferdinand and Isabella could count on the support of the common people who preferred a strong government to feudal anarchy. The monarchs then turned their attention to the reform of

Rise of royal power in Spain

the Spanish church, which had been thoroughly feudalized and rather lax in discipline. They acquired from Pope Sixtus IV the right to nominate all the higher ecclesiastical officers in Spain and used that right to fill the church with men of high character and unquestioned orthodoxy, who would also be devoted to the crown. As a result, the Spanish church became an instrument for the extension of royal power, and was to be the strongest bulwark of orthodox Catholicism in the religious conflicts of the sixteenth century. The Spanish Inquisition, founded in 1478 under the control of the monarchy, was used to crush all signs of heresy and to root out what elements of Moslem religion remained. The expulsion of Moors and Jews strengthened the religious and racial unity of the country, but was a sad blow to its commerce and industry. Finally, it was Ferdinand and Isabella who began the process of whittling away the authority of the Cortes of Castile and Aragon, now the sole remaining check on the authority of the crown. There were rebellions against Ferdinand's rule in Castile after the death of Isabella, but they had done their work so well that their successor was able to build up the most absolute monarchy in Europe.

Despite the union and expansion of its powerful neighbors, the little kingdom of Portugal on the western coast still retained its independence. **Portugal** Like the other kingdoms in the peninsula, it had played an unimportant part in European history until nearly the end of the fifteenth century. Then it, too, rose to sudden power, a change due almost entirely to the courageous energy of its great navigators. As we shall see when we come to deal with the explorations and discoveries of this era, Portuguese sailors vied with the Spanish in finding new trade routes through the Atlantic, and, like Spain, Portugal enjoyed a period of great if somewhat illusory prosperity.

SPAIN IN THE 15th CENTURY

2. ENGLAND

England had scarcely emerged from the Hundred Years' War (1453) when it was plunged into a long, intermittent civil strife by rival factions in the royal family and the higher nobility. The war had left England a dangerous legacy of disorder. The great nobles had become accustomed to keeping large bands of armed retainers, and accustomed also to violence and bloodshed. Every baron had a following among the knights and gentry of his neighborhood, who wore his livery (coat of arms) and would fight for him. He repaid their services by "maintaining" their interests in the law courts or in private quarrels. This custom of "livery and maintenance" frustrated the normal action of justice and restored something like the old condition of feudal anarchy. The weak government of the feeble-minded Henry VI utterly failed to keep order, as it had failed in the war against France. Moreover, the weakness of the king opened the way for quarrels between one faction or another of the baronage who sought to control the government. These factional disputes broke into open civil war in 1455 between the followers of Richard, Duke of York, next heir to the throne after Henry's infant son, and the supporters of the reigning house of Lancaster, though it was not till 1460 that York definitely claimed the throne. He was killed shortly after, but his son continued the struggle and succeeded in winning the crown as Edward IV (1461–83). The Lancastrian party was now in opposition to the king and the fight went on to an accompaniment of treachery and murder. On the death of Edward IV, his brother Richard III (1483–85) seized the crown from his infant nephew Edward V, and added to this fairly normal crime the more shocking one of having the young Edward and his brother murdered. This was more than the English people could stand, even in that callous age. They deserted Richard and welcomed Henry Tudor, a distant heir to the Lancastrian claims who made a successful bid for the crown in 1485. These frequent and rather petty civil wars are known collectively as the Wars of the Roses from the white and red roses that, according to tradition, were the badges of the houses of York and Lancaster respectively.

The civil wars had affected the majority of the population surprisingly little, save as they interfered with security and good government. The people generally were neutral. No principle of any kind was at stake. It was merely a party fight among the nobles and the royal family. But for that very reason the Wars of the Roses had one very important and lasting influence on the course of English history. They destroyed the old nobility. Each battle thinned the ranks of the old feudal families, and each turn of fortune was followed by executions and the confiscation of ancient family estates. From this time on, the monarchy would have little trouble with the barons. Feudalism in England, which had long been dying, had received its death blow.

A new era in England's history opened in 1485 with the reign of Henry VII, first of the Tudor sovereigns. Having no very sound hereditary claim to the throne, Henry knew that his only hope of keeping it lay in giving the people the kind of government they wanted, and they wanted, above all, peace, security for life and property, and an opportunity to carry on their business under favorable conditions. They were tired of factional strife and the violence of the nobles. In short, they wanted a strong government, devoted to the interests of the people. No one could have been better suited to the task of satisfying those demands than the quiet, self-contained, and hard-headed Tudor. There was nothing very colorful or dramatic about his personality, but he had a thorough understanding of the needs of his country and a remarkable ability to get things done. Under his canny guidance, England's transformation from a medieval to a modern state was well-nigh completed.

The most vital problem facing the new Tudor king was the restoration of order. This could be accomplished only by reducing the power of the remaining barons. Henry set about the task with great energy, excluding them from his royal council and using the court of the star chamber, which was the royal council in its judicial capacity, to suppress livery and maintenance, and to punish all attempts on the part of the lords to interfere with the prosecution of justice or to oppress their humbler neighbors. With the star chamber court, which could not be intimidated, to deal with the great lords, the local courts were left free to punish the lesser criminals. A task of this magnitude takes time, and something was still left to be done by his successors, but when Henry VII died he left England in a reasonably orderly condition, with the royal authority unquestionably supreme in the state.

Next to order at home, Henry needed peace abroad and recognition of his title by foreign powers. This he secured **Foreign alliances** by obtaining a marriage alliance with Spain, which was rapidly becoming one of the strongest of European states. The marriage of his son Arthur to Catherine of Aragon, daughter of Ferdinand and Isabella, was a diplomatic triumph. The death of Arthur shortly thereafter threatened to break the bond, but it was renewed by the remarriage of the widowed Catherine to Arthur's younger brother, the future King Henry VIII. The Tudor family thus gained the support of the powerful Spanish dynasty, which was already allied by marriage with the imperial Hapsburgs, who held, among other possessions, the Burgundian Netherlands. Not the least of the benefits accruing from this alliance was that it ensured to English merchants fair treatment in the ports of Spain and the Netherlands.

Henry VII, indeed, never forgot the interests of the merchants. English commerce, especially the rich trade in wool **Encouragement of commerce** and woolen goods, had been growing rapidly during the fifteenth century, but with very little help from the central government. Mostly it was handled by foreigners, some of whom, like the Hanseatic merchants, had greater privileges in English ports than the natives themselves. Moreover, lacking strong support from the state, English merchants had been unable to secure favorable treatment in other countries. Henry undertook to change all this as far as possible. At the beginning of his reign he passed legislation through Parliament designed to give English ships, manned by English sailors, a monopoly of carrying certain types of goods. Wherever possible, he cut down the privileges of foreign traders in England so as to give the advantage to their native competitors, and where the foreigners still held privileges in England, he sought treaties with their home governments to secure reciprocal privileges for English merchants. The commercial treaties, cemented by family alliances, with Spain and Burgundy, opened up great opportunities for English trade. All in all, Henry's economic policies were typically modern. Their chief characteristics — the protection of native trade and industry from foreign competition, the securing of commercial treaties with other states, the transference of economic control from the cities to the state government which all this implied, and the close alliance between the monarchy and the middle class — were all to be followed by English governments for the next three centuries.

It was a prosperous, orderly state and a strong royal government that Henry VIII inherited in the year 1509. The young king was active and ambitious. **Accession of Henry VIII** Under his rule England was to play a larger part in international affairs and to win a new national consciousness through the establishment of a separate national church. Henry VIII looms larger than his less spectacular father on the pages of English history, but it must not be forgotten that it was the elder Henry who laid the foundations of Tudor England.

3. FRANCE, BURGUNDY, AND ITALY

The successful conclusion of the Hundred Years' War was a triumph for the French monarchy. Charles VII was not the greatest of kings, but he had driven out the English and had saved his country from disintegration. The war had aroused a national consciousness in the French people and had taught them that the safety of the country depended on the king alone, for the great nobles had almost ruined France by their selfishness and the States General had proved incompetent. The people generally, and especially those of the commercial and industrial middle class, would welcome a strong royal government over the whole state; but before there could be such a government, the kings had still to complete the subjugation of the nobility and the consolidation of France by bringing the few remaining half-independent fiefs directly under their control. This task was barely begun by Charles VII. It was left for his son and grandson, Louis XI (1461–83) and Charles VIII (1483–98) to carry it to a successful conclusion.

The most powerful and independent of the French fiefs still outstanding was the duchy of Burgundy. Granted by King John to his son Philip in 1363, it became the nucleus of a rapidly growing state under the Burgundian branch of the royal family.[1] Philip's son, Duke John, who was assassinated in 1419, and his son Philip allied themselves with the English against the French kings and the Armagnacs in the later stages of the Hundred Years' War. Philip was, indeed, almost an independent sovereign, and his impetuous son, Charles the Bold (1467–77), was determined to be recognized as such and to break completely away from France. This ambition was not essentially unreasonable, for the Burgundian house had already acquired, by marriage, purchase, and conquest, extensive lands outside of France in addition to the original duchy. These included the Free County of Burgundy (Franche Comté), Luxemburg, and the rich states of the Netherlands, and to them Charles added Alsace and Lorraine. In reality, Charles ruled a kingdom in that debatable land between France and Germany, reminiscent of the ancient kingdom of Lothair, and it is not surprising that he should desire the title of king. His ambitions inevitably brought Charles into violent conflict with Louis XI. For a time he seemed to be having the best of it, but he had also aroused the enmity of his warlike neighbors, the Swiss, and it was they who finally brought about his defeat and death. His daughter Mary kept up the struggle

Louis XI and Charles the Bold

[1] See maps, page 336.

with France, aided by her husband, Maximilian of Hapsburg, son of the Emperor Frederick III, until her death in 1482. Maximilian then made peace with Louis. The duchy of Burgundy was surrendered and was brought directly under the French crown. Alsace and Lorraine were also returned to their former owners, but the rest of the Burgundian states were kept by Philip, the son of Mary and Maximilian, to make a formidable addition to the lands of the house of Hapsburg.[1]

Meanwhile, Louis XI was using his undoubted talent for diplomacy and intrigue to good effect in subjugating the other semi-independent feudatories of France. The character of this strange, cunning, and unscrupulous man will always be an enigma to historians. He was superstitious, treacherous, and cruel; yet he must be given credit for his invaluable services in making France a united nation. When he died in 1483, the duchy of Brittany was almost the only fief outside the royal domain. Charles VIII was still a boy, though officially of age, when he succeeded to the throne, but fortunately Louis had left his daughter, Anne of Beaujeu, with authority to act as guardian to her young brother until he should grow up. For nine years this princess, whom her wise if somewhat misogynous father had called "the least foolish woman in Europe," practically ruled France. It was her energy that put down the last rebellions of the French nobles and finally, after years of fighting, secured the union of Brittany with the royal domain by the marriage of Charles VIII to Anne, Duchess of Brittany, in 1491. With this acquisition the consolidation of France into a united territorial state was practically complete.

Consolidation of France

As in Spain, the territorial consolidation of France was accompanied by the centralization of power in the hands of an absolute monarchy. The nobles were robbed of almost all their political authority and the States General was reduced to a negligible position. During and after the war, the French kings had secured the right to levy taxes on their own authority throughout the state. With

Triumph of monarchy

[1] See map, page 394.

HENRY VII OF ENGLAND
The founder of the Tudor dynasty was an unspectacular but very competent ruler.

CHARLES THE BOLD OF BURGUNDY
This portrait scarcely suggests the recklessness that characterized the last Burgundian duke of the French line.

CHARLES VIII OF FRANCE
As this contemporary portrait indicates, Charles was not the most intelligent ruler in Europe.

LUDOVICO SFORZA, DUKE OF MILAN
Ludovico Sforza, called "Il Moro," was the man who first invited the French to invade Italy.

RULERS OF THE SECOND HALF OF THE FIFTEENTH CENTURY

this financial backing, they could maintain a standing army with which the nobles could not compete. Moreover, they could ensure the subjugation of the nobility by taking them into their pay. The nobles became courtiers and officers in the royal army. In compensation for their lost independence, they retained their social prerogatives and the more substantial privilege of practical immunity from taxation. Only occasionally hereafter, under very weak kings and when the country was torn by religious strife, would the nobles attempt to reassert their independence, and then with no permanent success. Meanwhile, the middle class in France, as elsewhere, profited by the restoration of order and the assumption of economic control by a strong government. At the end of the fifteenth century, France was prosperous and all classes looked to the king as the embodiment of the national state.

Charles VIII had scarcely taken over the government of his newly united kingdom from his wise sister before he began to dream of adding to his glory by wars of conquest. And Italy, rich and famous for its culture, but weakened by its fatal lack of unity, seemed a prize within the easy grasp of the absolute ruler of a great state. Moreover, he had inherited the old Angevin claim to the kingdom of Naples, and few monarchs in that age of dynastic greed could bring themselves to ignore such a claim when a favorable opportunity for pressing it was presented. In 1494, France was strong and united, while the political situation in Italy made any united resistance to an invader extremely unlikely. The balance of power in Italy, which depended on the alliance of Milan, Florence, and Naples, had been overturned after the death of Lorenzo de' Medici in 1492.[1] Alfonso II of Naples, who became king early in 1494, had turned against Ludovico Sforza, called "Il Moro," who had been ruling Milan since 1479 in the name of his feeble nephew, the Duke Gian Galeazzo. The latter was Alfonso's son-in-law, whence his demands that the powerful Moro should turn the government over to the titular duke, whom Alfonso could easily control. Piero de' Medici, forgetting his father's diplomatic policy, supported Alfonso's demands. To protect his usurped authority, Ludovico Sforza then turned to Charles VIII and offered to help him in the conquest of Naples. So began for France the long series of futile wars in Italy. For more than half a century French kings wasted men and money in the vain attempt to conquer and hold a land that had little in common with France, while neglecting the more possible and profitable aim of rounding out their frontiers to the north and east within the natural boundaries of the Rhine and the Alps.

The first French invasion of Italy was little more than a military parade, with some comic-opera effects. Charles VIII crossed the Alps in September, 1494, marched down through the peninsula without encountering serious opposition, and by the early spring of the following year had conquered the whole kingdom of Naples, still without fighting a real battle. However, Naples was easier to win than to hold. The tactlessness and brutality of the French soon made them unpopular in the kingdom, while to the north the other Italian states, belatedly alarmed at the presence of the foreign invader, began to unite. Charles was forced to withdraw from Italy, leaving a garrison in Naples which was easily driven out by Alfonso's son Ferrante in 1496. The only immediate result of the invasion had been the expulsion of the Medici from Florence by the indignant citizens, when Piero supinely surrendered the outlying Tuscan forts to Charles.

Charles's expedition, however, had shown the ease with which conquests could be won in Italy, and the next French king, Louis XII (1498–1515), had not been a year on the throne before he followed his example. Louis, who was a cousin of the late king, had inherited a claim to Milan through his grandmother Valentina Visconti, Duchess of Orléans. He therefore directed his attack against Milan, which he had isolated by winning over Venice and Pope Alexander VI with promises of aid for their own selfish ambitions. The French army made short

[1] See above, page 363.

work of the Milanese mercenaries. The duchy was conquered and Ludovico Sforza was taken prisoner. Louis then prepared to move against Naples. The major difficulty in that direction was the probable opposition of Ferdinand, King of Aragon and Sicily, who might resent the expulsion of his kinsmen of the lesser branch of the house of Aragon from Naples. Louis avoided this difficulty by inviting Ferdinand to become a partner in the conquest. Naples was again taken without serious opposition, and again the French found it impossible to hold what they had won. Almost immediately the two conquerors quarreled over the division of the spoils. War broke out between them in 1502, and before the end of the following year the French were driven out and Naples was added to the growing possessions of Spain.

The League of Cambray

With France holding the duchy of Milan in the north and Spain the kingdom of Naples in the south, the independence of Italy was sadly threatened, but still the other Italian states could not unite against the menace of foreign domination. The next few years were occupied by shifting alliances and cold-blooded land-grabbing on the part of both Italian and foreign states. Venice was the first to suffer. That rich republic had aroused the enmity and greed of the other powers by its unfortunate policy of landward expansion. Both the French king, now Duke of Milan, and Maximilian of Hapsburg, who had been elected emperor in 1493, claimed parts of the Venetian territory, as did also the warlike Pope Julius II (1503–13), whose determined ambition was to recover full control of all land that had ever belonged to the Papal States. These three formed the nucleus of the League of Cambray (1508), later joined by Ferdinand of Spain, for the partition of Venice. Most of the fighting was done by the French and papal troops, and with considerable success. The proud republic was on the verge of ruin when Julius II made a separate peace with it in 1510, on condition of receiving the lands taken by Venice from the Romagna.

Having won all he wanted from Venice, the pope then turned against his French allies who were becoming dangerous neighbors. In 1511, Julius succeeded in breaking up the League of Cambray and forming a new "Holy League," composed of the papacy, Venice, and Spain, and soon joined by the Swiss, Maximilian, and Ferdinand's son-in-law, Henry VIII of England. The purpose of the league was to drive the French out of Italy and, incidentally, to distract the attention of France while Ferdinand conquered Spanish Navarre. The French won an initial victory in the bloody battle of Ravenna early in 1512, but before the end of the year the Holy League had achieved its objective. The French were again forced to withdraw from Italy, leaving Milan to the Moro's son, Maximilian Sforza, under the protection of the Swiss. Florence was punished for her alliance with France by being handed back to the Medici.

The Holy League

For a brief period Italy was restored to something like its state prior to the invasions. But in 1515 a new king, Francis I, ascended the throne of France and immediately followed the example of his predecessors in seeking glory beyond the Alps. The young king swept down into Italy with a powerful army, defeated the combined Swiss and Milanese forces at Marignano, and within a few months had reconquered the duchy of Milan. One very important result of this invasion was the Concordat of Bologna, arranged in 1516 between Francis and the new pope, Leo X, whereby the king surrendered the "liberties" of the French church asserted in the Pragmatic Sanction of Bourges (1439) [1] but received in return the right to nominate all the higher clergy in France.

Francis I reconquers Milan

The wars in Italy had by this time lasted more than two decades. Italy had paid dearly for its lack of unity, and France had merely paved the way for a long and costly struggle with the house of Hapsburg, to whose rising fortunes we must now turn our attention.

4. GERMANY AND THE HOUSE OF HAPSBURG

Germany in this period presents the one

[1] See above, page 352.

Disunion of Germany — great exception, outside of Italy, to the general rule of territorial and political consolidation and the rise of strong central government that applies to the other European states. The amalgamation of the German monarchy with the impressive but impractical Holy Roman Empire and the disastrous conflict with the papacy had prevented the formation in either Italy or Germany of a unified state. In the middle of the thirteenth century the empire had seemed on the point of dissolution. It was revived, but with scarcely more than a nominal unity, and it grew no stronger. The emperors had still very little real authority. They could raise neither adequate revenue nor an effective army outside their own domains, nor were they strong enough to keep order and enforce justice save in their own family lands. The Diet of the empire — the assembly of princes and representatives from the free imperial cities — was equally powerless to secure obedience to its laws. The Emperor Maximilian I did make some attempt to strengthen the central government, but accomplished little, for like the other emperors of this period he was far more interested in advancing the position of his family than in adding to the imperial authority. This lack of unity in the empire, however, was made up for to some extent by the consolidation of the larger states within Germany. In these individual states, duchies, margravates, and the like, something like the same tendency toward centralization that we have noted in the monarchical states was taking place. Finally, it must not be forgotten that, despite political and social disorder, Germany was on the whole very prosperous in these years and was undergoing a spiritual and intellectual revival under the influence of the Christian Renaissance.

The most striking development in German political history during this period, and one that was to have a tremendous influence on the whole history of Europe, was the phenomenal rise of the Austrian house of Hapsburg. **Hapsburg emperors** After the election of Albert II (1438–39), the imperial title remained in the Hapsburg family generation after generation until it came to be considered almost as an hereditary right. Albert was followed by Frederick III (1440–93) and Maximilian I (1493–1519). It was the latter of these who was chiefly responsible for bringing into the Hapsburg family that vast collection of lands outside of Germany that was to make his grandson, Charles V, the greatest ruler in Europe in the next generation. Charming, cultured, and impractical, Maximilian played a part, usually pretty ineffective, in every international crisis of that crucial period when the monarchs of France and Spain were consolidating their territories and were turning to the conquest of Italy. Maximilian was the perpetual victim of magnificent and visionary schemes, for which his economic and military resources were ludicrously inadequate. His participation in the Italian wars brought him nothing but grief, while his devotion to his family interests and to foreign projects ruined his chances of building up a strong imperial government in Germany. His only success was due to the skill and good fortune with which he arranged a series of marriage alliances with other powers. But that alone was enough to make his house the most powerful in Europe.

The first of the marriages that was to do more for the Hapsburg family than conquest had ever done took place in 1477, when Maximilian himself married Mary of Burgundy, the daughter and sole heiress of that **Hapsburg marriage alliances** reckless duke, Charles the Bold, who had just met his death in battle with the Swiss. To this marriage was born a son, Philip the Handsome, who inherited the Burgundian estates, including the Free County of Burgundy, Luxemburg, and the rich provinces of the Netherlands, after his mother's early death. In 1496, Philip was married to Joanna, the daughter of Ferdinand and Isabella, under whom the kingdoms of Spain had been united. Within a year this marriage became unexpectedly important because of the death of Joanna's only brother, which left her the heiress to the combined territories of Castile and Aragon. Ten years after their marriage, Prince Philip died and his wife Joanna was adjudged insane. The hereditary claims of both were thus left to

from Maximilian I

TYROL · AUSTRIA · STYRIA · CARINTHIA · CARNIOLA

from Mary of Burgundy

NETHERLANDS · LUXEMBOURG · FRANCHE COMTÉ

from Ferdinand and Isabella

Baleares · Naples · SARDINIA · SICILY · Malta

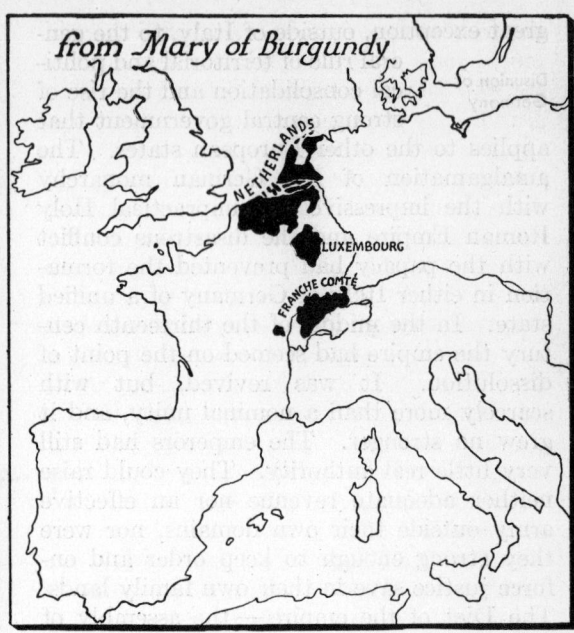

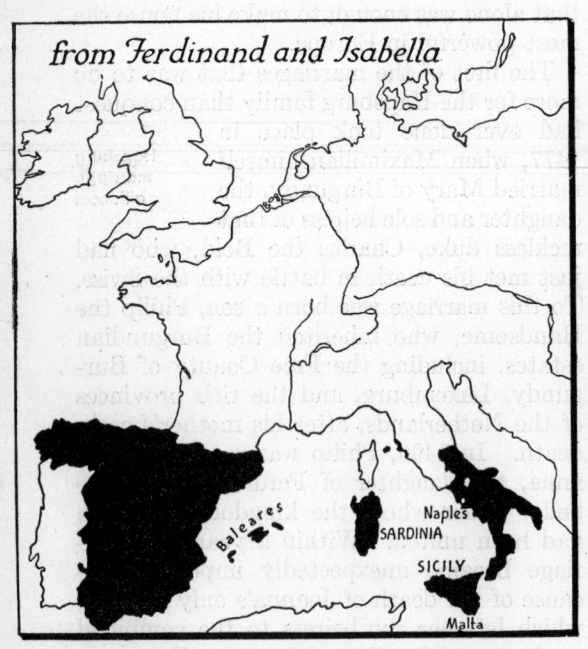

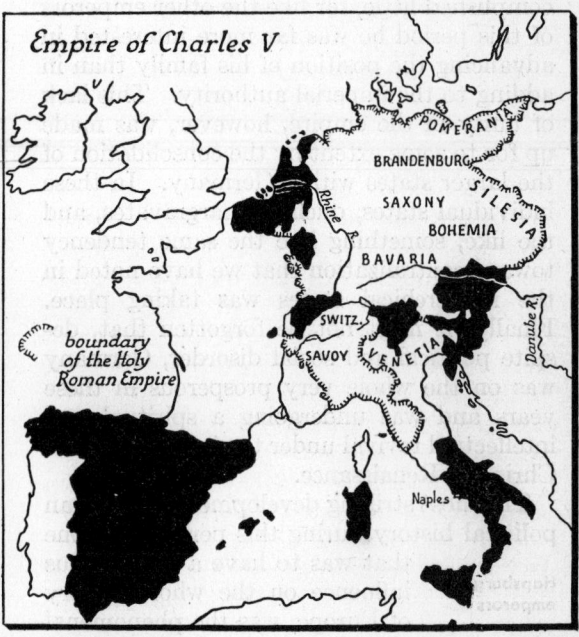

Empire of Charles V

POMERANIA · BRANDENBURG · SILESIA · SAXONY · BOHEMIA · BAVARIA · Rhine · SWITZ. · SAVOY · VENETIA · Danube R · boundary of the Holy Roman Empire · Naples

THE HERITAGE OF CHARLES V

their six-year-old son Charles, who immediately took over his father's Burgundian states. With the death of his maternal grandfather Ferdinand in 1516, the young Charles also inherited the united kingdom of Spain, plus the Aragonese kingdoms of Sardinia, Sicily, and Naples, and the Castilian claims staked out by Columbus and other explorers to the new world of the Americas. When, in 1519, his paternal grandfather Maximilian died, Charles added to these the hereditary Hapsburg lands in Germany, which included the duchy of Austria and the adjacent duchies of Styria, Carinthia, and Carniola and the county of Tyrol. In that same year he was elected emperor as Charles V, and thereby gained the imperial rights of government, such as they were, over all of Germany and northern Italy. With this vast accumulation of Burgundian, Spanish, Austrian, and imperial lands, Charles V, at the age of nineteen, became the ruler of a larger territory than had been collected under one monarch since the break-up of Charlemagne's empire.[1]

5. EXPANSION OF THE EUROPEAN HORIZON BY EXPLORATION

In this last part of the transitional period between the High Middle Ages and the beginnings of modern times, while the states of Europe were consolidating under the impulsion of economic forces to form strongly centralized units, the cupidity and economic rivalry of those states caused an eager search for new trade routes that resulted in a vast expansion of the horizon of Europe. Not only new trade routes but new lands were discovered, and a new world was opened up to European exploitation. The beginning of the modern age in Europe coincides with the beginning of the modern world.

What knowledge medieval Europe possessed of the world outside its narrow borders it had inherited mostly from ancient Greek geographers. This fund of information had been preserved and augmented by generations of Saracen scholars until the people of Latin Christendom

Early geographical knowledge

were prepared to take it over. But if the Saracens preserved the knowledge of Ptolemy, they preserved also many of his errors and ingenious guesses, including his calculation, much too small, of the size of the world. Their maps, which represented the tropical portion of Africa as an uninhabitable land of burning heat surrounded by boiling water and the Atlantic as an impassable sea of darkness, did as much to hinder as to help further exploration, though they were fairly accurate in their description of lands already known. Europe, northern Africa, western Asia, and the lands bordering on the Indian Ocean were shown fairly clearly. Much as the Moslems had done for the science of geography, however, the first great addition to western knowledge of the world during the Middle Ages was made by Christian explorers, who pressed eastward overland until they reached the rich and populous countries of the distant East.

Of these the most important were three members of an enterprising Venetian merchant family. In 1271, Nicolo and Matteo Polo, who had already traded in the western portion of the great Tartar Empire that covered all central Asia as well as eastern Europe, set out on a second expedition to the East. This time they took with them Nicolo's young son Marco, and they did not stop in the western lands of the Golden Horde. Instead, they pressed on through central Asia until they arrived at the court of the Tartar emperor, Kublai Khan, in the Chinese city of Pekin. They were kindly received and were given positions of honor in the Tartar government. Marco, especially, became a favorite of the great khan and was sent on numerous expeditions to almost every part of the Tartar Empire. For seventeen years he remained in the khan's service, visiting lands unknown to Europeans before his time and traveling roads where no European was to follow him until the nineteenth century. At last, wearied of exile, the Polos returned home, traveling this time by water around the eastern and southern coasts of Asia to India and thence by land to the Mediterranean.

Marco Polo

After his return, Marco Polo published his famous memoirs. His account of what he

---

[1] See map, page 394, and genealogical table, page xvii.

had actually seen is amazingly accurate, though to his contemporaries it seemed the wildest exaggeration. Still, if only a part of what "Marco of the millions" recounted were true, there was in the East wealth such as Europe had never dreamed of, and held, moreover, by a people who loved the arts of peace more than war. To Europeans, poor and warlike, Cathay (China) became the promised land of unbelievable wealth, an easy prey if only it could be reached, or at any rate the source of a fabulously rich trade. And aside from Marco Polo's story, the West had already ample evidence of the rich possibilities of the eastern trade. The trade in pepper, cinnamon, and other spices, which were so highly valued in an age when artificial means of preserving food were rare, in silk, precious stones and woods, etc., all luxury commodities that brought a very high price in proportion to their bulk and weight, had helped to found the fortunes of Venice, Genoa, and Pisa. But the Italians could not trade directly with the producers of these commodities. The Moslem middlemen, who commanded the land and water routes between India, where they met merchants from China and the Spice Islands, and the Mediterranean, took the lion's share of the profits. The long overland route through central Asia was impractical for regular trade. Was there not some other way of getting to India and China, a direct route by water that would enable western merchants to sail directly to the source of eastern wealth?

The lure of the East

It was the hope of finding such a route, either by sailing south around Africa or west to the coast of Asia, which was believed to be much less distant than it was, that inspired daring Portuguese, Spanish, French, and English seamen of the fifteenth century, and even earlier, to set out on perilous voyages of exploration into the unknown Atlantic. Fear of the Atlantic was ingrained in the minds of European sailors, accustomed as they were only to coasting voyages, though by the end of the Middle Ages the use of the magnetic compass as a guide in the open sea was generally known. Exploring voyages were expensive as well as hazardous, and for a long time they brought few results. Small wonder that progress was very slow. Had it not been for the authority of the great state governments, backed by the capital and the demands of the merchant class, the age of discovery might have been postponed indefinitely. It is doubtful, indeed, if it could have been achieved by the medieval system of guild and city economy. That discovery followed the rise of the centralized states and of the beginnings of capitalism was no coincidence; nor was it coincidence that the explorations were nearly all sponsored by the states along the Atlantic seaboard. For the people who faced the Atlantic felt the need of a new route to the East more keenly than the Italians, who were on the whole well enough content with their existing monopoly of the eastern trade, second-hand though it was.

Search for a new route to the East

The little kingdom of Portugal, situated at the southwest tip of Europe, took the lead in fifteenth-century exploration of the African coast and of the neighboring islands of the Atlantic. They were not the first to set out, but they were the most persistent, thanks in large part to the intelligent direction and unflagging enthusiasm of a prince of the royal family, Henry "the Navigator," who for more than forty years prior to his death in 1460 devoted himself to the encouragement of exploration. Henry's motives were a strange mixture of scientific curiosity, crusading zeal, and national ambition. Some of his ideas, such as his hope of reaching the upper Nile from the western coast by way of the Senegal River and thus outflanking the Moslems in North Africa, proved erroneous. Nevertheless, his explorers achieved important results. Before his death they had founded permanent settlements in the islands of Madeira and the Azores, had set up a regular trade, partly in slaves, with the Guinea coast, which so far as is known had never before been reached by water, and were already pushing farther south. The sure profits of the Guinea trade, however, tended to keep explorers from going farther, and twenty-six years passed before the first Portuguese ship, commanded by Bartolomeo

Portuguese sail around Africa

HENRY THE NAVIGATOR  CHRISTOPHER COLUMBUS  VASCO DA GAMA

THE POLO FAMILY ON THEIR WAY TO CHINA

The scene above is from an illumination in the Catalan Atlas of 1374.

THE GREAT EXPLORERS

Diaz, rounded the southern extremity of Africa in 1486. The way to India was now open, and in 1498 a Portuguese fleet under Vasco da Gama sailed into the Indian harbor of Calicut.

Having at last arrived at the long-awaited goal, the Portuguese threw themselves with the utmost enthusiasm into the development of the new commerce. **Portuguese trade with India** They did not establish themselves, however, without a bloody struggle with the Moslem traders who had hitherto enjoyed a monopoly of commerce in the Indian Ocean. The tale of Portuguese conquest of Indian trade is one of terrible bloodshed and brutal atrocities. Under the viceroy, Albuquerque (1509–15), the Moslem merchants were driven out of the Indian waters and permanent trading posts were established on the Malabar (western) coast of India and at Malacca on the Malay Straits. The latter served as a receiving-point for the spices from the islands of the East Indies and for the Chinese trade. The profits accruing from the new commerce were immense, and for a time Portugal became one of the great powers of Europe. The direct water route was cheaper than the old Moslem-Venetian route overland and through the Mediterranean, and the profits did not have to be split. Venice could not compete and gradually declined, never to recover.

In the meantime, while the Portuguese were still feeling their way down the African coast, other explorers were following the lure of the East out across the open Atlantic. **Discovery of America** The ancient error of the Greek geographers in underestimating the size of the world was still accepted. There were encouraging legends, too, of islands midway in the Atlantic that would serve as stepping-stones across the sea. Since they knew nothing of the two continents that barred the way (for the discovery of America by the Northmen had been long since forgotten), the explorers who sailed straight west into the Atlantic had every reason to believe that they were on the shortest and most convenient route to China or India. There was nothing novel in the plans of the Genoese captain, Christopher Columbus, who sailed westward with a charter from the Spanish government in 1492, except his determination to sail straight on till he encountered land, instead of turning back as his predecessors had done to look for the mythical islands of the Atlantic. The result of Columbus's epoch-making voyage is known to every schoolboy. Having touched the islands of the Greater Antilles, he returned with the assurance that he had found India. Later explorations brought disillusionment. In the next few years, Spanish explorers coasted the mainland from Florida to Brazil and found it to be an impassable barrier.

Despite their disappointment at not reaching the East, the Spanish adventurers settled down to the conquest and exploitation of the lands they had found. **Spanish conquests in New World** This process was accompanied by the most frightful cruelty to the helpless natives. Yet for all their brutal exploitation of the natives, the Spaniards found in the islands where they first settled no great or sudden wealth, though the colonies they founded proved permanently valuable. It was not till they reached Mexico that their dream of finding El Dorado was realized. The conquest of the Aztecs of Mexico by Hernando Cortez and a small Spanish force in 1519 brought to light a store of gold and silver such as no European had ever seen before. A few years later, a handful of Spaniards under Francisco Pizarro began the conquest of Peru, where they took from the peaceful Incas quantities of gold and silver that surpassed even the riches of Mexico. The importation of gold and silver from the New World into Spain, from whence it eventually circulated to other countries, revolutionized the economic state of Europe. The amount of money in circulation was greatly increased; as gold and silver became more common, prices rose in proportion; and the opportunities for the accumulation of capital became much greater. As for Spain, it became the leading power in Europe on the strength of its sudden wealth.

The Spanish government, meanwhile, had not given up all hope of establishing direct contact with the East and of cutting in on

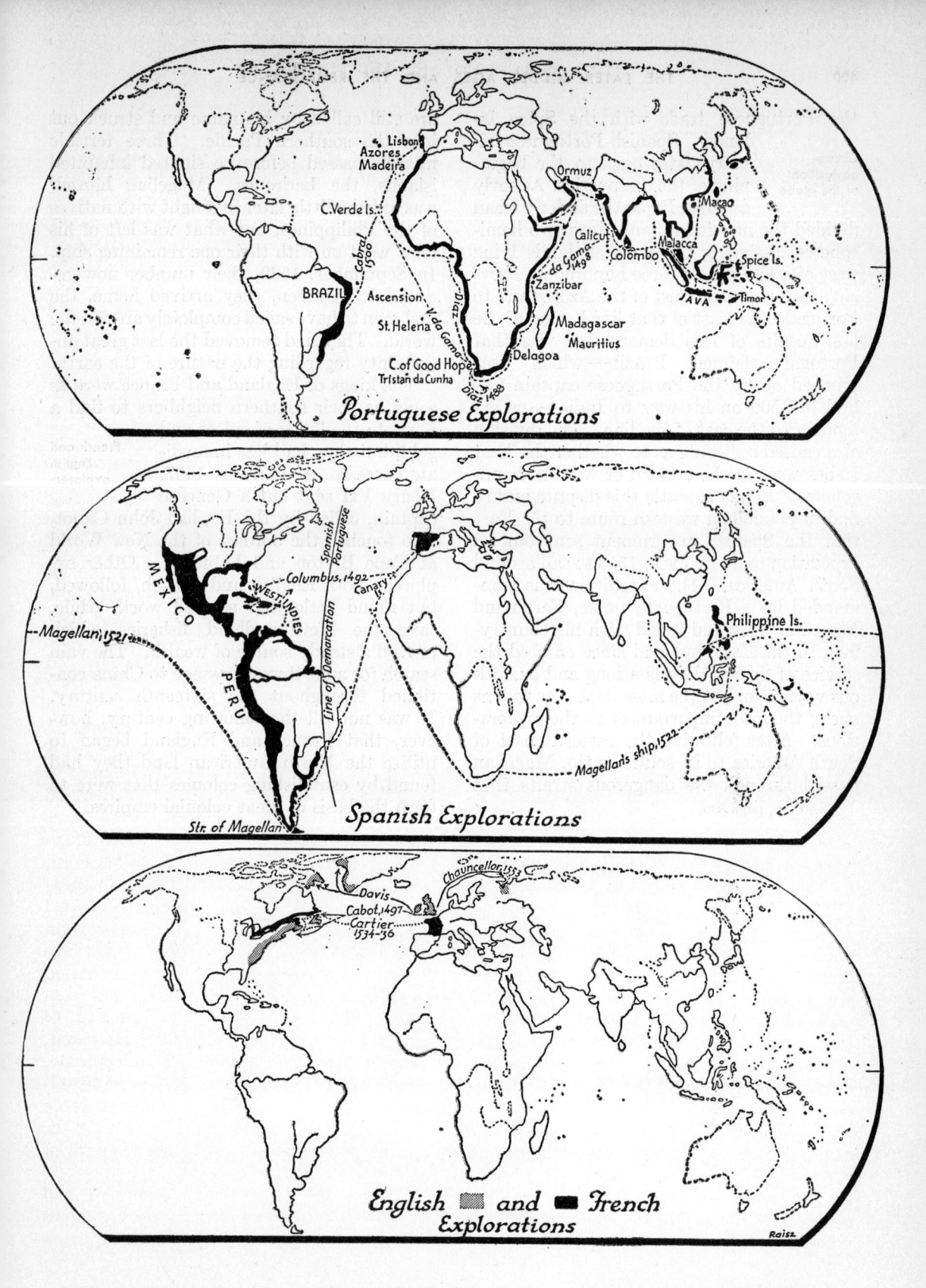

EXPLORATIONS OF THE FIFTEENTH AND SIXTEENTH CENTURIES

the Portuguese trade with the Spice Islands. Spanish-Portuguese rivalry dates back to the beginning of the discoveries. As early as 1493, Pope Alexander VI had divided the new-found lands into two hemispheres, assigning to Spain all lands lying west of a line drawn three hundred and seventy leagues to the west of the Azores and to Portugal those east of that line.[1] One of the first results of this demarcation was that Portugal claimed Brazil — which was touched on by the Portuguese captain Cabral in 1500 on his way to India — as extending to the east of the line. The division also caused a dispute as to whether the East Indies were in the eastern or western hemispheres. It was to settle this dispute and to find, if possible, a western route to the East that the Spanish government sent out an expedition of five ships in 1519 to sail around South America. The expedition was commanded by a Portuguese noble, Ferdinand Magellan, who had sailed with his countrymen to the East, but had since entered the service of Spain. It was a long and hazardous voyage, one of the most daring as well as one of the most important of all the explorations. After following the eastern coast of South America to its southern tip, Magellan passed through the dangerous straits that are still called by his name and struck out into the southern Pacific. Three terrible months passed before he sighted inhabited islands, the Ladrones. Magellan himself was killed a little later in a fight with natives of the Philippines, but what was left of his crew went on with their one remaining ship. In September, 1522, their number now reduced to eighteen, they arrived home, the first men to have sailed completely around the world. They had removed the last great uncertainty regarding the nature of the earth.

Circumnavigation of the globe

The kings of England and France were as eager as their southern neighbors to find a route to the lands of spices and gold, but they had less immediate success. As early as 1497, Henry VII sent out a Genoese captain, called by the English John Cabot, who touched the borders of the New World at Cape Breton and Labrador. Other explorers, both English and French, followed, but found little that seemed worth while, save the Newfoundland fisheries which proved a steady source of wealth. The vain search for a northwest passage to China continued throughout the sixteenth century. It was not till the following century, however, that France and England began to utilize the North American land they had found by establishing colonies that were to form the basis of great colonial empires.

French and English explorers

[1] See map, page 399.

SECTION F

The Reformation and the Wars of Religion

(c. 1517 — c. 1660)

In the first two decades of the sixteenth century, the transition from the medieval to the modern world was nearing completion. Feudalism had lost most of its independent political significance and the centralized territorial states were almost full grown. The corporate economic life of the High Middle Ages had almost disappeared, though the modern form of individual capital was not yet fully developed. The church still held the allegiance of all western Europe, but it was no longer the dominating institution that it had been in the twelfth or thirteenth century. Even that intellectual and artistic efflorescence that glorified the age of transition and which we call the Renaissance was passing its peak. Europe was again about to enter upon a new era with new problems. At the close of the second decade of the sixteenth century, two events signalized the nature of the coming age and revealed the problems that would most concern the people of Europe for the next century and a half. In 1517, Martin Luther nailed his ninety-five theses on the church door at Wittenberg, and thereby set in motion the forces that were to break up the universal church into warring sects and to make religious controversy the focal center for political rivalries, economic and social discontents, and intellectual activity. Two years later, Charles V was elected Emperor of the Holy Roman Empire, thus completing the accumulation of territory which brought the greater part of Europe under the rule of the house of Hapsburg and precipitating a century and a half of dynastic wars. Because of the dominating part played by the religious revolution and religious rivalry, we have called the period from about 1519 to 1660 the age of the Reformation and the Wars of Religion. But it was also an age of frequent dynastic wars; it witnessed the development of modern forms of state government and many modern forms of culture; and it saw the most important stages of that economic revolution which made capitalism the dominant factor in modern economic life.

EUROPE
AT THE BEGINNING OF THE 16th CENTURY
NORWAY
SWEDEN
SCOTLAND
Edinburgh
IRELAND
DENMARK
ENGLAND
London
TEUTONIC ORDER
Danzig
Lübeck
Hamburg
Bremen
NETHERLANDS
HOLY ROMAN EMPIRE
Cologne
GRAND PRINCIPALITY OF LITHUANIA
MOSCOVY
POLAND
BOHEMIA
Paris
FRANCE
FRANCHE COMTE
Munich
Vienna
AUSTRIA
TYROL
STYRIA
SWISS CON.
HUNGARY
MOLDAVIA
Bordeaux
SAVOY
VENICE
MILAN
AVIGNON
NAVARRE
GENOA
MODENA
FLORENCE
SIENA
PAPAL STATES
OTTOMAN EMPIRE
Constantinople
PORTUGAL
KINGDOM OF SPAIN
Madrid
Barcelona
Rome
Naples
KINGDOM OF SARDINIA
KINGDOM OF THE TWO SICILIES

28

The Reformation and the Founding of the Protestant Churches

(1517–55)

EUROPE was a very different place in the early years of the sixteenth century from what it had been in the thirteenth. In the intervening years the most characteristically medieval aspects of European civilization had disappeared or were rapidly disappearing, and modern society had begun to take recognizable shape. Yet one medieval institution, and that the greatest of all, still stood, unchanged in form though considerably shaken and with alarming fissures appearing here and there in its once solid masonry. The real unity of Western Christendom had been broken up; yet the Roman Church still maintained its traditional place as the embodiment of all religion in western Europe; the papacy still kept alive its claims to universal sovereignty, and the clergy still exercised their monopoly over the means of salvation. The church, it is true, had changed in some respects since the thirteenth century, but not as a rule in ways that made it a more satisfactory minister to the needs of the new age. Nothing could be more certain in this age of rapid change than that some of the people at least would demand changes in their religious life to fit the changes in their worldly existence. And such changes could not be effected without extensive changes in the church; for in that age religion was inseparable from the church, just as the church was inseparable from the state and society. The most devout churchmen recognized that a reform of the church was necessary and hoped to bring it about in ways that would leave the outward structure intact. They were too late. Before they could accomplish anything, the explosive forces of the new nationalism, the new ethical and moral interests of the bourgeois class and the new humanistic piety, combined with old grievances against Rome and discontent with the clerical system, were ignited by the fiery preaching of Martin Luther, and the resulting explosion split the unity of the ancient church beyond all hope of rebuilding. What occurred was in reality a religious revolution, and it is this revolution that is generally referred to by historians as the Protestant Reformation, or simply the Reformation.

1. CAUSES OF THE REFORMATION

The immediate acceptance of Luther's revolutionary doctrine by all kinds of people in all parts of northern Europe is sufficient proof that those who welcomed the new movement did so for a wide variety of reasons. No such spontaneous reaction of popular sentiment could have sprung from any single cause or have been inspired by a single motive. We must look for the causes of the Reformation, then, in the economic, political, social, and cultural, as well as religious, background of the age. These various causes have already been mentioned and explained in previous chapters. Here we can give only a brief summary to gather them together and to indicate their bearing on the problem of the Reformation.

The most obvious cause of the Reformation was the necessity of reforming abuses in the church, a necessity that had been widely recognized for the past two centuries or more, without much being done about it. The wealth and temporal power of the church; the special jurisdiction of ecclesiastical and papal courts; the appointment of foreign papal favorites to high ecclesiastical offices; the avarice, carelessness, ignorance, and immorality of some of the clergy; the evils of simony and the financial exactions of the papacy — all these served to arouse a strong feeling of discontent with the church as it was, particularly when they bore heavily on the purses of the laity.

Abuses in the church

Still the fact that there were abuses in the church would not in itself have caused such a widespread revolt from the Roman communion as took place in the Reformation. The need for reform was no greater when Luther nailed his theses on the church door at Wittenberg than in the days of William of Occam, Marsiglio, Wyclif, and Huss. Yet these earlier reformers failed, while Luther succeeded. Why? Aside from the fact that Luther provided a more satisfactory theological formula to justify revolt, it is clear that in the meantime conditions had changed so that more people were prepared to break with the church than before. The early critics of the church and the papacy had been voices crying in the wilderness. They had propounded many of the ideas later asserted by Luther, but they had secured only a relatively small following because the time was not yet ripe. They had not labored entirely in vain, however, for among the factors that prepared the way for the success of the Reformation the memory of their teaching, never wholly forgotten, must be given a prominent place.

Influence of earlier reformers

The sacramental system was the rock upon which the early revolts against the authority of the church had foundered. However much men might feel the need of reform, they felt still more keenly the need of those services that only the clergy could perform. When, more than a century after Wyclif and Huss, Luther reasserted their doctrine of the priesthood of all believers, one of the important reasons for his success was that in the meantime certain religious and social developments had combined to make a good many men less ready to admit dependence on the priests and the sacraments for their salvation. In Germany and the Netherlands, the mystics, whom we have already noted,[1] had preached an inner piety, a religion that consisted chiefly of an immediate communion between man and God and left little room for the mediation of a priest. During that time, too, in the cities where the seeds of both the Renaissance and the Reformation found their most fertile soil, the growing education, individualism and self-reliance of the prosperous middle class tended to make them resent the necessity of depending for their salvation on the ministration of the priests. This tendency to rebel against the church's most fundamental belief was more dangerous to it than any amount of criticism of abuses in the clerical system.

Revolt from the sacramental system

In other ways the changing spirit of the new age was causing men, especially of the bourgeois class, to lose interest in the beliefs, ideals, and traditions of the medieval church. The medieval ideal of the truly religious life, as embodied in monasticism, had stressed poverty, asceticism, and otherworldliness as among the prime virtues. But with increasing prosperity, money was playing a much more important part in men's lives, and by the beginning of the sixteenth century the age in which Saint Francis of Assisi had sung the praises of his Lady Poverty and had enrolled enthusiastic recruits in her service had long since passed. Practical business men had begun to think of poverty as a social evil rather than as a saintly virtue.

Changing spirit of the age

[1] See above, pages 377–380.

Other-worldliness made small appeal to men absorbed in the business of this world, and asceticism had few charms for the hard-working burgher who looked forward soberly to an old age spent in quiet enjoyment of the results of honest trade. Next to monasticism the strongest force in shaping the spirit as well as the form of the medieval church had been feudalism. And as feudalism lost vitality, the medieval church lost the social atmosphere that had been most congenial to it. To the middle class of city dwellers especially, whose temper was to shape the interests of the new age, the chivalric-feudal spirit of the crusading era which was also the great age of the medieval church had very little appeal. Saint Louis was no more akin to them than was Saint Francis. The elaborate and colorful ritual of the Catholic Church rather jarred on their sober minds. In some vague way, very difficult to express, they felt it to be more suited to the gilded and extravagant society of the feudal nobility than to their own business-like world. Added to that, of course, was the economic fact that the church conferred solid benefits upon the great nobles, whose sons became bishops, whereas the economic relations of the bourgeoisie with the church represented an unfavorable balance of trade.

But for the present we are discussing the failing appeal of the ideals of the medieval church, and in that connection one further factor must be noted. The saints themselves were losing something of their appeal to the popular imagination. Not only were the ideals they represented losing conviction, but the number of saints on the calendar had grown too great for the proper observance of saints' days, and their relics had been too freely peddled about the country. Perhaps they had grown too familiar to be given the respect formerly accorded them. Certainly, no feature of church practice was dropped with less resistance during the Reformation than the veneration of the saints.

The intellectual basis for the revolt against medievalism in the church was provided by the Christian humanists.[1] Whole-heartedly devoted to the study of antiquity, they had

Influence of humanists

[1] See above, pages 382-383.

learned to despise medieval traditions as products of "Gothic" barbarism. Erasmus was not the only one of them who ridiculed pilgrimages, the veneration of the saints, the supernatural power of relics, the practices of monasticism, and the temporal power of the papacy, on the ground that these things were not part of original Christianity. It was the humanist emphasis on the literal study and reinterpretation of the Bible from original sources that gave Luther his most potent weapon. It was a commonplace among the enemies of the Reformation that Erasmus had laid the egg which Luther hatched.

Among the other causes of the Reformation, the interests of the state governments and the strength of national opposition to papal authority must not be forgotten. Indeed, few if any of the changes that had taken place in the preceding century did more to make the break with Rome politically possible than the development of the centralized territorial states and the growth of national consciousness which we have noted in the last two chapters. As these grew stronger, both prince and people resented more and more keenly the payment of taxes to an Italian prince, the appeal of cases from the national courts to the papal court at Rome, and the interference of a foreign power in their national affairs. This was particularly true in England, Germany, and the Scandinavian countries, where the rulers had not secured such control of the national church before the Reformation as had the kings of France and Spain. The opportunity presented to the kings and princes of these countries to gain complete control of the church in their states, as well as the financial advantages that would result from the stoppage of papal taxation and from the confiscation of church lands, was a strong inducement to them to embrace the Reformation movement. Without the help of the secular governments, it is doubtful if the new churches could have been securely established in many of the northern states.

National opposition to Rome

2. LUTHER AND THE REFORMATION IN GERMANY

By the second decade of the sixteenth cen-

ALEXANDER VI
1492–1503

The worldly and ill-famed Borgia helped to give the papacy a bad reputation.

JULIUS II
1503–1513

Raphael's portrait gives a magnificent impression of the old fighting pope.

LEO X
1513–1521

The first Medici Pope was less violent, more cultured than his two predecessors, but scarcely less worldly.

CLEMENT VII
1523–1535

The second Medici Pope, who had to meet the full shock of the Reformation, is shown here as a young man.

POPES OF LUTHER'S TIME

tury, Germany was ready for a religious revolution. All that was needed was a leader who would unite men of varied interests and show them the way. That leader was Martin Luther (1483–1546). In his ringing phrases the inarticulate discontent with things as they were and blind gropings for a more satisfactory religious life found expression. And in his doctrine of salvation by faith alone, all who were ready to rebel against the authority of the church found for the first time a justification for revolt that carried conviction to their consciences. Luther did not cause the Reformation; but he gave the signal for its start and shaped its course. So far as any man can, Luther influenced the history of his age.

Martin Luther

Luther's parents were Saxon peasant folk, stern, hard-working, and pious, somewhat better off than the average, for they were able to give their son an excellent education. In 1501, at the age of eighteen, young Martin entered the famous Saxon university at Erfurt. There for four years he studied the Nominalist philosophy that still dominated the old school, but he also read the classics and talked to the enthusiastic group of young humanists who were known as the "Erfurt poets." Having completed his course in the faculty of arts, Martin began the study of law in accordance with the wishes of his practical father. Almost immediately, however, he changed his mind and entered the local monastery of the order of Augustinian Eremites. Two years later he was ordained priest, and in 1508 was moved to the house of his order at Wittenberg to teach in the new university recently founded there by the Elector of Saxony, Frederick the Wise. There followed nine years of outwardly peaceful academic activity, during which Luther lectured to students, preached in the castle church, and began to acquire a considerable local reputation. But quiet though they seemed, they were years of mental turmoil for the young monk, until the discovery of the doctrine of faith brought peace to his soul, and before long strife to all Christendom.

Early years

Since his entry into the monastery, Luther had been tormented by the fear that nothing he could do would be sufficient to merit salvation. Indeed, it was this fear that caused his sudden decision to become a monk, to the disappointment of his father and the astonishment of his fellow students. He had carried with him from the peasant environment of his childhood a conception of God as a stern, unforgiving judge, and he had accepted the current teaching of the church that salvation depended on "good works," which included the sacraments, prayer, fasting, and, if one would be sure, the ascetic practices of monasticism. But though he devoted himself to an excessive asceticism, he still found no assurance that he had merited salvation. His reading of Saint Augustine further shook his faith in his own efforts by the suggestion that only those who are predestined to receive divine grace will be saved. And who can know that he is among those chosen? The answer to all his problems came to him suddenly about the year 1515, from the reading of a verse in Saint Paul's Epistle to the Romans on which he was lecturing to the university students. It contained the phrase, "The just shall live by faith." He had often read it before, but now he saw in it a new meaning — that man may be justified, i.e., saved, by faith and by faith *alone*. Doubtless only those predestined for salvation would be given faith; but to possess faith, which is the means of salvation, is also to possess the conviction that one will be saved. It took some time for Luther to work out all the logical consequences of his doctrine, for he was not essentially a systematic thinker. Eventually, however, he was forced to the conviction that, if faith alone was needed for salvation, then the good works of the church, fasts, pilgrimages, and even the sacraments, were unnecessary, and that no man was dependent upon the services of pope or priest for his salvation.

Justification by faith

With these ideas running through his mind, it was inevitable that Luther should begin to criticize some of the practices of the church arising from the doctrine of good works. As it happened, the question that first aroused him to open protest was that represented by the papal indulgence proclaimed by Pope Leo X

Indulgences

to obtain money for the building of Saint Peter's Church in Rome. The granting of indulgences had been a common practice in the church for more than two centuries. It was an integral part of the church's scheme of salvation and had become an important source of papal revenue. In theory it was an elaboration of the penitential system, the origins of which date back to the early days of the church. Following confession and proof of contrition, the sinner received absolution for his sins through the sacrament of penance. He was then free from the guilt of sin and the fear of eternal damnation. But he still owed further atonement in the form of penance or punishment in this world and, after death, in purgatory. The first indulgences or remissions of further penance were granted by the popes, acting as the successors of Saint Peter, to the crusaders. Later, pilgrimages or other good works were substituted, until in the fourteenth century the Avignonese popes set the precedent of accepting money payments as constituting the major part of the necessary good works.

To Luther, however, convinced that faith alone could save men from the results of sin, it now seemed clear that indulgences were not only useless but actually harmful, since thereby men were encouraged to put their trust in something that could be of no help to them. He felt bound, therefore, to issue a warning to his people. As the simplest method of securing a hearing, he prepared a list of ninety-five theses or propositions on the subject, which he announced his willingness to defend in public debate. Following the usual academic practice, he posted these theses on the church door where all could read them, and awaited developments. To his surprise the theses aroused a perfect furor of interest. They were soon printed and circulated all over Germany. That they carried conviction to their readers was attested by a sharp decline in the sale of indulgences.

The ninety-five theses

In 1517, Luther had no thought of breaking away from the ancient church, but the next three years saw him forced step by step farther from it. In order to meet the arguments of the papal legates who were sent to demand

Luther drifts from the church

that he recant and of the orthodox theologian, John Eck, who engaged him in public debate at Leipzig in the summer of 1519, he had to work out his ideas to their ultimate conclusion. Almost against his will, for he had a natural respect for authority, the Wittenberg monk was forced to realize that his beliefs were contrary to many of those held by the church and that there was no place for him within the Roman communion. He had found in the Bible, however, as he interpreted it, a firm support for his convictions, and resting on that divinely inspired authority he confidently defied the authority of the pope.

Leo X was delayed in taking decisive action against Luther by what seemed to him the more important business of the imperial election in 1519. This hotly disputed election worked doubly to the advantage of Luther, for his prince, Frederick the Wise, was able to secure from Charles V, as the price of his support, a promise that the rebellious friar should not be condemned without a hearing before the imperial Diet. This meant further delay, and Luther used the time to good effect by writing a series of pamphlets with a view to publicizing his beliefs and winning the support of the German people. He was amazingly successful. The *Address to the Christian Nobility of the German Nation on the Improvement of the Christian Estate* was a stirring appeal to German patriotism against the tyranny of Rome. In it he called on the German princes to reform the church and outlined a comprehensive program. This popular pamphlet was followed by the *Babylonian Captivity of the Church*, a more scholarly exposition of his views on the sacramental and sacerdotal system. A third pamphlet, *The Liberty of a Christian Man*, explained in popular fashion for the common man the practical bearings of his doctrine.

The pamphlets of 1520

When at last the summons came calling Luther to appear before the Diet of the empire at Worms in the spring of 1521, he went with the assurance that he had the sympathy at least of the majority of the German people. He was at the height of his popularity. All who nursed grievances against the church

Luther at Worms

MARTIN LUTHER (1483–1546)

This portrait shows the German Reformer in the years just after the Diet of Worms. In the full strength of early middle age, his strong peasant face indicates something of the forceful character that lay behind it.

CATHERINE LUTHER

Luther's wife, the former Catherine von Bora, as she appeared in 1526 shortly after her marriage. The painting by Lucas Cranach was done at the same time as that of Luther opposite.

A SATIRICAL PICTURE OF THE SALE OF INDULGENCES

This contemporary wood-cut is a satire on the methods of the indulgence seller, John Tetzel.

or hoped for reform wished him well, for the split in the church had not yet gone so far that it was necessary to take definite sides. Nevertheless, it took real courage to walk into the lions' den, with the fate of John Huss at Constance as a warning of what might happen. It was a dramatic moment when the Saxon peasant monk faced the assembled dignitaries of state and church and firmly refused to recant. Next day he left Worms. Within a few days he was proclaimed an excommunicated heretic by the church and an outlaw by the empire. But by that time he was safe in the lonely castle of the Wartburg, where he had been conducted by the orders of Frederick the Wise. There he passed a year in enforced leisure, which he put to good use by translating the New Testament into German. The Old Testament he translated later, completing it in 1532. As his whole program rested on the authority of the Bible against that of church tradition, it was essential for his success that the Bible should be readily accessible to the people. The importance of his German Bible can scarcely be overestimated. It has often been called the most powerful Reformation tract, and it had almost as much influence on the development of the German language as on German religion. Luther was a master of his native tongue, and his Bible played a part as important in fixing the standard of modern German as Dante's *Divine Comedy* did for the Italian.

The peaceful interlude on the Wartburg marks a turning point in Luther's career as a reformer. Hitherto he had been a sturdy rebel against church authority and a champion of individual liberty of conscience. He was now to become the organizer of a church of his own and an increasingly conservative defender of established authority. Returning to Wittenberg in the spring of 1522, he began at once the task of reconstruction. His first action was to moderate the extreme changes put into effect by some of his more radical followers during his absence. He then set about the business of organizing a new church on as conservative a basis as possible. In the Lutheran Church as it finally took shape, a good deal of the old

The Lutheran Church

Catholic doctrine and practice was retained. Nevertheless, there were changes of vital importance. In accordance with Luther's denial of the doctrine of good works and hence of the validity of the sacramental and sacerdotal system, all of the sacraments were abolished except baptism and the Lord's Supper, which are specifically mentioned in the Bible, and even these lost their character as miraculous good works. Pilgrimages, fasts, veneration of saints and relics, and the rest of the traditional practices based on the doctrine of good works also went by the board. The clergy, no longer considered as having special sacramental powers, were permitted to marry and live the life of ordinary men. The monastic orders were entirely dissolved. Thus was broken down the barrier that had separated the clergy from the laity and had made them a separate caste with unique privileges. Finally, the church, in everything save questions of belief, was placed directly under the control of the state government. The superintendents, who replaced the former bishops, were practically state officers.

With the definite organization of a separate church, Luther lost the support of many who had sympathized with him before the Diet of Worms. Among these were the majority of the Christian humanists, including their leader, Erasmus. They had favored Luther's early demands for reform within the church, but were repelled by his violence and dogmatism. When the time for a final decision came, they found their loyalty to the ancient church too strong to be broken, especially as Luther's theological doctrine seemed to them no improvement on that of the old church. Erasmus was bitterly disappointed at the ruin of his hopes for a peaceful reform to be accomplished by education and without schism or turmoil, and he found it impossible to accept Luther's denial of man's free will or ability to work out his own salvation. The defection of the humanists was a serious loss to the new church, leaving it more conservative and dogmatic than ever.

Defection of the humanists

The Lutheran Church was scarcely begun before it lost the support of another and more numerous class, the majority of the

German peasants and poor city workers, who were alienated by Luther's conservative attitude toward the great social revolution which swept across Germany in 1525. The Peasants' War, as it was called, was a general rising of the downtrodden peasants, frequently joined by the discontented working classes in the towns, to demand justice and relief from crushing economic and social burdens. It had been preceded by a long series of similar revolts, extending over the past two hundred years, but becoming increasingly frequent since the turn of the sixteenth century. These earlier risings, however, had been confined to limited districts or individual lordships. What made the present rebellion at once more general and more radical was that the peasants had found, in Luther's assertion that the Bible is the only real authority, a justification for revolt and a program of social reform that would unite the discontented elements of different parts of the country in a common movement. Their dream of restoring the social conditions of evangelical Christianity was impractical, but it gave the necessary religious coloring to their demands. Beginning in Swabia, the revolt spread rapidly through central and southern Germany. For a time the old order seemed seriously threatened. Luther was as much alarmed as the princes at this revolt against established authority. With a singular lack of sympathetic insight, he urged the peasants to remember the Biblical injunction to obey the magistrates. Then, when they refused to listen, he called on the princes to crush and slay the "thievish, murderous hordes of peasants." The lords needed no such encouragement. The revolt was put down with appalling savagery. The peasants and artisans sank back into a hopeless economic slavery and looked no more to Luther for guidance.

Instead, great numbers of them joined one or other of the numerous little sects which now formed as independent groups apart from both the Catholic and Lutheran churches. Luther's example had been more potent than he could have wished, especially now that he was the active head of a triumphant state church. In the days when he was in rebellion against the Catholic Church, he had confidently asserted the right of the individual man to interpret the Bible and religion generally in the light of his own reason and conscience. And though he later denied that right to others in practice, and though the Lutheran Church, like all other Protestant state churches, persecuted dissenting opinion, yet the ultimate sanction of Protestant belief continued to be the reason and conscience of individual men rather than the authority of a universal, apostolic church, as was true with Catholicism. As a result, Protestants in every land continued to assert the right to individual judgment in opposition to the state church, whatever it might be, and to found dissenting sects. No matter how it might organize or become established with state support, Protestantism was essentially sectarian rather than universal in character.

In Germany the sectarian revolt took a great variety of forms, with wide divergence in creed as well as in moral and social teaching. Nevertheless, they all shared a few common characteristics, and since most of them refused to recognize the validity of infant baptism and insisted on rebaptizing their converts, they were generally known as Anabaptists. They were all recruited from the submerged and downtrodden classes; they refused obedience to the state church and sometimes to the state; they founded their doctrine, whatever it might be, on a literal, unhistorical interpretation of the Bible with a view to restoring the simplicity of primitive Christianity; and they were cruelly persecuted everywhere by Catholic and Protestant states alike. Ignorant they may have been, but they were deeply pious and their history is ennobled by an inspiring record of heroic constancy in the face of persecution. Despite every effort of the persecuting state churches, they continued to exist, and their modern descendants are to be found in the Baptist, Mennonite, Moravian, and other churches.

If Lutheranism lost heavily through the defection of the humanists, the peasants, and proletariat, that loss was compensated

Consolidation of Lutheranism

by the adherence of the middle and upper classes in an increasingly large number of the German states and free cities. Within Luther's lifetime, nearly half of Germany officially adopted his church. The princes found in it a valuable support for their governments, while the burghers found in Luther's teaching a moral and ethical ideal as well as an individual spiritual life more in harmony with their character than that provided by the medieval church. The victory of Lutheranism was in part the triumph of the territorial state over the universal church, but it was also the triumph of a new lay-bourgeois ethic over the feudal-clerical-monastic ideals of the Middle Ages. It was not the least important result of the Reformation that the good citizen — the pious layman, who was a good husband and father, honest, hard-working, and thrifty — supplanted the ascetic monk or the crusading knight as the ideal Christian.

The founding of Lutheran state churches inevitably caused grave political complications in Germany. Church and state were too closely united to admit of any degree of religious toleration. The Lutheran princes claimed the right to determine the religion of their states as Catholic rulers did, and when at the emperor's dictation, the Diet of Spires in 1529 passed a resolution denying that right, the Lutheran princes drew up a formal protest. It was from this that they came to be called Protestant, a name later applied to all non-Catholics. Shortly after this, both Lutheran and Catholic princes formed leagues for mutual protection and Germany was divided into two armed camps. Charles V was eager to restore religious unity to his empire for political as well as religious reasons, but was too busy elsewhere to bring strong pressure to bear on the heretics until 1546. He then declared war on the Protestant league, only to find that he had delayed too long. Though successful at first, he found that the new religion was too firmly established to be permanently crushed. Finally he was forced to agree to a compromise that left each prince free to make his state either Catholic or Lutheran as he

Religious war and peace

chose. This was the **Religious Peace of Augsburg**, signed in 1555.[1] It kept a rather uneasy peace in Germany for the rest of the century.

By this time, Lutheranism had gained nearly the whole northern half of Germany. It had also spread to the Scandinavian lands. The Reformation in Norway, Denmark, and Sweden followed much the same course as in the German states, the rulers taking the lead and establishing national churches directly under the control of the state, though here the episcopal system was retained.

Lutheranism in Scandinavia

3. ZWINGLI AND CALVIN AND THE REFORMATION IN SWITZERLAND

Luther's doctrine seems to have been peculiarly suited to the Teutonic mind. Outside of Germany and Scandinavia, pure Lutheranism never gained any permanent hold, though Luther's influence and example played a large part in the spread of the Reformation to other lands. Save in England where the Anglican Church grew up under a variety of influences, the Protestants in other countries, Switzerland, France, the Netherlands, and Scotland, to name the most important, followed the leadership of Zwingli and Calvin. The Protestant churches founded in these countries were generally known as the "Reformed Churches," to distinguish them from the Lutheran.

To the south of Germany, and closely connected with it by bonds of tradition, language, and trade, the thirteen cantons of the Swiss Confederation maintained an independent existence as the freest and most democratic states in Europe. Situated at the heart of Europe, Switzerland was in constant contact with her great neighbors, Germany, France, and Italy. Sturdy Swiss foot soldiers, the finest of their age, fought for pay in the armies of France and Italy, while the merchants of the city cantons grew rich on the trade that flowed through the Alpine passes from Italy to Germany. In the northern cities of Zurich, Basle, and Berne, Christian humanism of the northern type had taken firm root.

Zwingli's early environment

[1] See below, page 427.

Erasmus found at Basle a printer for his New Testament and a circle of congenial friends with whom he spent many of the later years of his life. It was in this stimulating intellectual atmosphere that Huldreich Zwingli (1484–1531) grew up and received his education. He entered the priesthood at about the time that Luther was taking his final vows in the monastery at Erfurt; but in the years when the German monk was seeking salvation in agony of soul, the future Swiss reformer was devoting himself to the study of the classics. He was a thorough humanist and Erasmus was his idol. It was due to his influence that Zwingli first turned to the study of evangelical Christianity, though for many years his interest in religion was fairly perfunctory.

In 1519, shortly after he had been transferred to the minster church in Zurich, Zwingli experienced a religious conversion. At the same time he began to read Luther's first pamphlets. **The Reformation in Zurich** He immediately became a reformer and preached to such good effect, appealing both to the desire for reform and the patriotic resentment of Roman domination, that he gradually won over the city council and a majority of the people to his views. In 1525, the last Catholic Mass was celebrated in Zurich. That event marked the completion of the Reformation in the canton. The "Reformed" religion, which now became the official doctrine of Zurich, was in many respects similar to Lutheranism. The sacramental system, the celibacy of the clergy, monasticism, fasts, and the veneration of saints and relics were abolished. Like Luther, Zwingli founded his teaching on the authority of the Bible, but he interpreted it more freely and with more radical results. The point on which he differed most widely from Luther was in his interpretation of the sacrament of the Lord's Supper, which he considered merely a symbolical commemorative service, whereas Luther, though denying the miracle of the Mass, insisted on the real presence of the body and blood of Christ in the elements of bread and wine. This distinction foiled all attempts at union between the two branches of Protestantism, but it was not the only difference. Zwingli was less mystical and less absorbed in theological dogma than Luther. He was a practical reformer with much of the Erasmian conception of religion as a philosophical guide to daily life.

From Zurich the reform spread to the other city cantons and even beyond the borders of Switzerland to Strasbourg and other German cities of the upper Rhine. **Spread and opposition** The five forest or rural cantons, however, were more conservative and remained loyal to Rome. In 1529 they united in alliance with Austria to oppose the Reformation. The bitter feeling between the two religious parties soon led to open war, which ended with the defeat of Zurich, left alone to face the Catholic forces, in 1531. The Peace of Cappel, which followed, was moderate, leaving each canton free to determine its own religion, but the Reformed Church had suffered a serious loss in the death of Zwingli, who was killed in the final battle. For a time it was left leaderless, until the arrival of Calvin opened the second period of the Swiss Reformation.

John Calvin (1509–64), the new leader who did more than even Zwingli had done to form the spirit of the Reformed Church in Switzerland and the **Calvin** other countries that adopted it, was by birth and training a Frenchman. He was born of moderately well-to-do parents in Picardy and educated at the University of Paris and in the law schools of Orléans and Bourges. At Paris he received a thorough training in the classics, which left him with an excellent Latin style and may have been in part responsible for the feeling for style in handling his native tongue that made him one of the greatest masters of French prose in his century. His legal training was equally important, for to the end of his days his thought on all religious and moral questions retained a strongly legal cast. Shortly after he had completed his studies, Calvin was converted to the new doctrine of the Reformation, through reading the works of Erasmus and Luther. But France at that time was no safe place for heretics and he was forced to flee. He took refuge in the Swiss city of Basle in 1534 and there began his first theological writing.

HULDREICH ZWINGLI

This portrait of the founder of the Reformation in Switzerland is from a painting by Hans Asper.

JOHN CALVIN

The grim austerity of Calvin's face was well suited to his character and creed.

CALVINIST ICONOCLASTS IN THE NETHERLANDS

The Calvinists were opposed to the decoration of churches with pictures or images of the saints, and sometimes destroyed them.

THE REFORMATION AND THE FOUNDING OF THE PROTESTANT CHURCHES 415

Calvinism

Two years later, Calvin published the first edition of his *Institutes of the Christian Religion*. From time to time thereafter he added to it in new editions and also translated it from the original Latin into French. When finished, this work contained a complete summary of that system of theology and morals generally known as Calvinism. More than any other book it was responsible for the spread of Protestantism to the non-Lutheran countries. Its clarity of thought and remorseless logic carried conviction more unescapably than did the mystical fervor of Luther. There was little that was really original in Calvinism, for the fundamental doctrines were Luther's almost without exception, and yet the total effect was very different from Lutheranism. The chief difference, aside from the more logical and consistent development of Calvin's thought, lay in a decided shift in emphasis. Starting with the same belief in man's inability to save himself by good works, Luther placed the greatest emphasis on the saving power of faith, whereas Calvin thought much more about the majesty and power of God, who predestines certain souls for salvation and assigns the rest of mankind to hopeless damnation. Calvin's was a sterner doctrine, and its sternness was reflected in his moral teaching and legislation. He considered it the duty of the church and state to make men moral in the strictest legalistic sense. No part of his teaching had a more profound influence on the life of the Calvinist countries than this. The civilization of America to this day shows traces of the Calvinist morality brought over to these shores by the Puritan immigrants who founded the early colonies in New England.

Calvinist morality

In the emphasis on strict morality lay the one apparent logical inconsistency in Calvin's doctrine. Yet if it did not follow logically from his doctrine of predestination, it was psychologically necessary. No serious man — and Calvinism appealed essentially to serious men — contemplating the awful majesty of God and the foreordained alternatives of eternal salvation or damnation, could remain indifferent to his own fate in eternity. And since no man could be sure that he was of the elect, and since nothing he could do of his own will could change the immutable decree of predestination, the Calvinist lived under the shadow of a terrifying uncertainty. According to all logic, the fact that he could do nothing to change his fate should have made him indifferent to his conduct in this world, but the doctrine of predestination had instead exactly the opposite effect. For it might safely be assumed that those whom God had chosen to be saved would be men who would lead good moral lives. The fact of living a strictly moral life did not prove that one was of the elect, but if one were leading an immoral life it did prove that one was not of those chosen. Hence there was at least a partial assurance in the former case, and it was a bold man who could spurn even such uncertain comfort. Further, Calvin and his followers tended to take their conceptions of God and of morality more from the Hebraic Old Testament than from the New. To the Calvinist moral laws were veritably laws, such as Jehovah had handed down to Moses on Mount Sinai, and in enforcing moral laws, including the strict observation of the Hebrew Sabbath, Calvinist rulers and ministers felt that they were carrying out the will of Jehovah. To understand the spiritual atmosphere of any Calvinist country, whether Geneva, Scotland, or New England, one must know the atmosphere of the Old Testament prophets and the Pentateuch.

Reformation in Geneva

The laboratory in which Calvin worked out the practical application of his doctrine was the city of Geneva. It lay in the French-speaking district on the borders of Switzerland and was not yet a fully fledged member of the Swiss Confederation when Calvin first entered it in 1536, though it was closely allied with the Protestant canton of Berne, which was supporting the Genevan citizens in their struggle for freedom from the rule of their bishop and count. The latter two, who shared the government of the city, were both members of the house of Savoy. Owing to the bishop's double authority, the rebellion against the domination of Savoy meant also rebellion against the church. The Reformation in Geneva, therefore, began partly as a political expedient. The chief Protestant preacher, William Farel, was finding grave difficulties in organizing the Reformed Church among the people who were not all converts by conviction. Such was the situation when Calvin came to Geneva for a brief visit and was commanded by Farel in the name of the Lord to stay and help him. For three years Calvin and Farel strove to organize and purify the new church, but aroused so much opposition by their unbending discipline that they were finally driven out. The new church, however, was hopelessly divided without their leadership, and in 1541 the people of Geneva begged Calvin to return on his own terms. For the remainder of his life Calvin was the real ruler of Geneva, though all opposition to him was not crushed until 1555. Under the new constitution, which Calvin helped to form, the government of Geneva was a sort of theocratic republic, with the administration of state and church so closely interwoven that it is difficult to determine which was responsible for the moral legislation that made Geneva the most moral city in Europe.

From Switzerland, Calvinism spread to other countries. In some sections of southern Germany it replaced Lutheranism, but mostly its converts were found in countries where the Lutheran reform had gained no strong foothold. The Reformation in France soon became thoroughly Calvinist, and largely through Calvin's influence it gained ground steadily, despite the royal persecution which prevented the organization of Reformed churches till about 1555. The history of the Huguenots, however, as the French Protestants were called, belongs mostly to the period of the Counter-Reformation and the religious wars in the second half of the century and will be treated more fully later. The same holds true for the Calvinist or Reformed churches in the Netherlands, Bohemia, Scotland, and such influence as Calvinism had on the Church of England. The organization of the Reformed churches in other countries, and their relation to the state, varied according to local conditions, but all showed the influence of the strict moral sense and rugged spirit of the Genevan reformer.

4. THE REFORMATION IN ENGLAND UNDER HENRY VIII AND EDWARD VI

In the English Reformation the same causes were present as have been noted in connection with the revolt from Rome in the continental states; but they were present in a very different ratio. National, political, and economic motives played a much more important part in the early stages of the movement in England than did religion. Under Henry VIII, little more was accomplished — or aimed at — than the transference of the political control and of the temporalities of the English Church from the pope to the king. The religious Reformation followed the political. It was not till after Henry's death that England became in any real sense Protestant.

Henry VIII was as nearly an absolute ruler as any English king ever became, and his will was the determining factor in bringing about the break with Rome at the time when it occurred, yet Henry could never have forced his people to throw off their ancient obedience to the pope had not a great many of them been already prepared to welcome the move. National opposition to papal interference in English affairs had found bold expression from time to time since the fourteenth century. England had suffered more than most countries from the financial exactions of the papacy and from the appointment of the pope's foreign favorites to high ecclesiastical offices. The wealthy and corrupt monks and priests were no more popular in England than elsewhere. Moreover, England had been the scene of Wyclif's daring attack on the wealth and temporal power of the clergy, and though his Lollard followers had apparently been crushed, the memory of his teaching had never been entirely forgotten. The Christian humanists, too, had done their share to prepare the way for the Reformation here as on the Continent. John Colet, Sir Thomas More, and the rest of Erasmus's circle of English friends, though most of them remained loyal Catholics, had made evangelical Christianity and the idea of a practical reform of church abuses familiar to the educated classes. Finally, Lutheranism had been brought over from Germany by merchants and wandering scholars, aided by the printing press, and was spreading slowly through the city middle class, where it found a congenial atmosphere as it had among the continental bourgeoisie. When Henry rebelled against papal authority, then, he could count on a considerable amount of popular support.

In the early years of Henry VIII, however, there was little to indicate his future rôle in England's church history. Indeed, he was generally considered a strong champion of orthodoxy. In 1521 he published a violent attack on the Lutheran heresy, for which the pope awarded him the title of Defender of the Faith. Besides, he was too much engrossed in his ambitious foreign policy, in which he was encouraged by his chief minister, Cardinal Wolsey, to pay much attention to the reform of the church at home. For years Wolsey and the king expended the resources of the kingdom in an attempt to make England a power in international affairs by holding the balance between the Emperor Charles V and Francis I of France. And though Henry apparently realized that clerical privileges, ecclesiastical courts, and papal jurisdiction were now the only remaining obstacles in the way of his complete control of his kingdom, Wolsey, who was papal legate in England and hoped to be pope, was always able to distract his attention and stave off any action against the rights of the church. More than once, papal ambassadors warned the pope that if Wolsey fell, the church in England would suffer, and by 1527 Wolsey was slipping. His diplomacy had accomplished nothing save to waste the accumulated treasure of Henry VII and to burden the English taxpayers. Henry was already losing confidence in the cardinal, when the affair of the divorce precipitated Wolsey's ruin and brought on the break from Rome.

In 1527, Henry had been married to Catherine of Aragon for eighteen years and, save for one daughter, Mary, was still childless.

Early years of Henry VIII

Therein lay the immediate occasion of all the momentous events of the next few years. Henry needed a male heir to preserve the Tudor line and there was apparently no hope from Catherine. The death of all Catherine's sons in infancy began to seem to the king a divine judgment upon him for having broken the Biblical injunction against marrying a deceased brother's wife, for Catherine had previously been married, briefly, to his elder brother Arthur. Henry had secured a papal dispensation at the time of his marriage, but now conscience and inclination running together were sufficient to convince him that the marriage had not been valid. He was eager to marry again and had already chosen as his future wife Anne Boleyn. He therefore instructed Wolsey to secure a divorce, or rather an annulment, from Pope Clement VII. But in 1527 the pope was in no position to take action against Catherine. She was the aunt of Charles V, and Charles was master of Italy. The imperial troops had just sacked Rome and the pope was in their power.[1] Negotiations dragged on until Henry lost all patience. In 1529 he called a Parliament that was to declare the English Church independent of Rome. Wolsey was deprived of his office and the following year was arrested on a charge of treason. Meanwhile, Parliament had begun to pass act after act reducing clerical privileges and papal authority. By 1533 it had so far separated the English Church from Rome that the new Archbishop of Canterbury was able to grant the king his divorce.

The royal divorce

The next year Parliament took the final step needed to establish the complete independence of the English national church. All relations with the papacy were severed and the king was declared by the Act of Supremacy to be the "supreme head" of the Church of England. This meant that one more kingdom had been lost to the once universal church. It was one more example of the triumph of central government over separate interests, of state over church, and of nationalism over the unity of Christendom that was characteristic of the age. The

The Anglican Church

[1] See below, page 421.

change was made with very little opposition because the majority were ready for it. Besides, it was a very conservative revolution. Save for the substitution of royal for papal authority and the loss by the clergy of their special legal status, there was no very marked change in the outward organization of the Anglican Church. The most radical change was the gradual dissolution of the monasteries and confiscation of their lands. Again Parliament willingly lent its authority to the king's will, for the monks had long been unpopular and the confiscation of the monastic lands enriched both the state and the wealthy burghers and gentlemen who purchased them from the king.

There was even less change in the official doctrine of the church than in its organization. Henry was still a champion of orthodoxy so far as was possible. A few earnest Catholics, like Sir Thomas More, were executed for their refusal to accept the king as supreme head of the church, but there were as many martyrs on the other side who suffered because they were too Protestant. Parliament authorized the use of the English Bible, and some changes were made in religious practice, but Henry was determined to keep the essentials of Catholic faith. In 1539, as a Catholic reactionary party gained ascendancy at court, Henry passed through Parliament an act defining the faith of the Anglican Church in six articles, all quite Catholic in tone, and this act was enforced by severe persecuting laws. The political break with the Catholic Church, however, inevitably opened the way for criticism of Catholic doctrine and, despite everything that Henry could do, Lutheran and Calvinist opinions were spreading rapidly in England.

Conservative doctrine

When Henry VIII died in 1547, he left his throne to his infant son Edward VI (1547-53) and the government to a Council of Regency headed by the Protector Somerset, the young king's maternal uncle. During the next six years a doctrinal Reformation was accomplished to supplement the political and constitutional Reformation of the previous reign. There can be no doubt that Protestants, whether Lutheran or Calvinist, or a compromise between the two, were still in a distinct minority, but they were an influential minority and strongly represented in the Council. The repressive laws of Henry VIII were repealed almost at once. The next step was to prepare an English liturgy and enforce its use by an Act of Uniformity in 1549. This was the first Book of Common Prayer, the work of Archbishop Cranmer, whose grand English cadences still are heard in the services of the Anglican Church. Three years later it was revised so as to make it more acceptable to the extreme Protestants, and at the same time the official creed of the church was defined in the Forty-two Articles of Religion. These were made as vague and general as possible so as to enable those who were almost Catholics, as well as Lutherans and Calvinists, to remain within the church. England was still far from unanimity in religion. All that the government was working for at the moment was a decent outward uniformity, while at the same time favoring a steady drift toward real Protestantism. But the question was still an open one when the premature death of Edward replaced his Protestant government by the Catholic régime of Mary Tudor.

The doctrinal Reformation

29

The States of Europe in the Age of Charles V

(1519–56)

DURING THE PERIOD dealt with in the preceding chapter, that in which the unity of the Catholic Church was broken and the three great Protestant churches, Lutheran, Calvinist, and Anglican, were founded, the rulers of Europe had often other and apparently more important problems to consider than the fate of religion, though that was something that could never be entirely forgotten. The outstanding factor in the relation of the European states to each other in this period was the existence of the vast dynastic empire of Charles V, which threatened the rest of Europe with the menace of Hapsburg domination. We have already seen [1] how this great accumulation of territorial states came to be united under the rule of the young heir to the Hapsburg, Burgundian, and Spanish dynasties, and have noted at the same time the development of strongly centralized states throughout Europe, under rulers who had acquired new national and dynastic ambitions with the acquisition of absolute authority in their own lands. Before the accession of Charles V, national and dynastic rivalry had embroiled the European countries in a greedy struggle for the spoils of Italy. That rivalry now took on a new character. The Valois king of France stood pitted against the mighty Hapsburg as his sole rival for the hegemony of Europe. They had too many conflicting interests to remain at peace with each other, and the destruction of either would have meant the domination of Europe by the victor. The other states, therefore, were drawn into the struggle in the hope of maintaining the "balance of power," that is, a state of international equilibrium. Meanwhile, within each territorial state, the rulers continued still further to centralize the government and to develop unhampered sovereign power.

These major themes of European history were repeated in miniature among the German states that made up the Holy Roman Empire. There the ambitions of Charles for centralized control and dynastic aggrandizement met the similar ambitions of the territorial princes. The German princes feared Hapsburg domination as much as did the rulers of the other European states. And in Germany, more than elsewhere, the situation was complicated by the religious revolution and by the constant threat of Turkish aggression from the east. The result here was the establishment of a temporary equilibrium among the German states that matches the larger equilibrium of Europe.

1. THE RIVALRY OF HAPSBURG AND VALOIS

In 1519, almost all of western Europe —

---

[1] See above, pages 393–395, and map, page 394.

the Scandinavian countries, Switzerland, and parts of Italy were the only exceptions — owed allegiance to one or other of three young and ambitious monarchs who for a generation were to remain the principal actors in the international drama. The youngest of the three, Charles V, had just been elected emperor of the Holy Roman Empire; but the shadowy imperial sovereignty over Germany represented only a small fraction of his real power. He was already the hereditary ruler of the Hapsburg family lands in and around Austria; of the Burgundian states of Franche-Comté, Luxemburg, and the Netherlands; as well as of the Spanish kingdoms of Castile and Aragon, Sicily, Naples, and Sardinia, and those new lands in the Americas whose store of gold the Castilian *conquistadores* were only beginning to touch. This imposing array of possessions made Charles the most powerful monarch in Europe; yet not so powerful as would appear on the surface, for in actual practice the available strength of his empire was always considerably less than the total strength of its component parts. It was a purely dynastic empire, accumulated by a series of family alliances. It lacked both national and geographical unity. The person of Charles was the only bond holding his scattered dominions together. To utilize the full resources of each in a common policy, or to satisfy their varying interests, would have taxed the genius and energy of a Charlemagne. And the nineteen-year-old ruler who accepted that appalling task was not a brilliant youth. He was not even personally attractive, being of a somewhat stolid nature and having inherited the more unfortunate Hapsburg features. But, as time went on, he proved that he possessed a large measure of sound common sense, industry, patience, and a degree of determination verging on stubbornness. These qualities in the long run served him better than the more brilliant and attractive traits of his rival of the house of Valois.

Francis I of France was a little older than Charles and had already won military glory by the conquest of Milan. He had a good deal of surface charm and culture; but his character was essentially frivolous, without depth or substance. Had he possessed any of the qualities of greatness, he might have fared very well in his contest with the Hapsburg, for, though he ruled less land, it was united in one compact national state, over which he had absolute control. Instead, he was vain, inconsequent, absorbed in selfish pleasures, and gifted with a fatal genius for snatching defeat from the jaws of victory.

Between these two monarchs stood the Tudor Henry VIII of England. His aim was to keep the balance between them so even that the influence of England, though a relatively weak state, might become the determining factor in European affairs. It was a sound policy, but Henry got less from it than might have been expected, for both he and his chief minister, Wolsey, too often mistook pointless duplicity for diplomatic skill and he was never prepared to back his promises by determined action.

It is a commonplace of history that war between Charles V and Francis I was inevitable, and certainly there were enough causes for friction to make peace between them impossible in that age when the personal or family interests of rulers were considered sufficient reason for war. In the first place, France was surrounded by Hapsburg territory,[1] and its king felt it necessary to break the Hapsburg power in self-defense. Then, too, Charles and Francis had conflicting dynastic claims to territory in half a dozen places. In the north, Francis held the duchy of Burgundy, which Charles claimed by right of descent from Charles the Bold, while Francis revived an old feudal claim to Charles's Netherland provinces of Flanders and Artois. In the southwest, Francis supported the claims of his kinsman the King of Navarre to the territory annexed by Charles's grandfather Ferdinand. Finally, both rulers hoped to dominate Italy. There, Francis held the duchy of Milan, which Charles claimed as a fief of the empire, while Charles ruled the kingdom of Naples, which Francis claimed as heir to the house of Anjou. And

[1] See map, page 402.

as if these various grounds for conflict were not enough, the two young rulers had been rival candidates in the imperial election, which created a strong personal animosity between them.

Of the two, Francis was better prepared for immediate war, since all his resources were concentrated in a single compact state. Charles had pressing problems to meet in Spain, threatened by a serious revolt, as well as in Germany, and he was in desperate need of money. He was fortunate, however, in being able to postpone hostilities until 1521. By that time he had met the imperial Diet at Worms, had disposed of his family interests in Germany by entrusting the Hapsburg lands there to his brother Ferdinand, and had gained allies, for what they were worth, in Henry VIII and Pope Leo X. The war opened with campaigns on three fronts, in the Netherlands, in Navarre, and in Italy, but throughout the war nearly all the serious fighting was concentrated in the last-named country. For four years the fortunes of war shifted from one side to the other, as did also the alliances of the papacy and the other Italian states. The French lost Lombardy and regained it. In the spring of 1525 their success seemed certain, when the situation was suddenly reversed. In a bloody battle fought before the walls of Pavia, the imperial troops destroyed the French army and captured the French king. It seemed like a decisive victory for Charles, but his resources were too far exhausted for him to take full advantage of it. He did not press the war, but contented himself with keeping Francis a prisoner in Spain until his resistance was so worn down that he would accept the terms dictated to him. By the Treaty of Madrid, January, 1526, Francis solemnly pledged himself to give up the duchy of Burgundy, as well as all claims to the disputed territories in the Netherlands, Navarre, and Italy.

Despite his solemn oaths and the pledge of his knightly honor, Francis had not the slightest intention of keeping the terms of the treaty. No sooner was he back in France than he was busy organizing the League of Cognac, composed, with France, of the Italian states, Venice, Florence, the papacy, and Milan, which had been given as an imperial fief by Charles to one of the Sforzas. All of these now became the natural enemies of the victorious emperor through their desire to keep the balance of power in Italy. Henry VIII declared himself favorable to the league, but did not join it. It was an alarming situation for Charles. As usual, he found it hard to raise enough money for foreign war from his scattered possessions and still harder to get the money to Italy. The Constable of Bourbon, a French prince who had deserted France and now commanded the imperial army in northern Italy, found it impossible to keep his troops in order without pay. In 1527 they mutinied and forced Bourbon to lead them to Rome, to collect their own pay from the pillage of the rich papal city. The sack of Rome, which followed, was as brutal and as thorough as any that the eternal city had suffered from the Goths or Vandals. The Spanish soldiers in the emperor's army left a bitter memory of cruelty and greed, while the German mercenaries, mostly Lutheran, took a special delight in deeds of sacrilege. The capture of Rome left Pope Clement VII helplessly in the emperor's power. Neither Rome nor the papacy would ever again enjoy the same wealth or freedom. For them the glory of the Renaissance was over. A new French invasion also marked the year 1527, but again Francis saw hope of victory turned to defeat. By 1529 both sides were ready for peace. The Treaty of Cambray was in main outline a repetition of that of Madrid, save that Francis was allowed to keep Burgundy, which Charles had learned he would not give up anyway. Like the former treaty, this was to prove no more than a truce. Nevertheless, it is an important milestone in the history of Europe. It marks the end of the first and most active stage of the war, and the beginning of that Hapsburg domination of Italy which was never seriously challenged till the nineteenth century.

The war dragged on through the remainder of the reign of Charles V, but intermittently. The emperor was left free from time to time to attend to the affairs of his

FRANCIS I OF FRANCE

This portrait possibly fails to do justice to the gallant king, who was regarded — at least by his courtiers — as a handsome man and more than a little of a dandy.

HENRY II OF FRANCE

Henry II, as painted by Jean Clouet, was an altogether grimmer person than his father. He belonged to the atmosphere of the Counter-Reformation.

various lands, to stem the tide of Turkish invasion, and to try to crush out the Lutheran heresy that was dividing Germany, but never for long enough to accomplish decisive results. The enmity of the Valois crippled him at every turn. More than once, the French king formed alliances with the Protestant princes of Germany and with the Turks against the emperor. Even the death of Francis I did not end the strife, for his son Henry II (1547-59) carried on the feud. The situation was still very much the same when, in 1556, Charles V voluntarily laid down the heavy scepter he had wielded so long. He left the Hapsburg lands in Germany and the imperial crown to his brother Ferdinand, his western states to his son Philip II of Spain.

The war, to 1556

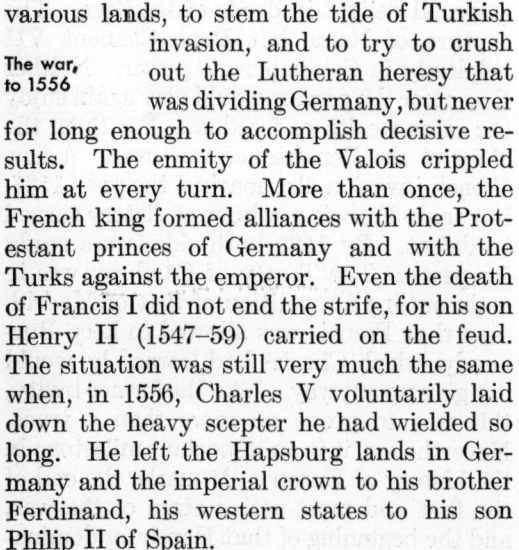

The concluding act of the long rivalry of Hapsburg and Valois is little more than a brief epilogue. In 1559, Philip II and Henry II signed the Treaty of Cateau-Cambrésis, the terms of which settled the

The Treaty of Cateau-Cambrésis

questions at issue between the two powers for the remainder of the century. France acquired some small additions of territory along her northeastern border, but in return finally renounced all claims to lands in Italy, the Netherlands, or Spain. This renunciation was in itself a solid gain for France. Her opposition to the encircling power of the Hapsburgs had perhaps been justified, but the men and money expended on the vain attempt to conquer territory in Italy, which could never have become an integral part of France, were wasted. They would have been better spent in an effort to round out the French frontiers to the north and east within the geographical limits of old Gaul. The final abandonment of the Italian dream removed one of the principal causes for war, while the splitting of Charles's empire between his brother and son reduced the fear of Hapsburg domination. A rough equilibrium among the European powers was thus established, which lasted for the most part during the coming half-century of internal religious wars.

2. CHARLES V AND HIS EMPIRE — THE PROTESTANTS AND THE TURKS

If the contest with the kings of the house of Valois formed the central theme of the reign of Charles V, it must not be forgotten that, along with this foreign problem, Charles had also to deal with a host of problems connected with the internal government of his various states. These states were so diverse in geographical position, race, language, economic and cultural interests, and even in religion, that no one consistent policy could be applied to all. No policy, that is, except the traditional policy of the Hapsburgs, which was to capitalize every opportunity for the aggrandizement of the family. Dynastic ambition was not a trait peculiar to the Hapsburgs; it was shared by most European rulers. But Charles could not identify it with national interests as could the kings of France or England. He was born and brought up in the Netherlands, yet his empire was too large for him to subordinate his major policies to Flemish interests. He was always a foreigner in Germany and Italy. In the latter he worked for Hapsburg domination rather than Italian unity, and in the former he allowed the interests of the Austrian Hapsburg states and the distractions of his dynastic war with France to thwart his efforts to rebuild a united imperial state. So far as Charles did identify himself with any country, it was with Spain.

Problems of Charles V

In the sixteenth century, Spain was the greatest state in Europe, with the possible exception of France. It was certainly the strongest of the states ruled by Charles, and it was there that he made his permanent residence, leaving it only when the pressing needs of his other possessions demanded his presence. He became in time a thorough Spaniard and won the loyalty of the Spanish people by convincing them that their country was the center of his empire and that their interests were his. His relations with them, however, were not at first happy. When he first came to Spain in 1517 as the heir of the late King Ferdinand, he was regarded as a foreigner and his Flemish ministers were distrusted and hated. The Spaniards resented the expenditure of Spanish gold to win the imperial election, which threatened to make Spain merely a province of a German empire. A widespread revolt, inspired by a mixture of social discontent with resentment of royal taxes and foreign ministers, broke out just as Charles was leaving for Germany in the spring of 1520. It collapsed, however, from lack of cohesion among its leaders, before Charles returned in 1522. For the next seven years, while the war with France raged most fiercely, the emperor stayed in Spain and gradually the Spanish people came to accept him as the embodiment of their national state. His victories were Spanish victories, won largely with Spanish gold and the incomparable Spanish foot soldiers. Moreover, his rigid Catholic orthodoxy, which tended to alienate him from his northern subjects, was perfectly congenial to the Spaniards, the most orthodox nation in Europe. They fully approved of his bloody conversion, or extermination, of the Moorish population in the southern provinces, though it meant the destruction of the most industrious class in the peninsula. There was here no conflict between church and state, but rather a strong mutual support.

Spain

In these years the wealth of Spain was a byword in Europe; yet for all its apparent prosperity, the economic strength of Spain was not so secure as it seemed. Before another generation had passed, it was destined to begin a rapid and permanent decline. The truth was that Spain was living on unearned increment, the gold and silver stolen from Mexico and Peru. This sudden wealth stimulated industry and commerce for a time, but in the end it proved a curse — the curse of Midas. There was too much gold. It raised prices to a higher level than in any other country, with the result that Spain bought more than it sold. The most lasting benefits, therefore, went to other countries. The tremendous expense of Charles's foreign wars, too, helped to drain the country of its gold, while bringing no economic return. Finally, the easy wealth of the Americas destroyed the industrious instincts of the people, such as they were, for they always had been more apt to war than

Prosperity of Spain

to trade. This wealth lasted about two generations. When it was gone, there was nothing left.

Next to Spain, Charles depended most on the wealth of the Netherlands and was most at home there. Under his rule the Netherlands prospered, despite heavy taxation, and the frontiers were rounded out by occasional conquests. Save for one serious rebellion at Ghent in 1539, the people remained loyal to their native prince. Nevertheless, there was a growing discontent under the surface, the fruits of which were to be reaped by Charles's son Philip II. There was reason for the suspicion that the emperor was exploiting their resources for his own advantage rather than theirs. The prosperity of the Netherlands was due more to the industry and keen trading sense of the people than to the government, and what advantage accrued to trade from the connection with Spain scarcely compensated for the heavy taxes to support Charles's foreign policies, in which the Netherlands had no real interest. Besides, the emperor's attempts to suppress heresy in all his dominions aroused resentment, for, despite persecution that kept them under cover, Lutheran, Anabaptist, and finally Calvinist opinions were gaining many converts.

The Netherlands

If the Netherlands were still a source of strength to the Spanish monarchy, though destined to be a ruinous expense in the next generation, Italy probably cost more than it was worth to Spain. Here the interests of Charles were purely dynastic. He made no attempt to establish national unity in Italy. All he aimed at was to acquire as much land as possible for his family and so to manage the remaining states as to bring the whole peninsula under Hapsburg domination. And this he accomplished. Milan was conquered, while Florence, Genoa, the papacy, and the smaller Italian states preserved their nominal independence only by subservience to the dominant power.

Italy

It was in Germany that Charles encountered his most difficult problems and met with the least success. Although it was the ancient home of the Hapsburg family, Charles was always a foreigner in Germany. He spent little time there, and constantly put off dealing with German problems until he had leisure from his more vital interests elsewhere. This, however, was not the only reason for his failure. It is doubtful if the most German of emperors could have revived the outworn Holy Roman Empire at this late date, or have preserved in it more than a formal unity. True, there had been of recent years a marked growth of German national sentiment, which Charles might have used if he had identified himself strongly with German nationality; but class jealousies, the petty independence of free cities and imperial knights, the territorial sovereignty of the princes, and, in addition, the new religious differences were centrifugal forces stronger than any feeling of national unity.

Germany

At his first imperial Diet, that of Worms in 1521, Charles took steps to meet the two most important problems of the empire, the reform of imperial government and the suppression of the Lutheran heresy. In neither was he successful. The solution of the former problem was attempted through the creation of a council of regency, which would rule during the emperor's absence, and which he and the electors hoped would hold the empire together. After Charles left, however, the council proved powerless to act in any important matter. It had no adequate military or financial power, and even the princes on the council ignored its decisions. It was completely discredited by its failure to suppress the rebellion of the Rhineland knights, led by Franz von Sickingen, in 1522, and the Peasants' Revolt three years later, both of which were put down by the independent action of the princes most concerned. These two rebellions prove how strong was the social discontent among all classes, a discontent that had its roots in the economic readjustment of the new age, but was given an additional impetus by the first impact of Luther's revolutionary teaching.

The council of regency

The emperor's legislation against Luther had no more effect than had the attempt to reform the imperial constitution, and largely for the same reason. The imperial authority

The Protestant party

THE EMPEROR CHARLES V

Titian did his best to give the emperor the appearance of imperial dignity, but even he could not make him handsome.

THE EMPEROR CHARLES V AND POPE CLEMENT VII ENTERING BOLOGNA, 1530

The scene above, painted by Brusasorci, was part of the ceremony that attended the imperial coronation of Charles V.

was not strong enough, especially with Charles engrossed in affairs elsewhere, to coerce the princes or the governments of the free cities. During his long absence no serious effort was made to enforce the Edict of Worms. The Lutherans were left free to organize their church wherever they had the support of the local government. The Diet of Spires in 1526, despite a Catholic majority, passed a law, called a "recess," declaring each state free to act as it chose in regard to the new church. This was not an edict of toleration, but rather a declaration of the independent sovereignty of the separate states, a principle with which even the Catholic princes sympathized. Three years later, the news that Charles had ended the war with France and was about to return influenced a second Diet of Spires to repeal the recess, whereupon a number of Lutheran princes and cities presented a signed protest. The Protestant party was born. The following year (1530) Charles was back in Germany and presided over the Diet of Augsburg. He was determined, now that he was free from foreign complications, to take vigorous action. After an attempt at reconciliation had failed, the emperor gave the heretics six months in which to return to the church, after which, he declared, he would suppress them by force. But before he could put his threat into effect, Charles was forced to temporize by the necessity of gaining all the support he could get against the Turks, and the opportunity for decisive action was lost.

For more than a century, Christian Europe had lived in fear of the Ottoman Turks. **The Turkish menace** In 1453 they had completed the conquest of what remained of the Byzantine Empire by the capture of Constantinople. During the succeeding generations their conquests had continued at the expense both of their Christian and fellow Moslem neighbors.[1] Their victorious armies seemed invincible. At the time when Charles V was elected emperor, they held nearly all the land of the ancient Byzantine Empire as it had been in the days of Justinian. All the Balkan states had been lost to Christendom, and before long Europe

[1] See map, page 323.

was shocked by the news of a further Turkish advance up the Danube, under the command of the new Sultan Suleiman II, "the Magnificent" (1520–66). In 1526 his army defeated the Hungarians and killed their brave king on the field of Mohács. In 1529 the Turks laid siege to Vienna; were driven back; and now, in 1532, were advancing on Austria again.

Hitherto, Charles's brother Ferdinand, to whom he had entrusted the German Hapsburg lands, had borne the brunt of the defense against the Turks. **Ferdinand and the Turks** On the death of his brother-in-law, King Louis II of Hungary and Bohemia, at Mohács, Ferdinand had been elected king of both countries. His attempts to defend his newly acquired kingdoms as well as his hereditary Austrian lands kept Ferdinand too busy to take any action against the Lutherans. The new Turkish advance of 1532 forced both Charles and Ferdinand to come to terms with the heretics. Charles dropped his plans for crushing Protestantism for the time being and came to his brother's aid, driving back the Turks and recovering part of Hungary. The demands of his other possessions, however, prevented Charles from following up his victory. Before the end of 1532 he was on his way back to Spain via Italy. Ferdinand was again left to carry on the struggle alone, which he did without much success. Finally, in 1547, he and the emperor secured a precarious peace by recognizing the Turkish possession of the greater part of Hungary.

Meanwhile, with Charles once more absent from Germany and absorbed in other interests, Protestantism spread rapidly, while the Protestant party formed a defensive organization against the time of the emperor's return. **The League of Schmalkalden** As early as 1531, when there still seemed a chance of immediate action by the emperor, the chief Protestant states — principalities and free cities — had joined together in the League of Schmalkalden for mutual defense. As other princes were converted to Lutheranism, they too joined the league. Though often weakened by petty jealousies, the princes of the league made a formidable force. More than once the kings of France and England sought alliance with them against the emperor. With each year it became increasingly clear that Charles must return and crush them, or all hope of restoring the political as well as religious unity of the empire would be lost. But, what with campaigns against the Algerian pirates in the Mediterranean, wars with France and the Turks (now allies), a rebellion in the Netherlands, and other troubles, fourteen years passed before Charles was once more free to take up the task he had abandoned in 1532. By that time, about half of Germany or more was Protestant, including four of the seven electors.

Nevertheless, when Charles at last opened war on the League of Schmalkalden in 1546, he had fair prospects of success. His army was smaller than that of the league, but it contained a large number of those Spanish foot soldiers who had proved themselves to be the finest fighting material in Europe, and it was commanded by the able and ruthless Duke of Alva. Also, he had won over the treacherous Maurice of ducal Saxony and one or two others of the Protestant princes. His chief advantage, however, lay in the lack of unity among the leaders of the league and in their equally fatal lack of military strategy. As the chief Protestant princes separated to protect their own lands, the emperor forced one after another of the smaller states to submit. Finally, only John Frederick, Elector of Saxony, and the Landgrave Philip of Hesse had strong forces outstanding. In the spring of 1547, the former was defeated and captured at Mühlberg, the latter at Halle. Charles then set about the suppression of Protestantism in the states of the vanquished princes. The next five years proved that it was easier to defeat the princes than to reconvert their people. They had been Lutheran too long to give up their religion at the command of even a victorious emperor. In 1552, the Protestant princes rebelled, aided by an alliance with Henry II of France. Three years more of anarchy at last persuaded the emperor to give up all hope of crushing Lutheranism in Germany, and to make peace.

Schmalkaldic War

The final settlement of the religious strife in Germany, at least for the sixteenth century, was arranged at the Diet of Augsburg of 1555. It is called the Religious Peace of Augsburg. It kept Germany free from further religious war for more than sixty years; but there were terms in the compromise that maintained a constant tension between the Protestant and Catholic parties and promised serious trouble at some future date. That promise was fulfilled in the following century in the frightful devastation of the Thirty Years' War.[1] Four major principles laid down by this treaty are worth remembering: (1) The princes of the various German states and the governments of the free cities were to be free to choose between the Lutheran and Catholic faiths. The princes were to have the right to enforce the religion of their choice upon their subjects, but the free cities on the Lutheran side could not expel a Catholic minority. This principle, which made the religion of the state that of its ruler, is generally known by the phrase *cujus regio ejus religio*. (2) This principle was to apply only to Lutheran and Catholic governments. It did not extend to Calvinists, though their number was increasing. (3) An "ecclesiastical reservation" made an exception of ecclesiastical princes (archbishops, bishops, and abbots), who ruled territorial states. In case any of these should become Lutheran, he was to surrender his state, which would remain under the control of the church; but Lutheran subjects of such princes were not to be forced to give up their religion. (4) Protestant states were to retain whatever church property they had confiscated prior to 1552. The Peace of Augsburg marks a definite stage in the disintegration of the empire, not only because it determined that Germany should remain divided between two religions, but because it recognized the sovereign authority of the princes in the important matter of religious control. It was a victory for the princes in their struggle for independence as much as for Protestantism.

The Religious Peace of Augsburg

The Religious Peace was followed shortly by the abdication of Charles V. His dealings with his German empire had been

[1] See Chapter 35.

Hapsburg Lands after 1556

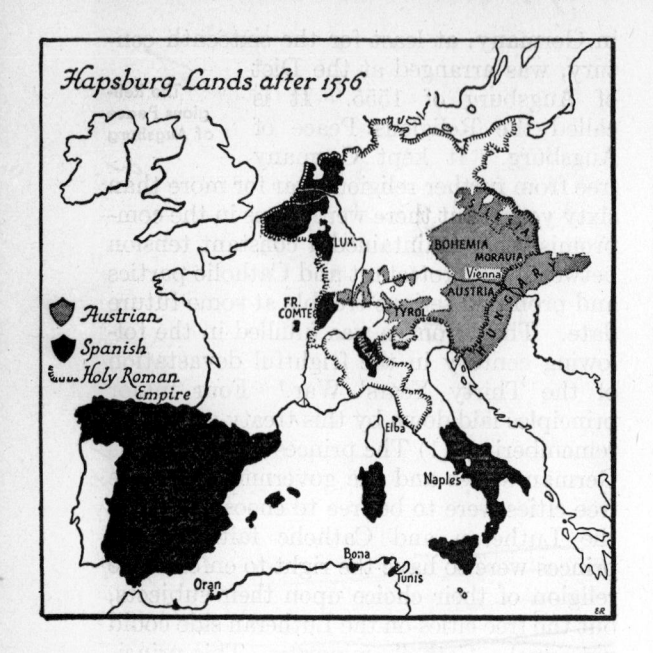

- Austrian
- Spanish
- Holy Roman Empire

generally unfortunate. He was embittered by one more failure at the end. He could not persuade the electors to accept his son Philip as his successor. He was forced, therefore, to split his inheritance. He surrendered the German Hapsburg lands to his brother Ferdinand, who had ruled them since 1521, and with them went the imperial crown. The remainder of his possessions, the Burgundian and Spanish inheritance, he left to his son Philip II. The abdication was completed in 1556. The weary emperor then retired to a Spanish monastery, where he died three years later. He was not an old man, but he had carried a tremendous burden of responsibility almost from childhood.

Abdication of Charles V

3. THE MONARCHY IN FRANCE AND ENGLAND

The kings of France who were the contemporaries of Charles V were rather less successful than he in foreign affairs, but, on the other hand, they had less trouble with the internal government of their state. We have already noted the triumph of the French monarchy over the nobles and the estates who might have checked its power. When Francis I came to the French throne, he took over a practically absolute government, and the royal power had grown still stronger when he handed it on to Henry II. It had been strengthened by one more generation of tradition, a generation in which the royal rights had been repeatedly asserted and stated in legal form by the school of legists who were trained in Roman law at the University of Toulouse. The treason of the Constable of Bourbon was the only indication that the great nobles who were related to the royal family might again be a menace to the crown; for the present at least, the nobility were obedient courtiers and soldiers in the king's pay.

Royal power in France

Like Charles V, Francis I and Henry II were often in need of money to carry on their foreign wars. What income the government had, however, was entirely at the disposal of the king, and with reasonable care it should have been sufficient, though the expense of a standing army was considerable. The French army was strong in artillery and cavalry, having the fighting nobility to call on for the latter arm, but was always weak in native infantry. For this wing of the service, the king had usually to depend in part on Swiss and German mercenaries, who were willing to fight under any flag so long as they were paid. In addition to the army, a good deal of money was spent in pensioning nobles and on the expenses of a luxurious court. The largest part of the royal income came from the *taille*, a direct tax, the amount of which the king could increase at will. Extraordinary expenses were often met by the sale of offices, many of them unnecessary ones created solely for the purpose of sale. This, of course, created a financial burden on the government for the future. On the whole, the financial system was awkward and wasteful. Later, during the Wars of Religion, its inadequacy came near ruining the monarchy.

Taxation and finance

The royal finances and royal authority were both strengthened by the power which Francis I acquired over the church in France. The terms of the Concordat of Bologna (1516) left the king with almost complete control of appointments to the higher ecclesiastical offices in the country. He used this

King and church

HENRY VIII, KING OF ENGLAND

Upper left: Henry is painted here (by Holbein) in later life, after he had lost much of his early vigor and abundant health; yet the face still shows the blunt strength and arrogant will that were characteristic of this bluff Tudor at any age.

THOMAS CROMWELL

Upper right: A Holbein portrait of the minister who was Henry's right-hand man during the years of the establishment of the Anglican Church.

CARDINAL WOLSEY

Left: This astute and ambitious prelate was the chief adviser of Henry VIII during the early years of his reign, but lost favor after failing to secure the king's divorce.

power freely to reward the loyalty of the nobles and also to pay the diplomats and ministers who served him, thus relieving the royal treasury of a considerable drain. A further extension of royal power over the church came in 1539, when the king transferred jurisdiction over the great majority of cases from the ecclesiastical courts to the royal courts. That the king had already acquired all the control of the national church and its wealth that he desired was one of the most important factors in deciding the fate of the Reformation in France. Had it been otherwise, Francis might easily have followed the example of other northern rulers in breaking with Rome. As it was, he remained strictly orthodox and persecuted heresy whenever he was on good terms with the pope, though neither he nor his son scrupled to ally themselves with the Protestant princes of Germany. Henry II was much more severe than his father in the persecution of French heretics, and, indeed, had more to work on, for despite persecution the Calvinist faith was spreading rapidly in France.

Across the Channel from France, Henry VIII inherited a government that was almost as absolute as that of the Valois kings, and, like Francis I, he handed it on still further strengthened to his son. England was now a full-grown national state. Most of the old medieval institutions still lived on in form, but the substance of their power had been transferred to the crown. The central government controlled commerce and industry, once the duty of the towns and guilds; it had taken over the full administration of justice, either through the royal courts or through the justices of the peace, who were the unpaid servants of the crown; and during the reign of Henry VIII the king also took over the supreme government of the English Church, thus completing his sovereignty over all institutions and all individuals in the state. Before this all-powerful monarchy, the old feudal nobility faded into insignificance. They were excluded from the king's council, which was the chief instrument of the central government, in favor of middle-class men or the **new nobility created**

Tudor absolutism

by the crown, men trained in legal and administrative service and wholly devoted to the king. At the same time, their local jurisdiction was superseded by that of the justices of the peace, who were recruited from the country gentry.

But if Tudor government was absolute, it was also popular, and scrupulously constitutional. Parliament never died out in England as the States General were dying out in France. Under Henry VIII, Parliament might seem little more than a subservient tool in the hands of the king; but it was a tool that he used constantly and kept in good condition. All Henry's major policies, for example his radical change in the government of the church and the dissolution of the monasteries, were carried out by act of Parliament. Henry VIII was, indeed, a master in the art of handling Parliament. Under his skillful guidance it became a dependable support to the royal authority by giving a legal coloring to the king's acts, rather than a check upon him. Yet all Henry's skill in avoiding the appearance of tyranny would have been useless had not the majority of his policies been genuinely popular, at least with that middle class of burghers and country gentlemen who made up the most influential class in the state. The success of the great Tudor monarchs, Henry VII, Henry VIII, and Elizabeth, depended in large part on the fact that they understood their people, that their policies were thoroughly English, and that they never forgot the economic interests of the middle class.

King and Parliament

The task of carrying on an absolute government in England was made easier by the fact that it was relatively inexpensive. High taxation would soon have destroyed the popularity of the government. But the kings of England in the sixteenth century were freed from many of the expenses that burdened the royal exchequer, and hence the people, elsewhere. There were not so many greedy nobles to pension as in France, and for some time Henry was able to take care of his favorites by means of the confiscated monastic lands. The administration of local justice cost nothing, being carried out by the unpaid

Tudor finance

justices of the peace. And, the greatest saving of all, the English kings did not need to maintain a standing army, as did the continental rulers whose borders were always open to invasion. Though Henry VIII was frequently drawn into continental complications, the number of English troops employed on the Continent was never very large. Instead of building up a strong permanent army, Henry devoted his attention to the more important, but less expensive, task of creating a royal navy. Not the least part of Henry's claim to be the founder of modern England lies in this realization of the importance of England's insular position and of defense by sea.

30

The Catholic or Counter-Reformation

FOR HALF A CENTURY after Luther nailed his theses on the church door at Wittenberg, the Protestant Reformation continued to spread, until the very existence of the Roman Catholic Church seemed threatened. At the end of that half-century, one or other of the three great Protestant churches was firmly established, with the active support of the state, in the three Scandinavian kingdoms, in about half of Germany and Switzerland, and in England and Scotland; Calvinism was in open rebellion against a Catholic monarch in the Netherlands and was fighting on fairly even terms in France; while the Catholic states of Germany, as well as Poland, Bohemia, and Hungary were honeycombed with the Protestant heresy, and signs of it had been seen even in Italy, the home of the Roman Church. Then the tide turned. The rising tide of Protestantism was checked and then gradually turned back. Within the next generation, the Catholic Church recovered much of the ground lost in Germany and the neighboring countries to the east, and made secure its permanent hold on the Latin nations to the south. This dramatic reversal was the work of the Catholic Reformation or Counter-Reformation, as it has been variously called, depending largely on the writer's point of view.

Historians have long debated whether the reformation of the Catholic Church in the sixteenth century was a spontaneous movement, springing from the desire of the Catholic peoples who were emerging from the age of the Renaissance for a deeper piety and a reform of ecclesiastical morals, or whether its inspiration was the necessity of rallying all the forces of the church against the growing menace of Protestantism by the revival of a more vital Catholic piety, by the strict definition and teaching of orthodox doctrine, and by the removal of those abuses that were so largely responsible for the defection of the north. The truth seems to be that it was both. That its origin was partly spontaneous is shown by the frequent and widespread demands for reform in the days before Luther was heard from, and in the following years before Lutheranism had become a serious danger to the church. A reform of clerical morality and a revival of piety within the church, a true Catholic reformation, would undoubtedly have taken place without the stimulus of the Protestant Reformation. But, lacking that stimulus, the Catholic Reformation would have followed a very different course from that which it actually took. As the Protestant menace increased, the efforts of the Catholic reformers were turned more and more toward the combating of heresy, so that in its mature form the Catholic Reformation was in very large part a counter-reform. The activity of the Council of Trent, the repressive measures of the Inquisition and the Index, and the work of the Jesuits, which were the chief agencies of the reformation, were directed principally to the defense of the church against heresy and to the recovery of those who were lost to it.

1. THE EARLY CATHOLIC REFORMATION

The spontaneous Catholic Reformation won its first and most complete success in Spain, and it was the Spanish spirit that dominated the movement later as it drifted into the Counter-Reformation. *The Spanish reform* The state of religion in the Spanish peninsula at the end of the Later Middle Ages was in many respects unique. The long crusade against the Moslems had tended to identify the defense of the orthodox faith with the growing sentiment of national patriotism, so that there was not a country in Europe where heresy was regarded with greater abhorrence. Spain had been less affected by the Renaissance revolt against medievalism and by those social changes that together helped to deaden the piety of Italy and to prepare the peoples of the north for new religious ideals and beliefs. The spirit of Spain was unquestioningly orthodox, and its piety of a type wholly in keeping with the ideals of medieval Christianity. Moreover, the monarchy had won control of the Spanish church and the interests of state and church were closely identified. Everything, therefore, favored the purely orthodox reformation, begun by Cardinal Ximenes in the closing years of the fifteenth century with the full support of the monarchy. The result was a marked improvement in the morals and educational standards of the clergy, which in turn led to a strong revival of piety among the people under their care. But the Spanish reform had also its darker side of persecution and intolerance. The Inquisition was introduced into Spain in a new and more effective form, to crush by force and terror all deviation of opinion from the strict lines of medieval orthodoxy.

In Italy, too, during the early decades of the sixteenth century, Catholic reformers were working earnestly to revitalize the spiritual life of church and people; but their efforts were isolated and did not meet with the immediate success achieved by the reform in Spain. *Catholic reformers in Italy* Indeed, in this late and rather decadent period of the Renaissance, Italy presented no very hopeful field for either clerical reform or religious revival. The upper classes were steeped in the semi-paganism of the classical revival, and some of them were prepared to give philosophical credence to the heretical ideas of the north; the great mass of the people were orthodox enough, but superstitious rather than pious; and in Italy, more than anywhere else, the papal *curia*, still headed by popes of the Renaissance type, was a perpetual stumbling-block to reform. Most of the abuses in the church had a financial reason for their existence and to remove them would cause a sharp decrease in the revenues of the pope and the members of his court. Hence the vested interests at Rome were opposed to reform. At the same time, Italy had received too many material benefits from the Italian papacy to rebel against it, as the northern states did, and there was no state government strong or independent enough to take the initiative in reform, as was done in Spain. Nevertheless, there were in Italy many earnest and devout men, some of them holding high offices in the church, who were sincerely interested in reform. In the later years of Pope Leo X, a number of these formed at Rome a loosely organized society known as the Oratory of Divine Love. Elsewhere similar groups were to be found. All were united in their hope of a Catholic reformation; but as time went on they drifted into two fairly distinct groups, separated by divergent ideas as to the policy to be pursued in regard to Protestantism. The one group, best represented by the Venetian humanist and statesman, Contarini, hoped for reconciliation with Protestant reformers on the basis of practical reform and a liberal interpretation of Catholic doctrine; the other, typified by the Neapolitan Bishop Caraffa, were equally eager for reform, but with no change or compromise in doctrine or usage, and favored the suppression of heresy by the means that had proved so successful in Spain.

Meanwhile, though efforts for practical reform were thwarted by lack of papal coöperation, considerable progress was made in the revival of religion among the masses of the people. Much of the credit for this work was due to new or revived religious orders, of which the most influential was the **Capuchin** order, founded in 1526 as a reformed branch of the Franciscan. The spirit of the new order was medieval rather than modern; its inspiration was a return to the ideals of Saint Francis. Like the early Franciscans, the Capuchins devoted themselves to preaching a simple piety among the poverty-stricken masses, and no group did more to gain popular support for the early Catholic Reformation than these kindly enthusiasts, whose pointed hoods soon became familiar sights in every marketplace. Good work, too, was done by the new Theatine order, founded by Bishop Caraffa in 1524 with the object of reforming the secular priesthood. It was composed of priests who had taken monastic vows, and had a wholesome influence on the clergy in all parts of Italy.

Revival of religious orders

With the accession of Pope Paul III (1534–49), following the death of the harassed and vacillating Clement VII, the Catholic reformers at last began to receive some co-operation from the papacy. Several of the most distinguished leaders of the reform party, including Contarini and Caraffa, were made cardinals, and a committee of cardinals was appointed to investigate conditions in the church. The report which they submitted showed so many abuses in the papal *curia* and throughout the government of the church that it was thought wise to suppress it, lest it give aid and comfort to the heretics. A beginning, however, was made in the reform of the *curia*, but as the energy of the aged pope declined, his zeal for reform also diminished and the results were disappointingly small. Still, the pontificate of Paul III marks an important turning point in the history of the church, the end of the Renaissance papacy and the beginning of the reforming popes.

The papacy takes up reform

In the early years of Paul's reign, the liberal reformers, led by Cardinal Contarini, seemed to be in the ascendancy at Rome. They were prepared to make some compromise with the spirit of the new age, as represented by both the Renaissance and the Reformation, and still hoped to re-establish the unity of the Catholic Church by a reconciliation of the Protestants. That accomplished, a general Catholic Reformation, free from the distractions of partisan strife and dogmatic controversies, would be possible. It was the policy proposed at the beginning by Erasmus, and it was doomed to failure now as then. Contarini and his friends failed to realize the fundamental nature of the differences separating the new churches from the old. They had, however, powerful support in Charles V, who was determined to restore religious unity to Germany and would have been glad to do so by peaceful means. In 1541, a serious effort was made to establish a mutual understanding at a religious colloquy, held at Regensburg (Ratisbon). Contarini was the chief representative of the Catholic Church and the liberal and conciliatory Melanchthon the principal spokesman for the Protestants. Thanks to Contarini's tactful diplomacy, both sides made surprisingly liberal concessions, yet they failed to come to any agreement on the fundamental question of the sacraments. The net result of the colloquy was to prove the impossibility of reconciliation even under the most favorable circumstances. The party of conciliation was discredited and quickly lost influence.

Failure of conciliation

Their place was taken by the conservative reformers, under the leadership of Cardinal Caraffa. This meant that hereafter the Catholic Reformation in Italy would follow the Spanish model and would become more and more a Counter-Reformation, directed against the growth of Protestantism. For more than a decade Spain had dominated Italian politics; from this time on the spirit of Spain was to dominate Italian religion as well. The reform of practical abuses in the church and the revival of popular Catholic piety continued, but they were coupled with strict medieval orthodoxy and stern repression of all deviating opinion. Before the death of Paul III, the Jesuits had become a powerful militia in the service of the papacy and the orthodox faith; the first

Opening of the Counter-Reformation

SAINT IGNATIUS LOYOLA

Upper left: The soldier saint who founded the Society of Jesus was a man of single-minded and passionate purpose.

POPE SIXTUS V

Lower left: One of the reforming popes of the sixteenth century, Sixtus V did much to restore discipline within the church.

TYPES OF SIXTEENTH-CENTURY CLERGY

Upper right: The idealized picture of the four Fathers of the Church shows the costumes worn by high church dignitaries in the sixteenth century. From left to right they are a bishop, a pope, a cardinal and another bishop.

LEADERS OF THE CHURCH IN THE SIXTEENTH CENTURY

session of a general council had been held at Trent; and the Inquisition had begun its work in Italy.

2. LOYOLA AND THE SOCIETY OF JESUS

Of the various agencies through which the Counter-Reformation was brought about, possibly none had a wider influence in retaining the loyalty of those who were still members of the Roman Church, or in winning back those who had deserted it, than the devoted preachers and skillful teachers who made up the Society of Jesus. In the Jesuits, as they were popularly called, "the most powerful missionary organization the world has ever seen was placed at the disposal of the papacy."

In the year when Martin Luther faced the Emperor Charles V at the Diet of Worms, the man who was to organize the church's best defense against Luther's teaching was fighting as an officer of Charles's army in the besieged city of Pampeluna in northern Spain. He was a noble from the Spanish Basque province of Guipuzcoa, one Don Iñigo Lopez de Recalde de Loyola, better known to history as Ignatius Loyola. He was wounded before the city was taken, and in the months of anguish that followed, his whole attitude toward life was changed. He determined to abandon his career as a soldier of the Spanish king for that of a soldier of Christ. Hereafter he would fight only with the weapons of the spirit, and would strive to emulate the deeds of the medieval saints, as in his earlier days he had imitated the heroes of chivalric romance. When he had recovered, save for a slight lameness that lasted through life, he set out on his new career with characteristic enthusiasm. As he himself tells us, he had still much to learn about the religious life. Some three years passed before he gave up the hermit life and extravagant self-denial he had begun, and determined to devote his life to aiding the salvation of his fellow men. For this purpose he realized that he would need more education, especially in theology. He therefore set about the difficult task for a man of his years of learning Latin, which was a necessary prerequisite to study in any university. In 1528, he matriculated in the University of Paris, where he remained for the next seven years, studying patiently and meanwhile gathering about him a group of disciples to aid him in his major purpose.

If Loyola never became a great scholar, he had other qualities that made men who were more learned than himself follow his leadership. Aside from his absolute sincerity, unswerving determination, and those indefinable gifts of personality that any leader of men must possess, Loyola's most valuable asset was his uncanny insight into the workings of the human mind. This was abundantly proved by his *Spiritual Exercises*, the book that helped to win his first followers and that later maintained the character of his order. Based on a detailed, introspective study of his own experience in the early days of his conversion, it gives directions for a period of intensive contemplation, lasting normally about four weeks, and designed to produce in the participant those soul-shaking emotional experiences that Loyola himself had undergone haphazard and over a much longer time. The *Exercises* left an indelible impression on the minds of those who passed through the course faithfully, and transformed them into devoted and obedient soldiers of the church.

Such was the training of the little group of companions who gathered about Loyola at Paris. There were six of them when, in 1534, they took an oath to go to Jerusalem, as soon as their studies were completed, there to do missionary work among the Moslems, or, if that proved impossible, to go to Rome and place their services at the disposal of the pope. The six had been carefully selected. They were all men of unusual character, ability, or learning. Among them was the Basque noble Francis Xavier, who was to become the most famous of the Jesuit missionaries, and the Spaniards, Lainez and Salmeron, who later exercised a decisive influence at the Council of Trent. In 1537, the companions, with three more added, met again in Venice, but, finding the road to Jerusalem blocked by the Turkish war, took the alternative course of going to Rome. The next two years were spent preaching and teaching in various parts of Italy. This experience showed them the crying need for work such as they were doing, and they determined to organize as a permanent order. After some delay, they received papal confirmation of their plan from Pope Paul III in 1540. The following year Loyola was elected first general of the order. The new order was called the Society of Jesus, but a more accurate translation of the Latin *Societas* would make it the "Company of Jesus," for Loyola intended the word to be used in the military sense. They were to be a company of spiritual soldiers, fighting under the banner of Jesus. During the next ten years, the rapidly growing society received many extensions of privilege from the pope, and these, together with a more complete draft of the constitution, were confirmed by a bull of Pope Julius III in 1550.

The purpose of the society was set forth clearly in the constitution, which Loyola finally completed just before his death, and in the bull of 1550. The best brief statement is in the latter: "The company is founded to employ itself entirely in the defense of the holy Catholic faith." In particular, that meant the defense of the church by helping to retain the allegiance of her people, by adding to her membership through the conversion of the heathen, and by winning back as many as possible of those who had been lost to the various Protestant sects. The order was not founded specifically for the combating of heresy, but that would be one of its chief duties. The method to be employed was fourfold: first, to educate the young in orthodox schools; second, to win influence with the doubtful through their services as confessors; third, to carry on missionary preaching in heathen or heretical lands; and fourth, to acquire diplomatic influence in international affairs by serving in the courts of nobles and princes. Unlike the earlier monastic orders, the society was not founded primarily for the salvation of its own members, though that was taken for granted, but to accomplish a definite purpose. For that reason, the keynotes of the constitution were efficiency and obedience. The spirit of the Jesuits was the spirit of their founder,

Its purpose

and Loyola was a Spaniard and a soldier. As a Spaniard he was unshakably loyal to the orthodox faith and to the traditional practices and authority of the organized church, whose head was the pope. As a soldier he never questioned the orders or policies of his superior officer, in this case the pope, and he expected equally unquestioning obedience from those under his command. In the *Spiritual Exercises* he had insisted on the necessity of mental obedience to the church, "always defending her teaching and never opposing it," and in the constitution he stressed above all else the necessity of absolute obedience, first to the pope and second to the general and other superiors of the order.

Loyola's emphasis on efficiency, which followed naturally from his conviction that the order was intended primarily to accomplish a definite purpose, was reflected in the military organization of the society and in the rules for the selection of new members. Novices were to be carefully chosen, with due regard to those qualities, such as good appearance, pleasing personality, intelligence, suitable character, and good social standing, that would make them most useful. Before becoming a full-fledged member of the society, the novice had to pass through a long period of spiritual training and education, during which he might be dismissed at any time. He was then assigned to one of the several different classes into which the society was divided, according to his ability or experience. All members took the customary monastic vows of poverty, chastity, and obedience, but there was an inner circle of the most experienced members who took an additional vow of special obedience to the papacy. From these "Professed of Four Vows" the executive officers were chosen. At the head of the whole order stood the general, elected for life, with absolute authority over all members. Under him were the provincials and a descending hierarchy of inferior officers, very much like that of a modern army. The Jesuits were a very mobile as well as a disciplined body. Any member could be dispatched at a moment's notice to whatever field seemed most in need of his services. As

Organization

a further innovation in the interests of efficiency, Loyola freed his order from those restrictions of dress, ascetic practice, regular hours, etc., which were common in the monastic orders, but which might interfere with the duties of missionary preachers and teachers.

The society thus formed grew with amazing rapidity and soon spread to every country of Europe as well as to the heathen lands beyond the seas. At the death of Loyola there were twelve provinces and some fifteen hundred members. Preaching and hearing confessions made up the largest part of their work, but their service as educators was perhaps more important. Jesuit schools and colleges soon sprang up in every Catholic country, and were regarded as among the most efficient of their age. The opportunity provided by their schools to shape the thought of the younger generation, in addition to their work as preachers and confessors, enabled the Jesuits to exert a very great influence on the people, the results of which were amply demonstrated in the success of the Counter-Reformation. In later centuries they were frequently charged with working more for the formal adherence to the church of the masses of the people than for their spiritual betterment, and their methods were subjected to a good deal of criticism. The emphasis on efficiency had its dangerous side. But in their early days, at least, the people saw in them only the most unselfish and devoted as well as the most effective servants of the church.

3. THE COUNCIL OF TRENT (1545–63)

The Jesuits had barely begun their work when the rulers of the church took steps to strengthen its defenses against the Protestant heresy by the calling of a general council, which was to determine the character of the Counter-Reformation. It met in the imperial city of Trent, just north of the Italian border, in three separate periods. The first period, 1545–47, fell in the reign of Paul III, the second, 1551–52, in that of Julius III, and the last, 1562–63, in the reign of Pius IV.

From the very beginning of the Lutheran movement, there had been frequent demands for a general council as a means of settling the great problem of the church. At first Luther and his followers had appealed from the authority of the pope to that of a general council, and later the Catholic reformers who hoped for reconciliation, as well as the Emperor Charles V, took up the cry. They were joined by the Spanish bishops and the conservative reformers of Italy, who agreed that a council was necessary for reform, but who were violently opposed to any policy of doctrinal compromise or reconciliation. In addition, all opponents of papal authority in the church worked for a council. The popes, however, were very loath to call one, for they had unhappy memories of the councils of Pisa, of Constance, and of Basle, and feared that the chief result would be an attempt to limit their authority. When Paul III finally agreed to summon a council, he did so as the result of a policy that few of those who demanded it would entirely approve. Since the failure of conciliation at Regensburg, the pope and the Counter-Reformation party, who were now in the ascendancy at Rome, had determined on a new policy, which was to recognize the loss of the Protestants as a whole as irremediable, and to concentrate on the defense of what remained, with the hope of winning back individual heretics wherever possible. This was to be done by an authoritative definition of Catholic doctrine on all disputed points, so as to clarify the differences between the old and the new churches; by active repression of heretical opinion in all Catholic countries; and by reform of those practical abuses that left the church open to reproach. This policy appealed to the Spanish churchmen, but not to the majority in France and Germany, who still hoped for some compromise with the new ideas; and even the Spanish reformers were opposed on one very important point. They had little hope of the papacy reforming itself and felt that reform should be carried out by the council, whereas the papal party felt that this part of the task should be left to the authority of the pope.

With all these divergent ideas as to the work the council was to do, it is not surpris-

EL GRECO

Upper left: A self-portrait of the painter, who seemed most deeply imbued with the spirit of the Counter-Reformation, at least in its Spanish form

PIETÀ, BY EL GRECO

Upper right: El Greco's conception of the dead Christ has a morbid and tortured quality.

ST. FRANCIS AND BROTHER RUFUS, BY EL GRECO

Like his Pietà, El Greco's conception of St. Francis was marked by a morbid asceticism that was foreign to the early Franciscan tradition.

THE SPIRIT OF THE COUNTER-REFORMATION

ing that its meetings were stormy, or that there were such long gaps between them. The political interests and animosities of the various states helped to complicate the situation still further. On the whole, however, the papal party was able to carry through its policy. At the very beginning, the pope secured a working control of the council by obtaining a decision that only bishops and heads of religious orders, who were present in person, should have the right to vote. This enabled him to maintain a loyal Italian majority, for Trent was close to Italy and the prelates from more distant countries were usually prevented by wars, expense, or other inconveniences from attending in large numbers. Still, the papal control was never very secure, and the papal legates were forced to compromise on the matter of reform, permitting its discussion, but on the condition that the definition of doctrine should be taken up at the same time. As a matter of fact, most of the time of the council was occupied with the latter question. All through the council, the Jesuits Lainez and Salmeron exerted a great influence on the members and were often instrumental in winning them over to agreement with the wishes of the papal party. During the last session, the diplomatic pope, Pius IV, took pains to secure the agreement of the great Catholic monarchs before submitting his projects to the council, and so won his way through what seemed an almost impossible situation. The final triumph of the papal authority was assured when the council in its closing session voted to present all its decrees to the pope for confirmation.

The council

The most important result of the Council of Trent was the final definition of Catholic doctrine. At a time when all religious opinion was in a state of flux, and when Protestantism was splitting up into antagonistic churches with irreconcilable differences in belief, the Roman Catholic Church was given a coherent and authoritative statement of orthodox faith which would prove a powerful instrument for the preservation of unity. The lines of demarcation between Protestantism and Catholicism were sharply drawn. Almost every one of the doctrinal decrees of Trent was designed to meet some Protestant dogma. Among the most important was the decree defining authority. Luther, Calvin, the Anabaptists, and other Protestants had appealed to the sole authority of the Bible against that of the church and the papacy. This was the authoritative foundation for Luther's fundamental doctrine of salvation by faith alone as well as for the general Protestant attack on the sacramental system, the secular power of the papacy and the clergy, monasticism, the veneration of saints, and the other practices of the church which had grown up in post-Biblical times and hence were not mentioned in the Bible. Forced to meet this argument, the council decided that the Bible and the tradition of the church were of equal authority, and that both could be interpreted only by the church, which in practice meant by the pope as head of the church. In addition, the traditional Latin translation of the Bible, the Vulgate, was declared to be the only authoritative version. This adherence to tradition as the best weapon against the innovators was the keynote of all the major doctrinal decrees of the council. By establishing the authority of tradition, however, the Council of Trent bound the modern Catholic Church to medieval precedent and made any later change in either doctrine or practice extremely difficult. Still, the very insistence on tradition had its value, for it gave to the Roman Church the prestige and authority of unbroken continuity with the past, which the newer Protestant churches necessarily lacked.

Definition of doctrine

The work of practical reform, so far as it was actually accomplished by the council, was of secondary importance. Still, it did outline a comprehensive program of reform abolishing the worst abuses and making provision for better discipline and higher educational standards among the clergy. The practical execution of these decrees, however, was beyond the power of the council, which ceased to exist as soon as its work was done. It had to be left to the executive authority of the pope and his successors. Fortunately, the majority of the later popes

Reform decrees

THE GRAND INQUISITOR, DON FERNANDO NINO DE GUEVARA

In one of his finest portraits, El Greco has made the Grand Inquisitor, who sentenced to death so many heretics, an entirely believable figure.

POPE PAUL IV

Cardinal Caraffa, later Pope Paul IV, was for many years the leader of the conservative wing of the Counter-Reformation. He was largely responsible for the introduction of the Spanish form of the Inquisition into Italy.

HERETICS BURNED BY THE INQUISITION

A contemporary representation of a scene which was an all too familiar sight in Spain during the Counter-Reformation

THE INQUISITION

proved worthy of the trust. The Catholic Church never again suffered from the lax discipline or worldly minded leadership that had left it so open to criticism during the period of the Renaissance.

4. THE COUNTER-REFORMATION IN ACTION

With the conclusion of the Council of Trent, all the forces of the Counter-Reformation swung into action, under the leadership of reforming popes. Without the support of papal authority, which was strengthened rather than otherwise by the council, no permanent success would have been possible. Even before the end of the council, the papacy had been responsible for a good deal of reform, in the reign of Paul III and still more under Paul IV (1555–59), who as Cardinal Caraffa had for years been the leader of the conservative Catholic reformers. After Trent, the spirit of the Counter-Reformation ruled at Rome. During the remainder of the sixteenth century, two popes in particular, Pius V (1566–72) and Sixtus V (1585–90), were zealous exponents of clerical morality and rigid orthodoxy. Under the former, the Catholic Church took on new vigor, crushed out all opposition in the lands it controlled, and began a remarkable period of reconquest. Catholicism was no longer on the defensive. It was carrying the war into the enemy's country. Under Sixtus V, as the power of Spain declined, the papacy took its place once more as the leader of the Catholic world, though no longer with the secular power that had hampered rather than helped its spiritual authority in earlier times.

Reforming popes

In the Latin countries of Italy and Spain, where the Counter-Reformation triumphed most completely, the work of reform was accompanied by savage repression of heresy. The Inquisition, which was the chief agent of repression, was not a new institution. It had been used with terrible effect against the heretics of southern France in the thirteenth century. In the closing years of the fifteenth century, it was revived and given new and more effective powers in Spain. Then, in 1542, when the Counter-Reformation first gained headway at Rome, Cardinal Caraffa persuaded Pope Paul III to reorganize the papal Inquisition in Italy on the Spanish model. Throughout the remainder of the Counter-Reformation period, the Holy Office, as the Inquisition was officially named, with its secret trials and its power to turn over condemned heretics to the secular government to be burned at the stake, maintained a reign of terror, completely successful in stamping out all open signs of heresy in Italy and Spain. North of the Alps and the Pyrenees it never gained a firm foothold, though Philip II at one time tried to introduce it into the Netherlands. A second and almost equally important agent for the suppression of unorthodox opinion was the Index of Prohibited Books, an elaborate system of censorship of the press, designed to prevent the publication or circulation of any book that might suggest to the people ideas derogatory to the church or to orthodox belief. One of the immediate results of the Council of Trent was the publication of the Tridentine Index, which superseded earlier lists, and was enforced wherever the co-operation of the civil government could be obtained. Later, a permanent Congregation of the Index was instituted by Pius V to keep the work up to date. The effect of this rigid control of the press in moulding the thought of the Spanish and Italian people can scarcely be overestimated.

Inquisition and Index

It is only fair to note that the persecution of heresy and censorship of heretical books were by no means confined to the Catholic Church. Tolerance of varying opinions in matters of religion was a virtue that found few champions in the sixteenth century. To both Protestant and Catholic theologians, the heretic who endangered men's souls was a deadly enemy of mankind. Moreover, in every country, church and state were so closely united that a dissenting religious sect was likely to become a seditious political party, and the persecution of heresy by the state often appeared as the punishment of treason or sedition. Nevertheless, the persecution of heretics was never as thorough or as savagely enforced in the Protestant countries as it was in Italy and Spain, for in none

Intolerance on both sides

of them was there a separate institution, with the terrible powers of the Inquisition, dedicated to that purpose.

However successful the negative measures of suppression might be in stamping out heresy in Catholic lands, they would never have accomplished the real revival of Catholic piety, much less the reconquest of doubtful or openly Protestant lands, which took place during the Counter-Reformation. For this, aside from the work of the Council of Trent and the reforming popes, credit must be given to the Jesuits. Their methods were positive and constructive. They preached, heard confessions and taught, reviving the piety of the indifferent, directing the consciences of the penitent, and instilling orthodox beliefs and devotion to the church into the minds of the young in their formative years. And they went out as missionaries to the lands that were drifting toward Protestantism. Some of their most effective work was done in Germany where, under the leadership of Peter Canisius, they brought about a revival of Catholic education and piety in the states whose rulers were still Catholic, but whose people were hovering on the verge of heresy.

By the end of the sixteenth century, the Counter-Reformation, like the Protestant Reformation, had spent its aggressive force. By that time the religious map of Europe was fairly definitely fixed. The church on both sides had become closely identified with the national, political, and governmental interests of the state, and could count on them for permanent support when the wave of religious enthusiasm died down. France had emerged from the Wars of Religion with a recognized Protestant minority, but with Catholicism assured as the national faith. Poland had been won back from Protestantism and Germany was evenly balanced between the two opposing creeds, with little chance of further conquest by either.

31

The States of Europe in the Age of Philip II

(1556–98)

THE FIRST HALF-DOZEN YEARS of the reign of Philip II marked the opening of a new era in the history of most of the states of Europe. The scenes shifted and new figures replaced the old on the European stage. In France, the death of Henry II left the government in the hands of his widow Catherine de' Medici and her weakling sons; in England, the last of the Tudors, Elizabeth, began her long and prosperous reign; the ill-fated Mary Stuart took over the government of Scotland in the midst of a religious revolution; and Charles V, about whom European politics had centered for nearly half a century, divided his vast empire between his brother Ferdinand and his son Philip II, who for the remainder of the century was to take his father's place as the focal center of European affairs. Nor were the changes of these momentous years merely changes of person. The strife of Lutheran and Catholic in Germany had just been settled by the Religious Peace of Augsburg, and the German states entered on a period of formal peace that makes it possible to ignore their history for half a century; in the next few years, Protestantism was permanently established in England and Scotland; the Netherlands were drifting fast toward open revolt against Spain; France gave up her claims to Italy, thus ending the long Hapsburg-Valois wars, and the French Huguenots opened the Wars of Religion that were to devastate France with civil strife for more than a generation; and in 1562 the leaders of the Catholic Church met in the final session of the Council of Trent.

These years set the stage for the history of Europe during the remainder of the sixteenth century. In many respects the age of Philip II was very different from that of Charles V. Both the Renaissance and the Reformation had passed their peak and other problems engaged the attention of the European peoples. The action is often confusing, the motives tangled and difficult to follow. But two or three main threads, often interwoven, run through the history of the whole period. They are: the Spanish-Catholic policy of Philip II, the driving force of the Counter-Reformation, and the rising commercial interests of England and the Netherlands.

1. SPAIN UNDER PHILIP II

The son of Charles V, who inherited the crown of Spain with its dependencies in the Netherlands, Italy, and the Americas, clung throughout his life to a consistent policy and to the conviction that it was God's purpose for

Policy of Philip II

the people of Europe. That policy may be briefly stated. It was, in the first place, to enforce absolute government and strict conformity to the Catholic faith in all his dominions; second, to use the unified force thus established to make Spain the dominating power in Europe; and finally, to use this Spanish hegemony as God's instrument for the restoration of religious unity under the Roman Catholic Church to Western Christendom. In essence it was the dream of Charles V in his later years, but narrowed and intensified in his son by the shearing away of the German half of the Hapsburg empire, by Philip's Spanish upbringing, and by the influence of the Counter-Reformation, which made Philip a more bigoted Catholic than his father had ever been. In short, where Charles had been a cosmopolitan emperor, to whom his family interests meant more than any country, Philip was a Spanish king, a Spaniard born and with a Spaniard's narrow patriotism, rigid orthodoxy, and relentless hatred of heresy. Philip's problems were made simpler than his father's by the loss of the German lands, but he had still a baffling variety of tasks to demand his constant attention, and, as in his father's case, his efforts were hampered at every turn by the utter inadequacy of the financial means at his disposal.

He was hampered, too, by fatal inadequacies in his own character and ability.

Character Philip had a very strong sense of duty, and he was an indefatigable worker. But, in an absolute ruler, industry may be nearer a vice than a virtue, when it is the product of a narrow, plodding mind, without understanding of men and lit by no spark of imagination. Philip's conscientious attention to every detail of government too often led to fatal delays. His best-intentioned efforts were often misdirected. His was the strength and weakness of the monomaniac. The conviction that his cause was the cause of God and Spain and he himself the chosen instrument of God's will held his spirit firm through countless trials, but it also closed his heart to mercy and his mind to counsel.

Philip was successful in carrying out the first part of his policy, at least in Spain. There the enforcement of universal orthodoxy was relatively easy, for the majority of the Spanish people were as stanch Catholics **Religious persecution** and as intolerant of heresy as Philip himself. The Inquisition had done its work well in the past half-century. Still there were alarming signs of heresy here and there in the last years of Charles V. Philip's first act, therefore, on his return to Spain in 1559, was to stimulate the Inquisition to renewed activity. The fires of the *auto-da-fe*, that terrible ceremony in which heretics were burned to death, spread across Spain. The persecution was thorough and effective. Even the suspicion of heresy was eradicated and it did not make its appearance again. There was still, however, in southern Spain one large group of very doubtful Catholics, the Moriscos of Granada. They were not heretics in the ordinary sense of the word, but descendants of the Mohammedan Moors who had been forcibly converted by Charles V. Philip had good reason to believe that their professed Christianity was no more than skin deep. Determined to crush out all signs of Mohammedan faith or practice, he instituted a series of repressive measures that finally goaded the Moriscos to a desperate rebellion. The revolt was put down with frightful thoroughness. The helpless Moriscos were massacred or transported into servitude in Castile. Granada, which had been the richest agricultural land and the most prosperous center of industry in Spain, was left a barren waste.

Religious unity was closely bound up in Philip's mind with the establishment of his own absolute authority in Spain. Each would help the **Absolute government** other and both were necessary in order to place the full resources of the country at the disposal of his greater purpose. The way had been prepared for him. He had only to carry on the work of Charles V in weakening the already feeble constitutional powers of the Cortes and in excluding the nobles from an active share in the civil government. His chief contribution was the development of a highly centralized bureaucratic administration, in which most of the offices were held by men of low birth who would be entirely dependent upon him. He

PHILIP II OF SPAIN

Titian has caught much of the essential character of his subject. The long pale face and heavy eyes indicate the cold and enigmatic character that made Philip respected by many but loved by very few.

THE DUKE OF ALVA

The Spanish general who tried to subdue the Netherlands by calculated cruelty was well suited by nature to carry out Philip's religious and political policies.

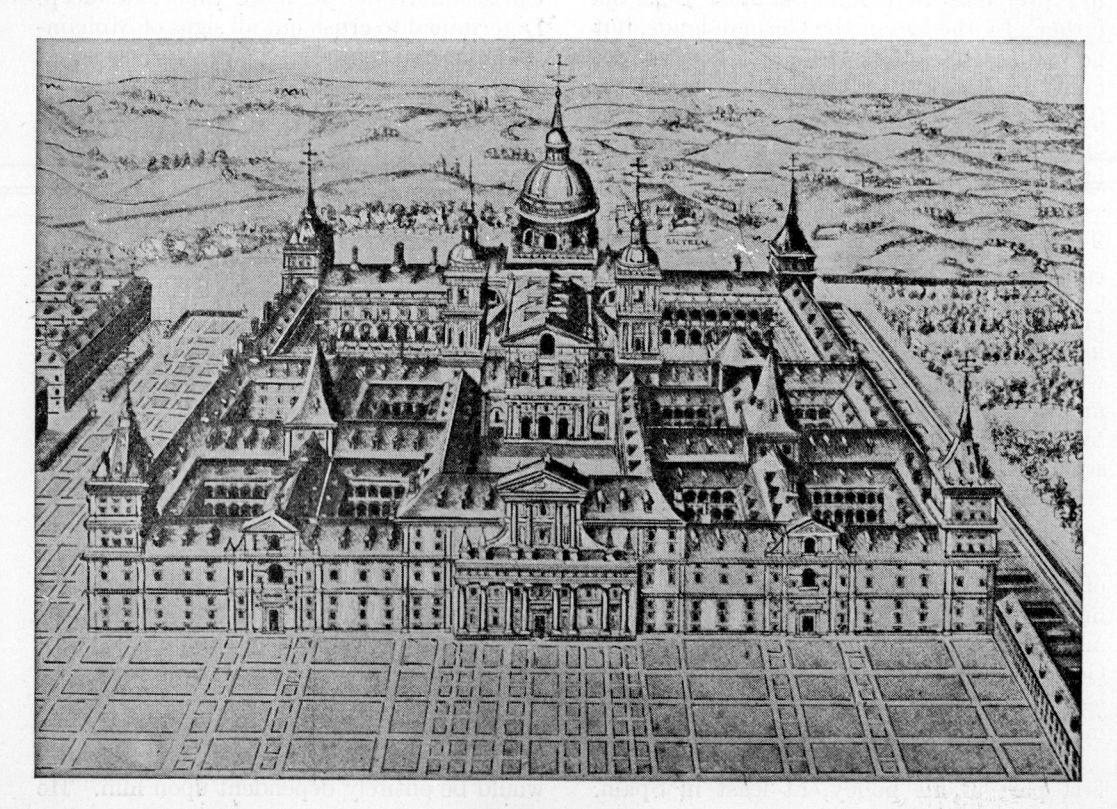

THE ESCORIAL

In the cold grandeur of this palace, built in the form of a grid in memory of the martyrdom of St. Lawrence, Philip II brooded upon death and the life eternal.

himself was the center of the whole system, supervising the work of all departments, often down to the most petty details.

So far, Philip succeeded in putting his policy into effect. But it did not have the desired result of making Spain a greater nation. On the contrary, both the country and the government grew steadily poorer, and when Philip died the fabulous wealth of Spain was fading to a memory. From the beginning, indeed, Philip was in constant financial straits. The ambitious foreign policies of Charles V had already reduced the government to the verge of bankruptcy, and Philip was forced to meet expenses almost as great from diminishing resources. Italy had never contributed much to the royal treasury, and the Netherlands on which his father had depended so heavily were in revolt during most of Philip's reign, thus making them a source of expense rather than of income. The whole burden, therefore, fell upon Spain. But even from this source, the amount that could be collected steadily decreased, as stupid economic legislation and a misguided system of taxation aggravated the decline of Spanish prosperity. The net result of Philip's financial policy was to kill the goose that laid the golden egg. The *alcabala*, a tax of ten per cent on every sale of goods, to mention but one of many burdensome taxes, was in itself enough to strangle the commerce of Spain and starve her industry, and to these were added innumerable hampering regulations and prohibitions, which in the end gave most of Spain's trade to the English or Dutch and drained the country of its gold and silver.

The results of Philip's unwise policy in Spain were not at once discernible. Thanks to the conquered wealth of the New World and to the apparent strength acquired through union with the great Hapsburg empire, Spain had become the greatest of the European nations during the reign of Charles V. For a long time after his death, she was able to maintain the appearance of greatness and an undiminished prestige, but under Philip the reality of Spanish power was crumbling. Two important successes, however, helped to hide this fact. In 1571, the Spanish fleet administered a decisive defeat to the Turks at Lepanto, and in 1580, Philip succeeded in making good an hereditary claim to the kingdom of Portugal, thereby uniting the whole peninsula under his rule and adding the great colonial empire of Portugal to that of Spain. Nevertheless, in summing up the results of Philip's government of Spain through nearly half a century, one must note more failure than success. He left his country impoverished, his people orthodox and proud, but unindustrious. Spain still seemed greater than it was, but it would not be long before the internal decay would destroy its prestige.

Meanwhile, Philip's attempts to carry out that part of his policy which concerned the rest of Europe had not met with even the partial success he had achieved in Spain. The Netherlands rebelled against his autocratic Spanish-Catholic government and the northern provinces broke away to form an independent Protestant state. Henry IV foiled his efforts to crush out Protestantism in France and to dominate the French government in alliance with the Catholic party. Finally, his hopes of restoring England to the Catholic Church and of gaining control of Spain's most dangerous commercial rival led only to the supreme disaster of the Armada.

2. THE REVOLT IN THE NETHERLANDS

In almost every respect, the Netherlands were very different from Spain and they could not be made to accept the same policies or methods of government. It was one of the tragedies of Philip's reign that he never fully understood or became reconciled to that fact. The sovereignty of the seventeen provinces that made up the Netherlands was his by hereditary right, but there was no other political bond to hold them together, and each province had its own cherished institutions and ancient privileges. Even racial or linguistic unity was lacking; for the northern provinces were predominantly Germanic and Dutch-speaking, while the southern were more nearly French in tradition and language. Situated at the commercial crossroads of northwestern Europe, the Netherlands were the home of a vigorous commercial and industrial people, prosperous and independent. Their position left them open to all the cultural and religious influences of the age and, despite persecution, many had adopted one or other of the current Protestant faiths. Lutheranism and Anabaptism had been the first to make an impression, but at the time when Philip began to rule, Calvinism was spreading rapidly in the northern provinces. The government of a people who were so divided, yet so prosperous and independent, would require a good deal of tact and understanding. Charles V, himself a native of the Netherlands and their own prince, had possessed those qualities in sufficient degree to retain their loyalty, though there was a good deal of discontent in his later years. Philip had neither tact nor understanding — and he was a foreigner.

Causes of the revolt

The causes of the revolt were inherent in the character of Philip and his Netherland subjects and in the irreconcilable opposition between his general policies and their economic, political, and religious interests. From the beginning they distrusted him as a foreigner who did not speak their language and had no sympathy with their point of view. Philip was, indeed, a Spaniard first and last. He regarded the Netherlands as satellites of Spain, to be used for Spanish interests. Economic grievances soon gave point to their resentment of this attitude. Philip was in desperate financial straits. He was forced to begin his reign by increasing the burden of taxation, already high enough under Charles V, and most of the money wrung from the Netherlanders was spent in Spain. Still worse, he strove to restrict their commerce so as to give the advantage to Spanish merchants. Political grievances fed their resentment still further, as Philip tried to force upon the Netherlands a centralized, absolute government like that of Spain, regardless of the ancient constitutional rights and traditional privileges of the separate provinces. Finally, Philip's determination to crush out heresy in all his dominions permanently alienated the growing number of Protestants, while his arbitrary reorganization of the church government (including the creation of a number of new bishoprics) aroused the opposition of many Catholics. Philip's rigid Catholic policy was not the sole cause of the revolt, but once the revolt had begun, it was the factor that made reconciliation of the provinces that were predominantly Protestant impossible.

Beginning of the revolt

Despite these various causes of discontent, the first ten years of Philip's reign passed before there were any signs of open rebellion. Following his father's abdication, Philip remained in the Netherlands until 1559, when he returned to Spain, never to visit his northern possessions again. From that time on, he left the government of the distant provinces to a series of regents, of whom the first was his half-sister, Margaret of Parma. He always insisted, however, on a vexatiously detailed supervision of the regent's activity from his cabinet in Madrid. So far as he gave independent authority to anyone, it was to his chief minister in the Netherlands, Cardinal Granvelle, who became so unpopular that Philip was forced to recall him in 1564. The power of this foreign minister was especially resented by the great nobles, who were accustomed to being consulted in affairs of state. The most important of these, Prince William of Orange, had been shown high favor by Charles V, but now found himself neglected. He was not, however, responsible for the first outbreak of the revolt, though he was later to be its greatest leader. In 1565, a group of young hotheads from the lesser nobility, together with some of the wealthy burghers, organized to protest against the arbitrary government, the foreign ministers, and the Inquisition. The following year, some two hundred and fifty of them gathered to present a formal petition to the regent. They accomplished nothing, but the incident is memorable because it was then that the rebels acquired the name of "Beggars," applied to them in derision by one of the regent's councilors and carried by them in defiant pride throughout the revolt. The protest of the nobles was followed by wild anti-Catholic riots and image-breaking on the part of the Protestant proletariat, and Philip began to lay plans for crushing the independence of his turbulent and heretical subjects. In 1567, William of Orange resigned his offices and retired to his German estates to organize resistance; the first army of the Beggars was defeated by government troops; and Philip sent a Spanish army to the Netherlands.

The arrival of ten thousand veteran Spanish troops under the Duke of Alva, who now replaced Margaret as regent, opened one of the darkest and most blood-stained pages in European history. Philip had ordered Alva to crush all opposition both to the government and to the Catholic faith, and he could scarcely have found a more perfect instrument for his purpose than this hardened campaigner, who shared to the full his blind Spanish patriotism and hatred of heresy. For six years (1567–73) Alva raged through the land, imprisoning, executing, and confiscating the property of those who were suspected of either rebellion or heresy. Even the greatest nobles were not spared. The gallant Lamoral of Egmont and the Count of Hoorn were among the first to fall. In addition, Alva levied crushing taxes (including the Spanish *alcabala* or ten per cent tax on sales), which almost ruined the commercial and industrial prosperity of the Netherlands beyond repair. All this was not accomplished without opposition, but the people of the Netherlands were cowed by fear, and the duke's Spanish veterans easily defeated the German and French mercenaries recruited by William of Orange and his brother Louis of Nassau. The only success of the rebels was won on the sea. From 1569 on, the "Sea Beggars," lawless privateers who hated Spaniards and Catholics as much as they loved fighting and plunder, preyed on Spanish shipping along the Atlantic coast. At first they had operated from friendly English ports, but in 1572 they acquired a base on the coast of Holland by capturing the harbor of Brill. This first success on land encouraged other towns in Holland and Zeeland to rebel. In July, the Estates of Holland proclaimed William of Orange their stadholder, and despite frightful sieges and massacres the northern provinces never again submitted entirely to Spanish authority. Even Philip could see that the reign of

Alva's reign of terror

terror had borne its logical fruit in bitter hatred of Spain, and in 1573 he recalled Alva, replacing him by the more pacific Don Luis Requesens.

Throughout these bloody years, William of Nassau, Prince of Orange, was the heart and soul of the rebellion. He was a German by birth and his title was derived from a principality in southern France, but he had large estates in the Netherlands and became a Netherlander at heart. He was a tolerant man who hated religious persecution, and after the beginning of the revolt he threw in his lot with the Protestant minority. It was his grim determination, his refusal to accept defeat, and his patient and skillful diplomacy that kept the spark of rebellion alive during the darkest years. A discreet capacity for keeping his own counsel was one of his outstanding gifts, whence the name William the Silent by which he is best known in the annals of his adopted country. His constancy was rewarded by success in the years following the removal of Alva. Sternly refusing all conciliatory offers short of complete religious freedom and restoration of the old political rights, he kept up the fight, meanwhile uniting the northern provinces under his leadership and working to win the co-operation of the south. This latter object he achieved in 1576 after the Spanish troops, who had been left unpaid and leaderless by the death of Requesens, mutinied and perpetrated the horrible massacre known as the "Spanish Fury" at Antwerp. Goaded by this final outrage, the States General of the southern provinces signed the Pacification of Ghent, a treaty with Holland and Zeeland to stand together against the Spanish tyranny.

William unites the provinces

The union, however, did not last long. The common hatred of Spain was offset by too many differences between north and south. They did not speak the same language, and the aristocratic governing class of the industrial southern provinces had little in common with the democratic commercial states of the north. The chief barrier between them, however, was the difference in religion. The years of persecution had driven the most stubborn Protestants from

Treaty of Arras and Union of Utrecht

the south to the more easily defended and rebellious northern provinces, which were now fanatically anti-Catholic, while the south was left fairly free from Protestantism. It would therefore not be difficult for an astute diplomat to stir up dissension between the provinces, and this was the aim of Alexander Farnese, Duke of Parma, who arrived with a new Spanish army to take over the regency in 1578. The famous Parma, already renowned as a soldier but equally skilled as a diplomat, was not long in getting results. Early in 1579, a group of the southern provinces signed the Treaty of Arras, forming a league for the protection of the Catholic faith. This was immediately answered by the Union of Utrecht, in which the northern provinces banded together to resist religious persecution and Spanish rule "with life, blood, and goods." These two treaties mark the final split between north and south. In the following years, Parma conquered or cajoled the remaining rebels in the south and restored the ruined land to the Spanish crown and the Catholic Church, while the little Protestant states in the north struggled on to maintain their independence and to form the Dutch Republic.

Philip never became reconciled to the loss of the most prosperous part of his Netherland possessions. Until he was assassinated in 1584, William the Silent was kept busy defending his country against Parma's armies and trying in vain to get substantial aid from France by offering the sovereignty of the United Provinces to the king's younger brother. After his death the danger increased. There was no strong central government in the new republic, and each of the provinces claimed independent sovereign powers. Aid from England helped them over the difficult period of the next four years until events elsewhere relieved the pressure. Parma's attention was distracted, first by Philip's plans for the invasion of England, then by wars with the French Huguenots, and later with France itself. Meanwhile, two new leaders appeared who united the provinces and shepherded them through two decades of war to final security. John van Oldenbarneveldt gave wise direction to affairs of state, while Maurice of Nassau, the brilliant son of William the Silent, became stadholder of the various provinces and led the Dutch army to victory after victory. A truce in 1609 practically ended the war, but Spain did not formally recognize the existence of the Dutch Republic as an independent state until 1648. Meanwhile, the Dutch had prospered mightily. Their seaborne commerce had not been wrecked by the revolt as had the industry of the southern provinces, and, though the long war with Spain was expensive, their expanding commerce more than made up the loss. Despite its small size, the Dutch Republic was now one of the greatest commercial powers in Europe with trade extending from the West Indies to the Far East. Together with England, it fell heir to the commercial supremacy that was slipping from the hands of Spain.

3. THE WARS OF RELIGION IN FRANCE

The Treaty of Cateau-Cambrésis and the death of Henry II, both in the year 1559, ended an epoch in French history — that of the long foreign wars against the encircling Hapsburg power and for the domination of Italy. For the next forty years, French history centered around new problems, as foreign wars gave place to the civil Wars of Religion.

The Reformation came to France as an importation from Germany and Switzerland, though the way had been prepared by some of the earlier French Christian humanists. From the first it had to make its way against the opposition of the monarchy, for the French kings had already acquired all the control of the church in France that they needed and regarded heresy as a menace to national unity. In the early years Francis I was fairly tolerant, but as Lutheranism gained ground, he commenced an intermittent persecution, which became more severe and constant in the last decade of his reign. Under Henry II, the persecution became still more severe. Nevertheless, Protestantism continued to spread, finding many converts among the burghers, gentry, and nobility, and took on a more aggressive character. The secret of this new energy was the influ-

THE "SPANISH FURY" AT ANTWERP

This engraving gives a vivid impression of the massacre of the people of Antwerp by the mutinous Spanish soldiers in 1567.

THE SURRENDER OF BREDA

In one of his finest paintings, Velasquez commemorated the surrender of the town in which William the Silent had his home. The Dutch commander is shown surrendering the key of the town to the Spanish general.

ence of John Calvin and the shift among French Protestants from Lutheranism to Calvinism. Calvin was himself a Frenchman and a master of French prose. His logical spirit made a more direct appeal to the French mind than did the mysticism of Martin Luther. Moreover, he maintained a personal supervision of the struggling Protestant communities from his stronghold on the eastern frontier, and gave them the benefit of his genius for organization. In the year 1559, which saw the death of Henry II, the first French Protestant Synod met secretly in the king's own city of Paris to work out a national organization for the Reformed Church in France.

The next step in the development of French Protestantism followed almost immediately. It became a political party, headed by a group of great nobles who were held together by family ties. Under the absolute monarchy of Francis I and Henry II, the majority of nobles were little more than courtiers and soldiers. Nevertheless, there were a few great nobles, divided into two family groups, both more or less closely related to royalty, who exercised great influence at court. Under the feeble rule of Henry's sons, they became rivals for the control of the government, and, as one group was Protestant, though of fairly recent conversion, the other extremely Catholic, their rivalry became an integral part of the religious struggle. On the Protestant side were the two foremost Princes of the Blood, Anthony of Bourbon, King of Navarre by virtue of his marriage to the Protestant Jeanne d'Albret, and his brother Louis of Condé. Allied to them by marriage was the able and deeply religious Gaspard de Coligny, Admiral of France, who, together with his two brilliant brothers, gave the soundest leadership to the Protestant party. Coligny was also related to the family of Montmorency, though the head of that powerful house, the aged constable, remained a Catholic. On the other side, the family of Guise headed the ultra-Catholic opposition to heresy. They were a younger branch of the ruling house of Lorraine and were closely connected by marriage with the royal families of France and Scotland. Duke Francis of Guise, the head of the family, had acquired a great military reputation and considerable popularity in the recent wars with Spain; two of his brothers were cardinals and royal ministers; his sister Mary was Regent of Scotland as widow of James V and mother of the young Queen Mary Stuart, and the latter now became Queen of France as the wife of Henry II's eldest son, Francis II (1559–60).

Rival noble families

As Francis II was still too young to rule, though he had passed the legal age of majority, the government fell naturally into the hands of the queen's uncles, the brothers Guise. They at once made use of the known Calvinist leanings of their rivals, the Bourbon-Coligny group, to drive them from court, thus forcing them into opposition as avowed leaders of French Protestantism. During the next year, the Guises redoubled the religious persecution, filling the prisons and keeping the executioners busy, while in self-defense the Protestants were forced to organize as a political-religious party. It was at about this time that the Protestants in France came to be known by the name of Huguenot. They were drifting rapidly toward rebellion when the Guise ascendancy ended for a time with the death of Francis II, after only a year's reign.

The Guise ascendancy

The crown now passed to Henry's second son Charles IX (1560–74), who was still a child. His mother, Catherine de' Medici, promptly seized control of the royal government as regent. Hitherto this daughter of the famous Florentine family had played a secondary rôle as the wife of Henry II and mother of the late king, but from this time on she was to be a principal actor in the hectic French drama. For a quarter of a century she directed the government of her remaining sons, and wielded whatever power was left to the French crown. Through it all she clung to a consistent policy, though it was one that had every appearance of inconsistency. Her aim was simply to maintain control of the government for herself and her sons and to keep the kingdom at peace so far as possible. To do that, she played off

Catherine de' Medici

Guise against Bourbon, extreme Catholic against Huguenot, and strove whenever possible to build up a center party of moderate Catholics who would be loyal to the crown and would help to keep the peace.

Catherine's first action was to stop the persecution of the Protestants and to issue an edict granting them a limited freedom of worship. If Catherine hoped that this would keep the peace or conciliate the Huguenots, she was mistaken. Calvinism had gained steadily and become increasingly militant under the weight of persecution. When the pressure was lifted, it spread with startling rapidity and remained as militant as ever. The Protestants were never more than a small minority of the population of France, perhaps not more than ten per cent, but their strength was far greater than their numbers would indicate. They were recruited chiefly from the most energetic and influential classes — the industrial and commercial townsmen and the fighting gentry from the country, to whom were added a few great nobles. They were characterized by a high morality and earnestness of purpose that made them in every way a respectable as well as formidable group. Filled with hope, they were now determined to win full freedom at all costs. Catherine's moderate edict failed to satisfy them. At the same time, it aroused strong opposition from the extreme Catholics. Fanaticism on both sides flared to fever heat. Catholics and Protestants alike rioted and desecrated each other's churches in every corner of France. In 1562, the Duke of Guise, placing himself at the head of a group of Catholic nobles, seized control of the government and forced Catherine to recall the edict of toleration. But the Protestants had gone too far to submit. They took arms to defend their faith and opened the Wars of Religion.

Protestant aggression

France now entered on a decade of alternate civil war and peace that was very little different from war. Despite their great inferiority in numbers and frequent defeats, the Huguenots held their own by virtue of able leadership and unshakable determination. The murder of Francis of Guise in 1563 weakened the Catholic party, and in the following years nearly all the original leaders on both sides fell, leaving Coligny the most outstanding figure in France. Meanwhile, Catherine pursued her vacillating course, alternating persecution with toleration, and striving to restore peace and keep control of the government. In the years 1570–72, she seemed about to obtain her objective. She arranged a peace treaty, granting a fair amount of freedom to Protestants in places where they were in the majority; summoned Coligny to court; and planned to win over the Huguenot leaders by marrying her daughter Margaret to young Henry of Bourbon, who had succeeded his father Anthony as King of Navarre and would in time become the natural chief of the Huguenots.

First Wars of Religion

As usual, however, Catherine had failed to reckon with the fanatical passions on both sides, which indeed she could never understand. The Huguenots were still unsatisfied and the Catholics were developing a strong opposition under the leadership of Duke Henry of Guise, the son of the old Catholic leader. Moreover, Catherine began to fear the influence of Coligny with the king, now of age, whom he was trying to persuade to help the Protestant rebels in the Netherlands and to seize the opportunity provided by the revolt to annex the French-speaking provinces. Peace seemed as far away as ever, and Catherine decided to throw in her lot again with the Guises. She persuaded herself that the admiral and the few remaining Huguenot chiefs were the principal obstacles to peace, and that if they could be removed, the Huguenot resistance would collapse. Their presence in Paris for the wedding of Henry and Margaret provided the opportunity, and on Saint Bartholomew's Eve, 1572, Catherine and the Guises laid the plans that led to the terrible massacre of the following day. They had probably intended no more than the murder of Coligny and the other chiefs, which Henry of Guise supervised himself, but, as news of the killing spread, the fanatical Paris mob rose to take a hand, and before morning some two thousand Protestants had been

Massacre of Saint Bartholomew

slain. Similar massacres in other cities soon accounted for thousands more.

Despite the loss of their leaders, the Huguenots still fought on, until in 1576 they won the most favorable peace yet accorded to them. Nevertheless, it was clear that they had passed the peak of their power and were losing ground. Their numbers had been cut down by war and massacre and it was only in the south and west of France that they were strong enough to hold their own. Protestantism was no longer spreading. On the contrary, a strong Catholic reaction had set in under the influence of the Counter-Reformation and the activity of the Jesuits. Moreover, the whole country had suffered terribly from the wars, and the ruined people not unnaturally blamed the stubborn Protestants. The royal government was almost bankrupt, and Henry III (1574–89), who succeeded his brother Charles IX two years after the massacre, was too feeble to control the situation. In 1576, the extreme Catholic party, headed by Henry of Guise, took matters into their own hands and formed the Catholic League, independent of the king, for the suppression of Protestantism. During the next few years, the league gained a wide following and also the assurance of support from Philip II.

The Catholic reaction

The death of Catherine de' Medici's fourth son, the Duke of Alençon, the last of the Valois line, brought about a crisis and precipitated the final struggle. Henry III was in feeble health and had no sons, and the nearest heir to the throne was now the Protestant Bourbon prince, Henry of Navarre, who for some years had been the most active leader of the Huguenots. Rather than accept him, the league was prepared to go to any lengths. In 1585, the leaguers signed a treaty with Philip of Spain in open defiance of their king. The war that followed is called the War of the Three Henrys. Lacking resources or the strength to use what he had, Henry III was caught between the league, led by Henry of Guise, and the Huguenots who followed Henry of Navarre. At first the unfortunate king submitted to the dictation of the league, then in a burst of futile energy he strove to free himself by the assassination of Duke Henry. Vengeance followed within the year. In 1589, he was himself assassinated by a fanatical leaguer, and Henry of Navarre proclaimed himself King of France as Henry IV (1589–1610).

War of the Three Henrys

The death of Henry III did not at once end the wars, for his successor had still to overcome the opposition of the league and of Spain. His religion was the chief obstacle in his path to the throne. Save for that, the French people would have accepted him willingly enough, for they were weary of war. After four years more of fighting, Henry IV finally realized that the obstacle was insurmountable. He submitted and formally adopted the Catholic faith. After that he had little trouble in reconciling the leaders of the league, though he had still to fight a war with Spain, for Philip II was loath to give up his dream of dominating France through the Catholic party. The war ended on terms favorable to France in 1598, the last year of Philip's reign. In the same year, Henry provided a settlement of the religious problem for France, which in main outline was to last for nearly a century. By the Edict of Nantes, he guaranteed freedom of conscience and full political rights to all Protestants. The Wars of Religion were ended. Protestantism in France had secured a legal status, but its great days were over. During the next century it faded slowly, as the interests of the age shifted. Meanwhile, with peace restored at home and abroad, Henry IV was free to turn his attention to the reconstruction of his shattered kingdom. But that is a story that must be left for another chapter.

Settlement under Henry IV

4. ENGLAND UNDER ELIZABETH AND THE SCOTTISH REFORMATION

Before Protestantism was finally established in England, there was a brief Catholic interlude. When the young King Edward VI died, the fate of religion in England was still far from certain. The English Reformation had begun as a political and national revolt against Rome, supported by economic motives, rather than as a primarily religious

Catholic interlude: Mary

movement. The people had acquiesced in Henry's establishment of a national Anglican Church, but neither king nor people had changed their doctrinal beliefs in any very marked degree. True, Protestant teaching of the various types emanating from Germany and Switzerland gained many converts, especially in the influential commercial class and among the gentry of the south, and under Edward doctrinal Protestantism made rapid progress. Still, there is reason to believe that when Edward's eldest sister Mary Tudor, the daughter of Henry VIII and Catherine of Aragon, came to the throne in 1553, the greater number of Englishmen were either still Catholic or were sufficiently indifferent to accept either church as the government should decide. The proof is that Mary, herself a devout Catholic, was able to restore Catholicism as the official religion with the aid of Parliament and to reunite the English Church to the Roman. There was no rebellion, and the Catholic restoration might have been successful but for two things. In 1554, Mary married Philip II of Spain and joined Spain in a close alliance that reduced England to the position of a Spanish satellite. And she persecuted Protestants with a harshness that won for her the name of Bloody Mary. The Spanish alliance, coupled with the persecution and the restoration of papal authority, aroused national resentment in England and hatred of Spain and the papacy. When Mary died, most Englishmen were formally Catholic, but Catholicism had become more unpopular. The issue was still to be decided.

The crucial decision was made by a young woman of twenty-five, Elizabeth (1558–1603), Anne Boleyn's daughter, and the last of the Tudors. The new queen had been raised as a Protestant, but she was no fanatic. What she wanted was a national church, free from Rome and subject only to the royal authority, Protestant in character, but liberal enough so that all but the most stubborn extremists might conform. She procured it by act of Parliament in 1559. In the matter of church government, Elizabeth followed the example set by her father. An Act of Supremacy re-established the Anglican Church under the supreme authority of the crown, with the old episcopal system otherwise unchanged. This was followed by an Act of Uniformity, which prescribed the use of a Book of Common Prayer, modeled on that of Edward VI, as the only legal form of worship. Having secured the outward uniformity that was so essential for political reasons, Elizabeth was prepared to leave a good deal of leeway in matters of doctrine. The creed as stated in the Prayer Book and the later Thirty-Nine Articles was predominantly Protestant, but the phrasing at crucial points was vague enough so that the more moderate Catholics, who did not hold strongly to the papal obedience, might attend the national church without too great a shock to their consciences, while almost all Protestants, whether they had taken their opinions from Wittenberg or Geneva, could interpret it to suit their own convictions. The Elizabethan settlement of the church was a characteristically English compromise and amazingly permanent. Elizabeth reigned long enough to see it firmly established and it has lasted down to our own time. Divergent parties soon arose within the church — but they remained there. Only the wilder Protestant sects and the extreme Catholics remained stubbornly aloof. They were punished and harassed by fines, but were not persecuted so severely as to arouse public sympathy for them.

The peaceful and permanent establishment of a Protestant church in England was closely bound up with the conversion of Scotland to Protestantism just at the time when Elizabeth was beginning her reign. The coincidence was of vital importance to both countries. United by a common religious interest, England and Scotland were both able to withstand the threat of domination by the great Catholic states of the Continent, Spain and France respectively.

Scotland was still a very backward country, almost medieval in its social and political structure. Its church was dominated by lawless nobles, was disproportionately wealthy for a poverty-stricken country, and was probably the most corrupt in Europe. It was an easy target for the attacks of the Protestant reformers. Moreover, the latter had patriotic national sentiment on their side. The Scottish people were growing restless under the rule of the French regent, Mary of Guise, while their queen, her daughter Mary Stuart, was living at the French court and in 1558 married the heir to the throne of France. They resented the treatment of Scotland as a dependence of France, and as the Guises were ultra-Catholic, Catholicism came to be associated in the popular mind with French domination. All the materials for a conflagration were present. All that was needed was the fiery preaching of John Knox, who returned from Geneva in 1555, to set the land ablaze. In 1557, a congregation of Scottish nobles signed the first Covenant for the defense of the Protestant faith. Two years later, Scotland was in armed rebellion against the French Catholic regent, and in 1560 Elizabeth sent aid to the rebels to help them drive out the French troops. That action was decisive. It secured the triumph of Protestantism in Scotland and ended the long-standing enmity between the two British countries.

Mary and the Presbyterians When Mary Stuart came to rule her Scottish kingdom in 1561, she found the Calvinist Presbyterian Church already firmly established. The fact that the Reformation had come to Scotland in the form of Calvinism and in opposition to the government made the religious situation in Scotland very different from that in England. The Presbyterian Church was founded as the result of a revolution that swept away the old episcopal system with the royal control. As was characteristic of Calvinist churches everywhere, its organization was essentially democratic, with the final authority vested in the congregations and their elders and ministers. Such a church could not be controlled by the state, but, on the contrary, could bring powerful pressure to bear on the government. This Mary Stuart soon found to her cost. Through seven years of folly and romantic adventure, she fought the power of the church, only to be beaten by it. At last she fled from the country to take refuge in England, leaving her infant son James VI to be brought up by Presbyterian divines.

Rise of English commerce We must turn now to other aspects of English history, of equal importance with the religious settlement. The age of Elizabeth was the age when England rose to the first rank among the commercial nations of the world and built up the sea power that was the foundation of her future greatness. The origin of England's opportunity was the shift, already noted, in the center of gravity of world trade from the Mediterranean to the Atlantic.[1] New trade routes, around Africa to India and the Spice Islands and straight west across the ocean to the Americas, were blazed out by Portuguese and Spanish seamen. As a result, Portugal and Spain acquired a monopoly of the rich commerce of the Far East, the African coast, and the New World. But they did not hold it long unchallenged. The Spaniards and Portuguese were great pioneers and colonizers, but they were indifferent merchants, and their methods of government were fatal to home industry and trade. It was inevitable that the hardy seagoing folk and canny merchants of England and Holland should seek their share in the New World trade — and almost as inevitable that they should get it. They had the advantage over their competitors of thriving native industries, like the woolen cloth industry, which gave them valuable goods to sell in foreign parts. Despite all prohibitions, English merchants poached on Spanish preserves in the New World, and carried on a profitable smuggling trade with the Spanish colonists, who needed the goods which they could supply to better advantage than could the merchants from the home country. Meanwhile, daring English sailors risked their lives in Arctic seas, in the hope of finding new routes to the Orient by the northwest passage around North America or by the northeast passage around Europe. The latter aim led to solid results through the discovery of the White Sea, which opened up a new and profitable trade route to Russia. English merchants, too, dared the Spanish control of the Mediterranean to carry on trade with the Levantine countries of the Near East.

[1] See above, pages 396–400.

QUEEN ELIZABETH
This portrait tells us more, perhaps, of the styles at the court than of the character of the "good queen" herself.

SIR FRANCIS DRAKE
For centuries Drake's name has been a symbol of the fighting tradition of the British navy.

THE GREAT ARMADA
A contemporary picture of the great Armada fighting the English fleet commanded by Sir Francis Drake

The fact that open trade with the Spanish and Portuguese colonies, united into one great empire by Philip II, was denied to them forced the English merchants to become armed smugglers and pirates, and made England a militant sea power. For years before there was formal war between England and Spain, merchant-privateers like Drake and Hawkins plundered the Spanish Main, captured treasure ships, and perfected a new technique of naval warfare. Religion added bitterness to the commercial rivalry. The English merchants were mostly Protestant, and they took a double satisfaction in every blow struck against the commercial monopoly of Catholic Spain. Nor were they the only Protestant seamen who combined profit with religious satisfaction in daring assaults on Spanish commerce. By an odd coincidence, the sea power of both the Netherlands and France was almost entirely in Protestant hands, that of the rebellious Dutch and Huguenots respectively, who held the best of the Atlantic ports and issued forth to prey on the shipping of Spain. From the North Sea to the Caribbean, militant Protestantism rode the seas and harassed the great Catholic state, whose land armies were still regarded as invincible. It was the English privateers, the Huguenots, and the Sea Beggars of Holland, who, by strangling Spanish trade and cutting Spain off from the Netherlands, made possible the success of the Dutch revolt. Or, if that were not enough, the aid, official and otherwise, sent from England to the Protestant rebels in the Netherlands may be considered a decisive factor. Small wonder that Philip II finally determined to crush the island kingdom which had become the chief menace to his cherished plans for the restoration of Catholicism to Europe and for the aggrandizement of Spain.

It is more surprising that he did not attack England earlier, when, indeed, he would have had a better chance of success. But there were a number of good reasons for his delay. At first he had hopes of restoring the ascendancy over England, which he had lost on the death of Mary, by marrying Elizabeth, or through the queen's fear that France would press the claims of Mary Stuart. And Elizabeth's astute diplomacy maintained the delusion as long as possible. Then the Netherlands revolted and Philip put off war with England until he should have regained control of his northern possessions. He lacked the sea power to land an army in England, so long as the English could count on the aid of Dutch and Huguenot privateers, and with every passing year the English themselves became more formidable opponents on the sea. Philip accordingly turned to conspiracy with English Catholics to rid himself of Elizabeth and to restore Catholicism in England by replacing the Protestant ruler with the Catholic Mary Stuart. The weak point in Elizabeth's position was that she was the last of the direct line of Tudors, that her legitimacy was disputed by all good Catholics, who had never recognized the validity of Henry's divorce from Catherine and marriage to Anne Boleyn, and that Mary Stuart, as great-granddaughter of Henry VII, was the next claimant to the throne. For years Elizabeth's life was in constant danger from Spanish-Catholic plots, which, incidentally, served to arouse in patriotic Englishmen an undying hatred of papal Spain. So long as Mary Stuart lived, neither English independence nor Protestantism was safe. Elizabeth protected the unhappy queen as long as she could, but at last, in 1587, she submitted to the popular demand and ordered her execution for treason. There was now nothing to delay Philip any longer. He declared open war immediately. It lasted until after the end of Elizabeth's reign.

Though the war dragged on for years, its fate was settled at the very beginning by the dramatic defeat of Philip's great Armada in 1588. He had strained the financial resources of Spain to the utmost in order to build a fleet great enough to crush the English navy and transport an invading army to England. But more than money is needed to build an effective navy. Philip listened too little to the advice of experienced sailors, and entrusted the command to landsmen and soldiers. From beginning to end, the history of the Armada is a story of short-sighted stupidity and hopeless bungling. No account was taken of the new technique of naval warfare, based on the use of heavy cannon in light, handy ships, which had been worked out by Drake, Hawkins, and other privateers and introduced into the small but efficient English navy. The story of how the "invincible" Armada was destroyed by the winds and water of the English Channel, ably assisted by the men and guns of the English navy, is too well known to need recounting. The destruction of the Armada marked a definite stage in the decline of Spain's power, while for England it was the beginning of a great era of ascendancy on the sea.

32

The Economic Revolution

IN PRECEDING CHAPTERS we have traced the history of Europe during the period of transition from medieval to modern civilization. We have noted the transformation of society and the state, together with the accompanying changes in the realm of thought and religion, and have suggested more than once that the motive force behind many if not all of these changes was the development of new and more potent forms of economic activity. It is time now, with the political, cultural, and religious background already before us, to study at greater length the nature of the transformation of European economic life that took place during these centuries. We shall find that it amounts to an economic revolution, and one that marks what are perhaps the most fundamental differences between the medieval and the modern ages. Indeed, it is very doubtful if any of the changes of this crucial period in Europe's history had more far-reaching consequences than the change in the methods of doing business. Because the change occurred at different times and in different degrees in different places — in isolated instances in the fourteenth century, more generally in the fifteenth, and almost universally in all parts of Europe in the sixteenth century — it is difficult to trace its history in any connected fashion. We have one clue, however, to guide us through the maze. Our main task will be to follow the development of capital and to discover what it did to commerce, industry, agriculture, the state, and society.

1. THE ACCUMULATION OF CAPITAL

The first prerequisite to the introduction of capital as a productive force in the business world was the existence of private fortunes, or accumulations of capital, large enough to furnish a surplus that could be invested in any profitable enterprise. *Rise of money economy* The problem of how such fortunes were accumulated, in occasional instances before the end of the High Middle Ages and with increasing frequency during the fourteenth and fifteenth centuries, is one that has led to a great deal of discussion among modern historians. One point, however, is clear. They could not have existed had it not been for the gradual spread of what we call "money economy," following the revival of trade that began about the middle of the eleventh century. In the purely feudal society of the earlier Middle Ages, there had been little use for money and but little cash in circulation. What trade there was in that age, when almost all men drew their living from the cultivation of the soil, was carried on by barter, and the obligations of man to man were usually fulfilled by personal services. With the revival of commerce, accompanied as it was by the revival of industry and town life, this primitive economic condition gradually changed. Merchants and artisans found it more convenient to buy and sell raw materials or goods for cash, and even the peasants who worked the land in time acquired the habit of buying and selling, as the growing towns offered a cash market for foodstuffs. The change from the "natural economy" of barter and personal services to the "money economy" of cash transactions took place very slowly and was not complete at the end of the Middle Ages. Moreover, the medieval organization of commerce and industry under the corporate guild system, which was designed to limit the activity of individuals in the interests of the whole city community, effectively prevented most business men from accumulating more money than they needed for a "decent" living and the current expenses of a small business. Nevertheless, by the end of the thirteenth century, a good deal of money was in constant circulation, and already some few fortunate individuals had succeeded in accumulating surplus capital that might be invested to produce a profit when opportunity offered.

Given the general use of money, we have still to answer the question of how such private fortunes or any considerable amount of surplus capital could be accumulated in the age before the feudal system had ceased to dominate agriculture and even before the guild system had lost its hold on commerce and industry. Leaving aside for the moment the fact that such long-distance commerce as that between the Italian cities and the Near East afforded unusual opportunities for individual profit even at the height of the guild régime, we shall find that most early accumulations of capital resulted from the use of political power, from money-lending, or from large mining operations.

Accumulation of capital

As has already been pointed out, the rise of money economy was closely associated with the rise of strong central governments in the European states.[1] It was the increasing possibility of raising money taxes that enabled the princes of the Later Middle Ages to hire standing armies and support a centralized administration, thus freeing themselves from dependence on the feudal nobles.

Through political power

[1] See above, pages 372–376.

At present, however, we are interested in another aspect of the collection and expenditure of the growing royal revenue. The collection of royal taxes meant the accumulation in one place of a sum of money larger than could be gathered together in the normal course of trade. And where any large sum of public money is gathered together, there are always opportunities for the diversion of considerable portions of it into private hands. Medieval governments were notoriously careless and inefficient in the handling of finance. The king might be in constant need of money, but the officials who were entrusted with the handling of the royal revenue frequently retired with sizable fortunes. It is said that the French superintendent of finance, Pierre Remy, left a fortune equivalent to $14,000,000 on his death in 1328. Similar opportunities were afforded by the revenues of great nobles, whose lands were petty states in themselves.

Another source of early fortunes, and one of the earliest ways in which surplus capital could be made to produce more capital, was the practice of usury, as the church called it, i.e., money-lending at high rates of interest. There had been money-lenders all through the medieval period, many of them Jews, who made large though uncertain profits, and in the Later Middle Ages an extensive banking and money-lending business, with ramifications reaching to every part of Europe, was built up first by Lombard and then by Tuscan and German bankers. The famous Augsburg banking house of the Fuggers and the Florentine bank of the Medici are but examples of a number of fifteenth-century firms engaged in what would today be called international finance, and even earlier the bankers had become a very real power in international affairs. The most important clients of the early bankers were the rulers of the European states, who needed large sums of money at short notice for the paying and equipping of armies or for other expenses of the government and the court. Edward III could not possibly have begun the Hundred Years' War had he not been able to borrow large sums from the Florentine bankers to pay his new type of non-feudal army, and

Money-lending and banking

JACOB FUGGER, THE RICH

This portrait, from a contemporary wood-cut, has every appearance of being a realistic picture of the richest man in Europe in the age of Charles V.

JACQUES COEUR

Merchant and finance minister to Charles VII of France, Jacques Coeur was one of the most prosperous capitalists in the fifteenth century.

LARGE-SCALE MINING

The silver mine shown above is one of the large operations financed by Fugger capital.

even his relatively peaceful contemporary, the Emperor Charles IV, is reported to have borrowed two million francs in one year. The new centralized monarchies were discovering the potential power of money. They regularly anticipated the income from revenues that could not be collected very rapidly, and were almost constantly in debt. The profits from this sort of money-lending were usually very high, but also very uncertain, for a prince might readily disown his obligations, as Edward III did, thereby ruining a number of Florentine bankers and causing a disastrous financial panic in Tuscany, and the heir to a throne would not always feel obliged to assume his predecessor's debts. Next to the rulers, the most constant borrowers were the feudal nobles, chronically improvident and hard-pressed for ready money, and the great ecclesiastical lords who built the magnificent cathedrals and monastery buildings on borrowed money, or squandered their incomes and all they could borrow in very much the same fashion as did the lay nobles. One thirteenth-century Archbishop of Cologne, for example, borrowed a million francs from the Italian bankers. In short, most of this early money-lending was for unproductive purposes. It did not bring profit to the borrower as well as to the lender. Hence the objections of church and people alike to the practice of usury. When money was lent, as it was beginning to be in the fifteenth century, for such productive purposes as the financing of large commercial ventures, there was little or no objection.

Before we consider the use of capital for commercial purposes, however, we must note

Mining

one exceptional method of accumulating a fortune, closely allied to political power and banking, yet more productive than official graft or the lending of money to impecunious monarchs and nobles. In the Later Middle Ages mining operations on a large scale were undertaken by men, mostly bankers or princes who had enough capital to enable them to introduce improved technical methods and enough political power or influence to secure a monopoly of mining rights in a given district. A fair share of the Fugger fortune came from the operation of German silver mines.

Mining and banking played a particularly important part in the rise of capitalism, because they helped to furnish the tools of capital — money and accounting — as well as to accumulate fortunes.

Money and accounting

In the age when modern business was just beginning, "hard" money — that is, gold and silver coinage — was a much more essential ingredient in every business transaction than it is in our own day of elaborately organized credit systems. Up to the middle of the fifteenth century, the amount of money in circulation in Europe seems to have increased fairly steadily, though slowly, as the general volume of business grew and the opportunities for profitable investment became more numerous, thus bringing hoarded money into active circulation. From the end of the thirteenth to the middle of the fifteenth century, however, the total amount of money in existence in Europe probably did not increase, or may actually have decreased; for there was a lull in mining operations and a good deal of gold and silver was drained out of Europe by the luxury trade with the East. The revival of mining on a large scale after the latter date, due to the investment of capital to finance difficult operations, was of great importance in adding to the supply of coinage, which was so necessary to the development of capital. This supply was still further augmented in the sixteenth century by the importation of gold and silver from the mines of Mexico and Peru.

Almost equally important was the work of the bankers, not only in mobilizing capital, but also in working out a technique of convenient and accurate accounting, which is one of the principal tools of active capital. Originating in Italy, the science of accounting by double-entry bookkeeping spread to all parts of Europe by the beginning of the sixteenth century. Its adoption marks a definite stage in the development of capitalist business. It made possible accurate estimates of profit and loss, which greatly facilitated the handling of a large business, and also had a profound psychological effect on the business man himself by clarifying his attitude toward his business and pointing out with unmistakable clearness the importance of profit as his chief aim. Moreover, the improved methods of bookkeeping enabled the bankers to work out a system of clearing or exchanging bills of indebtedness, so that international trade could be carried on with less dependence on the transfer of actual money.

In short, by the dawn of the modern age, a new type of wealth was already in existence, while a new technique for handling it and a new attitude toward its use were in the making. This new wealth was money wealth. Men had discovered the potentialities of capital and the truth of the axiom that money can make money. Business men were beginning to think in terms of investment of capital and to aim at the accumulation of profit rather than at the acquisition of a mere living. We must turn back now to trace the introduction of capital into commerce and industry, for it is investment in these productive enterprises that is the most essential characteristic of modern capitalism.

2. CAPITAL REVOLUTIONIZES COMMERCE AND INDUSTRY

Given the existence of fortunes large enough to leave a surplus for investment, the introduction of capital into commercial life awaited only the opening-up of opportunities for the investment in trade of money in sufficient quantities to be dignified by the name of capital. Such opportunities were very few in the period of the High Middle Ages. Most medieval commerce was handled by small merchants, working under guild or city regulations which usually limited them to dealing in one kind of goods and to a small quantity. True, they had a small working capital, but they could scarcely be called capitalists, for they seldom aimed at or achieved more than the making of a respectable living from their trade. Only in long-distance, seaborne trade, like that between the Italian cities and the East, was it possible for a merchant to deal in large enough quantities to leave room for the investment of any considerable amount of money or the making of any considerable profit. It was in this trade that the first purely commercial fortunes were founded. In the fourteenth and fifteenth centuries, however, opportunities for larger commercial ventures became steadily more numerous and more general in all parts of Europe. These were in part the result of the larger and more concentrated demand created by the rising territorial states and the growing cities. The rulers of the new centralized states entered the market for large supplies of goods to equip their armies or for the luxurious needs of a royal court. This demand could be met more profitably and more conveniently by merchants working on a more extensive scale than that of their medieval forerunners, and frequently a single merchant or a small group would be able to secure a monopoly. The phenomenal fortune built up by the fifteenth-century French merchant, Jacques Coeur, owed a good deal to his double position as merchant and controller of the royal finances, so that as the king's agent he bought the government supplies from himself. The growth of great cities had a similar effect on trade, by creating a concentrated market for large quantities of goods from distant parts.

Finally, and this is perhaps the most important single factor in creating new opportunities for the investment of capital in trade, at the end of the fifteenth century, the discovery of new ocean trade routes to Africa, India, and the Americas [1] opened up the most distant and most profitable trade that the world had yet seen. The Portuguese merchants, who brought back shiploads of spices, dyes, and silks from India, realized an almost incredible profit on their investment. Scarcely less profitable was the trade between Spain and the New World. Spanish merchants imported gold and silver, the priceless cochineal, dyes, and drugs, and sent out in return to the growing Spanish colonies all the necessities of life. Nor were the profits from these new trade routes limited to Portugal and Spain. The cargoes that came into the harbors of Lisbon or Seville were trans-shipped to the Netherlands for distribution, and before long, Dutch, Eng-

[1] See above, pages 396–400.

A FLEMISH GOLDSMITH

The painting of St. Eligius, patron saint of goldsmiths, by Petrus Christus, is in fact a picture of a fifteenth-century goldsmith's shop.

THE MONEY CHANGER AND HIS WIFE

This famous painting of a money changer, by Marinus van Roymerswaele, is a study in naked greed.

lish, and French merchants were competing for their share in the New World trade.

But if the profits from this new ocean commerce were great, the risks and the time involved in distant voyages were also considerable and the initial investment must be fairly large. Such commerce could not have been carried on under the primitive guild system. Nor, indeed, could the expanding volume of trade within Europe itself have been handled successfully by the old methods. It is extremely difficult to trace the exact relation between cause and effect in the gradual transition from the guild system to the conduct of trade by individual capitalists; but the net result is clear. A constantly expanding volume of trade on a world-wide scale was outgrowing the framework of a system which had been designed to meet the needs of a much more limited economic life. New conditions demanded new methods, and the tradition-ridden guilds were not sufficiently flexible or adaptable to survive in competition with the relatively unrestricted capitalists, who were prepared to seize every opportunity offered by the changing times. Those centers of trade where the medieval system was too firmly entrenched to be dislodged now began to decline, while other centers where capital could operate more freely took on new life. Among the other advantages enjoyed by capital was its freedom to migrate. It could be transferred easily to the new strategic centers created by the shift in the direction of world trade. In the sixteenth century many German capitalists shifted their investments to Antwerp to take advantage of the rising Atlantic trade. Capital, in short, was a fluid force, eminently adaptable. It could be moved, not only from place to place, but from one kind of business to another, as was demonstrated by the Fuggers, who kept their money working constantly in banking, mining, commerce, and industry, piling up profit by the modern method of a constant and rapid turnover.

Commerce outgrows the guild system

The new conditions of trade, with greater opportunities for carrying goods in large quantities and from distant sources, gave rise to a new figure in European commerce, the entrepreneur or wholesale middleman. In the Middle Ages, when most international trade was concentrated in the periodic fairs, commerce was carried on by small wandering merchants, who sold their goods in large part directly to the consumer. At the same time local trade was handled chiefly by masters of the craft guilds who made their goods and sold them at retail, across the counters of their shops. This system survived through the sixteenth century, but the increased bulk demand of the cities was rapidly rendering it obsolete. Trade was outgrowing local limits, and the transportation of goods from place to place was being taken over by wholesale middlemen, who stood between the producer and the retail merchant. Handling goods in bulk, the entrepreneur had to have considerable capital to invest, but having that, he had a great advantage over his smaller competitors. Because of his strategic position between supply and demand, and because he was often able to secure a monopoly of trade either from the state government or through association with others like himself, the entrepreneur was frequently able to control prices at both ends and thus make certain of a profit.

Rise of the entrepreneur

As compared to the medieval method of doing business, the investment of capital in wholesale trade was essentially an individual enterprise; yet the new type of merchant found that there were still many advantages to be gained from association. In this respect the familiar guild organization provided a model that could be adapted to new uses. The fifteenth and sixteenth centuries witnessed the formation of a number of merchant companies for the purpose of securing monopolies or special privileges for their members, though each member traded independently on his own capital. Such were the great London companies of Mercers, Drapers, and Grocers, who dealt in linen and silk fabrics, wholesale woolen cloth, and spices and drugs, respectively.

Partnerships and companies

More characteristic of the modern development of capital, however, were the merchant associations of another kind, partnerships, family firms, and eventually joint-

RETURN OF THE FIRST DUTCH FLEET TO TRADE WITH THE EAST INDIES, 1597

In the seventeenth century the Dutch founded a great commercial empire in the East Indies. The contemporary painting above shows the first fleet returning to Amsterdam.

THE EAST INDIA HOUSE

The great building above was the headquarters of the Dutch East India Company.

stock companies. As has already been suggested, the wholesale trade, and especially the long-distance trade, demanded the investment of a considerable sum of capital to finance each venture. Not every merchant had enough capital to buy a large cargo or to send a ship to distant parts. Or, if he did have it, he might not be willing to risk so much on one venture. This problem could be solved by the formation of a temporary partnership of several merchants, each of whom would contribute a share of the necessary investment and would receive his proportionate share of the profit when the enterprise was completed. Such partnerships, if repeated, might in time lose their temporary character and become permanent business firms. Partnerships or associations of capital within the limits of a family group were the most likely to assume this permanent character.

The most complete development of the principle of association was represented by the joint-stock company. Though fairly common in southern Europe before the first one was organized in England in 1553 for the exploitation of the newly discovered northeast trade route to Russia via the White Sea, they remained fairly rare in the north until the end of the sixteenth century. As a rule the joint-stock companies were organized only when it was necessary to open up new and especially expensive or hazardous trade routes to distant lands. On the surface, their organization looks very much like that of a modern corporation. Each investor purchased a share or shares of the joint stock, thus contributing to the capital of the company, which was managed as a whole by the company's officers. However, they still kept many of the characteristics of the simple partnership, for each shareholder was responsible for the entire debts of the company.

The rise of capitalist commerce led inevitably to the introduction of capital into industry. The artisan, or manufacturer to use a more modern word, supplied the goods in which the trader dealt, and, as the merchant began to handle goods in larger quantities and to carry them farther afield, there arose

Capital invades industry

opportunities for the production of goods in greater quantities than had been needed to supply a local market or the relatively small demands of the ordinary medieval merchant. This demand for a larger volume of production created openings for the investment of capital in industry, in the same way that the demands of a growing market had done in commerce, and the results were as revolutionary. Medieval industry had been essentially small industry, designed for the most part to supply a local market. The typical guild master was a retail merchant, who sold his goods in his own shop, as well as a manufacturer. Even when he sold his goods to a merchant for export, guild regulations usually limited him to a small quantity of production by prescribing the number of apprentices and journeymen whom he might employ. This system proved adequate for the needs of a relatively simple economic life. It could not meet the demands of a rapidly expanding market and a growing international trade. This was apparent first in those industries which manufactured goods chiefly for sale in distant parts. Here there was growing up a wholesale demand, which necessitated, or at least created opportunities for, wholesale production, and wholesale production meant the investment of capital. In some cases industry adapted itself to the use of capital by a natural internal growth. In others, the capitalist method was imposed upon it by the entrepreneur, who handled raw materials and goods in wholesale lots, and who found it more profitable to hire laborers to work up his goods than to sell raw materials to individual masters and buy the finished product from them. In any case, the commercial middleman tended to separate the manufacturer from the consumer, and so destroyed one of the most characteristic elements of the original craft guild system.

Radical as was the change wrought wherever capital invaded industry, it did not, as a rule, result in the immediate destruction of the guilds. Rather, it tended to transform them, until they had entirely lost their original character. There were two fairly common ways in which this was accomplished. The

Capital in the guilds

first occurred in those industries where a number of craft guilds in turn worked on the manufacture of a product intended for a foreign market, and where the merchant guild, which handled the finished product, succeeded in dominating the workers' guilds. The best example of this process is the cloth-making industry in Florence, England, Flanders, and elsewhere. Here there was a necessary division of labor. The wool passed through the hands of spinners, weavers, dyers, fullers, and shearmen, before it was finally bought and sold as finished cloth by the merchants of the *Arte di Lana*, as the merchant guild was called in Florence, or the drapers, as they were called in England. As the only large and constant customers, the cloth merchants, by working together, found it easy to control prices and methods of work. This the *Arte di Lana* of Florence succeeded in doing as early as the end of the thirteenth century. The next step was for the merchants, who were themselves rapidly becoming capitalist entrepreneurs, organized in merchant companies solely for the purpose of securing monopolies, to buy the raw wool in bulk and hire the members of the workers' guilds to make it into cloth. They were now large employers, who had invested considerable capital in industry; and the masters of the subordinate craft guilds had sunk to the position of mere wage-earners. Those masters who clung to their independence were forced out of competition, because cloth that had been bought and sold in small quantities by a series of independent masters cost the merchants, who were the only purchasers, more than it did under the new system, in which the merchant bought the raw wool and merely paid wages. The final step in the subjection of the workers was taken when, as occurred in England in the sixteenth century, the merchant employers began to give out their wool to workers who were not guildsmen and who, therefore, could not combine to keep up wages.

A second way in which capital invaded the guild system was demonstrated by the rise of capitalist masters within the guild itself, where there was a demand for quantity production. In the fifteenth and sixteenth centuries, particularly in the most thriving industrial centers in France, England, and Germany, many of the guilds were becoming very exclusive. The masters banded together to form a small oligarchy and to exclude all outsiders from mastership. Having full control of the guild, they were able to relax the rules regarding the number of apprentices and journeymen whom any one master might employ. Each master could thus produce a larger quantity of goods. The result was that the masters, who still retained their guild monopoly of the right to sell their product in the city, became in reality merchant employers, while the majority of the workers in the craft became permanent wage-earners, who would in all probability remain journeymen for life. The growing gap between worker and employer within the guilds is shown by the numerous attempts of journeymen in all parts of Europe during the fifteenth and sixteenth centuries to form guilds of their own for defense against the masters, and by the formation, as in the English "livery companies," of organizations of the wealthy masters inside the guild, for the purpose of controlling the workers and the sale of goods.

While capital, in these various ways, was reshaping the guild system and making it serve its own interests, there was also a steady growth of capitalist industry outside the guilds altogether. **Capital outside the guilds** The original capital for this type of industrial enterprise was nearly always furnished by commerce. An example has already been noted in the wool merchants who gave out their wool to non-guild workers as a means of escaping the restrictions imposed by such few privileges as the guildsmen still retained. This usually necessitated the moving of industry from old established centers with traditional guilds to new towns or villages where no guild was already in existence. There the capitalist employer could pay lower wages and hence make a larger profit. And as capital inevitably followed profit, the new unrestricted centers throve and took business away from the old guild towns. The decline of many old English towns and the rise of new industrial centers in the north and west of England are good indications of the geographical shift that often followed the capitalization of industry.

One final word of warning before we leave this subject: we must not forget, in concentrating our attention on the new developments of this age, that the transformation of industry by capital was a slow process and was not completed until two centuries or more after the end of the sixteenth century. Some parts of Europe lagged behind the rest, and there were almost everywhere some small guilds that survived with little change.

So far we have been dealing with the effect of capital on the economic life of the towns and cities. But what of the great majority of the population in every country, who still wrung their living from the cultivation of the soil? Their life was as yet almost untouched by the transforming power of capital. Agriculture was the most conservative form of economic activity, the most thoroughly bound by tradition. In most parts of Europe, the ownership of land was not yet regarded as an investment, like a commercial or industrial business. It was rather an inherited possession, handed down in noble or knightly families, and worked in small plots by peasants who were traditional tenants and who owed customary dues to the landlord. The peasant tenants had few opportunities to accumulate the capital that would have been needed to change their methods of cultivation or their economic status, and the hereditary tenant system afforded few chances to the lord for the investment of capital in technical improvement or large-scale production. In short, though political feudalism was declining, economic feudalism still persisted. Some changes, however, were taking place. Money economy had already spread from the towns to the country, and, in most places, the peasants had arranged to pay a cash rent to their lord as a commutation of the personal services they owed him. And this change, slight though it was, did something to shake the rigid structure of custom and left some openings for capitalist enterprise. In some parts of Germany, wealthy burghers were buying up land with a view to exploiting it at a profit, and in both Holland and England capitalist methods were beginning to invade this last stronghold of medieval tradition.

The first signs of this development can be observed most clearly in England, for there feudalism died earlier than in most continental countries. The popular outcry against "enclosures" in the sixteenth century points to one of the ways in which capital was changing agricultural methods at the expense of the hereditary peasant tenants. By this was meant the fencing-in of the open fields of the manor in order to use them for grazing sheep. This required an initial capital investment, but brought a larger profit to the landowner, first, because the price of wool was rising with the expanding English woolen industry, and second, because grazing required the employment of much less labor than did the cultivation of the soil. But, though profitable to the landlord, this was disastrous to the peasants who were driven from their ancestral lands and thrown out of employment. As a matter of fact, the amount of land actually enclosed was comparatively small, but it demonstrated a change in attitude on the part of the English landowners. Traditional rights were being less carefully observed. Before the end of the sixteenth century, in many parts of England hereditary tenancy was giving way to leases for life or for a term of years.

3. CAPITAL AND THE STATE

We have already commented, in this and previous chapters, on the close relation between the growth of capital and the rise of the national or territorial states. This relation was so important that it deserves some further discussion, even though it may be in part repetition.

The origins of that gradual centralization of power in the hands of a monarch or prince, which was characteristic of most of the states of Europe in the Later Middle Ages, can be traced back to a time before capital, in the modern sense, was a vital force in business, but not before money had become an important factor in economic life. The growing power of the monarch depended on his ability to collect money to pay and equip an army and to maintain an effective administrative system. Since money circulated most freely among the business class of the towns and cities, and since they were as a rule not a part of the feudal system, the monarch depended on them for a considerable share of his taxes. As the central governments grew stronger, and feudalism declined, kings were able to extend taxation to the rural districts, yet the commercial and industrial middle class still remained an important source of royal revenue. The growth of capital among this class, therefore, greatly increased the possibilities of royal taxation. Capitalist business increased the amount of money in circulation and, at the same time, it concentrated a large part of that money in the hands of a relatively small class, thus making the collection of taxes easier. The rulers of Europe soon realized the extent to which their own power, or that of the state, depended on the prosperity of the capitalist business men, and with that realization they began consciously to promote the interests of capital.

Before discussing the conscious promotion of business by the state, however, let us pause to note some of the ways in which the rise of territorial states unconsciously favored the early steps in the growth of capital. We have already explained how the development of central governments aided the accumulation of those large fortunes which were among the important prerequisites of capitalism. Moreover, the supplying of goods for the state armies and the royal courts furnished some of the earliest opportunities for the investment of capital in large-scale commercial transactions. More important than any of these factors, however, was the greater security and order which strong centralized governments alone could enforce. The free and safe circulation of trade that was essential to the success of capitalist business would have been impossible in the midst of the earlier feudal chaos. So, if the rulers of the European states realized their need of a prosperous business class, the capitalist merchants and manufacturers realized as clearly their need of a strong state government.

This close relation between the new type of state and the new type of business inevitably tended to make the territorial or national state the most important unit in economic life, just as the city had been in the High Middle Ages. **The state an economic unit** Medieval merchants and artisans had looked to the city government for protection, and it in turn had regulated their activity, either directly or through the agency of the guilds, in the interest of the whole city community. All trade outside the city was in a sense foreign trade, and was intermunicipal in character. Now, with broader economic interests to consider, the capitalist merchants and manufacturers began to look to the state for protection, and the state government in turn regulated trade and industry for the good of the whole state as they conceived it. One great advantage of this transference of economic control from the city to the state was the clearing-away of the economic barriers, set up by city exclusiveness, to trade within the state itself; a second was the greater protection which the state could give to its merchants in foreign parts.

The economic policy adopted by the European states when they took over the regulation of business was in many respects similar to that of the **Mercantilism** medieval cities, save that it was carried out on a much larger scale. The activity of the individual was still controlled, though not so rigidly, for the good of the whole community. This national economic policy is generally known as "mercantilism." It was developed to its fullest extent in the seventeenth and eighteenth centuries, but it was also generally practiced in the sixteenth century and signs of it were apparent at an even earlier date. Mercantilism consists essentially in the regulation of industry and commerce by the state government, with a view to making the state more prosperous and hence more powerful in relation to neighboring states. One of the primary aims of mercantilist policy, though by no means the only aim, was the accumulation in the state of as large a supply of money — i.e., gold and silver — as possible. Actual money played a much more important part in the conduct of business then than now. Moreover, in the days before the credit system had been so highly developed as to enable states to float large national debts, money was very necessary to pay the expenses of the growing national armies, on which the safety of the state depended. And the amount of money that the government could collect in taxes depended more or less on the amount in existence in the state. The government, therefore, regulated trade whenever possible, so as to encourage exports above imports. This was called maintaining a favorable balance of trade, for if a country sold more than it bought, more money would come into the state than would leave it. Another aim, closely allied to the first, was to increase the wealth of the state by founding colonies, as Spain and Portugal did in the sixteenth century and England, France, and Holland in the seventeenth, and to exploit them in the interest of the mother country. The mercantilist state always endeavored to maintain an exclusive monopoly of trade with its colonies, exchanging manufactured goods for raw materials of greater potential value. Since war was an ever-present possibility in the mercantilist age, the preparation for war was a regular part of every government's economic policy. This explains why some states, like France, frequently forbade the exportation of grain, so that the country would not be dependent on its neighbors for food in case of war, and why maritime states, like England, promoted the shipbuilding and fishing industries and issued navigation acts to encourage native shipping, thus building up a merchant marine manned by trained seamen as a sort of naval reserve.

If the purpose of state economic legislation was in many ways like that of the medieval cities, the theory which justified it was still more clearly a legacy from the Middle Ages. The right to trade was still not regarded as the natural right of every resident; it was rather a privilege to be granted by the government as it saw fit. From this it followed naturally that the government which granted the right to trade had full power also to regulate the method of trade. Every sixteenth-century state government exercised that power in a variety of ways, but nowhere was the theory of privilege and control demonstrated more clearly than in the granting of monopolies to companies or groups of merchants for some specific type of trade. Sometimes a state would grant a monopoly to foreign merchants when it needed the goods that only they could supply, or in order to secure reciprocal advantages for its own merchants in foreign countries. More commonly, however, the monopolies were granted to organizations of native merchants. Such were the monopolies given by the governments of England, France, and Holland to the companies that opened up trade with the Far East, or the earlier monopoly of exporting English cloth to the Netherlands granted to the Company of Merchant Adventurers. These monopolies served the double purpose of excluding foreigners from the trade and of encouraging the most effective native trading organizations by freeing them from both native and foreign competition. In addition, the government often profited directly by retaining a share in the profits of the monopolistic company.

In regulating industry, the mercantilist governments followed the same principles as motivated their commercial legislation. Indeed, the two cannot be separated. Realizing that the wealth of a state depended in large part on its productive power, the best rulers of the mercantilist age made every effort to stimulate manufacturing, especially of those goods that could be exported in order to maintain the favorable balance of trade or that might be useful to the state in time of war. With this in mind they granted monopolies and even subsidies to those companies, guilds, or localities that seemed best fitted to produce needed goods. Whenever possible they strove to introduce and foster new industries that would make the state more independent of other countries. Thus, in the late sixteenth century the silk industry was introduced into France with government aid, and the glass industry was founded with royal monopolies in both France (1551) and England (1567). Government regulation and aid, however, did not always serve their intended purpose, and not infrequently industries were more hampered than helped by the well-meaning efforts of a paternalistic state.

INTERIOR OF A SIXTEENTH-CENTURY KITCHEN

INTERIOR OF A WEALTHY MERCHANT'S HOUSE

EVIDENCE OF THE PROSPERITY THAT CAME WITH THE COMMERCIAL REVOLUTION

When the state took upon itself the task of controlling the economic life of its citizens, it was forced also to assume the responsibility for adjusting those social problems that arose from the working-out of economic conditions. This was a relatively new problem for state governments, but before the end of the sixteenth century state legislation designed to fix wages and regulate conditions of labor was fairly common. Such legislation was usually much more favorable to the capitalist employers, who could bring pressure to bear on the government, than to the unorganized laborers, yet the interests of the latter and of the unemployed were not entirely neglected. The Elizabethan Poor Laws and the famous Statute of Apprentices are but examples of numerous state laws that were intended, in part at least, to protect the laborers and care for the poor.

Employment and poor relief

4. CAPITAL AND SOCIETY

We have seen how the rise of capital caused an economic revolution and fostered a political revolution through aiding the rise of the territorial states. It was the fundamental cause also of a social revolution, which had only begun in the fifteenth and sixteenth centuries, but which when completed would have reshaped society from top to bottom. The rise of capital changed the character of wealth and the sources of power. In the Middle Ages power resulted usually from an inherited position in society, and wealth was the product of power. It was only in small part money wealth; in much larger part it consisted of the ability to command the services of men by virtue of hereditary contracts. In the modern world, on the other hand, wealth is the source of power, and modern wealth is essentially money wealth. It is money that creates the power to control the services of men. This is the essence of the social revolution that was beginning in these transitional centuries.

Capital reshapes society

As a result of this social revolution, two powers, closely allied, rose to dominate the rest of society. They were the monarchy, representing the power of the territorial state, and the wealthy middle class or bourgeoisie. The latter was eventually to triumph over the monarchy itself and was either to control or destroy it, but for the present they were content to serve its interests, secure in the knowledge that its interests were also their own. Meanwhile, as the state grew stronger and the wealthy bourgeoisie more influential, the power of the feudal nobility declined.[1] They still maintained their social prestige, their pride of class and many of their special privileges, but they were no longer the dominating class in European society.

Triumph of state and bourgeoisie

The nobles, however, were not the only class to suffer because of the rising power of money. Capital reduced to complete subjection the much more numerous class of industrial laborers. They were no longer included among the bourgeoisie and did not rise with them to power; for the introduction of capital into industry had driven an ever-widening wedge between the few who became rich employers and the many who became mere wage-earners, with little chance of ever rising above that position. This is perhaps the most significant of all the changes wrought by the rise of capital. In the High Middle Ages, when nearly all industry was confined within the limits of the guild system, no such permanent division between employer and worker had existed, for every apprentice and journeyman expected some day to become a master and an employer on a small scale, and every employer had been at one time a wage-earning journeyman. At the end of the sixteenth century, this might still be true in some places, especially in the smaller crafts; but in the large industries a very different condition existed. The great majority of industrial workers already formed a class in society by themselves — the proletariat. Unorganized, or with organization strictly controlled by the state, unrepresented in government, uneducated, and lacking the surplus capital that was the source of power in the new society, men of this class had little hope of bettering their condition, either individually or as a whole. They were the victims of the new economic system, reinforced

Subjection of proletariat

[1] See above, pages 372–373.

by the tacit alliance of their employers with the state.

In conclusion, we must note two striking results of the capitalist revolution, which are so important that they cannot be ignored, by the historian or by anyone else. The first is the vast increase in the total wealth of the world produced by the capitalist system; the second, the concentration of a disproportionately large share of that wealth in the hands of a few people, thus opening up a tremendous gap between the economic and social status of the rich minority and the poor majority. Whether the latter condition will remain permanently as yet remains to be seen.

33

The Reconstruction of France and the Establishment of Absolute Monarchy

(1598–1660)

THE SIXTEENTH CENTURY, which had opened with such brilliant promise for France, drew to its close in the midst of disillusionment and disaster. When the century began, France had seemed about to enter upon a new and glorious epoch of national strength. The monarchy had apparently won at last its long fight for centralized government and national unity against the independent feudal nobility, and the dream of extending French power across the Alps into the fabulous land of Italy seemed already an accomplished fact. But sixty years of foreign wars ended with the abandonment of the costly Italian dream; and a further generation of civil Wars of Religion left France distracted and desolate, powerless in foreign affairs and internally divided, with her people impoverished and her government bankrupt, and with the ancient specter of feudal independence once more raising its head to mock an impotent monarchy. Just as the century ended, however, there were signs of renewed hope. Henry of Bourbon, King of Navarre, had become King Henry IV of France, and under his strong hand, peace, unity, and order were restored to the troubled land. Once secure upon his throne, Henry devoted himself to the task of reconstructing his shattered country and restoring the power and prestige of the monarchy at home and abroad. Many of the results of his work were wasted in the years following his death, but the task of strengthening the state was taken up again by Richelieu and by Mazarin, to such good effect that when the young King Louis XIV took over the personal government of his kingdom he found France the foremost power in Europe and himself an absolute monarch, whose authority was questioned by neither noble nor commoner.

Meanwhile, keeping pace with the evolution of the national monarchical state, the national culture of France was taking form. In the midst of the foreign and civil wars of the sixteenth century, France reaped the late fruits of the Renaissance and utilized the legacy of antiquity to aid in the formation of her national tongue. And when peace and order were restored, the aristocracy and intellect of France combined to lay the foundations of that refined society and polished literature that were to be the envy and despair of Europe in the age of Louis XIV.

1. HENRY IV RECONSTRUCTS FRANCE (1598–1610)

Though Henry IV had inherited the royal title in 1589,[1] five years of fighting passed before he was officially crowned, and it was not till 1596 that he received the submission of the

Peace restored (1598)

[1] See above, page 454.

RECONSTRUCTION OF FRANCE AND ESTABLISHMENT OF ABSOLUTE MONARCHY

last of the Catholic League. Meanwhile, he had been forced into war with Philip II of Spain, and peace at home was very uncertain with the real issue of the Wars of Religion still unsettled. Born soldier though he was, Henry was eager to restore peace, so that his country might have an opportunity to recover from the devastating turmoil of the preceding generation. In 1598, he brought the war with Spain to an end by the Treaty of Vervins, and in the same year he issued the epoch-making Edict of Nantes, which accomplished the still more important objective of securing internal peace for France by a fair settlement of the vexatious religious problem. Henry had become a Catholic for reasons of state, because he was to be the ruler of a country that was predominantly Catholic, but he had not forgotten his old Huguenot friends. The Edict of Nantes granted them complete freedom of conscience, the right of public worship in all places where it already existed and in a number of other specified places, and the right to hold any public office. As a temporary guaranty that these rights would be respected, the Huguenots were also given the privilege of governing and garrisoning some two hundred cities, mostly in southern and western France. This was a dangerous concession and caused trouble later, but the establishment of religious toleration was wise and just. That part of the edict remained in force for nearly a century. It reunited the kingdom and made France the one country in Europe where men of two different religions could dwell together in peace and equal citizenship.

Edict of Nantes

With the restoration of peace at home and abroad, Henry IV was free at last to take up his colossal task of reconstructing France, restoring the power of the monarchy, and rehabilitating French prestige in Europe. It was a task that might well have daunted a lesser man, for it involved every aspect of government. In the first place, the government must be rescued from bankruptcy and its finances put on a firm footing. Next, the people must be aided to recover their lost prosperity. Then the authority of the central government must be strengthened and the nobles reduced to obedience. And finally, the king must use all the power of the revived state, with the aid of skillful diplomacy, to teach the other powers of Europe that France was still a nation to be reckoned with.

Henry's task

For the carrying-out of this great task, no king in French history was better suited by nature than Henry IV, or, perhaps it would be fairer to say, than Henry IV aided by that most careful, energetic, and honest of French ministers, the Duke of Sully. The restoration of France was the product of the cordial collaboration of these two men of very different character. They had been friends and companions in arms from their youth up. During the troubled years of the Wars of Religion, Henry had learned to depend on Sully, then Marquis of Rosny, for those compensating qualities which he himself lacked. They were both good soldiers, though Sully fought with a cold Calvinist fury that was in marked contrast to the king's reckless, swaggering gallantry, but it was in the council rather than in the field of battle that Sully proved his worth. For Henry needed someone to check his tendency to extravagance. He was genial, friendly, endowed with the personal magnetism and understanding of men's characters which are essential to a leader, but also inclined to be profligate. His best qualities of mind were clear intelligence, sound common sense, and the kind of constructive imagination that is needed to shape the general policies of a state. In short, Henry was a popular king and a wise statesman, but he had not the qualities that make an administrator. And France needed an administrator. Henry realized that need and knew that in Sully he had the man to meet it. A rigid Protestant, grim, cautious, economical, and unshakably honest, Sully would never be popular, but he could be trusted to the limit, and he had all the tireless energy and passion for detail that are the marks of the born administrator. Henry might conceive wise policies, but it was Sully who attended to the practical problems of the business of government.

Henry and Sully

Sully's most immediate and pressing problem was to free the government from its apparently hopeless financial embarrassment.

HENRY IV OF FRANCE
Henry of Navarre was a shrewd, yet dashing and gallant leader, and looked the part.

MARIE DE' MEDICI
Henry's wife, shown here from a painting by P. P. Rubens, lacked all of her husband's qualities as a statesman.

HENRY IV ENTERING PARIS IN 1594
The scene above marks the turning point in the Wars of Religion.

Years of foreign and civil wars, the weakness of the last Valois kings, and the confusion, inefficiency, extravagance, and corruption that pervaded every branch of the financial administration had combined to bring the state close to the verge of bankruptcy. The people were crushed by heavy and inequitable taxes; yet the royal income was utterly inadequate to meet current expenses. In part this was the result of a vicious financial system inherited from the Middle Ages. A badly organized multitude of officials and a criminally careless system of bookkeeping made waste and corruption almost unavoidable. Moreover, the method of levying taxes was unjust and terribly wasteful. The *taille*, a personal and property tax, which represented the largest part of the royal income, was paid almost entirely by the poorer classes, since nobles and clergy were exempt and the wealthy bourgeoisie could often escape their just share. In order to raise money quickly, this and other taxes were "farmed out" to private persons or corporations in return for a lump sum. The tax "farmers" then collected as much as they could — usually far more than they had paid the government — from the defenseless people. It has been reckoned that under a weak administration not more than twenty-five per cent of the taxes paid by the people ever reached the royal treasury. Sully made no serious effort to reform this vicious system, but he did try to ensure its being honestly administered. He imposed a reasonable amount of order upon the administration, insisted on a strict accounting for all income and expenditure, did away with a number of useless offices, forced dishonest officials to disgorge, and saw to it that the money collected in taxes did not disappear on its way to the treasury. By such measures, Sully was able to decrease the *taille*, while at the same time increasing the royal revenue, and by cutting down waste and extravagance he was able to provide plenty of money for all the legitimate expenses of government, including the cost of building up a strong army and financing public works and other measures for promoting general prosperity. By the end of Henry's reign, he had recovered much of the royal domain, alienated by his predecessors; had paid off nearly a third of the national debt; and had accumulated a substantial surplus for use in any emergency.

In his preoccupation with the finances of the royal government, however, Sully did not forget that the wealth of the state depends in the long run on the prosperity of its citizens. Careful though he was to keep down royal expenses, he spent money freely on the improvement of roads, bridges, canals, and harbors, thus stimulating the economic life of the state by providing safe and convenient means of communication. He was also greatly interested in the promotion of agriculture, which he believed to be the true basis of national prosperity. With characteristic energy, he undertook the draining of marshes, the reclaiming of wastelands, and the resettling of districts deserted during the late civil wars. In addition he opened up a foreign market for the farmers by removing the prohibition on the exportation of grain from the country. To all this the king gave his hearty support, and also added some important innovations of his own. Henry, indeed, was a sounder economist than Sully, and took an active interest in both industry and commerce, which his minister tended to ignore. It was the king who introduced the silk industry into France, stimulated other industries by subsidies and monopolies, made favorable commercial treaties with Spain and England, and founded the French colonial empire by sending out the first colonists to New France, the Canada of the future. And, most important of all, Henry gave to France a dozen years of peace and security, which was all a naturally industrious people needed to work out their own economic salvation. When Henry's reign ended, there was still much poverty in the country, but the general economic condition was vastly improved, and France had taken a long step in the direction of national recovery.

Meanwhile, Henry had to deal with other than economic problems. Equally important was the task of restoring the authority of the crown, on which the security of the state depended. The civil wars, which had come near to ruining the monarchy, had given a new lease on life to political feudalism. The great nobles had recovered a part of their old independence, and they were always a destructive and disorganizing force in the life of the nation, unless kept well in hand by a strong king. In his struggle for the crown, Henry had been forced to buy off the great nobles of the Catholic League, but once his position was secure he taught them that he was their master. More than once discontented nobles rebelled, but the rebellions were easily crushed. The mass of the people, and especially the solid middle class, were unshakably loyal to the king who had given them peace, security, and a chance to prosper. With their backing, Henry built up as strong a monarchy as France had yet seen. His government was an intelligent, unoppressive absolutism, and that was the best that France could hope for under the circumstances. France had no institutions capable of building up a constitutional monarchy, and the civil wars had proved that the only alternative to absolutism was anarchy.

Much of Henry's energy, too, was taken up with foreign affairs. He saw the issues clearly and pushed every advantage, so that the growth of France's prestige abroad kept pace with her internal recovery. The king's foreign policy may be summarized in a very few words. His main objective was to free France from the menace of the encircling Hapsburg powers, by weakening Spain and Austria in any possible way. The Hapsburg states were not as strong as they had been, but France still lay wide open to invasion from four different directions. To the south, Spain held Roussillon on the French side of the Pyrenees; to the north, she held Flanders, and to the east, Franche-Comté, both divided from France by indefensible frontiers; and to the southeast, Savoy, friendly to the Hapsburgs, opened the way to invaders from northern Italy. With her enemies inside her only geographical defenses, France would never be safe while the Hapsburgs remained strong enough for aggressive action. While giving his country time to draw its breath and recover its strength, Henry devoted himself to diplomacy. He won the alliance of the Duke of Savoy, thus blocking the road from Hapsburg Italy; and in Germany he succeeded in mobilizing a group of Protestant princes in opposition to the Hapsburg emperor. Meanwhile, he was building up a national army and waiting for the right moment to strike a more forcible blow.

When the moment came, Henry rushed to war with his old enthusiasm, but death stopped him before he could accomplish anything. The cause of the war was the death, in 1609, of the Duke of Cleves, Jülich, and Berg, three small but strategically important states on the lower Rhine, near the borders of France. There were two claimants to the succession, both Lutherans, though the people were Catholic. The Emperor Rudolf promptly sent an Austrian army to occupy the duchies, pending the settlement of the succession. Henry naturally considered this act a menace to France. He mobilized his troops at once and rallied his Protestant allies in Germany and Holland. It was to have been a general war against the Hapsburgs in both Germany and Spain. Everything was ready and Henry was about to join his army in the field when an assassin struck him down as he rode through the streets of Paris. The king's death paralyzed France. She withdrew from the war and the anti-Hapsburg alliance disintegrated.

2. RICHELIEU AND MAZARIN ESTABLISH ABSOLUTE MONARCHY (1624–61)

With the death of Henry IV, the character of French government changed abruptly for the worse. Fourteen years passed before France found again, in Richelieu, a strong hand to guide her destiny. Those years form an interlude of waste, misgovernment, rebellion, and a shiftless foreign policy, during which the best results of Henry's reign were frittered away. For the first half of that period (1610–17), France was ruled by a stupid and irresponsible woman, Henry's widow, Marie de' Medici, acting as regent for their young son Louis XIII, and by her worthless Italian favorites. The queen had no understanding of her late husband's policies. She reversed almost every

LOUIS XIII OF FRANCE

Upper left: The king, shown here in court dress, was far from brilliant, but had solid qualities of firm will and kindliness.

THE DUKE OF LUYNES

Left: The handsome Charles d'Albert, Louis's first minister, was also his first mistake as a king.

CARDINAL RICHELIEU

Upper right: The terrible cardinal, Armand de Richelieu, whom Louis chose to succeed Luynes and who remained Louis's chief minister until virtually the end of his reign, more than made up for the weakness of his predecessor.

one of them, with disastrous results. She discharged Sully and the rest of Henry's ministers; she wasted the money he had saved and allowed the administration to lapse back into its old state of inefficiency and corruption; she permitted the great nobles to rebel and bought them off, instead of crushing them by force; and finally, she reversed Henry's anti-Hapsburg policy and sought an alliance with Spain, the alliance to be cemented by the marriage of Louis XIII to the Spanish infanta.

Meanwhile, the young king was growing up, disregarded by his mother and humiliated by her all-powerful favorite, the Italian adventurer, Concini, who had become chief minister of the kingdom. In his loneliness, Louis turned for friendship and counsel to his royal falconer, who accompanied him on the hunting expeditions that were his favorite pastime. With this rather obscure gentleman he planned the overthrow of his mother's arrogant minister. The plot was put into effect in 1617. Concini was killed and the queen-mother was banished from the court. The king then took over the government in his own right, with the former falconer, now Duke of Luynes, as his chief minister. The change, however, did not bring any marked improvement in government, for Luynes was a fool and the king was young and inexperienced. So the interlude of disorder continued until 1624, when Louis handed over the government to the capable hands of Cardinal Richelieu, who remained his chief minister almost to the end of his reign.

Louis XIII

For eighteen years (1624–42) Richelieu was master of France. He dominated every branch of the government and shaped the policies of the state. Yet he could not have done so without the steady support of the king. Louis gave him complete authority because he was convinced that Richelieu was the most capable man in France. That Richelieu overshadowed the king does not prove that the latter was a weakling, for no weakling could have backed the terrible cardinal with such stubborn determination against the hatred of the royal family and the whole court. For Richelieu was never popular. Indeed, Louis himself never really liked his awe-inspiring minister, but he trusted him and approved his policies. Throughout his ministry, Richelieu devoted himself with fanatical energy to the accomplishment of two main objectives: first, the unification of the whole state under the absolute authority of the crown, and second, the raising of France to a dominating position among the nations of Europe. It was part of the policy of Henry IV, but only part; for Richelieu, though utterly devoted to the crown and the state, cared nothing for the welfare of the French people. He never realized, as Henry did, that the strength of the state depends on the prosperity of its people. He was prepared to sacrifice their interests ruthlessly to what he believed to be the good of the state.

Richelieu

That lack of human interest and understanding kept Richelieu from being a really great statesman, but in one respect at least his ruthlessness was justified. A stern hand was needed to control the great nobles, for under the weak rule of the regent and the young king they had resumed their old lawless ways. They must be crushed if the king was to be really king. In his devotion to the ideal of absolute monarchy, therefore, Richelieu became the avowed enemy of the nobles, and no name or title was too great to save a traitor from the executioner's block. He had spies everywhere, and one conspiracy after another ended in a series of executions before it could become a menace to the state.

Richelieu and the nobles

The same motives determined Richelieu to crush the political power of the Huguenots. He was not a religious fanatic and did not believe in the practical utility of persecution, but the Huguenots as a political party were a menace to the king's authority and to the unity of the kingdom. The Edict of Nantes had left them in armed possession of a number of walled towns and with a religious-political organization of their own. Moreover, they were prepared to use their privileged position to make a bid for further independence. They had rebelled once in 1621 before Richelieu came into power, and he had been minister for only a year when they rebelled again. This time he had to

Suppression of the Huguenots

make peace, for the government was not yet strong enough to crush them, but he was working busily so that when the next opportunity occurred he would be ready to take decisive action. He had not long to wait. In 1627, the irresponsible interference of England on the side of the Huguenots precipitated another rebellion. The war lasted for two years, with most of the action centering around the siege of the strongly fortified seaport of La Rochelle. It held out for a year, but when it fell the Huguenot resistance soon crumbled. In 1629, the rebels submitted, giving up all their fortified strongholds and the last of their special military and political privileges. Richelieu had accomplished his purpose, and having done so, he wisely refrained from religious persecution. The main body of the Edict of Nantes, which guaranteed the Huguenots freedom of conscience and equal citizenship with Catholics, was left intact. Shorn of their political organization, but otherwise untouched, the French Protestants settled down to become loyal and useful members of the state.

Having now nothing to fear from the Huguenots, and not much from the great nobles, Richelieu was free to **Foreign policy** turn his attention to the aggrandizement of France on the international stage. His foreign policy was a revival, *in toto*, of that of Henry IV. His aim was to win security for France and a possible expansion of territory by weakening the Hapsburgs. He was the natural ally of all enemies of Austria and Spain, and would aid them with money or arms as the occasion demanded. To this end he devoted the largest part of his energy in the later years of his ministry. That story, however, belongs more properly to a later chapter dealing with the Thirty Years' War, in which he played a conspicuous part.

At the end of his life, Richelieu might well look back upon his career of service to **Administration** the state with satisfaction. He had accomplished everything he really cared about. He had raised French prestige abroad; he had crushed all dangerous opposition to the monarchy at home; and he had built up a strongly centralized government. Yet Richelieu's administration was far from being an entirely successful one, and nothing shows the limitation of vision which kept him from being a really great statesman more clearly than his inability to realize the extent of his failure. His successes had been won at too great a cost to the state, and he left France miserable and impoverished. The people were ground down by the excessive taxes raised to pay for his foreign wars; commerce and industry languished with little aid from the state; and even the government was drifting perilously close to financial ruin. Compared to the standard set by Henry IV and Sully, he cannot be called a successful administrator. He not only neglected the economic interests of the people, but he failed to check extravagance, waste, and corruption in the royal administration, so that both the government and the people suffered more than was necessary even to meet the heavy expenses of the war.

In only one respect did Richelieu attempt to reform the unwieldy administrative system. He sent out royal officials, called "intendants," with **Intendants** arbitrary powers to take over many of the duties of the nobles, governors of the provinces, and other traditional local officials. This reform was in keeping with his general policy of centralizing the government of the state under the king's council and strengthening the authority of the crown at the expense of such feudal institutions as still survived. The intendants were usually well-trained, middle-class men, on whose loyalty the king could rely more securely than on that of the great nobles. Though not as systematically established under Richelieu as they came to be later, the intendants already formed the basis of a governmental bureaucracy that would be of great service in holding the country together in any political crisis.

The structure of central government which Richelieu had created was put to a severe test in the years following his death. For the king died **Mazarin and Louis XIV** within a few months after his minister (May, 1643), and the crown was left to a four-year-old child, Louis XIV, with his mother, Anne of Austria, acting as regent.

Such a situation almost inevitably spelled trouble, but Richelieu had bequeathed to the young king, with the centralized administration, an able minister to act as his successor, and together they saw the royal government through a troubled period of foreign war and rebellion at home to eventual triumph. The new minister was an Italian who had been for years in Richelieu's service, the Cardinal Mazarin. Until his death, early in 1661, he remained chief minister of France, and in that time he carried out most of Richelieu's policies to their final conclusion. Supple and conciliatory, where Richelieu was hard and ruthless, the Italian cardinal had not the awe-inspiring personality of his terrible predecessor, but he was intelligent and he walked faithfully in the path prescribed by his former master.

That path led him safely through the early years of the regency and to the conclusion of the Thirty Years' War in 1648. But Mazarin was an even worse financial administrator than Richelieu. The expenses of the war grew heavier by accumulation, and with each year the burden of taxation became more intolerable to the people. Moreover, the great nobles who had hated and feared Richelieu hated his successor also, but did not fear him so much. In 1648, a group of the great nobles took advantage of the economic discontent to break into open rebellion in uneasy alliance with the citizens of Paris. This was the first of the two rebellions that are collectively known as the Fronde. It was quickly ended by a compromise. The trouble, however, was not ended. The next year the rebellion was renewed on a broader scale. For two years (1650–52) it threatened the hated minister and the whole system of absolute royal government. The danger would have been greater if the rebels had been united in their interests or had had the backing of strong popular support. But the Fronde was not really a constitutional struggle. The princes who led it were irresponsible, motivated by nothing more praiseworthy than the desire to ruin the cardinal and to weaken the royal government to their own selfish advantage. The solid middle-class adherents of the Fronde were soon disillusioned, leaving the nobles and the mob to go their own reckless way until the rebellion crumbled. The futile activity of the Fronde was in reality the death flurry of political feudalism in France. Never again would the nobles take arms against their king. It left the monarchy stronger than ever, for it reinforced the conviction of the French people that the only hope for peace and security lay in the absolute authority of the king. One of the tasks begun by Henry IV and carried on by Richelieu was finished at last.

Another, however, still occupied Mazarin's attention. Although the Thirty Years' War had ended in 1648, France was still at war with Hapsburg Spain. Mazarin carried on the war with fair ability against a weakening enemy, and at last brought it to a successful conclusion with the Peace of the Pyrenees in 1659, whereby France acquired Roussillon and some other important bits of territory along her frontiers, in addition to that awarded her at Westphalia.[1] Mazarin had now not long to live, but he had the satisfaction of knowing that he had completed Richelieu's work. France was indisputably the first power in Europe; the Hapsburg states were tottering; and the young King Louis XIV, who was soon to take over the government into his own hands, would find himself the unquestioned master of his kingdom. If the French people still groaned under an insupportable burden of taxation; if the administrative system was still wasteful and inefficient; if the government was still not far from bankruptcy, that could not be helped. Richelieu's dream, if only a part of that of Henry IV and Sully, had been fulfilled.

3. GROWTH OF FRENCH LITERATURE AND CULTURE

The final establishment of absolute monarchy in a united state completed a long process of evolution. There was no doubt now that France was a nation, closely knit together and conscious of its national identity. The same period saw also the completion of another evolution, that of the national language, which had kept pace

---
[1] See below pages 508–510.

CARDINAL MAZARIN

Top left: The Italian cardinal who succeeded Richelieu, as the above picture suggests, had a keen and subtle mind.

TURENNE

Top right: This portrait of Henri de la Tour d'Auvergne, Vicomte de Turenne, gives a striking impression of the great general who came to the aid of the government during the Fronde.

ANNE OF AUSTRIA

Left: This picture can scarcely have done credit to the queen-mother who ruled France as the regent for Louis XIV with Mazarin's aid.

through the centuries with the evolution of the state. This development was no more peculiar to France than was the growth of nationalism. Every country in Europe had developed a vital literature in the tongue of the people, though still marred by a variety of dialects corresponding roughly to the local divisions inherited from the feudal régime, before the classical revival of the Renaissance temporarily checked the development of the "vulgar" literature. For a time the ancient Latin of the humanists' adoration displaced the more modern languages. But the age of the Renaissance was also an age of rising nationalism, as the great territorial states were consolidated under strong monarchies, and in the long run nationalism proved stronger than the international heritage of ancient Rome. When once the first enthusiasm for the literature of antiquity had spent its force, the national languages asserted themselves more vigorously than ever. The new art of printing helped, for it made books cheap and circulated them more widely. A wider reading public, not thoroughly versed in Ciceronian Latin, demanded books in their native tongue. The humanists had made Latin too perfectly classical, so that it had become difficult for any but the most learned to read, and still more difficult to write. With the passing of the Erasmian age of humanism, Latin gradually subsided into the status of a dead language, reserved for the use of scholars. The vigor of the Renaissance passed over into the modern languages. The lessons of style and taste that the humanists had learned from the classics were now applied to the refinement of the vernacular. Moreover, the freer circulation of books made possible by printing, together with the closer union of all parts of the state into a conscious nationality, gradually wiped out local differences of dialect and cleared the way for the development of truly national literatures.

The late Renaissance After the full daylight of the classical Renaissance in France had passed with the great age of the humanists, there was a long twilight in which the interests and influences of the Renaissance lived on in modified form to inspire the founders of modern French literature. Before the end of the sixteenth century, two Frenchmen of this late Renaissance left the indelible imprint of their style and personality on the literature of their country. The first, François Rabelais (1494?–1553), **Rabelais** belongs, almost, to the age of the humanists. He was a profound classical scholar, and his egregious enjoyment of life was typical of the Renaissance spirit at its highest tide. But he foreshadows the coming age in his determination to write in his native language and for the people rather than for the limited world of scholars. His fabulous tales of *Gargantua* and *Pantagruel*, which won instant and lasting popularity by their wild humor and lusty glorification of the physical universe, may be said to mark the beginnings of modern secular French literature. The second outstanding literary figure of the sixteenth century in France was a man of very different character, the thoughtful essayist Michel de Montaigne **Montaigne** (1533–92). He was a product of the troubled era of the Wars of Religion. That age of violent passions, however, had not made him a partisan. On the contrary, the conflict of dogmatic beliefs had suggested to his reasonable mind the possibility that neither side of the religious, or any other, argument was in possession of all the truth. With calm curiosity, he examined one after another the problems that vexed his age, and, having examined them from all sides, left them in his brilliant *Essays* illuminated but still unsolved. He was at once the heir to the inquiring critical spirit of the Renaissance and the father of modern rationalism. Nurtured on the classics, Montaigne brought to French prose a perfection of style that makes him as important a figure in the history of the language as in the history of thought.

Meanwhile, an earnest little group of Montaigne's contemporaries, raised like himself in the classic tradition, were working conscientiously at **The Pléiade** the task of refining and perfecting French poetry, by applying to it the lessons learned from the poets of ancient Greece and Rome. There were seven poets in the group, whence the name of the Pléiade which they took for themselves. Their leader, and the only first-rate poet in the group, was Pierre de Ronsard (1524–85). By both precept and example he set a new and more conscious style in French poetry, while his friend Joachim du Bellay (1522–60) set forth the aims of the group in a *Defense and Illustration of the French Language*, asserting its potential equality with the ancient tongues.

Thus ordered, purified, and expanded by adaptation of the classics, the national language was already approaching its modern form when Henry IV restored peace and began the rebuilding of the state. During the next half-century, the work of standardizing and perfecting literary French continued. Two generations of uninspired poets and second-rate writers devoted themselves to a laborious study of the rules of grammar, to perfection of form, and to precision and refinement in the use of words. This devotion to refined form won for them the name of "Précieux," originally a term of respect, but turned to one of ridicule when, having outlived their usefulness, they fell victims to the biting satire of Molière. The vigorous writers of the golden age of Louis XIV have overshadowed their less inspired predecessors, but they owed the excellence of the language they used in no small degree to the men who had worked so hard to perfect its form. The age of Richelieu, too, had provided French literature with a permanent tribunal of literary taste, consecrated to the standardization of the language, for the cardinal had founded the French Academy in 1635.

The Précieux and the Academy

The refinement of the French language was closely connected with the development of a more refined society. Freed from civil war, the French aristocracy turned their attention to the perfecting of social life and manners. In countless salons, under the watchful eye of aristocratic hostesses, of whom none was more brilliant than the Marquise de Rambouillet, high society devoted itself to the study of form and the elaboration of rules for both manners and language. The Précieux and their feminine counterparts laid the foundation for that perfection of formal etiquette which later made the court of Louis XIV the wonder of Europe.

Refinement of society

Respect for form and a growing consciousness of national unity under the absolute monarchy were the outstanding characteristics of French culture in the seventeenth century, and they carried over into the religious life of the people. Religion, however, now that the wars were over and the Edict of Nantes had established legal toleration for the Huguenots, no longer occupied the foreground of French thought. A not unnatural reaction followed the intense religious strife of the past century, leaving the majority of the people somewhat disillusioned and indifferent. Thanks to the skillful work of the Jesuits, they remained within the church, but those champions of the Counter-Reformation seemed now more successful in keeping the people orthodox church members than in arousing vital religious enthusiasm. Their methods, indeed, left them open to the charge that the former was all they aimed at achieving. At any rate, the religion of the court and the aristocracy, and perhaps that of the mass of the people, like the literature and manners of the age, was more distinguished by attention to form than by emotional content or spiritual disturbance. This was not, however, universally true. There are in all ages men to whom religion is an overpowering emotional experience and who cannot be satisfied with formal observance. In the first half of the seventeenth century, a group of such deeply pious and sternly moral souls, under the name of Jansenists, led a reaction against the formal religion of their age and especially against the facile methods of the Jesuits. Their fate was the common fate of enthusiastic minorities. They were declared to be heretics and were suppressed by royal edict. But if the majority of Frenchmen were formally orthodox, the French church was not always on the best of terms with the papacy. The growing spirit of nationalism and the absolute claims of the monarchy led to a revival of the "Gallican" tradition of a French church controlled by the state and in its political structure more or less independent of Rome. The reasser-

Religion

tion of the "Gallican liberties," first stated in the fifteenth century by the Pragmatic Sanction of Bourges, strained relations between the king and the pope almost to the end of the century.

Meanwhile, under the surface of good manners and formal religion, the skeptical rationalism of Montaigne was working quietly, to come to light again in the following century. And most important of all, the new scientific spirit, posthumous child of the Renaissance, was beginning its work of transforming modern thought.

Rationalism and science

34

The Decline of the Monarchy in England

(1603–60)

WHILE IN FRANCE the first two Bourbon kings and their ministers were busy restoring the unity of the country after prolonged civil religious wars and were building a firm structure of absolute monarchy, across the Channel in England events were following an almost exactly opposite course. There, the first two Stuart kings were effectively, if unconsciously, destroying absolute monarchy and were driving a united nation, which had grown strong and prosperous during years of internal peace and firm government, to disunity and the final outbreak of civil religious wars. The end of the sixteenth century saw England approaching the close of one of the most glorious periods of her history, the reign of Queen Elizabeth. This last representative of the house of Tudor had guided England through troubled waters to confidence and security. She had defended England's independence against the aggressive power of Spain and had defended English Protestantism against the driving force of the Counter-Reformation. She left to her Stuart successors a country that was prosperous, loyal to the crown, and with a strong national consciousness that had found expression in a magnificent national literature. Yet it was a country that would need very careful handling if the Stuart kings were to continue the absolute government established by the Tudors. The story of the next half-century is the story of their utter failure to carry on the Tudor tradition. In that crucial half-century, absolute monarchy was broken, never to be restored, and Parliament won for itself a permanent place in the government of England.

1. THE LEGACY OF THE TUDORS

The age of the Tudors came to an end in 1603 with the death of Queen Elizabeth. The crown then passed to the house of Stuart with the accession of James I. But if the reign of the Tudors was over, the results of their rule remained as a legacy to their Stuart kinsmen. One important part of that legacy was a tradition of absolute government. It was, however, absolutism of an unusual kind, dependent on conditions that were peculiar to England. The Tudors were satisfied with the practical exercise of royal power. They did not insist on defining their authority, nor did they put forward sweeping claims to unrestricted rule. On the contrary, they were scrupulously careful to cloak their absolute power in a decent covering of constitutional legality. Both Henry VIII and Elizabeth, whose reigns covered most of the sixteenth century, took great pains to secure the consent of Parliament for their most autocratic acts. This, in truth, had not been difficult, for their policies were for the most part popular with the majority of Englishmen; the people felt the need of a strong government in a time of general insecurity; and both Henry and his brilliant daughter were masters of the art of persuading the people's representatives in Parliament that what they wanted was for the best interests of the state.

Under this system of legal absolutism, Parliament, though it lost the habit of independent initiative, was actually consolidating its position. In practice, the act of Parliament was little more than the official seal affixed to the expression of the royal will; but the fact that the king's authority was repeatedly expressed through act of Parliament built up a tradition that Parliament might use against the king, if the two ever came into conflict. In short, the Tudors kept alive a subservient Parliament to give legal or constitutional sanction to the acts of their absolute government; and as a result of that policy they left, as part of their legacy to the Stuarts, a constitutional body which was not yet conscious of its power, but which might become a menace to the authority of less popular rulers.

Parliament

The potential power of Parliament depended largely on the peculiar structure of English society, and was increased by certain changes that took place under the strong and peaceful government of the Tudor monarchs. Following the destruction of the greater part of the old feudal nobility in the Wars of the Roses, Henry VII was able to rid England of the last remnant of independent feudalism. In time, the Tudors created a new peerage to take the place of the old; but England no longer had anything that could be called a noble class, such as existed in every country on the Continent. Only those few peers who sat in the House of Lords were legally recognized as noble. All the rest of the landowning aristocracy, including the younger sons of the peerage, were classed as gentlemen (or collectively as the gentry), and were represented in the House of Commons. These country gentlemen were roughly of the same social class as the lords, though with many gradations of social importance, yet they were not cut off by any impassable barrier from the professional or commercial burghers of the cities, for younger sons of the gentry often enough

Tudor society

sought their fortunes as apprentices in the business houses of the towns or entered the professions, and many a country gentleman owed his estate to some wool-trading ancestor whose daughter had married into a county family. It was from this class of the gentry that the great majority of the members of the House of Commons were chosen, whether as representatives of the country shires or of the towns. The English Parliament, then, was a body which represented all the influential classes in the state, and it was not split by any strong division of class interest between noble and common or between country and city.

There was a latent menace to absolute monarchy in such a Parliament, but during the Tudor period it remained steadfastly loyal to the crown. England in the sixteenth century developed a strong national consciousness and an aggressive patriotism, as it rose from a position of insecurity and comparative insignificance in European affairs to confidence and power. And that national patriotism came to be more and more closely associated with loyalty to the ruling house. More than anything else, the struggle against the combined forces of the Counter-Reformation and Spain during Elizabeth's long reign contributed to this mingled feeling of patriotism and loyalty. The reverse side of English national consciousness was hatred of Spain and the papacy; for the conspiracies of Philip II to place the Catholic Mary Stuart on the English throne, and his later attempt to invade England with the avowed intention of restoring the Catholic Church there, united Catholicism with the threat of Spanish domination in the minds of the English people, just as it made Protestantism synonymous with English independence and reinforced their loyalty to Elizabeth, who stood as the defender of both. After the victory over Philip's great Armada, Englishmen felt a new pride in their country, and were obscurely conscious that that pride included the queen and the Protestant religion.

National sentiment

But if the victory over Catholic Spain made Englishmen more patriotic and more loyal to the queen, it also made them feel less keenly the need of a strong monarchy. England had at last won a sense of security to which it had long been a stranger. Protestantism and English independence were safe now. There was no longer any serious threat of foreign invasion or internal division. And to this feeling of national security was added a growing sense of personal security among the well-to-do classes of country and city, as a result of years of orderly government and an increasing national prosperity. Thus, the last of the Tudors left a country in which the influential classes were patriotic and loyal, but also more secure and hence more independent.

National security

The Englishmen of Queen Elizabeth's day had good reason to be proud of themselves, their country and their queen, and out of that pride there grew, among other things, a great national literature, which was not the least enduring part of the legacy of the Tudors. As in France, a literature in the language of the people had grown up in England during the Later Middle Ages, had then been superseded for a time by the Latin of the classical Renaissance, and was now revived in a more modern form with the growth of national consciousness. But still more than in France, the literature of the Elizabethan age reflects the patriotic enthusiasm of the people, even though literary traditions and forms might be borrowed from Italy or from the Latin classics. Edmund Spenser (1552–99) borrowed the romantic-epic form for his great poem, *The Faërie Queene,* from the Italians and colored it with classical allusions, but its theme was praise of England and England's queen. Shakespeare, too, though his genius was far too universal in its scope to be limited to a single theme, devoted many of his plays to the glorification of English history, while at the same time his immortal work so dignified the English speech that it need never again fear comparison with that of ancient Rome.

National literature

2. DECLINE OF THE MONARCHY — JAMES I AND CHARLES I (1603–40)

The man who fell heir to the Tudor legacy was Elizabeth's cousin, James Stuart (1603–25), the son of the unhappy Mary Queen of Scots. Since infancy he had held the title of James VI of Scotland, and now in middle age he became also James I of England, thus uniting at last the two kingdoms of Britain. Few kings have entered upon the government of a country with better intentions than James, and few have ruled with more disastrous results. His character, ideas, and training made him singularly unsuited to the task of carrying on the Tudor tradition. Education he had in plenty. No more learned man ever sat on the throne of England. But his education was of a pedantic kind, and he was much given to theories of "kingcraft" that had very little relation to reality. He had had plenty of experience in government, too, but it was in the government of a country still partly medieval and certainly very different from England. For all his learning, he was hopelessly ignorant of the peculiar laws, traditions, and sentiments of the English people, or even of the fact that they had any. And if he never came to understand the temperament of the English people, he was equally unfortunate in his judgment of individual men. By a kind of fatality, he surrounded himself with friends who were either rogues or fools, and, because of the strong human affections that made him a lovable man, if an untrustworthy king, he allowed his worthless favorites to administer the government as they chose. James was not in any way a bad man. He was merely miscast for his royal rôle. Had he been a country gentleman with a taste for learning or a professor of philosophy and dialectic at one of the universities, he would have lived out a happy and useful life as an honored member of the community. But it is from such miscasting that human tragedies are made.

James I

The new king's most cherished theory was that of the "divine right of kings." That kings received their authority directly from God and that to oppose their will was to fly in the face of Providence was an idea already familiar on the Continent. It appealed to James because of its theoretical completeness, and also because his sad experience

Divine right of kings

with turbulent barons and stubborn Calvinist ministers in Scotland had persuaded him of the value of an absolute government which drew its sanction from some more stable source than popular consent. This theory he brought with him to England, and he never came to realize how antagonistic it was to the English tradition. Where the Tudors had ruled in fact, but had carefully preserved legal and constitutional forms, and had been satisfied with an authority that was all the more real for being undefined, James insisted on the extreme definition of his rights, and even when he was forced to make concessions in practice, he spoiled the effect by blatant assertions of his superiority to the law and to the will of the people as represented in Parliament.

The first three years of James's reign decided the fate of the Stuart monarchy, for in those years the new king committed himself to definite policies on all the most perplexing problems of government. One of his first actions was to announce a decided policy of opposition to the Puritans. It is difficult to say exactly what is meant by Puritanism, for the term has been very loosely used. It covers a variety of types and a variety of opinions on doctrine and church government. The Puritans whom James first met on his way down from Scotland were not the Puritans who later founded New England, nor yet those who made up Cromwell's godly cavalry. As yet, the term Puritan signified only the more extreme Protestants, more or less Calvinist in theology, who wished to "purify" the church of the remnants of Catholic ritual and practice that still remained as part of the Elizabethan settlement of the Church of England. That settlement had been essentially a compromise, and so long as the terms were not too rigidly defined, both "High Church" Anglicans, with a leaning toward ritual, and Puritans, who wished a simpler service, remained peacefully within the church. The Puritans, however, were anxious to have their position made more secure, and hence presented a petition to the new king asking recognition of their right to a modified service. James argued with the Puritan clergy, for he could never resist an argument, and in the end lost his temper. The real reason for his opposition was that he suspected them of wanting to adopt a democratic form of church government like that of the Presbyterian Church in Scotland, which had already caused him so much trouble. James realized that absolute government would be impossible unless the state church were ruled from the top through the bishops. To destroy the episcopacy would be to strike a death blow to absolute monarchy. Shouting his famous epigram, "No bishop, no king," James swore that he would make the Puritans conform or would "harry them out of the land." James's bark was always worse than his bite, and very little active persecution followed. But he had made permanent enemies of a constantly growing number of stern and pious men, most of whom belonged to the influential classes of city burghers or country gentry. They could not as yet be called a party, but they formed the backbone of the opposition to all the king's unpopular policies.

While James thus alienated the left wing of Protestantism, he was equally unfortunate in his dealings with the Catholics, who stood at the opposite end of the religious spectrum. True to his large ideas of kingcraft, he at first treated the Catholics leniently, in the hope of uniting all religions under his beneficent rule. But when the fines levied on those who did not attend the Anglican Church were lifted, so many stayed away that he became alarmed and re-enforced them. Embittered by this betrayal of their trust, a group of extreme Catholics hatched a plot to blow up the Parliament buildings at a time when the king, his council, and the whole Parliament would be assembled in November, 1605. This was the famous Gunpowder Plot. It was discovered in time, however, and its chief result was to renew in the minds of English Protestants the fear and hatred of Catholicism which had existed before the defeat of the Armada. James might have utilized that feeling, but instead he turned it against himself by seeking an alliance with Spain.

In foreign policy, James looked to find a perfect field for the exercise of kingcraft.

JAMES I

Upper left: This portrait must, from contemporary accounts, have been rather flattering to the first Stuart king.

CHARLES I

Upper right: This is one of several portraits of Charles I painted by Van Dyke. The king's regular and rather delicate features suited Van Dyke's style.

THE DUKE OF BUCKINGHAM

Left: George Villiers, the charming and brilliant but irresponsible favorite of the first two Stuart kings, is shown here from a portrait by P. P. Rubens.

His theories were often very sound, but they seldom worked out successfully, and about all he accomplished was the further exasperation of his already discontented subjects. His first move, the ending of the war with Spain in 1604, though entirely justified, was unpopular with the Protestant merchant class who had been carrying on an illicit trade with the Spanish colonies. The opposition to this move, however, was nothing to the sullen fury aroused by his negotiations, pursued from 1619 to 1623, for the marriage of his son Charles to the daughter of the King of Spain. These were the years when Spain was actively aiding the Austrian Hapsburg emperor in crushing Protestantism in Germany.[1] Protestant England looked on appalled, as the king deserted the German Protestants in their hour of need, stopped the persecution of Catholics in England, and worked to give England a Spanish Catholic queen, who might, in time, give England a half-Spanish and possibly Catholic king. Religious and national sentiment united in violent opposition. The negotiations failed, and young Charles returned from Spain, still a Protestant and a bachelor, to the great relief of the people. But the damage was done. "More than any other part of James's schemes ... this project of the Spanish match made the ordinary man a Puritan at least in his politics."

The general discontent with the king's foreign and domestic policies found a means of expression in Parliament. The time had come when that body, so long subservient to the Tudors, was no longer content to accept the dictation of a less popular ruler. The Commons was filled with men from just those classes that were most decidedly opposed to the government on religious, national, and commercial grounds. A majority of the members were Puritans, or at least strongly Protestant, and, though most of them were of the gentry, a large number held borough seats and represented the city merchants who regarded Spain as a commercial rival as well as a religious and national enemy. Independent, practical, and often austerely pious men, they openly resented the extravagance of the royal government, the incompetence of the king's favorites, and the evil reputation of the court, which seemed much more immoral than it really was to simple gentlemen unused to the ways of the capital. To make matters worse, James showed no tact in dealing with them, and from the first alienated Parliament by disregard for their traditional privileges. He lectured his first Parliament on the subject of the divine right. The startled Commons replied with a unanimous expression of dissent. Hitherto they had not troubled themselves greatly about the definition of their authority, but now they began a careful study of English history, gathering together, and occasionally distorting, every precedent that would strengthen their position. The king's extravagance gave them their best weapon. Lavish in his gifts to friends and surrounded by careless and corrupt ministers, James was unable to live within the independent royal revenue. Additional taxation was generally regarded as subject to the consent of Parliament. At any rate, the Commons now asserted that right, and threatened to hold up appropriations unless the king would redress their grievances. Time and again, James dismissed a stubborn Parliament, only to be forced to call another. The struggle was still going on when James died and left a sadly discredited monarchy to his son.

Perhaps it was not yet too late to undo the damage of James's reign, but Charles I (1625–49) did nothing to heal the breach between king and people. He heartily subscribed to his father's theories of divine right; he continued to govern through the ministry of worthless favorites; and he was even more strongly opposed than his father had been to Puritanism. Charles was a dignified, cultured, and kindly man, loyal to his friends, but woefully lacking in the kind of imagination that is essential to a statesman. Though brought up in England, he had no more understanding of the English people than had the Scottish James, and he had much less understanding of the Scots whom he was also called upon to rule.

The events of the early years of Charles's

---

[1] See below, pages 503–504.

reign ended all hope of co-operation between king and Parliament. Until he was assassinated in 1628, the Duke of Buckingham, favorite of both James I and Charles, was the power behind the throne. The new king could scarcely have made a more injudicious choice than to entrust the government to this brilliant but unstable man. Under his reckless guidance, England careered into a hopeless war with Spain, the fatal marriage of Charles to the Catholic sister of Louis XIII of France, and a brief war with France that could end only in humiliation for England. The war with Spain and that in aid of the Huguenots against the French king should have won the support of Parliament; but the utter incompetence of Buckingham served only to enrage the Commons, while the French marriage aroused all the old fear of Catholicism. Parliament, therefore, refused supplies and threatened to impeach Buckingham. The king dismissed one Parliament after another with nothing accomplished, and finally tried the experiment of raising money for the war by forced loans and martial law. In 1628, however, Charles was forced to call Parliament again, and as the price of its co-operation in raising taxes, he accepted the Petition of Right. This petition, one of the corner stones of British freedom, was a clear statement of the illegality of the exercise of absolute power on four crucial points, martial law, the billeting of soldiers on the civilian population, arbitrary taxation, and arbitrary imprisonment. The first two were a protest against the means used by the king to support an army without funds, a protest inspired in part by fear lest the army be used to coerce the people. The second two points were designed to protect the right of Parliament to control such taxes as were not a recognized part of the royal prerogative, and to protect individual citizens from arrest and imprisonment by the king for political reasons. These provisions, if respected, would have made absolute government impossible. Charles accepted them; then broke them; and when Parliament in protest again refused supplies, he determined to rule without it.

For eleven years, from 1629 to 1640, Charles tried the experiment of personal government without calling Parliament. To the king, it seemed the only possible alternative. If he could not rule with Parliament — and he could not without abandoning his principles — he would rule without it. He recognized in part what that decision meant. He would have to give up all thought of a vigorous foreign policy for lack of funds, and would have to strain every legal means of taxation within the royal power to the utmost. What he did not realize was that such a policy was doomed to failure. Had Charles possessed a strong army, he might have coerced the whole population into the payment of unparliamentary taxes. Lacking that, he chose rather to distort the laws, laying a heavy burden of taxes on the relatively small but very influential class of propertied gentry and burghers who fell within the scope of royal taxes. This policy aroused a deep resentment among just those people whom he could least afford to offend, while at the same time it did not bring in enough money to maintain an army with which to meet a rebellion. One factor, however, worked in the king's favor. So long as he could avoid calling Parliament, the general discontent had no means of expression. Without leadership, the English people, unused to rebellion, were sullenly but helplessly passive.

So they might have remained if Charles had not, in addition to economic and political oppression, trespassed upon their freedom of conscience. He gave a free hand to Archbishop Laud, the most thorough exponent of High Church Anglicanism, whose greatest ambition in life was to force all England to conform to the strictest form of Anglican ritual and practice. Laud's plan was to smother Puritanism by preventing every possible means of expression. He banished all clergy suspected of Puritan leanings from the church; he censored the press; and he used the authority of the government to suppress all meetings for religious purposes outside the established church. Under this steady pressure, the gap between Puritan and High Churchman widened and became a more conscious antagonism. Religious doctrines and political theories became curiously involved, as men of many different types silently ranged themselves in opposition to king and church. Puritanism now represented a complex of ideas, sentiments, and resentments, held in varying proportion. The men who sat sullenly through the prescribed services of the Anglican Church, and muttered threats against the government as they returned home to read their Bibles in privacy, were characterized by some or all of the following — by a Calvinist belief in predestination, which was directly opposite to the Arminianism common among High Churchmen; by a strict morality that showed itself in stern simplicity of life and disapproval of Sunday games; by a growing hatred of ritualistic church services, of all bishops and of Laud's hand-picked clergy; and by an equally strong hatred of royal despotism. Parliament had long been a Puritan body. Now that Parliament no longer met, all Puritans were Parliamentarians, and all who resented divine-right absolutism, as practiced by Charles Stuart, were, more or less, Puritans.

It was Scotland that gave the signal for rebellion and provided the opportunity. In 1637, Laud and the king determined to extend the enforcement of Anglican service to Scotland, to replace the traditional Presbyterian form. This was sheer madness, as James I, who knew his stubborn Scots even if he never learned to know his Englishmen, might have told them. More accustomed to the ways of rebellion than their law-abiding English neighbors, the Lowland Scots rose as one man, and swore to a Covenant to defend their religion. Charles then marched north with a meager army to force them to obedience, only to find a nation in arms awaiting the attack with a godly fervor. Lacking money and with his people heartily out of sympathy with his plans, Charles could not raise anything like an adequate army. The two "Bishops' Wars" of 1639 and 1640 were no more than futile demonstrations. The king was forced to make a humiliating peace with his northern subjects and to promise them a large indemnity as the price of the withdrawal of the Scottish army from England.

Revolt in Scotland

Absolutism without adequate financial resources had failed. In October, 1640, Charles summoned a Parliament to raise money to pay the indemnity. This was the Long Parliament, which lasted through years of opposition, civil war, and the experiment of the Commonwealth. It provided the long-awaited opportunity to organize the opposition to the king.

The Long Parliament

3. THE CIVIL WAR, THE COMMONWEALTH, AND THE PROTECTORATE (1640–60)

The members of the new Parliament were almost unanimous in their determination to curb the absolute powers of the monarchy. Led by John Pym, a Puritan gentleman of great ability, the Commons at once launched an attack on Laud and the Earl of Strafford, the two chief ministers of the king. Laud was sent to the Tower, while Strafford, more dangerous because more powerful, was condemned to death by an act of attainder. Parliament then proceeded by one act after another to strip the king of the powers that had made absolute rule possible. Provision was made for regular meetings of Parliament, which was not to be dismissed arbitrarily. The arbitrary and more or less extra-legal courts of star chamber and high commission were abolished, as were also those taxes which kings hitherto had been able to collect without consent of Parliament. In the course of a few months, this determined Parliament destroyed absolutism in England forever. For when the monarchy was restored in 1660, it was the limited monarchy left by these acts of 1640–41.

Parliament curbs absolutism

So far, Parliament had been nearly unanimous. The Puritan majority, however, were not content to stop there. They went on to a "root and branch" attack on the episcopal system in the church and to claim for Parliament powers over the army and the executive authority that would have made Parliament as absolute as the king had ever been. Divisions now began to appear in the ranks of the

Division of parties

Commons. Many men who had joined heartily in the acts to curb royal absolutism hesitated at proposals to transfer full authority from king to Parliament, contrary to constitutional precedent. And the same men, though willing enough to check the power of Laud's High Church bishops, suspected as they were of leaning toward Catholic practice, balked stubbornly at Puritan proposals to do away with the Prayer Book, endeared to them by years of familiarity. Parliament was dividing on religious and political grounds, with Puritans and Parliamentarians on one side, moderate Anglicans and rather reluctant Royalists on the other. At last in 1642 the crisis came, and men in Parliament and in the nation had to make a definite choice. In January, Charles made a frustrated attempt to arrest five members of Parliament who were recognized as the leaders of the opposition. In self-defense, the Commons took unconstitutional measures to raise an army. The king fled to Oxford, and with him went the Royalist minority in the Commons and a majority of the Lords. There was now open war between king and Parliament, or what was left of it.

All through the summer of 1642 the opposing sides were mustering their forces. In the long run, only a minority of the population took an active part, but they were the influential minority. The great mass of agricultural laborers remained neutral, save when pressed into the infantry on one side or the other. The volunteers were yeoman farmers, gentlemen, and the industrial and commercial classes of the towns. The line between Royalist and Parliamentarian, however, represented no clear class division. Yeomen and gentlemen fought on both sides, and, though London and the seaports were the strongholds of Parliament, there were Royalists in every city and a majority in some. In general the Royalists were stronger in the north and west, while Parliament could count on a majority in the eastern and midland counties. But even this geographical alignment was only partially valid. It was not a war of sections any more than it was a war of classes. In the final analysis it was a war of opposing political and religious principles or

Cavalier and Roundhead

sentiments. The ancient feeling of loyalty to the crown was the force that rallied men about the royal banner. Some of those who found that they could not desert the king in the face of a call to arms were Puritans, but most of them were Anglicans, Catholics, or men to whom religion was not a dominating passion. Among them were enough of the hard-drinking, hard-riding gentry to give the whole Royalist party the name of Cavaliers. On the other side were men in whom the memory of royal oppression was stronger than the sentiment of loyalty. For the most part they were Puritans, for it was the Puritans who had suffered most under the recent absolutism, and the stern determination to win religious freedom was one of the few sentiments strong enough to make Englishmen take up arms against their king. Yet not all Parliamentarians were Puritans, and not all Puritans were of the strict type painted by popular fancy. There were enough of the latter, however, to win for their party the name of Roundheads, from their refusal to wear the flowing curled wigs affected by their less godly opponents.

The war lasted four years (1642–46). The limits of space forbid our giving a description of the campaigns, nor would the attempt be particularly profitable. It was a strange, scrambled affair, with much aimless marching about. Only the Royalists had a definite strategy in the plan to converge on the city of London and capture it, which, however, never succeeded. Parliament had the advantage of holding the great seaports and controlling the wealthiest cities, so that they could draw supplies from abroad and could pay for superior equipment. The navy, too, was on their side, and Scotland was their ally. In the long run, though, the deciding factor was the New Model Army, recruited from among the most extreme Protestants and organized by the only real military genius whom the war produced, Oliver Cromwell. Well armed, well drilled, and kept under a strict military and moral discipline, the New Model were the shock troops of the Parliamentary army. Cromwell's "Ironside" cavalry proved their disciplined worth against Prince Rupert's wild Cavaliers at Marston Moor in 1644. By the

Civil war

OLIVER CROMWELL

Left: The plain stern face, shown in this picture, was well suited to the commander of the New Model Army and ruler of the Puritan Commonwealth.

A SESSION OF PARLIAMENT

Below: The English Parliament in session is shown here from a seventeenth-century engraving.

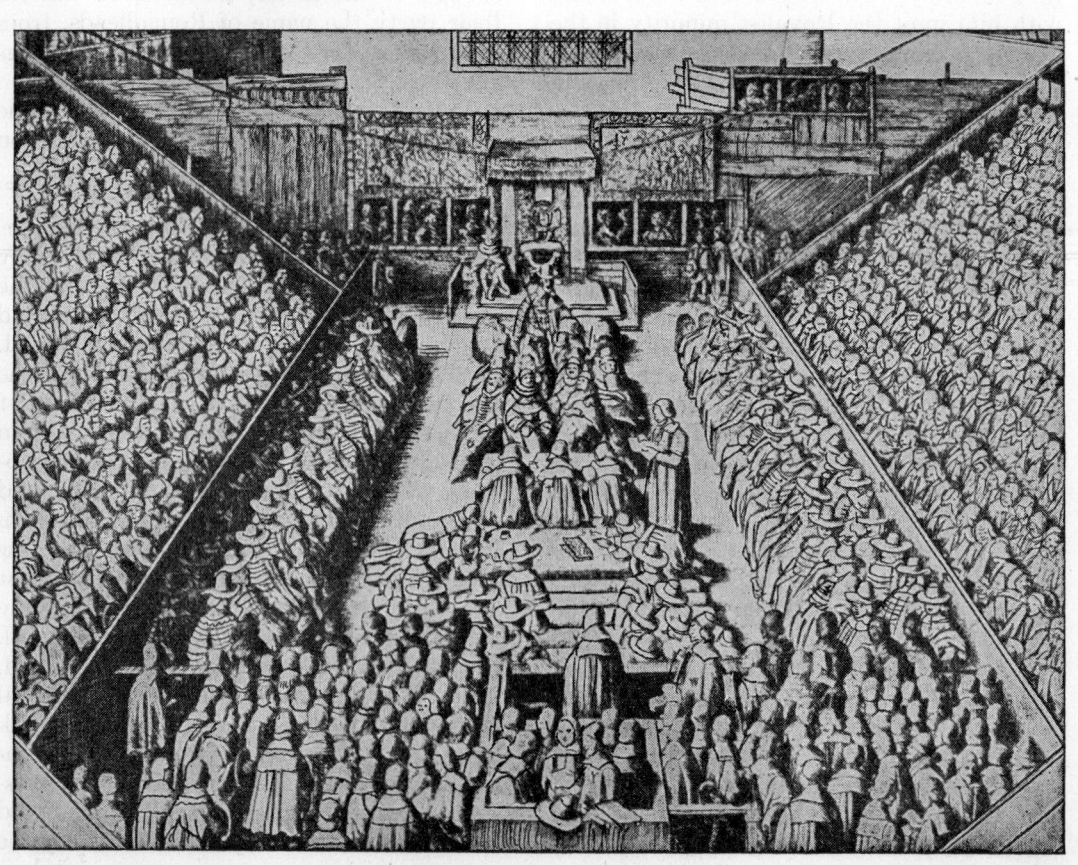

end of the war the New Model included about a fourth of the Parliamentary forces, and by far the most effective part.

With the surrender of the king in 1646, Parliament faced the difficult problem of arranging a permanent settlement. One question was what to do with the king. Few men were prepared to abolish monarchy. But could Charles be trusted to maintain a constitutional authority, limited by Parliament? And while Charles foiled all negotiations by his bewildering inconsistencies and double-dealing, another vital problem rose to the surface. As the price of the Scottish alliance, Parliament in 1645 had agreed to make Presbyterianism the state religion of England. It was a compromise that satisfied most Puritans, for some kind of state church was needed, though few were really Presbyterian in the Scottish sense. It did not, however, satisfy the New Model Army. This grim organization had been recruited from among the most extreme Protestants, men whose individualistic love of religious freedom made them oppose any state-controlled church. They were the Independents, differing among themselves in theological views, but united in the conviction that each congregation must be free to determine its own religion. Now, the Presbyterian Parliament, flushed with victory, made two serious mistakes. It persecuted Anglicans, on the one hand, thus embittering the defeated Royalists, and, forgetting who had won the war, it also passed persecuting acts against the Independents and proposed to disband the New Model without its back pay. The result was a second brief civil war, with Royalists, Parliamentary Presbyterians, and Scots in a curious alliance against the Independents. The latter, led by Cromwell, were again victorious. And, not to be cheated of the fruits of victory the army chiefs now took control. In December, 1648, they forcibly "purged" Parliament of its Presbyterian members, leaving only a small minority who could be trusted to do what the army wished. Two months later, this "Rump Parliament" abolished the House of Lords.

The Independent army was in the saddle, and in no temporizing mood. Parliament had betrayed their hopes of religious freedom, and they could not trust the king. All hope of a peaceful, amicable settlement that would preserve the things they had fought for seemed lost. They were riding the tiger, and there was nothing to do but to go on. Cromwell was now the undisputed leader of the army and what remained of Parliament. He had labored patiently to preserve a constitutional monarchy, but was now convinced that that was no longer possible. With grim courage, he accepted the logic of the situation and instituted the trial of the king. Charles Stuart met his death with dignity, while England staggered under the shock, and men who had fought against him united with those who had rallied round his banner to hail him as a martyr. The execution of the king wiped out the memory of his oppressive government and made the great majority of Englishmen Royalists at last. England was a republic now, but a republic ruled by a small minority of armed men who could not count on the support of the people.

During the next eleven years (1649–60), England passed from one experimental form of government to another. The first was the Commonwealth, a republic governed by a council chosen by the Rump of the Long Parliament, which still held the legislative authority. This was changed in 1653 by the forcible dissolution of the Rump, and a new constitution was substituted, making England a Protectorate, with Cromwell as Lord Protector and a carefully selected Parliament to hold the legislative authority. Even the most carefully chosen Parliament, however, could not co-operate with the army chiefs, and further changes followed, making Cromwell king in all but name. Whatever the form of constitution, in actual fact England was ruled by Oliver Cromwell with the backing of the army. It was not the kind of government that anyone wanted, perhaps least of all Cromwell. But it was apparently the only form of government possible at the time; the only form that could save the country from anarchy or further civil war. England was not yet ready to restore the Stuart monarchy, and there was still too much division of opinion to permit of a true republic. The rule of Cromwell and the army provided a working government, which, however, dared not permit a freely elected Parliament. Such a government could not last long; but under the capable guidance of Cromwell it lasted long enough to give England time to recover from the civil wars and to restore her prosperity and her prestige abroad.

The internal government of England under Cromwell was peaceful and orderly, but the warlike spirit of the Puritan army had plenty of opportunity to express itself in relation to Ireland, Scotland, and the neighboring states of the Continent. During the period of the Commonwealth, Cromwell had to crush strong opposition in both Ireland and Scotland. In the former, the Catholic majority rose in support of the Stuart heir, the future Charles II. The Puritan army invaded Ireland and put down the Catholic rising with a barbarous cruelty such as they had never shown in dealing with their Protestant enemies. To this day, the "curse of Cromwell" holds an unforgettable place in the memory of the Irish people. In Scotland, where the opposition was Presbyterian rather than Catholic, Cromwell was much more merciful. After defeating the Scots, he left them with a settlement that was eminently fair, though unpopular because it was forced upon them by the English and also because Cromwell insisted on the toleration of other Protestant sects. Having restored peace to the British Isles, the militant Commonwealth turned to war with the Netherlands, the chief commercial rival of England. More than any other group in the population, the new government represented the commercial class. Cromwell zealously fostered their interests, reviving trade with the colonies and striving by a new navigation act to build up England's carrying trade at the expense of the Dutch. The war with the Netherlands proved that England had not lost her mastery of sea warfare and left her once more mistress of the Narrow Seas.

Cromwell's foreign policy

Later, Cromwell, as Protector, launched another naval war against Spain for similar commercial reasons and with equal success. Before his death in 1658, he had made England a ranking power again among the nations of Europe.

On the whole, Cromwell accomplished a great deal, and much that was of permanent value, for many of his economic policies were carried on by the restored Stuart monarchy. Yet his government grew steadily more unpopular. Englishmen who had fought against the king had not fought to substitute a military despotism for the ancient monarchy. The new government had not given the people political freedom, and, though Cromwell guaranteed a large measure of religious toleration to all save Catholics and Anglicans, the Puritan government instituted a moral oppression as irksome as the religious oppression of Charles had been. Under the pressure of what would today be called blue laws, enforced by the army, many a former Puritan turned Cavalier and many a former Parliamentarian turned Royalist. When the death of Cromwell left the Protectorate to his feeble son, the nation was very nearly unanimous in its opinion that only one course lay before it — to restore the Stuart monarchy in the person of Charles II, with adequate guaranties that the powers of Parliament, as fixed by the acts of 1640–41, would be respected. This decision was put into effect without further civil war, thanks to the intervention of General Monk, now in command of the army, who used his power to secure a freely elected Parliament, which invited Charles II to return. In 1660, the new king was welcomed home with delirious demonstrations of joy. England had a legitimate king again; but he would not be an absolute ruler, nor would any king in the future successfully revive the claims of the first two Stuarts. The Anglican Church, too, was restored and for a time persecuted dissenters; but the principle of religious freedom was not lost sight of and was soon to come into its own at least so far as dissenting Protestants were concerned.

The Stuart Restoration

35

The Thirty Years' War

THE FIRST HALF of the seventeenth century witnessed the last and greatest of the religious wars, a war that for thirty years (1618–48) devastated Germany and involved, before it was over, nearly every state in Europe. For more than half a century before the war began, the Religious Peace of Augsburg (1555) had served to maintain an uneasy peace between the Protestant and Catholic forces in Germany. But conditions had changed since 1555, and with the opening years of the seventeenth century it became increasingly apparent that the settlement could not last much longer. The revived energy of Catholicism under the impetus of the Counter-Reformation, the rising power of militant Calvinism, the territorial greed and jealous independence of the German princes, the dynastic ambitions of the house of Hapsburg in both its branches, and the national interests of France, Sweden, and other European powers all tended to increase the tension and to produce a situation that menaced the peace of Europe. In these years, Germany was a vast powder magazine, which any chance spark might ignite with devastating results. For there were more than religious problems involved. Political and economic motives played their part in the war from the first, and as the war continued, religious issues sank into comparative insignificance before the greed and mutual hatred of territorial states and ruling dynasties. When the war was over, Germany lay prostrate; the Holy Roman Empire had been reduced to an empty shell; and out of the final settlement emerged the modern state system of Europe.

1. THE BACKGROUND OF THE THIRTY YEARS' WAR

The years immediately following the Religious Peace of Augsburg marked the high tide of Protestantism in Germany. For a time the momentum gained by the Lutheran Reformation in its early days carried it on to further conquests, especially in northern Germany. But as the century drew on, the tide turned. The Catholic Church in the period of the Counter-Reformation gained a new and aggressive energy and began to recover some of the lost ground. In every German state where the prince was still Catholic, the Jesuits set up their efficient schools and exerted a steady, tactful influence on both the people and their princes. One Catholic prince after another seconded their efforts by energetically enforcing the principle of the religious peace which gave the prince the right to dictate the religion of his subjects. Thus large sections of southern Germany, including Bavaria, the Austrian Hapsburg lands, and the ecclesiastical states of the Rhineland, were purged of their numerous Protestant population and became almost unanimously Catholic. By the beginning of the seventeenth century, German Catholicism had developed a decidedly militant spirit, and had found two powerful and devoted champions in the young

Counter-Reformation in Germany

Maximilian, Duke of Bavaria, and his contemporary, Ferdinand of Styria, cousin and heir of the Hapsburg emperor.

In contrast to this Catholic revival, Lutheranism seemed to be sinking into a state of passive apathy. All that was positive and aggressive in the Protestant faith was now concentrated in the growing Calvinism, which had established itself in several of the upper Rhineland states and in Bohemia, and had won over the Elector Palatine and the Elector of Brandenburg. The stern faith of Calvin provided the moral force needed to meet the revived energy of Catholicism, but the growth of Calvinism in Germany weakened rather than strengthened the Protestant cause, for Lutheran and Calvinist were divided by an antagonism almost as deep as that which separated Protestant and Catholic.

Calvinism in Germany

The growth of Calvinism, indeed, was one of the principal factors that tended to nullify the settlement arranged by the Religious Peace of Augsburg. In 1555, Calvinism had not yet become a power to be reckoned with in Germany, and the Calvinists had been excluded from the terms of the peace.[1] Thus, unlike their Lutheran neighbors, they had no legal status. But even the Lutherans were no longer fully protected by the religious peace. It had recognized the right of the Lutheran princes to hold those church lands which they had confiscated prior to 1552. A good deal of church land, however, was secularized (i.e., taken over by the Lutheran lay governments) after that date. So long as Protestantism was in the ascendant, no effective protest could be made, but as the Catholic forces gained new strength, they asserted that these lands were not included in the peace and still belonged to the church. A similar problem arose from the interpretation of that part of the peace known as the ecclesiastical reservation. According to this clause, ecclesiastical princes (bishops or abbots ruling territorial states) who became Protestant were to give up their land, which was to be retained by the church. This provision, however, had been violated on numerous occasions, and most of the bishoprics in northern Germany, as well as many smaller ecclesiastical principalities, had become secular Protestant lands.

Defects of the Peace of Augsburg

The growing feeling of insecurity among the Protestant princes led in 1608 to the formation of an armed league, the Evangelical Union, under the leadership of the Calvinist Elector Palatine. It was largely a Calvinist league, for they were in the most serious danger, but some Lutherans were included, though the sequel was to show how little they were prepared to sacrifice for their Calvinist allies. The following year, the challenge of the union was met by the formation of a Catholic League led by Maximilian of Bavaria. The Protestant and Catholic forces in Germany were now ranged in hostile armed camps. Peace was maintained only by the even balance of power. Should any circumstance upset that balance, war would be inevitable.

Evangelical Union and Catholic League

This intricate adjustment of forces in Germany was further complicated by the rather anomalous position of the Hapsburg emperors. Though they were all orthodox Catholics, the emperors (Ferdinand I, 1556–64; Maximilian II, 1564–76; Rudolph II, 1576–1612; and Matthias, 1612–19), whose reigns occupied the time between the abdication of Charles V and the outbreak of the Thirty Years' War, were not aggressive champions of Catholicism. Their interests were confined in large measure to the aggrandizement of their hereditary family lands, which included, besides Austria and the other Hapsburg territories in southern Germany, the kingdoms of Bohemia and Hungary. In addition, of course, they held such vague authority over the entire Holy Roman Empire as still adhered to the imperial title. The princes of Germany, however, both Catholic and Protestant, had already gained a good deal of independence, and desired more. This fact tended to prevent any whole-hearted co-operation between the emperors and the other Catholic princes. Indeed, the emperor was pointedly left out of the Catholic League. The league might join with him in a common effort against the

Position of the Hapsburgs

[1] See above, page 427.

Protestants, but the princes of the league would be careful to see that the imperial authority was not strengthened by a victory over the Protestant princes. In the long run, the only support on which the Hapsburg emperors could count without question, outside of their own territory, was that of their cousins of the Spanish branch of the family. Always intensely conscious of their dynastic solidarity, the Austrian and Spanish branches of the house of Hapsburg, though divided since the abdication of Charles V, had maintained a very close relationship, reinforced by frequent intermarriages. Any German war involving the Austrian Hapsburgs, therefore, would certainly involve Spain also. And Spain, though greatly weakened through internal decay, was still to all outward appearances the greatest power in Europe.

As it happened, the Hapsburgs were involved in the coming war, and that from the very beginning, for the spark that ignited the conflagration was the revolt of the Bohemian Calvinists against their Hapsburg ruler. The rebellion was motivated by a mixture of national and religious aspirations. Nowhere in Europe was national consciousness stronger than in this Slavic land, where a Czech population had for centuries been ruled by German kings, and heresy was ingrained in this people, whose ancestors two centuries before had defied the might of Catholic Christendom in memory of the martyred John Huss. Under the feeble rule of the emperors, Rudolph and Matthias, the Bohemian Protestants, the most aggressive of whom were Calvinists, had gained a measure of religious freedom. Their rights were guaranteed by a royal charter, but they depended in reality upon the weakness and tolerance of the emperor. This fact explains the consternation of the Bohemians when, in 1617, the childless Matthias designated as his heir his cousin Ferdinand of Styria, notoriously the most fanatical opponent of Protestantism in Germany. To make matters worse, Matthias forced the Bohemian Diet to accept Ferdinand as their hereditary king, in violation of the ancient tradition that the Bohemian crown was elective. Seeing both their religious and national freedom endangered, the Czech nobles determined to strike without delay, before Ferdinand could consolidate his power.

2. THE THIRTY YEARS' WAR (1618-48)

The story of the thirty years of warfare, which opened with the Czech-Calvinist rising in Bohemia, is a rather complicated one, but it is made somewhat easier to follow by the fact that it falls readily into four major periods: (1) the Bohemian revolt, beginning in 1618; (2) the Danish intervention, beginning in 1625; (3) the Swedish intervention, beginning in 1630; (4) the French intervention, beginning in 1635 and lasting till the end of the war.

The Bohemian revolt was begun with a dramatic gesture of defiance. Determined to commit their fellow countrymen irrevocably to rebellion, a group of Czech noblemen entered the royal palace at Prague and heaved the emperor's representatives bodily out of a window, from which they fell, with considerable loss of dignity, but with no fatal injury, into the moat below. There was now no turning back. The Bohemians organized an army, though with characteristic irresponsibility the nobles refused to contribute the money necessary to make it really effective, while on the other side, Ferdinand began to mobilize his forces. He could count on a certain amount of support from Spain, the pope, and the Catholic League, and early in 1619 the opportune death of the aged Matthias gave him the additional prestige of the imperial title as Ferdinand II (1619-37). Still he might have been left practically alone to deal with his rebellious subjects if the Bohemians themselves had not called in outside aid and turned the rebellion into a general religious war. In the summer of 1619, the Bohemian Diet elected Frederick, the Calvinist Elector Palatine, King of Bohemia, and that rash young prince accepted the dangerous honor. The choice of Frederick had been inspired largely by the hope that he would be able to secure aid from his father-in-law, James I of England, as well as from the other Protestant princes of Germany. But James, who was engaged in negotiations for a marriage alliance with Spain, contented himself with giving good advice, and the Lutheran princes had no desire to risk a war for the sake of Calvinism and the elector's territorial ambitions. On the other hand, the union of the Calvinist Palatinate with Bohemia threatened to upset the delicate balance between the religions, and drove Maximilian of Bavaria and the Catholic League to the assistance of the emperor. The campaign in Bohemia was brief and decisive. The combined army of the emperor and the league, commanded by Maximilian's veteran general, Tilly, routed the undisciplined Bohemians outside of Prague in the fall of 1620, and the unfortunate Frederick fled the country.

The net result of this first stage of the war was a triumph for militant Catholicism. Ferdinand proceeded to stamp out Protestantism in Bohemia with ruthless severity. The lands of the rebels were confiscated and a relentless persecution drove the Protestant populace to give up their religion or emigrate. Meanwhile, a similar fate befell Frederick's native County Palatine on the Rhine. Sincere Catholic though he was, Maximilian of Bavaria was not above demanding a high price for his services to his church. The emperor was forced to turn over to him Frederick's electoral title and with it his lands. The conquest of the Palatinate kept the war going till 1623, and the fear and indignation aroused among the Protestant princes by this high-handed act, coupled as it was with a threat to the rest of German Protestantism by swinging the balance of power to the Catholic side, ensured the continuation of the war on a still broader basis through foreign intervention.

Catholic triumph

For the present, German Protestantism seemed to have collapsed into a state of helpless passivity. But aid was soon forthcoming from outside Germany. England had broken off the marriage negotiations with Spain, and young Charles was eager to revenge his humiliation. The Dutch, too, were willing to co-operate in any Protestant alliance that would enable them to fight Spain. Finally,

Danish intervention

with the promise of aid from England and Holland, Christian IV of Denmark was ready to invade Germany and join hands with the Lutheran princes in a war against the emperor and the Catholic League. Christian's motives were partly religious, for he was a Lutheran; but in rather greater degree he was moved by the hope of winning territory and by the necessity of protecting certain secularized church lands already in the possession of his family. The Protestant princes of Germany, too, had lands as well as their religion to protect. The time seemed ripe for intervention as the Danes marched into northern Germany in 1625.

Meanwhile, the Emperor Ferdinand, unwilling to trust entirely to the army of the league and too impoverished to raise an adequate army himself, had turned for assistance to one of the most remarkable adventurers in the history of Germany, the enigmatic Wallenstein. This obscure Bohemian noble had fought his way to power, wealth, and titles by sheer ability and the driving force of an unscrupulous ambition. Born a Protestant, he had become a nominal Catholic, but was unencumbered by any religious loyalties. By skillful profiteering in confiscated lands after the Bohemian revolt, he had accumulated a colossal fortune, and he now offered to raise an army at no expense to the emperor, provided he were given a free hand to support it by plunder and to repay himself in conquered territory. His great military reputation, backed by promises of good pay and plunder, brought soldiers of fortune flocking to his banner from every country in Europe and representing every variety of religious creed. He had an army of over fifty thousand men when he marched north to co-operate with Tilly and the army of the league. Together they were too strong for Christian, who had found small support from his allies. The Danes were defeated at Lutter in 1626 and slowly withdrew from Germany. The Catholic-imperial forces were left in control of northern Germany, and Wallenstein proceeded to establish what amounted to an independent sovereignty in captured territory along the Baltic coast. It is not clear just what were the plans of this

Wallenstein

WALLENSTEIN

Upper left: The personal interference of this great mercenary general was more than once a decisive factor in the Thirty Years' War.

FERDINAND II

Upper right: The Emperor Ferdinand was a considerably less dashing figure than this picture would suggest.

GUSTAVUS ADOLPHUS

Left: Of all the leaders engaged in the Thirty Years' War this Swedish king was at once the most able and the most attractive.

inscrutable genius; but he seems to have offered Ferdinand a military despotism, based on religious toleration, that would make Germany a united state under an absolute Hapsburg monarchy. The emperor, however, was too irresolute, perhaps too suspicious of his powerful general, and certainly too strongly Catholic to accept such a proposal. He listened instead to the urging of the Catholic League that he use his victory for the Catholic cause.

The league had not forgotten the confiscated church lands nor the secularized bishoprics and abbacies. If the lost ecclesiastical states could be won back to the control of the church, the provision of the religious peace which empowered a prince to dictate the religion of his people would enable Catholic bishops or abbots to stamp out Protestantism in some of the richest cities and territories in northern Germany. It seemed too good an opportunity to be ignored, and in 1629 Ferdinand issued the Edict of Restitution, commanding the restoration to the church of all ecclesiastical lands secularized since the Peace of Augsburg. The edict was a fatal blow to peace, for it aroused Protestant feeling from passive resignation to bitter resentment and ensured the continuation of the war, just at the time when the Treaty of Lübeck with Denmark seemed about to end it. To have carried out the edict would have meant taking from princes and people land and religious freedom which they had held securely for two or three generations. It would have meant the end of Protestant territorial supremacy in northern Germany. Further, the enforcement of the edict depended largely on Wallenstein and his personal army, for it could be put into effect only by a powerful army and by methods of brute force. And Wallenstein, who disapproved of the edict because it meant the ruin of his larger plans, was fast drifting into open antagonism to the league. Ferdinand would have to choose between the two. He had, in fact, already chosen. In 1630 he submitted to the demands of the league and dismissed his great general.

Edict of Restitution

When Ferdinand thus gave up the only armed force strong enough to enforce his rash policy, a new champion of the Protestant cause had already landed in Germany. The decision of Gustavus Adolphus, King of Sweden (1611–32), to take up the cause of his fellow Lutherans in Germany opened the third period of the war, that of the Swedish intervention. The motives of Gustavus, like those of most of the participants in the war so far, were a mixture of religious partisanship and territorial greed, save that with this hero-king, "the Lion of the North," religion was a more sincere motive than with most and his territorial ambitions were but part of a long campaign to make his country secure and a power in the north. Ever since his accession, at the age of seventeen, to the throne of a beleaguered, impoverished, and divided kingdom, Gustavus had fought to consolidate his state and to win for it that supremacy in the Baltic upon which its economic and political life depended. His reign was from the beginning a perpetual war — war with Denmark, 1611–13, war with Russia, 1614–17, and war with Poland, 1617–29. As a result of each, he had won additional territory on the Baltic coast and a more complete control of the Baltic trade. Now all that he needed was a foothold in northern Germany to make the Baltic indeed a "Swedish lake." For years he had been watching the course of the war in Germany and biding his time. In 1630, he decided that the time for intervention had come. He was free from the threat of war elsewhere; the collapse of German Protestantism demanded instant action; and he had the promise of financial aid from France, whose cardinal-minister Richelieu was willing to forget religious differences in his eagerness to aid anyone who would indirectly serve France by weakening the Hapsburgs.

Swedish intervention

The Protestant deliverer received at first a cold welcome from the Lutherans whom he had come to defend. They had been overawed by the power of the emperor and the league and they were suspicious of the foreigner. The Electors of Brandenburg and Saxony maintained a stubborn neutrality, while the city of Magdeburg, which had declared for Gustavus, was captured and cruelly sacked be-

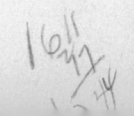

Protestant successes

cause the former would not permit the Swedish king to cross his territory to its relief. It was not till Gustavus had invaded Brandenburg and ranged his guns before the walls of Berlin that the elector finally consented to join forces with him. The imperialists under Tilly then tried to win over the Elector of Saxony by a similar show of force, but with the opposite result. The cautious elector was finally aroused to opposition and joined Gustavus with a force of some eighteen thousand men. Thus reinforced, the Swedish king fell upon the Catholic imperial army at Breitenfeld, not far from Leipzig, in September, 1631. The Saxon contingent proved worthless, but the Swedish army, which Gustavus had reorganized along entirely new lines, justified its reputation as the most formidable military machine in Europe. Outmaneuvered and outfought, Tilly retired with the shattered remnants of his army, while Gustavus proceeded on a triumphal march through the Rhineland into Bavaria, where Tilly was again defeated, and this time the old Bavarian general was left dead on the field. The Swedish king now dominated Germany, and the balance of power swung high in favor of Protestantism. In desperation the emperor turned again to Wallenstein. For months Gustavus and Wallenstein fenced carefully, but at last, in November, 1632, the two great generals met in a desperate battle at Lützen. The result was a victory for the Swedes; but it was a victory more disastrous than any defeat, for it cost them the life of their king. With his death the Swedish-Protestant cause lost direction and cohesion. Only Gustavus could have reaped the fruits of his brilliant victories.

For a time, however, the momentum of victory carried the Swedes on to further conquest under the guidance of the Chancellor Oxenstjerna, who acted for the child Queen Christina. But they were weakened by heavy losses and by the defection of the Elector of Saxony, who refused to co-operate any longer, though he continued the war as an independent party. Meanwhile, Wallenstein was leisurely refitting his army in Bohemia and refusing to take decisive action.

Peace of Prague

Perhaps he was plotting treason. Ferdinand, at any rate, grew suspicious and decided, now that the greatest danger was past, to rid himself finally of his dangerous general. In 1634, Wallenstein was assassinated by some of his own soldiers. In the same year the Swedes were defeated at Nördlingen by an imperial army. The tide was turning against them and they soon lost a large part of their conquered territory. The emperor was quick to take advantage of this favorable turn to make peace with Saxony and the other German Protestant princes, for both sides were tired of the war, and the emperor's own resources were nearly exhausted. According to the terms of the Peace of Prague (1635), all disputed ecclesiastical lands were to be restored to those holding them in 1627. This amounted to a revocation of the Edict of Restitution. With the signing of the Peace of Prague, the religious phase of the war ended. And the war itself might have ended, had France been willing to permit it.

The religious significance of the war had always been a matter of secondary importance to Cardinal Richelieu. Heir to the foreign policy of Henry IV, the cardinal's aims were clear and simple, however complex the methods he might see fit to use. He could never forget that France was still surrounded by Hapsburg territory. To make his country secure and powerful, the Hapsburg states must be reduced to impotence, and France must win defensible frontiers on the Rhine and the Pyrenees. So long as other powers — the German princes, Holland, England, Denmark, or Sweden — were engaged in the process of wearing down the resistance of Spain and Austria, Richelieu was content to wait, offering no more than diplomatic and financial aid to the enemies of the Hapsburg dynasty. After the Peace of Prague, however, the war seemed about to end with the Hapsburg power still not completely crushed. The Swedes were not included in the treaty, but they could not continue long alone. It was time for France to intervene with all her strength.

Richelieu's foreign policy

With the active intervention of France in 1635, the war broadened to truly European

THE SIGNING OF THE PEACE OF WESTPHALIA

The final scene of the great war is shown here from a painting by Terborch.

dimensions. Before declaring war on Spain and Austria, Richelieu had formed an alliance with the Swedes, the Dutch, who were to attack the Spanish Netherlands, and Savoy, which opened the gates to northern Italy. German princes were again involved in the war on one side or the other. For thirteen years the war continued, with few notable battles but terrible devastation of the occupied territory. Although there was fighting along the Pyrenees, in northern Italy, and in the Netherlands, it was still Germany that suffered most from the ravaging of native and foreign armies. During the early stages of their intervention, the French met with small success. In course of time, however, the undrained wealth and reserve energy of France began to tell against the already exhausted Hapsburg states. The French army became more efficient with experience and gained the additional advantage of able leadership when the command

French intervention

was given to two young generals, the Prince of Condé and Turenne, of whom the former was responsible for the decisive defeat of the Spanish army at Rocroi in 1643. Richelieu had died before this brilliant victory, but his successor Mazarin carried on the war with equal energy. As the war drew on, the French and Swedish armies joined forces, invaded Bavaria and closed in on the home territory of the emperor. Meanwhile, peace negotiations had begun. They dragged on interminably, but at last the terms were agreed upon and the Thirty Years' War ended in the Peace of Westphalia.

3. RESULTS OF THE WAR — THE PEACE OF WESTPHALIA AND THE PEACE OF THE PYRENEES

The Peace of Westphalia (1648) was the work of the first great European peace conference. It marks the end of the era of religious strife and the beginning of the new era of dynastic and national wars for economic or terri-

Peace of Westphalia

torial aggrandizement. In its adjustment of territorial boundaries and in the recognition of the sovereignty of states hitherto considered subject to the empire, it laid the foundations for the modern state system of Europe. Until the Napoleonic era, most of the further territorial changes were considered merely readjustments of the settlement of Westphalia.

The victors in the long struggle demanded, and received, additions of territory as compensation for their efforts. (1) **Territorial compensations** France, the laborer come late to the vineyard, profited most, receiving the strategically important bishoprics of Metz, Toul, and Verdun, and the "sovereignty" of Alsace except for the free city of Strasbourg, thus making a notable advance toward the Rhine. (2) Sweden obtained western Pomerania and some neighboring territory on the Baltic, as well as the bishopric of Bremen on the North Sea. (3) Brandenburg received, in return for the surrender of western Pomerania, three secularized bishoprics and the succession to the archbishopric of Magdeburg, and was confirmed in the possession of eastern Pomerania. (4) The problem of the Palatinate was solved by dividing it between the Duke of Bavaria and the son of the late Elector Palatine, both to hold an electoral title.

The peace also recognized certain important changes in the political status of the powers involved. (1) The Holy **Political provisions** Roman Empire, though continuing to exist as a formal entity, was practically dissolved, since each prince in Germany was recognized as a sovereign power, free to make peace or war and to govern his own state independently. As a result, the authority of the imperial Hapsburgs was limited more than ever to their own hereditary lands, and their policy became more and more a purely Austrian one. (2) France and Sweden acquired, with lands in the empire, the right to vote in the imperial Diet. (3) The accomplished fact of the independence of Holland and Switzerland was formally confirmed, and they entered the state system of Europe as free and independent powers.

The religious issues of the war, almost forgotten, were settled in the simplest possible way by recognizing the facts of the existing situation. (1) Secularized church lands were to remain in the possession of those holding them in 1624. (2) The Calvinists were admitted to the privileges of the Religious Peace of Augsburg with the right, accorded to Lutheran and Catholic princes, to determine legally the religion of their states. The Peace of Westphalia did not establish religious toleration, but Germany was too impoverished for any prince to risk the loss of subjects by enforcing religious uniformity. **Religious settlement**

The most important results of the war, however, were not of a kind that could be summarized in the terms of a peace treaty. For three decades the Four Horsemen of the Apocalypse had ridden through all the rich land of Germany, scattering death, disease, and destruction in their wake. Pitched battles were few and unimportant compared to the appalling loss of life from famine, disease, and the brutality of marauding soldiers. The armies on both sides plundered, burned, tortured, and killed, without regard to the supposed friendship or enmity of the helpless people. Such statistics as can be procured regarding the decrease in population in Germany and Bohemia during the war reveal an almost unbelievable situation. It is confidently asserted that the total population was reduced to two thirds and possibly to a half of what it had been. The relative loss of property was still greater. But even this shocking loss of life and property was perhaps less important in its lasting results than the complete moral and cultural degradation of a people who, in the preceding century, had given cultural and religious leadership to all northern Europe. It is a commonplace, all too true, to say that Germany was set back at least a century in the development of her civilization. **Effects of the war**

For Spain, too, the war was disastrous. She had been drained of her vitality and was to suffer still more, for she was not included in the Peace of Westphalia. She had already lost Portugal, which had taken advantage of the war to assert her independence, and had **France and Spain** lost Roussillon to the French. Moreover, her possessions in Italy and the Netherlands were threatened. Nevertheless, Philip IV still hoped to recoup some of his losses, and Mazarin was loath to make peace till he had completed the ruin of France's most dangerous enemy. The war between France and Spain, therefore, continued. At first it seemed certain that nothing could save Spain from a crushing defeat that would leave her shorn of her most valued possessions. She was saved just in time by the outbreak of the Fronde in France. That futile rebellion of the French nobles distracted Mazarin's attention, and when it was over France was too weak to carry on the war alone. In 1657, Mazarin made an incongruous alliance with the Protestant regicide, Cromwell. Thus reinforced, France had again the advantage over her enfeebled enemy. In 1659, Philip IV was forced to accept a peace, which was humiliating enough, but not as bad as it might have been if France had been able to push home her first successes.

Peace of the Pyrenees

The Peace of the Pyrenees ended the long struggle between the rival dynasties of France and Spain. It ended also the last vestige of Spain's claim to ascendancy in Europe and transferred that claim to France. By the treaty, France acquired Roussillon, which meant the winning of the Pyrenees as a southern frontier, and the county of Artois from the Spanish Netherlands. The peace was sealed by the marriage of the young king, Louis XIV, to Maria Theresa, the daughter of Philip IV. With the conclusion of this treaty, Mazarin could die content, for the greater part of the task begun by Henry IV and carried on by Richelieu was now complete.

Treaty of Oliva

The treaties of Westphalia and the Pyrenees restored peace to the greater part of Europe. But in the North war clouds still hung over the Baltic, where Frederick William of Brandenburg was exploiting the old enmity between Sweden and Poland with the aim of securing a free title to East Prussia. Even the warlike Baltic powers, however, were weary of war and in 1660 the intervention of England, Holland, and other great states was enough to bring the Northern struggle to a close. Brandenburg, Sweden, and Poland signed the Treaty of Oliva recognizing Frederick William's free sovereignty in East Prussia, and all Europe was at peace for the first time in more than a generation.

SECTION G

Europe in the Age of Louis XIV

(1660 — 1715)

There is no date of which it may be said: Here modern European history begins. The transition from medieval to modern times in Europe was a slow and painful evolution still far from complete in the middle of the seventeenth century, the point at which this volume opens. The political map of Europe, it is true, had already acquired a distinctly modern appearance, with England, France, Spain, and Portugal enjoying approximately the same boundaries as today. Dynastic and commercial rivalry had superseded religious and feudal disputes as primary incentives to war, and the unity of medieval Christendom had yielded to a system of national territorial states under secular control. But much that was characteristic of the medieval centuries — relics of half-discarded institutions, social distinctions, legal codes, customs and habits of thought — still profoundly influenced European society.

A political fact of importance that should be noted about this Europe of 1660 was the ascendancy of France. Spain was in decline, the Austrian Hapsburgs were embarrassed by the Turkish menace, the Germanies had not recovered from the devastation of the Thirty Years' War, and England had recently been disturbed by a revolution. These favoring factors made it possible for Louis XIV of France, as head of the strongest and most highly centralized state on the Continent, to play a dominant rôle in European affairs during his long reign. Because Louis, who began his personal rule about 1660, was supreme in France, and France was unquestionably the first state of Europe, the period from 1660 until his death in 1715 has been distinguished as the Age of Louis XIV. It is not the reign of Louis alone, however, which gives this period a claim to unity, as the next four chapters explain.

EUROPE AFTER 1648
SWEDEN
INGRIA
ESTHONIA
RUSSIA
LIVONIA
KURLAND
KINGDOM OF NORWAY AND DENMARK
SCOTLAND
IRELAND
ENGLAND
London
Copenhagen
WEST POMERANIA
EAST PRUSSIA
PRUSSIA
POLAND
Warsaw
BREMEN (SWEDEN)
UNITED NETHERLANDS
Berlin
BRANDENBURG
SAXONY
GERMAN STATES
SPANISH NETHERLANDS
Brussels
BOHEMIA
PODOLIA
Paris
Verdun
Metz
Toul
BAVARIA
AUSTRIA
Vienna
HUNGARY
MOLDAVIA
JEDISAN
TRANSYLVANIA
FRANCE
FRANCHE COMTE
SWITZERLAND
TYROL
STYRIA
BANAT
ITALIAN STATES
AVIGNON
OTTOMAN EMPIRE
BOSNIA
Constantinople
PAPAL STATES
CORSICA
Rome
SPAIN
Madrid
Lisbon
PORTUGAL
SARDINIA
KINGDOM OF THE TWO SICILIES

36

Europe in the Middle of the Seventeenth Century

> This is the Generation of that great LEVIATHAN ... to which we owe, under the Immortall God, our peace and defence.
>
> THOMAS HOBBES (1651).

IN 1660, after nearly a century of civil and international warfare, the peoples of Europe enjoyed once more the almost forgotten blessings of a general peace. By the Treaty of Westphalia (1648) the terrible Thirty Years' War in the Germanies had been brought to a close. Rivalry between the Bourbon and Hapsburg dynasties kept France and Spain in conflict for eleven years longer, until they reached an agreement which was embodied in the Peace of the Pyrenees (1659). So weary had the nations grown of warfare and its inseparable evils that the powers determined to stamp out the last embers of the general strife, and Sweden, Poland, and Brandenburg, which were still engaged in a three-cornered struggle among themselves, were persuaded to end their hostilities by the Treaty of Oliva (1660).

The era thus brought to a close, the century of tumult between 1560 and 1660, is often termed "The Period of the Religious Wars." It had opened with the revolt of the Dutch against their Spanish masters, had included the religious wars in France and the defeat of the Spanish Armada by the English, and it culminated in a great struggle which devastated the Germanies from 1618 to 1648. Religious fanaticism had done much to provoke these wars, but

Century of General Readjustment

trade rivalry and dynastic ambition had urged them on. It is obvious that a series of conflicts which spread across the breadth of a continent and lasted for generations must have gathered strength from many sources. The phrase "Religious Wars" emphasizes one issue unduly, an issue which, as the struggle matured, was overshadowed by the rivalry of Bourbon and Hapsburg and the dynastic ambitions of the German princes. A better title for this period might therefore be "The Century of General Readjustment."

For it becomes clear, from our point of observation in a later century, that what the European states passed through between 1560 and 1660 was a period of brutal and convulsive reorganization. During the fifteenth and sixteenth centuries tremendous forces were unloosed which broke up the ordered habits of the medieval world. In the Middle Ages land had been the chief source of wealth, but with the expansion of commerce and the voyages of discovery, merchants became more wealthy than feudal lords. This social and economic change brought such far-reaching results that it has been called "The Commercial Revolution." At the same time the intellectual revival which came at the close of the Middle Ages, the renewed interest in the classical

513

literature and art and in secular learning, which is known as the Renaissance or rebirth of the European mind, swept out a number of old ideas and swept in a multitude of new ones. In the sixteenth century the Protestant Reformation, following closely upon the impact of these earlier forces, shattered the unity of the Roman Catholic Church and divided Europe into hostile religious camps. By 1560 these three great movements — the Commercial Revolution, the intellectual revival, and the Protestant Reformation — had largely spent their force, but they had filled Europe with wreckage and confusion. The three foremost institutions of the Middle Ages, the Universal Church, the Holy Roman Empire, and the Feudal System, were crippled and disrupted. It required a hundred years of repair and readjustment, of civil and religious and dynastic struggle, to reduce European society to some degree of stability and order once more.

1. THE SYSTEM OF CENTRALIZED TERRITORIAL STATES

In the end a new Europe was hammered out upon the iron anvil of war. Turn to the accompanying map of Europe and note how modern it is in appearance. All the wars and revolutions from that day to this have changed the boundaries of the states surprisingly little, for by 1660 Europe was divided into territorial areas which correspond to the European states of today. No such centralized territorial states existed in the Roman Empire or during the Middle Ages. They had emerged slowly as the Middle Ages waned, and as slowly organized themselves. It was not until the seventeenth century that the concept of Christendom as a united whole yielded definitely to a state system composed of autonomous (that is, self-governing) territorial units, and for this reason modern history is often said to begin in the seventeenth century. To the political philosopher, Thomas Hobbes (1588–1679), the sovereign state appeared so portentous a social organism that he called it a *Leviathan*, a "mortall God." In his opinion citizens submitted to the authority of the state, wielded by an absolute monarch, because they realized that such despotism was their only sure protection against anarchy, and in a condition of anarchy the life of man would be "solitary, poore, nasty, brutish and short." Like most of his contemporaries, therefore, Hobbes considered monarchy the best form of government, and held that the sovereign expressed in his august person the concentrated will, authority, and majesty of the state.

Thus two important facts are to be noted about Europe in 1660. The first is the existence of these autonomous states. The second fact concerns the form of government common to these states: they are all, or almost all, absolute monarchies. The sovereign power, in the great majority of cases, is vested in a prince who claims to rule by divine right. It need hardly be explained that this triumph of the kingly power was not obtained without a struggle. In France, nobles tenacious of their independence resisted the growth of the royal authority until their last revolts were crushed by Richelieu and Mazarin and Louis XIV. In the Germanies, the dukes and electors subdued their subjects and fought their overlord, the Holy Roman Emperor, until they won what amounted to sovereign independence for each of them. In Spain and Portugal the people were taught to accept the will of the king without protest, even if he proved wicked or incompetent. Only the English had dared to flout the divine right of kings, but, although they sent Charles I to the block (1649), they received back his son Charles II eleven years later as "King by the grace of God." In 1660, monarchy was the accepted form of government everywhere in Europe, with the exception of Switzerland and some Italian states, which were republics, and Holland, where an elected officer exercised the power of a king under republican forms.

Divine-right monarchies

The new organization of Europe, consolidated during the Century of Readjustment, proved remarkably stable. For a hundred and thirty years the settlement endured without essential changes, while Europe continued to progress within the lines laid down by 1660. Though the balance of power between one state and another shifted from time to time, a general equilibrium was maintained. No civil wars or serious revolts threatened the European monarchs, who continued to rule by divine right, except in England where the ruler was made responsible to Parliament. The Century of Readjustment, it seemed, had produced an order of things that possessed the virtues of stability and permanence.

Unfortunately, the new order also brought grave evils. The most important characteristic which the national states held in common was a lust for self-aggrandizement. Though religion had been eliminated as a cause of international strife (the Thirty Years' War was the last of the religious struggles), war remained a persistent scourge none the less. Like the monster in the fable, it seemed to have grown three heads for one that was stricken off. If states no longer clashed over religious differences, they found more imperious issues, such as greed for territory, jealousy over each other's trade, or the desire to monopolize the new lands discovered across the seas. More than once an ambitious king plunged Europe into war to advance the claims of his dynasty. So bitter and so relentless have national antagonisms proved in the modern state system that the system itself has been called "Ishmaelitish nationalism," the term being borrowed from the story of Ishmael in the Old Testament, whose "hand will be against every man, and every man's hand against him."

Nationalism

The danger that as the states developed the wars between them would grow more frequent and more destructive alarmed farseeing statesmen and philosophers before 1660. Sully, the able minister of Henry IV of France, formulated in his master's name a "Grand Design" for uniting all the European states in a permanent alliance. General councils were to arbitrate all international disputes, and war was to be restricted to campaigns against the infidel Turks. In 1623, a French scholar, Émeric Crucé, in a book called *The New Cyneas*, proposed that armies should be abolished and a world court created to adjust disputes. Two years later, the great Dutch jurist, Hugo Grotius (1583–1645), published a treatise *On the Law of War and Peace* in which he attempted to distinguish between just and unjust wars, urging that if war proved unavoidable the nations engaged should at least pledge themselves to abstain from needless barbarities such as the massacre of the wounded. Unfortunately, to most practical statesmen the "Grand Design" and the suggestions of Crucé and Grotius appeared idealistic and unenforceable. Believing that no nation could expect to escape a war once in every generation, these men held it wisest to prepare for the stern eventuality by making their respective states as self-sufficient as possible, by building up armaments and seeking allies for the expected struggle.

The result was the formation of alliances for purposes of offense and defense, a process which often went forward until the states of Europe were aligned in two hostile groups. If these groups were evenly balanced, the outcome of a war between them was difficult to predict, a fact which the diplomats extolled as the best possible guaranty of peace. So long as a just balance of power was maintained, few states would be reckless enough to invite a war which they stood an even chance of losing. Moreover, small countries would be preserved from the rapacity of powerful neighbors by other powers interested in maintaining the international equilibrium. This somewhat optimistic ideal, which had been invoked in the sixteenth century (and earlier), became in the seventeenth century the guiding principle of international diplomacy.

Balance of power

The gravest flaw in the political state system of seventeenth-century Europe was this perpetual threat of war. A second defect was to be found within the states themselves, and was inherent in their form of government. Divine-right monarchy is successful if the monarch is equal to his task, but not otherwise. Political thinkers who had witnessed the evils that sprang up to plague a nation during a civil war or interregnum declared that people were safe and happy only when their ruler had adequate power to maintain order, and could hand on that power without interruption to his successor. As they found these two qualifications implicit in absolute monarchy, they praised it

Defects of absolutism

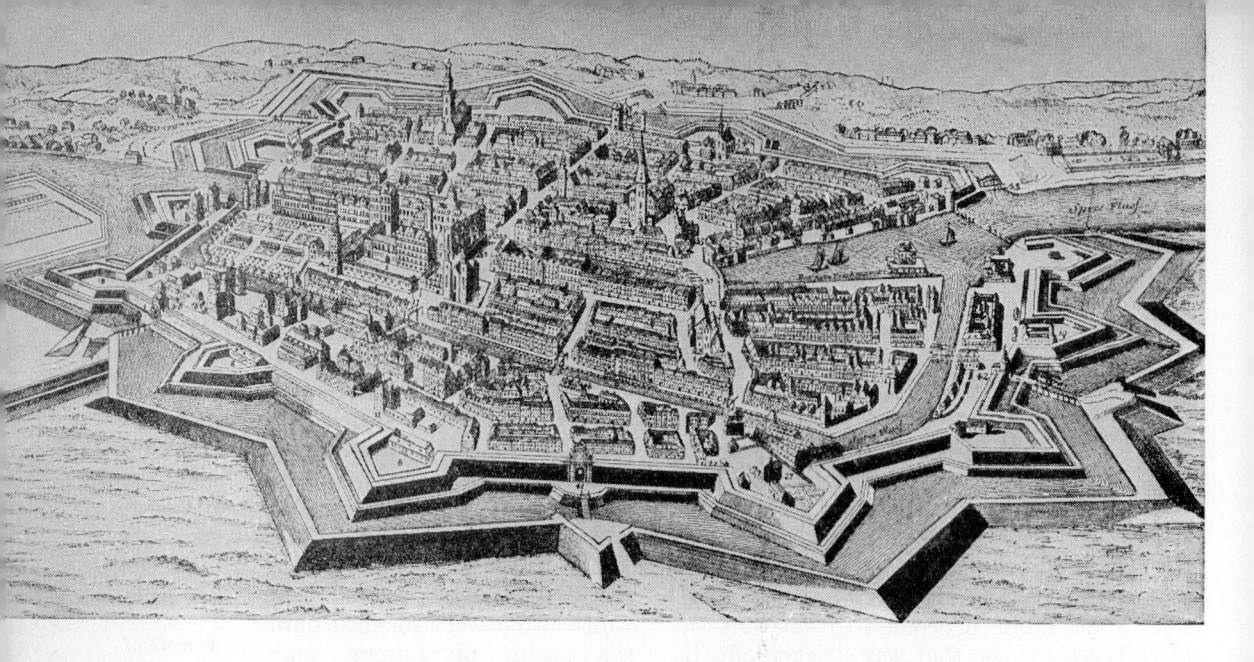

BERLIN IN THE LATER SEVENTEENTH CENTURY

The artist has exaggerated the defensive moat, counterscarp, and hollow bastions that represented the seventeenth-century answer to artillery and infantry attacks.

WARSAW IN 1656

When this engraving was made the Polish kings at Warsaw still claimed an area twice as large as the area of France.

A CANAL IN AMSTERDAM

Jan van der Heyden (1637–1712) loved Amsterdam and depicted the charm and prosperity of this comfortable Venice of the North.

A GARDEN IN ROME

Europe still imitated formal Italian gardens like this at Rome during the later seventeenth century.

as the best system of government. But there is a Latin proverb to the effect that the best, when corrupted, becomes the worst. Under a capable king monarchy might justify itself admirably, but under a bad one it was almost certain to prove execrable. Unfortunately, not every prince who inherited a throne also inherited a talent for ruling. For one king born with genius there were ten who were mediocre if not actively mischievous. If the ministers of a stupid or wicked king were too servile to restrain him, a whole nation might suffer for his mistakes. His subjects had no redress against the injuries he did them, for in theory the king was answerable for his acts to God alone. The people might pray to God to soften his heart and enlighten his understanding; but if their prayers proved unavailing there was nothing they could do, except, as one writer has wittily observed, "to give thanks for the evil which the king neglected to do."

2. THE EUROPEAN STATES IN 1660

Had an Englishman of 1660 decided to take advantage of the restoration of peace in Europe to make a grand tour of the Continent, he could have learned much in a year of travel and adventure. Desiring to visit as many countries as possible, he might plan to sojourn a month or two in France, travel through Holland to the Germanies and Scandinavia, and then turn south to Austria and Italy. From Genoa he could, if he wished, take a ship to Spain, explore the Iberian Peninsula until the time came to board a merchantman at Lisbon, and conclude his year of wandering by a sea voyage to London. The stages of his journey may be followed with ease by referring to the map that opens this chapter.

If we suppose our imaginary traveler to have started from London in June, 1660, he must have left behind him a city gay with flags. The English people were celebrating the return of Charles II. Weary of the grim austerities of the Puritan régime, the nation hailed the restoration of the monarchy as an omen that England was to be "Merrie England" once more. Theaters were reopened, dancing and card-playing came back into fashion, and fine clothes were no longer frowned upon as a mark of vanity. The wit and affability of the new king pleased his subjects and earned him the title "The Merry Monarch." Beneath his charming manners he concealed thoughts that were selfish but sagacious. England, with a population of some four and a half million people, together with Scotland and Ireland, formed a kingdom no monarch need spurn. Charles had determined to escape if he could from the limitations set upon his authority, but to defer to Parliament if necessary rather than "start again upon his travels."

England

Leaving London to welcome its new king, our traveler of 1660 caught a coach for Dover. Recently inaugurated, these coaches were introducing a revolution in land transportation, for they ran more or less on schedule and jogged men and baggage over the vile English roads at the surprising average of four miles an hour. The traveler was much relieved, after crossing the Channel, to find the French roads much better. A few days' journeying brought him to Paris, which was rapidly becoming the foremost city in Europe, as France was becoming the foremost state. In June, 1660, the Parisians were celebrating the marriage of their king, Louis XIV, to Maria Theresa, daughter of the Spanish king, Philip IV. This wedding was solemnized with a pomp and luxury remarkable even for an age which loved sumptuous display, for Louis XIV, then in his early twenties, was the most powerful monarch in Europe. For over half a century he was to maintain his position as the most dreaded, the most flattered, and the most troublesome figure on the European stage.

France

On the northeastern frontier of France lay the provinces of the Spanish Netherlands which Louis coveted; and beyond these the populous cities of the Dutch Republic whose inhabitants Louis despised. Yet his contempt for the Dutch merchants was mixed with envy, for they were the wealthiest merchants and traders in Europe. Our traveler, who paused a few days in Amsterdam, was amazed to see the harbor so dark with the masts of ships that it looked like a level for-

The Dutch Republic

est. It was said the herring trade alone brought the Dutch more wealth than Spain had drawn from all the mines of the Indies. All the nations shared the envy felt by Louis XIV at the spectacle of Dutch prosperity, but Louis had two additional reasons for disliking his neighbors. He disliked them because they were Protestant and he disliked them because they were republican.

Leaving Holland behind and ascending the river Rhine, the traveler soon found himself in the heart of the Palatinate. The Thirty Years' War had ended in 1648, but traces of its ravages were apparent everywhere, so that an Englishman might well be thankful his own country had escaped such a visitation. This wave of destruction which had overwhelmed the Germanies helps to account for the ascendancy gained by France in the seventeenth century. German civilization had been thrown back a hundred years; large areas were swept as clean as a desert, and millions of people throughout the empire had perished from the sword or plague or famine. With the re-establishment of peace, the German princes took up the task of restoring prosperity to their shattered domains, the most successful being Frederick William of Brandenburg, known to German history as the "Great Elector" (1640–88). By his political and military reforms Frederick William laid a foundation for a strong Prussian state in northern Germany. Settlers were drawn from all parts of Europe to people his depleted villages through the promise of good government and freedom from religious persecution. Hearing of the Great Elector's statesmanlike rule, our traveler decided to visit Berlin. He found the future capital of Germany a grim and cheerless town of ten or twelve thousand inhabitants, situated in the midst of a desert-like countryside, and his disappointment led him to hasten on for a view of the Scandinavian countries.

Five states disputed the control of the Baltic Sea in 1660: Sweden, Denmark, Russia, Brandenburg, and Poland. As a temporary truce had been concluded, the traveler was able to visit Copenhagen, the capital of the united kingdom of Denmark-Norway, and to linger in Stockholm, the capital of Sweden. It astonished him to learn that these kingdoms, which desired to play the rôle of great powers, had a population of only a little over a million each. Remembering how Brandenburg was developing, and pondering what he had heard of Russia, a vast and little-known country on the eastern fringe of Europe, the Englishman decided that Sweden and Denmark were unwise to waste their resources fighting each other when they might soon have such much more powerful rivals. Being tactful, however, he kept his opinion to himself, and resumed his journey down the Baltic to Danzig and thence across Great Poland on his way to Vienna.

In that ancient city on the Danube, the Emperor of the Holy Roman Empire, Leopold I, had recently celebrated his election. His reign (1658–1705) was to prove a critical half-century in Austrian history. Despite his grandiose titles, the emperor's power was crumbling: the Peace of Westphalia had virtually terminated his authority over the German princes, France was powerful and aggressive in the West, and the Turks, having overrun Hungary, were pressing up the Danube toward Vienna. Twenty years later, they were to besiege the city, from which Leopold fled in panic. Only the heroic action of John Sobieski, King of Poland, saved eastern Europe for the cross. With a small relief force of Poles and Germans, Sobieski hastened to the aid of Vienna, and routed a Mohammedan host that outnumbered his own by three to one (1683).

In the cathedral of Saint Stephen the grateful Viennese intoned the text, "There was a man sent from God whose name was John"; but for the timely aid Sobieski had rendered, the proud Hapsburgs showed scant gratitude. Poland, in 1660, was a loosely organized kingdom that occupied an area as large as France. A little over a century later, it disappeared from the map of Europe completely, partitioned and annexed by the rapacious rulers of Austria, Prussia, and Russia.

It is recounted that in the hour of their defeat before the walls of Vienna, the Turks

The Turks

were dismayed to behold the shadow of an eclipse blot out the ascendant moon from the evening sky. A crescent moon was the sign of Mohammedan power, and the Islamic Empire for a thousand years had stretched from Asia Minor across Africa to Spain, a menacing crescent with its horns closing on Christian Europe. The western pincer had been blunted at the battle of Tours (732) and broken off when the Spaniards ended the Moorish power in Spain (1492). But in the same century the fall of Constantinople (1453) saw the eastern horn of the crescent plunged into the heart of the Hapsburg Empire. The siege of Vienna in 1683 marked the farthest gain in this advance. Thereafter the Turkish power in the Balkan Peninsula was doomed to ebb with the centuries like a slowly receding tide.[1]

Italy

The summer of 1660 changed to autumn while the traveler lingered in Vienna, but before the snows could deepen in the Alps he hastened across the Brenner Pass, and saw the waters of the Adriatic for the first time at Venice. The city of the doges, once the greatest commercial port of Europe, had lost its supremacy with the development of the Atlantic sea lanes, and its glory was waning. At Rome, the traveler mused upon the fate of the ancient empire of the Caesars and the prestige which still invested the city as the capital of Christendom. Then he lingered in the lovely cities of northern Italy — Florence, Bologna, Mantua, Milan, Pavia — before he embarked at Genoa in a swift galley which carried him to Barcelona in Spain.

Spain

On his way across the valleys and plateaus which separate Barcelona from Madrid, the traveler came to understand why Spain, the dominant nation of Europe a century earlier, had fallen into decline. The peasants appeared lazy, disliking to work more than a few hours a day, although one day in four was a religious holiday. The irrigation systems by which, in Moorish times, farmers had coaxed produce from the arid soil were no longer tended. The only roads in many parts were the water courses, impassable after rains when streams had the right of way. Trade languished, for the government, which had driven out the industrious Moors and Jews, was also ruining Christian merchants by exorbitant taxes. Remembering how commerce was encouraged in his own country, the Englishman confessed his astonishment at this, but the noble hidalgo to whom he revealed his thoughts explained that in Spain shopkeeping was considered a mean pursuit in which no gentleman would stoop to engage. If the merchants were heavily taxed, he added with a shrug, they doubtless fared as well as they deserved.

Madrid proved to be a medieval city with a multitude of beggars in the narrow and noisome streets. The government was constantly in financial straits, while many noble families had little or nothing left except their pride. Even that had been damaged by the recent national misfortunes, such as the capture of Jamaica by the English (1655) and the concessions extorted by the French in the Peace of the Pyrenees (1659). A further reverse demanded acknowledgment, for Portugal, united to the Spanish crown in 1580, had revolted in 1640, and the Portuguese were making good their independence under John IV, a king of their own choosing. The Spaniards, however, remained loyal to their own royal line, although inbreeding and degeneracy were soon to bring it to an end. In 1661, an heir was born to Philip IV, a diseased and sickly prince who astonished his doctors by surviving the maladies of childhood. He was to astonish all Europe by living until 1700 as Charles II, last of the Spanish Hapsburgs.

An overland journey of some weeks carried the traveler from Madrid to Lisbon. The Portuguese, in their struggle for independence, had developed friendly commercial relations with England, and he had little difficulty in discovering a merchantman bound for London. A year of wandering had taught him much about the life led by the European peoples of his day. It will be interesting to imagine some of the conclusions he may have reached. The next paragraphs will summarize the conditions he had a chance to observe in Europe three centuries ago.

---

[1] Compare the map facing the first page of this chapter with the maps of Europe in the later sections.

PEASANT LIFE IN SEVENTEENTH-CENTURY FRANCE
This reproduction of a painting misses the squalor of most peasant homes at that time.

AN ENGLISH COTTAGE
As one inmate lived to 102, the dwelling must have been more durable than it appears.

THE PUBLIC LETTER WRITER
In an age when four people in five were illiterate every town had its public letter writer, whose stall was a haven for gossip. This writer holds his goose quill pen in the left hand.

THE COMMON PEOPLE

3. LIFE IN THE SEVENTEENTH CENTURY

From England to Italy and Prussia to Spain, the traveler must have found three fourths of the people leading miserable lives without leisure or luxury. In the cities most of the inhabitants subsisted on the verge of destitution, toiling as artisans or apprentices, as servants poorly paid and overworked, as porters or ostlers, linkboys or lackeys, peddlers or beggars. But there were few cities in Europe of even fifty thousand inhabitants, and the great majority of Europe's eighty or ninety million people lived amid rural surroundings, their horizon bounded by the limits of the local hamlet or feudal estate. The open countryside, when it did not begin at their doorsill, was within sight or walking distance and this was one great advantage which they possessed. But in most other respects their lives were wretched, burdened as they were by a host of inescapable hardships, by intermittent famines and plagues and unceasing toil.

The difficulty and cost of transportation confined the poor to their native community: thousands of people lived and died without traveling fifty miles from their birthplace. The roads were often no more than mud ruts, impassable for months in the year. This absence of easy means of transport or communication kept society in the country districts "frozen" as it were. Many hamlets still preserved the same qualities of self-sufficiency and isolation which they had possessed in the Middle Ages. Attention was confined to local affairs; the villagers had little incentive to speculate about the world beyond the horizon, for their days were filled with a multitude of duties, and when they paused to gossip it was of personal concerns. The passage of a regiment of soldiers on the highroad some miles away, and the sojourn of a nobleman overnight at the inn, were casual echoes of the great world that disturbed them little.

Hindrances to travel

In that era before the advent of labor-saving machinery, life presented an endless succession of inescapable tasks. The farmer had his stock to feed and his fields to tend. Tools called for resharpening, roofs had to be rethatched, there was always wood to be hewn or water to be drawn, so that little leisure was left for amusement or study. Few outside of the professional classes ever learned to read, but news circulated about the community by word of mouth or was announced at the church on Sundays, and the illiterate masses carried a store of ballads and tales, as well as the details of local history, in their memories. Everyone in a village knew everyone else, his uncles and his cousins and his aunts, and the fact that families had dwelt in the same neighborhood and intermarried for generations bound the community together. The status of each person was thus fixed by custom and known to all; few had the opportunity to rise above their class; and the occupation a man inherited from his forbears might determine, not only his place and duties in village life, but his name also, as the Bakers, Millers, Taylors, Smiths, and other common surnames still bear witness.

To hold some settled position, to "belong" in the community, was then a matter of pride, and families clung tenaciously to ancient privileges and pretensions however humble. The craving for distinctions and honors was particularly strong among the rising bourgeois class, and it has been estimated that in some towns one half the population purchased minor rôles or offices of one kind or another in the administration. In a society where the position of everyone is well known and defined, strangers are usually viewed askance, and it is not surprising to find in the seventeenth century that most localities maintained special laws against "rogues, vagabonds, and sturdy beggars." Gypsies, traveling tinkers, and strolling players were treated with suspicion as immoral and dishonest vagrants, a prejudice that has been slow in dying out. The wars of the seventeenth century flooded Europe with disbanded soldiers and other masterless men who begged or stole as the mood pleased them, and against such "sturdy beggars" the laws were particularly severe.

In the Middle Ages poverty, or at least a contempt for worldly riches, had been considered an admirable quality, and begging assumed the dignity of a profession. But this tolerant atti-

Harsh laws

WHEATFIELDS, BY JACOB VAN RUISDAEL (1628–1682)

Almost everyone, in seventeenth-century Europe, lived within a few minutes' walk of the open country.

THE GARDEN OF AN INN, BY JAN VAN STEEN (1626–1679)

Jan van Steen was the most prolific of genre painters and one of the most captivating. His casual merrymakers welcome all comers into their group.

tude toward mendicancy had changed by the seventeenth century, especially in Protestant countries. A new sense of the dignity of useful labor had developed, and merchants and guild masters who needed workers for their shops and factories urged severe laws against idleness. Able-bodied men who declined to work were cured by whipping, forced labor, or, if they proved incorrigible, by transportation to the colonial plantations. For graver crimes the laws were proportionately harsher. Thieves, bandits, smugglers, and murderers might incur penalties which ranged from a term in the galleys, branding or mutilation, to hanging or breaking on the wheel. Executions were public, the condemned were urged to make edifying speeches at the gallow's foot for the benefit of the audience, and the bodies of criminals were left hanging from the gibbets as a warning to other evildoers. Unfortunately, these cruel laws were administered in so clumsy and unequal a fashion that they proved more ferocious than salutary; yet few people protested against the stupidity of the system, for it was in the spirit of the time to take the evil with the good and accept the established customs in government or society without much questioning.

It must be remembered, too, that the coarseness and crudity of living conditions three centuries ago bred in the mass of the people an indifference to suffering which today would be considered inhuman. Some old European towns still preserve a whipping-post in the marketplace to recall the days when misdemeanors were punished by a public flogging. Bear-baiting and cock-fighting were popular sports, and the wretched inmates of the insane asylums were sometimes exposed in cages for the amusement of visitors who might poke and tease them as if they were animals. Pain and suffering were such commonplace things in an age before anesthetics, when surgical and dental methods were elementary, that people grew insensible to the thought of them. Death and disease carried off every second child before it was ten years old and struck down the strong man in his prime. The air was full of "farewells to the dying and mourning for the dead," and the resultant sense of helplessness, of the mystery of life and the imminence of death, partly explains why people then cherished their religion more closely, and felt a deeper sense of awe toward the supernatural.

The peasants and laborers who made up the larger part of the population in every European state clung to their established mode of life with dogged and unenlightened conservatism. The prejudice against changes and innovations was so strong that frequently new and better methods of doing things, of planting crops or breeding cattle, were rejected simply because they were new. Forks were a long time coming into fashion because people were accustomed to lift the food to their mouths with their fingers. The belief that night air was harmful led people to seal up doors and windows at night. All the members of a family often slept in a single room, huddled together on a straw mattress, or stretched on the level top of a brick oven for the sake of its comfortable warmth. The dwellings were frequently no better than barns, with earth floors and thatched roofs. Water had to be drawn from a well or stream; there were no baths, and bathing was a luxury it was easier to forgo. The poorer classes could not afford to buy meat and subsisted chiefly on cereals and coarse vegetables; inadequately nourished, they were less fitted to resist the diseases and plagues to which their unsanitary mode of life exposed them, and they lacked the reserve of energy and courage which might have moved them to rebel against their condition.

This picture of life in the seventeenth century, as it was lived by the majority, is a dark one, but there were signs even then that a change was coming, though it was coming *Signs of change* all too slowly. The era of exploration and expansion which had begun as early as the fourteenth century gradually brought to Europeans a widening horizon and a richer life. New dress materials, such as muslin and calico, were introduced from the East; cotton cloth was developed as an addition to wool; and new foods, such as potatoes, tomatoes, and sugar, supplemented the monotonous diet. Coffee and tea were added to the list of common beverages in the seventeenth century, and the habit of smoking, or "drinking tobacco" as it was called, was acquired from the American Indians. The rich were the first to enjoy these innovations, but, as they grew cheaper and more common, the new types of food and clothing became available for the poorer classes also.

Yet most of the wealth created by the revival of trade remained concentrated in a few — too few — hands. While the lot of the poor had improved but little since the close of the Middle Ages, the prosperous merchant had begun to enjoy luxuries unknown to princes a few centuries earlier. The clean and comfortable interiors of Dutch houses, with their handsome furniture, polished utensils, pictures on the walls and rugs on the floors, as they are preserved in many a seventeenth-century painting, prove that well-to-do people had learned in that day how to surround their lives with comfort and charm. The country château of many a noble, the town houses of many a merchant prince, were crowded with rich collections of silver plate, carved furniture, and woven tapestry. But the enjoyment of such possessions was a privilege reserved for the rich and the powerful, and for one man who drank his wines from a silver goblet and amused himself with the intricate variety of a thirty-course dinner there were a hundred who called themselves blessed if they had a chicken to put in the pot on Saturday night.

All these impressions and many others might have crowded through the mind of our imaginary traveler as he concluded his grand tour. But not the most thoughtful and intelligent observer could have been expected to detect in the Europe of 1660 the dynamic forces which were to enable Europeans, in less than three centuries thereafter, to dominate the world. Europe, the smallest of the continents and by no means the most ancient in its civilization, which in 1660 possessed less than one seventh of the world's population, was destined to reduce four larger continents to subjection and tribute. The story of this amazing expansion, which was to carry the impress of European civilization to every quarter of the globe, is the main theme of modern history. The Europeans had never been particularly noteworthy for meekness, but they were to come nearer than any other people had ever done to inheriting the earth.

37

Louis XIV Dominates France and Aspires to Dominate Europe

Homage is due to kings, they do what pleases them.
MAXIM FROM THE YOUNG LOUIS XIV'S COPYBOOK.

IT IS THE FORTUNE of some men to personify so fittingly the dominant spirit of the period in which they live that they give their name to their age. Louis XIV of France was such a figure. The spirit which he exemplified was royal absolutism, and so impressively did he play his part as king, by the grace of God, of the leading European state of the time, that the latter half of the seventeenth century is still called the Age of Louis XIV.

1. FRANCE AT THE ACCESSION OF LOUIS XIV

Louis's long reign lasted from 1643 to 1715, and fate ordained that its glory should exceed even its length. Three factors combined to heighten the unique prestige of the *Grand Monarque*. The first was the general state of Europe in the seventeenth century. As explained in the previous chapter the turmoil and dissension of the religious struggles, followed by the civil war in England and the internecine strife known as the Fronde in France, aroused a profound longing among European peoples for peace and stability. If a king sought to gratify this wish, he would have to maintain a balance between the turbulent nobles, ambitious bourgeois, and oppressed peasants, by proclaiming himself the symbol of the state and raising the state above faction. The century thus offered an astute monarch a rare opportunity to demonstrate the saving virtues of royal absolutism as a method of government, and Louis made the most of this opportunity.

The second factor which helped to augment his prestige was the happy combination of royal supremacy with national supremacy. With Germany ruined and half-depopulated by the Thirty Years' War (1618–48), England torn by civil war (1642–49), and Spain already in decline, France under Louis XIV stood forth as the leading European power. The labors of Richelieu and Mazarin in consolidating the royal power had made the authority of the French king more extensive and more absolute than that of any other contemporary monarch. Louis became arbiter of France at the moment that France was becoming arbiter of Europe, and this second factor largely explains his historical importance.

The third factor was the king's personality. Historians have long debated whether Louis XIV deserved to be called great, and the verdict, paradoxically enough, seems to be **Character of Louis XIV** that he was not a great man, but he was a great king. In appearance he was of average height, endowed with natural grace and dignity and by some accounted handsome. In youth he revealed no precocious talents and as a man he was by no means learned, for he possessed little more than a smattering of history and Italian and enough Latin to construe Caesar's *Commentaries*. But if his intelligence was mediocre, his character had elements of grandeur. A lonely and diffident childhood had taught him to be self-sufficient, to discipline his feelings and conceal his thoughts; and he reached manhood with the determination to devote all his faculties to the business of kingship. There is something attractive in the picture he has left of himself at twenty-two when Mazarin's death called him to command the ship of state. Outwardly, he knew, he must reveal nothing but calm resolution, but within he was beset with qualms and uncertainties. To his relief this timidity vanished once he set his hand to the task. "I really seemed to myself," he wrote later, "to be a king, and born to be one. I experienced a delight, in fact, which it is difficult to express." Unfortunately, years of flattery dissolved away his early sense of modesty and moderation, and made him selfish and bigoted.

Believing himself chosen as God's vicegerent to guide the destinies of France, Louis accepted his power as a serious responsibility. He schooled himself to evaluate character, to choose able subordinates, and to weigh decisions. If he lacked genius, he possessed the best substitute for it, which is an infinite capacity for taking pains. The multifarious details of the kingly trade engrossed him, he toiled at them relentlessly, and not even in sickness or defeat would he permit the routine of councils and ceremonies to be interrupted. For over fifty years Louis sustained without faltering the exacting rôle for which he had trained himself, and history, as a reward for the technical perfection of that performance, has awarded him the title of the "Grand Monarch." To contemporary Europe, his example was a practical proof of the divine right of kings, for no demagogue lifted to power by the will of the populace and no conqueror who might "wade through slaughter to a throne" could hope to sway a scepter with so sure a hand as this legitimate and consecrated king. Among a host of writers who flattered Louis by proving that

Divine right of kings

God had ordained kings to rule and endowed them with peculiar gifts for the task, the most eloquent was the Bishop of Meaux, Bossuet (1627–1704), who based his arguments on the Holy Scriptures. Those who presumed to criticize or resist the Lord's anointed were declared to be not only political rebels but heretics and blasphemers, for, as Bossuet proclaimed, the king's power was without limits and he was answerable for the use he made of it to no one on earth.

When Cardinal Mazarin, who had governed France during the minority of Louis XIV, died in 1661, the young king announced that he would thenceforth take upon himself the duties of first minister. He was determined to preside over the councils of government in person and guide with his own hand the destinies of the first state of Europe. There was no force in France strong enough to dispute his wishes. Louis XIV enjoyed greater powers than any of his predecessors because every faction in France which might have resisted him had been reduced to impotence or taught to serve the royal will. The king had become much more than the executive head of the state; he was the center of all authority and order, a sun radiating light and warmth to every corner of the realm. His most important vassals and ministers were no more than satellites, circling in their orbits about his august person, reflecting his glory, but forbidden to approach too near. Louis chose the sun as his symbol because it was a unique body of matchless power and radiance, and its dominant position in the heavens suggested the rôle which he felt himself called upon to assume in France. The methods by which he reduced the kingdom to an obsequious obedience offer a fascinating study in statecraft.

Absolutism of Louis

The threefold division of society into clergy, nobles, and commoners still survived in seventeenth-century France. The clergy were known as the First Estate, and occupied an anomalous position, for as Frenchmen they were subjects of the king, while as churchmen they were servants of the pope. It is not difficult to foresee that under a king as jealous of his power as Louis, the exact divi-

First Estate: the clergy

sion of authority between the king and pope was likely to become a subject of dispute. Louis was anxious to be esteemed orthodox, as befitted one who bore the title "His Most Christian Majesty," but he disliked to see the pope interfere in French affairs. His predecessors on the throne of France had wrung a number of concessions from the papacy, so that the Gallican Church (as the Roman Catholic Church in France was called) enjoyed a semi-independent position. Among the privileges assumed by the French kings was that of collecting the income from certain clerical offices whenever they were vacant, a custom extended so broadly by Louis XIV that in 1673 his claims were repudiated by Pope Innocent XII. As the quarrel deepened, Louis allowed Bossuet to draw up a declaration which defined the "liberties of the Gallican Church," asserted the king's independence of the pope in temporal affairs, and proclaimed that a general council was superior to the papal authority. To this declaration the French clergy gave their consent (1682), but the threatening schism was composed ten years later when Louis, having won his way in the matter of appointments, permitted the bishops to withdraw from the unorthodox position he had persuaded them to assume (1693). The strong can afford to be generous and Louis had come to the conclusion that the pope would be of more service to him as an ally than as an adversary.

Like the clergy, the nobles were taught to accept the royal authority. Under Louis XIV the great feudal vassals finally lost the power to rebel. They had been the architects of their own ruin, for the long story of their selfishness, treason, and dissension had converted the French people to the belief that the rule of one despot was preferable to the misrule of many. The days when a powerful noble could maintain his private army, wage his private wars, and even defy from his impregnable castle the anger of his impotent king, were past. Under Richelieu and Mazarin royal troops crushed the last revolts and royal orders leveled many of the provincial castles to the ground. The rebellion of the Fronde represented in its main

Second Estate: the nobility

aspect the last convulsive struggle of a decadent feudalism before it yielded definitely to the shackles of the kingly power. Throughout his reign Louis XIV was resolute in withholding from the nobles all political or military authority. Stripped of such power they were harmless, and he had no wish to humble them further. Their titles and honors he left intact and even multiplied, his policy being to domesticate these feudal lions rather than to destroy them. Summoning to his capital the leading nobles of France, he consoled them with pensions and flattered them with empty but impressive duties at court. Ruin or imprisonment would have made these erstwhile rebels the objects of popular sentiment and the heroes of a lost cause, so Louis bound them to him astutely with golden chains. Like the giant Antaeus in the Greek fable, their strength drained away when their feet no longer trod their native earth, for their real power was derived from their lands and their armies of loyal retainers. Cut off from these, they became parasites at the court of the Sun King. Like the orange trees in silver tubs which graced the Hall of Mirrors at Versailles, they were decorative and expensive, but they no longer served any useful purpose.

The Third Estate, although it included over nine tenths of his subjects, Louis found by far the easiest to manage, for the commoners had never been accustomed to the exercise of political power. From this class he drew his most trusted councilors and officials, knowing such men would be dependent upon his whim and powerless before his wrath. The subservience of the Third Estate in France is most interesting, especially when compared with the arrogance of the English Commons, which proved strong enough in the seventeenth century to get rid of two unpopular kings. In France, however, the continuous expansion of the royal power had stunted the growth of representative institutions. Yet the French monarchs, though not obliged to consult the wishes of their subjects, could not altogether ignore them. One organ through which they might learn of popular opposition to a new edict was the

The Third Estate

parlement de Paris. This body was not a "parliament" in the English sense. It was the most important of several similar legal courts, and one of its privileges was to register royal decrees. The councilors of the *parlement* interpreted this to mean that they might on occasion *refuse* to register a law which appeared to them contradictory or unconstitutional, but the king could silence all objection by summoning the councilors to a *lit de justice* (bed of justice) and commanding them to accept the disputed decree as an expression of his will. As further opposition would not hinder the promulgation of the law, the *parlement* usually yielded at this point, though occasionally the members persisted in their opposition and were banished from Paris as a sign of the royal displeasure. Louis XIV was so jealous of the royal prerogative that even this shadow of resistance annoyed him, and early in his reign the *parlement de Paris* was deprived of the right of protest.

Because he controlled the national income and well-paid clerical appointments, and was not dependent upon appropriations granted by a jealous parliament as were contemporary English monarchs, Louis XIV could bind the great nobles of France to him by gifts, reserving the most lucrative church offices for members of the leading families. The rising prices of the sixteenth and seventeenth centuries had impoverished many a knight and baron whose feudal income was fixed by custom, and many a titled bankrupt was happy to retrieve his fortunes through the king's generosity. But although Louis willingly bestowed sinecures at court upon such nobles, or rewarded younger sons with clerical appointments, he preferred to entrust political duties to able members of the Third Estate. More than one ambitious bourgeois served the king loyally as councilor or intendant, in the hope of winning a title thereby, and he usually paid a goodly sum into the royal exchequer in addition when he received the coveted coat of arms. These new "nobles of the robe" were scorned by the older "nobles of the sword," but they acted as a counterweight in preserving the social equilibrium, which answered the king's purposes excellently. Favored by circumstances, Louis XIV thus evolved a system in which the old nobility were paid to be subservient, the ambitious bourgeois, subservient and industrious, paid to become nobles, and the bishops and the abbots of the Gallican Church, chosen from the ancient nobility, subordinated the church to the accessory rôle which Louis intended it to play in his absolutist state.

2. HOW LOUIS XIV CONDUCTED HIS GOVERNMENT

The administrative system over which Louis presided was a highly centralized and complicated mechanism. The executive power was exercised through four royal councils, which met regularly each week and dispatched their business under the king's direction. The council of state decided questions of foreign policy, peace and war, etc. The council of dispatches regulated the internal affairs of the kingdom, but left matters of a fiscal nature, such as taxation and tariffs, to the council of finances. The privy council was a court of the king's justice, but possessed extraordinary powers so that it could act as a final court of appeal and could arrest or withdraw a case from the inferior courts at its discretion. The power of these councils reached into the farthest corners of the kingdom, where financial and judicial matters were entrusted to royal officials known as intendants, each of whom administered a province in the king's name, and corresponded regularly with the council of dispatches. All the business of the kingdom was thus supervised from Versailles; all important decisions (and many that were unimportant) came before the king for his signature, with the natural result that officials preferred to evade decisions and contented themselves with obeying orders. Thus summarized, the machinery of government sounds comparatively simple, but as it had grown up haphazardly there was actually an endless confusion and overlapping of authority; the lower officials lacked independence and initiative, and an increasing burden of details was thrown upon the central councils. An energetic king and capable ministers could force the machine to function with a certain majestic ponderosity, but it was,

Councils of government

THE PALACE OF VERSAILLES

Top: This engraving illustrates the elegance and order which distinguished French court life in the age of Louis XIV. The cost of laying out the palaces and gardens was so enormous that Louis ordered the accounts destroyed.

LOUIS XIV OF FRANCE (1638–1715)

Above: This portrait of Louis (from a painting by Rigaud) in his robes of state suggests the poise and self-confidence which made him a model for the lesser despots of his age.

JEAN BAPTISTE COLBERT

Above: Colbert worked indefatigably to make France prosperous.

MARQUESS DE LOUVOIS

Below: Louvois was minister of war and had great influence with Louis XIV.

for all that, a desperately wasteful and inefficient system.

In the first part of his reign Louis XIV was fortunate in commanding the services of Jean Baptiste Colbert (1619–83), perhaps the greatest financial administrator in French history. Appointed controller general of finance in 1661, Colbert doubled Louis's revenue within ten years, not by increasing the taxes, but by cutting down the wastage and defalcations. A dour and friendless man, consumed by a passion for work, Colbert had the acuteness to realize that most systems of raising revenue ended by killing the goose that laid the golden eggs. Too many finance ministers thought only of pleasing their royal masters by filling the treasury, and cared little where the burden fell; but Colbert worked with four aims in mind, directed to one end. He sought (1) to collect an adequate revenue by the most honest and efficient system; (2) to expend the sums collected wisely and economically; (3) to distribute the burden of taxation upon those classes best able to sustain it; and (4) to stimulate with exemptions and subsidies those branches of farming and manufacture in which the nation was deficient so that it might be more self-sufficing and independent of its neighbors.

Colbert

The last point embodies the most significant element in Colbert's policy. The doctrine that a state which is politically independent should make itself economically independent also is known as "mercantilism," or sometimes, in honor of its greatest exponent, as "Colbertism." As applied by Colbert, the theory rested upon two main suppositions: (1) In peace, and more especially in war, a state should be able to produce within its borders or draw from its colonies all the commodities necessary for its national existence. (2) To prosper, a state should sell its surplus commodities to foreign countries, but should buy as little as possible in return, for if the value of its exports always exceeds that of its imports, the difference must be paid by the purchasers in gold, so that a store of the precious metal will accumulate in the coffers of the state adhering to mercantilist principles.

Mercantilism

Mercantilism, though a selfish and egotistic policy, appealed strongly to the rulers of the new nationalistic states. To make France economically independent, Colbert imported skilled artisans from all parts of Europe so that they might teach the French workmen to manufacture Dutch cloth, Venetian lace, Flemish tapestries, English steel, Italian pottery and blown glass and mirrors. To protect the new industries from foreign competition, he erected high tariffs against foreign commodities; French subjects were warned that it was "unpatriotic" to buy abroad, and were forbidden to send gold out of the country. Colbert hoped to raise French manufactures to such a level of excellence that they would outsell Dutch goods in Amsterdam and Venetian goods in Venice. To hasten this end he enforced exacting regulations and punished careless workers. His paternal efforts stimulated French industrial processes enormously and French trade profited from his improvement of roads, canals, and harbors. But there were some qualities which he could not create by legislation, qualities of initiative, of imagination and daring, and for lack of these some of his greatest schemes went astray. The great trading companies which he founded in the fond hope that they would rival the Dutch and English East India Companies failed after a few years. The navy which he built up at great expense to extend the French colonial empire in India and Africa and America could not compete successfully with English and Dutch sea power. The tariffs he enforced to protect French industry provoked other nations to similar measures against French goods and created a tradition of economic hostility so intense that every war in which France has been engaged since Colbert's time has been in part at least a tariff war. But the basic cause for the failure of Colbert's grandiose schemes is to be found in the conflict between his aims and those of Louis XIV. The resources of France, though great, would not permit her to seek commercial supremacy on the seas and military supremacy on land at the same time. To lay the foundations of a world empire or to snatch at the military hegemony of Europe were the two courses open to Louis, and nursed upon traditions of conquest he chose the latter. For France, for Europe, and for the world it was a momentous decision.

The evil genius whose influence was largely to nullify the achievements of Colbert was the minister of war, Louvois (1641–91). Under his direction the French army became the most efficient in Europe. France was the first state to keep a standing army in the modern sense, drilled, uniformed, and paid by the government. To promote discipline Louvois held frequent inspections, punished breaches of order, and berated indolent officers. Every branch of the service felt the impulse of his brutal and dynamic spirit, and he increased the reserves until the French army reached the total of two hundred thousand effectives. Louis was delighted with the toy which his energetic minister had placed at his command. In Condé and Turenne he possessed the foremost generals of the age; in Vauban he had the greatest master of siege warfare in all time. A city defended by Vauban, ran a popular saying, is impregnable; a city attacked by Vauban is doomed. With such resources France was secure from any threat of invasion, but Louvois was not content to see his weapon rust in peace. He played upon the king's love of "glory" and urged him along the path that led to conflict, well knowing that war alone could demonstrate the excellence of the army he had fashioned and assure his triumph over his great rival Colbert.

Louvois

3. THE COURT OF THE SUN KING

To provide a suitable stage upon which the Grand Monarch might live and move and have his being, the foremost artists and architects of Europe were pressed into service. Henry IV had held his court in the Louvre, close by the Seine, but Louis XIV never liked Paris. He remembered from his childhood the insolence of the Parisians during the wars of the Fronde, and early in his reign he moved his residence to the small hamlet of Versailles, eleven miles southwest of Paris. There on a low crest of rising ground he had constructed a palace and gardens so vast they became the wonder of Europe, and so costly (the expense has been calculated at one hundred million dollars) that Louis ordered the accounts destroyed. At infinite labor water was pumped from a nearby river to supply the fabulous fountains and fill a "Grand Canal" two hundred feet wide and a mile long. The clipped hedges, statuary, arbors, and shaded walks made the garden an ideal setting for the fêtes and masquerades in which the courtiers delighted; while the palace itself, when finally completed, contained a theater, a chapel, a "marble court," with long connecting halls and glittering galleries, as well as sumptuous apartments for the king and his officials.

Versailles

The modern visitor is likely to find the desolate splendor of Versailles oppressive, and to feel disappointed at the monotony with which the palace and parks are laid out. Tastes change, and Versailles today is like a lantern with the light extinguished. Yet even in the seventeenth century there were critics courageous enough to declare that this royal residence (and the later palace built for Louis XIV at Marly) demonstrated nothing except the king's "invariably bad taste" and his delight in "doing violence to nature." To its admirers, however, the beauty of Versailles consists in the harmony and proportion of the whole design. The architect Mansart and the landscape artist Le Nôtre studied to subordinate each part to the classic ideal of order and restraint, so that nothing alien or exotic was introduced to mar the purity of the general pattern. Versailles embodies the spirit of an age. Its virtues were the virtues of Louis XIV himself: it was formal, orderly, and elegant; but its limitations reveal no less surely the limitations of Louis's character. Even at its best Versailles had grandiosity rather than grandeur; it was crowded with unoriginal artificialities; it was, in a word, dull, for it lacked cloudy perspectives, and the lift of distant horizons to set the spirit free.

As his reign advanced, Louis indulged his love of ceremony until his smallest daily acts were encrusted with ritualistic observances. On rising from bed in the morning (the king's *lever*) he was attended by a roomful of privileged nobles who esteemed themselves honored if they

Court ritual

THE CRIES OF PARIS
Street venders sang or yodeled to attract customers as they peddled their wares.

PARISIAN WORKERS, 1700
These workers are manufacturing playing cards on a wholesale scale.

PARIS IN THE EARLY EIGHTEENTH CENTURY
The Hôtel de Ville was the center of Paris city government. Note the importance of boats and horses as methods of transportation.

were awarded the distinction of holding one arm of his shirt or adjusting his shoe buckles. His meals, his drives, his promenades were each an affair of state; and when he retired, he was assisted to bed by courtiers eager to attend the king's *coucher*. The burden of such regulated pomp would have amused some men, and wearied most, but Louis found the business of kingship "grand, noble, delightful." He was at once the high priest and the idol in this cult of majesty and he succeeded in persuading his courtiers that they enjoyed their part in it, too, so that existence away from Versailles was "a living death." If a noble displeased him, Louis might banish the man to his country estate, where the poor wretch was likely to fill his days petitioning friends at court to secure a revocation of the sentence before he died of ennui. Flattery explains in part this exaggerated anxiety to remain close to the king; vanity explains it in part, too, for Versailles was the center of fashion; but greed was the most potent incentive. Only those who caught the king's attention could hope to profit by his generosity. When besought to aid some needy noble who seldom appeared at court, Louis was wont to answer, "That is a man I rarely see. I have forgotten him."

Seated at the pinnacle of the pyramid of state, and worshiped almost as a divinity, Louis must sometimes have found life a little lonely. Yet he allowed no inner doubts to ruffle the serenity of his manner; even in the darkest days his fortitude sustained him, and the hand that held the scepter, though it might grow weary, was never seen to waver. Nor was he always serious; in his younger days especially he delighted in entertainments and the court exhausted its resources to amuse him. His wife, the worthy but stupid Maria Theresa, daughter of Philip IV of Spain, was an uninspiring consort, and even before her death in 1683 Louis had permitted himself a succession of mistresses. The gentle Louise de la Vallière was followed by the dazzling Marquise de Montespan, who had wit and beauty and the taste necessary to encourage great artists. In 1679 there was a new favorite, a Mademoiselle de Fontanges; but by this time Louis was coming more and more under the influence of his children's governess, Madame de Maintenon. The king was growing sedate and middle-aged; he liked the grave demeanor and earnest piety of this unassuming woman, and in 1684 he secretly married her. "Madame de Maintenon," a witty historian has said, "was not so much Louis's last mistress as his companion in repentance, and it might almost be said, a part of his penance."

Margin note: Louis's mistresses

4. THE "GREAT AGE" IN LITERATURE AND ART

Louis XIV was not only the greatest king of his age, served by the most brilliant diplomats and the most invincible generals; he also patronized artists and writers whose work was the admiration of Europe. Pierre Corneille (1606–84), the greatest of French tragedians; Molière (1622–73), whose satirical comedies still delight audiences today, and Racine (1639–99), the noblest of French dramatic poets, brought such prestige to the French stage that it remained the model for over a century. The critical Boileau (1636–1711) helped to purge the language of barbarisms and laid down the rules of elegant diction. Before the reign of Louis XIV ended, French plays, French novels, and French manners had been adopted by cultured people everywhere, and a knowledge of the language was indispensable to those who hoped for a distinguished social or diplomatic career.

Margin note: Dramatists

There was one rôle which the polished nobles at the court filled with honor and distinction: they patronized — and sometimes created — great literature. Few annalists have wielded a pen so steeped in malice, so cruel yet candid in the details of its portraiture, as that with which the Duc de Saint-Simon wrote his memoirs of Louis and his court. The letters, too, which Madame de Sévigné composed for her daughter, relating with delicious wit and irony the gossip of Versailles, are still used as models of epistolary style. The *Fables* and *Contes* of La Fontaine are miracles of art for which he often compressed hours of labor into a single naïve but inimitable line; and the caustic, patrician wit of the Duc de la Rochefoucauld preserved the ob-

Margin note: Literary figures

servations of a lifetime in a book of *Maxims*, each polished like a jewel at the hands of a master lapidary. These, and a score of other writers whom there is not space to mention, helped to refine the French taste at the court of Louis XIV and to sustain the traditions of elegant intercourse for which French salons have long been famous.

Royal patronage profoundly influenced the art of the "Great Age." The indefatigable Colbert (among a host of other offices he held that of minister of fine arts) issued charters for an Academy of Painting and Sculpture, an Academy of Architecture, and an Academy of Music. Music was, indeed, the only art for which Louis XIV possessed any real taste, and the first French operas date from his reign. For the rest, the official, not to say officious, interest of the government in matters artistic, the rules and definitions laid down by the academicians, the prizes offered for poems in praise of Louis, and the pensions accorded men of art, stimulated the production of much sycophantic craftsmanship. Yet an age in which Mansart designed the dome of the Invalides, in which Lebrun produced his admirable battle scenes and portraits, and Poussin his poetic and delightful landscapes, must always rank high in the annals of art, nor must it be forgotten that all these men were pensionaries of the Grand Monarch.

5. WHY LOUIS XIV PERSECUTED THE JANSENISTS AND HUGUENOTS

To many European thinkers the Wars of Religion, so profitless in other respects, had taught one valuable lesson. They demonstrated conclusively that it was impossible to heal religious schisms by the sword. Persecution had failed to reunite all Christians in one belief; bloodshed had only intensified the hatred existing between the sects, until rulers were driven, reluctantly, to tolerate divergent creeds and make the best of it. But in the seventeenth century such tolerance was regarded, not as a virtue, but as a necessary evil. Where tolerance appeared, it was the fruit of exhaustion or of expediency, for religious passions were still narrow and strong and few men were really tolerant by conviction. The wise statesmanship of Henry IV, who consolidated France by extending protection and liberty to his Protestant subjects in the Edict of Nantes (1598), gained him many critics and few admirers. The absence, in the seventeenth century, of that genuine tolerance which recognizes every man's right to seek God after his own fashion must be kept in mind in judging the religious policy of Louis XIV.

To Louis the fact that a minority of his subjects clung to beliefs which he disliked indicated that they were self-willed to the point of treason. His desire to see all Frenchmen orthodox Catholics was not inspired by zeal for Rome; during most of his reign he was on hostile terms with the papacy; but he considered that to be one hundred per cent French and one hundred per cent royalist, a subject must share the religion of his king. His conviction that to be unorthodox was to be disloyal — a conviction, be it noted, that often had some foundation — goes far to explain why Louis persecuted both the Jansenists and the Huguenots.

The Jansenists were a group of austere and dogmatic enthusiasts who derived their name and much of their teaching from a certain Jansen, Bishop of Ypres (1585–1638). Their somewhat unorthodox views of salvation brought them into conflict with the Jesuits and were condemned by a papal bull in 1653. But the movement took on new life when Blaise Pascal, the famous scientist (1623–62), defended it in his *Lettres Provinciales* in 1656, so that the controversy between the puritanical doctrines of the Jansenists and the more worldly teaching of the Jesuits stirred all France. In 1661, Louis determined to suppress the Jansenists. He had little patience with their austere morality, considered them hair-splitting troublemakers, and knew that many of them had sympathized with the Frondeurs. The effort to silence them was only partly successful; Clement XI condemned the Jansenist doctrines in 1708 and again in 1713, while Louis had the convent at Port-Royal, a center of Jansenist piety near Paris, leveled to the ground. He preferred his subjects to be re-

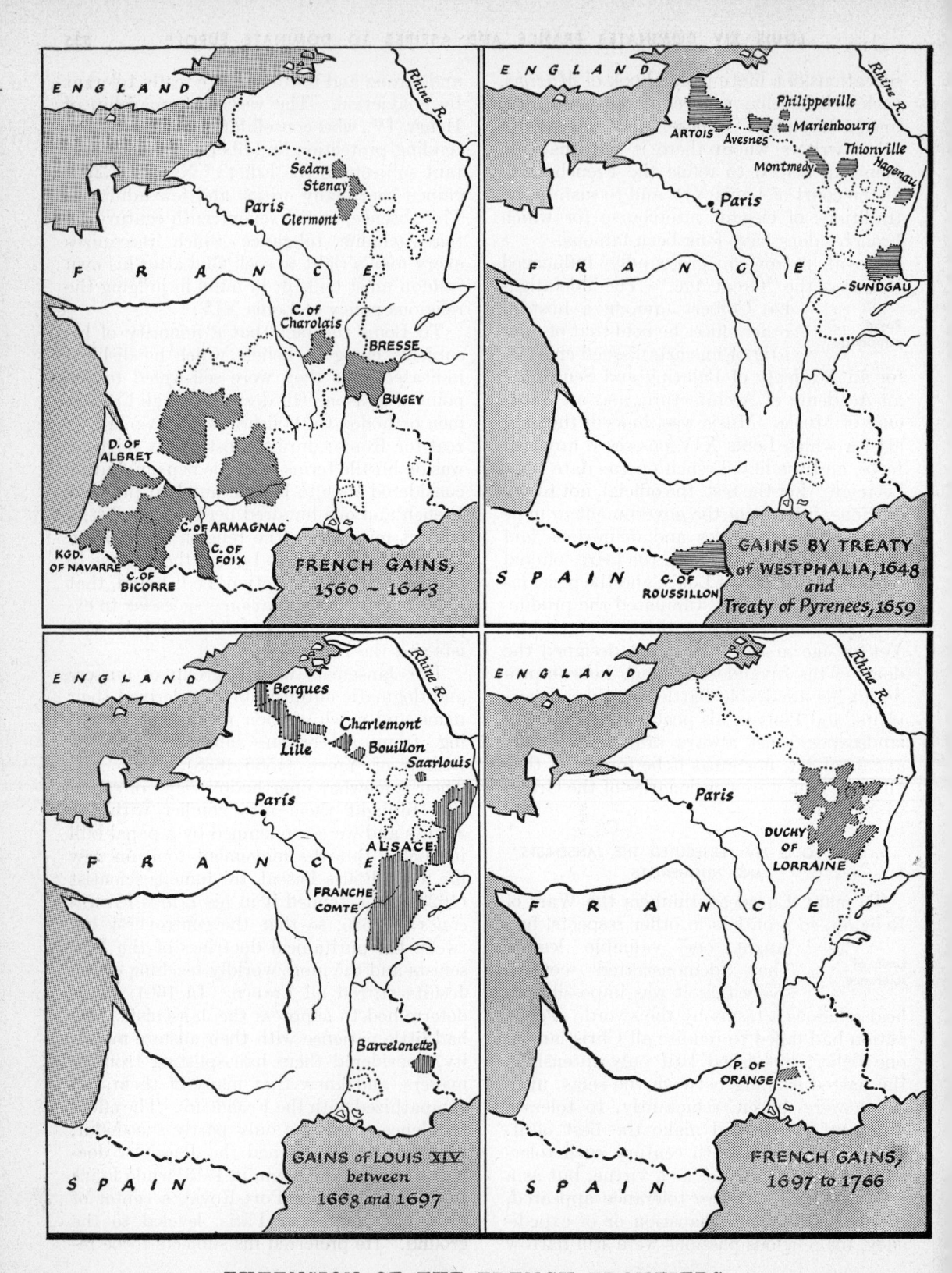

EXTENSION OF THE FRENCH FRONTIERS

ligious without too much enthusiasm; and he never forgot, as his memoirs attest, that some of the Jansenists had once engaged in antiroyalist activities.

The same spirit actuated Louis in his treatment of the French Protestants. The right to garrison a number of towns, a right which had been accorded these Huguenots by the Edict of Nantes (1598), had been rescinded by Richelieu, but they still retained their freedom of worship and the full liberties of French citizens. Unhappily, influences were at work which convinced Louis by 1680 that he owed it to his greatness to convert this recalcitrant minority among his subjects to the Catholic faith. He was engaged at the time in his controversy with the pope, and it was a politic method of proving that although he might disagree with Rome he had the propagation of the faith at heart. Moreover, his orderly mind disliked exceptions, and he was afraid that the Huguenots might find their loyalty divided when France was at war with a Protestant power. So he acquiesced in a campaign of conversion. The Huguenots were gradually stripped of their schools and places of worship. Gifts of money were offered those who accepted Catholicism but professional proselytes discredited this method by their repeated conversions. Then harsher means were invoked, and the minister of war, Louvois, encouraged his officers to quarter dragoons and other troops in Huguenot homes, with instructions to make their presence as unpleasant as possible. That Louis knew of the indignities to which many industrious and law-abiding citizens were subjected during these *dragonnades* is improbable. He was pleased at the number of reported conversions that followed, and in 1685, believing that there were few Huguenots left, he was persuaded to revoke the Edict of Nantes.

The result was a loss to France of some two hundred thousand of her worthiest citizens. They fled for refuge to Holland, to England, to Prussia, and even to America, taking with them what they could of their wealth, but taking also an even more precious gift to the countries they reinforced, their skill in trade and manufacture, their industry and their courage. The emigration of these trained artisans was a severe blow to the progress of French industry which Colbert had so zealously fostered, but this was not the only evil. The poorer Huguenots, who could not afford to flee, took up arms in defense of their faith and defied from their fastnesses in the Cevennes all the royal efforts to crush them. Their resistance did not end until after the death of Louis XIV, when they were finally pacified by a grant of toleration. The bigotry of the Great King not only failed to bring about that religious uniformity which he desired for his kingdom, but weakened France and enriched her enemies. Yet such was the spirit of the age that the Revocation of the Edict of Nantes was widely hailed in Catholic countries as the most statesmanlike, the most courageous, and the most glorious act of Louis's reign.

6. THE WARS OF LOUIS XIV

The greatest defect in Louis's character, greater even than the bigotry which impelled him to revoke the Edict of Nantes, was his love of martial glory. The predominance of France made that nation secure from foreign attack, therefore the wars which Louis precipitated were wars of deliberate and undisguised aggression. Where there is a will there is always a way to find a subject for international dispute: the most fertile cause of conflict in the seventeenth century was the Bourbon-Hapsburg rivalry, and Louis revived that by asserting the need of France to realize her "natural frontiers." The map on the opposite page will show that Nature has set certain geographical barriers which might be taken to represent natural boundaries for the French kingdom, the most important being the river Rhine, the Alps, and the Pyrenees. To appreciate how conveniently the doctrine of "natural frontiers" accommodated itself to the furtherance of Louis's dynastic policy, it should be noted that in order to reach the Rhine the French would have to annex Franche-Comté, the Rhenish Palatinate, the Spanish Netherlands, and about one fifth of the Dutch Republic, all of which (except the last-named) were territories under the sovereignty of Spanish or Austrian Hapsburgs.

War of Devolution

A clause in the Peace of the Pyrenees (1659) had provided that Louis XIV should marry Maria Theresa, eldest daughter of the Spanish king, Philip IV. Philip died in 1665, leaving one other daughter, and (by a second marriage) a sickly son who succeeded him as Charles II. Louis promptly claimed the Spanish Netherlands as his wife's share of the Spanish Empire, advancing a doubtful argument known as the "principle of devolution," which was based upon the legal rule that property (in some provinces of the Netherlands) descended exclusively to children of a first marriage. The Spaniards replied that an empire was not landed estate, and repudiated Louis's demands, whereupon he found stronger arguments. In 1667, he conquered a number of towns in the disputed territory, and the following year his armies overran Franche-Comté. The European states regarded these martial parades with growing apprehension. England and Holland forgot a trade war which they had been waging shortly before, and joined with Sweden in a Triple Alliance against the warlike French king. Louis decided to make peace before a general conflict ensued, and agreed to restore Franche-Comté, but retained eleven towns in Flanders, including Lille, Tournai, and Charleroi (Treaty of Aix-la-Chapelle, 1668).

Dutch War (1672–78)

The sturdy Dutch boasted somewhat arrogantly that their promptness in forming the Triple Alliance had checked the Sun King in mid-career. Louis had no love for these "maggots" whom he disliked for their republican institutions and their Calvinist theology. Moreover, the Dutch had recently introduced retaliatory tariffs damaging to French trade. So Louis shrewdly prepared his revenge. Sweden was detached from the Triple Alliance by liberal bribes; English neutrality was purchased by pensioning the venal Charles II (Treaty of Dover, 1670). In June, 1672, without warning, Louis hurled his well-trained army against Holland. The Dutch opened the dikes and flooded the countryside to delay the invaders, and in their desperation they murdered their grand pensionary, John de Witt, whom they blamed unjustly for their predicament. The defense of the republic was then entrusted to William, youthful head of the house of Orange, who was thus initiated at twenty-two into his lifelong task of humbling Louis XIV.

Treaty of Nijmegen

Sympathy for the Dutch and fear for themselves soon drove other European states to oppose France. The Emperor Leopold and the Elector of Brandenburg came to the aid of Holland; Denmark, Spain, and finally England joined the alliance; and by 1678, Louis was ready to make peace. Although the French soldiers under Condé and Turenne had won brilliant successes against the allies and earned the title of Huns by the ferocity with which they had devastated the Palatinate, France was suffering from exhaustion. By the Treaty of Nijmegen (1678) Louis retained Franche-Comté and exchanged some frontier positions in Flanders to his advantage. He had taken another step toward the Rhine, once more at the expense of Spain; but the Dutch had escaped his vengeance, and even managed, in the final treaty, to extort from France a more favorable tariff for their goods.

The "gnawing peace"

Changing his tactics, Louis now strove to establish legal claims to the territories which he sought to conquer. He appointed special courts, or "chambers of reunion," to resurrect forgotten titles of sovereignty on the strength of which his armies would quietly occupy the disputed ground. In 1680, the cities of Metz, Toul, and Verdun were declared annexed to France; in 1681, the imperial city of Strasbourg was seized; and in 1683, it was the turn of Luxemburg. To resist the unscrupulous projects of the French king, Spain, the Holy Roman Empire, Holland, Sweden, and Bavaria united to form the League of Augsburg (1686), and when Louis attempted to seize the Rhenish Palatinate (1687), he precipitated a third war.

The opening of the war in 1689 was marked by an event which augured ill for France. In 1688, the English drove out

THE FRENCH IN HOLLAND

FRENCH DEVASTATION IN ITALY

The French earned the title of Huns in the seventeenth century because of their military ruthlessness in Italy, the Germanies, and the Netherlands.

James II (who had succeeded his brother Charles II in 1685) and welcomed William of Orange as their king. This "Glorious Revolution," which is related in the subsequent chapter, united the resources of Holland and England under a man who had proved himself the most patient, the most skilled, and the most implacable of Louis's opponents. England promptly joined the League of Augsburg, and the struggle which ensued showed that the preponderance of France was passing. The French navy, which Colbert had dreamed of making the strongest in the world, was outfought by the English and Dutch; the French army failed in the later years of the war to repeat its early successes. In the Peace of Ryswick (1697), Louis was compelled to restore almost all the territories adjudged him by the chambers of reunion except Strasbourg; to abandon Lorraine and his claim to the Palatinate; to recognize William of Orange as King of England; and to concede a favorable commercial treaty to the Dutch.

League of Augsburg

In 1700, the long-expected demise of Charles II of Spain brought to the fore the question of the Spanish succession. With death at his elbow, Charles had summoned strength to dictate a testament naming Philip of Anjou, grandson of Louis XIV, as his successor. The will was a triumph of French diplomacy, but Louis knew that his enemies would never permit such aggrandizement to befall the house of Bourbon without a struggle. Nevertheless, he accepted the bequest, and bade his grandson mount the throne at Madrid. As if he was determined to make war unavoidable, he then seized some border fortresses in the Spanish Netherlands, and proclaimed the exiled Stuart Pretender (the son of James II) King of England. As a result his adversaries organized a "Grand Alliance" against him, which by 1702 included Austria, England, Holland, and Brandenburg. Thus opened the War of the Spanish Succession, the last and most exhausting of the wars of Louis XIV.

Spanish Bourbons

William of Orange (William III of England after 1689), who had been the moving spirit in forming the Grand Alliance, died at the opening of the war (1702), but the English possessed an even more brilliant soldier in John Churchill, Duke of Marlborough (1650–1722), whose victories at Blenheim (1704), Ramilies (1706), Oudinarde (1708), and Malplaquet (1709) drove the French out of the Germanies and wrested the Netherlands from their control. In the south the French halo of invincibility was likewise stripped away by the inspired tactics of Prince Eugene of Savoy, for the duchy of Savoy, which guarded the passes into Italy, had also joined the Grand Alliance. The resulting exhaustion and misery of France forced the Grand Monarch to sue for peace in 1709, but, finding the allies' terms too severe, he appealed to the French and Spanish people to continue the fighting. In 1710, the Whigs, the war party in England, were overthrown, and England practically withdrew from the struggle. The next year a worse embarrassment confused the councils of the Grand Alliance. They had been planning to place the Archduke Charles of Austria on the Spanish throne after expelling the Bourbon, Philip V, but by 1711 a succession of unexpected deaths in the Hapsburg family made Charles heir to the Austrian and imperial thrones also. The English and Dutch were profoundly dissatisfied to think that they had fought a ten years' war in order to replace a Bourbon preponderance by a Hapsburg hegemony.

In the peace settlement France profited by the disagreement among her enemies. The treaties which concluded the War of the Spanish Succession were negotiated in 1713 and 1714 and are known collectively as the Peace of Utrecht. The terms of this settlement, which brought Europe thirty years of comparative peace, may be summarized as follows.

Peace of Utrecht

(1) Philip V was allowed to retain the Spanish throne on condition that the crowns of France and Spain were never to be united.

(2) In compensation the Austrian Hapsburgs received the Spanish (henceforth to be known as the Austrian) Netherlands, and Milan, Naples, and Sardinia.

(3) The Dutch were reinvested with the "bar-

rier fortresses" against France, and were granted a trade monopoly of the river Scheldt.

(4) The Elector of Brandenburg acquired Spanish Guelderland, and was permitted to assume the title of "King in Prussia."

(5) The Duke of Savoy was rewarded with the title of king and the addition of Sicily to his domains. (In 1720 he exchanged Sicily for Sardinia and styled himself King of Sardinia.)

(6) England was not interested in continental lands, though she kept Gibraltar and Minorca which she had wrested from Spain. Her prizes were the French colonies: Newfoundland, Acadia, and Hudson Bay, supplemented by such commercial privileges as a preferential tariff with Spain, the right to send one ship a year to the Spanish colonies to trade, and a monopoly of the lucrative traffic in slaves.

France was still a great nation, but her ascendancy no longer threatened Europe. War had exhausted the state and impoverished the people. Louis XIV outlived his most capable servants, outlived his son and his grandson, and almost, one might say, outlived himself. "My child," the dying monarch exhorted his great-grandson, five years of age, "you are going to be a great king. Do not imitate me in my taste for building, nor in my love of war. Strive, on the contrary, to live in peace with your neighbors. ... Make it your endeavor to ease the burden of the people, which I, unhappily, have not been able to do." The sentiment was excellent, but it shared the fatality that attends most good resolutions in that it came too late. And Louis XV was too young to profit by it.

Louis XIV dies (1715)

38

The Triumph of Parliamentary Government in England

In all cases where government subsists, the legislature is the supreme power.

JOHN LOCKE (1690).

WHILE LOUIS XIV was dazzling Europe with his brilliant and irresponsible display of power, across the Channel in England the cause of royal absolutism suffered a reverse. The English had never taken kindly to the rule of a despot, and the same years which saw the French monarchy reach its apogee witnessed in England the triumph of the Parliament over the king. By 1715, France and England had come to represent two divergent types of government. In France an absolute king, with the support of the privileged aristocracy, claimed the right to make the laws by the will of God; in England, a Parliament controlled by the ruling classes of the kingdom limited the royal prerogative and allowed the sovereign to make laws only "by and with the consent of the lords, spiritual and temporal, and the commons."

It is not easy to account for this divergence. One important factor to note, however, is that the French had found it necessary to concede arbitrary power to their kings as the best security against the invasion or disunion of their country, and the greatness of the monarchy had come to symbolize for patriotic Frenchmen the glory of France. The English kings, although they furthered the national growth, were never in the same degree essential to it, for the island kingdom was practically secure from invasion and possessed a geographic unity. Hence, while in France the right of maintaining a large army, of collecting and spending the revenue, and even of borrowing and repudiating debts, were left to the king's discretion, in England these privileges were gradually curtailed by a critical Parliament. When Charles I, misunderstanding the situation, attempted to rule like a despot, he precipitated a civil war and paid for his misconception with his head (1649).

Yet the English people were royalist at heart. A decade of kingless rule under the stern and militaristic Protector, Oliver Cromwell, left the nation weary of the Puritan Commonwealth. Cromwell's death in 1658 prepared the way for the restoration of the Stuart line, and in 1660, Charles II (son of Charles I) was acclaimed king "by the grace of God." At the same time he agreed to limit his power and promised to summon Parliament regularly, with the understanding that he was to levy no taxes and make no changes in religion without parliamentary approval. This was a reasonable compromise and might have proved a durable one if Charles, and his successor James, had been honest in keeping their part of the bargain.

Restoration of Charles II

1. CHARLES II: A DESPOT IN DISGUISE

Charles II (1660–85)

The general desire for harmony prevalent in 1660 assured the settlement a fair trial, but its perpetuation until after Charles's death in 1685 is a tribute to that monarch's duplicity. Though he played the rôle of a Protestant and constitutional ruler, Charles was a Catholic and absolutist in his secret convictions — if so shifty a character may be said to have had convictions. This witty, affable, indolent king was one of the most capable conspirators who ever held a throne. Confined in his prerogatives by a jealous and watchful Parliament, he plotted for twenty years by bribery, by adroit encroachments, even by treason, to win to absolute power, and he had reached the point of success when death cut short the fruition of his plans in his fifty-fifth year.

The haughty Louis XIV chose for his motto, *Nec pluribus impar* (not unequal to many, or a match for all), but Charles II followed the more cautious precept, *Divide et impera*. To "divide and rule" the various political factions until he could play one against another and make himself master of all was the cue to his patient policy. There were four major factions in England under the Restoration: (1) The Anglicans, who wished to see the Church of England the state church, and opposed the tolerance of dissenters; (2) the "squirearchy," country squires and gentry who had, many of them, opposed the despotism of James I and Charles I, but, finding the civil war and the Puritan Commonwealth even less to their liking, had welcomed the restoration of Charles II. These first two groups were closely identified. In addition there were: (3) the merchant and trading classes of the cities which desired to control Parliament in order to supervise taxation and direct foreign policy; and (4) the "dissenters," a term applied to members of various Puritan sects who were denied civil and military offices because they "dissented" from the teaching of the Anglican Church. Nor must the Roman Catholics be forgotten, of whom a minority still persisted in England despite persecution, while by far the greater number of the Irish people were of that faith.

For the first ten years of his reign Charles trod warily, for he found the "Cavalier" Parliament, elected in 1660, loyal but headstrong. This Parliament was dominated by the squirearchy and the supporters of Anglicanism, who promptly applied their power, the country gentlemen to obtain remission of the remaining feudal dues levied on their lands and the Anglicans to restore the Church of England to its full privileges and to punish dissent. All who were not Anglicans were barred from a share in municipal government (Corporation Act, 1661); two thousand Puritan clergy were expelled from the church for refusing assent to the prescribed Prayer Book (Act of Uniformity, 1662); and dissenters who persisted in attending noncomformist services were condemned to imprisonment or transportation (Conventicle Act, 1664). Charles himself had little patience with this persecution; his secret desire was to make not Anglicanism but Catholicism triumphant; but he bent for the time to the wishes of Parliament.

"Cavalier" Parliament

In 1665, the "Great Plague" carried off thousands of people in London, to be followed a year later by the "Great Fire" which destroyed half the city. To many a Puritan these disasters were signs of God's anger against a wicked and immoral king, for Charles set the example for a licentious court and was held responsible, as well, for the persecution which Parliament enforced against the dissenters. In 1667, a third misfortune occurred when a Dutch fleet sailed up the Thames to London and burned a number of English ships.

England had begun a second trade war with Holland in 1665 (the first was fought in 1651–54 under Cromwell). The scepter of commercial supremacy was passing from the Dutch to the English and London had become the great trade rival of Amsterdam. In his languid way Charles helped to promote this development. The Navigation Acts, limiting British colonial trade to British ships, were renewed, the navy improved, new possessions acquired (Tangiers and Bombay), and in 1664, New Amsterdam was captured from the Dutch and renamed New York.

English trade rises

Dissenters, persecuted at home, swelled the population of the colonies, while city traders and courtiers eager for profit organized companies, such as the Honorable Company of Gentlemen Adventurers Trading into Hudson's Bay (better known as the Hudson's Bay Company), which was chartered in 1670. As the various companies, encouraged by the English, French, Dutch, and other national governments, often held conflicting charters, the traders frequently descended to acts of war and piracy at the expense of their rivals. In this somewhat unscrupulous contest the English were destined to outstrip all competitors and secure the lion's share of the spoils. And the spoils were a world empire.

The extraordinary prosperity of the Dutch in the seventeenth century made England and Holland inevitable trade rivals, but the two peoples had also two strong sentiments in common: both were Protestant and both feared and hated France. It was therefore logical that the two maritime powers should draw closer together as the lengthening shadow of a French hegemony spread across Europe. How deeply the English people feared France and Catholicism, Charles II failed to comprehend. By the secret Treaty of Dover (1670) he promised to aid Louis XIV in the attack the latter contemplated against Holland, and agreed to restore the Catholic faith in England in return for a subsidy that would make him practically independent of parliamentary grants. Charles's first step was to issue a declaration of indulgence for dissenters including Catholics (1672). To his surprise there was an immediate protest, rumors of a Catholic plot began to spread, and Parliament insisted upon the withdrawal of the indulgence. Though the English were hoodwinked into joining in the war on Holland (1672), their conviction grew that in so doing they were furthering the sinister designs of Louis XIV and in 1674 they withdrew from the conflict.

Third Anglo-Dutch war

Fear of a popish plot, once roused, continued to terrify the nation. James, Duke of York, brother of Charles and heir to the throne, confessed himself a Catholic and became the hope of that party, but Charles, more astute, took refuge in hypocrisy. In 1678, an adventurer named Titus Oates announced his discovery of a conspiracy to murder Charles and set his brother in his place with the assistance of a French army. Conspiring of a sort there had undoubtedly been, though it is doubtful if Oates knew anything about it, but his perjured testimony sufficed in the frenzy of popular fear to send a score of innocent Catholics to death. And Charles, who "believed not one word of what was called Oates's plot," signed the warrants.

The popish plot (1678)

In the tension of feeling excited by the popish plot, political leaders ranged themselves more definitely in two opposing parties and the shadow of a second civil war hung over the land. Those who supported the king and the Anglican Church were nicknamed Tories,[1] while the faction which favored a constitutional monarchy under a Protestant king, with toleration for dissenters, came to be known as the Whig Party.[2] In the elections of 1679, the Whigs swept the country, ending the eighteen-year rule of the Cavalier Parliament. They promptly proposed an exclusion bill to bar James from the throne as a Catholic. Charles thereupon dissolved Parliament; but a second Whig Parliament was elected and passed the bill (1680), only to see it thrown out by the House of Lords. A third Parliament met at Oxford with the Whigs blustering and arming. "Like father, like son," they declared, and prepared to fight for their liberties in the spirit of 1642. But they overreached themselves; hatred of military rule was still strong in England and the country was not prepared to follow the Whigs into another civil war. If war was the only alternative to despotism, the nation preferred the genial despotism of Charles and respected him when he dissolved the unruly Oxford Parliament as soon as it assembled.

Exclusion Bill (1679)

[1] Defenders of the royal power and the authority of the Anglican bishops were called Tories by their opponents, the term being borrowed apparently from the Irish, who applied it to certain outlaws professedly royalist.

[2] The Whigs were Scottish Presbyterians who defied the royal power in defense of their religion. Hence the name was applied derisively to the party which desired to limit the royal prerogatives and tolerate dissenters in England.

CHARLES II OF ENGLAND (1630–1685)

This Stuart monarch was indolent and sensual, but he had affable manners and a shrewd mind. The suit of armor was painted in for effect, and the long hair was considered elegant and aristocratic in the seventeenth century.

SIR ISAAC NEWTON (1642–1727)

Newton's "Mathematical Principles of Natural Philosophy" was the outstanding scientific treatise of the century.

ROBERT BOYLE (1627–1691)

The enunciation of "Boyle's Law" on the expansion of gases was a fundamental contribution to physics and chemistry.

WILLIAM HARVEY (1578–1657)

Left: By his discovery of the circulation of the blood, Harvey opened a new chapter in the study of anatomy.

JOHN LOCKE (1632–1704)

Right: Locke provided a philosophical justification for the Glorious Revolution of 1688, and thus for later revolutions in America and France.

FAMOUS ENGLISHMEN OF THE SEVENTEENTH CENTURY

The only point the Whigs had won in their campaign to limit the king's power was their passage of the Habeas Corpus Act (1679), which provided that no subject accused of crime was to be held at the king's pleasure, but must be brought before a judge within a specified time and the charge against him indicated.

After 1681, Charles felt strong enough to rule alone and refused to summon another Parliament. Left in this way without any constitutional means of resistance, some of the more desperate Whigs plotted to assassinate Charles and James and set the Duke of Monmouth, an illegitimate son of Charles, on the throne. The discovery of this Rye House Plot (1683) led to the execution or exile of the principal Whig leaders. With the opponents of the crown thus discredited, Charles was secure in his despotism and the Tories helped him to stifle self-government in the towns and suppress free speech. A subsidy from Louis XIV permitted him to meet expenses and increase his army. But the plan to re-establish Catholicism he dropped from his program: that was the price he had to pay for Tory support and Charles was too shrewd to miscalculate the temper of the nation a second time. After twenty years of trimming, he had found a way to rule without Parliament and without serious opposition from the country, but death cut short his triumph in 1685.

Charles rules alone

2. JAMES II: A DESPOT IN DIFFICULTIES

When James II (1685–88) ascended the English throne, he had many circumstances in his favor. Although he was known to be a Catholic, it was supposed that he would make his faith a private matter and confirm the privileges of the Anglican Church. In return for such protection, the churchmen were prepared to teach the doctrine of non-resistance, i.e., that it was wicked and blasphemous to resist the king, because he was ordained of God. So long as James was careful to retain the support of the Tory Party (the Anglican clergy and the country squires), his throne was reasonably safe; for many Whigs hesitated to oppose the legitimate king; others wanted the Duke of Monmouth in his place; while still others favored William of Orange, Stadholder of the Dutch Republic, who had married James's daughter Mary. Divided in this fashion, the Whig Party was powerless to prevent the coronation of James.

Nevertheless, in June, 1685, simultaneous revolts were organized in England and Scotland by followers of the Duke of Monmouth, Charles's illegitimate son. Both failed and were followed by the famous "Bloody Assizes" under Judge Jeffreys, in which over a thousand suspected persons were condemned to death or transportation. James rewarded Jeffreys's zeal with the lord chancellorship, and sent Monmouth, who had been taken prisoner, to the block. Nothing could have been better calculated to strengthen the cause of the opposition faction; the bloody reprisals disgusted many people, while the death of Monmouth left the Whig malcontents no choice but to unite in support of William and Mary. At the same time the Revocation of the Edict of Nantes sent thousands of French Huguenots to England, where the vivid tale of their sufferings filled Englishmen with alarm and sympathy.

Monmouth's rebellion

As if determined to alienate every element in the nation, James proposed to maintain a permanent standing army, to repeal the Test Act which barred Roman Catholics from office, and the Act of Habeas Corpus also. When the Parliament which he had summoned protested, he prorogued it (November, 1685). Catholics were admitted to the privy council, granted commissions in the army, and even appointed to high office in the Anglican Church and the universities. In 1687, James issued a declaration of indulgence offering all his subjects the free exercise of their religion. The High Church Tories, even those who had preached that it was wrong under any circumstances to resist the lawful sovereign, found that these proceedings overstrained their loyalty, and James thus alienated many who, aside from the religious issue, were his stanchest partisans. Nor were the dissenters grateful to him for the indulgence as he had hoped; in England and Scotland nonconformists joined in denouncing an act which granted freedom of worship to Catholics. Still blind to consequences, James persisted in uniting the realm against him. A second declaration of indulgence was issued in 1688, and when seven bishops of the Anglican Church ventured to draw up a petition against it, James had them tried for libel and sedition. All England waited anxiously for the decision, and the news that the jury had voted for acquittal was the signal for wild rejoicing. It was ominous for James that even the royal army, which he had assembled near London to keep his capital in awe, cheered the verdict.

In the same month (June, 1688) a son was born to James and the news crystallized the discontent into active opposition. Many had been prepared to endure James's misrule, because he was over fifty and would be succeeded on his death by his Protestant daughter Mary. The birth of a son who would be raised in the Catholic faith ended this hope, and political leaders from both the Whig and Tory Parties dispatched a secret invitation to William of Orange to come and take the throne. William's life purpose was to defend Holland against the attack of Louis XIV; as King of England he might be able to combine the forces of both countries against France, and this argument persuaded him to accept the challenge. It was a dangerous stroke; the odds appeared to be all against success; but he displayed prudence and decision. At the news that William had landed (November 5, 1688), the English turned to him as a deliverer and James found himself deserted. William purposely allowed him to escape to France, for he had no wish to make his father-in-law a prisoner.

3. THE GLORIOUS REVOLUTION OF 1688

James's flight enabled a Convention Parliament, which met promptly, to offer the throne to William and Mary on the pretext that "King James ... having violated the fundamental laws, and having withdrawn himself out of the Kingdom, had abdicated ..." But the English had no intention of giving themselves into the power of a new despot; Parliament had learned at last not to put too much trust in princes and drew up a settlement which was enacted into law as the Bill of Rights. It provided: (1) That the sovereign had no power to suspend or dispense with the laws, to erect special courts of justice, maintain a standing army, or levy taxes without the consent of Parliament. (2) That Parliament should meet frequently, the members to be freely elected and allowed freedom in their debates. (3) That subjects were entitled to petition the monarch without fear of prosecution, that those charged with crimes could not be refused jury trial, nor could they be exposed to cruel or unusual punishments.

Bill of Rights (1689)

The religious settlement was embodied in the Toleration Act (1689), which granted freedom of worship to all except Catholics and Unitarians. This act did not establish religious equality; the Anglican Church remained the privileged state church, and the Test and Corporation Acts still barred dissenters and Catholics from civil and military office. Nevertheless, a long stride had been made toward genuine toleration, for after 1689 the government ceased to persecute, imprison, or transport people on religious grounds and the mobs lost their zest for Jesuit-hunting.

Unfortunately, this statesmanlike moderation was not applied to Ireland. Cromwell, it may be recalled, attempted to keep the Irish in subjection by dividing the land among Protestant proprietors, thus reducing the native Catholic Irish to a position of social and economic bondage. The plan failed because the English settlers were too unpopular and too few in number. James II determined to restore the Catholics to power and his overthrow grieved his Irish subjects as deeply as it delighted the English. In 1689, an uprising of the Irish broke the Protestant yoke, and in 1690, James came over from France to lead the rebellion and if possible to invade England with a French and Irish force. William III realized that his newly won throne was in danger. The French fleet, having defeated the English and Dutch at the battle of Beachy Head (June, 1690), was free to land an army on the English coast itself. To control Ireland and restore James II were to Louis XIV but preliminary moves in his vast struggle for the hegemony of Europe. The success or failure of an Irish revolt was thus transformed into a matter of European significance, and when William defeated James at the battle of the Boyne (July 1, 1690), it meant that Louis XIV had lost the first round in the War of the League of Augsburg which was just opening.

For the Irish the battle of the Boyne spelled further subordination and exploitation at the hands of their stronger neighbors. Irish commerce was regulated and sometimes ruined for the advantage of English trade, while all but a minority of the inhabitants of the unhappy isle were shut out from a share in their own government because they were Catholics. This determination to hold the native Irish in subjection was founded in the fear that Ireland might otherwise join any European power that attacked England, a danger that invariably warped the Englishman's mind when he considered the Irish question. This sacrifice of justice to expediency sowed a bitter heritage of discord between the two countries and the Irish never forgot or forgave their centuries of tutelage and subjection.

The Irish problem

4. ENGLAND AND SCOTLAND BECOME GREAT BRITAIN

Between England and Scotland a happier settlement was achieved. Following the "Glorious Revolution" those Scottish clans still favorable to James were offered a chance to make peaceful submission and swear allegiance to William, although one which was dilatory in complying was given over to cold-blooded slaughter as an example — an infamous episode known as the "Massacre of Glencoe." The tie which united England and Scotland was in reality a frail one; an accident had made James VI of Scotland James I of England (1603), but each state retained its separate parliament and its peculiar laws. When William and Mary replaced James II, the dynastic tie was weakened and it appeared more than probable that the nations would drift apart. The Scots, who numbered less than a million, were distrustful and envious of their southern neighbors who had five times the population and a world-embracing trade, but the English, who dreaded lest Scotland desert to the side of France, were prepared to offer generous terms, to achieve a "more perfect union." Under William's successor, Anne, this end was attained by the Act of Union (1707), which provided that the two kingdoms were to be known as Great Britain, the Scots sending forty-five representatives to the English House of Commons and sixteen to the House of Lords. Presbyterianism was recognized as the established faith in Scotland.

The Act of Union, like most of the developments in English politics during these years, was an indirect response to the French threat. During twenty of the first twenty-five years that followed the expulsion of James, England was fighting Louis XIV, in the War of the League of Augsburg (1689–97) and the War of the Spanish Succession (1701–13). Throughout this period James II (and after his death in 1701, his son who took the title James III) threatened to invade England and regain the throne with the aid of a French army. A Stuart restoration thus became inseparable from the idea of national humiliation and defeat, a consummation few Englishmen were prepared to applaud. It is a fact not without irony that, by aiding the Stuarts, Louis XIV, the supreme absolutist of the Continent, did more than any other single individual to assure the triumph of Parliament in England.

Act of Union (1707)

The political leaders who had invited William and Mary to take the throne, in order "to save the liberties and the religion of England," felt it best to safeguard the revolutionary gains won through this act of usurpation by regulating the succession. It was provided that if William and Mary died childless, the throne should pass to Mary's sister Anne and her descendants. Unfortunately, Anne's children died young, and the fear that her own death would leave the crown to the Pretender moved Parliament to decree as her successor her nearest Protestant relative, the Electress Sophia of Hanover.[1] By this Act of Settlement, Parlia-

Act of Settlement (1701)

---

[1] See the Genealogical Table of English Rulers in the Appendix.

GREENWICH OBSERVATORY

Above: In 1675 Charles II granted £500 toward this observatory, which became the official point through which 0° longitude was reckoned. The observation made here helped Sir Isaac Newton to verify his famous laws.

THE ROYAL SOCIETY (1662)

Right: As patron of the Royal Society of London for Improving Natural Knowledge, Charles II is flanked by Francis Bacon (right) and Lord Bruncker, first president of the new society.

ment once again arrogated to itself the right to select the sovereign and to define the conditions under which he must rule. In an age of legitimacy, such an act appeared to many, even in England, an illegal and revolutionary decision. The Pretender had his partisans, and the whole revolutionary settlement still hung on the question whether, on Anne's death, the Tories would proclaim the Pretender as James III or the Whigs would bring in the Hanoverian line. In the outcome, despite Jacobite [1] plots, Whig principles triumphed. On Anne's sudden death (1714), George, son of the Electress Sophia, was proclaimed King of Great Britain and Ireland. A rising in Scotland in 1715 in favor of the Stuart Pretender was put down and the rule of Parliament assured under the king that Parliament had chosen.

5. SIGNIFICANCE OF THE SEVENTEENTH CENTURY IN ENGLISH HISTORY

In the century which ended in 1715 the English people had overturned, re-established, and remodeled their monarchy until they had reduced it to a pattern which satis-

[1] Those who favored the Pretender were called Jacobites from the Latin word for James, *Jacobus*.

fied them. In the same period they had fought strenuously on land and sea, laying the foundations of a colonial empire and commercial supremacy. It is not always easy for a student who follows the crowded events of these years to distinguish the main lines of development, so it may be helpful to pause at the date 1715 and decide what were the really significant and durable achievements of the seventeenth century in English history.

In politics the nation had succeeded after two revolutions in reducing the royal power within clearly stipulated limits. The sovereign had become dependent upon Parliament for his revenue, he could not raise an army without parliamentary approval, nor could he any longer deprive a subject of his liberty or property at pleasure, for the laws guaranteed anyone accused of crime a fair and public trial before a jury of his fellow citizens (Habeas Corpus Act, 1679; Bill of Rights, 1689). Citizens were no longer to be persecuted for their religious beliefs (Toleration Act, 1689); but the Bill of Rights provided that no one who was a Roman Catholic or married to a Roman Catholic might occupy

Political achievements

the English throne, and Parliament asserted this principle by excluding the legitimate Stuart claimants and choosing the Hanoverian line to succeed Anne (Act of Succession, 1701). When George I ascended the English throne in 1714, he became king by the will of Parliament, and he knew it; English sovereigns thenceforth were to *reign* but not to *govern,* and the rule of Parliament was assured. In analysis, this meant the rule of the nobles, the country gentry, and the merchant classes, for these were the groups which dominated Parliament. Under William and Anne it became the custom for the sovereign to select Whig or Tory leaders to compose the royal council, according to which party held a majority in the Commons, and the council thus chosen exercised the executive power in the king's name, but in response to the wishes and subject to the approval of Parliament.

The seventeenth century was also for England an age of swift economic development. New companies were chartered, new colonies seized or founded almost yearly. For the aid which the English rendered in checking the power of Louis XIV, they received a generous reward. The Peace of Utrecht transferred Acadia, Newfoundland, and the Hudson Bay region to English rule, as well as Gibraltar and Minorca. Great Britain was rapidly becoming the foremost mercantile and colonial power in the world, which helps to explain why the country was able to establish a dozen settlements in America, to challenge the maritime supremacy of the Dutch, and finally to endure the enormous burden of the struggle against Louis XIV, without serious privation, while France, a nation with more than three times the population of England, was reduced to the verge of bankruptcy.

Commercial expansion

Part of the explanation for the English victories must be sought in the financial expedients to which the government resorted to meet the cost of the wars with France. The annual revenue proving insufficient to cover the expenditures of the war years, borrowing was found to be the best solution, with the result that the national debt rose by 1715 to the hitherto unimagined sum of £50,000,000. As an aid, the Bank of England was founded in 1694, and invested with banking privileges in return for the loans it advanced to the government. At first sight this extensive borrowing might appear reckless and improvident, but it had certain advantages. Without it the nation could not have prosecuted the war to a successful conclusion and reaped the rewards of victory. A precedent was established and a credit structure developed which was to serve the government needs admirably in later wars; England's financial strength has often proved the mainstay of her allies. Moreover, the thousands of people with capital to spare who invested it in government bonds did so with the confidence that Parliament (which the moneyed class largely controlled) would see to it that principal and interest were repaid. Only defeat or a Stuart restoration could endanger the national debt, so these creditors had a powerful motive for supporting the existing régime. When a responsible Parliament backed a bond, it meant more than the word of an absolute king. The English government was able to borrow all the funds it required at six and seven per cent, while Louis XIV found it difficult to obtain loans even when he offered fifteen to twenty per cent. As observers began to contrast the success and prosperity of Great Britain with the losses and impoverishment of France, they grew less confident that absolutism was really the ideal form of government. In the eighteenth century, as we shall discover later, Frenchmen conceived a profound admiration for the system of government which the English had established. Their desire to reshape their own absolute monarchy until it resembled the English model was one of the causes which brought about the great French Revolution that broke out in 1789.

Financial solidarity

In literary achievement the close of the seventeenth century fell short of its opening years — "the spacious times of great Elizabeth." The political and religious controversies which absorbed the energies of the nation colored the work of even the greatest writers. John Milton (1608–74), who had given his best years and worn out his sight in the

Literature and art

JOHN CHURCHILL, DUKE OF MARLBOROUGH

Above: Marlborough commanded the English and Dutch armies in the War of the Spanish Succession.

THE OLD EAST INDIA HOUSE

Right: By the end of the seventeenth century the English were headed for commercial supremacy, and the East India Company was an instrument of empire.

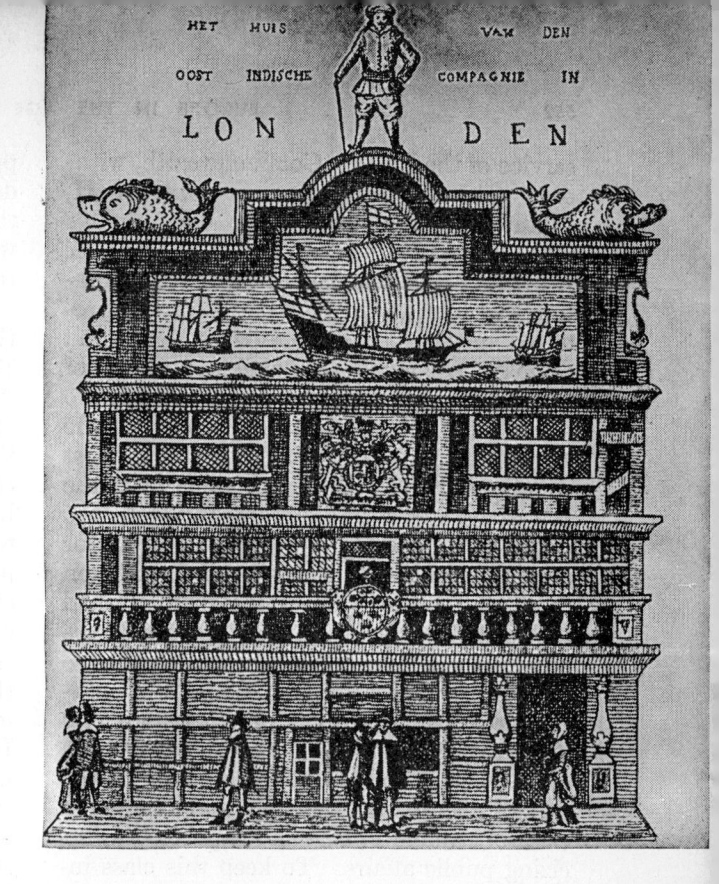

GIBRALTAR

The English and Dutch captured Gibraltar from Spain in 1704. This view, dated 1727, shows the less familiar back view of "The Rock."

service of the Puritan Commonwealth, withdrew at the restoration of Charles II, "blind, old, and lonely," to compose his majestic epics *Paradise Lost* and *Paradise Regained*. The poet laureate of the Restoration was John Dryden (1631–1700), who produced a number of poems, satires, and dramas to amuse the dissolute court of Charles II, at which it became the fashion to ridicule the sober habits and bigotry of the Puritans. Despite this mockery, the most widely read work of the age came from the pen of a Puritan tinker, John Bunyan, who wrote his *Pilgrim's Progress* while in jail for preaching without leave. The common sense and moderation which distinguished the civil and religious settlement of 1689 are admirably represented in the writings of the philosopher John Locke (1632–1704), particularly his *Letter on Toleration* and *Two Treatises of Government*. The controversies of the seventeenth century stimulated the rise of pamphlet literature and created a class of readers in England capable of criticizing public affairs. To keep this class informed was the task of the journalists, who consequently demanded "freedom of the press," and finally won it in principle after 1694. Pamphlets and periodicals multiplied, and by the reign of Anne they had attained a vast influence and a high standard of literary excellence, a development not surprising when it is remembered that the sardonic humor of Jonathan Swift (1667–1745), the author of *Gulliver's Travels*, as well as the wit of Joseph Addison (1672–1719), borrowed this means of expression.

In architecture the outstanding figure of the period was Christopher Wren (1632–1723), to whom the Great Fire of London in 1666 proved a generous patron, for it brought him innumerable commissions. He is credited with designing over fifty churches, including Saint Paul's Cathedral, where he is buried beneath the inscription, *Si monumentum requiris, circumspice* — "If you seek [my] monument, look about you." The arts of painting and music throve but meagerly under the Restoration, for Charles as a patron had little taste or discrimination, while the Puritan spirit which still animated the middle and lower classes was inimical to art. In England the true intellectual greatness of the late seventeenth century must be sought among those minds devoted to science and mathematics. The development of modern science, however, is not a national but an international movement. The achievements of such men as Sir Isaac Newton will be discussed in a later chapter on "The Intellectual Revolution," where they can be more conveniently linked up with the contributions of Newton's illustrious contemporaries in other lands.

39

The Declining Empire of the Hapsburgs

> The dear old Holy Roman Realm,
> How does it hold together ...
>
> GOETHE, *FAUST*, PART I, SCENE V.

AS ALREADY EXPLAINED, the aggrandizement of France in the seventeenth century involved a corresponding decline in the fortunes of the Hapsburg dynasty. Part of Flanders, of Lorraine, and the whole of Franche-Comté were seized by Louis XIV; and after 1700, Spain, under a Bourbon prince, became the constant ally of France, the two powers being bound together by a common hostility toward Austria and toward England. The title of Holy Roman Emperor, though still retained by the head of the Austrian Hapsburgs, had become an illusory honor, for the empire was little more than an historical fiction kept alive by the force of tradition. These vicissitudes in the fortunes of a once dominant dynasty have already been described in part. The present chapter will trace the history of the Hapsburg dominions in greater detail through the years 1660 to 1715, and relate at the same time the contemporary developments in Italy and eastern Europe.

1. THE AUSTRIAN HAPSBURGS

The Emperor Leopold I (1658–1705), whose long reign filled the greater part of the period under discussion, was a timid and irresolute man, no match in either war or diplomacy for his aggressive cousin Louis XIV. As Archduke of Austria, and King of Bohemia and of Hungary, Leopold was hereditary ruler of dominions which, had they been better organized, would have constituted a powerful state of some nine or ten million people. In addition, he enjoyed the elective title of Holy Roman Emperor, which meant that he was the nominal ruler of the twenty-five million people living within the boundaries of the empire.[1] In this rôle he symbolized the unity of Germany, and the Hapsburgs might, under happier circumstances, have transformed the empire into a national German state, the most populous and powerful in Europe. But two persistent forces frustrated this project, although it was a consummation toward which many patriotic German hearts secretly aspired. The first obstacle was the jealous particularism of the German princes (especially the rulers of Brandenburg-Prussia), who clung to their semi-independent status and would not sacrifice it to consolidate German-speaking peoples into one political whole. The second obstacle was the jealousy of France. It was a cardinal principle of French foreign policy to promote German disunity lest France be endangered by the formation of a powerful neighbor across the Rhine. In prosecuting this policy, France often allied herself with Prussia and other recalcitrant German states.

The machinery of government whereby the emperor sought to impose his will upon his federal empire had been out of joint since the Protestant Reformation. The imperial court (*Reichskammergericht*), to which the

[1] See the map of "Europe after 1648."

princes sent representatives, had grown insolent and unmanageable; the imperial council (*Reichshofrath*), appointed by the emperor himself, was more tractable, but its decrees were often evaded or disregarded. Concerning all important matters which related to the empire as a whole, it had become the custom to consult the Diet, a sort of parliament composed chiefly of the leading German princes and representatives from the free towns. But in this assembly likewise the princes held the real power and (fearing that they might give themselves a strong master) they never voted the emperor the quota of men and money which he demanded. Their contributions for the defense of the empire were so niggardly that the imperial army often took the field with less than one fourth of its nominal strength. Not even the emergency created by the Turkish advance up the Danube could subdue the selfishness of the princes, and Leopold was obliged in 1663 to accept the aid of thirty thousand men in French pay to repel the invaders; while in 1683 he had John Sobieski and his Poles to thank that Vienna was saved from capture. The lack of support offered by the princes can be explained in part by the fact that many of them were Protestant and saw no advantage in strengthening a Catholic emperor, who might, if he gained the power, suppress the Protestant faith as an earlier emperor had essayed to do in the Thirty Years' War.

Not even in his hereditary domains could Leopold exercise the control of an absolute monarch. The provinces most securely in his power were Styria, Carinthia, Carniola, the archduchy of Austria, and the county of Tyrol. In Bohemia he ruled as king, with the assistance of a Diet, while in Hungary (nine tenths of which was held by the Turks in 1660) he found it expedient to confirm the ancient liberties of the nobles. Ineradicable barriers of language, of custom, and of topography contributed to the disunity of the Hapsburg lands. The disruptive forces of feudalism had survived too long, the havoc of the religious conflict had left wounds too deep, the lure of imperial pretensions had distracted the emperors too persistently from the task of consolidating their local domains, until the opportunity of building up a national state escaped them. Certainly the problem of unifying these mosaic possessions defied the mediocre talents of Leopold I. He clung inertly to his throne through the vicissitudes of the late seventeenth century, and, if the closing years of his reign witnessed a revival in Hapsburg prestige, the credit for this must be given to Austria's allies for their aid, and to her enemies for their blunders, rather than to any vigorous activity within the Austrian lands.

2. THE TURKISH MENACE

From the fourteenth century to the seventeenth, the Danube Valley was a vast battlefield where it seemed as if the resistance of the Christian inhabitants was destined to be slowly crushed by the power of the Turkish invaders. The western European nations, preoccupied with their own politics, remained comparatively indifferent to this threat from the East. Had the Turks possessed the ability to *govern* as well as the ability to *conquer*, half of Europe might have been theirs for the taking, and the future of the European peoples profoundly altered, but fortunately for the Christian states the Mohammedan Empire was a prey to internal ills which frequently paralyzed its armies in the hour of victory.

The chief limitation from which the Turks suffered was an inability to assimilate and organize their conquests. They remained always an alien military caste in Europe, living on the tribute they extorted from the conquered in the form of money, recruiting their armies from the tribute they extorted in men: for it was their custom to conscript boy children whom they raised as Mohammedans and trained for military service. Knowing better how to destroy than how to create, they left matters of trade and details of local administration to their subject peoples. At its core their government was an oriental despotism in which the reign of a strong sultan was usually characterized by pitiless autocracy, the reign of a weak one by harem intrigue and military anarchy. Such a system

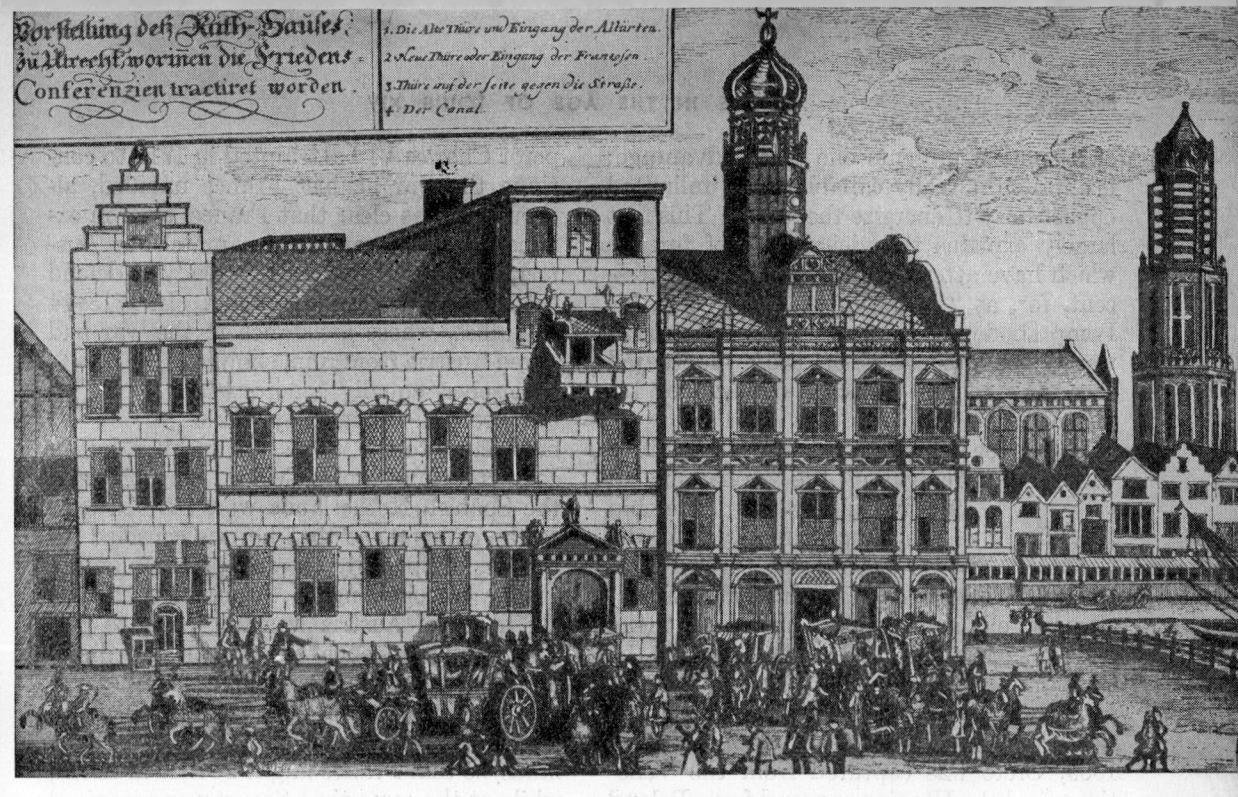

THE BUILDING AT UTRECHT WHERE THE TREATY WAS SIGNED

The peace concluded at Utrecht in 1713 ended the rule of the Hapsburg line in Spain and raised Brandenburg and Savoy to the rank of kingdoms.

THE GREAT ELECTOR

Frederick William, Elector of Brandenburg from 1640 to 1688, consolidated his realms and made Berlin rival Vienna as a center of influence in the Germanies. His successor took the title Frederick William I, King in Prussia, after 1713.

of despotism presents one great advantage: it affords the really capable ruler unlimited opportunity to energize the state. This fact largely explains the vicissitudes of fortune which have attended the march of the crescent, for, as "Sultan after Sultan with his Pomp abode his Hour or two and went his way," the prosperity of Islam fluctuated according to his capacity or that of his vizier.

The latter half of the seventeenth century witnessed a revival of the Mohammedan offensive under the leadership of the Kiuprili family. As the power behind the throne, Mohammed Kiuprili (and later his son Achmed) stamped out anarchy and united all "true believers" in a war to the death against the Christians. An attack on Hungary was repulsed at Saint Gothard (1663) by an imperial army aided by French troops; but in 1669, Crete was captured from the Venetians, and the Ukraine annexed from Poland in 1676. To crown these successes by a blow that would astonish Christendom, the grand vizier planned an irresistible drive against Vienna. With an army of one hundred and fifty thousand, he reached the walls of that city in 1683, but the arrival of John Sobieski with reinforcements led to the overwhelming defeat of the besiegers, and the Turkish tide ebbed as swiftly as it had risen. When peace was re-established between the emperor and the sultan by the Treaty of Carlowitz (1699), the Hapsburgs had recovered the greater part of the fertile Hungarian plain, and the suzerainty over Transylvania.[1] Corruption and anarchy had begun once more to devitalize the Mohammedan Empire and it settled into a slow decline. The crescent had made its last conquests from the cross.

Turk drive (1655–83)

In a second conflict — the dynastic duel with the Bourbons — the emperor was fortunate in finding powerful allies. Marlborough and Prince Eugene saved Vienna from the French in 1704 as Sobieski had saved it from the Turks in 1683. But, although the allies were victorious over France in the War of the Spanish Succession, the Hapsburgs lost the Spanish throne. Reluctant to acknowledge this reverse, the Emperor Charles VI [1] attempted in 1712 to continue the war against France unaided, although it was clear that France, even in exhaustion, was more than a match for Austria, and the Spaniards were ready to defend their Bourbon king devotedly. In 1713–14 the allies, whose assistance in the war had saved Austria from ruin, showed themselves equally generous in the peace.[2] Spain they could not restore to the house of Hapsburg, but in compensation Naples, Milan, Sardinia, and the Spanish Netherlands were handed over to the emperor, so that he was consoled for the loss of Spain by a practical hegemony in Italy. Recognizing at the same time that the house of Austria was too feeble to prevent further French aggression, the diplomats provided that the Dutch should garrison certain "barrier fortresses" in what were to be thenceforth the Austrian Netherlands, so that France might be held in check, while at the same time Savoy was organized as a buffer state between Bourbon and Hapsburg frontiers in the south.[3]

Peace of Utrecht

The house of Austria thus emerged, after the most critical half-century in its history, victorious over the Ottoman Turks, with extensive gains in Hungary, and suzerainty over half of Italy. Of his imperial pretensions little was left to the emperor beyond the shadow of a great name, the Holy Roman Empire having ceased, in Voltaire's famous phrase, to be either holy or Roman or an empire; but in compensation he found himself the personal ruler of some twenty million people dwelling in a federation of rich and lovely provinces which possessed almost every blessing save that of national unity. For two hundred years the Hapsburg monarchs were to dedicate themselves to the heroic task of preserving this mosaic "Empire on the Danube" from the dissolution to which it was predestined.

3. SPAIN IN DECLINE

In the sixteenth century, under Charles V

---

[1] See map, "Europe in 1789," opposite page 629.

[1] Leopold I died in 1705 and was followed by Joseph I, whose death in 1711 brought to the Austrian throne the Archduke Charles, Hapsburg claimant to the Spanish throne also.

[2] The treaties of Utrecht, Rastadt, and Baden are styled collectively the Peace of Utrecht.

[3] See map, "Europe in 1789," in Chapter 46.

GOTTFRIED WILHELM LEIBNITZ (1646–1716)

LEIBNITZ'S CALCULATING MACHINE

Leibnitz was the greatest German mathematician and philosopher of the seventeenth century. He strove to compose a mathematical language, and designed the calculating machine at the right.

CHRISTIAN HUYGENS (1629–1695)

Huygens invented the pendulum clock and so improved the telescope that he saw the moons of Jupiter and the rings of Saturn.

ANTONY VAN LEEUWENHOEK (1632–1723)

Van Leeuwenhoek developed microscopes that would magnify 270 times and was the first to see red blood cells and bacteria.

SCIENTISTS OF THE SEVENTEENTH CENTURY

and Philip II, Spain had played the dominant rôle in European politics, but before the end of the seventeenth century, the Spaniards had seen this ascendancy transferred to France, while their own country sank to the position of a second-rate power. After 1700, the reforms of the Bourbon kings induced a slight revival, but the Spanish nation did not recover the energy, the prestige, or the intellectual vigor which distinguished it in the age of gold. The explanation for this decadence appears to lie in the character of the Spanish people and in the unsound economic principles which the monarchy enforced to the detriment of Spanish trade.

For many of the ills afflicting Spain the misguided policy of the government may be held responsible. In 1609, His Most Catholic Majesty, Philip III (1598–1621), ordered the Moriscos (descendants of Christianized Moors) expelled from the country, a measure which strengthened the religious solidarity of the realm, but crippled many trades and handicrafts in which the Moors had specialized. Trade was further hampered by the *alcabala*, a tax of ten per cent on all sales, by the debasement of the coinage, and by the monopolies and restrictions enforced by the unenlightened sovereigns. By the reign of Charles II (1665–1700), all manufacture save that of a few necessities had come to an end; beggars multiplied and privation increased, until many, even of Spain's half-million nobles, were reduced to a degree of poverty the more tragic because their pride forbade them to confess it. Charles II, or Charles the Sufferer as he was named out of pity for his numerous ailments, the heritage of that inbreeding too long pursued by the Hapsburg clan, was the tragic symbol of a monarchy and a nation which appeared to have reached the nadir of exhaustion. Rapacious neighbors waited impatiently for Charles's death as a signal to partition imperial Spain and confiscate its possessions, while within the kingdom misery increased, trade and population continued to decline, and the credit of the state foundered in a sea of bankruptcy.

Economic decline

The decline in agriculture was no less serious. Too much property was owned by absentee landlords whose agents neglected it. Large areas which might have been rendered productive were used as pasture for sheep-raising, an occupation which attracted the indolent class of Spaniards and helped by its promise of easy profits to discourage the virtues of industry, thrift, and foresight required for successful farming. The agricultural districts were gradually deserted and the fields abandoned. The population of Spain declined steadily throughout the seventeenth century, for the colonies lured the most venturesome spirits in each generation, while the ten thousand convents and monasteries withdrew the most devout from the stream of national life. The result of this double depletion is clearly to be traced in the progressive deterioration of the Spanish character, a consequence more fatal in its ultimate effects than the twenty per cent loss in population.

Decrease in population

The most un-European of European peoples, the Spaniards clung tenaciously to their peculiar customs and revealed slight susceptibility to foreign influences. Little affected by the Renaissance, and still less by the Protestant Reformation, they kept a distinctive culture which in the sixteenth and early seventeenth centuries was imitated by other nations because of Spain's commanding position as a colonial and military power. This golden age of Spanish civilization was the prelude to a swift decline. Art degenerated, literature grew pompous and empty, the universities became strongholds of medieval theology, and the Spanish Inquisition discouraged free speculation and scientific inquiry. The great Spanish novelist Cervantes (1547–1616), writing at the opening of the seventeenth century, created in Don Quixote a character which exemplified many of the virtues and vices of his countrymen. Brave, loyal, and courteous, Don Quixote was also stubborn, superstitious, and impractical, and failed lamentably in the daily business of life because his fancy was encumbered with the lingering figments of fairy tales, feudal lore, and medieval superstitions. Like him, many Spaniards preferred

Intellectual decline

to live amid the ghosts of the past rather than grapple with the commercial and industrial problems of an age that had forsaken medievalism and chivalry. Bound by the dictates of a religious zeal corrupted by mysticism and materialism, they clung complacently to outmoded methods, and fortified themselves against the impact of newer forces or the winds of agnostic speculation.

The death of Charles II in 1700 and the accession of Philip V, followed by the European struggle over the Spanish succession, stirred the Spaniards rudely and awakened them to a show of resistance. The Portuguese, allied with the English,[1] invaded the western provinces, while to the east Catalonia was occupied and Madrid captured (1706). Spanish pride resented the attempt of the allies to force the Archduke Charles upon the nation. In the outcome Philip V remained, and his reign (1700–46) witnessed the introduction of some moderate reforms. The government of Spain and the colonies was better centralized, local laws and special statutes were abolished in favor of a national code, while trade restrictions were broken down somewhat by the *Asiento* Treaty (1713), which yielded a share in Spanish colonial trade to the English. Throughout the eighteenth century, Spain was to exhibit a slow but measurable progress.

4. THE ITALIAN STATES

Italy, the "Mother of arts, as once of arms," had, like Spain, subsided in the seventeenth century into a state of decadence. It seemed as if the initiative and fecundity of the great Renaissance masters had exhausted the race, for the gifted Italian people had declined by 1700 from a position of leadership in the arts and sciences to a condition of intellectual apathy and political impotence. Three causes influenced this decline: (1) the languishing trade of the Mediterranean ports which suffered when the discovery of the New World turned European commerce into the Atlantic sea lanes; (2) the Counter (or Catholic) Reformation, which consolidated the power of the Roman Catholic Church in Italy, producing an atmosphere less friendly to the license and paganism which had marked the Renaissance age; (3) the conflict in Italy of French, Austrian, and Spanish forces, each seeking to dominate the peninsula and transform the Italian states into pawns to be controlled by diplomats sitting in Madrid or Paris or Vienna. This third factor was the most evil in its effects, for it reduced Italy to a battleground to be ravaged by contending armies, reduced many Italian states to subject provinces that were "robbed rather than governed" by their alien masters, and condemned the Italian people to play an insignificant rôle, not only in the period 1660 to 1715, but throughout the eighteenth and a large part of the nineteenth century.

From the Treaty of Cateau-Cambrésis (1559) to the Peace of Utrecht (1713–14), the Spaniards dominated Italy, for they held the Milanese, Naples, and Sicily. Their oppressive rule produced two serious revolts in Naples and Messina during the seventeenth century, revolts which were followed by reprisals as stupid as they were ferocious. When the Spanish throne passed to the Bourbon line, Spain's Italian possessions were handed over to the Austrian Hapsburgs,[1] but the change involved little that was new for the Italian inhabitants in these states except that they were to be governed thenceforth from Vienna instead of from Madrid.

Spanish rule (1559–1713)

Of the Italian states which still managed to preserve their independence in this period, four — Tuscany, Genoa, Venice, and Savoy — deserve passing notice. Florence had degenerated from an intellectual center, the Athens of Italy in the high Renaissance, to a provincial capital where the later Medici princes held their court as Grand Dukes of Tuscany. The memory of Dante and Botticelli still shed luster upon the city of their nativity, and beauty still lingered untarnished, but the days of Florentine greatness

Florence and Genoa

---

[1] The Methuen Treaty (1703) allied Britain and Portugal in a friendly commercial and political understanding.

[1] The Hapsburgs acquired Milan, Naples, and Sardinia by the Treaty of Utrecht, but in 1720 they exchanged Sardinia for Sicily and thus held all of Spain's former possessions in Italy.

were done. Genoa fared little better, though it preserved its republican institutions, and its banking business still assured it a moderate prosperity. In 1684, a French fleet bombarded the city on slight justification, and Louis XIV rebuked the independent pretensions of the citizens by imposing a humiliating peace.

In spite of the fact that Venice had been declining for two centuries, the doge and his councilors managed by skillful diplomacy to maintain the dignity of the waning republic, and even carried on an intermittent war against the Turks from 1645 to 1699. Venice in decay was still "Europe's bulwark 'gainst the Ottomite," but the Turkish power also, it must be remembered, was on the wane, and although the Treaty of Carlowitz (1699) brought Venice a portion of Dalmatia, Greece, and the Aegean Islands, it was in reality a peace of exhaustion between crippled giants whose strength was spent. As the main stream of European commerce shifted more and more decisively to Amsterdam and London, the erstwhile "Queen of the Adriatic" became a city of empty palaces and desolate splendors, retaining to the last, however, the fantastic beauty which had crowned her in more prosperous days, when "the exhaustless East poured in her lap all gems in sparkling showers."

The only truly progressive and independent state in seventeenth-century Italy was Savoy, which had been welded into a compact duchy by the genius of its duke, Charles Emmanuel (1580–1630). With territory strategically placed so that it commanded both the coast route into Italy and the famous Mont Cenis pass over the Alps,[1] the dukes of Savoy could prove useful allies to any power which aspired to the control of Italy. Bargaining astutely between the French and Spaniards, they had strengthened their position and added to their territory. Victor Amadeus II joined in the War of the League of Augsburg against France to his profit; but it was the War of the Spanish Succession that gave him his real opportunity and raised Savoy to the position of a European state. Siding first with France, Victor Amadeus had the foresight to desert Louis XIV in 1703, and his army, brilliantly led by Prince Eugene, aided materially in the ultimate defeat of the French. For this assistance the allies rewarded Victor Amadeus with the island of Sicily and the title of king. In 1720, he exchanged Sicily for Sardinia, and the duchy of Savoy was generally known thenceforth as the Sardinian Kingdom. In the nineteenth century the house of Savoy was destined to head the movement for Italian unity and provide the first king of a united Italy.

The States of the Church in central Italy shared the general decline in papal prestige which made Rome less important as a diplomatic center in the seventeenth century than Paris, Vienna, or even London. Seven popes occupied the chair of Saint Peter in the years 1660 to 1715, but none was noteworthy. Innocent XI (1676–89) was the most upright and possibly the most capable. He defended his prerogatives against Louis XIV, and aided with subsidies in the defeat of the Turks in 1683. But the mediating power which the popes had once wielded over Europe had diminished; their pleas for peace passed almost unheeded in the clash of the dynastic wars that disfigured the seventeenth century. The eighteenth century held no better days in store for the papacy; indeed, it was to see the authority of the church still further weakened and that venerable institution reduced to the nadir of its fortunes.

5. SUMMARY OF THE PERIOD, 1660 TO 1715

When the major political developments that filled the period from 1660 to 1715 are passed in review, it becomes clear that the balance of power among the European states was perpetually shifting because several states were in decline and threatened to disintegrate. Thus Spain, the Holy Roman Empire, the Italian states (except Savoy), Sweden, Poland, Turkey, and even Holland were stationary or decadent. France, on the other hand, despite its reverses, was still an aggressive power of the first rank, while Great Britain was developing vigorously. It was not difficult to foresee that these two

[1] See map, "Europe in 1789."

THE MAGDEBURG HEMISPHERE

Otto von Guericke (1602–1686), a German physicist, demonstrated that atmospheric pressure was so great that two hemispheres, from which he exhausted the air with a pump, could not be pulled apart by sixteen horses.

A LESSON IN ANATOMY

The progress of medicine in the seventeenth century is indicated by this painting by Rembrandt van Rijn (1606–1669).

leading powers might clash severely; by 1688, England had recognized France as her most dangerous commercial rival, and a titanic struggle between the two for commerce and colonies was to provide the leading drama of the eighteenth century.

By 1715, religious issues had been subordinated to political expediency and no longer constituted a serious cause for war. On the other hand, trade rivalries had grown more intense. Dynastic greed remained an active force, ready as ever to promote hostilities for its own profit. The long duel between Bourbon and Hapsburg lost much of its bitterness with the decline of the Hapsburg power, but new antagonists were waiting to crowd upon the stage. In the Germanies the meteoric rise of Prussia was to upset the balance of power by adding a first-class military state to the European system, while farther east Russia was about to emerge and claim its share of influence. The five great powers of the eighteenth century include, therefore, three states already familiar to us — France, Austria, and England — and two new powers, Prussia and Russia. The wars of the eighteenth century grow out of the conflicting interests of these five powers. Their methods and motives will be found to differ little from those described in the preceding section. Each state seeks to consolidate and aggrandize itself, the weaker form alliances against aggressive neighbors, and the diplomats defend the principle of the balance of power as the surest guaranty of peace and equilibrium. In all this the eighteenth century differs scarcely at all from the period just studied. But the emergence of Prussia and Russia modified the structure of European politics so sharply that their entry marks a new period and merits a new section, while the progress of new ideas among the enlightened classes gave to the eighteenth century an intellectual temper distinct from that of the seventeenth.

SECTION H

The Eighteenth Century

(1715 — 1789)

Although the seventy-four years between the death of Louis XIV and the outbreak of the French Revolution filled in reality less than three fourths of "the eighteenth century," they constitute a distinct period in European history for which no better name suggests itself. This period was marked chiefly by a balancing of forces. The threat of French domination had been checked, and the diplomats labored to maintain a more or less stable equilibrium among the powers. This political equilibrium was preserved with fair success to the end of the period, despite such disturbing developments as the rise of Prussia to the rank of a first-rate power, the decline of Austria and Turkey, and the westward expansion of Russia.

It proved less easy, however, to preserve a balance of forces between the social classes. As the power and wealth of the middle class increased, and the influence of the privileged orders, the nobles and clergy, declined, stress and discontent developed which could only be eased by radical social and political readjustments. The failure to carry through the necessary reforms promptly and peaceably resulted, after 1789, in the outbreak of the Great Revolution in France, the prelude to a quarter of a century of tumultuous and far-reaching change which affected every country in Europe. The harbinger of this revolution was a widespread mood of impatience and optimism, always a dangerous blend.

GROWTH OF RUSSIA IN EUROPE
1462-1815

Baltic Sea

1795-1815

TERRITORY ACQUIRED 1462-1505

BOUNDARY OF THE GOLDEN HORDE TILL 1480

1670-1725

St. Petersburg

1505-1670

MOSCOVY 1462

Moscow

1517

TERRITORY ACQUIRED 1505-1670

1795-1815

1772-1795

Kiev

Black Sea

1795-1815

Caspian Sea

40

The Emergence of Russia

Our greatest enemy is space.
RUSSIAN PROVERB.

NO STUDENT who examines the map of Europe can fail to note how markedly the western part of the continent is divided into segments. The British Isles, Italy, and the Iberian Peninsula possess a geographical unity of their own, while for France the ocean, the Alps, and the Pyrenees form a natural boundary for the greater part of the frontier. Western Europe thus enjoys a wide diversity of scenery and of climate, and the rising national states there have found the seacoast and the mountain ranges a protection behind which each could develop its culture and its institutions more or less unmolested.

The geography of eastern Europe is surprisingly different. Instead of an irregular coastline and snow-capped peaks, there stretches a vast and monotonous plain. From the Baltic to the Black and the Caspian seas, from the Carpathian Mountains on the border of Hungary to the Ural Mountains on the border of Asia, this great inland plain extends, large enough to contain England, France, and Spain together. In the north there are many swamps and thick forests of coniferous trees; the central belt produces a mixed deciduous growth; the plains of the southland are semi-arid and bare. These bare, uncultivated steppes of the south, stretching above the Black and Caspian seas into the heart of Asia, provide an undefended route down which the Asiatic nomads have swept at intervals, to break like a destructive wave on the frontiers of eastern Europe.

The Great Plain

To the Romans the broad steppes beyond the Carpathian Mountains and the Black Sea were known as Sarmatia. The Romans traded with the natives for furs and amber, but they cared little what happened in such a cold and forbidding region which for them lay shrouded in a twilight beyond the bounds of their empire. In the fifth century the Huns rode out of this shadowy East, to devastate the weakened provinces of Rome, and, although they retired after the death of their leader Attila (453), other Mongols continued to threaten Europe with new invasions throughout the Middle Ages. Yet the trade routes in this region were kept open even after the fall of Rome; Viking adventurers from Scandinavia penetrated the steppes (the word *Rus* was probably derived from *Ruotsi*, a Finnish name for the Swedes); and Byzantine merchants from Constantinople continued to traverse the territory and to navigate the rivers. Throughout the dark ages the dwellers of the Great Plain were thus exposed to the stimulus of Norse enterprise and Byzantine culture. But it was difficult for them to raise cities or cultivate the arts in an area where Roman civilization had laid no foundations, where natural frontiers were lacking, and the possibility of new invasions from Asia was a constant threat.

It is not surprising, therefore, that the Slavic peoples of eastern Europe remained politically backward and semi-barbarous while the Latins and the Germans were making substantial advances. The original home of the Slavs is believed to have been the basin of the Pripet River, whence they migrated across the Great Plain, or filtered into the Balkan Peninsula. The earliest accounts picture them as an agricultural people, generous and hospitable in character, fond of music, and deeply religious. These characteristics still distinguish most of their descendants.

1. THE RISE OF MUSCOVY

In the ninth century the impact of a new wave of Asiatic invaders split the Slavs into several groups. The eastern Slavs, who were to lay the foundations of the Russian state, built up a principality with Kiev, on the Dnieper River, as its center, but after two centuries Kiev declined before a fresh wave of invaders from Asia. Thereupon the eastern Slavs established new cities within the forest zone to the north, of which Moscow proved the most important. Here they were better able to resist the horsemen of the plains, and Norse adventurers and traders helped them to organize a federation of feudal principalities. Until the fifteenth century, the Mongols, who had established their capital at Sarai on the Volga, continued to levy tribute on the eastern Slavs, but in 1480, Ivan the Great, Prince of Moscow, defied the Khan of the Golden Horde, and this Mongol ruler's supremacy was broken.

Ivan the Great (1462–1505) married Sophia Paleologus, niece of the last Byzantine emperor, Constantine Paleologus, who perished when the Turks captured Constantinople in 1453. Ivan considered himself heir to the Byzantine traditions, called himself Czar (Caesar) and successor of Augustus, and Protector of the Orthodox (Greek) Church. Moscow became the "Third Rome." This assumption of imperial dignity by a Slavic prince is more easily understood when it is realized that missionaries from Constantinople had converted the eastern Slavs to the Greek faith, and a strong Byzantine influence tinctured the culture of the Russians. Their architecture and their icons, their calendar, and even their alphabet, were borrowed from Constantinople. It was an interesting anomaly, this adoption of the outworn, sophisticated, and highly conventionalized art of Byzantium by a race of vigorous barbarians who still retained many of the oriental customs of their Asiatic conquerors. The blend of these diverse influences was to make the Russians unlike any other European people.

Byzantine influence

The slow task of consolidating and extending the principality of Moscow, or Muscovy, engaged the energies of successive czars. Ivan IV, also known as Ivan the Terrible (1533–84), subdued his boyars, or vassals, with ruthless cruelty, conquered the last Tartar strongholds in European Russia, and pushed his frontiers eastward beyond the Ural Mountains and westward until he clashed with the Poles and the Swedes. In the seventeenth century, under a new dynasty, the Romanovs, this westward expansion was resumed. The absence of any natural barrier made it possible for the Muscovite state to expand in all directions, but the nations of western Europe remained indifferent to this rise of a new power in the East. So long as Sweden and Poland stood as buffer states, the Russians could not interfere directly in European affairs, and the English, French, and Italians thought of Russia as an Asiatic rather than a European country.

By the close of the seventeenth century, however, Poland and Sweden were both in decline, and they yielded before the inexorable pressure of the Russian advance. A glance at the accompanying map will show how rapidly the Russians pressed forward. In 1660, they were still shut off from the Baltic Sea, for the Swedes held the littoral provinces from Finland to the mouth of the Dvina River, where the Polish dominions began. But Sweden, with a population of a little over a million, was unequal to the burden of guarding her empire. Even with the aid of French subsidies, the Swedish kings found it difficult to hold their Baltic provinces against the rapacity of Poland and Brandenburg.

PETER THE GREAT OF RUSSIA (1683–1725)

Top left: Peter the Great ruled Russia in the first quarter of the eighteenth century. As a despot this Muscovite giant was by turns pious, cruel, resourceful, and naïve, for he possessed a disharmonic but forceful personality.

CHARLES XII OF SWEDEN (1697–1718)

Top right: Charles XII of Sweden impressed the age by his inflexibility and daring, but he reduced his kingdom to ruin and defeat by his wars.

THE EXECUTION OF THE STRELTZI

Right: The mass executions after the streltzi revolt, and the barbarous modes of punishment employed, proved that Russia was still an oriental despotism rather than a European state.

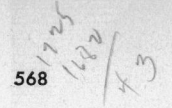

2. PETER THE GREAT OF RUSSIA

The decline of Poland and Sweden invited further Russian expansion, and the westward advance of the Muscovites was renewed under the restless and autocratic czar, Peter the Great (1682–1725). Ambitious to see his backward and semi-barbarous subjects acquire the culture and the institutions which made France, England, and Holland powerful and respected nations, Peter determined to hasten the "Europeanization" of Russia by opening "windows to the west." By windows he meant ice-free seaports through which European trade, European travelers, and European culture could enter Russia, and before he died in 1725, he had secured outlets on both the Baltic and the Black seas.

Peter's youth, and his later career, too, ran in channels of intrigue and violence. Moscow was the scene of much factional strife in the last years of the seventeenth century, and the impressionable young czar saw more than one of his friends murdered before his eyes. He was proclaimed joint ruler with his weak-minded stepbrother Ivan in 1682, but he had to wait until 1689 to overthrow the regency of his stepsister Sophia. The death of his mother in 1694, however, followed by that of Ivan in 1696, left Peter sole lord of Muscovy. Over six and one half feet in height, dexterous with his hands, and consumed with a quenchless curiosity concerning ships and navigation, machinery, and all technical processes, the new czar was destined to change the current of Russian history. His first taste of success came in 1696, when he captured Azov from the Turks with the aid of a fleet constructed by foreign shipwrights under his command. Although the Turks later regained this Black Sea port (1722), the czar's desire for further conquests was whetted by this campaign of 1696.

Peter the Great

The following year Peter set out on a tour to study the civilization of Europe for himself. Mathematics, physics, chemistry, anatomy, and engraving claimed his attention by turns, but it was the art of warfare and particularly naval warfare that absorbed him most. In Holland and England he worked in the shipyards, and he dispatched five hundred artisans to Russia to instruct his subjects in the newer technical methods. In Vienna his tour was interrupted by the news that revolt had broken out at home among the *streltzi*, or royal guards. Hastening back to Moscow, Peter revealed the less amiable side of his character by condemning two thousand of the rebels to torture and death, as a lesson to his subjects on the futility of resisting his will.

Revolt of the streltzi

Then the Russian people were startled from their fatalistic conservatism by a succession of imperial reforms. With his own royal hand Peter clipped the beards of his nobles, and tailors stood ready to shorten their long oriental robes, for the czar desired to initiate European dress and habits. The women were summoned to court from their domestic seclusion, but being unused to social freedom they huddled modestly at one end of the hall while their lords and masters drank themselves under the table at the other. Peter comprehended that his *ukases* or decrees, even when they were emphasized by knout and scaffold, could not change his people so swiftly as the penetrative influence of European ideas. To provide closer contacts he fostered trade agreements, sent young Russians abroad to study, and invited Europeans to sojourn in Russia. When his alien innovations led to conspiracies among his discontented subjects, he punished the rebels mercilessly, his own son being numbered finally in the list of victims. Believing many churchmen, and especially the monks, hostile to his reforms, Peter created a holy synod, or council, responsible to himself, placed it in charge of religious affairs, and abolished the office of patriarch (1700). Other departments of the government were likewise reconstructed and rendered more efficient, despite the fact that the czar possessed so few trained officials that he was compelled at times to employ Swedish prisoners of war in administrative posts.

It is difficult to exaggerate the importance of Peter's reforms. The calendar was improved, the western system of enumeration introduced, printing presses set up, and schools and hospitals established. Peter even

Peter's reforms

founded a Russian Academy of Sciences, composed, perforce, almost entirely of foreign savants. But there were some projects that could not be achieved by peaceful means. The annexation of a port where the ships of all nations might come freely to trade cost Peter twenty years of warfare, a hazardous struggle in which he was opposed by the most brilliant, the most daring, and the most erratic monarch of the age, Charles XII of Sweden.

3. THE GREAT NORTHERN WAR (1700–21)

The famous French writer, Voltaire, who composed an *Histoire de Charles XII*, observed shrewdly that Charles carried all his virtues to such an excess that they became more dangerous than their contrary vices. Charles crowned himself King of Sweden in 1697, at the age of fifteen, showing immediately a temper so imperious and abilities so precocious that the *Riksdag*, or Parliament, dispensed with a regency and voted him absolute powers. He thus became master of Sweden, with its million and a quarter inhabitants, at almost the same time that Peter assumed full control in Russia, and the stage was set for a contest between the two young autocrats and the two empires.

Charles XII of Sweden

In 1700, Russia, Saxony, and Denmark took advantage of Charles's youth and presumable inexperience to attack Sweden, but the boy-king speedily astonished Europe by the daring of his counterstrokes. In a single campaign he forced the Danes to sue for peace; then, marching with eight thousand men to the relief of Narva, in Esthonia, he hurled his veterans through a blinding snowstorm upon the Russian lines and routed the czar's army of forty thousand men. These victories won for Charles the sobriquet "The Lion of the North," but their ultimate effects were disastrous for his character and for Sweden. Instead of following up his victory at Narva, he chose to regard the Russians as vanquished, and turned to deal with his third enemy, Saxony.

Frederick Augustus I of Saxony (1694–1733) was also by election King of Poland (1697). Charles speedily deposed him from the latter throne and had a rival candidate, Stanislaus Leszczynski, elected in his place. The young Swedish king was now the arbiter of northern Europe, for the western powers were occupied by the War of the Spanish Succession (1702–13), but his blind and imperturbable self-confidence drove his enemies to unite and exasperated his friends. Moreover, the five years which he spent in reordering Polish affairs permitted Peter the Great the needed leisure to reknit the Russian armies, so that by 1707 they were able once more to press to the shores of the Baltic Sea.

This insolent advance of the Russians goaded Charles into attempting a project at which Napoleon was to meet disaster a century later: he marched on Moscow. Scattering a Russian army at Holowczyn (1708), the Swedes pressed on through a country stripped bare of provisions by the retreating foe. But to reach Moscow proved impossible, and rather than retreat, Charles turned his devoted army southward, and sought an alliance with the Cossacks of the Ukraine. The terrible winter of 1709 harassed his ragged veterans more pitilessly than the Russian horsemen, and when summer came, Peter was able to crush the remnant of Charles's army at Poltawa (1709). Charles took refuge with the Turks, stirred them up repeatedly to attack the Russians, and finally, after incredible adventures, returned to Sweden in 1714.

Battle of Poltawa

Although his country was exhausted, the defiant monarch insisted upon maintaining the struggle against Russia, Prussia, Poland, Saxony, Hanover, and Denmark. But in 1718 he was killed while attacking the Danes, and Sweden sank to the level of a third-rate power, while the victorious allies seized her empire. Russia was the last to make peace, and Peter had the satisfaction of adding Ingria, Esthonia, and Livonia to his empire by the Treaty of Nystad (1721).[1]

As early as 1703, Peter the Great had begun the construction of a new capital for his dominions on the marshy ground where the river Neva drained into the Gulf of Finland. Despite the constant danger of Swed-

Saint Petersburg (1703)

---

[1] See map, "Growth of Russia in Europe" in this chapter.

ish reconquest, of floods, and of fevers, Saint Petersburg rose slowly from the treacherous lagoons, and in 1712 it was recognized as the new seat of government. Moscow, symbol of the old Russia, was humbled before the splendor of this "western" city, where Peter established his court and assumed the novel and grandiloquent title "Emperor of all the Russias." Alone of all the great powers, Russia was to have its capital city, not near the center of the country, but upon the frontier; not in an ancient town with long traditions, but in a modern seat of administration, built upon conquered ground, the least Russian of all the Russian cities. Yet so well had Peter labored that not even his premature death in 1725 could undo his life-work, and for good or ill the destiny of Russia had been joined with that of Europe.

4. THE SUCCESSORS OF PETER THE GREAT

As Peter had married twice, and left descendants by both marriages, it is not surprising that the first sixteen years following his death were filled with disputes concerning the succession. In 1741, however, his daughter Elizabeth began a reign of twenty years and the empire regained a comparative degree of tranquillity. But there was still a deep conflict between the old and the new forces in Russia, and a deep resentment among the conservative classes at the spread of foreign ideas and the elevation of foreigners to high posts in the state. This opposition between a pro-Russian party and a pro-European party remained a permanent heritage in Russian politics from the time of Peter the Great, for many Russians felt that their country possessed a peculiar and distinct culture of its own which could not successfully be blended with or remodeled after that of the western European nations.

During Elizabeth's reign this conflict between old and new forces produced a deadlock, but foreign influences, particularly French, continued to win an ascendancy. Russian policy, both at home and abroad, gained during these years but mediocre successes. Despite the political stagnation, however, **the arts and sciences progressed, education was encouraged for the upper classes,** and

Elizabeth (1741–62)

the Czarina Elizabeth, though a dissolute woman herself, endeavored to elevate the morals of her subjects and to ameliorate the ferocious penal code.

A minor conflict with the enfeebled Swedish state brought Russia additional gains in Finland by the Treaty of Abo (1743); and in 1756, Elizabeth joined France and Austria against Prussia and England in the Seven Years' War (1756–63). The Russian armies penetrated East Prussia and won several victories, but their sacrifices were in vain, for on Elizabeth's death in 1762 her nephew and successor Peter III (grandson of Peter the Great) arbitrarily reversed the alliance, and came to the aid of Frederick II of Prussia in time to save that hard-pressed monarch from ruin.[1] Peter's admiration for Frederick and his readiness to fling away the fruits of Russian victories to gratify his personal whims speedily excited a palace revolution, and before the close of the year 1762 the erratic and vicious young czar had been deposed and murdered. In his place the guards acclaimed his wife Catherine "Autocrat of all the Russias."

5. CATHERINE THE GREAT (1762–96)

Sophia Augusta Frederica, better known to history as Catherine the Great, was the daughter of a Prussian general, Prince Christian Augustus of Anhalt-Zerbst. Married to the despicable Czarevitch Peter at the age of sixteen, and received into the Orthodox Church under the name of Catherine, this German princess passed several lonely years at the Russian court, where she had few friends and was shamelessly neglected by her husband. She consoled herself with wide reading, learned the Russian language, and identified herself so loyally with the interests of her adopted country that she was chosen to succeed her degenerate husband in 1762. Indiscriminate in her love affairs, and often Machiavellian in her politics, Catherine was none the less a woman of remarkable sagacity and proved an inspired ruler. Under her shrewd guidance Russia once again played a rôle equal to its importance, recaptured its waning prestige, and took a leading part in

Catherine's character

[1] See the following chapter, section 5.

CATHERINE II OF RUSSIA (1762–1796)

Catherine the Great was the executor of Peter the Great's program in her energetic promotion of Russian interests and Russian expansion.

SAINT PETERSBURG, 1749

This shows the Russian capital much as it must have appeared to Catherine when she wed the Czarevitch Peter in 1745.

RUSSIAN PEASANTS

Misery and serfdom increased in Russia while Catherine rewarded nobles and bureaucrats with lands and privileges.

FREDERICK AUGUSTUS III OF POLAND

It required a War of the Polish Succession (1733–1736) to establish Frederick Augustus as King of Poland and then he left both Saxony and Poland to the rule of incapable ministers.

POLISH PEASANT DWELLING

Poland was known as "the peasants' hell" for centuries.

the affairs of northern Europe. Whenever possible, Catherine appointed Russians rather than foreigners to office, and showed herself at all times deeply devoted to the glory and greatness of Russia. But she introduced reforms after the European pattern when she could do so without stirring up discontent, and proved herself, especially in her foreign policy, the real executor of Peter the Great's bequest.

Catherine's long reign (1762–96) lasted until after the outbreak of the French Revolution in 1789. She was thus a contemporary of Frederick II of Prussia (1740–86), Joseph II of Austria (1780–90), Gustavus III of Sweden (1771–92), and other rulers of the second half of the eighteenth century who are often styled the "enlightened despots." These monarchs were all inspired by a conscientious desire to improve their realms and to make their subjects happy, and something more will be told about their reforms later. Catherine was exceedingly anxious to be considered an "enlightened despot" herself, but her title to the honor is a little dubious. Of her good intentions there can be no question; she wrote to Voltaire, Diderot, d'Alembert, and other illustrious critics of society and government, inviting them to advise her how best to make her subjects contented and civilized. With her own hand she drew up a liberal plan for revising and codifying the Russian laws (1766), in the hope of making them at once more inflexible and more humane. She dreamed of establishing schools in every town and village in order to elevate her people to the responsibilities of citizenship. She encouraged artists and writers, and permitted radical books, which the authorities in France had condemned as dangerous and seditious, to circulate freely in Russia.

An enlightened despot

Among the noblest monuments to her kindliness of heart were the hospitals and orphanages erected under her patronage. She submitted herself to vaccination so that her subjects might be encouraged by her royal example to accept this newly discovered preventive against smallpox. For the millions of serfs toiling on the lands of Russia she expressed deep commiseration, and she hoped that some day they might be liberated. But she took no serious steps to free them. Between Catherine's wishes and her acts there was often a wide divergence, for she had a kind heart but a calculating mind, and it was the dictates of her shrewd brain that guided her. Her sympathy for the serfs did not prevent her granting large estates to her courtiers, which further increased serfdom. When she divided Russia into fifty provinces, she professed to wish each district to control its own local affairs, but she kept the real power in the hands of a governor appointed by herself. Thus, despite her pretensions of benevolence, the practical results of her administration revealed more despotism than enlightenment.

Catherine's reforms

For her failures in this respect Catherine must not be blamed too harshly. In politics one seldom does the best or even the next best thing: one does the best one can. Because her power rested upon the loyalty of the nobles she had to please them; hence the grants of land and the increase of serfdom. Her orders might be humane and wise, but if unsympathetic officials disdained to enforce them, she dared not rebuke them too sharply. Her desire to play the part, or at least to *appear* to be playing the part, of an enlightened ruler was genuine enough, but she was too clear-headed a realist to forget for a single moment that she had been called to govern an empire of barbarous peoples. She knew that she could best control them by the methods they had been trained to understand, the methods of an oriental despot.

6. THE DISMEMBERMENT OF POLAND

The expansion of Russia in the seventeenth and eighteenth centuries helped to weaken and finally to destroy the kingdom of Poland. When Catherine II ascended the Russian throne in 1762, Poland was already enfeebled and disorganized. The Poles, like the Russians, were of Slavic origin, but they had been converted to the Roman Catholic instead of to the Greek Orthodox faith, and were thus affiliated by ties of religion and culture with the western rather than the eastern European peoples. In the four-

Poland in decline

teenth century, Poland had been united to Lithuania, and by the sixteenth the Polish dominions extended across the plains between the Black Sea and the Baltic in a loosely knit kingdom almost twice as large as France. In that golden age of Polish history the able rulers of the Jagellon dynasty were strong enough to resist the pressure of the Muscovites in the east and the Turks in the south, but in the seventeenth century, Poland was weakened by the attacks of Turks, Tartars, Swedes, and Russians. Although King John Sobieski (1674–96) arrested the decline momentarily, and even rescued Vienna from the Turks (1683), the greatness of Poland had passed and the eighteenth century witnessed the extinction of the kingdom.

The decline and final dismemberment of Poland was the result of (1) indefensible frontiers and (2) political anarchy. The accident of geography which made their homeland a level plain left the Poles no natural

Political instability

barriers, such as high mountain ranges, behind which they could rally to check an invasion. The wide steppes, transected by slow-moving rivers which favored navigation, made it possible for Poland to expand rapidly in the days of her power, but also left her open to the inroads of her enemies in the days of her decline. Worse, however, than this territorial instability was the political instability of the kingdom. The government of the country was so wretchedly organized that it has been called "a legalized anarchy tempered by rebellion." The Polish Kingdom was in truth little more than a loose federation of feudal principalities somewhat like the Holy Roman Empire, and the people did not even possess unity of religious faith, being predominantly Catholic in Poland, Greek Orthodox in Lithuania, and Protestant in the area adjoining East Prussia. By the eighteenth century the royal authority had been dispersed, the power of the Diet all but nullified, and the state re-

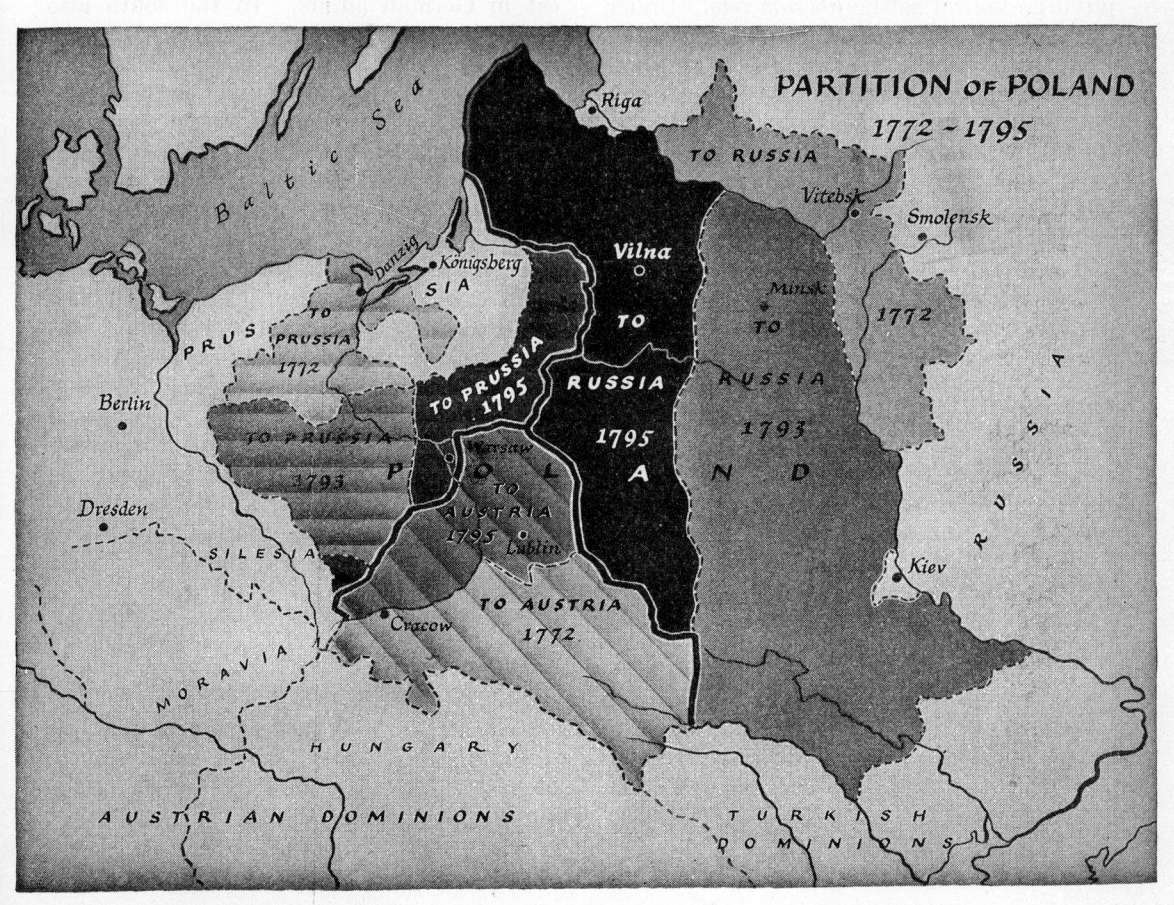

PARTITION OF POLAND 1772–1795

duced to impotence, a process deliberately hastened by the watchful and rapacious neighbors of Poland.

Perhaps the worst enemies of the unfortunate country were the Polish nobles. The monarchy was elective, and these vassals were unwilling to give themselves a master who might call them to account for their misrule. They saw to it that the elected king lacked sufficient authority to curb them, sometimes extorting pre-election promises from him, sometimes choosing a French, Saxon, or Swedish prince unfamiliar with Polish affairs. Denied an income or an army large enough to defend his position, the king was often a sorry figure. But if the royal rôle was ignominious that of the Polish Diet was even more futile. Controlled likewise by the nobles, the Diet was incapable of effecting any reforms because its decrees were binding only when they were passed unanimously. Any member might block a bill or dissolve the chamber by exercising a privilege known as the *liberum veto*. Under this fantastic constitution, the selfish nobles, who had nothing to fear from Diet or king, exploited their serfs mercilessly. Poland had been known as the "Peasants' Hell" in the Middle Ages and continued to deserve the title. The townsmen, also, lacking political power, were unable to protect their interests, and Poland drifted steadily toward economic and political ruin, with the nobles blocking every suggestion for reform.

With the rulers of Russia, Prussia, and Austria eager to acquire more territory, the fate of Poland could not long remain in doubt. In 1772, Catherine came to an understanding with Frederick II of Prussia and the Empress Maria Theresa of Austria that each should annex a small share of the enfeebled kingdom. Too disorganized to resist, the Poles saw a fourth of their territory

Partitioning of Poland

snatched away. Sobered by this experience, the nobles made a belated effort to strengthen the kingdom and repair the disorder, but the three neighboring powers deliberately encouraged further confusion in order to have an excuse for renewed intervention. In 1793, Russia and Prussia seized coveted sections in a second partition, and in 1795, Austria, Prussia, and Russia divided what remained, despite the heroic resistance offered by a small army of Polish patriots under Kosciusko. Few transactions, even in that age of callous diplomacy, could equal this heartless obliteration from the map of Europe of a proud and independent state, but it must be admitted that the Poles had invited such a fate by the suicidal anarchy to which they had reduced themselves.

By the successive Partition Treaties, six million subjects and 183,000 square miles of territory were added to the Russian Empire. Russia had become a neighbor of both Austria and Prussia, and had acquired an interest in German affairs. In the south also Catherine saw her power extended as the result of two wars against the Turks. By the Treaty of Kuchuk-Kainardji (1774) she won Azov, and the right to protect the Christian subjects of the sultan; ten years later the sultan ceded her the Crimea; and the Treaty of Jassy (1792) brought her the lands on the Black Sea lying between the Bug and Dniester rivers. With this Catherine had to content herself, although she had cherished the dream of expelling the Turks from Constantinople, and making the czars of Russia masters of the (Eastern) Roman Empire in the ancient Byzantine tradition. Her second grandson was baptized Constantine in anticipation of the hoped-for triumph, and the dream of reaching Constantinople, unrealized in Catherine's time, persisted as a glittering legacy to spur the ambition of later czars.

41

The Rise of Prussia

> It is the unfailing rule of princes to aggrandize themselves as greatly as their means permit.
>
> FREDERICK THE GREAT.

BY THE MIDDLE of the seventeenth century, it will be recalled, the medieval German Empire of the Holy Roman Emperors had crumbled into more than three hundred political fragments. The main causes for this dissolution may be traced to (1) the system of electing the emperors, which resulted in the passing of the imperial title from one princely house to another and prevented any one family from knitting the Germanies into a dynastic state; (2) the conflict between the popes and emperors, which weakened the imperial power and stimulated the disruptive forces of feudalism; (3) the Protestant Reformation, which might have developed into a movement for national unity under a sympathetic emperor, but encountered instead the stubborn opposition of Charles V. Left half-Catholic and half-Protestant, the Germanies were doomed to a century of religious strife which culminated in the terrible Thirty Years' War (1618–48). When the Peace of Westphalia ended this struggle, the country was half-devastated and wholly disorganized, with the emperor's authority damaged beyond repair. Thenceforth "Germany" or the "German Empire" as a political entity had no real existence and it is customary to speak instead of "the Germanies."

Inevitably, the lack of a central authority exposed the Germans to the attacks of aggressive and better organized neighbors. France took Alsace during the Thirty Years' War, and Sweden annexed Pomerania. At a time, too, when Spain, Portugal, France, England, and even Holland and Sweden, were establishing colonial empires beyond the seas, the Germans, because of this fatal lack of political cohesion, were denied a chance to participate. The seventeenth century was thus a melancholy interlude in German history, when the imperial machinery which had lent a ponderous grandeur to the medieval empire had finally broken down, when society itself appeared to be on the verge of dissolution, and the new forces which were to shape from this chaos a modern national state had not yet made themselves apparent.

1. THE ELECTORATE OF BRANDENBURG

Nevertheless, the forces of national reconstruction were already at work. The nucleus about which they centered was the little North German state of Brandenburg, where a competent prince, Frederick William I, better known as the Great Elector, had begun his reign (1640–88) toward the close of the Thirty Years' War. His forbears, of the Hohenzollern family, had been rulers of Brandenburg for over two centuries, but none had inherited problems more grave or discouraging. Like the rest of the Germanies, Brandenburg had been laid waste by the war. Frederick William's possessions were disorganized and disunified, for, in addition to his title of Elector of Brandenburg, he

The Great Elector

was Duke of (East) Prussia, and he had acquired by the Treaty of Westphalia the cities of Magdeburg and Minden and a part of Pomerania, and annexed shortly thereafter (1666) three little duchies near the Rhine — Mark, Cleves, and Ravensburg.[1] Being an administrator of patience and insight, he realized that his primary task was to link his scattered domains together as firmly as possible by means of a centralized bureaucracy, establish a single treasury to administer the revenue, and build up an army strong enough to maintain a vigorous defense. The chaotic state of the Germanies made the maintenance of a strong army an indispensable precaution, and the Great Elector spent every thaler he could spare upon his splendidly drilled regiments.

His prudence, economy, and skill made Brandenburg-Prussia the foremost state in the Germanies. In 1701, his son and successor, Frederick, took the title of King in Prussia, and the scattered Hohenzollern dominions came to be known thereafter as the kingdom of Prussia.[2] The grandson of the Great Elector, King Frederick William I (1713–40), was a bluff, soldierly disciplinarian, who continued the consolidation and annexed Swedish Pomerania from Sweden. When he died, he left Prussia with an army that ranked fourth in Europe, a well-filled treasury, and a deserved prestige. Destiny had selected the Hohenzollern dynasty to retrieve Germany from disintegration, and to point the way later toward a national resurrection. But the duties of such leadership are grave and the Hohenzollern princes no less than their subjects were sternly disciplined for their task. In its struggle to survive and expand in those anxious times, Prussia became (1) the most militaristic state in Europe, and developed (2) a highly efficient, centralized bureaucracy. Furthermore, the prominent rôle played by strong rulers in the rise of Prussia fostered (3) a deep-rooted tradition of paternal despotism.

Prussian organization

[1] See map, page 579.
[2] Frederick was styled "King *in* Prussia" because East Prussia lay outside the bounds of the Holy Roman Empire. Within the empire he was nominally Elector of Brandenburg. Under his successor the title "King of Prussia" came to be used indiscriminately.

It is highly important to bear these formative influences in mind in order to understand the trend of later German history.

2. FREDERICK THE GREAT (1740–86)

Exactly one hundred years after the Great Elector began his reign, his great-grandson ascended the throne as Frederick II. This keen-witted prince was to play an even more important rôle in the eighteenth century than his illustrious ancestor had played in the seventeenth. His brilliant talents, unceasing labors, and enlightened rule won him the title of Frederick the Great, for he not only raised Prussia to the rank of a first-class power, but he made the force of his personality and his example felt throughout the Germanies, so that his career, like that of a Richelieu or a Napoleon, is part of the history of his age.

There seemed little in Frederick's youthful character that was prophetic of future greatness. His father, bluff old Frederick William I, feared that his son would prove a disgrace to the house of Hohenzollern. *Der Fritz ist ein effeminerter Kerl* (Fritz is an effeminate fellow), he lamented, disgusted by the lad's preference for flute-playing and French poetry. When Frederick attempted flight, to escape the rigorous discipline which his father imposed, he was imprisoned for a year, and was compelled to witness the execution of a friend who had aided him. Then for ten years the youth suffered a drastic training in the business of statecraft, toiling like any clerk over minute details of civil and military administration. Few rulers have had such exemplary training, and fewer still have possessed the genius to profit by it. When Frederick ascended the Prussian throne at twenty-eight, he was admirably equipped for his duties, and the severe training had tempered and toughened him. The poet who had once planned to write great dramas had become a prince who aspired to act them, a Machiavellian prince who had learned to conceal his feelings and had grown daring and cynical. The change is not wholly to be regretted. Frederick made an inspired ruler: he would almost certainly have made an uninspired poet.

Frederick's youth

FREDERICK THE GREAT OF PRUSSIA (1712–1786)

Upper left: Frederick had a cynical mind, a bitter tongue, and a contemptuous opinion of what he called "this damned human race"; but he rose early and toiled late for the welfare of his subjects.

FREDERICK'S LIBRARY, POTSDAM

Upper right: Frederick designed this residence himself.

MARIA THERESA

Left: Maria Theresa never forgave Frederick for wresting Silesia from Austrian control in the first years of her reign.

It is a permanent rule with princes to aggrandize themselves to the limit of their power, the young prince decided in 1738. Even at twenty-seven his shrewd mind penetrated the web of European intrigue with an ease that surprised older statesmen. Austria, he perceived, was decadent and crumbling. A war between the Bourbons and Hapsburgs over the Polish Succession (1733–36) had demonstrated to all Europe the weakness of the Hapsburgs, who had purchased peace by sacrificing the duchy of Lorraine to France. Yet the decline of Austria, if carried too far, might leave Europe at the mercy of "these modern Romans" as Frederick styled the French. The lesser powers would be safer if they could preserve a balance between Austria and France, and so maintain an equilibrium in the body politic of Europe. "It is like the human body" — Frederick was drawing upon his dubious knowledge of physiology — "which can only subsist by the commixture of equal parts of acid and alkali. . . ." But secretly he hoped to raise the Hohenzollern prestige until he could claim an equal position with the two older dynasties, adding some Prussian iron to the French acid and the Austrian alkali, as it were. Within a few months of his accession he found an opportunity for a bold stroke of self-aggrandizement.

European balance

3. THE WAR OF THE AUSTRIAN SUCCESSION (1740–48)

In an age of keen dynastic rivalries a disputed succession is a fertile source of conflict. The death of Charles II of Spain, it will be remembered, plunged Europe into the War of the Spanish Succession (1702–13), a vacancy on the electoral throne of Poland precipitated the War of the Polish Succession (1733–36), and the death of the Hapsburg emperor, Charles VI, without a male heir, had the same melancholy result in 1740. Charles wished his daughter, Maria Theresa, to inherit the Hapsburg lands intact, and he labored during the last years of his life to assure her succession by means of a Pragmatic Sanction which he bribed or persuaded the European powers to accept. Two hundred thousand fighting men would have been a far better guaranty, in the opinion of the cynical Frederick II, who took prompt advantage of Charles's death to seize the province of Silesia. For Frederick saw no profit in keeping a pledge which other princes were plotting to break. His house held plausible titles to a part of Silesia, and this seizure of the upper valley of the Oder strengthened and enriched the Prussian kingdom.[1] To the Silesians he explained that he was guided by his concern for their liberties, which Austria (ironic truth) was not powerful enough to protect. These explanations were designed, of course, to conceal Frederick's true motive, which was a ruthless desire for self-aggrandizement. But this was something which he could hardly be expected to confess, even to himself. "We are all," he admitted, "the sophists of our passions." It is a permanent rule with princes, he might have added, to find good motives for bad acts.

Silesia occupied

Lured by the hope of spoil, France, Spain, Saxony, and Bavaria joined Prussia in attacking Austria. Great Britain, already at war with Spain,[2] thereupon became the ally of the empire of the Danube. The War of the Austrian Succession was therefore two wars in reality, (1) a commercial and colonial conflict waged by France and Spain against Great Britain, and (2) a continental struggle in which Maria Theresa fought to retain her hereditary dominions against the rapacity of Prussia, France, Spain, and some lesser states. In both contests the outcome of the fighting was surprisingly negative. The maritime struggle ended in a restoration of the *status quo* (Treaty of Aix-la-Chapelle, 1748), while Maria Theresa, "a woman with the heart of a king," repulsed her aggressors and emerged from the contest with her empire almost intact. Almost, but not quite, for Frederick, by the Treaty of Dresden (1745) retained possession of Silesia.

Peace of 1748

4. THE DIPLOMATIC REVOLUTION

Frederick's plan to advance Prussian prestige had succeeded almost too well, for the unscrupulous use which he had made of

---

[1] See map on the opposite page.
[2] The War of Jenkins's Ear. See below, page 593.

GROWTH OF BRANDENBURG-PRUSSIA TO 1795

his powerful army alarmed both Bourbons and Hapsburgs. The rise of a new power in northern Europe drove Austria and France together, and eight years after the Treaty of Aix-la-Chapelle these perennial enemies became allies. Maria Theresa's passionate desire to be revenged on Frederick made her welcome the new combination, and Louis XV of France was converted to the project by his strong-willed mistress, Madame de Pompadour, whom Frederick had antagonized. To seal Frederick's fate, the Czarina Elizabeth of Russia, who hated the Prussian king for his satirical verses, also joined the coalition. The mischief which these three women were plotting against him was no secret to Frederick: he felt, he declared maliciously, as if he were pursued by the Three Furies, and he placed his armies in readiness to meet an attack.

The machinations of his enemies had left him without an ally on the Continent, but Frederick hoped for assistance from Great Britain. For hostilities between the English and French had already broken out again in America with the commencement of the French and Indian War (1754), neither side being satisfied with the indecisive peace of 1748. The renewal of war with France, however, meant that French armies might embarrass the British government by invading the German electorate of Hanover, to which the English (Hanoverian) kings still retained the title. When Frederick the Great offered to protect Hanover with his veterans in return for a treaty of mutual defense with England, the British readily agreed (Convention of Westminster, 1756). Thus, between 1748 and 1756 a double reversal of alliances took place. In the War of the Austrian Succession (1740–48) England and Austria fought France and Prussia, whereas in the Seven Years' War (1756–63) England and Prussia were to fight France and Austria. This realignment of the powers, which brought France and Austria, enemies of two hundred years' standing, into the same camp, marked such a complete change of established policy that

"Diplomatic Revolution"

it is called the "Diplomatic Revolution."

The motives which inspired the powers to change their partners for the Seven Years' War are more easily understood when this second war is seen to be really two wars, just as the War of the Austrian Succession had been. Great Britain and France carried their struggle for colonial supremacy in India and America to a decision, while Austria and Prussia engaged once more over the disputed province of Silesia.

5. THE SEVEN YEARS' WAR (1756–63)

Frederick II was not the man to wait passively while Austria, Russia, and France prepared to dismember his kingdom. Instead, he forced the issue by a sudden descent upon Saxony, for he knew the elector of that state was plotting with the coalition. His hope was to crush the Austrians before the French could come to their aid, but a reverse in Bohemia compelled him to fall back on the defensive. What followed after that is too intricate to describe in detail. For five years Frederick campaigned back and forth across his ravaged dominions, as desperate and cunning as a wolf at bay. The English furnished him with subsidies but little military aid, and Prussia, with four and a half million people, had to hold off the forces of three empires with a combined population twelve times as great.

That Prussia survived the ordeal must be attributed to its possession of three great advantages: (1) The Prussian troops could be moved from one scene of battle to another more rapidly than those of the allies because they possessed what are termed the "inside lines." (2) The Prussian State was admirably organized and unified in its efforts, while the allies were often at odds and failed to concert their attacks. (3) The Prussian armies were commanded by one of the most audacious tacticians of the age in the person of Frederick II.

Advantages of Prussia

Having routed a French army at Rossbach (1757) and relieved the pressure in the west, Frederick swept east into Silesia in time to overwhelm the Austrians at Leuthen. Next it was the turn of the Russians, who were re-

Prussia survives

pulsed at Zorndorf (1758) after ten hours of bloody carnage. These were victories won by inspired generalship against odds that were never less than two to one, but they could not continue indefinitely. At Kunersdorf (1759) Frederick's daring overreached itself disastrously, but the Austrians and Russians neglected to profit by their victory, and complete his ruin. In the two years that followed he continued to slip back and forth between the encroaching armies with ever dwindling forces. Yet even when England withdrew her support, Frederick refused to capitulate, hoping against hope for a turn of fortune, until in 1762 it came. The death of the Czarina Elizabeth brought to the Russian throne the erratic Czar Peter III [1] whose admiration for Frederick led him to propose a generous peace. The coalition had shattered itself against the obduracy of the Prussian king and all the contestants were weary of war. By the Peace of Hubertusburg (1763), Frederick not only extricated his kingdom intact, but forced Austria to acknowledge permanently his title to Silesia. In the separate Treaty of Paris of the same year, England secured the greater part of the French colonial empire.[2]

6. FREDERICK THE GREAT IN TIME OF PEACE

In the years of peace after 1763, Frederick, who was already illustrious as the most brilliant general of his age, gained new laurels as the model of enlightened despots. To heal the wounds of war he remitted taxes in stricken districts, set cavalry horses to the plow, and distributed free seed grain to destitute farmers. Canals and roads were constructed, bridges built, and fifteen hundred square miles of marsh and waste land reclaimed under his direction, so that he could well boast that he had thereby "added a province to his kingdom." To increase the population new villages were founded, and settlers drawn to them from all parts of Europe, encouraged by the promise of just laws, religious toleration, and financial assistance.

In his efforts to stimulate manufacture, Frederick resorted to protective tariffs, and

---
[1] See above, page 570.
[2] See below, pages 593–594.

RECRUITING SOLDIERS FOR THE ARMY IN THE EARLY EIGHTEENTH CENTURY

Able-bodied men were sometimes persuaded to join the army while too drunk to know what they were doing.

MARIA THERESA'S PALACE AT SCHOENBRUNN

The formal gardens and long horizontal façade of this royal residence at Vienna recall the palace which Louis XIV constructed at Versailles half a century earlier.

encouraged backward industries by royal patronage. The results were not all uniformly successful. To gratify the king's desire to see Prussia economically self-sufficient, silkworms were imported, mulberry trees grown for them to feed on, and a silk industry artificially developed despite the unsuitable climate. But Frederick's attempt to discourage his subjects from drinking coffee because it could not be grown at home, and was not, as he assured them, so healthful as beer soup, led to wholesale smuggling and damaged his popularity. Money spent outside the country he regarded as lost, his idea being to make the Prussian people provide all their essential commodities, sell the surplus abroad, but import as little as possible in return. This was the one certain method of increasing the wealth of a state according to the precepts of Colbert, the minister of Louis XIV, who had extended the principles of the mercantile system in the previous century. All the states of Europe were striving, more or less successfully, to follow this system in the eighteenth century, and Frederick accepted the prevailing ideas.

Frederick's mercantilism

With inexhaustible patience Frederick forced himself to dispatch the tiresome details of administration. Often he was at work by five in the morning, and indolent or inefficient subordinates lived in terror of his critical eye which appeared to overlook nothing. The remotest corners of the kingdom were quickened by the energy of his example, for he visited all the provinces in person, checking errors and correcting abuses. To enforce the laws more firmly and justly, he had the legal codes unified and simplified, forbade the use of torture to extract confessions, and warned the judges that cases must not be permitted to wait indefinitely for a decision. Toward his subjects Frederick played the part of a kindly, though somewhat despotic, father, guarding the welfare of children who were well-meaning but ignorant and stupid. He labored, and expected others to labor, for the glory of Prussia as he saw it, never permitting himself to forget that his duties were proportionate to his rank, and that a king was "the first servant of the state."

Servant of the state

In 1772, the annexation of West Prussia from Poland added a new province to Frederick's kingdom, as large as Silesia and almost as valuable. The decline and dismemberment of Poland have been described in the previous chapter. The Prussian share in the First Partition, though considerably smaller than that of Austria or Russia, promoted the solidarity of the kingdom, for it united East Prussia to Brandenburg.[1] With a population swelled to five million, and an army of two hundred thousand, Prussia had become a first-class power, the dominant state of the Germanies and a rival of Austria. Frederick's prestige made him not only a Prussian but a German hero; his achievements wakened a patriotic pride among all the German-speaking people; and one of his latest triumphs, before his death in 1786, was the formation of a league of German princes, organized for mutual defense against Hapsburg aggression. In thus consolidating German sentiment, he was unknowingly establishing the foundation of a greater Germany, but another century was to pass before German political unity could be realized.

In the lighter intervals between his official labors, Frederick found time to compose melodies for his flute, to indulge his literary bent (his writings fill thirty volumes), and to enjoy the company of philosophers, poets, and scientists. "Philosophers should be the preceptors of the world and the masters of princes," he declared; and he invited the great French satiric genius, Voltaire, to be his honored guest at his palace, *Sans Souci*. There were amusing supper parties at which Frederick and his companions discussed life and literature in witty and often irreverent fashion, ridiculing the frailties and superstitions of men and exalting the advantages of a free, unprejudiced, rational mind. Unfortunately, Frederick and Voltaire discovered that even rational men do not always agree, and Voltaire's visit ended in a scandalous quarrel between them. But for Voltaire's writings Frederick retained the liveliest admiration, for strangely enough this Prussian king, who was a national hero to the German people, preferred to speak and write in

Frederick and Voltaire

[1] See map, page 579.

THIS CONTEMPORARY ENGRAVING SHOWS THE TROOPS OF FREDERICK THE GREAT ENTERING A TOWN IN SILESIA

French. He regarded his native tongue as uncouth and undistinguished, and his preference for the French classic style completely blinded him to the brilliant literary revival in the Germanies which marked the closing years of his reign. Compared with the tragedies of Corneille and Racine, the early work of the young Goethe seemed to him a "detestable imitation" of the "abominable plays of Shakespeare."

In 1786, Frederick the Great died quietly in his armchair at *Sans Souci*. He had raised Prussia to the rank of a great power, made it the acknowledged rival of Austria in the direction of German affairs, doubled the army and the area of the Prussian State, and afforded Europe a dazzling example of the success which a despot might achieve if his genius and industry were equal to his opportunities.

CHRISTIAN WORLD, c. 700 A.D.

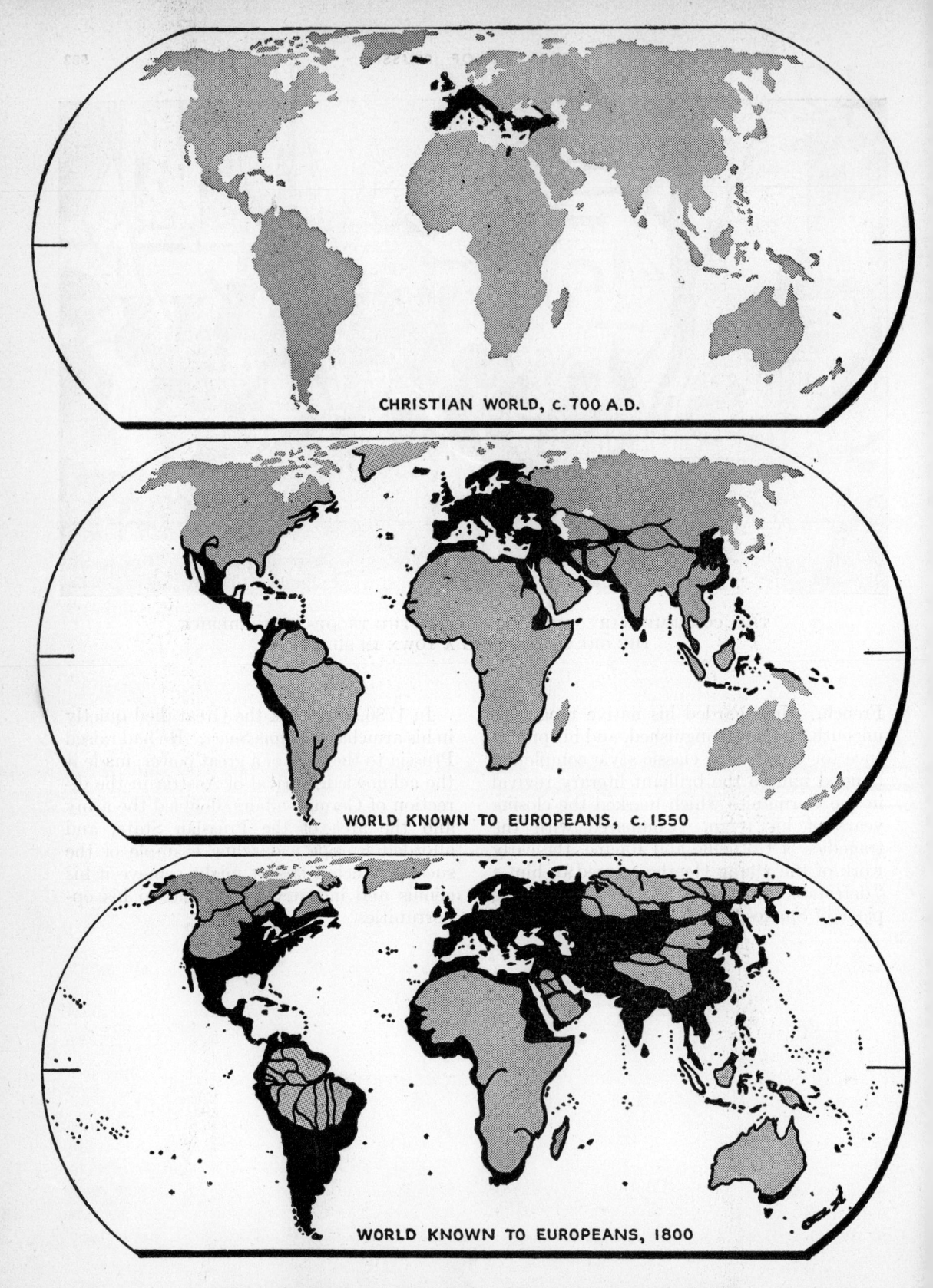

WORLD KNOWN TO EUROPEANS, c. 1550

WORLD KNOWN TO EUROPEANS, 1800

THE WIDENING OF THE EUROPEAN HORIZON

42

Overseas Expansion and the Struggle for Commerce and Colonies

We will go on, even if we have to eat the leather on the ships' yards.
FERDINAND MAGELLAN.

IN THE MIDDLE AGES the people of Europe did not speculate very much about what lay beyond the boundaries of their small continent. They knew less of geographical science than the ancient Greeks and Romans. India, with its millions of inhabitants, was a land of fable to them, and the vague wonders which they had heard of China (Cathay) and Japan (Cipango), they dismissed as travelers' tales. Of North and South America, and Australia, they knew nothing whatever. Their ignorance, of course, was due not so much to a lack of curiosity as to a lack of the means for gratifying it. Travel was slow, costly, and dangerous. Not until the revival of commerce made it profitable to visit distant lands for trade did the Europeans find it worth while to seek new continents.

1. A WORLD TO WIN

It is difficult for the historian to explain how, at the close of the Middle Ages, a handful of European states could suddenly undertake a program of world conquest. Developments *within* Europe which helped to make this possible have already been discussed. But this drama of world exploration and exploitation also depended upon conditions *outside* Europe, upon the state of civilization in America, Asia, and Africa. These conditions must now be sketched in brief form.

North and South America, when the Europeans arrived, were sparsely populated by natives still largely in a Neolithic stage of culture. Two regions, Mexico and Peru, were centers of Indian civilizations, but these empires of the Aztecs and the Incas were landlocked, self-centered, and easily destroyed. Thus, the conquest of the Western Hemisphere proved a relatively easy matter. In Asia, however, European adventurers found a very different situation. Asia contained three fifths of the human race, and the civilizations there had been well advanced when the inhabitants of Europe were still in the Neolithic stage themselves. Why, then, did the Asiatics not explore and exploit Europe instead of enduring European aggression?

America unlike Asia

There is no simple answer to such a question. It should be noted, however, that the vast population of Asia was mainly concentrated in two areas, India and China. The early history of the Indians and Chinese antedated that of Greece or Rome, and life in Asia had not changed fundamentally in two thousand years. Indian society was still stratified in the caste system, a permanent, inflexible division into hereditary

India open to invasion

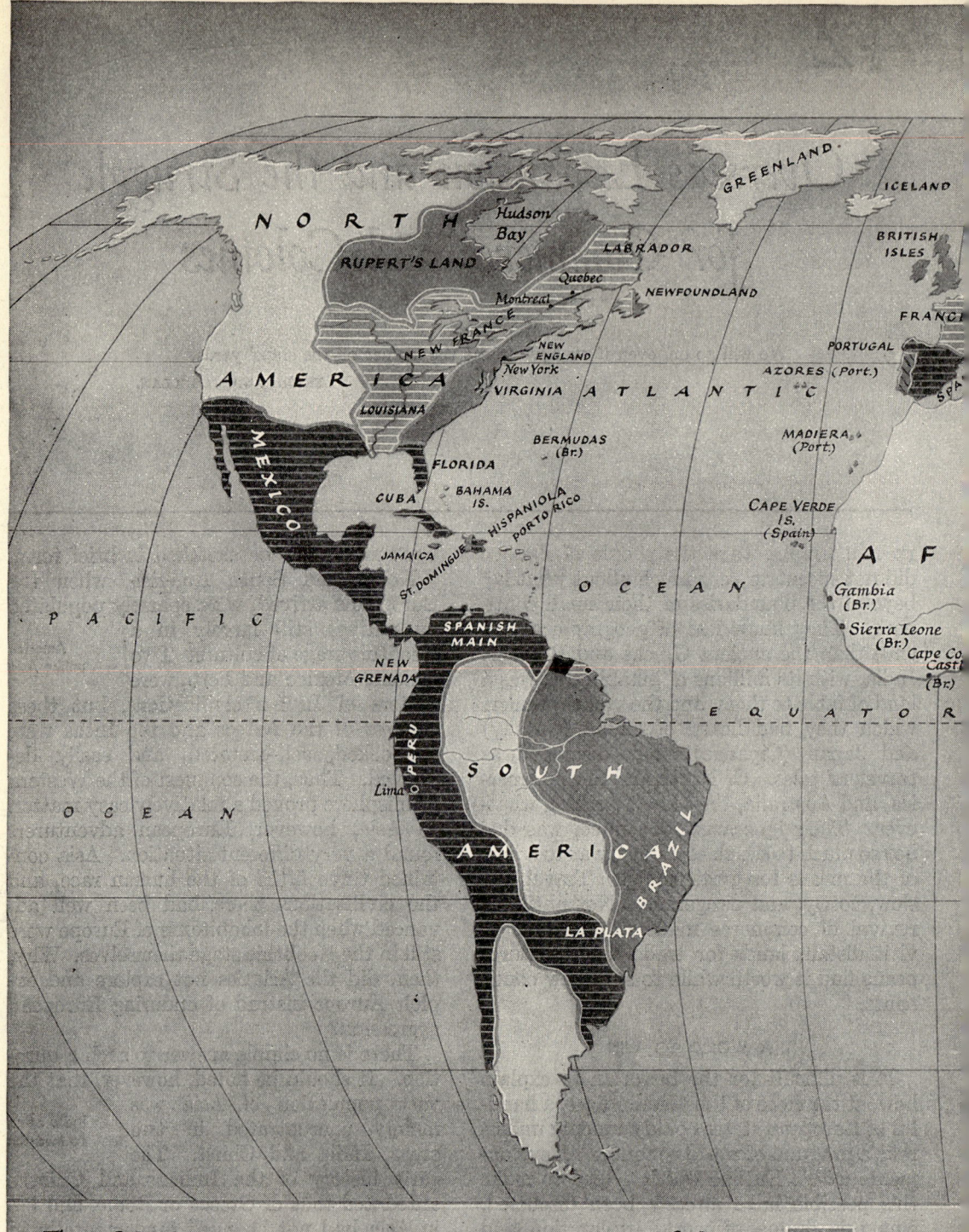

The COLONIAL SITUATION ABOUT 1689   BRITISH

FRENCH   DUTCH   SPANISH   PORTUGUESE

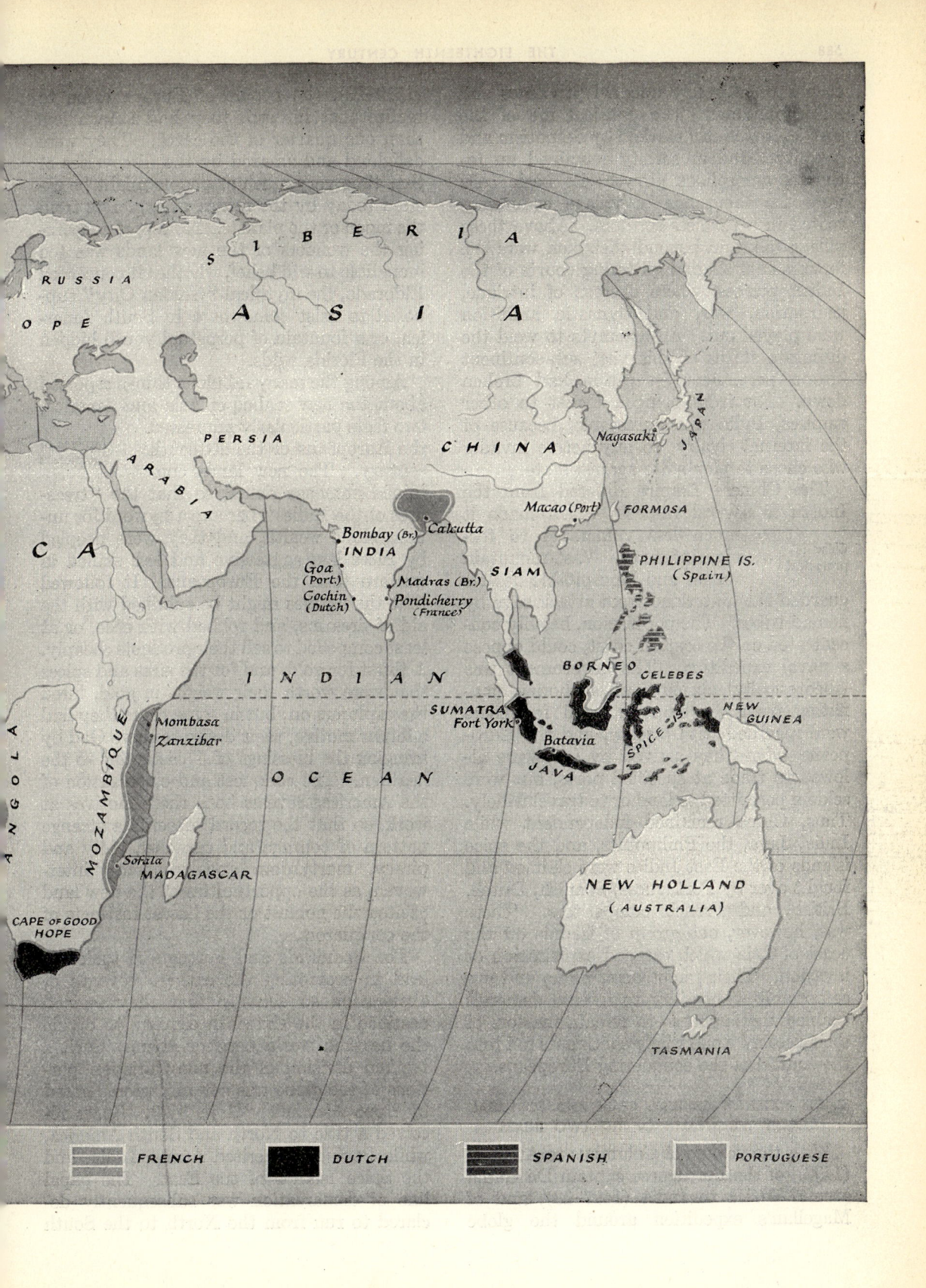

classes with grossly unequal privileges and fixed functions. The political life of the peninsula was still marked by despotism and disunity. Indian society remained an inchoate, amorphous growth; its basic cells were the thousands of village communes rooted in a timeless serfdom. Above these village folk and beyond their ken were the fortress capitals and glittering courts of the Indian princes, where dramas of intrigue, usurpation, war, and dynastic ambition were played out. All attempts to weld the disparate states of this vast sub-continent into a permanent federation had broken down. Far from being a threat to other empires, India was vulnerable, because of the internal rivalry, to any active invader who chose to play state against state.

The Chinese Empire differed from the Indian in several respects which made it much less vulnerable to foreign influence. Vast mountain ranges and inhospitable deserts guarded the hinterland from attack save by nomad tribes. The population, heavily concentrated on the eastern coast, could oppose a naval expedition. The government was (theoretically) absolute, all authority emanating from the emperor. All foreigners were regarded with disdain, and the Europeans, when they arrived by sea, were allowed to trade at specified ports, but were seldom permitted to land or to travel widely. Thus, China remained independent while India, Java, the Philippines, and the spice islands of the East Indies were claimed and fought over by Portuguese, Spanish, Dutch, British, and French competitors. There was, however, one group of islands off the coast of Asia which escaped exploitation or invasion. Their remoteness, pride, and uncompromising hostility to foreign demands enabled the Japanese to remain masters of their destiny while whole continents fell into the control of the conquering Europeans.

China protected

2. THE SIXTEENTH CENTURY: SPAIN AND PORTUGAL EXPLOIT THE WEALTH OF THE TWO INDIES

With the voyage of Columbus to America (1492), of the Portuguese captain Da Gama around Africa to India (1497–98), and of Magellan's expedition around the globe (1519–22), the people of Europe came to realize that hitherto they had known less than one quarter of the earth. They were delighted and amazed by the discoveries of that time very much as people might be excited today by the return of explorers from the moon or the planets. No report concerning the wonders of the new lands was too incredible to win belief, whether it concerned Eldorado, the mythical "Golden City" supposed to exist somewhere in South America, or a fountain of perpetual youth hidden in the Florida wilds.

Among the many fabulous things reported about the new realms of Asia and America, two facts particularly impressed the Europeans of the sixteenth century. The new lands contained immense riches, so that the "treasures of the Indies" became a byword for unimaginable wealth, and they were peopled by races less aggressive and less skilled in warfare than the Europeans. It followed that the natives might be subdued with the aid of firearms, and robbed with ease, or at least compelled to sell their products cheaply. A thirst for gold, and for the silks and spices that were worth their weight in gold, lured the explorers on; but in some cases they had a loftier motive, their desire to serve God by bringing the blessings of Christianity to the heathen. The conquest and colonization of the Americas reveals both these motives at work, so that the record presents a strange pattern of courage and cupidity, piety and piracy, martyrdom and massacre, interwoven, as the opportunities of the new land excited the noblest or the basest instincts of the conquerors.

Motives of explorers

The Spaniards and Portuguese took the lead in promoting the earliest voyages of exploration so actively that they seemed destined in the sixteenth century to divide the heathen world between them. Such a twofold division of the non-Christian portions of the globe was actually promulgated by Pope Alexander VI in 1493. Spain received a title to North and South America, while Portugal inherited Africa, India, and the Spice Islands of the East. The papal line of demarcation was subsequently declared to run from the North to the South

FORT NIEUW AMSTERDAM

*The earliest known view of the Dutch settlement of
New Amsterdam, which became New York after 1664*

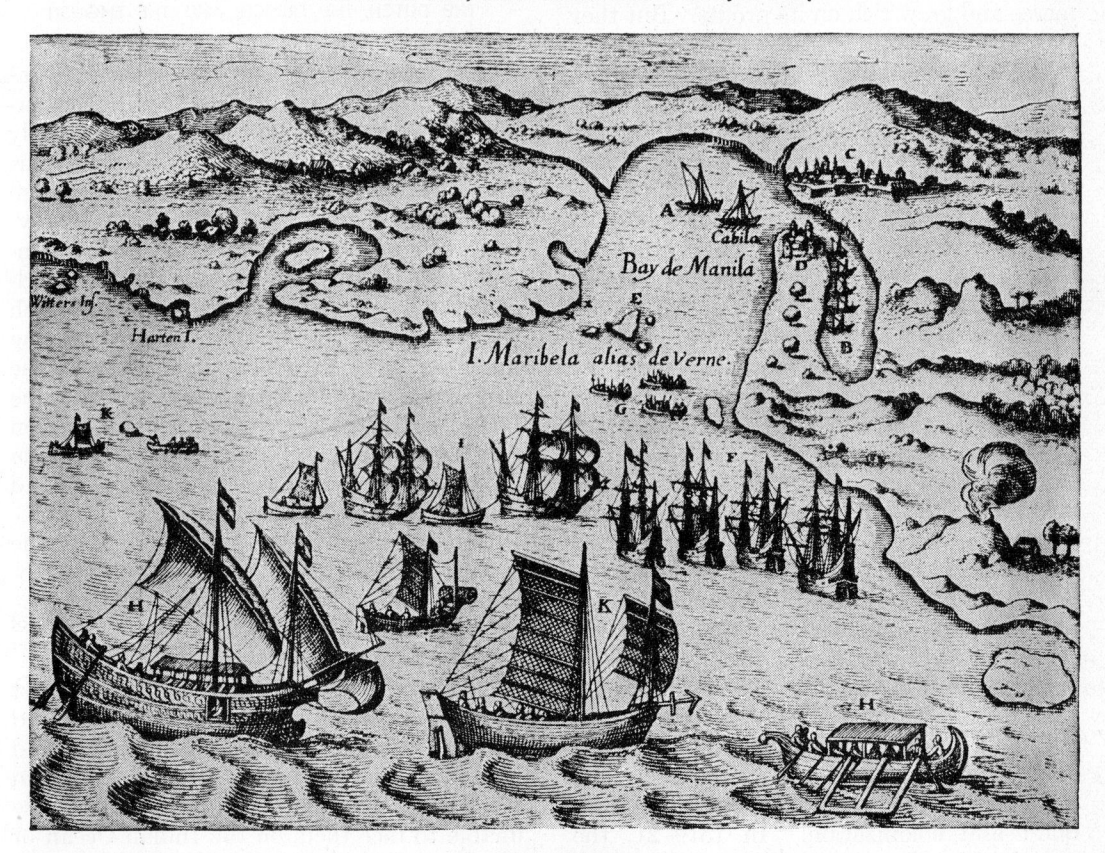

MANILA (1619)

*Manila, founded by the Spaniards in 1571, was destined
to pass to the United States three centuries later.*

Pole through a point three hundred and seventy leagues west of the Cape Verde Islands, and this gave Portugal the eastern half of Brazil also. These vast possessions brought enormous wealth to the Iberian peoples, but they also excited the envy of the Dutch, the French, and the English, who not unnaturally coveted a share of colonial trade and territory. By 1600, the Portuguese in the East and the Spaniards in the West had built up empires of measureless extent and wealth. It remained to be seen whether they could maintain their dual monopoly of the new lands.

The empire which the Portuguese established in the East Indies was an empire based upon trade. Fortifying themselves at convenient points — at Ormuz in Persia, at Goa in India, at Malacca, the Spice Islands, Java, and Sumatra — they monopolized the commerce and grew rich on its profits. But they sent out few white settlers, for the lands of the East were already densely populated, and their missionaries converted a very small proportion of the natives to Christianity. The "unchanging East" accepted their presence and their extortions, but their empire was an artificial one, without roots. It had been created by the genius of the viceroys, Almeida and Albuquerque, who broke the naval power of the Arabs in the Indian Ocean and substituted that of Portugal (1505–15). While their supremacy held, the Portuguese shipped yearly their rich cargoes to Lisbon, spices and rare fabrics from the East, gold and ivory from Africa, sugar, emeralds, and dyestuffs from Brazil. Then, after 1600, the Dutch and English tracked the Portuguese wealth to its sources, invaded the Indian Ocean with superior naval forces, and divided the vulnerable Portuguese Empire there between them.

During the same period the Spaniards in America were laying the basis of an empire of a different and more enduring kind. Finding the western world sparsely populated, they embarked upon a policy of wholesale conquest and colonization. In 1519–21, the redoubtable Cortez overthrew the Aztec Empire in Mexico; ten years later, Pizarro, with equal daring, made himself master of the Inca cities in Peru. The enormous treasure which these conquests yielded drew a stream of adventurers to the New World. Central and South America were parceled out as viceregal provinces; the Indians were subdued and converted to the Catholic faith; and the forests, mines, and plantations were soon yielding their tribute to Spain. When Philip II, coveting the Portuguese trade also, united the crowns of Spain and Portugal in 1580, he made himself master of an empire upon which the sun never set, and Europe trembled at the power of a monarch who could draw upon the wealth of the two Indies. But the vast imperial structure, reared by Spanish and Portuguese sea power in less than a century, lacked inward strength and was not destined to endure.

3. THE SEVENTEENTH CENTURY: COMPETITION OF THE DUTCH, THE FRENCH, AND THE ENGLISH FOR COLONIES AND TRADE (1588–1688)

The beginning of the Spanish decline was marked by the loss of the Dutch Netherlands. Many Dutch merchants had already grown wealthy as middlemen, buying cargoes of Portuguese spices and reselling them throughout Europe, before the Dutch provinces broke into revolt against Spanish control (1566). In their struggle for independence the Dutch found that they could enrich themselves and cripple their foe by preying upon Portuguese and Spanish shipping. The English, already jealous of Spanish maritime power, aided the Dutch, and the destruction which overtook Philip's Invincible Armada (1588) proclaimed the fact that Spain had passed the zenith of her greatness.

The first maritime nation to profit by the decline of Spain was the new Dutch Republic. By 1600, Dutch ships had rounded the Cape of Good Hope and the oriental empire of Portugal was at their mercy. A Dutch East India Company was formed (1602), and within ten years the hardy Hollanders had made themselves masters of the eastern trade. Spanish and Portuguese ships were unable to face them on the Indian Ocean or the Atlantic, and for a time a Dutch expedition even occupied the Brazilian coast.

These spectacular successes, and the commercial prosperity which they brought to the United Provinces, made the Dutch the envy of all Europe, but their supremacy lasted barely half a century. After 1650, England on the sea and France on land almost crushed Holland between them. In a series of trade wars (1652-54, 1665-67, 1672-74) the English captured a share of the eastern trade and annexed New Amsterdam, which they renamed New York. Further weakened by the attacks of Louis XIV, the Dutch were driven after 1674 to seek an alliance with their later despoiler, England, as the only means of resisting the French preponderance. The accession of a Dutch stadholder to the English throne, in the person of William III (1689), cemented this alliance, and the ambitions of Louis XIV were successfully curbed. But the Dutch had lost ground in the struggle and their maritime supremacy had passed to Great Britain.

The English colonial empire, which was ultimately to surpass all others, included in the seventeenth century only some islands in the West Indies and a strip of coast in North America stretching from Maine to South Carolina.[1] To this may be added a disputed claim to Newfoundland and to the little known regions of Hudson Bay. But the English, like the Dutch, took advantage of the Spanish decline to organize an East India Company (1600), and several associations were formed in the following years to promote English trade and colonization in North America. Religious persecution at home helped to swell the colonial population, for nonconformist exiles founded Plymouth in 1620, and Roman Catholics flocked to Maryland after 1632. By 1700, the English colonies on the mainland had a population of well over three hundred thousand souls, imbued with a hardy, aggressive, and independent spirit.

English settlements

The French colonists in North America were only about one tenth as numerous, but they had extended their settlements from the mouth of the Saint Lawrence River to the Great Lakes, and had established a claim to the Valley of the Mississippi. The accompanying map reveals how this extension of French influence confined the English settlements, preventing expansion to the north, the west, or the south. A thoughtful observer might easily have foretold, in 1700, that the century would bring a long struggle between France and Britain for the control of the Ohio and Mississippi Valleys.

The great Colbert, minister to Louis XIV of France from 1661 to 1683, had striven earnestly to build up the French navy and merchant marine in order to win control of the seas and their trade. But Louis, preferring the vision of European dominion, wasted his resources in continental wars, and England, victorious at sea, gained Acadia (Nova Scotia) and a clear title to Newfoundland and the Hudson Bay territory from France in the Treaty of Utrecht (1713-14), which ended the War of the Spanish Succession. From Spain, the ally of France, the English gained Gibraltar and Minorca in the Mediterranean, the right to send one ship a year to trade with the Spanish American colonies, and the highly lucrative privilege of supplying these colonists with negro slaves. This agreement was known as the *Asiento*.

The decline of Spain and Holland had left France and Britain to dispute for the crown of maritime supremacy. In this keen contest France had the advantage of a larger population, but the English were able to throw more energy into the struggle. They could devote all their resources to naval development because a strong fleet was at once the best defense from invasion and the best protection for their shipping. Great Britain possessed, moreover, a parliamentary government which was responsive to the demands of the influential merchant class. Parliament favored commerce and had freed it from the restrictions and the crippling supervision which still burdened French traders. In other words, England had evolved into a mercantile state, with the requisite economic machinery — banks, joint-stock companies, an independent merchant class, and a strong maritime tradition — while France remained an essentially continental state with rigid institutions un-

Primacy of the English

---

[1] See map, pages 586-587, "The Colonial Situation About 1689."

adapted to control and direct the new forces to the best advantage. The French colonies in Canada were laid out like transplanted feudal fiefs, and the settlers, despite brilliant leadership, never acquired the energy and initiative of the English colonists. Similarly, the French trading companies, organized and subsidized by royal decree, failed to compete profitably with rival ventures which owed their existence to the enterprise of Dutch or English merchants.

4. THE EIGHTEENTH CENTURY: THE DUEL OF FRANCE AND BRITAIN FOR COLONIAL SUPREMACY (1689–1763)

The French in India

In the quarter of a century which followed the Peace of Utrecht (1713–14), the French made the most determined efforts they had so far shown to check the British in India and America. Of the lost Portuguese Empire in the East, the Dutch had taken the islands while tacitly relinquishing India to British enterprise. Eager to gather some of the profits of the India trade themselves, the French entered the race, and speedily alarmed the English by their competition. They had organized a French East India Company (1664); now they established posts and factories in India, defended them with forts and garrisons, and concluded treaties with the native princes. Trade, however, was by no means the sole attraction which drew European adventurers to India. It was a much more lucrative venture to aid the Indian rulers in their wars against one another, for the presence of a small European force with its superior weapons could decide important campaigns, and the rajahs were ready to pay for such aid with a king's ransom. When, after 1741, the able and ambitious French governor general, Dupleix, began to recruit and drill Indian troops and meddle in the affairs of the Great Mogul's Empire, the British were convinced that he planned to make French influence supreme and expel them from the peninsula.

England vs. Spain

Between Spain and England also a hostile spirit reigned, for the Spaniards wished to monopolize the trade of their South and Central American colonies. The Treaty of Utrecht, which permitted the English to sell the colonists slaves, and to send one trading ship a year to the Isthmus of Panama, revealed to them how profitable commerce with New Spain might be, and they coveted more of it. Had it been possible, they would have seized the Spanish cities in the New World, but the empire of Spain was vulnerable only on its fringes. Stretching from the Rio Grande to the Rio de la Plata, with its

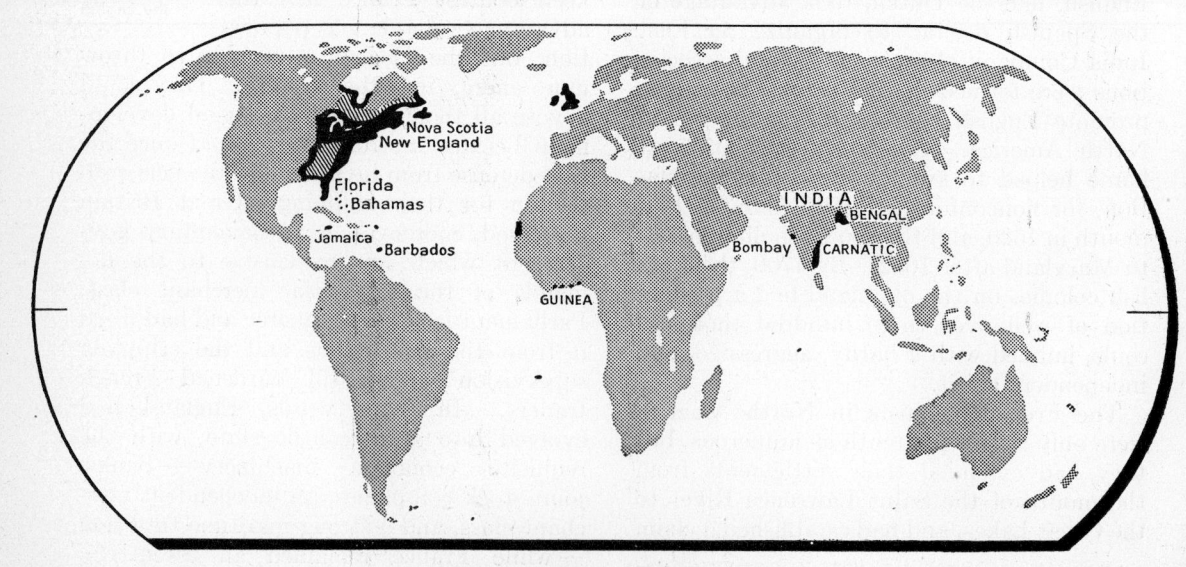

BRITISH COLONIAL EMPIRE IN 1763

ports of entry well guarded, New Spain has been compared to a tortoise which hides under its shell and defies its enemies. The English had to content themselves with the gains they made by bribing the Spanish authorities and so carrying on a smuggling trade with the colonists. This equivocal state of affairs created ill-feeling on both sides. When, in 1739, a Captain Jenkins came before the English Parliament avowing that his ship had been boarded and his ear cut off by the Spanish officials, a conflict developed between Spain and England known as the "War of Jenkins's Ear."

The following year (1740) Frederick II of Prussia seized the Austrian province of Silesia and plunged Europe into the War of the Austrian Succession, in which England and Austria were allied against Prussia, France, and Spain. The European aspects of this struggle, which left Prussia in possession of Silesia, have been described already.[1] In India and America the French and English fought with varying fortune but indecisive results. By the Treaty of Aix-la-Chapelle (1748), England, France, and Spain restored all conquests, and the English consented to abandon the *Asiento* in return for an indemnity of £100,000.

War of 1740–48

The interval of peace which followed 1748 was only a breathing spell in the colonial struggle, a preparation for a definitive test of strength between France and Great Britain. To the victor would go the mastery of the seas and a colonial empire without parallel in history, yet even this glittering prize failed to excite the French to a supreme effort. Under the indolent Louis XV, they turned their attention more willingly to Polish or German problems than to the needs of their colonies. Brilliant leaders like Dupleix in India and Montcalm in Canada worked heroically for the glory of France, with inadequate resources and scant encouragement, while the national revenue was being gaily squandered by the courtiers at Versailles. In America, especially, the French commanders displayed foresight and energy in their efforts to hem in the English by a line of forts stretching from the Valley of the Saint Lawrence down the Ohio and Mississippi rivers to the Gulf of Mexico. But too many Frenchmen thought with Voltaire that Canada was only "a few acres of snow," and failed to appreciate that the expenses of a single campaign on the Rhine might have secured half a continent across the ocean.

Hostilities between the French and English broke out again in America in 1754, where the new struggle was to be known as the French and Indian War. Its European phase began in 1756, and was marked by the heroic defense which Frederick the Great of Prussia maintained against France, Austria, and Russia.[1] While the Prussian king waged his desperate campaigns year after year, his ally, England, was concluding the colonial duel with France. Fortune proved unfavorable to British arms in the first campaigns; a force under General Braddock was ambushed and almost annihilated near Fort Duquesne on the Ohio River; and expeditions directed against the French forts at Niagara and Crown Point were unsuccessful. But in 1757 the British were inspired to new efforts by the great war minister, William Pitt (the Elder), and their victories broke the French resistance. In 1759, in a battle which cost both leaders their lives, Wolfe wrested Quebec from the French veteran Montcalm, and Canada, with its sixty thousand settlers, was lost to France. The British flag seemed destined to wave undisputed from the Gulf of Mexico to the Arctic Ocean.

The French lose Canada

In India the success of the English was no less complete. The ambitious projects of Dupleix were frustrated by the military skill and audacity of a young commander, Robert Clive, whose astonishing feats with insignificant forces broke the French influence. The southeast coast of India (the Carnatic) as well as the rich province of Bengal were brought under British control. When the Seven Years' War ended in 1763, French naval power had been shattered and French commerce had all but disappeared from the seas.

The stakes in this most arduous and exhausting colonial war yet fought had clearly

[1] See above, page 578.

[1] See above, page 580.

gone to the English. Yet it would be a mistake to imagine that the extension of British influence and the annexation of new lands benefited all Englishmen equally. The classes which profited directly were the investors who drew larger dividends from the fur trade with the American Indians, the colonists and land speculators who could exploit the rich territory beyond the Alleghanies now freed from French control, and the adventurous officials in India whose lucrative meddling in native affairs now met no serious competition. These were the classes which had done most to provoke the war, and had pressed Parliament most vigorously to carry the struggle to a victorious conclusion.

The Treaty of Paris (1763) reflected the magnitude of the British triumph. It left **Treaty of Paris (1763)** England in control of French Canada, and of Florida which was ceded by Spain. As compensation, the Spaniards received a title to the lands, only partly explored, lying between the Mississippi and the Pacific Ocean. In India the French retained some of their trading posts, but their activities were so restricted that they could no longer offer any effective opposition to British expansion. The Treaty of Paris assured Great Britain the position of the world's leading commercial and colonial power, a position which her less successful rivals found it difficult to contemplate without envy. Smarting from their losses, and from British arrogance, the French, the Dutch, and the Spaniards all nursed a hope of revenge. They were to find an opportunity to gratify it shortly by helping to disrupt the British dominions in America.

5. THE BRITISH COLONIES IN AMERICA WIN THEIR INDEPENDENCE

In the eighteenth century colonies were valued chiefly because they provided non-European commodities, such as rice, sugar, and tobacco, for consumption in the home country, and thus helped to render it independent of the products of other nations. This attitude toward colonies was an extension of the prevailing Mercantile System, formulated in the belief that a great power should accumulate gold by selling to its neighbors while buying as little as possible in return. As early as 1650, the English Parliament passed more stringent Navigation Acts, which declared that only English ships could bring colonial products to English ports. Later edicts commanded the English colonists to trade only with the mother country, and forbade them to compete with manufacturers in England. For instance, the colonists were forbidden to make hats for sale in England, while the English people were forbidden to raise tobacco which was a colonial monopoly. It irked the merchants of Boston and Philadelphia that they were expected to sacrifice potential profits by trading only with English firms, when they could obtain tea from the Dutch or molasses from the French at cheaper prices. The regulations were frequently evaded and a smuggling trade developed which the British government made little serious effort to repress. This tolerant attitude eased the friction which might otherwise have developed, and the colonists were reasonably satisfied as long as the government at London pursued a policy which has been defined as "salutary neglect."

After the Seven Years' War this tolerant state of affairs underwent a change, and the British government assumed a more despotic tone in matters **Colonists resentful** of colonial administration. With the establishment of peace in 1763, the prime minister, George Grenville, prepared to regulate colonial trade more vigorously. New import duties were imposed upon coffee, wines, calico, etc., entering the colonies, and although the duty on foreign molasses was reduced (1764), a determined effort was made to keep the American merchants from smuggling it in duty free as they had been doing. The colonists had been in the habit of selling their products in the foreign West Indies, buying in return the sugar and molasses from which they manufactured cheap rum to exchange for Indian furs and African slaves. When this form of exchange was checked by the British regulations, the colonists found themselves running short of hard money wherewith to buy British goods; and when they sought to issue paper cur-

WILLIAM PITT, EARL OF CHATHAM

William Pitt, the Elder, was the great British war minister of the Seven Years' War.

ROBERT CLIVE

By conquering Bengal, Clive laid a basis for British supremacy in India.

JAMES WOLFE

The daring assault by which Wolfe captured Quebec in 1759 delivered Canada into the control of the British.

CAPTAIN JAMES COOK

Cook rose from the rank of common seaman to become the greatest British navigator and explorer of the eighteenth century.

BRITISH ARCHITECTS OF EMPIRE

rency to supply the shortage, Parliament restrained them (Currency Act of 1765). To British statesmen, conscious that England had incurred heavy expenses in order to win the Seven Years' War, it appeared no more than just that the colonists should pay in part for their defense. The effort to suppress smuggling and increase the customs revenue reflected this policy, and the government sought to raise further funds by a Stamp Tax (1765), requiring all pamphlets, newspapers, and legal documents to bear a stamp. The colonists, however, argued that they could not legally be taxed by a Parliament sitting in London, to which they elected no representatives, and so loudly did they raise the protest of "no taxation without representation" that the Stamp Tax was withdrawn in 1766.

Nevertheless, the British government still insisted upon its right to levy duties if it saw fit to do so. The colonists were requested to provide for the maintenance of British garrisons stationed in America for local defense, and additional duties on imports were introduced to meet this expense (Townshend Acts, 1767). Twenty years earlier the colonists might have furnished such a contribution willingly, for they needed the protection of British regulars while the French still menaced their settlements. But the Seven Years' War had transferred Canada to England and broken the French power in the West. This newly won security fostered a spirit of independence and self-confidence in the British colonists, and they found it easy to convince themselves that the policy of George III and his ministers was a despotic infringement of their liberties.

When the British attempted to employ coercive measures, they excited armed resistance (1775). Both sides were determined not to compromise, and the colonists prepared to fight for their rights and if possible enlist outside support. In 1776, a Continental Congress representing all thirteen colonies assembled in Philadelphia and issued a Declaration of Independence. In taking this extreme step the delegates were strongly influenced by the knowledge that the French government might aid them materially if they gave proof

July 4, 1776

that they sought complete separation from England. But the new nation thus ushered into existence was at first neither free nor united. The British were determined to hold the empire together by all the armed force at their command, while in America many colonists, known as "loyalists" or "tories," were opposed to the complete separation demanded by the "patriots."

The Declaration of Independence attributed the outbreak of hostilities to the tyrannous rule of George III, but the true causes were deeper and more complicated. The colonists, a nation of some three million in 1775, were accustomed to managing their own affairs. By toil and daring they had subdued and colonized a strange land. To survive and prosper under such conditions required courage and initiative and bred a spirit of self-assurance and independence. A clergyman writing in 1781 estimated that the English settlers had killed eighty-six thousand Indians in fifty years; and on the lands thus cleared they had set busy towns and rich plantations. It was perhaps no more than natural that these Americans should resent the orders of a cabinet in London, which understood little about their problems and had long treated them with comparative indifference and neglect. The removal of the French menace, as already explained, gave the colonists a new sense of strength and security; the attempts of the British officials to regulate their trade and supervise their affairs more straitly crystallized their discontent; and the treatment accorded to the newly conquered French Canadians added a final grievance. For by the Quebec Act (1774) the British government extended the boundaries of Canada south to the Ohio River (territory the American colonists coveted for themselves), and promised the French Catholics the full privileges of their religion, customs, and laws, measures which gratified the Canadians as deeply as they affronted the New England Puritans. Thus the ties which bound the English colonists to the mother country had been progressively weakened before the Declaration of Independence broke them.

At first it appeared improbable that the Americans could maintain the independence

ADAM SMITH (1723–1790)

Adam Smith, the Scotch economist, indicted the old colonial system and advocated economic liberty in his "Wealth of Nations," published the same year as the Declaration of Independence.

THOMAS JEFFERSON (1743–1826)

As author of the Declaration of Independence and third President of the United States, Jefferson exemplified the faith in democracy, the vision, and the inventiveness which brought forth a new nation.

THE DECLARATION OF INDEPENDENCE, 1776

The expansion of the United States from a colony to a leading world power in a century and a half is the most remarkable epic in modern history.

which they had proclaimed. When, after three years of campaigning, the tide of success began to turn in their favor, France came to their aid (1778) and was joined by Spain (1779) and Holland (1780). Great Britain could not maintain a successful struggle against this coalition. The high-handed use which the British had made of their maritime supremacy had left them without a friend in Europe, and they were willing by 1782 to purchase peace at the price of concessions. The thirteen colonies were recognized as independent [1] and became the United States of America; the territories of the new nation extended from the Atlantic seaboard to the Mississippi, and from the Great Lakes to Florida. Florida itself Great Britain retroceded to Spain, while France regained some posts in India, two islands in the West Indies (Saint Lucia and Tobago), and Senegal and Gorée in Africa. The British had tasted the medicine of defeat and their prestige had been somewhat reduced, but Great Britain still remained the foremost colonial and maritime power of the world.

Anti-British coalition

6. THE ABATEMENT OF COLONIAL RIVALRY AFTER 1783

By the end of the eighteenth century, the Spanish, Dutch, French, and finally the English had discovered that it was easier to found settlements overseas than to retain them. Colonies, as one French statesman observed, were like fruits: they dropped from the parent tree as soon as they were ripe. To waste blood and treasure establishing such colonies, only to see them fall into other hands or assert their independence, seemed a dubious investment, especially because most of the islands and coastal areas in the New World had been claimed, and the further exploitation and colonization of the interior promised to be an even more costly and hazardous enterprise. This mood of disillusionment may explain in part why the powers relaxed their colonial rivalries for nearly a century after 1783. Wars were not for that reason less numerous or less destructive, but they were inspired by events in

[1] Treaty of Paris, 1783.

Europe itself and were little affected by colonial questions. Not until after 1870, as we shall note later, did new factors drive the nations to revive their interest in overseas empires, and the spirit of a "New Imperialism" make colonies once again a major source of armed conflict.

The reverses suffered in America might have provided British statesmen with valuable lessons in the art of colonial administration, but there is little evidence that they derived much conscious profit from them. Their attitude toward French Canada remained benevolent but conservative. The Quebec Act of 1774, as already explained, conciliated the *Canadiens* by preserving their customs and religion, and this statesmanlike treatment of the conquered kept French Canada loyal while the thirteen colonies revolted. In 1791, representative assemblies were established in Upper and Lower Canada (Ontario and Quebec), but the Canadians had to stage a minor rebellion (1837) before they obtained a measure of genuine popular government, and not until 1867 were the scattered provinces knit into a self-governing Dominion.

Colonial government

Ireland likewise, though granted a local parliament in 1782, was deprived of this privilege in 1801 when England was struggling against Napoleon, and the Irish remained bitterly discontented with British rule throughout the nineteenth century. In India a somewhat more liberal and conscientious policy prevailed after 1784, when the East India Company was brought under stricter government supervision lest it abuse its great power, but there also a bloody rebellion, the so-called Sepoy Mutiny of 1857, was needed to awaken the British administrators to the importance of reform.

The mercantilist philosophy, the application of which had helped to disrupt the British Empire in America, held its ground for some decades after 1783, but yielded slowly to the newer doctrines of free trade. Many economists, especially in France, had come to believe that governmental regulation of trade by means of monopolies, tariffs, and bounties was artificial and constrictive, creating

Decline of mercantilism

more evils than it cured. To govern better, they argued, it was necessary to govern less, for trade languished under arbitrary rules and could prosper to best advantage only when it was allowed to follow a normal or natural development. The most able exposition of the new theory was propounded by the Scotsman, Adam Smith (1723–90), in a monumental study entitled *An Inquiry into the Nature and Causes of the Wealth of Nations*. By a coincidence, Smith's work, which was to become a bible for those who advocated a liberal trade policy, appeared in 1776, the year the American colonists proclaimed their independence. The mercantilist theory thus received two blows, one in the practical and one in the theoretical field, during the same year. When the liberal bourgeoisie secured control of the English Parliament in the nineteenth century, they were to lead the way in advocating the doctrine of non-interference with trade, or *laissez-faire*, and to see their theories apparently vindicated by the unequaled prosperity which British commerce and industry enjoyed throughout the greater part of the century. But this prosperity was founded upon a combination of favoring circumstances which could not endure indefinitely, and in the twentieth century even the British, as we shall discover, found that free trade could become unprofitable in practice.

DUTCH SAILORS STUDYING NAVIGATION, 1661
The Netherlanders were the most enterprising navigators of the seventeenth century.

43

The Intellectual Revolution

> True philosophy expounds nature to us; but she can be understood only by him who has learned the speech and symbols in which she speaks to us. This speech is mathematics, and its symbols are mathematical figures.
> GALILEO GALILEI (1564–1642).
>
> If I have seen farther than Descartes, it is by standing on the shoulders of giants.
> SIR ISAAC NEWTON (1642–1727).

THE MOST SIGNIFICANT CHANGES in human history, developments fraught with incalculable results for the destiny of mankind, have sometimes passed all but unnoticed in their time. To European people in the seventeenth and eighteenth centuries the misery of the Thirty Years' War, the troublesome ambitions of Louis XIV, the rivalry of France and England for colonies or of France and Austria for conquests, seemed matters of the highest importance. And so, in their time, they were. But the historian who looks back on those centuries can detect a movement of another kind, a movement which proceeded without thunder of cannon or fanfare of trumpets, yet was destined to change the course of history more profoundly than all the wars from that time to the present. This development was the progress made in the study of natural science.

1. THE BEGINNINGS OF THE SCIENTIFIC REVOLUTION

Scientific spirit
The Italian Renaissance in the fifteenth century had liberated a remarkable outburst of creative energy, and the Protestant Reformation in the sixteenth had shaken the power of the universal church and weakened the hold of tradition. More men had begun to think for themselves, and by the seventeenth century they were looking about them with a new self-confidence, a new audacity, a new inquisitiveness. Rejecting accepted beliefs, natural philosophers in all parts of Europe turned to probe Nature for her secrets with sharpened curiosity, and the result was a flood of discoveries. In a few generations men learned more truths about the universe in which they lived than their ancestors had brought to light in all previous history. Linking one discovery to another, formulating bold hypotheses and then confirming them by observation and experiment, scientists created a new heaven and a new earth, sweeping into the discard many of the most venerable beliefs which they had inherited from previous ages. Compared with this revolution in thought, the social and political changes of the period were insignificant, but the new theories were unintelligible to most people and were consequently ignored by them. Then as now scientific speculation proved too abstruse to be grasped by the lay mind, and the progress of science depended upon the labors of a small class of experimenters and specialists.

Some of the earliest and most brilliant victories of the new scientific method were won in the field of astronomy. Although in ancient times several Greek astronomers had taught correctly that the earth revolved about the sun, during the Middle Ages the

NICOLAS COPERNICUS (1473–1543)

GALILEO GALILEI (1564–1642)

Five thinkers, a Pole, a German, an Italian, an Englishman, and a Frenchman, whose speculations dissolved the firmament.

JOHANNES KEPLER (1571–1630)

ISAAC NEWTON (1642–1727)

PIERRE SIMON DE LAPLACE (1749–1827)

people of Europe believed that the earth was the immovable center of the universe, and that round it the other heavenly bodies revolved once in twenty-four hours. This theory had been expounded so convincingly by an astronomer of Alexandria, Claudius Ptolemaeus, who lived in the second century of the Christian era, that it is still referred to as the Ptolemaic theory.

Copernicus
For thirteen centuries this fallacious view prevailed, until in 1543 a thoughtful Polish astronomer, Nicolas Copernicus (1473–1543), offered a new theory to explain the movements of the heavenly bodies. He suggested that the sun was the center of the system, that the earth and planets revolved about it, and that the earth also rotated on its axis once every twenty-four hours. This view, which we accept today as self-evident, is termed the Copernican theory because it was first advocated in the work Copernicus prepared *On the Revolution of the Heavenly Bodies*.

As this book was written in Latin, and was difficult to understand, only scholars paid any attention to it at first. Some found it convincing and declared that a more patient and exact observation of the heavens would confirm its thesis. Others rejected the whole theory as fallacious, even asserting that it was dangerous and blasphemous to publish views which seemed to contradict the Bible and the teaching of the church. But the stars in their courses were fighting for the new theory and an increasing number of astronomers became reconciled to the Copernican formulas.

Kepler
By the opening of the seventeenth century, the movements of the planets had been calculated so carefully that a German astronomer, Johannes Kepler (1571–1630), was able to formulate mathematical laws for them. He showed (1) that each planet in its orbit around the sun does not describe a perfect circle, but an ellipse of which the sun is one of the foci; and (2) that the speed of each planet changes, growing swifter as it passes nearer the sun and slower as it swings around the more distant segment of its orbit, so that its radius vector traverses equal areas in equal times. These conclusions led Kepler to his supreme discovery or third law. (3) The time interval which a planet requires to complete its journey around the sun depends upon its mean or average distance from the sun. This dependence Kepler reduced to the formula: the square of a planet's periodic time is proportional to the cube of its mean distance from the sun.

Galileo Galilei
The invention of the telescope at this time brought fresh evidence to support the Copernican hypothesis and justify it as a system. In 1610, the Florentine scientist, Galileo Galilei (1564–1642), turned this new instrument upon the heavens and disclosed a succession of marvels. For the first time the mountains of the moon, the rings of Saturn, the moons of Jupiter, and the phases of Venus were made visible to the eyes of men. Doubters who had found it easy to scoff at theories were shaken by observable facts. Yet to many it still appeared wicked to teach that the earth, far from being the center of things, created by God's special care as the stage for the drama of man's fall and redemption, was in reality no more than a ball of mud spinning on an endless spiral through infinite night. Galileo was warned by the Inquisition that in defending the new astronomy he was weakening Christian belief and the respect due to established authority. When he persisted, he was summoned before the Inquisition, compelled to forswear his belief in the movement of the earth, and forbidden to teach the theory thenceforth. Had he refused to yield, he might have been imprisoned for life or burned at the stake.

Despite discouragement and opposition, however, the scientists intensified their speculations and experiments, spurred on by the conviction that the heavens had further secrets to yield. The order and permanence which prevailed in the solar system drove them to ponder what force could hold the moons and planets to courses of such undeviating regularity. In 1600, an Englishman, William Gilbert (1540–1603), suggested that the earth might be regarded as a huge magnet which attracted bodies to itself by magnetism or gravitation. Kepler developed this idea, arguing that the force of attraction exercised by a body increased with its mass and extended far beyond that body, so that the earth, for example, must exert a constant attraction upon the moon which the moon resisted through some equivalent counterforce.

It remained for the English mathematician, Sir Isaac Newton (1642–1727), to reduce these inferences to order and explain the movements of all the celestial bodies as consequences of one general law of gravitation. In 1687, in his immortal *Principia*,[1] Newton formulated his conclusion that the force of attraction between two bodies varies directly as the product of their masses and inversely as the square of the distance between them. To test his hypothesis he applied it to explain the movement of the moon about the earth, and when he found his figures working out correctly, he was so deeply stirred by the splendor of his discovery that he had to ask a friend to finish the calculations for him. For further verification he extended his computations to the planets, to the tides, even to the apparent vagaries of comets, and found that all proclaimed the universality of the law his genius had discerned.

Sir Isaac Newton

In the century and a half following the death of Copernicus scientists had stripped most of the mystery from the heavens. Inexorable laws were found to govern the movements of all sidereal bodies, so that the smallest comet hurtling through the darkness of outer space could not vary a hair's breadth from the path prescribed for it by mathematical calculations. Edmund Halley, a friend and disciple of Newton, was able to compute the orbit of a comet which appeared in 1682 and predict its reappearance in seventy-seven years. Halley's comet not only justified this computation by reappearing in 1759; it returned in 1835 and 1910, and may be expected again about 1986. The medieval superstition that comets were sent to announce an approaching disaster or the death of a king was thus forced to yield, like many another superstition, to the matter-of-fact explanation of the scientists. It is not difficult to understand why opposition grew between those people who chose still to believe in omens and miracles and the rationalists who insisted there was no place for miracles in a universe governed by inflexible laws.

While the study of astronomy advanced thus with giant strides, the other sciences were not standing still. In physics, chemistry, anatomy, and a score of related fields, investigators only a little less illustrious than Galileo or Newton pressed on to new discoveries. In their search they found it necessary to invent tools more delicate and more accurate than the human senses, like the telescope, microscope, thermometer, and barometer. Unfortunately, there is no space to tell here how William Harvey (1578–1657) discovered the circulation of the blood, how Anton van Leeuwenhoek (1632–1723) first observed bacteria under his microscope, or how Robert Boyle (1627–91) formulated the law that the volume of a gas varies inversely with the pressure. Merely to list the outstanding discoveries of these eventful years would require several pages. So productive were the experiments of these fathers of modern science, so profound their speculations, that the seventeenth century has been well named "The Century of Genius." Of the many triumphs only the epic of the astronomers has been related in any detail because it reveals best of all two *habits* which the scientists had cultivated, to which they owed their amazing success. These were (1) the habit of translating all calculations whenever possible into a new and special language, the language of mathematics; and (2) the habit of basing all conclusions upon observation and experiment instead of appealing to ancient writers or to popular belief for the truth. Both these practices were so important and so revolutionary that they demand explanation.

"Century of Genius"

2. THE PROGRESS OF MATHEMATICS

The scientists of the seventeenth century first clearly perceived that "mathematics is the skeleton of God's plan of the universe." The most brilliant achievements of the astronomers, from Kepler's discovery of what he

"Language of Nature"

---
[1] The full title is *Principia Philosophiae Naturalis Mathematica*.

well named *The Harmony of the Heavens* to Newton's law of gravitation, were all expressed in mathematical formulas. It delighted these natural philosophers to think that they had at last stumbled upon the language in which Nature wrote her secrets. "This language," proclaimed Galileo, "is mathematics, and the characters are triangles, circles, and other mathematical figures." A peculiar charm invested this language of numbers, for it was flexible, accurate, and international.

The development of modern mathematics is the most original achievement of the human intellect. Although the ancients had laid down many of the first principles of the science, their legacy, in comparison with the progress of modern times, is like the simple melody of a flute contrasted with the intricate harmonies of a hundred-piece orchestra.

Advance in mathematics — To this science of numbers "The Century of Genius" made four pre-eminent contributions: (1) The introduction of decimals, first written with a decimal point in 1616, saved vast labors in the handling of fractions. (2) Of even greater value was the conception of logarithms, announced by a Scotsman, John Napier, in 1614. Because they offered a short cut through cumbersome calculations, logarithms doubled the lives of astronomers by halving their labors. (3) A further advance in method is associated with the name of the French philosopher, René Descartes (1596–1650). In 1637, Descartes revealed in his analytic geometry how facts ascertainable in geometry may be translated into algebra, and *vice versa*, thus offering a dual method of attack whereby stubborn problems could be outflanked. (4) A fitting culmination to these previous gains was the formulation after 1680 of the differential calculus, developed independently by Sir Isaac Newton and the German philosopher Leibnitz, and acclaimed as "perhaps the most important step in the progress of mathematical science."

3. THE EXPERIMENTAL METHOD

The second habit to which the scientists owed much of their success was their practice of appealing to observation and experiment as the surest test of truth. No statement, though repeated by ancient and venerable sages and long accepted by the mass of mankind as too obvious for argument, was to be accepted if it contradicted established facts. Copernicus, for instance, rejected the opinions of men of learning and the evidence of his own senses, all of which assured him that the earth was immovable. But because this theory failed to explain the motions of the planets, he abandoned it, observed the phenomena, pondered them, and then devised a new theory which would include and account for the motions of all the heavenly bodies. Reasoning in this way from a number of particular cases to a general conclusion is called *induction*. The triumph of Copernicus was one of the first in a long series of successes won by the method of experiment, observation, and induction.

Beliefs vs. experiments — Scholastic thinkers of the Middle Ages had been disposed to spin fine theories while ignoring facts, or to interpret facts in such a fashion that they would appear to support established theories. Believing, for example, that the sun was a perfect, unchanging body because the Greek philosopher Aristotle had said so, the later schoolmen offered this statement, which they could not prove, as a refutation of the Copernican theory. When the newly invented telescopes revealed spots on the sun which moved across its face, the Aristotelians declared the notion inadmissible and argued that the flaws must be in the telescope because they could not be in the sun. Similarly, the scientists demonstrated by dissection and experiment that accepted beliefs in anatomy and physics were wrong, but they found it difficult to convince conservative thinkers, who rebuked them for their irreverence and repudiated the evidence submitted to them. Some theologians affirmed that the Devil mixed himself in scientific experiments and falsified the results in order to confuse men and shake their faith in true principles. In the face of such objections it is not altogether surprising that advocates of the newer sciences learned to feel contempt for the scholastic philosophy and for its defenders.

The experimental method, on the other

hand, seemed to promise man infinite possibilities for bettering his lot and controlling his destiny. The English lord chancellor, Francis Bacon (1561–1626), thought so highly of it that he drew a prophetic picture of the glories of the future in his *New Atlantis,* and scorned the hoary errors of the past. In breaking with tradition the new thinkers came to prize independence of judgment above mere book learning. Thomas Hobbes (1588–1679), who sometimes acted as secretary to Bacon and later wrote dogmatic works on political philosophy, was wont to boast that if he had read as much as most men he would probably know as little. "Reasoning from the Authority of Books," he declared, in his caustic fashion, ". . . is not Knowledge, but Faith." Descartes found so many errors in the works on anatomy which he consulted that he turned to Nature for the truth. "These are my books," he told a visitor, pointing to the bodies of animals which he was dissecting. But these scientists, though they sometimes scorned the learning of earlier centuries, understood the value of sharing their discoveries with each other. "If I have seen farther than Descartes," admitted Newton, who lived half a century later, "it is by standing on the shoulders of giants."

4. THE SCIENTIFIC ACADEMIES

It was, therefore, by means of learned journals, correspondence, travel, and exchange of views that the earliest scientists sought to keep alive the flame of curiosity, which, while it sometimes burns brightly in one lonely genius, is never so productive as when it feeds upon the combined enthusiasm of many workers. In their impetuous search they were like mountaineers who attack a mighty peak from many sides, convinced that they were destined to converge until they met together at the summit and found that all truth was ultimately one. Newton had compared himself to a child playing on the seashore with the great ocean of truth all undiscovered before him, but many of his followers were less modest and more sanguine. Already they had learned how a discovery in physics might supply the clue to an obscure problem in astronomy, and this in turn depend for solution upon a recent advance in mathematics. The most versatile genius could not excel in all fields, but he might utilize the principles and proofs established by gifted contemporaries if he could avail himself of them. By such borrowing a scientist was in a position to follow experiments in a hundred laboratories at once, observe the stars from every corner of Europe on the same night, and help himself to the answers which the labor of others had wrung from arduous computations. Such collaboration speedily became a habit with the scientists, as fruitful in its results as the habit of using observation and induction to seek new truths and the habit of expressing them in mathematical terms when found.

The easiest way to share ideas is by personal contact, and societies organized for discussion and experiment were one of the first proofs that the scientific revolution had begun. **Academies of Science** An "Academy of the Lynx-Eyed" was formed at Rome in 1601, and an "Academy for Experiment" made its appearance at Florence in 1657. After 1660, when war ceased for a time to absorb the major attention of princes, several new societies were established under royal patronage. The most distinguished were the "Royal Society for Improving Natural Knowledge" incorporated at London in 1662, and the French "Académie des Sciences" chartered by Louis XIV in 1666. To record their deliberations and experiments these academies published scientific journals, and to encourage research they collected funds to build libraries and observatories and to purchase retorts and furnaces, telescopes and microscopes, chronometers, barometers, air pumps, and all the other paraphernalia which laboratory workers had discovered they needed in their pursuit of "Natural Philosophy."

By the eighteenth century, scientists were no longer persecuted; they were honored and rewarded. Galileo had been reproved by the Inquisition for his novel opinions, but when **Interest in research** Sir Isaac Newton died in 1727, less than a century later, he was buried with honors befitting a king. Science had begun to capture the popular imagination. Even people who

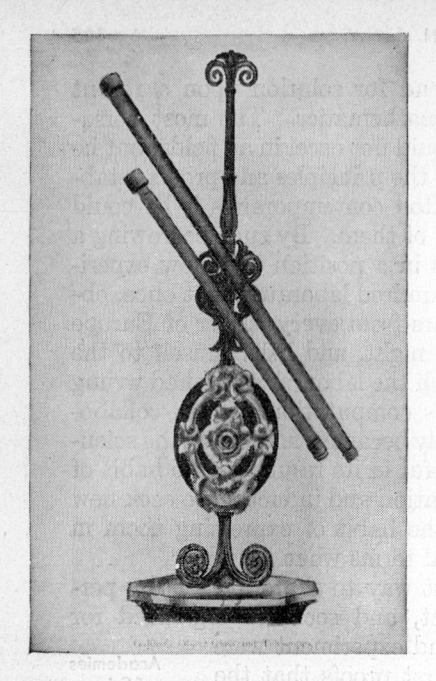

GALILEO'S TELESCOPES

The instruments with which Galileo and Newton worked seem trivial when measured against the revolution they wrought in astronomy.

NEWTON ANALYZING A RAY OF LIGHT

Newton considered his experiment with a prism, which analyzed a ray of sunlight into its primary colors, as "the oddest, if not the most considerable, detection which hath hitherto been made in the operations of Nature."

THE LABORATORY OF ANTOINE LAURENT LAVOISIER

Antoine Laurent Lavoisier (1743–1794), assisted by his wife, laid the basis of quantitative chemistry by his exact experiments and careful recordings.

GEORGE LOUIS LECLERC DE BUFFON
(1707–1778)

Top left: Buffon labored for years compiling a Natural History, completed in 44 volumes after his death.

CAROLUS LINNAEUS (1707–1778)

Center left: This great Swedish naturalist is known as the father of modern systematic botany.

NATURAL HISTORY CABINET

Upper right: This sketch of 1719 represents an idealized plan for a natural history museum, but it also reflects the deepening public interest in Nature.

JENNER'S FIRST VACCINATION

Right: The artist has pictured a famous medical event, when an English physician, Edward Jenner, used the virus of cowpox, from which the dairymaid suffered, to vaccinate a boy against smallpox (1796).

did not understand much about it were persuaded that it provided a new and marvelous method for unveiling Nature's secrets. Cultured ladies and gentlemen read books explaining Newton's laws and attended lectures on astronomy. Some wealthy men equipped laboratories of their own and conducted experiments in the hope of adding to the sum of human knowledge. And the sum of knowledge continued to grow. In chemistry the elements hydrogen, nitrogen, and oxygen were isolated and their general properties analyzed; in physics valuable progress was made in studying the nature of heat and sound; in zoology, Buffon (1707–88) and Linnaeus (1707–78) reduced the study of animals to a descriptive science. Benjamin Franklin demonstrated that bolts of lightning were discharges of electricity which could be turned harmlessly aside by a lightning conductor. Astronomy, anatomy, biology, geology, and mineralogy likewise had their triumphs and flourished apace, so that although the seventeenth century takes rank as "The Century of Genius," the eighteenth has been well named "The Scientific Renaissance."

5. THE INTELLECTUAL REVOLUTION

In every age the great majority of people are too absorbed in their private affairs, in trade, or crops, or home-making, to pay much attention to the progress of abstract ideas. Few Europeans in the seventeenth and eighteenth centuries, for instance, were aware that their habits of thought were changing, for the changes came in slow and subtle ways. Nevertheless, each generation brought some modification of ancient beliefs and outworn ideals, each decade contributed some new discovery, until all educated Europeans, without being aware of it, had passed through a revolution. This revolution was in no way sudden or violent, but it was a revolution none the less. For it overturned a hierarchy of intellectual values, freed civilized men from many obsolete prejudices, knocked the shackles from their minds, as it were, and turned their thoughts from the past to the future. Above all, it filled them with an intoxicating wine, the wine of a new self-confidence.

A very old and intelligent man, looking back let us say from the year 1760, might have observed that within his own lifetime people had altered many of their ideas. A man of unusual perception might even have noted that this change could chiefly be distinguished as "a waning of fear." With each generation it seemed as if men had less dread of the wrath of God, less reverence for the wisdom of the ancients, less awe respecting Nature and her unknown forces. How was this change coming about and what factors promoted it? Whence arose this skeptical and arrogant spirit in the hearts of men which is such a striking component of the modern temper? It will be an interesting task to try to answer these questions.

With the rise of natural philosophy, theology was displaced from its proud position as "Queen of the Sciences." The Great Schism, the Revival of Learning, and the Protestant Reformation had all tended to weaken the unity and authority of the medieval church, and the religious wars which racked Europe for a hundred years sapped by their futile fanaticism the faith of many Catholics and Protestants alike. By the eighteenth century religious fervor was yielding before the spirit of tolerance or indifference. It was no longer the custom to burn witches, or to martyr as heretics those who wished to seek heaven in their own fashion. Secular concerns and worldly pursuits had obscured the sense of intimate dependence upon religion which people had felt so keenly in earlier centuries. Some skeptics dared to repudiate all belief in an infinite power and to deny that the theologians were or ever had been the custodians of divine truths which could guide men to salvation.

Decline of theology

The new learning offered man a more vainglorious picture of himself, and rooted itself in his pride, whereas his religious beliefs had been the fruit of his humility. Man was a miserable creature, the theologians had taught, condemned, because of his corrupt nature, to err and suffer endlessly unless he were rescued by divine grace and intervention. But the rationalists were moved to question this view. Perhaps, they sug-

Rise of rationalism

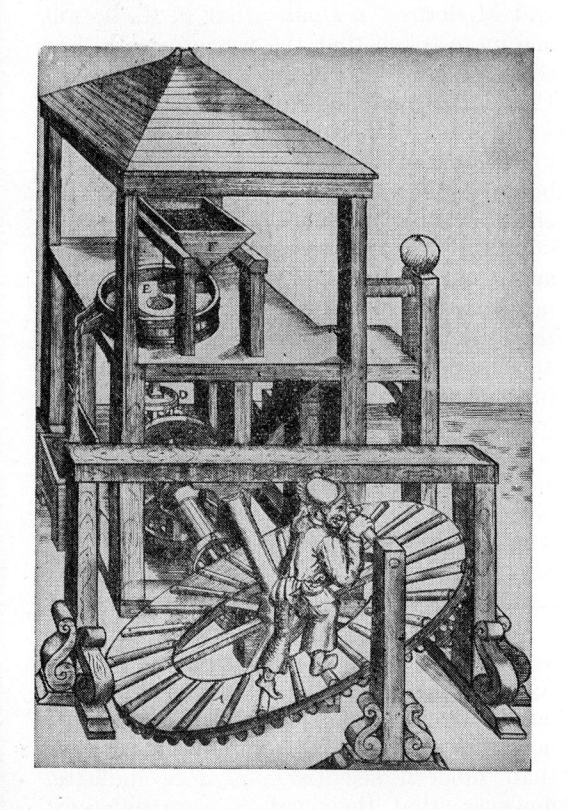

THE APPLICATION OF POWER

These plates, from a work published as early as 1598, prove that the application of power to machinery was well understood. What was needed was a form of energy more effective than men, animals, wind, or water could then provide.

gested, man was intended to control his own destiny, instead of bowing fatalistically to the will of an inscrutable Providence. If God granted him intelligence, there could be nothing blasphemous in using it. It might be that the plagues and miseries from which he suffered were not after all the righteous punishment for his sins, but only the logical consequences of his folly. Instead of being "born to trouble as the sparks fly upward," he might be born to improve his lot on earth far beyond his hopes or dreams. The "original sin" which brought woe to men might not be the sin of Adam, but the sin of their own stupidity. These and similar arguments of the philosophers, disseminated by a few bold minds, won converts and leavened the consciousness of European society because they were suited to the temper of the new age.

The decline of theology was reflected in the waning faith in miracles. If God had established majest and inflexible laws for the movement of the stars and other phenomena of the physical world, it seemed illogical to suppose that He would interfere arbitrarily with the working of them. To imagine that God could be swayed by human passions or prayers, so that He would make the sun stand still, conjure up a hurricane to punish a blasphemous sailor, or overwhelm a wicked city by a specially invoked earthquake, appeared to the rationalists both stupid and irreverent. They preferred to conceive of God as a remote and impersonal deity, a First Cause or First Principle, or an ideal constitutional monarch who never violated the laws which He had established for the government of the natural realm. Thinkers who embraced this view were termed deists, but some went so far as to deny the existence of a deity altogether, and thereby proclaimed themselves atheists.

Deism and skepticism

A waning reverence for the wisdom of the ancients has been cited as the second symptom of the Intellectual Revolution. In the general assault upon authorities and institutions long established, the reputation of the classical authors suffered considerably. Under Louis XIV some French savants, proud of the greatness of their own age, dared to challenge the title of superiority commonly accorded the great men of Greece and Rome. Half the conclusions of Aristotle, they pointed out, had been disproved by modern students of science; Plato, the "divine Plato," was after all no more than human; Virgil, for all his suavity, was somewhat cold and barren; and even the great Homer could sometimes nod — and make readers nod — with his tedious digressions. At this blasphemy the champions of the "ancients" sharpened their pens and hastened to combat these audacious "moderns." Seas of ink were spilled and the controversy dragged well into the eighteenth century without reaching a decision. But thinking men in general came to feel that the moderns were partly right; that in mathematical and scientific progress, and perhaps in music also, their own age was supreme, though they were willing to concede that ancient masterpieces in art and literature might remain unsurpassed. This "Quarrel of the Ancients and Moderns," a small affair in itself, was one more token that the western world had come of age. For over a thousand years Europeans had looked backward with a sense of nostalgia and tragic loss to the fading gleams of the Age of Gold. They had hoarded the crumbs of wisdom from the classical times as mankind's rarest heritage of culture, for, in the barbarism of the dark ages, such veneration was not altogether misplaced. Now they were escaping from this tutelage of the past and learning to anticipate such glorious progress in the future that all previous accomplishments would seem but a prelude to it.

Ancients and Moderns

The third and possibly the most important change which the Intellectual Revolution brought to western man was a new attitude toward Nature. Medieval students neglected the natural sciences, and few important discoveries in physics or chemistry, in astronomy or medicine, were made during the Middle Ages. This failure to investigate Nature does not prove that medieval thinkers were necessarily less intelligent or industrious than modern scientists; it does indicate, however, that their values were different,

Nature long neglected

that they reasoned from different premises and pursued a different aim. Undue concern with earthly affairs diverted the soul from God and might lead to damnation. The investigator who dabbled successfully in alchemy, astrology, or other pseudo-sciences, became to the popular mind a wizard or magician who had purchased his uncanny art by selling his soul to the devil. To the majority of people in the Middle Ages, the world was like a haunted house, in which they moved about cautiously and timorously, respecting the jealous whims of unknown beings, and trusting to the aid of the saints and angels to save them from the devils and goblins.

When the austere wind of scientific speculation blew away the mists of medieval fantasy, it disclosed a universe built on a grander scale and a different plan from that previously imagined. To the eye of the scientist Nature emerged as a vast and intricate machine of severe and geometric beauty. The great machine was governed by eternal and immutable laws. To suppose that such a universe could turn from its course to strike a man to earth for presumptuous questioning, or that the sea would part and allow him to cross it dry-shod in his need, was to the rationalist a naïve and implausible presumption. "In Nature there are neither rewards nor punishments, there are only consequences." And it appeared to follow that if man had faith in himself and in science, if he applied himself to the study of Nature and mastered her secrets, he could learn to avoid evil consequences and assure good ones, thus becoming the arbiter of his destiny. Such at least was the dazzling promise held out by many apostles of the new enlightenment.

This optimistic faith in man's capacity for progress inspired the Age of Reason. Liberal thinkers everywhere urged that manners, morals, modes of education, of government, of religion, should be analyzed rationally, brought to perfection, or discarded. Once the existing laws and institutions had been perfected, the rationalists felt confident that humanity would undergo a miraculous regeneration. This conclusion appeared to follow logically from the teaching of John Locke (1637–1704), who had proclaimed in his *Essay Concerning Human Understanding* (1690) that man's knowledge and beliefs are the fruit of his training and environment and are not predetermined by innate ideas or the curse of original depravity. The mind of a newborn child Locke compared to a blank sheet of paper. "Let us suppose the mind to be, as we may say, white paper, void of all characters, without any ideas — how comes it to be furnished?" he asked, and answered his own question with the one word "Experience." It appeared, therefore, that children born into a just and equitable society, children trained in right thinking under a rational régime, could not fail to grow into good citizens. The first step toward reform was to abolish all irrational practices, all abuses, all myths and superstitions, and to establish wise principles, just laws, and rational institutions.

In thus insisting that man must be freed from all myths and superstitions, the philosophers overlooked the possibility that to cling to myths and superstitions might be part of his nature, and in their relentless war against prejudice and error they failed to take account of their own delusions. They erred concerning the past, particularly the Middle Ages, the significance of which they misunderstood and underrated; and they erred even more seriously concerning the future, for they evinced a touching faith in human perfectibility and underestimated the obstacles to human happiness which still confronted them. They imagined that the millennium was at hand because they had found a fruitful method for investigating the physical sciences, and they leaped to the false conclusion that this method could be applied to the social sciences with the same success. Some ages ask questions, others answer them. The eighteenth century was of the latter type. Its intellectual leaders hoped to find the answers to all the problems of society, they burned to apply them, and infected all classes with their contagious enthusiasm. It is not difficult to understand why the century was loud with projects of reform, nor surprising that it should have ended with a revolution.

44

Government and Society under the Old Régime

> I should have wished to be born in a country in which the interest of the Sovereign and that of the people must be single and identical; to the end that all the movements of the machine might tend always to the general happiness.
>
> JEAN-JACQUES ROUSSEAU.

THE SYSTEM OF GOVERNMENT and the organization of society under which the European peoples lived before the great French Revolution broke out in 1789 is commonly spoken of as the *ancien régime* or old régime. It was an outmoded and inefficient system with glaring deficiencies. The wreckage of feudalism still weighed like an incubus upon society, and governments functioned in a makeshift and haphazard fashion, for none of the states had developed administrative machinery adequate to deal with the complexities of a mercantile era. It is the purpose of this chapter to reconstruct a picture of life under the old régime, and to emphasize the defects and abuses which incited the French people to rise against the system. As France was in many respects the typical land of the old régime, the discussion will deal with France in particular, but the student may think of the conditions described as prevailing with local variations throughout most of Europe.

1. DIVINE-RIGHT MONARCHY IN THEORY AND PRACTICE

In the Middle Ages two small but powerful classes, the clergy and the nobles, had come to dominate society. Above these, as the separate states organized themselves, rose the power of the king. By the seventeenth century, in almost all the European states, monarchs had made their authority supreme in theory and in fact. What the king willed was law; his peculiar function was to be at once the benevolent father of his people and the dread sovereign who animated and directed the life of the state. The laws were executed in his name, the coinage was stamped with his image, the nobles enjoyed his bounty and the priests offered prayers for his preservation. For a subject to refuse homage, or to question why one man, who might be endowed with no particular brilliance of mind or nobility of character, should enjoy royal honors, was considered sedition. The king held his office through hereditary right, an office glorified by tradition and sanctified by religion. The throne was revered as the altar was revered, because both were regarded as symbols of God's divine authority governing the world through His instruments.

In practice, needless to say, the absolute power of the king was modified by a thousand contingencies. He was dependent upon a host of subordinate officials who supplied him with information and exercised delegated powers in his name. Even an industrious monarch like Louis XIV of France, the model of absolute despots, could not

The royal government

supervise all the business of the state; under his indolent successor, Louis XV (1715–74), France was governed in reality by the ministers of the royal council. These councilors sometimes met together with the king presiding, but more often assembled in smaller committees, as the council of state, council of dispatches, council of finance and commerce, and council of war. As the functions of the councils were not very clearly defined, there was much confusion and business piled up more rapidly than it could be dispatched. The councilors were often compelled to waste their time on trivial matters while important issues waited, but they hesitated to delegate the decision to subordinates for fear of sacrificing their jealously guarded authority.

Chaos in the provinces
Confusion in the capital bred chaos in the provinces. The royal government in France had extended itself gradually, as it was superimposed by successive rulers upon the relics of feudalism and upon the vestiges of local institutions older sometimes than the monarchy. The kingdom had been acquired by fragments and organized by fits and starts. At one time it had been divided into *baillages* and *sénéchausées*, later into *gouvernements*, and finally, under Richelieu, into *généralités*. Each *généralité* was controlled by a royal official known as the intendant, and the power of the intendants had grown so great that they were called in the eighteenth century the "thirty tyrants" of France. Yet the governors of the provinces still held office, as relics of an older organization, and some of the provinces preserved a shadow of independence under their local assemblies, or estates, and were known as *pays d'état* to distinguish them from provinces which lacked this privilege, the *pays d'élection*. Finally, the country was further separated into segments for ecclesiastical administration, segments which bore little relation to the political subdivisions, and into judicial districts which bore little correspondence to anything, even to one another.

The centralization of authority in the hands of the bureaucracy had stifled the initiative and enterprise of local officials, who found it easiest to refer every difficult decision to their superiors. An army of civil servants was required to handle the flood of reports, dispatches, and petitions which poured in from the provinces. The royal government of France was no worse than that of Spain or Austria; it was served by many hard-working and intelligent administrators; but their efforts were of little avail in a system which seemed to have been specially devised to perpetuate confusion and procrastination. When advisers warned Louis XV that reforms were desperately needed, the pleasure-loving king replied that the machine would last out his day. He left it to his ministers to make minor repairs and readjustments and to keep the machine running.

Disorder in the courts
What the state required was a radical and exhaustive reconstruction in every branch of the administration. The partial and often capricious reforms instituted by the ministers in the hope of clearing a way through the disorder only added to the confusion. Their instructions were commonly so involved, so lengthy, and so loaded with amendments that their subordinates found it impossible to master them. Worst of all, where a sound and simple statute existed which might have served as a guiding principle, it was speedily corrupted by a list of exceptions each more complicated than the original. Critics of the old régime in every state in Europe were agreed that the reform of paramount importance was the preparation of a simple and unified code of laws. An absolute monarch, it was urged, might bring order out of the existing chaos by defining the duties and functions of his government in a few logical and invariable rules. Or, if the prince neglected his duty, the people themselves might prepare a constitution which would safeguard their liberties by establishing the government on true and inflexible principles. Throughout society, from the king's councilors to the petty tradesmen in provincial towns, irritation at the administrative disorder was growing into a passion.

2. THE PRIVILEGED AND UNPRIVILEGED CLASSES

The feudal stratification of society into three classes, the Clergy, the Nobility, and the Third Estate, had become iniquitous and illogical by the eighteenth century. In France, a country with perhaps twenty-five million people, the clergy and nobility together constituted less than two per cent of the population, yet they enjoyed the income from the richest lands of the kingdom, were exempted from the most onerous taxes, and occupied by right of rank the highest and best paid offices in the government, the army, and the church.

The Roman Catholic Church in France owned approximately one fifth of the land.

The French clergy
Its income was enormous, one half as great as the royal revenues according to some estimates, and was derived from two main sources. The estates of the church brought in the modern equivalent of $200,000,000 a year, and a sum almost as large was furnished by the tithe. This was a tax, theoretically one tenth but in practice more often one fifteenth or less, commonly levied upon the annual yield from land cultivated by laymen. The church itself paid no taxes to the king on its property, but the clergy voted "free gifts" to the royal exchequer from time to time as a partial substitute. Part of the revenue of the church went for charitable purposes, part as salary for the 130,000 clergy; but the salaries were very unevenly distributed. Many abbots and bishops, nobles by birth in most cases, disposed of princely incomes, but the humble and hard-working parish priests were often little better off than the peasants among whom they labored. The impending revolution was to prove that many village *curés* had less loyalty to the First Estate to which they nominally belonged than to the Third Estate whose grievances they understood.

The second privileged class, the nobles, numbered about 110,000 souls, and likewise

Privileged nobility
enjoyed the income from about one fifth of the land. As a rule this land was cultivated by tenants who paid the noble owner rent and services for the privilege. Some of the nobles did not even reside on their estates, preferring the more amusing and expensive life at court. Bailiffs collected from the tenants the income which these absentee landlords often squandered on gambling and display. There was a further injustice in the fact that the nobles who enjoyed this unearned revenue, amassed by the toil of others, were free from the more burdensome taxes which the impoverished peasant still had to pay. It was the dream of many a wealthy bourgeois to win his way into this privileged caste, and members of the Third Estate occasionally gained patents of nobility through purchase or distinguished service. Such newcomers were termed the "nobility of the robe" to distinguish them from the prouder "nobility of the sword" whose titles often dated from feudal times. In addition to their exemptions and the income from their estates, many nobles received pensions from the king, while others, who had ruined themselves through extravagance and failed to secure a share of the royal charity, had to retire to their mortgaged lands and a life of penurious obscurity.

The millions of unprivileged subjects who made up the Third Estate scarcely needed the writings of the philosophers to persuade them that the system under which they lived was

The Third Estate

out of joint. The simple peasant, who plowed his land and dreaded the visits of the tax collector, might not understand much about political economy, but he had grievances that were concrete and specific. It irked him that when he had scattered his seed in the furrows the pigeons from the lord's dovecote might scratch it up again; that he was forbidden to molest the deer when they nibbled his vegetable garden because they were maintained for the nobleman's pleasure; that when his tender crops which represented weeks of care and toil were trampled by a hunting party from the castle, he had no means of claiming compensation. It was troublesome, too, that he had to carry his grain to the lord's mill to have it ground, and leave part of it as payment when he had too little for himself, or that he might be summoned to work on the road (the *corvée*), or to draw wood to the castle, when his threshing was overdue and his apples were rotting in the orchard because he had no time to press the cider.

The heavy and unequal taxes were a spe-

LOUIS XV (1715–1774) **MADAME DE POMPADOUR**

When warned of the defects in his government, Louis XV is reputed to have said, "After us — the deluge!" Some memoirs attribute the remark to Louis's mistress, Madame de Pompadour.

FESTIVAL FOR LOUIS XVI AND MARIE ANTOINETTE TO CELEBRATE THE BIRTH OF THE DAUPHIN (1781)

Such costly displays when France was at war and the government insolvent were not wise.

cial source of bitterness. All the ranks of the unprivileged, the upper middle class, the lower middle class, the artisans, the servants, the peasants, down to the thieves and vagabonds of the highway, hated the fiscal system. This was not surprising since the burden of taxation rested most heavily upon those least able to support it and crushed the peasant most cruelly of all. For in addition to the rent and services paid to the lord of the manor, and the tithe paid to the church, poor Jacques had to discharge a land tax (the *taille*), a poll tax, an income tax, and a salt tax (the *gabelle*). Peasants too poor to buy food were still compelled to purchase salt at exorbitant prices, and if they attempted to smuggle enough for their need in order to avoid paying the royal revenue on it, they were punished with barbarous severity. Many of them deliberately sank into a state of destitution, knowing that to improve their dwellings or increase the yield of their lands would only expose them to higher assessments and heavier taxes.

The middle-class dwellers in the towns, though better off than the peasants, were even more critical and discontented. The professional and business classes, the bourgeoisie, included the most cultured, the most intelligent, and the most progressive elements in the nation. From the bourgeois class came the most competent officials in the king's service; it included the bankers who tided the government over its financial crises with their loans, and the business men who increased the prosperity of the state by their commercial and industrial enterprise. Yet this energetic and intelligent class was denied political power, and its members were forced to accept a position of inferiority, while the highest offices in the church, the army, the law courts, and the diplomatic service were bestowed upon men whose only claim to preference was their noble birth. Knowing their own worth and importance, conscious that in wealth, ability, and education they were the equals of the titled few, ambitious members of the bourgeoisie hated the system which denied them their deserts. They possessed both the intelligence and the motive for starting a revolution, and they

The bourgeoisie

fed their discontent by studying the abuses in the government, particularly those connected with the administration of law and the collection of taxes.

3. LEGAL AND FINANCIAL ABUSES

The confusion of authority under the old régime is well illustrated by the condition of the law courts. Instead of a uniform code of laws in force throughout the nation, France was burdened with some three hundred and sixty differing codes, with the inevitable result that jurisdictions overlapped, decisions conflicted, and litigation grew to interminable proportions. Moreover, an offense punishable in one court by a fine might earn branding or ten years in the galleys from another, although it was obvious, as the rationalists pointed out, that there could not be several penalties for the same crime and all of them just. The humane spirit of the age was further shocked by the barbarous practices of judicial torture, mutilation, branding, and breaking on the wheel. It was not unknown for judges to dismiss guilty criminals brought before them rather than inflict the brutal sentences prescribed by the statute books. But the worst terror in this legal jungle was the arbitrary power of the king and his ministers, who could imprison any citizen without warning, without trial, and without appeal, and on the sole authority of a royal *lettre de cachet* confine him in a secret dungeon "at the king's pleasure."

Harsh laws

Another active cause of discontent was the stupid and oppressive legislation which fettered the expanding trade and industry of the age. Interior customs lines restricted the normal flow of commodities, feudal overlords still levied toll on certain goods passing through their dominions, and town wardens stopped merchandise at the gate for an entrance fee. A load of wine on its way to Paris, for instance, might be assessed for duty over twenty times, with much consequent waste and delay. In industry, progress was checked by the obstructive and antiquated guilds, which guarded their monopolies jealously. Artisans were forbidden to change from one trade to another, and better

Industry and trade checked

and speedier methods of manufacture were frequently outlawed because of ancient ordinances which had outlived whatever usefulness they once possessed.

Had the government of Louis XV pursued an energetic and successful policy abroad, Frenchmen might have overlooked their domestic ills. But in the wars of the eighteenth century, France was singularly unfortunate, and by 1763 the country had lost all but a remnant of its colonial empire, and amassed a heavy debt. Frenchmen knew that their country was one of the most populous, most favored and wealthy in Europe, yet every year they saw the national indebtedness increase, until bankers hesitated to lend money to the state even at twenty per cent interest. One grave fault of the fiscal system was the custom known as "farming out the taxes." A group of wealthy men would advance a sum of money to the king in exchange for his permission to reimburse themselves by collecting the taxes due. As they often collected more than they had advanced, this practice of discounting the revenue meant in reality that it was carried to the king as it were in a leaking bucket. A second grave fault was the absence of a budget. The monarch treated the national revenues as a private credit account, and might squander upon his mistresses and his amusements the resources which should have been devoted to urgent national needs.

Evils of the tax system

4. THE CRITICISM OF THE PHILOSOPHERS

Against these numerous abuses the rationalists of the eighteenth century leveled a stream of brilliant, satirical, and destructive criticism. With the Intellectual Revolution a spirit of rationalism and skepticism had spread among the enlightened classes of society. In France the movement was particularly strong, for it was led by a unique group of writers who are known as the *philosophes*. No tradition or institution was sacred to these critics, who delighted in holding up to public ridicule the stupidity, hypocrisy, and irrationality of existing customs, and who pleaded, in the name of humanity and right reason, for a program of intelligent reforms.

The philosophers

The most famous of the *philosophes* was François Marie Arouet, better known as Voltaire (1694–1778). Like the other *philosophes*, Voltaire was not a philosopher in the English sense of a profound, original, and systematic thinker. Rather he was a popularizer of ideas, an inspired journalist, whose tireless and sarcastic pen never rested. The ninety volumes of his collected writings show him in every mood from delicate irony to thunderous denunciation and fully explain why he found it necessary to pass much of his life beyond the borders of France. Against the theologians in particular Voltaire delighted to turn the flood of his mockery. He was the self-appointed champion of all victims of bigotry and injustice and he made Europe a court which rang with his appeals. Religion had originated long before priests, he believed, but it had been exploited ever since "the first knave met the first fool." To expose the tricks of religious charlatans and break the power of narrow and intolerant sectarians Voltaire considered a service to humanity; he raised the battle cry, *écrasez l'infâme!* (destroy the infamous thing!) insistently, for to him intolerance symbolized all that was stupid, irrational, and degrading in the old régime. A "natural religion," he pointed out, was one that would "enjoin us to serve our neighbors through love of God," but we had been led by intolerance and bigotry into the monstrous error of "persecuting and butchering them to His greater glory."

Voltaire

Scarcely less influential than Voltaire was Denis Diderot (1713–84), who edited an encyclopedia to which almost all the philosophers contributed. The encyclopedia proved an arsenal of arguments for the rationalist cause and was completed in 1765 after repeated efforts had been made to suppress it by the clergy and the censors. While avoiding controversial subjects as far as possible, the encyclopedists wrote to convince the thoughtful reader that science, and the growth of a tolerant spirit, had contributed more to the happiness of mankind than the tenets of a thousand warring religious faiths. Theological doctrines were not excluded from the work, nor were

Diderot

JEAN-JACQUES ROUSSEAU (1712–78)

Morbid sensitivity and a feeling of personal maladjustment made Rousseau the most eloquent critic of eighteenth-century society with its artificialities and inequalities.

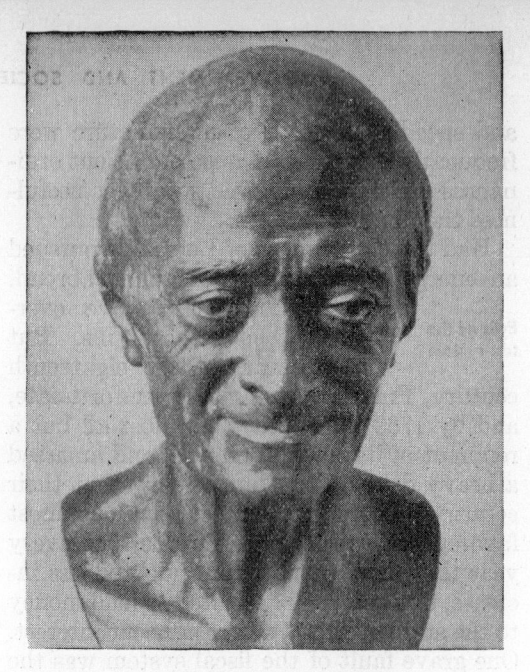

VOLTAIRE (1694–1778)

The sculptor, Jean-Antoine Houdon, has caught the keenness of wit, self-conceit, and genius for mockery which drove Voltaire to attack all irrational customs and stupid abuses.

BARON DE MONTESQUIEU (1689–1755)

Montesquieu wakened a more critical attitude toward government by his "Spirit of the Laws" (1748).

DENIS DIDEROT (1713–1784)

The editor of the famous "Encyclopédie" was an understanding friend and a man of virtue and sentiment.

FOUR CRITICS OF THE OLD RÉGIME

they openly combated, but they were overshadowed and robbed of significance by the space and emphasis devoted to more practical and secular matters.

No evil stirred the philosophers more profoundly than the inequality of the laws, for they were almost all members of the Third Estate and resented the immunities enjoyed by the privileged orders. Also, they had personal grievances, for several of them (like Voltaire) had been imprisoned for audacious writing, or (like Diderot) had seen their books burned by order of the censor. Furthermore, the spectacle of criminals going to execution was a constant reminder of the barbarous codes in force. In 1764, an Italian *philosophe*, the Marquis Beccaria, published *An Essay on Crimes and Punishments*, in which he denounced the use of torture and the infliction of cruel and outmoded punishments. Beccaria even ventured to urge the abolition of the death penalty, arguing that "crimes are more effectively prevented by the *certainty* than the *severity* of the punishment." His essay was translated into several European languages and exerted a strong influence on theories of criminal jurisprudence.

Beccaria

In view of the disorder prevailing in the national finances, it is not surprising that some of the philosophers were attracted to problems of political economy. François Quesnay (1694–1774), court physician to Louis XV, became the leader of a group of thinkers known as the *physiocrats* because they believed all governments should conform to "the natural order of things." They regarded most legislation as a curse rather than a benefit, insisting that trade, for instance, developed most vigorously when least interfered with, since artificial regulations constricted it. Hence, "To govern better, govern less." The mercantilist theory that a state grew wealthy by accumulating gold they declared unsound; the wealth of a society was the *produit net*, the surplus of agricultural, mineral, and other natural products accruing from the labor of its citizens. Agriculture they considered the most vital interest of a nation and they believed it important to improve the lot of the French peasantry because "poor peasants make a poor kingdom."

The physiocrats

To dedicate oneself to the task of rooting out abuses and destroying the obstacles to human happiness is a noble adventure. The philosophers liked to think of themselves as knights-errant of humanity, and could be flattered to tears at the picture of a grateful posterity raising a statue to their memory. They did not doubt that mankind was on the threshold of a new age, in which right reason would triumph, and all citizens would enjoy their natural and imprescriptible right to life, liberty, and the pursuit of happiness. Some oversanguine dreamers even anticipated the installation of a Utopian society which would assure prosperity and contentment to all classes under laws so reasonable and so just that the people "could not choose but be good."

This hope of achieving social harmony was based in part on the deepening reverence for natural law. It seemed impossible that Nature, or Nature's God, could have *intended* confusion and disorder to reign in human affairs, for the rest of the universe, to the orbit of the farthest star, obeyed majestic and inflexible laws. There must be a *natural* order of society, the principles of which had been lost or ignored, and it was the business of the legislators to regenerate society by discovering and applying these natural principles. Once enunciated, the new precepts would be accepted by all right-thinking people. Some of these natural and axiomatic laws the philosophers believed they had already discovered, but they lacked the authority to put them into force. They appealed, therefore, to the princes of Europe, urging them to employ their despotic authority to inaugurate the new régime. So successful was the appeal, and so readily did the rulers lend an ear to the proposed program, that in 1768 Diderot declared enthusiastically, "There is no prince in Europe who is not also a philosopher."

"Natural law" revered

5. THE ENLIGHTENED DESPOTS

Monarchy was to have a last chance to justify itself as "enlightened despotism." The European rulers of the later eighteenth century were for the most part earnest and benevolent princes. In recognition of their high sense of responsibility, and their sincere desire to improve the lot of their subjects, they have been styled the "enlightened despots," and the middle and later years of the eighteenth century constitute "the monarchs' age of repentance." These princes strove to undo in one century the mistakes their ancestors had committed in five. Had they succeeded, benevolent despotism might still be accepted as the ideal form of government in Europe, but their intelligence was not equal to their intentions, and several of them, in their attempts to improve matters, ended by making them worse.

The most brilliant exponent of enlightened despotism was Frederick II of Prussia (1740–86). Many of his reforms anticipated the writings of the philosophers, and, although he delighted to honor these illustrious thinkers whom he called the "masters of princes," his success as a ruler was due less to their advice than to his own practical sense, his energy, and his genius for administration. The improvements he wrought in Prussia have already been described,[1] as well as his military triumphs which won him the title of "the Great."

Frederick the Great

Catherine II of Russia and her attempts to pose as an enlightened despot have also been mentioned, as well as the obstacles which vitiated her reforming zeal.[2] The admiration which Catherine felt for the philosophers, and the interest she took in their recommendations, led her to invite several of them to her court. But Catherine, like Frederick II, was a practicing politician rather than a political theorist, and she never made the mistake of regarding the philosophers as seriously as they regarded themselves.

Catherine II of Russia

The most sincere and least successful of this group of benevolent princes was the Emperor Joseph II of Austria (1780–90). It was Joseph's ambition to transform the disunited Hapsburg possessions into a centralized military state on the Prussian model.

Joseph II of Austria

[1] See above, pages 576–583.
[2] See above, pages 570–572.

His program embraced many admirable reforms; he wished to liberate the serfs, codify the laws, balance the budget, and stimulate trade; but his personality and his methods stirred up a surprising opposition. "Joseph always wishes to take the second step before he has taken the first," was the shrewd judgment of Frederick the Great. In Belgium, Hungary, and the Tyrol the people revolted against the emperor's proposals to unify the imperial administration and make German the official language. The nobles resented his attacks upon their privileges, Pope Pius VI protested against his interference in religious affairs, and the jurists criticized his attempt to improve the legal code. Even his councilors grew discontented and insolent. The mounting opposition only increased Joseph's determination. "The father of a family," he declared, "who holds the welfare of his children at heart, must not allow himself to be turned from a salutary course because of ill-judged complaints."

Failure attended his foreign no less than his domestic policies. An attempt to exchange the Austrian Netherlands for Bavaria was frustrated by Frederick the Great who was ever vigilant to combat any extension of Austrian power in the Germanies. Seeking aggrandizement in another direction, Joseph allied himself with Catherine of Russia and commenced a war against the Turks in 1788. Lacking military talent, he met with reverses, and in 1789, broken in health, he returned to Vienna to die. The thought of his failures obsessed him and in his last months he withdrew all his reforms. "Here lies Joseph II" was the epitaph he composed for himself, "who, with the best intentions, was unsuccessful in everything that he undertook." The judgment of history has been more generous. Peasants long remembered him as their friend, and Protestants and Jews in Austria blessed his memory for his tolerance in lightening the restrictions under which non-Catholics labored.

Of the lesser European states, scarcely one escaped the rough hand of the reformer in the eighteenth century. In Spain the conscientious Charles III (1759–88) curbed the power of the Inquisition and expelled the Jesuits

Spain and Portugal

from the kingdom (1767). Pride, ignorance, bigotry, and lawlessness were too deeply rooted in Spanish life to be extirpated in a single reign, but Charles sought by wise legislation to reduce the effects of these evils. Like measures were pursued in the neighboring kingdom of Portugal by the autocratic Pombal, minister of Joseph I (1750–77). Pombal secured the expulsion of the Jesuits from Portugal in 1759, and the Society of Jesus, already widely unpopular, was suppressed by a papal decree in 1773. It was Pombal's patriotic aspiration to reinvigorate the Portuguese Empire by sending the life blood of trade coursing once more through its enfeebled frame, but his arbitrary temper won him many enemies and he fell from power in 1777.

The prestige of Sweden, which had suffered eclipse in the great northern war,[1] was partially restored during the enlightened reign of Gustavus III (1771–92). This versatile monarch possessed a magnetic personality and labored with zest to reform the finances, improve agriculture, promote education and religious tolerance, and ameliorate the harshness of the laws. Unfortunately, he excited the opposition of various privileged groups, and in 1792 he was assassinated by some discontented nobles.

Sweden

In Denmark-Norway,[2] Count Struensee, able minister of the king, Christian VII, likewise paid with his life for his presumptuous attempt to play the enlightened despot. As the power behind the throne from 1771 to 1772, Struensee reorganized the administration and attacked everything that was corrupt in the state of Denmark, until his enemies combined to impeach him and send him to the block. But the memory of his reforms survived him, for legitimate ideals and aspirations are more difficult to silence than their mortal advocates.

Denmark-Norway

It was a curious anomaly that while French writers everywhere led the attack upon the abuses of the old régime, and French philosophers taught the princes of Europe the axioms of good government, the glaring evils in French administration went unreformed. Louis XV (1715–74) was too selfish and too indolent to work at the arduous rôle of enlightened despot, and his ministers contented themselves perforce with a policy of palliatives and expedients. The peasants continued to groan beneath the burden of their taxes, the bourgeoisie murmured, and the government debt mounted steadily, while the privileged few continued to revel in the golden splendors of the court like butterflies which dream the summer has no end.

France

The accession of Louis XVI in 1774 brought a promise of better days, for one of his first acts was to appoint the able and courageous Turgot controller general of the finances. Turgot was a friend of the philosophers and favored many of the reforms which they had proposed. "Give me five years of despotism," is a saying attributed to him, "and France shall be free." The danger of insolvency he met with the bold policy: "No bankruptcy, no increase in taxation, no loans." Only a rigid curtailment of expenditures could make the plan a success, yet, when Turgot attempted to introduce economies in order to balance the budget, he created a host of enemies, from the extravagant young queen, Marie Antoinette, to the holder of the smallest sinecure. "There is no abuse that does not give someone a livelihood," he admitted bitterly, but he held to his course. Fresh opposition greeted his proposal to relieve the peasants of the hated *corvée* and to suppress the obstructive trade guilds; the clergy were unfriendly because he favored religious toleration; even the *parlement* of Paris, popular with the people because it was considered a check on royal absolutism, joined in blocking his reforms. Had Louis XVI supported him firmly, he might have fought his way through, but in 1776 his enemies won the king over and Turgot was dismissed after twenty months in office. "Do not forget, sire," was his final prophetic plea, "that it was weakness which brought the head of Charles I to the block." But Louis was too confused and too irresolute to profit by sage advice. Turgot's fall sealed the fate of the

Turgot

---

[1] See above, pages 569–570.
[2] The kingdoms of Denmark and Norway were united under the same crown from 1397 until 1814.

LES ADIEUX   LA GRANDE TOILETTE

The histrionic air which makes all the figures in a rococo drawing room seem like character actors was part of the theatricality of the period.

READING MOLIÈRE IN AN EIGHTEENTH-CENTURY FRENCH SALON

The finest blend of social and intellectual life in the eighteenth century was found in the Parisian salons.

A CARNIVAL IN THE STREETS OF PARIS

Above: The elegant manners affected in the eighteenth-century salons had little influence on the multitude. These Parisians are celebrating a carnival.

GIN LANE, BY WILLIAM HOGARTH
(1697–1764)

Below: Paris had no monopoly on misery and vice among the populace as Hogarth's views of contemporary London prove.

French monarchy, for under his successors in office the old expedients were revived, new loans were floated, expenditures increased, and the ship of state drifted steadily toward the rocks of revolution.

6. ROUSSEAU AND THE DOCTRINE OF POPULAR SOVEREIGNTY

When intelligent Frenchmen saw the king and his ministers delay so long in carrying through the needed reforms, they began to ask themselves whether there was not some other authority in the state to which they might appeal. They knew that in the previous century the English people had grown impatient with their monarchy, had sent Charles I to execution (1649), and later had driven James II from his throne and kingdom (1688). These acts had shocked Europe in an age when almost everyone accepted the principle of the divine right of kings, and the English revolutionists had endeavored to justify their unconventional procedure. The philosopher John Locke (1632–1704) argued very reasonably that governments were instituted by the people to protect their lives and property; that when a government failed to fulfill these functions, or a king abused his power, the sovereign people had the right to change their government for a better one. This was what the English had done in 1688–89 when they expelled the absolutist James II and invited William and Mary to reign in his place as constitutional monarchs.[1] They found comfort in Locke's doctrine, which assured them that, far from being rebels, they had in fact acted as honest and courageous citizens defending their natural rights.

John Locke did not originate this idea of the sovereignty of the people, but he was one of the first writers to present it clearly and make it popular. Any people desiring to throw off allegiance to an unpopular monarch could now find an argument to justify the act. In the American War of Independence, the "patriots" invoked Locke's philosophy to prove that the tyranny of George III had absolved the colonists from their allegiance to the English king, and that they were asserting no more than their "natural rights" in setting up an independent government. The idea that the people were not created to obey the king, but that kings were merely executive magistrates responsible to the sovereign people, was indeed a revolutionary concept. In France, where it was to precipitate the greatest revolution of all, the new philosophy found an eloquent advocate in one of the most moving and passionate spirits of the century, Jean-Jacques Rousseau.

Rousseau was born in Switzerland in 1712, but first achieved fame as a writer in Paris when he composed a prize essay in 1749. He followed this with several works wherein he attacked the evils of society and government, not coldly and rationally as more philosophical critics had done, but with a fresh and emotional style that charmed his readers. Rousseau's contempt for the frivolous and artificial society of the time was partly a defense to cover his morbid sensitiveness; his passion for quiet pastoral scenes and lonely walks verged on misanthropy, and his sympathy for the poor and unfortunate was sincere largely because they belonged to the one class he could find no reason to envy. To the *blasés* and superficial frequenters of the salons, however, his artistically written diatribes seemed outpourings of passionate honesty and they wrought a revolution in sentiment. Fine gentlemen neglected their cards and their dice to take lonely walks and commune with Nature, the queen and her ladies-in-waiting played at being dairymaids, and courtiers and commoners alike began to cultivate deep but voluble emotions like the characters in Rousseau's novels.

Rousseau (1712–78)

In *The Social Contract* (1762) Rousseau formulated his philosophy of government, and pictured the state as a corporate body of citizens who subordinate their individual aims to the "general will." The sovereign power resides in the citizens, but it is indivisible, and the government derives its authority from the consent of the governed. The concept of the "general will" baffled many readers, but they applauded Rousseau for his fearless defense of popular sovereignty, and understood his meaning without diffi-

The Social Contract

---
[1] See above, pages 547–548.

culty when he wrote: "The depositors of the executive power are not the people's masters but its officers . . . it can set them up or pull them down when it likes."

The revolutionary nature of his doctrines brought Rousseau into trouble with the authorities and he was obliged to flee from France. But the ideas he had voiced and the criticism poured out by the *philosophes* continued to circulate through men's minds, dissolving like a subtle acid the presuppositions upon which the old régime was founded. By 1789, people had been so widely converted to the new philosophy that a celebrated historian has ventured to declare: "The Revolution was accomplished in men's minds before they made it the work of their hands."

SECTION I

The French Revolution and Napoleon

(1789 — 1815)

The French people were the first to raise the cry of Liberty, Equality, Fraternity, and to challenge in radical fashion the right of a small group, the nobles and clergy, to enjoy wealth, privileges, and immunities while the vast majority of Frenchmen were shut out from such favors and from all political power. In 1789, the leaders of the middle class prepared to sweep away the old régime with its inequalities and abuses, but they ended by sweeping away the French monarchy also, and plunged their newly proclaimed republic into a war with the rest of Europe. The issues at stake in this struggle, the fashion in which the revolution influenced neighboring states, and the succession of events which made Napoleon Bonaparte master of France, and of a great part of Europe, form the subject matter of this section. Although the revolution failed to usher in the social Utopia of which its early protagonists dreamed, it broke through the entrenchments of the old régime, liberated the middle classes in the greater part of the Continent from irritating disabilities and obsolete restrictions and the peasants from the burdens of an outmoded feudal servitude. The revolutionary years marked the appearance in Europe of a new social order in which the middle class, the bourgeoisie, was destined to hold the dominant position and control the government.

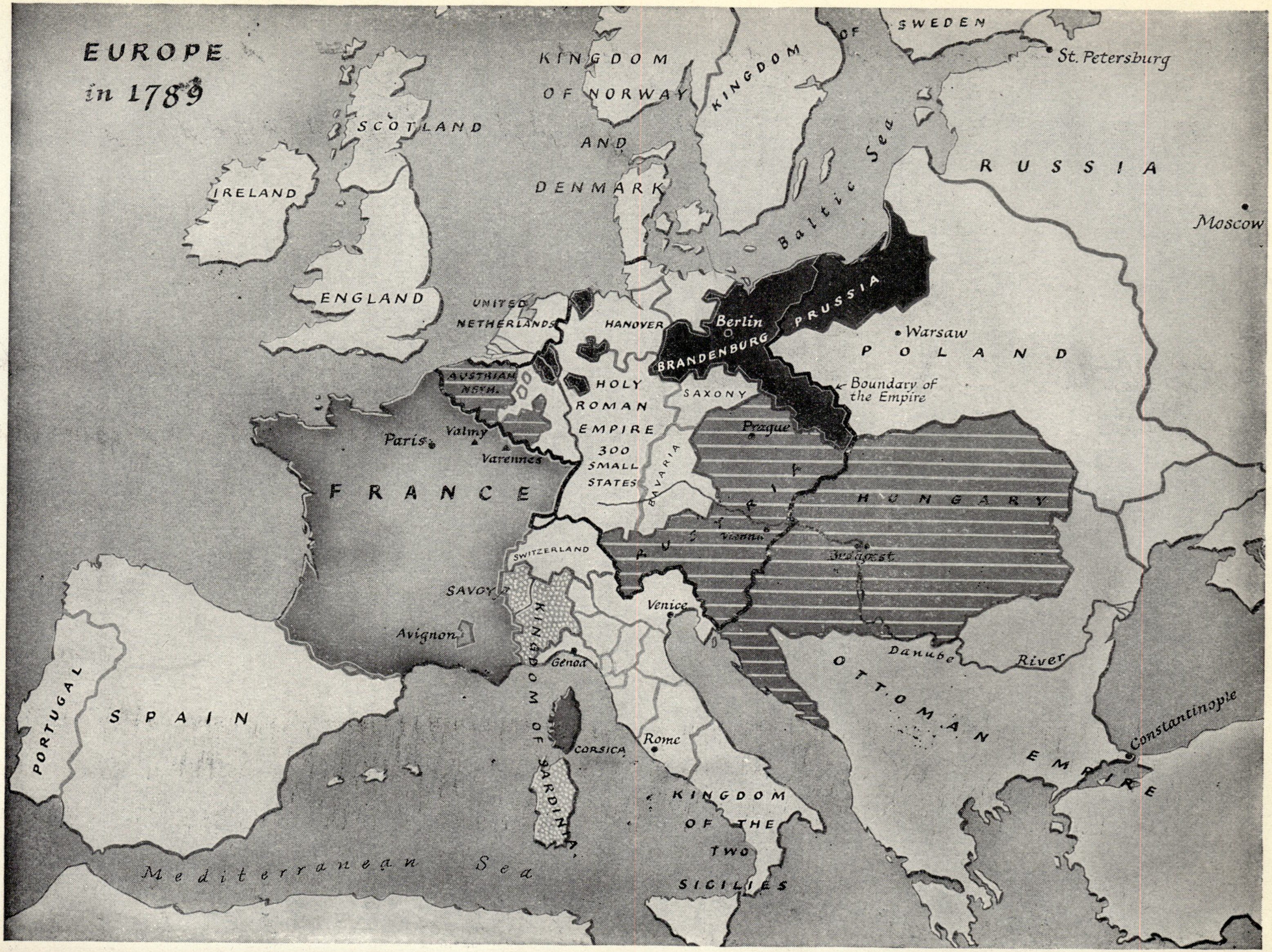

Europe in 1789

45

The French People Destroy the Relics of Feudalism and Overturn the Monarchy

> The end of every political association is the preservation of the natural and imprescriptible rights of man. These rights are liberty, property, security, and resistance against oppression.
> DECLARATION OF THE RIGHTS OF MAN AND THE CITIZEN (1789).

WHEN REVOLUTIONS OCCUR, they do not necessarily break out in the most backward countries, or among the most miserable and most oppressed people. As explained in the foregoing chapter, the inequalities and restrictions of the old régime weighed upon the unprivileged classes in every state on the continent of Europe. As it happened, the French people were the first whom a sense of injustice and a desire for reform goaded into revolution, but the reason for this was not that the French were the most brutally governed or the most unhappy nation, but rather that they were the most enlightened and most eager for reform. The unprivileged classes in France toward the close of the eighteenth century were on the whole better treated than in some neighboring states, and in general their lot was improving. But for this very reason they were less disposed to tolerate abuses, less inclined to put their implicit trust in princes, and less willing to wait indefinitely for the reforms which their leading thinkers had propounded with so much brilliance and conviction.

1. THE STATES GENERAL IS SUMMONED

By 1788, the French monarchy was threatened with bankruptcy. All other expedients for raising money having failed, Louis XVI yielded to the advice of his councilors and agreed to convoke the ancient representative body of the French nation, the States General. His finance minister, Necker, announced the decision to the people as "a New Year's gift" for 1789, and it excited fervent enthusiasm. For the first time in nearly two centuries the French people were to be consulted on the management of their national affairs. When it was learned that the "good king" had agreed in addition to grant the Third Estate double representation, the people "bathed the edict with tears of gratitude."

One hundred and seventy-five years had passed since the previous meeting of the States General in 1614. Dusty records were searched to discover the forgotten modes of procedure, and royal instructions were issued to the puzzled electors. From February to May, 1789, the elections went forward, in orderly fashion for the most part, although all classes of the nation were stirred by the flood of pamphlets and the passionate debates. They were stirred, too, by a spirit of loyalty to the king, their friend and counselor, and by a spirit of generosity which infected even the privileged orders. In this early and idealistic phase of the revolution the mutual enthusiasm frequently transcended class distinctions and some of the leading advocates of reform were men of noble birth. The Marquis de Lafayette, for instance, had fought in the American War of Independence, and had waited impatiently for the day when he might aid the French people also to gain their rights and liberties.

While choosing delegates the electors of the three orders, in each town or parish, were permitted to draw up instructions for them. The king had invited the people to list their grievances, and the result was a flood of memorials filled with advice, complaints, and remonstrances, which are known as the *cahiers*. The peasants begged for relief from the salt tax, from the hated *corvée* or forced labor on the roads, from the destruction wrought by the hunting privileges of the nobles, and from the feudal dues paid to the overlord. Men of the middle class had other grievances: the law courts were costly and often corrupt, trade and industry were checked by stupid restrictions, all high offices in the army, the church, and the government were reserved for the sons of noblemen. The *cahiers* suggest that the twenty-four or twenty-five million Frenchmen who constituted the Third Estate were in substantial agreement: (1) that the privileged orders, the clergy and nobles, would have to surrender their immunities and pay their full share of the taxes, and (2) that France must have a definitive constitution, a written charter of liberties which would limit the irresponsible powers of the government, guarantee each citizen against arbitrary arrest, assure him justice in the courts and protection of his life and property. On the other hand, the nobles and clergy, while approving the convocation of the States General, were disposed to argue that France already possessed an unwritten constitution sanctioned by custom and precedent. They favored some revision and minor concessions, but they expected to remain in a position to safeguard their interests and preserve their social pre-eminence.

As the spring approached, Louis XVI viewed with mounting distrust the wave of popular enthusiasm that his proclamation had called forth. Even his liberal minister, Necker, the idol of those who prayed for reform, was alarmed by the spirit of lawlessness that burst out frequently into acts of violence. Many of the courtiers who surrounded Louis in his palace at Versailles were hostile to the idea of change, and warned him not to make any definite promises. To them, the convocation of the States General was merely an expedient to raise money. If more gold could be found to grease the wheels, they felt certain that the old machine of government would run smoothly enough. But the friends of reform in the royal council had another aim. They hoped to use the indignation of the people as a threat whereby they could compel the nobles and clergy to tax themselves, and to this view they had more or less converted Louis. Tired of the selfishness of the privileged orders, he was prepared to coerce them a little, but his ideas went no further than that. If he could have brought himself to recognize the force of the popular movement, have deserted the elegant but useless nobility, and gone over whole-heartedly to the side of the Third Estate, he might have saved his throne. But such a step was no part of his program.

The truth is, he had no definite program. Slow-witted, irresolute, and unmanageable, Louis XVI was tragically unfit to command in a time of crisis. He had virtues of a high order, physical courage, morality, genuine religious conviction, and deep affection for his family. As a private citizen he might have rounded out an obscure and honorable life; but he had neither talent nor liking for the business of kingship. In council he found it difficult to keep awake; pageants and parades bored him; his chief enthusiasm was hunting, and his chief aptitude leaned apparently toward mechanics. Because he was troubled with a conscience he endeavored spasmodically to fulfill the duties of royalty, but he had neither the will nor the interest to sustain long the rôle which he had inherited and could not resign.

On the queen, Marie Antoinette, more severe judgments have been passed. Beauti-

LOUIS XVI

Louis XVI was not a kingly figure and took no pleasure in the exercise of power. In the Royal Council, where he found it difficult to keep awake, he sometimes hid his inattention by declaring, "I am of the same opinion as the last speaker."

MARIE ANTOINETTE

The elaborate coiffure and the gown reflect the character of the queen. She loved gaiety and luxury; but she was so poorly educated that she wrote an unformed script full of misspellings.

STORMING OF THE BASTILLE

The Bastille, part of which dated from the fourteenth century, was a gloomy fortress and prison standing in the suburb of old Paris known as the Faubourg Saint Antoine. As political and other prisoners were sometimes confined in its dungeons, the edifice acquired a sinister reputation, and the Parisians, looking up at its frowning walls, may well have come to regard it as a symbol of the old régime.

ful, extravagant, and indiscreet, she made herself the center of a coterie at court and the object of considerable scandal. By birth she was a daughter of Maria Theresa, and she had been betrothed to Louis to strengthen the Austro-French alliance which dated from the Seven Years' War.[1] The alliance had never been popular in France and neither was the Austrian-born queen. Her interference in affairs of state helped to split the court into cabals, whereby the queen, the king's brothers (the Count of Provence and the Count of Artois), and the ministers of state conspired and maneuvered to control the vacillating mind of Louis to their own advantage. This was a tiresome task, and as difficult, the Count of Provence admitted, as holding together a handful of oiled ivory balls. For Louis it was a species of martyrdom that drove him on occasion into fits of irrational obstinacy. His moods added the final erratic touch to policies already enfeebled by duplicities and contradictions.

Marie Antoinette

2. THE STATES GENERAL MEETS

On May 5, 1789, the deputies of the three estates assembled at Versailles to hear the proposals of the king and his ministers. In a short speech by Louis and a long speech by Necker, they were lectured on a fact which they already knew: that the government was faced by a financial crisis. But concerning the question of reforms and a constitution nothing definite was said; and the problem of the vote "by order" or the vote "by head" was left unsettled. For the Third Estate this last was a vital issue. Hitherto, the three estates, when assembled, had been in the habit of meeting separately, and presenting their separate petitions and responses to the throne. If this rule were maintained, the deputies of the Third Estate, although they represented over ninety-five per cent of the nation, might find themselves opposed and outvoted by the two privileged chambers. They had hoped that the "good king," in doubling their representation, had intended the deputies of the three orders to sit together and vote their decisions by head, for in a single chamber the six hundred delegates of the Third Estate, with the aid of friendly nobles and priests, would hold an assured majority. But this, they gathered, was not to be, and they left the royal session with a sense of injury and disappointment.

"By head" or "by order"?

Sullenly they declined to organize as a separate body. Twice they invited the nobles and clergy to meet with them. The offers were declined, but on June 13 three parish priests joined them. Others followed, and on June 17 the Third Estate took a momentous step: it proclaimed itself the National Assembly. The whole theory of a democratic revolution was implied in this step which set the dignity of numbers against the dignity of caste. Two days later, a majority of the clergy voted for fusion, and some of the nobles were yielding. The reactionaries at court decided to call a halt to these irregular proceedings. On the morning of June 20, when the deputies of the Third Estate assembled for their daily debates, they found their meeting-place closed while carpenters prepared it for a royal session to be held on the twenty-second. Alarm and indignation seized the representatives. Believing that their session had been intentionally prevented, they hastened to an indoor tennis court nearby, determined to hold it there. On the proposal of Mounier, one of their number, they swore that they would not separate, and would meet whenever necessary, until they had given France a constitution. This was the famous Tennis Court Oath of June 20, 1789.

The Tennis Court Oath

Louis, under pressure from conservative advisers, had resolved to be firm with his obstinate commoners. At the royal session held (a day late) on June 23, he scolded the deputies of the Third Estate for wasting time, and warned them that he might lose patience and send them home. There must be no further resistance to his decree. "Gentlemen," he stated in conclusion, in his rough, unmusical voice, "I command you to disband immediately, and to assemble tomorrow morning each in the chamber allotted to your order." He left the hall, the **nobles and clergy followed, but the Third**

[1] See above, pages 578–580.

Estate remained, irresolute yet defiant. Before them appeared suddenly the master of ceremonies, the Duc de Brézé, to remind them of their duty. "Gentlemen, you have heard the king's intentions." Then the tempestuous Mirabeau, a noble born, but sitting as a deputy of the people, poured out the accumulated indignation of his colleagues upon the startled functionary. "Go tell your master," he thundered, "that we are here by the will of the people, and that only bayonets can drive us forth." De Brézé sought the king to learn his wishes; the regiments were within call; but Louis as always was unequal to a decision. He allowed the commoners to hold their ground in defiance of his expressed orders. It was the first step on a road which was to carry him within three years to the guillotine.

It may be that Louis hesitated to call upon the soldiers because the government no longer trusted its own troops.

Counter-revolution Several of the regiments stationed in Paris had been infected with the revolutionary fever, and the soldiers declared openly that they would never fire upon the people. So four days after his unsuccessful attempt to overawe the deputies, Louis conceded their demands, and reversing his previous decision, he ordered the privileged classes to sit with the Third Estate. Meanwhile, fresh regiments were summoned to surround Paris, Swiss and German mercenaries whose discipline could be relied upon. By July 8, twenty thousand soldiers were encamped near Versailles, and the deputies of the Assembly, watching in apprehension, petitioned the king to withdraw them. Louis responded that the troops were there only to repress disorderly members of society. If *they* felt alarmed, they could remove themselves to some other city. The deputies thought the reply ironic, but Louis was probably sincere. The queen and the Count of Artois had persuaded him that it was necessary to curb the growing riots, and he had yielded to the argument that a large body of troops would be the surest guaranty against bloodshed. Secretly, the Count of Artois was less sanguine and less squeamish. "If you want an omelet," he confided to a friend, "you must not be afraid of breaking eggs."

Paris was in a ferment. Much still remains obscure regarding the disorder that spread among the people in the early days of July, but some historians have come to believe

Philip of Orléans

that anarchy was deliberately fostered. Rich bankers who had lent money to the government saw in the National Assembly the one power likely to stabilize the finances, and therefore urged the mob to defend it. There is some evidence to suggest that the food supplies in Paris were deliberately withheld, so that famine might add to the exasperation of the populace. One person who played a dubious rôle in the preliminaries to the revolt was the king's cousin, Philip, Duke of Orléans, the head of a collateral line of the Bourbons descended from Louis XIII. Orléans early espoused the people's cause and made the gardens of his residence, the Palais Royal, a rendezvous for the politically disaffected. Some of his adherents hoped to set him on the throne if Louis XVI were forced to abdicate, and they purposely aggravated the general discontent to further this end. It is unwise, however, to overemphasize such influences. Throughout the revolution there were many men who, like Orléans, sought to fish for their own advantage in the troubled waters. But the movement was too vast and too complicated to be charged to the designs of any individual, and the conspirator who attempted to control it for his own profit found himself in the position of a man who has summoned up an earthquake to grind his axe.

On the eleventh of July, the king, who had come under the influence of the reactionaries, curtly dismissed Necker and three other liberal ministers. The news stunned the Assembly, where the most radical deputies saw the shades of a prison house already closing about them. They protested earnestly, they debated eloquently, but they were bitterly depressed, for they knew that in reality they were powerless against a royal *coup d'état*. On the populace of Paris the news had a more stimulating effect. For weeks dark rumors had been spreading that the court planned a Saint Bartholomew's Massacre of the patriots, and through the hot July days the storm of revolt had been gathering. With the news of Necker's overthrow it burst.

3. THE CAPTURE OF THE BASTILLE

Word of Necker's dismissal reached Paris on July 12. At the Palais Royal a young journalist, Camille Desmoulins, harangued the people on their danger and the alarm spread rapidly. Mobs began to pillage the gunshops to secure arms, and were joined by mutinous soldiers from a friendly regiment, the French Guards. At the Hôtel de Ville a new municipal government organized itself, with the backing of the middle class, in an effort to curb the mounting anarchy. A civic militia, later to become famous as the National Guard, was created to patrol the streets, for many better-class Parisians felt with reason that they had as much to fear from the thieves and cutthroats running loose with the mobs as from the disciplined soldiery of a kindly though ill-advised king. The establishment of this illegal communal government, with a Parisian deputy, Bailly, as mayor, was the bourgeois reply to the mob violence on the one hand and the court project for a *coup d'état* on the other.

In their search for arms and powder the emissaries of the people, on the morning of July 14, demanded entrance to the prison of the Bastille. This ancient castle of the king was garrisoned by over a hundred soldiers; grim and ill-omened, it stood in the midst of a more modern Paris, a fit symbol of the old régime, with frowning walls and narrow dungeons, in the depths of which innocent victims of the royal displeasure were believed to languish. When the commander, De Launay, courteously declined to lower the drawbridge, the anger of the mob crystallized. An assault began and was carried on with considerable loss to the besiegers. The garrison could have held out, but agreed to capitulate, and the mob streamed in. Only seven prisoners, and none of them altogether innocent, were discovered, and De Launay and some of his men were massacred after they had been disarmed. This rather ugly episode of mob violence was immediately embroidered with legends and became one of the vital myths of the revolution.

July 14, 1789

The first news of the storming of the Bastille filled the National Assembly with deeper gloom. Nevertheless, the lawless citizens, by their audacity, had broken the force of the counter-revolution. Warned by the outbreaks, the Count of Artois left France, and a number of conservative nobles followed. The council of state was reorganized and Necker recalled to office. Realizing their debt to the populace whose violent intervention had saved them, the deputies resolved to applaud an act which filled many of them with secret misgiving; and they even condoned the butchery of defenseless men. "Was the blood that they have shed then so pure?" one deputy named Barnave demanded. Before long many of these legislators were to find smooth phrases for still less agreeable facts, and to speak unctuously of the salutary justice of the people, and the need of watering the tree of liberty from time to time with the blood of tyrants.

On July 17, Louis XVI paid a visit to his rebellious capital. He came in peace, once more the "good king," and he donned a red, white, and blue cockade to signify his acquiescence in the recent developments. The crowds, suspicious at first, cheered him when he reached the Hôtel de Ville, and restored him to a sort of conditional popularity. Had he possessed the art or the acumen he might still have deserted the privileged orders who were deserting him, have flung aside his empty feudal title of King of France, and become the King of the French, but the rôle was beyond his skill. He had taught the bourgeois to distrust him and had driven them into an alliance with the common people, an alliance fraught with grave implications, which threatened to carry the revolution farther than the average bourgeois had any real desire to see it go.

Louis condones revolt

4. THE DESTRUCTION OF FEUDALISM AND THE DECLARATION OF THE RIGHTS OF MAN

Not only in Paris, but everywhere throughout France, revolts seemed to break out spontaneously in the spring and summer of 1789. The storming of the Bastille gave this progressive disintegration of order a swift impulsion. The fabric of society appeared visibly to rend itself apart and the structure of government threatened to dissolve in the rising tide of anarchy. The peasants, many of whom had imagined that their feudal dues had been abolished with the election of deputies, grew impatient at the delay and rose to reckon with their masters, dragging out the records of their obligations in order to burn them, and sometimes burning the lord's château as well. Reports spread that bands of brigands were abroad; in some villages the inhabitants armed themselves for self-protection while in others they locked themselves in at nightfall, oppressed by a terror so vague yet so widespread that it has been called "The Great Fear." Without doubt, under cover of the disorder and dismay, real brigands were active; but in most cases the violence was a consequence of the unlimited expectations of the spring, of the hopes of reform too long deferred, and of the economic hardships which the political disruption had augmented.

"The Great Fear"

By the opening days of August reports of these disturbances were pouring into the Assembly from all quarters. To the anxious deputies it seemed as if the whole of France was lurid with the light of burning châteaux. Among the great landowners the conviction was growing that it would be a wise and humane move to surrender their personal privileges voluntarily, but they hoped to obtain adequate compensation for their real rights. On the night of August 4, while the Assembly was debating measures to calm the provinces, the Viscount de Noailles proposed that the nobles should renounce their seignorial privileges and so abolish the injustice of the feudal system by a single edict. Even the conservative leaders of the privileged orders were prepared to make some concessions, but as the evening advanced enthusiasm swept the Assembly into a series of extraordinary decrees which constituted the death warrant of the feudal system. Nobles vied with churchmen in renouncing traditional rights and immunities, but personal calculations were not entirely forgotten.

Session of August 4–5

The landlords anticipated financial compensation for their losses, and many consoled themselves with the thought that the peasant outbreaks had reduced their prerogatives to a dead letter in any case. At dawn, the deputies, with an enthusiasm as sincere as it was illogical, proclaimed Louis XVI the Restorer of French Liberties, and dispersed to their lodgings, drunk with fatigue and emotion.

The legislation of August 4 extended the scope of the revolution and added a social and economic program to the political reforms. For in abolishing feudal obligations, suppressing serfdom and the game laws, commuting taxes such as the *aides*, the *gabelle*, and the *tithe*, and proposing civil equality, equality of taxation, and an equal opportunity for public service to all Frenchmen, the National Assembly transformed the French people from subjects to citizens. If the full implications of these decrees were carried into effect, it meant the end of the old social system with its corporate groups and classes vested with special rights, and the end of the old economic system with its guilds, industrial monopolies, and feudal prerogatives. Finally, it meant that the National Assembly would have to prolong its session indefinitely in order to draft the detailed legislation required to carry through this complicated program.

Humanity, which had lost its birthrights, was now on the way to recover them, and it seemed wise that they should be written down for all men to read. In the remaining days of August the deputies prepared a table which listed the inalienable rights of free citizens. The formulas chosen for this famous Declaration of the Rights of Man and the Citizen were suggested in part by English and American models, and were permeated by the democratic philosophy of Rousseau. Every citizen was declared to be born free. He could not be arrested or imprisoned except by due process of law, and in the making of the laws which he had to obey he was entitled to participate directly or indirectly, since a valid law was the expression of the general will. Furthermore, the citizen was entitled to enjoy religious liberty and freedom of speech and of the press. All officials who

The Rights of Man

MARIE JOSEPH PAUL YVES ROCH GILBERT DU MOTIER, MARQUIS DE LAFAYETTE (1757–1834)

After fighting for liberty in the American War of Independence, Lafayette hoped to see a more liberal régime in France, but the Revolution soon moved too fast and he fled to the Austrians.

HONORE GABRIEL RIQUETTI, COUNT DE MIRABEAU (1749–1791)

Mirabeau was one of the few leaders in the first years of the Revolution who had qualities of statesmanship, but his acceptance of "gifts" from the king might have brought him to the guillotine if he had lived longer.

MARCHE DES MARSEILLAIS

A contemporary printing of the famous revolutionary march. The soldiers still move in the eighteenth-century manner, like marionettes.

LIBERTY, EQUALITY, FRATERNITY, OR DEATH

The Frenchman plays blindman's buff with Liberty, Equality, and Fraternity, while Death reaches for his hand.

helped to govern a state were the responsible servants of the sovereign people, and if they abused their trust, the people had the right to resist and to depose them, however exalted their rank. It is unnecessary to point out the conflict between such teaching and the theories of absolute despotism.

The Declaration of the Rights of Man and the Citizen was intended to serve as a preface to the constitution upon which the deputies were busily laboring. In the debates on this subject, however, certain differences of opinion had already betrayed themselves, suggestive of a cleavage between the ideals of the people of moderate wealth and the poorer folk who owned no property. The middle class, the bourgeoisie, desired the revolution to stop short with political and legal reforms, which would leave them in charge of a responsible constitutional monarchy. But the laborers in the towns and the peasants in the fields had been inspired by radicals and demagogues to hope for a social revolution, which would introduce a genuine egalitarianism. They had a confused idea that men were to be equal, not only in rights and liberties, but in education, in opportunity, and even in wealth. Among the deputies themselves there were some ecstatic dreamers who believed that it was possible by enlightened edicts to legislate poverty and ignorance out of existence, and to render all citizens virtuous and happy. Men engaged in a herculean effort, such as a war or a revolution, are often seduced by vague and shining ideals which help to blind them to the uglier aspects of the work they have to do. The French Revolution produced more than one leader who was prepared, in his attempt to construct a Utopia, to sacrifice his own head and a hundred thousand others with it. To such men, and to the credulous masses which heeded them, the revolution could not fail to bring the bitterness of disillusionment.

Rifts divide Third Estate

5. THE MARCH TO VERSAILLES

The National Assembly had traveled far in four months but not far enough to appease the impatient expectations of the populace. The fever in Paris, which had been eased a little by the blood-letting in July, threatened to mount again with the autumn. The National Guard, under the command of the Marquis de Lafayette, endeavored to hold the riotous elements of the populace in check, but the news from Versailles was disturbing. Louis, it was learned, had again been corrupted by evil counsels. He had withheld his approval to the Declaration of the Rights of Man and was furtively concentrating troops. In the last week of September, the Flanders Regiment arrived, and the officers demonstrated their loyalty to the king by trampling under foot the tricolor cockade of the Revolution. Marat, a popular leader and the editor of a journal called *The Friend of the People*, rushed out to Versailles to investigate for himself the truth of these rumors, and returned filled with alarm, "making as much noise," his fellow journalist Desmoulins wittily averred, "as four trumpets on the Day of Judgment." The crowds were ready to follow any leader, for back of these inflammable rumors was the hard reality of hunger, to render men and women furious at a king who vacillated and an assembly which theorized, while starvation stalked the streets. If the king dwelt in Paris it was argued, instead of twelve miles away in Versailles, he would understand better the needs of his people and do something to alleviate them.

Accordingly, on October 5, an unorganized mob composed largely of women started a march to Versailles to petition the king to reduce the price of bread. Louis made gracious promises, but the crowd remained encamped near the palace. In the evening Lafayette arrived with the National Guard, but the precautions which he took were insufficient to prevent assassins slipping into the palace before dawn in an unsuccessful attempt to murder the queen. The majority of the visitors, however, had no murderous intentions; they were appeased and gratified when Lafayette, acting a doubtful rôle as intermediary, persuaded the royal family to return with them to Paris, and they escorted the carriage back on the morning of October 6, shouting that they had brought with them "the Baker, the Baker's wife, and the Baker's little boy." By noon, Louis had taken up his residence at the Tuileries, in the heart of his capital. Thenceforward he was to be a hostage of the people.

This removal from Versailles to Paris exercised a profound effect upon the course of the revolution. For the National Assembly considered it expedient to follow the king, and a long bare riding-school near the Tuileries, the Salle de Manège, was furnished for its sessions. With its rows of mounting benches sweeping around the walls, and a cleared space in the center, the new home of the Assembly suggested an arena, and such it was to prove. In the upper galleries space was provided for visitors, and the common people soon swarmed there, to criticize the debates and applaud vigorously their favorite orators. During more than one grave crisis, in the days that were approaching, groups of disorderly onlookers, full of brandy and patriotism, were to render calm deliberation impossible and force the Assembly to measures from which a majority of the deputies secretly recoiled.

6. THE CIVIL CONSTITUTION OF THE CLERGY

The threat of bankruptcy, which had led to the convocation of the States General, proved one of the most difficult problems which faced the Assembly. In the general confusion taxes could not be collected, and the Assembly found it necessary to borrow over two million livres for current expenses. The economic plight of the government drove the deputies to undertake a measure which proved in many respects a serious mistake. The lands held by the church and by the various monastic orders in France were valued at about three billion livres, which was approximately the amount of the national debt. On November 2, 1789, the Assembly decided to appropriate these lands for the needs of the nation, and to issue paper currency, or assignats, for which the church property would serve as security.

Having in this way relieved the clergy of their wealth and their income, the Assembly then assumed responsibility for their support. As part of the political program, France was to be cut up into some eighty-three new *départements*, and the ancient ecclesiastical

State to pay clergy

dioceses were reconstituted to coincide with these new divisions. Priests and bishops became salaried servants of the state, and were to be chosen by election like other public officials, which meant that Huguenots, Jews, freethinkers, and other non-Catholics might help to choose them. Monks and nuns were urged to forsake their cloisters and find some secular occupation. All members of the clergy were required to swear an oath that they accepted the new settlement which was styled "The Civil Constitution of the Clergy," and those who refused were deprived of their offices and persecuted as non-jurors (French *jurer*, to swear). The civil constitution turned half the French clergy into non-jurors, and also made many laymen bitter opponents of the revolution. Unfortunately, too, the confiscation of the church property failed to solve the financial problems of the state, for the land sold slowly, and the assignats, which were issued with reckless prodigality, declined in value to fifty, then to thirty, and by 1795, to less than two per cent of their face value. However, the paper money helped somewhat to provide for government expenses during a critical period, and the sale of the lands, though slow, gradually created a class of landowners who could be counted upon to support the revolution because the restoration of the old régime would have meant the loss of their newly acquired estates. In its final effects this break-up of the landed estates and the transference of ownership to members of the middle and lower classes was perhaps the most significant change wrought by the revolution, and, coupled with the ultimate abolition of all feudal dues without redemption in July, 1793, it dissolved the economic foundations upon which the old régime had rested.

7. THE CONSTITUTION OF 1791

The members of the National Assembly had sworn in the Tennis Court Oath (June 20, 1789) to provide France with a constitution. The main features were settled in 1789, and by the spring of 1791 the momentous document, which was to transform France from an absolute to a limited monarchy, was

Monarchy limited

completed. The powers which the king had formerly exercised were transferred to a legislative assembly elected by the people. Louis was no longer to make laws or to collect taxes. He lost his right to appoint and dismiss at will the local administrative officials throughout France, for henceforth these men were to be elected by the people and paid by the nation. Nor could he declare war or make peace without the vote of the legislative assembly which represented the nation. This assembly was to consist of a single chamber, the members of which were to be chosen by election every two years, and the king had no power to dissolve it. A few rights, however, had been left to him. He could choose the ministers who composed his council; could supervise the conduct of foreign affairs; and might veto a law passed by the assembly if he disapproved of it. His veto, though termed suspensive, was all but absolute, for a law had to pass three successive legislatures to become effective in the face of his opposition.

Thus, in less than two years, the nobles had been stripped of their privileges, the church of its wealth, and the king of the greater part of his authority, which had passed to the representatives of the nation. Yet the nation as a whole was not satisfied. The humbler classes, the people who had no wealth or property, were beginning to suspect that they were being cheated, that the Revolution was not destined to fulfill their hopes. The new constitution established liberty for all, but it did not establish equality. Despite the assurance of the Declaration of Rights that every Frenchman was entitled to assist, directly or indirectly, in the making of the laws, the people found that only those citizens who paid a direct tax equal to three days' wages were to be given a vote, while none but citizens of comparative wealth would be eligible to sit in the legislative assembly. Popular leaders were quick to point out that under such a constitution the middle class would control the government. Some radicals even went so far as to denounce the deputies of the National Assembly as traitors, because they had betrayed the interests of the people as a whole into the power of the propertied classes.

Persistence of discontent

To a certain extent this charge was justified. The members of the National Assembly were nearly all middle-class men, loyal to their group and its traditions. Many of them sincerely believed the most ignorant class of citizens unfit, without further training, to exercise the responsibility of electors. "The veil that hides the dazzling figure of Liberty," they argued, "must not be torn away too suddenly." In the early days of the revolution, the deputies of the National Assembly had allied themselves with the people through fear of the court; but after the relics of feudalism had been destroyed and the royal power reduced, the middle class, the bourgeoisie, was left supreme in the state. The Constitution of 1791 represented an attempt of the bourgeoisie to arrest and stabilize the revolution at this point. The attempt failed (1) because Louis XVI was untrustworthy and hated the rôle of a constitutional monarch; (2) because the Parisian populace was determined to see the revolution continue until it brought equality as well as liberty; and (3) because a radical minority in the new assembly, as well as counter-revolutionaries in France or in exile, and the apprehensive princes of Europe, all desired (though for different reasons) to see the settlement fail.

Middle class dominates

Although Louis had accepted the reforms which had been forced upon him, he was not reconciled to them. On June 21, 1791, when their labors were almost completed, the deputies of the National Assembly were dismayed to learn that the king had fled from Paris. His plan was to join with loyal troops in the east and north of France, win the support of the provinces, and return to his capital as master once more. Such a step had been suggested to him earlier by the great orator Mirabeau, who had been brought secretly into the pay of the court. But Mirabeau died in April, 1791, and Louis had no other adviser with sufficient statesmanship to manage the project. The attempt at escape miscarried; the royal family were recognized *en route* and arrested at Varennes; and

The flight to Varennes

A POPULAR ASSEMBLY

French revolutionary leaders liked to declare that "the voice of reason and the voice of the people is the same thing." Another aphorism popular in these sanguinary days was that "justice can never harm the innocent."

ASSIGNAT FOR TWENTY-FIVE LIVRES

The paper money issued by the French Revolutionary Assemblies depreciated rapidly because it was printed too prodigally. The assignats fell from 98 per cent of their face value in 1789 to 2 per cent in 1795.

within a week they were brought back to Paris as prisoners.

The deputies of the Assembly were in a quandary. Their new constitution called for a king; if they definitely deposed Louis and set up a regency or a republic, the move might throw the revolution into the hands of the people. For the moment they compromised by suspending the king from his functions. When a crowd assembled on the Champ de Mars, on July 17, to petition for the removal of the king, the National Guard dispersed it with musketry. The Assembly, growing daily more conservative, decreed that Louis should be restored to his throne, and that there should be no further change in the constitution for at least ten years. Confident that these measures would check the democratic movement, the deputies resigned their places, and closed their last session with the announcement (ironic prophecy) that the revolution was at an end.

Republic or monarchy?

Reforms of 1789-91

Their labors had earned them the right to rest. In a session of a little over two years the National (Constituent) Assembly had inaugurated a remarkable program of destruction and reconstruction. (1) It had decreed the doom of feudalism and serfdom in France, although the liquidation of the old system remained incomplete. (2) It had obliterated the old, bewildering patchwork of provincial, judicial, fiscal, and ecclesiastical divisions in France and replaced them by eighty-three approximately equal departments. (3) It had suppressed the chaos of the conflicting legal tribunals, *parlements*, and feudal courts which had complicated the administration of justice under the old régime, and supplanted them by a graduated system of judicial courts with elected judges. (4) It had stripped the church and the monastic orders of their wealth and power and made the clergy the servants of the state. (5) It had relieved an absolute monarch of the greater share of his authority and confided it to an assembly of the sovereign people. The following months were to decide whether the constitutional monarchy would function and the revolution could be arrested at this point.

8. THE LEGISLATIVE ASSEMBLY (1791-92)

The retiring deputies of the National Assembly had decreed themselves ineligible for immediate re-election, with the result that the new legislature was composed very largely of obscure men with little political training. They arrived in Paris, as one observer noted, "discontented to find the farce over and the curtain down," for many of them "were eager to win glory by destroying something" — an ominous portent, since there was nothing great left that they could destroy except the throne. From its first sessions the Legislative Assembly found itself divided into a party of the Right, which sought to preserve the constitutional settlement, and a party of the Left, which criticized the king and sought to lead the revolution into greater extremes. Among the leaders of the Left were several brilliant young deputies from the Department of the Gironde, and from them the whole group, which was aggressive in its tactics and republican in its sentiments, came to be known as the "Gironde" and its adherents as the "Girondists."

The most momentous step which the Legislative Assembly took was to plunge France into a war with Austria and Prussia in the spring of 1792. The first reforms of the revolution had been greeted with applause from all parts of Europe, but as the months passed this early approval changed to doubt and then to hostility. Three issues in particular provoked ill-feeling between France and her neighbors. (1) The *émigrés* (French royalists who had "emigrated") found refuge chiefly in the Germanies, where they plotted a counter-revolution and intrigued for foreign aid. (2) The abolition of feudal tenure deprived some German landlords of their rights in Alsace and they demanded compensation. (3) The National Assembly, at the request of the citizens of Avignon, had annexed that city to France (1790), although it was a part of the papal possessions. When Austria and Prussia joined in a demand for satisfaction on the last two points, the Girondists decided upon a war. "It may be," one deputy opined complacently, "that the revolution has need of a war to consolidate

Era of war opens (1792)

it." The struggle so light-heartedly begun was destined to last, with breathing spells, for twenty-three years, and before it ended France was to send her armies through the capitals of all her enemies on the continent of Europe.

With the outbreak of hostilities the position of the royal hostages in Paris became desperate. Girondist orators openly accused the king and queen of sympathizing with the enemy, and the charge had a basis of truth. Louis hoped that the invaders would hasten to Paris and restore his powers, and Marie Antoinette transmitted information concerning the French plans to her Austrian fellow countrymen. Excitement and suspicion flamed up in Paris at the news of French reverses, and on June 20, 1792, a rowdy mob stormed into the Tuileries "to pay a visit to the king." Louis faced his unwelcome visitors calmly and courageously, drank a glass of wine to the revolution, and had the relief of seeing them finally disperse. Nothing had been smashed except a few windowpanes. The indignity to the king even caused a brief reaction in his favor, and the Assembly, which considered king-baiting its peculiar prerogative, stopped scolding Louis in order to scold the mob. These eloquent legislators, who loved to hurl audacious and inflammatory phrases from the tribune, were suddenly sobered when they saw a mob translate their suggestions into acts.

June 20, 1792

Louis's throne was already tottering when the *émigrés* decided to come to his aid, and all was lost. On July 25, these short-sighted partisans persuaded the Duke of Brunswick, commander of the invading armies, to issue a manifesto to the French nation. In bombastic language it warned all Frenchmen that, if they still refused to lay down their arms, they would be treated as rebels to their king, and promised, if any harm befell Louis or the queen, that Paris would be handed over to total annihilation. It seemed impossible to doubt any longer that the king was in collusion with the enemy. The Parisians decided that the monarchy would have to be destroyed; a revolutionary committee took charge and directed matters from the Hôtel de Ville; the sections poured forth their hordes of "patriots," and on August 10 the mob attacked the Tuileries.

Brunswick Manifesto

The royal family, having been warned in time, retired to the hall of the Legislative Assembly for protection, but the king's Swiss Guard, left to defend an empty palace, was sacrificed to the fury of the mob, which massacred and mutilated its victims in ghastly fashion. The leadership of affairs had passed into the hands of the revolutionary committee which had organized itself at the Hôtel de Ville, under the direction of a violent but patriotic lawyer named Danton. In obedience to this committee the Legislative Assembly suspended the king, and then summoned a new and special convention to decide the fate of France and construct a second constitution.

Fall of the throne (1792)

In the interval between August 10 and September 21, 1792, Danton and the insurrectionary commune provided the only real impetus behind the dislocated national government. With prodigious energy Danton spurred on the work of recruiting soldiers to resist the invading armies. To cow opposition all aristocrats and enemy sympathizers were sought out in a house-to-house search. The prisons of Paris were soon crowded, and the populace feared the prisoners might break out and massacre the good citizens while the soldiers were away at the battlefront. This served as an excuse to exercise "the salutary justice of the people." Self-appointed judges visited the prisons; hired executioners accompanied them; and over a thousand victims, after the shadow of a trial, were butchered in the prison yards. For three days the massacres went on, while the deputies of the Legislative Assembly waited nervelessly, and Danton with culpable negligence forbore all protest. The annals of the revolution offer no darker page or more sanguinary example of popular violence than these prison massacres of the first days of September, 1792.

September massacres

46

The First French Republic and Its Struggle to Survive

The French Republic is one and indivisible.
CONSTITUTION OF 1793.

BY OVERTURNING THE THRONE on August 10, 1792, the people of Paris ended the first phase of the revolution. The constitutional monarchy had failed and the king was a prisoner. To meet the crisis a National Convention was summoned and held its first session on September 21, 1792. Three problems of the utmost importance confronted the new assembly: (1) What was to be done with the dethroned king? (2) How was France to be saved from her invaders? (3) What form of government should be devised to replace the monarchy? The fate of France and of the revolution depended upon the answers which the members of the National Convention found for these questions.

1. THE NATIONAL CONVENTION (1792-95)

At their opening session the deputies of the Convention lost no time in declaring royalty abolished in France. A few days later, with considerably less enthusiasm, they decided to style France a "republic." Their hesitation reflected the general uncertainty of the time. Although some radical leaders in Paris had urged a republican form of government as early as 1791, after Louis's flight to Varennes, and most educated Frenchmen professed admiration for the city-republics of ancient times, the idea of transforming France into a republic did not appeal very strongly to the nation in 1792. Conservative members of the bourgeoisie feared such a step might deliver the government into the control of the populace, and many people in the provincial centers were still attached to the monarchy, although they had lost confidence in Louis XVI. The proclamation of the new régime was accepted as a more or less unwelcome but logical alternative to the discredited monarchy, but even the champions of the republic were constrained to admit that its birth occurred in a manner obscure and unpropitious.

France a republic

So long as the ex-king lived, it seemed inevitable that the royalists would plot to overthrow the republic and restore him to power, and this danger made it the more necessary to decide his fate promptly. An active group of deputies seated high on the benches of the left in the assembly hall (the "Mountain") were determined to condemn the king, and they found support in the Jacobin Club, a powerful political society dominated by ardent revolutionaries, which had affiliated itself with local groups throughout France. Maximilien Robespierre, popular and radical deputy of Paris, carried the verdict of the Jacobins to the Convention. "I demand," he proclaimed from the trib-

Louis XVI guillotined

une, "that Louis XVI be condemned to death." The Girondists, the party which had dominated the Legislative Assembly, made half-hearted efforts to win a reprieve, but were outmaneuvered by their Jacobin opponents on the "Mountain." In the final test vote, Louis was condemned to death by a small majority. His execution (January 21, 1793) deeply shocked the courts of Europe and made the new French Republic an Ishmael among the nations.

By this drastic solution of one problem, the Convention greatly aggravated a second, the question of national defense. The Austrian and Prussian forces had withdrawn from France temporarily after suffering a reverse at Valmy (September 20, 1792), but they planned a new invasion for the spring of 1793. After the execution of the king, Great Britain, Spain, Holland, and some lesser states joined the coalition against France. The allied monarchs pledged themselves to avenge the death of Louis and to destroy the revolution, believing that the superiority of their resources assured them an easy victory. Yet, although France was to fight alone against the greater part of Europe, the contest was less unequal than it appeared. Oppressed classes in every country were stirred by the French example, and to them the National Convention made appeals urging them to rise against their tyrants. It was against governments rather than against embattled nations that the revolution had to struggle in these early years. The allied powers, moreover, were far from maintaining a close accord, and the allied statesmen neglected at first to give the French situation the serious attention which it warranted.

First coalition (1793)

Nevertheless, the dangers threatening France in the spring of 1793 might have sobered the most sanguine patriot. They failed, however, to silence the quarrel in the Convention, where the two factions, the Girondists and the Jacobins, wasted precious months wrestling for leadership. The Girondists drew their chief support from the provinces, were opposed to the dominant rôle which Paris had assumed in the affairs of France, and were disliked by the Parisian populace. They accused their political opponents, the Jacobins, of currying favor with the mob and of planning to confiscate private wealth for the benefit of the indigent. The Jacobins retorted that the Girondists wished an "aristocratic republic"; that their project for exalting the departments would destroy the unity of France, and that at heart they were secretly royalist. These charges and counter-charges masked a quarrel which was at bottom a fight between two revolutionary groups for control of the new government. In the end the people of Paris settled the issue by a fresh insurrection (May 31–June 2, 1793) which crushed the Girondists. Several of the proscribed deputies escaped to stir up armed revolts in the provinces, but their cause was speedily compromised by royalist overtures. The victorious Jacobins consolidated their victory by drafting a popular constitution and submitting it to the voters. On obtaining a favorable response, they laid aside this Constitution of 1793 and chose to regard the result of the referendum as a justification of their high-handed rule.

Girondists overthrown

Thus, by the midsummer of 1793, the Jacobins had won control of the central government, but the republic appeared to be on the point of dissolution. The army was disorganized, for many of the officers (nobles by birth) had deserted. The administration was dislocated, the allied troops were advancing from the east while royalist or Girondist insurgents held the chief western departments. It seemed all but certain that Paris would fall before the converging forces and the revolution end in defeat and obloquy.

2. THE ORGANIZATION OF VICTORY

In this critical summer of 1793, the allies proved themselves the unintentional saviors of France. Coalitions are notoriously inept in concentrating their forces; each of the powers had selfish ends to serve and each preferred to let its allies bear the brunt of the fighting. Austria and Prussia were less interested in crushing France than in securing further remnants of Poland, for that unhappy kingdom had just suffered a second partition, and a third was imminent. As a

MARIE ANTOINETTE ON HER
WAY TO EXECUTION

*French painter, Jacques
is David, made this sketch
the tumbril passed.*

THE REVOLUTIONARY TRIBUNAL

Above: The dread headquarters where the arbitrary orders for arrests, searches, and confiscations were issued as part of the "salutary justice of the people."

THE EXECUTION OF LOUIS XVI

Below: The execution of Louis XVI on January 21, 1793, helped to plunge France into war with half of Europe.

result, the invaders advanced too cautiously, and failed to destroy the French armies and seize Paris while they had the chance. Twenty years were to pass before such a favorable opportunity recurred.

Strong winds extinguish a small fire, but they feed a large one, and the misfortunes which beset the French Republic in 1793 fanned the fervor of the revolutionaries to a white heat. Though civil war raged in the Vendée, though Lyons, Marseilles, and Toulon had risen against the Convention, though the fortresses of the north, Condé and Valenciennes, fell before the allied advance, these reverses proved to be hammer-strokes which fashioned a new France on the anvil of war. In their inconclusive attempts to blow out the torch of the revolution, the monarchs fanned it to a mighty conflagration. Patriotic Frenchmen of all classes flocked to the armies, prepared to die for *la liberté* and *la patrie*. Too late the allies were to learn they had excited a popular tumult that was to sweep across Europe.

The Spirit of '93

Fortunately for France, the National Convention, controlled by the Jacobin element, provided the iron leadership necessary for a nation in arms. An executive cabinet, the "committee of public safety," assumed dictatorial powers. It dispatched deputies to the departments to supervise the organization of the defense; it called all able-bodied men to the colors to swell the "fourteen armies of the republic," and appointed young and audacious generals to positions of command with the warning that a defeat might cost them their heads. This energetic policy swiftly turned the tide. By the close of 1793, the royalists in the Vendée had been checked, Toulon recaptured, and the Austrians and Prussians thrown upon the defensive. In 1794, the French armies swept on to further triumphs. France was cleared of her invaders, her generals took the offensive, and Lazare Carnot, the military genius of the committee of public safety who had directed the campaigns, was acclaimed "The Organizer of Victory." But the victory had been dearly bought. It will be well to pause here to note how the struggle for national defense in 1793 and 1794 militarized the revolution and deflected its aims.

"Organizer of victory"

3. THE JACOBIN DICTATORSHIP

Although the National Convention remained in power for three years (1792–95), it failed in the primary task for which it had been summoned; i.e., to provide a permanent and satisfactory constitution for France. The Constitution of 1791, it will be recalled, had been cast aside when the king was deposed. Consequently the National Convention was an "extraordinary" or "revolutionary" assembly with no constitutional limits to its authority. It conducted the affairs of the nation with despotic assurance, repressing criticism, crushing its opponents, and spurring the citizens to supreme efforts. The French people submitted to this tyrannical war-time régime because they believed it was "a bridge of bronze" by which they would pass from a corrupt monarchy to a regenerated republic.

But the war wrenched the revolution from its course and the "regenerated republic" remained an unrealized dream, though for this the war was not wholly to blame. Almost from the first an inner conflict checked the progress of reform measures, a conflict between the bourgeoisie and the classes without wealth or property. The bourgeoisie wished the revolution to end when the control of the government had passed from an autocratic king and a selfish nobility to the hands of an enlightened middle class; i.e., to themselves. But among the poorer classes there were many enthusiasts who construed liberty, equality, fraternity, more literally. They thought equality meant not only equality before the law, but equality of birth, of opportunity, and of wealth. A political revolution was not enough for them, they wanted a social revolution, which would extinguish poverty by distributing the property of the wealthy among the poor. Against such egalitarian doctrines the bourgeoisie fought relentlessly, asserting at every opportunity that private property must be considered sacred and inviolable.

Bourgeoisie guard wealth

Not even Robespierre, who posed as the champion of the poor, and earned by his

JEAN PAUL MARAT (1743–1793)

Top left: Marat's violent rabble-rousing helped to bring the Girondist deputies to their doom, and also inspired a Norman girl, Charlotte Corday, to assassinate him.

GEORGE JACQUES DANTON (1759–1794)

Top center: Danton was a man of great vigor and patriotism, but he was compromised by dishonest associates and swept under in the fury of 1794.

MAXIMILIEN MARIE ISIDORE ROBESPIERRE (1758–1794)

Top right: On his way to the guillotine, Danton swore that Robespierre would follow him. The prophecy was fulfilled within four months.

THE ACTOR CHINARD AS A SANSCULOTTE

Left: The change from the elegance of the old régime to the deliberate slovenliness of sansculotte garb may be judged from this popular painting of 1792.

scorn of wealth the title of "The Incorruptible," dared openly to attack the sanctity of private property. "Souls of mud," he upbraided those who accused him of such an aim, "I do not wish to touch your wealth however unclean its origin." Nevertheless, under the pressure of the war, he urged the National Convention to adopt measures which penalized the rich to benefit the poor. The assignats, the paper money so recklessly issued by the revolutionary assemblies, declined in value until it was almost worthless. To meet expenses the Convention seized the property of *émigrés* nobles, and forced rich citizens to "lend" money to the state, part of which was used to relieve the poverty of "indigent patriots." When the poor complained at the cost of bread, the Convention attempted to fix the price of necessities at a fair level, and threatened profiteering merchants with the guillotine. Such experiments in what, today, would be termed state socialism helped to placate the populace and were accepted by the bourgeoisie as temporary war-time measures.

In the same acquiescent spirit the French people accepted the extraordinary decrees passed against traitors and enemy agents. A special revolutionary tribunal was established (1793) to judge "enemies of the people," and as the struggle grew more intense the list of victims mounted. The queen, Marie Antoinette, the Duke of Orléans who had joined the revolutionaries and renamed himself Philippe Égalité, revolutionary generals accused of incompetence, leaders of the defeated Girondist Party, all took their turn on the guillotine. Nor did humbler victims escape. Seamstresses who ventured to sigh for the days of the monarchy when business was better, and loyal servants convicted of concealing a noble master, met the same fate. By the spring of 1794, the condemned were dispatched to the Place de la Révolution in batches of thirty and forty a day, there to make their bow before what Danton, with wry humor, referred to as the representative of the *executive* power.

The Reign of Terror

Danton's grim jest possessed its element of truth, for the executive committee of public safety was using the guillotine as a political weapon. In March, 1794, it destroyed the Hébertists, a radical group which desired to push the revolution to further excesses, under the leadership of Hébert, editor of a scurrilous journal *Le Père Duchesne*. A few weeks later the committee struck at an opposing group, the "Indulgents," because they sought to retard the revolution and arrest the Terror. Having dispatched Danton and other leaders of the indulgent faction to the guillotine (April, 1794), the committee of public safety was master of the field, and Robespierre was regarded in France and abroad as master of the committee. What use would the Incorruptible make of his extraordinary prestige?

In Robespierre's narrow mind one ideal burned clearly. He aspired to establish a Utopian republic in which all citizens would possess pure morals, high ideals, and unselfish patriotism. But France was growing weary of his exalted creed. As the victories of the republican armies dispelled the threat of invasion, Robespierre found himself blamed for maintaining the Terror when the excuse for it had passed. He felt the decline of idealism and the waning of his popularity, and it seemed to him that the revolution was losing momentum at the very moment when the goal was in sight. "My reason," he confessed, "though not my heart, is at the point of doubting that Republic of Virtue of which I have traced the plan." In July, 1794, he appealed to the Convention to support him in a further "purification" of the government, but the men of property were beginning to distrust him and his enemies declared he aspired to establish a dictatorship. The Convention voted him under arrest with several of his friends, and although the Parisian populace, through their representatives at the Hôtel de Ville, attempted an insurrection in his favor, the movement failed and Robespierre perished on the guillotine.

The Republic of Virtue

4. THE THERMIDORIAN REACTION

From 1789 to 1794 the revolution had been dynamic, gaining momentum with each year that passed. The overthrow of Robespierre on the Ninth of Thermidor, as the date was styled in the revolutionary calendar (July 27, 1794), was followed by a period of reaction.

Decline of idealism

From 1795 to 1799 the revolution appears "frozen" or "stagnant." The men who destroyed Robespierre had been concerned chiefly with saving their heads, but they found themselves hailed as heroes who had ended the Terror. The prisons were emptied, the committee of public safety and the scarcely less powerful committee of general security were stripped of their despotic authority, and the Jacobin Club was closed. A spirit of frivolity, extravagance, and dissipation supplanted the austere ideals of the Reign of Virtue. Fortunes which had been acquired by speculation and profiteering were spent in gambling and amusements. Social life in Paris had never appeared more vivacious, but the gaiety, the glitter, and the immorality disguised a mood of cynicism and disillusionment.

The destitute, however, had no superficial gaieties to alleviate the sharpness of their misery. Feeling that the revolution had betrayed their hopes, they began openly to regret the passing of Robespierre, and attempted to assert once more the "sacred right of insurrection." In April, 1795, and again in May, mobs invaded the Convention demanding bread and a constitution. But the nation as a whole was weary of radicalism and terrorism and breathed more easily when these outbreaks were crushed. The Jacobin ideals had been discredited, the leading terrorists of 1793 and 1794 were dead or in hiding, and a desire for a strong and permanent government inclined many Frenchmen to favor a restoration of the Bourbon monarchy. This sentiment was stimulated by priests and royalists, who, finding the laws against them somewhat relaxed after 1794, ventured to slip back into France.

Two powerful groups, however, opposed a return to the Bourbon rule. The first included men who had grown rich and acquired confiscated property during the revolution, and knew their fortunes would vanish if the republic fell. A second group, the regicides, stood to lose even more. For if the Count of Provence ever ascended the French throne as Louis XVIII,[1] those deputies of the Convention who had voted the death of Louis XVI would face death or exile. So these two groups, the speculators and the regicides, united to hold the revolution from retrograding. Clinging to power, they struck alternately at the radicals and the royalists, using the army to preserve their unpopular régime. From 1795 to 1799 the balance of power in the government remained in the hands of this coalition of trimmers.

Trimmers in power

Any subterfuge provided these opportunists with an excuse to remain in office.[2] When the National Convention was driven to prepare a constitution and dissolve itself (1795), it decreed that two thirds of its members must be re-elected to the chambers of the new assembly and would take their places whether they were elected or not. Furious at this parody of popular representation, the Parisian sections rebelled, but the insurrection was promptly suppressed by the army. Among the officers who aided materially in crushing this revolt of Vendémiaire 13 (October 5, 1795) was a young Corsican officer of artillery named Napoleon Bonaparte, to whose shrewd mind it must already have been clear that the real control in France was slipping slowly but surely into the hands of the army leaders.

5. THE DIRECTORY (1795-99)

So the great Convention which had guided France through three years of war and tumult passed into history and the nation sullenly accepted the new government provided by the Constitution of the Year III (1795). This new régime was known as the Directory because the executive power was vested in a committee of five directors. The legislative branch consisted of a Council of Ancients (with two hundred and fifty members) and a Council of Five Hundred, chosen by the voters who possessed the requisite property qualifications. The leading director was Paul Barras, a profligate and un-

---

[1] The dauphin, son of Louis XVI, died in Paris, in prison, a year and a half after his father's execution. Although he never reigned, the royalists styled him Louis XVII.

[2] The Constitution of 1793 (see page 644) had never been applied.

scrupulous man of mediocre ability, and, despite the fact that both chambers contained many deputies of patriotism and talent, the moral tone of the Directory was corrupt and sordid. Society became increasingly cynical, dissolute, and heartless as the revolution lost the impulse of its early ideals. Dishonest politicians and profiteers amassed fortunes at the public expense and spent them in wasteful display, while starving thousands cursed them. The directors did little to relieve the famine and suffering, for they were chiefly intent upon safeguarding their power against royalist intrigues and popular revolts. When the elections of 1797 returned a number of reactionaries to the legislature, the regicide directors called in the army once more to "purge" the chambers of royalists lest they muster a majority and invite the Bourbons back.

While the political prestige of the Directory sank, the army pursued its successes abroad. Trained and tempered in the school of war and condemned to be brilliant or to face the revolutionary tribunal, the young republican generals had developed a tactical audacity which numbed their opponents. As the French in their turn became the invaders, the proud coalition formed against France in 1793 fell to pieces. Prussia, Holland, and Spain made peace with France in 1795, and Napoleon Bonaparte, appointed to command the French army in Italy, brought Sardinia to terms (1796) and compelled the Austrians to sign the Treaty of Campo Formio (1797). Of the imposing combination of powers which had threatened to dismember France three years earlier, only Great Britain remained at war, and the British were on the defensive.

First coalition broken

France had thus secured for herself an ascendancy in Europe unequaled since the time of Louis XIV. The government of the Directory used this advantage to "revolutionize" neighboring states, surrounding France with a ring of sister republics. Belgium was annexed outright; Holland (the Batavian Republic) was bound to France by a close alliance; the left bank of the Rhine was in French hands, while in northern Italy French influence erected the Cisalpine Republic with Milan as its capital and the Ligurian Republic which included Genoa. These new states were not only tied to France by treaties; they paid a heavy indemnity and subscribed to the support of the French armies which had conquered (or "liberated") them. If the citizens complained that the burden of tribute was too heavy, the cynical directors assured them that the French had brought them liberty and "it is impossible to buy liberty too dearly."

6. THE ACHIEVEMENTS OF THE REVOLUTION (1789–99)

It will be useful at this point to enumerate the most important changes wrought in France by a decade of revolution. Feudal rights and titles had been canceled, the church stripped of its property, the monarchy abolished, the ancient historic provinces of the kingdom carved into new departments, the anarchy of the old legal system replaced by simpler codes and elected magistrates. Unfortunately, this mighty work of destruction had not always been followed by constructive labors of equal magnitude. Too often the new institutions remained impressive sketches, distinguished by nobility of concept rather than by practicality. The revolution had failed signally to establish a government founded upon liberty and equality, for liberty had little meaning under the Directory which was in reality a corrupt and unpopular oligarchy sustained by military power. The bourgeoisie had flouted the principle of equality by entrenching themselves in a position of social and economic privilege, while denying even a vote to the poorest citizens. But the protests, and even the revolts, of the masses had little effect. "The revolution is not finished," declared the popular leader Babeuf, "for the rich monopolize all the wealth and govern exclusively, while the poor toil like veritable slaves, languish in misery, and count for nothing in the state." Babeuf was voicing a protest which in the nineteenth century was to become the leading argument of the socialists, but his ideas were premature and the conspiracy which he organized against the Directory brought him to the guillotine (1797).

Rule of the middle class

Politically, therefore, the revolution had done little more than to shift the control of the government from an inept king and a selfish aristocracy to a vigorous bourgeoisie, but in other fields of endeavor the results were somewhat more heartening. Through the labors of enlightened thinkers like the philosopher Condorcet, a system of public instruction had been adopted which made the state responsible for the education of children. At first the new primary schools in particular were gravely handicapped by the insufficiency of funds and of teachers, but a start had been made in the great task of training all Frenchmen to become patriotic and literate citizens. Unspectacular reforms of this nature are the most easily ignored because they require many years to reveal their benefits; and the same is true of such innovations as the metric and decimal system of weights and measures, introduced by the National Convention to replace the confused standards of the old régime, but adopted all too tardily by a populace wedded to more cumbrous and diversified methods of calculation.

Educational reforms

Legal reform, that favorite project of the eighteenth-century rationalists, was likewise greatly advanced by the revolutionary assemblies, though it remained for Napoleon to cap with his codes the structure they erected. The new legislation recognized the peasant's freedom from onerous duties and the artisan's liberation from obsolete guild restrictions. Merchants and manufacturers were encouraged by the legal abolition of internal customs and the freedom allowed to business initiative. Perhaps most far-reaching of all in their social effects were the new laws of inheritance which assured all the children of a family a share in their father's estate, a policy which tended to break up large estates and foster the wider distribution of property.

Legal reforms

The printing of the assignats, continued by the National Convention with injudicious prodigality, reduced France to financial chaos, and by 1798 this paper money had become practically worthless. But the currency inflation, while it worked great hardship on many people, also furthered the sale of property confiscated from the church and from "enemies of the republic," and throughout the years of the revolution this property tended to pass into the possession of bourgeois and peasant purchasers until France numbered a larger class of independent landed proprietors than any other European country. The poorest peasants and day laborers were seldom in a position to profit by this unusual opportunity, but many a well-to-do farmer or townsman realized his dream of becoming a landowner and blessed the revolution for it. The comparative stability of French society since the revolution has been due in no small measure to the existence of this numerous and conservative group of citizens with "a stake in the country."

Economic reforms

The effects of these changes were not easily perceived in 1799 after a decade of tumult and confusion, and to most Frenchmen it appeared that the revolution had been a costly failure. But the dubious successes achieved at home were partly offset by the brilliant triumphs on the battlefield. The war of defense upon which France had entered in 1792 had been changed by 1794 into a vigorous offensive. Yielding to the lure of imperial conquests, the French speedily established a military hegemony which destroyed the balance of power in Europe. The government of the Directory, unpopular at home, sustained itself by the revenues extorted from Dutch, German, and Italian provinces, and prolonged the hostilities because the conclusion of peace would bring the republican generals back to Paris, victorious and insubordinate. The directors had no definite policy other than to postpone the day when they might be called upon to account for their corrupt and inadequate rule. The government was at the mercy of the army leaders, and the first ambitious general who fully comprehended this fact might brush aside the incompetent Directory and make himself master of France.

47

Napoleon and France

> We must not pass through this world without leaving traces which may commend our memory to posterity.
>
> NAPOLEON.

NAPOLEON BONAPARTE was born in 1769 on the island of Corsica, which had become a French possession the previous year. At the age of ten he was sent to a military school in France, a shy, uncouth boy, who spoke French awkwardly and envied his schoolmates their more polished manners and larger incomes. Lacking a title or a powerful patron, he would most probably have remained a lieutenant or captain under the old régime, but the revolution threw open the gates of opportunity. The desertion of the nobles created many vacancies in the staff of the republican armies, and Bonaparte, a second lieutenant of artillery in 1789, had been promoted to be a general of brigade by 1794, mainly as a reward for his services in the recapture of Toulon. Suspected as a partisan of Robespierre, he suffered a brief arrest after the latter's fall, but was soon released. In 1795, he was in Paris seeking a new appointment when the insurrection of Vendémiaire broke out. Called upon, with other available officers, to defend the Tuileries, Bonaparte collected some batteries of artillery and met the insurgents with "a whiff of grapeshot." There were, as he later explained laconically, "certain splashings," and the revolt collapsed. His presence of mind made a favorable impression on his superiors and his name was on everyone's lips. Napoleon had entered history with a salvo of artillery.

Napoleon's youth

1. THE ADVENT OF BONAPARTE

From the new government of the Directory, which he had thus helped into power, the young general received further promotion. Appointed (1796) to command the Army of Italy, he left his newly married wife, Josephine, and led his thirty-five thousand ragged French troops across the Alps. The Austrian and Sardinian armies holding northern Italy were taken by surprise, and the King of Piedmont speedily agreed to an armistice. Turning swiftly against the Austrians, who still outnumbered his forces two to one, Bonaparte laid siege to Mantua, captured it (February, 1797), after defeating the Austrian armies sent to its relief, and pursued the discomfited enemy to within a hundred miles of Vienna. Threatened by a second French army in southern Germany, the Austrians sought peace, and Bonaparte, turning diplomat, persuaded them to acknowledge the French annexation of Belgium, offered them Venice (which his troops had lately seized) as compensation for their losses, and demanded recognition for his Italian conquests which he organized as the Cisalpine and Ligurian Republics. When he returned to Paris, the populace turned out to see him present this successful Treaty of Campo Formio to the directors. France was delighted with this young general of twenty-eight who knew not only how to wage war but how to conclude peace.

Italian campaign

Bonaparte in Egypt

Finding his presence an embarrassment, the directors appointed him commander of the Army of England. But to cross the Channel with an army Bonaparte judged too hazardous. England and Russia were the "great intangibles": to the end of his reign both were to evade the full power of his smashing blows. Not yet strong enough to make a bid for supreme power, and fearful that he would be forgotten if he let his sword "grow rusty," Bonaparte proposed a plan to the directors whereby he might strike at Britain indirectly. His imagination turned to the East; he planned to conquer Egypt and thence attack the British posts in India. "I saw myself," he confessed later, "on the road to Asia, perched on an elephant, a turban on my head." But this romantic dream of following in the footsteps of Alexander the Great led him to the borders of disaster. Though Egypt was easily overrun, Bonaparte's fleet was destroyed by the English admiral Nelson (battle of the Nile, August 1, 1798), which severed his connections with France. His invasion of Syria carried him no farther than Acre. The proposal to invade India by land had been from the first a piece of incredible audacity as Napoleon now realized. "I allowed my imagination to interfere with my practice..." he admitted. "I shall take good care not to let it run away with my judgment again." He could appraise himself with the same cold rationality which he employed in judging his subordinates.

In Europe, meanwhile, the situation had changed to the grave disadvantage of France.

The second coalition

In 1798, Great Britain, most implacable enemy of the republic, drew Austria and Russia into a new coalition, designed to check French conquests in Italy and the Mediterranean. Within a few months the French forces in Italy had been routed by an Austro-Russian army (battle of Novi, 1799), and the Rhine frontier laid open to invasion. Then the French rallied. Masséna checked the Russians at Zurich; and to fire the reviving French hopes came the news that Bonaparte had landed at Fréjus, October 9, 1799. Leaving his marooned army to waste away in Egypt, he had slipped through the British blockade and returned at an auspicious moment. A month later he was to be master of France.

The government of the Directory was tottering. Discredited, bankrupt, and incompetent, it had thrown away the fruits of Bonaparte's Italian victories and involved France in new wars. Both Jacobins and royalists were plotting to overturn it, while moderate republicans under the lead of Sieyès looked about for a soldier to help them "revise the constitution." Bonaparte's arrival in October, 1799, could not have been better timed.

A plot was formed which called for Sieyès, Ducos, and Barras, three of the five directors, to resign (November 8).

Coup d'état (1799)

Under the pretense of checking a Jacobin conspiracy, Bonaparte's friends proposed that he should be given command of the Parisian troops. Then the Council of Ancients and the Council of Five Hundred were persuaded to adjourn to Saint-Cloud to deliberate on the crisis (November 9). The conspirators hoped to give their *coup d'état* the appearance of legality by persuading the two chambers to approve the necessary changes, but the Council of Five Hundred grew suspicious and were on the point of voting Napoleon's arrest when his brother Lucien, president of the Five Hundred, appealed to the soldiers to clear the chamber. Lucien's presence of mind and the bayonets of the guard saved the conspirators. Of this, however, no mention was made in the proclamation posted in Paris the following day, which announced to France that the constitution would shortly be revised, and that in the interval Bonaparte, Sieyès, and Ducos would act as consuls. From their first meeting Bonaparte assumed the lead.

The man who thus at thirty became master of France was to bestride Europe like a Colossus for fifteen years. In-

Napoleon's character

numerable books have been written to explain the peculiar genius and temperament of Napoleon Bonaparte, but there is space here for only the briefest summary of his character. In appearance he was short, with an olive com-

THE FIFTH OF OCTOBER, 1795

This engraving celebrates the repulse of a mob which assailed the National Convention on October 5, 1795. The occasion gave Bonaparte his chance to win fame with a "whiff of grapeshot."

THE YOUNGER PITT ADDRESSING THE HOUSE OF COMMONS IN 1793

Forgetting that they had been the "revolutionary" nation of Europe a century earlier, the British Parliament declared the execution of Louis XVI a crime without parallel and opened a twenty-year war against France in 1793.

plexion, sharply cut features, and a penetrating gaze. The qualities which make a ruler — knowledge of men, an untiring capacity for work, a rarely failing memory for detailed facts, the power of instant and inspired decision — he possessed in a unique degree, and these very largely explain the success of Napoleon the man. But he added to them a personal magnetism that could exact the utmost in devotion from his followers, an imagination incredibly romantic in its wild sweep, and a sense of the dramatic which made him the architect of his own legend. These help to explain Napoleon the myth. For a great many people the myth has obscured the man, transfiguring all his defects of judgment and character and investing him with attributes almost superhuman. "People will often give me credit," Napoleon prophesied, "for a great deal of depth and sagacity on occasions which were, perhaps, most simple in themselves; I shall be suspected of plans which I never formed." In his own lifetime people had begun to confuse the man and the legend.

That Napoleon was a master of military tactics and political finesse is conceded by almost all authorities. But he was no such universal genius on a throne as some admirers pretend. His taste in art and literature was mediocre; his knowledge of the sciences (aside from mathematics) was dubious and second-hand; his command of history was capricious and his economic beliefs were marred by disastrous errors. His character was inferior to his intellect and a deficient moral sense permitted him to stoop to ignoble deceptions and the basest tricks of Machiavellian polity. Nevertheless, with all his limitations he remains the most dominant and arresting personality in modern history, and the years from 1800 to 1815 are justly named the Era of Napoleon.

2. COLLAPSE OF THE SECOND COALITION

Frenchmen welcomed Bonaparte's ascent to power because they believed he would put an end to internal disturbances and conclude the war which had burdened France since 1792. Other republican generals — Hoche, Pichegru, Moreau, Masséna — had proved that they could win victories, but Bonaparte had crowned his Italian campaign with the Peace of Campo Formio. Knowing that the desire for peace was widespread, the First Consul opened his régime with proposals for a general truce. On Christmas Day, 1799, he dispatched conciliatory overtures to London and Vienna, but he strained every effort none the less to be prepared for further hostilities. The British response was vague, and the reply from Vienna left Napoleon in no doubt that the Austrians would never yield France the advantages she desired without a struggle.

The First Consul settled the issue with his customary speed. "Napoleon," admitted a contemporary, "is the only man in Europe who knows the value of time." Crossing the Alps in May, 1800, he snatched victory from defeat with the aid of Desaix and Kellermann at Marengo, and concluded a second Italian campaign even more decisive than his first. The following December, Moreau defeated the Austrian army in the Germanies at Hohenlinden and peace was assured. The Treaty of Lunéville practically recapitulated the terms arranged at Campo Formio four years earlier.

Marengo (1800)

The defeat of Austria broke the second coalition. Negotiations with the Czar Paul I (1796–1801) ended in the withdrawal of Russia in 1801, and Great Britain was left to carry on the struggle against France alone. For a year these wary adversaries bargained and finally signed a grudging peace (the Treaty of Amiens, 1802). The French Republic had established a political hegemony in Europe. Belgium, the left bank of the Rhine, and Piedmont had been annexed outright. Holland (the Batavian Republic) and Switzerland (the Helvetic Republic or Swiss Confederation) were bound to France by a close alliance that amounted to vassalage. In Italy, the Ligurian Republic (Genoa) and the Parthenopean Republic (Naples and Sicily) were under French control, while the Cisalpine Republic (renamed the Italian Republic) acknowledged Bonaparte as president. The French justified their acquisitions on the ground that the inhabitants of the annexed territories welcomed union with

French hegemony

France, and that the people of the subject states, the Dutch, the Swiss, and the Italians, regarded the French as allies and liberators. To a certain extent this was true; but the liberators were also conquerors, and the other European powers, disregarding subtler distinctions, complained that republican France had pursued with unexampled success the foreign policy of Richelieu and of Louis XIV.

The English in particular found it difficult to accept this French expansion. They deplored the fate of Belgium, for Antwerp in enemy hands was "a pistol pointed at the heart of England," as Napoleon clearly appreciated. The subjugation of the liberty-loving Swiss and the fall of the Venetian Republic after centuries of glorious independence inspired the poet Wordsworth to eloquent protests. The English merchant classes, disappointed that the Treaty of Amiens did not open Europe to their commerce, and alarmed because Bonaparte proposed to revive French colonial activity in the West Indies, in Louisiana, and in India, complained that peace was more disastrous than war. The French on their part likewise nursed grievances which they attributed to English perfidy, and neither party executed its treaty promises in full. It is not surprising, therefore, that the general peace with which Bonaparte gratified France proved to be an illusory peace of the briefest duration. The causes which led Britain and France to renew hostilities in 1803 will be discussed in the following chapter.

English hostility

3. NAPOLEON RECONSTRUCTS FRANCE

In December, 1799, the French people approved by 3,011,007 votes to 1526 the "Constitution of the Year VIII." This interesting document provided for a dictatorship under the guise of a democratic republic. As First Consul, Bonaparte was to wield the executive power for ten years. A second and third consul, a council of state appointed by himself, and a senate filled with his supporters, assisted in his decisions. To preserve the appearance of popular sovereignty for which Napoleon had no real sympathy — "Your Rousseau was a madman," he asserted privately — provision was made for two elective chambers, the tribunate and the legislature. The tribunate had the privilege of discussing laws, but could not vote on them; the legislature might vote, but could not discuss them. This arrangement, coupled with the fact that legislation was to originate with the First Consul and the council of state, placed the legislative as well as the executive power in Bonaparte's hands. This negation of popular rule, to gain which the French had just waged a revolution, was not easily apparent to the people because all male citizens retained the right to vote. But this, too, was rendered illusory. The electors of each commune chose one tenth of their number to form a communal list; members of all the communal lists in each department then chose one tenth of their number for the departmental list; and the departmental delegates chose one tenth of their membership for the national list. Public officials and members of the tribunate and legislature could then be appointed by Napoleon and the council of state from the national list, a system which left the voters free to cast their ballots and Napoleon free to promote only those men whose loyalty to himself assured their co-operation in his aims. Actually, most appointments were made before the lists were complete.

The Consulate

If the French people lost their political liberty and initiative, they gained a government of unparalleled efficiency and vigor. The farmer who had paid two and even three fifths of his income in taxes under the old régime now paid one fifth, yet the state revenues had doubled. New and more competent judges stiffened respect for the law, and special courts curbed the widespread disorder and brigandage. Ruined roads and bridges were restored, harbors dredged and canals deepened. The consolidation of the national debt and attainment of a balanced budget by 1801 revived business confidence, and trade expanded under an administration which proved it could assure tranquillity. After ten years of political vicissitude France enjoyed a competent, honest, and energetic government, and the merchant in the city and the peasant on the farm gave Bonaparte

NAPOLEON BONAPARTE (1769–1821)

Left: This portrait of Napoleon as a young man emphasizes the stern, relentless, and unsympathetic elements in his character. His likeness was not an easy one to transfer to canvas, for his moods shifted rapidly and he was a consummate actor. When it suited his purpose, few men could appear more frank, winning, or persuasive.

THE EMPRESS JOSEPHINE

Lower left: Napoleon's desire to have a son to succeed him induced him to divorce Josephine Beauharnais and marry the Austrian Archduchess Marie Louise in 1810. His son, known as the King of Rome (*lower right*), was born in 1811 and died in 1832.

the credit. To assure permanence for the new régime the constitution was amended (1802) making him consul for life with the right to nominate his successor, and the French people approved this extension of power by 3,568,885 "ayes" to 8374 "noes."

The First Consul's most popular reform was his solution of the religious problem.

Concordat (1801)
The breach between republican France and the papacy created by the Civil Constitution of the Clergy [1] grieved a majority of the French people who were still Catholic in sentiment. In 1801, a *concordat* was negotiated, whereby Pius VII agreed to renounce all claim to church property confiscated and sold by the revolutionary assemblies, and to permit the French government to nominate French bishops who would in turn appoint the lower clergy. In return the Roman Catholic faith was declared the religion of the great majority of Frenchmen and the constitutional clergy (i.e., those who had defied the pope and accepted the civil constitution) were replaced by priests duly consecrated. This settlement meant: (1) that the ten-year schism between Rome and the Gallican Church had ended with the spiritual authority of the pope unimpaired; (2) that the purchasers of confiscated church lands might for the first time consider their titles strictly valid; and (3) that the French clergy would prove submissive to the consular government because the selection of bishops and the payment of salaries had become a function of the state. Though ardent republicans disliked this compromise and called it a step backward, the mass of Frenchmen welcomed reunion with the Church of Rome. Those Catholics who had opposed the revolutionary settlement on religious grounds were mollified by the *concordat*, which remained in force for over a century.

Critics had frequently protested, both before and during the revolution, that France would never be tranquil until the laws had been reduced to a clearly formulated code. Napoleon considered it his chief claim to glory that under his direction this gigantic and confusing task was completed. He drove

The Code Napoléon

[1] See above, page 638.

his committee of lawyers relentlessly until by 1804 the main principles of the revolution concerning persons and property had been embodied in a civil code. Four additional digests followed, on civil procedure (1806), commerce (1807), criminal instruction (1808), and the penal code (1810). Of the five the civil code was by far the most influential and forms today the basis of civil law, not only in France, but in Belgium, Holland, Italy, and parts of Germany.

A law passed in February, 1800, went far to reconstruct the centralized bureaucracy familiar to Frenchmen from Bourbon times. In the departments the authority of elective councils created by the revolution was subordinated to that of a prefect appointed by the first consul. Similarly, a subprefect directed the affairs in each district and a mayor in each municipality. This relatively simple and centralized administrative system has survived in France up to the present day very much as Napoleon left it, demonstrating its efficiency through five changes of government.

Centralized control

The leaders of the revolution, having closed up the church schools, had planned to replace them by a system of national education. This project also Napoleon carried to completion with his customary genius for organization. The Imperial University (1808) crowned a state school system which embraced primary schools, high schools, and colleges. The curriculum was rigidly designed to train good citizens and the pupils learned their duty to the head of the state more thoroughly than they learned anything else. To Napoleon's mind the youth of France might have been so much raw material, to be manufactured into civil servants or soldiers as the need required. Even the adult population remained in a sort of tutelage, reading only censored journals and official *communiqués*, or attending plays specially designed to inculcate "sound principles." Napoleon was fulfilling the *philosophes*' dream of a paternal despot to a degree perhaps undreamed of in their philosophy.

Education

All his reforms — the legal codes, the centralized administration, the obedient church, the schools that trained his councilors, and the barracks that disciplined his cannon fodder — all had been erected to the greater glory of Napoleon. Moralizing in his captivity at Saint Helena, Napoleon declared his constant motto had been "Everything for the French People." But if he made France the most efficiently ruled and the most powerful state in Europe, it was less from love of France than from love of power. "Power is my mistress..." he confessed with truer insight. "I love it as an artist." So, despite the glory he won for France, his popularity waned. In reducing thirty million Frenchmen to be the instruments of his will, he did violence to human nature, for man does not wish to be regarded as a means to an end, but as an end in himself. Under Napoleon's barrack-room methods the finer flowers of the human spirit, art and literature, were slow to blossom. In the end his system failed in its primary purpose, for it did not provide administrators so efficient nor officers so inspired as the revolution had bequeathed to him. "The men of 1812 were not the men of 1792," he complained, criticizing his second generation of officials for their lack of initiative. Perhaps he had drilled it out of them.

4. THE IMPERIAL ADVENTURE

The Constitution of the Year VIII (1799) had made Bonaparte consul for ten years, the Constitution of the Year X (1802) made him consul for life.

Plots against Napoleon

His ambition, however, was not yet satisfied. He began deliberately to surround himself with a royal etiquette and ceremonial and took up his residence in the palace of the Tuileries where Louis XVI had held his court. In 1804, the obedient senate was persuaded to offer him the title of emperor. Several attempts had been made upon his life; agents of the exiled Bourbons and of the British government were plotting his removal; and the French people were troubled that such a beneficent régime should depend upon the safety of one man. To establish a Bonaparte dynasty appeared the surest way to perpetuate his reforms. At the same time, to deter conspirators, Napoleon had the Duke d'Enghien seized near the French borders, tried before a military court, and shot, a stroke which filled Europe with horror, but ended the plotting of the duke's Bourbon kinsmen. Several republican generals, including Moreau and Pichegru, were also arrested on the charge of conspiracy, and these drastic measures silenced all effective opposition to the establishment of the empire.

At Napoleon's invitation, Pope Pius VII journeyed to Paris to assist at the coronation of the first "Emperor of the French." The imposing ceremony took place in the Cathedral of Notre Dame (December 2, 1804), but instead of waiting to receive his crown from the pope, Napoleon set it upon his own head and then crowned his wife Josephine empress. High-sounding titles were invented to honor a new hierarchy of imperial officials. Napoleon's elder brother, Joseph, became grand elector. Leading generals were promoted to be marshals of France, leading statesmen became grand dignitaries with the title of "Highness," while even senators were to be addressed as "Excellency." The creation of a new order for distinguished service, the Legion of Honor, enabled Napoleon to flatter the vanity and reward the merit of loyal followers by distributing ribbons and medals carrying with them a comfortable annuity for the recipients. Thus, after purging itself of one privileged caste in the fires of revolution, the French people beheld the formation of another, but the new nobility differed in one important respect from the old. The aristocrats of the old régime claimed their titles and privileges by right of birth, but the imperial notables won their promotion on the basis of service. Napoleon's motto remained as it had been, "Careers open to talent," and he boasted that any private in his armies "might carry a marshal's baton in his knapsack." "It was my intention," he maintained, looking back on these crowded years from the loneliness of Saint Helena, "to put an end to all feudal institutions in Europe by reconnecting the idea of nobility with that of public service, and detaching from it all prescriptive or feudal notions."

Imperial hierarchy

Those who served the Emperor of the

WILLIAM PITT, THE YOUNGER (1759–1806)
Precocious political talents made Pitt prime minister in 1784 at the early age of twenty-five.

HORATIO NELSON (1758–1805)
Nelson's broad naval strategy and consummate audacity made him Napoleon's nemesis.

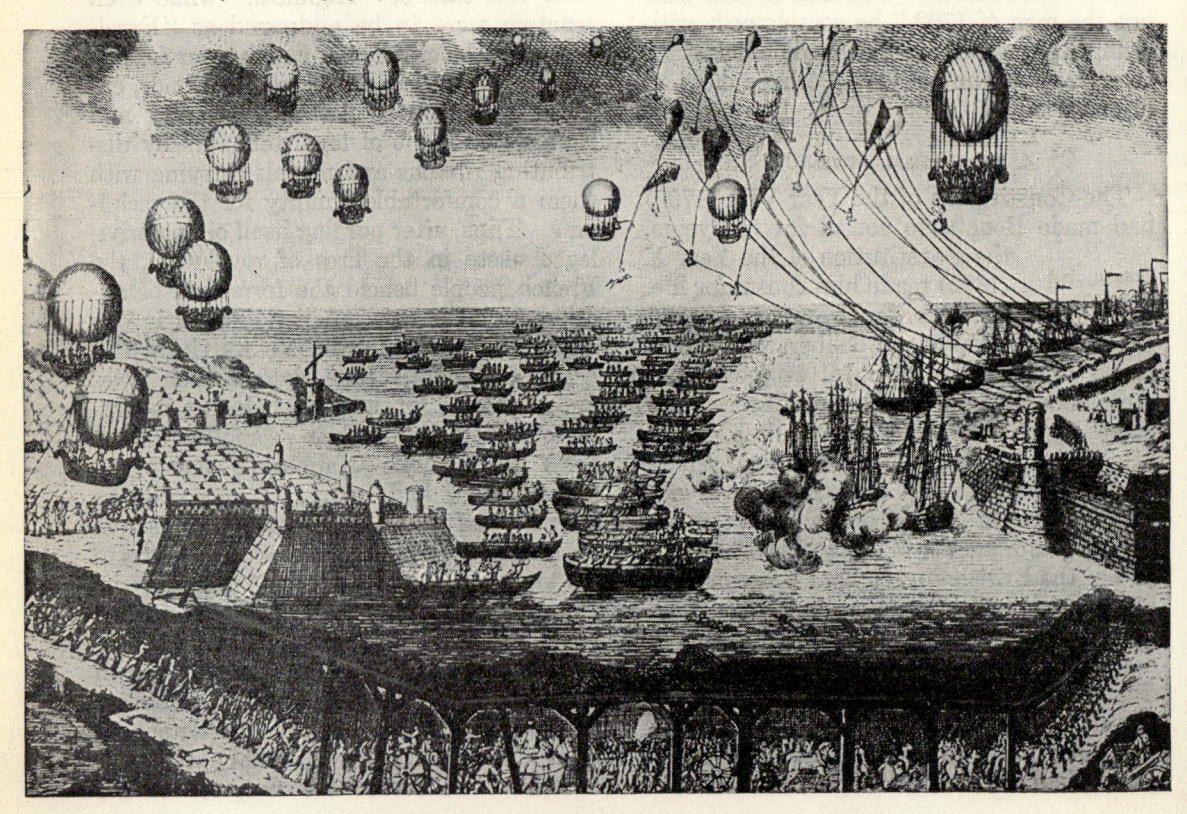

IMAGINARY PLAN FOR INVADING ENGLAND, 1804
The artist has pictured a triple-threat invasion of England, with Napoleon's forces coming by balloon, by tunnel, and by naval transports.

French successfully might hope for a title, a dukedom, even a royal crown. Not from France alone, but from all parts of Europe men hastened to learn the commands of the Man of Destiny whose aspirations seemed limitless, whose good fortune appeared inexhaustible. Napoleon in the plenitude of his power suggests Shakespeare's description of Mark Antony:

> in his livery
> Walked crowns and crownets, realms and islands were
> As plates dropped from his pocket.

But unlike Antony, he lacked magnanimity. Toward failure he had no pity, and he insisted that to serve him was to serve France, a presupposition which grew increasingly dubious as he staked the security of France and the lives of his soldiers more and more recklessly on his foreign ventures.

Nor was Napoleon always just in his distribution of awards. As his empire extended itself, he yielded to an excessive nepotism, showering undeserved honors upon the members of his family. His stepson Eugène (Josephine's son by her first marriage to General Beauharnais) he appointed Viceroy of the Italian Kingdom. One brother, Joseph Bonaparte, became successively King of Naples and of Spain, another brother, Louis, he made King of Holland, a third, Jerome, King of Westphalia. His sisters acquired titles and estates and his mother a princely income. As a family the Bonapartes possessed more than ordinary talents, but none to warrant such promotion. Moreover, Napoleon displayed partiality even in his nepotism, for Lucien, next to himself the ablest of the family, was left to languish in the cold shades of the imperial disfavor because he dared to marry against the emperor's wishes.

Napoleon's nepotism

It was a source of deep concern to Napoleon that his first wife, Josephine, bore him no children. In 1810, he divorced her for reasons of state, and married the Archduchess Marie Louise of Austria. In 1811, a son was born and received the title "King of Rome," for Rome had become the second city of Napoleon's international empire.

Imperial succession

With the imperial succession assured, Napoleon predicted that his reign was about to enter a second and even more glorious chapter. In reality his star was approaching a disastrous eclipse, the causes of which will be explained in the succeeding chapter.

5. RESULTS OF NAPOLEON'S RULE IN FRANCE

Napoleon called himself "the son of the revolution"; he even said, "I am the revolution"; and he never ceased to remind Frenchmen that they owed to him the preservation of all that was beneficial in the revolutionary program. It will be interesting to decide how far his claim was justified.

In the political sphere Napoleon's work was reactionary. He not only ended the republic; he re-established hereditary monarchy and revived many distinctive features of Bourbon rule. His prefects ("emperors on a small scale," he termed them) were replicas of the former intendants; his council of state was the royal council remodeled. His censorship regulations and his police agents had little to distinguish them beyond their greater effectiveness from those of the old régime. Behind a screen of popular deceptions he restored absolutism in France both in theory and practice, an absolutism buttressed by institutions more efficient and more highly centralized than those fashioned by Richelieu or Louis XIV. An incomparable army, a highly organized administrative bureaucracy, a state-controlled church, a standardized educational system — these were the instruments of his will, and the legacy he bequeathed to France. But these instruments were scarcely the product of the revolution, although the revolution had cleared the way for them. Rather they approximated to the ideal of government endorsed by Frederick the Great or Joseph II of Austria, just as Napoleon himself approximated to the ideal of an enlightened despot. The French people accepted him because he was successful and because his régime provided an escape from ten years of revolutionary strife, but they never quite forgot and never quite relinquished the democratic dreams of 1793 which had beckoned like an apocalyptic vision before the

Political reaction

clouds of disillusionment tarnished them.

Napoleon discarded liberty, but he preserved that other great revolutionary watchword, equality. The class privileges, the iniquitous taxation, the feudal obligations of the old régime, disappeared along with the archaic modes of punishment and the arbitrary administration of justice. The *Code Napoléon* assured all Frenchmen equality before the law regardless of rank, riches, or religion. Furthermore, proprietors who had acquired land confiscated from the church or from exiled nobles could thank Napoleon for confirming and legalizing their titles of ownership. Business men applauded the abolition of internal customs barriers, the improvements in roads and harbors, the benefits of a uniform system of weights, measures, and coinage, revolutionary projects which Napoleon perpetuated. The peasants were grateful for the abolition of feudal dues, for the suppression of disorder and brigandage, and for the restoration of the Catholic faith. In fact, there was no class in France which did not have some substantial reason for blessing Napoleon's régime. He undid much of the political work of the revolution, but he preserved and extended the civil and economic reforms.

Benefits retained

The revolution had killed feudalism in France: Napoleon buried it and reared a new order of society upon its tomb. But beyond the French borders feudalism was still alive, and the privileged classes would fight until their last battlement had fallen. For if the revolutionary notion of equality triumphed, it meant the ruin of the old aristocracy. The dues their peasantry paid them, the rent from inherited estates, the sinecures gained through family connections, and the promotions assured by right of birth — all these the spreading revolution would destroy. Even the laws which had long fortified the aristocrats in their pretensions would be changed to the advantage of the vulgar. Custom had hitherto reserved the most lucrative positions in the state, the church, and the army for the nobly born, but few aristocrats could hope to win such offices if the more capable commoners could compete for them on equal terms. It is not difficult to understand why the privileged classes throughout Europe resisted the revolution as an impious and subversive movement, or why Napoleon, in extending it, found them among the most implacable of his enemies.

As the son of the revolution, he was condemned to extend it, and he believed that "every man must fulfill his destiny." When the powers leagued themselves against his spreading influence, he fought and defeated them. "I always appear to be attacking," he complained more than once, "yet what I am doing is defending myself all the time." The student will be better able to decide how much reliance to place on this statement after reading about Napoleon's European projects and the campaigns he undertook to realize them.

48

Napoleon and Europe

> Throughout my whole reign I was the keystone of an edifice entirely new, and resting on the most slender foundations. Its duration depended on the issue of my battles. I was never, in truth, master of my movements; I was never at my own disposal.
>
> NAPOLEON.

IN 1802, the wars which had grown out of the French Revolution came to a momentary close. The French had proved by force of arms that they would suffer no interference from the other powers, and the monarchs of Europe, weary of bloodshed, abandoned their plan to crush the revolutionary movement and restore the Bourbons to the French throne. Unfortunately, this temporary truce did not endure. Fighting broke out again in 1803 and continued with mounting casualties until Napoleon was finally defeated and sent into exile. It is the purpose of the present chapter to explain why, between 1800 and 1812, Napoleon was able to extend his control over the greater part of Europe, and why, after 1812, his empire collapsed.

1. THE REVOLUTION SPREADS

When Napoleon became First Consul in 1799, the French Republic had already secured control of several states beyond its legitimate boundaries. Belgium and the left bank of the Rhine had been annexed, while Holland, Switzerland, and northern and southern Italy were regarded by the French as part of their "system" of allied republics. Napoleon had to maintain and defend this extension of French influence or risk his popularity. Because of his military genius he was able to conclude a general peace by 1802 without making any concessions, but the peace was not likely to endure if he attempted further conquests, for England and Austria were intensely jealous of the French success. If Napoleon had sincerely desired peace, he might well have rested content with the laurels won, but he had a passion for reconstructing and reorganizing things. One country was too small for his ambition, and looking abroad he decided that the people of Italy and Germany would be happier if he brought to them a few of the masterly reforms which had already been introduced in France. It was easy to find a pretext for interfering because many Italians and Germans admired Napoleon for what he had done in France and were willing to defer to him and to welcome his assistance.

So Napoleon disregarded the warnings of Austria, of England, of Prussia and Russia, and continued to extend his power by extending the work of the revolution. At first he had on his side the force of public opinion and the force of arms. Many Europeans outside of France sympathized with the ideals of the revolution and regarded Napoleon as its directing genius. People of the middle class in particular envied the French bourgeoisie who had thrown off the stupid and oppressive rule of privileged orders and made themselves the dominant class in the state. Of course kings and nobles everywhere were opposed to any extension of revolutionary principles, and they could set the armies of

France admired

Europe in motion, but Napoleon believed himself a match for them. The French battalions were the better organized and were commanded by a group of generals without equals in Europe, while at their head rode one of the greatest military strategists of all time. Moreover, Napoleon knew he would be fighting foreign governments rather than the nations they ruled and he believed he could easily turn his foes against one another.

2. THE RECONSTRUCTION OF ITALY

An Italian by descent, Napoleon knew that the people of Italy had learned during four centuries of oppression to hate the rule of the foreigner. He engaged their support by promising them liberty and self-government, and he prophesied that before long Italy would take her merited place among the powers as a strong and united nation. When he became president of the Cisalpine Republic (1802), he changed the title to Italian Republic, and the name stirred a patriotic response in the hearts of his new subjects. It seemed a further proof that the First Consul was working for Italian independence, and this hope long steeled the Italians to endure his exactions and to furnish men for his wars.

But in Italian affairs as elsewhere there was a wide divergence between Napoleon's pretended and his actual aims. Julius Caesar, it will be remembered, described Gaul when he first invaded it as divided into three parts. The modern Caesar returned the compliment, for he divided Italy into three parts and maintained the division. It had been a maxim of statecraft since Roman times that a country is more easily held in subjection when it is partitioned, and Napoleon feared that a strong and united Italian state, once formed, would prove difficult to control.

In 1805, the Italian Republic became the Italian Kingdom, but it still included only about one third of the peninsula. Napoleon came to Milan as a modern Charlemagne, to be crowned with the iron crown of the Lombard kings, and he designated his stepson, Eugène Beauharnais, as viceroy. In the following year the Parthenopean Republic was transformed into the Kingdom of Naples and Sicily with Napoleon's brother Joseph as king. The remaining Italian states were gradually annexed to France, Piedmont in 1801, the Ligurian Republic (Genoa), Parma, Piacenza, and Guastalla in 1805, Tuscany and the Papal States including Rome in 1809. The map in this chapter shows the limits of the Italian Kingdom, the Kingdom of Naples, and French Italy, in 1810, when Napoleon's power was at its height. Note that the Illyrian Provinces, seized between 1806 and 1809, were not added to the Italian Kingdom, but were annexed to France.

Though Napoleon treated Italy as a vassal state, he introduced many beneficial reforms. The Inquisition was abolished, the feudal régime swept away, taxation more equitably apportioned, and justice administered according to the new codes. The bands of brigands which had long terrorized sections of Italy, particularly Naples, were ruthlessly suppressed. An attempt was made to reduce the illiteracy and superstition of the Italian masses by establishing a state school system, improvements in agriculture and in public hygiene were introduced, and roads, bridges, and parks constructed for public use. But ten years of enlightened administration could not cure the corruption and inertia into which Italy had declined, and the French reforms, like the promise of national unity, remained more of a hope than a reality. With Napoleon's downfall Italy once again found herself chained by the forces of reaction.

Benefits of French rule

3. THE REORGANIZATION OF THE GERMANIES

The three hundred or more states, large and small, which composed "the Germanies" were likewise destined to benefit from Napoleon's passion for rearrangement. His plan at first was merely to weaken Austria by strengthening lesser German principalities such as Bavaria, Württemberg, Baden, and Hesse-Darmstadt. As France had annexed nearly a hundred small states on the left bank of the Rhine, he encouraged the German princes, dispossessed by these changes, to seek "compensation" by seizing

FRENCH SOLDIERS SEARCHING FOR ENGLISH GOODS

Right: To strike at the "nation of shopkeepers" Napoleon ordered the continent of Europe closed to English trade, but goods from London entered nonetheless.

THE BATTLE OF TRAFALGAR, 1805

Below: The greatest naval victory which the British won in their long war against revolutionary France came just six weeks before Napoleon's most spectacular military triumph at Austerlitz.

ecclesiastical lands and free cities on the right bank. After Austria had been induced to consent (Peace of Lunéville, 1801), the German Diet authorized the procedure by a decree known as the *Reichsdeputationshauptschluss* (1803), and by 1806 two hundred small German states, too weak to defend themselves, had been swallowed up by their larger neighbors. There were still nearly a hundred separate states in the empire, but a long stride had been taken toward a political consolidation of the Germanies.

Napoleon had no intention of welding Germany into a powerful and united empire any more than he planned to transform Italy into a single kingdom. But he knew that if the South German States owed their political aggrandizement to France, they would prove valuable allies in the event of a new war with Austria. He did not believe the Hapsburgs would allow him to usurp their leadership in German affairs without striking another blow, and when the new war came he wished to be prepared for it.

With Great Britain hostilities had broken out again in 1803. The English prime minister, William Pitt (the Younger), was a son of that resolute minister who had helped to strip France of her colonies in the Seven Years' War. The Younger Pitt proved an equally implacable foe of French ascendancy. Napoleon, when he found a renewal of war inevitable, determined to concentrate a fleet of transports at Boulogne and other French ports for a blow against England. "If we are masters of the Channel for six hours," he boasted with undue optimism, "we are masters of the world." To deflect the impending blow, Pitt stirred up resistance on the Continent, and pouring out gold with a lavish hand he persuaded Austria and Russia to join in the formation of a third coalition. Whether Napoleon seriously meditated a descent upon England has been doubted by some historians. If he did, he abandoned his campaign projects against his principal enemy without hesitation, and marching his divisions toward the Rhine with incredible rapidity he overwhelmed an Austrian army of fifty thousand men at Ulm on the headwaters of the Danube (October 20, 1805).

The third coalition

One day later (October 21, 1805) an English fleet under Admiral Nelson (1758–1805) destroyed the combined French and Spanish [1] squadrons off Cape Trafalgar, a victory which cost Nelson his life, but assured the English control of the seas to the end of the war. Once again, as in Egypt, Napoleon had felt the might of British sea power, and once again he pressed on undeterred. December 2, 1805, the anniversary of his coronation as emperor, he attacked an Austro-Russian army at Austerlitz and completely defeated it. For the third time he had forced Austria to a humiliating peace. By the Treaty of Pressburg the South German States which had aided France were enlarged and declared independent, Bavaria and Württemberg becoming kingdoms.

Napoleon now made his German policy clearer by organizing these new kingdoms and a dozen lesser states into the Confederation of the Rhine, with himself as protector. The princes of the confederation agreed to support France in the field with sixty thousand men, and to renounce all connection with the Holy Roman Empire. On Napoleon's assertion that he no longer recognized a Holy Roman Emperor, Francis II agreed to abandon that title and style himself Francis I, Emperor of Austria, instead (1806). Such was the ignominious end of that impressive medieval empire, the rulers of which had traced their authority to Charlemagne and Augustus.

Holy Roman Empire ends

The battle of Austerlitz shattered the third coalition and hastened the death of Pitt. "Roll up that map," he is reported to have said, pointing to a chart of Europe. "We shall not need it these ten years." Yet, as Napoleon complained, he had no sooner broken up the third coalition when a fourth threatened him. While pushing on his reorganization of the Germanies, Napoleon had kept Prussia neutral by promising Frederick William III Hanover and the leading rôle in a North German Confederation. Realizing by 1806 the hollowness of these promises, the Prussian war party persuaded Frederick William to defy France. But at

Intervention of Prussia

[1] Spain had been the passive ally of France since 1801.

NAPOLEONIC EMPIRE AT ITS HEIGHT

The Empire
Dependent States

Jena and Auerstädt, a double battle fought October 14, 1806, the Prussians learned that their army, famous since the days of Frederick the Great, was no match for the revolutionary tactics of the French. By the end of October, Napoleon was in Berlin. Pushing on he encountered a Russian force at Eylau (February, 1807) and fought it to a sanguinary draw. For the moment he was checked, but the following June he sought out the Russians again at Friedland and won a victory as conclusive though not so dramatic as that of Austerlitz or Jena.

The young Czar Alexander I was ready for peace, and Napoleon, who had learned to respect the fighting qualities of the Russians, was prepared to be generous. By flattering Alexander and offering him a free hand in dealing with Turkey and Finland, he won Russia to his side. But for Frederick William III of Prussia, who had so rashly yielded to warlike advice and defied him, he had no pity. Stripped of half its territory, Prussia became a second-class power with an army limited to forty-two thousand men. Prussian Poland Napoleon reconstructed as the "Grand Duchy of Warsaw," and the Prussian possessions west of the Elbe River he joined with some lesser states to form a new "Kingdom of Westphalia" for his brother Jerome. At the same time he secured control of the North German coastline to the Baltic, including the free cities of Hamburg, Lübeck, Bremen, and Danzig. North as well as South Germany was now in his control.[1]

Peace of Tilsit (1807)

The Peace of Tilsit marked the high tide of Napoleon's fortunes; after Tilsit, it has been said, he "began to attempt the impossible." Even his splendid mind was not immune to the insidious and corrupting influence of an unmeasured despotism. Hitherto he had extended his control less by conquest than by converting others to his projects, harmonizing their selfish aims with his own grand designs. Now he grew increasingly irritable at any form of criticism or opposition, and, while multiplying his own exactions, showed himself less willing to concede the desires of his allies and his vassals. He should have recalled how foreign interference after 1792 excited France to a militant protest, and have realized that his rough treatment of other nations must soon provoke them to a similar resentment. But this he failed to appreciate, misled very likely by the readiness with which the Austrian Netherlands, Italy, the Rhineland, and Poland had submitted to his control. These territories, disunited and misgoverned by their rulers, welcomed a change of masters, but when he humiliated independent national states such as Prussia, Spain, Portugal, and Russia, he unleashed the wrath of their people and united them behind their governments in a patriotic crusade.

Napoleon's despotism

4. NAPOLEON AND ENGLAND

The Nemesis of the Napoleonic Empire was Great Britain. With their colonial and commercial supremacy at stake, the English could not afford to compromise, and, as Napoleon found it impossible to strike at them directly, he decided to ruin this "nation of shopkeepers" by cutting off their trade. As master of the Continent he sought by his Berlin Decrees (1806) and Milan Decrees (1807) to close all European countries to English merchandise. By ruining the commercial classes which controlled Parliament he was confident he could bring the English government to sue for peace or face bankruptcy and revolution. He dared to stake the solidity of his empire on a test of strength and endurance, but the gamble was a gigantic one. It compelled him to close all the continental ports against England, and to stifle the hostility of Europe's millions who would be deprived of the English goods they desired to purchase.

Continental System

The British struck back by issuing decrees known as "Orders in Council," by which they hoped to regulate trade so as to force their own wares upon Europe while strangling the export trade of France and her allies. The French emperor believed that Britain, if unable to sell goods, would have to pay for necessary purchases abroad in gold, thus depleting her reserves, straining her credit, and dislocating her economic structure,

---
[1] See map on page 667.

THE RESISTANCE OF THE SPANISH PEOPLE

Napoleon imagined in 1808 that he could take Spain with 25,000 men, but by 1810 he had over 250,000 troops there and could not quell the resistance of the Spanish people. From a sketch by Goya.

while unsold products glutted her warehouses. The outcome belied his hopes. Though suffering severely from the curtailment of markets, British merchants and manufacturers still managed to defy the Continental System. Napoleon on his part found that the system was enormously difficult to maintain, and it led him into expedients which undoubtedly hastened his fall.

The principal points of entry for British goods were the German ports such as Hamburg, Lübeck, and Bremen, the Dutch ports, and Lisbon in Portugal. These Napoleon endeavored to control, but goods were still smuggled into Germany, Louis Bonaparte enforced the system leniently in Holland, and the Portuguese refused to drive the English ships from Lisbon. Napoleon, therefore, dispatched an army to Portugal (1807). The following year he forced the stupid Spanish king, Charles IV, to resign, and appointed his brother Joseph Bonaparte to the vacant throne. To subjugate Spain would require some twenty-five thousand men, he imagined, and take only a few months. But he underestimated three serious obstacles: (1) the mountainous nature of the country which favored guerrilla tactics; (2) the stubborn patriotism of the Spanish people; (3) the military assistance which Great Britain might render to the Spaniards. In the end Napoleon found ten times twenty-five thousand men insufficient to quell the Spanish resistance, although he came in person to supervise operations. The expeditionary force which the English sent to Spain, brilliantly commanded by Sir Arthur Wellesley, later Duke of Wellington, contributed in no small measure to the decline of Napoleon's military hegemony, particularly after 1810.

From Spain Napoleon was summoned

ARTHUR WELLESLEY, DUKE OF WELLINGTON (1769–1852)

The leading traits in Wellington's character were his remarkable self-discipline and moderation, which inspired the British poet laureate, Alfred Tennyson, to laud him as

> Rich in saving common-sense,
> And, as the greatest only are,
> In his simplicity sublime.

HEINRICH FRIEDRICH KARL, BARON VOM UND ZUM STEIN (1757–1831)

Baron vom Stein helped to revive Prussian power after the defeat of Jena. When Napoleon demanded his expulsion, he took refuge with Alexander I of Russia and helped to turn the czar against the French emperor. Stein had hopes that the recovery of Prussia would be followed by the national unification of Germany but this did not come until fifty years after his death.

hastily to the Danube (1809), where Austria, somewhat prematurely as it proved, had proclaimed a war for the liberation of the Germanies. Although he seized Vienna (May, 1809), Napoleon suffered a check at Aspern and had to call up reserves before he repaired his hazardous plight by the victory of Wagram. In the Treaty of Schönbrunn, Austria yielded territory to Russia, to Bavaria, and to the Grand Duchy of Warsaw, and acknowledged the French annexation of the Illyrian Provinces.

Austrian war of 1809

Nevertheless, Napoleon recognized that for a moment his fortune had wavered. He was impressed by the refashioned Austrian battalions (the Archduke Charles was learning by defeat) and angered at the bad faith of the Russians. Alexander had failed as an ally, for it was in his power to keep Austria harmless if he really willed it. These circumstances moved Napoleon to substitute Austria for Russia as the pivot of his European system. In 1810, after divorcing his first wife, Josephine, he married Marie Louise, daughter of the Hapsburg Emperor Francis I. Two years later, France and Austria contracted a defensive and offensive alliance, but this union of the youngest and the oldest dynasties in Europe had a touch of the fantastic about it. The Hapsburgs might overlook the humiliation of Campo Formio, of Lunéville, of Pressburg and Schönbrunn, but they could not forget the traditions of a thousand years wedding them to the old régime.

Alliance with Austria

5. THE RUSSIAN DISASTER AND THE WAR OF LIBERATION

The Franco-Russian Alliance, born at Tilsit in 1807, dissolved rapidly after 1810. Dislike of the Continental System and of Napoleon's Austrian marriage; resentment at the French annexation of the North German coast which dispossessed the czar's relative, the Duke of Oldenburg; apprehension at the choice of a Napoleonic marshal, Bernadotte, as heir to the King of Sweden — all these factors poisoned Alexander's friendship. But the gravest injury was the secret hope Napoleon held out to the Poles that they might recover their independence, for Russia held the greater part of Poland and Alexander had no intention of yielding it.

Nor did Napoleon lack grievances on his side. He reproached Alexander for failing in his promise to exclude all English products from his dominions, and he was alarmed when the czar stole a march on him by offering the Poles independence under Russian protection (1812). He had come to view his erstwhile friend as a "shifty Byzantine," and abandoning negotiations he concluded a military alliance with Austria and moved half a million men toward the Russian frontier. "What is the road to Moscow?" he demanded of the last of Alexander's envoys. "Sire," was the proud rejoinder, "one takes the road to Moscow at will. Charles XII chose the route by Pultava."[1] Napoleon knew the fate of the mad Swedish king who had marched on Moscow a century before, but he disregarded the lesson.

Rupture with Russia

Through the heat and dust of summer the Grand Army pressed forward, defeated the Russians at Borodino (September 7, 1812), and found Moscow a deserted city. For five weeks Napoleon camped in the Russian capital waiting for overtures of peace from Alexander which never came. Fires of mysterious origin leveled three quarters of the city, provisions ran low, and disorder spread through the ranks, until on October 18, Napoleon reluctantly gave the order to withdraw. The slow retreat became a nightmare of horror as hunger and frost decimated the ragged troops while Cossacks rode out of the blizzard to cut down the stragglers. When Napoleon recrossed the river Niemen in December, less than one fifth of the Grand Army remained to him. Some of his men were captives, many had deserted, but a quarter of a million had paid for his mad gamble with their lives.

Retreat from Moscow

The Russian campaign destroyed the myth that Napoleon was invincible. In 1813, with a hastily conscripted army, he found himself defending his hegemony in the Germanies against Russia, Prussia, and finally Austria. After their defeat at Jena in 1806, the Prussians had set quietly to work under the patriotic Baron vom Stein and Chancellor Hardenberg to reform their army, abolish serfdom and other social abuses, and prepare themselves, despite Napoleon's watchful eye, for a "War of Liberation." At the "Battle of the Nations" (or battle of Leipzig), October 16–19, 1813, Napoleon was decisively defeated by the allies and compelled to retreat across the Rhine. His grand empire collapsed almost overnight, his confederates deserted him, and the opening months of 1814 found him on the defensive in France itself, attacked at five different points by armies which totaled over four hundred thousand men.

"War of Liberation"

Before the battle of Leipzig, Napoleon might have had peace if he would have contented himself with retaining France and her natural frontiers; after that, with hope almost gone, he fought on in a defensive campaign as brilliant as it was desperate. His fortunes had changed, but not his character, and the egotism, the audacity, the gambler's faith in his luck which had extricated him from earlier dilemmas now became vices which betrayed him, lending a deeper truth to his boast that "Character is Destiny." On March 31, the allied forces entered Paris, and Napoleon, who was a few miles away at Fontainebleau, agreed to abdicate. He was granted a pension of two million francs a year and sovereignty over the little island of Elba, near his native Corsica in the Mediterranean Sea. The French Senate decreed the restoration of the Bourbon line, in the person of Louis XVIII, brother of the unfortunate Louis XVI who had been guillotined in 1793. The little dauphin, son of Louis XVI, who died in a Paris prison in 1795, had been styled Louis XVII by the royalists, although he had never reigned.

Abdication of Napoleon

---

[1] For the campaign of Charles XII, see page 569.

6. THE HUNDRED DAYS

This settlement satisfied the victorious powers, Britain, Russia, Prussia, and Austria. They allowed France to retain the boundaries of 1792, and imposed no indemnity, fearing to excite further resistance from that exhausted but still redoubtable nation. Moreover, since they had decided to restore the Bourbons, they could not very plausibly have offered them a dismembered state. Louis XVIII was urged to be moderate. He acknowledged the impossibility of undoing the work of the revolution and granted his new subjects a constitutional charter. There was to be a lower chamber elected by limited franchise and an upper chamber of hereditary peers after the fashion of the English Parliament. Louis retained the efficient bureaucracy established by Napoleon, and preserved almost unchanged the administrative centralization, the system of finance and taxation, and the legal codes which he found in force. He also did what he could to soften the hostility between the royalist followers who returned with him from exile and the imperial officials who had risen to power under Napoleon.

Many high dignitaries of the empire had foreseen Napoleon's fall in time to negotiate with his enemies. The urbane Talleyrand regained the portfolio of foreign affairs, although Louis XVIII could not forbear to remind him that he had dug the grave of three previous administrations. Talleyrand acknowledged the imputation. "There seems to be an inexplicable something in me, sire," he hinted, "that brings bad luck to governments that neglect me." But, however readily courtiers might turn their coats and serve a new master, the middle class and the peasants of France learned within a very few months to dislike and distrust the restoration government. They found Louis XVIII a colorless figure after Napoleon's fiery energy, and they feared to see the returning *émigrés* and high ecclesiastics regain the privileged position they had enjoyed before 1789. France had been thoroughly weary of Napoleon at the time of his abdication, but after nine months of Bourbon rule, people began to think more kindly of him, and to contrast his glorious achievements with the mediocre compromises of a king who had returned "in the baggage wagons of the allied armies."

This change in sentiment offered Napoleon the chance for a last fling at fortune. In February, 1815, he slipped away from Elba, and landing at Cannes, March 1, he started for Paris on what proved a veritable tour of triumph. The troops dispatched to arrest him deserted to his standard, the Bourbons fled at his approach, and by March 20 he was back in his capital. His belief that many Frenchmen would support him had proved right; his hope that the allies would not oppose him proved wrong.

Last flight of the eagle

For at Vienna, where the diplomats were already quarreling over the spoils, the news of Napoleon's escape brought swift unanimity. Prussia and Russia had been on the verge of war with Austria and England, but the four powers hastily composed their differences and concentrated their forces. Realizing that he must fight to keep his throne, Napoleon set feverishly to work organizing an army. To rally France to his side he outdid himself with promises. The Bourbons "had learned nothing and had forgotten nothing," but for himself he swore he had profited by past errors and would initiate a liberal régime and abandon wars of conquest. But he knew that his fate must first be decided on the battlefield, and that his only chance was to repulse his foes separately.

On June 16 he hurled back a Prussian corps advancing through Belgium, then turned to face a second army gathered near Brussels under the command of the Duke of Wellington. "I tell you Wellington is a poor general, the English are poor soldiers, we will settle the matter by lunch time," he insisted to his marshals. "I sincerely hope so," responded Soult, who had faced Wellington in Spain and knew better. Throughout the day Wellington held his position against the most desperate assaults, the Prussians under the redoubtable Blücher returned in time to aid him, and by nightfall Napoleon's army was completely routed. This was the battle of Waterloo, June 18, 1815.

Waterloo

Abdicating a second time, Napoleon chose to surrender to the English. "I come, like Themistocles," he wrote the prince regent, "to claim hospitality at the hearth of the British people." For the security of Europe, the British government decided, after consulting with other European powers, to imprison him on the lonely island of Saint Helena in the South Atlantic. There he beguiled the oppressive days dictating memoirs to explain and justify his career, and there, on May 5, 1821, he died.

NAPOLEON AT SAINT HELENA, AFTER A PAINTING BY PAUL DELAROCHE

49

The Vienna Congress

> Universal expectation has perhaps never been raised to such a pitch. Men had promised themselves an all-embracing reform of the political system of Europe, guaranties for universal peace; in a word, the return of the Golden Age.
>
> ... The real purpose of the Congress was to divide amongst the conquerors the spoils taken from the vanquished.
>
> FREDERICK VON GENTZ.

THE OVERTHROW of Napoleon brought the revolutionary era to a close. For twenty-five years Europe had been convulsed by war and social ferment, many landmarks of the old régime had been swept away, thrones had toppled, church lands had been secularized, nobles had lost their estates, while hitherto unprivileged commoners climbed to power and office. The new aristocracy which Napoleon created, as already pointed out, was an aristocracy of talent. His ablest marshals rose from the ranks, his officials won their promotion by ability and not by birth. It was largely for this reason that the administration of the empire functioned with an energy and efficiency unknown in the older governments of Europe, and it was natural that Napoleon, with his love of order, should have endeavored to extend the revolutionary reforms throughout the Continent. To do for Europe what had been done for France, to link the disparate states by a uniform code of law, a universal system of weights and measures and coinage, to free trade from frontier tolls and promote it by transcontinental highways, to end national wars by establishing a Roman peace under the hegemony of France — such was the imperial dream at which the Corsican had clutched. But the hostile powers had no faith in his design and refused to submit to it. His titanic struggle with Great Britain corrupted the scheme and the national resentment which he stirred up in Spain and the Germanies ruined it. Europe, weary of this inveterate trouble-maker with his mania for rearranging things, banished him to the lonely island of Saint Helena for the last six years of his life.

1. THE CONGRESS ASSEMBLES

In combining against Napoleon, the associated governments had proclaimed him the enemy of peace and of humanity, and laid upon his head all responsibility for the suffering and bloodshed. *Hopes deferred* In fighting him, the people were assured, they were fighting to end tyranny and social injustice. Many believed this, and made the sacrifices demanded of them in a high spirit of idealism. They looked to the Congress of Vienna not only to re-establish peace, but to remake European society and lay the foundations of a fairer world. Such idealistic hopes are needed to sustain men in the heat of a great struggle. Frederick von Gentz, a Prussian statesman who acted as secretary for the congress, noted these golden expectations in a passage quoted at the head of this chapter, and being a shrewd man he knew that they could never be fulfilled. Whatever settlement the congress reached was certain to disappoint a great many people. The evil that wars do lives after them, leaving a heritage of hatred and jealousy to becloud the peace discussions and corrupt whatever generous intentions the delegates may possess.

CHARLES MAURICE DE TALLEYRAND-PERIGORD (1754–1838)

Talleyrand's diplomatic gifts helped to secure easier terms for France.

KLEMENS WENZEL NEPOMUK LOTHAR, PRINCE VON METTERNICH (1773–1859)

Metternich represented the old order. With Napoleon's overthrow, he felt himself summoned to "prop a falling world."

THE CONGRESS OF VIENNA (1814–1815)

The decisions of the Vienna Congress were widely criticized, but it opened a period of almost forty years without a war among the European powers.

The Vienna Congress was no exception to this rule. It was, moreover, an assemblage of statesmen and rulers; the common people had no voice in it, no legitimate means to make their wishes known, or to show their approval or disapproval of the decisions taken. The princes and their ministers were to make the peace and the people would have to put their trust in princes.

For, with the tempest of war and revolution over, "kings crept out again to feel the sun," and many nobles and churchmen, remembering how pleasant life had been (for them) in the days before 1789, planned a return to the old régime. They hoped to re-establish the obsolete class distinctions of an older day, to rebuild the forts of privilege, restore society to its ancient foundations, and make the world safe from democracy. Europe, wearied by too many and too rapid changes, was to plunge from an era of revolution into an era of reaction.

In this temporary triumph of conservatism over liberalism, Austria played a leading part. The empire of the Hapsburgs was still a land of the old régime. Stricken repeatedly by Napoleon's swift blows, Austria had emerged toughened and consolidated by her reverses, and had been able to hurl her forces against the "Son of the Revolution" with decisive energy in 1813 when he was already wavering in the saddle. The choice of Vienna as the seat of the peace conference was a tacit recognition of this revival in Austrian prestige, for it seemed natural and fitting that a congress of reactionaries should choose for their sessions the capital of the most reactionary state in Europe.

Recovery of Austria

The leading Austrian statesman in 1814 was Klemens Wenzel Nepomuk Lothar, Prince von Metternich (1773–1859), the self-appointed spokesman of the reactionary forces of the day. As host to his fellow delegates at the conference, Metternich had an opportunity to display his unrivaled diplomatic gifts and to labor for a settlement which would undo the work of the revolution while exalting the position of his imperial master, Francis I. Metternich was an egotist who believed that he had been selected by Providence to re-establish the fortunes and the security of the Hapsburg Empire on a firm foundation. But as Austria was a land of the old régime, it could be preserved in tranquillity only if Europe were rendered as static as possible, with the privileged classes once more in power. Metternich sided, therefore, both by policy and inclination, with those who regarded the French Revolution as an unparalleled disaster inspired by false and irresponsible reasoning. Liberty and equality, as preached by the Jacobins, he recognized as subversive and disintegrating ideals which might have destroyed the Austrian Empire if they had not been checked. In politics, therefore, he argued that the safest methods were those which had been tried and tested; innovations, even when they promised great benefits, were likely to prove dangerous because they outran control and often destroyed what they sought to improve. As the old proverb had it, "the best is often the enemy of the good." Beguiled by the siren voices of demagogues and dreamers, the French people had attempted to introduce radical reforms with the result that Europe was plunged into twenty-five years of confusion and bloodshed. To repair the damage and to guard against a recurrence of such disorders, Metternich regarded as a practical duty. "To the dreamers," he admitted frankly, "I have never belonged."

Rôle of Metternich

With one notable exception his princely colleagues at the conference shared the Austrian chancellor's views. The exception was Alexander I of Russia (1801–25). A grandson of that enlightened empress, Catherine the Great, Alexander had been tutored in his youth by liberal thinkers. The desire of the Poles for national unity and of the French for constitutional government struck a responsive chord in his heart which caused Metternich grave apprehension. It seemed incongruous that a prince born to rule despotically over a great empire like Russia should harbor genuine sympathy for popular causes. To his fellow monarchs Alexander's character appeared a curious blend of piety and hypocrisy, of mystical concern for the welfare of humanity and hard-headed political acumen.

Alexander I

His importance compelled them to treat the whims of this "crowned Hamlet" with deference, but in private they distrusted and feared him.

The mediocre Prussian king, Frederick William III (1797–1840), was particularly subject to Alexander's influence. The czar had promised to help Prussia to obtain Saxony if Frederick William supported the Russian plans for Poland. The interests of Great Britain were ably defended at the congress by the astute foreign minister, Castlereagh, and by the Duke of Wellington, who was a statesman as well as a soldier. To represent France the newly restored Bourbon king, Louis XVIII, dispatched to Vienna the subtle and audacious Talleyrand. A bishop of the church under Louis XVI, and foreign minister under Napoleon, Talleyrand had offered his services to secure for France the best terms that could be wrung from defeat. For although loyalty to princes might be with him, as he confessed blandly, "a matter of dates," his loyalty to France did not falter. He had frequently advised Napoleon not to exceed the limits of the possible.

The delegates of the lesser states were doomed to play an insignificant rôle, for the representatives of the "Big Four," Austria, Russia, Prussia, and Great Britain, formed an inner circle and decided the most important questions with small regard for minority opinions. Into this charmed circle Talleyrand edged his way with the convenient principle of "legitimacy," a strange password in his mouth, but one which found favor with the victors. It should be the aim of the congress, Talleyrand suggested urbanely, to restore the states of Europe wherever possible to the control of their former rulers. This principle served France and the Bourbons well, for even after the "Hundred Days" the congress abstained from seizing territory "legitimately" French, and punished the nation instead by demanding an indemnity of seven hundred million francs on the payment of which all foreign troops were to be withdrawn. On the whole, this was generous treatment to accord a defeated power, especially if it be compared with the terms meted out to Germany by the victorious coalitions in the twentieth century.

2. THE POLITICAL SETTLEMENTS

It was not France, therefore, but her allies that paid a territorial forfeit. The great powers, while professing at Vienna their earnest desire for a just settlement, were in reality guided (1) by their greed for compensation to defray the enormous costs of the war, and (2) by their anxiety to erect safeguards against a fresh wave of French expansion. The final act of the congress, embodying these aims, was signed June 9, 1815, and a brief survey of its provisions will reveal how the spoils taken from the vanquished were divided among the victors.

Austria acquired once again a deciding voice in the affairs of Italy and the Germanies as well as increased territory. The Austrian Netherlands (Belgium) were not restored; but in compensation Austria gained Salzburg and the Tyrol, the Illyrian Provinces, and (in Italy) Venice and Milan and dynastic control over the duchies of Parma, Modena, and Tuscany.[1] No attempt was made to revive the defunct Holy Roman Empire. Instead, the thirty-eight German states were loosely organized into a Germanic Confederation at the Diet of which the Austrian delegate presided.

Austria

Many liberal and patriotic Germans had hoped to see their fatherland take its place among the powers as a strong and united empire. But the petty jealousies of the German princes and the ancient rivalry of Austria and Prussia rendered the fulfillment of this dream impossible at the time, although the cause of German unity had received a powerful stimulus during the revolutionary era. Politically, the Germanies had been reduced from over three hundred states to thirty-eight, a long step toward ultimate unity. A spirit of national patriotism had developed rapidly during the War of Liberation against Napoleon, and had found expression in the teaching of philosophers like Johann Gottlieb Fichte, in the poems of Theodor Körner and Ernst Moritz Arndt, and the broadvisioned labors of statesmen like the Baron vom Stein. Napoleon, by his aggressive interference, had hastened the political con-

The Germanies

---

[1] See map on page 680.

PIUS VII (1800–1823)

Upper left: Pius VII approved a concordat with France (1801) and anointed Napoleon emperor (1804). But after 1808, Napoleon seized Rome and Pius was taken to France as a prisoner. He regained the papal patrimony after Napoleon's fall.

ALEXANDER I OF RUSSIA (1777–1825)

Upper right: Alexander became Czar in 1801 after the murder of his father, Paul I. In his hours of liberal enthusiasm he was a "jacobin on a throne" and in his hours of mystic introspection he seemed a "crowned Hamlet."

ROBERT STEWART, VISCOUNT CASTLEREAGH (1769–1822)

Until his unfortunate suicide in 1822, Castlereagh labored patiently to restore and to preserve the European balance of power. His statesmanship was conservative and he was vilified by the liberals.

solidation and stimulated the national spirit of the Germans. Indirectly and unwittingly he had made himself the godfather of the later German Empire. But in 1815 the time was not yet ripe and the ideal of a united Germany remained a frustrated dream.

The peace conference was delayed for a time in its discussion of German affairs by the immoderate demands of Prussia. The Saxon king, Frederick Augustus, had been slow in deserting Napoleon, and to punish him the Prussian government proposed to annex the whole of Saxony. Austria, France, and Great Britain were prepared to oppose such a step by force of arms if necessary, and Prussia in the end received only two fifths of Saxony, but gained Swedish Pomerania on the Baltic and further possessions on the lower Rhine. It was hoped that these Rhineland annexations would make it possible for Prussia to maintain a "watch on the Rhine" and protect the German people from the danger of a new French invasion. The rulers of the house of Hohenzollern thus acquired a tutelary rôle in the affairs of the North German States which was equivalent to an international recognition of their leadership.

Prussia

The handsome and enigmatic young Russian czar, Alexander I, helped himself to an immodest share of the spoils. Finland, seized from Sweden in 1809, and Bessarabia, conquered from Turkey in 1812, he proposed to retain; while Poland was to be reconstructed as an independent kingdom under Russian protection, with himself as king. Austria firmly declined to cede her Polish territory for such a purpose, but the czar gained a slice of Prussian Poland, added it to the lion's share which he already possessed, and announced himself king of a united Poland. He even bid for the loyalty of his Polish subjects by granting them a constitution, to the disgust and apprehension of Metternich who distrusted such concessions to popular desires.

Russia

For Great Britain, as banker of the successive coalitions, the wars had proved enormously expensive. The British national debt quadrupled in a quarter of a century, largely as a result of loans to other countries which were never repaid. The British rewarded themselves, however, by expanding their trade and adding to their colonies. Malta and the Ionian Islands in the Mediterranean Sea, Tobago, Trinidad, Saint Lucia, Honduras, and part of Dutch Guiana in the New World, Capetown in South Africa, Mauritius and Ceylon in the Indian Ocean — all passed under the British flag. The Congress of Vienna failed to regulate the abuse initiated by British men-of-war of searching neutral vessels on the high seas. Nor, although this high-handed practice had precipitated a war between Great Britain and the United States in 1812, was the "right of search" defined when these two countries concluded the Treaty of Ghent in 1814. The British had secured an unparalleled predominance upon the Seven Seas, and they were determined to brook no curb upon the exercise of their naval supremacy.

Great Britain

In readjusting the claims of the lesser states, the diplomats evinced a callous disregard for national aspirations and popular preferences, bartering and subdividing densely inhabited areas as if they had been so much vacant real estate. To strengthen Holland, for instance, and compensate the Dutch for the loss of Capetown and Ceylon (which the English declined to restore), Belgium was joined to Holland to form the Kingdom of the Netherlands under William I of the house of Orange (1813–40). The Belgian provinces, which had been administered successively by Spain, Austria, and France, thus passed under Dutch control without consultation of their inhabitants. In the same fashion, Sweden received Norway, having lost Swedish Pomerania to Prussia and Finland to Russia; but in compensating the Swedes the diplomats paid scant attention to the wishes of the Norwegians. Norway had been administered by the Danish kings for over four centuries, but the Dano-Norwegian Kingdom was split as a punishment to the Danes for supporting Napoleon overlong. Even worse treatment awaited the Italian people whose desire for self-government and national unity was completely overridden. Only the Kingdom of Sardinia survived as an autonomous state under the

The lesser states

EUROPE IN 1815

house of Savoy, strengthened, indeed, by the addition of Genoa the better to serve as a check on French expansion in the south. Of the remaining Italian provinces, Venetia and Lombardy were in Austrian hands; Parma, Lucca, Modena, and Tuscany were restored to princes who looked to Vienna for their instructions; the States of the Church were restored to the papacy; while Naples and Sicily accepted the return of Ferdinand I, of the Kingdom of the Two Sicilies. The principle of legitimacy was extended to Spain also, where Ferdinand VII (1813–33) hastened to surround himself with all the symbols of despotism which the French had suppressed.

3. THE CONCERT OF EUROPE

To maintain peace and safeguard the Vienna settlement, Austria, Russia, Prussia, and Great Britain extended their wartime coalition into the post-war era, and pledged themselves to preserve a common agreement in international affairs by means of frequent congresses. After 1818, France was admitted to a sort of conditional membership and the Quadruple Alliance became in reality a Quintuple Alliance. This putative attempt at a League of Nations is usually called the Concert of Europe and it functioned with comparative success for several years after 1815. Congresses called under this plan assembled at Aix-la-Chapelle (1818), at Troppau (1820), at Laibach (1821), and at Verona (1822), but already by 1820 the divergent policies of the great powers had crippled the co-operative project, and it finally broke down for reasons to be explained in the following chapter. Great Britain, never friendly to the idea of permanent alliances, was the first of the powers to resume a position of diplomatic isolation; further rifts developed among the remaining members of the concert and by 1825 the British minister Canning was able to declare with satisfaction, "Europe is once more back to the situation in which every nation is for itself, and God for all." His words might serve as an epitaph for the Concert of Europe, and marked the dissolution of one more attempt at international co-operation.

Quadruple Alliance

Because it appeared to stand for the preservation of legitimacy and the *status quo*, the Quadruple Alliance was bitterly hated by all apostles of liberty and progress. In their denunciations they sometimes confused it with a second league formed at the same time and known as the Holy Alliance. The concept of the Holy Alliance, propounded by Alexander I in one of his more mystical and pious moods, was accepted by his deferential fellow monarchs with considerable skepticism. The czar proposed in all seriousness that the princes of Europe should pledge themselves "to take for their sole guide the precepts of the Holy Religion, namely the precepts of Justice, Christian Charity, and Peace..."; and that they should base their reciprocal relations as well as their conduct toward their subjects "upon the sublime truths which the Holy Religion of our Saviour teaches...." Unlike the Quadruple Alliance, which was a political compact among nations, the Holy Alliance was no more than a moral pledge subscribed to by the monarchs. Though Castlereagh expressed the general opinion when he called it "a sublime piece of mysticism and nonsense," all the princes of Europe endorsed the text except the Prince Regent of Great Britain, the pope, and the Sultan of Turkey. Despite its lofty phrases this "sonorous nothing" had no discernible effect upon the cynical diplomacy of the time, and liberals and republicans denounced it as a nauseating example of princely hypocrisy. Yet it would be unfair to Alexander and some of his colleagues to doubt that they were sincere in their wish to see a new era of human brotherhood succeed the slaughter and sacrifice of the war years. Great wars instill such a vivid impression of their horror and destructiveness that they are always followed by an earnest desire to avoid future conflicts. It is the tragedy of such good resolutions that they always come too late and are forgotten too early.

The Holy Alliance

In 1815, the tragedy of war had burned itself so deeply into the hearts and minds of men that the generation which had witnessed the retreat from Moscow and the slaughter at Leipzig could never be tricked into thinking of war as a romantic and chivalrous game. The impression of its horrors, however, faded with the years; already by 1830 a new generation was growing up to which Napoleon was almost a myth and war an untried adventure; but it was not until 1854 that Europe beheld again the outbreak of a major conflict between the great powers. That forty years' interval of comparative peace is the longest in modern European history. Part of the credit for it must go to the statesmen who shaped the Vienna settlement, for if the primary purpose of a peace conference is to make a peace as permanent as possible they were unusually successful. The merit of their work, however, has been ignored because it was overshadowed by the defects; the problems they solved are obscured by the problems they failed to solve or for which they found the wrong solution. This is natural, for it is the unsolved problems that focus attention on themselves and make subsequent history.

SECTION J

The Growth of Nationalism and Liberalism

(1815 — 1871)

Inspired by the example of the French revolutionists, the unprivileged classes in other European countries agitated for similar reforms during the turbulent era, 1789–1815, and the victories of the French armies spread the influence of the revolution across Europe. But in their struggle to preserve and to extend the new ideals, Frenchmen became extremely nationalistic. Napoleon's ruthless treatment of neighboring countries, even when it led to beneficial reforms, stimulated the patriotic resentment of Germans, Dutch, Spaniards, etc. When the revolutionary era closed with Napoleon's overthrow, it left behind as a heritage to nineteenth-century Europe an intensified and mounting spirit of nationalism, and a conquering faith in liberalism, which, though it was temporarily checked by the Restoration, was destined to revive and spread. When the bourgeois groups had rallied and consolidated their victory, they were to dominate nineteenth-century politics and impress their views and values on nineteenth-century society.

It is important to note, however, that the typical bourgeois, although liberal in principle when fighting for power, was generally conservative in his attitude toward the lowest classes, especially the city proletariat, when these in turn demanded full political recognition. This division of interests frequently paralyzed the liberal movement at critical moments. Note also that the sentiment of nationalism, which tended to grow more intense among all the European peoples during the nineteenth century, sometimes worked in harmony with, sometimes in opposition to, the spirit of liberalism.

ROMANTIC ARCHITECTURE

This synthetic nineteenth-century imitation of a medieval castle was built for an eccentric German prince, Ludwig II of Bavaria. Ludwig admired Richard Wagner and liked to picture himself as the knightly hero of a Wagnerian opera.

50

The Era of Restoration and Reaction

> In striving to reweld the chain of time, broken by a fatal interlude [i.e., the French Revolution], we have expunged from our memory — as we would that they might be expunged from History — all the evils which have afflicted the country during our absence.
>
> LOUIS XVIII, *PREAMBLE TO THE CHARTER OF 1814*.
>
> Yet, Freedom! yet thy banner, torn but flying,
> Streams like a thunder-storm against the wind;
> Thy trumpet voice, though broken now and dying,
> The loudest still the tempest leaves behind.
>
> LORD BYRON (1818).

WHEN THE NEWS of the capture of the Bastille first spread through Europe in 1789, it excited many favorable comments. Few contemporaries foresaw, in that bright dawn of the revolution, the profounder implications of the movement, or guessed that the thunder of its repercussions would soon shake the entire continent. But the mob violence, the Reign of Terror, and the long ordeal of the revolutionary wars brought discredit upon the whole movement and taught people to undervalue its real achievements. This change of mood made the more stable society of the old régime appear almost attractive in contrast to the turbulence and slaughter the revolution had brought with it, so that many people, after Napoleon's fall, were ready to welcome a period of restoration and reaction.

1. THE REACTION FROM THE AGE OF RATIONALISM

One of the first statesmen to sound a note of warning on the developments in France was Edmund Burke (1729–97), whose *Reflections on the Revolution in France* attacked the principles on which the revolutionary ideologists built their hopes. They erred, Burke submitted, in their conviction that society

Conservatism defended

could be radically transformed in a brief period, that ancient institutions could be remodeled overnight as it were. In their impatience with the old and their zeal for the new they had allowed themselves to be carried away by the belief that it was possible to tear out the scribbled pages of the past and start humanity afresh with a clean sheet. To confront this revolutionary or cataclysmic theory of reform, Burke offered the sober principle of the continuity of history. Each generation, he reasoned, is but one link in a lengthening chain. It is not for us, the creatures of a day, to decide what part of the heritage of the ages we will preserve, what part we will remodel or destroy. We are not the owners, but only the custodians, of humanity's baggage. It would be presumption on our part to discard old customs and institutions because their purpose is not clear to us; no one generation should set itself up as judge of society's future needs; the ties which knit together a state or a people have a mystical sanctity, and the rationalist who strikes right and left in a fanatical desire for progress may end by destroying the vital but intangible forces which preserve a civilization. To Burke, Reason did not seem an entirely safe guide.

"We ought to venerate where we are unable presently to comprehend," he insisted. He distrusted the revolutionaries because they envisaged man, not as he was, but as he might be or ought to be; they were ideologists who expected human nature to perfect itself to fit their formulas. But "the lines of morality are not like the ideal lines of mathematics," Burke pointed out, and his challenge marked the waning of the Age of Reason.

As the revolution spread and its excesses mounted, the conservative classes of Europe found Burke's arguments more and more convincing, and his masterpiece became a bible for the reactionaries. The revolution, its enemies contended, might seem to promise advantages, but experience proved them illusory, for in the outcome the sacrifices outweighed the gains. Revolutionists made the old mistake of the dog in the fable, which, crossing a bridge with a piece of meat in its mouth, saw reflected in the brook below another dog with a morsel even more juicy and attractive. Dropping its own prize, the dog plunged into the water, sacrificed the substance for the shadow, and emerged with neither. In similar fashion the Jacobins had clutched at the vision of liberty, equality, and fraternity, and plunged Europe into chaos.

Between 1789 and 1815 this distrust of radical experiments filtered through all classes and the people of Europe underwent a change of mood. The monarchs who returned to their thrones after Napoleon's downfall were convinced that Louis XVI had ended his life on the guillotine because he yielded to liberal advice. They blamed the enlightened despots of the eighteenth century also for preparing the way to revolution by experimenting with reform and encouraging the radical doctrines of writers like Voltaire and Diderot. That day was now past. After 1815, liberal writers who dared to comment freely upon political abuses were viewed with distrust. Princes no longer honored them nor read their books; instead they suppressed such criticism and persecuted the authors of it. Painters, sculptors, and musicians were tolerated because their work did not lend itself readily to propaganda, but so long as the fear of the great revolution endured (and it lasted far into the nineteenth century), all liberal poets, philosophers, and pamphleteers were viewed with suspicion and treated with official disfavor.

Intellectuals distrusted

The statesmen of the restoration believed likewise that the decay of organized religion in the eighteenth century, the prevalence of skepticism, deism, and atheism, had done much to weaken morals and promote revolution. In restoring Pius VII to his Italian domain, the Congress of Vienna sought to extend the authority of the Roman Catholic Church. Even in France, home of revolutionary principles, Catholicism had a powerful revival, the writings of François-René de Chateaubriand (1768–1848) and the arguments of Joseph de Maistre (1754–1821) converting many to the defense of papal authority. But ultramontanism — that is, the practice of appealing "beyond the mountains" (the Alps) to the pope at Rome as the supreme authority of the Catholic world — did not find favor with secular rulers. Monarchs might be anxious to renew the historic alliance of "altar and throne" against the forces of revolution which threatened both, but in reviving the spiritual authority of the church, they had no intention of restoring the political authority also, as it had functioned in medieval times. They regarded religion as a convenient handmaid of absolutism, and they expected the clergy, for favors received, to teach the people submissiveness and gratitude toward their rulers.

Revival of religion

In Protestant countries a new awakening of religious fervor had already stirred the common people in the eighteenth century. The German Pietists repudiated dogmatism and lifeless ritual in pursuit of a more intense and personal faith, and reanimated the Lutheran Church with their pure zeal for the Christian life. In England the passionate preaching of John and Charles Wesley spread the movement known as Methodism and induced many people to experience the sense of a "new birth." These religious revivals helped to elevate the morals of the poorer classes, to stir compassion for the sick

Protestant sects

and needy, and to direct attention to the wretched inmates of prisons and asylums. In their humanitarian zeal (though in little else) the revivalists were in harmony with the rationalists. "Humanitarianism" was the only tenet in the creed of the *philosophes* which survived the revolution unimpaired and won favor with the society of the restoration. The strength of the sentiment is manifested in the abolition of the slave trade by the Congress of Vienna, in the spirit animating the text of Alexander's Holy Alliance, and the abandonment of branding, flogging, and other "cruel and unusual punishments" in the prisons.

2. THE ROMANTIC MOVEMENT

Another reaction to the Age of Rationalism took the form of a vital outburst of artistic and creative energy known as the "Romantic Movement" or the "Romantic Revival." No simple formula will describe this dynamic outburst, which included revolutionary and reactionary elements and drew its strength from many sources. In one sense it was a revolt against the formal classical style of the seventeenth and eighteenth centuries. Poets of the romantic school deliberately broke away from the discipline of classical forms, turned back to Shakespeare with his "monstrous irregularities" and to the makers of medieval ballads for inspiration, extolled the joys and sorrows of the common man and the beauty and majesty of Nature as the authentic subjects of great verse. Sincerity and passion meant more to them than a precious style, for they sought to appeal to the emotions rather than the intellect. "For all good poetry," declared William Wordsworth, one of the first of the English romantic poets, "is the spontaneous overflow of powerful feelings...." Wordsworth chose characters from "humble and rustic life" and wrote about them in a simple, unadorned style, because, as he explained, "My purpose was to imitate, and, as far as possible, to adopt the very language of men."

Forewarnings of the romantic revolt appeared in the eighteenth century when tales of mystery and imagination achieved enormous popularity, and the generation which had worshiped the cynicism of Voltaire turned with even greater enthusiasm to the sentimentalism of Rousseau. As the claims of the heart reasserted themselves against the dominant rationalism, the century abandoned the pompous odes and "rocking-horse meter" of the classicists in favor of the "unpremeditated art" of the newer bards. Middle-class readers of average education could appreciate the common touch and the direct appeal of romantic poetry even better than sophisticated courtiers, and its democratic flavor pleased them. The spread of the Romantic Movement coincided with the rise of the bourgeoisie to social and political dominance. For in its reassertion of personal values and its emphasis on the dignity of the common man, romanticism harmonized with the political tenets of the revolutionary age. In Germany much of the early work of Johann Friedrich Schiller (1759–1805) and Johann Wolfgang Goethe (1749–1832) echoed revolutionary sentiments, and the English poets, George Gordon, Lord Byron (1788–1824), and Percy Bysshe Shelley (1792–1822), were ardent champions of political liberty.

Middle-class romanticism

The Romantic Movement also had its reactionary side. In the novels of Sir Walter Scott the old régime and the Middle Ages lived again under a veil of romantic glamour, for Scott had a "feudal soul" and found much to admire in the so-called "Dark Ages." The great French romanticist, Victor Hugo, likewise re-created the historic dramas of earlier centuries, suffusing characters and events with a color, intensity, and cloudy magnificence suggestive of the fabulous shapes, misty perspectives, and long red gleams with which the romantic painters, such as J. M. W. Turner in England or Kaspar David Friedrich in Germany, invested their landscapes. The neo-classical artists had shown a preference for the sharp contours and unshadowed brilliance of the noonday, but followers of the romantic vogue favored the mysteries of night, the magic of dawn and sunset, or the crepuscular shadows of an approaching storm for their effects. In music, likewise, the taste turned toward

Painting and music

more emotional compositions, lyrics and passionate extravaganzas, while in symphonies and operas the more formal patterns of the eighteenth century yielded to the originalities of Ludwig van Beethoven (1770–1827) and the titanic inventions of Richard Wagner (1813–1883). For his subjects, Wagner turned to the ancient Teutonic myths and the epics of crusading knights, a reversion to folklore and to medieval themes which was likewise a symptom of the Romantic Movement.[1]

Revival of Gothic This return to earlier models, and renewed enthusiasm for the achievements of the Middle Ages, led, in architecture, to a revival of Gothic art and Gothic structure. Reverence for the masterpieces of medieval style had never wholly languished, and much nineteenth-century architecture was modeled upon the cathedrals, castles, and town halls of the later Middle Ages. Castellated keeps, baronial halls, and ecclesiastic spires and naves of an earlier age reappeared, the revival being especially popular in England, where the romantic poets were regilding the romances of chivalry and the tales of knightly deeds. Much of the construction completed in the modern, synthetic style of neo-Gothic was anachronistic and oversentimentalized, so that after 1850 the whole movement came to be criticized as the production of artificial replicas and the indulgence of an affected enthusiasm. But it did stimulate a truer appreciation of the masterpieces of an earlier culture; induced William Morris and his school to challenge mass-production methods by an appeal to the beauty and satisfaction to be found in handmade articles; and inspired such outstanding edifices as the British Houses of Parliament.

Romanticism and nationalism The romantic interest in the past also linked itself readily with the deepening national sentiment of the age. The decades after 1815 saw the foundation of new state historical societies and the publication of great collections of official documents, as scholars and antiquarians labored to trace the slow and patient labor and the intricate processes whereby the national institutions, laws, and languages of the European peoples had been evolved. Men who realize how deeply all contemporary culture is rooted in the past hesitate to trust prophets or programs that call for sudden and revolutionary change. Thus, the study of historical continuity sometimes exerted a conservative influence upon social and political thought, an influence reflected in the observation that "a thousand years scarce serve to form a state, an hour can lay it in the dust."

Wide influence of the movement The wide range of the Romantic Movement, its search for new themes and novel forms, its tempestuous vigor and emotionalism, invaded and enriched all departments of art and speculation. The Utopian socialists of the first half of the nineteenth century, the humanitarian reformers and leaders of the evangelical sects, shared much of its mystical yearning and idealistic urge, and the revival of religious zeal among Catholics reflected another aspect of the same prevalent mood. Not until the third quarter of the nineteenth century did the artistic influence of the Romantic Movement diffuse itself into other channels and more realistic formulas, and the movement bequeathed a vital heritage. From Russia to Spain artists and thinkers had responded to a new intellectual quickening, so intense, so immediate, and so personal, that the Romantic Revival may almost be ranked with the Renaissance and the Intellectual Revolution in the richness and variety of its contributions to modern culture.

3. THE TRIUMPH OF CONSERVATISM: AUSTRIA AND RUSSIA

The distrust of "French ideas" after 1815, the revival of organized religion, and the shift toward more conservative lines of thought were related phases of the general reaction which found its most vigorous expression in the policies of the restoration governments. In this swing toward the right, Austria and Russia became the chief protagonists of conservatism for reasons which must now be more fully explained.

In the ill-assorted empire of the Hapsburgs, which lacked racial, geographical, and

[1] See illustration, page 684.

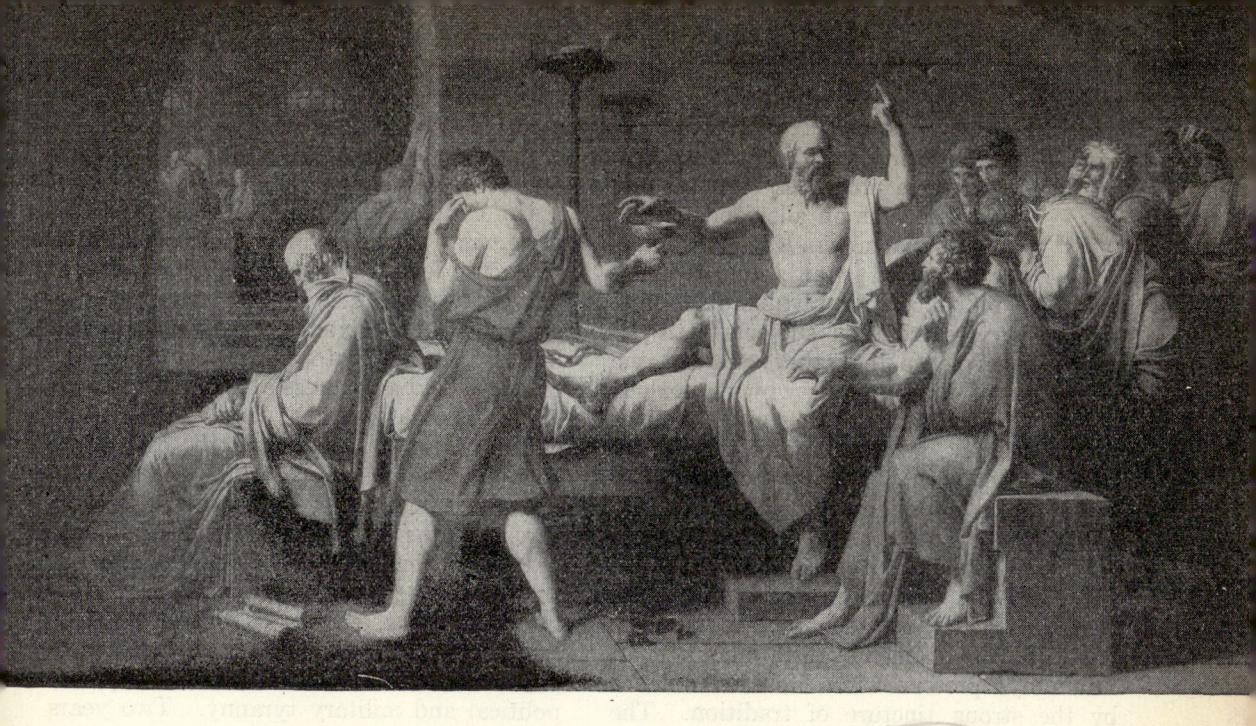

THE DEATH OF SOCRATES, BY JACQUES LOUIS DAVID (1748–1825)

The neo-classical spirit dictated the firm lines, the careful composition, and the theme of this famous painting by Jacques Louis David.

LAKE OF THUN BY JOSEPH MALLORD WILLIAM TURNER (1775–1851)

With the Romantic Movement artists turned to Nature, especially in her turbulent moods, and sought "the light that never was on sea or land."

even linguistic unity, the principal bond holding the diverse provinces together was their common allegiance to the imperial crown. Hapsburg rulers possessed "an almost inexhaustible influence and invulnerable prestige"; they treated their subjects with paternal benevolence, but they guarded the privileges of their dynasty with jealous hands. Austria remained, even in the nineteenth century, a feudal rather than a national state, with a nobility powerful and privileged, a middle class slight in number and influence, and a passive peasantry living chiefly as tenants on entailed estates. To foreigners the empire on the Danube appeared artificial, an anachronism with the dusty flavor of medievalism about it, a "mummy" preserved in a lifelike semblance by the strong tincture of tradition. The great personal authority of the ruler, the haughty and languid spirit of the officials, the disjointed and ponderous machinery of administration suggested an oriental satrapy rather than a European state. Even Metternich had been known to complain that "Asia begins on the *Landstrasse*," the eastern suburb of Vienna. Yet, despite handicaps, Austria possessed greater vitality than its enemies appreciated, and so long as the dissolving forces of nationalism and liberalism could be shut out it was capable of sustaining the rôle of a great power.

Austrian Empire

But Austria could not remain immune to revolutionary experiments if liberal agitation stirred again in neighboring states. The most rigid censorship of books and journals, the most careful scrutiny of travelers' baggage and papers, could not prevent ideas from filtering across a border. Self-preservation drove the Austrian government to urge the repression of radical movements everywhere, and Metternich, as the high priest of conservatism, labored to unite all the monarchs of Europe in a common resistance to revolutionary changes. He helped to dissuade Frederick William III from granting the Prussian people the constitution which they had been led to expect, and he constantly warned the other German princes, through their representatives in the Diet of the Germanic Confederation, to be perpetually on guard against secret revolutionary activities.

Unfortunately, minor disturbances in the Germanies soon provided Metternich with an excuse for further repression. In several universities the students had organized societies pledged to advance German liberty and unity. These fraternities, or *Burschenschaften*, held a congress at the Wartburg in 1817. The date was the fourth anniversary of the battle of Leipzig and the castle had been made famous by Martin Luther at the commencement of the Protestant Revolt three centuries earlier. After patriotic demonstrations, the students imitated Luther's burning of the papal bull, and flung into a bonfire the copies of several reactionary books, the *Code Napoléon*, and a corporal's staff, to indicate their contempt for political and military tyranny. Two years later an unbalanced student named Karl Sand assassinated the dramatist Kotzebue, believing him to be a Russian agent whose death would help to liberate Germany from the influence of the Czar.

Nothing more was needed to convince the German rulers that revolution threatened. They dissolved the *Burschenschaften* and ejected liberal-minded professors from the universities, while a council of ministers meeting at Carlsbad (1819) narrowed the laws of censorship and spurred the police on their hunt for radicals. These Carlsbad Decrees mark the high tide of repression in the Germanies and their stupid and unnecessary harshness added to the grievances of the discontented masses.

Carlsbad Decrees

In Russia, likewise, the pendulum swung toward reaction after 1815. Alexander I (1801–25) was a handsome and gracious prince, but he lacked the patient and inflexible character needed in executing the reforms of which he dreamed. With the aid of a practical minister, Michael Speranski, he opened his reign by consolidating the departments of government and even drafted a constitution for Russia. Face to face with fundamental issues of reform, however, his decision failed him. The intricacy of Russian affairs, and the dishonesty of the officials for

Reaction in Russia

GEORGE GORDON, LORD BYRON
(1788–1824)

e early nineteenth century Byron was
remely romantic figure, a superb and
c rebel, who died in the war for Greek
pendence.

JOHANN WOLFGANG VON GOETHE
(1749–1832)

In "Faust" Goethe created a character whose demonic lust for knowledge and power was typical of modern European man.

SIR WALTER SCOTT
(1771–1832)

Scott's historical novels cast a veil of glamour over earlier centuries and delighted a generation which enjoyed such romantic tales.

THE CHURCH OF THE MADELEINE, PARIS

This replica of a Greek temple, built in the late eighteenth century as a Christian church, represents the triumph of neo-classical taste.

which he could find no cure, drained away his enthusiasm. Not unwillingly he turned his attention from domestic difficulties to the long and absorbing duel with Napoleon. The annexation of Finland (1809), Bessarabia (1812), and further portions of Poland (1815) gratified the practical side of his nature, and it flattered his mystical temperament to picture himself as an instrument of the Divine Will in the stirring drama of Napoleon's downfall.

Yet a tincture of liberalism remained sufficiently strong in Alexander's complex nature to cause Metternich moments of uneasiness at the Congress of Vienna. The Holy Alliance, although it came to be viewed as a conspiracy of tyrants, originally reflected a sincere effort of the czar, under the influence of the religious mystic, Baroness von Krüdener, to infuse a more humane and Christian spirit into political affairs. But once again the pressure of events proved too strong for Alexander's unstable enthusiasms. The ingratitude expressed by the Poles at the constitution which he granted them, a mutiny in the imperial regiments, and the murder of his agent Kotzebue, cured him of his liberal fancies. At the Congress of Troppau (1820) he confessed his conversion to Metternich. "You are not altered. I am. You have nothing to regret. I have." Thenceforward, Alexander aligned himself with the protagonists of reaction until his death in 1825.

The Grand Duke Constantine, legitimate successor to Alexander I, preferred to resign his throne to the youngest of the three brothers, Nicholas.

Nicholas I (1825–55)

In the temporary confusion of the interregnum a group of Russian army officers organized a revolt at Saint Petersburg in favor of "Constantine and the Constitution" (December 26, 1825). Nicholas easily crushed this uprising of the "Decembrists" and punished the leaders with death or imprisonment. He had none of Alexander's sympathy for liberalism; trained as a soldier he based his faith upon discipline and autocracy; and he succeeded throughout a thirty-year reign in keeping political movements in Russia stagnant. To ensure this end he created the famous "Third Section," a special division of the imperial government organized to combat agitation and discontent. Nicholas could favor improvements in administration, as his codification of the Russian law (1832) and reform of the finances attest, but only if they left intact his autocratic powers. So successfully did he preserve his "system," even when his brother monarchs were driven to compromise, that he enjoyed the admiration of conservatives and the detestation of liberals throughout Europe.

Political stagnation, however, could not altogether dam the intellectual currents of the age. Russian writers escaped from their earlier dependence upon French and German models and developed in the nineteenth century a literature distinctively national. Wherever cultured people foregathered, at city salons or rural villas, new developments in music, painting, or architecture evoked animated discussion. New novels above all were read with emotion and criticized with tireless enthusiasm. For in the hands of such masters as Gogol (1809–52), Turgenev (1818–83), Tolstoi (1828–1910) and Dostoievski (1821–81) the Russian novel gave expression to the fervent political and social speculation of the day. Questions which could not be debated in parliament, because none existed, nor aired in the daily press, because of the censorship, found voice in works of fiction which were often political pamphlets thinly disguised. Permitted to indulge their mania for discussion, many Russian intellectuals developed radical and revolutionary theories, the more so because they were denied the opportunity to influence the government of the empire or to learn the sobering lessons of practical politics. It is an ominous portent for any régime when the intellectual classes become persistently hostile. In Russia, as in eighteenth-century France, the interminable discussions and philosophical ferment were to be the prelude to a revolution.

The Russian novel

4. THE BOURBON RESTORATION IN FRANCE

However greatly the statesmen of the restoration might desire to turn back the clock, the achievements of the French Revolution could never be wholly undone. Particularly in France too many momentous changes had intervened for Louis XVIII to see his wish realized that all the evils of the previous twenty years might be "expunged from history." Being an intelligent man, Louis recognized the facts and prepared to compromise. Napoleon's gibe that the Bourbons "had learned nothing and had forgotten nothing" was only partly true. The charter Louis granted his subjects in 1814 embodied the best of the revolutionary gains and made France the most liberal monarchy in Europe, for it promised a bicameral legislature consisting of a Chamber of Peers and a Chamber of Deputies, the latter to be chosen by about one hundred thousand voters. The best of Napoleon's achievements were likewise preserved; his centralized bureaucracy still functioned smoothly, the Bank of France continued to stabilize the admirable fiscal system, the schools were much as he left them, the *concordat* remained in force. Most important of all, the *Code Napoléon* assured all citizens equality before the law and all the children in a family a share in their father's possessions.

Nor could the church lands which had been confiscated and sold, and the estates of the nobles which had passed into other hands, be returned to their former owners. The revolution had created a solid class of peasant proprietors, men who held their farms free of feudal dues, conservative citizens desiring peace and order. The law of primogeniture had previously conserved entailed estates by transferring them intact to the eldest son or next male heir, but the revolutionary legislation provided that all the children must receive a share. By subdividing the land into smaller and smaller holdings, the new laws of inheritance induced an unexpected decline in the French birth rate. For a tradesman or peasant whose patrimony would barely provide for one family could not split it among several children and leave each an adequate means of livelihood. The most simple solution was to have only one or two children, and for this and other reasons large families became less common in France.

Results of the revolution

During the last hundred years the birth rate has steadily declined until the population has become almost stationary. In this way the French have achieved a social solidarity and compactness unrivaled by any other nation. Freed from the problems of an expanding population, France does not need to ship her surplus sons to the colonies, nor do many Frenchmen emigrate to other lands.

Thus the major social and economic results of the revolution proved remarkably effective and stable, but political stability was a goal more difficult to attain. Throughout the nineteenth century the French people oscillated between the opposing ideals of an autocratic monarchy and a democratic republic. Though Louis XVIII sought to steer a middle course as a constitutional monarch, the ultra-royalists (followers more royalist than the king) drove him toward a policy of reaction. In 1820, the Duke of Berry, the king's nephew, who stood in the line of succession to the throne, fell before the dagger of a fanatic, and the resulting wave of popular indignation brought the ultras into power. They proceeded to shackle the press and revise the electoral laws so as to strengthen the party of the Right, and having secured an overwhelming majority in the Chamber of Deputies, they decreed that the Chamber should remain in office for seven years.

The ultra-royalists

With the accession of the Count of Artois as Charles X (1824), the ultras found a king after their own hearts. More honest and more scrupulous than Louis XVIII, Charles was also more stiff-necked and despotic. The aristocrats, never reconciled to the loss of their confiscated estates, now pressed for reimbursement to the extent of a billion francs (1826). By converting the rate of interest on the national debt from five to three per cent, the government proposed to save twenty-eight million francs a year and apply it toward this indemnification. Capitalists and middle-class holders of national bonds would forfeit two fifths of their income from this source to benefit an undeserving nobility. A proposal to re-establish primogeniture in defiance of the Charter of 1814

Charles X (1824–30)

FERDINAND VII OF SPAIN (1808–1833)

Ferdinand typified the worst aspects of the Restoration Era, for he was a stupid, cowardly, and treacherous prince. Francisco Goya makes him look a sinister buffoon in ermine.

JOHN WESLEY (1703–1791)

As the founder of Methodism, John Wesley strove to make men better by touching their hearts and awakening their consciences.

SIMÓN BOLÍVAR (1783–1830)

Bolívar the Liberator did more than any other leader to free the people of Spanish America from the rule of Ferdinand VII of Spain.

JEREMY BENTHAM (1748–1832)

Bentham published his "Principles of Morals and Legislation" in 1789. In England his ideas fermented for half a century and helped to produce the Reform Bill of 1832.

increased the resentment of the bourgeoisie to the danger point, but Charles X persisted in his course, blind to the signs of popular discontent. In 1829, he attempted to override the parliamentary opposition by appointing as premier the stiff-necked and unpopular Prince de Polignac, thus violating the principle of responsible government. The consequences of his folly — the French Revolution of 1830 — will be described in the succeeding chapter.

5. TEMPORARY REACTION IN GREAT BRITAIN

Even in England, which Britons considered the historic home of political liberty, the period after 1815 proved an era of reaction. With the return of peace came economic depression and the evils of unemployment. The parliamentary system had ceased to be representative, owing to the shifts in population, and it had never been democratic, but distrust of the masses and of "French ideas" made the governing classes hostile to reform. When riots broke out in 1816, the government suspended the Habeas Corpus Act, the Englishman's guaranty of fair and speedy justice. When police and soldiers found it necessary to break up a mass meeting in Manchester with the loss of several lives (the so-called "Massacre of Peterloo"), the ministry succumbed to panic. They hastened to draft the Six Acts (1819), repressive enough to have pleased even Metternich, which curbed the long-established right of freedom of speech, muzzled the press, and limited the extent and purpose of public meetings.

Reaction (1815–22)

Not until 1822 did the panic wane and more liberal policies prevail. It was a sign of better times when the draconic penal code, which prescribed the death penalty for such offenses as stealing a sheep or picking five shillings from a pocket, was ameliorated in accordance with the more humane spirit of the age. Another concession long overdue was the removal of religious disabilities. Formerly candidates for almost all important offices in the state had to be members of the Church of England, a rule which excluded Roman Catholics and dissenters (members of Protestant sects other than the Anglican) from a share in the government. The abolition of these restrictions in 1828 and 1829 gave the English people, who had boasted religious freedom since 1689, the wider tolerance of religious equality. The Catholic Emancipation Bill (1829), passed reluctantly by the bigoted English Tories, was a particular boon to the Irish, for it enabled this predominantly Catholic people for the first time to elect representatives of that faith to the English Parliament.

Revival of liberalism

Though conservative at home during the years that followed Waterloo, Britain was often the champion of liberalism abroad. Such discrepancy between the domestic and foreign policies of a great power is not uncommon, and statesmen who sought to curb the popular demands in England actually aided the people of Greece and Belgium and South America to rebel against the governments that ruled them. In return Britain gained the gratitude — and the trade — of the liberated states, but displeased conservative powers like Russia and Austria. It was, in fact, Britain's refusal to co-operate with her late allies in suppressing revolutionary outbreaks that introduced the first serious schism in the councils of the Quadruple Alliance and prepared the way for the disruption of Metternich's system.

6. THE FIRST RIFTS IN THE CONSERVATIVE SYSTEM

Driven underground by the official repression, European liberals after 1815 planned new revolts in the name of liberty and democracy. Kings sat uneasily upon their thrones, remembering the fate which had overtaken Louis XVI, and spurred their police to burn revolutionary pamphlets and hunt down conspirators. Nor was this dread of secret societies without foundation. In Italy, the famous *Carbonari* (or "Charcoal Burners") numbered thousands of members pledged to abolish tyrants and establish a free and united Italy. In Spain, the attempt of the restored Bourbon monarch, Ferdinand VII, to reconquer his rebellious American colonies, led to a revolt among the troops embarking for that purpose. Thoroughly alarmed, Ferdinand hastened to grant his subjects a

Liberal agitation

constitution and made lavish promises of a liberal régime. Taking heart from this example, revolutionists in Naples compelled Ferdinand I of the Kingdom of the Two Sicilies to accept a constitution likewise. The following year the liberals of Piedmont won a smaller concession, forcing King Victor Emmanuel I of Sardinia to resign the throne to his brother Charles Felix.

Without loss of time the apprehensive monarchs united for a counter-offensive. At the Congress of Troppau (1820), **Troppau Protocol** to which all the great powers sent delegates, the governments of Russia, Prussia, and Austria pledged themselves to intervene, by armed force if necessary, in any state rent by a menacing revolt, and to restore the legitimate government to power if it had been overthrown by a revolution. The following year at the Congress of Laibach the Austrian government was commissioned to suppress the Neapolitan liberals, and Ferdinand I, restored to absolute power, took a barbarous revenge upon his late advisers, who paid with their lives for the folly of trusting their prince's oath. As the Sardinian government had failed to suppress the revolt in Piedmont, an Austrian army invaded that state also and extinguished the embers of rebellion. As a means of combating liberalism and maintaining the *status quo*, the principle of armed intervention had scored a brilliant success, and Metternich could congratulate himself that his system had shown itself "triumphantly fireproof." Because of its zeal in hastening to extinguish revolts, the Austrian army was derisively dubbed "the fire brigade of Europe."

Although Great Britain declined to endorse this international practice of armed intervention, the Congress of Verona (1822) decided to extend the principle to Spain. This time France received the mandate of the powers to intervene, for France had been admitted to the councils of the Quadruple Alliance in 1818 at the Congress of Aix-la-Chapelle. To prove that the French people had repented of their revolutionary debauch and had been converted to conservative ideals, Louis XVIII dispatched an army across the Pyrenees to subdue the Spanish liberals. In 1823, the French captured Cadiz, and Ferdinand VII, shamelessly revoking his promises, condemned hundreds of his subjects, who had been implicated in the revolt, to exile or execution. Master once more in his own house, he begged the powers to assist him further to bring his Central and South American colonies, which had broken away from Spain during the Napoleonic Wars, back under his control.

The prospect of extending their war on rebels and republicans to the New World was not unpleasing to the allied monarchs, but here for the first **British non-intervention** time their reactionary zeal encountered a definite check. The British government had protested with increasing force at the alacrity with which the allies rushed troops across Europe and disregarded national frontiers. Ignoring the British attitude, the autocrats had had their will upon the Continent, but to transport an army to South America might prove a hazardous undertaking if the Mistress of the Seas seriously opposed it. As the British had established a profitable trade with the independent Spanish-American republics, they had no inclination to permit a restoration of the Spanish monopoly.

Furthermore, the foremost power of the New World, the young United States of America, regarded an attempt of the allied monarchs to extend **The Monroe Doctrine** their repressive measures to this continent as a threat to all republics. In 1823, President James Monroe made it clear in a message to Congress that interference with the liberties of any independent American republic by a European power would be construed "as the manifestation of an unfriendly disposition toward the United States." In the face of British and American opposition, the absolutist powers did not venture to proceed.

The rift thus opened in the Concert of Europe steadily widened. The spirit of revolt could not be exorcised, and the fitful outbreaks of 1820 and **Greek War (1821–29)** 1821 had scarcely been suppressed when a new insurrection threatened. Embittered by centuries of oppression, the Greeks opened a sanguinary war against their Turkish masters. Cultured Europeans everywhere, who had received a classical education, felt a lively sympathy for these modern Hellenes, regarding them as the heroic descendants of the ancient Athenians and Spartans. Metternich insisted, however, that they were none the less rebels against their "legitimate" ruler, the Sultan of Turkey, and he urged that the revolt be allowed to "burn itself out beyond the pale of civilization." By 1826, the Greek resistance seemed broken, the murderous and energetic Ibrahim Pasha having depopulated the Morea in an apparent determination to make a solitude and call it peace. But the powers had finally decided to bestir themselves, Russia because of her traditional hostility toward the Turks, Britain from sympathy, and also because her bankers, having backed the Greeks, were anxious to collect, France because it had long been her policy to play a rôle in Mediterranean affairs, and all of them because none would trust another to intervene unsupervised. Having attempted in vain to resist the will of these powers, the sultan was forced to grant complete independence to the Greeks (Treaty of Adrianople, 1829).

The Greek Revolution illustrates better perhaps than any other event of the time the essential weakness of the Concert of Europe. Russia, as a signatory to the Protocol of Troppau, should have been willing to suppress the Greek revolt, but Russia was traditionally committed to the policy of hastening the dismemberment of the Turkish Empire. Great Britain, on the other hand, favored in a general manner the preservation of Turkish integrity, but the English statesmen, with their classical education, sympathized with the Greek insurgents, and English banking and shipping interests stood to profit if Greece became independent. The consequence of this division of motives and clash of national policies was a series of blunders and half-measures at the end of which Greece emerged as an independent state.

The guiding principle of the conservative system, the joint action of all the powers against any people which sought to change its government by revolutionary means, had broken down. The outcome of the Greek War of Independence displeased strict legitimists, but they found some consolation in the fact that the Greeks were not permitted to set up a republic, but accepted a monarchy instead, with a Bavarian prince mounting the new throne as Otto I of Greece. Nevertheless, it was an ominous portent for the defenders of the established order that the ideal of political immobility had been openly violated by governments pledged to maintain it. The system had suffered a serious blow, and the events of the year 1830 were to strain it still more severely.

51

The Bourgeoisie Secure Control in Great Britain and France

> In the silence one can hear a soft monotonous dripping. It is the dividends of the capitalist continuously trickling in, continuously mounting up. One can literally hear them multiply, the profits of the rich. And one can hear too, in between, the low sobs of the destitute, and now and then a harsher sound, like a knife being sharpened.
>
> HEINRICH HEINE (1842).

ANY FUNDAMENTAL CHANGE which affects a large number of people, altering their mode of living, their habits of thought, or their form of government, may be styled a revolution. The progress of natural philosophy in the seventeenth century was described in an earlier chapter as the "Intellectual Revolution" because it induced many people to revise their ideas about God and Nature. The action of the French nation after 1789 in destroying the monarchy and substituting a republic is an outstanding example of a political revolution. In this present section a third type of revolution is to be discussed, a revolution caused by the substitution of machinery for hand labor in many manufacturing [1] processes. The new machines changed conditions in the handicraft trades so radically and multiplied the output so enormously that they produced an Industrial Revolution the accelerating consequences of which still dominate our modern civilization.

1. THE INDUSTRIAL REVOLUTION

For reasons not yet fully understood, the eighteenth century brought an unusual increase of population to the European countries. This can be explained in part by the improvement in living conditions, the stricter sanitation and cheaper food. Between 1750 and 1800, the English population rose from six to nine million and the French from nineteen million to twenty-six. The same years saw a rise in the general standard of comfort, so that sugar, chocolate, coffee, tea, furs, and silks came to be looked upon as necessities rather than luxuries in the homes of the well-to-do, while even the poor were enabled to vary their diet with new vegetables like potatoes and carrots, and to afford cotton and linen clothing. The normal consequence of this increased demand was a marked quickening in trade, especially colonial trade, and a speeding-up of all business life. Anvils rang and spinning wheels hummed to a swifter tune, roads and canals were bettered so that goods might travel with greater dispatch, and sailing ships bound for distant markets crowded on more sail in the hope of a fleeter passage.

Quickening of trade

Rising demands meant greater profits, and the urge to speed production led manufacturers to experiment with new methods. When English foundry-owners discovered

---
[1] It is interesting to note that "to manufacture" meant originally, not to produce by machinery, but to make by hand. The word derives from the Latin *manus*, a hand, and *factura*, a making, from the verb *facere*, to make.

that they could not satisfy the orders for iron because sufficient wood was lacking to smelt the ore, they found a way to use coke instead. This meant more business for the mine-owners, but they were handicapped by the water in the mines, until they solved the problem with a steam-driven pump invented by Thomas Newcomen and improved by James Watt.

In like fashion, when spinning and weaving by hand proved too slow and costly a method of producing cotton fabrics for an expanding market, an improved loom was constructed by John Kay (1733) and a swifter method of spinning devised by James Hargreaves (1764). Five years later, Richard Arkwright invented a still better spinning frame, only to see it superseded within ten years by Samuel Crompton's mule, a machine which, under one worker, could equal the output of two hundred hand spinners. To eliminate the tiresome task of picking all the seeds from the raw cotton by hand, an American, Eli Whitney, invented the cotton gin (1793). For motive power to turn the spinning and weaving machines the owners first tried dogs and horses, then water power, and finally, where streams were lacking, Watt's steam engine was found to provide the needed energy. A fabulous increase in the production of cotton goods was the result. By 1790, Great Britain imported thirty million pounds of raw cotton a year, and the acceleration of the new processes was such that by 1810 this sum had quadrupled.

Effect of machinery

Similar mechanical improvements in the weaving of silk and woolen goods, and the knitting of hosiery and lace, came more slowly, but in these industries also Great Britain attained an unquestioned supremacy, possessing by 1812 more than twice as many knitting frames as could be found in the remainder of Europe. A unique combination of favoring circumstances explain this British leadership. (1) Nature had endowed the British Isles with the rich coal and iron deposits indispensable in the production of industrial machinery, and had provided in addition the damp climate most suitable for cotton spinning. (2) The wars of the eighteenth century left England with a colonial empire from which to draw raw materials and a maritime supremacy which enabled her ships to carry the manufactured product to every market. (3) Even before 1750, England led in the textile industry; her business men possessed surplus capital to purchase the new and costly machinery; and the extension of new farming methods, which drove many workers from the land, provided in this way a supply of cheap labor for the new factories. (4) Lastly, the disruption of economic life on the Continent resulting from the wars of the revolutionary era (1792–1815) favored British trade, spurring it to feverish activity and unparalleled expansion. Helped by these circumstances, Britain not only survived the financial burden of the struggle with Napoleon, but emerged in 1815 as "the workshop of the world."

Why England led in trade

2. THE FACTORY SYSTEM

Unfortunately, the Industrial Revolution possessed a dark as well as a bright side. In many trades, which had formerly demanded skill and craftsmanship, the introduction of machinery reduced the worker to an automaton, whose duties consisted of twisting together an occasional broken thread or periodically throwing a lever. The pride which an artisan had once felt in his handicraft vanished when he saw a machine supersede him and he became that machine's attendant, condemned to repeat motions of stultifying monotony all day long. Previously, under the so-called "domestic system," spinners and weavers had worked by their own firesides, receiving the raw material from merchants or middlemen who later called and paid for the finished product. But the factory system ended this casual part-time labor and herded the workers together for long hours in ugly and humid workshops. No longer their own masters, the spinners and weavers learned to hate the pitiless machines and their equally pitiless masters. Forced by the changing conditions to abandon the farming and other domestic activities which had brought them a living, and to toil for starvation wages in wretched factories, many workers held the machinery to

Evils of the system

blame for their plight and for the mounting unemployment after 1815. In a burst of vengeance as pitiful as it was futile, they fell to wrecking frames and power looms, and were speedily hanged or transported for their folly. They might as well have sought to sweep back the tide with a broom.

If men found the factory conditions cruel, for women and children they were all but insupportable. Yet women and children, it appeared, could tend machines as capably as men and would work for lower wages. Parsimonious employers hired wards from orphan asylums for their keep, and forced them to labor ten, fifteen, and even eighteen hours a day. It was not unknown for such children to be chained to their machines and locked up at night to prevent their running away. Overworked and usually underfed, without schooling, exposed to the brutal and promiscuous habits of the older hands, such children could hardly fail to grow up anemic and vicious. A few philanthropic employers attempted to better conditions, notably Robert Owen, who established a model industrial community at New Lanark in which the employees had a share in the ownership and profits of the factories. But the majority of owners were heartless or indifferent and the conscience of the nation remained numb.

Children overworked

Men who are growing rich, and who see their country growing rich, through their efforts, seldom fail to find good arguments to justify the existing conditions. Employers not only defended the factory system as wholesome and profitable; they fought all efforts of the government to investigate or improve the lot of the workers. Business prospered best when let alone, the economist Adam Smith had argued in his *Inquiry into the Nature and Causes of the Wealth of Nations* (1776). Business men pointed to the expansion of British industry as proof that a *laissez-faire* (i.e., non-interference) policy, without tariffs, regulations, or other trade restrictions, was the soundest course for a government to pursue. It was, they agreed, most regrettable that so many people lived on the margin of starvation, but inexorable economic laws ordained that it must be so.

Laissez-faire ideals

"Population," Thomas Malthus proclaimed in 1798, "has a constant tendency to increase beyond the means of subsistence." If war and disease failed to curtail a nation's growth, he went on to explain in his *Essay upon the Principles of Population*, actual starvation would keep it within the limits determined by the food supply. Another political economist, David Ricardo, applied similar reasoning to the problem of the laboring classes. If wages rose above the margin of subsistence, he argued, the workers took advantage of their increased income to raise larger families. This soon produced a surplus of unemployed laborers who, underbidding those with jobs, brought wages back to the subsistence level. It was not the greed of employers but the inexorable weight of economic laws which decreed that the poor must be damned for the greater glory of Mammon, a doctrine which naturally found favor with the governing classes.

Commencing as an economic phenomenon, the Industrial Revolution precipitated social and political changes of the highest importance. It raised two classes to new prominence and widened the gulf between them. On the one hand stood the men of wealth, men with the capital and the initiative to build factories, play for the high stakes offered by the rapidly expanding industries, and win for themselves the rank of an industrial aristocracy. On the other hand stood the workers, or proletariat, a class waxing in number, but without property, without any share or direction in the industry that employed them, and without the means to better their condition. In the years after 1815, years of economic adjustment and social strain, both these classes grew conscious of their importance and both began to seek political power.

Capital and labor

3. THE ENGLISH REFORM BILL OF 1832

Though admired by Europeans as the home of representative government and political liberty, Great Britain in 1815 possessed institutions far from liberal. The government may best be described as a "plutocracy," for the wealthy classes ruled the Parliament, particularly the city merchants, shipowners,

Social injustice

After 1779, Samuel Crompton's "mule" (left) greatly speeded cotton spinning by machinery; and Edmund Cartwright's power loom (right) mechanized the weaving.

In the eighteenth century, spinning, weaving, and textile printing were still done largely by hand.

In 1780 nine tenths of the English textile workers labored at home; by 1850, nine tenths were employed in factories.

THE MECHANIZATION OF THE TEXTILE INDUSTRY

landlords, and country nobility. As only one person in thirty-two had the right to vote, it was possible in many "rotten" boroughs to buy a seat in Parliament by bribing a majority of the local electors. In others, termed "pocket" boroughs, the most powerful local landowner controlled the election, nominating a candidate and persuading or intimidating the voters to support his choice. As the ballots were recorded publicly, a tenant openly invited his landlord's displeasure if he opposed the latter's selection. Under these circumstances it was inevitable that the House of Commons should represent the English governing classes rather than the English people. Nor must it be forgotten that two highly privileged groups, the peers and the bishops of the Anglican Church, sat in the House of Lords and exercised through that chamber a potential veto on all legislation. Clearly the plutocracy held all the entrenchments of power.

Projects for the reform of Parliament, designed to make it more popular and more truly representative, had been debated forty years earlier, but the outbreak of the French Revolution filled the ruling classes in England with panic and discredited democratic ideas. When the war with France ended in 1815, the Tory government embarked upon a policy of repression, fearing that any concessions might encourage revolts and revolts lead to revolution. Within a decade, however, as described in the previous chapter, this reactionary mood weakened. The amelioration of the penal code and the passage of the Catholic Emancipation Act [1] indicated that liberal sentiment was gaining the day.

At this point (1830) the Whig politicians, political opponents of the Tories, came forward as the champions of parliamentary reform. At heart the Whig leaders had little sympathy with democratic ideals, but they allied themselves with the discontented workingmen because they hoped by reform to keep themselves in power. The Tories drew much of their strength from the "rotten" and "pocket" boroughs, particularly in the south of England. They enjoyed the support of the great country landowners, and deserved it by the manner in which they favored and protected the agricultural interests in Parliament. The Whigs, on the other hand, were more closely identified with the middle-class dwellers of the cities, with merchants, traders, bankers, factory and mill owners. As already noted, the Industrial Revolution had rapidly increased the importance and wealth of the industrial aristocracy, causing factory towns to spring up around the coal-fields of the western counties. But the unreformed Parliament ignored this shift in population and denied important manufacturing centers, such as Manchester, Sheffield, and Birmingham, a single representative, although ancient and decayed boroughs, shrunken to a few families, continued to send a member to London. The first item on the Whig program was, therefore, a redistribution of seats, which would increase the representation of the new cities at the expense of depopulated counties.

Reform of Parliament

The second item of reform which the Whigs proposed was an extension of the suffrage. Hitherto less than four per cent of the population had enjoyed the right to vote. If this right were extended to all householders who paid the equivalent of ten pounds rent a year, many of the lesser bourgeoisie of the towns and leaseholders in the counties could share in the elections, increasing the number of voters from 435,000 to 656,000. As this was roughly one in twenty-two instead of one in thirty-two of the population, it will be seen that the measure stopped far short of genuine democracy. A majority of the laborers on the farms and workingmen in the cities were to be left no better off than before.

Extension of the suffrage

Nevertheless, the struggle for reform enlisted the ardent support of the city workers, who demonstrated, by mass meetings, riots, and occasional acts of violence, that they had reached a dangerous mood. The Whigs could also count upon the support of the intellectual radicals, a small but distinguished group of writers and scholars led by the philosopher Jeremy Bentham (1748–1832) and John Stuart Mill (1806–73). These Benthamites, or Utilitarians, believed

[1] See above, page 695.

GEORGE STEPHENSON (1781–1848) **STEPHENSON'S LOCOMOTIVE**

Stephenson labored to adapt steam engines to locomotion. The engine that is being stoked and oiled in this illustration of 1830 was known as "The Rocket."

ROBERT FULTON (1765–1815) AND THE "CLERMONT"

In 1807, Robert Fulton's steamboat, the "Clermont," made the trip from New York to Albany and back in five days.

STEAM POWER AND TRANSPORTATION

the purpose or utility of a government should be gauged by the degree to which it afforded "the greatest good to the greatest number." To fulfill this function it should be genuinely representative; hence the Utilitarians favored universal manhood suffrage, but they were willing to endorse the Whig program as a step in the right direction. Prospects brightened when the news that the French had driven out the absolutist king, Charles X, precipitated a cabinet crisis in England which caused the fall of the Tory Party and brought the Whigs into office (1830). The moment for an experiment in constitutional reform had arrived.

The Whig prime minister, Earl Grey, found the House of Commons divided on the merits of the proposed bill and called for a general election to discover the wishes of the electorate.

Reform Bill of 1832

The Whigs were returned to power with a large majority, but their second bill, though it passed in the Commons (1831), was rejected by the House of Lords. In 1832, therefore, the Commons passed a third reform bill. Again the Lords rejected it. Popular indignation had risen to the verge of revolution at this repeated frustration of the nation's expressed will. Yet when Earl Grey resigned as a protest, the stubborn king, William IV, called upon the Tory Duke of Wellington to take office. But not even the Iron Duke's resolution, which had defeated Napoleon at Waterloo, could stem the liberal tide. After a few days the king found it necessary to recall Grey to power, with the assurance that if no other means sufficed, the Crown would create enough new peers to break the deadlock in the House of Lords. The threat proved sufficient. Rather than see their august rolls defaced by a host of new titles minted for the occasion the Lords yielded, and the Reform Bill became law in June, 1832.

A revolution had been accomplished by constitutional means, and the strength of the old régime in England definitely broken. In effect, the Reform Bill of 1832 elevated the industrial aristocracy to a level with the older landed nobility and divided the control of the government between them. In a more final sense, however, it meant the triumph of the manufacturing interests over the agricultural. The clearest proof of this is to be seen a few years later in the repeal of the Corn [1] Laws. The tariff on grains had assured the great landowners a profit on their crops. The abolition of this tariff proved a blow to agriculture, but a boon to the city workers for whom it meant cheaper bread. And the city dwellers had to be served, for they had become the most important element of the population. By 1846, for the first time in English history, over half the people lived in towns, outranking in wealth and number the dwellers of the countryside. This rapid increase in the urban population was the most startling social change introduced by the Industrial Revolution.

4. THE CHARTIST MOVEMENT

Their somewhat hesitant espousal of the Reform Bill (1832) won for the Whigs the distinction of being the "Liberal" Party in England throughout the remainder of the nineteenth century, while their Tory opponents became known as the "Conservatives." The Liberals used their ascendancy after 1832 to hasten further reforms which reflect both the idealism and the selfishness of the middle class. Having won control of Parliament, the Liberals proceeded to reorganize the town governments also, to assure middle-class control in local affairs (Municipal Corporations Act, 1835). Trade and industry profited by a reduction in the tariff rates, by the construction of better roads and canals, the extension of steam railway lines, and the institution of a "penny post" system (1840). The abolition of slavery throughout the British colonies with compensation to the slaveholders (1833) stands out as a triumph of humanitarian sentiment, and the same spirit dictated further amelioration of the penal code and more humane treatment of criminals. But where the impulse toward kindliness warred too sharply with business profits, the middle-class legislators showed themselves less generous. A new Poor Law (1834) saved the taxpayers'

Reforms after 1832

---

[1] In England the term "corn" is applied to oats, barley, wheat, etc.

MANUFACTURE OF RAILROAD WHEELS IN FRANCE (1862)

INTERIOR OF A COAL MINE

Socialists complained that the age of machinery had substituted "industrial serfdom" for the agricultural serfdom of the old régime. The spread of revolutionary movements among the workers alarmed the ruling classes.

money, but subjected paupers to a régime so harsh that it made them feel that poverty had become a crime. Slaves on the plantations overseas might celebrate their liberty, but the factory workers at home too often appealed in vain for a lightening of their economic serfdom. Employers insisted that for the government to interfere in, or even to investigate, the lot of the workingmen, would be a violation of that *laissez-faire* policy under which business prospered best.

The workers who had paraded and petitioned for reform in 1832 thus found that they had gained little by it.

Workers disillusioned

Their hope that a further extension of the franchise would soon follow was rudely shattered, and Grey himself, who had sponsored it, declared the Reform Bill was "final." Too late the workers comprehended that they had helped to place in power a class actually hostile to their own interests. The "conservative" Tories were more disposed to help the factory workers than were the "liberal" Whigs. It was a Tory peer who proposed that children under ten years of age should not be worked over nine hours a day (Factory Act, 1833); and a Mines Act (1842) prohibiting the employment in the mines of women, or children under ten, passed with Tory support. Such reforms, however, were but feeble palliatives for a deep-rooted evil.

Though strong in numbers the working class was weak in organization. Since a Parliament dominated by landowners and business men might remain permanently indifferent to their needs, they determined to force further democratic reforms, secure the right to vote, and send their own delegates to Westminster. They drew up a People's Charter embodying six demands which became known as the "Six Points of Chartism" (1838). These were: (1) universal manhood suffrage; (2) secret balloting; (3) annual Parliaments; (4) equal electoral districts; (5) no property qualification for members of Parliament; (6) a salary for members of Parliament. This program would have transformed Great Britain into a genuine democracy, but the Chartists failed to secure its adoption by "moral" pressure and hesitated to resort to armed revolt. In 1848, the movement reached its climax. Several years of poor harvests and business depression had caused grave suffering among the submerged classes, and a monster petition, reported to bear six million signatures, was prepared for presentation to Parliament to support the Chartist demands. When Parliament rejected it, the resulting disorders were easily put down and the Chartist Movement collapsed.

Chartism

Yet it is interesting to note that the Six Points, considered radical in their day, have almost all been adopted since in all democratic countries. The Chartist Movement itself lost force largely because of the growing prosperity which affected all the leading industrial states after 1850. Railways and steam navigation quickened transportation. The construction of steel ships made England not only the workshop of the world, but the mistress of its carrying trade also, and so rapidly did capital increase that London became the banking center of the world. In this flood tide of prosperity the "benevolent bourgeoisie" conceded better terms to the workers and eased the tension between the two classes. The workers themselves, discouraged in their plans for political representation, turned instead to the formation of stronger trade unions and bargained directly with their employers.

5. THE FRENCH REVOLUTION OF 1830

In France, the Industrial Revolution developed later than in Britain and wrought no such swift and startling transformation. The English migration to the cities, which increased the population of Manchester and Birmingham forty per cent between 1820 and 1830, had no parallel across the Channel, where a majority of the French people continued to cultivate the fertile earth and to remain content with the rewards of agriculture.

It has been estimated that in 1815 no more than fifteen steam engines were serving French industry and that most of these had been set up to drive mine pumps. The importation of machinery from England was prohibited until after 1825, and the poor quality and scattered distribution of French coal offered a further difficulty, but by 1830 the fifteen engines had increased to six hundred, and a small group of factory-owners and a growing class of factory-workers added to the problems of the Bourbon régime. The owners reinforced the discontented bourgeoisie, the workers joined the discontented proletariat of the cities.

The reactionary policies of Charles X (1824–30) gravely displeased the French middle and lower classes.

Overthrow of Charles X Charles's unwise attempts to strengthen the privileges of the old nobility and to restore royal absolutism in France have been discussed in a previous chapter.[1] His policies, if fully successful, would have robbed the bourgeoisie of the broad advantages which they had gained since 1789. In 1829, Charles betrayed the principle of responsible government by appointing the Prince de Polignac prime minister despite the opposition of the Chamber of Deputies. Dissolving the obstinate Chamber, Charles called for an election (1830), but the new Chamber threatened to prove still more recalcitrant. Refusing to accept the verdict of the electors, the stubborn monarch prepared four summary ordinances: (1) The liberty of the press was severely limited. (2) The new Chamber was declared dissolved before it assembled. (3) Three fourths of the electors lost their right to vote. (4) A new election was decreed. The posting of these ordinances (July 26, 1830) stirred Paris to revolt, the royal forces proved unable to curb the movement, and after three days of fighting Charles fled to England.

Success so sudden and so unexpected left the Paris revolutionaries divided in their aims. Radical leaders of the

"Citizen king" populace demanded a democratic republic such as the Jacobins had attempted to establish in 1793. Bourgeois moderates urged a constitutional monarchy. A republic, they pointed out, could not hope to survive in a Europe dominated by the spirit of reaction, for the monarchs would unite their forces in opposition to it. The middle class won the day, and the Chamber of Deputies offered the vacant throne to Louis Philippe, Duke of Orléans.

[1] See above, pages 693–695.

Orléans was the son of the notorious Philip of Orléans of revolutionary fame who changed his name to Philippe Égalité, was elected a member of the National Convention, and voted for the death of Louis XVI. In 1830, the son was living quietly in Paris like any middle-class gentleman. His fellow citizens admired his simple tastes and bourgeois virtues; they recalled that he had fought for the French Republic in 1792, and they felt certain that if they placed him on the throne he would make an excellent "citizen king." The aged Lafayette, the hero of two worlds and three revolutions, had assumed leadership of the democratic, republican elements, but was duped into accepting the compromise which seemed happiest under the circumstances, and the "July Revolution" ended with the tricolor replacing the white flag of the Bourbons while Louis Philippe accepted the title "King of the French."

Like the English radicals after 1832, the Paris radicals and workingmen felt that they had been cheated. To shed their blood upon the barricades that the middle class might set up a bourgeois monarchy appeared to them a mockery of their hopes. They had not even secured to themselves the right to vote, since this privilege was restricted to some two hundred thousand "men of property." In 1830 they had to yield, however, because they realized that they were not strong enough to set up the republic they desired, but they continued to dream of democracy, and their discontent slowly undermined the foundations of the "July Monarchy."

Word that the French had again dethroned a legitimate king ran like an electric spark throughout Europe. Monarchs trembled on their thrones as if they had heard an echo of republican armies chanting the *Marseillaise*. "Gentlemen, saddle your horses," said Nicholas I when the news reached Saint Petersburg, "France is in revolution again." Liberals, on the other hand, hailed the event with delight, and prepared to rise in arms for a general war of liberation. The Poles, counting upon French aid, prepared to cast off the yoke of Russia, and the Belgians, who hated the union with

Holland decreed for them by the Congress of Vienna, proclaimed their independence. At this resurgence of liberalism the monarchs of Europe took hurried counsel, fearing France was about to loose a new wave of revolutionary fury upon them. But their apprehension proved groundless. The French middle class did not wish a war which might dislocate trade, and Louis Philippe assured his fellow monarchs that France would lend no aid to revolutionaries in other countries. This cautious policy proved a second disappointment to the French republicans, who, still fascinated by the great days of 1792, believed France owed it to her destiny and to Europe to take the lead in a general movement against the tyranny of kings.

This lack of French aid or intervention partly explains why the revolts of 1830 in the Germanies and Italy met with small success. A few secondary German states — Brunswick, Saxony, and Hanover — won limited constitutions, but Prussia remained unshaken, and Austria, the stronghold of reaction, stood so solidly amid the general unrest that Metternich was able to spare an Austrian army to quell the revolts in Italy. Rome was recaptured from the hands of a group of radicals who had proclaimed an Italian republic there; Parma and Modena received back their petty despots; and Italian liberals who had sprung to arms in the hope of liberating their country were hanged, imprisoned, or exiled.

Germanies and Italy

Even more tragic was the fate of Poland. The constitution granted by Czar Alexander I in 1815 failed to satisfy the Poles, and the news of the French Revolution of 1830 crystallized their discontent and spurred them into a futile stroke for freedom. Nicholas I (1825–55) had far less sympathy for Polish national aspirations than his brother Alexander had shown, and he encouraged his armies to crush the revolt without pity. When, after a brave and desperate defense, the kingdom lay at his mercy, he proceeded to punish the patriot leaders, abrogate the constitution, and incorporate Poland into the Russian Empire. Its cities acknowledged Russian garrisons, and Russian officials controlled the administration. As Prussia and Austria both held small fragments of Polish territory, their governments felt no regret at this extinction of Polish nationalism. France, under the citizen king, Louis Philippe, declined to interfere, and Great Britain, though sympathetic toward the Poles, possessed no adequate motive for intervention. The British government preferred to reserve its special attention for the troublesome question of Belgium.

Polish Revolt

In joining Belgium to Holland in 1815, the diplomats had sought to compensate the Dutch for colonies lost to England, and at the same time to strengthen them against a possible renewal of French aggression. The Belgians resented this union with a stronger, Protestant state, for they feared that their Catholic faith, their liberties, and their language might be endangered. The stern policies of William I, as King of the United Netherlands, increased these apprehensions. In 1830, therefore, the Belgians took their cue from the French and repudiated the rule of an unpopular king. Frenchmen of all classes favored the cause of Belgian independence, although the new bourgeois government was not prepared to risk a war in support of it. British merchants looked to Belgian independence to benefit their trade. Accordingly, in 1831, the great powers signed an agreement at London recognizing Belgium as a separate state. It was necessary to find a king for the Belgians, republics being in disfavor, and a German prince, Leopold of Saxe-Coburg, accepted the crown. William I of Holland clung to his Belgian provinces stubbornly until forced to yield by French military intervention and a British blockade. Holland did not, in fact, formally renounce her claims until 1839, whereupon Britain, France, Prussia, Austria, and Russia pledged themselves to respect the perpetual independence and neutrality of Belgium, a treaty which remained in force until the German government violated it in 1914.

The Belgian question

By 1830, the conservative system, or as it is often called, the system of Metternich, had suffered some severe reverses. The success of the Greek Revolt, the overthrow in France of the legitimate king, Charles X,

LOUIS PHILIPPE (1830–1848)

With Louis Philippe, the "citizen king," as constitutional monarch, the French middle classes secured a dominant voice in the government.

QUEEN VICTORIA (1837–1901)

The Victorian Age covered most of the nineteenth century and marked the political ascendency of the middle classes in England.

LIBERTY LEADING THE PEOPLE (1830), BY EUGÈNE DELACROIX

Throughout the nineteenth century the propertied classes remembered and feared the mob violence of the great French Revolution. Paris was torn by further civil strife in 1830, 1848, and 1870–71.

and the proclamation of an independent Belgium were all developments which violated the established order and the principle of legitimacy. For these setbacks the allied monarchs could largely blame Britain for lack of co-operation, for had the British government so chosen, its navy could have hindered the revolt of the Belgians and have assured the collapse of the Greek Revolt. But in each case the British government had thrown its influence on the side of the rebels, just as it had been the first to recognize Louis Philippe's usurpation of the French throne. It would be a mistake, however, to assume from these instances that the British cabinet was liberal and favored revolutions: on the contrary, its policy from 1815 to 1832 was, as already explained, one of repression and reaction. Nevertheless, the British government often found it profitable to press a liberal policy abroad in the interests of British trade. The creation of small independent states, in South America, in Greece, or in Belgium, favored British manufacturers and merchants who could not exploit these markets so easily while they were in the control of a strong and monopolistic power. In this sense, the exigencies of trade triumphed over political principles, and the Industrial Revolution became one of the most dangerous foes of the conservative system. The old feudal-monarchical order of society which the diplomats had labored to patch together at Vienna could not hold in check the growing pressure of national and liberal sentiment, especially when this sentiment was reinforced by the transforming influences of the factory system. The new forces, with time on their side, were destined to crack open a static society as irresistibly as a great tree pushes its way through the walls of a crumbling house.

It is interesting to study the gathering of the new forces, especially after 1830. Wherever factories increased the numbers of the urban workers, the republican party gained ground. Wherever railways spread across the countryside, they transformed and quickened the industrial and social life, facilitating travel and the interchange of ideas and goods. The new faith in progress, the increase in material wealth, the opening of new vistas and new opportunities made men more and more impatient with the obsolete class distinctions, outworn regulations, and inefficient methods of administration. The Revolution of 1830 and the Reform Bill of 1832 assured the new middle class the lead in the two most progressive European countries, France and Great Britain. A generation later the expanding forces gathered strength for a fresh explosion and another wave of revolution passed over Europe in the years 1848–49. How the wave gathered and how it broke will be described in the following chapter.

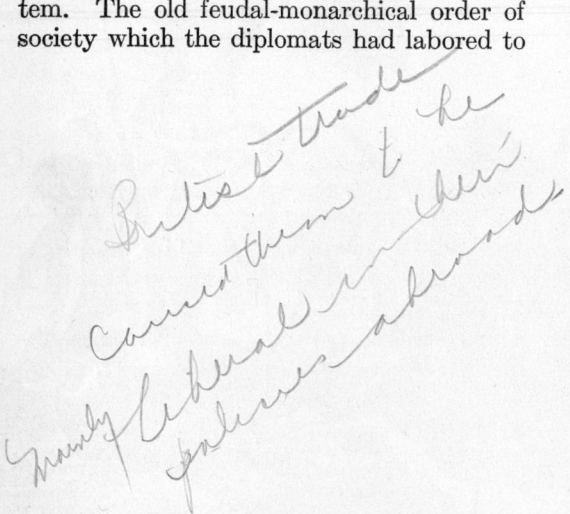

52

The Revolutionary Movement of 1848–49 and Its Collapse

The Revolution had come before its time.
PIERRE JOSEPH PROUDHON.

THE PARIS INSURRECTION of July, 1830, gave France a "citizen king" in the person of Louis Philippe,[1] but it did not go far enough to please the working classes or the republicans. The new régime represented, and was supported by, the bourgeoisie, and it made the promotion of business prosperity its chief aim. From 1830 to 1848, "Peace and Order" were to be the official watchwords in France. As war would have involved a disruption of trade, the government pursued a discreet and unaggressive foreign policy, and so far abandoned that authoritative stand customarily assumed by *la grande nation* in the affairs of Europe that ultra-patriots characterized the course as "peace without honor." In 1840, Louis Adolphe Thiers (1797–1877), who had attempted to revive French prestige by an aggressive policy in the Near East, had to resign his office to the more conservative François Guizot (1787–1874). The policy of caution had triumphed, and under Guizot's ministry, from 1840 to 1848, the unprogressive character of the régime became more and more apparent. Restrictions muffled all attempts at outspoken criticism, the government gratified the timid bourgeois with a foreign policy which eschewed glory but assured peace, and society grew daily more dull and respectable. The German poet Heinrich Heine shrewdly observed that Guizot's main qualification for office was the high degree to which he had perfected the art of immobility. "He does nothing," Heine wrote in 1842, "and that is his secret of preservation."

1. DISCONTENT IN FRANCE UNDER THE JULY MONARCHY

So long as its opponents remained divided, the government of Louis Philippe had little to fear. At least five factions desired its overthrow, but of these the Legitimist followers of Charles X and his line wasted no love on the Bonapartists who sought to revive the Napoleonic tradition, the Clericals resented chiefly the weakened authority of the church under a usurping king and had no sympathy for the Republicans who clung to the hopes betrayed in 1830, while the Socialists, though growing in number, alarmed all the other factions by their projects for establishing a communist society. Of the five groups the Legitimists counted least and had few serious adherents outside of the Faubourg Saint-Germain in Paris, where the ancient aristocrats lived in decayed elegance with their memories. The Bonapartists likewise lived on memories, but the Napoleonic legend had vitality, and

[1] See above, page 707.

when the ashes of the emperor were brought from Saint Helena to Paris in 1840, people could not help comparing the vigorous rule of Napoleon with the mediocre government of the citizen king.

The third group, the Clericals, were more than a political clique, yet could scarcely be termed a party. The clergy, who had formed the privileged First Estate under the old régime, regained a share of their lost power and wealth on the restoration of the Bourbons in 1814. They erred, however, in linking their fortunes to the legitimist line, for, with the fall of Charles X in 1830, they lost their chief protector and most of their privileges. When religious instruction was excluded from the curriculum, many pious people came to regard the schools as godless institutions which would corrupt the youth of France. The bourgeoisie paid little heed to such criticism, but the peasants still reverenced their priests and resented the official discrimination against them. Among them there grew up an intangible but powerful sentiment against the July Monarchy.

The Clericals

To the Republican standard rallied a number of young intellectual radicals disgusted with the existing government and its static ideals. The ministers of Louis Philippe turned a deaf ear to proposals for reform, and agitators who urged a wider franchise so that they might enjoy a share in the government won from Guizot the curt advice to work harder, grow rich, and so gain the ballot. As the administration solidified, the governing class became a closed official caste and the hope of constitutional reform steadily waned. It seemed as if nothing less than a revolution could break the torpid hold of the bourgeois régime, and young Republicans read eagerly the histories of the great French Revolution which poured from the press. Statesmen of that day prepared to make history by writing it. Thiers had first won fame by a *History of the French Revolution*, Alphonse Lamartine (1790–1869) composed a *History of the Girondins*, Louis Blanc (1811–82) wrote a *History of the French Revolution* and attacked the existing government in his *History of Ten Years*, while Guizot was the author of a voluminous *History of France* and a *History of the Revolution in England*. Reading of the great days of 1793 and 1794, the young republican idealists of the eighteen-forties were fired with impatience to emulate the heroes of the past.

The Republicans

Eager to find allies for an attack upon the royal government, the Republicans turned to the Socialists, and in 1843 the two groups joined forces in a fusion party. The Republicans sought a wider franchise and an abolition of the property qualifications which barred many of them from a part in politics. The Socialists had more radical demands and loftier dreams. The earliest Socialists, Henri de Saint-Simon (1760–1825) and François Marie Fourier (1772–1837), concocted visionary schemes for the reorganization of society, and dreamed of establishing ideal communities where the citizens would live lives of simplicity and harmony blessed by the dignity of labor. The working classes for whom these Utopian schemes were specially devised paid them scant respect, preferring the more practical suggestions of Louis Blanc, who understood their grievances and made himself the fearless champion of their hopes. The state, Blanc declared, was responsible for the welfare of the poor, and ought to abolish unmerited poverty by organizing the great industries of France on a co-operative basis as "national workshops," with employment assured to all who sought it. This doctrine violated the *laissez-faire* principles popular with the capitalist employers, but it seemed just and reasonable to the workers and the radical intellectuals.

The Socialists

2. THE FEBRUARY REVOLUTION IN FRANCE (1848) AND ITS SEQUEL

As its following increased, the reform party in France, like the Chartists in England, advertised their demands by monster petitions, mass meetings, and parades. By 1847, this agitation had taken the novel form of political banquets, and a "Banquet Campaign" grew to proportions that alarmed the government. Still true to his principle of immobility, Guizot refused concessions, and the civil authorities attempted to halt the

ADOLPHE THIERS (1797–1877)

Upper left: Thiers began his long career in French politics with the July Revolution of 1830 and served as a minister under Louis Philippe.

FRANÇOIS PIERRE GUILLAUME GUIZOT (1787–1874)

Upper right: Guizot, also an historian, succeeded Thiers as the leading minister of Louis Philippe from 1840 to 1848.

THE PEOPLE ON THE THRONE

Left: Thiers was more liberal than Guizot, but neither favored the extension of political power to the lower classes. This lithograph, by Honoré Daumier, stresses the bourgeois belief that the people were unfitted to exercise sovereignty.

agitation by forbidding a banquet scheduled for February 22, 1848. The thwarted populace reacted indignantly and the following day barricades blocked the streets of Paris. Too late, Guizot resigned, and Louis Philippe offered concessions, but the revolt grew more serious and on February 24 the king abdicated. The Chamber of Deputies yielded the control of the state to a group of popular Socialist and Republican leaders who formed a provisional government.

The success so speedily achieved as speedily revealed the anomaly of the Republican-Socialist coalition which had made it possible. Afraid at first to antagonize the working classes, the moderate Republicans admitted four Socialists to a place on the provisional government, and reduced the working day in Paris from eleven to ten hours. But it soon became apparent that the majority of the French people had little real interest in social experiments. Louis Blanc's demand for the immediate establishment of national workshops was held up by his less radical colleagues. Instead, a substitute program, a parody of Blanc's project, was entrusted to an unsympathetic minister who hired thousands of unemployed at two francs a day and set them to work digging ditches. The burden on the state of this wasteful and stupid work persuaded many taxpayers that Blanc's scheme was a costly failure, a deception easily propagated because the middle classes and the conservative farmers were already frightened by the nightmare of socialism.

In the elections of April, 1848, clericals and aristocrats, peasants and bourgeois united to choose a Constituent Assembly of distinctly moderate temper. Beaten at the polls, the Paris radicals resorted to the futile alternative of a bloody insurrection (June 23–26, 1848) which ended with the execution or deportation of eleven thousand of the insurgents, the suppression of the Socialist newspapers, and the abandonment of the plan for national workshops.

Socialists defeated

With the Socialists crushed, the Assembly soon completed a constitution for the Second French Republic. The right of free speech and a free press, security from arbitrary arrest, and permission to assemble peaceably and to petition the government, won legal recognition. The constitution further provided for a single legislative chamber of seven hundred and fifty deputies, to be selected by universal manhood suffrage, and a president to be chosen in the same broad and direct fashion. The moderates believed it safe to entrust the vote to all male citizens because they counted upon the peasant majority to offset the influence of the radical city proletariat and elect a "Party of Order."

The results more than justified these expectations. Of three leading candidates competing for the presidency, the Socialist Ledru-Rollin was feared as the standard-bearer of a party identified with the madness of the June revolt, while General Cavaignac, hope of the middle-class Republicans, was disliked because he had crushed that revolt by shedding the blood of Frenchmen. This illogical division of feeling, characteristic of electorates, defeated two capable men and opened the way to a third candidate, Louis Napoleon Bonaparte, who represented the Party of Order. He was (if legitimate) a nephew of the great Napoleon, his parents being Louis Bonaparte and Hortense de Beauharnais, the stepdaughter of Napoleon I through his marriage to Josephine de Beauharnais. The death in 1832 of Napoleon's son, born of his second marriage to Marie Louise of Austria, left Louis Napoleon Bonaparte heir to the imperial succession. In 1848, monarchists, Catholics, militarists, patriots, peasants, and workers combined to elect, by a majority of five and a half out of seven million votes cast, an adventurer about whom they knew little save that he bore the name Napoleon.

The nephew of Napoleon

It was an ominous portent for the stability of the Second Republic that the "prince-president" had already made two comic-opera attempts (in 1836 and 1840) to seize control of France by a military *coup d'état*. Imprisoned by the government of Louis Philippe after the second escapade, he finally escaped to England, where he was living in exile when the Revolution of 1848 brought him his opportunity. During the years of waiting, Louis Napoleon had published a book on *Napoleonic Ideas* in which his uncle emerged (somewhat unrecognizably) as the champion of peace and liberty. He also wrote on military science to prove that he had inherited soldierly interests, and even cultivated Socialist support by a work on *The Extinction of Poverty*. When, at forty, he assumed the executive rôle in the Second Republic, he felt himself under a fatal impulsion to follow in his uncle's footsteps. France had grown sated with mediocrity, and Louis Napoleon, if he would justify his name and his opportunism, was "condemned to be brilliant." But behind his enigmatic pose he possessed little of his uncle's genius or energy; his leading traits were a mystical faith in what he called his "destiny" and a fund of shrewd political sense.

From the outset of his rule, Louis Napoleon used his presidential office to build up a following for himself, especially in the army. As the Assembly declined to consider an extension of his term beyond the four years for which he had been elected, he prepared a military *coup d'état*. The date chosen was December 2, 1851, anniversary of the great Napoleon's coronation and of his victory at Austerlitz. Without warning, the leaders of the Monarchist and Republican parties in the Assembly found themselves arrested, and Paris awoke on December 3 to the rule of martial law. Despite resistance and bloodshed in Paris and some of the larger towns, the French nation ratified the president's stroke by an overwhelming plebiscite. In 1852, the Second Republic gave place to the Second Empire, and the European monarchs debated whether or not they ought to compromise their dignity by addressing Napoleon III, Emperor of the French, as "brother."

Coup d'état of 1851

The story of the Second Empire and the rôle which Napoleon III attempted to play in Europe between 1852 and 1870 will be related in the chapter which follows. First, however, it will be useful to note the repercussions which the French Revolution of 1848 exerted upon the rest of Europe. The Vienna settlement of 1815 had outlasted the mood of caution which inspired it and popular discontent had weakened its foundations.

3. THE GERMAN PEOPLE FAIL TO ACHIEVE POLITICAL UNITY (1848–49)

Attention has been called before this to the political disunion which weakened the Germanies. The breakdown of the Holy Roman Empire, the heritage of feudalism with its disruptive tendencies, the jealous independence of the German princes, and the rivalry of Austria and Prussia from the seventeenth century onward, combined to delay German unification until late in the nineteenth century. Napoleon I gave a great impetus to the work of consolidation by encouraging his allies among the more powerful German rulers to annex the smaller states, bishoprics, and free cities, a task which they performed with such alacrity that by 1815 three hundred and sixty states had been reduced to thirty-eight. But the Congress of Vienna showed no disposition to complete the amalgamation. Instead, it disappointed the friends of union by instituting a Germanic Confederation so loose and ineffectual in its structure that the thirty-eight fragments all enjoyed a practical autonomy. Poems and pamphlets pleading for closer political bonds were suppressed, and the princes displayed their loyalty to the spirit of the past by discouraging all sentiment in favor of liberty or unity.

German separatism

For a time these methods of repression proved successful. The German people could not have a revolution, as the poet Goethe humorously declared, because the police would not permit it. When the French rebelled in 1830 and drove out the unpopular Charles X, German liberals reacted in several states of the federation to the extent of demanding a larger share in the government and freedom of the press, but their agitation led to no serious violence and to few important reforms. Nor did it advance the national movement. The German people, because of their political impotence and disunion, seemed destined to forfeit indefinitely the important rôle which they deserved to play in European and world affairs.

Yet economic forces were drawing them together, though political bonds failed to knit. The multiplicity of tariffs erected by

KARL MARX (1818–1883)    FRIEDRICH ENGELS (1820–1895)

Marx and Engels collaborated in publishing the "Communist Manifesto" (1848) which closed with the challenge: "Workingmen of all countries, unite!"

LOUIS BLANC
(1811–1882)

CLAUDE HENRI, COUNT DE SAINT-SIMON 
(1760–1825)

Louis Blanc (left) projected an ideal society of workers in which the governing principle would be, "from each according to his abilities, to each according to his needs." Until the failures of 1848–49, most European Socialists were "Utopian" in their plans for a better world. The followers of Saint-Simon (right) turned his teachings into a mystic social cult.

The Zollverein

thirty-eight separate governments proved a severe hindrance to trade, so great that in 1818 Prussia adopted a uniform customs policy and invited her neighbors to merge their policies with hers. By 1834, seventeen German states had entered this *Zollverein* or customs union, and six others followed shortly. German manufacturers profited by the disappearance of internal trade barriers and by the common tariff which partly protected them from French and British competition. The exclusion of the Austrian Empire, with its mixed population, from this economic alliance, foreshadowed the unification of the strictly German states under Prussian leadership.

Frankfort Assembly

The success of the *Zollverein* convinced the business classes that political unification would prove a further boon to trade, for they saw that it would make possible a simpler postal, currency, and banking system and a single code of law. Professors urged it in the lecture room and journalists pleaded for it in the press. When, following the February disorders in France, a revolutionary wave broke over Europe in 1848, German liberals and nationalists believed that the auspicious moment had arrived to realize their hopes, and called an assembly at Frankfort to prepare a constitution for a federated commonwealth. All Germany anxiously followed the deliberations, but the delegates found themselves challenged from the first by two issues that defied a satisfactory solution: (1) Should the proposed German commonwealth be a republic or a monarchy? (2) Should the Austrian lands be included or excluded from the union? A third problem, which threatened for a time to precipitate a general European war, concerned the inclusion of Schleswig and Holstein, for these provinces, though largely German in population, were subject to the Danish king. Finally, the determination of the Prussian government to bring its segment of Poland into whatever German union might be formed raised another minority problem.

When, in the preliminary discussions at Frankfort, the delegates voted to make the greater Germany which they planned a constitutional monarchy, seventy-nine republicans walked out in disgust. From that point a fatal division weakened the national cause.

The failure of 1848–49

On the second problem, concerning the inclusion of Austria, the Assembly attempted to compromise. Since the Slavs, Magyars, Czechs, Poles, and Italians in the Hapsburg Empire could not properly be included in a Germanic union, only the German provinces of Austria were invited to join. The Austrian government, hostile to any federation it could not aspire to dominate, rejected the compromise and recalled its representatives from Frankfort. Still hopeful of forming a smaller German Empire under Prussian leadership, the Assembly offered the imperial crown to Frederick William IV of Prussia (March, 1849). His curt refusal, with the intimation that he might accept it from his fellow princes, but could not take a crown from the hands of a revolutionary assembly, extinguished the last hopes of the Frankfort delegates. Most of them dispersed in disillusionment, and the handful of extremists who attempted to resort to radical measures were driven out by force.

The aspirations of the German nationalists, so promising in 1848, had changed by 1849 to a sense of ignominious failure. In 1850, the old Germanic Confederation was re-established, a signal victory for Austria and for conservatism. Nevertheless, Germany had heard the call to union, and liberals could find a few grains of comfort in the fact that constitutional privileges had been extended in several states, while Prussia, hitherto a stronghold of autocratic principles, acquired a measure of representative government. For during the riotous days of 1848, Frederick William IV had been intimidated into promising his subjects a constitution, and he fulfilled his word, although the charter which he granted could not be called liberal. It created a House of Representatives, but the deputies possessed little power beyond the right to reject new taxes. It assured universal suffrage, but nullified its effect by dividing all the voters into three classes according to the amount of taxes they paid. As each class chose the same

Prussian constitution

REVOLUTIONARY OUTBREAKS OF 1848-49

number of deputies, the very rich and the moderately wealthy controlled the parliament, while the third group, including the millions of peasants and workers, had a minority representation. In 1854, Frederick William established an upper chamber, or House of Lords, the noble members of which were to hold their seats by hereditary right or by appointment for life. This constitution possesses more than passing interest because it preserved the autocratic principle in a democratic frame, an experiment which was to be repeated in the constitution of the German Empire after 1871.

The failure of the revolutionary movement of 1848-49 sobered the German liberals and turned their thoughts from finespun theories about the ideal form of union to a consideration of indissoluble, brute facts. They saw more clearly now that if Prussia was to unify the German-speaking people, it could only be accomplished in defiance of Austria, probably as the result of a military decision in which Austria suffered defeat. For such a test of strength between the two leading powers in the Germanies, the time was not ripe in 1849, but the problem had been clarified and the issue defined. Within twenty years the Germans were to unite their fatherland, despite domestic feuds, and in the face of French and Austrian opposition.

4. AUSTRIA RESTORES HER HOUSE TO ORDER

No European dynasty was more firmly wedded to conservative principles in 1848 than the house of Austria. From his palace in Vienna the ageing Metternich watched with disapproval the resuscitation of democratic ideas, as firmly convinced as ever that government by the people would lead to anarchy, and that the spirit of nationalism agitating the Italians, the Germans, and the subject peoples of the Hapsburg Empire formed the gravest threat to the peace of Europe. Like Guizot in France he sought to preserve his immobility in a world that ebbed and shifted, but his deep-seated conviction that any change in political or social relations was likely to prove dangerous can be ascribed to something more than prejudice. Metternich may well have foreseen, what subsequent history has made clear, that the triumph of liberalism would ultimately destroy the old régime in Austria and that the triumph of nationalism would result in the dissolution of the polyglot empire. He fought to preserve the dynasty he served, and the empire he administered, from forces which threatened both with destruction.

Despite all his precautions, however, the revolutionary fever of 1848 invaded Austria. A popular uprising in Vienna forced him into exile, while the liberals wrung the promise of a constitution from the feeble emperor, Ferdinand I (1835-48). In Bohemia the Czechs demanded local autonomy with their own elected Diet, while the Magyars prepared to establish Hungary as an almost independent kingdom. This last proposal roused opposition among the repressed Slavs who split the Hungarian Kingdom in two by proclaiming a Southern Slav State to include the Croats and Serbs. All the new governments demanded recognition from the paralyzed ministry at Vienna, and all adopted liberal programs, promising the peasants relief from feudal dues, the middle class freedom of speech and the press, and all the citi-

THE FRANKFORT PARLIAMENT

Above: The Frankfort Parliament (1848–1849), which was expected to create a constitution for a united Germany, is shown here in a contemporary etching.

BARRICADES IN VIENNA, 1848

Right: In Vienna, Berlin, and several other German and Italian cities, the news of the revolution in France in 1848 provoked similar uprisings of the populace.

zens the benefit of a representative government. Metternich's apprehensions had crystallized into facts; the bulwarks of absolutism in the Hapsburg Empire were tottering, and the empire itself seemed on the point of dissolution.

Then the tide turned. The insurgent factions fell to attacking one another and the conservative forces seized the opportunity to strike back. Rivalry between Germans and Czechs in Bohemia enabled Prince Windischgrätz to recapture Prague for the imperial government. In Italy the veteran Austrian general, Radetsky, suppressed the Italian outbreaks in Lombardy and Venetia. These victories encouraged the emperor's advisers to suggest a counterstroke against the liberals in Vienna. As a feud had already developed in the reform ranks between the middle-class moderates and the more radical workingmen, Windischgrätz found it possible to reoccupy the capital in October, 1848. Ferdinand resigned the throne to his nephew, Francis Joseph I (1848–1916), who dissolved the revolutionary assembly, threw out the newly completed constitution, and restored much of the conservative régime. The indifference with which the Austrian people accepted this defeat of the liberal experiment proved that the movement had excited little real support outside Vienna.

Reaction in Austria

Though threatened for a time, the old régime in Austria had demonstrated its capacity to withstand revolutionary change. Where the liberal cause had joined forces with the national urge, however, as in Hungary, a fiercer blaze had been kindled and one more difficult to extinguish. But the imperial court, long adept at the game of playing one national faction against another, cleverly selected Count Joseph Jellachich, leader of the Southern Slavs, to head a campaign against the rebellious Magyars. Windischgrätz followed with a second imperial army, and in 1849, Czar Nicholas I marched a Russian force to the aid of Francis Joseph and helped to destroy the Hungarian Republic in the interests of legitimacy. Weakened by dissensions and crushed by superior forces, the Hungarian patriots under the heroic Louis Kossuth were compelled to yield, and the Hapsburg ruler could congratulate himself that he was master in his own household.

The prestige which accrued to Austria from these triumphs over the forces of liberalism and separatism enabled the government at Vienna to adopt a decisive tone in German affairs also, and to oppose successfully the project for the unification of the Germanies under Prussian leadership. Austria had once again shown herself the vigilant champion of conservatism, and Metternich, though he did not resume the office of chancellor, returned to Vienna to write his memoirs, consoled by the assurance that his life-work had proved itself "triumphantly fireproof" in the years 1848 and 1849.

"Triumphantly fireproof"

5. ITALY REMAINS IN BONDAGE

In Italy as in Germany the events of 1848 roused the nationalists and liberals to action. Hatred of the rule of foreign despots had been growing steadily in the Italian states since 1815, but the revolutionary factions possessed no central committee and no concerted plan. In 1848, an uprising of the Milanese forced the Austrian garrison to withdraw, and the Venetians likewise expelled the Austrian authorities from their city and proclaimed it a republic. A surge of national defiance swept the peninsula as Charles Albert of Sardinia took the field and prepared to drive Radetsky's white-coated contingents from Italian soil. The pope, Pius IX, and the reactionary Neapolitan king, Ferdinand II, endorsed the War of Liberation. The Austrian administration, half-paralyzed at home by the liberal outbreak in Vienna and the revolts in Bohemia and Hungary, could hardly be expected to maintain a firm hold upon its Italian provinces.

Nationalism in Italy

Yet, despite these hopeful circumstances, the Italians signally failed to break the Austrian yoke. Pius IX and Ferdinand II soon recalled their contingents from the struggle, and Charles Albert of Sardinia, defeated by the Austrians at Custozza and again at Novara, resigned his throne (1849). Reaction swept Italy as it had swept central

Europe. Constitutions were revoked, popular assemblies dismissed, and Italian liberals hanged, jailed, or exiled. Austria had displayed unexpected strength, but the real fault for their failure lay with the Italians themselves. The excesses of the republican radicals in Milan, in Naples, and especially in Rome, where they drove the pope from the city and set up a Roman Republic, brought discredit upon the idea of "government by the people" and disgusted moderate-minded men. If the alternative to Austrian or papal administration was to be the murderous anarchy of a Roman mob or of Neapolitan brigands, sober citizens found that they preferred to live in reasonable security under princely despots. This division between the outlook of middle-class Italians who favored constitutional monarchy and radicals who sought to set up democratic republics so disrupted and crippled the national-liberal movement that the Austrians found it easy to reoccupy Milan and Venice, while a French expeditionary force (dispatched by the newly elected prince-president, Louis Napoleon Bonaparte) restored Rome and the Papal States to the rule of Pius IX. In Italy as elsewhere the revolutionary movement of 1848 had ended in failure in 1849.

6. THE LESSONS OF 1848-49

In fact, few upheavals of equal magnitude in the history of Europe have produced such apparently negative results. The Second French Republic, established in 1848 on the ruins of the monarchy, after destroying the Socialists was itself destroyed that an imperial adventurer, Napoleon III, might restore the throne. The Frankfort Assembly, summoned to unite the Germanies in 1848, closed its sessions in ridicule and failure in 1849. The widespread revolts in the Austrian Empire produced little in the way of permanent reform beyond the belated abolition of the remnants of serfdom in central Europe, while the Italian campaign for liberty and independence collapsed in defeat and anarchy.

Yet of these hopes betrayed in 1849 fully half were to be realized within a generation. By 1871, the French had proclaimed a Third Republic, destined to endure till 1940; the Germans had transmuted their dream of unity, so long deferred, into an actuality; the Italians had won their independence and a constitutional government. Note, however, that these were mainly nationalist causes, and that they triumphed largely because nationalism had the support of the industrial and mercantile classes. The social program of 1848, in so far as it sought the emancipation of the workingmen, ran counter to the powerful interests of employers and the prejudices of the wealthy, and this partly explains why socialism faltered while nationalism advanced. The propertied classes had, in fact, been so gravely alarmed by the socialist and communist menace in 1848 and 1849 that they cast about for measures to combat it, and in several states (France, Austria, Prussia) the government and the middle class repented the curbs which they had imposed upon the Roman Catholic Church and welcomed it again as an ally in the effort to curb socialist and anarchist influences.

Among Socialists and Republicans the collapse of their hopes produced a profound sense of disillusionment. Yet all the expense of blood and spirit had not been vain, for through defeat they achieved a more realistic and more practical comprehension of their task. The Russian liberal, Alexander Herzen, recorded this change of mood. "It is a strange thing: since 1848 we have all faltered and stepped back, we have thrown everything overboard and shrunk into ourselves, and yet something has been done and everything has been changed. We are nearer to the earth, we stand on a lower, that is a firmer, level, the plow cuts more deeply, our work is not so attractive, it is rougher — perhaps because it really is work." The romance of dreaming a social revolution was over; the work of preparing one had begun. But for some years after 1849, socialism languished, partly because it had suffered a setback, partly because the 1850's brought an era of business prosperity that exorcised the specter of unemployment and eased the lot of the worker.

Socialism discredited

Nor were signs lacking that the bourgeoisie might learn benevolence and soften the hostility between capital and labor by reasonable concessions. It was a favorable omen that the plight of the working classes had already attracted the sympathy of essayists and novelists who held up a mirror to society and pricked the consciences of the wealthy by descriptions of slum life and the degradation of poverty. In England the novels of Charles Dickens (1812–70) pleaded in all keys from humor to pathos the case of the wretched and impoverished. Thomas Carlyle (1795–1881), the Scottish historian and philosopher, launched flaming indictments against the evils of the factory system which rotted the hearts and souls of rich and poor alike. Across the Channel, Honoré de Balzac (1799–1850), perhaps the greatest of French novelists, depicted with dispassionate skill in his *Comédie Humaine* the ambition, selfishness, and avarice that infect a society ruled by the love of money, and revealed how petty and soulless life may become for people who know (like Oscar Wilde's cynic) the price of everything and the value of nothing.

The influence of such literature, though slow in its effect, could hardly fail in time to sensitize the rich to the problems of social justice. Books are more powerful than bombs in pleading a just cause. The violence of the radicals of 1848 and 1849, who sought to remake society by force, defeated its own aims because it welded the conservative classes together more solidly against the urban workingman. In all European countries the proletarian groups of 1848 were minority factions, and for this reason their successes, if they won any, were certain to be bloody and impermanent and to leave a heritage of obloquy upon their perpetrators. The anarchist Proudhon perceived this when he lamented that "the revolution had come before its time." It remained for established governments and conservative statesmen to make halting concessions to the popular demands after 1860.

53

The Establishment of the Second French Empire: Napoleon III

> I believe that from time to time men are created whom I will call providential, in whose hands the destinies of their countries are placed. I believe myself to be one of those men.
>
> LOUIS NAPOLEON BONAPARTE.

STUDENTS who delight in the conviction that history repeats itself often note remarkable similarities between the First French Empire created by the great Napoleon and its counterpart erected half a century later by Napoleon III. Like his more famous uncle, Napoleon III transformed a republic into an empire, allied himself with the Roman Catholic Church, promised peace and made war, nurtured vast colonial dreams, fought an Italian campaign against the Austrians, sent an army to invade Russia, attempted to interfere in the Germanies, lost his throne and empire on the battlefield, and died in exile. To insist too far, however, on these striking resemblances between the two reigns would prove dangerously misleading. History never repeats itself without significant variations. The Second French Empire was no more a re-creation of the first than Louis Napoleon was a reincarnation of Napoleon I. The points of comparison suggest a case of historic plagiarism rather than historic repetition, and the Second Empire as a political experiment can be most profitably judged if it is judged by itself.

Historic plagiarism

1. "THE EMPIRE IS PEACE"

As explained in the previous chapter, the *coup d'état* of December 2, 1851, by which Louis Napoleon made himself master of France, was confirmed by an enormous majority of the French voters. A second plebiscite, announced officially as 7,839,000 "ayes" to 253,000 "noes," sanctioned the establishment of an empire. In approving this move the French peasants remembered that an earlier Napoleon had secured them their property, reduced their taxes, and maintained public tranquillity; they forgot that he had also consigned their sons to slaughter on distant battlefields. The French middle class welcomed a strong government that would cope with the threat of socialism, though they dreaded that the name Bonaparte might spell military hazards for France and for business. Such fears the new emperor sought to dispel by a public denial. "In a spirit of mistrust certain people say 'The Empire is War.' I say 'The Empire is Peace.'" Whereupon he outlined the peaceful aims to which he hoped to dedicate his reign: the construction of railways, canals, and harbors which would create work for the unemployed, the expansion of commerce, the stimulation of agriculture, and the development of the French colonial empire. Nor did he forget the enrichment of culture and the propagation of the Catholic faith.

In his plans to promote the prosperity of

his subjects, Napoleon found himself favored by extraneous circumstances. The decade between 1850 and 1860 was a period of great business activity, especially in France. Prices rose steadily, farmers and manufacturers found a ready market for their commodities, and workers found employment without difficulty in the expanding industries or the public projects inaugurated by the imperial government. Frenchmen told themselves that they had lost nothing by surrendering some of their liberties to an autocrat, for at least the emperor knew how to give them security and prosperity. In actual truth, the business "boom" was due to many complicated economic factors, such as the quickening effect of the Industrial Revolution in France, improvements in the methods of manufacture and transportation, and the discovery of gold in California (1848) which increased the world supply of that precious metal and made commodity prices appear to rise as gold became cheaper. But as few people understood such complicated matters, Napoleon III received more credit than he deserved for his efforts on behalf of better business.

France had become bored, to borrow a famous expression of the poet and historian Lamartine, by the unimpressive appearance and mediocre policies of Louis Philippe. Napoleon III studiously avoided this danger by entertaining his subjects with lavish displays and dramatic actions designed to keep the person of the emperor constantly in their thoughts. He toured the country delivering political addresses full of high-sounding platitudes, dedicated town halls and hospitals and railway stations to the public service, and laid corner-stones with eloquence and dexterity. The Parisian populace soon learned to shout *Vive l'empereur* as he drove past with a clattering escort of guards, and crowded to watch him when, dressed in a brilliant uniform, his moustaches waxed to a point, he distributed decorations to his loyal soldiers.

To make Paris a more beautiful capital for the Second Empire, Napoleon had the city modernized under the direction of his able friend Baron Haussmann. At enormous expense

Modernization of Paris

beautiful boulevards and broad squares replaced many of the city's ancient and crooked streets. The program of reconstruction provided labor for the unemployed and made Paris the most elegant and spacious capital in Europe, but it also made the task of the troops easier in case of insurrection. Broad boulevards are less convenient to barricade than narrow lanes, and crowds in open squares are defenseless before gunfire or cavalry.

At an exposition held in 1855 to celebrate the progress of French art and industry, visitors were dazzled by the beauty and gaiety of the city. Paris had become once more what it had been under Louis XIV and Napoleon, the world center of art, fashion, and diplomacy. At the palace of the Tuileries the Empress Eugénie, a beautiful young Spanish girl whom Napoleon III married in 1853, presided gracefully over the imperial court. French writers, under the leadership of Gustave Flaubert (1821–80), set the standards for a new realist school of fiction which supplanted the romantic tradition of the preceding generation. All Europe acknowledged in Charles Augustin Sainte-Beuve (1804–69) the dean of literary critics. *Carmen* by Prosper Mérimée and *La Dame aux Camélias* by Alexandre Dumas the Younger, both destined to serve as the inspiration for famous operas, were written in these years, while Victor Hugo, a giant surviving from the romantic era, published his novel *Les Misérables* and much of his greatest poetry during the Second Empire. Frenchmen were proud to feel that their country had resumed again that leading position in art, literature, diplomacy, and military prestige to which *la grande nation* was entitled.

The Second Empire

2. ALL THINGS TO ALL MEN

It has been said of Napoleon III that even upon the throne he remained a conspirator at heart. His diplomacy always had a hint of the subterranean about it, and his idea of government was to divide the nation into a multiplicity of factions all bound to him by private understandings while he alone held the strings. There is some justice in this

NAPOLEON III, EMPEROR OF THE FRENCH

Napoleon III was a sphinx to many of his contemporaries. Bismarck decided he was a sphinx without a riddle, "a great, unrecognized incapacity."

EMPRESS EUGÉNIE (1826–1920)

Marriage to Napoleon III in 1853 made Eugénie de Montijo, a Spanish noblewoman, Empress of the French.

"A HOT DAY IN THE BATTERIES" DURING THE CRIMEAN WAR

From a lithograph after W. Simpson

criticism, but the same charge may be leveled with more or less truth against every successful politician. It is but another way of saying that Napoleon was a practicing politician upon a throne, and a very proficient one at that, until his many promises and diverse commitments combined to trip him up.

To win the support of the French Catholics, Louis Napoleon, before his *coup d'état*, had dispatched a military force to Rome to restore the Papal States to the rule of Pius IX after the outbreaks of 1848. In 1850, the Legislature of the Second Republic passed the Falloux Law which placed French schools under the supervision of the clergy. The panic created by the Socialist agitation in 1848 and 1849 had softened the hostility of the anti-clerical bourgeoisie toward the church and convinced them, as already noted, that religious instruction could best check the spread of radical and subversive doctrines among the masses. So the Empress Eugénie busied herself with Catholic charities, Napoleon acted as a champion of that faith, and felt confident that, so long as he maintained a garrison at Rome to safeguard the papal dominions and preserved the independent status of the clergy in France, he could count upon Catholic approval. Nor was he mistaken.

The bourgeoisie were disposed to endorse any government which promised peace and order. In addressing this class Napoleon disavowed any warlike intentions and promised economic prosperity and liberty of trade. Through the establishment of a sort of government bank, the *Crédit mobilier*, which lent large sums of money for business projects, Napoleon encouraged the extension of railway, steamship, and telegraph lines. Industry throve, profits mounted, and the business classes applauded the emperor for his sage administration throughout a decade of unparalleled expansion (1850–60). In 1859, largely on his own authority, Napoleon negotiated a free-trade agreement with Great Britain which speedily doubled French exports, but angered many French manufacturers because it swept away the tariff protection which had shielded them from British competition. Through this interference in trade he offended a group, numerically small, but powerful in the business world, an omen of the increasing difficulties which were to beset him in the later years of his reign.

The peasants had little fault to find with a régime which protected their religion and assured cheap transportation and a ready market for their produce. To them the fifty per cent rise in the cost of commodities which came after 1850 proved a blessing, for it meant a higher reward for their labors, but to the city working class it meant that food grew dearer while wages lagged. Napoleon succeeded to some extent in raising wages and reducing unemployment by his program of public works, and he sought to combat the evils of poverty by organizing insurance societies which would encourage the poor to save, and by rebuilding the tenement districts at public expense. The government reformed the pawnshops which had preyed upon the poor, the Empress Eugénie devoted herself to charity, the emperor constantly protested his deep concern with social problems. But socialism continued to spread among the city proletariat none the less, for the workers judged the régime less by its promises than by its fruits and saw that too few of the fruits fell to them.

Officers and men in the military services knew that with a Bonaparte at the head of the state they would not be forgotten. No dictator can afford to estrange his army; Napoleon had relied upon it for the *coup d'état* of 1851; and the beat of distant drums was to persist like a fateful chorus throughout the twenty years of his reign, growing louder and more ominous as the Second Empire drifted toward the final tragedy of Sedan. While protesting that the empire meant peace, Napoleon raised the prestige of the army and fed it with expectations. Nationalists, ashamed of the "peace without honor" policy that had been pursued by the government of Louis Philippe, applauded Napoleon when he dispatched troops to Rome (1849) to prove that France as well as Austria could meddle in the affairs of Italy. In 1853, he

THE EXECUTION OF THE EMPEROR MAXIMILIAN OF MEXICO

Napoleon III supported an attempt to set up an empire in Mexico, with Maximilian, brother of Francis Joseph of Austria, as emperor. The plan failed and Maximilian was shot by the Mexican republicans (1867).

ONE STEP IN THE OPENING OF THE SUEZ CANAL

A French diplomat and engineer, Ferdinand de Lesseps (1805–1894), brought glory to France by completing the Suez Canal in 1869. In this picture the Prince of Wales, later Edward VII, is letting the waters of the Mediterranean into the Bitter Lakes. From a woodcut in the London "Illustrated News."

sought to please Catholics and nationalists alike by challenging Russia in a dispute over the holy places of Palestine, a controversy which involved France in the Crimean War. At the same time an aggressive foreign policy led to an extension of the French influence in Algeria, the transformation of Cambodia (in Indo-China) into a protectorate, and the acquisition of islands in the Pacific, so that France came to rank second only to Great Britain as a colonial power, although the penalty of such imperialism was a constant danger of war. But Napoleon believed in his destiny, and destiny for a Bonaparte spelled war. Despite his own preference for peace and the assurances he had given that he would maintain it, war proved the deciding factor in his fortunes.

3. THE LIBERAL NEMESIS

The emperor's attempts to reconcile all factions failed to win over many clear-sighted intellectuals, or to appease the ardent republicans and socialists. These groups would not forgive Napoleon his usurpation of power, nor the bloodshed, the arrests, and the deportations by which that illegal usurpation had been consummated. Official manipulation of the elections, official supervision of the press, and official suppression of liberal courses in the universities reduced the opponents of the imperial régime to impotence, but intensified their resentment. France, the liberals held, had betrayed the high cause of Liberty, Equality, and Fraternity, and made herself the slave of one man. The army, the bureaucracy, the conservatives, and the men of property in general might support Napoleon the Little, as Victor Hugo named him, but an unreconciled minority of his subjects still insisted that his throne was built upon sand and must dissolve in the rising tide of European liberalism. France, "the queen of the world," would not remain "the slave of one man."

Napoleon was prepared, if he could, to conciliate the liberals also. In 1860, he compromised his absolutism by political concessions and opened the second phase of his reign, the Liberal Empire. A general amnesty for political prisoners freed the bitterest foes of

The Liberal Empire

his régime from captivity, an opposition press was permitted to appear, and the Chamber of Deputies gained the right to criticize Napoleon's ministers, to control the budget, and to make public its debates. This ingenious attempt to harmonize authoritarian with parliamentary government produced little except an opposition party supported by various discontented factions, by Legitimists and Orléanists, by Catholics antagonized when the emperor helped the Italians toward unity, by manufacturers who suffered by the commercial treaty with Great Britain, by the persistent Republican minority and the radical Socialists. Napoleon, prematurely aged, with his health failing, lost his faculty for reconciling discordant elements. He continued to make concessions to the growing liberal demands until his empire had become by 1870 a constitutional monarchy. Still the republicans and socialists harassed him, determined that the throne itself should be overturned and the republic restored. This rising menace which threatened his rule and the succession of his son, the prince imperial, was one reason why Napoleon in 1870 gambled on a war with Prussia in the effort to regain his waning prestige.

But in foreign as in domestic affairs fortune had deserted him after 1860. The subsequent pages will outline the foreign policies of the Second Empire, and endeavor to explain the complex motives which led Napoleon III to seek a war with Russia which added to his prestige, to provoke a war with Austria which added to his perplexities, and to accept a war with Prussia which overturned his throne.

4. THE SECOND EMPIRE AT WAR: THE CRIMEAN CONFLICT (1854–56)

Throughout the nineteenth century, European statesmen, particularly British statesmen, were haunted by an almost superstitious fear of Russia. The enormous size of the Muscovite Empire, larger in area than all the rest of the European states together, was in itself an alarming reflection. Napoleon's disastrous march on Moscow in 1812 furnished seeming proof of Russian invulnerability, and Alexander I, by his determined stand at the Congress of Vienna, had indicated that the great Slavic power was not yet satiated and lusted for more territory. As if driven by an irresistible pressure, the Russian frontier moved eastward until it reached the Pacific Ocean. By 1860, the province north of the Amur River had been wrested from China, and Vladivostok ("The Conqueror of the East") founded as a Russian port on the Sea of Japan. At the same time Russian armies in the Middle East pressed into Mongolia and overran Turkestan to the borders of Afghanistan and India. In the Near East the shadow of the Russian giant hung like a dark threat above the crumbling Turkish Empire, and the czar's forces waited only for a favorable opportunity to seize Constantinople.

British merchants were convinced that their Mediterranean trade would suffer if Constantinople fell to Russia, and the British people persuaded themselves that an army of Cossacks might soon be pouring through the passes of the Hindu Kush to compete for the control of India. A deeper knowledge of the internal weaknesses of the Russian Empire would have dispelled much of this anxiety, but few western Europeans had traveled there and the czar's subjects could not journey abroad without special permission. So to foreigners Russia remained shrouded with the vague menace which always invests an unknown and unpredictable force.

Even peaceful overtures from Saint Petersburg aroused misgivings. "We have a sick man on our hands," declared Nicholas I in 1853, referring metaphorically to Turkey; and he proposed to the British ambassador that, as chief beneficiaries of the Ottoman bequest, England should establish a claim to Egypt while Russia "inherited" the sultan's Balkan provinces. The British cabinet doubted the czar's good faith, but Nicholas apparently took their refusal for a diplomatic "yes."

"Sick man" of Europe

Thereupon Russian armies anticipated the "sick man's" demise by occupying the Turkish provinces comprising modern Rumania[1] and the British government prepared to aid the Turks. Meanwhile, a dispute had developed between France and Russia concerning the claims of Roman Catholic and Greek Orthodox monks to control and exhibit to pilgrims certain holy places in Syria. Napoleon III needed the prestige of a successful war; he was annoyed at Nicholas because the latter had declined to greet him as "my brother" when he made himself Emperor of the French; and he hoped to please the Catholics in France by claiming the right to protect Catholics in Turkey. So Napoleon deliberately fostered a conflict for which there was little cause and no justification, and Britain joined France in order to fight for the preservation of the Ottoman Empire in Europe.

In 1854, the two powers dispatched an expedition to the Black Sea to besiege the Russian fortress of Sebastopol on the Crimean Peninsula. After heavy losses and terrible suffering on both sides, Sebastopol was evacuated by the Russians (September, 1855) and the allies (France, Great Britain, Turkey, and the Kingdom of Sardinia, which had joined them in 1855) agreed to suspend hostilities. The British, who had conducted their share of the war with heavy casualties and tragic inefficiency, would willingly have continued it, but Napoleon III was satisfied with his victory such as it was. As for the Russians, they had never really desired the war, and had been disillusioned by the hostile attitude of the Austrian government, which had accepted Russian aid in crushing the Hungarians (1849), but failed to reciprocate in Russia's hour of need.

Siege of Sebastopol

So the Crimean War was terminated by a congress of diplomats who met at Paris to work out a new settlement for the Near-Eastern Question. To hold Russia in check the victors ordained: (1) That no great power should construct fortifications or maintain warships in the Black Sea. (2) That Moldavia and Wallachia (modern Rumania), which Russia had occupied in 1853, and later evacuated, should become an autonomous principality while remaining under Turkish suzerainty. (3) That the Danube River should be open to the trading ships of all nations. The

Treaty of Paris (1856)

---

[1] See maps on pages 680 and 730.

THE BALKANS

- - - - Boundaries before the Balkan Wars
─── " after " "
▨ Area of Turkey in Europe before the Balkan Wars 1912-13

Congress of Paris had the further significance of admitting Turkey for the first time to a recognized place in the European concert of nations, and of formulating a "Declaration" defining the rights of neutrals and the question of protecting neutral property in time of war. The attempt to limit the destructiveness of warfare and to impress a respect for certain humane conventions upon all the belligerents marked a distinct advance in the evolution of international law. Though frequently violated since, the "Declaration" of the Congress of Paris, because of the ban it placed upon privateering and the limits it set upon the right of blockade, has proved the most permanent benefit of the war.

For in so far as it represented an attempt to settle the Near-Eastern Question the Treaty of Paris proved a tragic failure. The sultan, after swearing to grant equal justice to his "Christian cattle," conveniently forgot his promise. After a few years Russia coolly ignored the provisions prohibiting armaments on the Black Sea, and a generation later a new congress had to be convoked to protect Turkey from the Russian advance. For this negative result, Britain, France, and Russia had shattered a truce which had restrained the great powers from war with one another for thirty-nine years; for this a sum equivalent to two billion dollars had been poured away, and half a million lives sacrificed to war, disease, and negligence. But Napoleon III had won the honor of presiding over a peace conference in Paris; British traders could sleep more soundly in their beds because for the moment the Russians ceased to threaten Constantinople; and Cavour, who had plunged Sardinia into an alien conflict to gain the friendly interest of Napoleon, could turn that interest to his own astute ends.

A new period of armed conflict had opened in Europe, for the Crimean War proved the first of five struggles which disturbed the great powers between 1853 and 1871. The second, which broke out in 1859, found Napoleon leading an army into Italy to expel the Austrians. Napoleon's reasons for engaging in this Italian war of 1859 were numerous and complicated. His mind was a strange crucible in which generous impulses and humanitarian ideals blended obscurely with dynastic aims and political calculations. As a youth he had campaigned with the Italian patriots in their ill-starred uprising of 1830, and as an emperor he continued to declare his sympathy for suppressed peoples, Poles, Germans, or Italians. To drive the Austrians from Italy and replace their influence by a French hegemony, as the first Napoleon had done, must certainly have appealed to him as an undertaking that would shed luster upon French arms and strengthen his throne. But he took no active steps to aid the liberals in Italy until, in 1858, an impatient Italian patriot named Orsini threw a bomb at his carriage to refresh his memory.

Far from deterring Napoleon, Orsini's conspiracy crystallized his resolution to aid the Italians. He knew that the only state in Italy strong and independent enough to take the offensive in a war to expel the Austrians was the Kingdom of Sardinia. With elaborate secrecy he arranged a meeting with Count Camillo di Cavour, the tireless and far-sighted Sardinian diplomat who was the most ingenious statesman of his time. The two agreed that Austria should be tricked into attacking Sardinia, whereupon a French army of two hundred thousand men would hasten to the aid of the Sardinians. Italy was to be freed from "the Alps to the Adriatic," and France as a reward would annex the province of Savoy and the city of Nice. Privately, Napoleon felt confident that a victory would enable him to make French influence supplant Austrian domination in the Italian Peninsula. He did not intend to make Italy a powerful independent kingdom.

It will be convenient at this point to pause in the discussion of the Second Empire, and turn back to trace the drama of Italian unification up to 1859 in order to appreciate better how skillfully Cavour had prepared the stage for Napoleon's entry.

54

The Political Unification of Italy

Italy is one nation; unity of customs, language, and literature must in a period more or less distant unite her inhabitants under one sole government, and Rome will without the slightest doubt be chosen by the Italians as their capital.

NAPOLEON I, at Saint Helena.

DISREGARDING the national aspirations which had stirred in Italy during the era of Napoleon I, the Congress of Vienna sought in 1815 to restore the Italian people to that condition of disunity and subjugation under which they had languished before the French Revolution. How well the congress succeeded may be seen by comparing the status of Italy in 1648 and in 1815. Old states and old governments reappeared, and princes long in exile returned to claim their privileges in the name of legitimacy. In the south Ferdinand I, despicable scion of the Spanish Bourbon line, assumed the crown of the Kingdom of the Two Sicilies. Central Italy, from Rome to Ravenna, was reconstituted as the States of the Church under the temporal rule of Pius VII. In the Grand Duchy of Tuscany and the neighboring duchies of Parma, Lucca, and Modena, petty despots, most of them Hapsburg dependents, returned to their thrones. North of the Po the new map differed slightly from that of 1789, because Austria now held both Lombardy and Venetia, while to the west the congress strengthened the Kingdom of Sardinia by incorporating with it the late republic of Genoa. Those patriotic Italians who cherished the dream of a free and united Italy in 1815 found the prospect disheartening. The nine fragments into which the peninsula had been redivided were not linked by even a loose confederative bond, and most of them were ruled by princes of foreign extraction who had no sympathy for the idea of Italian unity and independence.

Italy in 1815

1. THE NATIONAL SPIRIT STIRS (1815-48)

Nevertheless, though the map of Italy might be redrawn on the eighteenth-century model, the Italian people had acquired a new spirit, new memories, and new ideas. Everywhere in Europe the revolutionary epoch had quickened national feelings. The Poles, the Germans, and the Italians, who possessed no independent fatherland of their own, had grown fiercely conscious of their right to liberty and unity. In Russia and Spain the appearance of Napoleon's armies had aroused the people to deep patriotic resentment. The intensification of the feeling of nationalism during the years of war and revolution made it the most dynamic political force in the modern world. How this vital sentiment can spread among a people, converting them to a belief in their own uniqueness, their common historical and cultural heritage, and their right to political unity and self-government, is well illustrated by the story of the Italians.

Nationalism

The Italian people had never forgotten that in ancient times Rome was the mistress of the known world, and that a thousand years later the scholars and artists of the Renaissance made Italy the "mother of arts." Un-

The Risorgimento

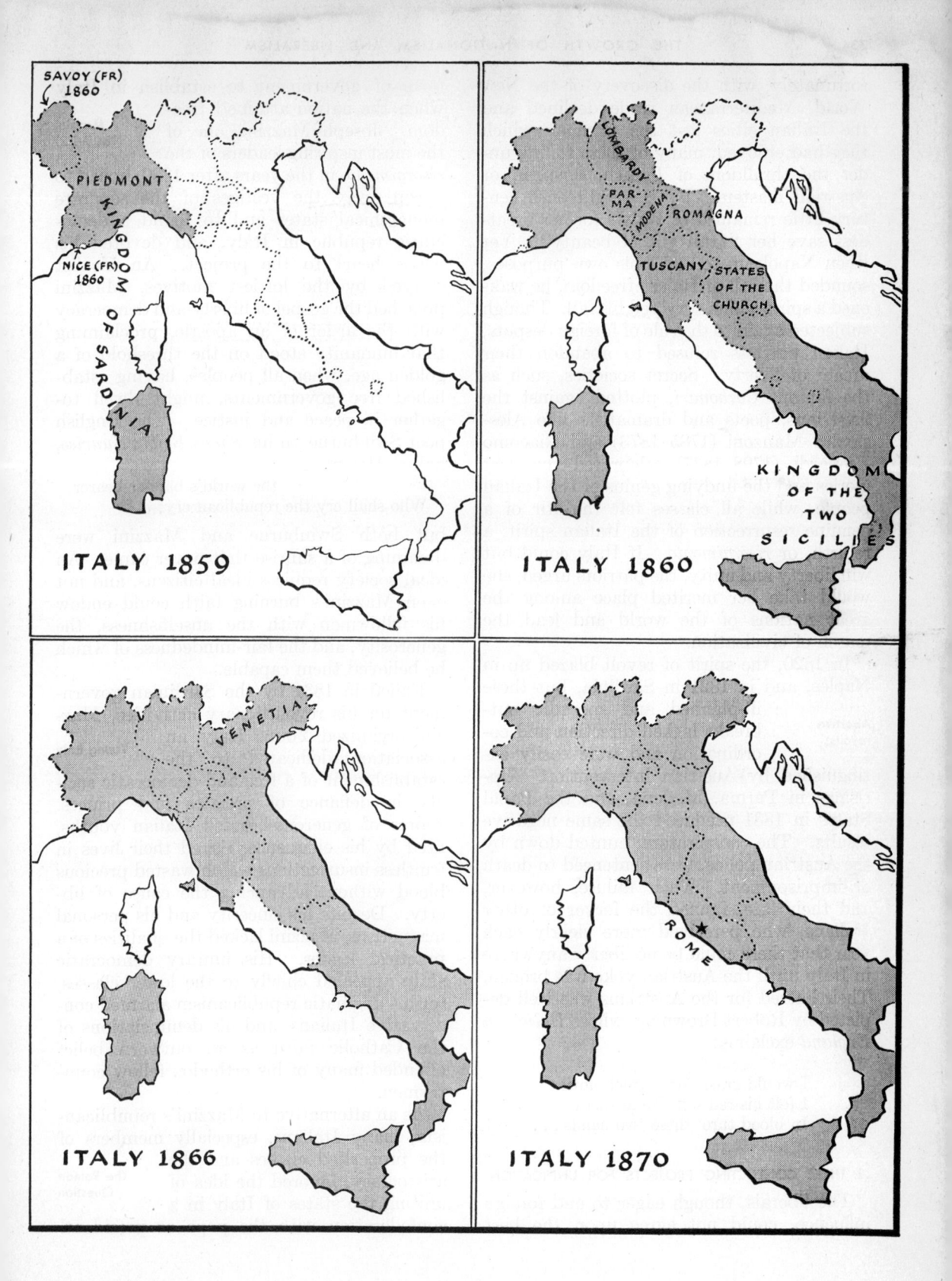

ITALY 1859

SAVOY (FR) 1860
PIEDMONT
KINGDOM OF SARDINIA
NICE (FR) 1860

ITALY 1860

LOMBARDY
PARMA
MODENA
ROMAGNA
TUSCANY
STATES OF THE CHURCH
KINGDOM OF THE TWO SICILIES

ITALY 1866

VENETIA

ITALY 1870

ROME

fortunately, with the discovery of the New World, Mediterranean trade declined and the Italian cities lost the primacy which they had enjoyed, many of them falling under the thralldom of French, Spanish, or Austrian masters. By the eighteenth century little remained of Italy's former greatness save her "fatal gift of beauty." Yet when Napoleon, to serve his own purposes, sounded the call of Italian freedom, he wakened a spirit which survived his fall. Though subjected again to the rule of foreign despots, Italian patriots refused to abandon their dream of liberty. Secret societies, such as the famous *Carbonari*, plotted against the Austrians, poets and dramatists like Alessandro Manzoni (1785–1873) and Giacomo Leopardi (1798–1837) celebrated the past glories and the undying genius of the Italian people, while all classes felt the stir of a genuine resurrection of the Italian spirit, a rebirth, or *risorgimento*. If Italy could but win liberty and unity, the patriots urged, she would take her merited place among the great nations of the world and lead the march of civilization.

In 1820, the spirit of revolt blazed up in Naples, and in 1821 in Sardinia, but these ill-planned and sporadic outbreaks lacked direction and coordination and were easily extinguished by Austrian intervention. Uprisings in Parma, Modena, and the Papal States in 1831 produced the same negative results. The conspirators, hunted down by the Austrian police, were sentenced to death or imprisonment. Their failure, however, and their fate, fanned the fervor of other Italians, who perceived more clearly each year that there could be no liberty anywhere in Italy until the Austrian yoke was broken. Their hatred for the Austrians was well depicted by Robert Browning, whose *Italian in England* exclaims:

Abortive revolts

> I would grasp Metternich until
> I felt his red wet throat distil
> In blood thro' these two hands

2. THREE CONFLICTING PROJECTS FOR UNIFICATION

The liberals, though eager to end foreign influence, could not agree upon the best form of government to establish in Italy when the nation attained freedom. Joseph Mazzini, one of the most inspiring leaders of the *risorgimento* in the years after 1830, hoped to sweep away the vestiges of the separate monarchical states and to found a democratic republic in Italy, and devoted his whole heart to the project. An idealist swayed by the loftiest motives, Mazzini preached the gospel of liberty and democracy with the ardor of an apostle, proclaiming that humanity stood on the threshold of a golden age, when all peoples, having established free governments, might dwell together in peace and justice. The English poet Swinburne, in his *Songs Before Sunrise*, hailed Mazzini as

Mazzini (1805–72)

> the world's banner bearer
> Who shall cry the republican cry;

but both Swinburne and Mazzini were dreaming of a sunrise that never came. An ideal society requires ideal citizens, and not even Mazzini's burning faith could endow his fellowmen with the unselfishness, the generosity, and the fair-mindedness of which he believed them capable.

Exiled in 1831 by the Sardinian government for his revolutionary activities, Mazzini organized Young Italy, an association dedicated to the establishment of a free and democratic society in defiance of prelates and princes. Scores of generous-hearted Italian youths, fired by his eloquence, risked their lives in fruitless insurrections which wasted precious blood without advancing the cause of liberty. Despite his sincerity and his personal magnetism, Mazzini lacked the qualities of a practical leader. His unitary democratic state appealed chiefly to the lower classes, for his dogmatic republicanism alarmed conservative Italians, and his denunciations of the Catholic faith as an outworn belief offended many of his orthodox fellow countrymen.

Young Italy

As an alternative to Mazzini's republicanism, many Italians, especially members of the propertied classes and the aristocracy, favored the idea of uniting the states of Italy in a confederation with the pope as president.

The Roman Question

This project found an earnest advocate in Vincenzo Gioberti, who wrote a lengthy and widely read work *On the Moral and Civil Supremacy of the Italians* (1843). The great virtue of Gioberti's plan lay in its solution of what was called "The Roman Question"; that is, the problem of founding a united Italy without dispossessing the papacy, for the papal government hesitated to surrender the States of the Church to the rule of a secular administration. By conferring upon the head of the church in perpetuity the office of president of the proposed Italian confederation, it seemed probable that this difficulty could be overcome, for in this way the pope could be assured of the power to maintain direction over his temporal dominions.

The election to the papal chair of the winning and charitable Pius IX (1846) gave a powerful stimulus to the plan. **Pius IX (1846–78)** Pius opened his pontificate by an amnesty for many political offenders, dismissed his Swiss Guard, and appointed popular ministers to his council. These reforms won him an enthusiastic following, particularly among liberal Catholics who were good churchmen and also good friends of Italian independence. But republicans and anti-clericals expressed a doubt that the pope's liberalism could be either deep or sincere, and continued to work for a secular state without religious affiliations.

Advocates of yet a third project of unification looked to the Kingdom of Sardinia [1] to lead the movement. As the only **The Sardinian Party** independent Italian principality ruled by a native dynasty, the Piedmontese state enjoyed a unique position in Italy. With its hard-working peasantry, influential middle class, and well-trained army, it ranked as a third-class power, and might aspire to play the rôle in Italy which Prussia was playing in the Germanies. Ardent revolutionaries like Mazzini distrusted the Sardinian king, the enigmatic Charles Albert (1831–49), believing him a traitor to liberal ideals because he had refused his subjects a constitution and hesitated to challenge Austria in a war for Italian liberation. To a large body of moderate liberals, however, the thought of unifying their country under the sober-minded Sardinian king seemed an admirable solution, for what they most desired for Italy was a secular government that would be independent of Austrian and of papal influence. Believing in the old Latin proverb that middle roads are safest, such men could be counted upon to support the Sardinian government if it steered a sane middle course between radical republicanism and clerical domination.

3. THE DEFEATED HOPES OF 1848–49

At the opening of 1848, that year of revolutions which saw the throne of Louis Philippe overturned in Paris and Metternich driven from office by an outbreak in Vienna, Italy **Uprisings of 1848** was shaken by spontaneous revolts from Venice to Sicily. Charles Albert at Turin, Ferdinand II at Naples, Pius IX at Rome, and the Grand Duke of Tuscany at Florence, all endeavored to pacify their rebellious subjects by granting constitutions. Nationalism and liberalism seemed on the point of obtaining a mutual triumph as the Venetian populace expelled the Austrian garrison and established a republic under the liberator Daniel Manin, while at Milan leaders of the national movement proclaimed the independence of Lombardy. The Austrian government was paralyzed at home by revolts in Vienna, Bohemia, and Hungary,[1] and this knowledge encouraged the Italians to attempt a general war of independence. Even the papal and Sicilian governments yielded to the popular fervor and contributed detachments to swell the gathering army of liberation.

With belated zeal, Charles Albert of Sardinia rallied to the head of the national movement. "*L'Italia farà da se*" (Italy will do it herself) **"L'Italia farà da se"** he announced proudly, and launched his army against the retreating Austrians. But the weakness and the un-

---

[1] The student should understand clearly that "Kingdom of Sardinia" refers not only to the island but also to Savoy and the Piedmont. See the map, "Italy, 1859," on page 733.

[1] See above, pages 718–720.

harmonized ideals of the Italians betrayed them. As the first flush of enthusiasm passed, the papal and Neapolitan contingents were recalled, for Pius IX and Ferdinand of Naples recollected their duties to the side of tradition and legitimacy. At the same time, the Austrians, rallying strongly under their octogenarian field marshal, Radetsky, defeated Charles Albert's mixed forces at Custozza (July 24, 1848). With the failure of moderate leadership, the more radical of the Italian insurgents swung to the left and set up republics (1849) in Florence and Rome. Pius IX fled from the Vatican as Rome passed under the control of a popular government headed by Mazzini and defended by the tireless knight of liberty, Giuseppe Garibaldi.

But the Italian people were unprepared for a sharp transition to democracy, and the Roman Republic could hardly have survived in any case amid the general reaction of 1849. Its death warrant, however, was signed by Louis Napoleon, newly elected president of the Second French Republic, who dispatched an expeditionary force to Rome which overcame the heroic resistance of Garibaldi's republican guard and re-established the papal government by means of French bayonets. At the same time Austria aided the lesser Italian despots to remount their thrones and revoke the constitutional guaranties which they had granted in the first months of the popular movement. By the close of the year 1849, the most determined and widespread effort yet made to free Italy from foreign oppression and domestic tyranny had ended in the blackest failure.

Collapse of republicanism

Yet one Italian state conserved its liberty even in defeat. Crushed by the Austrians at Custozza, and a second time at Novara (March 23, 1849), Charles Albert resigned his throne to his son Victor Emmanuel II, who made the best terms he could with Austria. A legend later grew up that Radetsky sought to coerce Victor Emmanuel into revoking the Sardinian *Statuto*, or constitution, proclaimed the previous year, and that the new king proudly refused. Actually, however, Radetsky softened his terms out of consideration for Victor Emmanuel, whom he considered more conservative than his father, and he did not criticize the *Statuto*.

Sardinia survives

Two lessons might be drawn from the failures of 1848–49. The first suggested that neither the Republican nor the Clerical Party would succeed in uniting Italy. The collapse of the Roman Republic left Mazzini and his colleagues, not exactly leaders without a party, but certainly leaders of a discouraged and diminished party. The Catholic liberals, on the other hand, now found themselves a party without a leader, for Pius IX had returned to Rome disappointed, like most Italians, with the disunity and failure of the liberal party. With the party of the Right and the party of the Left losing ground, it became clear that the party of the Center might yet win the day, and make the Kingdom of Sardinia the nucleus of a resurrected Italy. This was the first lesson to be learned from the events of 1848–49. But there was a second conclusion to be realized, a bitter one for Italian patriots to accept. Italy could not "do it herself." The Italian people possessed neither the forces nor the co-operation needed to drive out the Austrians; to attempt the task unaided was to invite further failure. Fortunately for the cause of Italian freedom, there was at least one statesman in Italy capable of appreciating both these lessons. His name was Camillo di Cavour.

The Center strengthened

4. CAVOUR CONTRIVES

Cavour was born in Turin in 1810, the second son of a noble family. After graduating from military school at the age of sixteen, he obtained a commission in the Sardinian army, but his dabblings in liberalism and his indiscreet comments upon the backward political condition prevailing in Piedmont got him into trouble, and after a brief imprisonment he resigned his commission. His liberalism had made him a marked man, and the Austrian police in nearby states were warned that he was "deeply corrupted in his political principles." From 1831 to 1848 he pursued private interests, experimented with new methods of agriculture, studied,

Camillo di Cavour

JOSEPH MAZZINI (1805–1872)

Mazzini was an inspiring leader, but he was deficient in capacity for organization and practical statesmanship.

CAMILLO DI CAVOUR (1810–1861)

Cavour was often careless in his dress and his appearance was not impressive, but he was the most astute diplomat of his day.

traveled, and accumulated a fortune, but his mind was constantly absorbed with political affairs in which he was denied a part. Then, in 1848, conditions changed abruptly. Charles Albert granted his subjects a constitution, and Cavour was elected to the recently created Sardinian Parliament. In 1850, the new king, Victor Emmanuel II, appointed him minister of commerce and agriculture, an office which permitted him to display at once his extraordinary grasp of political and economic questions.

Few people would have guessed from Cavour's appearance that he was one of the dominant personalities of the nineteenth century. With his stocky figure, plain garb, and metal-rimmed spectacles, he looked a shopkeeper or clerk. His life-purpose was to free Italy and give the Italian people a parliamentary government on the liberal English pattern, but he made no passionate speeches about the rights of man like Mazzini, nor did he lead the van of hopeless and heroic charges like the fearless Garibaldi. His unique talent consisted in his ability to grasp realities, to move only as fast as events permitted, to take practical advantage of the political forces at work in Europe and quietly direct them to his own ends.

The first step in Cavour's program was to make the Sardinian Kingdom known as a liberal and prosperous state to which all other Italians would look with pride and envy. His wide study and observance had made him an authority on commerce and agriculture, on railroads, finance, the methods of parliamentary government, and the conduct of foreign affairs. Once in office he pushed his reforms with implacable deliberation. The Sardinian Parliament ordained that marriage should become a civil contract, and forbade the gift of further property to the church, a policy aimed at curbing the influence of the clergy. Commercial treaties with other nations and a revision of the

Cavour's ministry

tariffs benefited the poorer classes. While assiduously cultivating the friendship of France and Britain, Cavour maintained a firm and cool attitude toward Austria, so that Sardinia came to be recognized as a state guided by liberal counsels where men dared to plan the liberation of Italy. This was precisely the impression Cavour wished to convey to the discontented citizens in other Italian provinces, and to Mazzini's republican insurgents.

Few of Cavour's contemporaries understood the intricacies of his foreign policy, yet his aim was comparatively simple. Believing that the Italians must have the aid of a great power to help them to expel the Austrians, he sought for such an ally and found it in France. How he joined Britain and France in the Crimean War has been mentioned already.[1] Sardinia had no real quarrel with Russia, but the intervention won Cavour a seat at the peace conference in Paris, where he had an opportunity to impress Napoleon III and to bring the Italian question before the European diplomats. Three years later, Cavour and Napoleon held a secret interview at Plombières, and the stage was set for the War of Italian Liberation. Napoleon insisted upon two stipulations: Austria must appear to be the aggressor, and France must receive the county of Savoy and the city of Nice as compensation for the aid rendered. Cavour hated to sacrifice a portion of the Piedmontese realm, but he knew that the population in the disputed sections was more French than Italian, and that France could not be expected to fight a war for pure altruism. Cavour was a realist and a man of business.

Cavour finds an ally

A policy of astute provocation incited Austria to declare war against the Kingdom of Sardinia in April, 1859, and Napoleon III fulfilled his promise by leading an army of two hundred thousand men into Italy. But after the Austrians had been driven from Lombardy in the bloody battles of Magenta and Solferino, and half Europe feared to see the French emperor follow up his successes as brilliantly as his uncle had done sixty years earlier, Napoleon III suddenly abandoned the campaign and signed a truce with the Austrians.

What were the motives which moved Napoleon to end the war before Italy had been freed from "the Alps to the Adriatic"? Well, for one thing, he had been appalled by the carnage of the battlefields. A second and weightier reason was the growing hostility of the Prussian government which had mobilized its army and could threaten France with an attack on the Rhine. Then, too, Napoleon had come to suspect that he had underrated the strength of the Italian movement for independence, which now seemed likely to create, not a loose Italian federation which he could dominate, but a unified state which might menace France in the south. Finally, if the Italians succeeded in forming a united kingdom, they would seek to include Rome as their capital, a course which must deprive the pope of his temporal possessions and cause French Catholics to blame Napoleon for endangering the papal patrimony after he had promised to safeguard it.

Napoleon makes peace

Accordingly, to prevent the developments from outrunning his aims, Napoleon made peace with the Austrian emperor, Francis Joseph (Treaty of Villafranca). As the Austrian forces remained strongly entrenched in the circle of fortresses known as the Quadrilateral (Mantua, Peschiera, Verona, and Legnago), Francis Joseph could still bargain, and although he agreed to surrender Lombardy he insisted that the rulers of Modena and Tuscany should retain their thrones. The two emperors also decided to promote the formation of an Italian federation under the presidency of the pope, a step which Napoleon counted upon to placate the French Catholics.

Overwhelmed with disappointment at this desertion of his ally before the successful completion of a war from which he had hoped so much, Cavour for once lost his good sense, demanded that Sardinia carry on the struggle alone, and, when Victor Emmanuel prudently refused, threw up his office. Equally chagrined at the developments, but more level-headed, the Sardinian monarch acqui-

Italy reconstructed

[1] See above, pages 729–731.

esced in the terms arranged at Villafranca, which at least promised to bring him Lombardy. But this inadequate settlement, so galling to Italian pride, was destined to be speedily superseded. Seized with patriotic enthusiasm, the people of Parma and Modena, as well as the population of the Romagna, in the Papal States, voted for unification with the Kingdom of Sardinia. The Romagna formed part of the patrimony ruled by Pius IX, which Napoleon had agreed to protect. Nevertheless, he offered to approve the enlargement of the Sardinian Kingdom on condition that France obtain Savoy and Nice, for, although he had failed to keep his full promise made to Cavour, Napoleon still desired his reward. After the inhabitants of the districts concerned had signified their approval through plebiscites, France incorporated Savoy and Nice, while Sardinia annexed Lombardy, Tuscany, Parma, Modena, and the Romagna (Treaty of Turin, 1860).

Cavour, recovering from the bitter mood into which Napoleon's separate negotiations had driven him, returned to office in time to complete these diplomatic exchanges with a masterly hand. His policy, though not wholly successful, since Venice still remained to the Austrians, had doubled the area and population of the Sardinian Kingdom. But many patriots, Garibaldi among them, denounced him as a traitor because he had relinquished Savoy and Nice to France.

5. GARIBALDI MARCHES

Giuseppe Garibaldi (1807–82) ranks with Mazzini and Cavour as the third in the great triumvirate of Italian liberators. While still in his twenties he joined Young Italy, and plunged, with the courage of a lion and the heart of a child, into the war against tyrants. In 1834, he was sentenced to death, but escaped to South America, where he fought for the liberty of alien republics until the outbreaks of 1848 afforded him another chance to strike a blow for Italy. The following year he defended Mazzini's Roman Republic, and barely escaped with his life, to resume his career of adventure and exile. The War of 1859 found him back in Italy, leading a free-lance company against the Austrians once more. The involutions of politics and the sagacious statesmanship of Cavour he neither understood nor approved. What he did understand was the nobility of taking up arms in the cause of liberty and fighting side by side with honest men. An alliance with a despot like Napoleon III, or the bargain by which Cavour traded Nice to France, appeared to Garibaldi, who had been born in Nice, an act of treason.

It is not surprising, therefore, that when Cavour wished to rest in 1860 and consolidate the Sardinian gains, Garibaldi insisted that the struggle must continue until all Italy was free. Organizing an expedition, the famous "One Thousand," he sailed from Genoa on May 5, to attack the Kingdom of the Two Sicilies. Francis II (1859–61) had an army of over one hundred thousand men, but many of his subjects hated him and his soldiers were half-hearted in their allegiance. Within six months Garibaldi's "red shirts" had conquered the island of Sicily in the name of Victor Emmanuel, and crossing to Naples they entered the city in triumph on September 7, after Francis II had fled. The south of Italy had been won for the Italian Kingdom, and the next step, logically, was to march on Rome. But Cavour, fearing that such an affront to the pope must bring a French army to his rescue, frustrated Garibaldi's impetuosity. With the tacit consent of Napoleon III, Victor Emmanuel led a Sardinian force across papal territory into the Neapolitan State, and completed the conquest of it; but at the same time he eased the tension by taking the leadership out of Garibaldi's hands. It is possible Garibaldi felt somewhat slighted, for, although he agreed to drive through the streets of Naples with Victor Emmanuel, the only favor he asked for his great services was that Cavour should be dismissed, and when this was refused, he retired to his farm on the island of Caprera.

By the close of 1860, Sicily, Naples, and the papal provinces known as the Marches and Umbria,[1] had voted for union with the other states now ruled by Victor Emman-

---
[1] See map on page 733.

uel, and the following March the Sardinian monarch was proclaimed king of a united Italy, although the kingdom remained incomplete. But the enormous labor, the hopes and the disappointments of the crowded years 1859 to 1861 had exhausted Cavour, and he died on June 6, 1861. In his last hours he consoled himself with the thought, *L'Italia è fatta* — Italy is made.

Death of Cavour

6. THE WINNING OF VENICE AND ROME

Italy was made, but it was not yet complete, for the papal government still ruled at Rome and the Austrians held Venetia. The successors of Cavour had to wait for a favorable moment to add these "unredeemed" segments to the Italian Kingdom. One such chance came in 1866, when Prussia fought Austria in the "Seven Weeks' War."[1] The Prussian statesman Bismarck arranged an alliance with the new Italian Kingdom, which joined in the attack and attempted to seize Venetia. Although they were defeated by the Austrians on both land and sea, the Italians received Venetia for their assistance when the triumphant Prussians negotiated the Treaty of Prague after their victory over the Austrians at Königgrätz.

To crown the new kingdom by the acquisition of Rome as its capital had now become "an inexorable necessity." Twice Garibaldi led a force of volunteers to seize the Eternal City, but he was checked by Victor Emmanuel's troops (wounded "by an Italian bullet" he complained) on the first attempt (1862), and defeated by the French garrison at Rome on the second (1867). Diplomacy seemed powerless to achieve a settlement of the "Roman Question," yet the Italian government feared that if the pope were dispossessed by force, the Catholic nations might come to his assistance. In 1870, however, the outbreak of the Franco-Prussian War directed international attention elsewhere, and compelled Napoleon III to recall the French guard at Rome for home defense. The moment was too auspicious to overlook. On September 20, 1870, Italian troops marched into Rome, and the citizens voted,

Occupation of Rome

[1] See below, pages 748–749.

by a majority of 134,000 to 1500, for incorporation into the Italian Kingdom. Cavour's great project had been completed nine years after his death.

7. THE ROMAN CATHOLIC CHURCH IN THE NINETEENTH CENTURY

Stripped of his temporal possessions, Pope Pius IX retired within the environs of the Vatican, where he chose to regard himself as a prisoner. In 1871, the Italian Parliament passed a Law of Papal Guaranties recognizing him as a sovereign within this tiny domain, and offering him a sum equal to $650,000 as compensation for the territory which had been seized. This offer Pius refused, and he and his successors[1] preferred to remain voluntary prisoners rather than recognize a government which they regarded as guilty of an act of inexcusable and illegal usurpation.

From the days of the great French Revolution, when the National Assembly confiscated all the church lands in France, the papacy had shown itself distrustful toward liberal and revolutionary doctrines. After the Congress of Vienna restored the States of the Church, which Napoleon had seized, to the rule of Pius VII, the influence of the clergy was invoked by the conservative governments of Europe during the Era of Reaction. Catholics were warned to be on their guard against the seduction of liberal notions, which, as experience had recently proved, often led to revolution and tragic social excesses. Yet, although liberals were sometimes denounced as atheists and enemies of society, liberal and national ferment continued to spread despite all efforts at repressing it. The outbreaks of 1848 and 1849, which shook conservative governments everywhere and drove Pius IX from Rome, not unnaturally convinced him that all revolutionists, whether they called themselves liberals, socialists, or republicans, were a danger to the established order. Nor was the pope alone in this opinion. Napoleon III greatly strengthened the position of the Roman Catholic clergy in France as the best defense against socialism. The

Liberalism distrusted

[1] Until 1929, see page 914.

PIUS IX (1846–1878)
After the seizure of Rome by the Italian government (1870), Pius spent his life in the Vatican because he could not compromise with the usurping power.

LEO XIII (1878–1903)
Intellectual keenness and kindliness of heart distinguished Leo XIII. His solicitude for the laboring classes was especially noteworthy.

SAINT PETER'S CATHEDRAL
Saint Peter's Cathedral in the Vatican City, Rome, is the center of the Catholic World.

Austrian government signed a *concordat* with the papacy (1855), and several lesser states restored to the clergy the control which they had previously exercised in matters of censorship and education. The panic over socialism which followed the revolutions of 1848 had modified the attitude of the bourgeoisie toward the church. The clergy, it was now felt, might prove invaluable allies in the combat with radical thinkers, who were misleading the people by their attacks upon religion and their demands for the confiscation of private property. When the liberals, socialists, and other rebels who dreamed of remaking society found the church entrenched upon the side of the propertied classes and the established governments, they assailed it as an obstacle to progress, and denounced it much as the eighteenth-century *philosophes* had done. Throughout the greater part of the nineteenth century, the liberals were inclined, not without reason, to regard the clericals as their most ingenious and most consistent opponents.

The policies of Pius IX (1846–78) did much to confirm this widespread impression that the church would always be found on the side of the conservatives and the traditionalists. In 1864, Pius issued an encyclical, *Quanta cura*, accompanied by a *Syllabus of Errors*, in which he reaffirmed the independence of the Catholic Church and its supremacy over all secular governments, condemned those who favored granting toleration to other sects, those who advocated civil marriage, lay schools, or curtailment of the privileges of the clergy, and those who sought to deprive the pope of his temporal possessions. Pius thus arrayed the church against liberalism and nationalism, the dominant social and political ideals of the day, at a time when a more cautious and more conciliatory diplomat might well have hesitated to antagonize and add to the anti-clerical forces.

Pontificate of Pius IX

For the opponents of organized religion in the middle of the nineteenth century had already opened a fierce and dangerous attack from another quarter. The spread of scientific doctrines concerning the age of the earth and the origin of man [1] appeared to contradict the teaching of the church, while a more critical study of history and of comparative religion led many people even in Catholic countries to question the authority of the pope, to deny the validity of religious dogmas concerning the fall of man and the divine revelations of the Gospels, to repudiate, in fact, the whole structure of theology, which supported the Christian faith, as a complicated mythology inadmissible to minds steeped in the truths of science. In every country a growing number of people, especially among the educated classes, found their faith weakened, and many became frank agnostics or atheists in matters of religion.

Growth of skepticism

In meeting this attack upon the intellectual front, Pius IX displayed the same firmness and consistency which had inspired his unequivocal condemnation of so many political and social currents of the age. The sharpest answer to those who presumed to question the papal authority was furnished by the Vatican Council which met at Rome in 1869. Before it was prorogued in 1870, the council declared it to be a dogma "divinely revealed" that when the pope officially pronounced upon a question of faith or morals he was endowed with infallibility. Thus, in the same year that his temporal possessions were reft away, Pius IX was invested with spiritual claims as absolute as any exercised by his mighty predecessors Gregory VII or Innocent III in the Middle Ages.

Vatican Council

To the theologians who proclaimed it, the dogma of papal infallibility was a definition of, not an addition to, the papal prerogatives. Among the laity, particularly among non-Catholics, it met with considerable distrust and opposition. The *Kulturkampf* in Germany, the breach between the Italian government and the papacy, and the conflict of church and state in France, as well as the feuds of clericals and anti-clericals elsewhere, were all intensified by the misapprehensions aroused by the papal claims. To Leo XIII, who succeeded Pius IX in 1878, fell the task of healing estrangements and harmonizing

Leo XIII (1878–1903)

---
[1] See below, pages 782–784.

the position of the church with the existing forces and realities of the modern age. While retracting nothing, Leo endeavored with tact and skill, and with considerable success, to reveal the possibility of a working compromise on the political and intellectual issues which had separated the church from most of the secular governments and dug a gulf between religion and science. The careers of Louis Pasteur and Gregor Mendel were cited as proof that it was possible to be a great scientist and a good Catholic, and the Vatican archives were opened to accredited historians in the hope that a more thorough study of the early centuries of the church would tend to reconcile the secular with the orthodox interpretations. In this way part of the opposition to clerical authority was skillfully dissipated, and the opening years of the twentieth century found the Roman Catholic Church performing its historic mission with renewed vigor, to the surprise of many prophets who had been prepared to predict its imminent collapse.

55

The Formation of the German Empire

... Not by speeches and majority votes are the great questions of the day decided — that was the mistake of 1848 and 1849 — but by blood and iron.

OTTO VON BISMARCK.

THE PANIC which seized the governing classes throughout Europe during the revolutionary outbreaks of 1848 and 1849 made itself felt with particular force in the Germanies. After 1849, the Austrian government, strengthened by its military victories over the Italians and the Hungarians, turned its forces to the familiar task of stamping out the last embers of revolt. The proposals for German unification sponsored by the Frankfort Assembly had fallen to the ground, largely because of Austrian hostility to the project; and a Prussian scheme to organize a federation of states excluding Austria met with the same haughty opposition, with the result that Prussia abandoned the plan (Humiliation of Olmütz, 1850). In 1851 the old inept Diet of the Germanic Confederation of 1815 resumed its sessions, and the Austrian chancellor, Schwarzenberg (Metternich's successor), advised the German princes how best to cancel the liberties which they had conceded to their subjects during the popular turmoil of 1848. In the test of strength between Prussia and Austria for leadership in central Europe, the hesitant Frederick William IV (1840–61) had been steadily outmatched by the purposeful Schwarzenberg, and the Prussians, unprepared for war, had been forced to concede the dominance of Austria and to stomach a diplomatic defeat. These facts made it self-evident that the unification of the Germanies would have to be undertaken in defiance of Austria.

1. THE DECADE OF REPRESSION AFTER 1848

For German liberals the decade from 1850 to 1860 was a tragic era. Their books censored, their letters opened, their homes searched, they endured the bitterness of official persecution until many of them were literally hounded out of the country because of their political convictions. Hardest to bear of all their misfortunes was the knowledge of their failure. They had come so near to establishing a constitutional government in a united Germany that the reaction covered them with the blacker discredit. Convinced in their disillusionment that democracy could never thrive in the poisoned soil of Europe, with its rooted prejudices and ancient hatreds, thousands emigrated to shape their lives anew in the freer air of the New World. Of these many found homes in the United States.

Those who remained behind found that a change came over the spirit of their dream. A harder note of cynicism, a readiness to face essential facts, replaced the tendency toward metaphysical speculation and sentimental eloquence which had paralyzed the Frankfort Assembly. The German people had long been noted for the dreamy and philosophical bent of their thought. "The English inhabit the sea, the French the earth, and the Germans the air," Napoleon observed at the opening of the nineteenth cen-

Realism in Germany

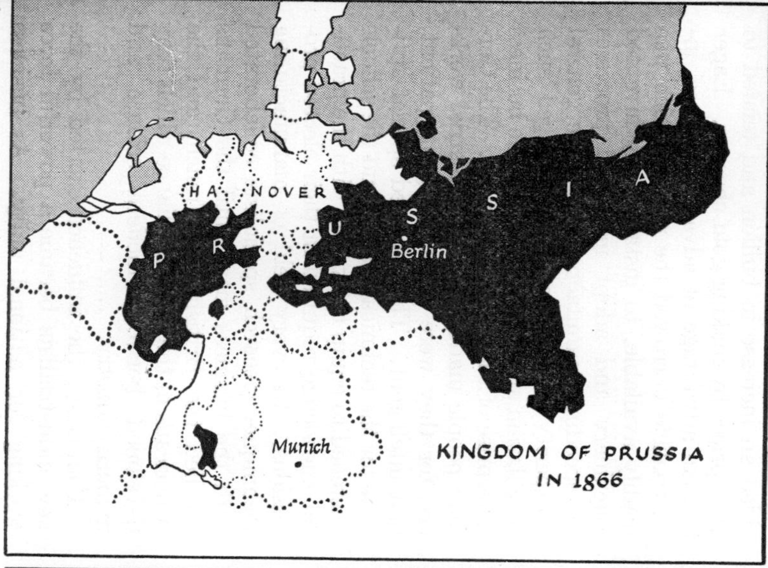
HA NOVER
P R U S S I A
Berlin
Munich
KINGDOM OF PRUSSIA
IN 1866

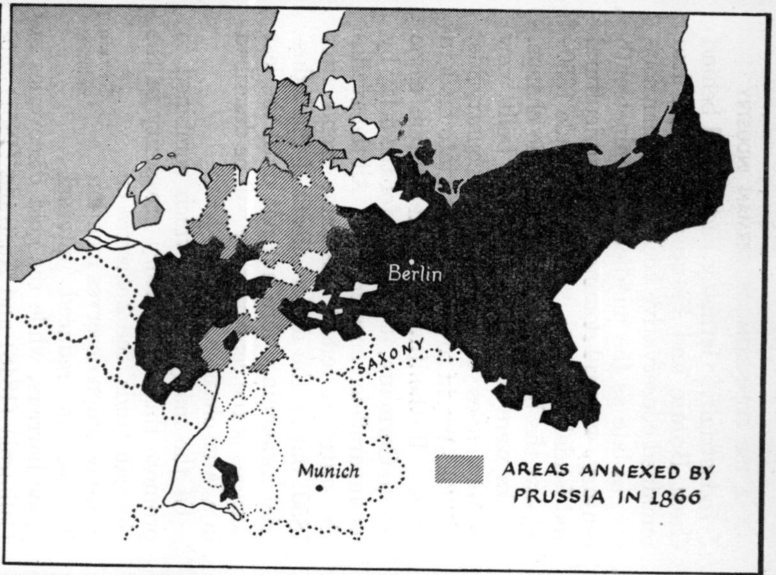
Berlin
SAXONY
Munich
AREAS ANNEXED BY
PRUSSIA IN 1866

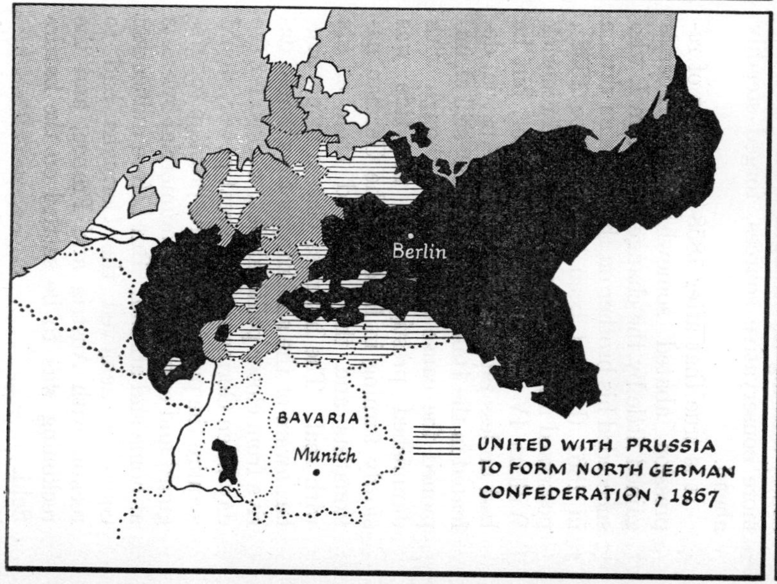
Berlin
BAVARIA
Munich
UNITED WITH PRUSSIA
TO FORM NORTH GERMAN
CONFEDERATION, 1867

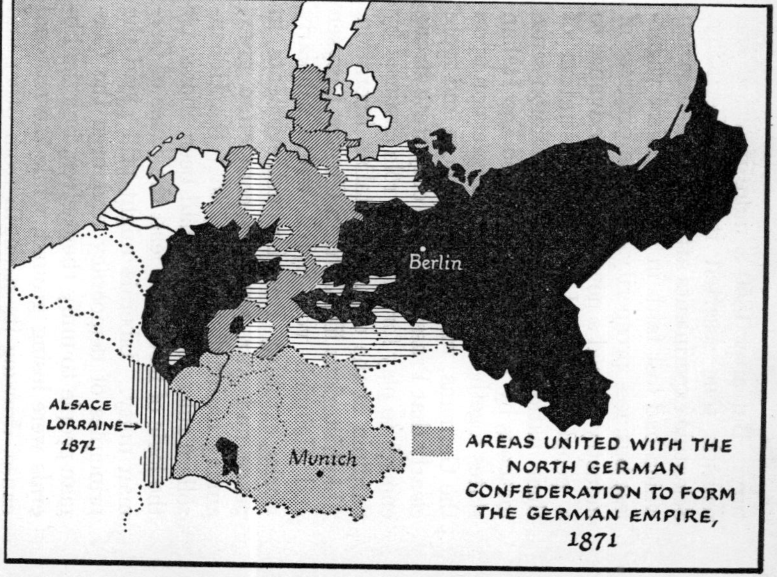
Berlin
ALSACE
LORRAINE
1871
Munich
AREAS UNITED WITH THE
NORTH GERMAN
CONFEDERATION TO FORM
THE GERMAN EMPIRE,
1871

tury. But after 1850 a more practical and realistic tone asserted itself in Germany. Scientific experiments attracted a generation which had lost faith in philosophical vagaries; business prosperity and the progress of industry opened a new avenue of advance to a people depressed by the frustration of their national hopes. The common-sense methods by which Cavour fused the Italian states together made a deep impression upon the Germans, who perceived more and more clearly that Prussia was the only state strong enough to play for them the rôle assumed by Sardinia in the drama of Italian liberation. Able historians like Johann Gustav Droysen and Heinrich von Sybel wrote scholarly works extolling Prussian achievements in peace and war, and the conviction grew, among nationalist groups, that the Hohenzollern rulers of Prussia had been chosen by the logic of history to lead the cause of German unity. Liberals might still plead the principles of democracy and urge the German people to unify themselves, but the liberals were losing ground, while the national cause, drawing its strength from other and more conservative sources, forged steadily ahead.

It is true that after 1858 the spirit of repression abated somewhat, but liberals gained little by the change. William I, who succeeded his brother on the Prussian throne in 1861 (he had been regent since 1858), possessed a more open mind than Frederick William IV and a firmer character, but he had no less faith in authority. Austria, defeated in the Italian War of 1859, still championed the cause of reaction, though with diminished prestige. Yet the tide was slowly turning in favor of the German nationalists and they renewed their efforts with zeal. The business classes in particular, aware of the advantages they would derive from closer political ties, worked for the day when Germany, as a great power, would acquire the position and the prestige to safeguard and extend their commercial interests at home and abroad. But before unification could be achieved the Germans had to reckon with Austria and France, and the reckoning was to be settled on the battlefield.

2. THE EXPANSION OF GERMAN INDUSTRY

Industrially, Germany had lagged behind Great Britain and France; the people had remained conservative because German society, as late as the middle of the nineteenth century, was still dominated by agricultural and feudal concepts. But the decade 1850–60 saw the beginning of a dynamic change. Banks were organized, factories built, new railway lines transected the countryside, and Old-World towns expanded into modern cities. If the Industrial Revolution came late to Germany, it made up for the delay by its unparalleled acceleration. All the available statistics reflect the same trend after 1850, but as the major effects of the industrial awakening were not felt until the last decades of the century they will be described in a later chapter.

Of the many factors which combined to promote this mid-century prosperity in the German lands, the *Zollverein* or customs union deserves mention because it reduced internal trade barriers, while the gold discoveries in California (1848) and Australia (1851) provided an increase in bullion and tended to raise prices by making gold cheaper. Eager to take advantage of advancing prices, industrialists borrowed the money which was readily available, to install newly invented machinery and adopt improved processes for speeding manufacture, and the general prosperity of the period encouraged such speculation and richly rewarded the business enterprise of the rising capitalists. The German people made excellent industrial workers, for they were frugal, diligent, patient, and intelligent. They showed special aptitude for the technical trades, and the schools hastened to equip the young with the practical knowledge required in their elected professions. In every field of manufacturing technique, research specialists collaborated with the business men, until the Germans excelled the British, the French, and the Americans in the fruitful alliance which they developed between modern science and modern industry.

Politically, the influence exerted by the new industrialists became a powerful force working for national unity. As business men, the manufacturers, mine-owners, steel barons, and railway builders desired the uniformity of laws, of taxes, tariffs, postal service, currency, weights and measures, which would follow political union, and they desired even more the support and protection in foreign lands which a powerful government could command for them. Familiar, moreover, with the traditional efficiency, economy, and vigor of the Prussian administrative system, the leaders of trade and manufacture were disposed to favor the establishment of a national government under the initiative of Prussia and on the Prussian model.

3. THE PRUSSIAN SYSTEM

What was this Prussian system to which its advocates pointed with such admiration? Since the days of the Great Elector (1640–88) the government of Brandenburg-Prussia had been a military and bureaucratic despotism in the best sense of the term. Supported by loyal and intelligent officials and a resolute army, the Hohenzollerns had transformed their scattered heritage into a powerful, well-governed state. Defeated and humbled by Napoleon, the Prussian ruling class profited by the lessons of adversity, rooted out abuses and remodeled the army, with the result that Prussia emerged after 1815 with territory increased and prestige restored. Yet how could this small kingdom continue to play the rôle of a great power when its population was less than eleven millions, its lands divided and largely unfertile, its industries backward, its merchant marine undeveloped? The answer was to be found in the Prussian System. A scrupulous economy in every department of government provided a surplus for the exorbitant expense of a first-class army, conscripted by compulsory military service. Even in time of peace Prussia remained a state disciplined for war, a militarized machine served by competent officers and obedient subordinates. The ranks were filled by the peasants, laborers, and artisans; the officers and administrators were drawn chiefly from the noble landowning families of East Prussia (the "Junker" class) or from the bourgeois group of the cities. At the threat of war the Prussian armies could take the field and strike with swift and deadly precision; but in a prolonged struggle the kingdom was certain to suffer from its lack of economic resources.

This inescapable deficiency in its economic reserves partly explains the inactivity of Prussia after the Napoleonic Wars: it was the quiescence of recuperation. From 1815 to 1848, Austria dominated the Germanies and Prussia followed the Austrian lead. But a rift developed between the two states in 1849 when Frederick William IV granted his subjects a constitution and maintained it in force despite Austrian disapproval. As a constitutional state and leader of the *Zollverein* (which excluded Austria) Prussia made a stronger appeal to German liberal and national sentiment than the Vienna régime, which was dedicated to reaction and anchored in the past. It is an error, however, to imagine that Prussia had become liberal in any true sense: the government remained intrinsically an enlightened military despotism. Under the new constitution the parliament consisted of an elected (but not truly representative) Chamber of Deputies and a permanent upper Chamber, but its powers remained exceedingly dubious.[1] The king continued to rule "by the grace of God" and retained the right to choose his ministers. He could levy established taxes, but could not impose new ones. Such an ill-defined compromise between king and parliament, between responsible government and absolute despotism, invited a crisis to determine on which side the real authority lay. The test came when William I ascended the Prussian throne in 1861, a test the outcome of which profoundly influenced the future of Prussia, of Germany, and of Europe.

Deceptive constitution

A soldier's training had confirmed in the mind of William I the belief that authority should come from above, and had given him a special fondness for the army. While still regent he nominated Helmuth von Moltke head of the Prussian general staff and Albrecht von Roon minister of war, and these

King vs. parliament

---
[1] See above, pages 717–718.

inspired appointments revealed his shrewd knowledge of men. In 1860 he approved a plan to reduce exemptions under the military service law and double the reserve period for conscripts, thereby increasing the Prussian army to 190,000 men in peacetime and 450,000 in war. The Chamber of Deputies fought this project stubbornly, agreed finally to vote the extra appropriation it necessitated for one year, but refused to extend it in 1862. Rather than yield on a measure which he considered indispensable if Prussia was to fulfill the destiny marked out for her, William I was prepared to resign his throne. His resignation had been already written out when he changed his mind and determined to hold resolutely to his course. For he had found a minister, Otto von Bismarck, who shared his views and was prepared to defy popular opinion and overrule the parliament in order to carry through the military reforms.

4. OTTO VON BISMARCK (1815-98)

The Bismarck family, dwellers in the Elbe Valley since the fourteenth century, had furnished many capable soldiers and servants of the state. The future chancellor of the German Empire inherited his faith in absolutism and militarism from ancestors who had learned to venerate those principles under the Great Elector and Frederick the Great. Even during the liberal days of 1848 and 1849, the young Bismarck remained a frank reactionary, openly voicing his contempt for parliamentary government and his admiration for the inflexible conservatism of the Austrian régime.

But this admiration faded when, as Prussian ambassador to the Diet of the Germanic Confederation, Bismarck studied Austrian diplomacy at closer range. Between 1851 and 1858 he came to view a war between Austria and Prussia for control of the Germanies as inevitable, and he pressed toward it so fervently that William I (then regent) "put him on ice," as he expressed it, by transferring him to Saint Petersburg. As ambassador to Russia, Bismarck set himself to strengthen the friendly feelings between Prussia and Russia, for he knew how invaluable the czar's friendship would be to the Prussians when the moment came for them to fight Austria.

Such was the determined and experienced man whom William I appointed as his chief minister in the crisis of 1862. For the next four years Bismarck overrode the opposition of the Prussian parliament, muzzled the press, and took from the treasury the funds required for army reform. Few men have been so fiercely denounced, so bitterly hated and vilified, but attempts at impeachment and even at assassination left him unmoved. He had set his talents to the task of making Prussia supreme in Germany and Germany supreme in Europe, and he held no illusion that such a triumph could be achieved by compromise or persuasion. The great questions of the day, he affirmed in a statement which became famous, were settled "by blood and iron."

5. THE AUSTRO-PRUSSIAN WAR

With such a man directing Prussian policy it is not surprising that the German Empire was forged in the flame of war, of three wars, in fact, all fought within a period of six years. In the first conflict Austria and Prussia united to wrest the provinces of Schleswig and Holstein from Denmark, cutting with the sword of war a Gordian knot of tangled diplomatic claims. The two duchies, though peopled largely by Germans, had long been subject to the Danish kings. But in 1864 they were overrun by the Austro-Prussian forces despite a courageous resistance, and Christian IX of Denmark had to relinquish his claims to the conquerors (Treaty of Vienna, 1864).

Although they had united temporarily for the purpose of despoiling Denmark, Austria and Prussia fell to quarreling again after the conclusion of peace. A sharp dispute over the disposal to be made of the conquered duchies brought them to an open breach in 1866. Austria controlled the Diet of the Germanic Confederation and could count upon support from the South German States. Prussia had a secret alliance with Italy, but even so the odds appeared to be against her, and few people doubted that Austria, so much superior in wealth, area, and population, would have the victory. But the Prussian troops carried a newly invented "needle gun" which was three times as deadly as the old muzzle-loading type, and their tactics were devised by the greatest strategist of the age, Helmuth von Moltke. What followed was a stunning demonstration of Prussian efficiency. Austria's German allies proved of little assistance, for the capitals of Hanover, Saxony, and Cassel fell within two weeks; the opposition of Bavaria, Württemberg, Baden, and Hesse-Darmstadt collapsed almost as swiftly. Three Prussian columns converged upon the Austrian army in Bohemia and shattered it on July 3, 1866, in the decisive battle of Königgrätz. Within five weeks the war was virtually at an end.

Instead of marching on to Vienna, Bismarck persuaded William I to offer Austria a generous peace. By the Treaty of Prague (August 23, 1866) the Italians, who had collaborated by attacking the Austrians in Venetia, received that province for their assistance;[1] Prussia annexed Schleswig and Holstein; and the Germanic Confederation was formally dissolved, leaving Prussia to control the Germanies. Bismarck spared the Hapsburgs all undue humiliation, anticipating a time when the friendship of Austria might prove helpful to his projects. Wisely he forbore to prolong the conflict or to take ruthless advantage of a victory which had already alarmed the other powers. Napoleon III, lulled into neutrality by the half-promise of Belgium or other territorial compensation on the Rhine, realized overlate that he had missed a rare chance to hold the scales between the combatants. To retrieve prestige he began to press for his "concessions," and Bismarck, who had no real intention of gratifying him, was happy to extricate the Prussian armies from Bohemia before a French offensive could materialize.

Peace of Prague

The "Seven Weeks' War" definitely ended Austrian interference in both Germany and Italy, the two countries which the Hapsburgs had so long sought to dominate for their own advantage. This curtailment of inflated pretensions, though a blow to their pride, actually strengthened while it constricted the empire on the Danube. Convinced at last of the need for internal reforms and liberal adaptations, Francis Joseph granted the seventeen Austrian provinces a constitution in 1867, establishing responsible parliamentary government with a bicameral legislature chosen by indirect suffrage. At the same time Count Beust, the Austrian imperial chancellor, and Francis Deák, a Hungarian leader, worked out an agreement whereby the relationship between Austria and Hungary was readjusted. This *Ausgleich* or Compromise of 1867 established Hungary as a semi-independent kingdom with a separate constitution and parliament. Francis Joseph remained Emperor of Austria and King of Hungary, and in addition to possessing the same monarch the two states were represented by a joint ministry for the conduct of foreign affairs, war, and finance. This curious Dual Empire established in 1867 survived for fifty years despite its seemingly cumbrous and impracticable form, for the settlement satisfied the German element, which retained a dominant position in Austria, while the Magyars controlled Hungary. But the subject races, the Czechs, Slavs, Poles, etc., grew increasingly restless as their national ambitions steadily mounted while the autonomy which they demanded was as steadily refused. This discontent, particularly among the Slavs, many of whom dreamed of uniting with Serbia and Montenegro to form a pan-Slav kingdom in the Balkans, had become a serious danger to the solidity of the Austro-Hungarian Empire by 1914. It will be explained later how the resultant antagonism between Austria and Serbia produced the incident which precipitated the First World War.

Austria after 1866

6. THE NORTH GERMAN CONFEDERATION

The strong can afford to be generous. Not only toward Austria, but toward the German liberals also, Bismarck displayed a spirit of patience and conciliation after the victory of Königgrätz had vindicated his policies. From the Prussian parliament, in which for

Bismarck's popularity

---
[1] See above, page 740.

ALBRECHT THEODOR EMIL, COUNT VON ROON

Above: As Prussian Minister of War and Marine, Von Roon carried through military reforms which brought the Germans victory over the Danes, Austrians, and French.

HELMUTH KARL BERNARD, COUNT VON MOLTKE (1800–1891)

Left: Von Moltke, as chief of the general staff, perfected the Prussian strategy.

the first time he enjoyed the support of a friendly majority, he requested a decree legalizing his former unconstitutional measures. It was voted at once, together with further appropriations for the victorious army, and substantial rewards and honors were heaped upon the leaders who had made the triumph possible.

The Peace of Prague, which closed the "Seven Weeks' War," left four South German States — Bavaria, Württemberg, Baden, and Hesse-Darmstadt — free to organize as they chose, but the remaining states, north of the river Main, were at the mercy of Prussia. Schleswig and Holstein, Hesse-Cassel, Nassau, the Kingdom of Hanover, and the free city of Frankfort, Prussia annexed outright, thereby acquiring some splendid ports on the North and Baltic seas, and a consolidated territory stretching from the Rhine to the Russian border. With a population raised to twenty-four million, the Prussian Kingdom after 1866 comprised two thirds of Germany and included nearly two thirds of the German people.

Prussian annexations

But Bismarck desired more than the aggrandizement of Prussia: he was aiming at the unification of Germany. At his invitation the twenty-one North German States joined Prussia in a new union to replace the defunct Germanic Confederation. After the rulers had consented, a convention elected by universal manhood suffrage approved the constitution of the alliance, and the King of Prussia became president of the newly formed "North German Confederation." This federal state was created with a popular chamber (the *Reichstag*) to represent the people, and an upper chamber (the *Bundesrat*) to represent the princes. Bismarck had been careful to leave the component states the illusion of independence and individuality, but the really vital matters, such as the direction of the military forces and the conduct of foreign affairs, had passed under the control of Prussia. Through his dynastic prestige, and his authority as president of the Confederation, the Prussian king could dominate the *Bundesrat*, for of its forty-three members seventeen were Prussian

North German Confederation

delegates and a sufficient number of the others subservient to his wishes to assure Prussia a majority control.

7. OPPOSITION OF FRANCE TO GERMAN UNIFICATION

Throughout the decade 1860–70, while he was laboring to prepare the way for the unification of the Germanies, Bismarck had constantly to be on his guard against the possible intervention of France. Since the time of Richelieu, French statesmen had encouraged the existing disunion in the Germanies by playing one state there against another, for the creation of a powerful and unified empire across the Rhine was likely to prove a disadvantage and a danger to France.

The spectacular rise of Prussian power and prestige under Bismarck's guidance filled many Frenchmen with alarm, and they blamed the government of Napoleon III for failing, either to prevent it, or to secure reciprocal compensations. Unfortunately, Napoleon's efforts to delay German unification brought him no advantage and even hastened the result which he desired to postpone. The Prussian victory over Austria in 1866 took him and many other European statesmen by surprise, but he hoped to derive one advantage from the Treaty of Prague, for it left the four South German States (Bavaria, Württemberg, Baden, and Hesse-Darmstadt) independent, and he believed he could make them allies of France. But Bismarck impressed upon the rulers of these states the dangers of isolation, showed them proofs of Napoleon's desire for German territory, and persuaded them to sign secret military treaties with Prussia (1867). At the same time they joined their commercial interests with those of the North German Confederation in a common *Zollverein* or customs union. Economically, therefore, Germany might be considered one empire after 1867, although distrust of the autocratic Prussian methods kept the South German States politically sundered for four years longer.

The diplomatic reverse which Napoleon thus suffered in the Germanies came at a time when his régime was growing more and more unpopular in France. The liberals had never forgiven his seizure of power, and his efforts after 1860 to reconcile their opposition by transforming an autocratic into a "liberal" empire failed to appease them. More than ever he felt the need of doing something truly Napoleonic.

The Polish insurrection of 1863 afforded him one chance, for French liberals and clericals sympathized with the desire of the Poles to liberate their fatherland, but Napoleon hesitated to offend Russia, Austria, and Prussia, all of which held fragments of Poland. Instead, he dispatched an expeditionary force to Mexico, where disturbed conditions provided the great powers with an excuse to intervene. Largely under French protection a Mexican Empire was set up (1863) and the Archduke Maximilian, brother of the Emperor Francis Joseph of Austria, accepted the crown. Napoleon hoped in this way to make Austria his ally, to conciliate Catholic sentiment by protecting church property in Mexico which the revolutionists threatened to confiscate, and to secure commercial benefits for France. The American government regarded the presence of a European army in Mexico as a violation of the Monroe Doctrine,[1] but could make no effective protest until the war between the States was concluded in 1865. Then, rather than risk the possibility of war with the veteran Union forces, fresh from their victory over the Confederate States, Napoleon withdrew his troops from Mexico, and Maximilian, who remained behind, was captured and shot by the revolutionaries. Instead of the brilliant *coup* which he had projected, Napoleon had precipitated a tragic fiasco.

In Europe, Napoleon's diplomacy proved equally disappointing after 1867. The possibility of a clash with Prussia made it at least advisable that France should come to a friendly understanding with one of the other powers, but despite negotiations nothing was achieved. The Italians would not join France so long as a French contingent remained at Rome, especially as this French garrison defeated an attempt of Italian patriots under Garibaldi to seize the Eternal City (1867). Between France and Russia

[1] See pages 696 and 891.

the question of Poland remained a source of friction which discouraged attempts at a friendlier co-operation. Austria remained as a possible ally, and should have proved a likely one, for Austria had suffered at the hands of the Prussians in 1866. Diplomatic overtures between Paris and Vienna dragged on from 1868 to 1869, but they resulted in nothing conclusive. Meanwhile, Napoleon's difficulties at home were increasing. In 1870 he offered further concessions by enlarging the powers of the Chamber of Deputies, but far from being satisfied, the liberals and republicans increased their criticism. Several of his closest advisers, ultra-imperialists who feared for the safety of his dynasty, urged him to do something forceful to retrieve his waning prestige, preferably some clever diplomatic stroke which would humiliate Prussia. The summer of 1870 brought the opportunity for such a stroke.

8. THE FRANCO-PRUSSIAN WAR

A revolution having driven Isabella II from Spain in 1868, the Spanish people decided, after two years of confusion, to offer the throne to a German prince, Leopold of Hohenzollern-Sigmaringen. Fearing the possibility of an alliance between Prussia and Spain if a relative of the Prussian king should don the crown at Madrid, the French government entered a protest. The news that the young prince, unable to secure his father's approval, had declined the honor, eased the tension, and should have satisfied the French, as it afforded them a tacit victory. But the ultra-imperialists who surrounded Napoleon III wanted to humiliate Prussia in some more signal fashion. They persuaded him to ask an assurance from bluff old William I that he would promise never to authorize the candidature of his kinsman at any future time should the Spanish offer ever be renewed. This unwise action played directly into Bismarck's hands.

The Spanish question

For behind the scenes Bismarck had been deliberately working for war. He knew that a struggle with France would consolidate the German nation and forge the bonds of a political union as nothing else could do, but it was essential for his plan that France appear the aggressor. He had privately encouraged the Spanish offer of a throne in order to alarm the French, and the news that Leopold of Hohenzollern had declined it (July 12) filled him with gloom because it wrecked his plans. Then the French envoy, Benedetti, sought William I at Ems, where the Prussian king was resting, and pressed the French demands for further assurances so insistently that William dismissed him with some abruptness. To Bismarck at Berlin the king dispatched a telegram recounting the incident (July 13), and in this Ems dispatch Bismarck saw his opportunity to retrieve his hopes. He condensed and published the telegram in curt phrases which persuaded the French that their ambassador had been repulsed, while patriotic Prussians were convinced that their venerable king had been insulted.

The Ems dispatch

Napoleon III did not want war, but he allowed himself to be pushed into it by the ultra-imperialists. Seemingly the advantage in the approaching conflict lay with France; actually the French had a doubtful cause (interference in a neighbor's affairs), an inferior army (courageous, but obsolete in tactics and equipment), and poor leaders (Napoleon III and his second-rate ministers and marshals). On July 15, 1870, the French prime minister, Émile Ollivier, announced the imminence of war to the Chamber of Deputies, and declared that the ministry accepted the prospect "with a light heart." Misled by incorrect information on the causes of the conflict, by jingoistic oratory, and by vague assurances of support from Austria or the South German States, the Chamber voted to declare war on Prussia (July 19) while the Parisian crowds cheered and shouted "On to Berlin."

The conflict which had been accepted "with a light heart" led France within six weeks to the *débâcle* of Sedan, where Napoleon III[1] was forced to surrender with 86,000 men (September 2, 1870). On October 27, General Bazaine handed over a sec-

---

[1] Napoleon III, released by the Germans in 1871, joined his wife and son who had escaped to England. He died there in 1873. Six years later his heir, the prince imperial, was killed while fighting with the British in Zululand.

OTTO VON BISMARCK (1815–1898)

In this portrait can be read the strong will, keen mind, and realistic outlook which distinguished the "Iron Chancellor."

PROCLAMATION OF THE GERMAN EMPIRE

Below: While the guns of Paris a few miles away were firing their last despairing volleys, his fellow princes proclaimed William I of Prussia German Emperor. The historic scene occurred in the Versailles palace of Louis XIV, January 18, 1871.

ond French army of 175,000 men which the Prussians had shut up in Metz. In Paris, where the régime of Napoleon III had been overthrown two days after Sedan, the newly proclaimed "Government of National Defense" prepared the city to resist an inevitable siege, but starvation forced the Parisians to surrender, January 28, 1871. The newborn republic had fought desperately for five months against the forces which had destroyed the empire in five weeks, but further opposition would only have prolonged a hopeless war.

A French National Assembly, convoked at Bordeaux, elected Adolphe Thiers "Head of the Executive Power" and authorized him to negotiate for a peace settlement. By the Treaty of Frankfort, May 10, 1871, France surrendered the provinces of Alsace and Lorraine to Germany and agreed to pay an indemnity of five billion francs (about one billion dollars). The Germans were to occupy French key fortresses until the last of the indemnity had been paid.

Treaty of Frankfort

It was not with Prussia but with a united German Empire that France concluded peace. The South German States had joined the North German Confederation in the struggle with the hereditary foe, and the common patriotic effort, as Bismarck had predicted, forged the bonds of union. In the Hall of Mirrors at Louis XIV's stately Versailles palace the German princes hailed William I as "German Emperor" (January 18, 1871) while the guns of Paris ten miles away were firing their last despairing volleys. After long delays and multiple discouragements, after peaceful projects had fallen through and liberal hopes miscarried, German unity had been finally sealed in the midst of war and under the direction of the conservative and autocratic Bismarck.

German Empire (1871)

Thus the Franco-Prussian War made Germany an empire and France a republic. Nor did this complete the changes of the historic year 1870–71. The withdrawal of French troops from Rome for service against Prussia made it possible for the Italians to occupy the Eternal City and complete the Kingdom of Italy by the acquisition of its predestined capital.[1] The entrance of Italy and Germany into the circle of great powers profoundly altered the pattern of European politics, and made it difficult for France to attempt again the rôle of *la grande nation*, interfering constantly in the affairs of her weak and divided neighbors across the Rhine and the Alps. Henceforth, until the World War, five first-class powers, France, Germany, Italy, Austria, and Russia, were to strain against each other in the narrow confines of Europe while Great Britain looked on and sought to preserve a balance of power among them for her own security.

The most significant development in the troubled years between 1848 and 1870 had been this triumph of nationalism. All the major conflicts of the period — the Italian and Hungarian revolts of 1848–49, the Polish insurrection of 1863, the Crimean War which grew in part from the Balkan ferment, the War of 1859 for Italian liberation, the Danish War of 1864, the Austro-Prussian War of 1866, and the Franco-Prussian War of 1870–71 — are traceable to the pressure of this movement for national consolidation. After 1871 the more powerful and legitimate national aspirations had been satisfied, the Germans and Italians had achieved unity and the Hungarians had been quieted by the Compromise of 1867. That a considerable measure of solidity had been attained is attested by the fact that the conflicts which had disturbed Europe on the average of one every three years from 1848 to 1870 are remarkable for their scarcity after the latter date. The remaining decades of the nineteenth century form the most peaceful period that Europe has enjoyed in modern times, although beneath the calm new antagonisms were deepening and frustrated national emotions gathering force, especially in the Balkans. The year 1870 is, therefore, an important date to remember, like 1815 or 1789, because: (1) it closed a broken period marked by frequent conflicts; (2) it signalized the establishment of a new relationship among the great powers; and (3) it opened a forty-three-year period of comparative peace, of great scientific progress, and of growing imperialistic tendencies.

[1] See above, page 740.

56

Russia in the Nineteenth Century

> The Russian government of this period is the most monstrous abstraction.
> ... The government exists for the sake of the government, the people for
> the sake of the state ... material force in place of an ideal, material power in
> place of authority.
>
> ALEXANDER HERZEN (1812–70).

IN THE NINETEENTH CENTURY as in the eighteenth the impressive expansion of the Russian Empire alarmed and disconcerted the other European powers. The costly victories achieved by France and Britain in the Crimean War (1854–56) checked the Muscovite ambitions in the West temporarily, and preserved Turkey from dismemberment, but Russian imperialism continued its drive to the east and south. In the twenty years that followed the Peace of Paris (1856), Russia gained the coastland opposite Japan and subjugated Turkestan.[1] This Asiatic territory, acquired in two decades, exceeded in area all the annexations that the Russians had won in Europe in two centuries. Clearly, the settled and civilized European states could withstand the Russian encroachments much more successfully than the backward and disorganized peoples of Asia.

1. THE AFTERMATH OF THE CRIMEAN WAR

Russia is a bridge between Europe and Asia, not only in a geographical sense, but in a cultural, historical, and military sense also. The Crimean War had demonstrated that the fighting forces of France and Britain surpassed the Russian armies in training, organization, and equipment as greatly as the Russians in their turn surpassed the Chinese. Throughout the czar's empire the blunders and defeats of the war produced a mood of disillusionment and discontent. The Russian army had been an object of special pride to Nicholas I (1825–55) and his last days were darkened by the reverses which it suffered on the Crimean Peninsula. These reverses could not be attributed to lack of manpower or of resources, for Russia possessed both in abundance. The common soldiers had fought stubbornly and bravely; but the collapse of the commissariat service, the breakdown of transport facilities, and the graft and corruption among high officials nullified the sacrifices of the rank and file. The war revealed defects in the Nicholas System which could not be covered up, and the army, the favorite instrument of the autocrat, lost much of the prestige which it had enjoyed since the struggle with Napoleon half a century earlier.

The spreading discontent encouraged the new czar, Alexander II (1855–81), to inaugurate an era of reforms. Autocracy, orthodoxy, and nationalism remained the watchwords, but Alexander proposed, within limits, to bring Russian institutions into closer harmony with the progressive and humanitarian spirit of the nineteenth century. He lacked his father's military firmness and had little experience in administrative tasks, but he was patient, cautious, and kind-hearted. People recalled how his uncle, Alexander I, had planned half a century earlier to play

Character of Alexander II

[1] See map on page 813.

the part of a reforming czar, but had gradually abandoned the ideal. Alexander II possessed a less ardent zeal but a firmer purpose, and he was destined to carry through an administrative revolution before he, too, wearied of the mounting difficulties and relapsed into conservatism.

2. THE EMANCIPATION OF THE SERFS

Alexander's greatest single achievement was his emancipation of some forty million Russian serfs, a deed which won him the title of the "Czar Liberator." To visit a rural Russian community in the earlier nineteenth century was like stepping back into the Middle Ages. Nine tenths of the land was held by something less than one hundred thousand noble families. The serfs, attached to the soil, could be sold with the estates to new landlords, conscripted into the nobleman's household to work as domestic servants, or even sent to the factories in the towns for their master's profit. Though some nobles exercised their authority in a kindly and paternal fashion, others overworked their serfs, flogged them cruelly for slight faults, and interfered insolently in their private affairs and family relations. A serf could not marry without his master's consent, could not leave the estate without permission, and might be pursued, brought back, and punished if he sought to escape. He lived at the mercy of his master's caprice.

Serfdom in Russia

This iniquitous and archaic system of human bondage was rightly resented by intelligent Russians as a stigma upon their civilization. As the landlords declined to modify the system voluntarily, Alexander II took the initiative, and after careful consideration he issued a *ukase* abolishing serfdom in 1861. Supplemented by further decrees in 1863 and 1866, this proclamation transformed the serfs into free citizens, and permitted them to retain their cottages, tools, and sufficient land for them to maintain themselves by their common efforts. The aristocrats ceded part of their estates to the peasant *mir* or community village, and for this sacrifice the government promised compensation. They also received some financial reimbursement for the loss of peasant dues and personal services, but instead of evincing gratitude for this settlement many nobles complained that they had been unjustly impoverished.

The peasants were dissatisfied also, but with greater reason. The land apportioned to the *mir* proved often an infertile tract, and the allotments inadequate. They discovered, moreover, that far from obtaining freedom they had in reality become serfs of the state, for the government expected them to pay off by a special "redemption" tax the enormous sums expended to reimburse the landlords. This meant in application that a serf was to purchase his land and liberty by annual payments extending over a period of forty-nine years. Many peasants found it difficult to believe that the "Little Father," as the czar was affectionately named, really intended to burden his children so heavily after treating the aristocrats so generously. It seems doubtful, however, if Alexander had it in his power to execute a fairer settlement. Despite the complaints of the landlords and the bitterness of the liberated serfs, the benefits of emancipation soon showed themselves in the form of larger crops, increased areas under cultivation, better living conditions for the peasants, and a rise in trade. The freeing of the serfs was without question the most important event in Russian history during the nineteenth century.

Emancipation terms

3. OTHER REFORMS OF ALEXANDER II

The emancipation edict had stripped the landlords of much of their judicial and paternalistic responsibility and had created many millions of new citizens. It appeared wise, therefore, to the czar and his advisers, to train the people in self-government by creating provincial and district assemblies, or *zemstvos*, composed of delegates representing the landlords, the townsfolk, and the peasants. Each *zemstvo* was to be a sort of local parliament, entrusted with the responsibility for maintaining the roads, schools, churches, and jails of the district. It had authority to levy taxes for local purposes and to relegate the execution of its decrees to a permanent committee. Admirable in theory, the *zem-*

The zemstvos

RUSSIAN LANDLORDS GAMBLING AWAY THEIR SERFS

This grim caricature shows Russian gentlemen of the nineteenth century gambling with bundles of serfs for counters. The serfs or "souls" changed ownership with the land.

A RUSSIAN VILLAGE IN THE NINETEENTH CENTURY

Russian village life remained agrarian and medieval by western European standards until the revolutionary changes of the twentieth century.

stvos proved a disappointment in practice. The members too often lacked political training, and the imperial officials, wedded to the methods of a centralized bureaucracy, distrusted and overruled the provincial legislators. Alexander recognized the defects in the system, but he hoped it would improve with time.

In all his attempted reforms, the czar found himself gravely handicapped by a lack of honest and experienced officials. This difficulty proved acute when he sought to reorganize the law courts. In place of the secret and arbitrary methods of the bureaucrats, he decreed (1862) a court system modeled on that of the western nations, with local justices of the peace, district tribunals, and a high court of final appeal. Criminals won the privilege of trial by jury and the proceedings in civil and criminal cases were opened to the public. Despite these improvements, the ignorance of the Russian masses left them still confused at the working of laws intended to guarantee their rights, and the ineradicable corruption and graft of the old legal system persisted and poisoned the new. Moreover, Alexander himself failed to make the new order either consistent or universal, for he preserved the infamous "Third Section" and the secret police tribunals organized by his father to punish political offenders. The Czar Liberator was like an architect who installs more spacious windows and widens the corridors in the upper floors of a feudal castle, while leaving unchanged the submerged dungeons with their dark secrets and instruments of torture.

Judicial reforms

While his zeal lasted, Alexander also sketched the plan for a system of public instruction, with primary schools, secondary schools, and colleges, supported and supervised by the state. He relaxed the strict censorship of the press, permitted Russians to travel abroad freely, and treated the Jews and other minority races in the empire with greater consideration and leniency than his father had shown. But the chorus of criticism which greeted his endeavors daunted and discouraged him. The conservatives denounced his policies as dangerously radical, the liberal intellectuals called them nervelessly moderate, while the peasants resisted all innovations with pious apathy. The fatalism that permeated the lower orders is reflected in the reply of an old *muzhik* who was urged to boil his drinking water because of the cholera epidemic. "If God wished us to drink hot water," he responded, "He would have heated the Neva." The indifference and the active opposition which he encountered checked Alexander's reforming efforts after 1865, although he still maintained a pretense of enthusiasm. But his liberalism had been more largely the fruit of expediency than of conviction and the mood had passed.

4. THE REACTION IN THE LATER YEARS OF ALEXANDER II

Undoubtedly one factor which turned Alexander II toward reaction was the Polish uprising of 1863. Stirred by the spread of liberal ideas and by their invincible dream of national independence, Polish patriots organized a revolt, but were defeated by the superior Russian forces. Determined to destroy this troublesome Polish nationalism once and for all, the Russian government executed or exiled the leaders of the revolt and sequestered their lands. Russian became the official language, and the Catholic Church in Poland was weakened by the loss of much of its land and the suppression of monasteries. From this harsh treatment one benefit resulted to the stricken people, for the confiscated lands were distributed among the peasantry, and Alexander remitted the feudal obligations in order to punish the disaffected ruling classes while securing the loyalty, or at least the gratitude, of the tenants and serfs.

Polish uprising (1863)

An attempt to assassinate him, made by a fanatic in 1866, dispelled Alexander's last liberal sympathies. Convinced finally that in tampering with the Nicholas System he had opened the door to anarchy, the czar turned his back on reform. Thenceforth the *zemstvos*, the law courts, the journals, and the schools found their privileges steadily curtailed; vigilant police spies circulated once more among all ranks of society; and teachers, writers, and others who had hailed the reform era too eagerly felt again the chill breath of imperial disfavor. Even the great novelist and philosopher, Count Leo Tolstoy (1828–1910), confessed that he felt surprise each morning on awakening to find that he was not on the road to exile in Siberia.

A considerable group of Russians, known as Slavophiles, or Nationalists, applauded the czar's resumption of the traditional policy of autocracy, orthodoxy, and nationalism. The Slavophiles held that Russia was a unique country, with customs, beliefs, and institutions peculiar to itself. To adopt the dress, the manners, the legal and political ideals of the western European states appeared disloyal to these ardent nationalists, whose dislike of the "westernizers" and their servile imitation of European culture dated from the days when Peter the Great had opened his "windows to the west." The innovations introduced by Alexander II, such as trial by jury and representative *zemstvos*, they were inclined to disdain as foreign importations, and when these reforms failed to work smoothly, when the Poles broke into revolt, and anarchists multiplied, they laid the responsibility upon the czar's liberal experiments instead of blaming the evils which those experiments were designed to cure. The Slavophiles themselves had little to offer in the way of a constructive program. Their ideals were for the most part vague and negative, but they had a strong following, for their insistence upon preserving the integrity of Holy Russia appealed alike to the reactionaries, the nationalists, the orthodox clergy, and the inertly conservative masses.

The Slavophiles

Placed upon the defensive, the "westernizers" tried to argue that the late reforms had proved disappointing, not because they went too far, but because they did not go far enough. They besought Alexander to continue his liberal efforts, but they lacked any constitutional means of action aside from the crippled *zemstvos* and their petitions brought no response. Turning, therefore, from the government to the people, they planned to make war upon the dense ignorance and superstition of the masses, as the chief obstacles to progress. Hundreds of ardent young intellectuals dedicated themselves to the work of instructing the liberated serfs, hoping by daily contact and kindly example to inculcate a gospel of enlightenment. But they soon grew discouraged at this seemingly hopeless task. Crushed between the hostility of the government and the apathy of the peasants, the liberals faced a crisis which split their ranks. The more moderate continued to hope that improvements might be introduced slowly through the spread of education and administrative reforms, but the more radical, losing patience with such dilatory methods, began to advocate more direct and desperate remedies.

The "westernizers"

The "Father of Russian Liberalism" and a leading protagonist of constitutional reform had been Alexander Herzen (1812–70). From his points of exile in France and Germany, Herzen had done much to encourage the liberal experiments that marked the period 1855–65, for his pamphlets and journals, smuggled into Russia despite the censorship, were read by many high officials including the "Czar Liberator" himself. But with Alexander's conversion to a more cautious policy after 1865 and Herzen's death in 1870, the more moderate program of constitutional reform lost its appeal, especially for the younger radicals, and many of them embraced new and more violent modes of revolutionary activity.

Alexander Herzen

5. THE SPREAD OF ANARCHISM, NIHILISM, AND TERRORISM

This change of temper after 1870 is reflected in the activities of the anarchists, nihilists, and terrorists. The word "anarchism" was first popularized by the French writer Pierre Joseph Proudhon (1809–65), who, believing that all government based upon physical force was iniquitous, urged an ideal order of society in which men would live together in peace and liberty without governments, without a police force, and without compulsion of any kind. Proudhon's theories, which might have sufficed to govern a community of saints, appeared utterly impracticable for the guidance of a society in which

Anarchism

most individuals are constantly seeking to enrich themselves by exploiting others. Nevertheless, his argument that the institution of private property, protected by the law, the police, and the government, is part of an iniquitous system whereby a favored group of individuals monopolize the wealth and power to the exclusion of the rest, struck a responsive chord in the heart of a Russian noble, Michael Bakunin (1814–76). If Herzen was the father of Russian liberalism, Bakunin may be considered the father of Russian radicalism.

Born in 1814, Bakunin visited Germany and France as a young man, and joined in the revolutionary movement of 1848. Arrested in Dresden and transported to Russia, he was exiled to Siberia, but escaped in 1861, and wandered thenceforth from land to land preaching his fanatical brand of anarchism. His hand was lifted against everything which imposed upon or restrained the liberty of the individual, against the God of the theologians, against marriage, and against the state. Kindly and simple in manner, Bakunin yet felt himself dedicated to a career of universal destruction and revolt, urged on by his pity for suffering humanity which he saw as crushed beneath the tyranny of existing institutions. That government, while it benefited some members of society more perhaps than others, might none the less be indispensable for the protection of all, he could not see, and in countries such as Russia, where the evils of despotism were more apparent than the advantages provided by the administration, his doctrines won many converts among the radical thinkers.

Michael Bakunin

The intelligent and educated minority among the Russian population tended to form, in the later nineteenth century, a curiously rootless, irreverent, and unconventional group. Isolated from the masses of peasants, denied participation in practical political affairs, the Russian intelligentsia indulged themselves in the pastime of criticizing existing conditions. Because they found little to commend in society, they repudiated government, religion, the sanctity of tradition, and the veneration usually accorded to that which is old. This iconoclastic attitude of mind, particularly admired among the younger members of the educated classes, came to be termed "nihilism," a nihilist being one who bowed before no authority without weighing its virtue, and accepted nothing on faith. The nihilists vented their disgust and ennui in passionate and pessimistic debates, arguing interminably and inconclusively upon the meaning of life, the purpose of government, and the tenets of religion. Most of them were harmless eccentrics, content to discuss philosophical dilemmas or invent theoretical projects, but a few, more ruthless and determined in their convictions, sought to compel reform by direct means. These swelled the group of the so-called terrorists.

Nihilism

The terrorists were apostles of action who believed that no orderly or legal cure could be found for the evils of the czarist régime. The government, irresponsible and autocratic, had failed to curb its own abuses, and stubbornly refused to let the Russian people institute reforms through a representative parliament responsive to their wishes. The only method which remained, the terrorist held, was to frighten the czar and his ministers into making reforms by a deliberate policy of violence and assassination. Secret revolutionary groups, working with extraordinary patience and cunning, plotted one assassination after another, despite the incessant activity of the police. In 1879 an attempt was made to blow up the czar's train; and shortly thereafter an explosion shattered part of the Winter Palace. Alexander II was no coward, and he insisted that these revolutionaries must be crushed; but he decided at the same time to satisfy some of the popular demands by drafting important reforms. Before the program could be completed, however, he fell a victim to a terrorist bomb (1881).

The terrorists

6. ALEXANDER III AND THE POLICY OF RUSSIFICATION

This drastic effort to temper despotism by assassination proved a failure. The revolutionaries gained no advantage from the violent death of the Czar Liberator, for his son and successor, Alexander III, showed himself a

Autocracy preserved

THE FIRST AND LAST ROMANOV

Above: The first Romanov czar, Michael, began his reign in 1613. In 1913, the Russian mint struck this medal to celebrate the 300th anniversary. Five years later, the execution of Nicholas II ended the dynasty.

ALEXANDER II OF RUSSIA (1818–1881)

Left: Some admirers of Alexander II professed to read in his haunted glance the tragedy of a ruler who was foredoomed to die by a terrorist bomb. His enemies declared that his fishlike eyes proclaimed the callous autocrat.

CONFERENCE ENDING THE RUSSO-JAPANESE WAR OF 1904–1905

Envoys of Russia and Japan, meeting through the mediation of the United States at Portsmouth, New Hampshire, ended the Russo-Japanese War on September 5, 1905.

strong-willed despot who promptly announced his intention to avenge his father's murder and to preserve the autocratic régime. In Constantine Pobiedonostsev (1827–1907) and Venceslas de Plehve (1846–1904) he found subordinates ready and willing to carry out this policy. Pobiedonostsev, as "Procurator of the Holy Synod," directed the affairs of the Russian Orthodox Church. He had rationalized his distrust of parliaments, popular education, and the press into a veritable philosophy of reaction, and he exerted a compelling influence over the mind of the new czar. For the more practical task of running conspirators to earth, Alexander III relied upon Plehve, who directed the state police with such ruthless efficiency that for several years revolutionary activity all but ceased.

Like most despots, Alexander III was disposed to favor a high degree of uniformity throughout his empire. This was the more difficult to attain because the advance of the Russian frontier had brought millions of alien people under the rule of the czar, until the minorities actually exceeded the real Russians of Great Russia in number. Alexander's ambition to promote cultural, linguistic, and religious unity pleased ardent pan-Slavists and "Russifiers," but it antagonized the Poles, Finns, Jews, and other racial minorities. The Poles, since their abortive revolt of 1863, had suffered bitterly under the policy of coercion designed to make better Russians of them. The Finns, Lutheran in religion and jealous of their vestiges of independence, suffered the same encroaching pressure until Nicholas II curtailed their constitution in 1899. But the most defenseless victims of this program of Russification were the Jews, for although they numbered over five millions, they were scattered throughout western Russia, possessed no one locality which they could call their own, and were subjected to periodic *pogroms*, or murderous persecutions, which were permitted, if not actually instigated, by the imperial authorities.

Russification

Naturally these abused minorities furnished numerous volunteers for the revolutionary cause. Had all the discontented factions in Russia discovered a formula upon which they could unite, the autocracy would not long have survived their onslaught. But the revolutionists were swayed by divergent ideals and interests. The peasants, constituting a majority of the Russian population, were primarily interested in the land question, and their hopes rested with the Socialist Revolutionaries or "S–R" Party. To destroy czardom, seize the landed estates of the aristocrats, and award a free farm to each peasant family was the S–R program, a program which any peasant could understand and support. The S–R leaders hoped to substitute a free association of communes for the existing bureaucratic tyranny, they accepted violence and assassination as a means of hastening this end, and they counted upon the assistance of the dissatisfied bourgeoisie and the workingmen of the towns in their war against autocracy.

The "S–R" Party

The workingmen of the towns, however, were formulating a revolutionary program of their own. Industrialism spread rapidly in Russia in the late nineteenth century, especially after 1890, and the construction of factories and railways brought trade unions, strikes, and the recurrent clashes between capital and labor which were already common in western Europe. The pan-Slavists opposed the new industrialism as a western importation, but it spread prodigiously under the direction of Sergei de Witte (1849–1915), who was minister of finance from 1893 to 1903. Witte favored a protective tariff for the benefit of the manufacturers and social legislation for the benefit of the workers, hoping thereby to keep both classes contented. But the growing ferment, the strikes, and the spread of Marxian socialism among the new proletarian classes greatly alarmed the reactionaries, as well it might, and Witte was forced to resign in 1903.

Industrialism in Russia

Witte's downfall could not check the spread of the Industrial Revolution, which, for good or ill, had struck Russia with its transforming magic. A new revolutionary class had emerged, a Russian workers' party, nursed on socialist doctrines, and more dangerous, more defiantly radical than the Socialists of

The Social Democrats

France or Germany. Organized as the "Social Democrats" the Russian workingmen prepared the way for the destruction of the czarist régime by means of strikes, propaganda, and mass action. They had little use for independent acts of terrorism and assassination, and they expected little help from the peasants. To these industrial proletarians the coming revolution was to be their revolution.

7. NICHOLAS II AND THE REVOLUTION OF 1905

Alexander III was succeeded by his son Nicholas II in 1894. Nicholas was an amiable man, but narrow in his outlook and his sympathies, intermittently stubborn without perseverance, despotic in principle yet weak in will. Like Louis XVI of France, he inherited a revolution and was destined to pay with his life for the mistakes of his ancestors as well as for his own. Although his father's policy of reaction and Russification had created mounting opposition, Nicholas made no concessions. He retained Pobiedonostsev in office and multiplied the powers of the hated pan-Slavist, Plehve, until the latter's assassination in 1904.

Nicholas II (1894–1917)

The Russo-Japanese War (1904–05), a consequence of the pan-Slavists' ambition to enlarge the Russian foothold on the Pacific Ocean, brought rude disasters which the rotten imperial system was ill-suited to endure. As one defeat followed another, and evidence of corruption and inefficiency in high official circles came to light, a ferment of complaint, criticism, and disorder swept the empire. Assassinations multiplied, armed revolt broke out in Poland, and in Saint Petersburg a procession of petitioners led by a priest, Gapon, was fired upon by the soldiers. Revolution threatened to engulf the imperial régime and Nicholas II agreed reluctantly to offer concessions. He proclaimed religious toleration for minority sects, cancelled the arrears which many peasants still owed for their communal lands, removed unpopular officials, and promised (June, 1905) to establish a Russian parliament. This promise he reaffirmed four months later in his "October Manifesto," which guaranteed popular liberties, a limited suffrage, and responsible government under a bicameral legislature.

Revolution threatens

By 1906, the revolutionary wave had begun to ebb. The Social Democrats in the cities and the Socialist Revolutionaries in the country could not combine their efforts; many middle-class liberals were satisfied with the October Manifesto (and were consequently known as "Octobrists"), while others (termed the Constitutional Democrats, or Cadets), wished to press on toward a genuinely democratic government. The reactionary classes, disconcerted in 1905, began to rally their forces, and, feeling confident that the threat of revolution was waning, they urged Nicholas to withdraw his promises.

The reaction in 1906

Under these circumstances it is not surprising that the first Russian Parliament, or Duma, which assembled in May, 1906, found itself powerless to control the czar's ministers. When the representatives of the empire demanded a responsible ministry, the Duma was dissolved by imperial decree. The Cadets, the most defiant group among the deputies, attempted to reassemble at Viborg in Finland, and appealed in vain to the Russian people to support their stand. A second Duma was summoned to meet in March, 1907, but when it showed the same independent spirit, it likewise was promptly dissolved. Nicholas now determined to revise the electoral system in such a way that the more radical elements were curbed or disenfranchised. The third Duma, in which the moderates and conservatives predominated, proved more conciliatory and was permitted to sit until 1912. But its rôle had been reduced from that of a legislature to the feeble dignity of an advisory or consultative body, and the Russian government continued to justify Herzen's indictment that it was "material force in place of an ideal, material power in place of authority."

Two Dumas dissolved

In 1906, Nicholas chose as his prime minister an able compromiser, Peter Stolypin (1863–1911). Stolypin was a man of firm character who dealt vigorously with political offenders, but he sought at the same time to render the gov-

Peter Stolypin

ernment more popular by improving the lot of the peasants and workingmen. After 1908, revolutionary agitation slowly subsided, acts of violence grew less frequent, police reprisals less severe, but this did not prevent Stolypin himself falling victim to an assassin in 1911. This act, however, did not disturb the comparative tranquillity of the empire.

In 1912, a fourth Duma was elected and evinced the same moderate disposition as its predecessor in compromising with authority. The activities of the pan-Slavists continued to alarm the national minorities, but one pan-Slav project, the enlargement and reorgani-

The fourth Duma (1912)

zation of the Russian army, was approved by the Duma because of the growing tension in Europe between the Triple Alliance and the Triple *Entente*. Russia had achieved a momentary balance between the forces of liberalism and despotism. It remained to be seen whether, under wise statesmanship, the empire would advance peacefully along the constitutional path, or whether a new crisis would precipitate a second revolution more radical, more sanguinary, and more destructive than the inconclusive effort of 1905. The hope for peaceful evolution faded when World War I opened in 1914, for war conditions halted all reforms. The result may be read in Chapter 66.

57

The Lesser States of Europe in the Nineteenth Century

> ...We know of no reason in the nature of things why a state should be any the better for being large....
>
> SIR JOHN R. SEELEY, *THE EXPANSION OF ENGLAND*.[1]

IN THE DRAMA of modern European history the great powers have tended more and more to usurp the center of the stage and to dwarf and obscure the significance of the secondary states. The peoples of the smaller countries justly resent this subordination, but a textbook which attempted to assign equal space to the history of France and Finland, or Britain and Belgium, in the nineteenth century, would develop abnormal and confusing proportions. Of the ten or more states discussed in the present chapter, several played dominant rôles in earlier centuries, but none has exerted a decisive influence in the last hundred years. For this reason their more recent annals, though intensely interesting in themselves, have been severely and perhaps unjustifiably compressed.

1. THE SCANDINAVIAN COUNTRIES

Sweden

The prominent part which Sweden played in European affairs during the seventeenth century came to an end with the Great Northern War of 1700–21.[2] Deprived of its hegemony in the Baltic, the kingdom declined into more peaceful days and economic decadence. The turmoil of the Napoleonic struggles, which left no part of Europe unstirred, drew Sweden into the later coalitions against France, and despite the fact that the Swedish campaigns were largely defensive the Congress of Vienna united Norway to Sweden as a reward (1814). On the death of Charles XIII (1809–18) without heirs, the Swedish throne passed to his adopted successor, the French general Bernadotte, as Charles XIV (1818–44). The Bernadotte dynasty still reigns in the northern kingdom.

Long a people of aristocratic traditions, the Swedes continued in the nineteenth century to accept the dominance of the great landowners and (with the development of mining and manufacturing activities) of the great industrialists. A constitution promulgated in 1863 did little to break this oligarchic rule, and the consequent discontent of the lower classes promoted the growth of socialism and helps to account for the phenomenal emigration. Over a million Swedes left their homeland between 1850 and 1900, the great majority of them settling in the United States.

Norway

The neighboring kingdom of Norway, united to the Danish crown from 1397 to 1814, was ceded in the latter year to Sweden. By approving this decision the diplomats at the Congress of Vienna hoped to console the Swedes for

[1] The Macmillan Company.
[2] See above, pages 569–570.

the loss of Finland (seized by Russia in 1808) and at the same time to punish the Danes for aiding Napoleon. This forced political union of Norway and Sweden left the Norwegians full control of their domestic affairs, but it irked this hardy and freedom-loving people none the less, for they cherished their distinctive speech and traditions. In 1905 the Norwegian Parliament, or *Storthing*, voted for complete independence and the people confirmed this decision by a plebiscite. The Swedish king, Oscar II, gave reluctant consent to the separation, and a Danish prince mounted the Norwegian throne as Haakon VII. Further democratic amendments to the constitution abolished the royal veto and permitted women to vote on the same terms as men (1913), Norway thus becoming the first state in Europe to accord women this right. Like Sweden, Norway has suffered heavy losses through emigration. The population at the opening of the twentieth century was less than two and one half million; but the Norwegians ranked fourth among the nations of the world in the tonnage of their merchant marine.

Denmark

The Danes, in their small seagirt kingdom of peninsulas and islands, endured two attacks by the British fleet (1801 and 1807) during the Napoleonic Wars, because they had been subordinated to French policy. The peace that followed brought a further injustice in the loss of Norway. In 1864, Austria and Prussia united to wrest the provinces of Schleswig and Holstein from the Danish monarch,[1] and the diminutive kingdom became the smallest of the Scandinavian states. Denmark retained, however, as tokens of those heroic centuries when Norse adventurers pushed their dragon-prowed vessels into unknown seas, the islands of Iceland and Greenland, forming a colonial empire fifty times the area of the Danish State, but sparsely populated with one hundred and twenty thousand settlers. In 1918, Iceland gained the status of a sovereign principality under the Danish king.

Farming, chiefly dairy farming, forms the principal source of wealth of the Danes, who export large quantities of butter, eggs, fodder, and animal products to England and Germany. The lack of mineral resources and of rivers suitable for providing hydroelectric power has retarded industrial development, but wood and textile manufactures are expanding. The campaign for political democracy, which made little headway in Denmark during the later nineteenth century largely because of the stubborn opposition of Christian IX (1863–1906), won a victory in the twentieth century with the

[1] See above, page 748.

OVERSEAS DEPENDENCIES OF THE NETHERLANDS, BELGIUM, DENMARK, AND NORWAY

SWEDISH CO-OPERATIVE ELECTRIC BULB FACTORY

This co-operative factory near Stockholm shows how successfully the Swedes have combined pleasant working conditions with industrial efficiency.

A HYDROELECTRIC STATION, SWITZERLAND

This station forms part of the huge Oberhasli hydroelectric development in the Bernese Oberland, Switzerland, and is operated by the water accumulated in the Grimsel Lake.

SOCIALIST DEMONSTRATION IN BRUSSELS

This wood-cut of 1886 shows a Socialist demonstration in Brussels when many middle-class people still confused Socialism with anarchism and violence.

extension of the franchise to all men and women of twenty-five or over who possess a fixed place of abode.

With their combined population of less than eleven million people, the three Scandinavian states could not play, or expect to play, a very ambitious rôle in the military, political, or economic affairs of nineteenth-century Europe. But if the material contributions of the Scandinavian peoples were modest, their intellectual influence was great. The foremost sculptor of the early nineteenth century, Albert Bertel Thorwaldsen (1770–1844), was a Dane, and Denmark could also boast of producing the greatest literary critic of his time in Georg Brandes (1842–1927). Still another Dane, Hans Christian Andersen (1805–75), made his name a household word in Europe and America by his exquisite fairy tales. The plays of the Norwegian, Henrik Ibsen (1828–1906), stirred widespread controversies by their unflinching diagnosis of social problems, and Norway also produced a world-renowned composer in Edvard Grieg (1843–1907). To list but one more name from many which might be included, the Swedish dramatist, August Strindberg (1849–1912), had no equal among his contemporaries in his capacity for bitter, pessimistic, and ironic characterization. The contribution which these men made to European culture is a fitting reflection of the high standards of intelligence and education prevalent among the Scandinavian nations.

Literature and art

2. HOLLAND, BELGIUM, AND SWITZERLAND

Endangered by the military might of France and the naval supremacy of Britain, Holland has invariably suffered when these two powers were at war. In the first years of the nineteenth century, Napoleon forced the Dutch into his Continental System, a step which afforded the British an excuse to deprive Holland of the Cape of Good Hope and Ceylon. But Dutch enterprise in the sixteenth and seventeenth centuries had built up an empire which still remains imposing despite such losses, and includes a native population (1931) of over seventy millions. It embraces Java, Sumatra, the Celebes, Dutch Borneo, and Dutch New Guinea in the East Indies, Curaçao and some lesser islands in the West Indies, and Dutch Guiana in South America. The immense volume of trade, both colonial and international, which flows in and out of northern Europe through the ports of Amsterdam and Rotterdam, lends the Kingdom of the Netherlands an economic importance out of proportion to its size (13,203 square miles) and population (9,048,529 in 1942).

Netherlands

The Congress of Vienna decreed in 1815 the junction of the Belgian provinces (previously the Austrian Netherlands) with Holland, thus forming the United Kingdom of the Netherlands under William I of the house of Orange. From this union the Belgians seceded in 1830. In 1848, the Dutch adopted a new constitution providing for a responsible ministry and a restricted suffrage, but the growth of democratic sentiment throughout Europe later led to cautious extensions of the franchise until today the electorate includes all men and women over twenty-five years of age. Fear of foreign aggression induced the Dutch to increase their naval and military forces considerably after 1890.

Upon proclaiming their independence of Holland (1830), the Belgians established a constitutional monarchy with a German prince, Leopold of Saxe-Coburg, as their first king. To protect the new state from the designs of more powerful neighbors, the leading nations of Europe, Great Britain, France, Austria, Prussia, and Russia, guaranteed the independence and neutrality of Belgium by solemn accord in 1839. The new kingdom was soon stirred by the quickening effects of the Industrial Revolution, with a consequent exploitation of its mineral resources, and a rise in population which has made it the most densely inhabited state in Europe (estimated population in 1944, 8,334,276). A liberal government, controlled after 1884 by the Catholic majority, promoted education, broadened the franchise, and improved the condition of the working classes through enlightened social legislation. In 1908, the immense Congo territory in Africa, which had been exploited largely through the business initia-

Belgium

tive of the astute Belgian monarch, Leopold II (1865–1909), and established as a free state under his sovereignty, was annexed to Belgium as a colony. Like the Dutch, the Belgians became increasingly apprehensive concerning their security in the tense years which preceded the outbreak of World War I in 1914 and followed the general trend in augmenting their armaments.

Until the middle of the nineteenth century, the Swiss Confederation was little more, politically, than a loose agglomeration of cantons, each practically autonomous. Their inhabitants were bound together by a common love of liberty and of republican institutions, but divided by differences in customs, language, and religion. In 1941, the population of Switzerland was estimated at 4,265,703 people, a majority of whom speak German, but French prevails in five of the twenty-two cantons and Italian in one, while some thousands of the country folk speak a Latin dialect known as Romansch. In addition to these linguistic barriers there are religious differences, for the Protestants predominate in twelve cantons and Roman Catholics in ten.

Switzerland

Yet, despite these racial and religious divergencies, the Swiss have found it possible in recent times to transform their loose association into a well-knit federal state. A constitution adopted in 1848 established an executive federal council and a bicameral legislature. Uniform coinage, tariffs, postal regulations, and law codes followed; and a federal militia, efficient but expensive, was created for national defense. Swiss citizens enjoy universal suffrage, manifest a lively interest in matters of cantonal and federal administration, and possess two novel constitutional prerogatives. They may, if they wish, demand a plebiscite on any important legislative measure (the referendum), or on any issue proposed and sponsored by fifty thousand voters (the initiative).

Farming, industry, and the tourist trade have combined to make Switzerland, with its four million inhabitants, one of the most prosperous states in Europe. The unrivaled Alpine scenery draws millions of visitors annually. Farming, particularly dairy farming, provides a living for almost one third of the Swiss people, while one half find employment in the manufacture of clocks, watches, silk articles, and other high-grade products. The plentiful water power supplied by the mountain torrents, a public utility controlled by the federal government, provides cheap electricity throughout the country, and permits the electrification of the greater part of the Swiss railway system, most of which is likewise state controlled.

3. SPAIN AND PORTUGAL

The history of Spain in the nineteenth century is largely a story of retarded economic development, maladministration, intrigue, and civil war. The secession of the South and Central American colonies [1] had deprived the Spanish government by 1820 of its major source of revenue, leaving it to stagger on as best it might under a burden of insolvency. As a considerable part of the Iberian Peninsula is a semi-arid plateau too infertile for easy cultivation, Spain lacked the agricultural wealth of France and has failed to develop an independent class of sturdy industrious peasant proprietors. Industry likewise, despite the existence of natural deposits of coal and iron, has made slow progress, for the Spaniards possessed little capital and less initiative. The devout and conservative temper of the masses, the widespread superstition and illiteracy, and the lack of modern facilities for internal communication have served to insulate Spanish society from the transforming effects of commerce and invention.

Spain

The strength of Spanish conservatism lay in the fact that it was a peculiar blend of patriotism and religious fervor. The rough attempts made by Napoleon to modernize Spanish institutions, after setting his brother Joseph on the throne (1808), intensified the national prejudice against liberalism as an alien and sacrilegious importation. Enlightened and enterprising Spaniards conceded the advantages of reform, but, in the absence of a powerful and progressive middle class, the reform movement drew its chief strength from the circle of the intellectuals

[1] See above, page 696.

THE PEACE PALACE AT THE HAGUE

Above: This impressive building recorded the unsuccessful effort of peace lovers to create machinery for international arbitration that would avert future wars.

ALFRED BERNHARD NOBEL (1833–1896)

Right: Alfred Nobel invented nitroglycerine and dynamite, but he is remembered better as the founder of the Nobel prizes for work in physics, science, chemistry, medicine, literature, and the cause of peace.

and the discontented army officers. These minority groups, while active enough to stir up occasional revolts and issue *pronunciamentos* (proclamations), could not awaken the masses from their lethargy. The enterprise of a firm and enlightened monarch might have turned the scale in favor of reform, but Spain has had few able or energetic rulers. The reign of the vindictive Ferdinand VII (1814–33) has been described already.[1] His decision to set aside the Salic law and transmit the throne to his daughter Isabella II (1833–68) led to the so-called Carlist Wars (1833–40), in which the supporters of Ferdinand's brother Charles contested the succession. Although Isabella finally made good her claim, her despotic rule and immoral life disgusted the Spanish nation and a revolutionary upheaval in 1868 drove her from the kingdom.

Between 1868 and 1875, Spain endured kaleidoscopic shifts as the Carlists, Liberal Monarchists, and Republicans battled for control. In 1870, the throne was offered to Prince Leopold of Hohenzollern-Sigmaringen, a move which excited a diplomatic crisis and precipitated the Franco-Prussian War.[2] Subsequently Prince Amadeo of Savoy, younger son of Victor Emmanuel II of Italy, was invited to become King of Spain, only to abdicate in discouragement three years later. Finally, in 1875, Alphonso XII (1875–85), son of the deposed Isabella, assumed the crown and restored peace to the distracted nation. With the aid of two remarkable statesmen, Marshal Martínez Campos and Antonio Cánovas del Castillo, Alphonso inaugurated a happier era under a moderately liberal constitution. Following his early death (1885), the throne passed to a posthumous son, Alphonso XIII, who was declared of age in 1902. In the interval the widow of Alphonso XII, Maria Cristina, acted as regent.

A stupid, tyrannical, and short-sighted colonial policy, which had already disrupted the once vast colonial empire of Spain, induced a stubborn revolt (1895–98) in the chief remaining dependency, the island of Cuba. With the intervention of the United States, Spain suffered a decisive defeat, and surrendered all title, not only to Cuba, but to Puerto Rico, and to the Philippine Islands and Guam in the Pacific, in return for twenty million dollars compensation. The loss of these last fragments of a shattered empire deeply wounded Spanish pride, and the nation entered the twentieth century with a heritage of defeat, impoverishment, and social unrest. Past colonial misfortunes, however, did not deter Alphonso XIII and the military chiefs

War of 1898

[1] See above, pages 695–696.
[2] See above, page 752.

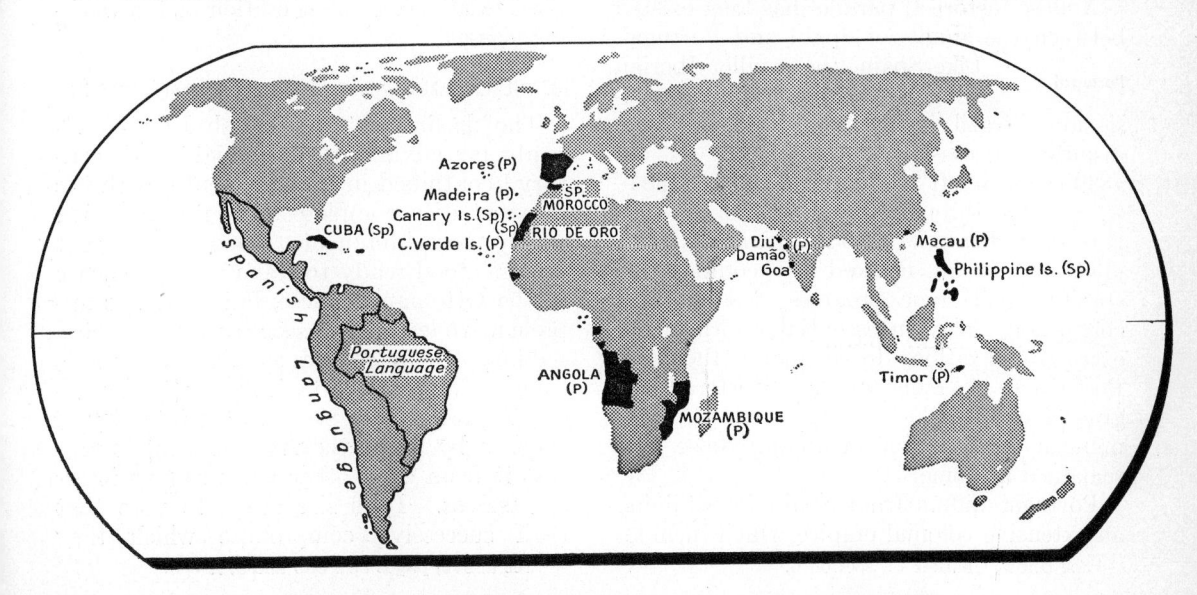

OVERSEAS DEPENDENCIES OF SPAIN AND PORTUGAL IN 1898

from embarking upon a campaign for the subjugation of the native tribes of Spanish Morocco, an essay in imperialism which brought expenses and defeats so ruinous that in 1923 revolution appeared imminent. For the moment it was averted by a *coup d'état* which established General Primo de Rivera as chief minister of the Spanish cabinet with dictatorial powers.

For eight years longer the amiable but extravagant Alphonso XIII clung to his shaking throne, but in 1931 the expected revolution broke out and the monarchy collapsed. A republican constitution, adopted December 9, provided for the confiscation of church property, suppression of religious instruction in the schools, and the expulsion of religious orders. The new government then attacked the land question, and plans were formulated for dividing the estates of the great landowners to provide farms for impoverished peasant families. But the attempt to push these reforms sharpened existing antagonisms, and in 1936 a group of army officers under General Francisco Franco organized a revolt against the republican government at Madrid. Germany and Italy supported Franco's "Nationalist" régime, Russia aided the cause of the "Leftists," and Spain was plunged into the agony of a pitiless and protracted civil war.[1]

<small>Revolution of 1931</small>

A close historical parallel has long existed between the annals of Spain and Portugal. Like Spain, the smaller Iberian Kingdom lost its American possessions (Brazil) in the 1820's, and suffered a disputed succession and civil war in the 1830's, which left a woman, Maria II (1834–53), on the throne. The reigns of Maria's two sons, Peter V (1853–61) and Louis I (1861–89), were marked by comparative stability and some progress, but political corruption, delay in essential reforms, and excessive taxation drove many thousand Portuguese to emigrate, and fostered the growth of anti-clericalism, socialism, communism, and anarchism among those who remained at home.

<small>Portugal</small>

Portugal differs from Spain in retaining an extensive colonial empire which includes the Azores, the Cape Verde Islands, Portuguese Guinea, Angola, and Mozambique in Africa, Goa, Damao, and Diu in India, Macao in China, and part of the island of Timor in the East Indies. The cost of administering an empire so widely distributed and estimated at twenty-six times the area of the mother country has strained the resources of the Portuguese treasury. Portugal entered the twentieth century with a heavy burden of debt, a population two thirds of which was illiterate, a heritage of political confusion and incompetence, and a government apparently blind to the need and demand for progressive reforms.

The not surprising result was the outbreak of a popular revolution in 1910. Manuel II (whose father, Charles I, and elder brother had been assassinated in 1908) fled from Lisbon, and a republic was proclaimed. The new constitution established a government resembling that of France, with a bicameral legislature, universal manhood suffrage, and a president chosen by the national deputies. The separation of church and state, confiscation of the property of religious orders, and the erection of a system of free popular schools followed; but in dealing with economic problems the new régime showed a bourgeois bent, and the government was more concerned to protect private property than to alleviate the condition of the working classes.

<small>Revolution of 1910</small>

4. THE CRUMBLING EMPIRE OF THE SULTAN (1815–78)

The decline of the Turkish Empire, already far advanced in the eighteenth century,[1] continued in the nineteenth, with the prospect of a complete dissolution growing yearly more imminent. Each of the great powers stood ready to claim a goodly share of the Ottoman bequest, but each was apprehensive lest a rival secure a more coveted section. As a consequence the diplomats frequently protested their hypocritical anxiety to protect and preserve the integrity of Turkey, by which they really meant to protect it from each other and preserve it for themselves. It is significant to note that each successive compromise which they

---

[1] See below, Chapter 71, section 6.

[1] See above, pages 554–556 and 574.

negotiated was preceded by a clause emphasizing the importance of preserving the Ottoman Empire intact, but each inevitably led to a further diminution of the sultan's possessions.

As a result of the Hellenic War of Independence [1] the Greek Peninsula slipped the Turkish yoke and was recognized as an independent kingdom by international agreement. The great powers considered Turkey then at the point of disintegration, and Russia pressed her military advantages so well that she was able to establish a protectorate over the provinces of Moldavia and Wallachia, and to annex the territory of Georgia in the region of the Caucasus (Treaty of Adrianople, 1829). At the same time the hardy Serbs, who had been in rebellion against their Turkish masters for years, won practical independence under their hereditary prince, Milosh I (1830). A comparison of the maps of Europe in 1815 and Europe in 1900 will reveal the extent of these Turkish losses. Note that Greece and Serbia were the first fragments of the Ottoman Empire to secede as independent principalities. Russia would readily have assumed a protectorate over both these states, the inhabitants of which were most of them of the Greek Orthodox faith, but the opposition of the other powers held the Muscovite ambitions in check.

The unhappy status of the sultan's remaining Christian subjects, oppressed by special taxes and denied civil equality, provided a constant motive for foreign intervention. Members of the Greek Orthodox Church in Turkey looked to Russia for protection, while Roman Catholics commonly sought sympathy for their lot from France. The solicitude which these two powers expressed for the welfare of the "Christian cattle" of the sultan was often no more than a cloak for moves aiming at the establishment of a protectorate. In 1854, as already explained,[2] mutual rivalries led France, in alliance with Great Britain, to attack Russia in the Crimea, and the Treaty of Paris, which closed this Crimean War, solemnly guaranteed the integrity of the Ottoman Empire, frustrated Russian designs for the moment, and protected British trade in the Near East. For this respite the sultan was grateful and he made eloquent promises of reform which as usual he forgot to redeem.

In thus preserving Turkey, Britain and France were playing a rôle suspiciously like that of the dog in the manger: they would not themselves free the Balkan peoples from the sultan's misrule nor permit Russia to do so.

Serbs and Rumanians

But the spirit of nationalism which fused Italy and Germany into unified states during the decade 1860-70 had penetrated the Balkans also, and drove the Serbs, the Rumanians, and the Bulgars to demand autonomy despite the procrastination of the western powers. In 1867, the Serbian ruler, Milan Obrenovich III, secured the withdrawal of the last Turkish garrison from Serbia, although the sultan refused to acknowledge the complete independence of that state until 1878. In the same years the peoples in what later became Rumania [1] voted to establish a common government, chose a nobleman, Alexander Cuza, as their prince, and proclaimed the union of the two Danubian provinces (1861). Like the Serbs, the Rumanians had to wait until the Congress of Berlin assembled in 1878 before they won acknowlegment of their status as a sovereign nation, the independent principality of Rumania.

The last of the Christian peoples of the Balkan Peninsula to escape from Turkish oppression were the Bulgars. A national and cultural revival

The Bulgars

preceded their demand for political freedom, and the Bulgars fought to emancipate themselves at one and the same time from the domination of the Greek clergy and the Turkish tax collectors. In 1870, the sultan permitted them to establish their own national church, but when they attempted to assert their political independence also (1876), they were punished by massacres so brutal and so sanguinary that all Europe was filled with indignation. Seizing the opportunity furnished by the general horror at these "Bulgarian atrocities," the Russian government intervened as the champion of

---

[1] See above, pages 696–697.
[2] See above, pages 728–731.

[1] See map on page 730.

TURKISH PRISONERS OF WAR

These Turkish soldiers were captured in 1912 when Greece, Serbia, and Bulgaria united to attack Turkey.

the Christian minorities and declared war on Turkey (1877).

Once more the Near Eastern Question had created a European crisis. As the Russian armies advanced with Constantinople as their ultimate objective, the British government dispatched a fleet to the Bosporus, and Austria mobilized an army to curb Russian activities in the Balkan States. To avoid a clash with either of these powers, and to secure the gains already made, the czar concluded the hasty Treaty of San Stefano with the sultan (1878). This provided for the creation of an extensive, free Bulgaria, and decreed complete independence for Serbia, Rumania, and little Montenegro. But the vigilant powers, particularly Great Britain and Austria, were not satisfied with this solution. They viewed with alarm the creation of a greater Bulgaria under Russian influence, and they insisted upon calling an international congress to revise the Treaty of San Stefano. Sullenly the Russians submitted. Berlin was chosen as the meeting-

Russo-Turk War (1877)

place for the diplomats, and Bismarck, who declared that Germany had no direct stake in the Near East and was therefore the best arbiter, proposed to play the part of an "honest broker" whose only desire was to reconcile his clients' interests.

Not since the princely delegates hastened to Vienna to celebrate the overthrow of Napoleon in 1814 had Europe beheld a diplomatic gathering of greater moment. The powers stood dangerously close to war, for, although the Russians had exacted fairly modest concessions from the Turks, British popular feeling was opposed to any compromise, and the audiences in the London music halls were chanting in belligerent fashion:

Congress of 1878

We don't want to fight, but, by Jingo, if we do,
We've got the ships, we've got the men, we've got the money too.

This spirit of "jingoism," as it came to be termed, made a judicious settlement of the dispute extremely difficult, but in July the leading British delegate to the congress,

Lord Beaconsfield (Benjamin Disraeli), was able to announce that he had brought back "peace with honor," and British "jingoists" applauded their returning prime minister and his imperialistic diplomacy. Later, however, his colleague, Lord Salisbury, was to confess that they had "backed the wrong horse" at Berlin, for, in checking Russia, Britain had not only helped to frustrate a possible solution of the Balkan tangle, embodied in the Treaty of San Stefano, but had encouraged the advance of Austria in the Balkans. Thirty years after the Congress of Berlin, the British had to ally themselves with the Russians to hold Austria, backed by Germany, in check.

For the moment, however, peace had been preserved by Russian concessions, and Great Britain and Austria mollified by the diplomatic device known as "reciprocal compensation." Russia was permitted to annex the province of Bessarabia on the Black Sea between the Danube and the Dniester deltas, and also the Armenian districts of Kars, Ardahan, and Batum. In return, Austria-Hungary received the right to administer the late Turkish provinces of Bosnia and Herzegovina, and Britain, by a separate convention with Turkey, assumed possession of the island of Cyprus. Thereupon the powers once more repeated their solemn determination to respect and to preserve intact the territorial unity of the Turkish Empire, or what remained of it.

The wishes of the Balkan peoples, who were most vitally concerned in the settlement, won scant and illogical consideration. Bulgaria was split into three parts, the northernmost section winning practical independence, the middle section administrative autonomy, while the southern section, including Macedonia, was restored to Turkish control. For Rumania, Serbia, and Montenegro, the congress decreed complete independence and some increases in territory, but the national aspirations of the inhabitants were far from being satisfied. The Greeks, who were permitted to add Thessaly to their diminutive peninsula-kingdom, had the most substantial reason for gratitude but were still dissatisfied.

The treaty of Berlin failed to solve the Near Eastern Question, failed to safeguard such Christian minorities as still remained under Ottoman rule, and failed to ensure the needed reforms which experience had shown the Turks might promise but would never execute. It may be that the problems involved were too intricate for solution, but in truth the diplomats revealed little honest desire to settle them equitably, being too deeply engrossed with their own plans for imperial aggrandizement to study the issues dispassionately. The Balkans remained a center of disorders, rivalries, and intrigues fermenting with national unrest, until two generations later they provided the spark which generated a World War.

SECTION K

The New Industrialism and Imperialism

(1871 — 1914)

In the twenty years preceding 1871, Europe had been shaken by no less than five wars, each involving two or more of the great powers. All these struggles — the Crimean War, the Italian War of 1859, the Danish War, the Austro-Prussian conflict, and the Franco-Prussian War — grew in large part out of the tension resulting from the progress of national consolidation. Italy, Germany, and to a less degree Russia, were striving to round out their territories and achieve a higher degree of political unity. By 1871, however, Italy had been organized into the Italian Kingdom, the Germanies had been welded together to form the German Empire, and Europe was permitted to settle down to a condition of relative peace and equilibrium. Twenty years of strain and frequent warfare were to be followed by over forty years of peace.

But history never stands still, and during these peaceful decades forces were at work which aggravated old problems and created new ones. The most impressive single factor affecting European civilization after 1871 was the rapid industrial development. Stimulated by new and revolutionary advances in science and technology, industry superseded agriculture as the main source of livelihood for a majority of the people in the industrialized states. But this further extension of the factory system deepened the conflict between the owners of the machines and the workers, while the steady accumulation of capital and the need for raw materials drove the powers to exploit backward countries and expand their colonial empires. As a consequence the period from 1871 to 1914 was characterized by social conflict and the rise of socialist parties *within* the industrialized states, and by keener commercial and colonial competition *between* the industrialized states. As the tension grew, the powers were driven into two competing systems of alliances, while the people suffered the burden of ever-increasing armaments. A succession of diplomatic crises culminated, in 1914, in the outbreak of one of the most tragic and destructive wars in European history.

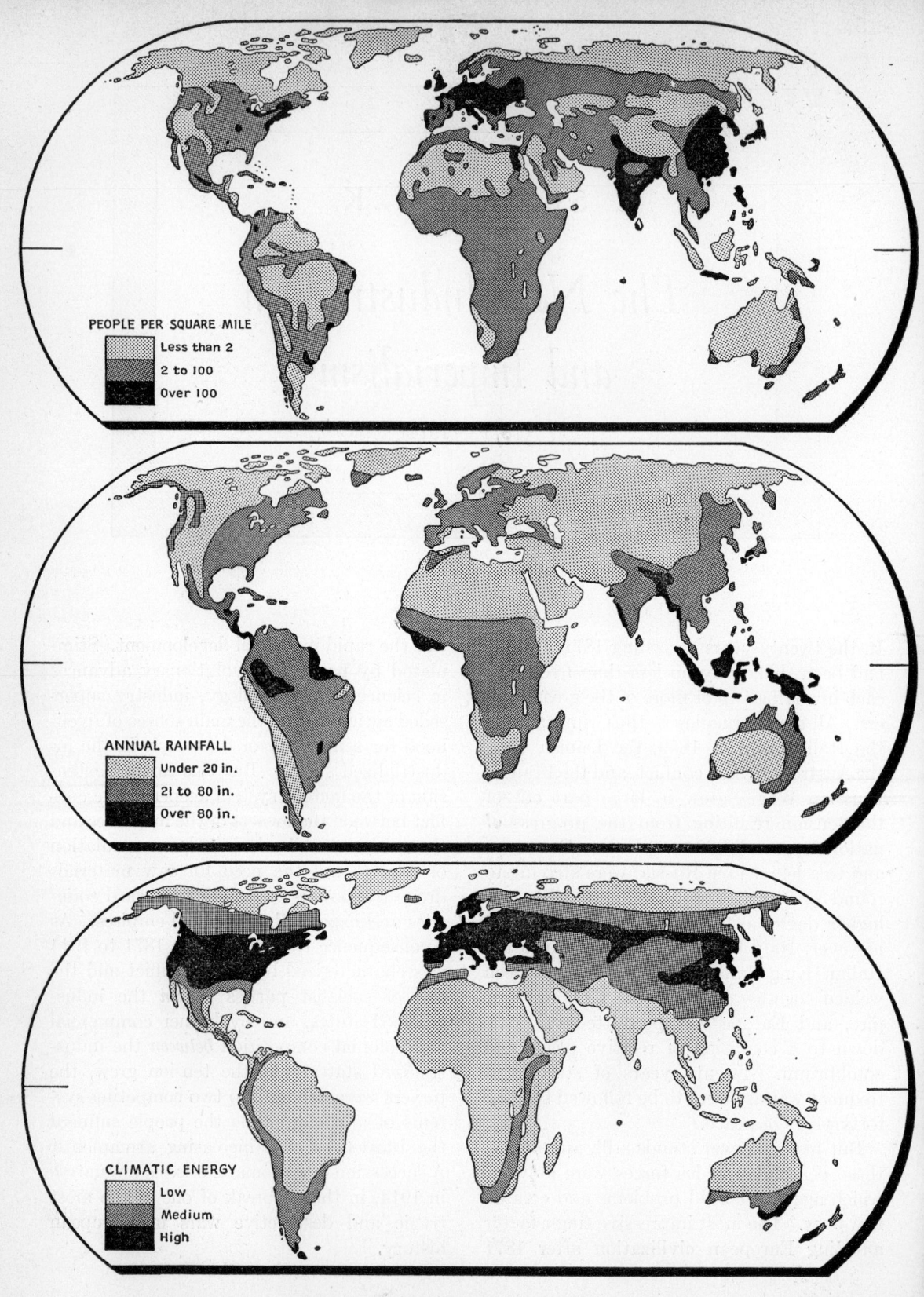

PEOPLE PER SQUARE MILE
- Less than 2
- 2 to 100
- Over 100

ANNUAL RAINFALL
- Under 20 in.
- 21 to 80 in.
- Over 80 in.

CLIMATIC ENERGY
- Low
- Medium
- High

FACTORS IN THE DISTRIBUTION OF WORLD POPULATION

The New World Which Science and Industry Created

Better fifty years of Europe than a cycle of Cathay.
ALFRED TENNYSON.

EVERY STUDENT OF HISTORY who peers back into past centuries will find himself drawn to certain periods with the conviction, "Here was an eventful age!" To have walked on the banks of the Nile when the Great Pyramid was rising, or through the streets of Athens in the fifth century before Christ; to have visited Cathay with Marco Polo and seen the court of Kublai Khan, or dwelt in Florence in the height of the Italian Renaissance, would doubtless have provided rich and stimulating experiences. Yet it is safe to say that at no point in the past could one find an age which, for eventfulness, for extension and diffusion of culture, rapidity of change, interest and complexity, might prove a rival to contemporary times. To have lived in Europe or America during the past half-century is to have lived in the most advanced civilization and the most extraordinary epoch in the recorded history of the human race, an epoch in which man's knowledge of the universe which he inhabits, his control over the forces of nature, his ability to produce the necessities of life and to prolong life itself, have increased more rapidly than in any comparable era of the past.

1. THE MARCH OF SCIENCE

The chief factor underlying the dynamic changes of recent years was the progress of science and industry. An earlier chapter described the beginnings of modern science in the sixteenth and seventeenth centuries, the advances in mathematical method, and the brilliant discoveries in astronomy, physics, and other fields of investigation. The scientists of the eighteenth century extended and systematized this new knowledge with such success that they made their period an Age of Rationalism, a Scientific Renaissance. But it was not until the nineteenth century that the fruits of their researches really made themselves felt in the life of the common man. A hundred and fifty years ago farmers still plowed their fields much as they had since Roman times two thousand years before. The horse provided the chief means of transportation on land, the sailing vessel on water. The swiftest method of communication was to signal a message from one hilltop to the next. Nevertheless, although the people of that age could not foresee its outcome, a revolution was at hand which speeded up the methods of communication, of transportation, and of production more effectively in a single lifetime than in all previous history. Men born in 1800 saw within the span of an average life the advent of the age of steam and steel.

Transport mechanized

In the eighteenth century it required as many days to travel the hundred and sixty miles from London to Manchester as now suffice for the crossing of the Atlantic or a journey from New York to San Francisco. Today goods can be shipped from England to Japan or Australia at less cost and labor than it demanded then to transport them from London to Edinburgh. The introduction of the steamship and the railway a century ago shrank this planet so surprisingly that distant continents became more accessible than neighboring states had been a few decades earlier. As a result, Europe was able to lay the world under contribution, drawing the products of every clime and every continent to her ports. The high speed and low cost of steam transportation made it possible for manufacturers to feed their factories with raw materials drawn from the ends of the earth, and to ship the finished articles back across the ocean to distant markets. The inhabitants, moreover, of the new industrial centers no longer cultivated gardens or raised their own food. For the whole world had become their garden, and from every part of it ships were racing toward them with the supplies of food which they no longer found it profitable to produce.

There is no easy comparison to be found in history for this revolutionary change. In days of old a king, perhaps, might obtain fresh fish from a lake in the next province by exhausting relays of fleet slaves, or draw melting snow from a mountain-top by the same means when he wished to cool his wine. Today every common man in a civilized community commands privileges which the king could not have imagined. The average Englishman, for example, will sit down unthinkingly to a breakfast gathered from five continents. He chooses casually between an apple from British Columbia and an orange from Tangier, coffee from Brazil or tea from Ceylon, lambs' kidneys from Australia or bacon and eggs from Denmark. The breakfast table may be of Venezuelan mahogany, the cloth of Egyptian cotton, the cutlery compounded perhaps of Canadian nickel, Swedish chromium, Chinese tin, and Mexican silver, all blended at Sheffield, England.

Cables link continents

The newspaper folded beside his plate likewise bears witness to a revolution, not in transportation, but in communication. From every part of the world the events of the previous twenty-four hours have been gleaned for his entertainment and information. News of an earthquake in Tibet, a fire in Buenos Aires, or a shipwreck off the Aleutian Islands is crowded together with market quotations from Chicago and Tokyo and messages from explorers in the Amazonian jungles or near the South Pole. To draw in this medley of details a wire net has been woven from a mileage of submarine cables long enough to girdle the earth a dozen times and a length of telephone wire that would reach to the sun. The more recent devices of wireless telegraphy and radio are already accepted as commonplaces by people whose tastes are jaded with so many scientific wonders. Yet the greatest marvel of all, and the one most frequently ignored, is the fact that the inventions which make this collection and diffusion of news possible, the telegraph, telephone, and wireless systems, the linotype, and the rotary press, have all been perfected within the memory of men yet living.

Production multiplies

While the conveyance of goods, passengers, and news was thus being speeded up, an equally momentous change took place in the methods of production. Industrial centers, able suddenly to draw upon the whole world for supplies, demanded them in prodigious quantities and doubled their demands every few years. The production of iron, an essential commodity of the machine age, increased a hundred-fold in the nineteenth century, and the output of coal kept pace with it. New inventions, such as the internal combustion engine, created new demands, and the world production of petroleum after 1900 leaped ahead one thousand per cent in thirty years. To satisfy the insatiable demands of expanding industries men learned to tap pools of oil miles below the earth's crust, to draw nitrogen from the atmosphere, and to extract bromine from the sea. Power for their engines was obtained by a reckless consumption of coal, oil, or gas, or by harnessing the tireless waterfalls.

CHARLES DARWIN (1809–1882)

Charles Darwin offered a theory to explain how the different species of animals, including man, might have originated through natural selection.

SIR CHARLES LYELL (1797–1875)

Sir Charles Lyell, the father of modern geology, sought to explain how the earth achieved its present appearance.

Nor did science lag in finding new ways to augment the food supply for the hungry millions. By the use of fertilizers, by experimenting with new and more nutritious types of grains and fruits, by the invention of agricultural machinery, power-driven plows, tractors, and threshing machines, the world's food supply has been augmented until in recent years the surplus has proved an embarrassment and its distribution a problem. By means of refrigerator cars and steamers millions of tons of fruit or meat can now be shipped from continent to continent, or, sealed in sterilized cans, may be preserved for years until needed. The dread specter of famine which had lurked like a lean wolf on the edge of every human community since the beginning of history seemed about to vanish at last.

This increase in material wealth has made the world a vastly more luxurious and amusing place for many people. Today the citizen of modest circumstances can afford luxuries which a Roman noble with a thousand slaves could not obtain. The electric light, telephone, and radio, the steamship, train, and automobile are at the disposal of millions. The Caesars carried no timepiece as accurate as a dollar watch, nor could their banquet table provide the variety of flavors obtainable at a modern soda fountain. Silk, once the apparel of princes, has become a household article, materials unknown or unprocurable to the ancients, such as rustless steel, aluminum, rubber, and a hundred synthetic products, have suddenly become so cheap that they are discarded after use as too worthless to salvage. Science and industry have accustomed civilized men to regard the supply of materials, raw and manufactured, as inexhaustible, so that they cast aside daily as rubbish the tons of newsprint, bottle glass, tin cans, old tires, or broken pottery which have served their purpose, indifferent to whether their mines and forests can long withstand such ruthless depletion.

2. NEW CONCEPTIONS OF MAN'S PLACE IN NATURE

While becoming richer and more interesting in the past hundred years, human existence has also become healthier and safer. The scientists did not rest content with exploring the inorganic universe from stars to atoms; they turned their investigations upon organic (that is, living) things as well. As a result of these researches they have been able to conquer many deadly diseases and prolong man's span of life, at the same time formulating new and revolutionary theories regarding his origin and place in nature.

In pursuing those branches of knowledge which concern man, however, such subjects as biology or psychology or politics, the scientists had to overcome a problem which had troubled them little in physics or chemistry. This problem might be called the human factor. It is an inescapable, and to the scientist a troublesome, fact, that man, who likes to put the rest of the universe under the microscope, objects to being put under it himself. For he has learned from experience that the results are likely to humiliate and bewilder him. It disturbs him little when the scientists dispute about the speed of light or the temperature of the sun, but his vanity is affronted when they tell him their evidence indicates that he is descended from the apes instead of from the angels. The poets may agree that "the proper study of mankind is man," but the scientists have found it is often considered an improper study. However warily they walk, however scrupulously they weigh their observations, they still find that their conclusions regarding man are apt to be distorted by popular prejudices and passions or invalidated by their own unsuspected loyalties.

One of the first shocks which modern science administered to human vanity was the Copernican theory.[1] If the universe was, indeed, nothing more than a vast machine, then all life on earth might be merely "the superficial phenomena of arrested radiation on the outer crust of a cooling nebula." Yet men clung to an inherited belief that the trees which bore fruits for them to eat, the lakes teeming with fish, the valleys which they plowed, and the hills to which they lifted up their eyes had been shaped to serve human needs by a benevolent Creator. How else could the mountains and the lakes, the river valleys and the fertile plains have achieved their present useful and familiar conformation?

In 1830–33, Charles Lyell attempted to answer that question in his *Principles of Geology*, explaining that the irregularities of the earth's surface were the result of natural processes still at work; that the actions of volcanic pressure, of winds and rain and rivers, the formation of strata, and the rising and sinking of the earth's crust would, in the course of sufficient time, produce all the results now apparent. The theories of this great English scientist, which won rapid acceptance, presupposed a much greater age for the earth than the six thousand years suggested by Biblical chronology. Some modern calculations have named a figure in excess of two thousand million years. *Geology*

Stimulated by Lyell's hypothesis, geologists began, by patient scrutiny and classification, to estimate the age of the various types of rock found in the earth's crust. Discovery of the fossil remains of plants and animals in some of these stratified formations provided a clue to the origin of life on this planet. The earliest indications revealed the most primitive forms of organic structures, successive later strata retained the impressions of shellfish, vertebrate fish, insects, trees, reptiles, mammals, and finally of man. In 1863, Lyell published a second important work on *The Geological Evidences of the Antiquity of Man*, in which he submitted that relics of human tools and skeletons had been traced back at least fifty thousand years. Thus the geologists and paleontologists (that is, students of fossilized animals and plants) discovered "books in the running brooks, sermons in stones," and opened up a new and amazing vista which stretched from the portals of written history back to the first algae in the proterozoic slime. *Paleontology*

The advances in geology set the stage for the most epoch-making conclusion of nineteenth-century thought, the theory of bio-

---
[1] See above, page 602.

LOUIS PASTEUR (1822–1895)

Pasteur demonstrated that many diseases in plants and animals are caused by minute organisms, and he found remedies against some of these bacilli.

MARIE CURIE (1867–1934)

Marie Curie and her husband, Pierre Curie, through their investigation of radium, speeded new discoveries in physics and medicine.

A BACTERIOLOGICAL LABORATORY IN THE BELGIAN CONGO

This bacteriological laboratory in the Belgian Congo suggests how science serves as the international handmaid of humanity in its fight against the great plagues.

logical evolution. Since the time of the Greeks independent thinkers had pondered the suggestion that all life might have developed originally from a simple cell, but the proposition appeared untenable because, so far as man could observe, all living things were divided into fixed species, each producing "after his kind," as the Book of Genesis had ordained. It followed that if species were, indeed, unchanging or *immutable*, they could not all have derived gradually from the same common ancestor. But the new calculations regarding the vast age of the earth, the discovery of prehistoric forms and species now extinct, and the variations found to exist between families of living animals and their fossilized forbears provided the clue that species were not immutable after all, but were, indeed, changing imperceptibly through vast periods of time.

How the variation, progression, and multiplication of life forms might have come about as a result of natural forces, occurred independently to two English naturalists, Charles Darwin and Alfred Russel Wallace, but Darwin reached his conclusion first and fortified it most carefully. Breeders of mice or pigeons, as Darwin knew, by mating only the dark- or light-colored offspring in successive generations, could produce in time a pure white or pure dark strain, and he reasoned that, if such a process of selection were carried on long enough, it could change the entire character of the stock. If the deer with the fleetest legs or the giraffes with the longest necks had been selected from each generation for millions of years, the cumulative effect would result in the emergence of new species. That such a process of *natural selection* had actually taken place, Darwin postulated as a corollary of the struggle for existence, explaining that the favored individuals of each species, the fleetest or the fiercest or the most intelligent, had the better chance to survive and propagate according as they were better adapted to their environment. In the course of time this principle of "the survival of the fittest" would bring about the evolution and differentiation of living organisms into an infinite variety of types and species. In 1859, Darwin offered

Darwin (1809–82)

this conclusion to the world by publishing his momentous work *On the Origin of Species by Means of Natural Selection*.

The Darwinian theories, as propagated in the philosophy of Herbert Spencer and the lectures of Thomas Henry Huxley, aroused deep opposition especially among theologians. Efforts to confirm or confute them led to a more intensive study of comparative anatomy and to a more careful classification of all forms of organic life. That all living bodies were built out of microscopic organisms or *cells* had been demonstrated as early as 1839. Further improvements in the microscope enabled Louis Pasteur to prove that the fermentation of wine and yeast and many diseases in plants and animals were caused by minute living organisms or *germs*. For the first time physicians were given the opportunity to recognize enemies which hitherto they had fought in the dark. Pasteur demonstrated that many dangerous disease germs could be killed by such a simple device as raising the temperature of their environment (pasteurization), and that others could be combated by inoculating or immunizing human beings against their ravages. A Prussian physician, Robert Koch (1843–1910), raised bacteriology into a science, and within a decade (1884–94) the bacillus of typhoid, tuberculosis, cholera, lockjaw, diphtheria, bubonic plague, and other scourges had been identified. Although the greatest scientists were generally the most modest in their claims, enthusiasts hoped that the twentieth century would see the passing of the great plagues.

Pasteur (1822–95)

In surgery the results of the germ theory were not less important. The knowledge that infection and suppuration of wounds was due to the presence of microbes emphasized the value of antiseptics and the importance of sterilizing all the implements, bandages, etc., used in operations (asepsis). At the same time the introduction of ether and chloroform as anesthetics not only spared the patient incalculable pain, but made possible longer and far more complicated investigations. The miracles of modern surgery would be impossible without these discoveries which now save the lives of hundreds of thousands of people yearly.

Throughout the civilized world the methods popularized by Pasteur, Koch, and others led to a concerted war against disease which has had spectacular results. The medical profession, the public health authorities, and a more enlightened public adopted measures of hygiene and sanitation which in many parts of Europe cut the death rate in half in fifty years. The result has been a phenomenal increase in population, due not only to the advances in medical science, but also to the new methods, already mentioned, of producing and distributing vast quantities of cheap food. Because of the mitigation of plague and famine, the population of Europe has more than doubled since 1800. But Europe is not the only continent affected. It is estimated that during the same period the population of the earth has trebled until it stands today at more than two billion people, a result made possible not so much by increasing the birth rate as by decreasing the death rate.

Increase in population

This unprecedented gain in population, stimulated by the achievements of modern science and industry, is the most arresting fact in modern history. It has created profound problems, for mere multiplication of the human race is not a blessing unless the newborn individuals are offered a chance to lead happy and profitable lives. It is pertinent to ask what sort of lives these added millions are condemned to live, what chance they have to find happiness, and what type of environment science and industry are providing for them. These are questions which the next section will endeavor to answer.

3. THE NEW ENVIRONMENT WHICH SCIENCE AND INDUSTRY HAVE PROVIDED: THE "CIVILIZATION OF CITY DWELLERS"

After 1870, the acceleration of the forces shaping modern life, the flood of inventions and the multifold discoveries, grew so rapid that it really constituted a second Industrial Revolution or what might better, perhaps, be termed a Technological Revolution. Successive innovations, such as the automobile, motion picture, airplane, and radio, led to the establishment of new industries overnight, industries which, like the older weaving and metallurgical trades, required hundreds of thousands of workers and were centered often in mushroom cities created to house their plants and their employees. The new methods of quantity production necessitated the co-ordination of all the processes of an industry, and of associated trades, so that the garment-makers tended to congregate in one locality, the makers of automobile parts in another. Miners crowded into dingy dwellings near the pit mouth, cotton spinners into congested towns where cheap power, a damp climate, or convenient transportation facilities had concentrated the factories. The machines required power to run them and raw materials to feed their tireless maw, hence it was most profitable to establish them where these essentials were easily available. Thus, in selecting the site of operations the machine was the master, and the workmen who had to tend it were condemned to live nearby. Too often this meant that thousands of mill hands had to pass their lives under the smoke-laden sky of a factory town, where the grass withered from the fumes of the blast furnaces and the streams were polluted with the wastage of tanks and vats. The migration of the population toward the new industrial centers, a shift already observable in England at the close of the eighteenth century, continued at an increasing rate throughout the nineteenth in all the leading European countries.

The result was the growth of cities at the expense of the country districts. The most notable feature about the population in the modern industrial state is the fact that it is predominantly an urban population. Until a century ago, and even later, the people of the British Isles, of France, or Germany lived chiefly on the land, supporting themselves by some form of agricultural labor. England was the first state to discover, about 1850, that the town dwellers had grown to outnumber the country folk. That process has continued inexorably until today four out of every five Englishmen live in cities of ten thousand or upwards. In France and Germany the same phenomenon is to be observed, induced by the same causes, but it

The growth of cities

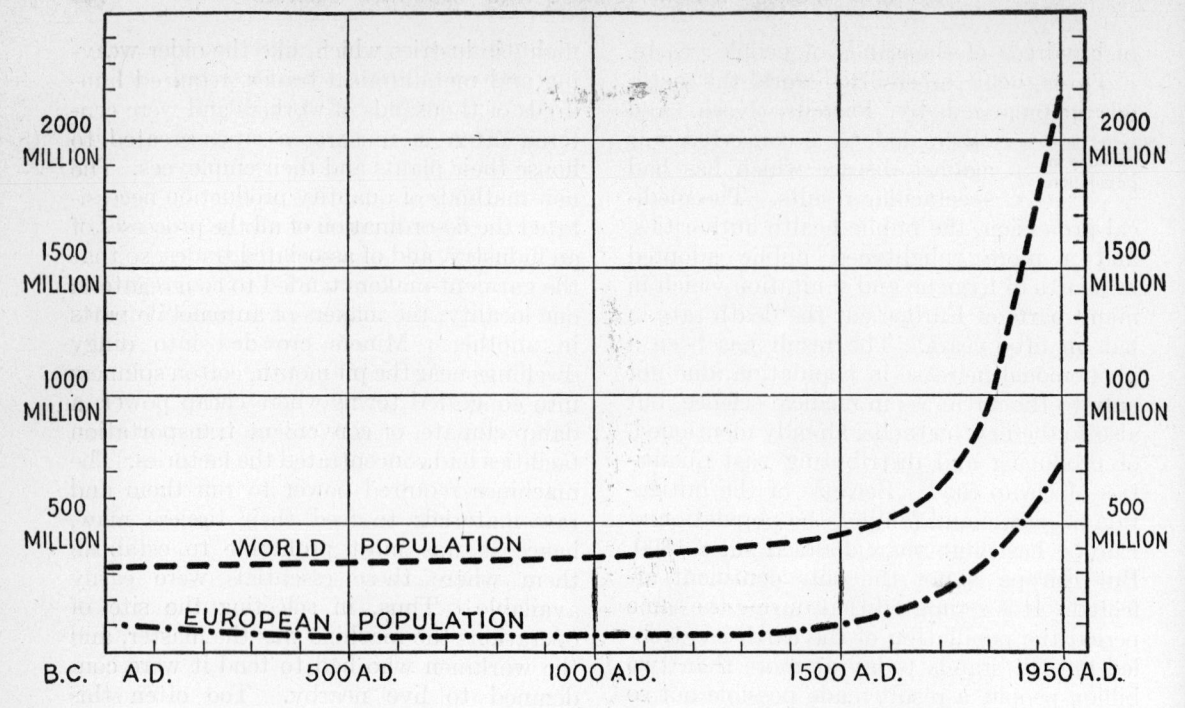

EUROPEAN AND WORLD POPULATION, 1 A.D. TO 1950 A.D. (ESTIMATED)

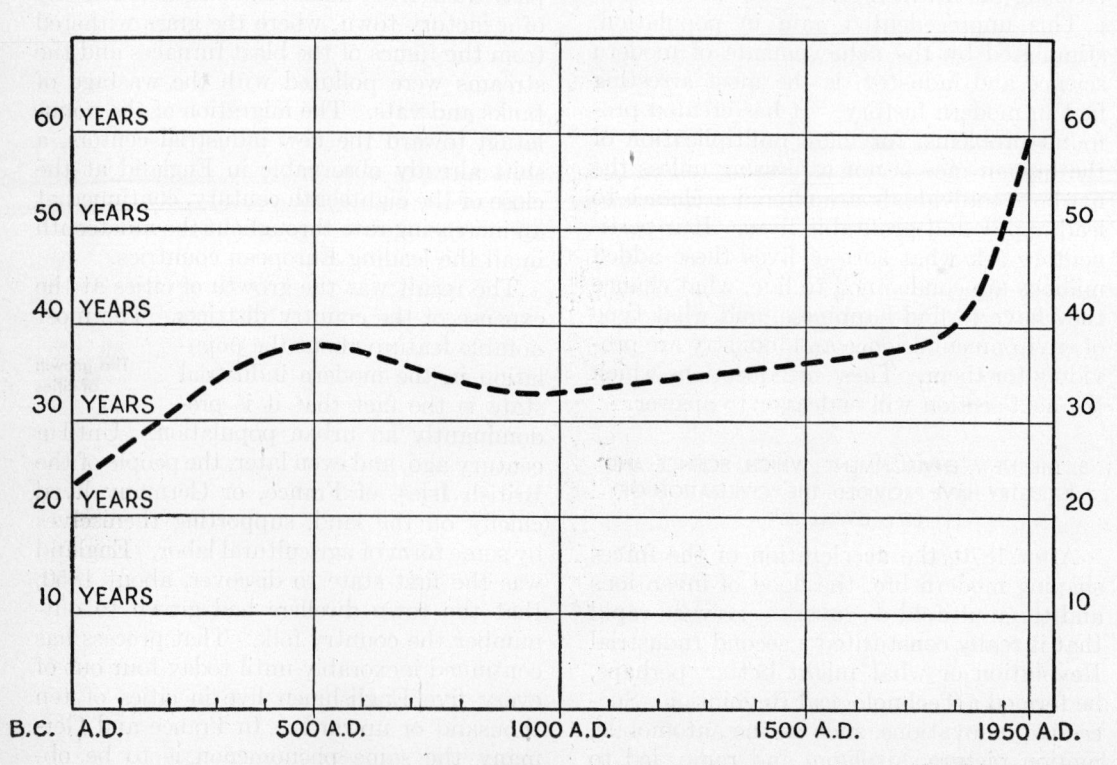

AVERAGE SPAN OF LIFE FOR EUROPEANS, 1 A.D. TO 1950 A.D. (ESTIMATED)

has not yet developed so far. The trend, however, which affects the whole of Europe, is startling enough. A century ago there were scarcely a dozen cities in Europe with a population over two hundred thousand. Today there are more than one hundred, and they are still growing.

Yet so swift has been the transformation, so recently has modern civilization become a civilization of city dwellers, that the thought, the language, the mental background of most urban inhabitants are still impregnated with rural images. City children who never visited a mill stream or plundered a farmer's orchard sing songs about the old swimming hole and the old gray mare, but they have little comprehension of these things. For most modern children know nothing of barefoot days or calling the cattle home; the world in which they are growing up has come to be a world of paved streets and angular buildings, of lighted shop windows and dark alleyways, of gasoline fumes and factory whistles. This is the environment in which the man of the twentieth century seems destined to pass the greater part of the twenty thousand days that fate allots him, divorced from the forests and the fields which were home to his grandfather, but in which a dwindling proportion of his fellow countrymen now dwell.

It follows that the proper regulation and development of those cities in which so large a part of the people elect to live must be of pressing concern to modern governments. Cities are vast agglomerations of unique and artificial growth. To police them, to safeguard their thousands or millions of inhabitants, to direct their traffic or dispose of their refuse, employs an army of public servants. Many modern cities have grown up so hurriedly and haphazardly that vast sums must later be expended to provide an adequate water supply, to create port and railway facilities, playgrounds, parks, and traffic speedways. A little foresight and foreknowledge might have solved many of these problems in advance, but the rapid changes of the machine era took governments by surprise and found even the experts largely unprepared to cope with the riddles of a dynamic civilization.

4. THE INDUSTRIALIZED SOCIETY: THE CONFLICT BETWEEN CAPITAL AND LABOR AND THE RIDDLE OF SOCIAL JUSTICE

In the Middle Ages, when land was the most important form of wealth, a man's power and riches were computed in terms of the number of fertile acres which he possessed. His income depended upon the produce raised on his estates, part of which was turned over to him by his tenants or serfs as rent. As the yield from the soil could not be greatly increased under existing methods of cultivation, medieval wealth and medieval society tended to remain the same from one generation to the next. By the thirteenth and fourteenth centuries, however, other factors introduced a change which helped to bring the Middle Ages to an end. The story has already been told of the improvements in communication, the slow revival of commerce, and the growth of the towns, which raised a new class to prominence, the class of manufacturers, bankers, and traders. The wealth of these men was not in land, but in the commodities which they sold, in bills of exchange, and in money. Though scorned at first by the feudal, landowning nobles, the merchant class gained steadily in power and wealth and influence. For whereas the landowner's income was limited by the yield of his land and the rents paid him by his tenants, the commercial classes grew wealthier as their business grew in volume. In time this emerging middle class became strong enough to challenge the privileged position of the feudal aristocracy, and in the end they succeeded, with the aid of the seventeenth-century revolutions in England and the great revolution in France, in dominating state policies. By 1832, as explained in an earlier chapter, the bourgeoisie, the class composed of manufacturers, merchants, traders, bankers, professional men, and shopkeepers, had secured control of the government in France and Great Britain.

Rise of bourgeoisie

At this point, when the leaders of the new "commercial aristocracy" were tasting the fruits of political power, they tapped a new source of economic gain through the wider application of machinery. The Industrial

Power of capital

Revolution had begun, and it proved the truth of the scriptural adage that to him that hath shall be given. For only men who already possessed surplus capital could afford to experiment with and to install the new spinning and weaving machines which revolutionized the production of cotton and woolen fabrics. Men with foresight and initiative, who had capital to invest or knew where to borrow it, made surprising profits, and those who utilized their dividends for the purchase of still more machines might multiply their fortunes and lift themselves to the rank of great industrial capitalists.

But the factory system not only enriched the capitalist class; it also multiplied vastly the number of unpropertied wage-earners, the class which has come to be called the industrial proletariat. The machines provided wide employment for the unskilled and semi-skilled laborer, but too often he found life in a factory little better than economic serfdom. In some respects his lot was even harder than that of a serf in the Middle Ages, for the medieval peasant could not be deprived of his land or his means of livelihood, poor as it might be, but a factory worker might be discharged at any time and face starvation if he found no other work. The peasants of the Middle Ages had usually accepted their lot with resignation, but the industrial laborers of the nineteenth century, living in larger groups, could combine and protest more effectively than their thirteenth-century forbears. They agitated for better working conditions and better wages, and organized themselves in order to fight for their rights. Dissatisfied and unemployed workingmen were among the first to raise the barricades in the Paris revolutions of 1830 and 1848, and they swelled the ranks of the Chartists in England.

Industrial proletariat

The attempts of the workers to organize trade unions to promote their interests met at first with strong opposition, and the unions were condemned and disbanded as "conspiracies in restraint of trade." Labor combinations formed for the purpose of gaining better hours, wages, or working conditions did not enjoy full legal protection in England until 1871. In France, although co-operative societies were permitted, workingmen's combinations formed to bargain with employers (*sociétés de résistance*) were first forbidden, then tolerated (1868), and finally given legal status (1884). In Germany, the laborers' right to combine for the purpose of winning more favorable wages and working conditions was not recognized legally until after 1890. It is to be noted that in all three countries the statutes which forbade the combination of the workers with the object of forcing wages *up* also contained clauses prohibiting combinations of employers for the purpose of forcing wages *down*, but these clauses frequently remained a dead letter.

Trade unions

After the middle of the nineteenth century, the deepening antagonism between the capitalist or bourgeois employers and the workingmen acquired new significance through the writings of Karl Marx. Born in Trier, Germany, Marx enjoyed an excellent education, but his political activities on behalf of the lower classes got him into trouble in his homeland and also in France, where he joined in the revolution of 1848. So he settled in London in order to devote himself to study and to the development of those theories which have earned him the title "the father of modern socialism."

Karl Marx (1818–83)

Armed with profound learning and a powerful intellect, Marx formulated a new philosophy of history, based upon his conclusion that the factor which is common to society in every age is the exploitation of one class by another. In modern society Marx found this "class struggle" exemplified in the contest between capital and labor, the capitalists being the "expropriators" and the workingmen the "expropriated," and he prophesied that the struggle would gradually split society into two hostile camps with no middle ground between. For the progress of the Industrial Revolution seemed destined to increase the profits of the machine-owners while the proletarians grew more numerous and more conscious of their violated rights. In the end the proletariat would take over the machinery of production to run it for the benefit of all, and the "expropriators" would be expropriated.

LABORATORY OF MICHAEL FARADAY (1791–1867)

Faraday discovered in his laboratory (1841) how to induce an electric current by rotating a wire around a magnet.

THE "GREAT EASTERN" ON ITS WAY TO AMERICA

A first transatlantic cable failed after three weeks (1858), but the tireless efforts of Cyrus West Field promoted a more successful attempt by the "Great Eastern" in 1866.

To its exponents the chief attraction of this "economic interpretation of history" lay in its logical prediction that the ultimate triumph of the proletariat must come about in the natural course of events. Critics have objected, however, that at this point Marx abandons his realistic approach and becomes almost as Utopian as Fourier or Saint-Simon. For he implies that the proletarian revolution will be followed by the creation of a co-operative commonwealth without expropriating or expropriated classes. Such a conclusion appears to presuppose either (1) that the class conflict is not a constantly operative and rigidly determined principle, or (2) that the human mind, by understanding it, can alter conditions and arrest the endless series of revolutions to which the class struggle has given rise — neither of which offers a wholly logical explanation. Most socialists were encouraged, however, by the Marxian prophecy that capitalism would dig its own grave, and that, although the advent of socialism might be delayed, it could not be prevented. Since the workers of all countries had the same general grievances, Marx urged them to unite in pressing the class war, disregarding national ties and boundaries, for all the workers of the world were "comrades."

Criticism of Marxism

In 1864, socialists from various countries attempted to organize an international movement for which Marx prepared a constitution. Weakened by the desertion of the moderates and the expulsion of the anarchists, this First International foundered in 1873, but a Second International was formed in 1889. Meanwhile, socialist groups in the leading European countries entered the political arena and socialist voters polled an increasing number of ballots. By 1914, the Socialist Parties in France and Germany had each over a hundred deputies in parliament, while in the British House of Commons the Labor Party held forty seats.

The Internationals

The spread of democracy in the period 1870–1914 and the extension of the suffrage to all classes naturally favored the expansion of the Socialist Parties. Their leaders hoped a time would soon come when the workers, as the most numerous class in each state, would control the parliaments through the deputies whom they elected, for when they secured this control they could transform the capitalist system by legislative decrees. All moderate-minded men naturally hoped that the ends of social justice might be realized by constitutional means and that the problems growing out of the class struggle would find an *evolutionary* rather than a *revolutionary* solution. The parliaments of the nineteenth century had generally avoided these problems, and, true to the bourgeois doctrine of *laissez-faire*, or "let alone," they had left the workers to the mercy of their employers. But there seemed good reason to hope after 1900 that the parliaments of the twentieth century would abandon this evasive course and grapple honestly with the task of reconciling the demands of capital and labor. Unhappily, this hope was to be jeopardized by the outbreak of two world wars and the crises which threatened democratic governments everywhere.

Evolution or revolution?

Like the "class struggle," the World Wars were very largely a product of the new forces which science and industry have let loose in society. The economic rivalries of imperialistic powers which helped to provoke war, the machine guns, submarine boats, and poison gas which multiplied its horrors, and the aircraft which dropped bombs on vulnerable cities were no less the products of the new world which science and industry have provided than the cheap food, the rapid transportation, and the protection against plagues. The Industrial Revolution not only helped to intensify the class struggle *within* the modern states; it also helped to intensify the jealousies existing *among* the modern states, as the next section will explain.

5. THE INDUSTRIALIZED STATE: THE COMPETITION AMONG THE GREAT POWERS FOR COLONIES AND MARKETS

In medieval times, when highways were few and poor and ships small and slow, the inhabitants of a village or dwellers on a barony had to raise the necessities of life in their own neighborhood. Meat and eggs,

SAMUEL F. B. MORSE (1791–1872)    THOMAS ALVA EDISON (1847–1931)

Samuel F. B. Morse (left) demonstrated his electric telegraph before Congress in 1844. Thomas Alva Edison (right) invented the first practical electric light (inset) in 1878, and helped to erect the first public electric-light power plant (below) in 1881.

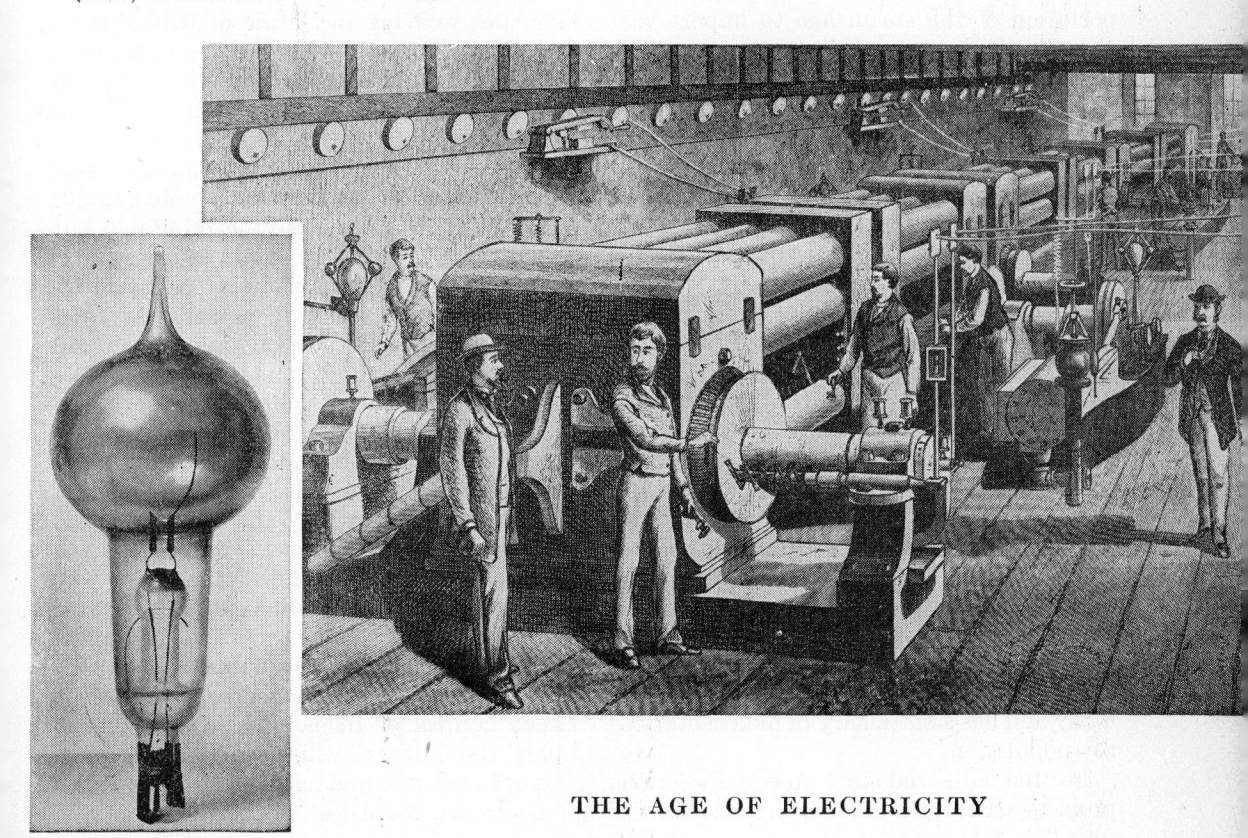

THE AGE OF ELECTRICITY

fruit and grain, wine and olives, were largely consumed where they were produced, for it was costly and difficult to preserve or to transport them. The same principle applied to almost all the commodities of existence. Traders had to limit their load to light and precious wares, such as salt, spices, silks, and jewels. After the revival of commerce and the voyages of exploration in the fifteenth and sixteenth centuries, the European peoples learned to enjoy many foreign products, such as coffee, tea, cocoa, tobacco, etc., but until the nineteenth century the European states still remained to a high degree self-sufficient and self-supporting.

Agriculture vs. industry

The Industrial Revolution tended to destroy this economic equilibrium. A modern industrial state such as England, with four fifths of the people living in towns, would find it impracticable if not actually impossible to raise at home the food required for its urban millions. Instead, the English people have learned to utilize the cheap and rapid transportation of the steam age to import vast supplies of wheat from Canada or Argentina and tons of frozen mutton from Australia. For this food, which makes good their own deficiency, they pay with shipments of manufactured articles from their humming factories, and so satisfactory did the method of exchange appear that British agriculture has been permitted to languish. In 1840, British farmers grew enough wheat to supply ninety per cent of the population of the United Kingdom, but by the close of the century their crops sufficed for only ten per cent. The German population has tended since 1870 to outgrow the domestic food supply in the same way, and, despite state encouragement and subsidies to the farmers, Germany has become partly dependent upon imported foodstuffs. On the other hand, France still demonstrates the balance which may be maintained between agriculture and industry, and has remained the most self-sufficient of the three powers, but France is not so highly industrialized as England or Germany and has a stationary or almost stationary population.

For the industrial state an equally serious problem arises from the fact that the insatiable capacity of the machines tends to outrun the domestic supply of raw material. England, long famous for the quality and quantity of her domestic wool, was able until a century ago to provide her mills with home-grown fleece. But industrial development rendered the local supply insufficient, and today four fifths of the wool utilized in the British textile trades comes from overseas. Where the raw materials of a trade cannot be raised in England, as in cotton manufacturing, the dependence upon foreign sources may be even more complete. Great Britain's imports of raw cotton have increased from a few million pounds a year in the eighteenth century to something over a billion, and her re-exports of cotton textiles have been valued at six hundred million dollars for a single year. Yet this gigantic industry, like many others in the British Isles, is dangerously dependent upon the vicissitudes of world trade. The ships which carry these cargoes back and forth are the indefatigable shuttles weaving the fabric of British commercial greatness. If they ceased to operate, even for a few weeks, British industry would face economic paralysis, and if the tie-up lasted several months, the British people would suffer the severest privation. This danger faces all states which devote a major part of their energies to the profitable but precarious hazards of modern industry.

The web of empire

Under these circumstances the great industrial powers must be prepared to safeguard their communications and to maintain contact with the foreign markets and sources of supply without which their home industries would languish. The incoming tide of raw materials and food, the outgoing flood of manufactures, these are the life blood of empire, and the railway and steamship lines are the channels through which this life blood ebbs and flows. This is the reason why modern governments often subsidize private transportation companies, why they build railways along strategic routes in the battle for trade, and are prepared to go to war to keep control of them. It also explains in part the interest which the great powers show in colonies and markets in the so-called "backward countries" of the world.

EXPERIMENTAL STREET CAR

Top: Cars driven by electricity were developed in several countries after 1880. This one ran near Berlin, Germany.

FIRST AIRPLANE FLIGHT (1903)

Center: Orville and Wilbur Wright conducted the first successful flights by a power-driven plane at Kitty Hawk, North Carolina.

DURYEA'S HORSELESS CARRIAGE

Inset: In the 1890's several inventors applied gasoline engines to drive a "horseless carriage."

But there is a second and less obvious reason which drove the powers to engage in an undignified scramble for control of the less civilized portions of the globe, especially after 1870. In all the industrialized states capital was accumulating as a result of business enterprise, and as the opportunities for highly profitable investment at home were narrowed by competition, the masters of this disposable capital looked abroad for new fields which might promise higher returns. They "exported" their capital to the backward countries, using it to open up untapped natural resources, to build roads and railways, and to develop new enterprises under favorable conditions which assured them a high rate of interest. Frequently the local rulers, like the Khedive of Egypt or the Sultans of Turkey and Morocco, invited this influx of capital because it helped to modernize their domains. The profits to be reaped from thus opening up backward and often anarchic countries were great, but the risks were great also, for local disturbances might endanger the plant or property which the investors' money had established. It was but natural, therefore, that British investors, for example, should appeal to their government to safeguard their investments by establishing a protectorate over the area they were exploiting. In its hidden but effective fashion, this pressure which British or German or American investors might bring to bear upon their respective governments to safeguard their exported capital provided a more persistent impulse toward imperialist expansion than either the profits of colonial trade (which were often negligible to the mother country) or the need to obtain raw materials (which could usually be purchased in the world's markets).

Backward countries

These several motives help to explain why the vast and half-unknown continent of Africa was parceled out among the European powers in little more than a decade after 1880, and the ancient but feeble Chinese Empire carved into "spheres of influence" as the Russians, British, French, Germans, and Japanese vied for control of the oriental resources. Even scattered islands in the seas, hitherto ignored as of no value or interest, were annexed as possible naval bases or sites for a cable or wireless station. Not since the colonizing ventures of the seventeenth century had Europeans shown such zeal in planting their flags on alien shores as in this era of the New Imperialism.

The native peoples of Africa and Asia frequently resented the imposition of foreign control, and all the colonizing powers became involved in frontier wars which were settled in almost all cases by the superiority of the white man's weapons. The New Imperialism brought with it, however, a threat of more serious conflict, of an armed struggle among the great powers themselves growing out of their clashing activities and claims. The tension already existing among the European nations was intensified by colonial rivalry and commercial competition; the result was a mutual increase in armaments which in turn increased the fear and suspicion. The consequences of this spirit of jealousy and of international covetousness were to be global conflicts, fought on a scale and with resources hitherto unimagined. The roots of the first of these wars will be examined in the two following chapters which discuss the class struggle within the industrialized states and the national antagonism among the industrialized states during the period 1871–1914.

Threat to world peace

59

The Social Conflict within Three Industrial States: Great Britain, France, and Germany

(1871–1914)

> ... Proclaiming social truth shall spread,
> And justice, ev'n though thrice again
> The red fool-fury of the Seine
> Should pile her barricades with dead.
>
> ALFRED TENNYSON, *IN MEMORIAM*, CXXVI.

THE MIDDLE YEARS of the nineteenth century were years of exceptional prosperity for the British people. As the greatest manufacturing, colonizing, and naval power of the world, Britain enjoyed a unique position in world affairs, a position which the Whig leader, Lord Palmerston, influential in foreign affairs throughout the period from 1830 to 1865, maintained vigorously by brandishing a "big stick" over the lesser nations. A spirit of complacency permeated the British ruling classes during this "Palmerstonian Era," which neither the blunders of the Crimean War nor the murmurs of the exploited masses could seriously disturb. The poet laureate, Alfred Tennyson, might lament "the faithless coldness of the times," but the rapid industrial expansion provided employment for all who sought it, and brought wealth to a growing number of business men, who were disposed to agree that all was for the best in the best of possible worlds.

British prosperity

1. THE MARCH OF DEMOCRACY IN GREAT BRITAIN (1867–1914)

The Chartist Movement had collapsed in 1848, but the prophets of democracy, the liberal and radical reformers, still raised their voices to demand the franchise for all adult males. Heartening reports of progress came from abroad. The establishment of a liberal monarchy in Italy (1859–61), the emancipation of the Russian serfs (1861), and the liberation of Negro slaves in the United States (1863), were events hailed by English liberals as milestones on the road to democracy. They demanded that England, the historic land of freedom, should lead the way in vindicating the rights of man and extend the vote to the common citizen. But the ruling classes remained hostile or indifferent to the idea of parliamentary reform. When, in 1866, William Ewart Gladstone (1809–98), the most popular and eloquent leader in the Liberal Party after Palmerston's death the previous year, proposed to add some four hundred thousand voters to

WILLIAM EWART GLADSTONE
(1809–1898)

Gladstone was a leading figure in British politics for over half a century.

BENJAMIN DISRAELI, EARL OF BEACONSFIELD
(1804–1881)

Disraeli first became Prime Minister in 1867 as head of the Conservative Party.

THE HOUSE OF COMMONS

The British House of Commons, shown here in a late session, preserved throughout the nineteenth century the air of a gentlemanly club.

the lists, his bill was rejected and the Liberal ministry resigned from office.

The Reform Bill of 1867
The defeat of Gladstone's bill created an outburst of popular indignation and was followed by threatening demonstrations in London and elsewhere. The brilliant and versatile Benjamin Disraeli (1804–81), who succeeded to the leadership of a Conservative ministry, decided that if the Conservatives wished to remain in power they would have to make concessions. So in 1867, Disraeli introduced a moderate reform bill and blandly permitted Gladstone, and the aggressive Liberal, John Bright, to amend it until it became more radical than the defeated bill of 1866. As finally passed, the Reform Bill of 1867 (supplemented by similar measures for Scotland and Ireland) added a million voters to the rolls and almost doubled the electorate. Disraeli's admitted purpose was to "dish" the Whigs (i.e., Liberals) by stealing their thunder, and he hoped that the workingmen whom he had enfranchised would vote for the Conservative Party out of gratitude. In obeying such selfish calculations, Disraeli did not stand alone, for many of the Whig members also had compromised with their prejudices and supported reform in order to attract the new voters. The vitriolic Thomas Carlyle, a friend of the oppressed but not of democracy, declared in a pamphlet on the bill — which he called ominously *Shooting Niagara: and After?* — that "Traitorous Politicians, grasping at votes, even votes from the rabble, have brought it on." Stanch reactionaries, who still clung to the time-hallowed conviction that the people who own a country, the propertied classes, were the only ones sane and stable enough to be trusted with political power, viewed the change with alarm and despondency.

Whatever their several motives, Gladstone, Disraeli, and Bright had advanced the British people a long stride on the way to complete democracy. Many tenant farmers in the country and all householders in the city, as well as all lodgers paying the equivalent of ten pounds a year for rent, won the ballot. Disraeli's argument that the Conservatives had shown themselves the true friends of the people, and his attempt to build up a "Tory-Democracy," met, however, with dubious success. The growing radical party in Parliament, including many delegates of the laboring classes, preferred to collaborate with the Liberals, who returned to power in 1868.

Third Reform Bill
In 1884, Gladstone introduced a further reform, extending the suffrage to include some two million agricultural laborers. The following year a Redistribution of Seats Bill enacted that each member of the House of Commons should represent a constituency of approximately fifty thousand inhabitants, but, as this provision was not consistently applied and no device included for redrawing the constituencies in obedience to the shifts and changes in population, proportional representation continued to be an ideal rather than a reality.

After 1884, four out of five adult Englishmen possessed the right to vote and the House of Commons might be considered to be fairly representative of the nation. But the House of Lords remained a stronghold of class privilege. Its membership was composed of several hundred hereditary English peers, two score elected peers chosen to represent the aristocracy of Scotland and Ireland, and the leading prelates of the Anglican Church. As all legislation had to be approved by both chambers, this aristocratic body enjoyed a virtual power of veto over the acts of the lower house. Usually, as in the case of the Reform Bill of 1867, the Lords showed the good sense to yield to the popular will, but their occasional opposition to liberal measures irritated many people who had come to consider the House of Lords a feudal anachronism.

Parliament Act (1911)
In 1909, the upper chamber excited particular indignation by throwing out a fiscal measure, although by custom all legislation concerning the budget had long been regarded as secure from such treatment. The Liberals, then in office, decided that the time had come to curtail the Lords' prerogatives, and despite Conservative resistance they passed the Parliament Act of 1911. Under this act all money bills voted by the House of Com-

mons were to become law after the lapse of one month, with or without the approval of the House of Lords. Other measures which the Lords opposed would become law after two years if passed by three successive sessions of the Commons. The members of the upper house could hardly be expected to approve the Parliament Act, but had they persisted in rejecting it the Liberal prime minister, Herbert Asquith, would have called upon George V to create enough new peers to change the balance, a move to which the king had pledged his agreement. As in the case of the Reform Bill of 1832, the threat sufficed and the Lords yielded.

In 1914, the Liberal program was interrupted by the outbreak of World War I.

Woman suffrage A vote for every adult male was assured, however, by the Reform Bill of 1918, and also for every woman over thirty provided that either she or her husband was eligible to vote in local elections. Full legal equality for women followed in 1919, a tribute to their varied services during the war, and in 1928 they obtained the ballot on the same terms as the men enjoyed. Great Britain had become, in theory at least, a land where the will of the people was the supreme law. The major demands of the Chartists, considered so dangerous and radical in the 1830's, had been adopted as matters of common practice less than a century later.

Of the Six Points of the Chartist program,[1] the abolition of the property qualification for members of Parliament had

Chartism vindicated first been enacted into law (1858); then followed the introduction of the secret (sometimes called the Australian) ballot (1872), the establishment of approximately equal electoral districts (1885), a salary for members of Parliament (1911), and universal adult male suffrage achieved through the successive reform bills of 1832, 1867, 1884, and 1918. The provision for annual Parliaments has not yet been adopted, but a five-year period has been set as the maximum interval that may elapse between elections.

This onward march of democracy is one of the most significant developments in British

[1] See above, pages 704–706.

history during the past hundred years. Without revolution, without serious disorder or bloodshed, the English liberalized their institutions and made their Parliament, once a stronghold of the privileged ruling classes, a flexible and responsive instrument of the people's will. This was a truly remarkable achievement, unmarred by violence or persecution, and Englishmen have reason to boast that theirs is a land "Where freedom broadens slowly down from precedent to precedent." If, as many of its protagonists had sworn, democracy held the answer to the ancient riddle of social justice, then a government which represented all classes should have been able to resolve the conflicts between those classes, and the legislators at Westminster, as democracy progressed, should have seen their way more and more clearly as they sought a remedy for the evils of the class struggle. To some extent they did; but in several important respects they failed. The story of that quest for social justice and its indeterminate outcome must now be told.

2. GREAT BRITAIN (1871–1914): THE QUEST FOR SOCIAL JUSTICE

From the beginning of the Industrial Revolution, the English workingmen had been confronted by two alternative programs for bettering their condition. The first was a political program. They might agitate for a more democratic franchise, elect delegates to Parliament, and work through their delegates for legislation that would assure them shorter hours, easier working conditions, and better wages. But such a workers' party had little chance to develop while the unpropertied classes still lacked the vote, and at first the English workingmen, especially in the years of depression which followed the Napoleonic Wars, gave little thought to politics. Instead, they favored a second program calling for more direct action. They organized trade unions or combinations whereby the metal-workers or the weavers or the papermakers might band together and extort more favorable terms from an employer by threatening a strike that would tie up his business. The law was hostile to such combinations, but they continued to operate, and the workers placed more confidence in such direct methods of bargaining than in tedious and uncertain political action. They were confirmed in this opinion when the Chartist Movement, despite the support that it received from the masses, failed to secure any parliamentary gains and broke up ignominiously after 1848.

Nevertheless, the occasional successes won by the trade unions did not obviate the fact that their members might be exposed to prosecution and their funds to confiscation under the existing laws. This difficulty did not disappear until after 1871, but with the passage of the Trade-Union Act of that year the organization of labor in Great Britain entered a new, legalized, and aggressive phase. Strikes became frequent, employers were thrown upon the defensive, and in 1899, the British Labor Movement was consolidated by the creation of a Federation of Trade Unions.

Trade-Union Act (1871)

Then came a serious setback. In 1901, the House of Lords, sitting as a court of final appeal, sustained a decision awarding the Taff Vale Railway Company £23,000 damages against the Amalgamated Society of Railway Servants for loss and destruction of property resulting from a strike. At a stroke of the pen the accumulated savings of all the trade unions, collected penny by penny to sustain the members through the possible privation of a strike, were placed in jeopardy. By this decision the unions would be exposed to possible suits for damages whenever their leaders ordered the members to lay down their tools.

Taff Vale decision

Leaders of the Trade-Union Movement now realized that perhaps organized labor had erred in avoiding the field of practical politics. If the existing laws worked against them, the existing laws would have to be changed by act of Parliament, for otherwise the gains of many years and many strikes might be undone by a few adverse verdicts. As early as 1893, a small Independent Labor Party had been organized by Mr. Keir Hardie, and there was in addition a Social Democratic Federation pledged to work for Marxian socialism. Furthermore, the members of the Fabian Society, a group of advanced thinkers which included the witty dramatist George Bernard Shaw, H. G. Wells the novelist, and writers on political and economic questions like Sidney and Beatrice Webb, were winning a strong following among the intellectuals and had begun to popularize socialist ideas among the liberal middle-class thinkers. These associations pressed their campaign so energetically between 1901 and 1906 that by the latter year Labor controlled twenty-nine seats in Parliament and had become a force in national politics.

Labor enters politics

The election of 1906 also brought the Liberal Party back into power after a decade of Conservative rule. By combining forces with the Laborites and with the Irish Nationalists (a parliamentary group seeking Home Rule for Ireland), the Liberals were in a position to control 514 seats against 156 held by the Conservatives. Under the leadership of the cool-headed Herbert Asquith, prime minister from 1908 to 1916, and the eloquent, mercurial Welshman, David Lloyd George, this *bloc* carried through a series of daring social reforms.

Reform era (1906–14)

One of the first fruits of the Liberal-Labor coalition was the Trades-Disputes Act (1906), which protected trade-union funds from the menace of the Taff Vale decision. Then the "New Liberals," having partly abandoned the old *laissez-faire* principles, attacked the evils of the industrial system with legislation which their opponents rightly termed "socialistic." A Workingmen's Compensation Act (1906) compelled employers to compensate a worker (or, in fatal mishaps, his family) for injuries incurred at his trade. Stringent regulations for the health and schooling of the young, and state pensions for the indigent old, followed in 1908. To relieve unemployment a government employment office was opened in 1909 to assist able-bodied workers to find occupations suited to their talents, and the same year a Trade Boards Act established commissions to regulate the wages and protect the employees from undue exploitation

Social legislation

BRITISH WORKERS' HOMES

The phenomenal industrial development of the nineteenth century crowded millions of British workers into ugly factories and monotonous homes.

in the so-called "sweatshops." The crowning achievement of this program of social reform was the adoption (1911) of a National Insurance Act. From premiums subscribed in part by the workers, in part by the employers, and in part by the state, a fund was established which gave the assurance to over two million workers that in case of unemployment they would receive an allowance of seven shillings a week. A much larger number were guaranteed free medical attention and weekly allowances in case of sickness, thus exorcising to some extent the cruelest fear that haunts people of small income and no resources.

To meet the mounting state expenditures resulting from the Old Age Pensions Act, the extension of education, and other items in the list of social reforms, the fiery crusader, Lloyd George, proposed to tax the rich. As chancellor of the exchequer he brought in a budget in 1909, which he frankly designated

The Budget of 1909

"a war budget" in the campaign against poverty. It not only increased the existing income and inheritance taxes, but laid a heavy strain upon the great landowners. In parts of England where land had recently increased in value, often through no effort of the owner, the government proposed to appropriate twenty per cent of such unearned increase. Idle land, particularly acreage set aside for private parks or game preserves, incurred a two per cent levy, and royalties derived from mineral deposits discovered on private property paid a five per cent tax. The House of Lords opposed this attempt "to lay the heaviest burden on the broadest back," a stand which moved the Liberals, as already explained, to reduce the obstructive power of the upper house to little more than a temporary or suspensive veto.

To rectify an old injustice and satisfy the Irish Nationalist Party, which had over eighty members in Parliament, the Liberals also passed a Government of Ireland Bill embodying a project for limited home rule. The bill excited frantic opposition from the inhabitants of Ulster, most of them Protestant descendants of English or Scottish settlers in northern Ireland, who feared that Home Rule would leave them at the mercy of the Irish Catholic majority. The Ulsterites and the Irish Nationalists were on the verge of armed conflict when the outbreak of World War I overshadowed their dispute and caused the suspension of the Government of Ireland Bill until the close of hostilities.

The war also brought to a close the era of the New Liberalism. In the progressive years, 1906–14, the political leaders had waged an energetic campaign against social injustice, relieving poverty, educating and elevating the masses, and distributing more equitably the burden of taxation. Yet these significant innovations had been fitted, with characteristic British caution, into the existing framework of government and society. The new architects had sought to compromise with, not to uproot, the old traditions, and even the emergence of a well-organized political group, pledged to socialist principles, had alarmed conservative opinion less than it might have been expected to do, perhaps because the new group called itself, not the "Socialist," but the "Labor Party."

Viewed as a triumph of political compromise, the reforms of 1906–14 might be called a success; but measured against the high hopes which a Thomas Jefferson or a Joseph Mazzini had reposed in the possibilities for good which would lie within the reach of a genuinely democratic government, they left much to be desired. Not in England only, but in all Europe, the decade before 1914 provided the best chance democratic statesmen had ever enjoyed to solve the conflicts within and between the different states. Some thinkers would have it that democracy failed to meet the test. Some are disposed to believe it succeeded as well as could be expected. Still others have argued that government by the people was never honestly tried, or that it failed to bring the peace and harmony expected of it because democratic institutions had been conceived in the eighteenth century when all nations were predominantly interested in agriculture, and applied in the nineteenth and twentieth centuries when the Industrial Revolution was remolding society on different lines. All these are speculations which the student might profitably ponder as he compares the social legislation introduced in France and Germany after 1871 with that which was passed in England.

Democracy on trial

3. FRANCE (1871–1914): CONSOLIDATING THE BOURGEOIS REPUBLIC

After the government of Napoleon III disappeared like an "insubstantial pageant faded" in the *débâcle* of Sedan, the French people pursued for six months longer a war that was already lost. Hostilities between the newly born French Republic and the newly proclaimed German Empire were formally closed by the Treaty of Frankfort (May 10, 1871), whereby France yielded the best part of Alsace and Lorraine and an indemnity of five billion francs.[1]

Not yet, however, were the misfortunes of "the terrible year" at an end. The National Assembly, which had been convoked at Bordeaux in February, 1871, was monarchist and bourgeois in temper, and the radical elements of the Parisian populace, led by Republicans and Socialists, repudiated its authority. Then followed a second siege of Paris, in which the defenders of the Commune, as the radical city government was termed, massacred their hostages and set fire to important buildings before they were suppressed in desperate street-to-street fighting by the national troops. The victims of this fratricidal strife exceeded fifteen thousand, and all Europe stood aghast at "the red fool-fury of the Seine." The merciless suppression of the *communards*, with the wholesale executions and deportations which followed, temporarily crushed the Socialist movement in France and left the bourgeois middle class securely entrenched, but it bequeathed a heritage of hate which continued to divide the workers from the propertied classes.

Paris Commune, 1871

Having restored order at this terrible cost,

[1] See above, page 754.

the National Assembly should have lost no further time in fulfilling its task and creating a permanent government for the republic. But the deputies were by no means certain whether they wished to make France a republic or a monarchy. The Monarchists, it is true, outnumbered the Republicans 500 to 200, but they were themselves split into Legitimists, Orléanists, and a few Bonapartists. In their dilemma they compromised by naming Adolph Thiers "President of the French Republic," as a temporary expedient, but when Thiers frankly defended the Republic as "the form of government which divides us least," the Monarchist majority replaced him (1873) by a stanch royalist, Marshal MacMahon, who could be counted upon to make way for a king at the right moment. The Legitimist pretender, the Count of Chambord (grandson of Charles X), might have mounted the throne as Henry V, but his insistence that before he did so the white flag of the Bourbons must replace the revolutionary tricolor proved a stumbling-block. Slowly the tide turned in favor of the Republican cause, which was championed indefatigably by the fiery and eloquent Léon Gambetta (1838–82). In 1875, the reluctant Assembly passed five constitutional laws which clarified the status of the quasi-republic, but the danger of a monarchist *coup* did not really wane until the elections of 1879 gave the Republicans control of the Senate as well as the Chamber of Deputies.

Deadlock (1871–75)

The Third Republic, established in this indefinite fashion, proved the most stable and enduring régime that France had known in a century. A Senate, the members of which were chosen through electoral colleges, and a Chamber of Deputies elected by universal manhood suffrage assured popular control. The president, elected for a seven-year term by the senators and deputies jointly, possessed a minimum of executive authority, the real power resting with the ministry or cabinet responsible to the Chamber of Deputies. In general, from 1879 to 1914 the successive *blocs* or coalition groups which controlled the Chamber and the cabinet represented the moderate republican point of view. The powerful middle class which had created the Third French Republic held it true to bourgeois principles.

Third French Republic

This middle-class rule was not maintained without a struggle. Two factions in France, the Clericals and the Royalists, were definitely hostile to the republican régime. They sought to discredit the leading Republican deputies by charges of dishonesty and incompetence, some of which were well deserved. Many Frenchmen, disgusted with the graft and intrigue that disfigured party politics, yearned for an efficient dictator of the Napoleonic type, a leader who would unite France and perhaps wage a war of revenge against Germany. From 1886 to 1889 General Georges Boulanger, minister of war, courted popularity and posed as the man of destiny, but Boulanger was no Napoleon and hesitated to gamble upon a *coup d'état*. When the republican government ordered an investigation of his activities, he fled from France, and the Boulangist Movement collapsed in ridicule, to the discomfiture of its supporters.

"Man on horseback"

Five years later the rivalry between the friends and foes of the republic provided the passionate and dramatic setting for a new dispute. In 1894, Captain Alfred Dreyfus, a Jew and an officer in the French army, was convicted by a military court of communicating important secrets to a foreign power, and sentenced to life imprisonment in a penal colony off the coast of French Guiana. Members of Dreyfus's family and others who had convinced themselves of his innocence (among them the famous novelist, Émile Zola) demanded a new trial, but the anti-Dreyfusards, led by high military officials, Clericals, and Monarchists, were satisfied of his guilt. Many of them regarded him as a symbol of the corruption, treachery, and commercialism which they conceived to be ruining France under the republican rule. But when subsequent revelations (1897–99) proved that the real culprit, a Major Esterhazy, had been shielded, and evidence exonerating Dreyfus withheld from those who sought to reopen the case, lest the prestige of

The Dreyfus case

the army staff should suffer, French public opinion underwent a profound reversal. Dreyfus, brought back from Devil's Island for a retrial (1899), was again found guilty by his hostile judges, but President Loubet pardoned him, and the supreme court of France finally exonerated him completely (1906). Royalism, clericalism, and militarism had been so thoroughly discredited by the revelations of this famous case that, from 1899 until the outbreak of the war in 1914, Republicans and Socialists controlled the Chamber of Deputies.

One of the first steps taken by the Republican-Socialist "Cabinet of Republican Defense" of 1899 was to "purify" the army, too long a stronghold of royalist sympathizers, and subordinate it to the civil authority. Having thus "republicanized" the military institutions, the cabinet attacked the more difficult task of curbing clerical activity. By the *concordat* of 1801,[1] which still remained in force, the government of the Third Republic was committed to an agreement to pay the salaries of the clergy. Furthermore, the clergy had continued to supervise the training of the young, and might, some liberals feared, teach them to grow up reactionary Monarchists instead of ardent Republicans. The first blow struck against this clerical influence was the Associations Law (1901), which had the effect of dissolving most of the religious orders engaged in teaching and charitable work in France, and of curbing religious instruction in the schools. The second blow followed in 1905 with the repeal of the *concordat*. A Separation Law stripped the Catholic Church of its advantages, ended the payment of state salaries to the priests, and the state appointment of bishops. The Roman Catholic Church in France was left to stand on practically the same footing as other religious cults.

Though its birth had been ill-omened and its early decades inauspicious, the bourgeois republic had attained at the end of its first thirty years a position of remarkable strength and solidity. Despite frequent cabinet crises caused by party shifts in the Chamber of Deputies, France had evolved a régime

The republic triumphs

[1] See above, page 658.

which appeared to meet her needs, with the army and the civil administration subservient to the rule of the middle class. But in France as in England this rule of the middle class was threatened at its foundations by the growth of an organized labor movement and the spread of socialism. This development must now be considered.

4. FRANCE (1871–1914): THE SPREAD OF SYNDICALISM AND SOCIALISM

The bloody suppression of the Paris Commune in 1871 shattered the Socialist Party in France for a generation. French workingmen retained, however, the privilege of forming labor unions and could call a strike to enforce their demands. In 1876, a labor congress convened at Paris, representing unions or *syndicats* from all parts of France, and in 1884 the government granted the *syndicats* full legal recognition. Unfortunately, the labor leaders could not agree among themselves concerning their aims or their methods. Some favored the idea of working with the Socialists for legislation that would reduce the hours of labor and compel employers to improve the conditions in mines and factories. But a majority of the French workers, like the English trade-unionists, were persuaded that they could do best for themselves by direct bargaining. If we elect leaders to the Chamber of Deputies, they argued, we shall have no control over them if they choose to compromise our interests and go over to the side of our masters.

So the members of the *syndicats* told the Socialists to go ahead in their own fashion, but for themselves they considered it more profitable to organize their forces in a General Confederation of Labor (1895). In this way they planned to work for the day when they would be strong enough to bring their capitalist employers to terms through a general strike, and expropriate the expropriators as Karl Marx had prophesied that they would do.

Several times between 1900 and 1910 the *syndicats* attempted to test their strength by strikes, and several times they gained concessions, but the results were not conclusive. Their most ambitious effort, a strike of the railway

Organized labor

Railway strike (1910)

workers, proved their most signal defeat. To tie up all railway transportation even for a few days would not only cripple the industries of a modern state, but would also cut off the food supplies from the great cities. The syndicalists believed that they would have the government of France at their mercy, but when they called their strike, the government struck back cleverly and effectively. The prime minister, Aristide Briand, had formerly been a Socialist, but his sympathy for radical measures did not restrain him from proclaiming a national emergency and calling in military aid to keep the trains moving. The strikers were faced by a difficult dilemma. As soldiers in the class war, their duty was to preserve a passive resistance, but as soldiers in the French army (all able-bodied Frenchmen were liable for military service), they could be ordered to drive the trains or face a court martial. In the test military discipline triumphed over syndicalist solidarity and the strike collapsed (1910).

Through this lesson the French syndicalists learned, as the English trade-unionists had discovered a few years earlier, that they had little chance of scoring a decisive triumph with the forces of law and government against them. But, as in England, their Socialist allies had been gaining political recognition during these same years, and were in a position to win concessions by less revolutionary means. In 1905, a United Socialist Party was organized in France and polled a million votes the following year. By 1910, the Socialists counted 105 delegates in the Chamber of Deputies, led by the patriotic Alexandre Millerand and the profound and witty historian and journalist Jean Jaurès. All the important measures which succeeded the *dénouement* of the Dreyfus affair, the "republicanization" of the army and the separation of church and state, were passed by a *bloc* composed of the parties of the Left — that is, of Republicans and Socialists. As a reward for their cooperation, the Socialists asked the adoption of old age insurance. Between 1905 and 1910 a compulsory pension system was worked out to assure all men and women workers a retirement allowance when they

Socialist legislation

reached the age of sixty, the premiums to be subscribed by the workers, their employers, and the state. The state also encouraged the introduction of accident and liability insurance on a large scale, but left the management of it to private associations. A ten-hour day in the factories, more sanitary conditions to safeguard the workers' health, and strict injunctions against overworking children to the detriment of their welfare and education, were further legislative achievements resulting from the initiative of the Socialists.

These concessions to the proletariat, in so far as they were designed to improve social conditions, often won the approval of Catholic deputies on the Right as well as Socialist deputies on the Left, though for a different reason. Heeding the advice offered by Pope Leo XIII in 1892, a section of the French Catholic Party rallied to the support of the republic and were known in consequence as *Ralliés*. Organized after 1901 as the Party of Liberal Action, this group pledged its representatives in the Chamber of Deputies to accept the republican régime instead of opposing it as some clericals and monarchists still insisted upon doing, to labor for the protection of the Catholic faith in France, and to promote legislation favorable to the working classes. It was the hope of these leaders of liberal clerical opinion that the spread of socialism might be curbed if the conflict between capital and labor were eased by means of remedial legislation which reflected a spirit of Christian charity. Despite their efforts, however, the Socialist Party continued to grow, and in 1914 there were over 130 deputies in the Chamber who might be considered as Socialists, although only 102 belonged to the United Socialist Party. In France as in Great Britain this rising influence of the proletariat was the outstanding political development of the pre-war era. The socialists defended their platform on the ground that it would assure a larger share of the profits of industry to the workers, and they also hoped to reduce the danger of war by curbing ruthless commercial competition and negotiating with other socialist governments for a general reduction of armaments.

Liberal Action

SACRÉ COEUR

Above: The hill of Montmartre in Paris was a stronghold of the Communards in the fratricidal struggle of 1871. It is now crowned by the spires of the Church of the Sacred Heart.

ÉMILE ZOLA (1840–1902)

Upper left: This portrait of Zola is by the French painter Édouard Manet. Zola risked liberty and reputation to champion the falsely convicted Captain Dreyfus.

LÉON GAMBETTA (1838–1882)

Lower left: Gambetta labored to establish the Third French Republic until his death in 1882.

British and French socialists were encouraged by the fact that in Germany, also, socialism was advancing, although there it pursued a somewhat dissimilar course.

5. THE GERMAN EMPIRE (1871–1914): FOUNDATION AND EXPANSION

Bismarck's pronouncement that the great questions of the day would be decided by blood and iron rather than by speeches or majority votes had proved true of the events which led to the forging of the German Empire. The Danish War (1864) had cut short the argument whether Schleswig and Holstein should or should not be incorporated in the new Germany. The Austro-Prussian War (1866) and the Franco-Prussian War (1870–71) had repulsed and excluded outside influences, leaving Bismarck at liberty to organize the Germanies into a powerful state under Prussian leadership. These conflicts were the birth-pangs of a new international order, for the sudden emergence of the German Empire, which was created, like the goddess Athena, full grown and fully armed, replaced the existing balance of power in Europe by what amounted to a German hegemony.

Unlike Cavour, who died before Italian unity had been fully realized, Bismarck enjoyed the opportunity to direct for nearly twenty years the policies of the empire which he had helped to create. The leading German princes, it will be recalled, proclaimed William I of Prussia "German Emperor" on January 18, 1871, at Versailles. The constitution of the new federation was not promulgated until some months later and proved to be a severely practical document. The states previously allied in the North German Confederation (1867) were now joined by the four South German States. All twenty-five [1] members of the new *Bund*

German Constitution

[1] The states composing the German Empire in 1871 included the four kingdoms of Prussia, Bavaria, Saxony, and Württemberg; the six grand duchies of Baden, Hesse, Mecklenburg-Schwerin, Saxe-Weimar, Mecklenburg-Strelitz, and Oldenburg; the five duchies Brunswick, Saxe-Meiningen, Saxe-Altenburg, Saxe-Coburg-Gotha, and Anhalt; the seven principalities of Schwarzburg-Sonderhausen, Schwarzburg-Rudolstadt, Waldeck, Reuss (older line), Reuss (younger line), Lippe, and Schaumburg-Lippe; and the three free cities

were to send delegates to a federal council or *Bundesrat* of 58 members, a body comparable in some respects to the United States Senate, with the difference, however, that the members were not elected, but appointed, and the state representation varied from Prussia, which held seventeen votes, to the smallest states with one apiece. There was also a popular lower chamber, the *Reichstag*, made up of 382 deputies. Outwardly, the imperial German government corresponded to the bicameral legislative systems of Britain and France, but there was one significant point of difference. Instead of providing for a cabinet of ministers responsible to the *Reichstag*, the constitution vested all ministerial authority in a single official, the president of the *Bundesrat*, who, as imperial chancellor, held his office at the emperor's pleasure and was not answerable for his actions to the assemblies. This all-important chancellery post Bismarck reserved for himself.

It was a matter of grave import for German and European history that this constitution failed, despite appearances, to establish a government that was representative of the German people or responsible to them. The chancellor was not a prime minister obedient to the will of a parliamentary majority. Furthermore, the *Bundesrat*, the members of which were nominated by the German princes, was superior to the *Reichstag* elected by the German people. Thus the *Reichstag*, though freely elected by all male Germans over twenty-four (a more democratic franchise than the three-class system of Prussia),[1] could not control cabinet policy as surely as the British Commons or the French Chamber of Deputies did. In this respect the new German government remained an autocracy or oligarchy rather than a democracy. A second point to note is the dominant position assumed by Prussia, a position so commanding that it is scarcely an exaggeration to say that the Germanies

Irresponsible government

of Hamburg, Bremen, and Lübeck. Alsace-Lorraine ranked as an imperial territory and remained without representation on the *Bundesrat* until 1911.

[1] See above, pages 717–718.

MODERN INDUSTRIAL PLANT, BREMEN

The iron sinews which made Germany powerful in peace and terrible in war grew from industrial plants like these at Bremen and Pilsen.

STEEL AND IRON WORKS, PILSEN

had been conquered and "Prussianized" by that militant kingdom. Bismarck had been solicitous to leave the smaller states the illusion of sovereignty; but the facts were that the King of Prussia had become German Emperor, and he appointed the all-powerful chancellor, who in turn selected the chief functionaries of the imperial government. In the *Bundesrat*, Prussia held 17 of the 58 votes and could as a rule dominate the deliberations.[1] The union of states was indissoluble and the Prussian vote could defeat any amendment to the constitution.

Powers not specifically delegated to the imperial government were reserved by the component states, which continued to handle their own fiscal, religious, educational, and administrative problems. So tactfully had Bismarck gathered the reins of power into his own hands that the minor states were unaware of the degree to which they had compromised their independence. The coinage, the banking system, the railways, telegraphs, and mails, and later the codes of civil and criminal law, were all harmonized and subjected to the regulation of the imperial bureaucracy. Although several states, notably Bavaria, Württemberg, and Saxony, maintained their separate army contingents and even their separate consular services, these survivals of particularism steadily lost significance as the authority and efficiency of the imperial government increased.

States rights

As the disparate segments of the empire were knit into an indissoluble whole, the German merchants and manufacturers discovered that political unity was a boon to business. The federal administration of the transport and communication services made them the nerves and sinews of a new economic order, and Bismarck counted upon the effects of the industrial expansion to vindicate and strengthen his political architecture.

For the German people after 1871 encountered the full transforming force of the Industrial Revolution, that irresistible ferment stirred by mechanical innovations, which had appeared in England a century earlier and had modified French society during the reigns of Louis Philippe and Napoleon III. The effects of the factory system and of machine production came still later to Germany, but for that reason they came with accelerated force. In Great Britain the mechanization of industry had been achieved in successive stages, from the eighteenth-century improvements in spinning and weaving to the technical inventions which multiplied in all trades after 1850. But in Germany the Industrial Revolution did not really manifest itself until approximately the middle of the nineteenth century. Then, borrowing the experience and the machinery of the British and French, German industrialists proceeded to overtake their rivals. In this they were enormously aided by the scientific progress made after 1870. Thus, the first wave of the Industrial Revolution (which had introduced the steam engine and the factory system in England a century earlier) and the second wave (for such the flood of technological inventions, electrical devices and chemical discoveries that began about 1870 may be called) both struck Germany in the same years. This largely explains the phenomenal development of German industry under the empire, but it must not be forgotten that the political consolidation achieved in 1871 smoothed the way for the industrial expansion which was already overdue.

Industrialism in Germany

6. THE GERMAN EMPIRE (1871–1914): ECONOMIC AND SOCIAL PROBLEMS

As in England and France, the spread of the factory system created in Germany a class of proletarian workers who organized trade unions to protect their rights and adopted socialistic views in politics. Until 1875, the German workingmen were divided, some adhering strictly to the teaching of Karl Marx, while others joined a Socialist Party formed in 1863 by Ferdinand Lassalle (1825–64). The union of these two factions into a single Social Democratic Party (1875), pledged to seek immediate legislation for the relief of the workers, and ultimate socializa-

The Social Democrats

---

[1] Subsequent to 1871, Prussia acquired the vote of Waldeck, and the two votes of Brunswick, raising her total for all practical purposes to twenty.

tion of industry, alarmed the forceful Bismarck. As he had no liking for democracy or socialism, he determined to destroy the Social Democratic Party before it grew strong enough to constitute a menace.

Although the constitution rendered the chancellor independent of the *Reichstag*, Bismarck knew that he could not rule without the approval of some powerful political groups. From 1871 to 1879, while he was consolidating the new imperial régime, he leaned upon the National Liberals, a party chiefly representing the upper middle class, the business men, bankers, lawyers, doctors, professors, etc. To satisfy the National Liberals, who favored free trade and responsible parliamentary government, Bismarck proposed low tariffs and pretended to have more patience for the ideals of free speech and freedom of the press than he really felt. The National Liberals supported him in his task of strengthening the central government and he joined them in making war upon the Catholic Church in Germany. The story of Bismarck's clash with the church is interesting for the light it throws upon his prejudices and his ability to profit by his mistakes.

National Liberals

The German Catholics, finding themselves a minority in the new empire, organized a strong Center Party after 1871 to protect their interests. The Center Party drew most of its support from the South German States, where many people were inclined to be distrustful of Protestant Prussia and of the centralizing policy pursued by Bismarck and the National Liberals. The Catholics in Germany, however, were themselves divided in sentiment, for the pope had recently been proclaimed infallible in matters of faith and morals by the Vatican Council, a decree not altogether popular in Germany. As one group of German Catholics, known as the "Old Catholics," declined to accept the decree of papal infallibility, Bismarck encouraged this schism by supporting them against the orthodox bishops, and this opened a conflict honored by the grandiose title of the *Kulturkampf* or "struggle for civilization." In 1872, the Jesuits were expelled from Germany and diplomatic relations severed between Berlin and the Vatican. In 1873 and 1874, the Prussian government prohibited the appointment of anyone to a clerical office in Prussia unless he were a native German and had attended a German high school and university, and declared all clerical appointments subject thenceforth to state approval. When the Catholic clergy opposed these decrees, they were expelled or arrested, and within a few years two thirds of the Prussian Catholic bishops had been driven from their dioceses and four hundred parishes lacked pastors. But instead of disintegrating, the Catholic resistance throve under this persecution and the Centrists increased their representation in the *Reichstag*. Awake to the danger which might result if the Centrists and Socialists fused their forces in an opposition *bloc*, Bismarck decided to change his tactics and halt the *Kulturkampf*. His enemies declared that, like the headstrong emperor, Henry IV, eight hundred years earlier, he had "gone to Canossa" — that is, yielded to the pope — but it would be more just to say that, like Henry IV, he had escaped from a threatening situation by an adroit move.

The *Kulturkampf*

For, dropping his war on the Catholics after 1878, Bismarck freed his hands for a struggle with the Socialists. His aims were: (1) to cripple the Social Democratic Party by repressive decrees; (2) to placate the discontented workingmen who voted Socialist by introducing legislation which would ease their grievances; and (3) to make the imperial government financially independent of state contributions by erecting a high protective tariff on imports. To follow this new course meant a break with the National Liberals, who disliked repressive legislation and opposed high tariffs. But the chancellor believed that he could win the Center Party to his side, and he counted upon the support of the landowners and manufacturers who would profit by a tariff which would protect them from the agricultural and industrial competition of other lands.

Two attempts at assassination made against the venerable William I (1878) provided an excuse for harsh measures against all radical trouble-makers. They were forbidden to publish or propagate their doctrines, or to hold meetings, and were exposed to arbitrary arrest. To reconcile the working classes and give them a motive for supporting the state, Bismarck drafted a comprehensive code of social insurance. The Sickness Insurance Law (1883) provided a fund, to which the employers contributed one third of the premiums, whereby workers were assured half-pay and medical attention for six months in case of illness. By the Accident Insurance Law (1884) employers were compelled to establish a fund providing compensation to workers partially or totally disabled through accidents of their trade, and a pension of one fifth the annual wages to the dependents of a worker killed while working. Most ambitious of all was the Old Age Pension Act (1889). Compulsory contributions from employers and workers, augmented by the state, provided a retirement annuity for all workers who reached their seventieth birthday or became incapacitated before that age. Although Socialist leaders denounced these measures as a means of insuring the capitalist system rather than the workers, and exhorted their followers not to be lulled by such pretended charity into a forgetfulness of their rights, the state insurance laws in Germany did much to alleviate the misery and anxiety of the poorer classes. Moreover, the extraordinary prosperity of German industry enabled the employers to carry their contributory burden with ease. It is not without interest to note that the autocratic and conservative Bismarck anticipated by more than twenty years the social legislation later enacted by the Liberal-Labor coalition group in Great Britain and by the Republican-Socialist *bloc* in France.

William I died in 1888 and was succeeded by his son, Frederick III, who reigned only a few months. On the latter's death in the same year the throne passed to William II (1888–1918), a prince of versatile talents, but unstable and impetuous moods. Determined to be his own chief minister, William II relieved Bismarck of his office in 1890, and the great chancellor retired with bitterness and foreboding in his heart. His successors in office, the rigid and pious Caprivi (1890–94), the aged Prince Hohenlohe (1894–1900), the supple Prince von Bülow (1900–09) and the ill-starred von Bethmann-Hollweg (1909–17), were none of them men of Bismarck's stature, and German policy, domestic and foreign, lost much of its earlier unity of will and direction.

Disapproving of Bismarck's harshness toward the Socialists, William II allowed the repressive legislation against them to lapse, and the Social Democratic Party, which had elected 9 deputies to the *Reichstag* in 1878, and 35 in 1890, increased its representation to 81 by 1903. By 1912 the Social Democrats held 110 seats and constituted the largest party in the *Reichstag*.

Thus, despite repression, and despite the paternal legislation intended as a sop to the workers, the Socialists had gained ground as their doctrines appealed to a wider and wider circle of voters. The class which Bismarck had called "the disinherited" appeared to be headed for ultimate control in Germany as in Great Britain and France. It is important to note, however, that as socialism became more popular in these three countries it became less radical, and Socialists abandoned the call to revolution in favor of more cautious and constitutional reforms. In this way they attracted many liberal-minded people who approved of remedial legislation for the benefit of the workers, higher income and inheritance taxes aimed at the rich, and a policy of progressive socialization of industry. With respect to foreign policy, Socialists were disposed to "view with alarm" the excessive growth of armaments and to denounce the methods by which most governments acquired and exploited the lands of backward peoples principally for the benefit of capitalists and business men at home. But the acquisition of colonies and the possession of a strong army and navy pleased so many unthinking people and flattered their patriotic pride so much that the Socialist leaders met with little success when they sought to reduce armaments and curb the aggressive imperialism of the era 1871–1914. In matters of foreign policy nationalism proved a stronger force than socialism.

60

The Competition among the Industrialized States: The Race for Colonies and Markets

(1871–1914)

The day of small nations has passed away; the day of Empires has come.
JOSEPH CHAMBERLAIN (1836–1914).

THE NINETEENTH CENTURY witnessed an exodus of European peoples to other parts of the globe in a remarkable migration surpassing anything of its kind in previously recorded history. Accurate statistics are lacking on many phases of this mass movement, but competent estimates place the number of European emigrants who took up permanent residence in the Americas, Asia, or Australia between 1800 and 1900 at forty to fifty millions. The greater number of these emigrants settled in the United States or the republics of Central and South America, lands dominated by European culture, but no longer attached politically to any European empire. But part of the tide also flowed to the colonies and dependencies of the European powers and helped to build up their overseas dominions. It is the purpose of the present chapter to describe the empires overseas which were acquired by Great Britain, France, Germany, and Italy, how they were governed, and especially how the rival powers clashed more and more frequently as they competed for the unclaimed areas of the earth and sought to win them as fields for imperial exploitation.

1. THE NEW IMPERIALISM AFTER 1871

As already explained in an earlier chapter,[1] Spain, Portugal, Holland, France, and England all established overseas empires in the sixteenth and seventeenth centuries. By the close of the Seven Years' War in 1763, Great Britain had usurped the lion's share of both colonies and trade, and her rivals, defeated and discomfited, largely lost interest in the competition. For the first three quarters of the nineteenth century, the European peoples gave their chief attention to the problems arising from the French Revolution, and to the national movements which culminated in the unification of Italy and of Germany. After 1871, the question of colonies came again to the fore, and Europe entered a new and dynamic phase of overseas expansion often referred to as the "New Imperialism." Like the growth of cities or the rise of socialism, the New Imperialism will be found upon examination to derive its strength from the forces let loose by the Industrial Revolution. For the highly industrialized state, colonies had sud-

[1] Pages 585–599.

denly acquired a new value as fields for the investment of surplus capital, as sources of raw material, as potential markets which could not be closed by foreign tariffs, and as reservoirs for the excess population of the home country.

2. THE BRITISH EMPIRE IN 1871

Following the loss of the thirteen American colonies, the slow growth of more liberal policies and democratic ideals in England inspired British statesmen to administer the colonial dependencies more tactfully. In Canada, which had been conquered from France (1763), the settlers, predominantly Catholic and French, had been reconciled by the assurance that they might retain their language and religion undisturbed (Quebec Act, 1774). Friction between the French and incoming English colonists was difficult to avoid and discontent with the royal administration led to small revolts, but a measure of local self-government eased the tension (1840), and Canada was later raised to the status of a confederated state by the British North America Act (1867). A bicameral legislature modeled upon the British Parliament assured the Canadian people control of their own affairs, and a governor general appointed from London fulfilled the constitutional and largely nominal duties discharged in England by the king. As a self-governing dominion in the British Commonwealth of Nations, Canada has developed her vast natural resources, linked up her scattered provinces with transcontinental railways, and increased her population to twelve million (1945).

Dominion of Canada

The island continent of Australia first became substantially known to the English when it was visited in 1770 by the famous navigator, Captain James Cook. The first settlement was established (1788) as a place of banishment for criminals, but during the nineteenth century five separate areas were colonized, with a sixth colony on the nearby island of Tasmania, and a seventh on New Zealand, twelve hundred miles to the east. The discovery of gold about 1850 and the profits of sheep-raising drew an increasing stream of immigrants to Australia, and in 1900 the separate provinces on the mainland joined with Tasmania to form the Commonwealth of Australia, the second largest self-governing dominion within the British Empire. As in the case of Canada, the Australian Parliament consists of a bicameral legislature and a governor general appointed by the British crown. As in Canada, manufacturing in Australia has overtaken and now exceeds in value the output of all agricultural activities. The population, including Tasmania, is over seven and a half million (1945).

Australia

The separate group of islands known as New Zealand attained dominion status in 1907. Politically the colonists have distinguished themselves chiefly by their democratic and socialistic experiments. Universal suffrage, state ownership of railways, state departments for life, accident, and fire insurance, old age pensions, and compensation for workers injured at their trade were all introduced in New Zealand before 1900. Both Australia and New Zealand have adopted a rigid immigration policy, so that their population is drawn almost exclusively from peoples of European ancestry. The population of New Zealand is approximately two million.

New Zealand

In India the British extended their influence inland from the trading posts, established in the seventeenth and eighteenth centuries, until they controlled the whole country with its teeming millions. Until 1858, the management of this empire, continental in its vast extent, was left in the hands of the British East India Company under the supervision (after 1784) of a royal board of control known as the "India Office." The sudden outbreak of a serious revolt in the Ganges Valley (1857), headed by native troops or *sepoys* and consequently termed the Sepoy Mutiny, led to cruel reprisals by the British, but also to a more enlightened type of rule. A secretary of state for India in the British cabinet and a governor general at Calcutta, assisted by a council and by provincial governors, superseded the régime of the East India Company (1858). In several hundred states, comprising perhaps two fifths of India, the native potentates continued to govern under Brit-

India

ASIA 1914

ish supervision, but in the larger part of the peninsula the white conquerors took charge of the administration.

The benefits conferred by British rule in India, in the form of better agricultural methods, irrigation systems, highways, canals, and railways, might be more deeply appreciated by the native population if the British had shown equal solicitude in promoting education and training for self-government. But to interfere with the social and religious customs of an oriental people is a dangerous experiment, and the British have allowed nine tenths of India's four hundred million people to remain submerged in a state of illiteracy and often of degrading superstition. In defense of this policy many Englishmen have argued that western ideals of education and democracy are unsuited to the eastern mind; that, despite the influence and prestige of the British administrators, they could not, even if they would, change the habits of an ancient and unprogressive people. Their position in India, like that of white men everywhere among less aggressive and less civilized peoples, has brought them a sort of "bewildered omnipotence" which they scarcely know how to use.

Since 1900, a growing body of Indian nationalists have demanded a greater measure of self-government so that the Indian peoples may learn to modernize themselves in their own way. Limited representative assemblies were conceded to most of the provinces of British India in 1909, but, despite this beginning of reform, nationalist sentiment has grown steadily and has led to acts of violence, the assassination of British officials, and consequent measures of repression. India is "the brightest jewel in the British crown," not only because of the valuable crops of cotton and wheat raised there, but also because it provides a market for textile and factory products. As a self-governing dominion, India might attempt to exclude British goods or even to secede from the empire. Naturally the possibility of such a grievous economic loss makes it difficult for the British people to view the Indian nationalist movement in a candid and impartial fashion, and they find it easy to believe that the nationalists represent only a noisy and discontented minority of India's millions and that the inarticulate masses are truly grateful for the benefits of British rule.

Indian nationalism

The lesser portions of the British Empire in 1871 included a number of crown colonies and protectorates scattered about the globe, as Gibraltar and Malta in the Mediterranean; British Guiana, British Honduras, the British West Indies, Bermuda, and the Falkland Islands in the New World; Aden, Ceylon, Lower Burma, and Hongkong in Asia; and Gambia, Sierra Leone, Cape Colony, and Natal in Africa. This impressive heritage, which the British had built up in the course of two hundred and fifty years of conquest and colonization, was destined to undergo further expansion under the stimulus of the New Imperialism.

3. BRITISH ACQUISITIONS (1871–1914)

In 1875, the imperialistically inclined Disraeli was able to increase British influence in the Mediterranean by purchasing a considerable share in the Suez Canal, the completion of which six years earlier had opened a new and shorter sea route to India. To safeguard the canal became one of the guiding motives of British foreign policy. When the Khedive (or ruler) of Egypt defaulted on his debts to European bankers, France and Britain established a condominium over that country (including the canal), despite the fact that technically it formed part of the Turkish Empire. The French government was only passively interested, but the British increased their military control, repressed an insurrection of the Egyptians (1882), and soon enjoyed a protectorate in everything but name. Anglo-Egyptian forces subdued the fierce Mohammedan tribes of the Sudan after several reverses and by 1900 the upper valley of the Nile had been marked out as a sphere of British influence.[1]

Egypt

At the headwaters of the Nile the area known as Uganda, lying to the north of Lake Victoria, was proclaimed a protectorate in 1894, and the following year the territory between Uganda and the Indian Ocean, which had already been chartered by the

[1] See map on page 819.

British East Africa Company, became a protectorate also. Though bisected by the Equator, British East Africa proved suitable for white settlers in the elevated sections. Less healthy, but valuable because of the tin, rubber, palm oil, and ivory produced there, was the lower Niger Valley, proclaimed a British protectorate in 1914, and the hinterland of the Gold Coast (Ashanti), annexed in 1886. British Somaliland, at the mouth of the Red Sea, became a protectorate in 1884, and the territory lying back of Sierra Leone was delimited as a sphere of British influence in 1889.

The most important area which the British won in the partitioning of Africa remains to be mentioned last. Since 1806, when they conquered Capetown from the Dutch, the British had made it a port of call for their ships on the long sea voyage to India. Preferring to keep their independence, the Dutch settlers, or Boers, moved inland and established the Orange Free State and the Transvaal Republic. But discoveries of gold and diamonds in South Africa after 1886 brought an influx of British colonists and precipitated an armed conflict between the Boer Republics and the British Empire. Such a war could end only one way, but unequal as it seemed, the struggle cost the British three years of fighting before they could break the resistance of the Boers, whose stubborn courage won the admiration of the world. By granting favorable terms, including $15,000,000 for the farms destroyed, the British government endeavored to placate their late adversaries. Seven years after the conclusion of peace, the provinces of Cape Colony, Natal, Orange Free State, and the Transvaal united to form the self-governing Union of South Africa (1909).

Boer War

Under the inspiration of an indefatigable empire-builder, Cecil Rhodes, the British pressed inland from their South African settlements to establish a protectorate over Bechuanaland (1885) and occupy the area traversed by the upper Zambesi River, now known as Rhodesia. With the proclamation of a protectorate over Nyasaland (1891) and the submission of the Boer Republics (1902), Rhodes's dream of a railroad that would run from Capetown to Cairo without leaving British territory seemed at the point of realization. But the proclamation of a German protectorate over the East African mainland opposite Zanzibar (1890) and the extension of this protectorate inland until it linked itself with the Belgian Congo at the head of Lake Tanganyika effectively broke the contiguity of the British possessions.[1]

In Asia, British expansion since 1871 has been largely confined to the task of consolidating and extending the frontiers of the Indian Empire. To forestall Russian interference, the Indus Valley from Sind to Kashmir had been occupied between 1840 and 1850; Beluchistan was added in 1876, and Afghanistan transformed into a buffer state under British influence.[2] In 1904, the Chinese province of Tibet likewise became a "sphere of British influence"; and in 1907, Persia was subdivided into a northern (or Russian) zone, a neutral center zone, and a southern (or British) zone. The compromise over Persia reflects the more amicable spirit which developed between England and Russia after 1905. As Russia had suffered a defeat at the hands of the Japanese, and the British were alarmed at the growth of German power, the diplomats at London and Saint Petersburg were more disposed to reach an agreement over Indian frontier problems than they had been earlier.

Rivalry in Asia

On the northeastern boundaries of India, the British had already conquered Assam and Lower Burma before 1871. In 1886, the native ruler was deposed, and the whole of Burma, a kingdom larger in area than the State of California, became part of the British Indian Empire. Holding in addition the Malay States, the Straits Settlements, and the northern coast of Borneo, Britain enjoyed a dominant position on the South China Sea.

Burma

A war with China (1840–42), occasioned by the efforts of the Chinese government to forbid importations of opium, delivered the island of Hongkong into British hands. The trade in opium, which was raised in India

Hongkong and Canton

---

[1] See map on page 819.
[2] See map on page 813.

and sold in China to the considerable profit of the British East India Company, helped to produce a second Chinese War (1856–60). By a joint offensive, Britain and France compelled the Chinese to pay a further indemnity, open new ports to trade, admit and protect Christian missionaries, and permit the traffic in opium. As a consequence of this "Second Opium War" the British gained a foothold at Canton and established another "sphere of influence" in the Yangtze Valley.

4. FRENCH COLONIAL ENTERPRISE

Since the days of the crusaders the French have maintained a persistent interest in the conditions affecting the eastern Mediterranean and the seaboard of northern Africa. Bonaparte's expedition to Egypt (1798) intensified this interest, although his conquests were speedily abandoned. In 1830, however, the dispatch of a punitive expedition against an insolent Dey of Algiers brought the French the control of several Algerian ports. Years of economic penetration and military campaigns gradually subdued the great Sahara Desert, and in 1881 Tunis as well as Algeria became a protectorate of France. The impotent protests of the Sultan of Turkey, who claimed a feeble suzerainty over northern Africa, failed to delay the march of events and served but to advertise the decline of the Turkish power.

Algeria and Tunis

The French were in some respects more successful than the British in consolidating their African conquests, for in 1885 they linked their expanding posts on the Congo (French Equatorial Africa) with their West African dominions by way of the Ubangi River. Morocco, established as a French protectorate in 1912, rounded out the northwest corner of their African Empire. Including the island of Madagascar, which was proclaimed a French colony in 1896, the French African possessions had come by 1914 to exceed even those of Great Britain in area. The scramble for territory on the Dark Continent had provided France with a colonial empire larger than the whole of Europe, and much of it adjacent to the mother country.

Morocco

Nor were the French possessions in Asia insignificant. In the middle of the nineteenth century, France held no more than two hundred square miles of Asiatic territory surrounding five small posts on the Bay of Bengal, the most important of which, Pondicherry, had been established by the French East India Company two centuries earlier. In 1858, however, the government of Napoleon III dispatched an armed expedition to Cochin China to avenge the murder of some Christian missionaries, and this province, nominally a part of the Chinese Empire, became a French protectorate five years later. A successful policy of war and diplomacy brought Annam, Tonkin, and part of Cambodia under French control in the decades which followed. The Chinese government was forced to renounce its shadowy sovereignty over these regions, concede favorable tariff rates on goods from Tonkin, and permit the French special privileges on the railroads of southern China. In less than fifty years the French had acquired an Asian Empire as large as Texas, with an industrious population half that of France itself. By agreement with Great Britain, the Kingdom of Siam was recognized as an independent buffer state between British Burma and French Indo-China.[1] Toward the east, however, France might aspire to enlarge the boundaries of Tonkin, and the lease of Kwang-chow (1898) near the island of Hainan hinted at such intentions.

French Indo-China

5. ITALY ENTERTAINS IMPERIALISTIC DREAMS

When the Italians achieved political unity in the decade 1860–70, they found their national government burdened with debt, embarrassed by an unresolved dispute with the papacy, and confronted with the problem of educating a largely illiterate population. Yet these domestic difficulties did not deter them from the attempt to play an imperialistic rôle in imitation of older established powers. Italian patriots not only regarded the Istrian Peninsula and part of the Austrian Tyrol as territory to be "redeemed," but cast covetous eyes across the Mediterranean Sea to Tunis on the North African coast.

[1] See map on page 813.

PAUL KRUGER (1825–1904)

As president of the South African Republic Paul Kruger opposed Rhodes' plans and defied the might of the British Empire.

CECIL JOHN RHODES (1853–1902)

Rhodes believed that Anglo-Saxon rule would benefit backward peoples. He admitted, "I would annex the planets if I could."

THE HEART OF A WORLD-WIDE EMPIRE

London was the commercial and financial capital of the world throughout the nineteenth century.

When the French thwarted their aspirations in this direction by annexing Tunis (1881), the act created a deep and lasting resentment between the two Latin powers.

Worse fortune awaited the Italians in Abyssinia. After establishing a colony at Massowah on the Red Sea (1885), the Italian government attempted to secure control of the inland empire of Abyssinia, or Ethiopia, a state lying between the Nile Valley and the Red Sea, ruled by the Ethiopians, a Hamitic tribe which professed Christianity. But the Italian hopes of creating a sphere of influence in East Africa went down to defeat in 1896 when the Abyssinians overwhelmed their expeditionary force in catastrophic fashion at the battle of Adowa. The protectorate was abandoned, and Abyssinia remained independent under the rule of Menelek II, the only native African ruler who had successfully repelled a European army. Italy retained, however, two strips of coastline in the neighborhood, Italian Somaliland and Eritrea.[1]

Restrained for the moment by this costly and humiliating reverse, Italian imperialists proceeded more cautiously in their next African venture. The provinces of Tripoli and Cyrenaica were marked out as fields for Italian exploitation by 1901, but it was not until ten years later that Italy took the initiative and wrested them from Turkey after a brief struggle.[2] The expense of improving the new conquests and subjugating the desert tribes of the interior proved a heavy burden for the Italian taxpayers, but their pride was gratified by this evidence that Italy could compete successfully with the older nations in the scramble for colonies. They named their new possession Libya.

6. GERMANY ENTERS THE RACE FOR COLONIES

Distracted by their own dissensions and handicapped by the lack of a competent central government, the German people took little share in overseas exploration and colonization before 1871. While Spain, Portugal, Holland, France, and England were fighting to found and maintain colonial empires, the German princes remained absorbed in the petty play of central European politics. Even after national unity had been achieved and the victory over France had made the new empire the leading European power, Bismarck displayed little inclination to compete for colonies. His chief concern was to consolidate the position which Germany had won for herself on the continent of Europe. To participate in the scramble for backward countries, when the best areas suitable for white men to live in had already been pre-empted, seemed to him a dubious game offering few rewards and likely in the end to embroil Germany with Great Britain, the leading colonial power of the world.

Nevertheless, the expansion of German industry and the growth of the German maritime interests prepared the way for a more aggressive colonial program. In 1884, after negotiations with Great Britain, the German government proclaimed a protectorate over South-West Africa, and annexed in the same year a strip of coastline on the Gulf of Guinea which shortly expanded into the German Cameroons. In 1885, German East Africa was acquired, and proclaimed a protectorate in 1890. Though less favorable for colonization or trade than the choicer sections of Africa already claimed by other nations, the new German colonies were by no means negligible in either wealth or area.

Once embarked upon the imperialistic race, the Germans pressed forward with energy. The murder of two missionaries (1897) provided an excuse for armed intervention in Shantung, and the Chinese government was compelled to lease the port of Kiaochau to Germany with some two hundred square miles of territory attached. In Oceania, a portion of the island of New Guinea was recognized as a German protectorate (1884); the two largest Samoan Islands were acquired in 1899; and the Caroline and some lesser groups of Pacific islands purchased from Spain in the same year. These far distant ports and islands provided bases and coaling stations for the new German high seas fleet.

---

[1] See map on the opposite page.
[2] The Turko-Italian War, 1911–12. See below, page 820.

AFRICA 1914

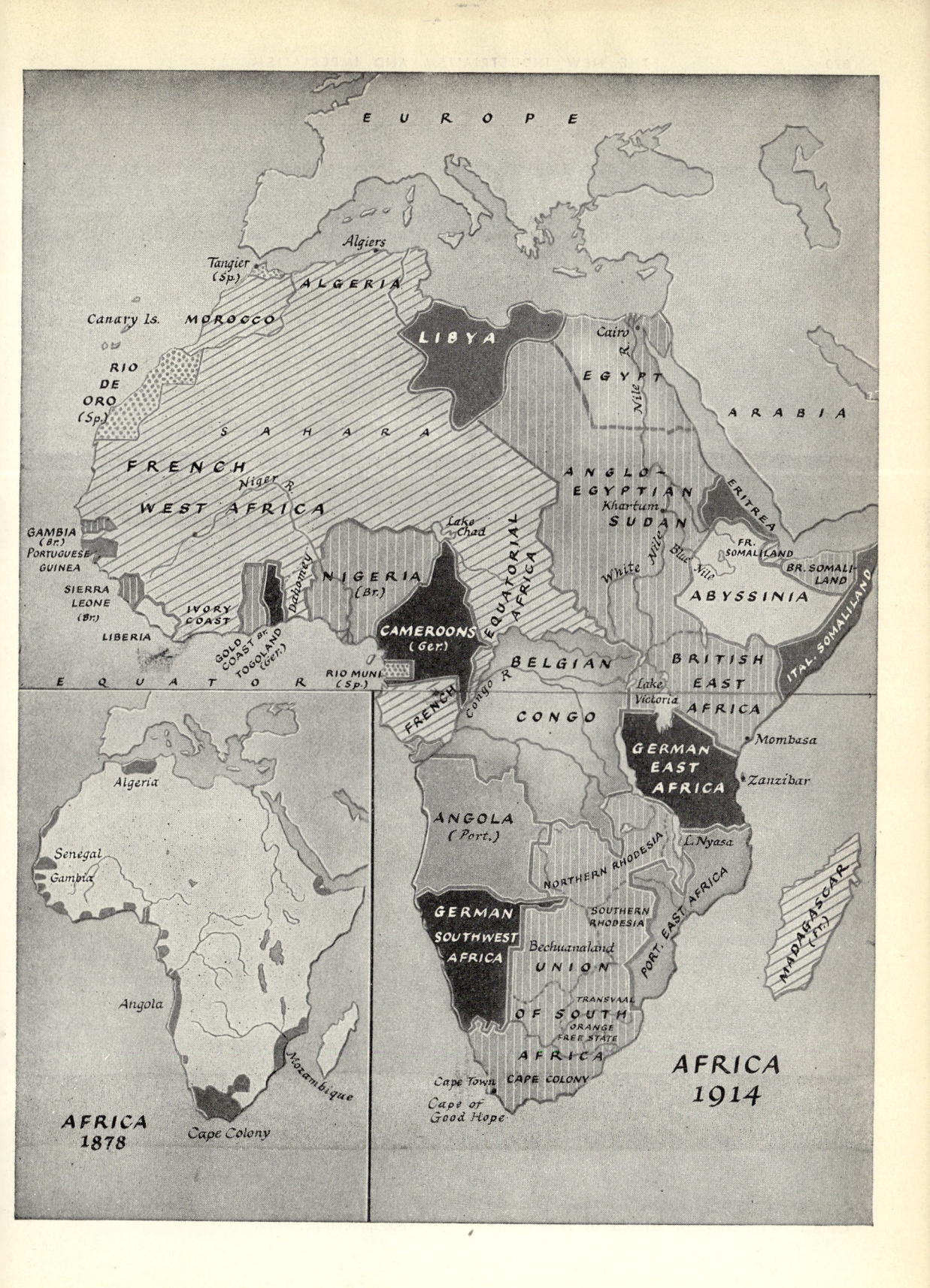

AFRICA 1878

7. THE RIVALRIES OF THE POWERS IN AFRICA

The competition for colonies quickened the jealousies of the great powers, and more than once, particularly during the partitioning of Africa, their rivalry brought them to the verge of war. Between 1880 and 1914, scarcely a year passed without its diplomatic incident or minor crisis concerning some disputed sphere of influence on the Dark Continent. But African protectorates were a little too remote from the knowledge and interest of the average European citizen to appear worth a war to him; and Austria and Russia, which held no African territory, had no wish to be drawn into a struggle over colonial questions by their allies. But although the acrid disputes arising from African rivalries were all settled by negotiation or arbitration, they added considerably to the international animosity.

When France established a virtual protectorate over Tunis in 1881, disappointment and irritation induced the Italians to sign a treaty of alliance with Germany and Austria the following year. This Triple Alliance, directed against France in particular, assured Italy of support if she became involved in a war over the disposal of North African territory. Five years later (1887), Italy and Great Britain agreed to respect each other's rights in the Mediterranean; and after 1901, Italy and France achieved a partial compromise whereby Tripoli was marked out as a potential sphere of Italian exploitation, while the French strengthened their hold on Morocco. In 1911, judging the moment opportune, the Italians seized the Tripolitan ports and compelled the Sultan of Turkey to acknowledge their right of control. This acquisition of a colony five times as large as Italy provided some compensation to Italian pride for the loss of Tunis and reduced the Franco-Italian rivalry.

Between France and Great Britain, the two powers most active in dividing Africa, an even sharper antagonism had risen and waned. While far-sighted Englishmen were dreaming of carrying the Union Jack from Egypt to Cape Colony, energetic Frenchmen were pressing eastward from the region of Lake Chad. The map of Africa in this chapter shows that these conflicting lines of advance must clash in the upper Nile Valley. In 1898, General Herbert Kitchener, fresh from his victory at Omdurman, where he had reconquered the Sudan for the Khedive of Egypt (and for England), learned that the intrepid Captain Marchand had hoisted the French flag at Fashoda, where the White Nile parallels the Abyssinian border. With the control of the upper Nile region at stake, both nations drifted dangerously close to a war mood, but the crisis passed when the French finally agreed to recall Captain Marchand. Following this incident, both rivals made an effort to improve their relations and avert such threats to peace in the future. The terms of the Anglo-French *Entente* of 1904 included a compromise affecting African questions, Great Britain retaining Egypt and the Egyptian Sudan, while acknowledging the right of France to win Morocco as compensation.

Fashoda incident

The active participation of the German government in the scramble for African territory may be dated from 1884, when an international congress was held in Berlin to delimit spheres of influence and provide for the adjustment of rival claims. The congress erected an international Congo Free State under the sovereignty of King Leopold II of Belgium, but sought to preserve freedom of trade and navigation on the Congo River. At the same time (1884–85), Germany took possession of Togoland and the Cameroons, secured a block of coastland farther south which became German South-West Africa, and proclaimed the German East African Protectorate.[1] As already explained, these German annexations struck a sharp blow at British hopes. South-West Africa had been considered of little value, but in German hands it might become a threat to British South Africa. German East Africa, extending inland to the shores of Lake Tanganyika, prevented the British from linking Rhodesia with their Uganda protectorate at the head of the Nile. With good grace, however, they suppressed their disappointment and concluded an agreement recognizing the new German claims (1890). In addition, Ger-

English vs. Germans

[1] See map on page 819.

many received the island of Helgoland in the North Sea in return for recognizing the British claims to Uganda, Nyasaland, and Zanzibar.

It will be noted that three of the lesser European states also developed African colonies, more or less under the sufferance of the great powers. The Portuguese, once foremost in exploring the coastline of the Dark Continent,[1] still preserved some trading posts in the nineteenth century which they enlarged into the protectorates of Angola and Mozambique. The Congo Free State, established as a neutral concession under international sanction (1884), was annexed as a Belgian colony in 1908. The Spaniards held, as remnants of ancient claims, a small Guinea protectorate, a stretch of northwestern coastline, the Rio de Oro, and a diminutive slice of Morocco opposite Gibraltar. Had their resources permitted the effort, the Spaniards would no doubt have subjugated the whole of Morocco, but this enterprise devolved upon the French instead. Britain was acquiescent, but Germany sought to block this French design, the result being a series of diplomatic clashes which brought the European nations close to war on three occasions.

By 1905, Morocco was entirely hemmed in on the landward side by French territory, but the sultan was still a nominally independent ruler. The German government wished him to remain independent, or, failing that, favored some system of international control. In 1906, a conference held at Algeciras (Spain) sustained the German view, but conceded France and Spain "police powers" to enable them to maintain order in the semi-civilized sultanate. Morocco had become a pawn in a dangerous diplomatic game, for the duel between France and Germany over Moroccan independence was at bottom a test of prestige between the Triple Alliance (Germany, Austria, and Italy) and the Triple *Entente* (France, Russia and Great Britain). A second Moroccan crisis developed in 1908 when French military police invaded the German consulate at Casablanca and arrested deserters from the

The Moroccan question

[1] See above, pages 588–590.

French Foreign Legion. The German government entered a vigorous protest against the use the French were making of their police power, but were partly placated by an assurance that the trade of all nations would be equally protected in Morocco. The French, however, continued to push their plans for a systematic conquest of the country, and in 1911 the German government protested a third time. On this occasion Great Britain ranged herself firmly at the side of France, demonstrating that the Anglo-French Alliance had acquired new force, and the Germans agreed to a compromise. In return for one hundred thousand square miles of the French Congo they permitted the French government to declare a protectorate over nine tenths of Morocco (1912).

All the colonizing powers advanced laudable motives to justify their annexation of African land, but the real forces which drove them into this form of imperialistic gambling remained hidden. Not even the citizens who paid their taxes and aided their governments in the task of conquest comprehended the cost or understood precisely who benefited when new protectorates were established. They were pleased in a general way to see new areas on the map marked out as part of their empire, and they supposed that they were doing a noble and progressive thing in bringing the Christian religion and the advantages of a higher civilization to backward peoples. But the strongest motive in most of these ventures was economic, and behind each diplomatic crisis or tribal war in which a government engaged there lurked the shadow of the bondholders and the investment brokers who were the chief and sometimes the only beneficiaries of the imperialistic game.

For by 1875, not only in Great Britain, but in France, Germany, Italy, and the United States, surplus capital had accumulated, and bankers and brokers were turning the golden flood toward foreign fields where the interest return promised to be high. Only a comparatively small group in each country drew a real profit from these imperialist enterprises — the investors who owned stock

Profits of imperialism

in the business or trading companies, or who bought the bonds which the Khedive of Egypt or the Shah of Persia might float in Europe, the investment bankers who made a good commission handling the bonds, and the civil and military officials who supervised or defended the undertaking. To the great majority of the people in England or France or Germany, however, these ventures brought no dividends, and might even mean higher taxes if their government yielded to the persuasion of the interested minority and fought a war or proclaimed a protectorate in order to safeguard the capital of a small group of investors. Because most of the profits derived from the imperialistic exploitation of Africa and Asia went to a small upper-class group, the socialist leaders in every European country opposed such expansion, while the bondholders, militarists, bankers, munition-makers, and others were likely to support a conservative *bloc* which would fight for an aggressive foreign policy, for imperialism, and (since interference in other countries often breeds war) for militarism. Thus the Industrial Revolution not only aligned the proletariat and the capitalist class on opposite sides in questions of domestic politics, it also separated them in much the same fashion on matters of foreign policy.

No small minority, however influential, can long control the foreign policy of a great power unless it wins some support from the masses. In every country there were citizens, sometimes well-meaning, sometimes stupid, who played the imperialists' game for them. Many devout people thought chiefly in terms of Christianizing the heathen. Many jingoists applauded their government's foreign policy, right or wrong. The self-sacrificing missionaries, like David Livingstone (1813–73), and the courageous explorers, like Henry Morton Stanley, who made Africa known to Europeans, were inspired by altruism or the lure of adventure rather than any hope of gain. But shrewd business men with a sharp eye for profits built on their labors and organized commercial ventures with attractive titles, such as the International African Association (1876), the

Colonial conflicts

German African Society (1878), the British East Africa Association (1885), and the British South Africa Company (1889). On the basis of concessions secured from the native chiefs, the agents of these companies exploited African resources, and, when blocked by rival companies or by native resistance, they appealed to their governments for protection. The result was the long succession of international disputes and rivalries already described, some of which missed war by the narrowest margin. With the native population the colonizing powers found it impossible to avoid hostilities. The French conquest of West Africa was a saga of unsung strife; the Germans had to suppress costly uprisings in South-West Africa and in East Africa; the British fought a score of frontier wars between 1871 and 1914 against the Zulus, Basutos, Ashantis, Swazis, Matabeles, and other African tribes; while the Belgian officials in the Congo Free State exploited and massacred the Bantu peoples there with a cruelty that finally aroused international protest. Yet, despite harsh incidents, the white man has brought many benefits to the native Africans, for he has curbed their tribal wars, reduced plagues, suppressed cruel and degrading practices, improved communications, and, in some colonies, fostered education.

8. THE RIVALRIES OF THE GREAT POWERS IN ASIA

As a field for imperialistic effort, the continent of Asia differed from Africa in several important respects. It had a population six times as large, and the level of civilization among the Asiatics was considerably higher than among the Negroes. Moreover, the Asiatics, notably the Japanese, revealed a marked capacity for assimilating the European arts of war and peace, and might learn in time to resent and to resist alien intervention in their affairs. But this possibility did not deter aggressive Europeans from exploiting Asia for their own purposes. The twentieth century will reveal whether in so doing they have created a Nemesis for themselves, for Asia holds one half the world's population, and the Asiatics, if trained in the use of modern weapons of war and in the arts of machine production, could offer a

RUSSIAN TROOPS IN MANCHURIA, 1905
The Russians' first effort to secure Manchuria failed when they were defeated by the Japanese in 1905.

THE BOXER REBELLION, 1900
The American Marines forced open the gates on the wall of Peking for the entrance of American and British troops.

serious challenge to the supremacy of the white races.

During the greater part of the nineteenth century, the chief protagonists of European imperialism in Asia were Russia and Great Britain. The Russian advance to the Pacific and to the borders of Persia and India has already been described.[1] The British, while consolidating their Indian Empire, opposed the Russians in the Near and Middle East, fought them in the Crimean War (1854-56), and resisted their demands on Turkey at the Congress of Berlin (1878). In the Far East, Russia and England did not clash directly, but both established spheres of influence in the Chinese Empire, the British making Tibet and the Yangtze Valley a field of special interest, while the Russians penetrated Mongolia and Manchuria.

Britain vs. Russia

These encroachments, supplemented by the French conquest of Indo-China, made it seem probable in the last quarter of the nineteenth century that China would suffer the same fate as Africa and pass completely under the domination of foreign powers. In 1894, a new claimant to the spoils appeared when Japan wrested the Korean Peninsula and the island of Formosa from the feeble sovereignty of the Celestial Empire. This Sino-Japanese War of 1894-95 also gave the Japanese a foothold on the Liaotung Peninsula, but this the other powers compelled them to relinquish. The evident helplessness of China invited a race for concessions. Germany seized the bay of Kiaochau in Shantung Province (1897), Russia secured Port Arthur (1898) and began to construct a railway across Chinese Manchuria, while the British occupied the harbor of Wei-hai-wei. A glance at the map of Asia in this chapter will show how these acquisitions on the Yellow Sea threatened the Chinese capital at Peking. Meanwhile, the French obtained the port of Kwang-chow in southern China, close to their Tonkin protectorate.

The hatred that developed in China against the "foreign devils" led to an uprising in 1900 known as the Boxer [2] Rebellion. It had been fomented with the approval of the reactionary empress, Tzu-hsi, but was crushed by an international force sent from Japan, Russia, Britain, France, Germany and the United States. Europeans besieged in Peking were relieved and the capital occupied by the allied troops until the Chinese government promised an indemnity of about $330,000,000 and commercial concessions to the victors. This salutary lesson convinced even the dowager empress of the need for reform, and projects were introduced for modernizing the military, political, and educational institutions of China. A proposal sustained by the United States (1899) had inaugurated an "open-door" policy in regard to Chinese trade, whereby all nations were to receive equal opportunity, even in those ports leased by foreign powers. The attitude of the United States, which had respected the integrity of China, and the jealousy of the other great powers, each eager to block the others, delayed the further dismemberment of China after 1900.

The astonishing rise of Japan also furnished a curb upon the spread of European imperialism in the Far East. Until 1853, the Japanese had little contact with Europeans and desired less; but the visit of a naval squadron under Commodore Perry forced them to open some of their ports for trade with the United States (1854) and later with other nations. Recognizing the superiority of western methods in war and peace, the Japanese embarked upon a program of modernization unique in history. Having organized a splendid army, modeled partly on that of Prussia, and an effective navy on the British type, the Japanese could feel secure from foreign aggression. The rapid spread of industry increased the population and strained the limited resources of the island kingdom, so that Japanese merchants and manufacturers looked to China as a market for their products and a source of raw material. Imitating European methods, the Japanese made war upon China in 1894,

The rise of Japan

---

[1] See above, pages 728-729.
[2] The Chinese patriots who were most active in the attempt to drive out all foreign barbarians were called "Boxers" because many of them belonged to secret societies, the most important being "The Fists of Righteous Harmony," or, as it is sometimes translated, "The Society of Harmonious Fists."

freed Korea, which was later annexed to Japan (1910), gained the island of Formosa, an indemnity of one hundred and eighty million dollars, and commercial privileges in four Chinese ports (Treaty of Shimonoseki, 1895). But the Japanese remained dissatisfied because the European powers compelled them to restore Port Arthur and the Liaotung Peninsula, to "preserve Chinese integrity."

Russo-Japanese War — If the Russians once made good their hold on Manchuria and fortified it, the Japanese knew that they would lose their fairest field of expansion on the mainland of Asia. The growing tension between the two powers brought on a war in 1904 which demonstrated how competently the Japanese had learned their lesson. The Russians suffered defeat on land and sea, and by August, 1905, were ready to agree: (1) to transfer their lease of Port Arthur to Japan; (2) to evacuate Manchuria; (3) to recognize the special Japanese interest in Korea; and (4) to cede to Japan the southern half of the island of Sakhalin (Treaty of Portsmouth). The European nations noted with amazement this discomfiture of the Russian giant by an Asiatic state with one third the population and one fiftieth the area of the czar's empire.

The scramble among the nations to seize and exploit backward countries reached its climax about 1900. By that year almost all of Africa, a large part of Asia, Australasia, and the far-scattered islands of the Pacific Ocean had been divided among the powers. In North and South America the European states had made no recent annexations out of deference to the position taken by the United States, which had made it clear that such intervention would be viewed as an unfriendly act.[1] But, in assuming this preponderant and protective rôle in the New World, the United States had in reality manifested a form of imperialism. In 1898, the question of Cuban independence brought on a war between the United States and Spain which ended in a Spanish defeat. Cuba became a republic under American protection, and Spain also transferred the Philippine Islands to the United States. The Hawaiian Islands were annexed the same year.

The Spanish-American War, the Boer War, and the Russo-Japanese War, the Boxer Rebellion, the Italian defeat in Abyssinia, and the English conquest of the Sudan all fell within the years 1895–1905. Occurring in widely separated parts of the globe, these events reflect how completely the whole world had been caught within the net of imperialism. There was no longer a country so obscure or so remote that it might not serve to awaken the spirit of covetousness and become the object of international conflict.

The competition for colonies was a grave threat to world peace because it sharpened antagonisms already existing among the European powers. The next chapter will explain why the period 1871–1914 has been named "The Armed Peace." Throughout Europe fear and misunderstanding between the states were fed by jingoistic patriots and intensified by the competition in armaments until the period ended in the most destructive war that had theretofore threatened modern civilization.

[1] See above, page 696.

61

The Growth of Alliances: International Tension and the Armed Peace

(1871–1914)

The factors which really constitute prosperity have not the remotest connection with military or naval power, all our political jargon notwithstanding.

NORMAN ANGELL, *THE GREAT ILLUSION*.[1]

THE FRANCO-PRUSSIAN WAR OF 1870–71 did much more than end an empire (that of Napoleon III) in France and consolidate a new empire (that of William I and Bismarck) in Germany. It shifted the center of gravity in European politics, increased the international tension, and augmented the spirit of militarism. Berlin superseded Paris as the diplomatic capital of Europe, and the new German Empire emerged as the dominant nation on the Continent. The old balance of power had been destroyed with disconcerting suddenness. For the neighbors of Germany it became a matter of the utmost importance to discover what use the Germans planned to make of their ascendancy. Would the Prussian forces, after winning three wars in seven years, be content to put away their weapons now German unity had been secured? And if not, which state would prove their next victim? The rapid industrial expansion, the increasing population, and the unrivaled military efficiency of the Teuton Empire filled weaker nations with jealousy and apprehension. In the tense and suspicious atmosphere of modern statecraft, a powerful neighbor is likely to be viewed as a perpetual threat.

1. THE GERMAN HEGEMONY AFTER 1871

Bismarck appreciated the general distrust

[1] G. P. Putnam's Sons.

which the Prussian victories had aroused. As chancellor of the German Empire he desired peace, and after 1871 he labored to prevent war as successfully as he had sought it hitherto. For he knew that the prevalent fear of Germany might easily favor the growth of a hostile coalition, and it lay in the logic of things that France, so brutally humbled in the process of German advancement, would furnish the nucleus for such a combination. Standing alone, France constituted no very grave danger, but Bismarck did not underrate the skill, patience, and patriotism of French statesmen, nor the jealousy which German success had fostered in international circles. He was haunted by the presentiment that sooner or later France would secure allies and assume the rôle of a Nemesis fated to destroy his life-work. The rapidity with which the French paid off their indemnity and restored their national prosperity after 1871 increased his misgiving so strongly that in 1875 he was supposed to have entertained the thought of inflicting a second and more crushing defeat upon France before that nation won wider support. Bismarck's friends chided him for entertaining a "nightmare of coalitions," but history has revealed that his fears were later to materialize as grim realities.

That Germany was able, under such circumstances, to keep France diplomatically isolated for twenty years and to build up friendly relations with all the other continental powers, was partly the result of circumstances, partly a tribute to Bismarck's moderation and astuteness. He arranged treaties of alliance and goodwill with Austria, Russia, and Italy before France could turn to them for aid or encouragement. These agreements, consolidating the recent Prussian military triumphs, rendered the position of Germany unassailable during the years that Bismarck remained in office. It will be useful to examine the Bismarckian system of alliances in detail, because they largely determined the diplomatic history of the period 1871–1914.

Isolation of France

Bismarck's first endeavor after 1871 was to unite Germany, Austria, and Russia in a cordial understanding. Although the Austrians had been defeated by the Prussians in 1866, they had been generously treated by the victors and were ready to forgive and forget; while the Russians had found Prussia friendly during the Polish Rebellion of 1863 and after. The three governments had several important interests in common: they were all concerned in keeping the Poles in subjection, they were all monarchies with an absolutist bent, and they were all hostile toward republican ideas. It was not a matter for great surprise, therefore, when Francis Joseph of Austria, William I of Germany, and Alexander II of Russia established a friendly compact known as the "Three Emperors' League" in 1873. Confident that this accord would assure a more stable peace, Bismarck turned his attention to projects for the internal consolidation of the German Empire, a complicated task which he was anxious to carry through undisturbed.

Three Emperors' League

Unfortunately for his hopes, the Three Emperors' League soon dissolved. Jealousy between Austria and Russia in the Balkans almost brought these powers to war in 1877. How a temporary settlement of this Near-Eastern Question was worked out at the Congress of Berlin the following year is told elsewhere.[1] Here it is sufficient to explain that Bismarck, though he strove to be impartial, leaned to the side of Austria in the controversy and so forfeited for a time the friendship of the Russians. The Three Emperors' League lost its force, Russo-German relations grew cold if not actually hostile, and Bismarck was denounced in Saint Petersburg as a false friend.

2. THE TRIPLE ALLIANCE

Wasting no time in fruitless efforts to soften the hostile mood of the Russians, Bismarck hastened to Vienna and arranged a dual alliance between Germany and Austria-Hungary which was destined to endure for forty years. This highly important treaty of 1879 provided that Germany and Austria would make war together should either of them be attacked by Russia; if either were to be attacked by France, the other promised to observe benevolent neutrality. The effect of this agreement was to bind Germany and Austria in a close understanding directed against Russia and France, but the two latter powers were carefully left in ignorance of the arrangement. The "High Contracting Parties" specifically agreed that "This Treaty shall, in conformity with its peaceful intentions, and to avoid any misinterpretation, be kept secret . . ."

Dual Alliance

Three years later the Dual Alliance was expanded into the Triple Alliance by the admission of Italy (1882). The Italians had been irritated by the French annexation of Tunis the previous year, and welcomed the assurance of German support in the event of a war developing with France over the North African littoral. The terms of the Triple Alliance provided that if Italy or Germany were attacked by France, the three allied powers (Germany, Austria-Hungary, and Italy) would fight together, or if any one of them were attacked by two other great powers, all three would provide mutual assistance. The treaty might be renewed after five years, and its terms were to remain secret. The Italians stipulated, however, that its provisions should not be regarded as directed against Great Britain.

Triple Alliance

Still Bismarck was not satisfied. In 1881, he had succeeded in resurrecting the Three

[1] See above, pages 774–775.

Emperors' League, Germany, Austria, and Russia pledging each other not to join any fourth power (France, for instance) against any member of the league. But this second Emperors' League proved no more permanent than the first, and when Czar Alexander III declined to renew it in 1887, Bismarck agreed instead to a secret Reinsurance Treaty between Germany and Russia. Each party promised to remain neutral if the other were attacked by a great power. Stripped of their ambiguities, the commitments which Bismarck had negotiated bound Austria, Italy, and Russia not to join France in a war of aggression against Germany. So long as the Bismarckian system of alliances remained in force, the French, if they opened a war of revenge, would have to enter it alone.

Reinsurance Treaty

Even the Balkan States, Serbia and Rumania, were drawn into Bismarck's system, Serbia by a secret treaty with Austria-Hungary (1881) and Rumania by an agreement for mutual support negotiated with the members of the Triple Alliance (1883). When the Emperor William II relieved Bismarck of his office (1890), the Iron Chancellor retired with the knowledge that he had consolidated the preponderant position of Germany and successfully frustrated for the moment the composition of a counter-alliance. Yet within the Bismarckian system dangerous rifts were already widening. Austrian pressure in the Balkans was almost certain, sooner or later, to estrange both Russia and Italy. The Reinsurance Treaty between Germany and Russia was not renewed in 1890. The loyalty of Italy could not be depended upon — "her promise will have no value if it is not in her interest to keep it," Bismarck had predicted shrewdly. Great Britain, though friendly toward Germany, might easily be alienated if the Germans pressed their commercial and naval rivalry, and their quest for colonies, too aggressively. To resolve these problems would have taxed even Bismarck's skill, and his successors in office were not his equals in diplomacy. By 1914, little remained of the Bismarckian system save the Dual Alliance of Germany and Austria, and a counter-coalition had been formed to oppose the Central Powers, a coalition more dangerous, more powerful, and more circumscribing than Bismarck's darkest apprehensions had foreshadowed.

Triple Alliance weak

3. FRANCE SEARCHES FOR ALLIES

Shamed by defeat, without friends, and weakened by the internal conflict between republicans and royalists, France played a minor part in international affairs from 1871 to 1890. Bismarck approved of a republican government in France for the precise reason that he opposed it in Germany, because he believed that republican institutions were unstable and unsuited to military enterprise. The political quarrels of the French factions and the frequent cabinet crises at Paris left foreign courts in doubt whether the Third Republic could long endure, but by 1890 the republican régime had acquired an appearance of permanence and French policies were accorded more serious attention as they gained in firmness and continuity.

Between 1891 and 1894, France secured her first ally, Russia. It might appear surprising that a liberal republic and a conservative autocracy should reach a "cordial understanding," but the exigencies of foreign policy often forge strange alliances. The Russo-German Reinsurance Treaty had lapsed in 1890 and the German government was disinclined to renew it. Russia, in need of capital for railroad construction and other industrial enterprises, found the French government benevolently inclined and French bankers obliging. The friendly feeling thus engendered was confirmed by a secret convention (1894) which stipulated:

France and Russia

(1) If France should be attacked by Germany, or by Italy supported by Germany, Russia would employ all her available forces against Germany.
(2) If Russia should be attacked by Germany, or by Austria supported by Germany, France would employ all her available forces to attack Germany.

This "rigorously secret" convention was to endure as long as the Triple Alliance remained operative, a condition which proved that it was intended as a counterweight to that alliance, which French and Russian statesmen feared the more because they were ignorant of its precise terms. It was also important to France and Russia in 1894 to present a united front in the face of British imperialism, particularly as there were rumors that Great Britain also might be drawn toward the Triple Alliance.

In 1898, the year of Bismarck's death, Théophile Delcassé became French minister of foreign affairs. He was to retain that important post for the unusually long period of seven years, and during that interval (1898–1905) he helped to bring about a diplomatic revolution which nullified much of Bismarck's labor. It was Delcassé's conviction that the security of France depended upon the creation of a coalition powerful enough to defy the Triple Alliance. Faced, when he took office, by the Anglo-French crisis concerning the occupation of Fashoda,[1] he sought a peaceful solution for the affair, and after France had yielded, he strove to obliterate the memory of the clash of interests and to promote closer relations with Great Britain. The accession in 1901 of Edward VII (1901–10), who liked the French and admired Delcassé, helped to create a friendlier feeling between the two powers. Irksome colonial disputes were smoothed away by negotiation, Great Britain agreeing in 1904 to recognize French interests as paramount in Morocco, while the French in return agreed to insist no longer that the British vacate Egypt. In its secret clauses this convention of 1904 further provided that France and Britain should afford each other diplomatic support on all questions concerning North African territory.

Because of the strong British prejudice against entangling alliances, this understanding with France was termed an *entente*, and no formal treaty was signed, but the *rapprochement* was full of significance nonetheless. The British government, like the French, had come to feel that the peace of Europe might be rendered more secure if the preponderance of Germany and her allies could be offset by a counter-combination of powers. As Germany, Austria, and Italy had formed a Triple Alliance, France, Russia, and England might form a Triple *Entente*. Yet as late as 1900 an alliance which would bind England to her erstwhile foes, France and Russia, seemed no more than a remote possibility, and few people in England or on the Continent would have prophesied such a development. Ten years later, however, the alliance was an actuality. The motives which inspired this "diplomatic revolution" may be traced to the sharp competition which developed between Britain and Germany in commercial, colonial, and naval affairs.

4. ANGLO-GERMAN RIVALRY

Throughout the greater part of the nineteenth century, the British had been content to maintain a policy of "splendid isolation." By 1900, however, isolation began to seem less splendid. The Boer War (1899–1902) revealed to the British people their military unpreparedness and their wide unpopularity. A sense of insecurity clouded the mood of complaisant superiority which they had derived from their industrial and maritime supremacy, for that supremacy was definitely passing. After 1880, British trade had begun to falter while that of Germany forged ahead. In all the world's markets, even in the British Isles, German goods sold in mounting quantities. Germany was the most enterprising, the most aggressive, and the most successful competitor, but the British monopoly suffered further reverses through the progress of industrialization in France and the United States.

It has been said that "race hatred is founded upon international covetousness." For a few years the British endeavored to preserve an attitude of "fair play" toward their chief rivals. They acknowledged the right of Germany to acquire colonies, and they clung to the belief that British commerce could meet all competition. But when the Germans continued to overtake them, when the German steel production surpassed their own, and German ships transported German manufactures that undersold the British in their own colonies, the

[1] See above, page 820.

note of sportsmanship yielded to one of anxiety. Unofficial British suggestions for a friendly agreement were coolly received in Berlin. After 1898, a race in naval armaments added to the tension, for the young kaiser, William II, declared that, in order to protect her growing commerce, Germany must construct a first-class navy. This challenge was promptly met by the British, who determined to launch two warships for each keel that the Germans laid down, in order that the British navy might continue to be a match for any other two fleets in the world combined. This two-power standard imposed an enormous strain upon the British taxpayer, but he accepted it as indispensable to his security, for the British Empire was founded upon sea power and any nation which could destroy its shipping in time of war could starve the island kingdom into surrender.

Between 1900 and 1914, the British admiralty steadily concentrated its forces in the North Sea to meet the German threat. Warships which had been scattered around the world to protect British interests, and had lain anchored in Rangoon, or Nanaimo, or the Bermudas until they "had grounded on their own beef bones," as one authority phrased it, were either scrapped or remodeled and recalled to home waters. A treaty of friendship and alliance, signed between Britain and Japan in 1902, enabled the British to withdraw a portion of their Pacific squadron with the assurance that the Japanese would watch over their interests in the Far East. After the establishment of the Entente cordiale with France in 1904, the naval defense of the Mediterranean Sea was largely relegated to the French in order that the British might further strengthen their North Sea fleet. Although the public remained generally ignorant of this redisposition of naval forces, it was fraught with a deep significance for the peace of Europe, and was a part of the tragic process which was aligning all European powers into two hostile camps.

Naval rivalry

5. THE TRIPLE ENTENTE

The formation of a Triple Entente including France, Russia, and Great Britain was indirectly hastened by the result of the Russo-Japanese War (1904–05). France as the ally of Russia and Britain as the ally of Japan were both anxious to prevent the war from spreading, lest they should be drawn into it on opposite sides. The defeat of Russia proved to the English that their long-nursed fear of the Muscovite power had been largely unnecessary and exaggerated. At the same time the Russian reverse showed the French that their only ally had feet of clay and would prove no match for Germany in case of war. The revelation of Russian weakness inspired the Germans to a new truculence, while France labored to draw Russia and England to her side and unite the three in a firm understanding in order to meet the Central Powers on a more equal footing.

The outcome was the negotiation of the Anglo-Russian Entente of 1907. As in the case of the Anglo-French Entente, arranged three years earlier, no definite treaty of alliance was signed, but the British and Russian governments smoothed away longstanding difficulties by an agreement to demarcate their spheres of influence in Persia and arbitrate any disputes that might arise concerning the frontiers of India. English sentiment toward Russia had been warmed by the promises of liberal reform made by Nicholas II after the revolutionary movement of 1905–06,[1] and the accord was further strengthened by a meeting of the English and Russian monarchs at Reval, the naval base of the Russian Baltic fleet, in 1908. Edward VII of England took a much more active part than usually falls to a constitutional monarch in the creation of the Triple Entente, which re-established the balance of power in Europe on a clearly defined basis. When he died in 1910, he was mourned by his subjects as "Edward the Peacemaker."

The Triple Entente

To German eyes, however, the Triple Entente wore anything but a peaceful aspect. It seemed rather a deliberate attempt to "encircle" Germany and Austria and stifle their free development. Everywhere that the Germans turned for expansion, they ap-

German ill-success

[1] See above, pages 763–764.

peared to find themselves hemmed in by the insidious encroachments projected by Entente diplomacy. In reality the agreements existing between France, Russia, and England were extremely vague, and were designed to operate only in the face of German aggression. Unfortunately, in a situation which would have taxed Bismarck's astuteness, the kaiser and his associates pursued a contradictory policy of overtures nullified by truculence and compromises inspired by pacific intentions, but marred by indiscreet saber-rattling. The blustering, touchy, and ill-advised attitude of the German foreign office helped more effectively than the machinations of the Entente statesmen to forge the links in the chain that was being drawn about the Central Powers. A dozen times between 1906 and 1914, when the interests of the Triple Alliance and the Entente powers clashed over some minor issue, the Germans had the melancholy success of driving England, France, and Russia closer together, and cementing the nebulous entente into an effective alliance by the very methods which they had adopted in the hope of dissolving it.

6. INTERNATIONAL CRISES: MOROCCO

In the ten years that preceded the outbreak of World War I, the increasing tension between the Triple Alliance and the nations which combined to form the Triple Entente gave rise to a series of diplomatic shocks which might be likened to the premonitory tremors which presage a violent earthquake. Several of these incidents were connected with the French penetration of Morocco. In 1900, France and Italy reached a secret agreement relegating Tripoli (renamed Libya) to Italian enterprise while the French sought supremacy in Tunis and Morocco. This understanding eased the Franco-Italian feud over North African territory, and two years later, Delcassé won a secret promise that the Italians would not join in a war of aggression against France. Spanish possessions in Morocco were delimited by a Franco-Spanish accord of 1904, and the same year Great Britain assented to the French designs in the convention establishing the Anglo-French Entente.

Suspecting the bent of Delcassé's intrigues, and annoyed by the conviction that German interests had been ignored, William II intervened brusquely in Moroccan affairs in 1905. The German government had selected a favorable moment to oppose France, for Russia had suffered a disastrous defeat at the hands of the Japanese, and the French dared not risk a war until their ally had recovered some strength and morale. Reluctantly the French cabinet yielded to the German demand for an international conference on Moroccan affairs, and acceded to the German hints that Delcassé's resignation of the portfolio of foreign affairs would ease the situation. The conference met at Algeciras (Spain) in 1906, and the delegates agreed solemnly that the sovereignty and integrity of the sultanate of Morocco must remain intact. At the same time, however, France and Spain were authorized to direct the police force, protect foreigners, and maintain order.

Moroccan crisis

To carry out this mandate, the French soon found it necessary to land troops in Morocco (1907). The following year French military police, searching for deserters from the Foreign Legion, invaded the German consulate at Casablanca and precipitated further trouble. A settlement was effected after the affair had been submitted to the Hague Tribunal, a permanent court of international arbitration which had been established in 1899. Germany conceded that her interests in Morocco were economic, not political, and the French government gave assurances that it would not abuse its privileges there to favor the commerce of any nation unduly. This compromise displeased many Germans, who perceived that "the power of France had spread... like an oil stain," until the greater part of Morocco had been subordinated to French control despite German vigilance.

When French forces occupied Fez, the chief city of Morocco, in 1911, the German government dispatched the warship *Panther* to the Moroccan port of Agadir as a protest. For several months the threat of war hung over Europe, but the British government showed its determination to support France, and

Compromise on Morocco

EUROPE IN 1900

Nations of the Triple Alliance

Germany accepted a compromise. The French were permitted to establish their long-sought protectorate over Morocco, and Germany received two strips of the French Congo as compensation. This settlement removed one dangerous subject of dispute which had exacerbated the mood of French and German patriots, but a heritage of ill-will remained, and the enmity between the two powers, though transferred to other issues, was not appreciably lessened by the compromise.

7. INTERNATIONAL CRISES: THE BALKANS

The Bagdad Railway

While France and Germany quarreled over the disposition of Moroccan territory, Russia and Austria pursued their tortuous rivalry in the Balkans. Although Bismarck had once declared that the Near-Eastern Question did not interest Germany sufficiently to be worth the bones of one Pomeranian grenadier, his successors in office modified this judgment. With the spread of industry and of transportation facilities German business men awoke to the possibility of exploiting the Turkish Empire as a commercial field of considerable importance. In 1902, they obtained concessions from the sultan's government for the construction of a railway from Constantinople to Bagdad and thence to Basra on the Persian Gulf. By linking up such a line with the German and Austrian railway system they hoped to develop important trade relations with the East, for the new overland route to the Indian Ocean would be shorter and speedier than the British or French maritime connections through the Suez Canal. (See the map of Asia on page 813.)

The Drang nach Osten

The German directors of the Bagdad Railway were willing to have the project financed and controlled as an international venture, but the British and French declined to co-operate. Fear of the German *Drang nach Osten,* or "drive to the east," was growing keener in British business circles by 1902. German diplomatic influence had become paramount at Constantinople, German officers were drilling Turkish regiments, and German manufacturers were demanding preferential tariffs in order to win the markets of Asia Minor. British jingoists, who had been loud in their declaration twenty years earlier that the Russians should not have Constantinople, suddenly perceived that German control of the Bosphorus had become an even more imminent danger. A century earlier, Napoleon had affirmed (with picturesque exaggeration) that the power which controlled Constantinople could control the world. After 1900, it seemed likely that this key position of the eastern Mediterranean would fall under the sway of the Central Powers. The British lion and the Russian bear neglected their ancient rivalry to watch the shadow of the Prussian eagle, and the two-headed eagle of Austria, sweeping toward the Dardanelles.

The Pan-Slav dream

A glance at the maps of Europe in 1900 and Asia in 1914 will show that the fear of German influence in the Near East was somewhat exaggerated. Direct communication between Berlin, Vienna, and Constantinople depended upon the attitudes of the Balkan States, particularly Serbia and Bulgaria. The Serb population, which was predominantly Slavic, looked to Russia as the "Big Slav Brother" for sympathy and support, and Serb patriots nursed dreams of creating a Pan-Slav state in the Balkans which would include their fellow nationals living under Austrian administration in Bosnia and Herzegovina. It is scarcely necessary to point out that such a project, the success of which would threaten the integrity of the Hapsburg Empire, was resented and resisted at Vienna. Any attempt either to expand or to constrict Serbian territory was certain to bring Russia and the Central Powers face to face in a duel of prestige, and as the Pan-Slav enthusiasts were constantly active, such a clash was likely to come at almost any time.

Near East crisis (1908)

The spirit of nationalism which had stirred the Balkan peoples spread to Turkey also. Turkish patriots were disgusted by the signs of decadence and disintegration in the Ottoman Empire, which in less than a century had lost control of most of its European provinces, and allowed France to seize Tunis and

Punch

THE TUG OF PEACE

The Second Hague Peace Conference, which met early in 1907, failed to induce any of the great powers to curtail their armaments.

Punch

KAISER WILHELM'S PANTHER LEAP

The German government sought to coerce the French into concessions by sending a gunboat, the "Panther," to Agadir (1911). Britain backed France, proving that the "Entente cordiale" had solidity.

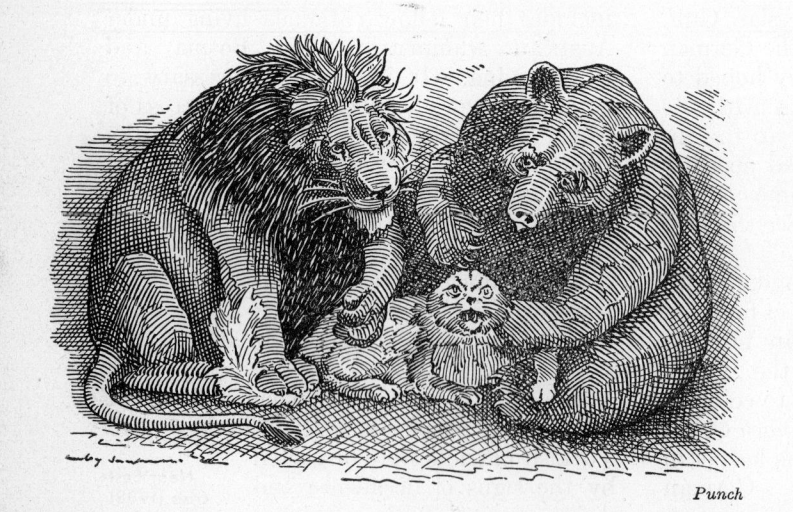

THE HARMLESS NECESSARY CAT

In 1907, Russia and Britain settled outstanding difficulties to form the Triple Entente with France. One compromise provided that Persia should be divided into a British, a Russian, and a jointly shared central zone.

Punch

Morocco while Britain occupied Egypt. In 1908, a Young Turk Association, inspired by the motto "Union and Progress," organized a revolutionary movement and compelled the reactionary sultan, Abdul Hamid II (1876–1909), to grant a constitution. This apparent rejuvenation of Turkey alarmed the Austrian government, for the Young Turks wished to take over Bosnia and Herzegovina which Austria had administered by virtue of the decision reached at the Congress of Berlin in 1878.[1] To forestall the Young Turk claim, Austria annexed the two provinces (1908), a move which displeased the Turks and infuriated the Serbs. For the Serbs regarded the Bosnians as fellow nationals destined to be incorporated into a greater Serbia, and the Austrian action dealt a fatal blow to their aspirations. They hastened to arm, counting upon Russian aid, but Russia had not yet recovered from the conflict with Japan, and found France and England cool toward the Serbian demands for aggrandizement. Advised "to avoid everything that might lead to an armed conflict," the Serbs yielded in sullen impotence, and the crisis passed.

Three years later, a situation of grave tension developed in the Near East as a consequence of the Turco-Italian War of 1911–12. The success of the Italians in seizing Tripoli proved to the world that Turkey was still feeble and could be attacked with impunity. Furthermore, as both the combatants, Italy and Turkey, were nominal allies of Germany and Austria, this dissension within the ranks of the Triple Alliance provided secret satisfaction for the Entente powers. Waiting for the repercussions that were certain to follow upon the Turkish defeats in North Africa, the European diplomats turned their scrutiny upon the Near East once more.

The repercussions soon displayed themselves and provided a second Near-Eastern Crisis in 1912–13. Heartened by the evidence of Turkish enfeeblement, the Balkan states, Greece, Serbia, Montenegro, and Bulgaria, launched a campaign against the Ottoman forces. Their victories were as surprising as their co-operation, and within a few months

Near East crisis (1912)

the allied armies had almost driven the Turks from Europe. But when the time came to divide the spoils of this First Balkan War of 1912, the Bulgarians, dissatisfied with their share, attacked their late allies, and were severely defeated in the Second Balkan War of 1913. Rumania, hitherto neutral, and even Turkey, entered the conflict against Bulgaria, which was stripped of the greater part of its earlier gains. Throughout the peace negotiations, in which the great powers insisted upon taking a hand, Austria showed a firm resolve to check the aggrandizement of Serbia as far as possible. By insisting that the liberated Turkish province of Albania must be organized as a separate independent principality, Austrian statesmen denied Serbia an outlet to the Adriatic Sea.

In Vienna, the Pan-Slav Movement, with the potential might of Russia behind it, was viewed with mounting alarm. In fighting it the Austro-Hungarian government was fighting to preserve the Hapsburg Empire from disintegration, for if the Austrian Slavs were permitted to secede, other minority races would demand similar privileges. Germany was constrained to support Austrian policy because she could not afford to alienate her only firm ally. Russian statesmen saw in the Pan-Slav Movement an opportunity to harass Austria and extend their own influence in the Balkan Peninsula. The French and British governments were anxious to preserve the existing balance of power in the Near East and to prevent either Austro-German or Russian influence from becoming paramount. With so many conflicting forces concentrating their effects in a small area, and with all the great powers ready to utilize the local rivalries and feuds to further their own designs, it is easy to understand why writers in 1913 constantly described the Balkans as "the powder magazine of Europe." Sooner or later a chance spark was likely to set off an explosion that would bring the old order in Europe crashing down in the chaos of a general war.

Balkan tremors

8. THE GROWTH OF ARMAMENTS

Nothing reflects the growing fear and ten-

[1] See above, page 775.

sion in Europe between 1900 and 1914 more clearly than the increase in armaments. Following the Franco-Prussian War of 1870-71, all the European powers except Great Britain enforced the principle of compulsory military training for practically all able-bodied male citizens, thus building up huge conscript armies, with a still larger reserve. The expense of drilling and equipping millions of men imposed a staggering burden upon the national budgets, and a secondary loss resulted because these men were necessarily withdrawn from peace-time occupations during some of the most important years of their early manhood. Yet the spirit of fear and of international distrust defeated all proposals for a limitation of armed forces, and led instead to a constant increase in the number of effectives, to extensions in the period of service, and additions to the military appropriations. In 1913, on the eve of World War I, all the great powers increased their expenditures for defense, and even lesser states like Belgium and Switzerland found it expedient to augment their forces.

Military conscription

Such gigantic preparations made it certain that any war which might develop would involve an unprecedented number of combatants. Wars were no longer to be waged between small professional armies, but with all the available manpower of great and populous states. Civilians might likewise be mobilized and compelled to produce food and munitions, and the danger and destruction would not be confined to the battlefields. For the new weapons which science and invention were producing promised to add new horrors to the ancient art of human massacre. Mines and torpedoes which would explode on contact, dreadnoughts with guns that hurled projectiles weighing a ton, new and deadly high-explosive shells, and machine guns that sprayed bullets as a hose sprays water, had all been brought to a high degree of effectiveness. With the invention of the airplane and the submarine boat, it became possible for men to slay each other, not only on land and sea, but beneath the waves and above the clouds. Troops far back of the firing line might now be bombed in their billets and cities destroyed with the concussion of explosives dropped from the skies.

New weapons

The deepening conviction that war would certainly come if the nations continued to prepare for it, and the belief that it would bring nothing but loss and tragedy to all concerned, led many earnest men and women to organize peace societies and to advocate a limitation of armaments and the arbitration of international disputes. The most important result of this widely diffused sentiment for peace was an international conference held at The Hague in 1899, at the suggestion of Czar Nicholas II of Russia. The delegates designed a formula whereby disputes between sovereign states might be submitted to arbitration, and a second conference (1907) strengthened the Hague Tribunal as an international court of justice. There was no power, however, aside from public opinion, which could compel nations to submit their quarrels to this impartial court, nor did the court have any means whereby it could enforce its decisions. Governments evinced little faith in its efficacy as an instrument for the prevention of war, and the efforts made at the Hague Conferences to effect a limitation or reduction of armaments came to nothing.

Peace societies

For side by side with the advocates of peace, who denounced war as unchristian or argued that under modern conditions it would ruin victor and victim alike, there stood an opposing group of thinkers who defended it as a harsh necessity of the struggle for existence. These realists, as they liked to style themselves, pointed out that history revealed that men had fought each other since the dawn of time, that in the animal world Nature showed herself "red in tooth and claw," and that mankind could not escape the call to strife because competitive struggles were an inherited biological necessity. The contemporary clash and rivalry of the imperialistic powers they held to be the modern application of the ancient law of battle. Peace-loving peoples, averse to war and unprepared for it, would be herded to the wall by those nations which had conserved the military virtues and had

WILLIAM II, GERMAN EMPEROR
1888–1918

EDWARD VII OF ENGLAND
1901–1910

NICHOLAS II OF RUSSIA
1894–1917

RAYMOND POINCARÉ, PRESIDENT OF
THE FRENCH REPUBLIC, 1913–1920

THE HEADS OF FOUR GREAT POWERS BEFORE WORLD WAR I

arrayed their warriors to conquer. Since war, regrettable and destructive though it might be, was nonetheless a visitation likely to confront each nation at least once in a generation, the sane course for a state was to prepare for it, to maintain a large and well-trained fighting force, and if possible to secure allies. For the fate of the unprepared peoples could be read in the history books, and it was written, not in black and white, but in red.

The belief that impressive armaments, and particularly a far-flung navy, helped a power to control and exploit the backward regions of the earth, and so increase its prestige and prosperity, was a political maxim so generally accepted at the opening of the twentieth century that few people undertook to dispute it. The fact that a small state like Switzerland could hold its own in the commercial race, although surrounded by four great military powers, or that Norway, with an insignificant navy, ranked fourth among the nations of the world in the extent of its maritime tonnage, did not shake the faith of the militarists in the efficacy of armed force to promote the prosperity of a nation. Precisely how battleships or howitzers captured trade was not made clear, but the belief that they were necessary to guarantee a nation's prestige and security, and to extend its commercial and colonial ambitions, appeared to be sufficient justification for their expense. It was even argued in all seriousness that the more heavily the nations armed, the less likely they were to fight, because the more destructive war became, the less profit there would be in it for the victor. And if war did come, some militarists averred, it would be over sooner if the states were fully prepared for it; unpreparedness only delayed the decision and so prolonged the agony. A painful operation should be complete and swift.

As a consequence of this contradictory and muddle-headed attitude, the European peoples prayed for peace and prepared for war. Each nation built up its armaments under the impression that its neighbor meditated an attack, and in so doing inspired its neighbor with the same dread. These mounting fears were stimulated by the patriotic and militant utterances of such writers as Frederick von Bernhardi, who declared it to be the law of life that the strong must vanquish the weak, and urged his fellow Germans to prepare for war. But German writers were not alone in defending militarism: in Russia, France, Austria, Italy, and England writers and teachers were active, fixing in the minds of the young men and boys the belief that to risk their lives on the battlefield in defense of their country was a supreme privilege and duty. Of course, the war envisaged was always a war of defense, for no people and very few leaders had any wish to provoke a conflict if war could be honorably avoided, but military strategists were in general agreement that the best defensive was an offensive, and the high command in each state developed plans for hurling an army across its neighbor's frontier as the first measure of self-defense. As rumors of new and secret weapons and plans for sudden attacks filtered back and forth, they created a nightmare of suspicion and fear from which there seemed to be no possible escape. If one power increased its military budget, its opponents matched the increase and lengthened the period of conscript service; a strategic railway leading toward the frontier was countered by the construction of a new line of fortifications. By 1914, all Europe was tense with the strain and the expense of the long-drawn-out competition, and for some the bursting of the storm came almost as a relief.

The armed peace

SECTION L

Two World Wars and the Years Between

(1914–1947)

The outbreak of a general European war in 1914, which ultimately involved almost all the nations of the globe, marked the opening of a new and unsettled era. Despite the enormous destruction and the tragic sacrifices which it caused, the First World War solved few problems and created many. Both victors and vanquished suffered irremediable losses, and the heritage of hate which the conflict bequeathed made a satisfactory settlement difficult.

From the nightmare of war the European peoples emerged into a scarcely less desperate era of political turbulence and economic confusion. Although all classes earnestly desired to safeguard the world from future conflicts, the post-war years brought a general increase in armaments and a growing fear that Fate held even more destructive wars in reserve unless the machinery of peaceful arbitration could be greatly strengthened. Politically, the most significant development of the twenty-year interval from 1919 to 1939 was the challenge to democracy afforded by the establishment of a new régime in Russia founded upon communist principles, and new governments in Italy and Germany which substituted the authoritarian rule of a single well-disciplined party, headed by a dictator, for the parliamentary rule of a popularly elected and representative assembly.

EUROPE
AFTER WORLD WAR I

------- Boundaries 1914
———   "   1926

62

The First World War

> We are glad, now that we see the facts with no veil of false pretence about them, to fight thus for the ultimate peace of the world and for the liberation of its peoples...
>
> WOODROW WILSON (1917).

THE INCIDENT which precipitated the long-dreaded war between the European powers in 1914 originated in the Balkans. A dispute which broke out between Austria and Serbia drew in Germany, as the ally of Austria, and Russia, as the protector of the Serbs. France was bound to Russia by treaty, and Britain chose to stand by France and Russia under the terms of the Entente. Thus the system of alliances which was supposed to preserve a balance of power not only failed to prevent war, but made it, when it came, an all but universal tragedy.

1. THE COMING OF THE WAR

Austria and Serbia

For more than a decade before 1914, the governing classes in Austria-Hungary had grown increasingly alarmed at the spread of nationalist sentiment among the Slavic peoples of the Balkan lands, and they were particularly hostile toward the Serbs, who had taken the lead in urging the creation of a Slavic state to include if possible all the Balkan Slavs. The Austrian annexation of Bosnia and Herzegovina in 1908 had dealt a severe blow to these Serbian aspirations, and Austrian opposition prevented Serbia acquiring all the territory she desired after the Balkan Wars of 1912–13.[1] In revenge the Serbs waged a tariff war against Austria, their newspapers stirred up anti-Austrian feeling, and Serbian secret societies strove to excite the Slavs within the Austro-Hungarian Empire to rebellion, despite the fact that the Serbian government had pledged itself to restrain such unfriendly activities.

The Serbian plots to disrupt the Hapsburg Empire would not have constituted a serious menace if the Slavic subjects of Francis Joseph had been contented with their lot. But, although half the fifty million people living in Austria-Hungary were of Slavic origin, they possessed little political power, for the Germans and Magyars practically controlled the government and were unwilling to relinquish their privileges. Some Austrian statesmen agreed that the best way to placate the Slavs and consolidate the empire was to extend greater political power to the subject Slavs, perhaps to transform the empire from a dual into a triple monarchy so that the Slavs might enjoy equality with the Germans and Magyars. Among the leaders believed to favor such a compromise was the Archduke Franz Ferdinand, nephew and heir of the Emperor Francis Joseph.

The first shots

But Franz Ferdinand was not destined to mount the Austrian throne. On June 28, 1914, he was assassinated while visiting the town of Sarajevo in Bosnia. The assassin was a Bosnian youth, Gavrilo Princip, but it was later proved that the act had been plotted in Belgrade and that officials in the Serbian army and the Serbian government had helped to provide the means. There is even some evidence to suggest that more than one member of the Serbian cabinet knew in advance of the conspiracy.

The Austrian government, already hostile

[1] See above, page 835.

to the Pan-Slav Movement in the Balkans, could hardly fail to take advantage of the opportunity thus offered for a reckoning with Serbia. On July 23, the foreign minister of Austria-Hungary, Leopold von Berchtold, dispatched an ultimatum demanding in substance: (1) that the Serbian government suppress all anti-Austrian activity in Serbia and dismiss officials guilty of fomenting it; and (2) that Austrian officials be permitted to aid in this work of suppression and in the punishment of the conspirators who had planned the archduke's death. A reply to this ultimatum was demanded within forty-eight hours. The Serbian government yielded to the greater part of the Austrian demands, but the conciliatory tone of the reply was contradicted by a simultaneous mobilization for war. The Austrian government, proclaiming the reply evasive and unsatisfactory, declared war against Serbia July 28.

Austrian ultimatum

The belligerent attitude of Austria was founded (1) on a promise of support from Germany, and (2) on a conviction that Russia, the natural protector of Serbia, would not intervene. But this time the Russian government was confident of French aid, for the president of the French Republic, Raymond Poincaré, had visited Saint Petersburg in July, 1914, and assured the Russian minister of foreign affairs, Serge Sazonov, of Franco-Russian solidarity. The Russians, therefore, began preparations for a general mobilization as early as July 25.

Failure of diplomacy

After July 28, the Serbian issue was completely overshadowed by the German alarm over the progress of Russian mobilization, officially decreed July 29 (a preparatory state of war had been proclaimed four days earlier). Mobilization made hostilities all but inevitable, and Kaiser William telegraphed Nicholas II entreating him earnestly to withdraw his order. The harassed czar thereupon "suspended" the order for mobilization against Germany, but his advisers persuaded him to renew it the following day (July 30). The kaiser, though proclaiming a "state of imminent danger of war," had delayed German mobilization while making his appeal to Nicholas. On July 31, he offered the Russians twelve hours in which to countermand their continued mobilization, waited twenty-four hours for a reply, and then, on August 1, announced that a state of war existed between Germany and Russia. From France, where mobilization had been going quietly forward since July 30, the German government demanded a statement of policy, and as no clear answer was obtainable (France had already promised Russia to fulfill her obligations as an ally), Germany declared war against France also (August 3).

If Germany and Austria fought Russia and France, could Great Britain remain neutral? The British were bound by no formal treaties, but the British fleet was pledged, by private agreement between the governments, to protect the northern French coasts while the French warships patrolled the Mediterranean. Sir Edward Grey, who had negotiated this "gentlemen's agreement," considered that Britain was bound in honor to aid France, but would the British Parliament and the British people see the matter in this light? On August 2, Grey's painful dilemma was solved by German ruthlessness, for on that date the German government demanded permission to march its armies through Belgium to attack France. This permission the Belgian government courageously refused. On August 4, the British government notified the German government that a state of war would commence at midnight unless Germany promised to respect Belgian neutrality. There was no reply, and Britain considered herself at war.

The British attitude

Thus, within a week five great powers had plunged into a war of unpredictable dimensions. Italy deserted the Triple Alliance and issued a declaration of neutrality on the ground that Austria and Germany were engaged in an offensive, not a defensive, conflict. But a sixth power came into the struggle on August 23, when Japan declared war against Germany; and one week later, Turkey joined the "Central Powers." At first glance the "Allies" or "Entente Powers," Britain, France, and Russia, together with Japan and Serbia, appeared to have a great advantage over the Central Powers, Germany and Austria and their dubious ally Turkey. For the Allies possessed the world's greatest sea force, the British navy, and a combined potential manpower three times that of the Central Powers. But in modern warfare, training, equipment, and generalship count more than numbers, and here the superiority lay with the Central Powers and encouraged them also to look for an early victory. Only a few farsighted realists anticipated that the struggle might last three or four years, or apprehended the full magnitude of the tragedy which had overtaken European civilization.

From the outset each side endeavored to lay the full responsibility for the war upon the other, and each government in turn published an official explanation to justify its course of action. These accounts, the British Blue Book, the German White Book, the French Yellow Book, etc., were presented as impartial diplomatic surveys of the events leading to the outbreak of hostilities, but in actuality they were subtle instruments of justification and propaganda. Supported by a carefully censored and not infrequently a subsidized press, they convinced the people in each belligerent country that their government was in the right, and that they were fighting for their liberties against an unprovoked attack by scheming and unscrupulous foes. No people and no government (a few reckless individuals aside) had planned or desired war; but once war came, a wave of patriotic fervor swept the rival populations into a maelstrom of enthusiasm and self-sacrifice. This spirit was deliberately intensified by carefully circulated tales of enemy perfidy and brutality manufactured for purposes of propaganda by the governments participating. Some of the atrocities recounted were true, for war is a brutal and brutalizing affair, but most of them were inventions. In justifying their own acts and blackening the case of the Central Powers, the Allied governments enjoyed an important advantage, for they controlled the sea routes and the ocean cables of the world and were enabled to impress their version upon the neutral nations. As the war progressed, neutral opinion turned steadily against Germany until it was overwhelmingly hostile.

2. THE WAR ON LAND (1914-17)

The plan of the German high command called for a vast enveloping movement which would destroy the French armies in the west before the dilatory Russians could concentrate their forces in the east. Five German armies were to advance through Belgium and northern France, the First Army sweeping past Brussels on a semicircle which would carry it west and south of Paris, the Second, Third, Fourth, and Fifth Armies pivoting with it on concentric arcs with Metz as a center. Enveloped by this prodigious flanking movement, the French armies were to be herded against the Alsatian frontier, where the Sixth and Seventh German Armies formed an anvil upon which they could be pounded to pieces. Time was the most vital factor in this plan, time and a powerful right wing, for the First and Second Armies on the extreme right had the longest arc to follow and the heaviest resistance to overcome. Despite the heroic opposition of the Belgian forces, the Germans swept rapidly forward, driving back the French and a small British expeditionary force of one hundred thousand men. By September 5, the German First Army was within thirty miles of Paris and ahead of its schedule. But it was weaker than the original plan, designed by Count von Schlieffen in 1906, had ordained, and the troops were wearied by long marches. On September 6, the French attacked it desperately. In defending his right, the German general, von Kluck, opened a gap twenty miles wide between his forces and the Second Army on his left. French and British troops were hurled into this opening, making the position of the Germans still more hazardous, and after four days of fierce conflict they retreated. This first battle of the Marne (September 6-12) had not only saved Paris, but had irreparably dislocated the Schlieffen plan.

Throwing up entrenchments, the Germans quickly fortified a line against which the Allied troops pounded in vain (battle of the Aisne, September 13-21). By October this line stretched from the North Sea coast near the Franco-Belgian frontier to neutral Switzerland. The Germans hoped to capture the French seaports, Dunkirk, Calais, and possibly Boulogne, in order to cripple communications between France and Britain, but they were blocked by the stubborn British resistance at Ypres. Before the close of 1914, the struggle in the west had changed from a war of movement to a war of position. Both sides constructed intricate systems of trenches fortified with barbed-wire entanglements and machine guns against which cavalry regiments were useless and infantry battalions hurled themselves in vain. The armies were unprepared for this type of warfare, and the commanders clung to the belief that, by wasting enough men in concentrated attacks, it would prove possible to break through the enemy lines and open a rapid deployment. In March, 1915, the British advanced one mile on a three-mile front at Neuve Chapelle, after an unprecedented bombardment, but the German lines held and the gain was dearly bought with thirteen thousand dead. A month later, the Germans surprised the Allied forces at Ypres with waves of poison gas, but this new and horrible instrument of war failed to drive the defenders from the city and increased the reputation of the Germans for treachery and inhumanity.

The year 1916 brought still further tragic proof that the western battle-line could not be broken. From February to June, the Germans assailed the great French fortress of Verdun. They gained over one hundred square miles of shell-torn ground, throwing in reserves until their casualties exceeded a quarter of a million, but the French had sworn, "They shall not pass," and Verdun still stood. In the north the Allies attacked in their turn, winning an equivalent area of tortured ground at twice the cost. In these prolonged battles the defenders suffered almost as heavily as the attackers, and the terrible slaughter weakened the morale of soldiers and civilians on both sides. There seemed, at the opening of 1917, to be little hope of forcing a decision on the western battle-front.

On the eastern front the campaigns had been more dramatic, but had proved even less favorable to the Allies. As the Russians had mobilized first, and with unexpected rapidity, they were able to invade East Prussia on the outbreak of war. To check their advance, the kaiser called from retirement General Paul von Hindenburg (1847–1934), a clear-headed strategist of sixty-seven, who possessed an intimate knowledge of East Prussian topography. With a Napoleonic gesture, Hindenburg hurled his forces between two larger Russian armies, and won, at Tannenberg, the most decisive victory of the war. Driving the Russian Second Army into the morasses of the Masurian Lake region, he practically destroyed it, taking ninety thousand prisoners and two hundred guns; then turning against the Russian First Army, which was advancing on his left, he forced it to retreat behind the frontier. The losses suffered by the Russians were enormous, but their early drive had caused the German high command to recall several divisions needed on the western front and this depletion helped to weaken von Kluck's First Army in its decisive encounter on the Marne.

Battle of Tannenberg

Against the Austrian armies the Russians continued for a time to compete with greater success, capturing the province of Galicia and one hundred thousand prisoners in September, 1914. But the tide turned when German reinforcements under von Hindenburg and von Mackensen came to the relief of the Dual Monarchy. Between May and September, 1915, the Russians were driven from Galicia and Poland with losses so catastrophic they appear incredible; at least one million of the czar's soldiers were made prisoner, and the list of killed and wounded must have been correspondingly large. From this drain of men and material Russia never recovered. Bulgaria decided the moment had come to join the Central Powers (October, 1915), and Serbia, vulnerable from three sides, was easily overrun. Before the end of 1915, the armies of Austria and Germany dominated the Balkans and had secured a direct land communication with their ally Turkey.

German victories

Strategically the Central Powers possessed several important advantages, for they held

AIR VIEW OF KRUPP WORKS AT ESSEN

Above: The industrial might which made Germany strong in World War I was centered in the famous Krupp Works at Essen.

BRITAIN'S NAVAL MIGHT

Right: The battleship was still monarch of the seas in World War I before air power seriously threatened it.

the "inside lines" and could move their forces from one sector to another with rapidity and ease. Also, they were in a position to cut Russia off from easy communication with France and Britain by blocking both the Baltic and the Black Seas. The Allies, hoping to force their way to Constantinople and open the Black Sea to their ships, prepared an attack on the Dardanelles early in 1915, but were compelled to abandon the project after a year of costly blunders. A British expedition which advanced from the Persian Gulf toward Bagdad in 1915 was likewise defeated. To offset these serious reverses on the eastern and Turkish fronts, the Allies had the meager satisfaction of repelling several assaults which the Turks directed against the Suez Canal.

Dardanelles campaign

One other important development of the year 1915 was the intervention of Italy in the conflict. On May 23, after eight months of bargaining with the opposing camps, the Italian government declared war against Austria. In return for this assistance the Allied Powers promised her all those sections of "unredeemed Italy" to the north and east of the Adriatic Sea which she coveted, and more if she could take it, for in disposing of enemy territory the Allies could afford to be generous. Among themselves, the Allies had already agreed that when the war had been won Russia should have Constantinople, France should reoccupy Alsace and Lorraine, and Great Britain should acquire the lion's share of the German colonies. But as 1916 succeeded 1915, bringing victory no nearer, the optimism of the Allied nations began to fade. In the west the indecisive carnage of Verdun and the Somme decimated the conscript armies. In the south the Italians were hard-pressed to hold their own against the Austrian offensives. In the east a valiant Russian drive in Galicia (June–July, 1916) raised undue hopes and encouraged Rumania to declare for the Allies, whereupon the armies of the Central Powers swiftly overran the kingdom and seized the Rumanian harvest. Thus the closing months of 1916 found the Central Powers holding Belgium, part of northeastern France, Poland, Serbia, Montenegro, and most of Rumania. So far as land operations were concerned, the Germans and Austrians appeared to be winning the war despite their costly failure at Verdun.

Italy joins the Allies

3. THE WAR ON THE SEA

The operations on land, however, did not tell the whole story. On the sea the Allies had applied their superior naval forces with immediate effect, capturing, sinking, or driving into port all ships flying the flags of the Central Powers. Great Britain then declared all enemy territory in a state of blockade and attempted to seize as contraband all materials useful in the prosecution of the war. As the months passed, the British government increased the list of goods liable to confiscation, and even restricted the importation of merchandise into neutral countries like Holland and Denmark on the ground that any surplus was intended for Germany. The United States and other neutral nations protested vigorously against the British actions, which violated international agreements, and the Germans complained with justice that the Declaration of Paris [1] and later declarations concerning the seizure of contraband in time of war were being flouted daily. To this the British replied that the German government had been the first to disregard international laws and treaties, and insisted that it must bear the responsibility if its civilian population suffered hardships because the supply of fuel, cotton, and foodstuffs had been curtailed by the blockade.

The naval blockade

In addition to the strangling effect of this state of siege, which steadily reduced the morale and resistance of the German people, the Allies took advantage of their control of the sea to isolate and capture the German colonies, to transport their own supplies and men to the scene of conflict, and to maintain the shipments of food and raw material without which British industry and the British population would have slowly starved. Furthermore, England and France could purchase munitions in the United States, where factories were kept running

[1] See above, page 731.

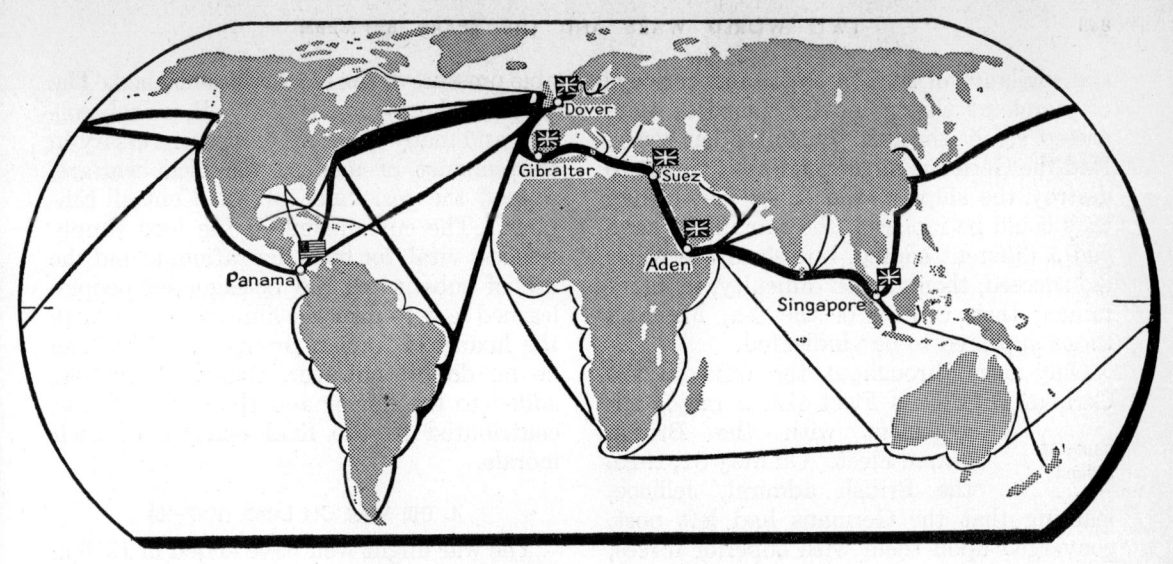

OCEAN TRADE ROUTES AND CONTROL BASES

day and night to fill their orders, while Germany and Austria were cut off from this important source of supplies. Under the circumstances it is not altogether surprising that the Germans decided upon a program of retaliation against Allied shipping, planning by means of submarine boats to enforce a counter-blockade.

Early in 1915, the German government pronounced the waters surrounding the British Isles a "war zone" in which any merchant ship of the Allied nations might be torpedoed without warning. This application of a new naval weapon, the submarine boat, proved at first highly successful; British ships were sunk almost daily, the most important being the giant liner *Lusitania* which was torpedoed on May 7, 1915, with a loss of over eleven hundred lives. But the campaign of the undersea boats failed to stop the flow of Allied commerce, although it seriously depleted the supply of merchant ships. Moreover, it injured the German cause by inflaming neutral opinion against the Central Powers. The arrogance of the British, in searching ships on the high seas and confiscating their cargoes, appeared almost pardonable in comparison with the inhumanity of the German U-boat commanders who sank ships, cargoes, and passengers indiscriminately. Strong protests from the United States after the sinking of the *Lusitania* impelled the German government to modify its procedure for a year, but in January, 1917, it announced a policy of "unrestricted submarine warfare" under which any ship, belligerent or neutral, which entered the danger zones surrounding the coasts of the British Isles, France, or Italy, would expose itself to destruction without warning. The Germans hoped by this defiant course to destroy one million tons of shipping a month and cripple the Allied transportation system beyond salvation, but they failed in their objective and sealed their fate by drawing the United States into the war on the side of their opponents.

Submarine blockade

In the years preceding the war, an American naval historian, Captain (later Admiral) Alfred Thayer Mahan, had written several widely read books to prove that in warfare a power which controls the sea possesses a decisive advantage over its adversary, an advantage which, if it be maintained, must almost certainly assure victory in the end. The Allied peoples found this argument a consolation during the darkest days of World War I; but some German theorists retorted that, even if Mahan's conclusions had held true in the past, the submarine had changed conditions, for it gave the Central Powers a means to control the seas also. Before the war ended, however, the destructiveness of the submarine boats had been severely curtailed by the improved tactics and vigilance of surface craft, and convoys of merchant ships, heavily guarded, were passed safely through the forbidden zones. Had the Germans made good their threat to destroy the ships of the Allies faster than they could be replaced, the war might have had a different ending, but since the Allies did succeed, though with difficulty, in maintaining their control of the sea, Mahan's thesis appeared to be vindicated.

Only once throughout the war did the German High Seas Fleet risk a major engagement with the British Grand Fleet. On May 31, 1916, the British admiral, Jellicoe, learning that the Germans had left port, converged upon them with superior forces, and attempted to draw them into a trap by advancing his cruiser squadron as a lure. When the German admiral, von Scheer, discovered the ruse, he extricated his slower fleet with exceptional skill, and after darkness had fallen slipped through a British destroyer screen to safety. Both sides claimed a victory, the Germans because they inflicted losses double their own upon a superior enemy force, the British because they remained masters of the scene of combat and held their supremacy without a second direct challenge until the end of the war. In marksmanship, maneuvering, and night fighting, however, the Germans had displayed a technical superiority which won the admiration of their foes.

Battle of Jutland

The battle of Jutland probably represents the only occasion when the war could have been won or lost in a single afternoon. Had the British destroyed the German High Seas Fleet, they could have opened the Baltic and secured their sorely needed communication with ice-free Russian ports. On the other hand, a striking German success which broke the blockade and exposed Allied merchant shipping to the risk of capture and destruction by German cruisers would have proved more paralyzing than the submarine campaign at its worst. But because Britain continued to rule the waves, and because the arrival of American naval reinforcements after April, 1917, made a further sally by the German fleet an unwise gamble, the inexorable pressure of the blockade continued. The growing shortage of rubber, oil, nickel, cotton, and many other substances necessary in the conduct of modern technical warfare, sapped the resistance of the Central Empires. The curtailment of the food supply was less vital, for by strict rationing and the use of substitutes the beleaguered peoples learned how to dispense almost entirely with the luxury of foreign products. There can be no doubt, however, that malnutrition, added to the horror and the strain of war, contributed to the final collapse of their morale.

Effects of the blockade

4. THE WAR ON LAND (1917–18)

The war might well have ended in 1916 in a general stalemate and a compromise peace. Allied mastery on the sea largely nullified the successes won by the Central Powers on land, and all the belligerents had come to realize that a decisive victory would demand disproportionate slaughter and ruinous expense. Yet, when the German government proposed "to enter into peace negotiations" (December 12, 1916), the Allied Powers returned a joint refusal, declaring the offer a ruse designed to create dissension in the Allied countries, and stigmatizing it as "empty and insincere." In the same month President Wilson dispatched a note through the state department of the United States, urging the adversaries to draw up an outline of their war aims. Wilson pointed out that the precise objectives for which the nations were fighting had never been definitely stated, and he suggested that an interchange of views might clear the way for a conference. To this friendly overture the Central Powers responded that they had themselves proposed an interchange of views a few days earlier. The Allied nations replied at greater length with a general but not entirely frank definition of their objectives, including "the restoration of Belgium, Serbia, and Montenegro ... evacuation of the invaded territories in France, in Russia, and in Rumania ... liberation of the Italians, as also of the Slavs, Rumanes, and Czecho-Slovaks from foreign [i.e., Austro-Hungarian] domination, [and] the setting free of the populations subject to

Peace overtures of 1916

WORLD WAR I COMMANDERS

Top left: Marshal Ferdinand Foch was Commander-in-Chief of the Allied Armies.

Top right: Field Marshal Paul von Hindenburg was the most renowned German general.

Right: Sir Douglas Haig commanded the British, and General John J. Pershing the American expeditionary force.

the bloody tyranny of the Turks...' The Allies also demanded compensation and indemnities, and adequate guaranties for the future peace of Europe.

Only definite defeat could bring the Central Powers to accept such terms, for they involved the break-up of the Hapsburg Empire. The insistence of the Allied governments that Germany and Austria were exclusively responsible for the war, and the rejection without thanks of the German peace overture, destroyed all hope of an early conference and condemned Europe to nearly two more years of bloodshed.

Following the rejection of the peace proposals, Germany turned to new and more ruthless methods of submarine warfare, for more than ever Time had become the enemy of the Central Powers. The Allies planned to make 1917 a year of synchronized attacks from all sides, but their hopes were betrayed through the collapse of Russia. Demoralized by the terrible slaughter, the failure of supplies and of munitions, and the despair which had followed on their disastrous reverses, the Russian armies and the Russian people broke into a popular revolt and the forces of government dissolved in spontaneous anarchy. Nicholas II abdicated (March 15, 1917) and a provisional government was established. For several months the French and British clung to the illusion that the new Russian government would press the war with fresh vigor, but after a second revolution in November, 1917 (which is discussed in a later chapter), the radical faction known as the Bolsheviki secured control and arranged a truce extremely favorable to the Central Powers. The withdrawal of Russia from the war was formally confirmed by the Treaty of Brest-Litovsk which was signed in March, 1918.

Revolution in Russia

While losing one ally, however, the Entente nations found another and more powerful one. The campaign of unrestricted submarine warfare, opened by the Central Powers in February, 1917, imperiled the lives of such American citizens as chose to sail on ships entering the war zones. Hostility toward the Central Powers had grown steadily in the United States. It was fostered by Allied propaganda, by sympathy for France and Belgium, and by the ill-advised activities of German agents who attempted to prevent the shipment of munitions from the United States to the Entente nations. The fact, too, that American financiers had advanced a billion and a half dollars in credits to the Allied governments played its part in shaping sentiment toward intervention. On February 3, 1917, the United States broke off diplomatic relations with Germany, and on April 6, Congress voted to declare war. This action meant that the enormous wealth, the industrial equipment, the natural resources, and the undepleted manpower of the American people would be available for the French, British, and Italians to draw upon. Sweeping measures were rushed through Congress extending loans to the Allied governments, mobilizing millions of men for military service overseas, and speeding up the production of ships, shells, guns, airplanes, and all the other forms of material and equipment essential to the vigorous prosecution of a modern war.

United States at war

Fortune was clearly deserting the Central Powers, but the German general staff, now dominated by Erich von Ludendorff, was still confident of victory and decided to risk everything upon a gambler's chance. With Russia in collapse, and the United States unprepared to train and dispatch large forces to Europe for at least a year, the Germans possessed a numerical superiority on the French and Italian fronts at any point where they chose to concentrate their reserves. In October, 1917, they launched a drive against the Italians at Caporetto, and the resulting *débâcle* cost Italy three quarters of a million men and all but drove the nation out of the war. Then the Germans prepared for a spring offensive on the western front, a drive of unparalleled proportions by which they hoped to bring the French and British to terms. All the nations were war-weary, the spirit of defeatism had infected soldiers and civilians alike, and both the French and Italian governments had crushed serious mutinies among the troops by summary executions. The Germans believed that the mo-

New German offensives

AN AMERICAN SQUAD NEAR VERDUN

The intervention of the United States turned the scale in World War I. Here is a section of the American manpower which reversed the balance on the western front.

AMERICAN OBSERVERS SCAN THE HORIZON FOR SIGNS OF THE RETREATING GERMANS

rale of the Allied armies would break under a new assault before July, 1918, so that the American reinforcements, even if they escaped the hazards of submarine attack, would reach France too late to turn the tide of war. In March, 1918, von Ludendorff delivered his first blow in this "Victory Drive," shattering the British Fifth Army, but stopping just short of the important railway junction of Amiens. A second blow parted the British lines before Lille. The numerical preponderance which the Germans enjoyed had given them two important though not decisive victories, but the cost exacted was half a million casualties. Their third drive, against the French this time, carried them forward thirty miles to the Marne River, so that they were almost as close to Paris as during their first rush of 1914. Ludendorff now prepared his fourth stroke, which was designed to capture Reims and dislocate the Allied front so completely that it would end the war.

This supreme offensive opened in mid-July, 1918. The Allied armies, recently unified under the command of General Ferdinand Foch, were learning to concert their resistance to better effect; they held firm against the fury of the German assault, and after three days they counter-attacked so energetically that the whole aspect of the war changed in two weeks. This second battle of the Marne (July 15—August 2, 1918) was even more decisive than the first. With American reinforcements coming into line by the hundreds of thousands, Foch gave orders to General Haig, who directed the British expeditionary force, and to General Pershing, who commanded the American army in France, to attack the enemy along the whole line. With the advantage of numbers now turning against them, the Germans were driven slowly back, in a rearguard action of such magnitude that it cost them another half-million casualties by the middle of September. The tide had turned irreversibly and the end was in sight.

Germans checked

In September, Bulgaria sued for peace. An Allied army, operating from Salonica, had reconquered Macedonia and Serbia, and was threatening the Bulgarian capital. A few weeks later, the Turkish Empire collapsed. The British had entered Jerusalem (December, 1917), and, after joining forces with rebellious Arab leaders, General Allenby opened a campaign in 1918 which overthrew the Turkish strongholds from Bagdad to Aleppo. With her southern allies dropping out of the war, Austria-Hungary could not hope to resist invasion. Her subject peoples were rising in revolt and her armies falling back before the Italians when the Dual Monarchy capitulated on November 4, 1918. In reality, even while the envoys were signing the armistice, the proud Austro-Hungarian Empire had ceased to exist, for the same day the Emperor Charles I (who had succeeded Francis Joseph in 1916) renounced his throne and the Poles, Czechs, Croats, and Slovenes were organizing independent states.

Collapse of Austria

Fully aware that the war was lost, but preserving their admirable discipline throughout the retreat, the German armies fought on stubbornly while their allies fell away from them and Foch's unremitting attacks multiplied from day to day. In the end it was the civilian population of Germany which first broke under the strain of defeat, malnutrition, and disillusionment. Repudiating the imperial government which had promised victory and now stood forsworn, the inhabitants of Munich and Berlin, and the sailors in the naval squadrons at Kiel, raised republican flags during the first week of November. On the tenth, William II fled to Holland, and the following day the German delegates, who had been sent to ask for an armistice, signed under protest the terms of surrender which Foch had drawn up. The reversal of fortune in the final months of the war had been so swift that the Allied Governments chose to regard the Germans' acceptance of a truce as an unconditional capitulation. Firing ceased at eleven o'clock on the morning of November 11, 1918.

5. THE COST OF THE WAR

For over three years the leading nations of the world had strained their resources to the breaking point in the work of slaughter and destruction. Before its close World War I had involved over thirty states and left no part of the planet or its population unaffected. The magnitude of the struggle blunted the comprehension even of those who lived through it, and no later description can give more than a feeble suggestion of its horrors. Statistics are but a ghostly residue of what were once flaming facts, and it is better perhaps that no ciphers on a page can ever borrow the power to clothe with reality for later eyes this tremendous modern tragedy.

Ten million soldiers, the finest of their generation, had perished, over six thousand a day for each day that the war continued. **Loss of life** Twenty million had been wounded, some in such ghastly fashion that they took their own lives rather than survive as blinded, crippled, or paralyzed invalids. Losses of life among the civilian population from shell fire, air raids, submarine attacks, the hardships of the blockade, and other causes, cannot be easily estimated; and it is still less possible to find any measurement for the spiritual anguish endured, the waiting for word from the missing, the disruption of family life, the shock and the grief as the friends and relatives of ten million men faced the knowledge that the dead would not return.

For the material costs of the war the figures are too vast to bear any recognizable relation to familiar things. The **Material costs** property destroyed, mines flooded, trees shattered, buildings razed, ships and cargoes sunk, have been valued at one hundred and fifty billion dollars. Modern methods of fighting proved far more expensive than anyone had conceived and grew more so daily, until the combatants were spending ten million dollars *an hour*, and piled up a grand total of war expenditure by November, 1918, which has been estimated at one hundred and eighty-six billion dollars. But when, to the cost of mobilizing sixty-five million men for military service, one adds the sacrifice entailed by withdrawing them from profitable and productive occupations, the loss to civilization becomes vastly greater. This expense of energy and of gold, turned into channels of peaceful accomplishment, might have replaced all the tenements in all the cities of Europe and America by model houses; might have curbed disease and provided medical service which would have saved as many lives as the war cost; might have banished illiteracy among the civilized nations and endowed free libraries in every town. Applied to more prosaic purposes, these billions would have cancelled the national debt of all the belligerent states and eased the burden of taxation, instead of leaving the governments in a state scarcely distinguishable from bankruptcy.

The scientists and inventors who had done so much to enrich and extend the life of man in recent generations were summoned by the warring governments to devise new methods of mass murder and new safeguards against it. Guns remained the principal weapons, but all types, from the light machine guns to the German long-range cannon which shelled Paris from a point seventy miles away, were developed to an extraordinary pitch of efficiency. Of new devices the most terrifying was poison gas, first utilized by the Germans, and the most effective the cumbersome armored tractors or "tanks," a British invention designed for smashing a way through entrenchments and barbed-wire entanglements impassable for infantry. The airplane was used chiefly for reconnaissance work and for directing artillery fire, for aerial bombing had not yet proved very effective. The construction of underground defenses, often reinforced with sheet iron and concrete, and of fortified machine-gun stations led to a much wider demand for high-explosive shells, which were used to destroy these positions as completely as possible before the infantry attempted to pass.

In sea fighting the most novel diversion of World War I was the submarine boat, but it is a truism in warfare that new weapons are met by new defenses. Before the conflict ended, the British and their allies had perfected methods for the detection and destruction of undersea craft which seriously curbed their activities. The question whether the giant battleships, which were the pride of all the pre-war navies, could survive the threat of airplanes and submarines remained open to debate, but most naval experts were satisfied that the dreadnought would preserve its relative invulnerability, and they continued to repose their trust in these floating fortresses with their armor plate a foot thick and their guns which hurl one-ton projectiles.

World War I taught other important lessons. More than any previous conflict it proved itself a war of steel and gold. Only nations which possessed huge financial reserves, and commanded the industrial equipment to supply the munitions required, were capable of waging a modern war successfully. The day had past, also, when a state could entrust its defense to a small professional army while the people went about their daily business. Not only the able-bodied men, but all the citizens of a society, were liable to be conscripted for war service of one sort or another in the modern state. Nor were all the casualties confined to the firing line, as the British discovered when their merchant ships were torpedoed and German aircraft dropped bombs on London. With no fireside secure, and the pervasive force of official propaganda reaching every quarter of the country, it was practically impossible for any citizens to preserve an indifferent or an open mind on the issues of the struggle. Patriotism triumphed, and on both sides, as the casualties mounted, a sense of loyalty to the heroic dead demanded further sacrifices from the living.

To maintain their peoples in this exalted mood, governments resorted to every device which could stimulate a waning morale. Indeed, the "propaganda offensive" waged by all the belligerents was perhaps the most significant weapon which the war developed. Official spokesmen of the Allies and the Central Powers consistently idealized their own acts and objectives while unscrupulously misrepresenting the aims and actions of their enemies. In this deceptive art the governments of Great Britain and France displayed a marked superiority, impressing not only their own nationals, but many neutral observers also, with the unimpeachable justice of their cause. They emphasized the war as a struggle between the forces of autocracy and democracy, between despotic rulers swayed by lust for conquest and free peoples defending their liberties, this despite the fact that Russia, most autocratic of the European governments, fought on the side of the Allies. World opinion was further impressed by the Allied claims after the United States joined in the war in the spring of 1917. Woodrow Wilson proclaimed with stirring phrases that the free peoples of the world were fighting to make the world "safe for democracy" and to secure a just and lasting peace. In warfare slogans are sometimes more effective than shells. The idealization of Allied war aims which Wilson presented as his "Fourteen Points" (January 8, 1918) not only inspired the people in all the Allied countries, but influenced the German and Austrian nationals also. When, in the autumn of 1918, the war-weary German people sued for an armistice, it was to Wilson that they appealed, and to his program. But Wilson referred their request for a peace based upon the Fourteen Points to the Allied and Associated Powers, and these powers accepted it "subject to ... qualifications." What these qualifications were will be explained in the next chapter.

War propaganda

63

The Peace Settlement of 1919

> The day of conquest and aggrandizement is gone by; so is also the day of secret covenants entered into in the interests of particular governments and likely at some unlooked-for moment to upset the peace of the world.
> WOODROW WILSON (January 8, 1918).

NO PEACE CONFERENCE has an easy task to perform, for the disputes which precipitate a war are seldom settled by the strife and the bloodshed, and new problems are certain to be created during the struggle. The student will recall the high hopes with which the people of Europe waited for the Congress of Vienna to assemble in 1814, and the disillusionment which followed as they concluded that the chief interest of the diplomats was not to secure a just settlement, but "to divide among the conquerors the spoils taken from the vanquished." After World War I ended in 1918, the nations, victors and vanquished alike, passed through a similar transition from hope to bitterness, and their dissatisfaction over the peace settlement of 1919 was even more profound and more general than the disappointment which succeeded the Napoleonic Wars a century earlier.

1. IDEALS AND REALITIES

There were many complex reasons why the delegates who met at Versailles in 1919 could not justify the hopes reposed in them. The chief difficulty, perhaps, was the gulf which had been dug between ideals and realities. While the World War raged, neither the Allied governments nor those of the Central Powers had admitted frankly and publicly the concrete advantages which they hoped to derive from victory. When, in April, 1917, the United States declared war against Germany, Wilson insisted that the American people had no selfish ends to serve. "We desire no conquest, no dominion," he averred. "We seek no indemnities for ourselves, no material compensation for the sacrifices we shall freely make. We are but one of the champions of the rights of mankind." By implication, the other "champions of the rights of mankind," Great Britain, France, and Italy, were likewise fighting to put an end to armaments and the spirit of militarism, to assure the principle of self-determination to all oppressed peoples, and to organize a world league of free nations pledged to live together for the future in peace and harmony. But unfortunately, these ideals were above the level of events, as the pre-election promises of politicians are above the predatory machinations of a party eager for the spoils of office.

David Lloyd George, prime minister of Great Britain after December, 1916, and the fiery French premier, Georges Clemenceau, recognizing the enthusiasm which Wilson's peace program evoked among the war-weary population, identified themselves with it and allowed Wilson to appear the spokesman for all the Allied and Associated governments. Everywhere people came to think of Wilson's Fourteen Points as embodying the generous aims for which the Allies were fighting, and even the Germans and Austrians trusted that the United States would contribute its powerful influence to assure a just treaty in accordance with Wilson's program. It is time, therefore, to examine the famous Fourteen Points in detail, before seeking to explain what happened to them when the congress finally assembled. A summary of them follows.

    I. Open covenants of peace, openly arrived at ...
   II. Absolute freedom of navigation upon the seas ... alike in peace and in war ...
  III. The removal, as far as possible, of all economic barriers ...
  IV. Adequate guaranties given and taken that national armaments will be reduced to the lowest point consistent with domestic safety.
   V. A free, open-minded, and absolutely impartial adjustment of all colonial claims ...
  VI. The evacuation of all Russian territory and such a settlement ... as will secure [for Russia] ... an unhampered and unembarrassed opportunity for the independent determination of her own political development and national policy ...
 VII. Belgium ... must be evacuated and restored ...
VIII. All French territory should be freed and the invaded portions restored, and the wrong done to France in the matter ... of Alsace-Lorraine ... should be righted.
  IX. A readjustment of the frontiers of Italy should be effected along clearly recognizable lines of nationality.
   X. The peoples of Austria-Hungary ... should be accorded the freest opportunity of autonomous development.
  XI. Rumania, Serbia, and Montenegro should be evacuated; occupied territories restored; Serbia accorded free access to the sea ...
 XII. The Turkish portion of the present Ottoman Empire should be assured a secure sovereignty, but the other nationalities which are now under Turkish rule ... autonomous development ...
XIII. An independent Polish state ... should include the territories inhabited by indisputably Polish populations ... [and should] be assured a free and secure access to the sea ...
XIV. A general association of nations must be formed under specific covenants for the purpose of affording mutual guaranties of political independence and territorial integrity to great and small states alike.

These were lofty and unselfish aims which would, many people hoped, remove the causes that were responsible for past wars, and safeguard the world from armed conflict in the future. Of course, it was easy to foresee that some of the points, such as the demarcation of Italian or Polish frontiers "along clearly recognizable lines of nationality," might prove more complex in practice than in theory, but it was hoped that any hasty or unwise decisions compounded in the hurry of a general settlement could be rectified later by an appeal to the League of Nations. The creation of such a league, though not mentioned until the last clause of Wilson's program, remained to him the point of first importance.

What the advocates of a "just peace" failed to allow for were the national passions which propaganda and sacrifice had fanned to an irrational pitch; the distorting effect of the "war-guilt" thesis, which had convinced millions of people in the Allied countries that William II and his responsible subordinates ought to be punished for their "crimes against humanity"; and the malign influence of those secret agreements which Britain, France, Italy, Greece, and Rumania had already concluded with respect to the disposal of the Rhineland, the Adriatic littoral, the Turkish Empire, and the German colonies. Allied expeditionary forces, chiefly British and Japanese, had conquered all the German colonies by 1918, and possession is nine tenths of international law. French statesmen had informed London and Saint Petersburg of a project to detach the left bank of the Rhine from the German Empire in the interests of security. Russia had been promised control of Constantinople and the Straits, but guaranties made to Russia might conveniently be revoked because that country had made a separate peace and was in no condition, after the revolutions of 1917, to insist upon the bargain. But the other parties to the secret treaty of London (April 26, 1915), to the secret accord with Rumania (August 17, 1917), and the secret conventions which drew Greece to the side of the

Allies were not likely to renounce their promised rewards. Wilson had been too sanguine in his assumption that the day of "secret covenants," of "conquest and aggrandizement," had gone by. The cause for which he strove was lost in advance before he sailed for Paris, and the "war to end war," as an embittered humorist remarked, seemed likely to be followed by "a peace to end peace."

2. THE TREATY OF VERSAILLES

In defiance of customary diplomatic usage, the four defeated nations, Germany, Austria-Hungary, Turkey, and Bulgaria, were excluded from any share in shaping the treaties of peace. Nor did any of the lesser states among the thirty-two "Allied and Associated" victors play a significant rôle. The real masters of the conference were the "Big Four," the representatives of Great Britain, France, Italy, and the United States. Lloyd George, who was the idol of his countrymen and had guided England through the last two years of the war; Clemenceau, whose fierce resolution had silenced the "defeatists" in France when they abandoned hope of victory; Vittorio Orlando, prime minister of Italy; and Woodrow Wilson, the first president of the United States to visit Europe while he was in office and participate personally in a peace congress — these were the men who formed the real deliberative committee which decided the peace.

The "Big Four"

By May, 1919, the treaty had been drafted and the Germans were summoned to sign it. In the Hall of Mirrors at Versailles, where the German Empire had been proclaimed on January 18, 1871, the representatives of the nations assembled forty-eight years later to signalize the ignominious defeat of that empire. Stunned by the severity of the terms, Count von Brockdorff-Rantzau, head of the delegation, entered an earnest protest at the contradiction between the draft of the treaty and the assurances granted the Central Powers when the armistice was negotiated. The Allied governments, however, were adamant in their hour of victory, and on June 28, yielding to necessity, the Germans accepted the treaty, acknowledging "the responsibility of Germany and her allies for causing all the loss and damage to which the Allied and Associated governments and their nationals have been subjected as a consequence of the war imposed upon them by the aggression of Germany and her allies" (Article 231).

The terms of the armistice, supplemented by the peace treaty, condemned the Germans to make restitution for property destroyed by their armies in the occupied regions. They turned over thousands of locomotives, railway cars, automobile trucks, farm machines, horses, swine, sheep, and cattle to the Allied governments. They also surrendered the best part of their merchant marine as compensation for Allied shipping sunk by their submarines, and promised to construct up to one million tons of new ships for the same purpose. Substantial payments in the form of coal, dyestuffs, chemicals, etc., were likewise required of them, and the German-owned ocean cables passed under the control of the victors.

Material surrendered

The Treaty of Versailles reduced the area and population of the German Empire by approximately one tenth. The provinces of Alsace and Lorraine were restored to France; some small districts (Eupen, Moresnet, and Malmédy) were transferred to Belgian sovereignty; and the Saar Valley, with its valuable coal-mines, was placed in pawn for fifteen years, after which the inhabitants might vote for independence, for union with France, or for reunion with Germany. In the east, Germany surrendered almost all the segments of Poland which she had gained by the earlier partitioning of that state. To provide Poland with an outlet to the Baltic Sea, a "corridor" was created which separated East Prussia from the remainder of Germany, while Danzig, with a population predominantly German, was incorporated in the Polish tariff system as a (nominally) free city. Germany also lost part of Upper Silesia to Poland although a plebiscite (1921) indicated a German majority throughout the greater part of the disputed territory. The city of Memel was finally allotted (1924) to the Lithuanian Republic; and a plebiscite in the province of Schleswig gave part of Schleswig back to Denmark.

Territorial concessions

DAVID LLOYD GEORGE

GEORGES CLEMENCEAU

WOODROW WILSON

THE "BIG THREE" OF 1919

David Lloyd George was adroit and resourceful. Georges Clemenceau was a hard-bitten realist. Woodrow Wilson was the idol of peace-loving multitudes throughout the world. These three shaped the Versailles settlement. When Vittorio Orlando sat with them, as representative of Italy, the group was known as the "Big Four" but Orlando was soon reduced to a secondary and ineffective rôle.

Colonies. Article 119 of the treaty declared that "Germany renounces in favor of the Principal Allied and Associated Powers all her rights and titles over her overseas possessions." Japan acquired the German posts and privileges in Shantung Province, China, and all the Pacific islands north of the Equator where the German flag had flown in 1914. Islands south of the Equator passed into British control, and the British also took over German East Africa and German South-West Africa. The French added the German Kamerun territory north of the Congo to their empire in Equatorial Africa. A suggestion put forward by the Germans that the computed value of these colonies might reasonably be deducted from the reparations total was disallowed by the Allied governments.

Reparations. Unable, in the few months at their disposal, to compute the total bill for reparations, the peacemakers contented themselves with stipulating that "Germany undertakes that she will make compensation for all damage done to the civilian population." A reparations commission, created to assess the damages and to examine the capacity of the Germans to pay, set the sum (1921) at thirty-three billion dollars. Although economists pointed out that there was no precedent for such a huge indemnity, and insisted that it could never be collected, the politicians and the Allied peoples were more sanguine, for the treaty entitled the victors to take punitive measures if the Germans fell behind in their payments, and the slogan that Germany should be made to pay to the last penny had been reiterated too long to be easily relinquished. Ten years of economic confusion and a world-wide depression in trade and manufacturing activities supervened before the Allied governments could be persuaded to reduce the German obligations to a sum which might be transferred without dislocating the machinery of international finance.

Guaranties. The Germans had surrendered their navy to the British under the terms of the armistice, and Allied troops held the left bank of the Rhine and the bridgeheads on the right bank at Mainz, Coblenz, and Cologne. The Treaty of Versailles exacted further guaranties that Germany would keep the peace, reducing the German army to one hundred thousand men and the navy to a handful of small or obsolete ships. No submarines or military aircraft were to be maintained, and all fortifications dismantled in the areas occupied by Allied troops and up to a line drawn forty kilometers to the east of the Rhine. Provision was made for the gradual evacuation of the occupied districts, to be completed within fifteen years, but the Allies retained the option of delaying, or even of reoccupying the left bank "to the extent regarded as necessary for the purpose of obtaining the required guaranties" (Article 429).

The Weimar Assembly. Repeatedly during the war the Allied spokesmen had emphasized the point that their quarrel concerned the imperial government of Germany rather than the German people. Wilson had reaffirmed this view. "We have no quarrel with the German people," he declared on April 2, 1917. "We have no feeling toward them but one of sympathy and friendship. It was not upon their impulse that their government acted in entering this war." Such protestations had encouraged the Germans to hope that, after they had overthrown the kaiser (November, 1918) and adopted a republican constitution (February, 1919), they would be permitted to join in the peace discussions, and to enter the League of Nations as an equal. The Socialist majority in the National or Weimar Assembly elected Friedrich Ebert provisional president of the German Republic, and this choice of a man who had begun life as a saddler, together with the democratic guaranties which distinguished the new constitution, advertised to the world that the German people had repudiated their late masters. But this hasty espousal of democracy gained them little appreciable advantage in terms of a more lenient peace. The Allied statesmen, who had professed a desire to see Germany a democratic republic, dealt the new government a deadly blow by forcing it to assume the onus of concluding a peace which patriotic Germans could never remember without a sense of humiliation. The Weimar Régime, as the republican ex-

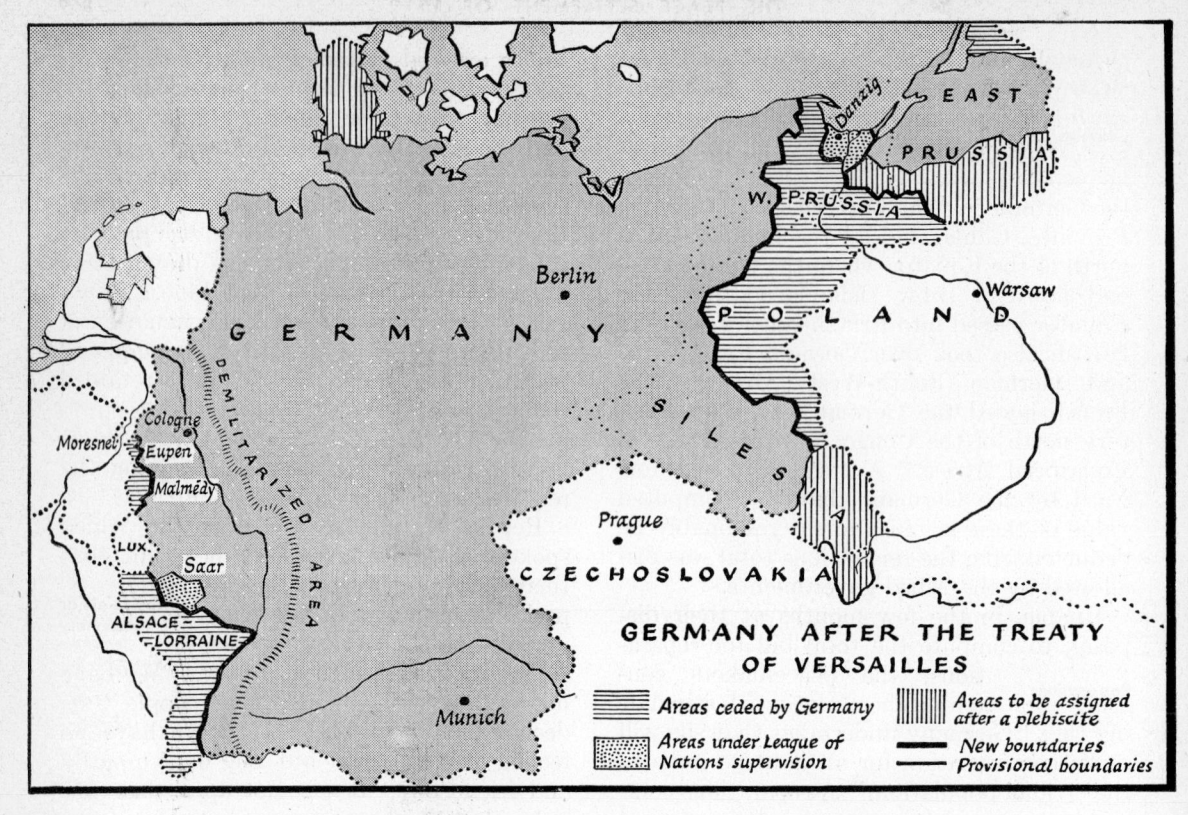

GERMANY AFTER THE TREATY OF VERSAILLES

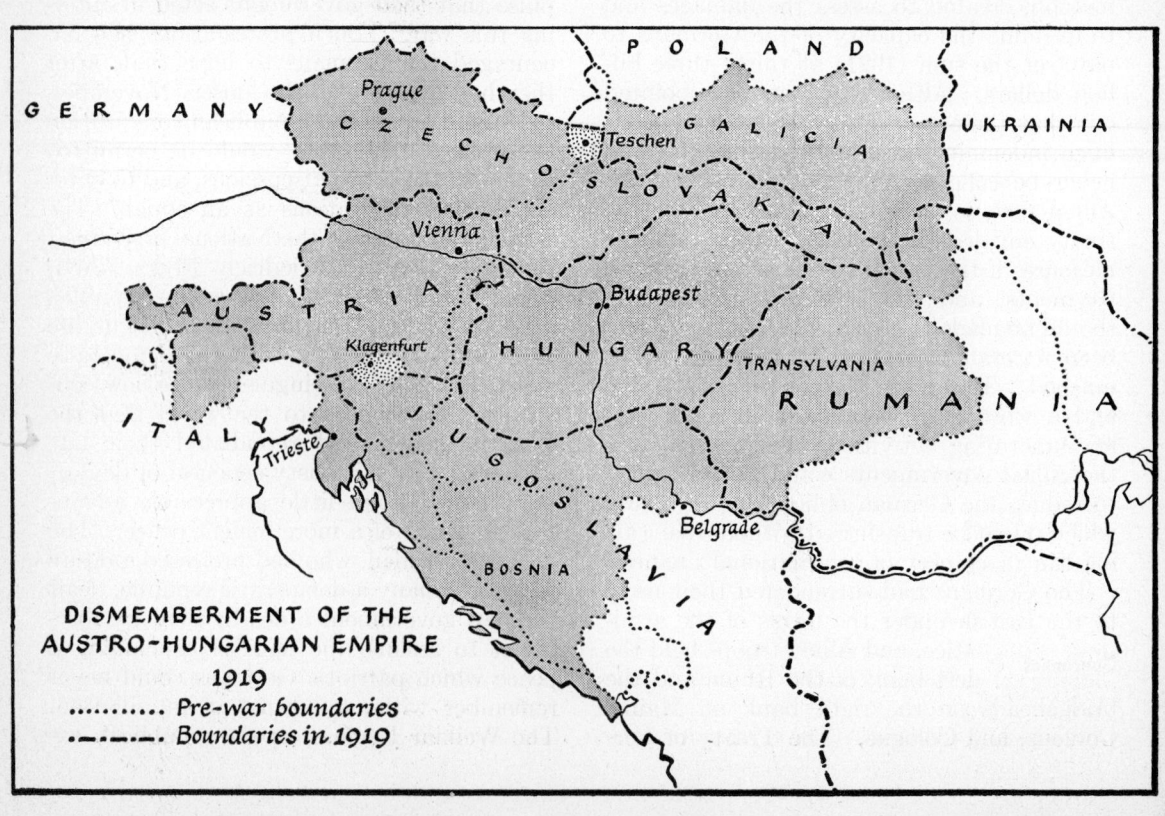

- ▭ Areas ceded by Germany
- ▦ Areas to be assigned after a plebiscite
- ⣿ Areas under League of Nations supervision
- ━━ New boundaries
- ─── Provisional boundaries

DISMEMBERMENT OF THE AUSTRO-HUNGARIAN EMPIRE
1919

- .... Pre-war boundaries
- ─·─·─ Boundaries in 1919

periment was called, never succeeded in clearing itself before the bar of German opinion for its inescapable part in "the betrayal of 1919."

3. THE SETTLEMENT WITH AUSTRIA-HUNGARY, BULGARIA, AND TURKEY

Before the Peace Conference assembled in January, 1919, the Austro-Hungarian Empire had ceased to exist. The subject peoples of the Hapsburg domains had felt little enthusiasm for the war, and the defeat of the Central Powers brought them a chance to assert their independence. It devolved, therefore, upon the Peace Conference to draw geographical boundaries for the nascent states in accordance with the principle of the self-determination of nations.

The Allies embodied their terms to Austria in the Treaty of Saint-Germain (September 10, 1919), which limited the Austrian Republic to an area one tenth the size of the former Hapsburg Empire. The six and a half million Austrian Germans who inhabited the diminutive state realized that a free national existence under these restricted conditions was impracticable because of economic problems. They asked to be united to Germany, but France feared to permit this aggrandizement of her defeated foe and the treaty specifically prohibited such a fusion. Hungary suffered a similar fate by the Treaty of the Trianon (June 4, 1920), the once proud Magyars retaining control of a small state comprising some thirty-six thousand square miles and nine million people. Like Austria, Hungary was called upon to bear part of the burden of reparations, although the ability of either country to pay, or even to survive, in its mutilated condition was open to doubt. As the Allies refused to permit the Hungarians to recall a Hapsburg to the throne, Hungary remained a kingdom without a king.

Fate of Austria and Hungary

From the peripheral areas of the defunct empire the peacemakers constructed one new state and enlarged four others. The new state, the Republic of Czechoslovakia, included over three million Germans, Magyars, and Slovenes, for the Allied statesmen proved more generous toward the demands of the Czechs and Slovaks than just toward the German and Magyar minorities. The violence done to the principle of nationality in this and other cases was excused on the basis of strategic necessity. The province of Galicia, lying to the north of Czechoslovakia across the Carpathian Mountains, was transferred to Poland; and Rumania received, as a reward for joining the Allies, the extensive province of Transylvania and part of the district known as the Banat. The remainder of the Banat and the late Austrian provinces of Bosnia and Herzegovina were united to Serbia and Montenegro to form the Kingdom of Yugoslavia. Finally, the Italians received the district known as the Trentino, and claimed all the Istrian Peninsula, including the cities of Trieste and Fiume. These claims were based upon the secret understandings which Italy had reached with her allies; but President Wilson refused to approve the cession of Fiume, and the Italian delegate, Orlando, withdrew from the conference in protest. A separate agreement between Italy and Yugoslavia (Treaty of Rapallo, 1920) finally divided the disputed area and established Fiume as a free city.

By the Treaty of Neuilly (November 27, 1919), the Bulgarians paid for their mistake in joining the side destined for defeat, by losing part of the gains which they had saved from the Balkan Wars and also their World War conquests. Greece and Yugoslavia (Serbia) were the principal beneficiaries, and the Bulgarians, in addition to promising reparation payments and reducing their armed forces, were obliged to see a million of their fellow nationals placed under foreign rule.

Bulgaria

Of the four defeated powers, the Turkish Empire, which had been the first to crumble, was the most truculent in adversity. The Allies planned to divide the greater part of the Ottoman possessions among themselves in the form of protectorates, but the Treaty of Sèvres (August 10, 1920), embodying these intentions, proved unenforceable. The Turks were stirred to national resistance by the severe terms, denounced the treaty, and repudiated the hapless sultan at Constantinople who had accepted it. In 1919, the

Revival of Turkey

Greeks, who had been promised a share of Anatolia, landed an army at Smyrna to help in carving up the Ottoman possessions, but in 1922, this expeditionary force was driven into the sea by the armies of the newly organized Turkish Republic. The English were chagrined, the French secretly gratified by this development, for the two powers were already pursuing divergent aims in the Near East, and the Turks profited by this divergence to reaffirm their hold on Constantinople and demand recognition of the complete independence of the Turkish Republic. Even the humiliating "capitulations," which had previously defined the special privileges enjoyed by foreigners in Turkey, were abolished. Though limited to the Anatolian Peninsula and a small strip of European territory,[1] the new Turkish State, with its capital at Ankara, entered upon a remarkable transformation under the inspiring and progressive dictatorship of Mustapha Kemal Pasha.

Over the Arabian Peninsula, where the Arab tribes had been encouraged during the war to rise against their Turkish masters, France and Great Britain were more successful in establishing a tutelary control. On a rough basis of self-determination the victors carved new states from the disintegrating Ottoman realm. The French acquired a mandate over Syria, including Lebanon, the British over Palestine and Iraq. The Arab principality of Trans-Jordania and the little-known hinterland which stretches from Aden to the Persian Gulf were also placed under British supervision and protection.

4. THE FATE OF THE FOURTEEN POINTS

To demonstrate how far the final peace terms diverged from the principles laid down in Wilson's Fourteen Points, it will be of interest to consider these points one at a time and to note the fate which overtook each.

I. *Open covenants, openly arrived at.* The peace discussions of the Big Four were so rigidly guarded that many of the lesser delegates were ignorant of the settlement until the treaty had been completed. Even Wilson conceded that treaties could not always be openly arrived at.

II. *Freedom of the seas.* Out of deference to British prejudices on this point, it was dropped before the conference assembled.

III. *Removal of economic barriers.* The effect of the treaties was to increase the number and augment the importance of economic frontiers.

IV. *Adequate guaranties for disarmament.* Only the vanquished were disarmed. The victors continued to maintain armaments, more costly in some cases than those of 1914.

V. *Impartial adjustment of colonial claims.* The victors divided the spoils.

VI. *Evacuation of Russian territory and an opportunity for independent political development to be granted the Russian people.* The Allied governments interfered repeatedly in Russia (1918–20) in their efforts to overthrow the Soviet régime.

VII. *Belgium to be evacuated and restored.* This point was carried out.

VIII. *All French territory to be freed and restored, and Alsace-Lorraine returned to France.* This point was likewise carried out.

IX. *Readjustment of the Italian frontier along recognizable lines of nationality.* The final compromise placed over half a million Germans and Yugoslavs under the Italian flag.

X. *Autonomous development for the peoples of Austria-Hungary.* Carried out in the main, with the Slavs winning most disputed areas at the expense of the Germans and Magyars.

XI. *Self-determination for the Rumanians, Serbians, and Montenegrins.* Vindicated in general.

XII. *A secure sovereignty for the Turkish portion of the Ottoman Empire, and self-determination for the subject races.* The Turks finally achieved a stable régime despite interference. The self-rule permitted the subject races by the French and British was more nominal than real.

XIII. *An independent Polish State with access to the sea.* This point was realized.

XIV. *A general association of nations.* The Covenant of the League of Nations was incorporated in the Treaty of Versailles.

---

[1] See map on page 840.

DEFEATED GERMANY

German motor trucks, passing through the unravaged German countryside, to be surrendered to the United States Army of Occupation, 1920

VICTORIOUS FRANCE

A French peasant woman in front of her wrecked home in the Marne district, 1919

In his anxiety to assure the principle of self-determination to subject peoples, and to win general acceptance for the idea of a League of Nations, President Wilson found it necessary to acquiesce in five significant compromises which violated his program in fact and spirit: (1) Some three million people, formerly subjects of the Austrian Empire, but German in speech and sentiment, were included within the boundaries of the newly created state of Czechoslovakia. (2) Several hundred thousand Germans and Yugoslavs were incorporated into the Italian Kingdom, many against their will. (3) The German colonies were parceled out among the victors without any honest regard for an "impartial adjustment of colonial claims." (4) Instead of the just peace between equals which Wilson had envisaged, the treaty condemned the Germans and Austrians to assume the sole guilt for the war and to pay as much as they could in restitution. (5) Reduction of armaments to the lowest point consistent with domestic security (Point IV) was enforced upon the Central Powers, but evaded by the victors.

The failure to disarm provided a particular disappointment for lovers of peace throughout the world, the more acute because the Allied governments, throughout the duration of hostilities, had blamed the pre-war armament race upon the initiative of the Germans, and had excused their own preparations for war as unavoidable measures of self-defense. Yet with Germany reduced to impotence they still maintained, and even increased, their military forces. It was possible to hope, however, that the sober judgment of conscientious men, exercising itself through the agency and the decisions of the League of Nations, might yet retrieve the ground lost through the unavoidable compromises, and that for each problem a final solution might be found in which the claims of justice would triumph over the forces of expediency.

5. THE LEAGUE OF NATIONS

More than once, in earlier centuries, proposals had been drawn up which aimed at the establishment of a permanent group or league of nations pledged to promote peace in Europe. The Duke of Sully, minister of the French king, Henry IV, drafted such a plan; Napoleon aspired to end war by organizing Europe into one great empire under French leadership; and the diplomats who assembled at Vienna after Napoleon's downfall proposed to maintain peace by calling frequent congresses of the powers. But the spirit of co-operation which inspired this last suggestion, and evoked the more mystical experiment known as the Holy Alliance, soon yielded to the older anarchic spirit of each nation for itself. Although advocates of peace continued to plead the advantages that would flow from an international court created to adjust disputes between states, the only important result of their efforts was the establishment (1899) of a permanent court of arbitration known as the Hague Tribunal.[1]

The failure of the diplomats, with their system of competitive alliances and balance of power, to prevent the World War, and the casual violation by the belligerents of many existing treaties and conventions, convinced thoughtful people more completely than ever that some organization was essential for the amelioration of this condition of international anarchy. In 1917, Wilson gave the concept new force by including the proposal for "a general association of nations" among his Fourteen Points. When the Peace Conference assembled in Paris in 1919, the organization of a League of Nations found a place on the agenda and the Covenant of the League was incorporated in the Treaty of Versailles. But here again the clash between ideals and realities compelled a number of compromises. The French statesman, Clemenceau, while endorsing the League, wished to see it an association dominated by the victors, pledged to preserve the Versailles settlement against all who might seek to disturb it. Although the French stand was later modified, the League as first constituted included none of the defeated powers and was too largely dominated by France and Britain. A second curb upon its efficiency and universality was imposed out

[1] See above, page 836.

SIGNING OF THE TREATY OF VERSAILLES

On June 28, 1919, the delegates of the German Republic signed a humiliating peace in the Hall of Mirrors at Versailles, in which the German Empire had been proclaimed in 1871.

THE LEAGUE COUNCIL IN SESSION AT ST. JAMES'S PALACE, LONDON

The gravest weaknesses of the League of Nations were the absence of the United States and the fact that many peoples saw it as a Franco-British syndicate to preserve the existing inequalities.

of deference to the United States, and concerned "regional understandings." American statesmen had stood by the Monroe Doctrine for a century and had consistently opposed European interference in New-World affairs, and American public opinion was not disposed to welcome League intervention in questions arising between American countries. The Monroe Doctrine was, therefore, recognized as a "regional understanding" which would be respected by the League. Other points upon which the framers of the Covenant were compelled to modify their objectives were: (1) disarmament, (2) the recognition of the racial and religious equality of all member nations, and (3) the proposal to endow the League Council with authority to execute its decisions against recalcitrant states by invoking force. Because of the grave difficulties which had to be overcome in any attempt to settle these issues, all three were compromised or abandoned.

By the Covenant or constitution of the League of Nations the member states agreed not to resort to war, and promised to observe open, just, and honorable relations, and a scrupulous respect for treaties, in their dealings with one another. The original list of members included some forty-two states, later increased to sixty, the leading British dominions, Canada, Australia, New Zealand, South Africa, and India, receiving individual representation. Any self-governing state was declared eligible for admission, and any member might withdraw after serving two years' notice of its intention to do so. The cost of administration was to be met by contributions levied upon the members in proportion to their national budgets, and Geneva was chosen as the permanent seat of the League bodies.

The Covenant

The machinery of the League provided for (*a*) an Assembly, (*b*) a Council, (*c*) a Secretariat, and (*d*) a Court of Arbitration. The Assembly included representatives from all the member states, large and small, each state casting but one vote. The Council was composed of one member each from Great Britain, France, Italy, and Japan, and one each from four (later increased to nine) lesser nations, and as originally constituted was little more than an executive cabinet dominated by the Allied Powers. Because the United States declined to join the League and the Soviet government of Russia had not been accorded official recognition, the places reserved for these powers on the Council remained vacant; but Germany was granted a permanent seat on her admission to the League in 1926. In 1933, Japan and Germany announced their intention to withdraw from membership, and in 1934, Russia was admitted, and received a permanent Council seat. The Council met at Geneva, official headquarters of the League, at least once each year, and could deal with "any matter within the sphere of action of the League or affecting the peace of the world." Its decisions, unless otherwise specified, had to be unanimous, a rule which also applied to the resolutions of the Assembly.

The Assembly and Council

Much of the current work of the League was conducted by the permanent Secretariat, or by commissions. A secretary-general appointed by the Assembly directed the work of the Secretariat in conducting correspondence, investigating disputes, and registering treaties. In addition, commissions were nominated under the League to investigate international evils, such as the traffic in narcotics, to curb the spread of malaria, cancer, and tropical diseases, to promote intellectual co-operation, to further the codification of international law, to abolish slavery and to protect minorities. Responsibility for the welfare of backward peoples was also entrusted to special commissions, and the powers which acquired control over former German colonies, or any other regions, by the Treaty of Versailles, administered these areas as "mandates" of the League, subject to the supervision of the Commission on Mandates.

The Secretariat

To settle disputes having to do with the legal claims of states under existing treaties and conventions, the Covenant provided for an International Court of Justice which was established in 1921. Like the Hague Tribunal, this World Court accepted cases referred to it for decision, and its verdicts contributed to

The World Court

the growing body of international law. All members of the League agreed to submit their quarrels to arbitration, and to abide by any decision endorsed unanimously by the Council members and accepted by the other party to the dispute. The real strength and significance of the League, therefore, depended upon the degree to which the members observed this compulsory arbitration clause (Article XII), and upon the effectiveness of the measures taken by the League to punish those members which ventured to flout it.

In the first fifteen years of its existence, the League arbitrated a number of disputes, arising between lesser states, with a creditable degree of firmness and impartiality. In sharp territorial conflicts which involved Sweden with Finland, Poland with Lithuania and with Czechoslovakia, and Greece with Albania and with Bulgaria, hostilities were averted, or were arrested after they had broken out, by judicious intervention. But the League proved less effective in dealing with the great powers. The reason for its failures in these major cases, failures which gravely diminished its prestige and impaired its effectiveness, will be outlined in a subsequent chapter entitled "Two Decades of International Tension (1919–1939)."

64

The Impact of European Civilization on Asia

The life blood of Japan is the water of the sea.

JAPANESE PROVERB.

BY THE TWENTIETH CENTURY the impact of European civilization had penetrated to the heart of Asia and was transforming Oriental society. As the Japanese, Chinese, and Hindus became acquainted with the weapons, technology, and political formulas of the European peoples, they rebelled against European imperialism and aspired to self-government and a position of equality among the world powers. This "revolution in Asia" concerned three fifths of the human race and provided one of the most critical problems of modern world politics.

The history of Asia has been shaped by four major factors. (1) *Topography*. The Asian land mass contains the loftiest mountains, some of the most inhospitable deserts, and the most intensively cultivated lowlands of the globe. (2) *Climate*. Asia includes some of the hottest and the coldest, the wettest and the driest regions of the earth. Much of it is almost destitute of plant or animal life, for the rainfall is ill-distributed. Only India, southeastern Asia, eastern China, and Japan receive more than twenty inches annually. (3) *Accessibility*. The interior of Asia has remained inaccessible because of poor roads and mountain or desert barriers. India and the East Indies, approachable by sea, were exceptions, and this fact largely explains why they fell under European control. (4) *Population*. Since prehistoric times Asia has apparently supported the greater part of the human race. The map on world population (page 778) suggests how largely this population is confined to regions which have a rainfall of twenty to eighty inches annually. In the valley of the Ganges and the Yangtze-kiang there are more than two hundred and fifty people to the square mile. A thousand miles inland, where the rainfall is under ten inches annually, there are less than two people to the square mile.

1. MODERN INDIA

The dominant influence in modern Indian history came from without: it was the influence of British administration. The English East India Company was chartered in 1600, and its power expanded until its officials became the most influential figures in Indian politics. Until 1858 the direction of this growing empire, almost continental in extent, was left to the Company, although after 1784 a board of control, known as the India Office, supervised its rule. In 1857 the outbreak of a serious revolt in the Ganges Valley, led by native troops or *sepoys*, and con-

British rule in India

Growth of British Power in India

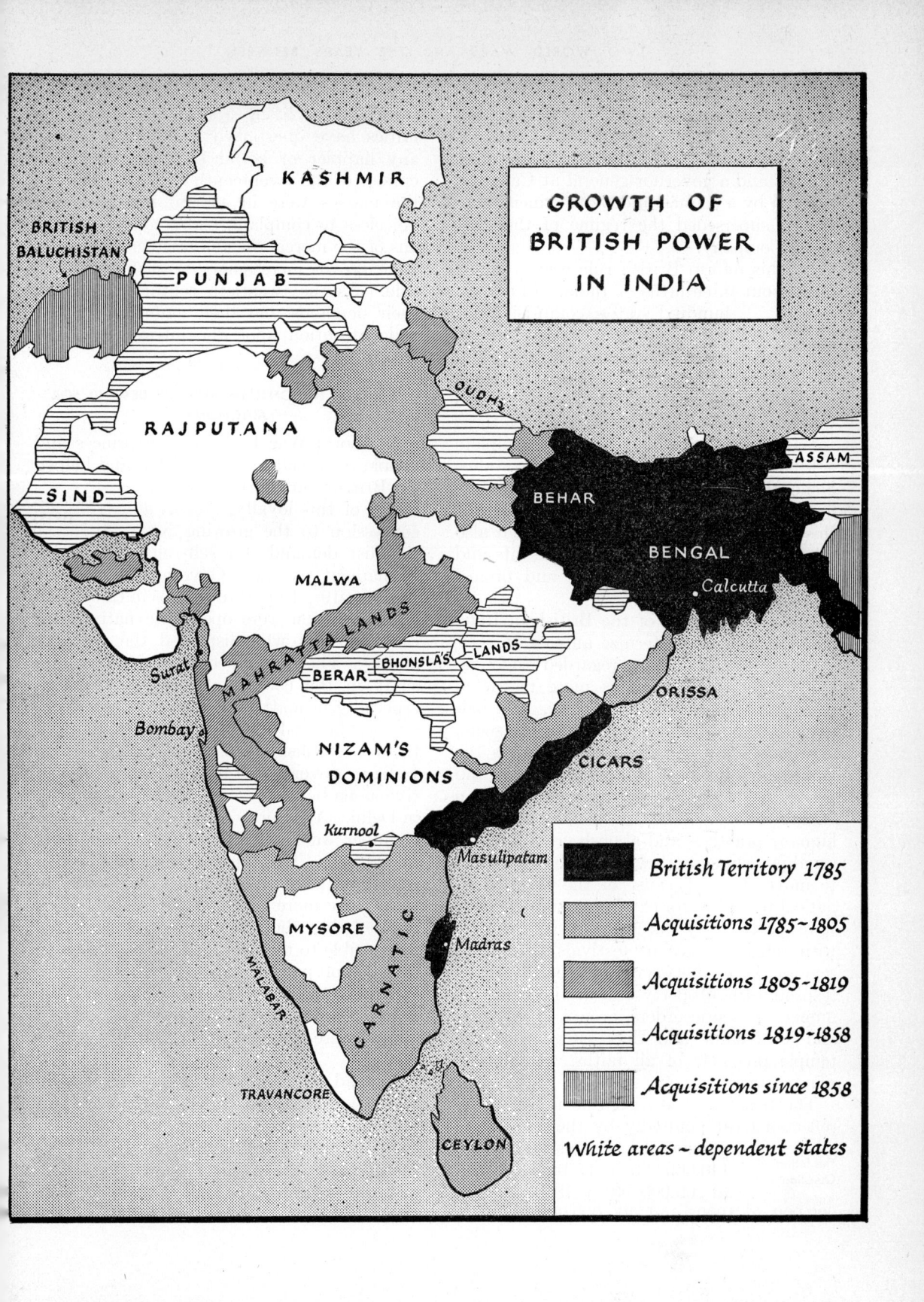

sequently termed the Sepoy Mutiny, provoked drastic reprisals by the British, but led to a more enlightened mode of rule. A Secretary of State for India in the British cabinet and a governor-general at Calcutta, assisted by a council and by provincial governors, superseded the régime of the East India Company.

By this reform British rule was extended over about three fifths of India. In several hundred states, comprising the remaining two fifths, Indian princes continued to govern under British protection. Their right to make war and to negotiate with foreign powers was abridged, but otherwise most of these Indian rulers retained almost complete autonomy within their hereditary states. Some, though not all, contributed voluntarily to the cost of the general defense, but for this and other fiscal needs the British also raised revenues by taxing the peasants and the small but active business and professional groups.

The Indian princes

The chief concern of the British in India has not been to westernize an eastern society. They regarded their responsibility as more restricted and more pragmatic. By balancing the power of the various states, sects, and classes, by keeping peace between the landowners, business groups, townsmen, and peasants, they preserved an equilibrium in Indian society. When they could check inhumane practices and abolish cruel and unusual punishments they did so, but they had to move slowly because of the Hindus' fanatical reverence for existing customs. They were particularly careful not to interfere with religious rites or festivals (except to repress clashes between rival sects). They respected the property and privileges of the numerous ascetic orders, groups of votaries, and local cults, and they safeguarded the temple precincts of all faiths without discrimination.

Policing a sub-continent

The benefits of British rule in India are reflected most pointedly by the rise in the population. From an estimated 140,000,000 in 1750, it climbed to 200,000,000 in 1850, to 330,000,000 in 1900, and 400,000,000 in 1945.

The Indian Question

For many of these millions, however, the standards of living are so low that some critics have questioned whether they were any happier or better off than their precursors of the seventeenth century. Though the masses were in general too inert and voiceless to complain, many educated Indians of the mercantile and aristocratic groups have grown increasingly critical of British rule. As the twentieth century advanced, their demands and their agitation focused wide attention upon the intricacies of the Indian Question.

2. INDIAN NATIONALISM AND THE DEMAND FOR AUTONOMY

In World War I, the Indian princes and people remained loyal to Britain and helped the British war effort. In recognition of this loyalty, and as a concession to the growing Nationalist demands for self-rule, the British Parliament passed a Government of India Act in 1919. Important offices in the Indian administration were opened to native-born civil servants who displayed the requisite ability. The Indian people received a larger share in the control of local government, especially in matters of taxation, education, and public health. Most important of all, the act established a national parliament for India, a government to consist of a legislative assembly and a council of state to meet in Delhi. A majority of the members in each chamber were to be elected, the remainder appointed. This approach toward representative government failed, however, to satisfy the more ardent Nationalists. They insisted that the new régime was not truly responsible to the people of India. For by a division of powers, termed "diarchy," the control of the police, the law courts, and the army, as well as the direction of foreign affairs, were reserved to the British authorities.

India Act (1919)

Instead of moderating, therefore, Indian opposition increased under the diarchy. An unofficial assembly, known as the National Assembly, became the popular parliament of India and the focal center of the national resistance. The most influential leader of the

Mohandas K. Gandhi

HINDU MASSES OF INDIA

MOHANDAS KARAMCHAND GANDHI

For the Hindu masses of India Gandhi united the authority of a religious saint and a political prophet. His aims were to win self-government for the Indian people and to improve the status and condition of the oppressed classes. But his methods — non-co-operation and non-resistance — demanded too much restraint, and his followers often advanced from passive strikes to active rioting and violence.

Nationalist cause was Mohandas Karamchand Gandhi, known to his followers as the *Mahatma*, the holy or saintly man. Gandhi adjured the Indians to seek independence by passive resistance, and he organized (1920) a movement of non-co-operation whereby all British goods, courts, laws, and institutions were to be passively boycotted. Despite Gandhi's injunctions against violence or rioting, disturbances inevitably broke out, and he was jailed as an agitator (1922). From his prison he continued to exhort his followers to practice non-co-operation and non-resistance. After his release, finding that the British government still refused further concessions, he advocated complete independence for India. In 1930 he defied the authorities by extracting salt from sea water (the manufacture and sale of salt in India was a government monopoly). This ostentatious act of defiance was followed by renewed disturbances perpetrated by his less manageable followers, and Gandhi was again imprisoned.

New factors were complicating the troubled Indian situation. The world economic depression after 1929 caused increased suffering, and unemployment speeded the formation of labor unions among Indian workers. The growth of factories was creating an Indian proletariat which might become a revolutionary party if strongly organized. Late in 1930 a Round Table Conference was called in London, and after protracted consultation a new "Government of India Act" was pieced together. It passed the British Parliament in 1935 and was put into partial operation in 1937.

The new act provided for an Indian federation. The Governor's provinces, Chief Commissioner's provinces, and such Indian states still under local rulers as might elect to join, were to constitute the federation. A governor-general (to represent the King-Emperor in London), a council of state, and a legislative assembly, were the chief organs of government. Some members of the council and the assembly were to be elected, some appointed, and a council of ministers, responsible to the legislature, would advise the governor-general. Subject to certain re-

India Act (1935)

strictions, the legislature was empowered to make laws for all persons in British India.

In *form* this act made India a self-governing dominion, but in *fact* its provisions were negated by the confused condition of Indian politics. A legislature which represented India truly would mirror diversity, not unity. The 400,000,000 Indians are not a nation; they speak seven distinct languages, with at least twenty-four subdivisions, and scores of local dialects. They are split into opposing religious faiths; the Hindus are separated among themselves by their caste divisions; and the Mohammedans, Sikhs, Parsees, Buddhists, and Christians are divided into multitudinous minor sects. There is in India neither racial, religious, linguistic, cultural, nor traditional uniformity to help fuse the will of the citizens into a patriotic unity of purpose. This lack of unity makes the phrase "Indian Nationalism" an idea for which there is no corresponding reality.

Diversity not unity

A second obstacle to self-rule is the fact that the Indian masses have not yet been trained to exercise or even to understand the responsibilities of democratic self-government. British India, which comprises more than half the peninsula, is divided into seventeen provinces, some with legislatures, but most of them administered by commissioners and deputy commissioners with wide discretionary powers. Politically, British India is a mosaic. The two hundred and thirty districts into which the provinces are divided are the real units of administration, and authority rests in the hands of a small number of experienced officials. For the British to resign this authority before a popular régime was ready to exercise it efficiently seemed an invitation to anarchy.

Training necessary

The Indian princes provide a third obstacle to self-government for India. These rajahs and maharajahs are independent rulers, enlightened despots many of them, but despots nonetheless by the force of tradition. They naturally hesitated to compromise their sovereignty and merge their domains with the seventeen British-ruled provinces in a federal union. In 1939 fifty of these princi-

The princes stand aloof

palities had refused to join the proposed federation, the rulers finding the terms of accession "fundamentally unsatisfactory."

During World War II India remained orderly but restive, and the demand for independence grew. The British Labor Government which assumed office in 1945 dissolved the imperial bonds and India became an autonomous member of the British Commonwealth in 1947. The predominantly Mohammedan sections in the north formed a separate entity (Pakistan), provinces of British India were organized as Hindustan, and the princely states decided their own political future.

Thus Anglo-Indian ties were relaxed but not wholly ruptured. India has been described as the largest foreign market any nation ever controlled, and the British stockholders have £1,000,000,000 invested there. Indian industry, stimulated by two world wars, has made remarkable advances in the twentieth century. Where other forces have failed, the industrial revolution may prove the agent which can transform Indian society. But so long as the capital essential to the industrial program, to the shipping, railways, communications, machinery, and raw materials, rests in the control of British bankers, or of Indian industrialists loyal to British rule, the tie between India and Britain will remain strong. Anglo-Indian economic collaboration is, and seems likely to remain, indispensable to both peoples.

Economic bonds

3. THE REMAKING OF CHINA

The civilization of China, like that of India, has persisted for thousands of years, conservative, tradition-bound, and self-contained. China differs from India, however, in four important respects. (1) The climate is less hot, less humid, and more stimulating in the daily and seasonal ranges of the temperature. (2) The Chinese population is predominantly Mongoloid and homogeneous, and lacks the large admixture of Caucasoid and Negroid types found in India. (3) The society of China never became stratified into religious castes. (4) Unlike India, China survived into the twentieth century as a sovereign state, although several outlying provinces had been lost and numerous humiliating concessions were extorted by alien powers.

In the past hundred years China was assailed by new forces, unique in its history, which promised to remold the Chinese way of life. Between 1840 and 1900 the armed attacks of "foreign barbarians" forced open the ports of the Celestial Empire and threatened to split East Asia into spheres of influence dominated by half a dozen European powers. After an unequal contest known as the Opium War (1840–42), the British annexed Hongkong and won trade concessions at five ports. Other nations speedily demanded similar privileges, and in 1856 the British and French jointly attacked China, won an extension of the profitable opium traffic, and gained special safeguards and privileges for European residents. In the same years the Russian government compelled the Chinese to cede a coastal province on the Asiatic mainland opposite Japan. There they promptly founded Vladivostok (1861) on a fine natural harbor which provided a Pacific base for the Russian navy.

Assault on the Orient

Once begun, the spoliation of China proved difficult to arrest. A new claimant appeared in 1895, when Japan defeated the Chinese with little difficulty, annexed Formosa, and demanded full independence (a prelude to Japanese annexation) for Korea. In 1898 the Russians (who had refused to allow Japan the Liaotung Peninsula in 1895) obtained a lease on this area for themselves, and marked out Manchuria as their special field of interest. The Germans followed promptly with demands for a port at Kiauchow and economic concessions in Shantung Province. The French, already masters of Indo-China, secured Kwangchow, with commercial rights in the provinces of Kwangsi and Yünnan. The British then added Weihaiwei and further land at Hongkong to their leaseholds, while asserting a special interest in the Yangtzi River Valley (see map, page 813).

Multiple intervention

Resentment at this repeated intervention finally aroused the Chinese people. In 1900 a patriotic group, known as the Society of the Harmonious Fists (rendered into English as "Boxers"), led attacks against the European residents, murdered some, and demanded the expulsion from China of all "foreign devils." In prompt retaliation the great powers dispatched a joint expeditionary force which captured Peking and exacted a heavy indemnity. It was evident that if the Chinese were to survive as an independent nation they would have to reform their unrealistic government and strengthen their antiquated defenses.

Boxer Rebellion

The first decades of the twentieth century saw the old China dissolve in the confusion of a civil war, and a new China come to birth amid the heroism and travail of 400,000,000 people. Two outstanding leaders symbolized the aims and efforts of the nation during these critical decades of discord and development. The first was Doctor Sun Yat-sen, a patriot and a philosopher. When a revolution ended the rule of the Manchu dynasty in 1912, a group of Chinese reformers proclaimed Sun Yat-sen president of the Chinese republic. The Nationalist Party, the Kuomintang, was pledged to establish a government of the people, but Sun Yat-sen foresaw that years must elapse before China would be ready for a constitutional, democratic régime. First, he predicted, there would be a period dominated by military operations while the Nationalist government secured control of the divided country. Secondly would follow a stage of political education under the dictatorship of the revolutionary party, the Kuomintang. Thirdly would arrive the desired stage of constitutional government. When Sun Yat-sen died in 1925, China had suffered fifteen years of civil war and was still unready for an experiment in free democratic government on the Western model. But the dead leader had defined the goals of the revolution: National Independence, Democratic Government, Economic Security. These aims were accepted as the three cardinal principles of the revolution.

Sun Yat-sen

The second leader who helped to remake China was General Chiang Kai-shek. As in all revolutions, the early period of lofty idealism yielded to a more practical mood, and was followed by a program of rigorous organization and discipline. Chiang was less of a philosopher and more of a soldier than his great predecessor. He built up and trained an army to assure the government the power essential for repressing bandits and guarding the frontiers. By 1927 his energy had brought most of China under the Kuomintang. Then, unfortunately, a split developed in the revolutionary ranks. Some of the more radical leaders sought to establish a communist régime and invited Russian aid. Chiang opposed the Communist group, and the feud between the factions spread, delaying the program of reform and the revival of Chinese economic prosperity.

Chiang Kai-shek

Foreign nations watched with interest this Chinese struggle for unity and independence. A strong Chinese government was certain to abrogate the leases and cancel the concessions which the powers had imposed. To Japanese militarists and industrialists in particular the promised revival of China offered a grave threat. The rapid overexpansion of Japanese economy made it essential to Japan that the resources and markets of Asia remain open. A strong, armed, independent Chinese government might exclude Japanese capital and commerce. The Japanese, therefore, hastened their preparations, for they were determined to penetrate and subdue China to their plans before the Kuomintang could complete its program of reconstruction. In 1931, on a feeble excuse, a Japanese army marched into Manchuria, opening an undeclared Sino-Japanese war. The future of the Chinese Republic was at stake, for the Japanese planned to bring all East Asia into a new order, a gigantic sphere of influence dominated by Japanese leadership.

Japanese interference

4. THE RISE OF JAPAN

The character of the Japanese people, like that of the Chinese, was molded by geography and climate. The two most powerful factors in the Japanese environment have been the lack of arable land and the proximity of the sea. These mountainous volcanic islands, less than 150,000 square miles in area, contain

Farming and fishing

few plains and only short shallow rivers. But Nature gave them a temperate ocean climate and abundant rainfall, so that by terracing the hillsides the Japanese farmers made every available acre into field or orchard land. Like the Chinese, therefore, the Japanese perfected the arts of intensive cultivation of the land, but unlike most Chinese they drew a second and more abundant harvest from the sea. Boatloads of fish served them with food and fertilizer, so that farming and fishing became equally important activities. The dilemma of a growing population and limited land, the problem of communication among the thousands of islands that are their homeland, the compulsion to venture farther from shore as local waters were fished out — all these factors impelled the Japanese to become sailors. Through the centuries when Chinese artists were drawing with loving care their safe, familiar landscapes, Japanese painters learned to limn stormy seascapes in which indomitable fishermen in their flimsy craft fled before the curling crests of gigantic waves.

The Japanese made their first acquaintance with Europeans when the Portuguese and the Dutch came seeking trade in the sixteenth century, and Saint Francis Xavier introduced Christian missions (1549). The movement spread until there were possibly a quarter of a million Japanese converts, but in the seventeenth century the missionaries were expelled and the Japanese Christians practically exterminated by official persecution. All European traders were likewise excluded after 1639, except the Dutch, who were permitted to maintain a single post at Nagasaki. As Japanese were forbidden to travel abroad, this tiny area of docks and warehouses on the island of Deshima was the one guarded window through which Japan maintained a tenuous contact with the European world for over two centuries.

A kingdom sealed

This era of isolation was abruptly ended after 1853. In that year Commodore Matthew Calbraith Perry entered Tokyo Bay with four ships, to negotiate for a trade treaty between the United States and Japan. By 1856, when the treaty was concluded, Great Britain, Russia, and the Netherlands had also obtained commercial privileges, extorted from the Japanese under the guns of the European warships. Japan faced a crisis which proved a turning-point in its history. The policy of exclusion had broken down; the alternative, if the islands were to remain independent, meant that the Japanese must learn the European mode of warfare and compete on equal terms with the aggressors.

End of exclusion

The result was a revolution in Japanese diplomacy, politics, industry, and education. For centuries the *Shogun*, an all-powerful hereditary official at Tokyo, had been the real ruler, but in 1868 a political overturn restored to the Emperor his long neglected rôle of supreme despot. A seven-hundred-year period of military feudalism was abruptly terminated, the shogunate superseded, and the new emperor, Mutsuhito (1867–1912), granted supreme power. Brief rebellions (1868 and 1877) were easily repressed and a program of "westernization" was inaugurated under imperial leadership. It is important to note that the Japanese *adopted*, they did not *develop*, the institutions and machines which had been perfected by the western nations. The result was a curious amalgam of feudalism, industrialism, militarism, and modernity which made Japan unlike any other nation in the world.

Revolution and reform

Seeking the best that they could borrow, the Japanese patterned their parliament and their navy on British models; their army was built up on Prussian formulas; their schools and banks copied largely from those of the United States; their law courts and codes designed by French and German jurists. Railways, telegraph lines, laboratories, technical schools, the Gregorian calendar were introduced by imperial edict. But it was noteworthy that as the reforms progressed the Japanese political and military edifice began to appear more authoritarian than democratic. The conscript army, decreed in 1872, was trained by German officers; the constitution (1889) resembled in operation the Prussian rather than the English mode

Adopted institutions

SUN YAT-SEN   CHIANG KAI-SHEK

Doctor Sun Yat-sen, the father of the Chinese Republic, bequeathed the task of welding China into one nation to the more practical, military-trained Chiang Kai-shek.

THE JAPANESE IN MANCHURIA

In 1931, Japanese forces opened a drive which detached Manchuria from China.

JAPANESE SEASCAPE, BY HOKUSAI

Top: The Japanese did not build a Great Wall against invaders, for they trusted to the sea as a defense.

THE GREAT WALL OF CHINA

Right: The earliest portions of the Great Wall of China date from the third century B.C., before the Romans established their empire in Europe.

of government. Most important of all, however, was the economic development of this energetic and extraordinary nation. A startling expansion of trade and industry enabled the Japanese to equip a large and powerful army with modern weapons, and to build an efficient navy. Though it was not yet widely realized at the time, Japan at the opening of the twentieth century was already a great power.

5. JAPAN OVER ASIA

The claim of Japan to a leading rôle in the Orient was vindicated by three striking successes within ten years. The first was a brief war which the Japanese waged with China (1894-95), a war which brought them Formosa, and a dominant influence in Korea which they annexed fifteen years later. The second milestone on their road to empire was a flattering alliance with Great Britain (1902). Each party agreed to maintain a friendly neutrality if the other went to war with *one* adversary, but to aid if the other were attacked by two or more powers. This treaty gave Japan a diplomatic standing among the great powers; and proof that the Japanese also had the military and naval standing of a great power speedily followed. The third milestone was the surprising victory which the Japanese won over Russia in 1904-05.

Three triumphs

Fear of Russian intentions had been the main motive which drew the British and Japanese into an alliance. The British regarded the Czar's armies as a constant threat to Turkey, Persia, Afghanistan, and even India. The Japanese knew that Russian imperialists coveted Manchuria and Korea. When negotiations failed, the Japanese staked their future on a surprise attack against the Russian military forces in the Far East (February, 1904). Port Arthur was besieged and finally captured, and the Russian armies were defeated at Liaoyang and Mukden. On the sea the Japanese were even more successful, destroying two Russian fleets in Far Eastern waters. This critical and audacious war provided a model for later Japanese moves. The Treaty of Portsmouth, which closed it (September, 1905), granted Japan Port Arthur, a lease on the Liaotung Peninsula, and the southern half of Sakhalin Island. Manchuria was restored to China.

Russo-Japanese war

The rivalry of the European powers, notably of Britain and Russia, had provided the alert Japanese with this chance for a swift and successful stroke. Henceforth their leaders watched events in Europe closely, waiting another favorable occasion. It arrived in 1914, when the tension between the Triple Alliance and the Triple Entente culminated in World War I. As an ally of Britain, the Japanese government seized German concessions and properties in the Far East, occupied Kiauchow and German Pacific islands, and pressed on the economic penetration of Shantung. While European production was checked and dislocated by war, Japanese business men did a lively trade, and Japanese imperialists judged the occasion opportune for the subjugation of China. In 1915 the cabinet at Tokyo issued Twenty-One Demands designed to bring the Chinese government under Japanese dominance, and in 1916 this policy of penetration was extended, with Manchuria and Inner Mongolia as specific fields of Japanese exploitation. By 1918, when World War I ended, the position of Japan had been notably improved. German Pacific islands north of the Equator (the Marshall, Marianas, and Caroline groups) were retained as Japanese bases. The revolution and civil war which had paralyzed Russia seemed to promise an easy Japanese penetration of Manchuria and northern China. The Washington Naval Conference of 1922 recognized the Japanese fleet as the third in rank, providing for a 5:5:3 rating in capital ships for Britain, the United States, and Japan respectively. The other Asiatic peoples looked on with astonishment and not without pride, to see a non-European nation rise to such power and prestige.

Expansion facilitated

The rise of Japan had indeed been phenomenal. In the half-century following the revolution of 1868, the Japanese population had almost doubled and was increasing a million a

Industrial momentum

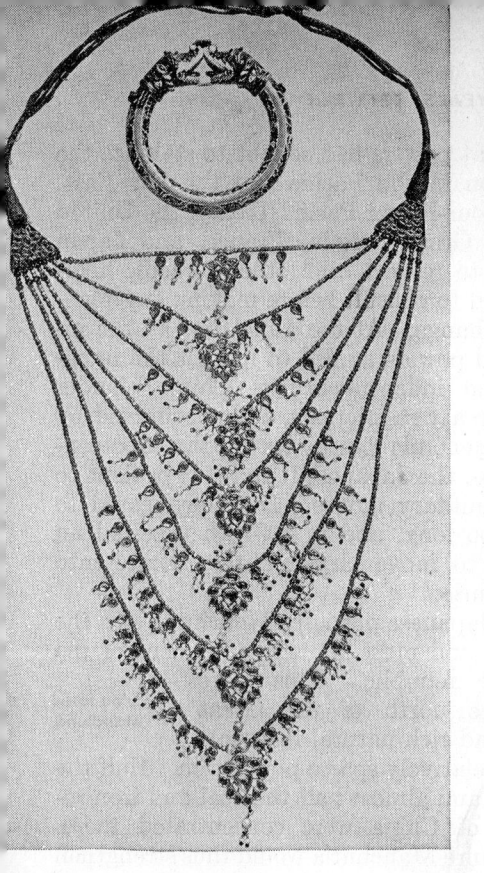

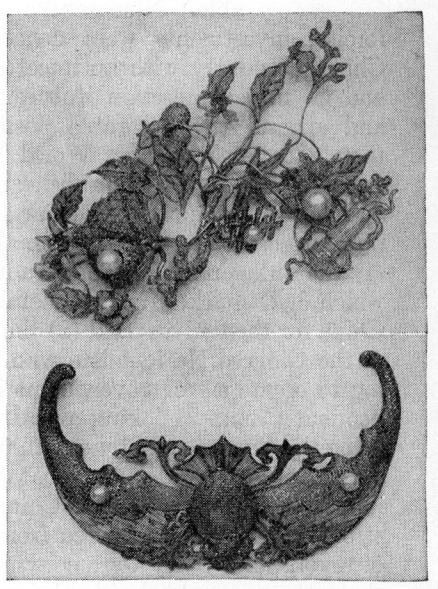

RICHES OF THE EAST

The informal robe of silk tapestry in upper right suggests the delicate beauty of much Chinese weaving and needlework. The examples of jewelry above from the Sung (960–1280) and Ming (1368–1644) periods were produced by Chinese craftsmen while Europe was passing through medieval and early modern times. The necklace is Indian workmanship of the eighteenth century.

year. The merchant marine, like the navy, ranked third among the nations. Helped by the low wages and low standard of living of Japanese workers, the manufacturers were able to undersell European and American competitors. Japanese industries expanded with extraordinary rapidity, and Japanese trade, which had doubled between 1900 and 1910, doubled again between 1910 and 1920. To many Japanese leaders it appeared as if an irresistible tide were sweeping them toward an imperial destiny. They were persuaded, however, that it was not enough to win markets, it was necessary to fight for them. After 1929, when the world-wide economic crisis caused acute suffering in Japan as elsewhere, the militarists gained control of the government. This shift in power was particularly dangerous because in Japan the army and navy ministers were privileged to report directly to the emperor and were to a large degree independent of the civil cabinet.

Militarism was a dangerous element in Japanese politics, but it was not the only danger. The Japanese business empire was dangerously vulnerable. Nine tenths of Japanese foreign investments were concentrated in China, a country with an uncertain present and a more uncertain future. To hold and expand the favorable position which they had gained during World War I, the Japanese planned to establish an economic "Monroe Doctrine" in the Far East. This policy forced them to face two major threats: (1) the antagonism of other trading nations which had marked out economic areas in China for themselves; and (2) the opposition of the Chinese Nationalists who were striving to create a free government in an independent China. Looking ahead, and measuring the progress of Chinese unification, the Japanese leaders decided that they must intervene decisively before China grew too strong and Russia recovered from the chaos of revolution. They were convinced that in the end war would decide the issue, and in preparation for it they had increased their armaments 400 per cent between 1914 and 1924.

Progress and peril

At the Washington Conference (1922–23), the great powers had sought to stabilize the situation in the Pacific and the Far East. By a Four-Power Pacific Treaty, the United States, Great Britain, France, and Japan agreed to respect each other's Pacific holdings and to consult before making any territorial change. At the same time all the interested powers agreed to respect the integrity and independence of China. Under these treaty restrictions, and encouraged by their economic prosperity in the nineteen-twenties, the Japanese found it expedient to avoid military moves. But they feared to wait too long, and in 1931 they seized an excuse to move large military forces into Manchuria.

For Japanese purposes Manchuria was the nearest and most attractive segment of the Chinese republic. This large province north of the Great Wall had rich natural resources and a relatively sparse population. Half the timber and almost half the coal and iron reserves of China were concentrated there. To acquire Manchuria would thus strengthen Japan, and cripple China, as an industrial power. The Nationalist government at Nanking knew the importance of Manchuria, and a million Chinese settlers a year were moving into the region to occupy and develop it. The pattern of conquest pursued by the Japanese proved that they had studied European precedents to advantage. They took over the Manchurian railways and garrisoned the towns on the excuse of restoring order. Insisting that the "incident" did not concern other powers, they avoided a declaration of war with China. But they established a puppet régime in Manchuria which declared the province an independent sovereign state under the name of Manchukuo. The government of Manchukuo then "invited" the Japanese to grant it "protection." Throughout China this serious loss had a stiffening effect upon the Nationalists. A patriotic campaign to boycott all Japanese goods drove the Japanese to retaliate by attacking Shanghai. There, however, they met with unexpected resistance from Chinese forces; after a few months they withdrew, and the boycott was rescinded.

China loses Manchuria

JAPANESE EXPANSION
1895-1945

By their military intervention in Manchuria the Japanese had clearly violated the Nine-Power Treaty of 1922. They had also disregarded their pledges as a member of the League of Nations. The League Council, after investigation, condemned Japan as an aggressor, whereupon the Japanese government announced that it would withdraw from the League. The powers took no positive steps to restrain Japan, however, and it was evident that the Chinese would have to defend themselves. At Nanking the Nationalist leaders played for time, acknowledging the loss of Manchuria, but holding off further Japanese advances while strengthening their forces. Financial reforms (1932), a plan for military training (1935), new highways, railroads, airlines, and a steady expansion of modern mechanical and industrial techniques were pressed through by General Chiang Kai-shek. But the very progress of these reforms was a challenge to the Japanese and made them more anxious to strike again. They waited only for a crisis in Europe which would occupy the attention and reserves of the great powers; then, as in World War I, the Japanese planned to open their drive for empire.

The League impotent

By 1937 they judged it safe to proceed. Moving forces into North China by several routes, the Japanese invaders took over the railways, blockaded the ports, and confiscated foreign-owned banks, factories, and public utilities. Foreign capitalists, they assured the Chinese, were "ghosts who drank the blood and sweat of the people." Japanese intervention was represented as liberation: the Japanese were about to create a "Co-Prosperity Sphere" to include all East Asia. Counting upon the outbreak of war in Europe, they completed elaborate and detailed plans, preparing to press their advantage to the full as soon as British, French, and Netherlands forces were withdrawn from the Far East for action nearer their homelands. The situation in Europe justified their hopes. When World War II opened in 1939, Japan had already allied herself with the aggressor powers, Germany and Italy, and was prepared to risk its previous conquests and its national existence upon an ambitious bid for control of East Asia and Indonesia. The consequences of that gigantic gamble, which involved Japan in war with the United States, Great Britain, and Russia, are summarized in Chapter 72.

The war comes

65

The Rôle of America

I like the dreams of the future better than the history of the past.

THOMAS JEFFERSON.

BY THE CLOSE of World War I the center of gravity of the modern world had shifted from Europe to America. The United States had become, economically, the most powerful nation on earth, and its wealth, industry, resources, and relative immunity from attack meant that it would continue to hold the balance of power in a divided world. The rôle which England had long discharged in Europe, standing outside continental politics but intervening when the preponderance of any one state threatened the balance of power, now fell to the United States. In the contracted world of the twentieth century, however, American diplomacy inherited the task of balancing, not European only, but global combinations. The future of European countries and of European civilization could no longer be predicted without weighing the mood and policies of the American people as a deciding factor. Although the United States declined to join the League of Nations and resumed an attitude of isolation after 1920, this diplomatic withdrawal was merely a denial, not a cancellation, of its preponderant influence in world affairs.

1. THE "MIRACLE OF AMERICA"

A new nation The growth of the United States in six generations from 3,000,000 to 140,000,000 people, from thirteen colonial states to a continental empire, has no parallel in history. Europeans, with the scars and wreckage of their destructive wars around them, are often more astonished by the "Miracle of America" than Americans themselves. The wisdom of the founding fathers, who devised durable institutions for an unfledged nation, yet made them elastic enough to meet an unpredictable evolution, is profoundly impressive, and it becomes more so with the tests of time. The speed and sureness with which the young United States spread westward, incorporating areas which had been explored and partly settled by French, Spanish, Russian, and English colonists, has provided further astonishment for observant Europeans, cramped and confined by their rigid frontiers and jealous rivalries. Most remarkable of all was the success with which the United States absorbed the flood of immigrants from Europe, peoples of differing nationalities, classes, faiths, languages, and traditions, forging them into a new social amalgam, a strong, proud, and united nation.

Frontier spirit It is estimated that from the Revolutionary War to the present nearly forty million people have sought new homes in the United States. For over a century the nation's area expanded at the rate of fifty square miles *a day* as frontiersmen pushed from the Alleghenies to the Mississippi, crossed the Great Plains to the Rockies, and deployed upon the shores of the Pacific. Frontier life passed with the nineteenth century, but the frontier spirit persisted, bequeathing a heritage of initia-

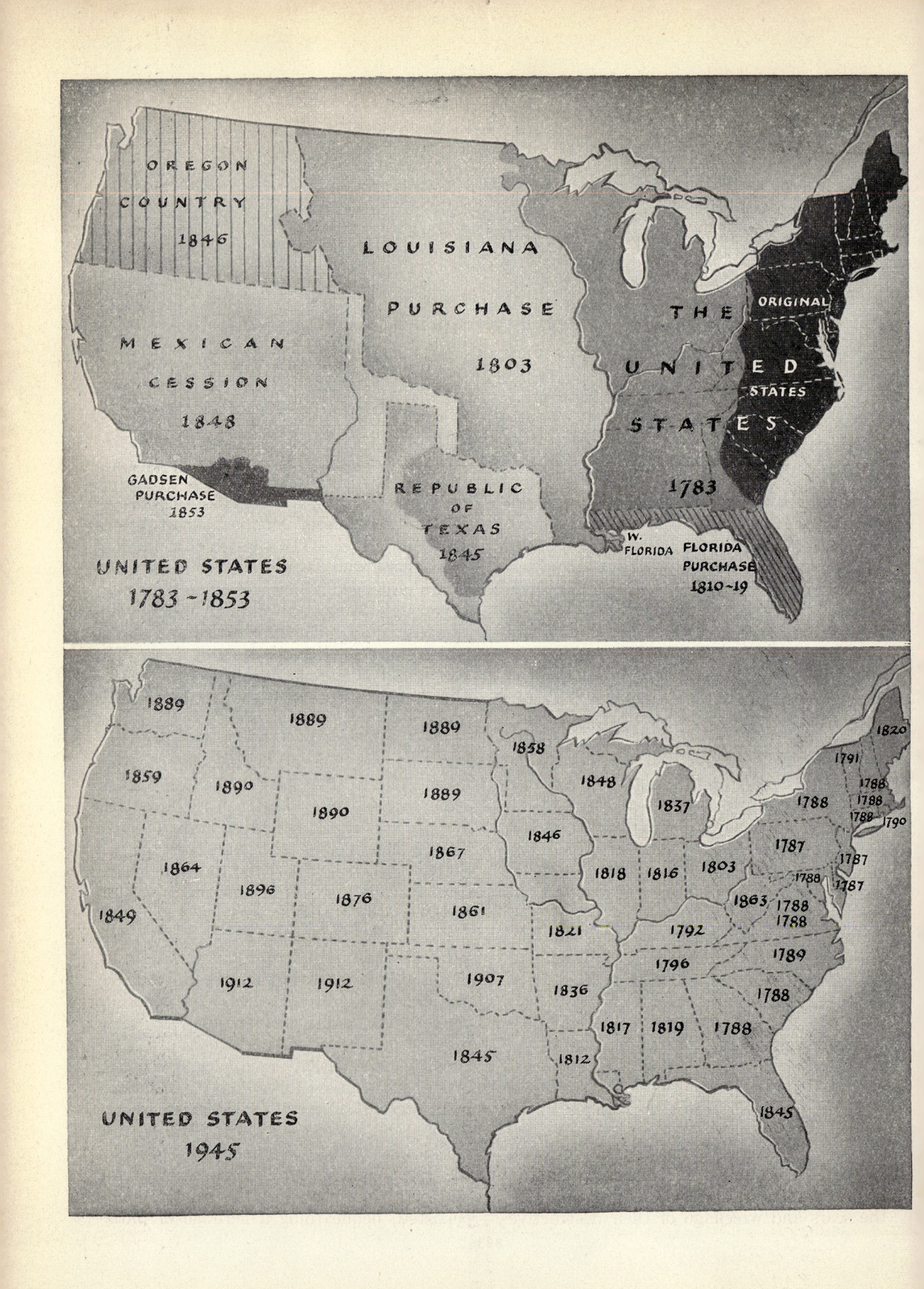

UNITED STATES
1783–1853

- ORIGINAL THE UNITED STATES 1783
- LOUISIANA PURCHASE 1803
- OREGON COUNTRY 1846
- MEXICAN CESSION 1848
- GADSEN PURCHASE 1853
- REPUBLIC OF TEXAS 1845
- W. FLORIDA
- FLORIDA PURCHASE 1810–19

UNITED STATES
1945

CYRUS HALL McCORMICK (1809–1884) DEMONSTRATING HIS MECHANICAL REAPER

With inventions like McCormick's reaper and the later power-driven farm machinery (below) reaping and harvesting underwent the most revolutionary change since the days of the Pharaohs.

tive, optimism, self-reliance, and independence to Americans unborn. For the earliest settlers were condemned to be resourceful and inventive, matching themselves against an environment where pertinacity counted more than pedigree. To land-hungry farmers from Europe the free soil of the West promised livelihood and liberty, and they marched by millions into the vastness of the plains to stake out their patrimony in the promised land.

At a critical point in the growth of the United States, when regionalism might have divided the republic, and the settlements scattered across the continent would have been stunted by longer isolation, the railway came to knit the nation together. Cheap and rapid transportation made the country an economic as well as a political unit. In the first century of the railway age one third of the world's trackage was laid in America and the lines which linked the forty-eight states together became the arteries of an economic empire.

Rôle of the railway

Nineteenth-century America was predominantly rural and agrarian, twentieth-century America is predominantly urban and industrial. The transformation, in full swing by 1900, was so swift that few citizens caught its implications. Industry forged ahead of farming as the leading activity, city dwellers multiplied, equaled, finally outnumbered the rural population. Arriving immigrants no longer sought the land; they found work in factory and mining towns. In 1870 fifty-three per cent of the workers were still engaged in agriculture, but by 1940 the proportion had dropped to seventeen per cent. The rise of cities, and the rapid appearance of an urban proletariat, raised problems which most European governments had already faced for decades. Industrial unrest, labor unions, strikes, class antagonism, the growth of great trusts and corporations — these were all symptoms of a new age and a new phase in American history.

Rural to urban

2. SOCIAL WELFARE AND NATURAL RESOURCES

The stimulating climate and more adequate food supplies available in the United States improved the physical condition of most European settlers; the children born in this country proved on an average nearly an inch taller than their forbears. Better medical care and sanitation reduced the death rate, which fell from twenty to ten and one half per thousand between 1890 and 1940. The American child born in 1800 had a life expectancy of only thirty-five years, but by 1940 its probable life span had almost doubled, reaching sixty-five years. The declining death rate, moderately high birth rate, and flood of immigration accounted for the exceptional rise in the population of the United States, but after 1920 the ratio of increase subsided. The birth rate dropped from twenty-three to eighteen per thousand in twenty years (1920–40). The tide of immigrants, which had reached a million a year in 1905, declined with World War I, and was checked after 1924 by an Immigration Act which established rigid quotas.

Longer life

The high living standards, abundant food, and ingenious mechanical services available to Americans could be matched nowhere else in the world. The pioneer spirit of colonial days, a talent for mechanical invention, and unrivaled natural resources enabled the American nation to outstrip all others in developing a lavish material civilization. In the interval between the world wars, forty per cent of the radios in existence, fifty per cent of the telephones, eighty per cent of the automobiles, and ninety per cent of the bathtubs were concentrated in the United States. Over four fifths of the monetary gold of the world was held by the Treasury Department. American wage-earners enjoyed the highest rate of pay of any nation, and they consumed five times as much electrical energy and used ten times as many labor-saving devices in their households as the average European. Frugal-minded inhabitants of the Old World found the accounts of American prosperity and prodigality disturbing and fantastic.

Material benefits

Almost all the essential raw materials needed to feed the factories could be found within the forty-eight states. Coal, iron, oil, timber, cotton, and most other commodities required for manufacturing, were available in abundance. These alone, however, would not have created great industries. American manufacturers enjoyed a further advantage: they had an assured market of over a hundred million customers, an integrated market, guarded for them by protective tariffs. Had the United States, like Europe, been split into a score of political fragments, with diverse laws, currencies, languages, tariffs, copyrights, and patents complicating the movement of goods at each frontier, American business expansion would have been greatly hindered. Mass consumption encouraged mass production. Mechanization of industry, by multiplying and greatly reducing the cost of standard products, brought them within the purchasing power of an ever-widening circle of consumers. It was an accelerating process.

Mass production

No other great power was as self-contained and self-sufficient as the United States had become by 1900. American agriculture was as rich, varied, and productive as American industry. The climate, ranging from sub-arctic to tropical, a generally adequate rainfall over large areas, a topography of infinite contrasts, enabled the farmers and herdsmen to feed the nation and produce a surplus for export. The wide plains, without fences, dykes, or buildings to obstruct the plow, were ideally suited to mechanized methods, and power-driven tractors, reapers, and harvesters transformed the ancient occupation of the husbandman. The yield exceeded the demand: good harvests came to mean a literal embarrassment of riches. The disposal of the crop surplus created problems solved only in part by canning, freezing, dehydrating, and storing for later use. As in the case of manufactured wares, statistics best reveal the extent of this triumph in food production. In the United States one sixth of the population raises a plentiful diet for 140,000,000 people. In Asia, where five sixths of the workers toil on the land, the population is fed perhaps one tenth as adequately. The extraordinary advantage enjoyed by the Americans is due to their machinery.

Ample crops

3. POLITICAL LIBERTY

From colonial times class distinctions and inherited rank meant less in America than in Europe because the frontier created its own gradations. Life was more varied, society more porous, men mastered half a dozen trades because skilled artisans were often lacking, and the dissatisfied workman, free of guild restrictions, could set up for himself or take up farming. The system of free business enterprise, the exceptional opportunities for self-advancement and self-enrichment, provided the economic foundations for American democracy.

Free enterprise

A second great advantage which distinguished the United States from most European countries was the absence of powerful and militant neighbors. This was a vital factor in preserving the high degree of personal liberty which Americans prized. Save for the War Between the States, Americans were spared long and exhausting conflicts. They did not have to maintain a large standing army, nor tax themselves to support a centralized, authoritarian government to rule them like a garrison state. In this respect the English colonists in America were favored from the first. In the Spanish vice-royalties, the colonial officials were ruled by instructions from Madrid, and the French settlements, controlled by the ministry of marine, were governed "like frigates lying at anchor." After France and Spain lost their American colonies, and the United States became a nation, it enjoyed a century of development without exhausting foreign wars, without conscription, without indemnities, and the wealth and manpower thus saved were turned to productive enterprises. Taxation, federal and state, remained remarkably low, and the freedom from restraint which Americans treasured and were ready to defend remained theirs in large measure because they were seldom constrained to defend it.

Militarism absent

Europeans who emigrated to the United States left behind many of the inherited habits, class prejudices, local feuds, and outworn allegiances which had enmeshed them in the Old World. For European society resembled the European landscape: it was partitioned and segre-

Spacious ways

CONTINUOUS STRIP AND SHEET MILL

The men who worked the mills were not always as obedient as the machines, and strikes increased in the United States as organized labor became more powerful and more united. Police were stoned by strikers and retaliated with their sticks and tear gas bombs.

PITTSBURGH STEEL MILL (*above*)
AND THE HOOVER DAM (*right*)

The rapid development of natural resources and multiplication of machinery made the United States the greatest industrial nation of the world by the first quarter of the twentieth century.

gated, with ancient hedges, dykes, tollgates, and town walls dividing farm from farm and hamlet from hamlet. In America the immigrant learned more spacious ways as inevitably as he learned American speech, because the new environment stimulated and challenged him. He found that political liberty in the New World had a positive and a negative aspect: on becoming a citizen he acquired the right to vote for the legislators and so shared in shaping the laws and policies he must accept. But the negative side of American government appealed to many Europeans even more. The absence of irrational regulations, of official intimidation, of excessive taxes and military conscription seemed a fulfillment of the adage "to govern better, govern less."

This account of American life has stressed the advantages. There were penalties also, arising from the novel conditions; there were severe hardships to be endured in half-built homes; there was violence and lawlessness and cultural crudity. With the end of the nineteenth century, however, and the "passing of the frontier," much of the roughness and romance of the early days disappeared. Within a few decades society ceased to be predominantly rural and became preponderantly urban. A majority of the wage-earners turned to the mechanical trades, manufacturing, mining, transportation, or office work for their living. This shift was responsible for the rise of trade unions: between 1910 and 1920 membership in the unions doubled to over five million. Problems which Great Britain and Germany had encountered fifty years earlier suddenly confronted American statesmen: problems of unemployment, of factory legislation, social security, the growing pressure of working-class movements. These issues, which reflected a deepened sense of opposition between capital and labor, were sharpened in times of economic stress, especially in the years after 1907 and after 1929. Minimum-wage laws, anti-trust legislation, the introduction of a federal income tax by constitutional amendment (1913), and the creation of a federal department of labor the same year, indicated that the government was preparing to regulate the social and economic activities of the citizens to a much greater degree in the twentieth century. After World War I, the extraordinary powers granted the federal bureaus in 1917 and 1918 were largely withdrawn, but the great depression of 1929-33 evoked a fresh demand for a national program of social and economic reform. In response, President Franklin D. Roosevelt, swept into office with a large Democratic Party majority controlling the Senate and House of Representatives, inaugurated a "New Deal" in 1933. Legislation empowering the government to deal with the crisis in unemployment, agriculture, labor, banking, transportation, and power control greatly increased the authority of the federal departments. An act raising the surtaxes on individual incomes (1935), and a "Wages and Hours Law" (1938), prohibiting child labor and establishing minimum wages and maximum hours of work in those industries subject to interstate commerce control, marked a further departure from the negative *laissez-faire* spirit of nineteenth-century government.

The standards of living in the United States were the highest in the world, but in the interval between the world wars most Americans became sharply critical of their institutions. The economic collapse of 1929 focused attention on the lack of order, the waste, and the exploitation of national resources for immediate profit which marred the system of free competitive enterprise. The evidences of inequality and discrimination in American society, and the suffering, often undeserved, caused by financial misjudgments and greed for profit, dimmed the optimism of the nation. It was clear that there were sick industries and sick areas. The reckless exhaustion of forest reserves, the depletion of rich farm land, the prodigal misuse of oil and mineral deposits, and the lack of legislation that might have prevented such abuse of the national heritage, persuaded most citizens that government regimentation, though contrary to the American tradition in the political, and especially in the economic, sphere, was nonetheless indispensable. Local boards and private charities were inadequate to deal with evils which affected whole regions. The dilemma of many rural families, working submarginal lands, the condition of tenant farmers and sharecroppers, especially in the southern states, and the slum sections in many factory towns, mocked the general boast of American prosperity. Even more disturbing was the squalor prevailing among migratory workers and their families as they drifted from state to state, seeking occupation at seasonal labor in canneries, orchards, and packing houses. Lacking permanent income, without savings to draw upon, or even homes, these marginal classes became stranded and destitute when times grew hard, and constituted a problem and a threat.

The remote, inexpensive, *laissez-faire* type of government which had served in the nineteenth century no longer served in the twentieth. Instead, there was a popular demand for control of working conditions, for accident, sickness and old-age insurance, for the safeguarding of public health, the prevention of waste, and the more equitable distribution of wealth. In surrendering to the government the powers necessary to promote these aims, American citizens also surrendered a part of their personal independence. For only by vastly increasing the authority, the agencies and personnel, and the expenditures of the federal government, could the taxpayers assure it the means to execute the program demanded. Thus, the New World was affected, though less acutely, by the dominant political trend of the twentieth century which was transforming European society. All groups and units in the modern industrialized state had become interdependent; the economic and productive activities had grown so complex, the maintenance of public services, communication and transportation so essential, that the major functions of the social organism could no longer be left to unregulated private initiative. The maxim popular in the eighteenth century, "To govern better, govern less," was yielding in the twentieth to the alternative formula, "To govern better, govern more." The American people were facing regimentation.

Federal power increased

4. FOREIGN RELATIONS

The United States became a world power without most of its citizens being aware of the fact. Throughout the nineteenth century its rôle in international affairs had been conservative and defensive. The Monroe Doctrine, proclaimed in 1823, warned European governments not to interfere in the internal affairs of the American republics, and promised in return that the United States would not seek to intervene in the affairs of Europe. This formula had the effect of turning the Western Hemisphere into a "sphere of influence" reserved to the United States. Yet, while proposing that all other powers must maintain a "hands-off" policy toward the Americas, the United States government failed to equip a fleet or train an army strong enough to repel a serious invasion. Fortunately, while Britain controlled the seas, no foreign power could dispatch an expedition to the Americas without its lines of communication becoming vulnerable, with the result that the British Navy formed, in a sense, America's first line of defense.

Monroe Doctrine

By 1900 the United States had come of age. It had largely mastered the titanic problems of integrating a continent, and was preparing to face outward as well as inward. The Spanish-American War of 1898 proved the strength of the United States Navy and brought distant dominions — the Philippines, Puerto Rico, Guam, and Cuba — under American protection. Awakening to the necessity of defending a coastline that stretched from Alaska to Cape Horn and from Cape Horn to Labrador, the nation approved a program of naval expansion. But the essential factor for effective sea defense is the ability to concentrate forces quickly at a threatened point, and for this purpose the United States Fleet needed a more rapid route between the Atlantic and Pacific areas. This implied the construction and control of an interoceanic waterway, and the Panama Canal, constructed by the United States government at a cost of half a billion dollars, was opened in 1914. As the Republic of Colombia had hesitated to yield the concessions asked, the province of Pan-

Naval expansion

ama was set up as an independent state under the protection of the United States, and its revolutionary government, promptly recognized at Washington, ceded the Canal Zone in return for $10,000,000 and a payment of $250,000 annually (1903). The Republic of Colombia was later compensated by a grant of $25,000,000, finally ratified by the United States Senate in 1922.

Guardianship of the Philippines gave the United States an interest in Far-Eastern affairs. In 1899, the secretary of state, John Hay, proposed that Great Britain, Germany, and Russia endorse an "Open-Door" policy in China, in order to maintain equality of economic opportunity for all. With the Russo-Japanese War of 1904–05, it became apparent that Japan was more likely to threaten Chinese independence than Russia had done, and the outbreak of World War I, ten years later, confirmed this danger. A state of tension developed between Washington and Tokyo over the Far-Eastern Question. But the conclusion of World War I in 1918 left the United States and Britain with powerful forces and trained reserves. Japan, therefore, agreed to avoid a naval race in the Pacific and accepted an invitation to the Washington Conference of 1922. There a Nine-Power Pact was approved by all the nations interested in the status of China. Japan returned Kiaochow, agreed with the other powers that Chinese territorial integrity and administrative independence should be preserved, and accepted a 5 : 5 : 3 ratio which fixed Japanese battleship tonnage at three fifths that of the British and American. This limitation offended the pride of the Japanese, and they were also humiliated by the total exclusion of Japanese immigrants from the United States under the Immigration Act of 1924.

Japan and China

The American people were largely unaware of the degree to which their policies might affect or offend foreign nations. A profound disillusionment with war and the international anarchy which caused and followed the struggle of 1914–18 had left them eager to avoid entanglements and happy in their isolation. This mood was still strong when the Japanese invaded Manchuria in 1931. The efforts of the League of Nations to check Japanese aggression had diplomatic support from Washington, and the State Department announced (1932) that the United States would recognize no conquests achieved by force in defiance of the Briand-Kellogg Peace Pact of 1928. But when diplomatic protests failed to halt the Japanese, neither the United States government nor the League members were prepared to offer positive resistance. The problems created by the great economic depression had not yet abated and none of the powers was prepared to undertake the risk of attempting to restrain Japan by force.

Isolationism

The mood of isolationism continued to rule American foreign policy throughout the nineteen-thirties. The fact that all the European states (except Finland) defaulted on their intergovernmental debts further persuaded most Americans that they had been too generous and too gullible in World War I, and in 1934 Congress passed the Johnson Act, affirming that no government which had defaulted on its obligations to the United States could float further loans in this country. Fear that the United States might be drawn into another European war stimulated several "Neutrality Acts" between 1935 and 1939, all designed to limit the sale of arms to warring nations. A compromise measure (1937) provided, however, that nations at war might purchase articles (not otherwise under embargo) if they paid for them in cash and carried them away in their own ships. This "Cash-and-Carry" plan revealed the desire of American merchants to retain the profits of international trade while avoiding the risk of international commitments. In reality, however, America was already committed by circumstances and by sentiment. For as Germany, Italy, and Japan grew more aggressive, and Britain, France, and Russia failed to check them, the people of the United States grew more hostile toward the aggressor nations. Even the neutrality legislation was not really neutral in effect, for in the event of war it was self-evident that only Britain and her allies, with control of the seas, would be in a position to carry

Neutrality legislation

away the product of American armament factories in their own ships. When war finally developed in 1939, the United States held the world balance of power. The Axis nations should have remembered that the attitude, the unmatched productive capacity, and the military potential of the United States had decided the outcome of World War I. The same factors were to determine even more conclusively the course and consequences of World War II.

5. LATIN AMERICA

The American Declaration of Independence of 1776 opened an era of wars and revolutions. The half-century which followed saw Europe wracked by the French Revolution and the campaigns of Napoleon, while in South America the strategy of Simón Bolívar and José de San Martín gradually liberated the provinces from royalist control and broke the ties with the Spanish government at Madrid. Brazil provided a refuge for the exiled royal family of Portugal in 1808, and became a constitutional empire, independent of Portugal, in 1822. By 1825 a score of self-governing states had arisen out of the New-World empires of Spain and Portugal.

New republics

The Latin-American nations differ from the "United States of the North" in several important respects. One characteristic that distinguishes most of them is the mixed racial heritage of the people. Save in Uruguay and Argentina the native Indians have survived in large numbers, sometimes with an admixture of African Negro strains, and in most Latin-American republics they form the larger proportion of the population. A second factor of contrast in Latin America is the lower standard of living. Two thirds of the people of Central and South America are undernourished and one half suffer from infectious or deficiency diseases. A third factor is the general lack of adequate transportation, which limits trade and compels the inhabitants to depend upon a few marketable crops or commodities. A fourth factor common to almost all these states is the land problem. Large plantations owned by a few wealthy families occupy the areas best fitted for cultivation or pasturage and many of the Indians and mestizos exist in a state of peonage. A fifth condition which lays a heavy burden on the masses is the heavy foreign debt. This weighs so heavily on all the Latin-American republics (save Venezuela) that some pay one half their revenue to alien bondholders. Lumber, mining, and transportation franchises are also, to a large degree, in the financial control of foreigners.

Latin-American problems

The demand for raw materials and minerals, especially heavy during the world wars, has speeded the economic development of Latin America and induced momentous social changes. An urban business class of growing power and influence is challenging the historic position of the great landholders, while the laborers in the mines and the great oilfields, and also on the coffee and sugar plantations, are beginning to ask for legislative protection and better standards of living. Programs of reform have been debated widely and introduced in some of the republics. In Mexico, since the revolution of 1911, and especially since 1924, popular leaders have distributed land among the peasant villagers on a communal basis, repossessed the oil, mining, and other monopolies obtained by foreign companies, and pressed a campaign of education and cultural development. In Brazil the improvement of transportation and control of infectious diseases are major concerns. But two serious handicaps make long-range planning difficult in Latin America. One is the political instability: régimes often have short lives and a military or political *coup* may interrupt reforms before they take effect. The second handicap is economic insecurity. Many of these republics are "one-commodity countries" which depend upon a single crop or product for foreign trade. Petroleum, for example, accounts for ninety-five per cent of the Venezuelan export total; in Bolivia tin makes up ninety per cent of the exports; Chile once furnished nine tenths of the world's nitrates; Costa Rica, Guatemala, and Salvador have three fourths of their export trade in coffee, and a poor market price means ruin to the producers. Until these

Reform programs

SOUTH AMERICA
IN THE
20TH CENTURY

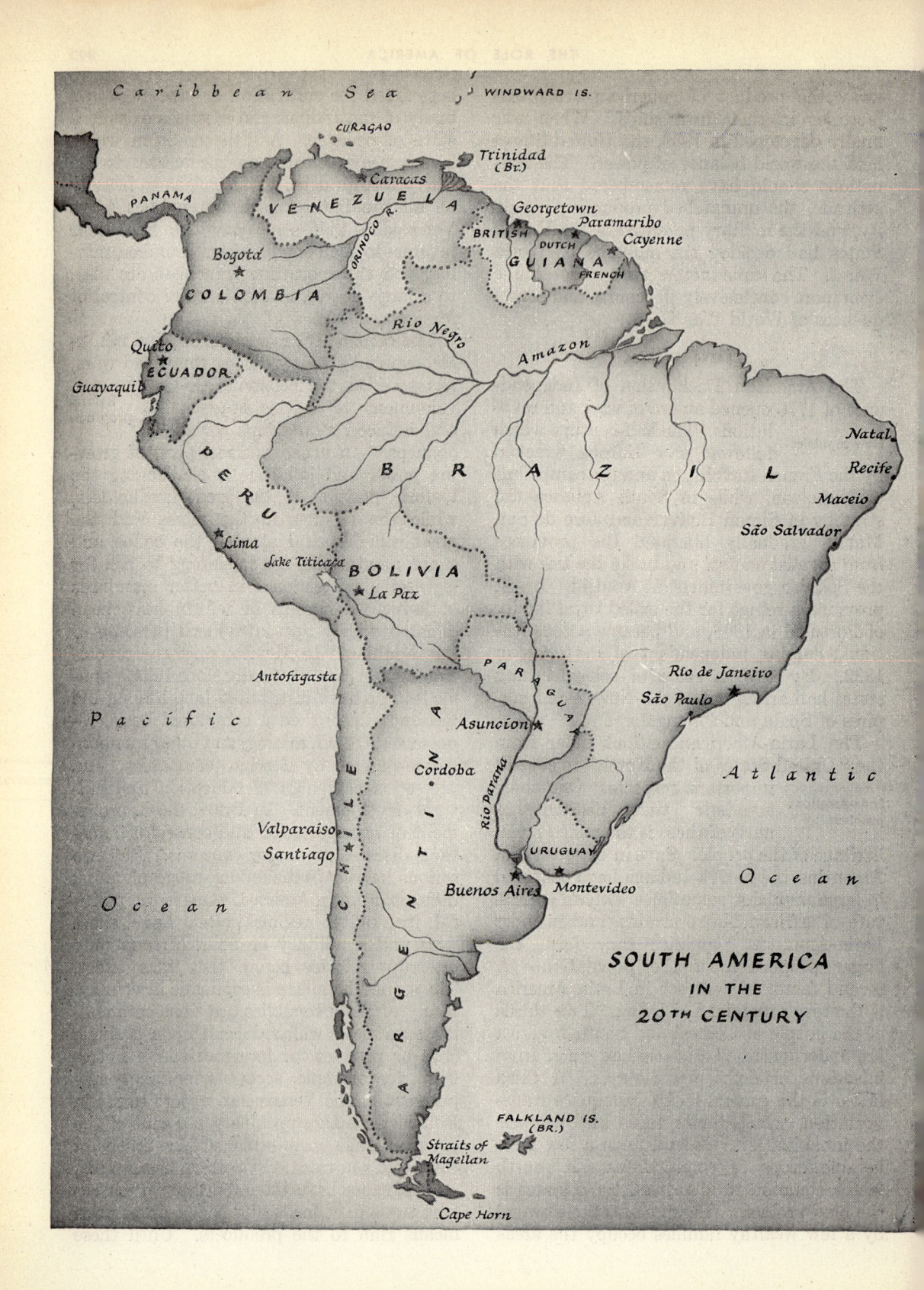

countries develop a better-balanced economy, their governments cannot easily plan ahead or undertake extravagant projects of reform.

The vulnerable economy of these states makes them particularly dependent upon the bankers who handle their bonds and upon the nations which purchase their exports. During World War I and the years that followed it the United States absorbed and dominated Latin-American trade to a preponderant extent. North-American dealers bought seventy-one to ninety-six per cent of the exports and furnished seventy-three to eighty-seven per cent of the imports of Latin-American states on the eve of World War II. This economic interdependence was one-sided, for if a tariff feud or other disagreement broke the trade connection, the United States could complete its purchases elsewhere, but a Latin-American nation might find no other market open and so face ruin. If the peoples of the Western Hemisphere were to collaborate, it was essential to dissipate the fear of the "Colossus of the North" which made the lesser republics distrustful, and to convince them that their sovereignty would be respected.

Unequal partners

To meet this situation the United States government initiated a "Good Neighbor" policy after 1933 and sought to develop a plan of hemisphere solidarity. Pan-American Conferences had met from time to time since 1889, and the member states, the twenty-one American republics, had formed a Pan-American Union. In 1928, through an exchange of agreements, the members pledged themselves to a pacific settlement of disputes by arbitration. In 1936 the twenty-one republics further agreed that they would consult on measures of general safety in the event of war in Europe or Asia; and in 1938 they approved the Declaration of Lima which affirmed the absolute sovereignty of the American states and provided for a joint maintenance of the peace, security, and territorial integrity of the lands of the Western Hemisphere.

Hemisphere solidarity

66

Russia under the Rule of the Soviets

> We shall have a soviet government, without the participation of bourgeoisie of any kind...
>
> NICOLAI LENIN.

THE SUPPRESSION of the revolutionary movement of 1905–06 in Russia left a heritage of hatred and ferment behind which the stupid and stubborn attitude of Nicholas II did little to dissipate. Although the Russians rallied loyally to their government in the fervent patriotism of the first months of World War I, distrust soon began to undermine their allegiance. The stupendous losses which their armies suffered on the eastern front, the lack of war materials and munitions, and the graft and corruption which disgraced many sections of the high command and the supply services, ripened the mood of rebellion. Rumors that alien influences were at work in the court, the malign power which the monk Rasputin was known to exercise over the czar and czarina, and the suffering caused in many cities by the virtual blockade of Russian trade resulting from the war, combined to destroy the last foundations of the monarchy.

1. THE MARCH REVOLUTION

Abdication of Nicholas II

In March, 1917, strikes broke out in Saint Petersburg. Nicholas, who had remained blind to the realities of the situation, and had refused to heed the advice of his own ministers or the remonstrances of the Duma, believed that the old methods of repression would once more prove effective. From his headquarters with the army he telegraphed orders to suppress the rioters and dissolve the Duma. But the troops refused to fire on the crowds, the Duma declined to dissolve, and the Autocrat of all the Russias suddenly found himself abandoned and helpless. On March 15, he abdicated a throne which had already collapsed.

The Kerensky régime

Habits of thought often lag behind events. The Russian people did not recognize at once the magnitude of the changes which were occurring, a fact which is not surprising when the size, complexity, and apathy of the Russian population is borne in mind. But even the political leaders at Saint Petersburg were slow at first to comprehend the depth of the movement which they had unchained. A provisional government was proclaimed, headed by a liberal nobleman, Prince Lvov, and the eloquent revolutionary, Alexander Kerensky, but it was out of touch with the masses, its bourgeois affiliations excited distrust, and its program for continuing the war against the Central Powers aroused little enthusiasm. Kerensky's efforts to galvanize the armies for a new drive broke down before the war-weariness of the soldiers. The peasants, who coveted the estates of the nobles, grew impatient with a régime which hesitated to attack private property, and the workers in the towns began to demand a genuine social revolution instead of a mere political shift. By the autumn of 1917, it was clear that the provisional government would have to ally itself firmly with the propertied classes and defy the "confiscators" or else swing definitely to the Left and

NICOLAI LENIN (1870–1924)

To those who stood in his way, Lenin seemed a modern Tamerlane, ready to sacrifice millions of victims without reason or compunction; but today his mausoleum in the Red Square, Moscow (above), is a shrine to the Russian people.

appease the land-hunger of the peasants by dispossessing the nobles. Kerensky's failure to strengthen his government played into the hands of the more radical revolutionaries. Even before 1914, the Russian Socialist Party had divided into two groups, the Mensheviki (minority) who hoped to introduce socialism by peaceful reforms and the Bolsheviki (majority) who planned to establish the "dictatorship of the proletariat" by a sudden and violent change.

After the outbreak of the revolution in 1917, the Bolsheviki urged the immediate introduction of socialistic measures, and they remained defiant in their refusal to join or to compromise with the bourgeois provisional government. The most important points in their program were: (1) the immediate conclusion of peace, (2) confiscation of large estates without compensation, and (3) control by the workers of the means of production. Their most intelligent leader was Vladimir Illyich Ulyanov, better known as Nicolai Lenin (1870–1924), a student of the writings of Karl Marx and a prophet of the proletarian revolution. With the collapse of czardom, Lenin had returned from his exile in Switzerland to put his profound understanding of social forces to practical use. Before his death seven years later, he was to make his name known throughout the world, and impress his ideals more forcibly upon the thought of the twentieth century than any other contemporary leader.

Nicolai Lenin

Throughout the summer of 1917, under the shadow of the shaky provisional government, the framework of a new order was being reared. The unit of the new organization was the *soviet* or council. Soviets of soldiers and workers and peasants were spontaneously organized in every regiment, factory, or village in the land, each sending delegates to higher committees, and these in turn choosing a national congress. At the First Congress of Soviets (June, 1917) the Bolsheviki were in the minority, but their strength grew rapidly. By October, Lenin's demand, "All power to the Soviets," had become a rallying cry, and the promise of land, peace, and bread made an irresistible appeal to the land-hungry peasants, to soldiers weary of war, and to workers threatened with famine. Kerensky had called for the election of a constituent assembly on November 25, but the events were moving too fast for legal formalities.

The soviets

2. THE BOLSHEVIKI IN POWER

At the beginning of November, the Bolsheviki prepared to seize control. They were still a minority organization of perhaps one hundred thousand members, but they were resolute and unscrupulous, while their opponents, the dwindling factions of Mensheviki, and the more cautious Social Revolutionaries, were still seeking a middle path. Kerensky attempted to call in troops from the front to sustain his régime, but the railway employees refused to transport them; and on November 7 Lenin was able to tell the Second Congress of Soviets that the provisional government was at an end. A resolution was immediately adopted calling for a three months' armistice with the Central Powers and a peace with no annexations and no indemnities.

November Revolution

Unfortunately for the Bolsheviki, the Germans were in dire need of supplies and determined to press every advantage. With the Russian front crumbling, they were in a position to write their own terms, and the Treaty of Brest-Litovsk, signed March 3, 1918, was a peace-at-any-price to the Russians and appeared an act of betrayal and desertion to their disconcerted allies, England and France. Russia abandoned her claim to one fourth of her pre-war European territory, including Poland, Lithuania, Esthonia, Livonia, and Finland, and conceded valuable commercial and economic privileges to the Central Powers. Kars and Batum were restored to Turkey. Many Russians likewise felt that this ignominious treaty was a betrayal, and the Bolsheviki found themselves menaced by a campaign of resistance and terrorism, but they clung defiantly to power. The National Constituent Assembly which assembled in January, 1918, declared the Soviet régime illegal, whereupon the Bolsheviki dissolved the Assembly by

Brest-Litovsk

force. A department of secret police, the dreaded *Cheka*, was organized to frustrate all "reactionary" activity and Lenin pressed on to establish the dictatorship of the proletariat.

The peasants were invited to cultivate the land they worked free of further rent, all private ownership having been abolished. Workingmen took over the management of the larger factories; the railways, banks, mines, and other enterprises became the property of the state; and the wealth of the Russian Orthodox Church was confiscated without compensation. The debts of the czarist administration, domestic and foreign, were repudiated, to the alarm and indignation of the foreign governments which had helped to finance Russia since pre-war years. Even in normal times such profound economic changes could not fail to disrupt the life of a nation, and their effect upon Russia, which had suffered more grievously than any other power from the shattering effect of the war, was to plunge the nation into a chaos from which there seemed no escape.

Nor were the Bolsheviki left free to work out a solution in peace. Their late allies, the French and British, grew steadily more hostile to the revolutionary régime, until they instituted an unofficial blockade and used the expeditionary forces which they had landed at Vladivostok, at Archangel, and on the Black Sea, to attack the Soviet government under the pretense of protecting Russian minorities. Disaffected classes in Russia organized a militant resistance and "White Armies" appeared in half a dozen sections. By the fall of 1919, the Bolshevik control had been reduced to the area around Moscow and the collapse of the Soviet régime appeared to be a matter of weeks.

The struggle to survive

Then the picture changed. A Red Army directed by Leon Bronstein (better known as Trotsky) and by Joseph Stalin began to check the advances of the "White" generals. Kolchak, who had established a provisional government at Omsk, was overtaken and executed; Yudenich, operating in the Baltic area, and Denikin, who advanced from the south, were both forced back by the close of 1919. But the struggle was not yet over. In 1920, Poland declared war against the Soviet government, and a White Army from the Crimea, commanded by General Wrangel, advanced upon Moscow. Trotsky agreed to a sacrifice peace with the Poles, which left him free to turn his Red Guards against Wrangel's forces and destroy them. The Allies had abandoned their blockade early in 1920, and two years later the Japanese withdrew their forces from eastern Siberia. Soviet Russia had demonstrated its right to survive, but the sacrifice had been great. Wholesale execution of suspects and hostages by Red and White forces alike had marred the records of every campaign in the civil war, the most illustrious victims being Nicholas II and his entire family, executed at Ekaterinburg on July 16, 1918.

While crushing insurrections and consolidating their power, the Bolsheviki attempted to carry out their program to nationalize all land and industry in Russia, but by 1921, Lenin recognized that the task was too great for immediate execution. In many industries production had fallen to less than one fifth of the pre-war output. The peasants, eager enough to take over confiscated lands, were disillusioned when the government demanded that (as part of the collectivist experiment) they surrender their crops to feed the city workers. Agriculture, like industry, seemed on the point of foundering when Lenin sponsored a compromise known as the New Economic Policy, or more briefly, as the NEP. The NEP restored the smaller plants, employing no more than fifteen to twenty workers, to private control, and permitted the peasants to sell their grain for profit. Furthermore, capital was obtained by extending concessions to foreigners and commerce began to revive. With economic conditions improving, the Communist Party, as the Bolsheviki had named themselves (1919), grew more and more popular, and when Lenin died in 1924 the desperate experiment which he had directed during seven perilous years was on the road to success. As the Communist régime represents the most interesting social experiment so far undertaken in the twentieth century, it will be useful to examine its ideals and methods.

The NEP (1921)

3. THE PHILOSOPHY AND PROGRAM OF THE RUSSIAN COMMUNISTS

In proclaiming the dictatorship of the proletariat, the Russian Communists sought to establish a state in which the workers would be the controlling and the favored class. They accepted the teaching of Karl Marx that wealth is the product of human labor, and they believed that the workers, instead of piling up surplus profits for their capitalist masters, should themselves be the chief recipients and beneficiaries of the wealth created by their efforts. The so-called non-producing members of society — aristocrats, capitalists, employers of labor, and those who declined to work — were refused a vote, and received smaller rations of food than the "workers." Society was thus deliberately turned upside down. Ex-nobles, ex-officials of the czarist government, rich bourgeois, and churchmen now formed the unprivileged class, while peasants and workers were preferred to them, receiving better food, readier accommodations on the state railways, more habitable dwellings and lighter taxes.

Proletarians preferred

Needless to say, the members of what had been the property-owning classes were embittered by the change. But they were too small a minority to offer any effective protest, for no powerful and well-entrenched middle class had developed in Russia comparable to the bourgeoisie of England or France. Furthermore, all those who had been dispossessed were known and were watched by the secret police. Conspiracy against the Soviet government, or even unguarded criticism of it, was likely to be followed by arrest, a secret trial and a secret execution. The "Extraordinary Commission" created in 1917 for combating counter-revolutionary activity proved remorselessly efficient, hunting down the disaffected even more competently than the czarist police had done. By 1922 this commission, or *Cheka*, under the command of Felix Djerzinsky, had served its purpose so well that it was replaced by a new organization of political police known briefly as the *Ogpu*. A calculation of the number of counter-revolutionaries condemned to death in Soviet Russia since 1917 is difficult to make, for estimates have varied from a few hundred to over a million. Since 1922, however, exile to Siberia has largely replaced the death penalty, and has been invoked even more extensively than in czarist times.

Secret police

No institution of the old régime excited more criticism from the Communist leaders than the Russian Orthodox Church. At first the Bolsheviki were content to confiscate the property of the church, expecting that religion would soon lose its force if deprived of wealth and official support. Finding, however, that the clergy continued to be active and even to increase their following, the government adopted repressive measures, circumscribing the activities of priests in educational and charitable work, and inaugurating a campaign among the people to free them from "superstitious beliefs." The hostility felt by the Bolshevik leaders toward religious dogmas was due in part to their conviction that faith in miracles and the efficacy of relics was contrary to the modern, realistic, and scientific attitude toward life which they desire to instill. But they advanced another and profounder objection. They had accepted the doctrine of Marx that "Religion is the opium of the people," and they wished to extirpate it because they held that the spirit of humility and resignation which the Russian priests long urged upon the masses was a device of the ruling group to keep the people fatalistically resigned to their lot. According to this view the Russian Church was a subtle and successful instrument of propaganda for perpetuating the enslavement of the credulous peasants and proletarians by teaching them to accept their suffering as imposed by the will of God.

The war on religion

The children of Soviet Russia are undergoing a careful training in a new social philosophy. To fit them for a practical share in the duties of a proletarian state, they receive free instruction, are promoted on a basis of merit, and will take their places as artisans, engineers, laborers, or peasants according to their aptitudes. They are being trained also to compete with one another in the quality and quantity of their work, but to scorn the thought of toiling solely for material advan-

Education

JOSEPH STALIN

After the death of Lenin, Joseph Stalin won a commanding influence in the Russian Communist Party and the councils of government.

RUSSIAN INDUSTRIAL PLANTS

In 1931, Stalin warned the Russians that they were fifty or a hundred years behind the advanced countries. "We must make good this distance in ten years. Either we do it, or they crush us."

tage or profit. Whether, under changed conditions, the Russian workers can be persuaded to take such pride in their labor that they will give as much effort and attention to ordinary tasks as the workers in other lands, who are stimulated by the desire for material gain, is not yet certain. The Russians, however, are indoctrinated with the belief that their fellow toilers in capitalistic countries are heartlessly exploited under an unregulated system of ruthless and selfish competition, and they believe that the proletarians everywhere, when they realize this, will take heart from the Russian example, throw off their chains, and unite in a World Federation of Workers' Republics. Because they travel very little, and have no means to contrast what they are taught with the actual conditions elsewhere in the world, most Russians believe that in the western states of Europe society is honeycombed with dry rot and the capitalistic system is on the point of collapse. The morale and faith of two hundred million people in the Union of Soviet Socialist Republics is maintained by means of the campaign of education, and is fortified through radio, journals, traveling lecturers, and pictorial propaganda circulated for this purpose.

4. THE STRUCTURE OF THE SOVIET GOVERNMENT

The Union of Soviet Socialist Republics (or U.S.S.R.) is not a centralized empire but a federation of sixteen semi-autonomous states bound together by constitutional treaties. In area the Union embraces 8,350,000 square miles, almost one sixth the land area of the globe, and it includes 200,000,000 people, one tenth of the world population (1945). The largest of the constituent republics, the Russian Soviet Federal Socialist Republic, includes two thirds of this area and half the population, and its capital, Moscow, is the center of Soviet administration. Its first constitution, adopted by an All-Russian Congress in 1918, and revised in 1924, was supplanted by a new charter in 1936. This new Constitution provided for a bicameral legislature, consisting of a Council of the Union of some 570 elected deputies (one for each 300,000 of the population), and a Council of Nationalities of 571 delegates, the latter to be chosen by local governing bodies of the various constituent republics.

The executive functions of the government are exercised by a smaller council, or Presidium, elected by the twin legislative bodies, and the Presidium in turn entrusts great power and responsibility to a Council of People's Commissars with twenty-four members. These Commissars direct the state trusts which exploit the natural resources of Russia, as well as the railway, postal, telegraph, and telephone services. Under this system of state ownership private industries have almost entirely disappeared.

Two interesting points should be noted about this somewhat intricate political machine. The first is the concentration of legislative, executive, and judicial functions in the hands of the central executive committee and subcommittees. There is no provision for a separation of power between a legislative chamber which enacts the laws, a supreme court which interprets them, and an executive which enforces them. The second point to note is that the constitution does not tell the whole story because it makes no mention of the Communist Party. This energetic organization of some three million members is controlled by a central committee which in turn appoints a political bureau. Three fourths of the delegates to the All-Union Congress are members of the party, and so firm and effective is the influence which the political bureau exerts upon the government that, after Lenin's death, Joseph Stalin, secretary-general of the Communist Party, became the practical dictator of Russia, although for years he held no important political office.

In a land where all national resources, lumber, minerals, etc., are held in trust by the government for the benefit of the people, the power of the commissars who control the exploitation of the resources is almost unlimited. With no opposition party to criticize their acts, and no system of administrative checks and balances to delay their projects, the council of commissars could coordinate their efforts and apply with ruthless determination the plans which Stalin and his economic advisers worked out for the expansion of Russian industry and the improvement of Russian agriculture. The Communists not only sought to transform the social philosophy and ideals of the Russian people within a generation, but they sought in the same space of time to modernize Russia, exploit her natural wealth, and make the Soviet state one of the richest and most productive of the great powers.

5. ECONOMIC PROGRESS AND THE FIVE-YEAR PLAN

The New Economic Policy which Lenin instituted in 1921 represented a compromise between capitalist and Communist practices. But the Russian leaders did not intend to halt halfway on the road to socialism, and in 1928, Stalin and his advisers decided that the hour had come for a new advance. The result of their determination was the First Five-Year Plan, a gigantic project calling for the expenditure of over twenty billion dollars to speed up Russian industry, develop electric power, multiply mineral output, and create new factories capable of providing the tractors, automobiles, railway engines, airplanes, and other mechanical equipment necessary to a modern state. All lines of activity were to be co-ordinated, each mine or factory was given a quota to fill, and so keen was the enthusiasm of the workers that the government held out hope of realizing the First Five-Year Plan in four years. The goal set for Russian industry was a general increase of 133 per cent within five years. Engineers and technicians were hired from Germany, England, and America to supervise the establishment of new factories and train Russian workers in processes hitherto unfamiliar to them.

A state planning commission kept the records, and cast a balance each year, commending those branches of industry which achieved their quota, and investigating those which had failed. The Communist leaders have extolled their system as a signal improvement upon the unco-ordinated competition which distinguishes the march of industry under a *laissez-faire* régime, for they deliberately planned the future, regulating in advance the miles of railway to be built, the output of iron, coal, oil, electrical power, etc., which will be required each year, and the number of workers and of working hours needed in each unit of the gigantic whole.

Planning commission

For the peasants the Five-Year Plan entailed a progressive socialization of agriculture, the wholesale introduction of machinery, and the creation of state farms. The Communists had been displeased to find that their plan to divide the land into small holdings of some ten acres for each family had failed to work satisfactorily. In each rural community the more energetic and farsighted farmers had prospered, increasing their acreage, hiring helpers, and emerging as men of property, so that ten years after the great estates of the nobles had been confiscated a new class of landowners was in process of formation. Against these well-to-do peasants or *kulaks* the government opened a campaign of intimidation and suppression. Peasants were urged to merge their private holdings in collective farms, a movement which made rapid progress despite the opposition of many *kulaks*, who disliked to lose their improved status and see their farms submerged in the collective experiment.

By 1940 less than five per cent of the harvest was listed as raised on private farms. Under modern conditions it is much more profitable to manage large farms with power-driven machinery, and the Soviet government from the first years of revolution made enormous efforts to supply the tractors, reapers, harvesters, and threshers needed to supplant the primitive methods previously followed by the peasants. To stimulate the trend toward collective management and demonstrate the efficiency of mechanized agriculture, state farms have been established in all parts of the country. Some of these include hundreds and even thousands of square miles of farmland. The workers live in model villages, possess their own newspaper, motion-picture hall, library, hospital, and recreation grounds, and share, through the delegates they elect to the local soviet, in shaping the policies of the management. But they have lost the freedom of choice which they knew briefly as independent farmers,

Agriculture socialized

UNION OF SOVIET SOCIALIST REPUBLICS, 1939

Gains, 1939 to 1945

A SOVIET HEALTH RESORT

Former estates of the nobility and modern sanitariums are maintained by the Soviet government to care for the health of the workers.

and not all of them are happy in the change.

On December 31, 1932, a little over four years after its inception, the first Five-Year Plan was officially terminated. Not all the objectives had been achieved, but the results appeared encouraging. Unemployment had been greatly reduced, the increase in the manufacture of machinery was gratifying, and the production of coal and minerals, which had lagged behind, was speeding up. In the development of collective farms the results had exceeded all hopes. A second Five-Year Plan was drafted which projected the complete socialization of agriculture by 1937, with a fifty to two hundred per cent increase in the various crops, a doubling of the output of basic industries, and a sixfold increase in the production of electric power. These achievements were to be reflected in the living conditions of the Russian people, who were promised a six-hour working day and a threefold increase in the amount of the goods to be utilized for domestic consumption.

Five-Year Plans

6. FOREIGN RELATIONS OF RUSSIA AFTER 1917

At the time of its creation in 1917, the Soviet government stood without friends in a hostile world. Not only the Central Powers with which Russia was still at war, but also the Allied nations, France, Britain, and Italy, refused their recognition to the Bolshevik régime, and lent their aid to the counter-revolutionary forces. It is not difficult to find reasons for this opposition. The Bolsheviki repudiated the debts of the czarist government, published the secret treaties to which it had been a signatory, and proclaimed a world revolution of the working classes against their capitalist masters. The Allied statesmen were embittered at the Russians because they made a separate peace with Germany, and they became alarmed when the Communists attempted to inspire proletarian uprisings in other lands. In proclaiming a blockade of Russia, the Allied governments sought both to punish the Russians and to prevent their dangerous doctrines from spreading. Even after the Soviet régime had defeated the "White" forces and proved its strength and stability, it was still refused international recognition.

Very gradually this unfriendly attitude changed. The Communists learned that the "Third International," which they organized at Moscow in 1919 for the purpose of furthering a world revolution of the working classes, made them feared and distrusted by other nations, and they found it expedient to deny any official connection between it and the Soviet government. The need of reviving Russian trade moved the Bolshevik leaders to seek commercial understandings with neighboring states; political recognition followed, first from Germany (1922), then from Great Britain (1924). By 1933, when the United States re-established formal diplomatic intercourse, Russian foreign relations were normal and friendly once more. In addition to trade agreements the Soviet government had signed non-aggression pacts with fourteen states, and had ratified the Kellogg Pact (1928) renouncing war as an instrument of national policy.[1] In 1934, Russia joined the League of Nations and accepted a permanent seat on the Council.

In the Far East the relations of the Soviet government with Japan proved less amicable, and a non-aggression pact proposed by Russia was not ratified. The chief source of contention continued to be the Chinese province of Manchuria. When Japan defeated the czar's forces in 1904–05, the Russians abandoned their claims to Manchuria which remained technically a part of China. The victory of the Japanese, however, enabled the latter to persevere in their economic penetration and establish a disguised protectorate.

Japanese in Manchuria

Their aim was to make Japanese influence paramount throughout the Chinese Republic before other powers could forestall them or the Chinese Nationalist Party (the Kuomintang) could organize an effective national resistance. In the midst of World War I (1915), Japan presented twenty-one demands which would have subordinated the vast Chinese realm to Japanese designs had not the other powers protested. Frustrated for the moment, the Japanese imperialists moderated, but did not abandon, their aims. The surprising victories of General Chiang Kai-shek (1926), which established the power of the Kuomintang throughout the greater part of China, warned the Japanese that a strong Chinese Nationalist government would seek to reknit Manchuria to China proper. The increasing friction moved the Japanese to launch a sudden attack on Mukden, the Manchurian capital, in 1931, and they rapidly expelled all Chinese forces from the province. In retaliation the Chinese proclaimed a boycott of Japanese products, whereupon the Japanese attacked Shanghai (still without a formal declaration of war), but withdrew after encountering a stubborn and surprising resistance.

Japanese in China

Spurred by an appeal from China, the League of Nations investigated and condemned the aggressive tactics of the Japanese in Manchuria and Shanghai (1933). To disguise their suzerainty over the conquered province, the Japanese organized Manchuria as the independent state of Manchukuo under the rule of Henry Pu-yi, the boy emperor who had been deposed from the throne of the Chinese Empire by the revolution of 1911. Although the powers declined to recognize Manchukuo, the Japanese continued to consolidate and enlarge the new state, to the grave concern of the Russians, who operated the Chinese Eastern Railway across Manchuria to Vladivostok.[1] After prolonged and critical negotiations, the Russians agreed to sell their share in the railway (1934) and the tension in the Far East relaxed, but further clashes between Russia and Japan were certain to develop if the Japanese persisted in their efforts to dominate the Chinese Republic.

Tension with Russia

[1] See below, page 932.

[1] See map on page 904.

67

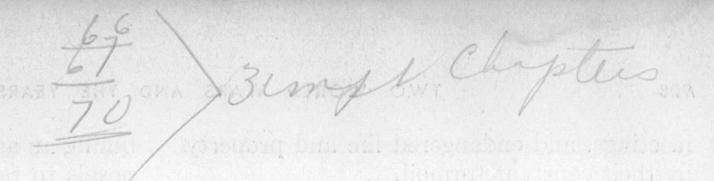

Fascist Italy

> For Fascism the state is an absolute before which individuals and groups are relative.
>
> BENITO MUSSOLINI.

AMONG THE ALLIED POWERS which emerged as victors from World War I, the Italians were the least satisfied with the results and the most deeply infected by the post-war mood of disillusionment. The war effort and war losses had dislocated the economic and social life of the nation, for Italy was less highly industrialized than France or Britain and less fitted to endure the financial strain of a war. The re-establishment of peace was followed in 1919 and 1920 by growing poverty and unemployment. The cost of living rose, and the government, unable to balance the budget, drifted toward bankruptcy. Italian industry was crippled by the necessity of importing coal from foreign sources, and Italian agriculture did not produce a food supply sufficient to feed a nation of forty million people. As conditions grew worse, the failure of the government to alleviate the distress or devise remedies for the economic situation aroused widespread discontent.

1. POST–WAR CONFUSION IN ITALY

Many patriotic Italians were further incensed by what they considered the inadequacy of Italy's war gains. The Trentino and the southern portion of the Tyrol, Trieste and the Istrian Peninsula, had been added to the kingdom by the Versailles Treaty,[1] but these territorial conquests did not satisfy the ardent nationalists who had hoped in addition for the port of Fiume and the Dalmatian coast. Moreover, they had another and more legitimate grievance concerning the division of colonial spoils, for France and Britain took possession of the German protectorates and choice portions of the Turkish Empire, and established their control over these mandates while ignoring the claims of the Italians for an equal share.

For several years after the war the tide of Italian discontent continued to rise, fed by the protests of the thwarted nationalists, by Socialists dissatisfied with the bourgeois régime, and by Communists who hoped to overturn the government and establish the rule of the proletariat. The nerveless and inefficient government failed signally to check the growth of opposition or to satisfy the popular demands. In 1919, the Socialists won 156 seats in Parliament, the largest number held by a single party, for the spirit of war-weariness, combined with the misery of the workers and the agricultural laborers, had turned many people toward socialism as a remedy. But in 1920 when strikes tied up the metal industries, and peasants, stirred by Communist ideals, began to seize and divide the landed estates, the fear of communism turned moderate citizens conservative, and the property-owning classes fought to protect their interests. In the midst of strikes and disorders, which affected all the larger cities of northern Italy, opposing factions rioted in the street, broke up each other's

Growth of disorder

[1] See map on page 860 (lower half).

907

meetings, and endangered life and property by their constant turmoil.

Out of this national chaos, a new political group, the Fascists, rose to power. The Italian people desired a firm and efficient government, which would save the country from communism, re-establish industrial peace, promote national prosperity, and gratify national aspirations. After almost four years of post-war turbulence the moment was ripe for a party professing these aims to take over the government. Such a group, commanded by an energetic leader, Benito Mussolini, was already in existence and a dramatic revolution placed it in control in 1922.

Desire for stability

2. BENITO MUSSOLINI

Born near Forli in 1883, the son of a blacksmith, Benito Mussolini rose to prominence through his own efforts. By working and saving, he managed to enter the University of Lausanne, but was expelled from Switzerland in 1904 as a Marxian Socialist. When World War I broke out ten years later, he had risen to a high post in the Italian Socialist Party, and was editor of the Socialist journal *Avanti*, published at Milan. His associates bitterly opposed the idea that Italy should enter the war, but Mussolini changed his views on this point, advocated war, and thereby lost favor with the revolutionary and Socialist groups with which he had been affiliated. Starting a new paper of his own, *The People of Italy*, he appealed to the patriotic sentiment of the Italians, and when Italy entered the war he fought in the ranks until wounded and discharged in 1917.

With the eye of a realist, Mussolini had perceived that nationalism was too powerful a force in Italian life to be ignored. The Socialists had won wide support by their demands for social justice and improved conditions for the workers, but they had also offended Italian patriots by their indifference toward the question of "unredeemed Italy," by their frank espousal of pacifistic ideals and their pleas for disarmament. The formula for a successful political party, Mussolini realized, might be found by blending elements of socialism and nationalism, by combining an aggressive foreign policy with proposals to tax the rich and benefit the poor. The impotence and extravagance of the representative parliamentary régime made a strong, even a despotic, rule seem preferable, and Mussolini strengthened his appeal by demanding a moral and administrative reform of the Italian State which would purge it of bolshevism and other foreign or corrupting influences. The nation was to be purified, regenerated, and dedicated to the task of regaining that historic leadership in arts and arms which the people of Italy had attained in the days of the Roman Empire and of the Renaissance. Few patriotic Italians could remain cold to such a national appeal; Mussolini's condemnation of bolshevism and communism reassured the property-owners, and the element of socialism in his program won over many members of the working classes. He preached a composite, but a conquering faith.

The formula of Fascism

In the chaotic days which followed the war, Mussolini organized aggressive groups pledged to promote the new faith. Many of his followers were, like himself, ex-soldiers and Socialists, and the Society called itself the *Fascio di Combattimento*, or "Union of Combat." Frequently resorting to violence, the Fascists attacked their political opponents, particularly the Communists, breaking up their meetings, smashing their printing presses, combating strikes, and in some cases compelling the strikers to return to work. It is not clear that Italy was ever in very grave danger of becoming a Communist state; the attempt to seize the factories for the benefit of the workers and set up soviets had already failed by 1922; but the Fascists claimed the credit of saving the nation from bolshevism, denounced the ineffective ministry headed by the premier, Luigi Facta, and prepared to march on Rome and take over the administration by direct action. At this point (October, 1922) the king, Victor Emmanuel III, offered Mussolini the post of prime minister, which he accepted. Although the *coup d'état* which placed the Fascists in power was irregular and perhaps illegal, it was a popular demonstration rather than a triumph of force.

"March on Rome" (1922)

BENITO MUSSOLINI (1883–1945)

The personal qualities which carried Mussolini to power in Italy were self-confidence, ruthless will, and a gift for vehement eloquence.

THE SONS OF THE WOLF

Under Fascism Italian boys were taught military ideals from an early age.

Declaring that the Parliament had failed ignominiously at the task of government, Mussolini demanded and obtained a grant of autocratic powers from the intimidated deputies.

Constitution changed

A vigorous policy of economy and efficiency was adopted, Mussolini himself assuming the portfolios of foreign affairs, and of the interior, to which he later added five other cabinet posts. A new electoral law, forced through the Parliament in 1923, provided that the political party obtaining the largest number of votes cast in an election (providing these amounted to twenty-five per cent of the total) would receive two thirds of the seats in the Chamber. The following year, after some official pressure, the Fascist or government party won the election by a large majority. The Socialist minority, however, continued to oppose and criticize the Fascist dictatorship. When a Socialist deputy, Giacomo Matteotti, threatened to make public some discreditable facts concerning Fascist methods of rule, he was abducted and murdered (1924). This act produced "a profound moral oscillation" in Italy, as Mussolini himself admitted, and almost overturned the new régime. Nevertheless, the Fascists continued to consolidate their control and press forward their designs for the reorganization of the state.

The policy of silencing political opponents by violent methods, the most revolting phase of Fascist activity before the March on Rome, continued to disfigure the record of Fascist success.

Fascist repression

Systematic beating, dosing with castor oil, and even worse barbarities, awaited those rash enough to oppose the new government. Newspapers survived at the price of a humiliating subservience; teachers in schools and universities took an oath to instill Fascist ideals into their students, or lost their positions; obdurate foes of the Fascist Party who had fled the country were punished by the loss of their rights and property, while many who failed to escape were transported to a prison colony on the Lipari Islands off the coast of Sicily. As head of the state, responsible to the king alone, Mussolini ceased to be dependent upon a Fascist-controlled Parliament and could issue decrees with the effect of laws. The cabinet members were his appointees, and the *podeste*, or local officials placed in control of the communes, were dictators in miniature executing his orders. Thus the minority opponents of Fascism were left without protection and without a court to which they might appeal.

3. THE CORPORATE STATE

Between 1925 and 1928, sweeping reforms initiated under the Fascist dictatorship transformed the government of Italy into a new type of political organism which was termed the "corporate state." From the first the Fascists had made clear their desire to control or dissolve all clubs, unions, or other associations outside their own ranks, to replace the confused tangle of political parties by a single National Party (Fascist), and to bring the political, economic, social, and intellectual life of the nation into harmony with Fascist ideals. By a decree issued in 1926, the National Syndicates or unions of Italian workers were legalized by the government, and a second decree established a ministry of corporations to control their activities. Six employers' associations and seven workers' associations were to be co-ordinated under the minister of corporations, but this reorganization meant that the workers would lose the right of independent action, the syndicates would no longer have the power to declare a strike, and no new or unofficial associations could be formed. Not only industry, but agriculture, commerce, banking, etc., were to be regimented by these enactments, which made it possible for the government to curb the conflict between workers and employers, and regulate the vital productive activities of the entire nation. The liberal philosophy of the nineteenth century, which had taught that business prospered best when left alone, and that governments should interfere as little as possible in the disputes of capital and labor, had thus been abandoned in favor of a policy of strict regulation which subordinated all the individuals and enterprises of a society to the welfare of the state as an entity. Critics of the Fascist régime have objected, however, that the corporations were never really organized, except on paper, and that they did not function, so that the workers lost the advantage of collective bargaining and gained little in return.

The final transition from the parliamentary to the corporative system of government was not proclaimed until 1928.

New electoral system In that year a new electoral law went into effect which made the hierarchy of official syndicates, directed by the minister of corporations, the "organs of the state." Universal manhood suffrage was discarded, and the right to vote limited to those men who could prove they were members of a recognized syndicate, paid one hundred *lire* in taxes, or held a position of responsibility. These provisions disfranchised some three million voters out of twelve million. The most striking innovation, however, concerned the nomination of the candidates for election. The Chamber of Deputies was reduced to four hundred members, electoral districts disappeared, and Italy became one great constituency. These measures were designed to curb the spirit of sectionalism, with the inevitable compromises and petty political bargaining which had disfigured the parliamentary régime before the Fascists came into power. Henceforth each deputy would represent, not one local district, but the Kingdom of Italy as a whole. Finally, the task of preparing a list of eight hundred candidates was confided to the executive councils of the thirteen national employers' and workers' federations. Two hundred additional nominees were chosen by professional associations, teachers, authors, artists, etc., and this list, now comprising one thousand names, was turned over to the Fascist National Grand Council (the central executive committee of the Fascist Party), which drew upon it in composing a final reduced list of four hundred "deputies designate." In the first election held under the new system (1929), the voters were invited to record their acceptance or rejection of the list of designated deputies as a whole. Out of some 8,650,000 ballots cast, only 136,000 had been marked "no."

The vigor and apparent success of the Fascist experiment in Italy encouraged the growth of Fascist movements in other European countries. Citizens who viewed with alarm the economic dislocation which followed the war, or grew disgusted with the mediocrity of professional politicians, re-echoed Mussolini's pronouncement that good government was more important than representation, and were disposed to agree that the parliamentary system, devised by theorists in the eighteenth century who envisaged the state chiefly as an agrarian democracy, was dilatory in dealing with the complex administrative problems of a modern industrial commonwealth. The Fascist doctrines appealed particularly to those people who,

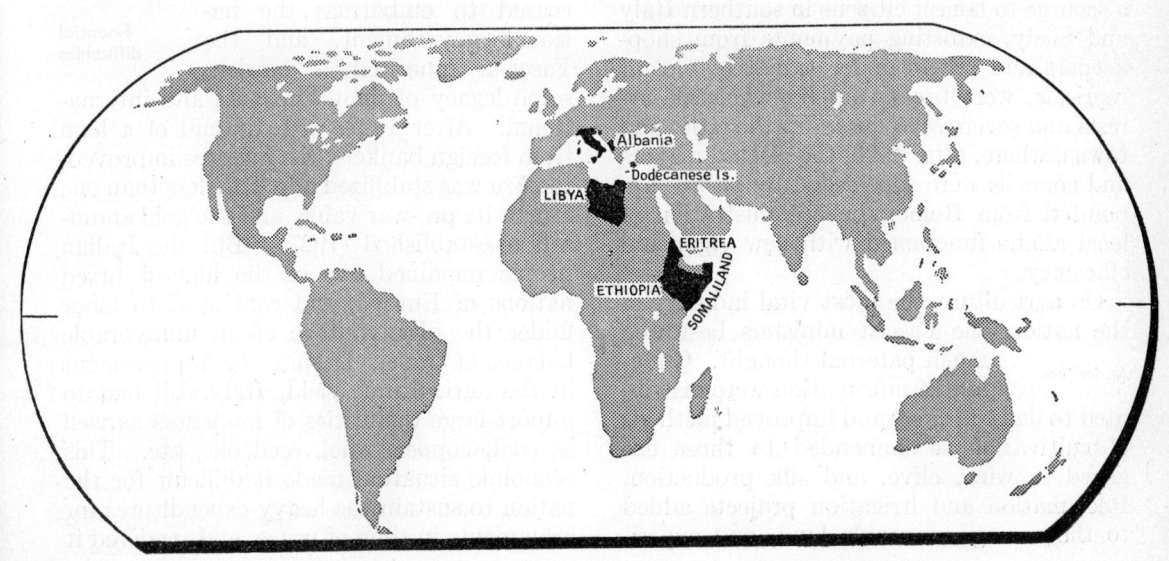

ITALIAN COLONIAL EMPIRE, 1939

for one reason or another, were most strongly opposed to Socialism and Communism. Thus Russia and Italy provided Europe and the world in the post-war era with two dynamic and antagonistic political faiths, Communism and Fascism.

4. EFFECTS OF THE FASCIST ADMINISTRATION

Under Fascism the Italian people were stirred by a new spirit of pride and accomplishment. Monster mass meetings, parades, and demonstrations, inspired and directed by the authorities, kept their patriotic enthusiasm aflame; the young boys were trained by courses in group calisthenics, maneuvers, and games to prepare themselves for military service; subsidiary organizations taught the girls to perfect themselves in those accomplishments which would make them good wives and mothers. A renewed sense of the purpose and dignity of life, a renewed faith in the grandeur and destiny of the country, and a deeper and more aggressive nationalism was bred in the hearts of Italian youths by the Fascist ideals and training.

The methods of Fascist rule were designed to impose social and industrial peace upon the Italian nation. Strikes and lockouts were forbidden and all labor disputes settled by compulsory arbitration. The secret societies, such as the *Mafia* and the *Camorra*, which had long been a scourge to honest citizens in southern Italy and Sicily, extorting payments from shopkeepers and others under threat of violent reprisals, were broken up by wholesale arrests and severe sentences. In the cities and towns, where, after 1926, the elected mayors and councils were superseded by *podeste* appointed from Rome, the administration of local affairs functioned with new vigor and efficiency.

Justice

On agriculture, the most vital industry of the nation, the Fascist ministers bestowed much paternal thought. Circulars of information were distributed to dairy farmers and improved methods of cultivation recommended to those engaged in wine, olive, and silk production. Reclamation and irrigation projects added to the acreage of arable land, and experiments with new types of grains and fruits were conducted by government experts. An agricultural credit bank, established to assist farm proprietors through their financial difficulties, enabled many farmers to expand their holdings and enlarge their crops.

Agriculture

In attempting to stimulate the mechanical trades the Fascist government faced serious obstacles. To offset the dependence upon foreign coal and petroleum supplies, new power stations harnessed the rivers, and three fourths of the power available for industrial purposes was drawn from hydroelectric sources. In comparison with England or Germany, however, Italy remained a backward nation in this respect, for the industrial establishments provided work for less than one tenth of the population. Unemployment proved a severe and stubborn problem, the number of jobless workers passing the million mark in 1932. Despite the best efforts of the government to provide work rather than doles, and to stimulate business by regulations and subsidies, the decline in world trade after 1929 had a serious effect upon Italian exports. By 1934 the annual deficit in the national budget promised to reach half a billion dollars, and this was a serious defect in a state which aspired to embark upon imperialistic conquests.

Industry

Since the proclamation of the Italian Kingdom in 1861, fiscal problems had never ceased to embarrass the national government, and the Fascists inherited a burdensome legacy of debts, internal and international. After 1922, with the aid of a loan from foreign bankers, the finances improved, the *lira* was stabilized at a little less than one fourth its pre-war value, and the gold standard re-established (1927). But the Italian people remained one of the highest taxed nations of Europe, and continued to labor under the disadvantage of an unfavorable balance of trade. Despite the improvement in the agricultural yield, Italy still had to import large quantities of foodstuffs as well as coal, copper, wool, seed oils, etc. This economic situation made it difficult for the nation to sustain the heavy expenditures for armaments in time of peace, and rendered it

Financial difficulties

ITALIAN WAR IN ETHIOPIA: ARMED ABYSSINIANS ON THE MARCH

The Italian conquest of Ethiopia in 1936 added to the African empire which the Fascists lacked the naval strength to defend. Like their merchant marine it was a liability in war.

THE ITALIAN LINER "REX"

The Italian Fascist government subsidized luxury liners like the "Rex" in an effort to capture more of the Atlantic passenger trade.

5. THE FASCIST STATE AND THE PAPACY

One achievement of Mussolini's régime was the conclusion (1929) of an accord between the Italian government and the papacy. After 1870, each succeeding pope had accepted the precedent set by Pius IX and had regarded himself as the prisoner of the Vatican. The student will recall that when the forces of the new Italian Kingdom occupied Rome, Pius IX refused to sanction this infringement of his authority or to accept compensation for the loss of his temporal possessions. This papal policy of nonrecognition, awkward alike for the Italian government and for the papacy, prevailed for nearly sixty years. After 1922, the aggressive and multifarious activities of the Fascists threatened to create new emergencies and to widen the existing rift, until in 1927 Pius XI found it necessary to condemn the Fascist theories concerning the supremacy of the state.

Two years of negotiation followed during which the Fascist chiefs succeeded in softening the papal displeasure. Mussolini recognized that the opposition of the church might prove a serious threat to his authority in a state where nine tenths of the people professed the Catholic faith. A mutual desire for reconciliation resulted in the Lateran Treaty of 1929, which recognized the pope as temporal sovereign of the Vatican City. This minute state of about one hundred acres in the heart of Rome was to enjoy complete independence, with its own rail, postal, and coinage facilities, and its own radio station. As compensation for the loss of that larger patrimony which former popes had ruled, the Italian government agreed to make restitution to the extent of 1,750,-000,000 *lire* (about $92,000,000). The government further consented to declare the Roman Catholic faith the official religion of the state, to provide for religious instruction in the schools, and to enforce the canon (church) law throughout Italy. In return the Holy See formally recognized the Italian Kingdom with Rome as its capital. To many people it appeared that the Fascists lost more than they gained by this *concordat*, but the Fascist régime was strong enough to afford concessions and the settlement helped to tranquillize Italian society.

Moreover, Catholicism and Fascism could serve the social order better as allied forces, for they possessed some common aims and common enemies. In successive encyclicals, Pius XI upheld the sanctity of private property and defended the claims of capital, while insisting with equal force that real progress in the industrial sphere must rest upon an equitable adjustment of the burdens and rewards of industry between the owners and the workers. Pius further stressed, as Leo XIII had done, the mutual interdependence of capital and labor, and adjured the wealthy to remember and exercise the sacred duty of charity toward the victims of economic pressure. His denunciation of birth control and divorce coincided with the Fascist drive to raise the Italian birth rate. Nor must it be overlooked that the church and the Fascist State were engaged in a common battle against the principles of communism, for both condemned the communistic program for the abolition of private property, the socialization of industry and agriculture, the suppression of organized religious bodies and the confiscation of their wealth.

The Fascists could not, however, derive an unmixed satisfaction from the papal pronouncements. For Pius denounced the competition in armaments and the national rivalries which threatened the peace of the world in phrases which lashed the more militant Fascists no less sharply than the ultra-patriots and jingoists of other nations. Mindful of the great influence for peace which the church exercises throughout the world, the pope issued an apostolic letter (1931) urging a crusade for the relief of the suffering and the indigent, in the hope that social and national rancors might be quenched by the pure zeal of a great religious and humanitarian effort, and that part of the funds expended so lavishly upon armaments might be diverted to more humane services.

68

The United Kingdom and the British Empire Commonwealth

> No Act of Parliament of the United Kingdom passed after the commencement of this Act shall extend, or be deemed to extend, to a Dominion... unless... that Dominion has requested, and consented to, the enactment thereof.
>
> STATUE OF WESTMINSTER (1931).

TO THE UNDISCERNING EYE it might well appear that Britain had gained more by World War I than any other great power. Her most dangerous trade rival had been crushed, her naval position strengthened by the destruction of the German fleet, and the major share of the German colonies had passed under the British flag. Although nearly seven hundred thousand British soldiers had lost their lives in the various theaters of conflict, the civilian population had escaped the horrors of invasion, and the fatalities from German air and naval raids totaled less than fifteen hundred. Britain had no shell-torn fields or ruined towns to reclaim, and her vast industrial plants had expanded under the stimulus of the war demands.

1. THE BRITISH ECONOMIC DILEMMA

But there was another and less hopeful picture to be drawn. Millions of tons of British shipping had been destroyed by submarines. Government indebtedness had risen enormously, and the loans which Britain had advanced to her allies in the war were largely uncollectible. The prosperity of the United Kingdom before the war had been a result chiefly of the Industrial Revolution, which had made Britain the workshop of the world. In addition, there was the large annual return on British capital invested abroad, and the profits derived from the British merchant marine which transported half the world's trade. Dependence upon these sources of wealth, however, made it impossible for Britain to recover from the exhaustion of the war years until world trade revived, and the political and economic chaos of the post-war era delayed such a revival. With Russia in revolution and Germany prostrate, with the reconstructed European states raising new tariff barriers, and the Indian Nationalists boycotting British goods, the anticipated revival had little chance to materialize.

Nor were these the worst features of the dilemma. In the decades before the war, British manufacturers had already found themselves embarrassed by the industrial progress of other nations and even of the British Dominions. Following the war this rivalry grew more serious. Japanese textiles competed with the product of British looms for the markets of China and India; merchandise from the United States undersold British manufactures in South America. The British coal exports, long an important source of revenue, declined rapidly, for motors driven by electricity or gasoline were supplementing the steam engine. Even at sea the British encountered a new spirit of competition, and soon express liners built in Germany and Italy were capturing the best of the Atlantic passenger trade while the

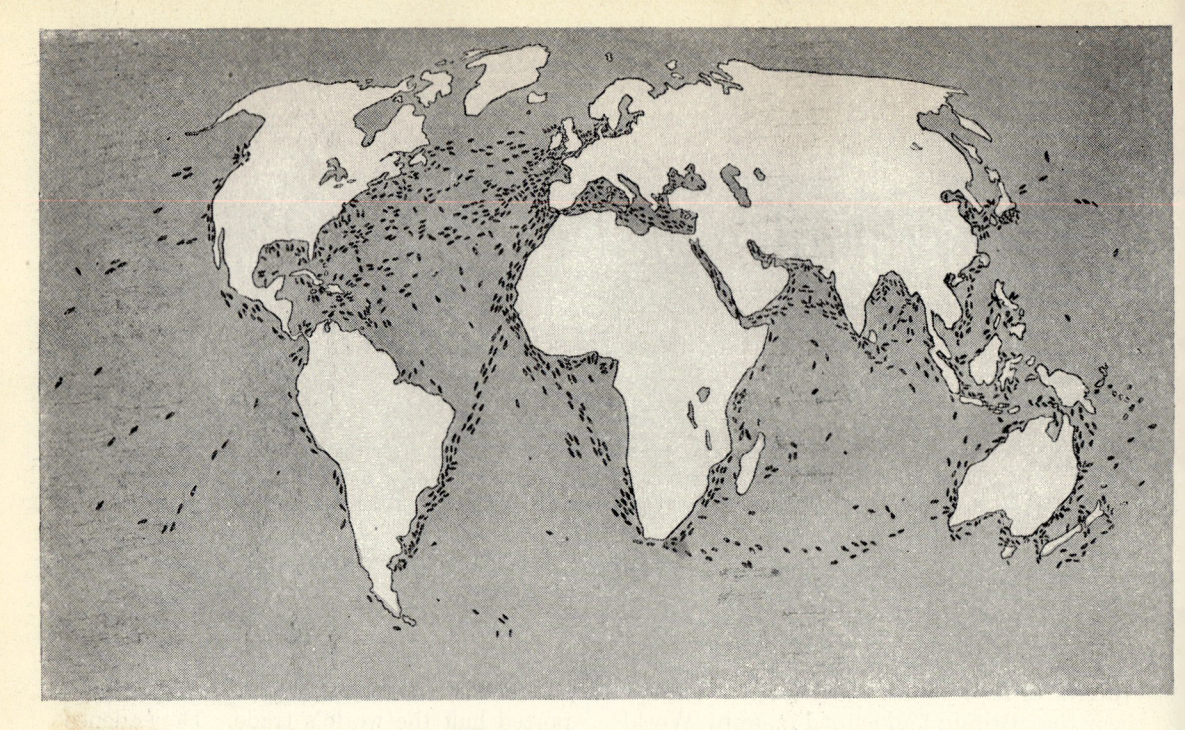

SEA SPACES OF THE WORLD

The hundreds of British merchant ships crawl like ants around the coasts of the world. This homolographic projection shows their position at a given moment as registered in London.

shipyards on the Clyde and the Mersey lay idle. By 1921, two million workers in England were without occupation; during the decade which followed, the number was to vary from three quarters of a million to approximately three million registered unemployed, as the business tide ebbed and flowed. The problem of providing relief for these victims of economic circumstances became the gravest issue of the post-war years.

Under the stress of these abnormal conditions the social insurance acts passed by the Liberals between 1909 and 1911 [1] proved lamentably inadequate. Although in 1921 nearly three million people were receiving annuities under the Widows', Orphans', and Old-Age Pension Acts, while another million were the recipients of poor relief, and upwards of two million more received war pensions, the government found it necessary to assume the burden of relieving the unemployed to the further extent of fifty million dollars. Within

<small>Unemployment relief</small>

[1] See above, pages 799–800.

ten years this aid to the unemployed had increased fivefold; and the total annual cost of social services amounted (1931) to nearly two billion dollars. The increased taxes necessitated by this expenditure augmented the burden and the difficulties under which British industry already labored, while the income, inheritance, and land taxes drove many property-owners to sell their estates or transfer their investments to other countries.

As four fifths of the inhabitants of the United Kingdom had become town dwellers by the twentieth century, British farmers were a neglected minority and the urban millions depended upon the food supplies imported from other lands. How to pay for these imports, and for the raw materials consumed by the factories, when the British export trade was languishing, became a problem of the utmost gravity. The world-wide economic depression which set in after 1929 reduced British trade and credit to such a serious extent that the government abandoned

<small>Free trade modified</small>

the gold standard (1931) and the pound sterling depreciated thirty per cent in terms of gold currencies. This financial crisis was followed by a frank abandonment of the free-trade principles which had dominated British commercial practices for nearly a century. With other nations raising their tariff walls against British manufactures, it became inevitable that Britain should retaliate. The Import Duties Act (1932) levied a ten per cent duty on foreign goods entering British ports, but left the government at liberty to negotiate a lower tariff accord with countries which accepted British products on favorable terms; and to raise the import duty as high as one hundred per cent on goods produced by those nations which discriminated against British exports.

The mounting economic pressure also proved an important factor in modifying British naval ambitions. Before World War I, Great Britain had attempted to maintain a fleet equal to any two other navies in the world combined, but by 1922 the naval forces of the United States and Japan had increased to such a point that Britain was driven to abandon this policy. The destruction of the German High Seas Fleet, the ships of which were sunk by their own crews after their surrender, left the British an unquestioned superiority in European waters; but their Pacific squadron could no longer compete with the American and Japanese forces. Great Britain, therefore, welcomed the proposal for a conference on naval limitation set forth by the American government in 1922. The most important treaty resulting from this Washington Naval Conference provided that Great Britain, the United States, and Japan should accept a quota regulating the tonnage of their respective navies in the proportions of 5 : 5 : 3 for capital ships. At the same time the three powers agreed to maintain their fortifications in the Pacific at their existing status. The Japanese were the least satisfied with the agreement, which permitted them a quota only three fifths as large as the two leading naval powers, but the treaty achieved its main purpose in that it postponed an unrestricted naval race.

Washington Conference

2. BRITISH POLITICAL PARTIES AFTER 1919

During the last two years of World War I, Great Britain was governed by a coalition cabinet, resting chiefly upon Conservative support, but headed by the indefatigable Liberal leader, David Lloyd George. This fiery Welshman was one of the few British politicians who emerged with enhanced prestige from what he later described as "our bloodstained stagger to victory," but his popularity waned in the troubled post-war period. The mounting economic distress after 1920 found British opinion divided regarding the best course to follow, the Conservatives generally favoring a tariff to protect the manufacturers, while a growing Labor Party demanded increased government relief for the unemployed and the progressive socialization of industry. In the national election of 1922, the Conservatives secured a majority of the seats in the House of Commons, but Labor also gained and became the official opposition party. A second election (1923) gave the Conservatives 258 seats, the Laborites 192, and the waning Liberal Party 158. By combining forces, the Laborites and Liberals were enabled to control Parliament, and James Ramsay MacDonald became the first Socialist prime minister to direct the destinies of Great Britain.

This first British Labor government lasted less than a year. MacDonald sought to lower duties, to modify the more aggressive features of British imperialism (work on a naval base at Singapore was arrested), and to conclude trade treaties with Soviet Russia. But the British electorate declined on appeal to support his policies and returned the Conservatives to power with a majority of two hundred members in the election of 1924.

First Labor government

For the next five years the Conservative government wrestled with the problems of trade and unemployment under the premiership of Stanley Baldwin. Business taxes were reduced and the pound restored to par value (1925), a victory for the bankers and the creditor class generally. But the Conservatives found themselves compelled to augment the "dole" to the unemployed, from fear of revolution if

Tory rule

not from more humanitarian motives. For a time the sinking coal industry was buoyed up by government subsidies, but when these were curtailed (1926), and the mine-owners attempted to cut wages, the miners went out on strike and were joined by unionized transport workers. For over a week business stood still, while the British people endured with rare common sense and good humor the discomforts of the gravest and most costly labor crisis in their history. The outcome proved a defeat for the miners; and public opinion endorsed the prompt passage of a new Trade Disputes Act which prohibited further "general" strikes, forbade picketing, and weakened the influence of the workers' combinations.

In the general election of 1929, the Labor Party came into power a second time, but once again the control of Parliament depended upon the co-operation of the Liberal group. In the face of the international business depression which set in almost immediately, Ramsay MacDonald, as prime minister, found it increasingly difficult to obtain a balanced budget, and heavy withdrawals of gold from the Bank of England in the summer of 1931 precipitated a financial crisis in London. On September 21 Britain abandoned the gold standard and the pound fell from $4.86 to $3.40.

Labor cabinet

In a general election the following month, a newly formed National Party won 554 of the 615 seats in Parliament on a platform of retrenchment, protection, and economic nationalism. The new government represented a coalition *bloc*, predominantly conservative, and guided the country through a critical period under successive prime ministers, the ex-Labor leader, Ramsay MacDonald (1931–35), being followed by the conservative, Stanley Baldwin, who was succeeded in 1937 by another conservative, Neville Chamberlain. The major domestic crisis which this coalition government had to surmount occurred in 1936, when Edward VIII, who had succeeded his father George V in January of that year, resigned the throne after the cabinet declined to approve his decision to marry a commoner and a *divorcée*. Edward was succeeded by a younger brother, who took the title George VI.

Edward VIII

After 1936 the trend of foreign affairs became the dominant concern of the British people. The aggressive attitude of Italy threatened their communications in the Mediterranean, German rearmament jeopardized the balance of power in Europe, and the Japanese invasion of China endangered British interests there, particularly at Hongkong. At an imperial conference held in London in 1937 the prime ministers of Britain and the self-governing dominions planned concerted measures for the defense of the empire. The budget for 1937–38 was increased to include a billion dollar estimate for rearmament of the land, sea, and air forces. Orders for war planes were placed with American firms, and closer relations between Britain and the United States fostered by a mutual reduction of tariffs in 1938.

British rearmament

3. THE IRISH FREE STATE

Although, to the people living in post-war Britain, the crises in domestic affairs appeared to outweigh all other issues, the Parliament at Westminster was forced in these same years to decide questions which concerned the empire at large. For London is the center of a commonwealth of nations which includes one fourth of the habitable area of the world and more than one fourth of the world's population. Decisions of momentous consequence for the inhabitants of Ireland, of India, and of other portions of the British Empire were reached between 1919 and 1939, and these must now be discussed.

No problem in British history has excited more bitterness of feeling than the Irish Question. The ill fate which has frequently frustrated attempts to settle the difficulties between England and Ireland did not fail to attend the Government of Ireland Bill which the Liberals passed in 1914.[1] This act was suspended because of the outbreak of World War I, and the hostility between the inhabitants of Ulster, who were largely Protestant and pro-British, and the Irish Catholic ma-

The Irish Question

---
[1] See above, pages 800–801.

TRADE-UNION CONFERENCE
The strength, sober leadership, and growing political influence of the British trade unions provided a foundation for the Labor Party.

THE GENERAL STRIKE, 1926
The gravest labor crisis in modern British history came in 1926 when a general strike paralyzed communication and production. This London bus was wrecked by strikers.

jority in the remaining four fifths of Ireland remained unappeased. Irish national feeling found its most vigorous expression in the movement known as "Sinn Fein" (Gaelic for "we ourselves"); and in 1916 a group of reckless patriots attempted to proclaim an independent Irish Republic. The swift and deadly measures adopted by the British in crushing this attempted "Easter Rebellion" made reconciliation between England and Ireland all but impossible. A majority of the Irish members elected to the British Parliament in 1918 refused to take their seats, and set up instead an independent Irish Parliament at Dublin, under the presidency of a stanch member of the Sinn Fein group, Eamon de Valera. The Irish situation had reached a point indistinguishable from civil war.

Stubbornly refusing to acknowledge the right of the Irish to self-determination, the British government endeavored to crush the irregular forces of the Irish Republic during three years (1918–21) of savage ambushes, assassinations, and reprisals. The struggle, which was characterized by acts of ferocity and treachery disgraceful to both sides, ended in the negotiation of a treaty between the Republicans and the British government on December 6, 1921, and the following year the Irish Free State was organized. Although fanatic Republicans favored the forcible inclusion of Ulster and repudiation of all ties with Britain, a more moderate settlement was worked out. The Irish Free State achieved Dominion status with its own Parliament (the *Dail Eireann*) and membership in the League of Nations, but deputies to the Irish Parliament were to take an oath of allegiance to the British king, and the military and foreign policy of the Free State remained a matter of proprietary concern to the British government.

Irish Free State

It was further provided that no religious legislation should be enacted which discriminated against citizens of the Free State or Ulster. As the six counties of Ulster refused to join the Free State, they were granted a separate government. The capital of Northern Ireland is Belfast, and the six Unionist counties which thus remained loyal to the British tie contain thirty per cent of the total population of Ireland, or approximately 1,300,000 of the 4,300,000 inhabitants of the two sections (1941).

Northern Ireland

The active head of the Irish Free State was not a governor general appointed by the British crown, but the prime minister, or president of the executive council, as he was termed. From 1922 to 1932, this office was filled by William T. Cosgrave, a leader of statesmanlike moderation who guided the new Dominion through its first decade of tense and troubled history. The agitation of an irreconcilable minority led by Eamon de Valera continued to disturb Anglo-Irish relations. In the general election of 1932, De Valera's party (the *Fianna Fail*) obtained a majority, and he replaced Cosgrave as president of the council. The *Fianna Fail* had pledged itself to abolish the oath of loyalty to George V, and De Valera's new administration repudiated the annuities due the British government under financial agreements ratified by the Cosgrave régime. The British government retaliated by imposing a tariff on imports from the Irish Free State, whereupon the Free State taxed imports from Britain. The chief burden of this economic war fell upon the Irish peasantry whose produce was thus excluded from its normal (British) markets. In 1937 a new constitution was adopted for Eire (as Ireland was officially renamed), proclaiming it a sovereign, independent, democratic state. In 1939 it manifested its free status by remaining neutral when the rest of the British self-governing dominions joined in the war against Germany.

4. EGYPT, IRAQ, AND PALESTINE

Great Britain had controlled Egypt for thirty years before World War I, but did not declare the ancient land of the Pharaohs a British protectorate until 1914. The resentment felt by the Egyptians at this domination led to increasing disorders, until the British consented to end the protectorate (1922), withdraw their armed forces, and permit the native population to set up a constitutional monarchy under their own ruler, who took the title

Egypt

Fuad I, King of Egypt. In 1936 Fuad was succeeded by his son Faruk. Egypt is not, however, an entirely independent state, for the British government continues to scrutinize its policies and has reserved the right to fortify and guard the Suez Canal. Moreover, the vast hinterland of the Sudan, stretching from the twentieth parallel north latitude almost to the Equator, remains under joint British and Egyptian control.

Iraq As a result of military operations in the valleys of the Tigris and Euphrates, the British were able to claim Mesopotamia as a mandate after World War I ended. The native Arab tribes, however, which had welcomed British aid in throwing off the Turkish yoke, did not wish to exchange one conqueror for another and demanded complete independence for their homeland, which they termed Iraq. Accordingly, after the Emir Feisal had been proclaimed King of Iraq (1921), the British agreed to recall their armed forces provided their interest in the rich Mesopotamian oilfield was safeguarded. In 1930, the official mandate was replaced by a treaty of alliance between Iraq and Great Britain, and in 1932 the Kingdom of Iraq became a member of the League of Nations. Iraq has a population of almost three million, and its capital is located at Bagdad, the ancient city of the caliphs.

Palestine When British forces conquered Palestine from the Turks in 1917, the foreign secretary, Arthur Balfour, declared that Great Britain favored "the establishment in Palestine of a National Home for the Jewish People...." At the conclusion of the war, the British received Palestine as a mandate under the League of Nations with the understanding that the Jewish people would be encouraged to settle there, but the discontent of the Arabs, who desired self-government and resented the immigration of Jews, led to constant turmoil. By 1938 the Jewish minority had swelled to forty per cent of the population, but the dissensions continued with increasing loss of life. Divided between its desire to honor the Balfour Declaration and its fear of further antagonizing the Mohammedan Arabs (who enjoyed the sympathy of their hundred million co-religionists within the British Empire) the cabinet at London sought desperately for some plan for dividing Palestine between the Jewish and Arab factions. The probability that the Arabs were receiving secret encouragement from Italy and Germany added a further danger to a threatening situation. For a spirit of na-

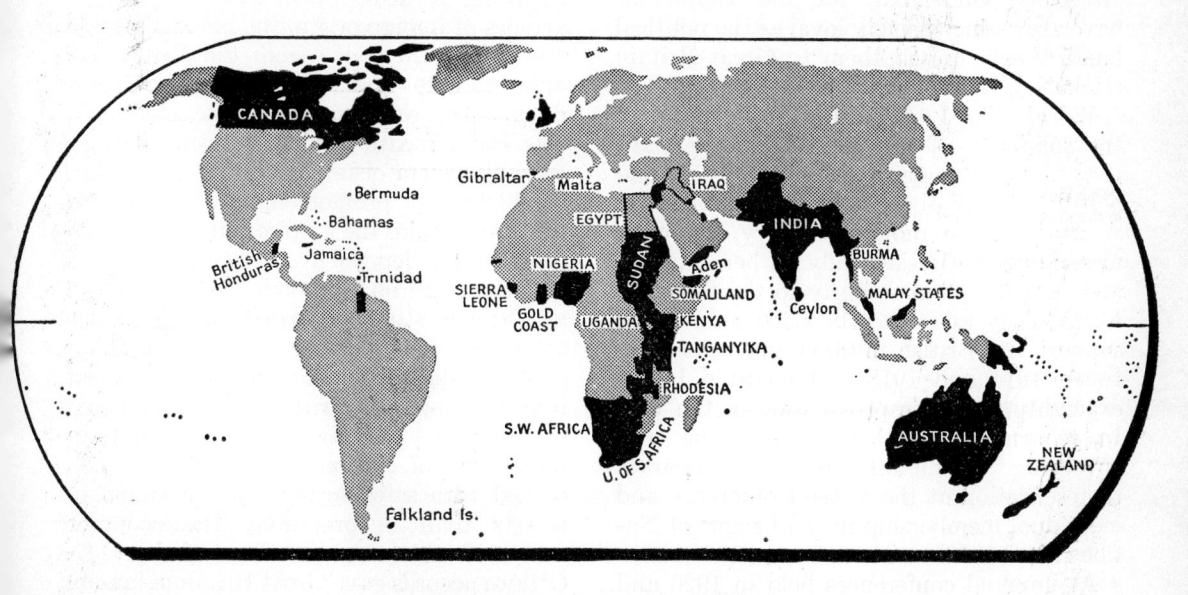

THE BRITISH EMPIRE IN 1939

tionalism was spreading through the Arabian world, and the state of Saudi Arabia, with a population of possibly 10,000,000 and an area of 1,000,000 square miles, was taking shape in the Arabian peninsula. The demand of the Arabs to incorporate the whole area from Yemen to Syria created one more threat to the peace of the Near East.

5. THE SELF-GOVERNING DOMINIONS

The political tie which binds Great Britain to the self-governing Dominions, Canada, Newfoundland, Australia, New Zealand, the Union of South Africa, and the Irish Free State, has been largely transformed in recent years into an empire partnership between semi-autonomous states.[1] As early as 1897, the prime ministers of the British Dominions (as then constituted) assembled in London for the first Imperial Conference, and numerous meetings of this empire cabinet have been held since that date. Its resolutions are recommended to the separate Dominion governments, which may or may not adopt them, and the divergent interests of the sister states not infrequently make cooperation difficult and complete agreement impossible. Nevertheless, the wisdom of allowing these major colonies to assume complete control of their own affairs has been strikingly vindicated, for the Dominions have grown increasingly loyal as the political bonds which united them to Great Britain slackened to a nominal tie.

World War I afforded effective proof of the solidarity of the British Empire. Although not technically bound by the treaty commitments of the mother country, the colonies rallied enthusiastically to her support, and contributed generously to the final victory. They raised nearly 1,500,000 men to support the British military operations between 1914 and 1918 and incurred heavy expenditures in the prosecution of the war. In recognition of these efforts, the self-governing Dominions received separate representation at the Peace Conference and individual membership in the League of Nations after 1918.

Dominions in the war

At imperial conferences held in 1926 and 1930, the question of the precise status of the British self-governing Dominions was further elaborated, and subsequently defined in the Statute of Westminster passed by the House of Commons in 1931. Henceforth the Dominions were to be recognized as "autonomous communities within the British Empire, equal in status, in no way subordinate one to another in any aspect of their domestic or foreign affairs, though united by a common allegiance to the Crown, and freely associated as members of the British Commonwealth of Nations...." In virtue of their new dignity, the Dominions have the privilege (with reservations) of contracting treaties with foreign states, and may establish direct diplomatic relations by appointing ministers to foreign capitals. As the white population of the empire overseas is increasing much more rapidly than the population of Great Britain, it is possible to envisage a time, a few years hence, when the Dominions will achieve an equality in numbers, in wealth, and in power, which will accord logically with their equality of rank.

Statute of Westminster

New economic forces working for imperial unity have come into play since 1931 when Great Britain abandoned the principle of free trade. While imposing a tariff upon many articles of foreign origin, the new regulations still permitted goods from the British colonies to enter the United Kingdom free of duty. The co-operation of the Dominions was invited with a view to establishing a general system of imperial preference which would help to promote imperial trade relations and make the empire largely self-sufficient and independent of foreign markets. But the Imperial Economic Conference held at Ottawa (1932) revealed the difficulties attending such a course, for the Dominions showed a disposition to protect their nascent industries against British competition, and as individual partners in the British Commonwealth of Nations they were more concerned with safeguarding their national interests than in promoting the economic unity of the empire. Nevertheless, the Ottawa accords gave Great Britain a favored position as a market for such products as

Imperial preference

---

[1] For India see pages 868–873.

HOUSE OF PARLIAMENT, CANBERRA, NEW SOUTH WALES, AUSTRALIA

Left:

HOUSE OF PARLIAMENT, OTTAWA, CANADA

Below:

HOUSE OF PARLIAMENT, CAPE TOWN, UNION OF SOUTH AFRICA

The Statute of Westminster (1931) recognized Canada, Australia, New Zealand, and the Union of South Africa as self-governing dominions in the British Commonwealth of Nations. Like Eire (Ireland) they became sovereign states.

Canadian wheat and Australian mutton, while the Dominions agreed to accept British coal, iron, and steel, and various commercial products, in preference to similar exports from foreign sources.

Increased liberties involve increased responsibilities, but the Dominion governments sometimes have been slow to realize this and reluctant to acknowledge their dependence upon the protection afforded them by the British fleet. The forty-seven million inhabitants of the United Kingdom support by their taxes the naval, military and air forces which constitute the empire's line of defense, while the thirty million people living in the self-governing Dominions devote a much smaller proportion of their revenues and their attention to the problem of imperial armaments. Australia and New Zealand, through fear of Japan, have displayed a greater readiness to co-operate with the mother country in these matters than Canada or the Union of South Africa, but in general the attitude of the emancipated colonies has been one of acquiescence in benefits received. Their people felt, perhaps rightly, that in founding new provinces and subduing new lands to the uses of British civilization, they were serving the empire in an original fashion and in adequate measure, and they continued to rely on British protection.

Imperial defense

69

France Seeks Security

> If Germany will not pay up, the Treaty of Versailles affords us a remedy. Article 248 gives the Allies a priority claim against all the property and resources of the German Empire and the German states.
>
> RAYMOND POINCARÉ (1922).

> The High Contracting Parties solemnly declare, in the names of their respective peoples, that they condemn recourse to war for the solution of international controversies and renounce it as an instrument of national policy in their relations with one another.
>
> BRIAND-KELLOGG PEACE PACT (1928).

THROUGHOUT WORLD WAR I the French people fought for their national liberties in the profound conviction that they were defending their fatherland against an unwarranted and premeditated attack. This assumption that Germany and her allies were responsible for the war, that they had plotted it in a desperate gamble for European hegemony, and fought it with the systematic intention of crippling France, in particular, beyond the possibility of recovery, colored the outlook of the French people after 1914 and settled their stand on questions of foreign policy. Believing themselves to have been the innocent victims of Teutonic fury, they emerged from the war of 1914–18 with two fixed ideas: that Germany must be made to pay to the utmost possible limit for the loss and damage which France and her allies had suffered, and that Europe must be safeguarded in future from the danger of a second conflict precipitated by German lust for conquest.

1. THE WORK OF RECLAMATION

By 1918 the French war losses, in proportion to the population and wealth of the country, were heavier than those of any other great power. The war dead numbered 1,385,000; the war expenditures exceeded $26,000,000,000; and the property destroyed in the devastated regions was estimated at a further $20,000,000,000 or more. Ten of the richest departments of the republic, the heart of industrial France, had suffered for over four years from the destructive effects of warfare and enemy occupation. Forests had been cut down, mines flooded, factories wrecked, thousands of towns, villages, farms, wells, and bridges destroyed, and an area as large as the State of Maryland transformed into a waste region of ruin and desolation.

Upon the conclusion of peace, the French people devoted themselves with admirable decision and energy to the work of reclaiming the devastated regions. Trenches and barbed-wire entanglements were removed, fortifications and gun emplacements demolished, hidden mines extracted, and the poisoned earth of shell-torn fields restored to productive uses. The replacement of ruined factories and wrecked machinery provided an opportunity for remodeling and modernizing many of the industrial plants, with results highly beneficial and stimulating to French manufacturing methods. Moreover, the colossal task of rebuilding and refurnishing three quarters of a million private dwellings and other edifices provided employment for millions of workers and induced a wave of

The devastated regions

The work of reclamation

prosperity in many lines of trade. In less than ten years the scars left by the war had all but vanished and the countryside of northeastern France once more supported five million industrial workers and farmers. Only a few square miles of desert, preserved in all their desolate horror as mementoes of the conflict, bore witness to man's ingenuity in the art of destruction and served as a warning to future generations.

The extravagant outlay required for this work of reclamation greatly increased the French national debt. German reparation payments were expected to cancel the expenditure, but unfortunately for the French hopes it proved impossible to make Germany pay the sums anticipated. A large portion of the French people, convinced that the Germans were deliberately defaulting, favored strong measures, and clung to the belief that full reparation could be exacted if the Allied governments preserved an implacable attitude. A stubborn conviction that Germany could pay and should pay for the devastation wrought by the invading armies blinded Frenchmen to the realities of the situation, and greatly complicated the whole question of war debts and reparations from 1919 to 1932.

2. THE REPARATIONS TANGLE

When the Treaty of Versailles was signed in June, 1919, seven months after the war ended, the Allied governments had not yet filed their complete claims for indemnification against Germany. The Germans were ordered to commence payments in money and materials, but they did not learn until 1921 their total liability, which the reparations commission fixed at approximately $33,000,000,000.[1] Financial experts pointed out that no precedent existed for the transfer of such an enormous sum, and that even if the payments were spread over many years the attempt to collect them would dislocate the framework of international finance, but the cupidity of the victors rendered them deaf to the cautions of the economists. The French had a major interest in forcing payment because they were to receive fifty-two per cent of the total reparations payments.

The German nation was crippled by the strain of war and the long blockade, by the loss of valuable colonies and shipping and the cost of supporting an army of occupation.

Germany defaults

Moreover, the Germans regarded the demand for reparations as totally unjust and had no will to contribute more than they were compelled to yield. In 1922, instead of the $180,000,000 in gold marks demanded, they paid only $112,000,000; and their payments in goods, estimated at $550,000,000, likewise fell behind. Recognizing that Germany had been brought to the verge of a ruinous financial collapse, the British government proposed a revision of the reparations terms; but France, dominated by a Nationalist *bloc* headed by the intractable Raymond Poincaré, favored punitive measures. Declaring Germany in default, Poincaré ordered French troops to seize the Ruhr Valley, the nerve-center of German industry, and hold it until payments were forthcoming.

A catastrophic collapse of German credit followed. The mark, already inflated when the French entered the Ruhr (January, 1923), fell faster than the printing presses could operate, until notes for a billion marks were needed to pay for a single meal. Since the stabilization of German currency was an indispensable preliminary if Germany was to resume payment, the late Allies agreed to reduce the burden of reparation temporarily to $250,000,000 a year, and to arrange for a foreign loan of $200,000,000 to promote the recovery of German industry. The international committee which devised this compromise was headed by an American, Charles Gates Dawes, and the project was subsequently known as the Dawes Plan. Under this arrangement Germany paid $1,896,860,-000 between 1924 and 1929. The French and Belgian troops which had occupied the Ruhr Valley were withdrawn in 1925.

The Dawes Plan (1924)

In 1929, the Dawes Plan was superseded

---

[1] This was an approximate sum, which was to be increased if it were found that the capacity of the Germans to pay had been underrated. The Allied governments had demanded (January, 1921), a total of $56,000,000,-000.

by a new project which took its title from another American adviser, Owen D. Young. The Young Plan fixed the sum which Germany still owed on reparations at $9,000,000,000 and provided for a scale of annual payments to run for fifty-nine years. Ratification of this new pact was followed (1930) by the withdrawal of the last Allied forces from the Rhineland, and Germany indicated her good faith by continuing her payments to the extent of $685,916,000.

The Young Plan (1929)

In 1931, however, the world-wide economic depression led President Hoover of the United States to suggest a one-year moratorium on all intergovernmental debts, a proposal which the debtor nations readily adopted. Recognizing that Germany would not be in a position to renew reparation payments when the moratorium expired, the Allies concluded a fresh agreement known as the Lausanne Settlement (1932). The reparations total still outstanding was cut drastically to about $2,000,000,000, a sum which the German government might reasonably discharge in time. But subsequent developments in Germany, which will be discussed in the following chapter, made it improbable that any further remittances on the reparations account would be forthcoming.

Lausanne Settlement

With the Lausanne Settlement the Allied governments finally acknowledged the impossibility of making the defeated nations pay the indemnity demanded. Reparations ceased to be a vital problem in international affairs, and the fierce and acrid controversy which had beclouded the issue for thirteen years passed into history. Yet even in the ledgers Allied and German estimates continued to clash, for the Germans calculated the value of their total remittances at nearly $13,000,000,000, while their late foes credited them with less than $5,000,000,000. This eight-billion-dollar discrepancy was traceable to divergent estimates regarding the value of the "tangible assets" — ships, cars, cattle, munitions, manufactured and raw material, etc. — which Germany had surrendered.

In releasing Germany from nine tenths of the obligations specified in the Young Plan, the delegates of Great Britain, France, Belgium, and the other nations represented at the Lausanne Conference, were influenced by the hope that the United States in turn would cancel the loans advanced to the Allies during the World War. These obligations the American government had already reduced from eleven to seven billion dollars, but the debtor states sought to make further repayment conditional upon the collection of the reparations demanded from Germany. In other words, France, Britain, Belgium, etc., would pay the United States when and if Germany paid them. It followed from this argument that since Germany in 1932 was relieved of all but a small fraction of her reparation liabilities, the debts owed by the Allies to the United States should be cut in the same proportion. This confusion of reparations and intergovernmental obligations the United States refused to sanction, with the result that after 1932 all the European nations in debt to America (except Finland) made reductions in their payments, and many of them defaulted altogether.

The war debts

3. THE SEARCH FOR SECURITY

After 1924, the French attitude toward Germany was characterized by greater moderation and a more conciliatory spirit. The intransigent policy of Poincaré and the Nationalist *bloc* having failed to solve the reparations tangle, a new French cabinet was formed from the parties of the Center and Left. The portfolio of foreign affairs was entrusted to Aristide Briand, whose efforts from 1924 to 1931 to promote more cordial relations among European states won him the Nobel peace prize.

But to solve the financial dilemma created by the cost of reconstruction and by official extravagance, the French turned again to Poincaré in 1926. The franc had fallen from its prewar value of nearly twenty cents to less than two, and France hovered on the verge of that bottomless pit of inflation which had engulfed German credit three years earlier. Poincaré's firm policies, as head of a Nationalist government, saved the day, and the

Savior of the franc

franc was stabilized at approximately four cents. By 1927, France revealed signs of a brisk business recovery, and by 1931 French prosperity excited the envy of the world. With little unemployment, humming factories, a good wheat and potato crop, and an enormous gold reserve, the republic appeared immune to the general depression which had set in. But Poincaré, the "savior of the franc" as he had been named by the grateful bourgeoisie, was forced to retire in 1929 because of ill-health, and the National Union ministry which he had headed fell from power.

Despite the recovery of Alsace and Lorraine, World War I left France weaker in manpower than in 1914. The consciousness that their fatherland had a smaller population than any other great power, and that the death rate equaled, when it did not exceed, the birth rate, filled Frenchmen with apprehension for their future security. As better protection against a new invasion from Germany, they demanded that the left bank of the Rhine should be ceded to France, or at least erected into a neutral state. But Lloyd George and Woodrow Wilson opposed these claims at the Peace Conference, and Clemenceau was driven to accept instead the promise of a treaty whereby the United States and Great Britain would guarantee France against any future threat of unprovoked aggression. This Wilsonian pledge was repudiated by the United States Senate and subsequently disallowed by Great Britain. In chagrin and disillusionment the French turned to more practical measures of protection.

The war divided the European states into two main groups: those which had gained by the peace settlements and those which had lost by them. French statesmen decided, in realistic fashion, that the nations which had gained territorially, especially those which had acquired more perhaps than their just share, would be eager to stand with France against any power or combination of powers that favored revision. To encircle Germany with a coalition of states pledged to oppose any renewal of the Teuton threat became once again, as before the war, the cardinal aim of French diplomacy.

With Belgium, France concluded a secret defensive alliance in 1920. Comrades in war, the French and Belgians were also united in peace, for they had substantial interests in common, including fear of a German revival and the claim to a major share of the expected indemnity.

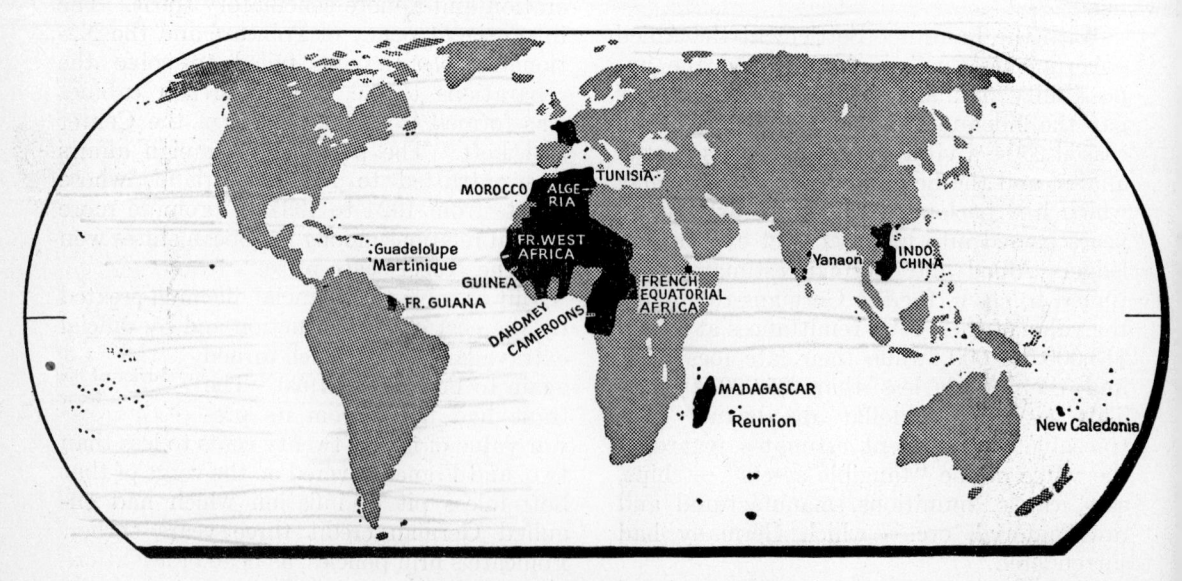

Belgium

FRENCH COLONIAL EMPIRE, 1939

FRENCH CHAMBER OF DEPUTIES

The Chamber of Deputies was a scene of factional strife as cabinet after cabinet failed to keep sufficient strength to steer France on a steady course.

TWO STATESMEN OF THE PERIOD: ARISTIDE BRIAND (*left*) AND LÉON BLUM (*right*)

FRENCH POLITICS, 1919–1939

Poland

Poland, re-created by the peace treaty from territory which before the war had belonged to Russia, Germany, and Austria, likewise anticipated with misgiving the day when Germany would arise from her defeat. A Franco-Polish Pact was concluded in 1921, providing for a common policy in foreign affairs and a concerted defense if either of the signatories were attacked. The following year France strengthened the alliance with gold links, advancing several hundred million francs for the construction of Polish armaments and other national projects. France was buying allies.

The Little Entente

The three states which profited most extensively from the dismemberment of the Austro-Hungarian Empire — Czechoslovakia, Rumania, and Yugoslavia — were particularly concerned to avert the possible return of the Hapsburgs to Vienna and the resurrection of the Dual Monarchy. In 1920, these succession states formed a protective alliance known as the Little Entente. Poland, already allied with France (1921), entered into an understanding with the Little Entente later in the same year. A new network of pacts and protocols was thus rapidly taking shape, to replace that which had preceded the war. France definitely bound the Little Entente powers to her side by contracting formal treaties with Czechoslovakia (1924) and Yugoslavia (1927). Loans for the purchase of French munitions were advanced with a lavish hand, and French officers were commissioned to assist in organizing the armies of the new allies. In knitting together this band of armed and vigilant states, which stretched from the Baltic Sea to the Adriatic, French statesmen served two purposes at once. They believed that the threat of the hostile band encircling their borders could be relied upon to keep the defeated nations (Germany, Austria, and Hungary) neutral and quiescent. But a further service of the league, no less important in French eyes, was the exclusion of Russian revolutionary influences from Europe. The student should study the map of Europe after World War I, and note how successfully the French system of alliances served both these aims. Poland, reconstructed chiefly at Russian expense, and Rumania, which had seized Bessarabia without Russian consent, could be counted upon to maintain a jealous guard and to constitute a *cordon sanitaire* which would check the infiltration of Bolshevist propaganda into Europe.

Nor did the French neglect, while securing allies, to augment their own military forces. Their army in the post-war decade was the most powerful in the world. Their air force was the largest and perhaps the best equipped. Their armament appropriations were more extravagant than in pre-war years. They spent billions of francs for the construction of defenses along their German border (the "Maginot Line"), and after 1930 they strengthened the fortifications along their Italian frontier also. Although Germany had been disarmed, and France had inherited the military hegemony of Europe, French statesmen were harassed by the fear that secret projects would be formed for a war of revenge, just as Bismarck, after the Prussian triumph of 1870–71, was haunted by his "nightmare of coalitions."

French armaments

Uneasy lies the head that wears a victor's crown. From 1919 on, a succession of fears harried the French public: fear that Germany would become a communist state and join Bolshevist Russia in proclaiming a world revolution; fear that the Germans were secretly rearming; fear that Italy would support Germany in demanding a revision of the Versailles Treaty. It was such alarms that made a rational consideration of the reparations problem impossible, and precipitated the seizure of the Ruhr Valley (1923), with the subsequent collapse of the German mark. In 1931, a projected customs union between Germany and Austria, which might have relieved the desperate economic plight of the Austrian people by linking them commercially to their stronger neighbor, was frustrated largely through French opposition. Such a pact, it appeared to the enemies of Germany, might easily prove the prelude to a political union of the two German states, and the Treaty of Versailles had specifically prohibited such an *Anschluss*. The precaution proved futile after 1933.

MODERN FRANCE

The beauty of the French châteaux, suggested by Chenonceau (above, left), has attracted millions of tourists; and Paris with its Arc de Triomphe (above, right) has long been a mecca for artists. The painting, "Anemones and Mirror" (right), is by Henri Matisse, a leading French post-impressionist.

4. THE PEACE PACTS

Since it was the earnest desire of French statesmen to maintain the *status quo* as established by the Treaty of Versailles, they stressed the defensive character of the alliances which they negotiated, and affirmed that France was ready at all times to enter any wider accord that would guarantee greater security and tranquillity to the nations of Europe and the world. France, and Italy also, sent delegates to the Washington Naval Conference of 1922,[1] and both these states agreed to a limitation of naval armaments on a ratio of 5 : 5 : 3 : 1.67 : 1.67 for Great Britain, the United States, Japan, France, and Italy, respectively. France also supported the League of Nations in its efforts to promote peace and arbitrate disputes (so long as the League did not recommend any revision of the Versailles Pact), and the League's repeated attempts to find an acceptable formula for the limitation of armaments enjoyed French approval "in principle." In 1924, Premier Edouard Herriot of France and Ramsay MacDonald of Great Britain formulated a project (the Geneva Protocol) for the pacific settlement of international disputes, but the agreement failed to thrive after MacDonald's Labor ministry in England was overthrown by the Conservatives a few months later.

In 1925, abandoning for the moment the search for a general formula against war, Aristide Briand of France and Gustav Stresemann of Germany joined in urging a conference to settle some of the outstanding controversies which threatened European peace. At Locarno, Switzerland, representatives of France, Germany, Great Britain, Italy, Belgium, Poland, and Czechoslovakia concluded five treaties of arbitration, the most important of which bound France, Germany, Great Britain, Italy, and Belgium to guarantee the existing boundaries between Germany and Belgium and Germany and France. By this Rhine Pact, the French abandoned any proposal to set up a buffer state in the Rhineland and the Germans acknowledged the permanent loss of Alsace-Lorraine, a compromise which did much to mollify the bitterness between the two nations. Furthermore, France, Germany, and Belgium pledged themselves to refer their future disputes to arbitration, and Germany made a similar agreement with Poland and Czechoslovakia. Lovers of peace everywhere hailed these "regional understandings," and pledges to negotiate, as cornerstones for the temple of peace, but in actuality the Locarno treaties were monuments to a momentary good-will rather than enduring evidence of a new spirit or policy. The French, at least, saw nothing inconsistent in signing at the same time pacts of mutual defense with Poland and Czechoslovakia.

Briand's efforts to curb war did not end at Locarno. In 1928, as a result of diplomatic conversations which he had conducted with Frank B. Kellogg, secretary of state for the United States, an anti-war pledge was devised and submitted to the representatives of fifteen nations meeting in Paris. This Briand-Kellogg Pact (or Paris Pact as it is often termed) was accepted within a short time by nearly fifty nations. The contracting governments pledged themselves to renounce war as an instrument of national policy in their relations with one another, and to seek a solution for any disputes which might arise among them by pacific means and pacific means only. In adopting this solemn and definitive agreement to outlaw war, however, each nation reserved to itself the right to take up arms in its own defense, or in order to punish a state which had violated the pact or flouted the Covenant of the League of Nations. As civilized states never resort to war save on the pretext that they are defending their rights, these reservations all but invalidated the purpose of the earlier clauses.

How little genuine trust the governments of the European states placed in the various peace pacts which they negotiated was grimly reflected in their armament budgets. With the exception of Germany and Austria, compulsorily disarmed after their defeat, all the great powers increased their military and naval defenses during the decade 1920–30. Great Britain, France, and Italy had expended approximately $900,000,000 on ar-

---

[1] See above, page 917.

maments in the year before World War I opened, pleading fear of German militarism as their chief excuse; yet in the ten years which followed a peace treaty which left Germany prostrate, they not only failed to reduce their expenditures for war purposes, but raised them to a total of $1,250,000,000, an increase of almost forty per cent. The secondary powers likewise felt obliged to strain their resources in the same desperate competition.

After 1933, the fear which had haunted French minds since 1919, the fear that Germany would rearm and demand a revision of the Versailles Treaty under the threat of war, became a reality. In a series of dramatic strokes, Adolf Hitler as the leader of a resurgent nation, reintroduced compulsory military service, occupied and fortified the demilitarized Rhineland zone, organized a fleet of war planes the equal of any in the world, and enlarged the German Reich by absorbing Austria and invading Czechoslovakia. This rapid emergence of Germany as the leading European power (which will be discussed more fully in the second chapter following) greatly weakened the position of France. Of the lesser states which French statesmen had courted, Belgium affirmed her neutrality, Poland drifted into the German orbit, Austria ceased to exist as an entity, Czechoslovakia, stripped of defenses, made terms with Germany, and the surviving members of the Little Entente, Rumania and Yugoslavia, adopted a more conciliatory attitude toward Berlin. By 1938 France was reduced almost to a passive attitude in foreign affairs, following obediently the hesitant and ambiguous rôle of Great Britain, while pressing with grim fatalism her program of defensive armaments.

French power wanes

70

Germany Seeks Equality

> And in this moment I can only repeat, within the hearing of the world, that no threat and no force will ever induce the German nation again to renounce those fundamental rights which no sovereign state can be denied.
>
> ADOLF HITLER (January 30, 1934).

THE REVOLUTIONARY OUTBREAKS in Germany during the last days of World War I,[1] which overturned the imperial régime and drove the kaiser into exile, delivered the fate of the empire temporarily into the hands of the Socialists. Had the Social Democratic Party remained united, it might have commanded an unquestioned majority in the subsequent elections, but during the war it had been split into three groups. The Majority Socialists headed by Friedrich Ebert and Philip Scheidemann favored a moderate program aiming at the progressive socialization of industry; the Independent Social Democrats insisted upon the immediate socialization of industry by constitutional decree; while the radical Spartacists clamored for the dictatorship of the proletariat on the Russian model. From the resulting struggle for control after the armistice, the Majority Socialists emerged in the lead. A Spartacist revolt was harshly suppressed, and an assembly elected to prepare a constitution (January, 1919). This Weimar Assembly accepted the peace treaty dictated by the Allies, and organized a government for the German Republic.

1. THE ORGANIZATION OF THE GERMAN REPUBLIC

The Weimar Constitution Under the Weimar Constitution, proclaimed in August, 1919, Germany became a democratic republic of federated states. The executive authority was vested in a president, elected by direct ballot for a period of seven years. The legislature consisted of the Reichstag, a popular chamber of more than five hundred members chosen by universal suffrage, and the Reichsrat, a federal council or senate of some seventy members in which the eighteen states composing the new Germany were represented in the order of their importance. The constitution confided the control of foreign affairs, national defense, tariffs and taxation to the central parliament at Berlin, ordained that the local governments in the component states should be republican and democratic in form, guaranteed freedom of speech and of the press, and promised equality before the law to all citizens. Popular rule was supposedly safeguarded by permitting the Reichstag to overrule the Reichsrat by a two-thirds vote, and by making the federal chancellor and ministry responsible to the lower chamber. In an emergency, however, the president had power to suspend the constitutional guaranties and the chancellor might rule by decree, provided the Reichstag consented. This provision left open a portal through which a popular dictator might enter and take over control if the Reichstag deputies were hypnotized or overawed and yielded him emergency powers which they could not reclaim.

Friedrich Ebert became the first president of the German Republic and Philip Scheidemann its first chancellor. A *bloc* made up of Majority Socialists, Christian Democrats (the former Catholic Center Party), and Democrats (Bourgeois Republicans) domi-

[1] See above, page 852.

nated the cabinet, while the Independent Socialists on the Left Wing (the People's Party) and the Nationalists on the Right Wing (Conservatives and Monarchists) sat as a divided opposition. Public opinion shifted steadily away from the proletariat to the bourgeoisie, and the more radical promises of the revolutionary days were not fulfilled, but earnest attempts were made, despite the financial confusion of the post-war years, to construct public parks, swimming pools, gymnasiums and libraries for the workers, to shorten hours and improve labor conditions, and to replace slum districts with model homes available at a reasonable rental.

This moderate program, a "betrayal" of the proletariat in the opinion of uncompromising radicals, incited the Communists to abortive plots against the government which the police suppressed without grave difficulty. More threatening were the Nationalist demonstrations, sponsored by ex-army officers disgusted with the rule of Socialists and Liberals who had "betrayed" Germany by signing an ignominious peace. Two leading liberal statesmen, Matthias Erzberger and Walter Rathenau, who had earned the hatred of the Nationalists, were assassinated, and several attempts were made to overturn the republic by militarist uprisings. In 1920 a group of soldiers headed for Berlin, but were foiled by a general strike of the railway workers. Three years later, General Erich von Ludendorff, and a vigorous political orator, Adolf Hitler, sought to organize a *coup* to overthrow the "inglorious republic," but were likewise unsuccessful. Hitler and other collaborators in the Munich "Beer Hall *Putsch*" were arrested and sentenced to prison.

2. ECONOMIC CHAOS AND RECOVERY

The Munich *Putsch* marked a crisis in the difficult days when inflation was ruining millions of Germans, when reparations were an acute issue, and the French seized the Ruhr Valley in an effort to make Germany pay. Economic and psychological factors rather than political ideals were shaping German destiny and would make or unmake the precarious Weimar régime established in 1919. After 1924 economic conditions improved steadily and political agitation declined until a new economic crisis revived the popular discontent and resentment after 1929.

The German financial situation after World War I would have been serious even without the problem of reparations. For the credit of the imperial government had been overtaxed, and before the fighting ended in 1918 the mark had declined to half its value. The peace terms, the sequestration of the Rhineland, deprivation of colonies and shipping, and imposition of reparations made German economic recovery almost impossible. The paper mark, nominally worth about twenty-four cents in gold, continued to fall in value until by 1923 it became literally worthless, and a new currency had to be issued for which the agricultural and industrial wealth of Germany was pledged as security. The Dawes Plan,[1] which provided for a foreign loan of $200,000,000 to stimulate the recovery of German industry, marked a turning point in the tide of economic distress. Thereafter business conditions improved slowly, but the inflation had ruined a large creditor class, and millions of Germans had seen their bonds, mortgages, and other securities repudiated or else paid off in paper marks which were finally redeemed at one billionth of their normal value.

The inflation

Yet all was not lost. Despite the suffering, the sacrifices, and the financial *débâcle*, the German people still possessed their habits of industry and efficiency, the workers had not lost their craftsmanship nor the experts their technical training. With the stabilization of the currency, business revived, industrial plants expanded, and exports increased rapidly. The annual reparations tribute of $250,000,000 payable under the Dawes Plan, though galling to national pride, was lighter than the cost of maintaining first-class armaments. Factories and shipyards worked overtime to replace the goods and ships surrendered to the Allies, unemployment decreased, and the frugal

Economic recovery

[1] See above, page 926.

GUSTAV STRESEMANN (1878–1929)

Above: As German minister for foreign affairs from 1923 to 1929, Stresemann strove to co-operate with other powers for the resettlement of Europe.

FRIEDRICH EBERT (1871–1925)

Left: Ebert, a saddler, and a leader in the German Social Democratic Party, was elected first president of the German Republic in 1919.

EINE MILLIARDE MARK

In 1923, the French declared Germany in default on reparations and seized the Ruhr district. German currency, already inflated, became worthless. This note would correspond to $240,000,000 under the 1914 value of the mark, but it was small change when put into circulation.

living standards in Germany enabled the manufacturers to produce their wares more cheaply and invade foreign markets despite discriminatory tariffs. By 1929, the German merchant marine was approaching the total of its pre-war tonnage, the industrial output exceeded that of 1913, and for the first time in fifteen years the value of Germany's exports surpassed that of her imports.

After 1929, however, this promising expansion of German industry suffered a series of checks. Domestic replacement and reconstruction was largely at an end; world trade declined sharply under the blight of the economic depression; foreign loans to Germany practically ceased; and several foreign nations inflated their currencies and offered sharper competition in the world markets. By 1934, the German trade balance had once more turned passive; that is, German exports fell short of German imports in value. One reason for this economic decline was the spirit of distrust and antagonism which the Germans excited among their neighbors after 1932. The political vicissitudes in Germany which gave rise to this international suspicion must now be discussed.

3. STRESEMANN AND THE SPIRIT OF CONCILIATION

The heritage of hate left by World War I, and the grievance felt by all Germans at the heavy terms of peace, made it difficult for Germany to re-establish normal relations with neighboring states. Bitterness over the reparations issue culminated in 1923 when the French, declaring Germany in default, seized the Ruhr Valley. With the adoption of the Dawes Plan the following year, however, and the subsequent evacuation of the Ruhr, Franco-German relations improved. The German people continued to resent the "guilt clause" in the Versailles Treaty and to condemn the extortion of reparations; they denounced the confiscation of their colonies without compensation and deplored the humiliating and defenseless status to which the treaty had reduced them; but their economic recovery after 1924 made them more philosophical about these injustices, and they sought for peaceful means whereby they might recover the equal place among the great powers to which their population, culture, and industrial progress entitled them.

From 1923 to 1929, the portfolio of foreign affairs in the German cabinet was held by Gustav Stresemann, a statesman who displayed remarkable tact in restoring Germany's international prestige. As a patriot and a realist Stresemann comprehended that a policy of conciliation might win favorable revision of the peace terms, whereas a policy of recalcitrance would only aggravate the evils of an irksome settlement. In 1925, he proposed that France and Germany abandon their watchful hostility by negotiating a security pact through which both would guarantee to respect the existing frontiers. Fortunately, Stresemann found in Aristide Briand, French foreign minister, a statesman no less eager to improve international relations, and the fruits of their joint labors were the Locarno treaties.[1] Germany agreed to arbitration pacts with France, Poland, and Czechoslovakia, and renounced all claim to Alsace-Lorraine. The spirit of cordiality which prevailed at Locarno proved that there could be peace among men of goodwill and seemed a hopeful augury for the future of European tranquillity.

The Locarno Pacts (1925)

The admission of Germany to membership in the League of Nations (1926) marked a further triumph for Stresemann's diplomacy, for, in assuming an equal status and a permanent seat on the League Council, the German Republic cast off much of the stigma of isolation and defeat which since 1919 had excluded the nation from its merited place among the European states. When the Briand-Kellogg Peace Pact was proposed in 1928,[2] Germany was one of the first to concur in renouncing war as an instrument of national policy. In the year of Stresemann's untimely death (1929), he was able to perform a final service for his country by facilitating the negotiation of the Young Plan,[3] winning a promise that the last Allied forces of occupation would be withdrawn from the Rhineland by the following year.

The honesty and moderation of Strese-

[1] See above, page 932.
[2] See above, page 932.
[3] See above, page 927.

mann's policies had thus wrung some notable concessions from the victor powers, and the stability and responsibility of the German Republic seemed to be assured. The German people were by no means reconciled to the position of disarmament and economic vassalage imposed by the Versailles Treaty, but they were disposed to emancipate themselves by peaceful and diplomatic means provided these promised them relief within a reasonable period. To ardent German nationalists, however, the concessions gained by Stresemann appeared too meager and too dilatory. As the memory of the war dimmed, the mood of socialism and pacifism which had dominated the first years of the republic waned also, and a mounting nationalistic fervor replaced it.

The election (1925) of Field Marshal Paul von Hindenburg as president of the republic revealed a latent veneration among the masses for those principles of discipline and authority which had distinguished the imperial régime. Hindenburg served the republic in his new capacity with the same rugged fidelity and dignity with which he had once served his emperor, and in 1932 the German people re-elected him, at the age of eighty-five, for a second presidential term. But it was significant that the monarchists and militarists, who had supported him in 1925, found his loyalty to his oath of office and to moderate republican principles a disappointment, and in 1932 he owed his re-election to the votes of Socialists and bourgeois republicans.

Hindenburg as president

4. HITLER AND THE SPIRIT OF RECALCITRANCE

Hindenburg's chief opponent in the election of 1932 was Adolf Hitler, a popular leader whose spectacular rise to power gave a new direction to German politics. Born in Austria in 1889, Hitler had served in the German armies during World War I, and after the peace had plunged into a career of political agitation. For his share, with Ludendorff, in an attempt to overthrow the republic (1923), he was imprisoned for a short term, but on his release he renewed his efforts to organize a party modeled on the pattern of the Italian *Fascisti*. Like Mussolini, Hitler recognized that nationalism and socialism were the two strongest political forces of the day, and he attempted to fuse them into a National-Socialist program. His propaganda and his plan of operations were proclaimed in a remarkable, vehement, and widely read book which he had dictated during his imprisonment and named *Mein Kampf* (My Struggle). By his impassioned oratory, and his denunciation of the "pacifist traitors" who had "stabbed Germany in the back" in 1918, and crowned their infamy by accepting a dishonorable peace, he awakened a fierce response, particularly among youthful enthusiasts, and discredited the Weimar Constitution. Organized bands of National-Socialist (or "Nazi") agitators carried Hitler's banners throughout Germany, attacked his political opponents, especially the Communists, with violence, and committed many brutal and disorderly acts. The Jews were marked out for systematic persecution on the ground that they had evaded their patriotic duties during the war and had enriched themselves in unscrupulous fashion amid the national misery that followed it. The Nazis' use of violence, terrorism, and even assassination to promote their aims made them abhorrent to many observers, particularly outside Germany, but they continued to increase their following by exploiting the inflamed spirit of German nationalism, and by a shrewd appeal to the German middle class which had been largely reduced to ruin and impotence by the war, the currency *débâcle*, and the taxes imposed by the Socialist régime.

Adolf Hitler

The successive election totals tell the story of the National-Socialist triumph. In 1928, the Nazis held only 12 seats in the German Reichstag. But the mounting economic difficulties deepened the indignation of the electorate, and the business depression multiplied the number of unemployed to over four million by 1930. The election of that year raised the National-Socialist representation to 107. The cabinet, resting chiefly upon the support of the Center and the People's Party, under the chancellorship of Heinrich Brüning, steadily lost ground. Had France

National-Socialists

A HITLER SPEECH

The German National-Socialists stressed the leadership principle and the power and discipline of the Party; and Hitler's impassioned oratory had an extraordinarily hypnotic effect upon the German people.

and Britain proved more prompt in easing the reparations burden, or made some other substantial concessions to German pride, the Brüning régime might have survived; but instead, the projected customs union between Germany and Austria [1] was frustrated chiefly through French opposition, and the Germans, thus forcibly reminded once again of their ignominious vassalage, listened the more readily to the defiant proposals of the National-Socialists. In 1932, the latter doubled their vote, winning 230 seats in the Reichstag, and emerging as the strongest political party of the republic. Hindenburg, who distrusted Hitler as a demagogue, hesitated at first to invest him with the chancellorship; but in January, 1933, he yielded, and a cabinet was formed under Nazi direction.

With their advent to power the National-Socialists undertook a complete reorganization of the republic. A new election, ordered in March, 1933, confirmed their supremacy, increasing their parliamentary lead to 288, which gave them a clear majority, as they could count upon the support of 52 Nationalist deputies. A fire of incendiary origin which destroyed the Reichstag building on the eve of the election was promptly blamed upon the Communists. In retaliation the government applied the "emergency clause" of the Weimar Constitution, suspended civil liberties, suppressed opposition newspapers, and invoked coercive measures against recalcitrant voters. Although the Communist leaders denounced the Reichstag conflagration as a Nazi plot, and denied all responsibility for it, they were imprisoned and their party dissolved. The following June, the Social Democratic Party (the Majority Socialists), which had elected 118 representatives, was likewise suppressed and its deputies unseated. Thereupon the Nationalists fused with the Nazis, and the Center Party voluntarily dissolved, leaving but one political organization, the National-Socialists, in control of the government, the Reichstag, and the republic.

The Reichstag fire

5. THE TOTALITARIAN STATE

At its first session after the Nazi triumph

[1] See above, page 930.

in the election of March, 1933, the Reichstag voted Hitler and his cabinet dictatorial powers for a period of four years. Hitler's avowed purpose, after silencing opposition in the peremptory fashion already described, was to weld Germany into a centralized national state under the domination of one party. The vestiges of particularism which even Bismarck had respected were to be stamped out, the semi-autonomous powers reserved by the leading component states under the federal empire of 1871 and the federal republic of 1919 lapsed, and local diets yielded up their authority to the central government in order that Germany might become a truly unitary state. As a means of increasing the efficiency, economy, and absolutism of the government, this consolidation of federal, state, and local institutions had much to recommend it. But when the leaders of the new régime sought to extend their control over the Reichswehr (the small but highly efficient German army), and attempted to reduce youth leagues, labor unions, and even the German Evangelical Church to state control, they awakened apprehension and opposition, and were forced to make some minor compromises. In general, however, the German people supported the Nazi policies with enthusiasm, and accepted Hitler's eloquent assurances that loyalty, unity, and discipline would restore the Reich to a position of power and dignity among the nations and ease the economic distress through a planned revival of industrial and agricultural activities.

In Germany as in other industrial states the gravest social and economic problem of the post-war era was the necessity of providing relief for the millions of unemployed workers. The National-Socialist government attacked this problem aggressively, portioning the Reich into thirteen sections under the control of thirteen labor trustees, all supervised by a supreme economic council. Trade unions and strikes were prohibited, for the establishment of wage scales, hours, and conditions of work, and all other regulations governing the relationship between employer and employee, had passed under the supervision of the state. By shortening the work-

Unemployment relief

THE REICHSSPORTSFELD, BERLIN

Hitler planned to beautify Berlin with many new structures, but the preparations for war, as shown in the realistic mock tank attack below, absorbed the national revenue.

GERMAN ARMY MANEUVERS

ing day more jobs were created, and a nation-wide drive raised funds to care for the indigent. Yet the workers were not wholly satisfied with the new system. Like the Italian laborers under the Fascist régime, they found their freedom of action greatly diminished and their welfare relegated to the paternal but bureaucratic care of a committee of experts. Many workers had rallied to the National-Socialist cause in the earlier years because they were attracted by the more radical phrases in the Nazi program, such as "the abolition of all income acquired without work," and "the distribution of the profits of large industries." But the National-Socialist leaders, who had secretly accepted financial aid from the great industrialists in order to achieve their victory, could not afford to alienate such powerful allies by adhering to radical projects which called for an attack upon private and corporate wealth.

By the spring of 1934, the realization that the National-Socialist program was likely to prove more "nationalist" than "socialist" in operation had roused secret discontent among the radical members of the Nazi Party. At the same time the "storm troopers," the thousands of uniformed youths who had formed the "shock troops" in the National-Socialist campaigns, were bitterly disillusioned by the report that their leader, Hitler, planned to dissolve them after they had raised him to power by their efforts. Whether a genuine conspiracy had been organized among storm troop officers to precipitate a "second revolution" is not clear, but in June, 1934, Hitler struck a sudden and deadly blow at the suspected malcontents. Scores, and possibly hundreds, marked for vengeance were shot down in their homes or executed without trial. Following this paralyzing lesson on the dangers of insubordination, Hitler prepared to reduce the number, privileges, and duties of the storm troopers, and transferred his dependence to the Reichswehr instead, the officers and soldiers of which had long resented the favors shown the semi-military storm troop detachments.

The "June Purge"

With Hitler's advent to power, President von Hindenburg, already in failing health, had been forced somewhat into the background of affairs. On August 2, 1934, he died, and a decree of the cabinet invited Hitler to assume the duties of president of the Reich in addition to those of chancellor. The German electorate, in a plebiscite held August 19, approved the step by a ninety per cent majority, and *Der Führer*, as Hitler was termed, assured in this fashion of the undiminished loyalty of the German people, accepted the presidential office. No previous German leader had been vested with more extraordinary powers.

6. GERMAN FOREIGN POLICY AFTER 1932

In their climb to power the spokesmen of the National-Socialist Movement had insistently proclaimed their determination to free Germany from the stigma of the "War Guilt Clause" in the Treaty of Versailles,[1] to repudiate further reparations payments, and to demand parity in armaments for Germany or an equal degree of disarmament for her neighbors. When the League of Nations refused to countenance the demand for parity in arms, Hitler announced the resignation of Germany from the League (October, 1933), and the German people, on appeal, sustained his act by a plebiscite majority of over ninety per cent. Thereupon the German government proceeded to ignore the treaty restrictions and took active steps to enlarge the military, naval, and aerial defenses of the Reich.

In the matter of reparations the attitude of the new German government proved equally firm, and no further payments were made after the adjournment of the Lausanne Conference in 1932.[2] By 1933, German export trade had declined sharply, partly as a consequence of the general economic depression and partly as a result of a world-wide boycott of German products which many anti-Fascists supported as a protest against the treatment accorded Jews and Communists under Nazi rule. This cancellation of credit and fall in trade helped to induce a perilous reduction in the German

Economic stalemate

[1] See above, page 857.
[2] See above, page 927.

gold reserve. Payments on all German foreign debts were suspended, and the government declared that Germany could pay neither principal nor interest to foreign bondholders until more favorable terms could be wrung from their respective governments. For the German people the adverse balance of trade meant a condition of enforced self-sufficiency, and they were urged by their government to find domestic equivalents for the curtailed imports, to the end that Germany might become self-sustaining in peace or war. This ideal of economic self-sufficiency for the nation was extolled under the name of autarchy.

To restore Germany to a position of full equality with other powers in the matter of armaments and prestige was a task calling for a rare combination of audacity and calculation. Hitler demonstrated his possession of these qualities by the skill with which he timed his moves, and by his masterly use of what may be termed the strategy of the limited objective. Recognizing that, if Germany's late opponents, Britain, France, Italy and Russia, chose to defend the Versailles stipulations, it would be folly to defy such a quadruple alliance, he labored to divide these four powers, while consolidating the German people into a unified and disciplined nation under his undisputed leadership. The success which attended this policy may be seen from a short summary of his moves.

Hitler's objectives

In 1933, the year he became chancellor, Hitler demanded revision of the Versailles Treaty and equality in arms for the German Reich. When this was refused he withdrew Germany from the League of Nations, and the German people demonstrated their confidence in his policy by an affirmative vote of 93.5 per cent. His next step showed his skill in disposing of one issue at a time. To

GERMAN ESTIMATE OF GERMAN MINORITIES, 1938

ADOLF HITLER (1889–1945)

No dictator since Napoleon I had so overawed Europe as Hitler succeeded in doing between 1933 and 1945.

dispel the fear of the Poles that a rearmed Germany might seize the Polish Corridor, he negotiated a pact with the Polish Republic (January, 1934) guaranteeing the existing Polish-German frontiers for ten years. Germany was not yet armed, however, and still lacked a powerful ally, and Hitler hesitated to embark upon his plans for German expansion in Europe at the risk of war. This was demonstrated in July, 1934, when a group of National Socialist agitators in Vienna assassinated the Austrian chancellor, Engelbert Dollfuss, and attempted to seize control. Germany was prepared to support the insurgents, had their *coup* proved successful, but Hitler disowned connection with it when it failed. This disavowal, however, did not altogether reassure the governments of Britain, France, and Italy, and the three powers in a conference at Stresa (April, 1935)

The "Stresa Front"

formally declared that the independence of Austria should and must be preserved.

The lesson was not lost upon Hitler. He had been encouraged in January, 1935, by the plebiscite held in the Saar Basin, where the population, after fifteen years of enforced separation, voted for reunion and was reincorporated with Germany on March 1. This act of restitution, conceded by the League of Nations, augmented Hitler's popularity in Germany, but his triumph was clouded by the disposition Britain, France, and Italy had displayed to unite against German encroachments, and by a Franco-Russian military alliance signed May 2. To weaken and if possible break the "Stresa Front," Hitler declared Germany had no intention of annexing Austria, and he softened British apprehension at the rearmament of the Reich by pledging in a naval accord (June 18, 1935) that the German navy would be restricted to 35 per cent of that of Great Britain.

Naval agreement

So long as the Rhineland, demilitarized by the Treaty of Versailles, remained unfortified, Germany was peculiarly vulnerable to attack. In March, 1936, when Italy was engaged in conquering Ethiopia, and Britain, France, and the League of Nations had all lost prestige through their abortive efforts to check Italian aggression, Hitler ordered German troops to reoccupy the Rhineland in defiance of the terms of the treaty. The stroke was skillfully timed. Britain hesitated to oppose it and France dared not act alone. Nevertheless, for a few tense hours peace or war hung in the balance, and Hitler thought it advisable to remind Europe that this step implied nothing more than the inalienable right of a sovereign state to protect its own frontiers. Germany, he declared, had no territorial claims to make in Europe. This assurance satisfied many people, especially in Great Britain, where it was generally conceded that the Versailles settlement had imposed excessive and humiliating restrictions upon Germany. The removal of these restrictions, it was hoped, would make possible a more equitable and more harmonious balance of power.

Rhineland refortified

71

Two Decades of International Tension

(1919–1939)

> Germany must soon either expand or explode.
> WINSTON CHURCHILL.

AMONG THE PRINCIPAL CAUSES of World War I, trade rivalry took a leading place, especially the keen competition that developed between Great Britain and Germany. After 1919 such economic competition remained an acute problem, for the industrial powers had grown more dependent than ever on the raw materials which they imported and the manufactures which they sold abroad. The results of such economic rivalry are often subtle, indirect and difficult to analyze. But economic needs and pressures so largely dominated world history in the twenty years between the two world wars that an attempt must be made here to suggest how these needs and pressures operated.

1. ECONOMIC IMPERIALISM

In the modern world all the great powers are *industrialized* states. The nations which still subsist by raising crops or exporting the products of their pastures, mines, and forests have a secondary, and sometimes a very unimportant, place in world politics. For the process of industrialization, once it gains momentum, carries a society ahead swiftly, transforms, vitalizes, and urbanizes it. The United States, Japan, and Russia have all developed phenomenally in the twentieth century through machine production. Even countries like Canada and Australia, where crops, herds, mining, fishing, and forestry were major sources of wealth a generation ago, now derive more than half their national income from manufacture. One reason why machine industries expand rapidly is that they create new needs and opportunities as they develop. The internal-combustion engine, for instance, not only made the automobile and airplane possible; it created an insatiable demand for gasoline and lubricants. The petroleum industry met this demand, but to do so new and deeper wells had to be opened, and the drilling machinery invented for the purpose tapped buried pools of sulphur, gas, salts, and minerals, creating additional wealth and more intricate problems. A second reason for the expansion of industry is that the men at the head of the great manufacturing corporations, the iron and steel mills, the textile factories, the communication and transportation systems, are alert to world conditions and to political trends. Because their industries soon become indispensable to the prosperity of the state they can induce the legislatures to favor them with subsidies and tariffs, and they press for a foreign policy which will promote trade, win concessions, and safeguard their markets and foreign investments. In so doing, however, the business classes may involve their government and nation in controversies with other countries where the business groups are pursuing the same methods of political pressure and economic imperialism.

All trade is, fundamentally, an exchange

Marginal note: Importance of industry

of goods and services for mutual advantage. Some forms of trade, however, enrich one party to the exchange more than the other. Nations such as Great Britain, which first adopted machine production and developed the factory system, grew almost too wealthy as a result. The British in the nineteenth century were able to pay for raw materials and imported food by selling the product of their factories, and the demand for their wares was such that each year their accumulation of capital increased. To business men money is not an end in itself, but a means for promoting new economic activity. As the British soon had more capital than they required for their own domestic development, they used the surplus to open and exploit gold, copper, or tin mines in other countries, to finance tea or rubber plantations in tropical regions, to build railways or harness hydroelectric power in retarded or economically backward states. From such investments the nation which had thus "exported" its surplus capital drew interest payments which could be reinvested. Such multiplication of profits built on profits helps to explain why the power, prestige, and influence of industrialized *creditor* nations expand so rapidly and dynamically. It also helps to explain why the classes which hold large foreign investments, or are interested in foreign trade, usually favor a strong fleet and army and a firm foreign policy. They want their government to have the power to guard their "property" in other lands.

Export of capital

Because they are geared to supply an "expanding market," industrialized states do not stand still: acceleration for them is the normal tempo of economic life. Sooner or later, however, they are certain to find the market glutted, or discover that their foreign customers, though eager for their wares, lack money to pay for them. To hold the market open and keep their goods moving, the manufacturers may sell on credit, or extend loans. But as investors they are likely to tender advice along with the loans, suggesting, perhaps, that the consumer nation use part of the money to produce wheat, coffee, sugar, minerals, or any other commodity which can be readily raised and offered as payment. Thus, the loans, which likewise bear interest, become one more means of profit-taking, and furnish a form of control whereby the economy of the debtor nation is subordinated to the requirements of the wealthier state. Some small nations have fallen so heavily into debt through these and similar transactions that one half the taxes are diverted to the payments on their funded obligations. This places them in a position of economic dependence, and some colonial or subject peoples resent their condition as "economic vassalage." In many cases, however, it is difficult for them to escape from their dilemma because the country to which they owe money is likewise their best customer, and may absorb as much as ninety per cent of their exports while furnishing ninety per cent of their imports. Thus, to rebel would almost certainly make small nations subject to reprisals which might dislocate their finances and plunge their precarious economy into chaos, whereas the great powers, to which they are merely one sphere of "economic interest," would suffer only minor loss or inconvenience from their revolt.

Economic satellites

In general, however, most secondary states gain as well as lose by their dependence upon a great power. They are likely to lean upon the protection of its army or navy, to look to it for diplomatic support in a controversy, or for financial support in a crisis. The main profits of economic imperialism may go to the great power. But its satellites and colonies benefit through a quickening of trade contacts, through the development of communication and transportation, the interchange of products, the surveys conducted by specialists opening up half-explored territory to which the protecting power has obtained a title or concession in return for a promise to share the profits but shoulder the losses. In essence, however, the system remains unfair and unequal because the small nation has little chance to obtain redress or even to plead its cause if it is treated unjustly.

Benefits of trade contacts

World War I increased the evils and inequalities of economic imperialism. Much

SPHERES OF INFLUENCE OF THE GREAT POWERS 1939

BRITISH | UNITED STATES | FRENCH | JAPANESE | RUSSIAN | ITALIAN | GERMAN

of the surplus capital which had made Europe "the world's banker" was exhausted in the conflict. All the belligerents (except the United States) accumulated such heavy debts, internal and external, that they could not balance their budgets or maintain their currencies at the level of 1914. The Russian Soviet government repudiated the debts of the czarist régime. Italy and France owed Great Britain, and all three owed the United States billions of dollars on war loans. These and other international obligations were funded and the total sum due the United States after World War I was set at $11,671,400,000. But the debtor nations insisted that they could not meet *their* scheduled payments unless the Germans discharged their reparations promptly. In the outcome the United States received a little over $2,000,000,000, less than one tenth of the total funded debt which interest charges swelled to $22,000,000,000 by 1933. Yet American investors, despite the default or reduced installments on these earlier loans, continued to subscribe heavily to foreign bonds, and by 1930 they held certificates for over $15,000,000,000 invested in other countries. Of this sum $2,500,000,000 had been advanced to the German government, German municipalities, and German corporations. A part of this huge credit the Germans used to retire their inescapable reparations payments, but much of it went to reconstruct their industries. Most of the principal was later lost to American investors through default. Thus, the people of the United States helped the Germans to pay their reparations, revive their shattered economy, and, indirectly, to prepare for a new war. It should be noted, however, that these credits were advanced because Americans held surplus capital, because the Germans offered tempting interest rates, and because American exporters wanted to sell the Germans American goods while German wares which might have been shipped in payment were largely excluded from the United States by the high protective tariff.

This brief summary may help to suggest how complicated the course of economic imperialism may become, how readily debts can be misrepresented as extortion, and how likely they are to awaken a sense of envy and antagonism. It should also suggest how involved a nation's economy can become when it must lend its customers the money to buy its goods or else face a recession of trade and loss of markets. The expedients to which a creditor nation is sometimes reduced appear utterly paradoxical at first view. It may, for instance, itself propose the cancellation of debts, in order to promote trade by restoring a more equal economic balance. The British government, after 1920, suggested an all-around renunciation of war loans. In 1931, President Hoover suggested a general moratorium, or postponement, of intergovernmental payments, to check the business depression. As the United States was the chief loser by this proposal, it was a one-sided accommodation which merely granted official sanction to the default on the funded debts from World War I. A further illustration of the seemingly paradoxical methods invoked to adjust the economic system when business declines is the deliberate devaluation of the currency. Embarrassed by its own high standards of living and high wages, a creditor nation may depreciate the value of its currency in terms of gold or of world prices, so that quotations on its products will fall. In this way its wares, reduced in terms of world prices, may find customers who could not afford them at their costlier level. All these expedients were tried after 1919, and especially after 1929, but the effect was to increase rather than to reduce the economic chaos of this turbulent era.

2. THE "HAVES" AND THE "HAVE-NOTS"

When a wealthy group or corporation invests millions of dollars, pounds, or francs in an undeveloped region of the globe, either to stimulate commerce or to exploit the natural resources, the investors commonly seek to safeguard their capital. One way to do this is to persuade their national government to proclaim the region a "sphere of influence" or a "protectorate." The inhabitants usually continue to manage their own local affairs, but the maintenance of order, protection of property, defense, diplomatic decisions, and economic policies are directed by the great power which assumes control over the region and the fate of its people.

No other nation in history has equaled the achievement of the British in extending political and economic control over dispersed populations and disparate realms. By 1919, the British Empire embraced over 13,000,000 square miles, or approximately one fourth of the land area of the globe, and included 500,000,000 people, one fourth of the earth's population. The second largest empire in point of area was the Union of Soviet Socialist Republics, which controlled some 8,000,000 square miles of territory and a population which already exceeded 170,000,000 in the nineteen-twenties. The French Empire ranked third in size, with 4,000,000 square miles and 100,000,000 inhabitants. Thus, three great nations, Britain, Russia, and France, dominated almost half the earth's land area and directed the destinies of more than two fifths of the human race. A fourth great power, the United States, dominated the Americas, and held sovereignty over an area totaling 3,735,000 square miles with a population of 130,000,000.

Modern empires

These "satiated" powers, which could command the resources of climes and regions stretching from the Arctic Circle to the tropics, and possessed empty areas in reserve for their excess population, aroused the envy of the "Have-not" powers, Germany, Italy, and Japan. For this latter trio together held less than 1,500,000 square miles, although their home population was roughly equivalent to that of Britain, France, and European Russia. This inequality stirred German, Italian, and Japanese patriots to demand a revision of the existing territorial settlement. In other words, the "Have-not" nations were prepared to favor a disruption of the established order, by war if necessary, because they felt this order to be unjust and unrealistic. The business men and economists of these powers which had lagged behind in the race for colonies pointed to the higher standard of living enjoyed by British and French workers as proof that colonies did pay. The German artisan who knew himself as skilled and industrious as his British colleague, the Italian merchant or manufacturer who lacked capital to compete with French or American firms, found it easy to believe that if his government adopted a more enterprising foreign policy and won a larger empire, this would assure national prosperity. As matters stood, the average German owned less than half the material goods at the disposal of an Englishman of equivalent status, and the German artisan, clerk, or laborer received only one half to two thirds as much pay in real wages for equivalent work. The Italian was even less fortunate economically; and the Japanese worker accepted a scale of wages and endured a level of living which would have seemed semi-starvation by British or American standards.

Unequal conquests

3. COLLECTIVE SECURITY

After 1919, not only the great powers, but almost all the nations of Europe tended to fall into one of two classes: those which favored the peace settlement and those which hoped to revise it. The states which had benefited favored the retention of existing frontiers and the adoption of guaranties against armed aggression. The states which had lost, or had received less than they sought in European or colonial territory, demanded a more equitable distribution and more liberal access to world markets. In Europe, France led the first group, for the French Army and French gold were the main bulwarks of stability and security. Lesser states, which had come into existence or gained additional areas by the peace settlement (Poland, Czechoslovakia, Rumania, Yugoslavia), formed alliances with one another and with France for the purpose of maintaining the existing order. In general accord with them might be found the secondary states with overseas empires, or valuable foreign trade (Holland, Belgium, Portugal, Switzerland, Denmark), although the first three looked to the British Navy rather than the French Army for protection.

Conservers and revisers

The leader of the revisionist group of

European states was Germany. The Germans, having been shorn of all their colonies, one eighth of their European territory, and one tenth of their population by the settlement of 1919, were wholeheartedly dedicated to the task of reversing the Versailles *Diktat*. The Austrians and Hungarians, formerly the privileged groups in the once proud Hapsburg Empire, shared this German aspiration. Had Europe remained solidly united against them, these three states could not have achieved very much. But Europe was not united. Many Italians were disappointed because their war efforts had not been rewarded with larger gains or a more extensive colonial empire, and were willing to see the peace terms upset. France and Britain, allies during the war, were also rivals in the Near East and in Africa, and could not be counted upon to stand together on all matters affecting treaty revision. Russia, emerging from the grim cataclysm of a ruthless but vitalizing revolution, had a dual rôle, as both a satiated and a revisionist power, with unpredictable intentions.

Rôle of Germany

The Russian "enigma" was all the more impenetrable because Russia was the crucible of a social experiment inspired by the Marxian program of expropriating the expropriators, nationalizing all property and means of production, and creating a classless society. In the nineteen-twenties Moscow was the home of the Third International (or *Comintern*), an organization which communicated with communist groups in other lands, and sought to undermine capitalist régimes and hasten a world revolution of the working classes everywhere. Such revolutionary plotting, never formally or officially admitted as a principle of Soviet foreign policy, was gradually abandoned, especially after the influence of Joseph Stalin became powerful (1927) and Leon Trotsky was exiled from the Union of Soviet Socialist Republics. While thus modifying their more extravagant revolutionary aims, however, the Russian leaders resumed the traditional foreign policy of expansion pursued by earlier Russian governments. From Finland to the Black Sea and from Rumania to Vladivostok the drive of Russian expansion was felt once again, a strong, inexorable pressure which disturbed all the smaller states bordering upon the Soviet Union, and alarmed the governments of the western European powers.

Soviet Russia in dual rôle

So far as loss of territory was concerned, the Russians had obvious reasons for demanding a revision of the peace settlement that emerged from World War I. Russia had forfeited larger areas in Europe than any other power. Finland, Esthonia, Latvia, Lithuania, the larger section of the re-created Polish republic, and the province of Bessarabia annexed by Rumania had all formed part of the Russian Empire in 1914. As patriotic pride once more stirred the hearts of the Russian people, Russian imperialistic ambitions tended to revive. It is true that they revived under a new form, for the communists denounced the older methods of imperialism as capitalist exploitation, but the new Russian program of penetration and amalgamation of contiguous areas differed from the old chiefly in its greater effectiveness. As the Soviet Union grew more powerful, more stable, and more highly industrialized, it became increasingly certain that sooner or later the Russian leaders would demand the return of the territories in the West which had been reft away during the critical days of civil war, revolution, and political enfeeblement. These circumstances made it difficult to foretell whether, in a diplomatic crisis, the Russian government would stand with Germany for a revision of the Versailles Treaty, or with France in support of peace and the existing balance of power and existing frontiers.

Russian losses

After 1918, French diplomats took the lead in successive attempts to "freeze" the settlement and erect a permanent and stable international order. The first attempt was born with the Versailles Treaty itself: it was the League of Nations, the covenant of which constituted the opening section of all the treaties which closed World War I. But the League, though pictured by its loyal advocates as a universal society of nations, became, in the view of hostile and unsympathetic critics, an

French rigidity

instrument for confirming the power of the victors and obstructing legitimate demands for change. The fact that the United States Senate declined to ratify the Versailles Treaty or approve the League, and the absence, likewise, of Germany (until 1926) and of Russia (until 1934), left the League too long and too largely under the domination of France and Britain. It is noteworthy that the only great powers which the League attempted to call to account as disturbers of the peace were the "Have-not" or revisionist states, Germany, Italy, and Japan, and all three resented the League action as unjust and resigned rather than suffer a rebuke or submit their claims to League arbitration. This meant that they did not trust the League to view issues impartially. Nations, like individuals, do not readily defy a court and invite popular condemnation as lawbreakers if they are confident that their claims will receive fair consideration.

A second attempt to organize a system of collective security against war, aggression, and violent change was sponsored by the French in 1924, after the failure of their military occupation of the Ruhr Valley. The bitter controversy over German reparations had been temporarily adjusted by the inauguration of the Dawes Plan (see page 926). In 1925, at Locarno, a number of treaties were negotiated in an effort to fix frontiers and guarantee a peaceful settlement of international disputes, not on a world-wide but on a limited, regional basis. Arbitration and non-aggression pacts became remarkably popular between 1925 and 1929, and if a cordial conference and conciliatory phrases could have solved antagonisms, the "spirit of Locarno" should have opened a new international era of peace and good will. But pledges and written guarantees have little strength or validity in the international sphere once the will to support them wanes.

Quest for guaranties

This truth was made manifest by a third effort to end war and assure the peaceful arbitration of all disputes likely to arise between civilized nations. In 1928, under the joint inspiration of the French statesman, Aristide Briand, and the United States secretary of state, Frank B. Kellogg, a Peace Pact was drawn up at Paris whereby some fifty nations agreed to renounce war as an instrument of national policy and to arbitrate disputes which might lead to hostilities. These diplomatic agreements suggest that ten years after World War I ended, some of the bitterness and maladjustment it engendered had been dissipated and a will to agreement was growing among the peoples of Europe. But this interpretation, popular at the time, was false to the facts. Too sincere a reliance upon the efficacy of phrases and formulas to perpetuate peace actually endangered that peace, because the pacts served as a screen which obscured the precarious condition of the peace structure.

Pact of Paris (1928)

For if there was a softening of resentments and antagonisms by 1928, this was due to the general rise in prosperity rather than to any change in fundamental international rivalries. Between 1924 and 1929 production increased in all the leading countries, prices rose, wages followed, unemployment declined, and business expanded, until a mood of confidence and optimism prevailed. French industrial output increased by almost one third; German by one fifth; British by one seventh; while in Soviet Russia, under state management, the industrial index was officially stated to have doubled in five years. It is significant, however, that despite the marked rise of international trade, which soared by 1929 to twice its 1914 valuation, no real solution had been submitted to equalize the uneven distribution of colonies, capital, markets, raw materials, and purchasing power. An era of relative prosperity is usually an era of good feeling; it is the sharp reverses of fortune, sudden impoverishment, and deflated hopes which try a people's magnanimity and uncover latent enmities. Unhappily for the principle of collective security, the years after 1929 were to be years of economic dislocation, disillusionment, and despair.

Prosperity and peace

4. THE GREAT DEPRESSION (1929–33)

The many complex causes of the economic collapse which struck the nations after 1929 are not yet fully understood. It is possible, however, to isolate four or five trends which weakened the shaky edifice of world prosperity. (1) By 1929, production had outrun consumption: there was actually a surplus of many crops and commodities, not because consumers lacked the desire for them, but because they lacked means to pay for them. (2) The financing of further sales by advancing credit to classes and countries which could not otherwise have continued their purchases was widening the inequality between debtors and creditors. The American people and the American government, for instance, had exported over $25,000,000,000 to foreign countries between 1914 and 1929. Such extravagant injections of capital had a stimulating effect upon business almost everywhere, but it encouraged overexpansion in many fields. (3) Much of the "prosperity" which encouraged nations and individuals to spend liberally and consume confidently was based upon "paper profits." Investors who watched their stocks and bonds climb on the market lists, where many quoted issues doubled and even trebled in a few years, imagined that they were actually the possessors of that much extra wealth. But the moment that any considerable number of investors tried to transform their holdings into tangible assets, they were certain to discover that their certificates did not correspond to any real or durable goods or values. (4) Commencing with the failure of several European banks, a wave of panic struck the New York stock market in September, 1929; investors who had borrowed the money to buy "on margin," making a partial payment only because they counted upon a continued rise, were ruined when stocks fell. Banks called in their loans, customers annulled orders, consumers ceased purchases and ceased installments on those already delivered, and prosperity suddenly collapsed. (5) When no more capital, especially American capital, was exported, the debtor nations, Germany in particular, ended payments and purchases. Other nations followed a similar course, declaring that they could not meet their intergovernmental obligations, and by 1930 reparations and war debts alike were hopelessly in default and international finance in a state of general insolvency.

The effect upon world trade was swift and disastrous. By 1932 it had declined to one third the 1929 level. As orders failed, factories closed, ships rusted at their docks, crops were left to rot in the fields, stores, hotels, theaters, and restaurants stood empty. All this meant that millions of machinists, stevedores, farmhands, clerks, and building employees were discharged. Without wages they soon exhausted their savings and lost purchasing power, which induced a further decline in consumption, wider unemployment, and a still sharper recession. Among all classes a mood of profound pessimism and futility succeeded the shallow optimism of the inflation period, and the public in Europe and America, obsessed with a sense of panic and impotence, demanded that the governments undertake energetic measures to arrest the fateful decline. But emergency measures imply emergency powers. The effect of the Great Depression was similar to that of a war: the general panic and despair led to a strengthening of the executive power in most states, and among peoples who lacked a strong democratic tradition this situation offered a unique opportunity for leaders with dictatorial ambitions to seize power.

5. RECOVERY AND REARMAMENT

In the United States, the Great Depression was followed by the repudiation of the Republican Party in the election of 1932, by the inauguration of a "New Deal" and the "Roosevelt Revolution" of 1933. In many European countries the people reacted in a similar fashion, but much more violently and decisively. The German elections of 1930 saw the "moderates" discredited. Leaders who had counseled co-operation with the League of Nations and the fulfillment of the peace terms and reparations payments were denounced as weak-kneed conciliators, while the defiant chauvinism of the National-Socialists, under the inspiration of Adolf Hitler, electrified the German masses. For Hitler had discovered that discontented

HEADLINES AND BREADLINES

The printing press, the radio, and the newsreel opened a new era of mass indoctrination. People in all civilized countries were swiftly affected by good or bad news, as when the Depression of 1929 threw millions out of work.

Above: PRINTING PRESS

Left: STOCK QUOTATIONS

Below: THE UNEMPLOYED

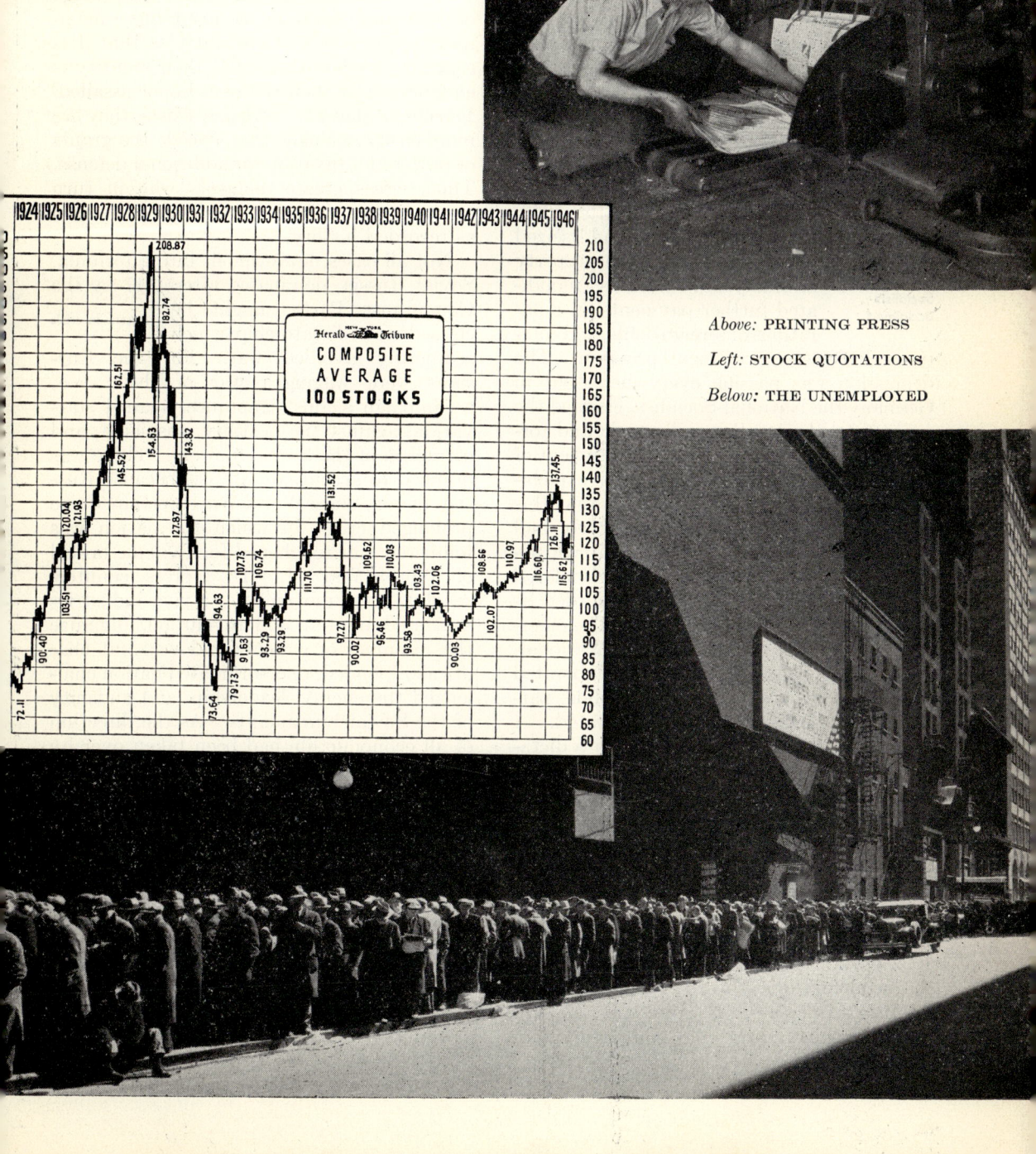

and envious groups are easily knit by their grievances, and all Germans felt keenly the ignominy of their inferior status and limited armament. A great nation, denied an army, a navy, or an air force of any consequence, and condemned to pay a humiliating tribute to its conquerors, is easily stirred to indignation. When, in addition to such resentment against foreign impositions, the people suffer the disaster of a currency inflation, the loss of their savings, insurance, and annuities, followed by widespread unemployment, their bitterness grows until they may readily be converted to a mood of defiance and recklessness. Such a spirit spread rapidly among the German people with the onset of the Great Depression.

When recovery set in, as it did after 1933, the National-Socialist Party had seized power, confiscated the property of many Jewish firms, repudiated further payments on reparations or foreign debts, and commenced a vast rearmament program. The depression was passing everywhere, but in Germany the National-Socialists claimed the credit, and their policies, domestic and foreign, received the passionate endorsement of the German electorate in successive plebiscites. It was ominous, however, that this economic recovery and patriotic fervor had been accompanied by sinister political, social, and juristic measures which violated principles of individual liberty regarded as inalienable in democratic states. The emergency powers demanded by the National-Socialist régime were retained and elaborated until all vestiges of a free, responsible, parliamentary democracy were obliterated. A totalitarian one-party régime, under a dictator who ruled by decree, replaced the representative government created in 1919 by the Weimar Constitution.

National-Socialists acclaimed

The Italian people had already traveled the road to totalitarianism under the rule of the Fascist Party. As explained in an earlier chapter, the rise to power of Benito Mussolini in 1922 curtailed the liberal constitution, and the economic crisis of 1929 led to further totalitarian decrees. Because a people will submit to dictatorial rule more readily in time of crisis, most dictators are under a persistent temptation to prolong their mandate by prolonging the crisis which provoked it. This is one reason why a dictator almost always assumes personal direction of foreign affairs and pushes the nation into an adventurous foreign policy. For in international affairs a people have a minimum of control over the minister, a minimum of knowledge of the issues said to be involved, but a maximum sensitivity and credulity, so that it is easy to persuade them that their security is endangered or their national honor assailed. Persuaded that an emergency exists, they are more easily persuaded to concede the grants of power and taxation for additional defense. Thus, crises create dictators who in turn create crises. The formula is almost as old as recorded history.

Italian totalitarianism

Not all cases, however, fit into a formula. Soviet Russia, dominated after 1917 by the Communist Party, might be classed as a dictatorship which sedulously avoided war. For the Russians were waging a war of their own, a campaign against ignorance, against starvation, against the hostility, suspicion, and ostracism of the leading powers. There was no need to accentuate a crisis because Russian history since World War I remained one prolonged crisis, in which the nation was tempered and toughened for the epic ordeal of World War II. To repress counter-revolutionary movements, revive industries shattered by war and revolution, organize the resources of a richly endowed but chaotically blended, unco-ordinated nation challenged the energy, leadership, and audacity of the Soviet bureaucrats. As the direction of all economic life had been taken over by the state, it was possible for the ministers (or commissars) in charge of the government departments to grapple with the problems of industrialization, mining, agriculture, transportation, and education on a national, a continental, scale. The result was a succession of "Five-Year Plans" of expansion, vast, concerted campaigns designed to extract and utilize the resources of Russia and the energies of the Russian people for the defense of the country and the improvement of the standard of living. With his gift for

Russia in crisis

EUROPE IN 1939

Dark areas show the Axis Powers and their European acquisitions to September 1, 1939

slogans, Lenin had summed up this program as early as 1920 in the sentence: Communism is Soviet government plus the electrification of the whole country.

Because Russian economy was largely self-concentrated, the Great Depression retarded the ambitious program of development very little. There was no serious increase in unemployment, and the scheduled expansion of crops, coal output, electric power, mining, lumbering, and manufacturing continued unabated. But the predicted rise in the Russian standard of living did not manifest itself, for the Soviet leaders found it expedient to divert the efforts and resources of the nation to a far-reaching, thorough, inspired, but unadvertised campaign of military preparedness. German rearmament after 1933 disturbed the balance of power in Europe, and the Russian strategists, with a militaristic Japan in the East and a belligerent Germany in the West, dared not relax or hope for an indefinite period of peace in which to complete the modernization of Russian economy and institutions.

Russian rearmament

For Britain and France the Great Depression proved a severe trial. By 1932, it was fairly apparent that Germany would pay no further reparations; indeed, it was doubtful whether the Germans would pay the debts which they had voluntarily contracted after repudiating those imposed upon them. French control in Europe was diminishing with French credit, and British power and prestige declined when the government abandoned the gold standard in 1931 and the pound sterling fell from $4.86 to about $3.40. To combat unemployment and win better trading concessions, the British also abandoned their historic principle of free trade and introduced a system of inter-empire tariffs, or "imperial preference" accords, designed to weld the commonwealth together as a stronger economic unit. After 1933, Britain, like Germany, Italy, France, and the United States, began to experience a business revival. But a British commentator, noting that orders for armaments had been a leading stimulus in the revival of the heavy industries in these countries, and that unemployment declined as preparations for war advanced, posed the significant question: "Is industry, then, a sick giant, which can rouse itself only to kill?"

British difficulties

6. THE FAILURE OF COLLECTIVE SECURITY (1933–39)

The attempts initiated in the nineteen-twenties, to preserve peace by arbitration treaties and guaranties against aggression, broke down in the thirties. The peace pacts had never been, in reality, more than paper promises. For the real test was the nations' willingness to renounce war, or at least to limit their armaments, by mutual agreement. The Treaty of Versailles had decreed the disarmament of the vanquished, forbidding the Germans an air force, and reducing their army and navy to a paltry one hundred thousand men and a few ships. The treaty also proposed a reduction of the French, British, and Italian armed forces, but this provision was not put into effect. The British, it is true, agreed to limit the building of capital ships, and Great Britain, the United States, and Japan declared a naval holiday at the Washington Naval Conference (1922). A ratio of 5 : 5 : 3 : 1.67 : 1.67 was established for Britain, the United States, Japan, France, and Italy respectively, each power accepting the proposed limitation of capital ship tonnage. But military armaments the French did not consider it safe to reduce. Indeed, they subsidized the arming of Polish, Czechoslovak, Rumanian, and Yugoslav divisions, and the forces of these allied states, under French inspiration, maintained a military hegemony in Europe after 1919.

Limitation of arms

During the years of relative prosperity, before the depression reduced national revenues after 1929, the burden of maintaining large armies was heavy but endurable. But in the depression years, when income fell and unemployment relief taxed the resources of all governments, many people asked (as the Germans had asked for ten years) why France and her satellite states did not reduce their military expenditures. Plans to call a disarmament conference had been discussed at sessions of the League of Nations since its inception, for reduction of

Disarmament Conference, 1932–33

armaments was recommended in the Covenant (Article VIII). Not until 1932, however, did the conference finally assemble. Many projects were considered for the reduction of existing forces and the scaling-down of military expenditure, and proposals were submitted to limit the new and frightful weapons of destruction which science had provided. But no broad or constructive measures were adopted. The preparatory labors of this conference had stretched over five years, the discussions, with several adjournments, extended over two years, yet progress was nullified from the outset by the insincerity, prejudice, and partiality implicit in the reservations of the leading powers. The French insistence upon "security" (which in essence meant the preservation of French armed supremacy), and the German demand for "parity" (which meant French disarmament or German rearmament), held up all real solutions. When the German demand was not conceded, the delegates of the Reich were recalled, and the German foreign minister announced that Germany might resign from the League. This threat was translated into action in 1933 after Adolf Hitler had assumed power. On appeal, the German people approved the action of their government by a plebiscite majority of over ninety per cent.

The failure to promote disarmament in these critical years after 1929 was not the only failure the League had to acknowledge. It failed even more ignominiously to curb a deliberate campaign of aggression launched by a great power. At the darkest hour of the economic depression, when Britain was driven to abandon the gold standard while struggling against unemployment and loss of trade; when France was hard pressed to hold her position; when Russian leaders were preoccupied with the First Five-Year Plan; and the American people were preparing for the historic election of 1932, the Japanese militarists seized the chance to strike a sudden but obviously premeditated blow against China. In September, 1931, Japanese troops invaded Manchuria, took over the railway lines, garrisoned the towns, organized a puppet government, and confiscated foreign-owned properties and concessions. The invasion was part of a concerted move to subjugate the rich provinces of northern China and transform them into a Japanese protectorate (see map, page 881). The Chinese government appealed to the League of Nations, and the League Council and Assembly agreed to dispatch a commission to investigate. The findings of this commission, known as the "Lytton Report," affirmed that the Japanese were guilty of acts of aggression. But beyond adopting the report and naming Japan as the aggressor, the League members did nothing purposeful, and by 1933 Manchuria, reorganized as the puppet state of Manchukuo, was completely under Japanese control, and the Japanese forces were turning their attention to other North China territories.

Japan had demonstrated to the world that the way of the transgressor was far from hard and that a great power might defy the League with impunity. Weak or undefended nations, it was clear, faced a precarious future, for the peace pacts, non-aggression treaties, and League guarantees were proving a flimsy defense against modern armies on the march. Mussolini in Rome and Hitler in Berlin drew the obvious lesson from the League's failure and both grew more bellicose. Dazzled by dreams of empire, the Italians began preparations as early as 1932 for a campaign of conquest in Ethiopia, the only African state not yet subjugated by a European power. Troops were concentrated in the Italian border colonies of Eritrea and Somaliland, and by the close of 1934 frontier incidents had been multiplied as a prelude and warrant for armed intervention. In the autumn of 1935, the Italian columns, supported by tanks and airplanes, penetrated and easily overran the backward and anarchic kingdom and it was annexed to Italy by proclamation (May 9, 1936).

Ethiopia had been an independent sovereign state, a member of the League of Nations, and the government, headed by the Emperor Haile Selassie, appealed no less than four times to the League for protection and for arbitration of the Italo-

Ethiopian dispute. Faced with such an unequivocal test, the League Council and League Assembly declared Italy an aggressor and voted "economic sanctions" to restrain the Italian invaders. A partial and ineffectual boycott by those states most ardent in defense of League principles was the consequence; but the resulting loss of trade was not acute enough to restrain Italy; and the boycott was not applied to those indispensable imports (such as gasoline) without which the Italian invasion would have been impossible. Nor was any attempt made to close the Suez Canal, through which the Italian troops and supplies had to pass to reach the area of combat. The real decision, in this half-hearted effort to halt aggression, lay with the diplomats in Paris and London. Fearful of driving Italy and Germany into an alliance, they sacrificed Ethiopia to the principle of power politics and selfish expediency.

How futile all calculations based upon such appeasement must prove was promptly demonstrated. Adolf Hitler had already announced (March, 1935) that Germany would rearm in defiance of the Versailles Treaty. One year later (March, 1936), when it was evident that the League sanctions had been more of a threat than a reality, Hitler marched his troops into the Rhineland and began to fortify this demilitarized zone which had insulated France from Germany. The British, French, Belgians, and Americans had opened the way for this step by withdrawing their forces of occupation from the German Rhine provinces ahead of schedule, one more gesture of appeasement which had failed to appease.

Rhineland refortified

The hopes inspiring French and British statesmen that some concessions to Italy might avert an Italo-German alliance proved vain. In July, 1936, a civil war broke out in Spain. Conservative forces, led by a group of army officers, attacked the republican régime which had been established there after the revolution of 1931 had driven out Alphonso XIII. From the first days of this new revolt, the "Nationalists," as the insurgents styled themselves, received arms, planes, artillery, and military aid from Germany and Italy. The Russian Soviet government, alert to the threat implied in German rearmament, had joined the League of Nations in 1934. It now sought to assist the Spanish Republicans against the combined efforts of the Fascist powers. But the mood of appeasement still dominated the diplomats in Paris and London and their moves were cautious, ambiguous, and ineffective. They sought to pledge all the powers to a neutral policy of non-intervention in the Spanish civil war, and they preserved the farce, although Hitler sent ten thousand and Mussolini one hundred thousand Fascist soldiers and technicians to fight with the insurgents. Valuable assistance was furnished the insurgent cause by German airmen, who leveled towns held by the Republicans as a demonstration of Teuton air superiority. Spain thus became a testing field where Fascist (Italian and German) arms and methods could be tried out. Russian experts, and some Russian tanks, planes, and supplies reached the Republicans, but after thirty months of cruel and destructive warfare, massacres, and reprisals, the insurgents (or Nationalists), under the command of General Francisco Franco, emerged as victors. In March, 1939, the sanguinary struggle, which had cost three quarters of a million lives, ended with the fall of Madrid, and the German and Italian contingents were withdrawn. But before this "solution" was attained, democratic statesmanship had been discredited by worse rebuffs and more signal defeats, and the events in Spain were eclipsed by German moves in central Europe. These must now be summarized.

Spanish civil war

7. AGGRESSION AND APPEASEMENT

The humiliation of a military defeat may chasten a proud nation temporarily, but it is almost certain to excite a delayed reaction which, when it grows strong, will manifest itself in arrogant and dynamic forms. One illustration of this was the invasion of France by allied armies in the first years of the great French Revolution, an invasion that alarmed and mortified French patriots, but led to the creation of those magnificent armies with which Napoleon dominated Europe ten

Defeats breed resentments

years later. Similarly, the defeat of Prussia by Napoleon in the campaign of 1806 quickened Prussian pride, inspired army reforms, and made possible the sacrifices and victories won by the Germans in the War of Liberation against the French after 1812. The French, in turn, defeated by the Germans in the War of 1870-71, experienced a strong mood of chauvinism in the eighties, when General Boulanger, a sort of prefigurement of Hitler in some respects, advocated a war of revenge. Such parallels made it predictable, and almost inescapable, that when Germany recovered from the losses, exhaustion, and dislocation caused by World War I, the nation would yield itself to a mood of overcompensation, and indulge in willful acts of self-assertiveness and aspiration for power. That eighty million Germans would willingly remain politically divided, financially penalized, disarmed and impotent, was highly improbable. A mood of revolt was in the making, and the fact that Germany had no "wild west," no empty frontier lands, no colonies to beckon adventurous and turbulent youths, meant that the most headstrong and impetuous adolescents remained to join in violent political agitation.

One principle most frequently emphasized by the peacemakers of 1919 was the right of all nations to self-determination. New political frontiers were drawn, six new states (Finland, Estonia, Latvia, Lithuania, Poland, and Czechoslovakia) appeared on the European map, and three lesser states previously in evidence (Serbia, Rumania, and Greece) were enlarged. These changes were justified by the treaty-makers on the ground that they assured national minorities maximum independence. But it is impossible to separate mixed populations by a mathematical line. In disputed areas "islands" of the defeated peoples, the Germans in particular, were divided rather than united by the redrawn frontiers. Austria, reduced to a small republic of six million people, German in speech and sentiment, was in reality a political and cultural fragment of the Reich. In the Sudeten area of Czechoslovakia, three million Germans, citizens of the Austro-Hungarian Empire before 1918, were discontented when they found themselves a minority in a predominantly Slavic republic. The German minority in Poland, in the Free City of Danzig, and in the Tyrolean areas transferred to Italy, were all susceptible to patriotic appeals and responsive to arguments that they would be happier if incorporated into a Greater Germany. It was a clever and persuasive move on Hitler's part to disguise the program of German expansion in Europe as a simple and legitimate desire to see the principle of self-determination vindicated by assembling all true Germans under one government.

German minorities

This campaign to redeem all German minorities registered its first notable triumph when the population of the Saar Basin, independent under the supervision of the League of Nations for fifteen years, voted for reincorporation with Germany in 1934. Encouraged by this proof of German solidarity, the National-Socialists began to press for an *Anschluss* or amalgamation of Austria with Germany. The first effort (1934) proved a failure, but by 1938 the program had been better concerted and a demonstration in Austria, followed by prompt support from German tank columns, transformed Austria into a province of Greater Germany. Although such a change of status was specifically prohibited by the treaties of 1919, no effective protest came from French or British quarters.

Austria

With Austria under German control the military position of the Czechoslovak Republic became highly vulnerable if not actually indefensible (see map, page 955). Pursuing adroitly the strategy of the limited objective, Hitler had forborne agitation among the Sudeten Germans, and had negotiated a ten-year non-aggression pact with Poland (1934) to quiet Polish apprehensions. But once Austria was joined to Germany, the "redemption" of the Sudetenland became an urgent object of National-Socialist policy. The only question in doubt was the resistance which France, Britain, and Russia might offer to this further German aggrandizement.

Czechoslovakia

Convinced that his opponents would neither combine to check him nor risk armed resistance, Hitler pressed on relentlessly. Six months after the Austro-German *coup*, a German-Czech crisis flamed up. But by this time (September, 1938) the attitude of the western democracies had grown a little more firm. The French mobilized part of their reserves. But the British were unprepared for war, and Prime Minister Neville Chamberlain suggested a conference. Twice Chamberlain flew to Germany only to find that Hitler raised his demands with each concession. When Hitler demanded the immediate annexation of the Sudetenland to Germany, the Czechs mobilized, British and French leaders consulted with Russian diplomats, and a concerted opposition to German demands seemed probable. Throughout Europe people scanned the skies for the bombing planes which would announce hostilities, and a mood of fascination and fatality gripped them. President Roosevelt from Washington, Prime Minister Chamberlain from London, Premier Daladier from Paris urged Hitler to withhold his armies until a diplomatic conference could draft a settlement. When Mussolini from Rome added his voice, Hitler agreed to a four-power conference (September 29, 1938). He received Chamberlain, Daladier, and Mussolini at Munich and won his demands that German troops occupy the disputed Sudeten regions within a few days. The truncated Czechoslovak state was then to receive a guaranty from Britain, France, Germany, and Italy that its revised frontiers would be respected.

Munich "cession"

A breath of relief passed over Europe as the tension eased, and Chamberlain, back in England, announced, "I believe that it is peace for our time." But the sacrifice of Czechoslovakia and the fact that Britain and France had accepted Mussolini's intervention while ignoring Russia appeared ominous to many observers. For it suggested that the British and French government leaders were prepared to acquiesce in Hitler's aggressive moves if they drew him *eastward*, to Vienna, Prague, and possibly into Poland. This *Drang nach Osten* was a threat to Russia and might involve Germany in a war with the Soviet Union, while the British behind their sea-wall and the French behind their Maginot Line watched in safety the struggle of the two great military powers of eastern Europe.

Confused aims and expectations

Such calculations cannot have been wholly absent from the minds of the British and French diplomats, and may help to explain their nerveless irresolution as Hitler's forces pressed into Czechoslovakia and served notice to the world that one more small nation had been sacrificed to expediency. For the guaranties promised the Czechs at Munich proved hollow and hypocritical. One third of the population and almost one third of the territory of the helpless republic were divided among Germany, Poland, and Hungary, and the remaining segments, Bohemia, Slovakia, and Ruthenia were split into autonomous units. By March, 1939, the Czechoslovak state was a fiction and German domination a fact. Bohemia and Moravia were declared German protectorates and Slovakia likewise submitted to German guardianship.

Czechoslovakia absorbed

This *dénouement* demonstrated beyond escape the falsity of Hitler's pretension that he wished no annexations, but only the incorporation of German-populated areas into Greater Germany. The National-Socialist foreign policy was revealed as one of unlimited aggression which threatened all the states of Europe. Scarcely had Czechoslovakia disintegrated before the Germans seized Memel from Lithuania and demanded Danzig and the Polish Corridor. The defense of Czechoslovakia had become precarious when Austria fell; the defense of Poland grew even more hazardous with Memel and Czechoslovakia and Danzig passing under German control (see map, page 955). The policy of the limited objective (which Frederick the Great had called "eating an artichoke one leaf at a time") was becoming an inexorable march of conquest under Hitler's dynamic direction.

Technique of "limited objectives"

At this critical moment, when Germany was intimidating all the northern European nations, Italy seized the opportunity to invade and annex Albania (April, 1939). The Nationalist government in Spain proclaimed

GUERNICA, BY PABLO PICASSO

The defeat of the Spanish Republicans by the Nationalist insurgents, who had the aid of Italian and German contingents, was a prelude to a vaster war between the totalitarian states and the democracies. (Painting on extended loan to the Museum of Modern Art, New York City.)

THE BRITISH STILL HOPED FOR PEACE

Prime Minister Neville Chamberlain returned from Munich with the message, "I believe that it is peace for our time."

its sympathy and alliance with Italy, Germany, and Japan. It seemed as if the international structure of Europe which had been set up in 1919 was falling into chaos, and lesser nations looked about for protection, and looked in vain. For no firm combination of the democratic or satiated powers had crystallized to check the aggressive policies of the "Have-not" states. Germany and Italy, joined by the "Rome-Berlin Axis," had concerted their moves with paralyzing effect. A triangular pact uniting Berlin, Tokyo, and Rome in the so-called "Anti-Comintern Pact" against Russia, further protected the aggressors and enabled them to apply pressure where and when they would. The hesitation and timidity of the French and British statesmen, with their policy of appeasement and their readiness to sacrifice small states, had encouraged the aggressors instead of placating them. Finally, the dubious negotiations and the distrust manifested by the British toward the Russian régime had convinced Hitler that no alliance of Britain, France, and Russia was likely to materialize. The weak Franco-Russian Accord of 1935 did not seem a prelude to a new equivalent of the Triple Entente which had defeated the Germany of William II, and in the absence of such a triad of powers Germany was the dominant power in Europe.

Berlin, Rome and Tokyo unite

In all the European capitals this truth was recognized. Europe waited to learn which country was to be the next victim of the dictator at Berlin. When it became clear that Poland was threatened, the French and British governments pledged their assistance to the Polish Republic (March, 1939); but in May and June they also pledged Turkey their aid, a move which suggested (as at Munich) that they feared Russian designs as much as they distrusted Hitler's projects. This suspicious and ambivalent attitude of the western democracies toward the Soviet Union becomes more understandable when it is realized that throughout the summer of 1939 negotiations were conducted for a tripartite Russo-Franco-British alliance, but the parleys failed to prosper. At the same time, the Soviet government was weighing offers from Germany for economic concessions and a non-aggression treaty. It is probable that Hitler, and his foreign minister, Joachim von Ribbentrop, offered the Russians their consent for a Soviet reannexation of Esthonia, Latvia, and Lithuania, and proposed a division of Poland between Russia and Germany. These were moves which the French and British negotiators could hardly be expected to discuss and could not possibly approve, a fact which may help to explain why the hope for an accord between London and Moscow languished. Instead, on August 23, 1939, the Soviet Union entered into a non-aggression pact with Germany. This "diplomatic revolution" threw the small nations into a state of consternation, confused the Japanese, and sealed the fate of Poland. Though the British renewed their recent pledge of aid and the French likewise prepared to intervene if Poland were attacked, it was evident that they could not prevent a division of Poland if Germany was to attack and Russia to acquiesce. Hitler wasted less than a week in preliminaries, once the German-Soviet Pact was completed. On September 1, 1939, German land and air forces opened an irresistible series of drives against the Polish armies, attacking from the west, north, and south. On September 3, when demands on Berlin that the German armies halt remained unanswered, the British and French governments declared war on Germany. The Second World War of the twentieth century had commenced, and was to prove longer, more tragic, more destructive, and more truly global in its scope than World War I.

German pact with Russia

72

The Second World War

(1939–1945)

> We are fifty or a hundred years behind the advanced countries. We must make good this distance in ten years. Either we do it or they crush us.
> JOSEPH V. STALIN (1931).

> The enemy [Russia] is already broken and will never rise again.
> ADOLF HITLER (1941).

IN MODERN WARFARE the increasing part played by intricate and expensive weapons, producible in vast quantities by mass production, gives the aggressor nation a great initial advantage. A campaign, launched without warning by a government which has built up large armaments, tanks, aircraft, self-propelled guns, submarines, explosives, bombs, may crush a weaker neighbor in a few days or weeks. In a protracted struggle, however, the side which possesses the greater resources in men, money, machinery, and material must outmatch an opponent deficient in reserves and supplies. This truth, demonstrated in World War I, was emphasized anew in World War II.

1. FROM THE FALL OF POLAND TO THE FALL OF FRANCE (SEPTEMBER, 1939 — JUNE, 1940)

Poland crushed

Though Poland in 1939 had a population of thirty million and a large conscript army, there was little hope that the Polish state, lacking defensible frontiers, could resist an attack by German mechanized units and air power. The British and French could provide no direct material aid, and the Russians, by their new compact with Germany, had become opponents instead of allies. Within a month the Polish armies had been encircled and broken to pieces; Germany held the western half of the defunct republic; and the eastern half was occupied by Russian troops.

Stalemate

It is probable that Hitler hoped at this point to arrange a peace settlement with the French and British, for fighting almost ceased. The Germans, ensconced behind their newly constructed "West Wall," the French holding their supposedly impregnable Maginot Line, and the British across the North Sea, measured one another carefully. The long and lethal deadlock of trench warfare which so often immobilized armies in World War I had created the belief that a strong defensive position was almost unassailable, and the swift Polish campaign taught the French little about the risks they might run in open mobile warfare. For six months the French and British waited, trusting that a sea blockade would weaken Germany and win the war.

Germany strikes

The Germans, however, had built up reserves of necessary military commodities, their chemists had learned how to produce synthetic nitrates, quinine, rubber, and gasoline, and their war strength was steadily increased throughout the winter of 1939–40. On April 9, they struck again, without warning, and again they found their chosen opponents unready and distracted. A lightning thrust into Denmark, an air and sea-borne invasion of Norway, delivered these two countries into their power within a few weeks. British and French landing forces held a few Norwegian ports briefly, but were forced to

963

abandon them, and the Germans swiftly constructed air and submarine bases from the Skagerrak to the Arctic Circle (see map, page 966). Then, as spring dried the fields for tanks and cleared the skies for bombing planes, the Germans wheeled westward. One month after the blow at Denmark and Norway (May 10, 1940) they struck Holland, Belgium, and Luxemburg. Some aid was furnished by spies and German sympathizers within these smaller states, but the real victory was achieved by speed, strength, and ruthlessness. Holland was crushed in less than a week, largely by air-borne paratroopers dropped at vital communications centers. The Belgian army, despite the arrival of some French and British support, was split, surrounded, and forced to capitulate (May 28).

France capitulates

Not strength and swiftness alone, but the inspired use of mechanized divisions explained the German victories. The French had prepared for a war of siege and were bewildered by a war of movement. When the famed Maginot Line was pierced at the Sedan Gap and an army of giant tanks and mechanized infantry raced through the breach to sweep across Belgium and northern France, resistance collapsed. Uncertain which way the German columns would turn, outfought, outgeneraled, and broken in morale, the French and British divisions fell back in disorder. Within ten days (May 11-21) the Germans had sliced through their center, racing down the Somme Valley to the sea. With Belgium conquered and communications with Paris cut, the British expeditionary force recoiled upon Dunkirk. All heavy equipment had to be abandoned, but most of the men were saved by a mass evacuation completed June 4. For the shattered French divisions, however, no way of escape was open. On June 10, one month after the German drive had commenced in the west, Italy declared war and invaded southern France. On June 17 the French high command asked for an armistice, and on June 25 the fighting ceased. Two thirds of France was held by the Germans. The remaining third, ruled from Vichy by an extemporized régime under Marshal Henri Pétain, retained a shadowy independence until November, 1942, when the Germans occupied the whole country.

2. THE BATTLE OF BRITAIN

By the end of June, 1940, Great Britain stood alone against a continent where Hitler was the master. Not since Napoleon's day had one despot controlled such a wide European empire or commanded such awesome military superiority. The continental seacoast, harbors and bases, from Norway to Spain, were in German hands. Gibraltar might be assailed from the rear with Spanish collaboration. Italy threatened the Mediterranean Sea routes; Italian armies in Libya and Ethiopia were preparing to invade Egypt, close the Suez Canal, attack Aden, or invade Tunis and French Morocco. More immediate and dangerous was the threat to British supply routes to London, Southampton, Liverpool, and Glasgow, for German sea and air power might block these shipping lanes. Even if ships could get through, supplies might fail. The Scandinavian states, Holland, France, and French North Africa had provided three fourths of the British imports of iron ore and paper, half to three fourths the butter and eggs, and a major proportion of other vital commodities. With the Germans controlling these sources of supply the British had to look abroad and provide ships for the long haul from Canada, the United States, South America, and Australia. In World War I, German U-boats had cut British shipping and imports to a margin so narrow that in 1917 only six weeks' supply of food and raw materials remained on reserve. With many more strategic harbors available for submarines and surface raiders, with advanced bases and fields for aerial attack and reconnaissance, it seemed almost certain that Hitler could isolate, cripple, and starve Britain where William II had failed.

It had taken the Germans only four weeks to crush Poland, a state of thirty million. The resistance of Norway, Denmark, the

Britain isolated

FRANKLIN DELANO ROOSEVELT (1882–1945)

WINSTON CHURCHILL

Both Roosevelt and Churchill received early training in naval affairs. They were competent to grasp the global strategy of World War II.

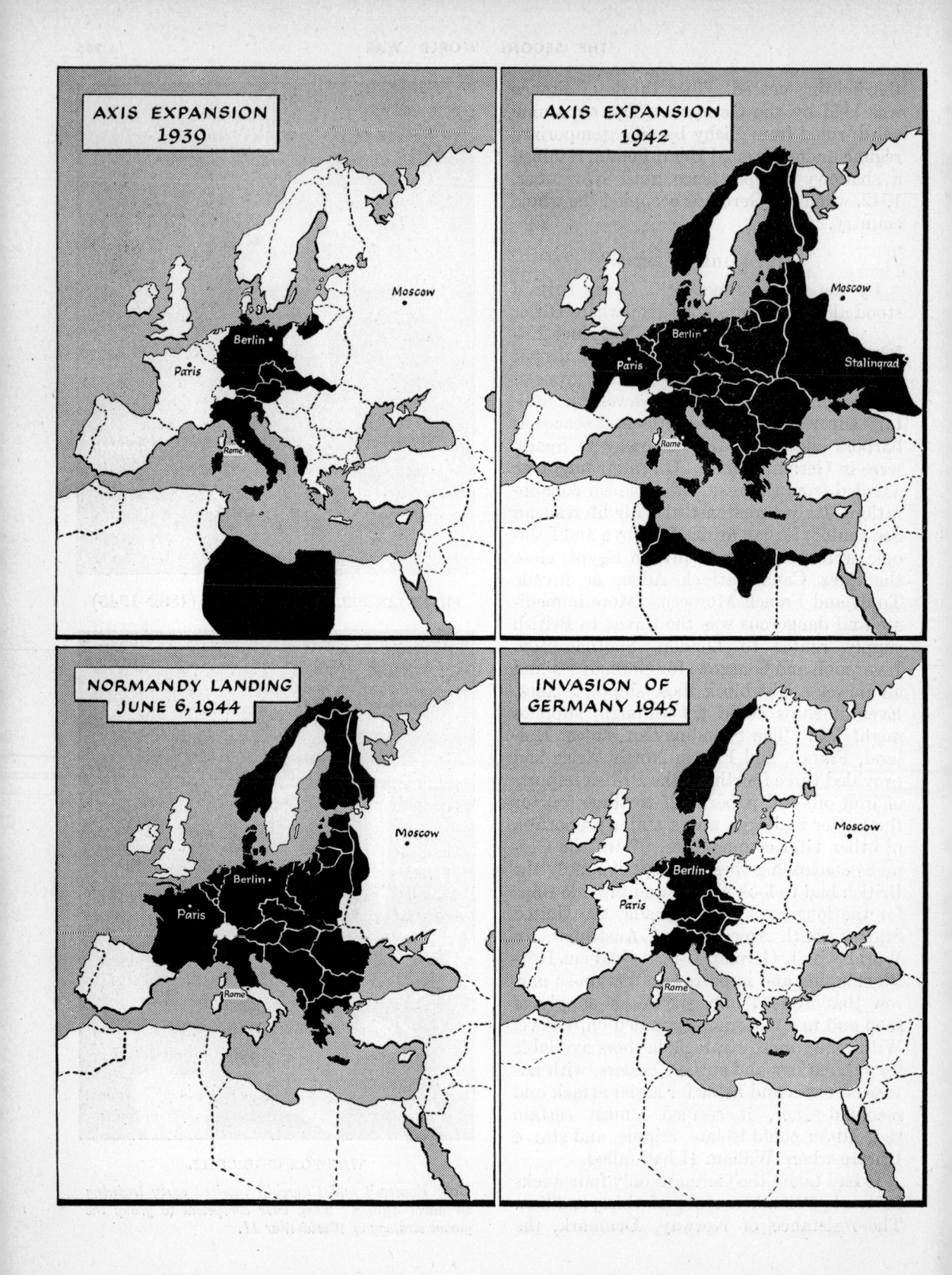

AXIS EXPANSION 1939	AXIS EXPANSION 1942
NORMANDY LANDING JUNE 6, 1944	INVASION OF GERMANY 1945

Netherlands, Belgium, and France, with a combined population exceeding sixty million, had been overcome in eight weeks. Could Great Britain, alone and vulnerable, expect to survive? The British themselves did not know the answer, but they faced the emergency with extraordinary courage and confidence. On the day that Holland and Belgium were attacked (May 10, 1940), the Chamberlain ministry resigned, and the energetic Winston Churchill became prime minister of a coalition war cabinet. Under his forceful and inspiring leadership the British prepared to fight to the last for their national existence.

Churchill in power

Three circumstances favored the British defense. (1) The Germans were not prepared to attempt an immediate invasion of the British Isles at the most favorable moment after France fell. The suddenness of their success threw their armies out of gait; they had prepared for land, not for naval or amphibious operations, and they could not cross the Channel while the British fleet remained intact. (2) Their submarine fleet was limited to a few hundred boats and they were unable to open at once the ruinous undersea warfare against British shipping for which, ironically, they now possessed superfluous bases. (3) German air power, still superior to all opposition, had been developed primarily to operate in combination with the ground forces and functioned less effectively when used as an independent arm of attack. The British, on the other hand, though late in arming, had specialized on fighter planes which could close swiftly with the German bombers when the latter were far from their bases and lacked a defensive escort.

British assets

Six weeks after the fighting ceased in France, the German air force commenced mass daylight bombing raids over England (August 8, 1940). It was their hope to dislocate British industry and shatter British morale. But they suffered such heavy losses that they failed to destroy the planes, air bases, hangars, and factories or break the British spirit. In ten weeks the attackers lost nearly twenty-four hundred aircraft to the defender's eight hundred. British Spitfire and Hurricane fighters, directed by secret methods of detection and communication, provided an answer to German mass bombing. After October, 1940, the German attacks weakened, and winter skies and cloudy weather helped to shroud the stricken land. Britain survived, but at the cost of many gallant pilots, thousands of civilian casualties, and the damage or destruction of one home in every five.

Air power fails to win

3. THE BATTLE OF RUSSIA

One compelling reason why the German commanders hesitated to risk further losses in the air, or to take the gigantic gamble of flinging an army into England, was their distrust of Soviet Russia. The Russo-German Pact of August 23, 1939, had saved Germany from a two-front war, but the advantage which resulted lay primarily with Russia. Not only did the pact permit Soviet troops to move into the eastern half of Poland in September, 1939, thus establishing direct contact with German-held territory; in March, 1940, after a brief Russo-Finnish conflict, Russia annexed over 16,000 square miles of Finnish territory in order to strengthen the approaches to Leningrad. Esthonia, Latvia, and Lithuania, with a combined area of 60,000 square miles and a population of 6,000,000, became members of the Union of Soviet Socialist Republics on August 3, 1940; and Bessarabia and northern Bukovina were annexed from Rumania on June 26, 1940. These gains added about 100,000 square miles and 10,000,000 subjects to the Soviet Union, and constituted a *restoration* in Russian opinion, rather than expansion, because all the territory (save northern Bukovina) had formed part of the Russian Empire in 1914. In reclaiming it, Russia, like Germany, was acting as a "revisionist" power, but the Russian advance brought Russia and Germany nearer to possible conflict because it brought them nearer together.

Russo-German tension

Thus, to the masters of Nazi Germany, Soviet Russia constituted a persistent threat and a persistent temptation: a threat because the growing Russian forces and dynamic Rus-

German calculations

sian industries increased the danger of a Russian attack if German strength were dissipated elsewhere. But Russia was also a temptation because Russian oil, coal, timber, minerals, wheat, and livestock were needed to feed German workers and German machines. An additional factor, which may have influenced the military specialists at Berlin who had perfected the theory of mechanized war, was the fact that the vast Russian plains offered an ideal field for *Blitzkrieg* tactics with motorized columns. To repeat the Polish campaign on a continental scale, with the prospect of greater glory and proportionately greater booty, was a seductive project. Then, with Russia broken and prostrate, the Germans could undertake an attack on Britain, a drive through Spain, or the penetration of Africa, Asia Minor, or even India. In Moscow the inclinations of the German militarists were no secret and the Russo-German Pact was accepted as an astute device to gain precious time. Russian experts pondered the lessons revealed by the opening campaigns of World War II, adapted their defensive measures to offset or neutralize the deadly innovations of scientific warfare, and freed themselves (as Hitler had tried to do) from the risk of a two-front war, by concluding a Russo-Japanese accord, a non-aggression treaty signed on April 13, 1941.

It is probable that Hitler in turn was aware of the Russian moves. On June 22, 1941, without warning or declaration of war, German armies smashed across the Soviet frontier from the Baltic to the Black Sea. Finland, Hungary, Bulgaria, and Rumania had been reduced to satellite states in the German system, and were persuaded to yield their roads, supplies, and armies to Hitler's direction. The invincible *Wehrmacht* hurled back the Russian armies, engulfed a million prisoners, and captured Smolensk and Kiev, Odessa, Kharkov, and Rostov (see map, page 966). In less than four months the Germans had achieved successes so impressive that Hitler proclaimed the Russian military power had been permanently destroyed.

Germany strikes east, 1941

This confident boast proved for the Germans a disastrous miscalculation. The Russians had yielded territory for time, falling back until the German lines were stretched and far extended. When the Soviet strategists decided to hold a defensive position, the Russian soldiers proved their heroism and high morale by grim defiance. Rallying before Leningrad, Moscow, and Sevastopol, they checked the Teuton tide, while guerrilla forces in the rear of the enemy's lines attacked supply trains and harassed the garrisons. With winter weather the Russians regained the initiative, for they were enured to the climate and familiar with the terrain. Skilled in winter fighting and transportation problems, they struck with vigor and recaptured one fifth of the lost area before spring. Moscow and Leningrad were relieved, and trainloads of machinery, withdrawn in time before the onsweep of the battle tides, were reassembled in newly constructed factories in the Ural region, a thousand miles behind the combat zone. Napoleon once described Britain and Russia as the "great intangibles" — Britain because of the Channel, Russia because of its vast area. Hitler was learning the significance of these obstacles.

Yielding territory for time

With the summer of 1942 the German armies renewed their attack, but this time they turned south. More than ever, the oil of the Caucasus had become a prize for which either side would sacrifice a million men. But the prize escaped the invaders' grasp. Though Sevastopol and Rostov fell to them, Stalingrad on the Volga, through which the oil was shipped, held out for months against titanic assaults. With the coming of the second winter, the Germans were stalled once more, and the Russians, turning upon them with fury, obliterated their summer gains and pushed back the lines which threatened Stalingrad and Leningrad. This Russian capacity to renew the offensive astonished the world. For in yielding the occupied zone the Soviet Union had forfeited seemingly indispensable sources of supply — twenty per cent of its oil, thirty per cent of its population, forty per cent of its coal and machine-tool industry, fifty per

Germany strikes south, 1942

AIR ROUTES 1945

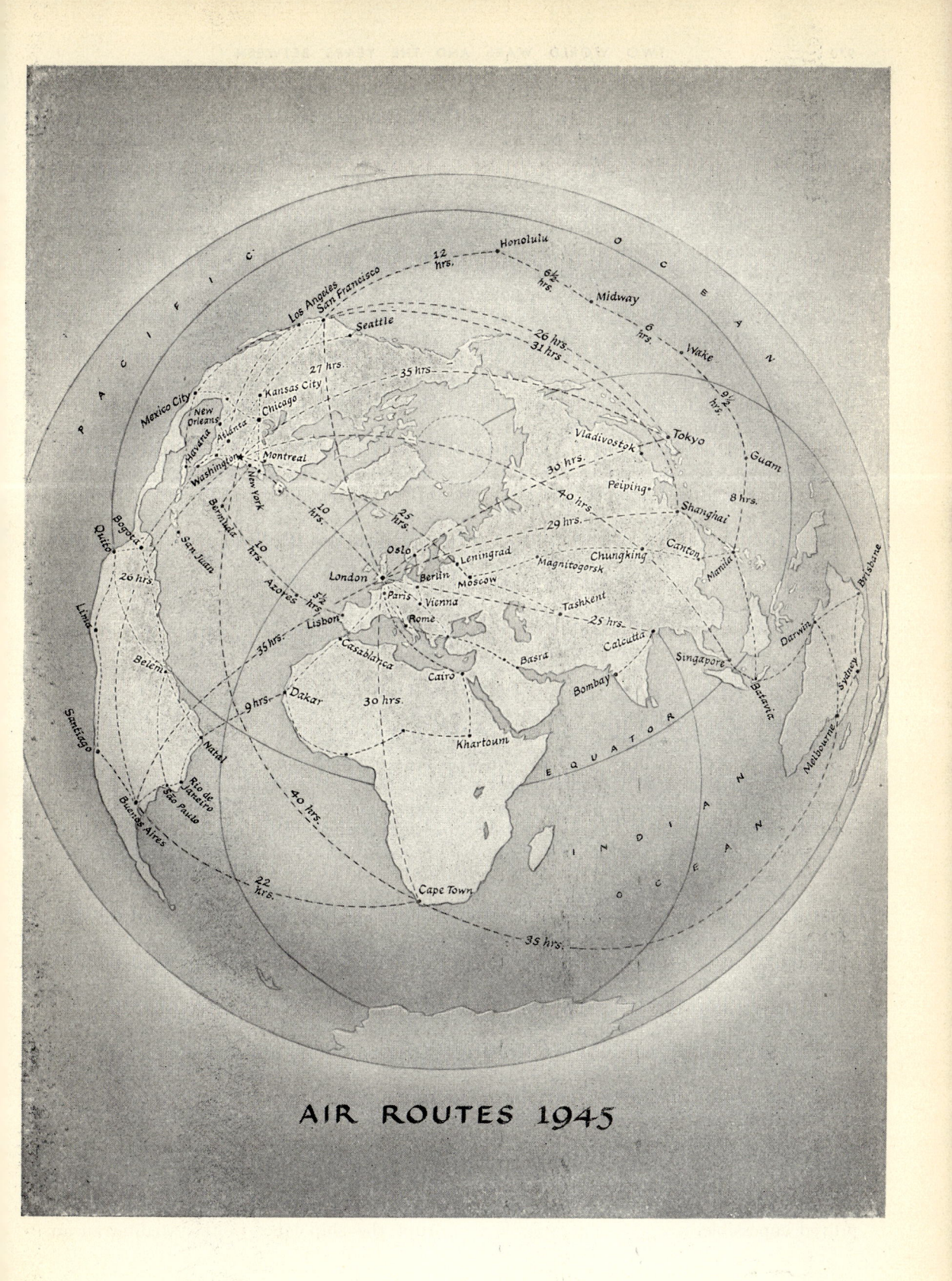

cent of its richest wheatfields, livestock, and farm areas.

But no hardship, no sacrifice, and no reprisals by the baffled invaders could quench the ardor of the Soviet population. The troops were reorganized in new mobile units better adapted to modern mechanized warfare and the Russian strategists defeated the best generals of the *Wehrmacht* at their own game. The summer of 1943 found the Soviet divisions, not the German armies, opening the offensive and driving forward to victory. Winter (1943–44) brought no relaxation of the deadly thrusts; and by the spring of 1944 the Germans and their allies were battling desperately to defend their own borders. From Finland to East Prussia, through Poland, Hungary, and Rumania, the eastern front was ablaze, moving forward like a prairie fire fanned by a relentless wind. The opening months of 1945 saw the irresistible holocaust engulf Germany and her satellite states, until all eastern Europe was overshadowed by the dust of the Soviet columns, and all opposition died away to silence before the thunder of the Russian guns.

Russia revives, 1943–44

Some realization of the leading part Russia played in the military defeat of Germany may be gained from the estimate that until 1945 probably four fifths of the total German losses in killed, wounded, prisoners, and missing, were casualties of the eastern front. But the contribution of the British and Americans in making possible this Russian resurgence should not be discounted. Though indirect and secondary as factors in the actual fighting, the shiploads of machinery, guns, tanks, trucks and planes which were dispatched from British and American ports played an essential part in keeping the Russian armies supplied and in the field. Furthermore, the steady bombing of German factories cut the supply of German war material, and the economic blockade starved the once dominant German industries until all German divisions were deficient in equipment, mobility, and morale. Without this sapping of the German strength, the Russian recovery and ultimate triumph might have proved impossible.

The Soviet contribution

4. GLOBAL STRATEGY: GIBRALTAR TO SINGAPORE

While two to three hundred divisions, the equivalent of three to four million men, Russian and German, were locked in exhausting combat from the White Sea to the Black, the British government was marshaling the resources of a world empire and calculating the moves in a six-year campaign of global strategy designed to block the German-Italian-Japanese bid for dominion. This aspect of World War II is the most complex and most difficult to summarize in a brief analysis. The plans of the United Nations depended in essence upon the problem of *supply*, the problem of producing and transporting the men, war materials, and food needed for long campaigns in all parts of the world. In war the calculation of supply and transportation is known as *logistics*, and there are important differences to consider in the mobility and reinforcement of armies which are supplied by *land routes* and those mobilized, moved, and maintained by *sea power*. World War II provided an historic example of a struggle between land power and sea power, for Britain and the United States maintained control of the ocean routes, or most of them, while the German and Italian forces were limited more and more inexorably to the land. Whenever they crossed salt water, the Axis armies exposed their supply lines to attack. This fact dictated Anglo-American strategy. The weakest sectors of the German-Italian battle-front were those held by the Italian troops in Libya and Ethiopia, second came the Italian islands in the Mediterranean Sea, Sicily and Sardinia, which had likewise to be supplied by ship, and third came the Italian Peninsula, for Italy imported oil, coal, and wheat by sea in normal times, and the long coastline was vulnerable to naval invasion in war. These three concentric and exposed "zones" were assailed in turn by the Anglo-American forces.

British long-range plans

The Germans, Italians, and Japanese were not wholly deficient in sea power: on the contrary, Germany could control the Baltic Sea and part of the North Sea, Italy could interrupt the ship lanes in the Mediterranean,

Bottlenecks of trade

BRITISH TANKS ROLLING OUT FROM
THE FACTORIES OF THE MINISTRY OF
SUPPLY

UNITED STATES FLYING FORTRESSES
OVER A NAZI FIGHTER BASE IN FRANCE

Their vast resources and machinery for mass production gave the United Nations a material superiority which in the end proved overwhelming.

and Japan, an island kingdom, dominated the coastal routes of the Far East to the East Indies. But none of these powers depended for its day-to-day existence upon keeping the high seas open, as Great Britain did. A study of the map on page 847 will indicate how farsighted British naval policy has been, for of six vital "bottlenecks" in the world trade routes, all save the Panama Canal were under British control in 1939, and the far southern routes around South America, Africa, and Australia could be controlled from British bases or supply stations in the Falkland Islands, Capetown, Hobart, or Wellington. To deal British trade and prestige a deadly blow, an enemy had only to close some of these "bottlenecks." The Straits of Dover, Gibraltar, Suez, Aden, or Singapore under hostile guns would involve a serious dislocation of British naval power and commercial economy. When Germany, Italy, and Japan united for World War II, their general staffs worked out plans for simultaneous attacks on all these gateways of commerce. German planes, submarines, and long-range cannon were to seal the English Channel. A thrust through Spain (with the consent of the Nationalist régime which the Axis nations had helped into power there) might close the Straits of Gibraltar. Pantelleria, a small island between Sicily and Tunis, had been heavily fortified by the Italians to bisect the Mediterranean, and an attack upon Egypt and Aden from the new Italian conquest, Ethiopia, might close both ends of the Red Sea. Finally, a Japanese descent upon Singapore would curtail sea traffic to the Far East and cut off China.

When the fall of France placed continental Europe under German control, the British cabinet did not hesitate, in the midst of the Battle of Britain, to ship an armored division all the way around Africa to reinforce the defenses of the Suez Canal. The spring of 1941 found British expeditionary forces pressing a steady campaign against the Italian East African Empire. No longer able to supply the army marooned in Ethiopia, because the British were astride the communication route through Suez, Mussolini saw his proud conquest crumble. Eritrea, Italian Somaliland,

Africa first

and Ethiopia fell before the British attacks between March and May, 1941. An Italian attempt to reach Egypt through Libya in 1940 was hurled back. Renewed with German aid early in 1941, it was hurled back a second time. The difficulty of supplying their African forces across the mid-Mediterranean helped to explain these Axis failures, and in April, 1941, the Germans drove at Suez more directly. Pressing into the Balkans, they overran Yugoslavia and Greece, and seized the island of Crete with air-borne divisions (April–May, 1941). But there they stopped, hesitating again to dispatch more forces into Asia Minor or Africa with Russia unconquered and menacing on their flank. Meanwhile, the British, to forestall a land drive through Constantinople and Turkey and so to Suez, occupied French Syria, Iraq, and Iran (May–September, 1941). Sea power had once more frustrated land and air power, and air attack failed to redress the balance. Though the Germans dispatched their specially trained and equipped *Afrika Korps* to Libya and the British were driven back almost to the gates of Alexandria, the outcome was delayed, not averted. In May, 1943, the last German resistance in Tunis and Bizerte collapsed; the United Nations controlled all Africa; and the Mediterranean was reopened to their shipping. The slow but inexorable pressure of sea power was turning the scale, and Axis forces were confined thenceforth to the "Fortress of Europe."

5. THE AMERICAN ACHIEVEMENT

While soldiers and sailors of the United Nations were fighting these desperate campaigns to reopen and keep open the vital sea lanes, other battles were going forward with less drama but equal success; the battle of shipping, the battle of industry, and the battle of finance. Modern wars, if they are lost on the assembly line, cannot be won on the firing line. The contribution of the United States as "the arsenal of democracy" was the decisive force in forging the victory of the United Nations.

Without a "bridge of ships" the sea powers could not have survived or continued the

Assembly line vs. firing line

struggle. Had Germany concentrated more heavily upon U-boat construction before 1939, the threat to the British life lines might have proved more conclusive than the abortive Italo-German thrusts at Suez or Gibraltar. In six years of war (1939–45) the United Nations destroyed some seven hundred U-boats. Most of these submarines, however, were built after the commencement of hostilities, and the constant losses kept the total at any one time within manageable limits. The giant British liner *Queen Mary* transported over two hundred thousand soldiers in five years of war and no submarine was sighted. Slower vessels sailed in guarded convoys, which so minimized losses that of seventeen thousand vessels sailing under American naval protection only seventeen were sunk, or one in one thousand. Air patrol, new detection devices, and depth bombs finally provided the answer to submarine warfare. But many ships were lost, especially in the first years of war, when unescorted freighters fell victim to mine, torpedo, or gunfire, and German surface raiders attacked and broke up convoys. The shipping crisis remained a grim problem throughout the conflict, for the long hauls to Archangel, Vladivostok, or around Africa threw an extraordinary strain upon world shipping. While the Mediterranean remained closed, and Britain was importing from other continents the supplies once secured in Europe, the problem of ocean transportation dominated and conditioned all others.

The solution was found in American mass production. To replace the sea losses of 21,000,000 gross tons of shipping, the United States yards built 28,000,000 after January 1, 1942, more shipping tonnage than Britain and the United States together possessed in 1939. This replacement was indispensable: before great expeditions could be undertaken or armies transported, the shipping crisis of 1941 and 1942 had to be eased. By cutting the construction period for a freighter from thirty weeks to seven, inventing new designs for amphibious operations, and standardizing production so that ships could be put together in sections, American engineers made possible the global strategy of World War II. Within three years the United States became the leading shipbuilding nation of the world.

The second item in the American achievement was the impressive expansion of air power. German air superiority and aircraft were reduced by persistent attacks, German replacements cut by systematic bombing of factories, assembly plants and air fields; and all enemy camps, industrial centers, railway yards, and bridges became vulnerable targets as Anglo-American aviation won a clear ascendancy and dominated the European skies.

The third great factor in the American achievement was the organization, equipment, and training of an army of ten million men, which proved equal in all respects to the long-established military forces of the Old World. The American military successes, including the triumphs of the supply and medical services, proved that the superb organization of the American Expeditionary Force in World War I was no chance accomplishment, for it was surpassed in every important respect in World War II. To this swift and remarkable program of military development was joined a naval program of construction equally impressive. The phenomenal growth of American wealth, production, and power, and the sudden emergence of the United States as one of the three "super powers," and the only one equipped to maintain parity of armaments on land, at sea, and in the air, opened a new era in the international balance of power. American influence, based upon vast economic reserves, and reinforced by the acquisition of air and naval bases dotting the Atlantic and Pacific Oceans, became a paramount force in world affairs.

Most difficult to measure, of all modes of war strategy, was the effect of the Anglo-American blockade on German industry and economy. By issuing ship warrants to all merchant captains who co-operated with them, and by issuing "navicerts" or permits which assured clearance to certified cargoes, the British Ministry of Economic Warfare and the United States Foreign Economic Administration combined their activities, and could speed or delay all ocean shipping. A special board, the Anglo-American Blockade Committee, systematically starved German economy by cutting off all supplies of certain key commodities. So desperate did the German government become in its search for irreplaceable industrial items, such as diamonds for jeweled bearings and cutting tools and the rare minerals platinum and tungsten, that it offered ten to one hundred times the peace-time price and still could not purchase adequate supplies. Neutral nations which produced and might have furnished such materials — Spain, Portugal, Turkey, Switzerland, Sweden — were deterred by the knowledge that their business firms would be placed on the United Nations black list for trading with the enemy. When other methods failed, American and British wealth provided an additional lever, and even goods which the United Nations possessed in abundance were bought in, regardless of price, to keep them from reaching the enemy. This costly mode of blockade is known as "preclusive purchasing." Its effectiveness proved that in war as in peace superior financial resources are a powerful weapon. The efficiency of German industry declined steadily as these restrictive measures were tightened, and the problem of replacing depleted supplies, joined to the problem of rebuilding bombed factories, became a nightmare to the German manufacturers.

In Great Britain, on the other hand, and to a much greater extent in the United States, the expansion of production under the stimulus of war requirements was extraordinary. By 1945 the industrial plants of the United States, secure from air attack, and guaranteed priority on essential supplies, were turning out more war material than all the rest of the world. This marshaling of American resources and multiplication of American production was a guaranty of victory to the United Nations and a prophecy of doom to Germany, Italy, and Japan. But the American achievement, planned with audacity and decision, and carried out with prodigious energy, imposed a grave burden upon American credit. Between 1940 and 1945 the national debt rose from approximately fifty to over two hundred and fifty billion dollars, and the annual budget from some ten to one hundred billion. This enormous increase in expenditure was almost all war expenditure. In 1940 almost nine tenths of the national revenue had been allotted to civilian needs, but in 1945, out of a budget ten times larger, nine tenths was being diverted to war needs. The change in tax rates which these outlays must involve for the American people will help them to comprehend more clearly the pressures and limitations under which most European peoples have lived for decades or centuries. By 1945 the annual *interest* charges on the national debt cost the American people more than the *total* federal budget of twelve years earlier.

6. THE LIBERATION OF EUROPE

The expansion and collapse of the German military hegemony in Europe, built up in five years of annexation and conquest (1938–43) and broken in two (1943–45) is the most arresting historical epic of recent times. Only a succession of maps, vitalized with statistics, which present graphically the relentless march of the German armies, can suggest the power and ruthlessness of the machine which the Germans perfected in their bid for domination.

After one year of open hostilities (September, 1939—September, 1940), Germany controlled the continent of Europe west of Soviet Russia. Italy, though a partner in theory, was a subordinate state. From the frontiers of Russia to the frontiers of Portugal, from Scandinavia to Sicily, conquered or intimidated peoples bowed before German might, or faced the probability of mass deportation and the possibility of mass extermination in the appalling concentration camps. Outside Europe, all North Africa, from the Atlantic coast to the Egyptian border, was likewise under the shadow of the Teuton and Italian legions. Moreover, the tide of conquest was still rising. After two years of war, Finland and the Balkan Peninsula had been added to the German-dominated sphere, and Russia was invaded. After three years of fighting, the German armies held a segment of European Russia *three times* the area of Germany itself. They had almost circled the Black Sea and were striving to enclose the Mediterranean, approaching within a few hundred miles of the Caucasus and of the Suez Canal. The fortunes of Adolf Hitler and the *Wehrmacht* were at full flood. But in 1943 they began to ebb, slowly at first, then more swiftly. Systematically, despite reverses, the United Nations reduced North Africa, then leaped the Mediterranean to Sicily and thence to Italy. The Russian armies, mauled but unsubdued by the tremendous German thrusts, counterattacked with a superb combination of fury and finesse. Throughout Europe subject peoples were stirring restlessly under German exactions and reprisals and a net of underground conspiracy was being woven by patriotic groups in all the conquered countries.

When the year 1944 opened, World War II had already lasted longer than World War I.

German collapse

As in 1918, after successful but exhausting campaigns and conquests, the German armies were facing an encroaching ring of steel, with their enemies multiplying until more than fifty nations had severed diplomatic contact and united against them. An Anglo-American expeditionary force had landed in Italy a few months earlier (September, 1943) and was advancing on Rome. In June, 1944, a second Anglo-American expeditionary force leaped the English Channel, achieving in reverse what Hitler had not dared in 1940, and a steadily augmented army pushed into France. Aided by secondary landings on the Mediterranean coast, and by the heroic and carefully timed uprising of French insurgent groups, the invasion progressed rapidly. By the close of 1944, France was free after four years of military occupation and systematic terrorism. Forced back to the Rhine in the west and to the Vistula in the east the German armies awaited the destructive blows which they no longer possessed the strength to parry. Their cities were deserts of crumbled stone and twisted iron, their elaborate net of railways and highways, which had given them the benefit of "inside lines," had been blown apart, their manpower was depleted by the toll of battle, and millions of "slave laborers," imported from conquered countries to operate the industrial plants and raise the crops, were sullen and mutinous. Each week the bombers came over in greater numbers, dropping heavier cargoes with increasing devastation.

As signs of German exhaustion multiplied, the attacks were doubled and redoubled, for war is as much a battle of morale as of military force. Propaganda leaflets and daily radio broadcasts informed the peoples of Europe of the victorious progress of the United Nations. In the Balkans the Russian advance liberated Rumania, Bulgaria, and Yugoslavia, and Russian armies also turned north to capture Budapest and Vienna. Through Poland and East Prussia the claws of the Russian offensive closed in upon Berlin. Caught in a vise, with Anglo-American forces driving across the Rhine until they met the Russian spearheads in the Elbe Valley, the German armies split into fragments and disintegrated. Despite Hitler's repeated orders to fight on, despite the fanatical efforts of suicide battalions and the punitive measures of the secret police, the dreaded *Gestapo*, many German commanders opened direct negotiations with Russian, British, and American headquarters. Shattered divisions of the *Wehrmacht*, herded into pockets, laid down their arms. Mechanized units and tank battalions, lacking gasoline, surrendered impotently. The end came in May, 1945, when the Russians fought their way into Berlin. Hitler committed suicide among the ruins of the Reichschancellery, and the German high command ordered the Reich forces still in action to capitulate. All German territory was immediately divided into occupation zones under Russian, British, American, and French military administration, and the United Nations announced that "Victory in Europe" had been achieved.

Fall of Berlin

7. THE WAR IN THE PACIFIC

The Japanese bid for domination in the Far East was rendered possible by the conflict in Europe. After 1931, with the fall in trade and the German rearmament, and after

The Japanese opportunity

1939, with open warfare engaging the attention of the leading powers, Japan enjoyed a free chance to expand in a semi-vacuum. For Britain, France, the Netherlands, and Portugal could no longer spare the armed forces needed to defend their imperial commitments in Asia, and it fell to the United States to play the major rôle in protecting the prestige, property, and colonies of the white peoples in Asiatic and Pacific areas. The Japanese attack on the American base at Pearl Harbor (December 7, 1941) forced the American naval and military forces into a war almost wholly novel in their experience, a long, costly, amphibious struggle on a scale new in history. American ingenuity, initiative, and endurance were to be taxed by problems and conditions of unique complexity.

There are four conditions worth particular attention in analyzing the campaign in the Pacific. (1) The Japanese had made long and careful preparations for their drives, and they were able to seize at the outset a strong defensive area, to control essential sources of supply, and to count upon several years in which to consolidate and fortify their conquests. (2) The peoples of Southeast Asia, of Thailand, Burma, Indo-China, Malaysia, and Indonesia resented the exploitation to which they had been exposed as a result of European imperialism, and they were in general receptive to the Japanese promise of a "New Order" and to the slogan "Asia for the Asiatics." (3) The curve of Japanese conquest coincided with the rise and fall of the German and Italian fortunes in Europe and Africa. Japan enjoyed practically a free field in a remote quarter of the globe because the European powers and the United States had to deal first with a crisis threatening them near at hand. (4) The vast emptiness which is the Pacific Ocean, starred with its numerous constellations of islands, offered the Japanese a rare chance to seize and fortify far distant, concentric rings of defense which could be reduced only with great difficulty. But the development of air power, which has shrunk Pacific travel from weeks to hours, largely destroyed the effectiveness of the Japanese outposts, and made their conquests, sea lanes, and cities vulnerable to direct attack. This meant that, once their own naval and air power weakened, they might be unable to defend or even to withdraw their overexpanded forces.

With these facts in mind, and a map of the Pacific and the Far East at hand (see page 881), it is easy to see that the Japanese campaign was a gigantic gamble against time. When World War II opened in 1939, the Japanese held Korea and Manchukuo on the Asiatic mainland, and were pushing slowly into China from Peking and Shanghai. Chinese resistance proved more tenacious than they anticipated, and necessity forced them to postpone the subjugation of China and to leap to Southeast Asia, in order to secure the oil and rubber of the East Indies. By 1941 they controlled French Indo-China and Thailand (Siam). But they dared not risk an invasion of Sumatra, Borneo, Java, and the Celebes while the British maintained a fleet at their naval base in Singapore and the Americans possessed the Philippines. Accordingly, the Japanese staked their imperial destinies on a swift and crippling blow that would destroy the United States fleet in the Pacific, and they came perilously close to success. Their surprise attack on Pearl Harbor sank or damaged all the American warships at that naval base, and left American striking power, naval and aerial, almost wholly paralyzed until repairs and replacements could create a new fleet. Knowing that every day would count, the Japanese lost no time in attacking the Philippines, Singapore, and the Dutch East Indies, and within three months these valuable areas were in their control.

No power ever made more extended or more lucrative gains in less time. At a stroke the Japanese secured adequate oil supplies while depriving the United States of almost all its rubber and tin imports. From the Aleutians to the northern coasts of Australia, Japanese sea power was supreme; British India was threatened with invasion from Burma, and Ceylon faced Japanese naval raids. But this critical spring of 1942 marked the limit of Japanese success. In 1942 the resistance of

THE BATTLE OF STALINGRAD

When Russian forces cut off and destroyed the German Sixth Army at Stalingrad, at the opening of 1943, the tide of battle turned on the eastern front.

THE MEETING OF THE RUSSIAN AND UNITED STATES INFANTRY AT THE ELBE RIVER

the United Nations stiffened on all fronts. With its naval strength replenished and its air power magnificently augmented, the United States opened a Pacific offensive which swept inexorably forward, leaping a thousand miles of ocean at a stretch. From Guadalcanal (August, 1942) to the Gilbert Islands (November, 1943), from the Marshall Islands (January, 1944) to the Marianas (June, 1944), the advance continued. With the reconquest of the Philippines and the capture of bases in the Bonin Islands, American bombing planes commenced a devastating attack upon Japanese cities, shipping, and military forces in China. The vulnerability of the Japanese position became rapidly apparent. Densely populated Japanese cities, peculiarly vulnerable to fire hazards, were mercilessly gutted by fires ignited by thousands of tons of incendiary bombs, and factories were leveled, as the German factories had been, by shattering explosives. Under this pitiless reprisal the common people endured and died as the outnumbered Japanese garrisons were doing, fatalistically, firmly, without hope and without rebellion.

As the Soviet government continued to honor its non-aggression pact with Japan, negotiated in 1941, Russian bases were not available for American planes or ships. A land attack upon the Japanese forces in East Asia was difficult to undertake because the ports were in Japanese control. A trickle of supplies continued to reach the embattled Chinese by air from India, and the government at Chungking, despite heavy losses, inadequate arms, and tragic suffering, maintained the unequal struggle, but the war against Japan was not won on land, it was won at sea.

The German surrender in May, 1945, ended hostilities in Europe and left the British and American governments free to concentrate their forces in the Pacific. In Burma, British, American, and Chinese divisions had destroyed three Japanese armies by May 5. By June, United States forces, in desperate fighting, captured Okinawa, providing bombing planes with a base three hundred and twenty-five miles from Japan. Within one month the Twentieth Air Force dropped forty thousand tons of explosive, while American battleships moved inshore to shell industrial and military targets. These deadly blows at their home islands made it difficult for the Japanese high command to reach or reinforce its troops isolated in China, on Pacific islands, and in Southeast Asia. By August, Japan's air force was almost eliminated, its warships sunk or immobilized, its sea communications cut by submarine blockade and minefields. The morale of the nation was already weakening when two terrible blows ended their will to resist. On August 6, 1945, a single atomic bomb, secretly prepared by British and American scientists, was dropped on Hiroshima, destroying three fifths of the city. On August 8, Soviet Russia declared war on Japan and commenced a powerful invasion of Manchuria. On the 9th, a second atomic bomb leveled Nagasaki. The Japanese cabinet decided to abandon the struggle and capitulated on August 14. United States forces landed in Japan two weeks later and the formal terms of surrender were signed at Tokyo on September 2.

8. THE COST OF WORLD WAR II

Although many years would be required to compute the total costs and casualties of the second world war of the twentieth century, it was apparent before hostilities ended that they would surpass the figures for World War I. General estimates suggested that the number of combatants slain in all theaters of operation might approximate 15,000,000. A gruesome feature of the newer modes of warfare was the large proportion of missing, equal in some engagements to the known dead. The list of civilian casualties, from air raids, firing squads, starvation, and mass murder in the slave battalions, on the gallows, or in the gas chambers of the Axis concentration camps, was thought to equal, and might even exceed, the military casualties.

Casualties

The estimated war expenditures for all belligerents (China excepted) was placed at more than one thousand billion dollars. The destruction of property — ships, docks, bridges, roads, factories, churches, schools, libraries,

Property damage

VICTORY AND ITS PROBLEMS

Victory solved only a few problems and left the Security Council of the United Nations a heritage of grave responsibilities.

EXPLOSION OF THE ATOMIC BOMB AT NAGASAKI (*above*)

THE SECURITY COUNCIL OF THE UNITED NATIONS (*below*)

and dwellings — defied computation, and left millions of refugees in Europe and the Far East destitute and homeless. The terrible destructive power of aerial bombs, rocket bombs, and the new and revolutionary atomic bombs, made exposed cities uninhabitable targets. More urgently than ever, the nations recognized the need to reduce the likelihood of war and promote international understanding and co-operation. Peace and war had become indivisible and any future conflict between nations was a threat to every nation. The new methods of communication, the swifter means of transportation, and the economic interdependence of all countries, had shrunk the planet and pressed the nations together in a global society. Never before in history had it been so evident that, for good or ill, a common destiny was uniting all mankind. This realization, quickened by the first world war of 1914–1918, had produced the League of Nations as an instrument of international arbitration, but the League had failed in its major function. Before the outcome of World War II had been determined, statesmen were already shaping a new international league, the United Nations. Its organization and program will be described in the next chapter.

73

The Post-War World

I do not believe in a real danger of a "new war."

JOSEPH STALIN (1946).

I believe that it must be the policy of the United States to support peoples who are resisting attempted subjugation by armed minorities or by outside pressures.

HARRY S. TRUMAN (1947).

1. THE UNITED NATIONS

IN THE SPRING OF 1945, when the American, British, and Russian armies were crushing the last German resistance in Europe, the delegates of fifty nations assembled in San Francisco to plan a new world order. Within two months they completed and approved a "Charter of the United Nations." Six years of war, with more than twenty million military and civilian dead, had filled the peoples of the world with an ardent will to preserve peace. They believed that a way could be found to solve international disputes without an appeal to arms and without bloodshed. The League of Nations, formed in 1919 after World War I, had failed to prevent a more costly and destructive war twenty years later. It was hoped that the United Nations, organized by the victors of World War II, might succeed where the League of Nations had failed.

The framework of the United Nations closely resembled the parliamentary machinery of the earlier league. All member nations were recognized as sovereign, independent states, equal in rights, and all were accorded one vote in the General Assembly. Corresponding to the Council of the League of Nations, there was a Security Council of eleven states. Five of these states — Great Britain, the Union of Soviet Socialist Republics, the United States, France, and China — held permanent seats; the remaining six were to be elected for two-year terms by the General Assembly. The Security Council was to function continuously and was invested with "primary responsibility for the maintenance of international peace and security." To check an aggressor, it might advise all other states to sever diplomatic relations with the recalcitrant government; it might propose the infliction of economic penalties and blockade; and as a final resort it might call upon members of the United Nations to furnish armed forces to be used against the aggressor nation.

In theory, therefore, the United Nations was an impressive international parliament and police agency, but in actuality its authority was almost exclusively moral. It had neither the funds nor the armed forces to match against an aggressive national state. Small nations might be brought to obey its decisions, but the great powers, particularly the five permanent powers represented on the Security Council, would not be easily coerced by judicial formulas. It was, moreover, highly improbable that the Security Council would adopt any restraining action against one of its members, for all important decisions required seven affirmative votes including the concurring votes of the five permanent members. This rule of concurrence gave each of the permanent five what was, in effect, a veto power, for by declining to endorse a proposal any one of the five could prevent a decision of the Security Council from going into effect.

These limitations made it difficult to predict how effective the United Nations would prove in a critical test. The governments of the leading powers hesitated to reduce their armaments or to entrust an international force to the command of the Security Council and relax their own defense measures. Until the United Nations became a world authority, with vigilant officials scanning the armed strength (especially the atomic weapons) of all nations, and until a reliable international police force existed, strong enough to restrain any aggressive state from warlike action, the peoples of the world would continue to put their main trust in their own armaments.

The United Nations had other important functions besides the supervision and reduction of military weapons. Its vast charitable labor began early in World War II, and by 1946 the United Nations Relief and Rehabilitation Administration (UNRRA) had spent over $4,000,000,000 to feed the starving in Europe and Asia, and to provide shelter for 12,000,000 displaced persons and war refugees. After January 1, 1947, UNRRA was dissolved, and its duties transferred to other agencies of the United Nations, in particular the International Refugee Organization, the Food and Agricultural Organization, and the World Health Organization. Other departments and commissions of the new world organization were created to protect human rights, to survey social and economic conditions, to promote a higher standard of living among depressed groups and classes, and to foster higher educational opportunities and closer cultural relations among the nations.

2. THE RECONSTRUCTION OF EUROPE

The death of Adolf Hitler in 1945, and the collapse of German resistance, produced a "vacuum of power" throughout central Europe. In Berlin, Vienna, Budapest, Bucharest, and Sofia the leaders who had collaborated with the German Nazis were dead or in hiding. Allied troops patrolled the streets, and the Allied Military Governments divided the conquered territories into Russian, British, American, and French zones of occupation.

The chief responsibility for the reconstruction of Europe after 1945 lay with the victors of World War II: no nation was strong enough to dispute the ascendancy won by the three "super-powers," Russia, Britain, and the United States. But these three great empires, which had worked together effectively to win the war, were soon deadlocked in opposition over the peace settlements. Russian foreign policy was directed by Marshal Joseph Stalin and the Commissar of Foreign Affairs, Vyacheslav M. Molotov. British foreign policy was formulated (after July, 1945) by a new Labor Cabinet under Prime Minister Clement R. Attlee, with Ernest Bevin as Secretary of State for Foreign Affairs. In the United States the sudden death of President Franklin D. Roosevelt in April, 1945, brought Harry S. Truman to the presidency. Cordell Hull, who had served as Secretary of State from 1933 to 1944 was followed briefly by Edward R. Stettinius, Jr., and James F. Byrnes, before General George C. Marshall accepted this post at the close of 1946. All the major decisions and compromises involved in making the peace treaties rested with the foreign ministers of Russia, Britain, and the United States, assisted by the corps of experts and assistants who held posts in their departments. The lesser powers among the United Nations exercised only minor influence on the discussions and the vanquished nations were permitted no voice at all.

The method and machinery for the peacemaking was announced in August, 1945. Meeting in captured Berlin, Marshal Stalin, Prime Minister Attlee, and President Truman declared that the foreign ministers of Russia, Britain, the United States, France, and China would be entrusted with authority "to draw up, with a view to their submission to the United Nations, treaties of peace..." In actuality, China did not participate in the European settlements, and France (reorganized as the Fourth French Republic) was not always consulted. Nor were the treaties submitted to the United Nations before they were signed: the terms for each of the defeated nations were drafted by the Council of Foreign Ministers, and only such other states as had been actively at war with the vanquished were invited to approve the conditions formulated. The "piecemeal" pacts which followed World War II were in this sense an imposed victors' sentence rather than a negotiated international settlement.

Because the foreign ministers found it difficult to agree, and postponed many decisions from one to two years, local conditions in many parts of Europe and Asia hardened into what might be called a "peace by default." Slowly and painfully, through compromises, plebiscites, and the fumbling of provisory governments, the lesser nations of Europe regained a measure of self-rule. The premiers or chancellors who headed provisory régimes in the conquered or liberated lands had to mediate between the Allied Military Governments and the bewildered populace. The people in occupied regions, when they were invited to vote, usually sought to please the dominant occupying power and the elections commonly took their color from the conqueror's flag. In Poland, Czechoslovakia, Rumania, Bulgaria, and Yugoslavia, where Russian influence was paramount, Communist groups led in the elections. In Norway, Denmark, Sweden, the Netherlands, Belgium, the British and American zones of Germany and Austria, and in Italy and Greece, the Communist vote was small. The post-war plebiscites in general indicated that the 400,000,000 European people west of the Soviet frontier preferred to work out their social and economic problems by some middle road rather than by embracing the extreme form of collectivism which the Communist leaders had established in Russia.

In the year which followed the surrender of Germany, the Council of Foreign Ministers met over two hundred times, in London, Moscow, Paris, and New York, and by the close of 1946 they had completed and approved treaties for Italy, Rumania, Bulgaria, Hungary, and Finland. The nations which had been at war with any or all of these five states criticized the treaties at a conference in Paris, and the drafts were finally signed, without ceremony, in January, 1947.

The terms imposed upon Italy were the most severe. The Italians lost their entire African empire, ceded the Dodecanese Islands to Greece, yielded the territory of Venezia Giulia (except Trieste) to Yugoslavia, and surrendered small border areas (Briga and Tenda) to strengthen French control of Alpine passes. The Italian Army was reduced to 250,000 men, the Navy to 22,500, and the Air Force to 25,000; and Italy was condemned to pay indemnities totaling $360,000,000 to Yugoslavia, Greece, Ethiopia, Albania, and the Soviet Union. The Anti-Fascist *coup* of July, 1943, whereby Mussolini was overthrown and Italy joined the United Nations as a "co-belligerent," did not save the country from the harsh terms reserved for the vanquished. Thus the Italian Republic (the monarchy was abolished in 1946) entered the post-war era with a bitter heritage of defeat, debt, and discouragement.

The Balkan satellites of Germany — Rumania, Bulgaria, and Hungary — suffered similar penalties. Rumania confirmed the cession of northern Bukovina and Bessarabia to Russia, and southern Dobruja to Bulgaria, but gained Transylvania in exchange from Hungary. The Rumanian armed forces were limited to 138,000 men for all services, and Rumanian reparations, all of which went to Russia, were fixed at $300,000,000. Bulgaria lost no territory and was enlarged by the acquisition of southern Dobruja, but Bulgarian armed forces were reduced to 55,500 men, and an indemnity of $70,000,000 was divided between Greece and Yugoslavia. Hungary was reduced to the limits of 1938, retroceding a slice of its northern frontier to Czechoslovakia and resigning Transylvania to Rumania. An indemnity of $300,000,000 completed the economic ruin of the Hungarian state, for its currency had already dissolved in a sea of inflation by 1946. The last of the five treaties fixed the status of Finland. The Finns were likewise assessed $300,000,000 in reparations for the benefit of the Russians. In addition, Finland ceded to

Russia the port and province of Petsamo in the extreme north, and the right to build and maintain a Soviet naval base at Porkkala Udd at the entrance to the Gulf of Finland.

The problem of reconstructing Germany, Austria, and Poland, and fixing their frontiers, was postponed to the last by the Council of Foreign Ministers. The first act of the victorious allies had been to carve Germany into several zones (Russian, British, French, and American) with separate administrations, separate economies, obstructive tariffs, and conflicting passport rules to emphasize the dismemberment. This deliberate segmentation of the Reich was the first and most obvious safeguard the victors could invoke to postpone the day of German recovery and rearmament. In each zone all German forces were disbanded, fortifications leveled, weapons confiscated, and arsenals abolished. Even the manufacture of such items as military maps and model airplanes was prohibited. To bring to justice those members of the National-Socialist régime most directly responsible for the war and for the mass-murder of millions of political prisoners, evidence was collected, lists compiled, and special courts established to try the accused. Twenty-one of the most prominent political and military leaders who had served Hitler were arraigned before an international tribunal at Nürnberg; eleven were sentenced to death, seven to prison, and three were acquitted. This prosecution of war criminals, which established the principle that conspiracy to make war and the instigation of crimes against humanity were indictable offenses, set a new precedent in international jurisprudence. Throughout the liberated and the ex-enemy countries, from Norway to Greece, local agents who had aided the German *Gestapo* were denounced and hunted down, and hundreds of "collaborators" were put to death with or without due process of law.

So long as German industry remained crippled and Germany dismembered there could be no normal economic revival in Europe. But a logical settlement of the German question was obstructed by the mutual jealousy and suspicion which divided Russia from the western powers, and by the widespread fear that Germany would seek revenge as soon as the fetters of military occupation were loosened. The French, recalling their deep forebodings of 1919 and the fulfillment of those fears in 1940, favored a permanent dismemberment of the Reich. The Poles knew that they could not retain German areas which reached almost to Berlin if Germany ever recovered national vigor. The Russians, who had suffered more loss of life and more property damage than any other people because of German pillage and devastation, demanded that Germany pay economic reparations from a captive economy. At the same time they carried away much German machinery and railway stock, and kept millions of German prisoners of war to work Soviet fields and factories. Other millions of Germans, including the young, the old, and the sick, were expelled from East Prussia, Silesia, and other regions of eastern Europe, and driven to seek asylum in their ruined fatherland. For these "displaced persons" no friendly United Nations Relief and Rehabilitation Administration provided aid: they were the belated dupes of Hitler's crusade for Pan-Germanism. Because, ten years earlier, German minorities in neighbor states had demanded reunion with the Reich, all Germans were now distrusted, and neighbor nations seized the excuse to despoil and then expel all who had shown pro-German loyalties. It was clear that whatever frontier lines might finally be drawn and whatever terms the victors might enforce, the peoples of central Europe would seethe for years with a passionate resentment and an indelible sense of injustice. It was ominous that the German people appeared to have no feeling of guilt for the crimes which the National-Socialist Government had committed, no awareness that their support of the Hitler régime had involved them, morally at least, in an enormity without parallel in modern history: the intentional and systematic extermination of five million victims in the concentration camps. Although Germans might forget or ignore these horrors, the groups and nations which had suffered from German arrogance and brutality were not likely to forget them, and the heritage of hate

Fear of Germany

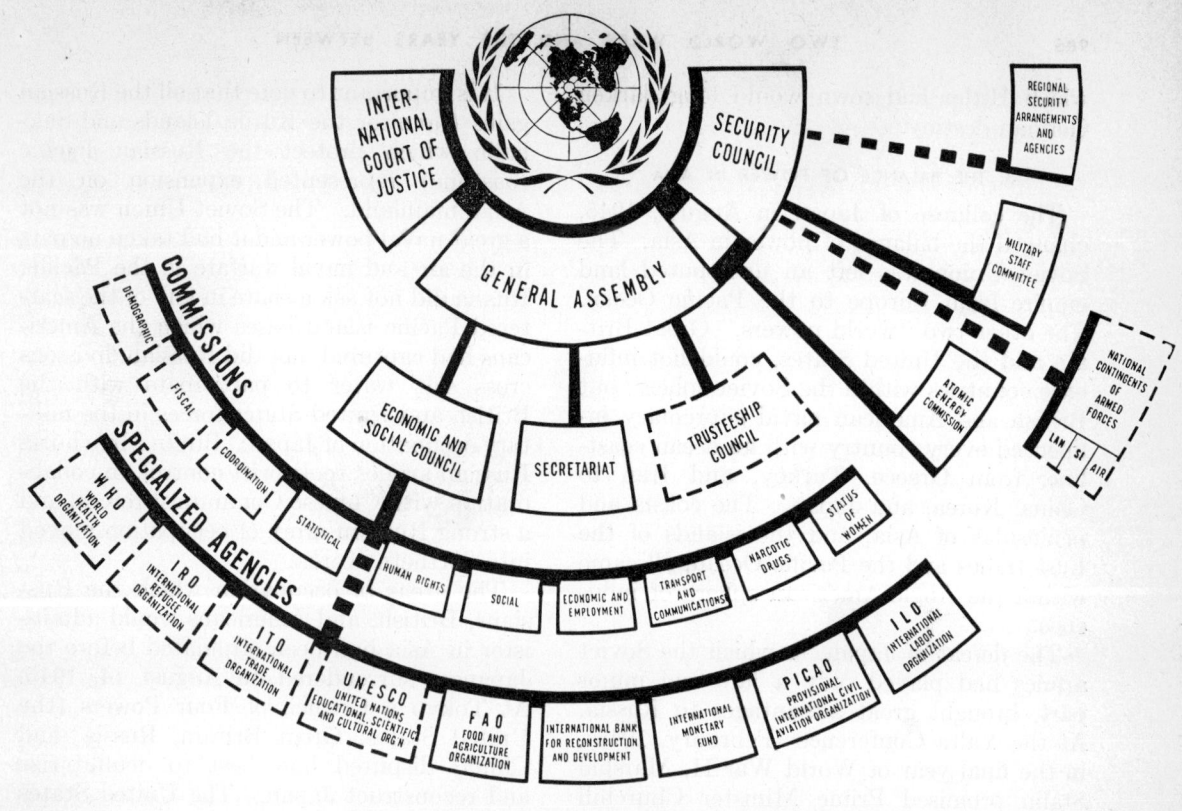

ORGANIZATION OF THE UNITED NATIONS

THE NÜRNBERG TRIALS

After the defeat of Germany in 1945, and the suicide of Adolf Hitler, twenty-one leaders of the National-Socialist régime (in prisoners' box) were brought to trial and eleven were hanged.

which Hitler had sown would long darken German destiny.

3. THE BALANCE OF POWER IN ASIA

The collapse of Japan in August, 1945, changed the balance of power in Asia. The Soviet Union was left an undisputed land empire from Europe to the Pacific Ocean. The other two "world powers," Great Britain and the United States, could not influence countries within the Soviet sphere, but British and American naval supremacy influenced every country with an ocean coastline, from Greece, Turkey, and Iran to China, Korea, and Japan. The coasts and peninsulas of Asia, and the islands of the East Indies and the Pacific Ocean, all came within the Anglo-American sphere of influence.

The defeat of Japan, in which the Soviet armies had played only a late and minor part, brought great advantages to Russia. At the Yalta Conference (February, 1945), in the final year of World War II, Marshal Stalin promised Prime Minister Churchill and President Roosevelt that the Soviet Union would join Britain and America in the war against Japan after the Germans surrendered. The Russian price for this co-operation was not announced at the time, but the Soviet armies fulfilled the agreement by opening a wide attack on the Japanese in Manchuria in August, 1945. Following the Allied victory over Japan, the Russians occupied the Kurile Islands and the southern half of Sakhalin. Dairen was internationalized and Port Arthur leased to Russia as a naval base. A joint Russo-Chinese corporation took over the Chinese Eastern and the South Manchuria Railways. Manchuria was restored to Chinese sovereignty, but the pre-eminent Russian interests there were guaranteed. Outer Mongolia remained under Russian influence as the (independent) Mongolian Peoples' Republic. These developments were not wholly pleasing to the Chinese Nationalist Government headed by Generalissimo Chiang Kai-shek, but the Chinese yielded to British and American advice and concluded a treaty of "friendship and alliance" with the Soviet Union (August, 1945).

It is important to note that all the Russian gains (save for the Kurile Islands and Sakhalin which protect the Russian Pacific coastline) represented expansion on the Asian mainland. The Soviet Union was not a great naval power and it had taken no part in the air and naval warfare in the Pacific. Russia did not ask a share in any of the scattered Pacific island bases which the Americans had captured, nor did Russian divisions cross salt water to participate with the British and United States forces in the military occupation of Japan. But in Manchuria Russian armies took swift control, in collaboration with Chinese Communist forces, and a strong Russian army of occupation moved into northern Korea.

The areas of occupation which the Russians, British, and Americans would administer in Asia had been stipulated before the Japanese surrendered on August 14, 1945. At Tokyo a Council of Four Powers (the United States, Great Britain, Russia, and China) disputed how best to demilitarize and reconstruct Japan. The United States established 250,000 soldiers at strategic centers in the Japanese homeland, the southern half of Korea, the Philippine Commonwealth, and the Pacific islands. Russian military forces of approximately equal strength dominated northern Korea and Manchuria. British forces reoccupied Hongkong, the Malay States, Singapore, and Burma. French forces battled stubbornly to regain control of Indo-China where popular leaders proclaimed an independent republic in 1945. The Dutch, with British aid, suppressed a revolt of the Indonesians in the Netherlands East Indies, but promised to grant the Indonesian Commonwealth self-government and dominion status.

Thus the Japanese program of "Asia for the Asiatics" was partly reversed with the Japanese defeat, and Japan itself, temporarily, came under the domination of the western powers. The Supreme Allied Commander at Tokyo was General Douglas MacArthur, and he labored to demilitarize and democratize Japanese society. Emperor Hirohito remained on the imperial throne, but he announced to his subjects that the divinity attributed to him was a myth, and he gave his royal assent to the new, liberal constitution for Japan which was drafted with American assistance. The Japanese House of Peers and House of Representatives were "purified" by disqualifying all members who had been active in the Japanese program of aggression. The right of free speech, freedom of the press, equal legal rights for women, and equality before the law were guaranteed, and the workers were permitted to strengthen their unions for collective bargaining with their employers. Great trusts and corporations which had collaborated in the Japanese war plans were dissolved, and all armament plants and fortifications were dismantled.

In Japan as in Germany the most urgent post-war problem which faced the victors was the problem of reviving trade sufficiently to feed a ruined nation. The Japanese islands, with a population of almost 80,000,000, increasing 800,000 a year, were not economically self-sufficient. Like Great Britain, modern Japan had become a vast workshop with millions of overseas customers. Exports of pottery, metalware, toys, electrical equipment, and especially textiles, had paid for the essential imports of food and raw materials which the Japanese needed. By 1945, however, the disasters of war had almost extinguished this trade. Three fourths of the Japanese merchant shipping was lost; three fourths of the cotton spindles had been destroyed; fuel and oil were desperately scarce, and fertilizer was lacking for the fields. To save some of the Japanese people from starvation in the first year of peace it was necessary to ship five hundred thousand tons of food from America. To General MacArthur and his advisers it was clear that until Japanese trade revived and the people were safe from hunger it would be difficult to make democratic institutions take root in Japan. The problem was to restore some fair measure of Japanese industrial prosperity without re-creating the spirit and machinery of Japanese militarism.

4. POLICING THE POST-WAR WORLD

The governments of the United States and Great Britain found the burdens of occupation costly and were willing to reduce their forces in Japan, Germany, and elsewhere as soon as they considered it safe to do this. They hoped to see the peoples of the defeated Axis nations become again self-governing and self-supporting, with adequate guarantees provided that they would not renew their aggressive plans. There were, however, two dangers which might threaten world peace and security if British and American forces stationed abroad were recalled too suddenly. The defeated nations might evade the terms of their surrender and prepare a new war if supervision were relaxed; or Russian influence and Russian armies might expand into the spheres from which the British and American forces retired. These fears help to explain why, a year after the fighting in World War II came to an end, more than three million Russian, British, and American soldiers were still lingering on foreign soil. The location and concentration of these armies of occupation provided a clue to the "danger spots" in the post-war world. For great powers post armed forces only at points where tension is high and an outbreak of violence seems probable.

About half the Russian, British, and American forces of occupation at the close of 1946, approximately 1,500,000 men, were stationed in Germany and Austria. The Soviet forces there totaled 800,000, the British 380,000, and the United States divisions 305,000. The Soviet Government kept an additional 800,000 troops scattered through Poland, Czechoslovakia, Hungary, Rumania, Bulgaria, Yugoslavia, and Albania. The British and Americans had a joint force of 70,000 safeguarding Trieste, and the British also kept 50,000 soldiers in Greece. This brought the British total for all Europe close to half a million men, and another quarter million British imperial troops occupied strategic areas outside the empire in North Africa and Asia Minor. In Asia (aside from defense forces in India, Burma, and Malaysia) the British kept 20,000 men in the Netherlands East Indies until they had helped the Dutch to repress a revolt of the Indonesians in 1946. An additional British contingent of 38,000 served in

Japan as part of the Allied army of occupation.

American forces outside the United States in 1946 totaled 700,000. In addition to 330,000 soldiers in Europe, the United States maintained 140,000 in Japan, 50,000 in Korea, 50,000 in the Philippines and Pacific island bases, and 29,000 in China. Some 25,000 American troops in Alaska, and 50,000 guarding the Caribbean and Panama Canal Zone, completed the list of United States forces on garrison or occupation duty outside the forty-eight states. A substantial part of these widely scattered forces, such as those holding the fourteen hundred Pacific islands captured during World War II, might be considered permanent garrisons overseas. The cost and the problems that are involved when a nation maintains a sizable peace-time army formed but one of the many burdens the United States had assumed when it became a world power with global responsibilities.

Whether the government of the United States would assume a leading rôle in world politics after 1945 was one of the gravest uncertainties of an uncertain era. After World War I the American people had withdrawn from Europe and Asia, preferring a vulnerable isolation to active participation in the imbroglio of power politics abroad. If the American people resumed this aloof attitude, after playing a decisive part in World War II, this abstention would have a profound negative effect upon the course of events in Europe, Asia, and Africa. The United States Secretary of State, General George C. Marshall, warned the American people in 1947 that they had not yet realized the new responsibilities which faced their nation: "You should fully understand the special position that the United States now occupies in the world, geographically, financially, militarily, and scientifically, and the implications involved. The development of a sense of responsibility for world order and security, the development of a sense of the overwhelming importance of this country's acts, and failures to act, in relation to world order and security — these, in my opinion, are great 'musts' for your generation."

The new responsibility which faced the people of the United States was indicated even more clearly by President Harry S. Truman in a message to Congress dated March 12, 1947. "I believe," he affirmed, "that it must be the policy of the United States to support peoples who are resisting attempted subjugation by armed minorities or by outside pressures." The President concluded by asking Congress for an appropriation of $400,000,000 to aid Greece and Turkey. The British, who had long championed such key states in order to maintain a balance of power in the Near East, were no longer able to sustain the cost, and the United States seemed destined to take over part of the British burden and share this British rôle.

Truman Doctrine

5. CONCLUSION

Even in relatively tranquil years the tensions and inconsistencies in western civilization had provoked grave misgivings in all thoughtful minds, and two world wars had advertised the need to seek wiser and more humane solutions. It was true that the material achievements of the modern age surpassed those of any preceding epoch, and it is perhaps no more than just to pay tribute to these achievements before attention is turned to the darker side of the picture. The triumphs of modern science in prolonging and enriching human life have been outlined in earlier chapters, and the progress has continued at an accelerating pace. Each year advances the war against disease, introduces new labor-saving devices, marks the attainment of higher speeds, the construction of longer bridges, the erection of taller towers, and the measurement of more distant nebulae. These marvels of science are the chief glory of the contemporary era and it is impossible to overpraise the labor, the devotion, and the inspiration which have made them possible. Nor is there much reason to doubt that the immediate future will prove to be an age of technological development so outstanding that the present will be reduced in comparison to a period of apprenticeship. Machines are destined to become immeasurably more intricate and more powerful, and the marvels and complexities of this machine-dominated civilization cannot fail to increase yearly.

Yet this development imposes a vast responsibility upon the masters of the machines, a responsibility which, it may well prove, they are not prepared for and are not competent to accept. There is a mounting disparity observable between the limitless capacity of the engines and the limited faculties of their human managers. It is easy, for example, to treble the speed of a motor vehicle, but the deliberations and reactions of the driver are limited by his mental and muscular inheritance and cannot be greatly accelerated. This failure of the human machine largely explains why there have been one hundred thousand automobile fatalities in the United States within three years. Similarly, the rotary press and the radio have recently combined to bring the news of the world to the attention of every interested citizen, but the capacity of the average man to select, analyze, and pass judgment upon that news has not expanded in proportion as the information multiplied, and he has found that knowledge spells bewilderment. A third example, perhaps the most ominous, of this growing disparity between the acceleration of mechanized processes and the lag of human adaptation involves the menace of warfare. Few modern diplomats can aspire to reach a decision as quickly as Napoleon was in the habit of doing more than a century ago, yet Napoleon in his swiftest campaign required six weeks to seize the enemy's capital, whereas today any city in the world can be bombed from the air *two hours* after the declaration of war, if indeed the formality of declaring war is observed. With danger of war and destruction thus reduced to a matter of hours, deliberation becomes impossible, the human machine breaks down and abandons its rôle of arbiter. The diplomats, as custodians of peace, cannot hope to evolve solutions in such emergencies, and it becomes a matter of the utmost importance to anticipate crises and prepare a channel for the arbitrament of international disputes in advance.

War and poverty remain the most desperate enigmas confronting western civilization, and in democratic countries the solution to them lies in the creation of a more enlightened and more humane citizenry. It seems possible to hope that the patience and ingenuity which have won so many triumphs for European man will not fail him here. Of the four horsemen enumerated in the apocalyptic vision as the four principal scourges of mankind, two, Famine and Pestilence, have been strikingly curbed in their ravages by modern productive methods and medical skill. Even Death, the rider on the pale horse, has been persuaded to allow the average European to live out at least his twenty thousand days. But the rider on the red horse still raises his sword above the nations, and the conquest of war remains the supreme challenge facing modern man. Only the spread of international goodwill, transmuting fear to fair-mindedness and national greed to national co-operation, can brighten the hope for peace. The growth of such a spirit will depend upon many factors, but the most important must be the will of anonymous millions in every country who seek to distinguish and to support policies of reason, humanity, and justice.

APPENDIXES

Chronological Outlines
The Preparation of History Reports
Genealogical Tables
A List of European Rulers to the Middle of the Seventeenth Century
A List of European Rulers since the Middle of the Seventeenth Century
Suggestions for Further Reading

Section E. The Later Middle Ages

	ASIA	AFRICA	EUROPE
1270	←——— Last Crusade (1270) ———→		Holy Roman Empire revives after an interregnum (1254)
	Mongol Empire of Kubla Khan disintegrates after his death in 1294		*Growth of constitutional government in England*
			Swiss confederation (1291)
			Centralization of the French monarchical government
1300			
	Tartars rule Russia		Hundred Years' War begins (1337-1453)
			The "Black Death" (1348-50)
1350			**SPIRIT OF NATIONALISM GROWS IN ENGLAND, FRANCE, SPAIN, AND PORTUGAL UNDER NATIONAL MONARCHS**
	Turks conquer Byzantine Provinces and invade Balkans		
1400			*Later phases of Hundred Years' War*
			Joan of Arc executed (1431)
1450	Turks capture Constantinople (1453)	*Portuguese navigators explore Atlantic coast of Africa*	*Age of the Despots in Italy*
			America discovered; Africa circumnavigated, and the route to India found.
1500			The French invade Italy (1494)
1517			*Spain reaches the height of her power*

d the Renaissance, 1270-1517

Religion and Culture	Social and Economic Life	Science and Technology	
	Population continues to increase	*Mariner's compass in use* *Astrolabe and quadrant*	1270
Papal power shrinks "Babylonian Captivity of the Church": the popes at Avignon (1305-77)	*Period of city republics in Italy*		1300
German universities founded	*North-German cities organize the Hanseatic League*	*Clocks improved*	1350
		Gunpowder introduced into Europe	
e Great Schism (1378-1417)	SOCIAL STRUCTURE CHANGES; *Feudal nobility declines*		
ncil of Constance (1414-18)	*Influence of bourgeoisie rises* *Power of capital mounts*	*Anatomy studied* *Perspective in art developed*	1400
ouncil of Basle (1431-49) *Spanish Inquisition* ALIAN RENAISSANCE: Humanism The New Learning Painting and Literature	*First national standing armies organized*	First printing done from movable type (c. 1447) *Astronomical tables evolved*	1450
e Renaissance crosses the Alps		*Double-entry bookkeeping used throughout Europe*	1500
			1517

Section F. The Age of the Reformati[on]

	ASIA	EUROPE	AMERICAS
1517	*Portuguese trading ships sail the Indian Ocean* *Magellan's voyage gives Spain a claim to the Philippines*	PROTESTANT REFORMATION BEGINS IN GERMANY *Charles V elected Holy Roman Emperor* Turks defeat Hungarians (1526) and besiege Vienna (1529) *Reformation introduced in England* *Bourbon-Hapsburg rivalry*	*Spaniards conquer Mexico and Peru* *Portuguese in Brazi[l]*
1550		Spain ascendant under Philip II (1556-98) Queen Elizabeth rules England (1558-1603) Netherlands revolt against Spain (1566) *Civil and religious wars in France* English Navy defeats Spanish Armada (1588)	
1600	*Dutch and English establish trade in East Indies* *Turkish advance threatens Danube Valley*	Thirty Years' War (1618-48) *Richelieu consolidates the French Monarchy* *The Germanies devastated by war* Civil War in England (1642-48) Peace of Westphalia (1648) ends Thirty Years' War Anglo-Dutch trade wars (1652-74)	*French in Canada* *First English settlem[ent]*
1650			
1660		Peace of the Pyrenees (1659) The Restoration in England (1660)	

d the Wars of Religion, 1517-1660

Religion and Culture	Social and Economic Life	Science and Technology	
PROTESTANT REFORMATION BEGINS *Lutheranism* *Calvinism* *Anglicanism* Council of Trent (1545-63) Religious Peace of Augsburg (1555)	*Peasants' War in the Germanies (1525)* *Prices rise* *Hanse towns and Italian cities decline*	 Copernicus (1473-1543) offers new theory of astronomy Vesalius (1514-64) lays foundations of modern anatomical study	1517 1550
Reformation in Scotland and the Scandinavian kingdoms *Counter-Reformation* Shakespeare (1564-1616) Cervantes (1547-1616)	NATIONAL TERRITORIAL STATES EMERGE *Trade shifts to Northern Europe, especially the Netherlands*	William Harvey (1578-1657) discovers circulation of the blood *Telescope invented* THE NEW PHYSICS: Galileo (1564-1642) Kepler (1571-1630) Napier announces concept of logarithms (1614) Decimals introduced (1616) Descartes (1596-1650) evolves analytic geometry	 1600
French Academy founded (1635) *French drama develops*			 1650 1660

Section G. The Age

	FRANCE	SPAIN	AUSTRIA	ENGLAND	NETHERLANDS
1660	Louis XIV (1660-1715)	Charles II (1665-1700)	Leopold I (1658-1705)	Charles II (1660-85)	

War of Devolution (1667-68)

| 1670 | | | | Treaty of Dover (1670) | French invade Holland (1672) |

Dutch War (1672-78) — FIRST COALITION TO CHECK FRENCH EXPANSION

French take Franche-Comté from the Spanish Hapsburgs

Treaty of Nijmegen........(1678).........Treaty of Nijmegen

| 1680 | French annex Strasbourg (1681) and Luxemburg (1683) | | Turks repulsed before Vienna (1683) | Habeas Corpus Act (1679)
Exclusion Bill (1679)

James II (1685-88)
"Glorious Revolution" (1688-89)
William III, king and stadholder | |

| 1690 | War of the League of Augsburg (1689-97) |

SECOND COALITION TO CHECK FRENCH EXPANSION

Treaty of Ryswick.........(1697).........Treaty of Ryswick

| 1700 | Philip of Anjou becomes Philip V (1700-46) | | | Act of Settlement (1701) | |

War of the Spanish Succession (1702-13)

France and Spain allied under the Bourbons — GRAND ALLIANCE AGAINST THE BOURBONS

Act of Union (1707)

Hapsburgs gain Naples, Milan, Spanish Netherlands, and Sardinia

British capture Gibraltar and Minorca

| 1710 | | | | | |

Peace of Utrecht..............(1713-14)..............Peace of Utrecht

| 1715 | | | | | |

ouis XIV, 1660-1715

OTHER STATES	COLONIES	SOCIETY	Religion and Culture	SCIENCE	
	English take New York (1664)	ABSOLUTE MONARCHY PREVAILS *Equilibrium of classes—a balanced society*	*Great age of French literature:* Corneille (1606-84) Racine (1639-99) Moliere (1622-73) John Milton (1608-74) Great Fire of London (1666) *Christopher Wren rebuilds London's churches*	Royal Society founded in London (1662) French Academy of Sciences chartered (1666)	1660 1670
mark and Brandenburg join Coalition		Mercantilism: Colbert (1619-83)			
	Explorers give France claim to Mississippi valley	*Middle class grows powerful in Holland and England*			1680
en and Bavaria join eague of Augsburg		Parliament triumphs in England: Bill of Rights (1689) Bank of England founded (1694)	Revocation of Edict of Nantes (1685) John Locke (1632-1704) England's Toleration Act (1689)	Sir Isaac Newton (1642-1727) Principia (1687) *Leibnitz (1646-1716) and Newton independently formulate differential calculus* *Leeuwenhoek (1632-1723) discovers bacteria*	1690
at Northern War (1700-21)					1700
NS adenburg and Piedat join the Grand Alliance			Jonathan Swift (1667-1745) Joseph Addison (1672-1719)		1710
	English take Acadia, Newfoundland, and Hudson's Bay				1715

Section H. The Eighteen[th]

	GREAT BRITAIN	FRANCE	AUSTRIA	PRUSSIA	RUSSIA
1715	George I (1714-27)	Louis XV (1715-74)	Charles VI (1711-40)	Frederick William I (1713-40)	Peter the Great (1689-1725)
1720					
	George II (1727-60)				
1730					
		War of the Polish Succession (1733-36)			
			Maria Theresa (1740-80)	Frederick II (1740-86)	
1740	WAR OF THE AUSTRIAN SUCCESSION (1740-48) *England and Austria oppose France and Prussia* Peace of Aix-la-Chapelle (1748)				Elizabeth (1741-
1750					
	SEVEN YEARS' WAR (1756-63) *England and Prussia oppose France, Austria, and Russia* Treaty of Paris (1763) - Peace of Hubertsburg (1763)				
1760	George III (1760-1820)				Catherine the G[reat] (1762-96)
1770					Treaty of Kuch[uk] Kainardji with T[urkey] (1774)
		Louis XVI (1774-92)			
1780		*France aids colonies against England in War of American Independence*	Joseph II (1780-90)		
				Frederick William II (1786-97)	
1789		French Revolution begins (1789)			

ntury, 1715-1789

THER STATES	COLONIES	SOCIETY	Religion and Culture	SCIENCE	
					1715
y acquires Sardinia (1720) eden defeated in at Northern War (1721)					1720
		Voltaire (1694-1778)	*Period of Rococo art*		1730
			The vogue of Deism	Linnaeus (1707-78) and Buffon (1707-88) advance study of zoology	1740
	King George's War (1743-48)				
h I of Portugal (1750-77)		Montesquieu, *Spirit of the Laws* (1748)		*Factory machines multiply*	1750
	French and Indian War (1754-63)	AGE OF REASON AND ENLIGHTENED DESPOTISM			
les III of Spain (1759-88)	The British win Canada and dominate India Stamp Tax (1765)	Rousseau, *Social Contract* (1762) *Agrarian revolution in progress*		Watt's improved steam engine (1764) Hargreaves' spinning jenny (1764)	1760
					1770
t Partition of oland (1774) n and Holland ar with Britain	War of American Independence begins (1775) American Declaration of Independence (1776) Thirteen American colonies become the United States (1783) First British settlements in Australia (1788)	Adam Smith, *The Wealth of Nations* (1776)	Pietism flourishes in Germany Wesleyan Methodism spreads in England	Oxygen discovered (1774) Crompton's "mule" (1779) Hutton, *Theory of the Earth* (1785) Crompton's power loom (1785)	1780 1789

Section I. The French Revolution

	FRANCE	BRITAIN	AUSTRIA	PRUSSIA	RUSSIA
1789	FRENCH REVOLUTION (1789-99)	George III (1760-1820)	Leopold II (1790-92)	Frederick William II (1786-97)	Catherine II (1762-96)
	First French Republic (1792)		Francis I (1792-1835) rules as Francis II, Holy Roman Emperor, to 1806		
		←―――――― FIRST	COALITION	AGAINST ⋯⋯⋯⋯⋯	
			Treaty of Basel (1795)		
	Directory (1795-99)				Paul I (1796-180…)
			Treaty of Campo Formio (1797)	Frederick William III (1797-1840)	
		SECOND COALITION	AGAINST ⋯⋯⋯⋯⋯⋯		FRANCE
1800	*Consulate* Napoleon Bonaparte the First Consul		Treaty of Lunéville (1801)		Peace restored ( )
		Peace of Amiens (1802)			Alexander I (1801-25)
	NAPOLEON I, EMPEROR OF THE FRENCH (1804-14)	THIRD COALITION	AGAINST ⋯⋯⋯⋯⋯⋯		FRANCE
		Battle of Trafalgar (1805)	Battle of Austerlitz (1805) Treaty of Pressburg (1805)	Napoleon defeats Prussia (1806)	Peace of Tilsit ( )
	Napoleon's Continental System directed against Britain		End of Holy Roman Empire (1806)		
	War with Austria ⋯⋯⋯⋯⋯⋯⋯⋯⋯⋯⋯ War with France (1809)				Finland annex⋯ (1809)
1810					
					Bessarabia anne⋯ (1812)
	Napoleon's retreat from Moscow (1812) Abdication of Napoleon (1814)				
	"The Hundred Days"	FOURTH	COALITION	AGAINST	FRANCE
1815	Battle of Waterloo (1815)				
	←――――― Congress	of	Vienna	(1815) ―――――	

d Napoleon, 1789-1815

THER STATES	COLONIES	ASIA AND AMERICA	Religion and Culture	SCIENCE	
		United States Constitution adopted (1789)	Neo-classical period in art	Lavoisier (1743-94) founds quantitative chemistry	1789
ond Partition of oland (1793)			Schiller (1759-1805)		
NCE → in and Holland in Coalition Treaties (1795)				French adopt metric system	
annexes Austrian Netherlands rd Partition of oland (1795)			Beethoven (1770-1827)		
e dominates Italy	French expedition to Egypt (1798-99)		Romantic Movement in literature begins: Wordsworth and Coleridge	Electrical investigations in progress First steam railway Fulton's steamboat Cuvier (1769-1832), naturalist	1800
	British extend their control in India	French sell Louisiana territory to U.S.	Concordat of France and the Papacy (1801) Code Napoléon formulated (1804-10)		
ederation of the hine (1806) ch invade Spain nd Portugal ninsula War (1808-14) annexes Holland (1810)	British take Cape Town (1806)	Latin American colonies agitate for independence War of 1812 Treaty of Ghent (1814)	Goethe, *Faust* (1808) Restoration of the Papal States New stimulus to organized religion	Laplace, *Mécanique Céleste* Dalton propounds atomic theory	1810 1815

Section J. The Growth of Nationali[sm]

	GREAT BRITAIN	FRANCE	AUSTRIA	PRUSSIA	RUSSIA
1815		Louis XVIII (1814-24)			
1820			←———— Troppau Protocol (1820) ————→		
		Charles X (1824-30)		*The Zollverein*	Nicholas I (182[5-])
1830	First Reform Bill (1832)	Revolution of 1830 Louis Philippe (1830-48)	Ferdinand I (1835-48)		
	Victoria (1837-1901)				
1840	Penny Postage established (1841)				
	Corn Laws repealed (1846)				
	Chartist Movement (1848)	←——— Revolutionary Outbreaks of 1848-49 ———→			
1850		Second Republic (Louis) Napoleon III Second Empire (1852)	Francis Joseph I (1848-1916)		
	Crimean War with Russia (1854-56)				Crimean War (18[54-56])
					Alexander II (18[55-])
1860		Italian War of 1859		*Expansion of German industry*	Liberation of [Serfs] (1861)
			Danish War of 1864		
	Second Reform Bill (1867)		Austro-Prussian War of 1866		
			Ausgleich with Hungary (1867)		
1870		Franco-Prussian War (1870-71)		Franco-Prussian War (1870-71)	

d Liberalism, 1815-1871

THER STATES	COLONIES	ASIA AND AMERICA	Religion and Culture	Science	
nanic Confederation *orway joined to Sweden (1814)*	*Spanish American colonies secede* *Brazil gains independence*		*Romantic Movement continues:* *Scott, Byron, Shelley, Victor Hugo*		1815
ench intervene in nish liberal revolt		The Monroe Doctrine (1823)	*Rise of the factory system* *Liberal reforms begin in England*	*Beginnings of photography*	1820
reeks win inde- endence (1829) *h revolt (1830-31)* *um separates from Holland (1831)* *ist Wars in Spain (1833-40)*	French invade Algeria (1830)			Lyell, *Principles of Geology* (1830-33) *McCormick's reaper*	1830
		First "Opium War" in China (1840-42)	*Oxford Movement*	*Schwann's cell theory* *Electric telegraph*	1840
ungarian revolt (1849)	Gold discovered in Australia (1851)		*Growth of the novel of ideas* Count Leo Tolstoy (1828-1910)	*Anesthetics used* *Law of the Conservation of Energy* *Kinetic theory of gases*	1850
itical unification in Italy *sh revolt (1862)* *ish War (1864)*	Canada becomes a Dominion (1867)	Japan opened up to Western trade (1854) Sepoy Mutiny (1857) Second "Opium War" in China (1856-60) U.S. Civil War (1861-65) Indo-China becomes a French protectorate (1863) Maximilian becomes Emperor of Mexico (1863) Revolution in Japan (1867)	Pope Pius IX issues *Syllabus of Errors* (1864) Karl Marx, *Das Kapital* (1867) *Growth of realism in art and literature* Vatican Council (1869-70)	Darwin, *Origin of Species* (1859) *Bessemer steel process* *Antiseptic surgery developed* *Transatlantic cable laid* Suez Canal completed (1869)	1860
e occupied; Italian gdom completed (1870)					1870

Section K. The New Industriali[sm]

	GREAT BRITAIN	FRANCE	GERMANY	AUSTRIA-HUNGARY	RUSSIA
1871	Trade Union Act (1871)	Third Republic (1870-1940)	Germany becomes an Empire (1871)		
			←——Three Emperors' League (1873)——→		
					Russo-Turk[ish]
	←———Congress of Berlin (1878)——→				Bessarabia annex[ed] (1878)
1880			Dual Alliance (1879)		Alexander III (1881-94)
			Triple Alliance (1882)		
			Social insurance introduced		
	Third Reform Bill (1884)				
			William II (1888-1918)		
1890			Bismarck dismissed (1890)		
		Franco-Russian.. Dreyfus Case (1894)			Nicholas II (1894- ..Alliance (18[94])
	Boer War (1899-1902)		*Naval expansion*		
1900	Anglo-Japanese Alliance (1902)				
	Dual Entente (1904)				Russo-Japanese [War] (1904-05)... Revolutionary mov[ement] (1905-06)
	The Triple..Entente			Bosnia-Herzegovina annexed (1908)	
	Era of liberal reforms				
1910					
1914	←————————————FIRST WORLD W[AR]				

nd Imperialism, 1871-1914

THER STATES	COLONIES	ASIA AND AMERICA	Religion and Culture	Science	
	Revival of imperialism		Kulturkampf in Germany (1872-79)		1871
		Rise of industrialism in the United States			
r (1877-78) nania, Serbia, and ntenegro become lependent (1878)	Britain acquires Cyprus (1878)		Pope Leo XIII (1878-1903)	*Rapid technical progress: telephone, phonograph, electric light invented*	1880
cludes Italy	French claim Tunis (1881) British in Egypt (1882)			Louis Pasteur (1822-95)	
		Britain acquires Burma (1886)	*Urban life induces a megalopolitan spirit*	*Internal combustion engine invented* *Steam turbine invented*	
	Europeans explore and partition African hinterland		*Growth of Socialism*		1890
		Sino-Japanese War (1894-95)		*Diphtheria serum discovered*	
	Italians defeated in Ethiopia (1896)				
ish-American War (1898).........	Australia becomes a Commonwealth (1900)	Spanish-American War ....(1898) Boxer Rebellion (1900) Anglo-Japanese Alliance (1902) Russo-Japanese War ....(1904-05)	First Hague Peace Conference (1899) *Rearmament increases throughout Europe* Pope Pius X (1903-14)	*Wireless telegraphy perfected* *First airplane flown*	1900
	New Zealand achieves Dominion status (1907)		Second Hague Peace Conference (1907)	*First dreadnaught built*	
g Turk Revolution (1908) guese Revolution (1910) ko-Italian War (1911-12) Balkan Wars (1912-13)	Union of South Africa (1909) Italians in Libya (1911) Morocco a French Protectorate (1912)	Revolution in China (1911)			1910
14-1918)———————→					1914

Section L. Two World Wars a[nd]

GREAT BRITAIN	FRANCE	GERMANY	ITALY	RUSSIA

1914 ← ——————————— FIRST WORLD W[AR]

	First Battle of the Marne (1914)		Italy joins Allies (1915)	Battle of Tannenb[erg] (1914)
Battle of Jutland (1916)	Battle of Verdun (1916)	U-Boat Warfare		
			Defeat at Caporetto (1917)	Russian Revoluti[on] (1917)
	Second Battle of the Marne (1918)	Weimar Assembly (1919)		Treaty of Brest-Lit[ovsk] (1918)

PARIS PEACE CONFERENCE.....(1919)

1920

Irish Free State proclaimed (1921)				New Economic Po[licy] (1921)
			Fascists gain power (1922)	
First Labor government (1923-24)		Ruhr occupied (1923)		
		Dawes Plan (1924)		
General Strike (1926)		Germany joins League (1926)		
	Briand-Kellogg Pact (1928)			Five-Year Plan (19[28])
		Young Plan (1929)	Concordat with the Papacy (1929)	

1930 ← ——————— WORLD ECONOMIC DEPRESSIO[N]

Statute of Westminster (1931)				
				Second Five-Year [Plan] (1932)
		Hitler becomes dictator (1933)		
Rearmament				

← Rome-Berlin Axis (1936) →

| | | *Anschluss with Austria* | | Third Five-Year P[lan] (1938) |
| Munich Conference (1938) | | | Italians in Albania (1939) | |

1940 SECOND WORLD WAR.....(1939-45)..........

Battle of Britain (1940-41)	Fall of France (1940) *Vichy regime* *"Free French" government*	Greece invaded (1941) Russia invaded (1941) Axis drive in North Africa (1942)	Italy attacks France (1940)	Germans invade R[ussia] (1941)
Air and submarine warfare			Italy surrenders to United Nations (1943) *German armies in Italy*	
	Liberation of France (1944)	Berlin captured (1945)	Allies invade Italy (1944) Italy liberated (1944)	Russians in Balkan[s] Germany (1944)

1945 ← ——————————— PROBLEMS OF PEACE A[ND]

e Years Between, 1914-1947

THER STATES	COLONIES	ASIA AND AMERICA	Culture and Political Thought	Science	
(1914-1918) ———		Japan joins Allies (1914)	Freudian psychology		1914
rkey joins Central Powers	*German colonies fall to Allies*		Impressionism in art	Radio developed Tanks invented by British	
nania joins Entente llies occupy Greece		United States enters war (1917)			
				Motion pictures perfected	
e Little Entente: Czechoslavakia, ugoslavia, Rumania, Poland (1920)	*Mandate System*		League of Nations (1919)	Progress in nuclear physics	1920
		Washington Naval Conference (1922)	Nationalism and Socialism intensified		
	Egypt independent (1922)	Turkey becomes a republic (1922)	Postwar disillusionment		
				Rapid progress in aviation	
			Locarno Pacts (1925)	First talking pictures	
		Gandhi leads India's Nationalist cause	Criticism of democratic ideals		
			RISE OF TOTALITARIAN REGIMES	Planet "Pluto" sighted	
			Economic insecurity	New inventions revolutionize industry	
AFTER 1929 ———		Japanese in Manchuria (1931)			1930
olution in Spain (1931)			World Disarmament Conference (1932-33)		
il War in Spain (1936)		Japan invades China (1937)			
mans in Czechoovakia (1938)	*Italians conquer Ethiopia (1938)*				
				Television and radar evolved	
COND WORLD WAR		(1939-45)			1940
land conquered (1939)	*Japanese occupy British, French, Dutch colonies in Far East*	U.S. Lend-Lease Act (1941)			
amark, Norway, erlands, Belgium, goslavia, Greece upied (1940-41)	*Axis drive in North Africa (1942)* *Axis forces driven from North Africa (1943-44)*	U.S. and Japan at war (1941) Japan surrenders (1945)	Atlantic Charter (1942)	Sulfa drugs used Jet propulsion evolving	
RECONSTRUCTION ———			First United Nations Conference (1945)	**ATOMIC ENERGY FIRST USED**	1945

THE PREPARATION OF
History Reports

IT IS NOT DIFFICULT to learn the forms which give written reports a professional character and value. The first helpful point to keep in mind is that most of the difficult work has already been done; the information needed has been assembled and is waiting in any average library. The second point to ponder is why so many thesis writers collect masses of material they won't need, omit to note down the source of valuable data they will want, and then spend hours hunting for half-remembered passages. Some of this waste of time is unavoidable, but it may be surprisingly reduced by system and experience.

A specific example will best indicate how a purposeful approach saves time and simplifies decisions. Suppose you were assigned a theme of three thousand words on *The Capitularies of Charlemagne*. Remind yourself that three thousand words means ten or twelve pages, $8\frac{1}{2}$ by 11 inches, in double-spaced typing, and that this would correspond, probably, to some fifteen pages of handwriting. Next, *define your subject*. The dictionary will inform you that a capitulary is: "1. A member of a chapter, esp. of an ecclesiastical or a masonic chapter. 2. An ordinance; chiefly, in *pl.*, a collection of ordinances." If your textbook has not told you which type of capitulary you are investigating, turn to the encyclopaedias. Look up Charlemagne, note that he is also called Charles the Great, copy his dates, and the fact that the Capitularies were ordinances or decrees issued by this great Frankish monarch in the eighth century. You now have material for an effective opening paragraph which will identify your topic for your readers. But it will do much more than that for you. If you keep this paragraph in mind, it will save you three fourths of the errant reading you might otherwise do, for it will remind you that you are seeking, not information merely, but *relevant* information.

The index shows what your textbook offers on Charlemagne and his times. Copy the suggestions for further reading, noting in particular any biographies of Charlemagne. Your next goal is the library. On your way there, try quizzing yourself on your topic. Why did Charlemagne issue ordinances? What particular problems were his Capitularies designed to meet? How were they registered and enforced? Did they improve his administration and benefit his subjects? Were they imitated by other rulers or preserved in later centuries? Such questions are not a waste of time: they will speed your research, for a question intelligently asked is half-answered. They will serve another purpose, too: they will make you think *organically* about your theme. Listed in succession they suggest a skeleton plan of procedure. Some students write out a synopsis *after* composing an essay and call this a plan. It is more constructive to survey your project, outline a tentative organization, then revise your strategy later if you must. Never forget that you are engaged in a limited operation. Your subject is specific, the length of your theme is indicated, the due date and the time you have for the assignment are set. The great poet and critic, Goethe, a shrewd judge of genius, affirmed that the superior mind first reveals itself by this ability to recognize limits, to construct a frame, and to work within it.

In the library your first and most valuable aid is the card catalogue: studied carefully the index cards tell you in advance several facts about a book. When you draw out a work on your subject, *it will save time* to copy exactly the author's name, the title of the work, the number of volumes (if more than one), the place of publication, the publisher's name, and the date of publication. If you use a loose-leaf notebook or filing cards, you will find it a simple matter, afterward, to arrange all your references alphabetically by the author's surname. Thus, without more labor, you have a "bibliography" of books consulted with which to close your theme. If you think to add a word of comment to the card, characterizing each book, you will have a "critical" bibliography.

There is another reason for listing exactly all the books which you find useful. Any direct quotation, and any very significant statement or statistics which you incorporate in your theme, should be accompanied by a notation to indicate the source. Place a numeral after the quotation or statement and include a reference with the same number in a footnote, giving the author, work, and page where the information may be found. Such footnotes, whether inserted at the base of the page or listed at the close of the essay, should be numbered consecutively throughout.

A competently prepared history theme incorporates these five features: (1) A plan setting forth the main points or divisions in the order of development. (2) A foreword, or opening paragraph, defining as clearly and crisply as possible the scope and significance of the subject. (3) Footnote references acknowledging the sources and authorities drawn upon. (4) A list of the works consulted, preferably with a phrase or two describing each. (5) A logical presentation in readable prose of the information gathered.

To pause here would leave the impression that the writing of a satisfactory theme for a history course is mainly a matter of system and mechanics. Good writing, of course, demands much more than that: it demands talent and individuality. Not only does each student respond to and evaluate material in a unique manner, the mood and personality of the writer colors the information acquired. For instance, in reading about Charlemagne you might be interested to discover that he was a contemporary of Haroun al Rashid of Bagdad, the Caliph of the *Arabian Nights*. Or you might be surprised to read that he lived in a society so unlettered that he never learned how to write. These facts, at first thought, you might discard as not relevant to a discussion of the Capitularies. But on second thought you might decide to include them, not for their logical but for their psychological value. You might feel they were worth mention because they would enliven your description, supply background and atmosphere, add a human touch. This impulse to "humanize" your facts is part of your effort to realize them more intensely, and it is a legitimate and fascinating aspect of history study. But it cannot be prescribed by any easy rule or formula. It is well to remember, too, when breathing life into the past and giving your imagination play, that fancy abhors footnotes and dramatizing data often distorts the truth. The ascertainable facts of history are usually so interesting and often so extraordinary that there is little need to apply artificial color to make them vivid.

REFERENCE WORKS

Of the many guides helpful to the history student only a few are listed here, but they will show the way to others.

Making Books Work, by Jennie M. Flexner (1943), tells the reader how to find what he needs in a library. Works of general reference in every field   Materials are classified in the *Guide to Reference Books*, 6th edition (1936), compiled by I. G. Mudge, and in *Basic Reference Books* (1939) compiled by Louis Shores. Students seeking to learn the scope and value of standard history studies and biographies will find *A Guide to Historical Literature* (1931), prepared by G. M. Dutcher and associates, a ready help. For historical facts and dates and lucid summaries of events the best one-volume reference is *An Encyclopaedia of*

World History, edited by W. L. Langer (1947). Every student makes his own acquaintance with the various encyclopaedias and biographical dictionaries; the history student will probably find the *Britannica* and the *Encyclopaedia of the Social Sciences* most convenient. M. G. Mulhall, *Dictionary of Statistics*, has useful data to 1899; for more recent history the yearbooks, such as *The World Almanac* and *The Statesman's Year-Book*, and the supplementary volumes issued annually by the leading encyclopaedias, are full of facts and tables. To locate articles which appeared in journals or periodicals, the *Reader's Guide to Periodical Literature* is invaluable. In the popular field where history and fiction blend, Jonathan Nield's *Guide to the Best Historical Novels and Tales* is a convenient aid.

Methods

The Gateway to History, by Allan Nevins (1938), describes the aids, the problems, and the pitfalls on the historian's path; no serious history student should overlook it. John C. Almack, *Research and Thesis Writing* (1930), and William G. Campbell, *A Form Book for Thesis Writing* (1939), explain in detail how to gather and present information correctly and effectively.

Man's changing concepts of the earth are traced by W. W. Jervis, *The World in Maps: A Study in Map Evolution* (1938). W. R. Shepherd, *Atlas of Medieval and Modern History* (1932), and R. Muir, G. Philip, and R. M. McElroy, *Putnam's Historical Atlas, Medieval and Modern* (1927), are standard history aids. There is charm and value in *A Literary and Historical Atlas of Europe* in the *Everyman's Library* edition, and the maps supplementing the *Cambridge Ancient, Medieval,* and *Modern History* series are detailed and valuable. For the United States C. L. and E. E. Lord, *Historical Atlas of the United States* (1944), is useful. The contemporary world is depicted with a wealth of detail in *The University Atlas*, edited by G. Goodall and H. C. Darby, 3d ed. (1944), and the *Atlas of Global Geography* by Erwin Raisz (1944) has colorful and arresting projections. W. L. Godshall has prepared a helpful set of *Map Studies in European History and International Relations* (1940), with full references and instructions for the student on marking and coloring the base maps included. The troublesome question of the preferred spelling for geographic names may be solved in many cases by reference to the *Sixth Report of the United States Geographic Board,* issued by the Government Printing Office, Washington, D.C. (1933). There are frequent supplements.

Geography

Genealogical Tables

THE PATRIMONY OF CHARLES V, SHOWING THE ANCESTORS FROM WHOM HE INHERITED HIS LANDS

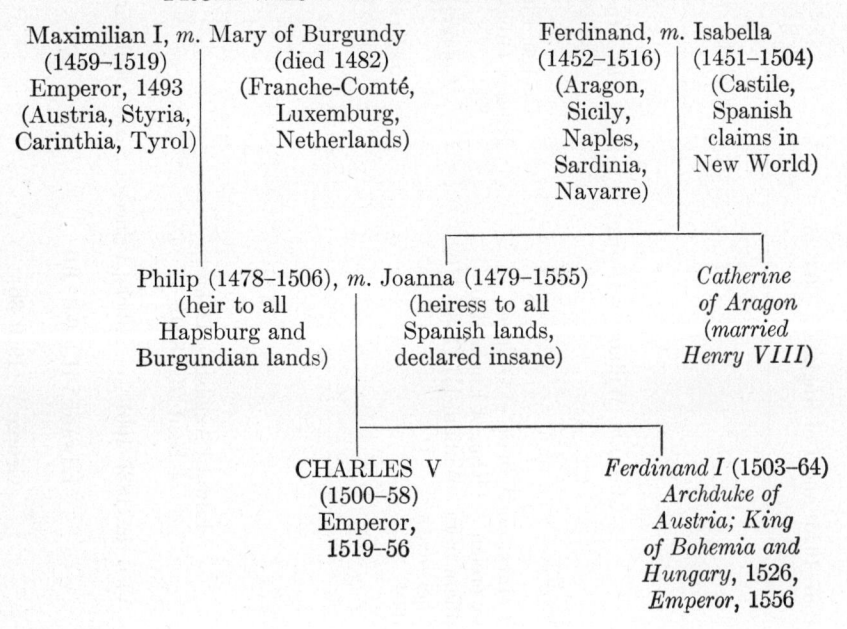

Maximilian I, *m.* Mary of Burgundy
(1459–1519)   (died 1482)
Emperor, 1493   (Franche-Comté,
(Austria, Styria,   Luxemburg,
Carinthia, Tyrol)   Netherlands)

Ferdinand, *m.* Isabella
(1452–1516)   (1451–1504)
(Aragon,   (Castile,
Sicily,   Spanish
Naples,   claims in
Sardinia,   New World)
Navarre)

Philip (1478–1506), *m.* Joanna (1479–1555)
(heir to all   (heiress to all
Hapsburg and   Spanish lands,
Burgundian lands)   declared insane)

*Catherine
of Aragon
(married
Henry VIII)*

CHARLES V
(1500–58)
Emperor,
1519–56

*Ferdinand I (1503–64)
Archduke of
Austria; King
of Bohemia and
Hungary, 1526,
Emperor, 1556*

GENEALOGICAL CHART OF THE ENGLISH SOVEREIGNS AFTER 1603

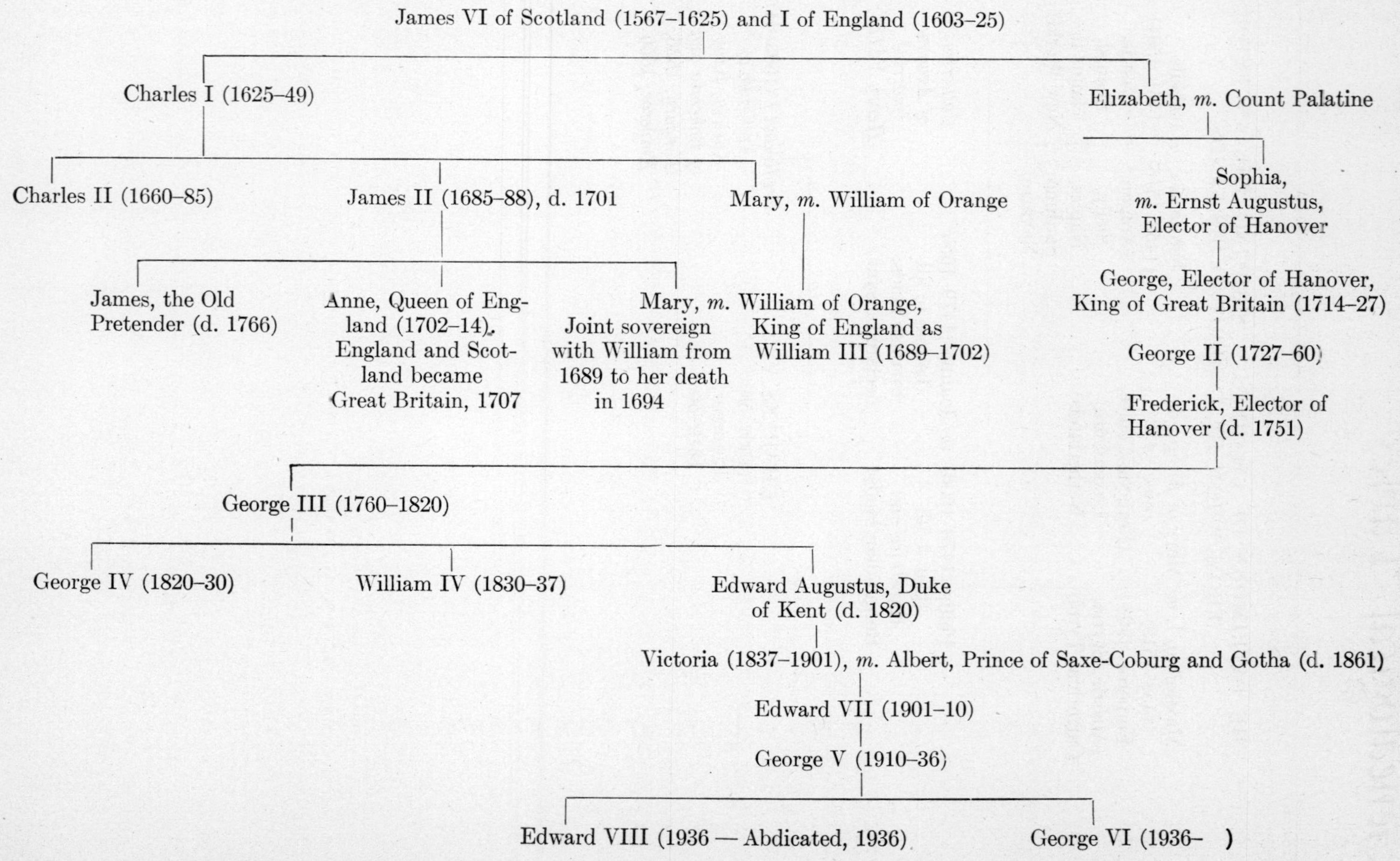

James VI of Scotland (1567–1625) and I of England (1603–25)
- Charles I (1625–49)
  - Charles II (1660–85)
  - James II (1685–88), d. 1701
    - James, the Old Pretender (d. 1766)
    - Mary, m. William of Orange as William III (1689–1702), Joint sovereign with William from 1689 to her death in 1694
    - Anne, Queen of England (1702–14), England and Scotland became Great Britain, 1707
- Elizabeth, m. Count Palatine
  - Sophia, m. Ernst Augustus, Elector of Hanover
    - George, Elector of Hanover, King of Great Britain (1714–27)
      - George II (1727–60)
        - Frederick, Elector of Hanover (d. 1751)
          - Mary, m. William of Orange
          - George III (1760–1820)
            - George IV (1820–30)
            - William IV (1830–37)
            - Edward Augustus, Duke of Kent (d. 1820)
              - Victoria (1837–1901), m. Albert, Prince of Saxe-Coburg and Gotha (d. 1861)
                - Edward VII (1901–10)
                  - George V (1910–36)
                    - Edward VIII (1936 — Abdicated, 1936)
                    - George VI (1936–)

GENEALOGICAL CHART OF THE FRENCH KINGS AFTER 1610

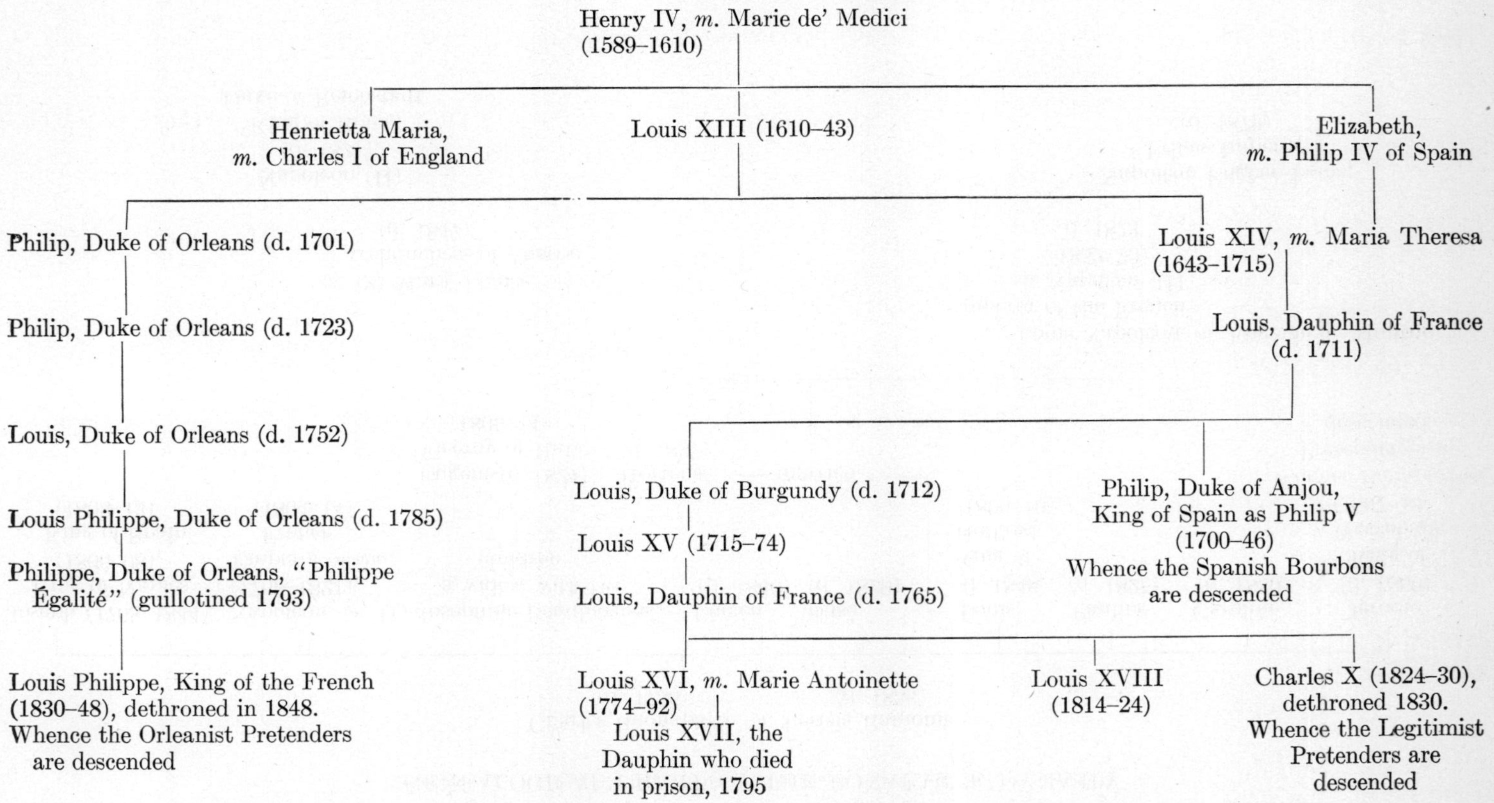

Henry IV, *m.* Marie de' Medici (1589–1610)
┬
├── Henrietta Maria, *m.* Charles I of England
└── Louis XIII (1610–43)
    ├── Louis XIV, *m.* Maria Theresa (1643–1715) ── Elizabeth, *m.* Philip IV of Spain
    │   └── Louis, Dauphin of France (d. 1711)
    │   ├── Louis, Duke of Burgundy (d. 1712)
    │   │   └── Louis XV (1715–74)
    │   │   └── Louis, Dauphin of France (d. 1765)
    │   │   └── Louis XVI, *m.* Marie Antoinette (1774–92)
    │   │   ├── Louis XVII, the Dauphin who died in prison, 1795
    │   │   ├── Louis XVIII (1814–24)
    │   │   └── Charles X (1824–30), dethroned 1830. Whence the Legitimist Pretenders are descended
    │   └── Philip, Duke of Anjou, King of Spain as Philip V (1700–46) Whence the Spanish Bourbons are descended
    └── Philip, Duke of Orleans (d. 1701)
        └── Philip, Duke of Orleans (d. 1723)
            └── Louis, Duke of Orleans (d. 1752)
                └── Louis Philippe, Duke of Orleans (d. 1785)
                    └── Philippe, Duke of Orleans, "Philippe Égalité" (guillotined 1793)
                        └── Louis Philippe, King of the French (1830–48), dethroned in 1848. Whence the Orleanist Pretenders are descended

GENEALOGICAL CHART OF THE BONAPARTE DYNASTY

Charles Buonaparte, *m.* Letizia Ramolino
(d. 1785) (d. 1836)

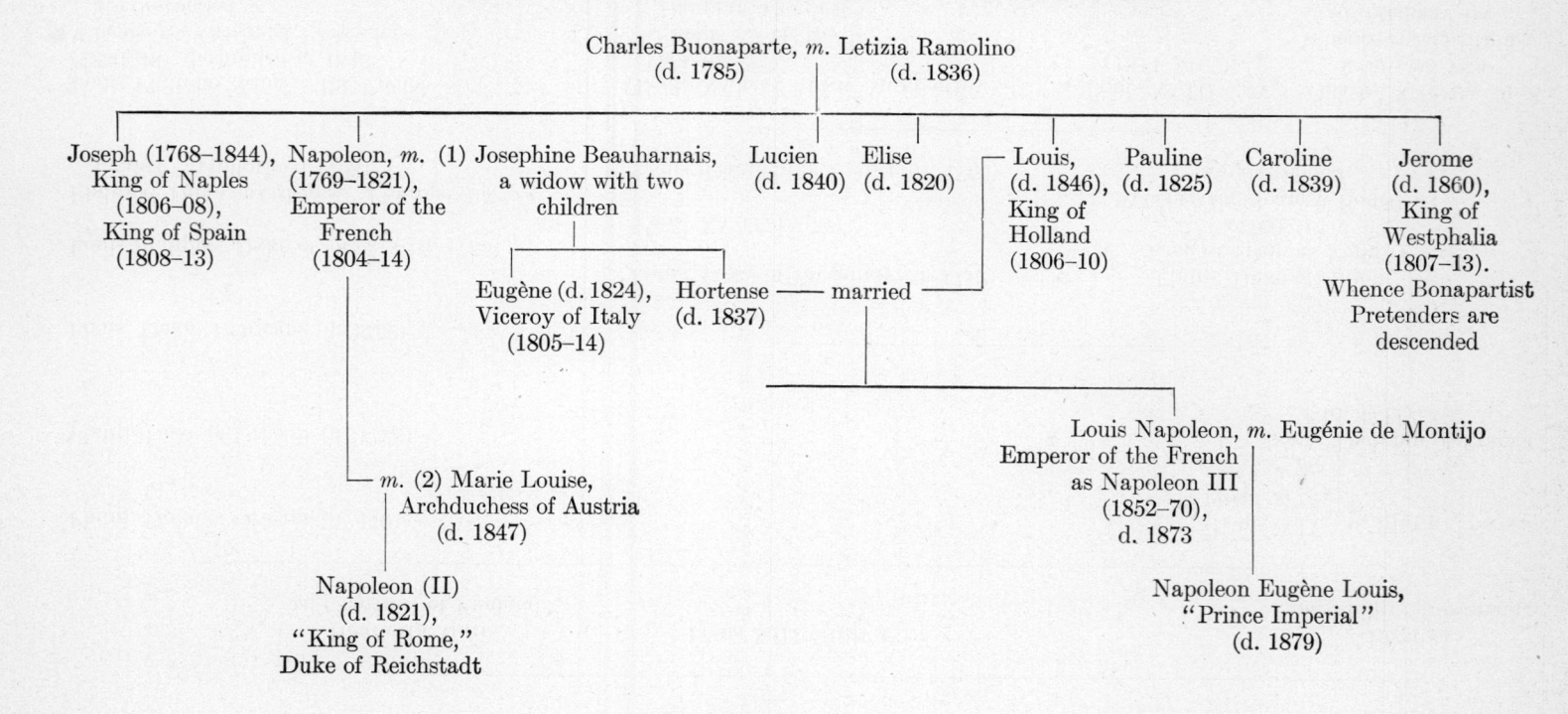

- **Joseph** (1768–1844), King of Naples (1806–08), King of Spain (1808–13)
- **Napoleon**, *m.* (1) Josephine Beauharnais, a widow with two children
  - (1769–1821), Emperor of the French (1804–14)
  - Eugène (d. 1824), Viceroy of Italy (1805–14)
  - Hortense (d. 1837) —— married —— Louis Napoleon, *m.* Eugénie de Montijo, Emperor of the French as Napoleon III (1852–70), d. 1873
    - Napoleon Eugène Louis, "Prince Imperial" (d. 1879)
  - *m.* (2) Marie Louise, Archduchess of Austria (d. 1847)
    - Napoleon (II) (d. 1821), "King of Rome," Duke of Reichstadt
- **Lucien** (d. 1840)
- **Elise** (d. 1820)
- **Louis** (d. 1846), King of Holland (1806–10)
- **Pauline** (d. 1825)
- **Caroline** (d. 1839)
- **Jerome** (d. 1860), King of Westphalia (1807–13). Whence Bonapartist Pretenders are descended

A List of European Rulers TO THE MIDDLE OF THE SEVENTEENTH CENTURY

RULERS OF THE CAROLINGIAN FAMILY

Pepin of Heristal, Mayor of the Palace, 714
Charles Martel, Mayor of the Palace, 715–41
Pepin I, Mayor of the Palace, 741, King, 751–68
Charlemagne, King, 768, Emperor, 800–14
Louis "the Pious," Emperor, 814–40

WEST FRANKISH KINGDOM

Charles "the Bald," King, 840–77, Emperor, 875
Louis II, King, 877–79
Louis III, King, 879–82
Carloman, King, 879–84

MIDDLE KINGDOMS

Lothair, Emperor, 840–55
Louis (Italy), Emperor, 855–75
Charles (Provence), King, 855–63
Lothair II (Lorraine), King, 855–69

EAST FRANKISH KINGDOM

Louis "the German," King, 840–76
Carloman, King, 876–80
Louis, King, 876–82
Charles "the Fat," Emperor, 876–87, reunites empire, 884, deposed 887

THE EMPERORS OF THE HOLY ROMAN EMPIRE

SAXON EMPERORS
  Otto I, King, 936, Emperor, 962–73
  Otto II, 973–83
  Otto III, 983–1002
  Henry II, 1002–24
FRANCONIAN EMPERORS
  Conrad II, 1024–39
  Henry III, 1039–56
  Henry IV, 1056–1106
  Henry V, 1106–25
  Lothair III (of Saxony), 1125–37
HOHENSTAUFEN EMPERORS
  Conrad III, 1138–52
  Frederick I "Barbarossa," 1152–90
  Henry VI, 1190–97
  { Philip of Swabia, 1198–1208
  { Otto IV (Welf), 1198–1215
  Frederick II, 1211–50
  Conrad IV, 1250–54
INTERREGNUM, 1254–73
EMPERORS FROM VARIOUS HOUSES
  Rudolf I (Hapsburg), 1273–91

Adolf (Nassau), 1292–98
Albert I (Hapsburg), 1298–1308
Henry VII (Luxemburg), 1308–13
Louis IV (Wittelsbach), 1314–47
Charles IV (Luxemburg), 1347–78
Wenceslas (Luxemburg), 1378–1400
Rupert (Wittelsbach), 1400–10
Sigismund (Luxemburg), 1410–37
HAPSBURG EMPERORS
  Albert II, 1438–39
  Frederick III, 1440–93
  Maximilian I, 1493–1519
  Charles V, 1519–56
  Ferdinand I, 1556–64
  Maximilian II, 1564–76
  Rudolf II, 1576–1612
  Matthias, 1612–19
  Ferdinand II, 1619–37
  Ferdinand III, 1637–57
  Leopold I, 1658–1705

HAPSBURG KINGS OF SPAIN

Charles V, 1516–56
Philip II, 1556–98
Philip III, 1598–1621
Philip IV, 1621–65

APPENDIXES

THE KINGS OF FRANCE FROM HUGH CAPET

CAPETIAN KINGS
  Hugh Capet, 987–96
  Robert II, 996–1031
  Henry I, 1031–60
  Philip I, 1060–1108
  Louis VI, 1108–37
  Louis VII, 1137–80
  Philip II "Augustus," 1180–1223
  Louis VIII, 1223–26
  Louis IX (Saint Louis), 1226–70
  Philip III, 1270–85
  Philip IV "the Fair," 1285–1314
  Louis X, 1314–16
  Philip V, 1316–22
  Charles IV, 1322–28
VALOIS KINGS
  Philip VI, 1328–50
  John, 1350–64
  Charles V, 1364–80
  Charles VI, 1380–1422
  Charles VII, 1422–61
  Louis XI, 1461–83
  Charles VIII, 1483–98
  Louis XII, 1498–1515
  Francis I, 1515–47
  Henry II, 1547–59
  Francis II, 1559–60
  Charles IX, 1560–74
  Henry III, 1574–89
BOURBON KINGS
  Henry IV, 1589–1610
  Louis XIII, 1610–43
  Louis XIV, 1643–1715

THE KINGS OF ENGLAND FROM THE NORMAN CONQUEST

NORMAN KINGS
  William I, 1066–87
  William II, 1087–1100
  Henry I, 1100–35
  Stephen, 1135–54
ANGEVIN KINGS
  Henry II, 1154–89
  Richard I, 1189–99
  John, 1199–1216
  Henry III, 1216–72
  Edward I, 1272–1307
  Edward II, 1307–27
  Edward III, 1327–77
  Richard II, 1377–99
LANCASTRIAN KINGS
  Henry IV, 1399–1413
  Henry V, 1413–22
  Henry VI, 1422–61
YORKIST KINGS
  Edward IV, 1461–83
  Edward V, 1483
  Richard III, 1483–85
TUDOR KINGS
  Henry VII, 1485–1509
  Henry VIII, 1509–47
  Edward VI, 1547–53
  Mary, 1553–58
  Elizabeth, 1558–1603
STUART KINGS
  James I, 1603–25
  Charles I, 1625–49
INTERREGNUM, 1649–60

A List of European Rulers SINCE THE MIDDLE OF THE SEVENTEENTH CENTURY

THE PAPACY

Alexander VII, 1655–67
Clement IX, 1667–69
Clement X, 1670–76
Innocent XI, 1676–89
Alexander VIII, 1689–91
Innocent XII, 1691–1700
Clement XI, 1700–21
Innocent XIII, 1721–24
Benedict XIII, 1724–30
Clement XII, 1730–40
Benedict XIV, 1740–58
Clement XIII, 1758–69

Clement XIV, 1769–74
Pius VI, 1775–99
Pius VII, 1800–23
Leo XII, 1823–29
Pius VIII, 1829–30
Gregory XIII, 1831–46
Pius IX, 1846–78
Leo XIII, 1878–1903
Pius X, 1903–14
Benedict XV, 1914–22
Pius XI, 1922–39
Pius XII, 1939 —

AUSTRIA

Leopold I, 1658–1705
Joseph I, 1705–11
Charles II, 1711–40
 (as Holy Roman Emperor he ranked as Charles VI)
Maria Theresa, 1740–80
Joseph II, 1780–90
Leopold II, 1790–92

Francis I, 1792–1835
 (as Holy Roman Emperor until he abandoned the title in 1806 he ranked as Francis II)
Ferdinand I, 1835–48
Francis Joseph, 1848–1916
Charles I, 1916–18
Republic, 1918–38
United to Germany, 1938–45
Republic, 1945 —

FRANCE

Louis XIV, 1643–1715
Louis XV, 1715–74
Louis XVI, 1774–92
Republic, 1792–1804
Napoleon I, Emperor of the French, 1804–14
Louis XVIII, 1814–24

Charles X, 1824–30
Louis Philippe, 1830–48
Second Republic, 1848–52
Napoleon III, Emperor, 1852–70
Third Republic, 1870 —

GREAT BRITAIN (ENGLAND AND SCOTLAND UNTIL 1707)

Charles II, 1660–85
James II, 1685–88
William III, 1689–1702, and Mary II, 1689–94
Anne, 1702–14
George I, 1714–27
George II, 1727–60
George III, 1760–1820
George IV, 1820–30

William IV, 1830–37
Victoria, 1837–1901
Edward VII, 1901–10
George V, 1910–36
Edward VIII, 1936
 (Abdicated 1936)
George VI, 1936 —

PRUSSIA

Frederick William, Elector of Brandenburg, 1640–88
Frederick II, Elector of Brandenburg, 1688–1701
  King of Prussia, 1701–13
Frederick William I, 1713–40
Frederick II, 1740–86
Frederick William II, 1786–97
Frederick William III, 1797–1840

Frederick William IV, 1840–61
William I, 1861–88
  German Emperor after 1871
Frederick III, 1888
William II, 1888–1918
Republic, 1918–33
Third Reich, 1933–45
Military occupation, 1945 —

RUSSIA

Alexius, 1645–76
Theodore II, 1676–82
Ivan V and Peter I, 1682–89
Peter I "the Great," 1689–1725
Catherine I, 1725–27
Peter II, 1727–30
Anna, 1730–40
Ivan VI, 1740–41
Elizabeth, 1741–62

Peter III, 1762
Catherine II "the Great," 1762–96
Paul I, 1796–1801
Alexander I, 1801–25
Nicholas I, 1825–55
Alexander II, 1855–81
Alexander III, 1881–94
Nicholas II, 1894–1917
Union of Soviet Socialist Republics, 1917 —

SPAIN

Philip IV, 1621–65
Charles II, 1665–1700
Philip V, 1700–46
Ferdinand VI, 1746–59
Charles III, 1759–88
Charles IV, 1788–1808
Joseph Bonaparte, 1808–13

Ferdinand VII, 1813–33
Isabella II, 1833–68
Amadeo, 1870–73
Republic, 1873–75
Alphonso XII, 1875–85
Alphonso XIII, 1886–1931
Republic, 1931 —

Suggestions for Further Reading

INTRODUCTION: EUROPE IN THE MIDDLE AGES

G. B. Adams, *Civilization During the Middle Ages* (rev. ed. 1914).
J. B. Bury, *History of the Later Roman Empire* (1923).
Cambridge Medieval History, 6 vols. (1911–29).
H. A. L. Fisher, *A History of Europe*, vol. I (1935).
E. Gibbon, *History of the Decline and Fall of the Roman Empire*, ed. by J. B. Bury. 7 vols. (1896–98).
E. M. Hulme, *The Middle Ages* (1929).
L. C. MacKinney, *The Medieval World* (1938).
M. Rostovtzeff, *A History of the Ancient World* (1928).
C. Stephenson, *Medieval History* (1935).
G. C. Sellery and A. C. Krey, *Medieval Foundations of Western Civilization* (1929).
T. W. Wallbank and A. M. Taylor, *Civilization — Past and Present*, vol. I (1942).

LONGER STUDIES. E. Eyre (editor), *European Civilization: Its Origin and Development*, vol. III, *The Middle Ages* (1938); S. Baldwin, *Business in the Middle Ages* (1937); C. R. Beazley, *The Dawn of Modern Geography, a History of Exploration and Geographical Science*, 3 vols. (1897–1906); J. Bryce, *The Holy Roman Empire* (rev. ed. 1886); E. P. Cheyney, *The Dawn of a New Era, 1250–1453* (1936); G. G. Coulton, *The Medieval Village* (1926); C. Dawson, *The Making of Europe: an Introduction to the History of European Unity* (1939); E. Faure, *History of Art: Medieval Art* (1937); A. C. Flick, *Rise of the Medieval Church and its Influence on the Civilization of Western Europe from the First to the Thirteenth Century* (1909); C. H. Haskins, *The Renaissance of the Twelfth Century* (1927); F. J. C. Hearnshaw (editor), *Medieval Contributions to Modern Civilization* (1921); J. Huizinga, *The Waning of the Middle Ages* (1937); N. Neilson, *Medieval Agrarian Economy* (1936); R. A. Newhall, *The Crusades* (1927); C. W. C. Oman, *History of the Art of War During the Middle Ages* (2d rev. ed. 1924); H. Pirenne, *Medieval Cities: Their Origins and the Revival of Trade* (1925); H. Pirenne, *Mohammed and Charlemagne* (1939); E. Power, *Medieval People* (1924); E. K. Rand, *Founders of the Middle Ages* (1929); H. Rashdall, *The Universities in the Middle Ages*, 3 vols. (1936); C. Seignobos, *Feudal Regime* (new ed. 1926); H. O. Taylor, *The Medieval Mind*, 2 vols. (4th ed. 1925); L. Thorndike, *History of Magic and Experimental Science during the First Thirteen Centuries of our Era*, 2 vols. (1923); G. G. Walsh, *Medieval Humanism* (The Christendom Series), (1942).

25. THE AGE OF THE RENAISSANCE IN ITALY

J. W. Thompson, *Economic and Social History of Europe in the Later Middle Ages, 1300–1530* (1931), chap. IX.
E. M. Hulme, *Renaissance and Reformation* (rev. ed. 1917), chaps. IV–VI.
H. O. Taylor, *Thought and Expression in the Sixteenth Century* (2d ed. 1930), vol. I, chaps. I–V.
H. A. L. Fisher, *A History of Europe* (1935), vol. II, chap. II.
W. K. Ferguson, *The Renaissance* (1940), chap. II.
Cambridge Medieval History, vol. VII, chap. XXV.
Cambridge Modern History, vol. I, chaps. V, VI, XVI.

LONGER STUDIES. J. C. L. S. de Sismondi, *History of the Italian Republics in the Middle Ages* (edited by W. Boulting, 1906); M. V. Clarke, *The Medieval City State* (1926); H. S. Lucas, *Renaissance and Reformation* (1934); J. A. Symonds, *Short History of the Renaissance in Italy* (1894); J. A. Symonds, *Renaissance in Italy*, 7 vols. (rev. ed. 1887–88); J. Burckhardt, *Civilization of the Period of the Renaissance in Italy* (new ed. 1929); E. Emerton, *Humanism and Tyranny* (1925); G. F. Young, *The Medici* (Modern Library, 1933); J. B. Fletcher, *Literature of the Italian Renaissance* (1934); R. Roeder, *Man of the Renaissance* (1933); E. P. Cheyney, *The Dawn of a New Era* (1936); F. Schevill, *History of Florence* (1936). BIOGRAPHIES. E. Armstrong, *Lorenzo the Magnificent and Florence of the Fifteenth Century* (1896); W. Boulting, *Aeneus Silvius* (1908); L. G. Gardner, *Cesare Borgia* (1913); P. de Nolhac, *Petrarch and the Ancient World*

(1907); E. Müntz, *Leonardo da Vinci*, 2 vols. (1878); E. McCurdy, *Raphael Santi* (1917). SOURCES. L. Landucci, *A Florentine Diary from 1450–1516* (trans. 1927); N. Machiavelli, *The Prince* (1897); B. Castiglione, *The Book of the Courtier* (1900); B. Cellini, *Autobiography* (Modern Library); J. H. Robinson, *Readings in European History* (1904), vol. I, chap. XXII; F. A. Ogg, *A Source Book of Medieval History* (1907), chap. XXVI.

26. THE WANING OF THE MIDDLE AGES AND THE RENAISSANCE IN THE NORTH

H. S. Lucas, *Renaissance and Reformation* (1934), chaps. IX, XI, XXIX.
E. M. Hulme, *Renaissance and Reformation* (rev. ed. 1917), chap. XI.
P. Smith, *Age of the Reformation* (1920), chap. I.
H. O. Taylor, *Thought and Expression in the Sixteenth Century* (2d ed. 1930), vol. I, chaps. VI, VII.
H. A. L. Fisher, *A History of Europe* (1935), vol. II, chap. IV.
J. H. Randall, Jr., *The Making of the Modern Mind* (1926), chaps. VI, VIII.
W. K. Ferguson, *The Renaissance* (1940), chap. I.
Cambridge Modern History, vol. I, chap. XVII.

LONGER STUDIES. J. Huizinga, *The Waning of the Middle Ages* (1924); Mrs. J. R. Green, *Town Life in the Fifteenth Century*, 2 vols. (1894); E. Power, *Medieval People* (1924); A. Tilley, *The Dawn of the French Renaissance* (1918); A. Hyma, *The Christian Renaissance* (1925); F. Seebohm, *The Oxford Reformers* (1867); A. Tilley, *Literature of the French Renaissance*, 2 vols. (1904); P. S. Allen, *The Age of Erasmus* (1914). BIOGRAPHIES. P. Smith, *Erasmus, a Study of his Life, Ideals and Place in History* (1923); E. M. G. Ruth, *Sir Thomas More and his Friends* (1934). SOURCES. D. Erasmus, *The Praise of Folly* (1913); D. Erasmus, *Familiar Colloquies* (1900); Thomas à Kempis, *The Imitation of Christ* (numerous editions); J. F. Scott, A Hyma, and A. H. Noyes, *Readings in Medieval History* (1933), no. 85; J. H. Robinson, *Readings in European History* (1904), vol. II, chap. XXIV.

27. THE STATES OF EUROPE AT THE DAWN OF THE MODERN AGE

C. J. H. Hayes, *A Political and Cultural History of Modern Europe* (1932), vol. I, chap. I.

J. W. Thompson, *Economic and Social History of Europe in the Later Middle Ages, 1300–1530* (1931), chaps. XX–XXII.
C. Stephenson, *Medieval History* (1935), chap. XXVI.
F. Funck-Brentano, *The Middle Ages* (1926), chap. XX.
W. E. Lunt, *History of England* (1928), chaps. XV, XVI.
E. F. Henderson, *A Short History of Germany* (new ed. 1927), vol. I, chap. X.
Cambridge Modern History, vol. I, chaps. II, IX, XI, XII, XIV.

LONGER STUDIES. W. T. Waugh, *A History of Europe from 1378 to 1494* (1932); A. J. Grant, *A History of Europe from 1494 to 1610* (1932); R. Lodge, *The Close of the Middle Ages, 1273–1494* (new ed. 1924); A. H. Johnson, *Europe in the Sixteenth Century, 1494–1598* (7th ed. 1928); R. B. Merriman, *Rise of the Spanish Empire* (1918), vols. I, II; J. S. C. Bridge, *History of France from the Death of Louis XI*, 4 vols. (1921–29); R. E. Dickinson and O. J. Howarth, *The Making of Geography* (1933); C. R. Beazley, *The Dawn of Modern Geography*, 2 vols. (1897); J. B. Brebner, *The Explorers of North America, 1492–1806* (1933). BIOGRAPHIES. P. Champion, *Louis XI*, 2 vols. (1927); J. Gairdner, *Henry VII* (1889); S. Zweig, *Conqueror of the Seas: Life of Magellan* (1938); S. E. Morison, *Admiral of the Ocean Sea: A Life of Christopher Columbus*, 2 vols. (1942); C. R. Beazley, *Prince Henry the Navigator* (1895). SOURCES. J. H. Robinson, *Readings in European History* (1904), vol. II, chap. XXIII.

28. THE REFORMATION AND THE FOUNDING OF THE PROTESTANT CHURCHES

P. Smith, *Age of the Reformation* (1920), chaps. II, III.
C. J. H. Hayes, *A Political and Cultural History of Modern Europe* (1932), vol. I, chap. IV.
E. M. Hulme, *Renaissance and Reformation* (rev. ed. 1917), chaps. XII, XV.
H. A. L. Fisher, *A History of Europe* (1935), vol. II, chaps. VIII, IX, XI.
E. F. Henderson, *A Short History of Germany* (new ed. 1927), vol. I, chaps. XI, XII.
G. M. Trevelyan, *History of England* (1926), part III, chaps. III, IV.
Cambridge Modern History, vol. II, chaps. IV, V, X, XI, XIV.

LONGER STUDIES. H. S. Lucas, *Renaissance and Reformation* (1934); T. M. Lindsay, *History of the Reformation*, 2 vols. (1906); F. A. Gasquet, *The Eve of the Reformation* (1900); W. Walker, *The Reformation* (1900); O. A. Marti, *The Economic Causes of the Reformation in England* (1928); J. Gairdner, *The English Church in the Sixteenth Century* (1904); M. Creighton, *History of the Papacy* (new ed. 1897), vol. V; E. B. Bax, *The Peasants' War in Germany* (1889); G. Baskerville, *English Monks and the Suppression of the Monasteries* (1937). BIOGRAPHIES. P. Smith, *Life and Letters of Martin Luther* (1914); G. Harkness, *John Calvin, the Man and his Ethics* (1931); S. M. Jackson, *Huldreich Zwingli* (1900). SOURCES. P. Smith, *Luther's Correspondence*, 2 vols. (1913–18); J. H. Robinson, *Readings in European History* (1904), vol. II, chaps. XXV, XXVII.

29. THE STATES OF EUROPE IN THE AGE OF CHARLES V

C. J. H. Hayes, *A Political and Cultural History of Modern Europe* (1932), vol. I, chap. V, sec. 1.
A. H. Johnson, *Europe in the Sixteenth Century, 1494–1598* (7th ed. 1928), chaps. III–V.
H. A. L. Fisher, *A History of Europe* (1935), vol. II, chaps. X, XII.
E. F. Henderson, *A Short History of Germany* (new ed. 1927), vol. I, chaps. XIV, XV.
L. Batiffol, *The Century of the Renaissance* (*National History of France*) (1916), chaps. II–IV.
W. E. Lunt, *History of England* (1928), chap. XVII.
Cambridge Modern History, vol. II, chaps. II, III, XIII.

LONGER STUDIES. A. J. Grant, *A History of Europe from 1494 to 1610* (1932); R. B. Merriman, *Rise of the Spanish Empire* (1918), vol. II; W. L. McElwee, *The Reign of Charles V.* (1936); N. B. Adams, *The Heritage of Spain* (1943); J. R. M. MacDonald, *History of France* (1915), vol. II; P. J. Blok, *History of the People of the Netherlands* (1900), vol. III; H. A. L. Fisher, *History of England from the Accession of Henry VII to the Death of Henry VIII* (1906); A. D. Innes, *England under the Tudors* (1911); J. Haller, *The Epochs of German History* (1930). BIOGRAPHIES. A. F. Pollard, *Henry VIII* (1905); F. Hackett, *Francis I* (1935); K. Brandi, *The Emperor Charles V.* (1939); R. B. Merriman, *Sulieman the Magnificent, 1520–1566* (1944). SOURCES. J. H. Robinson, *Readings in European History* (1904), vol. II, chap. XXVIII, sec. III.

30. THE CATHOLIC OR COUNTER-REFORMATION

P. Smith, *Age of the Reformation* (1920), chap. VIII.
H. S. Lucas, *Renaissance and Reformation* (1934), chaps. XLVII, XLVIII.
E. M. Hulme, *Renaissance and Reformation* (rev. ed. 1917), chap. XXI.
C. J. H. Hayes, *A Political and Cultural History of Modern Europe* (1932), vol. I, chap. IV, sec. 3.
A. H. Johnson, *Europe in the Sixteenth Century, 1494–1598* (7th ed. 1928), chap. VI.
H. A. L. Fisher, *A History of Europe* (1935), vol. II, chap. XIII.
Cambridge Modern History, vol. II, chaps. XII, XVIII.

LONGER STUDIES. T. M. Lindsay, *History of the Reformation* (1906), vol. II; L. von Pastor, *The History of the Popes from the Close of the Middle Ages* (1891–1930), vols. X–XIII; P. Sarpi, *The Historie of the Councel of Trent* (1620); A. W. Ward, *The Counter-Reformation* (1910); A. R. Pennington, *The Counter-Reformation in Europe* (1899); Father Cuthbert, *The Capuchins, a Contribution to the History of the Counter-Reformation*, 2 vols. (1929); H. Boehmer, *The Jesuits* (1928); T. J. Campbell, *The Jesuits, 1534–1921* (1921); M. P. Harney, *The Jesuits in History* (1941). BIOGRAPHY. P. Van Dyke, *Ignatius Loyola, the Founder of the Jesuits* (1926). SOURCES. J. H. Robinson, *Readings in European History* (1904), vol. II, chap. XXVIII, secs. I, II; J. F. X. O'Connor (editor), *The Autobiography of Saint Ignatius* (1900).

31. THE STATES OF EUROPE IN THE AGE OF PHILIP II

C. J. H. Hayes, *A Political and Cultural History of Modern Europe* (1932), vol. I, chap. V, sec. 2.
H. S. Lucas, *Renaissance and Reformation* (1934), chaps. LI, LII.
E. M. Hulme, *Renaissance and Reformation* (rev. ed. 1917), chaps. XXV, XXVI.
A. H. Johnson, *Europe in the Sixteenth Century, 1494–1598* (7th ed. 1928), chaps. VII–IX.
H. A. L. Fisher, *A History of Europe* (1935), vol. II, chaps. XIV–XVI.
L. Batiffol, *The Century of the Renaissance* (1916), chaps. V–VII.
W. E. Lunt, *History of England* (1928), chaps. XVIII–XX.
Cambridge Modern History, vol. III, chaps. I, VI, VII, XV.

LONGER STUDIES. M. A. S. Hume, *Spain, its Greatness and Decay, 1479–1788* (2d. ed. 1899); C. E. Chapman, *History of Spain* (1918); P. J. Blok, *History of the Peoples of the Netherlands* (1908–09), vol. III; J. L. Motley, *Rise of the Dutch Republic* (new ed. 1913); J. R. M. MacDonald, *History of France* (1915), vol. II; A. F. Pollard, *History of England from the Accession of Edward VI to the Death of Elizabeth* (1910); A. D. Innes, *England under the Tudors* (1911); J. A. Williamson, *The Age of Drake* (1938); J. B. Black, *The Reign of Elizabeth* (1936); E. M. W. Tillyard, *The Elizabethan World Picture* (1944). BIOGRAPHIES. J. E. Neale, *Queen Elizabeth* (1934); M. A. S. Hume, *Philip II of Spain* (new ed. 1911); E. Maas, *The Dream of Philip II* (1944); C. V. Wedgewood, *William the Silent* (1944); P. Van Dyke, *Catherine de Médicis*, 2 vols. (1922). SOURCES. J. H. Robinson, *Readings in European History* (1904), vol. II, chap. XXVIII, secs. V–VIII; R. D. Bodilly, *Fighting Merchantmen* (1927) (Extracts from Hakluyt).

32. THE ECONOMIC REVOLUTION

J. W. Thompson, *Economic and Social History of Europe in the Later Middle Ages, 1300–1530* (1931), chaps. XVII–XIX.
P. Smith, *Age of the Reformation* (1920), chaps. X, XI.
M. M. Knight, H. E. Barnes, and F. Flügel, *Economic History of Europe* (1928), part II, chap. II.
C. J. H. Hayes, *A Political and Cultural History of Modern Europe* (1932), vol. I, chap. II.
W. J. Ashley, *The Economic Organization of England* (1921), chaps. III–V.
E. P. Cheyney, *The Dawn of a New Era* (1936), chaps. I–III.
Cambridge Modern History, vol. I, chap. XV.

LONGER STUDIES. F. L. Nussbaum, *History of the Economic Institutions of Modern Europe* (1933); R. Ehrenberg, *Capital and Finance in the Age of the Renaissance* (1928); W. Cunningham, *The Growth of English Industry and Commerce in Modern Times* (6th ed. 1909), part I; E. Lipson, *The Economic History of England* (1930–31), vols. II, III; W. J. Ashley, *An Introduction to English Economic History and Theory* (3d ed. 1898), vol. II; H. H. Tawney, *The Agrarian Problem in the Sixteenth Century* (1912); M. Weber, *The Protestant Ethic and the Spirit of Capitalism* (1930); C. Day, *History of Commerce* (rev. ed. 1922); L. B. Packard, *Commercial Revolution* (1927); H. Sée, *Modern Capitalism, its Origin and Evolution* (1928); N. S. B. Gras, *An Introduction to Economic History* (1922); F. C. Lane, *Andrea Barbarigo, Merchant of Venice, 1418–1449* (1945); H. Heaton, *Economic History of Europe* (1936); J. U. Nef, *Industry and Government in France and England, 1540–1640* (1940).

33. THE RECONSTRUCTION OF FRANCE AND THE ESTABLISHMENT OF ABSOLUTE MONARCHY

C. J. H. Hayes, *A Political and Cultural History of Modern Europe* (1932), vol. I, chap. IV, sec. 1.
H. O. Wakeman, *European History, 1598–1714* (1894), chaps. II, VII.
D. Ogg, *Europe in the Seventeenth Century* (1925), chaps. II, V.
H. A. L. Fisher, *A History of Europe* (1935), vol. II, chap. XVIII.
J. Boulenger, *The Seventeenth Century* (National History of France) (1920), chaps. I, II, IV, VI.
Cambridge Modern History, vol. III, chap. XX; vol. IV, chaps. IV, XXI.

LONGER STUDIES. J. B. Perkins, *Richelieu and the Growth of French Power* (new ed. 1926); J. B. Perkins, *France under Mazarin*, 2 vols. (1886); L. Batiffol, *Marie de Médicis and the French Court in the Seventeenth Century* (1908); A. J. Grant, *The French Monarchy, 1483–1789*, 2 vols. (1900–05); J. R. M. MacDonald, *History of France* (1915), vol. II; G. W. Kitchin, *History of France* (4th ed. 1899–1903), vol. III; C. Hugon, *Social France in the Seventeenth Century* (1911); A. Tilley, *Literature of the French Renaissance*, 2 vols. (1904). BIOGRAPHIES. P. F. Willert, *Henry of Navarre* (1893); R. Lodge, *Richelieu* (1920); A. Hassal, *Mazarin* (1903). SOURCES. J. H. Robinson, *Readings in European History* (1904), vol. II, chap. XXXI, sec. I.

34. THE DECLINE OF THE MONARCHY IN ENGLAND

C. J. H. Hayes, *A Political and Cultural History of Modern Europe* (1932), vol. I, chap. X, secs. 1–2.
W. E. Lunt, *History of England* (1928), chaps. XXII–XXIV.
G. M. Trevelyan, *History of England* (1926), part IV, chaps. I–IV.
J. A. Williamson, *The Evolution of England* (1931), chaps. V, VI.
E. Wingfield-Stratford, *The History of British Civilization* (2d ed. 1930), chaps. IV, V.

G. B. Adams, *Constitutional History of England* (1920), chaps. XI–XIII.
Cambridge Modern History, vol. III, chap. XVII; vol. IV, chaps. VIII–IX, XV.

LONGER STUDIES. G. M. Trevelyan, *England under the Stuarts* (1914); F. C. Montague, *History of England, 1603–60* (1907); G. P. Gooch, *History of English Democratic Ideas in the Seventeenth Century* (1898); H. H. Henson, *Puritanism in England* (1912); W. H. Hutton, *The English Church, 1625–1714* (1903); C. H. Firth, *Cromwell's Army* (1902); J. N. Figgis, *Theory of the Divine Right of Kings* (2d ed. 1914); E. Barker, *Oliver Cromwell and the English People* (1937). BIOGRAPHIES. H. D. Traill, *Lord Strafford* (1889); W. H. Hutton, *William Laud* (1895); John Buchan, *Cromwell* (1934); C. H. Firth, *Oliver Cromwell* (1900). SOURCES. T. Carlyle, *Oliver Cromwell's Letters and Speeches*, 5 vols. (1871–72); S. R. Gardiner, *The Constitutional Documents of the Puritan Revolution* (1899); J. H. Robinson, *Readings in European History* (1904), vol. II, chap. XXX.

35. THE THIRTY YEARS' WAR

C. J. H. Hayes, *A Political and Cultural History of Modern Europe* (1932), vol. I, chap. V, sec. 3.
H. O. Wakeman, *European History, 1598–1714* (1894), chaps. IV–VI.
D. Ogg, *Europe in the Seventeenth Century* (1925), chap. IV.
J. Boulenger, *The Seventeenth Century* (1920), chap. III.
E. F. Henderson, *A Short History of Germany* (new ed. 1927), vol. I, chaps. XVII, XVIII.
H. A. L. Fisher, *A History of Europe* (1935), vol. II, chap. XVII.
Cambridge Modern History, vol. IV, chaps. I, III, VI, VII.

LONGER STUDIES. S. R. Gardiner, *The Thirty Years' War* (1874); A. Gindeley, *History of the Thirty Years' War*, 2 vols. (1884); C. V. Wedgewood, *The Thirty Years' War* (1939); F. H. Naylor, *The Civil and Military History of Germany from the Landing of Gustavus Adolphus to the Treaty of Westphalia*, 3 vols. (1816); R. N. Bain, *Scandinavia* (1905); W. Coxe, *History of the House of Austria*, 4 vols. (1893–95). BIOGRAPHIES. G. R. L. Fletcher, *Gustavus Adolphus* (1890); F. Watson, *Wallenstein: Soldier under Saturn* (1938). SOURCES. J. H. Robinson, *Readings in European History* (1904), vol. II, chap. XXIX.

36. EUROPE IN THE MIDDLE OF THE SEVENTEENTH CENTURY

W. C. Abbott, *The Expansion of Europe* (rev. ed. 1938), chap. XXIV.
C. J. H. Hayes, *A Political and Cultural History of Modern Europe* (1932), vol. I, pp. 260–77.
C. P. Higby, *History of Europe, 1492–1815* (1927), chap. VI.
D. Ogg, *Europe in the Seventeenth Century* (1925), chap. I.
J. Boulenger, *The Seventeenth Century* (1920), chap. IV.

LONGER STUDIES. H. D. Traill and J. S. Mann, *Social England* (1909), vol. IV; G. Renard and G. Weulersse, *Life and Labor in Europe, XV to XVIII Century* (1926); C. Hugon, *Social France in the Seventeenth Century* (1911); H. O. Wakeman, *The Ascendancy of France, 1598–1715* (1915); W. E. Sidney, *Social Life in England, 1660–1669* (1892); E. Trotter, *Seventeenth Century Life in the Country Parish* (1919); E. Godfrey, *Home Life under the Stuarts* (1903). GENERAL SUBJECTS. J. McSorley, *An Outline History of the Church by Centuries* (1944); H. Hoffding, *A History of Modern Philosophy*, 2 vols. (1920); G. H. Sabine, *A History of Political Theory* (1937); Sheldon Cheney, *The Story of Modern Art* (1941); P. H. Lang, *Music in Western Civilization* (1941).

37. LOUIS XIV DOMINATES FRANCE AND ASPIRES TO DOMINATE EUROPE

C. J. H. Hayes, *A Political and Cultural History of Modern Europe* (1932), vol. I, pp. 290–319.
J. E. Gillespie, *A History of Europe, 1500–1815* (1928), chap. XV.
T. W. Riker, *A Short History of Modern Europe* (1935), chap. II.
W. C. Abbott, *The Expansion of Europe* (1938), chap. XXVII.
R. Ergang, *Europe from the Renaissance to Waterloo* (1939), chap. XVI.
M. B. Garrett, *European History: 1500–1815* (1940), chaps. XXIV–XXV.
W. L. Langer (editor), *Encyclopaedia of World History* (1940), IV, B3. (References to this encyclopaedia are cited by period, section, and subsection.)
D. Ogg, *Europe in the Seventeenth Century* (1925), chap. II.
H. O. Wakeman, *The Ascendancy of France, 1598–1715* (1915), chap. II.

A. Guérard, *The Life and Death of an Ideal* (1928), pp. 150–222.

LONGER STUDIES. J. Boulenger, *The Seventeenth Century* (1920); L. B. Packard, *The Age of Louis XIV* (1929), and *The Commercial Revolution* (1927); J. Farmer, *Versailles and the Court under Louis XIV* (1905); A. Guérard, *France: A Short History* (1945); P. J. Blok, *History of the People of the Netherlands*, 5 vols. (1898–1912), vol. IV; E. F. Heckscher, *Mercantilism*, 2 vols. (1935). BIOGRAPHICAL WORKS. A. Hassall, *Louis XIV* (1901); L. Bertrand, *Louis XIV* (English ed. 1928); E. K. Sanders, *Bossuet* (1921); B. Matthews, *Molière, his Life and his Times* (1910). SOURCES. J. H. Robinson, *Readings in European History* (1906), vol. II, chap. XXXI; J. H. Robinson and C. A. Beard, *Readings in Modern European History* (1908), vol. I, chaps. I–III; H. Webster, *Historical Selections* (1929), nos. 505, 506.

38. THE TRIUMPH OF PARLIAMENTARY GOVERNMENT IN ENGLAND

Cambridge Modern History, vol. V, chaps. V, VI, VIII–XI, and XV.

C. J. H. Hayes, *A Political and Cultural History of Modern Europe* (1932), vol. I, chap. X.

T. W. Riker, *A Short History of Modern Europe* (1935), chap. V.

A. Hyma, *A Short History of Europe, 1500–1815* (1928), chap. VI.

J. E. Gillespie, *A History of Europe, 1500–1815* (1928), pp. 344–59.

A. L. Cross, *A Shorter History of England and Greater Britain* (1921), chaps. XXIX–XXXVI.

W. C. Abbott, *The Expansion of Europe* (1938), chap. XXV.

R. Ergang, *Europe from the Renaissance to Waterloo* (1939), chap. XVIII.

M. B. Garrett, *European History: 1500–1815* (1940), chaps. XXI–XXIII.

W. L. Langer, *Encyclopaedia of World History* (1940), IV, B1.

LONGER STUDIES. A. Hassall, *The Restoration and the Revolution* (1912); G. M. Trevelyan, *England under the Stuarts, 1603–1714* (1910), and *England under Queen Anne*, 3 vols. (1930–34); D. Ogg, *England in the Reign of Charles II*, 2 vols. (1934); G. N. Clark, *The Later Stuarts, 1660–1714* (1934); Agnes M. Mackenzie, *Scotland in Modern Times, 1720–1939* (1941); M. M. Knappen, *Constitutional and Legal History of England* (1942); G. M. Trevelyan, *English Social History: a Survey of Six Centuries, from Chaucer to Queen Victoria* (1942). BIOGRAPHICAL WORKS. O. Airy, *Charles II* (1901); H. D. Traill, *William III* (1911); C. T. Atkinson, *Marlborough and the Rise of the British Army* (1921); M. R. Hopkinson, *Anne of England* (1935); Arthur Bryant, *Samuel Pepys: the Saviour of the Navy* (1939). SOURCES. J. H. Robinson, *Readings in European History* (1906), vol. II, pp. 259–63; E. P. Cheyney, *Readings in English History* (1908), chaps. XVI, XVII; H. Webster, *Historical Selections* (1929), nos. 392–95, 511–12.

39. THE DECLINING EMPIRE OF THE HAPSBURGS

Cambridge Modern History, vol. V, chap. XI.

C. J. H. Hayes, *A Political and Cultural History of Modern Europe* (1932), vol. I, chap. VII.

J. E. Gillespie, *A History of Europe, 1500–1815* (1928), chaps. XII, XIII.

W. C. Abbott, *The Expansion of Europe* (1939), chap. XXV.

W. L. Langer, *Encyclopaedia of World History* (1940), IV, B4–7.

LONGER STUDIES. W. S. Whitman, *Austria* (1906); L. Leger, *A History of Austria-Hungary* (1889); W. Coxe, *History of the House of Austria*, 3 vols. (Bohn ed. 1847), vol. III; J. Bryce, *The Holy Roman Empire* (1904); C. E. Chapman, *A History of Spain* (1922); M. A. S. Hume, *Spain, its Greatness and Decay, 1479–1788* (1898); K. D. Vernon, *Italy from 1494 to 1790* (1909); F. Eckhart, *A Short History of the Hungarian People* (1931); S. Harrison Thomson, *Czechoslovakia in European History* (1943); F. Schevill, *The History of the Balkan Peninsula from the Earliest Times to the Present Day* (1922). SOURCES. J. H. Robinson, *Readings in European History* (1906), vol. II, pp. 312–15.

40. THE EMERGENCE OF RUSSIA

Cambridge Modern History, vol. V, chaps. XVI–XIX; vol. VI, chaps. X, XIX.

C. J. H. Hayes, *A Political and Cultural History of Modern Europe* (1932), vol. I, chap. VIII.

T. W. Riker, *A Short History of Modern Europe* (1935), chap. IV.

J. E. Gillespie, *A History of Europe, 1500–1815* (1928), chap. XXI.

A. Hassall, *The Balance of Power, 1715–1789* (1925), chaps. V, XI, XIII.

F. Nowak, *Medieval Slavdom and the Rise of Russia* (1930), chaps. II, III.

A. Hyma, *Europe from the Renaissance to 1815* (1937), chap. XIV.

R. Ergang, *Europe from the Renaissance to Waterloo* (1939), chaps. XVII and XX.
M. B. Garrett, *European History, 1500–1815* (1940), chap. XXVIII.
W. L. Langer, *Encyclopaedia of World History* (1940), IV, B9–11.

LONGER STUDIES. R. N. Bain, *Slavonic Europe: a Political History of Poland and Russia from 1447 to 1796* (1908); R. N. Bain, *The Pupils of Peter the Great: a History of the Russian Court and Empire from 1689 to 1740* (1897); R. N. Bain, *The Last King of Poland and his Contemporaries* (1909); R. N. Bain, *Charles XII and the Collapse of the Swedish Empire, 1682–1719* (1895); S. F. Platonov, *History of Russia* (1925); C. Hallendorff and A. Schück, *History of Sweden* (1929); O. Halecki, *The History of Poland* (1942); J. S. Martin, *Russia: a Picture History* (1945); W. F. Reddaway and others (editors), *Cambridge History of Poland* (1941); R. B. Mowat, *A History of European Diplomacy, 1451–1789* (1928). BIOGRAPHICAL WORKS. F. Schuyler, *Peter the Great*, 2 vols. (1894); K. Waliszewski, *Peter the Great*, 2 vols. (1897), and *The Story of a Throne: Catharine II of Russia*, 2 vols. (1895); K. Anthony, *Catharine the Great* (1925); E. A. B. Hodgetts, *Catharine the Great* (1914). SOURCES. J. H. Robinson, *Readings in European History* (1906), vol. II, chap. XXXII; J. H. Robinson and C. A. Beard, *Readings in Modern European History* (1908), vol. I, chap. VI.

41. THE RISE OF PRUSSIA

Cambridge Modern History, vol. V, chaps. XX, XXI; vol. VI, chaps. VIII, IX, XX.
C. J. H. Hayes, *A Political and Cultural History of Modern Europe* (1932), vol. I, pp. 329–56.
T. W. Riker, *A Short History of Modern Europe* (1935), chap. III.
J. E. Gillespie, *A History of Europe, 1500–1815* (1928), chap. XX.
A. Hyma, *Europe from the Renaissance to 1815* (1937), chap. XIII.
R. Ergang, *Europe from the Renaissance to Waterloo* (1939), chap. XIX.
M. B. Garrett, *European History, 1500–1815* (1940), chap. XXIX.
W. L. Langer, *Encyclopaedia of World History* (1940), IV, B7.

LONGER STUDIES. E. F. Henderson, *A Short History of Germany*, 2 vols. (1916), vol. II; G. M. Priest, *Germany Since 1740* (1915); C. T. Atkinson, *A History of Germany, 1715–1815* (1908); W. L. Dorn, *Competition for Empire,* *1740–1763* (1940). BIOGRAPHICAL WORKS. R. Ergang, *The Potsdam Führer: Frederick William I* (1941); N. Young, *Life of Frederick the Great* (1919); W. F. Reddaway, *Frederick the Great and the Rise of Prussia* (1904); J. F. Bright, *Maria Theresa* (1897). SOURCES. J. H. Robinson, *Readings in European History* (1906), vol. II, pp. 315–28; J. H. Robinson and C. A. Beard, *Readings in Modern European History* (1908), vol. I, chap. V.

42. OVERSEAS EXPANSION AND THE STRUGGLE FOR COMMERCE AND COLONIES

Cambridge Modern History, vol. V, chap. XXII; vol. VI, chaps. II, VI, XV; vol. VII, chaps. I–VIII.
C. J. H. Hayes, *A Political and Cultural History of Modern Europe* (1932), vol. I, chap. IX.
T. W. Riker, *A Short History of Modern Europe* (1935), chap. VI.
J. E. Gillespie, *A History of Europe, 1500–1815* (1928), chap. XVIII.
C. P. Higby, *History of Europe, 1492–1815* (1927), chap. X.
W. C. Abbott, *The Expansion of Europe* (1938), chaps. XVIII, XX, XXVI, XXIX, XXXIV, XXXV.
R. Ergang, *Europe from the Renaissance to Waterloo* (1939), chap. XXII.
A. Hyma, *Europe from the Renaissance to 1815* (1937), chap. XII.
G. Bruun, *Europe in Evolution* (1945), chaps. XXII–XXIII.
W. L. Langer, *Encyclopaedia of World History* (1940), IV, D.

LONGER STUDIES. Howard Robinson, *The Development of the British Empire* (1936); A. L. Cross, *A Shorter History of England and Greater Britain* (1939); W. P. Hall and R. G. Albion, *A History of England and the British Empire* (1937); W. T. Sellery, *England in the Eighteenth Century* (1934); Basil Williams, *The Whig Ascendency 1714–1760* (1939); A. T. Mahan, *The Influence of Sea Power upon History, 1660–1783* (new ed. 1944); J. E. Gillespie, *A History of Geographical Discovery, 1400–1800* (1933); Leonard Outhwaite, *Unrolling the Map: the Story of Exploration* (1935); J. N. L. Baker, *History of Geographical Discovery and Exploration* (1931); L. H. Gipson, *The British Empire before the American Revolution*, 10 vols. (1936–   ); V. Steffanson (editor), *Great Adventures and Explorations* (1946); C. H. Haring, *The Spanish Empire in America* (1947); L. D. Baldwin, *The Story of the Americas* (1943); J. B. Brebner, *The Explorers of North America, 1492–1806* (1933); F. A. Kirkpatrick, *The Spanish Conquistadores* (1934); B. W. Diffie, *Latin American Civilization: The Colonial Period* (1945); P. A. Means, *The Spanish Main, 1492–1700* (1935); A. H. Buffington, *The Second Hundred Years' War, 1689–1815* (1929); C. Becker, *The Eve of the Revolution* (1921); C. M. Andrews, *The Colonial Background of the American Revolution* (1924); C. H. Van Tyne, *The American Revolution* (1905). BIOGRAPHICAL WORKS. I. B. Richman, *Spanish Conquerors; a Chronicle of the Dawn of Empire Overseas* (1919); H. M. Stephens, *Albuquerque and the Portuguese Settlements in India* (1892); H. W. Van Loon, *Golden Book of the Dutch Navigators* (1916); A. Kitson, *Captain James Cook, the Circumnavigator* (1907); W. T. Waugh, *James Wolfe, Man and Soldier* (1928); F. Parkman, *Montcalm and Wolfe*, in *Works*, 13 vols. (1922); B. Williams, *Life of William Pitt, Earl of Chatham*, 2 vols. (1913); G. B. Malleson, *Lord Clive and the Establishment of the English in India* (1895). SOURCES. J. H. Robinson, *Readings in European History* (1906), vol. II, chap. XXXIII; J. H. Robinson and C. A. Beard, *Readings in Modern European History* (1908), vol. I, chaps. VI, VII; H. Webster, *Historical Selections* (1929), nos. 424–26, 459–61.

43. THE INTELLECTUAL REVOLUTION

Cambridge Modern History, vol. V, chap. XXIII.

C. J. H. Hayes, *A Political and Cultural History of Modern Europe* (1932), vol. I, chap. XI.

J. E. Gillespie, *A History of Europe, 1500–1815* (1928), chap. XXII.

C. P. Higby, *History of Europe, 1492–1815* (1927), chap. XIII.

P. Smith, *A History of Modern Culture* (1930), vol. I, chap. VI; (1934), vol. II, chap. IV.

T. W. Wallbank and A. M. Taylor, *Civilization — Past and Present*, vol. II (1942), pp. 35–37.

R. Ergang, *Europe from the Renaissance to Waterloo* (1939), chap. XIV.

G. Bruun, *Europe in Evolution* (1945), chaps. XI, XVIII, XXV.

LONGER STUDIES. J. H. Randall, Jr., *The Making of the Modern Mind* (rev. ed. 1940); W. T. Sedgwick and H. Tyler, *A Short History of Science* (rev. ed. 1939); W. C. D. Dampier, *A History of Science* (3d ed. 1942); Charles Singer, *A Short History of Science to the Nineteenth Century* (1941); F. R. Moulton and J. J. Schifferes, *The Autobiography of Science* (1945); F. Cajori, *History of Physics* (1899); D. E. Smith, *History of Mathematics* (1925); L. Hogben, *Mathematics for the Million* (rev. ed. 1940), and *Science for the Citizen* (1938); J. M. Stillman, *The Story of Early Chemistry* (1924); V. Robinson, *The Story of Medicine* (1932); H. B. Lemon, *From Galileo to the Nuclear Age* (1947); H. Shapley (editor), *A Treasury of Science* (enlarged ed. 1946). BIOGRAPHICAL WORKS. E. S. Haldane, *Descartes* (1905); J. W. N. Sullivan, *Isaac Newton, 1642–1727* (1938); Morris Bishop, *Pascal, the Life of Genius* (1936); F. Masson, *Robert Boyle: a Biography* (1914); H. W. Carr, *Leibniz* (1929); B. Faÿ, *Benjamin Franklin* (1929); P. de Kruif, *The Microbe Hunters* (1926). SOURCES. J. H. Robinson and C. A. Beard, *Readings in Modern European History* (1908), vol. I, chap. IX; H. Webster, *Historical Selections* (1929), nos. 527–34.

44. GOVERNMENT AND SOCIETY UNDER THE OLD RÉGIME

Cambridge Modern History, vol. VIII, chaps. I, II.

C. J. H. Hayes, *A Political and Cultural History of Modern Europe* (1932), vol. I, chap. XII.

T. W. Riker, *A Short History of Modern Europe* (1935), chap. VII.

C. P. Higby, *History of Europe, 1492–1815* (1927), chap. XV.

J. E. Gillespie, *A History of Europe, 1500–1815* (1928), chaps. XXIV, XXV.

L. Gershoy, *The French Revolution and Napoleon* (1933), chaps. I–IV.

L. R. Gottschalk, *The Era of the French Revolution* (1929), pp. 1–115.

A. Hyma, *Europe from the Renaissance to 1815* (1937), chap. XV–XVI.

M. B. Garrett, *European History, 1500–1815* (1940), chap. XXXI.

R. Ergang, *Europe from the Renaissance to Waterloo* (1939), chap. XXIII.

LONGER STUDIES. E. J. Lowell, *The Eve of the French Revolution* (1892); A. H. Johnson, *The Age of the Enlightened Despot, 1660–1789* (1925); H. E. Bourne, *The Revolutionary Period in Europe* (1914); G. Bruun, *The Enlightened Despots* (1929); D. Mornet, *French Thought in the Eighteenth Century* (1929); P. Smith, *A History of Modern Culture* (1934), vol. II; especially chaps. VI and XI; F. J. C. Hearnshaw (editor), *The Political and Social Ideas of Some Great French Thinkers of the Age of Reason* (1930); Lewis Mumford, *The Story of Utopias* (1922); Leo Gershoy,

From Despotism to Revolution (1944); H. E. Sée, *Economic and Social Conditions in France during the Eighteenth Century* (1927); S. B. Clough and C. W. Cole, *Economic History of Europe* (1946); E. L. Bogart, *Economic History of Europe, 1760–1939* (1942); N. S. B. Gras, *History of Agriculture in Europe and America* (1925). BIOGRAPHICAL WORKS. J. F. Bright, *Maria Theresa* (1897), and *Joseph II* (1905); J. Addison, *Charles III of Spain* (1900); A. D. White, *Seven Great Statesmen* (1927), essay on Turgot; L. Say, *Turgot* (1888); J. Morley, *Voltaire* (1871), and *Rousseau* (1873); M. Josephson, *Rousseau* (1931); A. Sorel, *Montesquieu* (1888); S. K. Padover, *The Revolutionary Emperor, Joseph II of Austria* (1934); J. W. Krutch, *Samuel Johnson* (1944). SOURCES. J. H. Robinson, *Readings in European History* (1906), vol. II, chap. XXXIV; J. H. Robinson and C. A. Beard, *Readings in Modern European History* (1908), vol. I, chaps. VIII–XI; J.-J. Rousseau, *The Social Contract* (Everyman's Library ed. 1913), especially Books I and II; Louis-Sébastien Mercier, *The Waiting City: Paris 1782–88* (translated by Helen Simpson) (1933).

45. THE FRENCH PEOPLE DESTROY THE RELICS OF FEUDALISM AND OVERTURN THE MONARCHY

Cambridge Modern History, vol. VIII, chaps. V–VIII.

C. J. H. Hayes, *A Political and Cultural History of Modern Europe* (1932), vol. I, pp. 596–629.

T. W. Riker, *A Short History of Modern Europe* (1935), chap. VIII.

C. P. Higby, *History of Europe, 1492–1815* (1927), chap. XVI.

J. E. Gillespie, *A History of Europe, 1500–1815* (1928), pp. 494–527.

A. Hyma, *Europe from the Renaissance to 1815* (1937), chap. XVII.

R. Ergang, *Europe from the Renaissance to Waterloo* (1939), chaps. XXIV–XXV.

M. B. Garrett, *European History, 1500–1815* (1940), chaps. XXXIII–XXXV.

W. L. Langer, *Encyclopaedia of World History* (1940), V, B1–3.

SHORT HISTORIES OF THE FRENCH REVOLUTION. L. Gershoy, *The French Revolution, 1789–1799* (1932); L. Gershoy, *The French Revolution and Napoleon* (1933); L. R. Gottschalk, *The Era of the French Revolution* (1929); C. Brinton, *A Decade of Revolution, 1789–1799* (1935); A. Mathiez, *The French Revolution* (1928); L. Madelin, *The French Revolution* (1928); R. M. Johnston, *The French Revolution; a Short History* (1909); S. Mathews, *The French Revolution, 1789–1815* (rev. ed. 1923); E. D. Bradby, *Short History of the French Revolution, 1789–1795* (1926); C. D. Hazen, *The French Revolution*, 2 vols. (1932); Pierre Gaxotte, *The French Revolution* (1932); J. M. Thompson, *The French Revolution* (1945). BIOGRAPHICAL WORKS. H. D. Sedgwick, *La Fayette* (1928); L. Barthou, *Mirabeau* (1913); H. Belloc, *Marie Antoinette* (1923); S. Zweig, *Marie Antoinette* (1933); E. D. Bradby, *Life of Barnave*, 2 vols. (1915); S. K. Padover, *The Life and Death of Louis XVI* (1939); J. M. Thompson, *Robespierre*, 2 vols. (1936); for further biographical works see the chapter following. SOURCES. J. H. Robinson, *Readings in European History* (1906), vol. II, chap. XXXV; J. H. Robinson and C. A. Beard, *Readings in Modern European History* (1908), vol. I, chaps. XII and XIII; F. M. Anderson, *Constitutions and Other Select Documents: France, 1789–1901* (1904), pp. 1–253; H. Webster, *Historical Selections* (1929), nos. 397–403; E. L. Higgins, *The French Revolution as Told by Contemporaries* (1938); Gouverneur Morris, *A Diary of the French Revolution*, 2 vols. (1939); J. A. Hawgood (editor), *Modern Constitutions Since 1787* (1939).

46. THE FIRST FRENCH REPUBLIC AND ITS STRUGGLE TO SURVIVE

Cambridge Modern History, vol. VIII, chaps. IX, XII, XV.

C. J. H. Hayes, *A Political and Cultural History of Modern Europe* (1932), vol. I, chap. XII.

T. W. Riker, *A Short History of Modern Europe* (1935), chap. VIII.

J. E. Gillespie, *A History of Europe, 1500–1815* (1928), pp. 527–50.

L. Gershoy, *The French Revolution and Napoleon* (1933), chaps. XI, XII.

L. R. Gottschalk, *The Era of the French Revolution* (1929), pp. 215–304.

R. Ergang, *Europe from the Renaissance to Waterloo* (1939), chap. XXV.

M. B. Garrett, *European History, 1500–1815* (1940), chaps. XXXVI–XXXVII.

W. L. Langer, *Encyclopaedia of World History* (1940), V, B4–6.

SPECIAL TOPICS. W. B. Kerr, *The Reign of Terror, 1793–94* (1927); C. Brinton, *The Jacobins; a Study in the New History* (1930); R. W. Phipps, *The Armies of the First French Republic and the Rise of the Marshals of Napoleon*, 3 vols. (1926–31); M. Minnigerode, *The Magnificent Comedy: Days of* the *Directory* (1931); W. M. Sloane, *The French Revolution and Religious Reform* (1901); R. R. Palmer, *Twelve Who Ruled* (1942). BIOGRAPHICAL WORKS. L. Madelin, *Danton* (1914), and *Figures of the Revolution* (1929); H. Belloc, *Danton* (1899), and *Robespierre* (1927); L. R. Gottschalk, *Jean Paul Marat; a Study in Radicalism* (1927); C. Young, *A Lady Who Loved Herself: the Life of Madame Roland* (1930); G. G. Van Dusen, *Sieyes: His Life and Nationalism* (1932); H. Beraud, *Twelve Portraits of the Revolution* (1928); J. M. Thompson, *Leaders of the French Revolution* (1929); W. W. Stephens, *Women of the French Revolution* (1912); J. S. Schapiro, *Condorcet and the Rise of Liberalism* (1934); G. Bruun, *Saint-Just, Apostle of the Terror* (1932). SOURCES. J. H. Robinson, *Readings in European History* (1906), vol. II, chap. XXXVI; E. L. Higgins, *The French Revolution as Told by Contemporaries* (1938).

47. NAPOLEON AND FRANCE

Cambridge Modern History, vol. IX, chaps. I, V–VII.

C. J. H. Hayes, *A Political and Cultural History of Modern Europe* (1932), vol. I, pp. 647–59.

T. W. Riker, *A Short History of Modern Europe* (1935), chap. X.

J. E. Gillespie, *A History of Europe, 1500–1815* (1928), pp. 550–60.

L. Gershoy, *The French Revolution and Napoleon* (1933), chaps. XIII–XV.

L. R. Gottschalk, *The Era of the French Revolution* (1929), part II, book I, chaps. I, II.

R. Ergang, *Europe from the Renaissance to Waterloo* (1939), chap. XXVI.

M. B. Garrett, *European History, 1500–1815* (1940), chap. XXXVIII.

A. Hyma, *Europe from the Renaissance to 1815* (1937), chap. XVIII.

G. Bruun, *Europe and the French Imperium* (1938), chaps. I, II, IV.

W. L. Langer, *Encyclopaedia of World History* (1940), V, B7–8.

BIOGRAPHIES OF NAPOLEON I. J. H. Rose, *The Life of Napoleon I* (1913); H. A. L. Fisher, *Napoleon* (1924); R. M. Johnston, *Napoleon; a Short Biography* (1910), and *The Corsican: a Diary of Napoleon in his own Words* (1930); E. Tarlé, *Bonaparte* (1937); A. Fournier, *Napoleon the First*, 2 vols. (1911); F. M. Kircheisen, *Napoleon* (1932); S. Wilkinson, *The Rise of General Bonaparte* (1931). SOURCES. J. H. Robinson, *Readings in European History* (1906), vol. II, chap. XXXVII; F. M. Anderson, *Constitutions and Other Select Documents: France, 1789–1901* (1904), pp. 208–451; J. H. Robinson and C. A. Beard, *Readings in Modern European History* (1908), vol. I, chaps. XIV, XV.

48. NAPOLEON AND EUROPE

Cambridge Modern History, vol. IX, chaps. III, IV, IX–XVII.

C. J. H. Hayes, *A Political and Cultural History of Modern Europe* (1932), vol. I, pp. 659–717.

T. W. Riker, *A Short History of Modern Europe* (1935), chap. X.

J. E. Gillespie, *A History of Europe, 1500–1815* (1928), chap. XXVI.

L. Gershoy, *The French Revolution and Napoleon* (1933), chaps. XVI–XX.

L. R. Gottschalk, *The Era of the French Revolution* (1929), pp. 356–456.

M. B. Garrett, *European History, 1500–1815* (1940), chap. XXXIX.

W. L. Langer, *Encyclopaedia of World History* (1940), V, B9–16.

F. Schevill, *The Making of Modern Germany* (1916), chap. III.

E. F. Henderson, *A Short History of Germany* (1916), vol. II, chaps. VI, VII.

G. M. Priest, *Germany Since 1740* (1915), chaps. IV–VII.

LONGER STUDIES. A. T. Mahan, *The Influence of Sea Power upon the French Revolution and Empire*, 2 vols. (1919), vol. II; especially chaps. XV, XVI, and XVIII; F. H. Heckscher, *The Continental System* (1922); H. A. L. Fisher, *Studies in Napoleonic Statesmanship: Germany* (1903); R. M. Johnston, *The Napoleonic Empire in Southern Italy*, 2 vols. (1904); G. B. McClellan, *Venice and Bonaparte* (1931); H. Deutsch, *The Genesis of Napoleonic Imperialism* (1938); G. Bruun, *Europe and the French Imperium* (1938); R. B. Mowat, *The Diplomacy of Napoleon* (1924); Eugene Tarlé, *Napoleon's Invasion of Russia: 1812* (1941); Arthur Bryant, *Years of Endurance: 1793–1802* (1942), and *Years of Victory: 1802–1812* (1945). BIOGRAPHICAL WORKS. For biographies of Napoleon see the preceding chapter; J. R. Seeley, *Life and Times of Stein, or Germany and Prussia in the Napoleonic Age* (1897); E. F. Henderson, *Blücher and the Uprising of Prussia Against Napoleon, 1806–1815* (1911); J. H. Rose, *The Life of William Pitt* (1923); A. T. Mahan, *Life of Nelson*, 2 vols. (1897); P. Guedalla, *Wellington* (1932); G. Lacour-Gayet, *Talleyrand, 1754–1838* (1930), vol. II; J. McCabe, *Talleyrand* (1906); N. Forssel, *Fouché, the Man Napoleon Feared* (1928); A. D. White, *Seven Great Statesmen* (1927), essay on

Stein. SOURCES. J. H. Robinson, *Readings in European History* (1906), vol. II, chap. XXXVIII; R. M. Johnston, *The Corsican: A Diary of Napoleon in his own Words* (1910).

49. THE VIENNA CONGRESS

Cambridge Modern History, vol. IX, chaps. XIX, XXI.
C. J. H. Hayes, *A Political and Cultural History of Modern Europe* (1932), vol. I, chap. XIV.
T. W. Riker, *A Short History of Modern Europe* (1935), chap. XI.
C. P. Higby, *History of Modern Europe* (1932), chap. II.
J. S. Schapiro, *Modern and Contemporary European History* (1929), chap. IV.
F. C. Palm and F. E. Graham, *Europe Since Napoleon* (1934), chap. III.
E. Achorn, *European Civilization and Politics Since 1815* (1934), chap. II.
W. L. Langer, *Encyclopaedia of World History* (1940), V, B15.

LONGER STUDIES. C. K. Webster, *The Congress of Vienna, 1814–1815* (1919); Harold Nicolson, *The Congress of Vienna: 1812–1822* (1946); C. D. Hazen, W. R. Thayer, and R. H. Lord, *Three Peace Congresses of the Nineteenth Century* (1917); W. P. Cresson, *The Holy Alliance* (1922); W. A. Philips, *The Confederation of Europe* (2d ed. 1919); *Cambridge History of British Foreign Policy* (1921), vol. II; R. B. Mowat, *History of European Diplomacy: 1815–1924* (1924); for biographical studies on the leading statesmen at the Congress of Vienna see the close of the following chapter. SOURCES. J. H. Robinson, *Readings in European History* (1906), vol. II, chap. XXXIX; J. F. Scott and A. Baltzly, *Readings in European History Since 1814* (1930), chaps. I, II; J. H. Robinson and C. A. Beard, *Readings in Modern European History* (1908), vol. I, chap. XVI; (1909), vol. II, chap. XVII; H. Webster, *Historical Selections* (1929), no. 436.

50. THE ERA OF RESTORATION AND REACTION

Cambridge Modern History, vol. X, chaps. I, II, IV–X, XIII.
C. J. H. Hayes, *A Political and Cultural History of Modern Europe* (1932), vol. I, chap. XIV.
T. W. Riker, *A Short History of Modern Europe* (1935), chap. XI.
C. P. Higby, *History of Modern Europe* (1932), chap. V.
J. S. Schapiro, *Modern and Contemporary European History* (1929), chap. IV.
E. Fueter, *World History, 1815–1920* (1924), chaps. VII–XI.
F. C. Palm and F. E. Graham, *Europe Since Napoleon* (1934), chap. IV.
W. J. Bossenbrook and others, *The Development of Contemporary Civilization* (1940), chap. V.

LONGER STUDIES. F. B. Artz, *Reaction and Revolution, 1814–1832* (1934); A. May, *The Age of Metternich, 1814–1848* (1933); C. K. Webster, *The Foreign Policy of Castlereagh, 1815–1822* (1925); H. W. V. Temperley, *The Foreign Policy of Canning* (1925); D. Perkins, *The Monroe Doctrine, 1823–1826* (1927); W. A. Philips, *The War of Greek Independence* (1897). FOR THE ROMANTIC MOVEMENT. I. Babbitt, *Rousseau and Romanticism* (1917); C. H. C. WRIGHT, *A History of French Literature* (1925); K. Franke, *A History of German Literature* (1909); O. Elton, *A Survey of English Literature, 1780–1880*, 4 vols. (1912–20); D. G. Mason, *The Romantic Composers* (1926). BIOGRAPHICAL WORKS. A. Herman, *Metternich* (1932); A. Cecil, *Metternich, 1773–1859; a Study of his Period and Personality* (1933); E. L. Woodward, *Three Studies in European Conservatism* (1929); Leonid I. Strakhovsky, *Alexander I of Russia* (1947); W. P. Cresson, *Diplomatic Portraits* (1923); J. Lucas-Dubreton, *Louis XVIII* (1927); A. Hassall, *Viscount Castlereagh* (1908); P. Guedalla, *Wellington* (1932); H. W. V. Temperley, *Life of Canning* (1905). SOURCES. J. H. Robinson and C. A. Beard, *Readings in Modern European History* (1909), vol. II, chaps. XIX, XX; J. F. Scott and A. Baltzly, *Readings in European History Since 1814* (1930), chaps. II, III; M. Spahr, *Readings in Recent Political Philosophy* (1935), chaps. II, IV; Columbia University, *Introduction to Contemporary Civilization: A Source Book*, vol. II (1946), chap. II.

51. THE BOURGEOISIE SECURE CONTROL IN GREAT BRITAIN AND FRANCE

Cambridge Modern History, vol. X, chaps. II, III, XV, XVIII–XX.
C. J. H. Hayes, *A Political and Cultural History of Modern Europe*, vol. II (1936), pp. 61–117.
F. C. Palm and F. E. Graham, *Europe Since Napoleon* (1934), chap. VI.
T. W. Riker, *A Short History of Modern Europe* (1935), chap. XI.

C. P. Higby, *History of Modern Europe* (1932), chap. V.
E. Achorn, *European Civilization and Politics Since 1815* (1934), chap. III.
J. S. Schapiro, *Modern and Contemporary European History* (1929), chap. V.
H. E. Barnes, *The History of Western Civilization*, 2 vols. (1935), vol. II, chaps. IV, VII.
T. W. Wallbank and A. M. Taylor, *Civilization — Past and Present*, vol. II (1942), chap. IV.
W. J. Bossenbrook and others, *The Development of Contemporary Civilization* (1940), chaps. VI–VII.
S. B. Clough and C. W. Cole, *Economic History of Europe* (rev. ed. 1946), part III.
W. L. Langer, *Encyclopaedia of World History* (1940), V, C2–4.

LONGER STUDIES. J. Lucas-Dubreton, *The Restoration and the July Monarchy* (1929); F. B. Artz, *France under the Bourbon Restoration, 1814–1830* (1931); E. Halevy, *A History of the English People, 1815–1841*, 3 vols. (1924–27); M. Hovell, *The Chartist Movement* (1918); F. C. Dietz, *The Industrial Revolution* (1927); Gilbert Slater, *The Growth of Modern England* (1915); G. D. H. Cole and R. Postgate, *The British Common People, 1746–1946* (1947); E. L. Woodward, *The Age of Reform: 1815–1870* (1938); G. M. Trevelyan, *British History in the Nineteenth Century and After, 1782–1919* (1938); P. Mantoux, *The Industrial Revolution in the Eighteenth Century* (1929); E. W. Byrn, *The Progress of Invention in the Nineteenth Century* (1900); J. A. Hobson, *Evolution of Modern Capitalism* (1928); M. M. Knight, H. E. Barnes, and F. Flügel, *Economic History of Europe in Modern Times* (1928). BIOGRAPHICAL WORKS. G. M. Trevelyan, *Lord Grey and the Reform Bill* (1920), and *John Bright* (1913); G. D. H. Cole, *Robert Owen* (1925); P. Guedalla, *Palmerston* (1926); H. C. F. Bell, *Lord Palmerston* (1936); J. A. Hobson, *Richard Cobden, the International Man* (1919); J. M. S. Allison, *Thiers and the French Monarchy* (1926); *Dictionary of National Biography* for short lives of James Watt, John Kay, Richard Arkwright. SOURCES. E. P. Cheyney, *Readings in English History* (1908), pp. 679–98; J. F. Scott and A. Baltzly, *Readings in European History Since 1814* (1930), chaps. III–V.

52. THE REVOLUTIONARY MOVEMENT OF 1848–49 AND ITS COLLAPSE

Cambridge Modern History, vol. XI, chaps. II–VII.
C. J. H. Hayes, *A Political and Cultural History of Modern Europe*, vol. II (1936), pp. 117–50.
F. C. Palm and F. E. Graham, *Europe Since Napoleon* (1934), chap. V.
T. W. Riker, *A Short History of Modern Europe* (1935), chap. XI.
C. P. Higby, *History of Modern Europe* (1932), chaps. VIII, IX.
E. Achorn, *European Civilization and Politics Since 1815* (1934), chap. IV.
J. S. Schapiro, *Modern and Contemporary European History* (1929), chap. XII.
E. Fueter, *World History, 1815–1920* (1924), chaps. XXI, XXIII.

LONGER STUDIES. A. de Lamartine, *History of the French Revolution of 1848* (1875); F. A. Simpson, *Rise of Louis Napoleon* (1909); G. M. Priest, *Germany Since 1740* (1915); E. F. Henderson, *A Short History of Germany* (1916), vol. II; J. A. R. Marriott, *The French Revolution of 1848 in its Economic Aspects*, 2 vols. (1913); Veit Valentin, *1848: Chapters in German History* (1940); Donald C. McKay, *The National Workshops: a Study in the French Revolution of 1848* (1933); G. F.-H. and J. Berkeley, *Italy in the Making*, 3 vols. (1932–40); C. E. Maurice, *The Revolutionary Movement of 1848–49 in Italy, Austria-Hungary and Germany* (1887); C. M. Knatchbull-Hugessen, *The Political Evolution of the Hungarian Nation* (1908), vol. II; R. M. Johnston, *The Roman Theocracy and the Republic, 1848–49* (1901); G. M. Trevelyan, *Daniel Manin and the Venetian Revolution of 1848* (1923), and *Garibaldi's Defense of the Roman Republic* (1907); L. B. Namier, *1848: The Revolution of the Intellectuals* (1947). SOURCES. J. H. Robinson and C. A. Beard, *Readings in Modern European History* (1909), vol. II, chap. XX; J. F. Scott and A. Baltzly, *Readings in European History Since 1814* (1930), chap. V; Columbia University, *Introduction to Contemporary Civilization: A Source Book*, vol. II (1946), chaps. V–VI.

53. THE ESTABLISHMENT OF THE SECOND FRENCH EMPIRE: NAPOLEON III

Cambridge Modern History, vol. XI, chaps. X, XVII, XXI.
C. J. H. Hayes, *A Political and Cultural History of Modern Europe*, vol. II (1936), pp. 183–214.
F. C. Palm and F. E. Graham, *Europe Since Napoleon* (1934), chap. VII.
T. W. Riker, *A Short History of Modern Europe* (1935), chap. XIII.

C. P. Higby, *History of Modern Europe* (1932), chap. XII.
E. Achorn, *European Civilization and Politics Since 1815* (1934), chap. V.
J. S. Schapiro, *Modern and Contemporary European History* (1929), chap. XIII.

LONGER STUDIES. A. L. Guérard, *Reflections on the Napoleonic Legend* (1924); G. L. Dickinson, *Revolution and Reaction in Modern France* (1927); H. A. L. Fisher, *Bonapartism* (1908); E. B. Hamley, *The War in the Crimea* (1890); P. F. Martin, *Maximilian in Mexico: the Story of the French Intervention, 1861–1867* (1914); P. Guedalla, *The Second Empire* (1922); Octave Aubry, *The Second Empire* (1940); S. B. Clough, *France: a History of National Economics, 1789–1939* (1939). BIOGRAPHICAL WORKS. F. A. Simpson, *Louis Napoleon and the Recovery of France* (1923); L. F. Mott, *Ernest Renan* (1921), and *Sainte Beuve* (1924); H. Gorman, *The Incredible Marquis: Alexandre Dumas* (1929); I. Babbitt, *The Masters of Modern French Prose* (1912); A. L. Guérard, *French Prophets of Yesterday* (1913), and *Napoleon III* (1943). SOURCES. J. H. Robinson and C. A. Beard, *Readings in Modern European History* (1909), vol. II, chap. XIX, sec. 59; J. F. Scott and A. Baltzly, *Readings in European History Since 1814* (1930), chap. VII, sec. 1.

54. THE POLITICAL UNIFICATION OF ITALY

Cambridge Modern History, vol. XI, chaps. IV, XIV, XIX, XXV.
C. J. H. Hayes, *A Political and Cultural History of Modern Europe*, vol. II (1936), pp. 214–25.
F. C. Palm and F. E. Graham, *Europe Since Napoleon* (1934), chap. VIII.
T. W. Riker, *A Short History of Modern Europe* (1935), chap. XIII.
C. P. Higby, *History of Modern Europe* (1932), chap. XI.
J. S. Schapiro, *Modern and Contemporary European History* (1929), chap. XIV.
W. L. Langer, *Encyclopaedia of World History* (1940), V, C6.

LONGER STUDIES. B. King, *A History of Italian Unity*, 2 vols. (1899); P. Orsi, *Cavour and the Making of Modern Italy* (1923); R. de Cesare, *The Last Days of Papal Rome* (1909); H. R. Whitehouse, *The Collapse of the Kingdom of Naples* (1899); W. Barry, *The Papacy and Modern Times* (1911); J. W. C. Wand, *A History of the Modern Church from 1500 to the Present Day* (1930); R. C. Binkley, *Realism and Nationalism, 1852–1871* (1935), chap. X; Luigi Salvatorelli, *A Concise History of Italy* (1940). BIOGRAPHICAL WORKS. B. King, *Mazzini* (1902); S. Barr, *Mazzini: Portrait of an Exile* (1935); J. A. R. Marriott, *Makers of Modern Italy* (1901); G. M. Trevelyan, *Garibaldi and the Thousand* (1912), and *Garibaldi and the Making of Italy* (1912); E. L. H. Martinengo-Cesaresco, *Cavour* (1898); W. R. Thayer, *The Life and Times of Cavour*, 2 vols. (1911); M. Paleologue, *Cavour* (1927); A. D. White, *Seven Great Statesmen* (1927), essay on Cavour. SOURCES. J. H. Robinson and C. A. Beard, *Readings in Modern European History* (1909), vol. II, chap. XXI; J. F. Scott and A. Baltzly, *Readings in European History Since 1814* (1930), chap. VII, sec. 3; P. Hughes, *The Popes' New Order: Social Encyclicals and Addresses of Leo XIII, Pius XI, Benedict XV, Pius XII* (1944).

55. THE FORMATION OF THE GERMAN EMPIRE

Cambridge Modern History, vol. XI, chaps. XV, XVI.
C. J. H. Hayes, *A Political and Cultural History of Modern Europe*, vol. II (1936), pp. 226–48.
F. C. Palm and F. E. Graham, *Europe Since Napoleon* (1934), chap. IX.
T. W. Riker, *A Short History of Modern Europe* (1935), chap. XIII.
C. P. Higby, *History of Modern Europe* (1932), chaps. XIII, XIV.
E. Achorn, *European Civilization and Politics Since 1815* (1934), chap. V.
J. S. Schapiro, *Modern and Contemporary European History* (1929), chap. XV.
W. L. Langer, *Encyclopaedia of World History* (1940), V, C9.

LONGER STUDIES. A. W. Ward, *Germany, 1815–1870*, 3 vols. (1916–18); M. Smith, *Bismarck and German Unity* (1923); W. Oncken, *Napoleon III and the Rhine* (1928); J. W. Headlam, *Bismarck and the Foundation of the German Empire* (1901); G. B. Malleson, *The Refounding of the German Empire, 1848–1871* (1904); R. H. Lord, *The Origins of the War of 1870* (1924); R. C. Binkley, *Realism and Nationalism, 1852–1871* (1935), chaps. XI, XII; George N. Shuster and Arnold Bergstrasser, *Germany: a Short History* (1944). BIOGRAPHICAL WORKS. C. G. Robertson, *Bismarck* (1918); E. Ludwig, *Bismarck* (1928); A. D. White, *Seven Great Statesmen* (1927), essay on

Bismarck; W. Morris, *Moltke* (1894); A. Forbes, *William of Germany* (1888); J. Redlich, *Emperor Francis-Joseph of Austria* (1929). SOURCES. J. H. Robinson and C. A. Beard, *Readings in Modern European History* (1909), vol. II, pp. 142–65; J. F. Scott and A. Baltzly, *Readings in European History Since 1814* (1930), chap. VII.

56. RUSSIA IN THE NINETEENTH CENTURY

Cambridge Modern History, vol. XI, chaps. IX, XXII; vol. XII, chap. XII.

C. J. H. Hayes, *A Political and Cultural History of Modern Europe*, vol. II (1936), pp. 252–70.

F. C. Palm and F. E. Graham, *Europe Since Napoleon* (1934), chap. X.

C. P. Higby, *History of Modern Europe* (1932), chaps. X, XIX.

E. Achorn, *European Civilization and Politics Since 1815* (1934), chap. VIII.

J. S. Schapiro, *Modern and Contemporary European History* (1929), chaps. XXIII, XXIV.

P. W. Slosson, *Europe Since 1870* (1935), chap. VIII.

W. L. Langer, *Encyclopaedia of World History* (1940), V, D2.

LONGER STUDIES. M. Karpovich, *Imperial Russia, 1801–1917* (1932); G. Vernadsky, *History of Russia* (1930); F. H. B. Skrine, *The Expansion of Russia, 1815–1900* (1904); A. Rambaud, *The Expansion of Russia* (1904); M. Baring, *The Russian People* (1914); D. M. Wallace, *Russia* (1912); B. Pares, *Russia and Reform* (1907); B. Pares, *A History of Russia* (1928); Donald Henderson, *From the Volga to the Yukon* (1944); D. S. Mirsky, *A History of Russian Literature* (1927); P. A. Kropotkin, *Ideals and Realities in Russian Literature* (1915); W. A. Philips, *Poland* (1915); W. R. Morfill, *Poland* (1903); O. Halecki, *The History of Poland* (1942).

57. THE LESSER STATES OF EUROPE IN THE NINETEENTH CENTURY

Cambridge Modern History, vol. XI, chaps. VIII, XX, XXIII, XXIV; vol. XII, chaps. IX–XI.

F. C. Palm and F. E. Graham, *Europe Since Napoleon* (1934), chap. XII.

C. P. Higby, *History of Modern Europe* (1932), chap. XX.

J. S. Schapiro, *Modern and Contemporary European History* (1929), chaps. XIX, XXII.

W. L. Langer, *Encyclopaedia of World History* (1940), V, C3, 5, and 8; D1, E1–2.

NATIONAL HISTORIES. R. N. Bain, *Scandinavia: a Political History of Denmark, Norway and Sweden, from 1513 to 1900* (1905); C. Hallendorff and A. Schück, *History of Sweden* (1929); K. Gjerset, *A History of the Norwegian People*, 2 vols. (1915); P. J. Blok, *History of the People of the Netherlands* (1912), vol. V; G. Edmundson, *History of Holland* (1922); A. J. Barnouw, *The Making of Modern Holland* (1944); H. Riemens, *The Netherlands: Story of a Free People* (1944); B. H. M. Vlekke, *Evolution of the Dutch Nation* (1945); J.-A. Goris (editor), *Belgium* (1945); H. vander Linden, *Belgium, the Making of a Nation* (1920); L. van der Essen, *A Short History of Belgium* (1916); W. Oechsli, *History of Switzerland, 1499–1914* (1922); M. A. S. Hume, *Modern Spain* (1923); H. D. Sedgwick, *Spain: a Short History* (1925); W. H. Koebel, *Portugal, its Land and People* (1909); H. M. Stephens, *Portugal* (1908); W. Miller, *The Ottoman Empire and its Successors, 1815–1921* (1921); W. Miller, *The Balkans: Rumania, Bulgaria, Serbia and Montenegro* (1908); W. Miller, *History of the Greek People, 1821–1923* (1923); F. Schevill, *The History of the Balkan Peninsula* (1922); J. Buchan (editor), *Bulgaria and Rumania* (1924); M. W. Childs, *Sweden: The Middle Way* (3d ed. 1947).

58. THE NEW WORLD WHICH SCIENCE AND INDUSTRY CREATED

Cambridge Modern History, vol. XII, chap. XXIV.

C. J. H. Hayes, *A Political and Cultural History of Modern Europe*, vol. II (1936), chap. XVIII.

H. E. Barnes, *The History of Western Civilization*, 2 vols. (1935), vol. II, chaps. VIII, IX, XII, XX.

T. W. Riker, *A Short History of Modern Europe* (1935), chap. XIV.

E. Achorn, *European Civilization and Politics Since 1815* (1934), chap. XII.

J. S. Schapiro, *Modern and Contemporary European History* (1929), chaps. XXVI, XXVII.

V. L. and M. H. Albjerg, *From Sedan to Stresa: Europe Since 1870* (1937), chaps. XI–XII.

F. A. Ogg, *The Economic Development of Modern Europe* (1926), XXI–XXIII.

C. Hodges, *The Background of International Relations* (1931), parts II, VI.

S. B. Clough and C. W. Cole, *Economic History of Europe* (rev. ed. 1946), chaps. XVI–XX.
W. L. Langer, *Encyclopaedia of World History* (1940), V, A.

LONGER STUDIES. F. S. Marvin, *The Century of Hope* (1919); A. H. Buck, *The Dawn of Modern Medicine, 1750–1850* (1920); C. E. A. Winslow, *The Conquest of Epidemic Disease* (1943); C. L. and M. A. Fenton, *The Story of the Great Geologists* (1945); E. W. Byrn, *The Progress of Invention in the Nineteenth Century* (1900); Lewis Mumford, *Technics and Civilization* (1938); A. P. Usher, *A History of Mechanical Invention* (1929); Harlow Shapley, *A Treasury of Science* (1944); J. A. Thompson, *An Introduction to Science* (1911); O. W. Caldwell and E. E. Slosson, *Science Remaking the World* (1927); E. C. Jeffrey, *Coal and Civilization* (1925); S. Chase, *Men and Machines* (1931); J. A. Hobson, *The Evolution of Modern Capitalism* (1926); R. H. Tawney, *The British Labor Movement* (1925); J. R. Macdonald, *The Socialist Movement* (1911); H. E. Barnes, *An Intellectual and Cultural History of the Western World* (1937), chaps. XXI–XXVII. BIOGRAPHICAL WORKS. G. T. Bettany, *Charles Darwin* (1887); R. Vallery-Radot, *Pasteur* (1923); P. de Kruif, *The Microbe Hunters* (1926); S. P. Thompson, *Faraday* (1898); G. S. Bryan, *Edison: The Man and his Work* (1926); P. Frank, *Einstein: His Life and Times* (1947). SOURCES. J. H. Robinson, *Readings in European History* (1906), vol. II, chap. XLI; C. Spahr, *Readings in Recent Political Philosophy* (1935), chaps. VIII–XI; H. Webster, *Historical Selections* (1929), nos. 473, 474.

59. THE SOCIAL CONFLICT WITHIN THREE INDUSTRIAL STATES: GREAT BRITAIN, FRANCE, AND GERMANY

Cambridge Modern History, vol. XII, chaps. III, V, VI, VII.
C. J. H. Hayes, *A Political and Cultural History of Modern Europe*, vol. II (1936), chap. XX, and pp. 533–71 and 598–619.
F. C. Palm and F. E. Graham, *Europe Since Napoleon* (1934), chaps. XVII–XIX.
T. W. Riker, *A Short History of Modern Europe* (1935), chap. XIV.
C. P. Higby, *History of Modern Europe* (1932), chaps. XV, XVI, XXI.
E. Achorn, *European Civilization and Politics Since 1815* (1934), chaps. VI, VII, IX.
J. S. Schapiro, *Modern and Contemporary European History* (1929), chap. XXVIII.

P. W. Slosson, *Europe Since 1870* (1935), chaps. III, IV, VI.
J. W. Swain, *Beginning the Twentieth Century: a History of the Generation that Made the War* (1933), pp. 1–200.
S. B. Clough and C. W. Cole, *Economic History of Europe* (rev. ed. 1946), chaps. XIX, XX.
C. J. H. Hayes, *A Generation of Materialism, 1871–1900* (1941), chaps. II, III, IV, V.
W. J. Bossenbrook and associates, *The Development of Contemporary Civilization* (1940), chaps. X, XI, XII.

LONGER STUDIES. C. J. H. Hayes, *A Generation of Materialism* (1941); L. G. Chiozza-Money, *Riches and Poverty* (1911); C. W. Pipkin, *The Idea of Social Justice* (1928); B. G. de Montgomery, *British and Continental Labor Policy* (1922); M. Beer, *A History of British Socialism* (1942); D. W. Brogan, *France under the Republic* (1940); D. C. McKay (editor), *The Dreyfus Case* (1937); P. Sabatier, *Disestablishment in France* (1906); A. L. Guérard, *French Civilization in the Nineteenth Century* (1914); C. Tower, *Germany of Today* (1913); J. C. Clapham, *Economic Development of France and Germany, 1815–1914* (1921); W. H. Dawson, *Bismarck and State Socialism* (1891); A. Rosenberg, *The Birth of the German Republic* (1931); W. F. Brook, *A Social and Economic History of Germany from William II to Hitler, 1888–1939* (1939); H. T. Laidlaw, *History of Socialist Thought* (1927); P. O. Ray, *Major European Governments* (1931); F. A. Ogg, *The Governments of Europe* (1917). BIOGRAPHICAL WORKS. O. Burdett, *W. E. Gladstone* (1928); Sir E. Clarke, *Benjamin Disraeli: the Romance of a Great Career* (1926); A. Maurois, *Disraeli* (1927); L. Strachey, *Queen Victoria* (1921); Sir F. T. Marzials, *Life of Léon Gambetta* (1890); C. G. Robertson, *Bismarck* (1918); J. H. Jackson, *Jean Jaurès* (1944); G. Bruun, *Clemenceau* (1943); F. Mehring, *Karl Marx, The Story of his Life* (1935). SOURCES. J. F. Scott and A. Baltzly, *Readings in European History Since 1814* (1930), chap. IX; Columbia University, *Introduction to Contemporary Civilization: A Source Book*, vol. II (1946), chap. IX.

60. THE COMPETITION AMONG THE INDUSTRIALIZED STATES: THE RACE FOR COLONIES AND MARKETS

Cambridge Modern History, vol. XII, chaps. XV–XX, XXII, XXV.
C. J. H. Hayes, *A Political and Cultural History of Modern Europe*, vol. II (1936), pp. 691–749.

F. C. Palm and F. E. Graham, *Europe Since Napoleon* (1934), chaps. XXII–XXIV.
H. E. Barnes, *The History of Western Civilization*, 2 vols. (1935), vol. II, chap. XV.
T. W. Riker, *A Short History of Modern Europe* (1935), chap. XV.
C. P. Higby, *History of Modern Europe* (1932), chaps. XXII, XXIII.
E. Achorn, *European Civilization and Politics Since 1815* (1934), chap. X.
J. S. Schapiro, *Modern and Contemporary European History* (1929), chaps. XXX, XXXI.
P. W. Slosson, *Europe Since 1870* (1935), chaps. V, IX.
P. W. Slosson, *Twentieth Century Europe* (1927), chaps. VI, VII.
C. Hodges, *The Background of International Relations* (1931), parts VI–VIII.
J. W. Swain, *Beginning the Twentieth Century* (rev. ed. 1938), chap. XII.
P. E. Eckel, *The Far East Since 1500* (1947), Introd. and part I.

LONGER STUDIES. J. A. Hobson, *Imperialism: A Study* (3d ed. 1938); P. T. Moon, *Imperialism and World Politics* (1926); R. Muir, *The Expansion of Modern Europe* (1923); H. L. Hoskins, *European Imperialism in Africa* (1930); C. K. Hobson, *The Export of Capital* (1914); Sir H. H. Johnston, *A History of the Colonization of Africa by Alien Races* (1913); N. D. Harris, *Europe and Africa* (1927), and *Europe and the East* (1926); Sir Valentine Chirol, *India* (1922); V. A. Smith, *The Oxford History of India* (1928); K. S. Latourette, *The Development of China* (1929); H. A. Giles, *The Civilization of China* (1911); H. H. Gowen, *Outline History of Japan* (1927); J. H. Gubbins, *The Making of Modern Japan* (1922); K. S. Latourette, *The History of Japan* (1947); D. G. E. Hall, *Europe and Burma* (1946); E. R. Hughes, *The Invasion of China by the Western World* (1937); H. M. Vinacke, *A History of the Far East in Modern Times* (4th ed. 1941). BIOGRAPHICAL WORKS. Sir H. H. Johnston, *Livingstone* (1890); H. W. Little, *Stanley* (1890); B. Williams, *Cecil Rhodes* (1921); E. Hahn, *Raffles of Singapore: A Biography* (1946); A. Maurois, *Lyautey* (1931).

61. THE GROWTH OF ALLIANCES: INTERNATIONAL TENSION AND THE ARMED PEACE

Cambridge Modern History, vol. XII, chaps. I, VI.
C. J. H. Hayes, *A Political and Cultural History of Modern Europe*, vol. II (1936), pp. 749–83.

F. C. Palm and F. E. Graham, *Europe Since Napoleon* (1934), chaps. XXVI–XXVIII.
T. W. Riker, *A Short History of Modern Europe* (1935), chap. XV.
C. P. Higby, *History of Modern Europe* (1932), chaps. XXIV, XXV.
E. Achorn, *European Civilization and Politics Since 1815* (1934), chaps. XIII, XIV.
J. S. Schapiro, *Modern and Contemporary European History* (1929), chaps. XXXIII, XXXIV.
P. W. Slosson, *Europe Since 1870* (1935), chaps. X–XIII.
J. W. Swain, *Beginning the Twentieth Century* (rev. ed. 1938), part II.
C. J. H. Hayes, *A Generation of Materialism* (1941), chaps. I, VI, VIII.
W. L. Langer, *Encyclopaedia of World History* (1940), V, F.

LONGER STUDIES. H. Feis, *Europe, the World's Banker* (1930); J. V. Fuller, *Bismarck's Diplomacy at its Zenith* (1922); W. L. Langer, *European Alliances and Alignments* (1931); A. C. Coolidge, *The Origins of the Triple Alliance* (1926); B. E. Schmidt, *Triple Alliance and Triple Entente* (1934); B. E. Schmidt, *The Coming of the War*, 2 vols. (1930); S. B. Fay, *The Origins of the World War*, 2 vols. (2d ed. 1930); H. E. Barnes, *The Genesis of the World War* (2d ed. 1927); R. J. Sontag, *European Diplomatic History, 1871–1932* (1933); G. L. Dickinson, *The International Anarchy, 1904–1914* (1926); Hans Kohn, *The Idea of Nationalism* (1944); Ross J. S. Hoffman, *Great Britain and the German Trade Rivalry, 1875–1914* (1933); A. W. Salomone, *Italian Democracy in the Making* (1945). BIOGRAPHICAL WORKS. C. W. Porter, *Career of Théophile Delcassé* (1936); G. M. Trevelyan, *Grey of Fallodon* (1937); G. Bruun, *Clemenceau* (1943); Sir Sidney Lee, *Life of King Edward VII*, 2 vols. (1925–27). SOURCES. W. H. Cooke and E. P. Stickney, *Readings in European International Relations Since 1879* (1931), part I.

62. THE FIRST WORLD WAR

C. J. H. Hayes, *A Political and Cultural History of Modern Europe*, vol. II (1936), chap. XXIV.
F. C. Palm and F. E. Graham, *Europe Since Napoleon* (1934), chaps. XXIX, XXX.
H. E. Barnes, *The History of Western Civilization*, 2 vols. (1935), vol. II, chap. XVII.
T. W. Riker, *A Short History of Modern Europe* (1935), chap. XVI.
W. C. Langsam, *The World Since 1914* (1943).
F. L. Benns, *Europe Since 1914 in its World Setting* (6th ed. 1946).

G. N. Steiger, *A History of the Far East* (1936).
Owen Lattimore, *Solution in Asia* (1945).
Bruno Lasker, *Asia on the Move* (1945).
G. F. Hudson and Marthe Rajchman, *An Atlas of Far Eastern Politics* (1943).
H. M. Vinacke, *A History of the Far East in Modern Times* (4th ed. 1941).
E. J. Jurji (editor), *The Great Religions of the Modern World* (1946).

INDIA. *The Cambridge Shorter History of India* (1934); W. H. Morland and A. C. Chatterjee, *A Short History of India* (1944); F. R. Morae and R. Stimson, *Introduction to India* (1943); Penderel Moon, *Strangers in India* (1945). CHINA. W. H. Mallory, *China: Land of Famine* (1926); K. S. Latourette, *The Chinese, their History and Culture* (1934); O. and E. Lattimore, *The Making of Modern China* (1944); E. R. Hughes, *The Invasion of China by the Western World* (1937); L. K. Rosinger, *China's Crisis* (1945). JAPAN. J. A. B. Scherer, *Romance of Japan through the Ages* (1927); J. F. Embree, *The Japanese Nation: a Social Survey* (1945); E. H. Norman, *The Emergence of Japan as a Modern State* (1940); T. A. Bisson, *Japan in China* (1938); A. J. Grajdanzev, *Modern Korea* (1944). SOUTH-EAST ASIA. B. Lasker, *Peoples of Southeast Asia* (1944); B. H. M. Vlekke, *Nusantara: a History of the East Indian Archipelago* (1943); Amry Vandenbosch, *The Dutch East Indies* (2d ed. 1941); J. R. Hayden, *The Philippines: A Study in National Development* (1942). BIOGRAPHICAL WORKS. E. J. Thomas, *The Life of the Buddha as Legend and History* (1927); W. E. Soothill, *Analects of Confucius* (1910); C. F. Andrews (editor), *Mahatma Gandhi: his own Story* (1930); Jawaharlal Nehru, *Towards Freedom* (1941); S. Chen and R. Payne, *Sun Yat-sen: A Portrait* (1946); R. Berkov, *Strong Man of China: the Story of Chiang Kai-shek* (1938).

Thomas C. Cochran and William Miller, *The Age of Enterprise: a Social History of Industrial America* (1942).
V. L. Parrington, *Main Currents in American Thought*, 3 vols. (1927–30).
S. F. Bemis, *A Diplomatic History of the United States* (rev. ed. 1942).
Allan Nevins and L. M. Hacker (editors), *The United States and its Place in World Affairs, 1918–1943* (1943).
H. U. Faulkner, *American Economic History* (5th ed. 1946).
A. D. Hansen, *America's Role in World Economy* (1945).
Nicholas J. Spykman, *America's Strategy in World Politics* (1942).

LATIN AMERICA. M. W. Williams, *The People and Politics of Latin America* (rev. ed. 1945); W. S. Robertson, *History of the Latin American Nations* (3d ed. 1943); D. R. Moore, *A History of Latin America* (rev. ed. 1944); S. E. Harris, *Economic Problems of Latin America* (1945); J. F. Rippy, *Latin America and the Industrial Age* (1944); S. G. Inman, *Latin America: its Place in World Life* (rev. ed. 1942); W. R. Crawford, *A Century of Latin American Thought* (1944); P. Henriquez-Ureña, *Literary Currents in Hispanic America* (1945); J. A. Crow, *The Epic of Latin America* (1946); H. B. Parkes, *A History of Mexico* (1938); J. P. Calogeras, *A History of Brazil* (1939); Hudson Strode, *Timeless Mexico* (1944); Ysabel F. Rennie, *The Argentine Republic* (1945); P. T. Ellsworth, *Chile: an Economy in Transition* (1944). SOURCES. H. S. Commager, *Documents of American History* (3d ed. 1942); United States Department of State, *Treaties in Force: a list of Treaties and other International Acts of the United States in Force on December 31, 1941*. Government Printing Office, Washington (1944); N. Cleven (editor), *Readings in Hispanic American History* (1927).

65. THE RÔLE OF AMERICA

C. A. and M. Beard, *Rise of American Civilization* (1934).
S. E. Morison and H. S. Commager, *The Growth of the American Republic*, 2 vols. (3d ed. 1942).
J. D. Hicks, *A Short History of American Democracy* (1944).
H. C. Hockett and A. M. Schlesinger, *Land of the Free* (1944).
H. Wish, *Contemporary America: the National Scene Since 1900* (1935).

66. RUSSIA UNDER THE RULE OF THE SOVIETS

C. J. H. Hayes, *A Political and Cultural History of Modern Europe*, vol. II (1936), pp. 906–30.
F. C. Palm and F. E. Graham, *Europe Since Napoleon* (1934), chap. XXXIII.
H. E. Barnes, *The History of Western Civilization*, 2 vols. (1935), vol. II, chap. XXV.
T. W. Riker, *A Short History of Modern Europe* (1935), chap. XIX.

W. P. Hall, *World Wars and Revolutions* (1943).
F. P. Chambers, C. P. Grant, C. C. Bailey, *This Age of Conflict, 1914–1943* (1943).
C. P. Higby, *History of Modern Europe* (1932), chap. XXVI.
E. Achorn, *European Civilization and Politics Since 1815* (1934), chap. XV.
J. S. Schapiro, *Modern and Contemporary European History* (1929), chap. XXXV.
P. W. Slosson, *Europe Since 1870* (1935), chap. XIV.
P. W. Slosson, *Twentieth Century Europe* (1927), chaps. X–XII.
J. W. Swain, *Beginning the Twentieth Century* (rev. ed. 1938), part III.
W. L. Langer, *Encyclopaedia of World History* (1940), VI, A1–36.

LONGER STUDIES. M. E. Durham, *The Sarajevo Crime* (1925); J. F. Scott, *Five Weeks* (1927); C. J. H. Hayes, *A Brief History of the Great War* (1920); W. S. Seaver, *Colossal Blunders of the War* (1930); W. S. Churchill, *The Unknown War* (1931); H. D. Lasswell, *Propaganda Technique in the World War* (1927); Sir H. J. Newbolt, *A Naval History of the War, 1914–1918* (1920); J. E. T. Harper, *The Truth About Jutland* (1927); L. Guichard, *The Navy Blockade, 1914–1918* (1930); B. H. Liddell Hart, *A History of the World War* (1934); C. R. M. F. Cruttwell, *A History of the Great War, 1914–1918* (1936); Alfred Vagts, *The History of Militarism* (1938); J. R. Newman, *The Tools of War* (1942); E. M. Earle (editor), *Makers of Modern Strategy* (1943); Bernard Brodie, *A Guide to Naval Strategy* (1944); F. P. Chambers, *The War behind the War, 1914–1918* (1939). BIOGRAPHICAL WORKS. R. Recouly, *Joffre* (1931); B. H. Liddell Hart, *Foch, the Man of Orleans* (1932); C. R. Ballard, *Kitchener* (1930); K. Tschuppik, *Ludendorff, the Tragedy of a Military Mind* (1932); M. Goldsmith and F. Veigt, *Hindenburg, the Man and the Legend* (1930); C. Seymour, *Woodrow Wilson and the World War* (1922).

63. THE PEACE SETTLEMENT OF 1919

C. J. H. Hayes, *A Political and Cultural History of Modern Europe*, vol. II (1936), pp. 854–71.
F. C. Palm and F. E. Graham, *Europe Since Napoleon* (1934), chaps. XXXI, XXXII.
T. W. Riker, *A Short History of Modern Europe* (1935), chap. XVII.
C. P. Higby, *History of Modern Europe* (1932), chap. XXVII.
E. Achorn, *European Civilization and Politics Since 1815* (1934), chap. XVI.

J. S. Schapiro, *Modern and Contemporary European History* (1929), chap. XXXVI.
P. W. Slosson, *Europe Since 1870* (1935), chaps. XVIII, XIX.
P. W. Slosson, *Twentieth Century Europe* (1931), chaps. XV, XVI, XVIII.
F. L. Benns, *Europe Since 1914 in its World Setting* (6th ed. 1946).
W. C. Langsam, *The World Since 1914* (1943), chaps. IV–VI.
F. H. Soward, *Twenty-five Troubled Years: 1918–1943* (1944).
C. G. Haines and R. J. S. Hoffman, *The Origins and Background of the Second World War* (1943).
J. H. Jackson, *A Short History of the World Since 1918* (1939).
A. J. May, *Europe and Two World Wars* (1947).

LONGER STUDIES. A. C. F. Beales, *The History of Peace: a Short Account of the Organized Movements for International Peace* (1931); C. H. Haskins and R. H. Lord, *Some Problems of the Peace Conference* (1920); J. M. Keynes, *The Economic Consequences of the Peace* (1920); G. B. Noble, *Policies and Opinions at Paris, 1919* (1935); Paul Birdsall, *Versailles Twenty Years After* (1941); T. A. Bailey, *Woodrow Wilson and the Lost Peace* (1944); J. S. Bassett, *The League of Nations* (1928); P. J. N. Baker, *The League of Nations at Work* (1926); C. Eagleton, *International Government* (1932). RECONSTRUCTED STATES. S. H. Thomson, *Czechoslovakia in European History* (1943); R. J. Kerner (editor), *Czechoslovakia* (1940); J. H. Jackson, *Estonia* (1941), and *Finland* (1938); B. E. Schmitt (editor), *Poland* (1945); O. Halecki, *The History of Poland* (1942); T. G. Chase, *The Story of Lithuania* (1946). BIOGRAPHICAL WORKS. D. Lloyd George, *Memoirs of the Peace Conference*, 2 vols. (1939); E. M. House, *The Intimate Papers of Colonel House arranged as a Narrative by Charles Seymour*, 4 vols. (1926–28); H. C. F. Bell, *Woodrow Wilson and the People* (1945); G. Bruun, *Clemenceau* (1943); R. S. Baker, *Woodrow Wilson, Life and Letters*, 8 vols. (1927–39). SOURCES. W. H. Cooke and E. P. Stickney, *Readings in European International Relations Since 1879* (1931), part IV; W. C. Langsam, *Documents and Readings in the History of Europe Since 1918* (1939).

64. THE IMPACT OF EUROPEAN CIVILIZATION ON ASIA

G. B. Cressey, *Asia's Lands and Peoples* (1944).
P. H. Clyde, *A History of the Modern and Contemporary Far East* (1937).

C. P. Higby, *History of Modern Europe* (1932), chap. XXX.
E. Achorn, *European Civilization and Politics Since 1815* (1934), chap. XVII.
J. S. Schapiro, *Modern and Contemporary European History* (1929), chap. XXXVII.
P. W. Slosson, *Europe Since 1870* (1935), chap. XXI.
F. L. Benns, *Europe Since 1914* (1931), chaps. III, XVII.
W. C. Langsam, *The World Since 1914* (1943), chap. XVIII.
V. L. and M. H. Albjerg, *From Sedan to Stresa: Europe Since 1870* (1937), chap. XXIX.
J. W. Swain, *Beginning the Twentieth Century* (1933), chap. XXX.
W. P. Hall, *World Wars and Revolutions* (1943), chap. V.
W. L. Langer, *Encyclopaedia of World History* (1940), VI, B12.

LONGER STUDIES. W. H. Chamberlain, *The Russian Revolution, 1917–1921*, 2 vols. (1935); W. H. Chamberlain, *Soviet Russia* (1930); G. Vernadsky, *The Russian Revolution, 1917–1931* (1932); L. Trotsky, *The History of the Russian Revolution*, 3 vols. (1932); J. Mavor, *The Russian Revolution* (1928); W. R. Batsell, *Soviet Rule in Russia* (1929); H. N. Brailsford, *How the Soviets Work* (1927); C. V. Hoover, *The Economic Life of Soviet Russia* (1931); M. Doble and H. C. Stevens, *Russian Economic Development Since the Revolution* (1928); M. G. Hindus, *Humanity Uprooted* (1929), and *The Great Offensive* (1933); Walter Duranty, *U.S.S.R.: The Story of Soviet Russia* (1944); S. N. Harper, *Civic Training in Soviet Russia* (1929); G. B. Cressey, *The Basis of Soviet Strength* (1945); Edgar Snow, *The Pattern of Soviet Power* (1945); W. H. Chamberlain, *The Russian Enigma* (1943); Harriet L. Moore, *Soviet Far Eastern Policy* (1945); A. Baykov, *The Development of the Soviet Economic System* (1946); F. Lorimer, *The Population of the Soviet Union* (1946); W. Mandel, *A Guide to the Soviet Union* (1946); E. J. Simmons (editor), *U.S.S.R.: A Concise Handbook* (1947). BIOGRAPHICAL WORKS. L. Trotsky, *My Life: An Attempt at an Autobiography* (1930), and *Lenin* (1935); D. S. Mirsky, *Lenin* (1931); G. Vernadsky, *Lenin, Red Dictator* (1931); I. D. Levine, *Stalin* (1931); B. Souvarine, *Stalin: A Critical History of Bolshevism* (1939). SOURCES. W. H. Cooke and E. P. Stickney, *Readings in European International Relations Since 1879* (1931), nos. 159–62; F. A. Golder(editor), *Documents of Russian History 1914–1917* (1927); W. C. Langsam, *Documents and Readings in the History of Europe Since 1918* (1939), chap. X.

67. FASCIST ITALY

T. W. Riker, *A Short History of Modern Europe* (1935), chap. XIX.
C. P. Higby, *History of Modern Europe* (1932), chap. XXVIII.
F. C. Palm and F. E. Graham, *Europe Since Napoleon* (1934), chap. XXXIV.
E. Achorn, *European Civilization and Politics Since 1815* (1934), chap. XIX.
J. S. Schapiro, *Modern and Contemporary European History* (1929), chap. XXXIX.
P. W. Slosson, *Europe Since 1870* (1935), chap. XXVI.
F. L. Benns, *Europe Since 1914 in its World Setting* (6th ed. 1946).
W. C. Langsam, *The World Since 1914* (1943), chap. XIII.
V. L. and M. H. Albjerg, *From Sedan to Stresa: Europe Since 1870* (1937), chap. XXVIII.
W. L. Langer, *Encyclopaedia of World History* (1940), VI, B6.

LONGER STUDIES. H. Finer, *Mussolini's Italy* (1935); H. W. Schneider, *The Fascist Government of Italy* (1936); H. A. Steiner, *Government in Fascist Italy* (1938); H. L. Mathews, *The Fruits of Fascism* (1943); M. H. H. Macartney and P. Cremona, *Italy's Foreign and Colonial Policy 1914–1937* (1938); E. B. MacCallum, *Rivalries in Ethiopia* (1935); E. J. Hughes, *The Church and the Liberal Society* (1944); W. Teeling, *Pope Pius XI and World Affairs* (1937); J. W. Naughton, *Pius XII on World Problems* (1943). SOURCES. M. Spahr, *Readings in Recent Political Philosophy* (1935), chap. XVII; W. H. Cooke and E. P. Stickney, *Readings in European International Relations Since 1879* (1931), nos. 180, 182; W. C. Langsam, *Documents and Readings in the History of Europe Since 1918* (1939), chap. VII.

68. THE UNITED KINGDOM AND THE BRITISH EMPIRE COMMONWEALTH

H. Robinson, *The Development of the British Empire* (rev. ed. 1936), chaps. XXIV–XXVII.
E. Achorn, *European Civilization and Politics Since 1815* (1934), chaps. XVIII, XX.
C. P. Higby, *History of Modern Europe* (1932), chap. XXVIII.
J. S. Schapiro, *Modern and Contemporary European History* (1929), chap. XXXII.
P. W. Slosson, *Europe Since 1870* (1935), chap. XXIX.

F. L. Benns, *Europe Since 1914 in its World Setting* (6th ed. 1946).
W. C. Langsam, *The World Since 1914* (1943), chaps. X, XI.
F. C. Palm and F. E. Graham, *Europe Since Napoleon* (1934), chap. XXXVIII.
V. L. and M. H. Albjerg, *From Sedan to Stresa: Europe Since 1870* (1937), chap. XXV.
W. L. Langer, *Encyclopaedia of World History* (1940), VI, B2.

LONGER STUDIES. A. Siegfried, *England's Crisis* (1931); W. P. Hall, *Empire to Commonwealth* (1928); R. G. Trotter, *The British Empire Commonwealth* (1932); Albert Viton, *Great Britain, an Empire in Transition* (1940); Seumas Macmanus, *The Story of the Irish Race: a Popular History of Ireland* (4th ed. rev. 1944); N. Mansergh, *The Irish Free State* (1934); Carl Wittke, *A History of Canada* (rev. ed. 1941); D. G. Creighton, *Dominion of the North: a History of Canada* (1944); C. W. de Kiewiet, *A History of South Africa, Social and Economic* (1941); R. Peattie, *Struggle on the Veld* (1947); G. L. Wood, *Australia: Its Resources and Development* (1947); C. Hartley Grattan, *Introducing Australia* (1942); P. Soljak, *New Zealand: Pacific Pioneer* (1946); Walter Nash, *New Zealand: a Democracy that Works* (1943). SOURCES. E. M. Violette (editor), *English Constitutional Documents Since 1832* (1936); W. C. Langsam, *Documents and Readings in the History of Europe Since 1918* (1939), chap. V.

69. FRANCE SEEKS SECURITY

T. W. Riker, *A Short History of Modern Europe* (1935), chap. XX.
C. P. Higby, *History of Modern Europe* (1932), chap. XXVIII.
E. Achorn, *European Civilization and Politics Since 1815* (1934), chap. XVIII.
J. S. Schapiro, *Modern and Contemporary European History* (1929), chap. XXXVIII.
P. W. Slosson, *Europe Since 1870* (1935), chaps. XXV, XXVIII.
F. L. Benns, *Europe Since 1914 in its World Setting* (6th ed. 1946).
W. C. Langsam, *The World Since 1914* (1943), chaps. VIII, XII.
F. C. Palm and F. E. Graham, *Europe Since Napoleon* (1934), chap. XXXVII.
W. L. Langer, *Encyclopaedia of World History* (1940), VI, B4.

LONGER STUDIES. D. W. Brogan, *France under the Republic* (1940); A. Wolfers, *Britain and France between Two Wars* (1940); A. Werth, *Which Way France* (1937); P. Vaucher, *Post-War France* (1934); C. J. H. Hayes, *France: a Nation of Patriots* (1930); R. H. Soltau, *French Parties and Politics, 1871–1930* (1930); C. Gide (editor), *The Effects of the War upon French Economic Life* (1923); S. Huddleston, *France* (1927); W. MacDonald, *Reconstruction in France* (1922); W. F. Ogburn and W. Jaffé, *The Economic Development of Post-War France* (1929); F. Alexander, *From Paris to Locarno and After: the League of Nations and the Search for Security* (1928); P. J. N. Baker, *Disarmament* (1926); D. H. Miller, *The Peace Pact of Paris: a Study of the Briand-Kellogg Treaty* (1928); J. T. Shotwell, *War as an Instrument of National Policy, and its Renunciation in the Pact of Paris* (1929). SOURCES. W. H. Cooke and E. P. Stickney, *Readings in European International Relations Since 1879* (1931), nos. 166, 170, 173–76, 181; W. C. Langsam, *Documents and Readings in the History of Europe Since 1918* (1939), chaps. IV and VI.

70. GERMANY SEEKS EQUALITY

T. W. Riker, *A Short History of Modern Europe* (1935), chap. X.
C. P. Higby, *History of Modern Europe* (1932), chap. XXIX.
E. Achorn, *European Civilization and Politics Since 1815* (1934), chap. XVIII.
J. S. Schapiro, *Modern and Contemporary European History* (1929), chap. XXXIX.
P. W. Slosson, *Europe Since 1870* (1935), chap. XXVII.
F. L. Benns, *Europe Since 1914 in its World Setting* (6th ed. 1946).
W. C. Langsam, *The World Since 1914* (1943), chap. XV.
F. C. Palm and F. E. Graham, *Europe Since Napoleon* (1934), chap. XXXV.
W. L. Langer, *Encyclopaedia of World History* (1940), VI, B8–9.

LONGER STUDIES. R. H. Lutz, *The German Revolution of 1918–19* (1922); R. H. Lutz, *The Fall of the German Empire*, 2 vols. (1932); J. F. Carr, *The Old and the New Germany* (1924); K. Kautsky, *The Labour Revolution* (1925); J. W. Angell, *The Recovery of Germany* (1932); A. Fabre-Luce, *Locarno: a Dispassionate View* (1928); R. Martel, *The Eastern Frontiers of Germany* (1930); C. B. Hoover, *Germany Enters the Third Reich* (1933); K. Heiden, *A History of National Socialism* (1934); F. L. Schuman, *Germany Since 1918* (1937); H.

Lichtenberger, *The Third Reich* (1937); William Eberstein, *The Nazi State* (1942); Albert Brecht, *Prelude to Silence: the End of the German Republic*, (1944); K. Heiden, *Hitler's Rise to Power* (1943); S. W. Halperin, *Germany Tried Democracy* (1946); W. M. Knight-Patterson, *Germany from Defeat to Conquest* (1947); F. Neumann, *Behemoth: the Structure and Practice of National Socialism* (1942); M. MacDonald, *The Republic of Austria, 1918–1934* (1946). BIOGRAPHICAL WORKS. H. von Kessler, *Walther Rathenau: His Life and Work* (1930); R. Olden, *Stresemann* (1930); R. Weterstetten and A. M. K. Watson, *The Biography of President von Hindenburg* (1930); A. Hitler, *My Battle* (1933); S. Wallach, *Hitler* (1933); K. Heiden, *Hitler* (1936), and *Der Fuehrer* (1944). SOURCES. W. H. Cooke and E. P. Stickney, *Readings in European International Relations Since 1879* (1931), nos. 167, 177, 183; W. C. Langsam, *Documents and Readings in the History of Europe Since 1918* (1939), chap. IX; A. Hitler, *The Speeches of Adolf Hitler, April, 1922–August, 1939*, 2 vols. (1942).

71. TWO DECADES OF INTERNATIONAL TENSION

C. G. Haines and R. J. S. Hoffman, *Origins and Background of the Second World War* (1943).
Dwight E. Lee, *Ten Years: the World on Way to War, 1930–1940* (1942).
W. C. Langsam, *The World Since 1914* (1943).
F. L. Benns, *Europe Since 1914 in its World Setting* (6th ed. 1946).
W. P. Hall, *World Wars and Revolutions* (1943).
W. J. Bossenbrook and others, *The Development of Contemporary Civilization* (1940).
A. Nevins and L. M. Hacker, *The United States and its Place in World Affairs, 1918–1943* (1943).
K. Ingram, *Years of Crisis: An Outline of International History, 1919–1945* (1945).
G. M. Gathorne-Hardy, *A Short History of International Affairs, 1920–1938* (1938).
H. Beukema and W. M. Geer, and associates, *Contemporary Foreign Governments* (rev. ed. 1946).
W. L. Langer, *An Encyclopaedia of World History* (1940), VI, B1.

LONGER STUDIES. W. E. Rappard, *The Quest for Peace Since the World War* (1940); J. P. Day, *An Introduction to World Economic History Since the Great War* (1940); F. H. Simonds, *The A.B.C. of War Debts* (1933); L. Robbins, *The Great Depression* (1936); G. T. Garratt, *Mussolini's Roman Empire* (1938); W. S. Churchill, *While England Slept: a Survey of World Affairs, 1932–1938* (1938); E. P. Allison, *The Spanish Tragedy* (1936), and *Spain in Eclipse* (1943); Gerald Brenan, *The Spanish Labyrinth* (1943); Antonin Basch, *The Danube Basin and the German Economic Sphere* (1943); Hugh Seton-Watson, *Eastern Europe between the Wars, 1914–1941* (1945); Bernard Newman, *Balkan Background* (1944); Elihu Horin, *The Middle East: Crossroads of History* (1943); Ernest Jackh, *The Rising Crescent: Turkey* (1944); O. Lattimore, *Manchuria, Cradle of Conflict* (1935); H. L. Stimson, *The Far Eastern Crisis* (1936); H. Rauschning, *The Revolution of Nihilism* (1939); M. Fuchs, *Showdown in Vienna: the Death of Austria* (1939); V. M. Dean, *Europe in Retreat* (1939); J. H. Simpson, *The Refugee Problem* (1939); W. M. Jordan, *Great Britain, France, and the German Problem* (1944); H. V. Hodson, *Slump and Recovery, 1929–1937* (1938); B. Mitchell, *The Depression Decade, 1929–1941* (The Economic History of the United States, vol. IX) (1947); K. London, *Backgrounds of Conflict: Ideas and Forms in World Politics* (1945); Sir H. Richmond, *Statesmen and Sea Power* (1947). SOURCES. W. H. Cooke and E. P. Stickney, *Readings in European International Relations Since 1879* (1931); W. C. Langsam, *Documents and Readings in the History of Europe Since 1918* (1939); A. B. Keith (editor), *Speeches and Documents on International Affairs, 1918–1937*, 2 vols. (1938); *Events Leading up to World War II, 1931–1944* (U.S. Government Printing Office, 1945).

72. THE SECOND WORLD WAR

R. C. K. Ensor, *A Miniature History of the War* (1945).
E. W. McInnis, *The War: First Year* (1940), *Second Year* (1941), *Third Year* (1942), *Fourth Year* (1944), *Fifth Year* (1946), *Sixth Year* (1947).
Francis Brown, *The War in Maps* (4th rev. ed. 1946).
H. S. Commager (editor), *The Story of the Second World War* (1946).
W. P. Hall, *Iron out of Calvary: An Interpretative History of the Second World War* (1946).
F. T. Miller, *History of World War II* (1945).
R. W. Shugg and H. A. DeWeerd, *World War II: a Concise History* (1946).
W. L. Langer, *Encyclopaedia of World History* (1946), VI, H.

MORE SPECIALIZED STUDIES. John Goette, *Japan Fights for Asia* (1943); O. D. Tolischus, *Tokyo*

Record (1943); L. K. Rosinger, *China's Wartime Politics, 1937–1944* (1945); Walter Kerr, *The Russian Army* (1944); Robert E. Anderson, *The Merchant Marine and World Frontiers* (1945); Fletcher Pratt, *The Navy's War* (1944); Theodore Draper, *The Six Weeks War: France, May 10–June 25, 1940* (1944); Raphael Lemkin, *Axis Rule in Occupied Europe* (1944); E. R. Stettinius, Jr., *Lend-Lease, Weapon for Victory* (1944); George C. Marshall, *Biennial Report of the Chief of Staff . . . to the Secretary of War, July 1, 1941 to June 30, 1943* (1943), and *Biennial Report . . . July 1, 1943 to June 30, 1945* (1945); Sumner Welles, *An Intelligent American's Guide to the Peace* (1945); Camille Cianfarra, *The Vatican and the War* (1944); W. L. Langer, *Our Vichy Gamble* (1947); S. E. Morison, *The History of United States Naval Operations in World War II* (1947–); G. Cant, *The Great Pacific Victory* (1946); D. M. Nelson, *Arsenal of Democracy: the Story of American War Production* (1946); F. A. Southard, *The Finances of European Liberation* (1946); J. B. Schechtman, *European Population Transfers, 1939–1945* (1946); J. P. Baxter, *Scientists Against Time* (1946). BIOGRAPHICAL WORKS. H. A. DeWeerd, *Great Soldiers of World War II* (1944); P. Guedalla, *Mr. Churchill* (1942); Francis Martel, *Petain: Verdun to Vichy* (1943). SOURCES AND DOCUMENTS. Nathan Ausubel, *Voices of History* (1940–45); M. B. Schnapper (editor), *United Nations Agreements* (1944); L. M. Goodrich and Marie J. Carroll (editors), *Documents on American Foreign Relations, 1943 and 1944* (1945); B. D. Zevin (editor), *Nothing to Fear: The Selected Addresses of Franklin Delano Roosevelt, 1932–1945* (1946); *The Collected Wartime Messages of Generalissimo Chiang Kai-shek*, 2 vols. (1946); W. Churchill, *Blood, Sweat and Tears* (1941), *The Unrelenting Struggle* (1942), *The End of the Beginning* (1943), *Onwards to Victory* (1944), *The Dawn of Liberation* (1945).

73. THE POST-WAR WORLD

THE UNITED NATIONS. V. M. Dean, *The Four Cornerstones of Peace: the Aims and Achievements of the United Nations Conferences* (1946); A. Boyd (editor), *United Nations Handbook* (1947); L. Dolivet (editor), *The United Nations: a Handbook on the New World Organization* (1946); H. Finer, *The United Nations Economic and Social Council* (1946); *United Nations: Report of the Secretary General on the Work of Organization* (1946); *United Nations Documents* (Royal Institute of International Affairs, 1946). EUROPE. E. H. Carr, *The Impact of the Soviet Union on the Western World* (1947); P. E. Cobbett, *Britain: Partner for Peace* (1946); C. C. Brinton, *The United States and Britain* (1946); R. H. Jackson, *The Nuremberg Case* (1947); S. V. Valkenburg, *Peace Atlas of Europe* (1946); J. Parkes, *The Jewish Problem in the Modern World* (1946). UNITED STATES. J. F. Dewhurst and associates, *America's Needs and Resources* (1947); O. L. Nelson, *National Security and the General Staff* (1946). THE NEAR EAST. E. A. Speiser, *The United States and the Near East* (1947); W. H. McNeill, *The Greek Dilemma* (1947); F. Stark, *The Arab Island: the Middle East* (1945); A. H. Hourani, *Syria and Lebanon* (1946); K. S. Twitchell, *Saudi Arabia* (1947); *Great Britain and Palestine* (Royal Institute of International Affairs, 1945). FAR EAST. H. F. McNair (editor), *China* (1947); Chih Tsang, *China's Postwar Markets* (1945); D. G. Haring (editor), *Japan's Prospect* (1946).

INDEXES

Persistent Factors in European Civilization

List of Maps

Index of Charts and Illustrations

General Index

Persistent Factors in European Civilization

AGRICULTURE, 470, 522–25, 792, 890, 903, 912.

ART AND ARCHITECTURE, 367–71, 535, 552, 577, 684, 687–91, 724, 877, 933, 961.

COMMERCE AND INDUSTRY, 373–74, 376, 460–75, 531, 543–44, 550, 580–82, 590–92, 598–99, 616–17, 668–69, 698–708, 746, 762, 792.

GEOGRAPHY (MIGRATIONS AND EXPLORATIONS), 395–400, 585–92, 786, 847, 868, 873, 883. (*See also* List of Maps.)

GOVERNMENT (POLITICS, ADMINISTRATION, THE STATE), 357–58, 375–76, 470–74, 489–90, 496–97, 514–18, 529, 543–49, 553–54, 576, 598, 612–13, 629–42, 646–48, 656–58, 661–62, 688–90, 692–95, 702–08, 714–15, 747–48, 749–51, 756–58, 763–64, 795–98, 801–03, 890–91, 902, 910–11, 917–18, 938–40.

INTERNATIONAL RELATIONS, 515, 655–56, 663–73, 674–82, 695–97, 728–31, 732, 738, 774–75, 811, 814, 821, 826–35, 841–43, 855–67, 891–92, 905–06, 922–23, 931, 957, 981–82, 987.

LAW AND JURISPRUDENCE, 515, 547, 613–19, 634–39, 658, 717–21, 758, 934, 985.

LITERATURE, LEARNING, AND EDUCATION, 363–67, 380–83, 484–87, 534–35, 550–52, 658, 687, 691–92, 721–22, 803.

MEDICINE AND PUBLIC HEALTH, 524, 784–85.

POPULATION, 518–19, 558, 698, 785, 886, 905.

RELIGION AND THEOLOGY, 377–80, 382–83, 403–18, 432–43, 450–56, 487–88, 492, 535–36, 547, 658, 681, 686–87, 740–43, 809, 900, 914.

SCIENCE, NATURAL, 549, 557, 561, 600–11, 777–85.

SOCIAL CONDITIONS, 353–57, 372–73, 411, 487, 490, 522–25, 571–72, 613–16, 622–25, 648–51, 685–86, 698–708, 711–22, 726–28, 787–90, 798–801, 803–06, 808–10, 870, 886–87, 893, 907–08, 951–54.

TECHNOLOGY (TOOLS, MACHINERY, TECHNIQUES), 381, 606–09, 698–708, 808–10, 888–90, 901, 945.

TRANSPORTATION AND COMMUNICATION, 522, 585–93, 792–93, 847, 886, 916, 969–73.

WARFARE AND WEAPONS, 358, 532, 537–40, 569–70, 578–80, 593–98, 641, 643–46, 652–56, 666–72, 728–31, 748–49, 752–54, 824–25, 835–38, 843–54, 864, 877–78, 891–92, 917, 930–32, 944, 956, 963–80.

List of Maps

Physical Map of Europe, Title page
Medieval Trade Routes, facing page xxv
Italy in the Fifteenth Century, 359
Spain in the Fifteenth Century, 386
The Heritage of Charles V: from Mary of Burgundy; from Ferdinand and Isabella; from Maximilian I; the Empire of Charles V, 394
The Great Explorations and Discoveries: Portuguese; Spanish; English and French, 399
Europe at the Beginning of the Sixteenth Century, 402
Hapsburg Lands after 1566, 428
Europe after 1648, 512
Extension of the French Frontiers, 1560–1766: French Gains, 1560–1643; Gains by Treaty of Westphalia, 1648, and Treaty of the Pyrenees, 1659; Gains of Louis XIV Between 1668 and 1697; French Gains, 1697 to 1766, 536
Growth of Russia in Europe, 1462–1815, 564
Partition of Poland, 1772–1795, 573
Growth of Brandenburg-Prussia to 1795, 579
The Widening of the European Horizon: Christian World, c. 700 A.D.; World Known to Europeans, c. 1550; World Known to Europeans, 1800, 584
The Colonial Situation about 1689, 586–87
British Colonial Empire in 1763, 592
Europe in 1789, 628
Napoleonic Empire at Its Height, 667
Europe in 1815, 680
Revolutionary Outbreaks of 1848–1849, 718
The Balkans, 730
The Unification of Italy: Italy, 1859; Italy, 1860; Italy, 1866; Italy, 1870, 733
The Unification of Germany: Kingdom of Prussia in 1866; Areas Annexed by Prussia in 1866; Areas United with Prussia to Form North German Confederation, 1867; Areas United with the North German Confederation to Form the German Empire, 1871, 745

Overseas Dependencies of the Netherlands, Belgium, Norway and Denmark in 1900, 766
Overseas Dependencies of Spain and Portugal in 1898, 771
Factors in the Distribution of World Population: People per Square Mile; Annual Rainfall; Climatic Energy, 778
Asia, 1914, 813
Africa, 1914; Africa, 1878 (inset), 819
Europe in 1900, 832
Europe after World War I, 840
Ocean Trade Routes and Control Bases, 847
Dismemberment of the Austro-Hungarian Empire, 1919, 860
Germany after the Treaty of Versailles, 1919, 860
Growth of British Power in India, 869
Japanese Expansion, 1895–1945, 881
United States, 1783–1853, 884
United States, 1945, 884
South America in the Twentieth Century, 894
Union of Soviet Socialist Republics, 1939; Gains, 1939 to 1945, 904
Italian Colonial Empire, 1939, 911
Sea Spaces of the World, 916
The British Empire in 1939, 921
The French Colonial Empire, 1939, 928
German Estimate of German Minorities in Neighboring Lands, 943
Spheres of Influence of the Great Powers, 1939, 947
Europe in 1939, 955
Poland after World War II, 964
Advance and Retreat of the Axis Powers, 1939–1945: Axis Expansion, 1939; Axis Expansion, 1942; Normandy Landing, June 6, 1944; Invasion of Germany, 1945, 966
Air Routes, 1945, 969

Index of Charts and Illustrations

Airplane, first flight (1903), 793
Alexander I, of Russia, 678
Alexander II, of Russia, 761
Alexander VI, Pope, 406
Alva, Duke of, 446
American marines at Peking (1900), 823
American observers scan the horizon for signs of retreating Germans (1918), 851
American squad near Verdun (1918), 851
Amsterdam, in seventeenth century, 517
"Anatomy Lesson," painting by Rembrandt van Rijn, 561
"Anemones and Mirror," painting by Henri Matisse, 931
Anne of Austria, Queen of France, 485
Arc de Triomphe, Paris, 931
Architecture, Romantic, nineteenth century, 684
Armada, 457
Assignat for twenty-five *livres*, 640
Atomic bomb, at Nagasaki, 979
Automobile, early model, 793

Bacteriological laboratory in the Belgian Congo, 783
Bastille, storming of the (1789), 631
Beaconsfield, Benjamin Disraeli, Earl of, 796
Bentham, Jeremy, 694
Berlin, in later seventeenth century, 516
Berlin, the *Reichssportsfeld*, 941
Bible, Gutenberg, 379
Bismarck, Otto von, 753
Blanc, Louis, 716
Blum, Léon, 929
Bolívar, Simón, 694
Borgia, Cesare, 361
Botticelli, Sandro, 368
Boxer Rebellion (1900), 823
Boyle, Robert, 545
Breda, Surrender of, 451
Briand, Aristide, 929
Britain's naval might, 845
British armored tanks, 971
British general strike (1926), 919
British trade-union conference, 919
British workers' homes, 800
Buckingham, Duke of, 493
Buffon, George Louis Leclerc de, 607
Byron, George Gordon, Lord, 691

Calvin, John, 414
Calvinist iconoclasts, 414
Canberra, Australia, House of Parliament, 923
Cape Town, Union of South Africa, House of Parliament, 923
Carnival at Paris (1781), 623
Carpaccio, 365
Cartwright, Edward, loom invented by, 701
Castiglione, Baldassare, 355
Castlereagh, Viscount, 678
Catherine II (the Great), of Russia, 571
Cavour, Camillo di, 737
Chamberlain, Neville, 961
Charles the Bold, Duke of Burgundy, 390
Charles V, Emperor, 425
Charles I, of England, 493
Charles II, of England, 545, and Royal Society, 549
Charles VIII, of France, 390
Charles XII, of Sweden, 567
Chenonceau, French château, 931
Chiang Kai-shek, 876

China, the Great Wall of, 877
Christus, Petrus, 465
Church of the Madeleine, Paris, 691
Churchill, Winston, 965
Clemenceau, Georges, 858
Clement VII, Pope, 406, 425
Clergy, sixteenth century, 435
"Clermont," the steamboat constructed by Robert Fulton, 703
Clive, Robert, 595
Clouet, Jean, 422
Coal mine, interior of a, 705
Coeur, Jacques, 462
Colbert, Jean Baptiste, 530
Columbus, Christopher, 397
Conference ending the Russo-Japanese War (1905), 761
Congress of Vienna (1814–15), painting of, 675
Cook, Captain James, 595
Copernicus, Nicolas, 601
Cottage, English, seventeenth century, 521
Cranach, Lucas, 409
Crime and punishment, seventeenth century, 567
Crimean War, "A Hot Day in the Batteries" (lithograph), 725
Crompton, spinning machine invented by, 701
Cromwell, Oliver, 498
Cromwell, Thomas, 429
Curie, Marie, 783

Danton, George Jacques, 647
Darwin, Charles, 781
Daumier, Honoré, lithograph by, 713
David, Jacques Louis, painting by, 645, 689
Declaration of Independence (1776), 597
Delaroche, Paul, painting by, 673
Diderot, Denis, 618
Donatello, 369
Drake, Sir Francis, 457
Dürer, Albrecht, 378
Dutch East India House, 467
Dutch sailors studying navigation (1661), 599

East India Company, British, headquarters of, 551
Ebert, Friedrich, 936
Edison, Thomas Alva, 791
Edward VII, of England, 837
Eine milliarde mark, 936
Electric light and power plant (1881), 791
Elizabeth, Queen of England, 457
Empress Eugénie, of France, 725
Engels, Friedrich, 716
England, imaginary plan for invasion of, 660
Engraving, seventeenth century, 498
Erasmus, Desiderius, 379
Escorial, 446
Ethiopian army (1936), 913

Factory, textile, nineteenth century, 701
Faraday, Michael, studio of, 789
Federigo da Montefeltro, Duke of Urbino, 355
Ferdinand II, Emperor, 505
Ferdinand VII, of Spain, 694
Festival at Paris (1781), 615
Fifth of October, 1795 (engraving), 654
Flying fortresses (United States Air Force), 971
Foch, Ferdinand, 849
Fortifications, in seventeenth century, 516
Francis of Assisi, Saint, 439
Francis I, of France, 422

INDEX OF CHARTS AND ILLUSTRATIONS

Frankfort Parliament (1848), 719
Frederick Augustus III, of Poland, 571
Frederick the Great, of Prussia, 577
Frederick William, of Brandenburg, the "Great Elector," 555
Frederick's library, Potsdam, 577
French army, in Holland, seventeenth century, 539
French army, in Italy, seventeenth century, 539
French Chamber of Deputies, 929
French Revolution, "A Popular Assembly" (caricature), 640
French soldiers enforcing Napoleon's Continental System, 665
Fugger, Jacob, 462
Fulton, Robert, 703

Galilei, Galileo, 601
Galileo's object class and telescopes, 606
Gambetta, Léon, 805
Gandhi, Mohandas Karamchand, 871
"Garden of an Inn," painting by Jan van Steen, 523
Gattamelata, 369
Gérard, François Pascal, portrait by, 654
German army, 939
German army maneuvers, 941
German Empire, proclamation of (1871), 753
Germany, defeated (1920), 863
Ghiberti, Gian Matteo, 369
Ghirlandaio, 355, 361, 365
Gibraltar, Fortress of, in 1727, 551
"Gin Lane," painting by William Hogarth, 623
Giotto, 368
Gladstone, William Ewart, 796
Goethe, Johann Wolfgang von, 691
Goldsmith, fifteenth century, 465
Goya, Francisco, etching by, 669
"Great Eastern," on its way to America, 789
Greco, El, 439, 441
Greenwich Observatory, seventeenth century, 549
Guericke, Otto von, experiment with air pressure, 561
Guérin, Pierre Narcisse, portrait by, 654
"Guernica," painting by Pablo Picasso, 961
Guevara, Fernando Nino de, Grand Inquisitor, 441
Guizot, François Pierre Guillaume, 713
Gustavus Adolphus, of Sweden, 505

Hague, peace palace at The, 770
Haig, General Sir Douglas, 849
"Harmless Necessary Cat" (cartoon from *Punch*), 834
Harvesting machine, 885
Harvey, William, 545
Henry the Navigator, Prince of Portugal, 397
Henry VII, of England, 390
Henry VIII, of England, 429
Henry II, of France, 422
Henry IV, of France, 478
Heyden, Jan van der, painting by, 517
Hindenburg, Field Marshal Paul von, 849
Hindu masses of India, 871
Hitler, Adolf (1889–1945), 944
Hitler speech, 939
Hogarth, William, painting by, 623
Hokusai, painting by, 877
Holbein, Hans, 378, 379, 429
Hoover Dam, 889
Hôtel de Ville, Paris, early eighteenth century, 533
Houdon, Jean-Antoine, portrait bust of Voltaire by, 618
House, fifteenth century, 355; sixteenth century, 473
House of Commons, British, 796
Humanists, 365
Hunting, late medieval, 374
Huygens, Christian, 557

Hydroelectric station, Switzerland, 767

Indulgence selling, 409
Industrial plant, Bremen, 807
Industrial plants, Russia, 901
Inquisition, 441
Italian liner, "Rex," 913

James I, of England, 493
Japanese in Manchuria, 876
"Japanese Seascape," by Hokusai, 877
Jefferson, Thomas, 597
Jenner's first vaccination, 607
Josephine, Empress of the French, portrait by François Pascal Gérard, 657
Julius II, Pope, 406

"Kaiser Wilhelm's Panther Leap" (cartoon from *Punch*), 834
Kepler, Johannes, 601
Kruger, Paul, 817
Krupp Works at Essen, Germany, 845

Labor strike in the automobile industry, 888
Lafayette, Marquis de, 636
La Grande Toilette (painting), 622
"Lake of Thun," painting by Joseph M. W. Turner, 689
Laplace, Pierre Simon de, 601
Lavoisier, Antoine Laurent (in his laboratory), 606
Lawrence, Sir Thomas, portrait by, 654
League of Nations Council in session, 865
Leeuwenhoek, Antony van, 557
Leibnitz, Gottfried Wilhelm, 557
Lenin, Nicolai, 897
Leo X, Pope, 406
Leo XIII, Pope, 741
Letter writer, a public, 521
Liberty, Equality, Fraternity (French revolutionary cartoon), 636
"Liberty Leading the People," painting by Eugène Delacroix, 709
Life Span of Europeans, 1 A.D. to 1950 A.D. (chart), 786
Linnaeus, Carolus, 607
Lloyd George, David, 858
Locke, John, 545
London, nineteenth century, 817
Louis XIII, of France, 481
Louis XIV, of France, 530
Louis XV, of France, 615
Louis XVI, of France, 631; execution of, 645
Louis Philippe, King of the French, 709
Louvois, Marquess de, 530
Loyola, Saint Ignatius, 435
Luther, Catherine, 409
Luther, Martin, 409
Luynes, Duke of, 481
Lyell, Sir Charles, 781

Machine, calculating, seventeenth century, 557; driven by horse power, 609; driven by man power, 609; driven by water power, 609
Magdeburg hemispheres, engraving of, 561
Manet, Édouard, portrait by, 805
Manila (1619), 589
Manuscript illumination, 374, 397
Marat, Jean Paul, 647
Marche des Marseillais (French revolutionary cartoon), 636
Maria Theresa, Empress of Austria, 577; her palace at Schoenbrunn, 581
Marie Antoinette, of France, 631; on her way to execution, 645

INDEX OF CHARTS AND ILLUSTRATIONS

Marlborough, John Churchill, Duke of, 551
Marx, Karl, 716
Matisse, Henri, painting by, 931
Maximilian, Emperor of Mexico, execution of, 727
Mazarin, Cardinal, 485
Mazzini, Joseph, 737
McCormick, Cyrus Hall, demonstrating his reaper, 885
Mechanization of the textile industry, 701
Medici, Cosimo de', 361
Medici, Giuliano de', 365, 369
Medici, Lorenzo de', 361
Medici, Marie de', 478
Metternich, Prince von, 675
Michelangelo Buonarroti, 369
Mill, continuous strip and sheet process, 888
Mining, sixteenth century, 462
Mirabeau, Count de, 636
Moltke, Karl Bernard, Count von, 750
Mona Lisa, 368
Money changer, fifteenth century, 465
Montesquieu, Baron de, 618
More, Sir Thomas, 379
Morse, Samuel F. B., 791
Moscow, the Red Square, 897
Mussolini, Benito, 909

Napoleon I, Emperor of the French, portrait by Pierre Narcisse Guérin, 657; at Saint Helena, painting by Paul Delaroche, 673
Napoleon II, King of Rome, portrait by Sir Thomas Lawrence, 657
Napoleon III, Emperor of the French, 725
National Socialist Party rally, 939
Natural history exhibit, early eighteenth century, 607
Nelson, Horatio, 660
Newton, Isaac, 545; analyzing a ray of light, 606
Nicholas II, of Russia, 837
Nobel, Alfred Bernhard, 770
Noble society, late medieval, 374
Nürnberg trials, 985

Ottawa, Canada, House of Parliament, 923

Painting, Renaissance, 355, 361, 365, 368, 378, 379, 390, 406, 409, 414, 422, 425, 429, 465; early modern, 439, 451, 478, 493, 508
Palmesano, 361
Paris, early eighteenth century, 533
Parliament, 498
Pasteur, Louis, 783
Paul IV, Pope, 441
Peasants, French, seventeenth century, 521; Polish, 571; Russian, 571
Peddler, seventeenth century, 533
"People on the Throne," lithograph by Honoré Daumier, 713
Pershing, General John J., 849
Peter the Great, of Russia, 567
Philip II, of Spain, 446
Picasso, Pablo, painting by, 961
Piero della Francesca, 355
Pinturicchio, 406
Pitt, William, Earl of Chatham, 595
Pitt, William, the Younger, 660; addressing the House of Commons, 654
Pittsburgh steel mill, 889
Pius VII, Pope, 678
Pius IX, Pope, 741
Poggio Bracciolini, 365
Poincaré, Raymond, 837
Poliziano, Angelo, 365
Polo family, 397

Pompadour, Marquise de, 615
Pontormo, 361
Population, European and World, 1 A.D. to 1950 A.D. (chart), 786
Primavera, 368
Printing, the Gutenberg Bible, 379
Printing press (modern), 953
Prussian troops entering a Silesian town, 583

Railroad wheels, manufacture of, 705
Raphael Sanzio, 355, 406
"Reading Molière in an Eighteenth-Century French Salon" (painting), 622
Recruiting soldiers (early eighteenth century), 581
Rembrandt van Rijn, painting by, 561
Revolutionary Tribunal, the, 645
Rhodes, Cecil John, 817
Richelieu, Cardinal Armand de, 481
Riches of the East, 879
Robespierre, Maximilien, 647
Roman garden, seventeenth century, 517
Romano, Gian Cristoforo, 361
Roon, Albrecht Theodor Emil, Count von, 750
Roosevelt, Franklin Delano, 965
Rousseau, Jean-Jacques, 618
Royal Society, foundation of the, 549
Roymerswaele, Marinus van, 465
Rubens, Peter Paul, 478, 493
Ruisdael, Jacob van, painting by, 523
Russian and United States infantry at the Elbe River (1945), 977
Russian landlords gambling away their serfs, 757
Russian troops in Manchuria (1905), 823
Russian village in nineteenth century, 757

Sacré Coeur, Paris, 805
Saint Peter's Cathedral, Rome, 741
Saint Petersburg, in 1749, 571
Saint-Simon, Claude Henri, Count de, 716
Sansculotte, the actor Chinard as a, 647
Schoenbrunn Palace, Vienna, 581
Scott, Sir Walter, 691
Sculpture, Renaissance, 361, 365, 369
Sebastiano del Piombo, 406
Sforza, Francesco, Duke of Milan, 361
Sforza, Ludovico, Duke of Milan, 390
Ships, Dutch merchant, 467
Signing of the Treaty of Versailles, 865
Sixtus V, Pope, 435
Smith, Adam, 597
Socialist demonstration in Brussels (1886), 767
Socrates, death of, painting by Jacques Louis David, 689
"Sons of the Wolf" (Italy), 909
Soviet health resort, 905
Spain, resistance against Napoleon's army, etching by Francisco Goya, 669
Spanish Fury, 451
Spinning, weaving, in the eighteenth century, 701
Stalin, Joseph, 901
Stalingrad, battle of, 977
Steam power and transportation, 703
Steel and iron works, Pilsen, 807
Steen, Jan van, painting by, 523
Stein, Baron vom und zum, 670
Stephenson, George, 703; his steam locomotive, 703
Stock quotations, 1924–46 (chart), 953
Street car, electric (1880), 793
Streltzi, execution of the, 567
Stresemann, Gustav, 936
Suez Canal, opening of, 727
Sun Yat-sen, 876
Surgery, in seventeenth century, 561

INDEX OF CHARTS AND ILLUSTRATIONS

Swedish co-operative electric bulb factory, 767

Talleyrand-Périgord, Charles Maurice de, 675
Terborch, 508
Textile printing, eighteenth century, 701
Thiers, Adolphe, 713
Titian, 425, 446
Tournament, 374
Trafalgar, the battle of (1805), 665
"Tug of Peace" (cartoon from *Punch*), 834
Turenne, Vicomte de, 485
Turkish prisoners of war (1912), 774
Turner, Joseph Mallord William, painting by, 689

Unemployed workers, in depression era, 953
United Nations, plan of organization (chart), 985; Security Council of, 979
Utrecht, in seventeenth century, 555

Vasco da Gama, 397
Velasquez, 451

Versailles, palace of, 530
Victoria, Queen, of Great Britain, 709
Victorious France (1919), 863
Vienna, barricades in, 1848, 719
Vinci, Leonardo da, 368

Wallenstein, Prince, 505
Warsaw, in 1656, 516
Weapons and armor, late medieval, 374
Wellington, Duke of, 670
Wesley, John, 694
Westphalia, Peace of, 508
"Wheatfields," painting by Jacob van Ruisdael, 523
William II, German Emperor, 837
Wilson, Woodrow, 858
Wolfe, James, 595
Wolsey, Cardinal, 429
Workers, seventeenth century, 533
Writing, in seventeenth century, 521

Zola, Émile, 805
Zwingli, Huldreich, 414

General Index

PRONUNCIATION KEY

āle, chăotic, câre, ădd, ȧccount, ärm, ȧsk, sofȧ; ēve, hẽre (27), ĕvent, ěnd, silĕnt, makẽr; īce, ĭll, charĭty; ōld, ȯbey, ôrb, ŏdd, sôft, cŏnnect; fōod, fŏŏt; out, oil; cūbe, ūnite, ûrn, ŭp, circŭs, menü; chair; go; sing; then, thin; nat̯ūre, verd̯ūre (118); ᴋ = ch in G. ich, ach; ʙoɴ; yet; zh = z in azure.

(The numbers in parentheses refer to the Guide to Pronunciation in *Webster's New International Dictionary*.)

The system of respelling for pronunciation is used by permission of the publishers of *Webster's New International Dictionary*, Second Edition, copyright, 1934, 1939, 1945, by G. & C. Merriam Co.

Abo (ä′bō), treaty of (1743), 570
Abyssinia (ăb′ĭ·sĭn′ĭ·ȧ). *See* Ethiopia
Acadia (ȧ·kā′dĭ·ȧ), ceded to Great Britain, 541, 591
Academy, French, 487
Accounting, origins of, 463–464
Act of Supremacy (1534), 418
Act of Uniformity (1534), 418; (1662), 543
Acre (ä′kẽr), 653
Act of Settlement, English (1701), 548
Act of Union, England and Scotland (1707), 548
Addison (ăd′ĭ·s'n), Joseph, 552
Adowa (ä′dṓ·ȧ), battle of (1896), 818
Adrianople (ā′drĭ·ăn·ō′p'l), treaty of (1829), 697, 773
Aegean Islands (ė·jē′ăn), 560
Aeneus (ē·nē′ăs), Silvius, 362. *See* Pius II
Afghanistan (ăf·găn′ĭ·stän), 729, 815
Africa (ăf′rĭ·kȧ), trade with, 396–398; in 16th century, 588, 590; in 19th century, 815; in 20th century, 972; and European powers, **818–822**
Age of Reason. *See* Rationalism
Agricola (ȧ·grĭk′ō·lȧ), Rudolph, 381
Agriculture, in Spain, in 16th century, 470, 479, 558; in Great Britain, 808; in Italy, 912; in Russia, 903–905; in United States, 886–887
Air power, in 20th century, 973
Aix-la-Chapelle (ĕks′là·shà′pĕl′), Congress of (1818), 681, 696; treaty (1668), 538; treaty (1748), 578, 579, 593
Albania (ăl·bā′nĭ·ȧ), annexed to Italy (1939), 960–961
Albret (àl′brē′), Jeanne d', 452
Albuquerque (ăl′bū·kẽrk), Alfonso de, 398, 590
Alcabala (äl′kä·bä′lä), 447, 558
Alençon (à′läɴ′sôn′), Francis Duke of, 454
Alexander I (ăl′ĕg·zăn′dẽr) of Russia, 668, 671, 676, **679**, 681, **690–692**, 708, 728
Alexander II, of Russia, **755–764**, 827
Alexander III, of Russia, **760–762**, 828
Alexander VI, Pope, 359, 362, 391, 400; and papal line of demarcation, 588
Alfonso (ăl·fŏn′sō) of Aragon and Sicily, 363
Algeciras (ăl′jĕ·sē′ràs) Conference (1906), 831
Alfonso of Naples, 391
Algeria (ăl·jēr′ĭ·ȧ), French occupation of, 816

Almeida (äl·mā′dȧ), Francisco de, 590
Alphabet, Russian, 566
Alphonso XII (ăl·fŏn′sō) of Spain, 771
Alphonso XIII of Spain, 771–772
Alsace (ăl′săs), 389; acquired by France, 575
Alva (äl′vä), Fernando, Duke of, 427, 449
America. *See* Colonies, United States, North America, South America
America (ȧ·mẽr′ĭ·kȧ), Latin, 893–894
America, North, in 16th century, 585, 588; in 17th century, 591–592; in 18th century, 592–598
America, South, in 16th century, 585; in 17th century, 590; in 20th century, 891–892, 893–894. *See also* America, Latin
American army, in France, 850
Amiens (à′myăɴ′), treaty of (1802), 655, 656
Amsterdam (ăm′stẽr·dăm), in 17th century, 560; in 20th century, 768
Anabaptists, 411, 448
Anarchism, 299
Anatomy, study of, in 17th century, 603–604, 610
Andersen (än′dẽr·s'n), Hans Christian, 768
Angevin (ăn′jė·vĭn) family, in Sicily and Naples, 362–363, 420
Anglican Church, in 16th century, 417–418, 430, 454–455; in 17th century, 492–497, 499, 500, 543, 546, 547
Anglo-Dutch wars, 544
Anglo-German rivalry, 829–830
Anglo-Japanese alliance (1902), 830, 875
Anne of Austria, regent of France, 483
Anne of Beaujeu (bō′zhû′), daughter of Louis XI of France, 389
Anne, Queen of England, 548, 549, 550
Anschluss (ahn′shlŏŏss), 932, 944. *See also* Austria, after 1918
Anthony of Bourbon, King of Navarre, 452
Anti-Comintern Pact (1936), 962
Antwerp (ănt′wûrp), 449, 466
Arabs (ăr′ăbz). *See* Mohammedanism
Aragon (ăr′ȧ·gŏn), Kingdom of, 385–386
Architecture, 535, 552, 566, 684, 688–691, 724, 877, 929, 933; in Renaissance, 370–371
Argentina (är′jĕn·tē′nȧ), 893

Ariosto (ä′rĕ·ôs′tō), Ludovico, 367
Aristocracy. *See* Nobles
Aristotle (ăr′ĭs·tŏt′'l), 367, 604, 610
Arkwright, Richard, 699
Armada, Spanish, 458–459, 590
Armaments, modern, 835–838, 852, 931–932, 944, 988
Arminianism (är·mĭn′ĭ·ăn·iz'm), 496
Army, French, 428, 480, 726; German, 576, 747–749
Arndt (ärnt), Ernst Moritz, 677
Arras (ăr′ăs), Treaty of (1579), 449–450
Art, in Renaissance, 367–371; decline of, in Spain in 17th century, 558; in 18th century, Russia, 572. *See also* Architecture, Literature, Painting, Music, Sculpture. *Also* Index of Charts and Illustrations
Arte di Lana, in Florence, 469
Arthur, son of Henry VII of England, 388
Artois (àr′twà′), Count of (Charles X of France), 632, 634
Artois, province of, 420, 510
Asia, and European powers, 585, 588, 815, 822–825, 868
Asiento (äs·ē·ĕn′tō), Treaty (1713), 559, 591, 593
Aspern (äs′pẽrn), battle of (1809), 670
Asquith (ăs′kwĭth), Herbert, 799
Assignats (ăs′ĭg·năt), 638
Associations Law, France (1901), 803
Astronomy, in the 16th century, 600, 602–604, 610–611
Atomic bomb, first use of, 978
Attila (ăt′ĭ·lȧ), 565
Attlee (ăt′lē), Clement R., 982
Auerstädt (ou′ẽr·shtĕt) battle of (1806), 668
Augsburg (ouks′bōōrᴋ), League of (1686), 538, **540**; War of (1689–97), 548, 560
Augsburg, Diet of (1530), 426, 427
Augsburg, Religious Peace of, 412, **427**, 501–502, 506
Augustine (ô′gŭs·tēn), Saint, 407
Augustus, Prince Christian, 570
Ausgleich (ous′glīᴋ). *See* Austria-Hungary after 1867
Austerlitz (ôs′tẽr·lĭts), battle of (1805), 666, 668
Australia (ôs·trāl′yȧ), 585, 812
Austria (ôs′trĭ·ȧ), in the 16th century, 395, 413; in 17th century, 503, 508, 553–554, 562, 563, 570, 574, 579–580, 583, 593; in 18th century, 578; and the French Revolution, 644–646; and Napoleon, 664, 676; in 19th

lviii

GENERAL INDEX

century, 666, 670, 677, 681, **687–689**, 696, 718, 720, 774–775, 827, 833; and World War I, 833–835, 841–842, 861; in 20th century, 959; Republic of, after 1918, 861, 944; united with Germany (1938), 959. *See also* Holy Roman Empire, Hungary, Austria-Hungary, Bohemia
Austria-Hungary (1867–1918), 751–752, 827, 841
Austrian Succession, War of (1740), 578, 579–580, 593
Auto-da-fe, 445
Avignon (ä'vē'nyôn'), annexed to France, 641
Azores (a·zōrz'), islands, 396
Azov (ä'zŏf), 568, 574
Aztecs (ăz'tĕks), 398

Babylonian (băb'ĕl·lō'nĭ·an), Captivity of the Church, 362
Babeuf (bȧ'bûf'), François Émile, 650
Backward countries. *See* Colonies, Imperialism
Bacon (bā'kŭn), Sir Francis, 605
Baden (bä'dĕn), 664; in 19th century, 749
Bagdad (băg'dăd), Railway, 833
Bailly (bȧ'yē'), Jean Sylvain, 634
Bakunin (bŭ·kōō'nyĭn), Michael, 760
Balance of power, 515–518, 578
Baldwin, Stanley, 917–918
Balfour (băl'fōōr), Arthur, 921
Balfour Declaration (on Palestine), 921
Balkan War (1912), 835, (1913), 835
Balzac (bȧl'zȧk'), Honoré de, 722
Bank of England, 550
Banking, in Later Middle Ages, 461–463
Barras (bȧ·ras'), Paul, Vicomte de, 649–650, 653
Bastille (bȧs·tēl'), capture of the, 634, 685
Battle of the Boyne (boin) (1690), 548
Battle of the Nations. *See* Leipzig, battle of
Bavaria (bȧ·vâr'ĭ·ȧ), in 17th century, 501, 507, 508; in 18th century, 578, **664–666**; in 19th century, 749, 808
Beachy Head, battle of (1690), 547
Beauharnais (bō'är'nē'), Eugène, 661, 664
Beauharnais, Hortense, 714
Beauharnais, Josephine. *See* Josephine, French Empress
Beccaria (bĕk'kä·rē'ä), Cesare, 619
Beethoven (bā'tō·vĕn), Ludwig, van, 688
"Beggars" of Holland, 448–449, 458. *See* Sea Beggars
Belgium (bĕl'jĭ·ŭm), in 18th century, 650, 655, 656, 663; in 19th century, 679, 708, 710, **708–710**, 768; in 20th century, **842–844**, 846, 928, 931, 933, 964, 967, 983. *See also* Netherlands, Spanish; Netherlands, Austrian; Netherlands, Kingdom of the United
Bellay (bĕ'lā'), Joachim du, 487

Benedetti (bā'nȧ·dāt'tē), Vincent, Count, 754
Bentham (bĕn'thăm), Jeremy, 702
Berchtold (bĕrĸ'tŏlt), Leopold von, 842
Berlin (bĕr·lēn'), in 17th century, 519; in 19th century, 826; in 20th century, 975
Berlin Decrees (Napoleon's), 668
Bernadotte (bûr'nȧ·dŏt'), Jean Baptiste Jules. *See* Charles XIV, of Sweden
Berne (bûrn), 415
Bernhardi (bĕrn·här'dē), Frederick von, 838
Berry (bĕ'rē'), Duke of, 693
Bessarabia (bĕs'ȧ·rā'bĭ·ȧ), 679, 931; annexed to Russia (1940), 967
Beust (boist), Friedrich Ferdinand Freiherr von, 749
Bevin, Ernest, 982
Bible, Greek New Testament, 383; and the humanists, 382–383; and the reformers, 349–350, 404, 408, 413, 440
Bill of Rights (1689), **547**, 549
Bishops' Wars, 496
Bismarck (bĭz'märk), Otto von, **748–754**, 774, 806, 808, 809–810, 818, 826–829, 833
Blanc (blän), Louis, 712
Blenheim (blĕn'ĭm), battle of (1704), 540
Blockade, Naval, in Napoleonic Wars, 668–670; in World War I, 847–848; in World War II, 970–978
"Bloody Assizes," 546
Boccaccio (bŏk·kät'chō), Giovanni, 364, 366
Boer (bōōr) War (1899–1902), 815, 825
Bohemia (bō·hē'mĭ·ȧ), in 17th century, 502–504, 507, 554; in 19th century, 718. *See also* Austria, Czechoslovakia
Boileau (bwȧ'lō'), Nicolas, 534
Boleyn (bōōl'ĭn), Anne, 417
Bolivar (bō·lē'vär), Simon, 893
Bologna (bō·lō'nyä), Concordat of (1516), 392, 428
Bolsheviki (bōl'shĕ·vē'kē), 850, **898–900**
Bombay (bŏm·bā'), acquired by the English, 543
Bonaparte (bō'nȧ·pärt), Jerome, 668
Bonaparte, Joseph, 661, 664
Bonaparte, Louis, 661, 671, 714–715, 721
Bonaparte, Lucien, 653, 661
Bonaparte, Napoleon. *See* Napoleon I, Emperor of the French
Borgia (bôr'jä), Cesare, 362
Borgia family, 362
Borodino (bō'rō·dyĕ·nô), battle of (1812), 671
Bosnia (bŏz'nĭ·ȧ), annexed by Austria-Hungary, 835
Bossuet (bō'sü·ē'), Bishop of Meaux, 527
Botticelli (bŏt'tē·chĕl'lē), Alessandro, 370, 559
Boulanger (bōō'län'zhā'), Georges, 802, 969

Boulogne (bōō'lôn'y'), 666
Bourbon (bōōr'bŭn), Charles, Constable of, 421, 428
Bourbon (bōōr'bŭn) Restoration (France), 672, 677, 693
Bourgeoisie, in Later Middle Ages, 373, 376; in the 16th century, 404–405, 412, 430; growing power of, 474–475; Dutch, 448; English, 490, 494–495; in 18th century, 616; in 19th century, 687, 698–700
Boyne (boin), battle of (1690), 548
Boxer Rebellion, China (1900), 825, 873–874
Boyle (boil), Robert, 603
Braddock (brăd'ŭk), Edward, British general, 593
Bramante (brä·man'tā) (Donato d'Agnolo), 371
Brandenburg (brăn'dĕn·bûrg), in 17th century, 507, 513, 519, 553, 566–575; in 18th century, 582. *See also* Prussia
Brandes (brăn'dĕs), Georg, 768
Brazil (brȧ·zĭl'), 400, 590, 893
Breitenfeld (brī'tĕn·fĕlt), battle of (1631), 507
Bremen (brā'mĕn), bishopric of, 509; city of, in 19th century, 668
Brest-Litovsk (brĕst'lyĕ·tôfsk'), treaty of (1918), 850, 898
Brethren of the Common Life, **380**, 383
Briand (brē·äɴ'), Aristide, 804, 927, 931–932, 937, 951
Briand-Kellogg (brē·äɴ'kĕl'ŏg), Peace Pact (1928), 892, 931, 937, 951. *See* Paris Peace Pact (1928)
Bright (brīt), John, 797
Brill, 449
Britain. *See* England, Scotland, Great Britain (after 1707)
British East India Company. *See* East India Company, British
British Empire, 591–592, **812–815**, **915–924**, 956, 965–967. *See* England, Great Britain
British North America Act (1867), 812
Brittany (brĭt'ȧ·nĭ), brought under French crown, 389
Browning, Robert, 734
Brunelleschi (brōō'nĕl·lĕs'kē), Filippo, 371
Bruno (brōō'nō), Giordano, 602
Brunswick (brŭnz'wĭk) Manifesto (1792), 642
Buckingham (bŭk'ĭng·ăm), Duke of, 495
Buffon (bü'fôn'), George Louis Leclerc, Comte de, 608
Bulgaria (bŭl·gâr'ĭ·ȧ), in 19th century, 773–775; in 20th century, 835, 844, 852, 861, 968, 983
Bundesrat (bōōn'dĕs·rät') of North German Confederation, 749; of German Empire, 806
Bunyan (bŭn'yȧn), John, 552
Burgundy (bûr'gŭn·dĭ), family, 389; duchy in the Middle Ages, 389; in the 16th century, 419–421; Free County of. *See* Franche-Comté
Burke (bûrk), Edmund, 685–686

Burma (bûr′mȧ), 815, 976
Burschenschaften (bōōr′shĕn·shäf′-tĕn), 690
Byrnes, James F., 982
Byron (bī′rŭn), George Gordon, Lord, 685, 687
Byzantine (bĭ·zăn′tĭn) Empire and Ottoman Turks, 426; influence on Russia, 566
Byzantium (bĭ·zăn′shĭ·ŭm). *See* Constantinople

Cabot (kăb′ŭt), John, 400
Cabral (kȧ·bräl′), Pedro Alvarez, 400
Cahiers (kȧ′yā′), 630
Calendar, Russian, 566, 568
Calvin (kăl′vĭn), John, **412–413**, 416, 452
Calvinism, in Switzerland, 413–416; spread of, 416; in England, 418; in France, 430, 452; in Germany, 427, 502, 509; in the Netherlands, 448; in Bohemia, 502. *See also* Reformed Church, Presbyterian Church
Cambodia (kăm·bō′dĭ·ȧ), 257
Cambray (käm′brĕ′), League of (formed 1508), 392; Treaty of (1529), 421
Campo Formio (käm′pŏ·fôr′mĕ·ō), treaty of (1797), 650, 652, 653, 655, 670
Campos (käm′pōz), Martinez, 771
Canada (kăn′ȧ·dȧ), French colonization, 592–593, 598; under British rule, 596, 598; Dominion of, 812, 922–924, 965
Canisius (kȧ·nĭsh′ŭs), Peter, Saint, 433
Canning (kăn′ĭng), George, 681
Cánovas del Castillo (kä′nŏ·väs thĕl käs·tē′ly·ō), Antonio, 771
Cape Verde (vûrd) Islands, 590
Capital, rise of, 370, **460–464**; and exploration, 464; revolutionizes commerce and industry, 466–470; and the state, 470–474; and society, 474–475; and the factory system, 699; conflict with labor, **787–790**; export to backward countries, 794, 946
Cappel (kȧ′pĕl′), Peace of (1531), 413
Capuchin (kăp′ū·chĭn) order, 434
Caraffa (kä·rä′fä), Cardinal, 433–434. *See* Paul IV, Pope
Carbonari (kär′bŏ·nä′rĕ), the, 695, 734
Carinthia (kȧ·rĭn′thĭ·ȧ), duchy, 395, 554
Carlowitz (kär′lō·vĭts), treaty of (1699), 556, 560
Carniola (kär·nyô′lä), duchy, in 17th century, 314, 395, 554
Carnot (kär′nō′), Lazare, 646
Carlsbad (kärlz′băd) Decrees (1819), 690
Carlyle (kär·līl′), Thomas, 722, 797
Castiglione (käs′tēl·yō′nȧ), Baldassare, 356
Castile (kăs·tēl′), kingdom of, 385
Catalonia (kăt′ȧ·lō′nĭ·ȧ), 559
Cateau-Cambrésis (kȧ′tō′ käN′brä-zē′), Treaty of (1559), 422, 450, 559

Catholic Church, abuses, 403; definition of doctrine at Trent, 440; in France, 428, 452–454; in the Netherlands, 448; in Scotland, 455; in Spain, 445; lands of, secularized in Germany, 501–503, 504, 507, 509; in 17th century, 543–550, 559; in 18th century, 572, 573, 574, **614**; and French Revolution, 638; and Napoleon, 658; in 19th century, 686, 695, 712, 726, **742–743**, 803, 809; in 20th century, 914. *See also* Papacy
Catholic Emancipation Bill (1829), 695, 702
Catholic League, in France, 454, 477; in Germany, 502, 503–506
Catholicism in England, in 16th century, 418, 455, 458; in 17th century, 492, 500
Catherine II (the Great), of Russia, **570–572**, 620
Cavaliers, English Royalist party, 497–499
Cavour (kä·vōōr′), Camillo di, 731, **736–737**, 739, 746
Cellini (chĕl·lē′nē), Benvenuto, 357
Center Party, in Germany, 809–810
Central powers, in World War I, 842–854. *See also* Germany, Austria
Cervantes Saavedra (thĕr·vän′täs sä′ä·vä′thrä), Miguel de, 558
Chamber of Deputies, French, 693; 706, 714, 747
Chamberlain (chām′bĕr·lĭn), Arthur Neville, 918, 960, 967
Charles Albert, of Sardinia, 720, 735–736, 737
Charles, Archduke of Austria, 540, 556, 559, 670, 671
Charles the Bold, Duke of Burgundy, 389
Charles Emmanuel, Duke of Savoy, 560
Charles I, of England, **494–499**, 504, 514, 542, 543, 624
Charles II, of England, 500, 514, **518**, **538**, 540, **542–546**
Charles II, of Spain, 520, 540, 558–559, 578
Charles III, of Spain, 620–621
Charles IV, of Spain, 669
Charles V, of Spain, 556, 575
Charles IV, Holy Roman Emperor, 463
Charles V, Holy Roman Emperor, 393, 395, 408, 411, **420–428**, 434, 438, 444–448
Charles VI, Holy Roman Emperor, 540, 556, 578
Charles VII, of France, 388–391
Charles VIII, of France, 363, **389–391**
Charles IX, of France, 452–454
Charles X, of France, **693–695**, 704, 707–708, 712
Charles XII, of Sweden, **569**, 671
Charles XIII, of Sweden, 765
Charles XIV, of Sweden, 671, 765
Charter of 1814 (French), 693
Chartist Movement (England), 704–706, 798–799

Chateaubriand (shȧ′tō′brē′äN′), François-René de, 686
Chemistry, in 18th century Russia, 568
Chemistry, in 17th century, 603, 610; in 19th century, 782
Chiang Kai-shek (jĕ·äng′ kī′shĕk′), 874, 882, 986
China (chī′nȧ), 395–396; in middle ages, 585, 588; in 19th and 20th centuries, 815–816, 818, 824, 873–882, 906, 918, 976, 978, 986
Chivalry, ideals of, 356
Christian (krĭs′chăn) IV, of Denmark, 504
Christian IX, of Denmark, 748, 766–767
Christian humanists, 381–383
Christianity. *See* Church, Catholic Church, Protestantism, etc.
Christina (krĭs·tē′nȧ), of Sweden, 507
Chrysoloras (krĭs′ŏ·lō′rȧs), Manuel, 366
Church, in Spain, 386; decline of, in Later Middle Ages, 375, 377. For Modern Period, *see* Catholic Church. *See also* Papacy, Heresy.
Church of England. *see* Anglican Church.
Churchill (chûrch′(h)ĭl), John, Duke of Marlborough, 540
Churchill, Winston, British Prime Minister, 967, 986
Cisalpine (sĭs·ăl′pīn) Republic, 650, 652, 655, 664
Cities, during Renaissance), in Italy, 424–425, 428–430 growth of, in modern times, **785–786**; in United States, 886
Civil Constitution of the Clergy (French), 638–639
Civil War, English, 497–499
Clemenceau (klā′mäN′sō′), Georges, 855, 857, 864, 928
Clement (klĕm′ĕnt) XI, Pope, 535, 560
Clergy, French, 527–528, 563, 613–614, 712–714, 726; German, 809
Clericalism, in 19th century, 742–743, 802–803
Cleves (klēvz)-Jülich succession, 480
Clive (klīv), Robert, 593
Code Napoléon (nȧ·pō′lĕ·ŭn), 658–659, 693
Coeur (kûr), Jacques, 464
Cognac (kō′nyăk), League of, 421
Colbert (kôl′bâr′), Jean Baptiste, 531, 535, 540, 582, 591
Colet (kŏl′ĕt), John, 382–383, 416
Coligny (dē kŏ′lē′nyē′), Gaspard de, 452–454
Collective Security, after World War I, 949–951, 956–958
Colonies, 707, 818–821; competition for, 590–592; British, 594, **812**, 918–922; Dutch, 590; French, 591–592, **816**; German, 818, 859; Italian, 816, 818, 911, 957–958, 983; Portuguese, 590–592, 771; Spanish, 590–592, 771, 891

GENERAL INDEX

Colonization, in 17th and 18th centuries, 590–592; in 19th century, 790–792, 811, 821; disputes, 820–825
Columbus (kŏ·lŭm′bŭs), Christopher, 385, 398, 588
Commerce, Saracen, 396; 354, 385, 388, 396–398, 464–470; introduction of capital, 468–469; in 16th century, English, 428, 456, 495; Dutch, 450, 458; French, 479; Spanish, 447; in 17th century, English, 500; French, 483, 543, 544, 548; in 18th century, 550, 558, 559, 560, 562, 565, 582, 585, 588–590, 591, 594, 599, 616–617, 698; in 19th century, 699, 726, 790, 792. *See also* Mercantilism
Commons, House of, contrast with Third Estate, 542; in 17th century, 548. *See also* Parliament
Commonwealth, in England, 499–500
Communist Party, founding of, 899; philosophy and program of, 900; 902–906; in Italy, 907; after World War II, 983. *See also* Bolsheviki, Soviets
Companies, business, origin of, 466–468
Concert of Europe (after 1815), 681–682, 695–697
Concordat (kŏn·kôr′dăt) (1801), 658, 803
Condé (kôN′dā′), Louis II, Prince of, 508, 532, 538
Condorcet (kôN′dôr′sĕ′), Marquis de, 651
Condotteri. *See* Mercenaries
Congo (kŏn′gō), Belgian, 768, 816, 820
Congress of Berlin (1878), 773, 827
Congress of Paris, 731
Congress of Vienna, 674–682, 686, 687, 692, 708, 732, 765, 855
Conservative Party, British, 704, 797, 917–918. *See also* Tories
Constantine (kŏn′stăn·tīn), Grand Duke, 692
Constantinople (kŏn′stăn·tĭ·nō′p'l), captured by Turks, 366; fall of, 520; captured by Turks, 566; and Russia, 574, 731; and Germany, 833; in World War I, 846; in World War II, 972
Constitutional government. *See* Parliament
Consulate, French (1799–1804), 655–656
Contorini (kōn′tä·rē′nĕ), Cardinal Gaspero, 433–434
Continental System (of Napoleon), 669–670
Conventicle Act, English (1664), 543
Convention of Westminster (1756), 579
Cook (kook), Captain James, 812
Copernicus (kŏ·pûr′nĭ·kŭs), Nicolas, 602, 604
Corn Laws, British, 704
Corneille (kôr′nâ′y′), Pierre, 534, 583
Corporation Act, English (1661), 543, 547
Cortez (kôr′tĕz) Hernando, 398, 590

Cosgrave (kŏz′grāv), William Thomas, 920
Cossa (kôs′sä), Baldassare. *See* John XXIII, Pope
Cotton, 524. *See also* Spinning, machines for
Council of Ancients, France, 649
Council of Five Hundred, France, 649
Counter-Reformation, defined, 432–433; effects of, 440–443, 453, 501–502. *See also* Reformation, Catholic Church, Society of Jesus, Trent, Council of
Covenant, in Scotland, First, 456; Second, 496
Cranmer (krăn′mĕr), Thomas, Arch., 497–500, 510
Crete (krēt), captured by Turks (1669), 556
Crimea (krī·mē′ȧ), ceded to Russia, 574, 754, 755
Crimean War (1854–56), 728–731
Cromwell (krŏm′wĕl), Oliver, 497–500, 510, 542, 547
Crompton, Samuel, 699
Crucé (croō·sā′), Émeric, 515
Culture, in Spain, 558; in Russia, 565, 566, 759
Currency Act (1765), 596
Custozza (koōs·tōt′sä), battle of (1848), 720, 736
Czar Liberator. *See* Alexander II, of Russia
Cyprus (sī′prŭs), 775
Czechoslovakia (chĕk′ŏ·slŏ·vä′kĭ·ȧ), 861, 864, 930–933, 959–960, 983. *See also* Bohemia, Austria

Daladier (dȧ′lȧ′dyā′), Edouard, 960
d'Alembert (à′läN′bâr′) Jean Le Rond, 572
Dalmatia (dăl·mā′shĭ·ȧ), 560
Danes (dānz). *See* Denmark
Danish War (1864), 751, 754, 806
Dante (dän′tĕ), Alighieri, 363–364, 559
Danton (däN′tôN′), Jacques, 642, 648
Danzig (dän′tsĭk), 857, 960
Dardanelles (där′dȧ·nĕlz′), in World War I, 846
Darwin (där′wĭn), Charles, 784
Dawes (dôz), Charles Gates, 926
Dawes Plan (1924), 926, 935, 937, 951
Deák (dĕ′äk), Francis, 749
Declaration of Independence (1776), 596
Declaration of Indulgence (1672), 544; (1687), 546; (1688), 547
Declaration of Lima (1938), 895
Declaration of Paris (1856), 731, 846
Declaration of the Rights of Man (1789), 629, 635
Deism, 610
Delcassé (dĕl′kȧ′sā′), Théophile, 829, 831
Democracy, in France, 802–803; in Germany, 806; in Great Britain, 795; in Italy, 732–740; 907–908; in the United States, 883–891. *See also* French Revolution, Parliament, Reform Bill, British
Denmark (dĕn′märk), in 17th cen-

tury, 504–506, 519; in 18th century, 569, 621; in 19th century, 679, 766–768; in 20th century, 763–764, 963, 965, 983
Depression, Economic (1929–33), 951–952
Descartes (dā′kärt′), René, 604–605
Desmoulins (dā′mōō′lăN′), Camille, 634, 637
Despots, in Italy, 357–358
De Valera (dĕv′ȧ·lâr′ȧ), Eamon, 920
Diaz (dē′ăs), Bartolomeo, 396–398
Dickens, Charles, 722
Diderot (dē′drō′), Denis, 572, 617–619, 686
Diet, of the Holy Roman Empire, 509, 554; of Germanic Confederation, 748
Diplomatic Revolution (1756), 580
Directory, French, 649–650, 653
Disarmament Conference (1932–33), 931, 956
Disease, in 17th century, 524; in 19th and 20th centuries, 786
Disraeli (dĭz·rā′lĭ), Benjamin (Earl of Beaconsfield), 775, 797, 814
Dissenters, English, 543, 546
Divine rights of kings, 491–492, 514–515, 518, 527, 612–613
Dollfuss (dŏl′foōs), Englebert, 944
Donatello (dŏn′ȧ·tĕl′lō) (Donati de Betto Bardi), 371
Donation of Constantine, 367
Dostoievski (dŭ·stŭ·yäf′skŭ·ĭ), Fedor Mikhailovich, 692
Dover (dō′vĕr), treaty of (1670), 538, 544
Drake (drāk), Sir Francis, 458–459
Dramatists, of 17th century, 534; of 19th century, 768
Dresden (drĕz′dĕn), treaty of (1745), 578
Dreyfus (drā′fŭs), Captain Alfred, 802–803
Droysen (droi′zĕn), Johann Gustav, 746
Dryden (drī′d'n), John, English poet, 552
Dual Empire. *See* Austria-Hungary
Ducos (dü′kō′), Pierre Roger, 653
Duma (doō′mä), Russian, 763, 764, 896
Dumas (dü′mȧ′), Alexandre, the younger, 724
Dupleix (dü′plĕks′), Joseph Francis, Marquis, 592, 593
Dutch Republic, 518–519, 590. *See also* Netherlands, Greek Orthodox Church
Dutch War (1672–78), 538

East India Company, British, 531, 591, 598, 812, 816, 868; Dutch, 531, 590; French, 592
East Indies, in the 20th century, 976; after 1945, 986
Ebert (ā′bĕrt), Friedrich, 934
Eck (ĕk), John, 408
Eckhart (ĕk′härt), Master, 380
Economic legislation, and Henry VII of England, 387–388
Economic Theory, 529, 700. *See also*

GENERAL INDEX

Mercantilism, *Laissez faire*, doctrine of, etc.
Education, in France, 651, 658–659, 724; in Germany, 690, 809; in Italy, 912–914; in Russia, 568, 572, 758, 900–902; in Scandinavian States, 768; in Spain, 558; in United States, 886–887; in 19th century, 782–785
Edward (ĕd′wĕrd) III, of Great Britain, 461, 918
Edward IV, of England, 387
Edward V, of England, 387
Edward VI, of England, 416, 418
Edward VII, of Great Britain, 829, 830
Egmont (ĕk′mônt), Lamoral of, 449
Egypt (ē′jĭpt), in 18th century, 653; in 19th century, 814–815; in 20th century, 920–921, 972
Elizabeth, Czarina of Russia, 570, 579–580
Elizabeth, Queen of England, **455–458**, 489
Emancipation of the serfs (1861), in Russia, 756
Ems (āms) dispatch, 752
Enghien (däN′gäN′), Duke d', 659
England, **387–388**, 400; in the 16th century, 416–418, 428–431, 454–459, **464–466**, 468–470, 472–474; in 17th century, 489–500, 518, 540, **542–552**, 559, 562, 590–591; in 18th century, 592–599; for period after 1707, see Great Britain
English East India Company. See East India Company, British
Enlightened despots. See Frederick II, of Prussia; Catherine II, of Russia; Joseph II, of Austria; etc.
Entente (äN′tänt′) Powers, and World War I, 842–843
Entrepreneur, rise of the, 466–468
Erasmus (ĕ·răz′mŭs), Desiderius, **383**, 405, 410, 413, 416
Eritrea (ĕr′ĕ·trā′ä), 957, 972
Estates, in 16th century, of Holland, 449. See States General.
Este (ĕs′tā), family, 363
Estonia (ĕs·tō′nĭ·à), added to Russia (1721), 569; united with U.S.S.R. (1940), 967
Ethiopia (ē′thĭ·ō′pĭ·à), 957–958, 965; Italian influence in, 818; in World War II, 972
Eugene (ū·jēn′), of Savoy, Prince François, 540, 556, 560
Eugénie (ū′zhā′nē′), French Empress, 724, 726
Evangelican Union, 502
Exclusion Bill (1679), English, 544
Exploration, in 15th and 16th centuries, **395–400**, 464–466, 585, 588, 590
Eylau (ī′lou), battle of (1807), 668

Factory system, 699–700; Act (1833), 706. See also Industry, modern
Falloux (fa·lōō′) Law (1850), France, 726
Famine, reduction of, in modern period, 781
Farnese (fär·nā′sà), Alexander, Duke of Parma, 450

Fascism, Italian, 907–914. See Italy, in the 20th century
Fashoda (fä·shō′dä) affair, 820
Federigo, Duke of Urbino, 356
Ferdinand (fûr′dĭ·nănd) of Aragon, 385–386, 392, 395
Ferdinand I, Holy Roman Emperor, 426, 428, **502**
Ferdinand I, of the Two Sicilies, 681, 696, 718, 720
Ferdinand II, of the Two Sicilies, 720, 735, 736
Ferdinand VII, of Spain, 681, 695–696, **771**
Ferrara, duchy of, 359, 363
Feudalism, in England, 387; in Castile, 385; decay of, 373–375, 405; destruction of, in France, 634–635. See also Nobles Monarchy
Feudal warfare, 373
Fichte (fĭĸ′tĕ), Johann Gottlieb, 677
Ficino (fĕ·chē′nō), Marsilio, 366
Finland (fĭn′lànd), 570, 679, 762, 766, 959, 967–968, 974, 983
First Estate. See Clergy
Five-Year Plan, Russia, 903–905
Flanders (flan′dĕrz), in 16th century, 420–421, 469, 480
Flaubert (flō′bâr′), Gustave, 724
Florence (flŏr′ĕns), in the Age of the Renaissance, 356, **360–362**, 366, 370, 421, 424, 469; in 17th century, 559–560. See also Italy
Florence, Council of (1439), 366
Florida (flŏr′ĭ·dà), 398
Foch (fôsh), General Ferdinand, 852
Formosa (fôr·mō′sà), 873
Fourier (fōō′ryā′), François Marie, 712
"Fourteen Points," in World War I, 454, 855–856, **862–863**
France (fràns), 590–591, 950, 956; in the High Middle Ages, 359; in the Later Middle Ages, **388–392**; in the 16th century, 400, 419, 428–430, **450–454**, 464; in 17th century, **476–488**, **507–510**, 518, 526–553, 558, 560, 562; in 18th century, 568, 570, 575, 578, 579–580, 591–593, 596, 598, 612–620, 621, 627; in Revolutionary era, 629–639; under Napoleon, 652–662; in 19th century, 681, 698, 707, 711–714, 728, 749, 773, 801–806, 816, 826–828, 831, 833, 842–844; in 20th century, 925–933, 964–965, 967; after World War I, 949–951; empire of, 592–594, 831; foreign relations, 828; liberation of (1944), 974; natural frontiers of, 597
Franche Comté (fräNsh′kôN′tà′), in the Later Middle Ages, 389–391, 393; in the 16th century, 420, **480**; in the 17th century, 461, 538
Francis I, of Austria, 666, 670, 676, 677
Francis II, Holy Roman Emperor. See Francis I, of Austria
Francis II, of the Two Sicilies, 739
Francis, Duke of Guise, 452
Francis Joseph I, of Austria (1848–

67), and of Austria-Hungary (1867–1916), 720, 738, 749, 852
Francis I, of France, 392, 417, 420–422, 428, 452
Francis II, of France, 452
Franciscan (frăn·sĭs′kăn), order, 434
Franco (fräng′kō), General Francisco, of Spain, 772, 958
Franco-Prussian War (1870–71), 751, 754, 826
Franco-Russian Accord of 1935, 962
Franco-Russian Convention (1894), 828–829
Frankfort (frăngk′fĕrt) Assembly (1848–49), 717
Frankfort, treaty of (1871), 754, 801
Franklin, Benjamin, 608
Franz Ferdinand (fränts fûr′dĭ·nănd), Archduke of Austria, assassinated, 841
Frederica, Sophia Augusta. See Catharine II (the Great) of Russia.
Frederick I, of Prussia, 576
Frederick II (the Great) of Prussia, 570, 572, 574, **576–578**, 579, **580**, **582–583**, 593, 620, 661, 960
Frederick II, Holy Roman Emperor, and King of Sicily, 363
Frederick III, German Emperor, 810
Frederick III, Holy Roman Emperor, 393
Frederick Augustus I, of Saxony, 569, 679
Frederick William, of Brandenburg (the "Great Elector"), 519, 538, **575–576**
Frederick William I, of Prussia, 576
Frederick William III, of Prussia, 593, 666, 668, 677, 690
Frederick William IV, of Prussia, 717, 718, 744, 746–747
Frederick the Wise of Saxony, 407–408
Freedom of the press, in England, 552; in France, 706
French and Indian War, 593. See Seven Years' War
French Revolution (1789), 550; 629–642; (1830), 706–709; (1848), 712–715
Friedland (frēt′länt), battle of (1807), 668
Friedrich (frē′drĭĸ), Kaspar David, 687
Fronde (frôNd), the, 484, 532
Fugger (fōōg′ĕr) family, bankers, 461–463, 466

Galilei (gä′lĕ·lâ′ĕ) Galileo (gä′lĕ·lâ′ō), 600, 602–603, 605
Gallican Church. See Clergy, French
Gallican liberties, 487–488
Gama (gä′mà), Vasco da (dà), 398, 588
Gambetta (găm·bĕt′à), Léon, 802
Gandhi (gän′dē), Mohandas K., 870–872
Garibaldi (gär′ĭ·bôl′dĭ), Guiseppe, 736–739, 751
General Confederation of Labor, French, 804
Geneva (jĕ·nē′và), 415–416, 866; in 17th century, 559

GENERAL INDEX

Genoa (jĕn′ō·à), 360, 424, 559–560. *See also* Italy
Gentz (gĕnts), Frederick von, 674
Geography, early knowledge of, 395–400, 585
George I, of Great Britain, 550
George III, of Great Britain, 596, 624
George VI, of Great Britain, 918
German Empire. *See* Germany
German government. *See* Germany
German language, 583
Germanic Confederation, in 19th century, 690, 717, 750
Germanies, the. *See* Germany
Germany (jûr′mȧ·nĭ), in the Later Middle Ages, **392–395**; in the 16th century, 405–412, 424, 428, 443; in 17th century, 509, 519; in 18th century, **575–583**; 620; and French Revolution, 642–646, 677; and Napoleon, 664–673; in 19th century, 677, 708, 715, 744–754, 806; after 1871, 806–810, 826–831, 833, 856–859, 934–944; after World War I, 841–854, 857–859, 934–944, 950–955, 958–959, 974–975; in World War II, 963–975; after 1945, 984–986. *See also* Austria, Prussia, Holy Roman Empire
Ghent (gĕnt), 511
Ghent, Pacification of (1576), 449
Ghibellines (gĭb′ĕ·lĭnz), in Italy, 357, 359
Ghiberti (gē·bĕr′tē), Gian Matteo, 371
Gibraltar (jĭ·brôl′tēr), acquired by British, 541, 591; as control port, 970
Gilbert (gĭl′bẽrt), William, 602
Gioberti (jō·bĕr′tē), Vincenzo, 735
Giotto (jôt′tō) di Bondone, 370
Giovanna (jō·vän′nä) II, of Naples, 363
Gironde (zhē′rônd′), party of the, 641–642, 644, 674
Gladstone (glăd′stōn), William Ewart, 795, 797
"Glorious Revolution" of 1688–89 (England), 540
Goethe (gû′tẽ), Johann Wolfgang von (fŏn), 583, 687, 715
Gogol (gô′gŭl·y′), Nikolai Vasilievich, 692
Gonzaga (gŏn·dzä′gä), family of, 363
Gothard (gŏth′härd), Saint, battle of (1663), 556
Government of India Act (1919), 870; (1935), 872
Government of National Defense, French (1870), 746
Granada (grȧ·nä′dȧ), Kingdom of, 385
Grand Alliance (1702), 540
Grand Duchy of Tuscany. *See* Italy
Grand Duchy of Warsaw. *See* Poland
Granvelle (gräɴ′vĕl′), Cardinal, 448
Great Britain. For period prior to 1707, *see* England
Great Britain, in 18th century, 568, 570, 575, 578–580, 591–592, 624;
and French Revolution, 644; and Napoleon, 653, 655, 656, 666, 668; in 19th century, 679, 681, 696, 698–706, 729–731, 773–775, 792, 794, 795–801; in 20th century, 829–830, 833, 835, 842, 915–924, 949, 970; in World War I, 841–854; in World War II, 963–978; empire of, 592–594, **812–816**, 821, 946; foreign policy of, 695, 708, 829; and naval blockade, 965–967. *See also* England
Great Elector. *See* Frederick William, of Brandenburg
"Great Fear, the," (1789), 635
Great Northern War, 569, 765
Greece (grēs), and Treaty of Carlowitz, 560; and War of Independence, 697–698; in 19th century, 696–697, 710, 773–775; in 20th century, 861, 959, 972, 983, 988
Greek culture, revived in Renaissance, 366–367
Greek Orthodox Church, in Russia, 566, 568; in Lithuania, 573; and the Catholic Church, 352, 366
Grenville (grĕn′vĭl), George, 594, 722
Grey (grā), Charles, 2d Earl, 704, 706
Grey, Sir Edward, 842–843
Grieg (grĭg), Edvard, 768
Groote (grōt), Gerard, 380
Grotius (grō′shĭ·ŭs), Hugo, 515
Guadalcanal (gwä·tʜäl·kä·näl′), 978
Guarino da Verona (gwä·rē′nō dä vä·rō′nä), 356
Guelfs (gwĕlfs), in Italy, 357
Guicciardini (gwēt′chär·dē′nē), Francesco, 367
Guild system, break-up of, 373–375; survivals of, in 18th century, 621
Guise (gēz) family, 452–453
Guizot (gē′zō), François, 711–712, 714
Gunpowder Plot (1605), 492
Gustavus (gŭs·tā′vŭs) III, of Sweden, 506–508, 572, 621
Gutenberg (gōō′tĕn·bĕrк), John, 381

Haakon (hô′kŏn) VII, of Norway, 766
Habeas Corpus Act (1679), 546, 549; suspended, 695
Hague (hāg) Conference, 836; Tribunal, 864
Halley (hăl′ĭ), Edmund, 603
Hamburg (hăm′bûrg), 670
Hamid Abdul (hä·mēd′ äb′dül), II, of Turkey, 835
Hanover (hăn′ō·vẽr) and Sweden, 569; in Seven Years' War, 579; annexed to Prussia, 749
Hanoverian succession (England), 548–549
Hapsburg (hăps′bûrg), family in the Later Middle Ages, 393–395; in 16th century, 421–426; in 17th century, 480–483, 484, 553–559, 562; in 18th century, 577–582; in 19th century, 718–720, 738, 748–749; in 20th century, 841–842, 861
Hardenberg (här′dĕn·bĕrк), Karl August, Prince, 671
Hardie (här′dĭ), Keir, 799
Hargreaves, James, 699
Harvey (här′vĭ), William, 603
Hawkins (hô′kĭnz), Sir John, 458
Hay, John, 892
Hebrew language in Renaissance, 382
Heine (hī′nĕ), Heinrich, 698, 711
Henry of Bourbon, King of Navarre, 453–454. *See also* Henry IV, of France
Henry, Duke of Guise, 453–454
Henry the Navigator, Prince, 396
Henry VI, of England, 387
Henry VII, of England, 387–388, 400
Henry VIII, of England, 388, 416–418, 420–421, 430–431
Henry II, of France, 422, 427, 450, 452
Henry III, of France, 454
Henry IV, of France, 447, 453–454, 476–480. *See also* Henry of Bourbon
Henry VII, Holy Roman Emperor, 359
Heresy, in the 16th century, 367, 430, 445
Hermandad (ĕr′män·däth′), 385
Herriot (ĕ′ryō′), Edouard, 932
Herzegovina (hĕr′tsĕ·gŏ·vē′nä), annexed by Austria-Hungary, 835
Herzen (hĕr′tsĕn), Alexander, 721, 759
Hesse-Darmstadt (hĕs′ĕ därm′shtät), 664; in 19th century, 749
Hindenburg (hĭn′dĕn·bōōrк), Paul von, 844, 938, 940, 942
Hirohito (hē·rō·hē·tō), Emperor, 986–987
Hiroshima (hē′rō·shē′mà), bombed, (1945), 978
Hitler (hĭt′lẽr), Adolf, 933, 935, **938–944**, 952–954, 957–960, 965, 968, 975, 982
Hobbes (hŏbz), Thomas, 514, 605
Hohenlinden (hō′ĕn·lĭn′dĕn), battle of (1800), 655
Hohenzollerns (hō′ĕn·tsŏl′ernz). *See* Brandenburg, Prussia
Holland. Dutch Republic in World War II, 964. *See* Netherlands, Dutch Republic
Holowczyn, battle of (1708), 569
Holstein (hŏl′shtīn), in 19th century, 717, 748
Holy Alliance, The, 681
Holy League, formed by Pope Julius II, 392
Holy Roman Empire, in the Later Middle Ages, 392; in the 16th century, 421; in 17th century, 502, 509, 575; dissolved, 670, 677. *See also* Germany, Italy, Hapsburgs
Homer (hō′mẽr), 610
Hongkong (hŏng′kŏng′), 873
Hospitals, in 18th century Russia, 568, 572
Hoorn (hōōrn), Count of, 449
Hoover, Herbert, 927, 948
House of Commons. *See* Commons, House of, Parliament, etc.
House of Lords. *See* Lords, House of, and Parliament

Hubertusburg (hōō·bĕr′tōōs·bōōrĸ), Peace of (1763), 580
Hudson Bay Territory, 541, 591
Hudson's Bay Company, 544
Hugo (hū′gō), Victor, 687, 724
Huguenots (hū′gĕ·nŏts), in the 16th century, 453, 477; in the 17th century, 482–483, 495; expelled from France, 535, 537; flight to England, 546. See also Nantes, Edict of, Protestantism in France, etc.
Hull, Cordell, 982
Humanism, in Italy, 364–366; in northern Europe, 380–383, 413, 486; Christian, 404, 410, 416
Humanitarianism, 687
Hungary (hŭng′gȧ·rĭ), in the 16th century, 502; in 17th century, 554, 556; in 19th century, 717–720; in 20th century, 861, 983
Huss (hŭs), John, 410
Hutton (hŭt′'n), Ulrich von, 382
Huxley, Thomas Henry, 784

Ibsen (ĭb′s'n), Henrik, 768
Iceland (īs′lănd), 766
Illyrian (ĭ·lĭr′ĭ·ȧn) Provinces, 670
Imperialism, 585–599, 811–825, 868–882, 920–922, 928, 943, 945–949
Incas. See Indians, Peru
Index of Prohibited Books, 442
India (ĭn′dĭ·ȧ), 585–594, 598, 653, 812–815, 868–873
Indians, in 16th century, 585; in 18th century, 596
Indies, West and East, in 16th century, 588; in 17th century, 590–591; in 18th century, 598
Individualism, in Renaissance, 356, 367–370, 375
Indo-China (ĭn′dō·chī′nȧ), French, 816
Indulgences, 407–408
Industrial Revolution, 698–699, 706, 746, 788, 790, 792, 808, 915. See also Industry, modern
Industry, modern, 698, 700, 779, 788, 945; in 16th century, 428, 468–470; in 17th century, 479, 483; in Belgium, 768; in France, 706, 726; in Germany, 746–747, 808–810, 937; in Great Britain, 698–700, 779–780; in Italy, 912; in Russia, 762, 899–905; in the United States, 886, 890, 951, 972–974
Inner Mongolia (mŏng·gō′lĭ·ȧ), 878
Innocent VIII, Pope, 362
Innocent XI, Pope, 560
Innocent XII, Pope, 528
Inquisition, in Spain, 386, 433, 558, 621; after Trent, 442–443, 445
Insurance Laws, in Germany, 810
Intellectual Revolution, 600–603. See also Science, modern
Intendants, 483
Intergovernmental debts, 946
International, First and Second, 790
Iraq (ē·räk′), in 20th century, 921, 972
Iran (ē·rän′), in 20th century, 972. See also Persia

Ireland (īr′lănd), in 17th century, 500, 547, 548; in 18th century, 598; in 19th century, 598; in 20th century, 801, 918–920
Irish Free State. See Ireland
Irish Nationalist Party, 800–801
Irish Nationalists, in British Parliament, 800
Isabella (iz·ȧ·bĕl′ȧ) of Castile, 385–386
Isabella II, of Spain, 752, 771
Islam. See Mohammedanism
Israelites. See Jews
Italian Somaliland (sȯ·mä′lē·lănd′), 958
Italy (ĭt′ȧ·lĭ), in the Renaissance, 391–392; in the 16th century, 420, 421, 424, 440; in 17th century, 520, 556, 559–560; in 18th century, 559–560, 652, 663; and Napoleon, 650, 655, 664; in 19th century, 677, 679–681, 708, 720–721, 732, 795, 827–828; in 20th century, 842, 846, 907–914, 949, 950, 954, 957–958, 960–962, 964, 970–972, 975, 983
Ivan (ē·vän′) III (the Great), of Russia, 566
Ivan IV (the Terrible), of Russia, 566, 568

Jacobin (jăk′ȯ·bĭn) Club, 643–644, 649, 686
Jagellon (yä·gĕl′ŭn) dynasty, 573
Jamaica (jȧ·mā′kȧ), 520
James I, of England, 491–494, 503–504, 543, 548
James II, of England, 540, 544, 546–547, 548, 624
James III, of England, 548
James VI, of Scotland, 548. See James I, of England
James, Duke of York. See James II, of England
Jansenists, 487, 535, 537
Japan (jȧ·păn′), 585, 824–825, 830, 842, 873, 874–882, 892, 906, 917, 949, 957, 970–972, 975–978, 986–987
Japanese Mandates (1919), 878
Jassy (yäs′ē), treaty of (1792), 574
Java (jä′vȧ), in 16th century, 588; in 17th century, 590
Jeffreys (jĕf′rĭz), George, Baron, 546
Jellachich (yĕl′ȧ·chĭch), Joseph, Count, 720
Jellicoe (jĕl′ĭ·kō), Admiral John Rushworth, 848
Jena (yā′nä), battle of (1806), 668, 671
Jenkins's Ear, War of (1739), 593
Jesuits. See Society of Jesus
Jews, 386, 461, 762, 921–922, 938, 954
Joanna, daughter of Ferdinand and Isabella, 393–395
John IV, of Portugal, 520
Johnson Act, United States (1934), 892
Joseph I, of Austria, 556 n
Joseph II, of Austria, 572, 620, 661
Josephine, Empress, of the French, 652, 661, 670, 671
Jugoslavia. See Yugoslavia

Julius (jōōl′yŭs) II, Pope, 359, 370, 392
Julius III, Pope, 437, 438
Justices of the peace, 430–431
Jutland (jŭt′lănd), battle of (1916), 848

Kapp (käp), Waldmar, 935
Kay, John, 699
Kellogg (kĕl′ôg), Frank B., 932; Kellogg Pact, 932
Kempis (kĕm′pis), Thomas à, 380
Kepler (kĕp′lẽr), Johannes, 602–604
Kerensky (kĕ·rĕn′skĭ), Alexander, 896–898
Kiauchow (jyou′jō′), 878
Kiev (kē′yĕf), 566
"King of Rome," son of Napoleon I, 661
Kingdom of the Netherlands. See Netherlands, Dutch Republic
Kingdom of the Two Sicilies, united to the Italian kingdom, 739
Kingship. See Monarchy
Kitchener (kĭch′ĕ·nẽr), General Herbert, 820
Kiuprili (kōō′prē·lē′), Mohammed, 556; Achmed, 556
Knights, of the Holy Roman Empire, Chivalry
Knox (nŏks), John, 456
Koch (kōk), Robert, 784, 785
Königgrätz (kû′nĭk·grĕts′), battle of (1866), 749
Korea (kō′rē·ä′), 873, 878, 986
Körner (kûr′nẽr), Theodor, 677
Kosciusko (kŏs′ĭ·ŭs′kō), Thaddeus, 574
Kossuth (kŏ′shōōt), Louis, 720
Krudener (krü′dĕ·nẽr), Baroness von, 690
Kublai Khan (kōō′blī kän′), Tartar Emperor, 395
Kuchuk-Kainardji (kü·chük′kī′-när·jȧ), treaty of (1774), 574
Kulturkampf (kōōl·tōōr′kämpf′), 742, 809
Kunersdorf (kōō′nẽrs·dôrf), battle of (1759), 580
Kuomintang (gwō′mĭn·täng′), Chinese Nationalist Party, 874

Labor Movement, British, 799
Labor Party, British, 799, 801, 917
Lafayette (lȧ′fī·ĕt′), Marie Joseph Motier, Marquis de, 630, 637, 707
La Fontaine (lȧ fôɴ′tĕn′), Jean de, 534
Laibach (lī′bäĸ), congress of (1821), 679, 681, 696
Lainez (lī·näth′), Diego, 436, 440
Laissez faire (lĕ′sā′fâr′), doctrine of, 599
Landcastrian family, 387
Landtage. See Estates
Language, English, in the 16th century, 491
Lamartine (lȧ′mȧr′tēn′), Alphonse, 712, 724
Language, French, development of, 486–487; elegance of, 534
Lassalle (lä·säl′), Ferdinand, 808

GENERAL INDEX

Lateran (lăt′ẽr·ăn), Treaty (1929), 914
Latin America, in 19th and 20th centuries, 893–895, 959
Latin literature, in Renaissance, **363–367, 380–383**. See Literature
Latvia (lăt′vĭ·å), 959; united with U.S.S.R. (1940), 967
Laud (lôd), William, Archbishop of Canterbury, 495–496
Launay (lō′nā′), Bernard René, 634
Lausanne (lō·zăn′) Settlement (1932), 927, 942
La Vallière (lā vä′lyâr′), Louise Françoise de, 534
Law, Russian, 572
League of Nations, 864–867, 880, 892, 938; Germany's withdrawal, 942–943, 950–951, 956–957, 981
Lebrun (lẽ·brûɴ′), Charles, 535
Leeuwenhoek (lā′věn·hōōk), Anton van, 603
Lefèvre d'Étaples (lẽ·fě′vr' dả·tá′pl'), James, 382–383
Legion of Honor, 659
Legislation, criminal, 522–524, 616, 658, 695
Legislative Assembly, French (1791–92), 642
Leibnitz (līp′nĭts), Gottfried Wilhelm von, 604
Leipzig (līp′sĭk), battle of (1813), 672
Lenin (lyā′nyĭn), Nicolai, 898–899, 903, 956
Leningrad (lěn′ĭn·grǎd), 968
Le Notre (lẽ·nō′tr'), André, 532
Leo X, Pope, 362, 370, 392, 407–408, 421, 433
Leo XIII, Pope, 742–743, 804, 914
Leopardi (lā′ō·pär′dě), Giacomo, 734
Leopold I, Holy Roman Emperor, 519, 538, 553–554, 556
Leopold I, of Belgium, 768
Leopold II, of Belgium, 769
Leopold of Hohenzollern-Sigmaringen, 752, 771
Lepanto (lě·păn′tō), battle of (1571), 447
Leuthen (loi′těn), battle of (1757), 580
Liberal Party, British, 704, 797
Liberalism, French, 696, 728
Liberum veto, in Polish Diet, 574
Libya (līb′ĭ·å), 818, 911, 965, 972
Ligurian (lĭ·gū·rĭ·ăn) Republic, 652, 655, 664
Linnaeus (lĭ·nē′ŭs), Carolus, 608
Lisbon (lĭz′bǎn), 520, 669
Literature, English, in 16th century, 489; French, in the Age of Louis XIV, 484–487, in 17th century, 534–535, 550–552, 558; in 18th century, 572, 582–583, 610–611, 617–619, 624–625; in 19th century, 687–692, 722, 724, 768; in 20th century, 799
Lithuania (lĭth′ū·ā′nĭ·å), 573, 898, 959, 960, 967
Livingstone, David, 822
Lloyd (loid) George, David, 799, 855–858, 917, 928

Locarno (lō·kär′nō) Conference (1925), 951
Locarno Pacts (1925), 931, 937, 951
Locke (lŏk), John, 552, 611, 624
Lollards (lŏl′ẽrdz), 377
Lombardy. See Italy
London, in 17th century, 543, 560; in 19th century, 817
London, treaty of (1832), 773; secret treaty of (1915), 856
Lords, House of, in the 16th century, 490; abolished by the Rump Parliament, 499; powers curtailed, 797, 800
Lorraine (lŏ·rān′), duchy of, in the Middle Ages, 389; acquired by France, 578; annexed to German Empire, 754; reannexed to France, 856–857. See also Alsace
Lotharingia. See Lorraine
Louis I (lōō′ĭs), of Portugal, 772
Louis II, King of Hungary and Bohemia, 426
Louis IV, Holy Roman Emperor, 345
Louis XI, of France, 389
Louis XII, of France, 391
Louis XIII, of France, 480–482
Louis XIV, of France, 483–484, 510, 511, 518, **526–541**, 543, 544, 546, 547, 548, 550, 553, 560, 591, 593, 600, 610, 612–613
Louis XV, of France, 541, 579, 613, 617, 621
Louis XVI, of France, 621, **629–639**, 643, 686
Louis XVII, the dauphin, 649 n., 671
Louis XVIII, of France, 649, 671–672, 677, 685, 693
Louis, Duke of Orléans, 360
Louis of Nassau, 449
Louis Napoleon Bonaparte. See Napoleon III
Louis Philippe (lōō′ĭs fē′lēp′), King of the French, 707–710, 711, 714, 724
Louvois (lōō′vwå′), François Michel le Tellier, Marquis de, 532
Louvre (lōō′vr'), Palace of the, 532
Loyola (lŏ·yō′lä), Saint Ignatius, 436–438
Ludendorff (lōō′děn·dôrf), Erich von, 850–852, 935
Lunéville (lü′nå′vēl′), treaty of (1801), 655, 664, 666, 670
Lusitania (lū′sĭ·tā′nĭ·å), torpedoed, 847
Luther (lōōt′ẽr), Martin, 380, **403–412**, 424–426, 440, 690
Lutheran Church, organization, 410–411
Lutheranism, compared with Zwingli's doctrines, 413; compared with Calvinism, 415; in England, 417, 418; in France, 434; in Germany, 424–426, 437, 502; in Scandinavia, 412. See Protestantism
Lutter (lōōt′ẽr), battle of (1526), 504
Lützen (lüt′sěn), battle of (1632), 507
Luynes (lü·ēn′), Duke of, 482
Luxemburg (lŭk′sěm·bûrg), 389, 393, 420, 538, 964

Lyell (lī′ěl), Sir Charles, **782**
Lytton (lĭt′'n) Report (1932), 957

MacArthur, General Douglas, 986–987
MacDonald, James Ramsay, 917–918, 932
Machiavelli (mä′kyä·věl′lě), Nicolo, 358, 367
MacMahon, Marshal, Duke of Magenta, 802
Madrid (măd′rĭd), 559
Madrid, treaty of (1526), 421
Magdeburg (măg′dĕ·bûrg), archbishopric of, 506–507, 509
Magellan (må·jěl′ăn), Ferdinand, 400, 588
Maginot (mä′jĭ·nō′) Line, 963
Magyars (măg′yär), in 19th century, 749. See also Hungary
Mahan (må·hăn′), Alfred Thayer, 847–848
Maintenon (măɴ′t'·nôɴ′), Madame de, 534
Maistre (dẽ mâ′tr'), Joseph de, 686
Majorca (må·jôr′kå), 385
Malabar (măl′å·bär), 398
Malacca (må·lăk′å), 398
Malplaquet (mål′plå′kě′), battle of (1709), 540
Malthus (măl′thŭs), Thomas, 700
Manchukuo (män′jō′kwō′). See Manchuria
Manchuria (măn·chōōr′ĭ·å), 873, 878, 880, 892, 906, 957, 986
Manfred, King of Sicily, 363
Manor, **190–194**. See also Feudalism, Agriculture
Mansart (mäɴ′sär′), Jules Hardouin, 532, 535
Mantua (măn′tů·å), battle of (1797), 652
Mantua, marquisate of, 359, 363
Manuel (mä′nōō·ěl) II, of Portugal, 772
Manuscript, 366
Manzoni (män·dzō′ně), Alessandro, 734
Marat (må′rå′), Jean Paul, 637
March Revolution (1917). See Russia, in 20th century
Marengo (må·rěng′gō), battle of (1800), 655
Margaret of Parma, 448
Maria (mä·rē′ä) II, of Portugal, 772
Maria Theresa, of Austria, 574, 577–579
Maria Theresa, Queen of France, 518, 534, 538
Marie Antoinette (må′rē′ äɴ′twå′-nět′), Queen of France, 621, **630–632**, 648
Marie Louise, wife of Napoleon I, 661, 662
Marignano (mä′rē·nyä′nō), battle of (1515), 392
Marne (märn), first battle of the (1914), 843; second battle of the (1918), 852
Marshall, George C., 982, 988
Marsiglio (mär·sē′lyǒ) of Padua, 404

GENERAL INDEX

Marston (mär′stŭn) Moor, battle of (1644), 497
Marx (märks), Karl, 788–790, 803, 808, 900
Mary of Burgundy, 393
Mary of Guise, Regent of Scotland, 452, 456
Mary, Queen of England with William III, 546–547, 548, 624
Mary Stuart, Queen of Scotland, 452, **456–458**
Mary Tudor, Queen of England, 417, 418, **455–458**
Masaccio (mä·zät′chō) Tommaso Guidi, 370
Massacre of Glencoe, 548
Mathematics, in 17th century Russia, 568; modern, 603–604
Matteotti (mät′tä·ôt′tē), Giacomo, 910
Matthias (mă·thī′ăs), Holy Roman Emperor, 502–503
Maurice (mô′rĭs), Duke of Saxony, 427
Maurice of Nassau, 450
Maximilian (măk′sĭ·mĭl′ĭ·ăn), Emperor of Mexico, 749
Maxmilian, Duke of Bavaria, 501–502, 504
Maxmilian I, Holy Roman Emperor, 389, 392–393
Maxmilian II, Holy Roman Emperor, 502
Mazarin (mȧ′zȧ′răN′), Cardinal, 476, **483–484**, 508–510, 514, 526, 527, 528
Mazzini (mät·sē′nē), Joseph, 734–735, 736
Medici (měd′ē·chē), Catherine de', Queen of France, **452–454**
Medici, Cosimo de', 356, 362, 366
Medici, Lorenzo de', 356–357, 362–363, 366–367
Medici, Marie de', Regent of France, 480
Medici, Piero de' (the elder), 362
Medici, Piero de' (the younger), 362, 391
Medici family, 362–363, 391, 392, 461
Medicine, modern, 784
Medieval civilization, decline of, 354–359, **372–375**
Melanchthon (mē·langk′thŭn), Philip, 434
Mendel (měn′děl), Gregor, 743
Mercantilism, **471–474, 531**, 582, 594, 598–599
Mercenaries, Italian, **358–360**; German, 421, 428, 449; Swiss, 428
Merchant Guilds. See Guild system
Mérimée (mȧ′rē′mȧ′), Prosper, 724
Methodism, 686
Methuen (mě·thū′ěn) Treaty, The (1703), 559 n.
Metternich (mět′ěr·nĭκ), Klemens Wenzel Nepomuk Lothar, Prince von, 676–677, 679, 690, 692, 697, 708, 718, 720
Metz (měts), 538, 752
Mexico (měk′sĭ·kō), 398, 585, 590, 749, 893

Milan (mī′lăn), in seventeenth century, 540, 556, 559; in 18th century, 650. See also Italy
Milan Decrees (1807), 668
Militarism. See Armaments
Military conscription, 836
Mill, John Stuart, 702
Milosh (mē′lŏsh) I, of Serbia, 773
Milton (mĭl′tŭn), John, 550, 551–552
Mines Act (1842), 706
Minorca (mĭ·nôr′kȧ), 541, 591
Mirabeau (mē′rȧ′bō′), Honoré Riquetti, Comte de, 633, 639
Mohammedans. See Turkey
Moldavia (mŏl·dā′vĭ·ȧ), 729
Molière (mō′lyâr′), (Jean Baptiste Poquelin), 534
Molotov (mô′lŏ·tôf), Vyacheslav M., Russian foreign minister, 982
Moltke (mōlt′kě), Hellmuth von, 747
Money, increase in circulation of, 724
Mongolia (mŏng·gō′lĭ·ȧ), 729, 906. See also Inner Mongolia, China
Monmouth (mŏn′mŭth), Duke of, 546
Monroe Doctrine (1823), 696, 751, 866, 891
Monroe, James, 696
Montcalm (mŏnt·käm′), Louis Joseph, Marquis de, 593
Montenegro (mŏn′tě·nē′grō), 774
Montespan (mŏn′těs·păn′), Marquise de, 534
Moriscos (mō·rĭs′kōz), in Spain, 445, 558
Morocco (mō·rŏk′ō), 816, 820–821, 831–833
Morris, William, 688
Moscow (mŏs′kō), 566, 568, 569, 570, 672, 968, 983
Moslem See Mohammedanism
Mounier (mōō·nyā′), Jean-Joseph, 632
Mühlberg (mül′běrκ), battle of (1547), 427
Mukden (mōōk′děn′), 878
Munich (mū′nĭk) Conference (1938), 960
Municipal Corporations Act (British) (1835), 704
Muscovy (mŭs′kō·vĭ), 568. See also Russia
Music, in 17th century, 535, 552; in 19th century, 687–688, 768
Mussolini (mōōs′sō·lē′nē), Benito, 908–914, 954, 957, 960, 972, 983
Mutsuhito (mōōt′sōō·hē′tō), Emperor of Japan, 824, 875
Mystics, German and Dutch, **377–378**, 404

Nagasaki (nä′gȧ·sä′kě), 875
Nantes (nants), Edict of (1598), 454, 477, 483, 535; revocation of (1685), 537, 546
Napier (nā′pĭ·ēr), John, 604
Naples (nā′p'lz). Kingdom of, 359, **362–363**, 395, 420. See Italy
Napoleon (nȧ·pō′lě·ăn) Bonaparte, Emperor of the French as Napoleon I, 569, 598, 627, 649, 650, **652–673**; 674, 683, 692

Napoleon III, Emperor of the French, 714, 723–724, 726, 728–729, 731, 736, 738, 739, 740, 751, 752
Napoleonic legend, 711–714
Napoleon's family, 653, 661, 664, 670, 714–715, 721
Narva (när′vȧ), battle of (1700), 569
National Assembly, French (1789–91), 632–639; (1871), 801–802
National Convention, French (1792–95), 643–644
National Guard, 637
National Insurance Act (British), 800
National Liberal Party, German, 809–810
National Socialist Party, German, 938–944
National Workshops (French), 712
Nationalism, growth of, 388, 424; in 17th century, 490–491, 503, 515; in 19th century, 732; German, 744; Nature, modern attitude toward, 610–611
Naval blockade, in 20th century, 973
Navarre (nȧ·vär′), Kingdom of, 385–386, 392, 420
Navigation Acts, British, 388, 543, 594
Navy, Russian, 568; British, 830
Near Eastern Crisis, 833–835
Near Eastern Question. See Turkey, Crimean War, Congress of Berlin
Necker (ně′kâr′), Jacques, 629, 632–633, 634
Nelson, Horatio, 653, 666, 668
Netherlands (něth′ěr·lăndz), in 15th century, 377–380, 389, 393; in 16th century, 420, 421, 422, **447–450**; Dutch, revolt against Spain, 444, 466, 543–544; Spanish, 508, 510, 538 540, 556; 560, 590–692; Austrian, 621; and French Revolution, 650; and Napoleon, 655, 663, 671; in 17th century, 500, 504, 508; in 19th century, 679, 708, 768; and American War of Independence, 598; in 20th century, 964, 967, 983; and Japan, 875, 976; colonies, 589–592, 766–768, 987; Kingdom of the United (1815–30), 768–769
Neuilly (nû′yē′), treaty of (1919), 861
Neuve-Chapelle (nûv′shȧ′pěl′), battle of (1915), 844
New Amsterdam (nū ăm′stěr·dăm) (New York), 543, 591
Newcomen (nū′kŏ·měn), Thomas, 699
New Deal, in United States, 890
New Economic Plan, Russia, 899–900
New World, discovery of, 398–400
New Zealand (zē′lănd), 812, 922–924
Newfoundland, 400, 541, 591–592
Newton, Sir Isaac, 552, 600, 603–604, 605, 608
Nice (nēs), ceded to France (1860), 739
Nicholas I, of Russia, 692, 707, 720, 728, 755
Nicholas II, of Russia, 763, 830, 836, 842, 850, 896; executed, 899
Nicholas V, Pope, 362
Nihilism, 760

GENERAL INDEX

Nijmegen (nī'mä'gĕn), treaty of (1678), 538
Nile (nīl), battle of the (1798), 653
Nine-Power Treaty (1922), 881
Noailles (nô'à·y'), Viscount de, 635
Nobles, French, in Later Middle Ages, 354, 373, 474; in 16th century, 428–431, 445, 448, 452, 455; in 17th century, 479–480, 482, 483, 484, 528, 563, 613–614, 639; Polish, 574
Nördlingen (nûrt'lĭng·ĕn), battle of (1634), 507
North German Confederation, 806
Norway (nôr'wā), in 18th century, 621; in 19th century, 679, 766; in 20th century, 963, 965, 983
Novara (nŏ·vä'rä), battle of (1849), 720, 736
November Revolution (1917), Russia, 898
Novi (nō'vē), battle of (1799), 653
Nystad (nü'städ), treaty of (1721), 569

Oates (ōts), Titus, 544
Obrenovich (ŏ·brĕ'nŏ·vĭch), Milan III, of Serbia, 773
"October Manifesto" (1905), Russia, 763
Okinawa (ō'kĕ·nä'wà), 978
Oldenbarneveldt (ŏl'dĕn·bär'nĕ·vĕlt), John van, 450
Old Régime, in France, 612–616
Oliva (ō'lĕ·vä), treaty (1660), 513
Ollivier (ô'lē'vyā'), Émile, 752
Opium Wars, China, 816, 873
"Orders in Council," British, 668
Orlando (ŏr·län'dŏ), Vittorio, 857
Orléans (ôr'lā'äɴ'), Philip, Duke of, 633, 648
Orsini (ŏr·sē'nē), Felice, 721, 731
Oscar II, of Sweden, 766
Otto I, of Greece, 697
Ottoman Turks, 426, 447
Oudenarde (ou'dĕ·när'dĕ), battle of (1708), 540
Owen, Robert, 700
Oxford Parliament (1681), 546

Padua (păd'ŭ·à), 360
Painting, in Renaissance, 370–371; in 17th century, 535, 552; in 19th century, 687
Palatinate (pà·lăt'ĭ·nāt), Rhenish, 502, 503–504, 509, 540
Paleologus (pā'lĕ·ŏl'ŏ·gŭs), Constantine, 566
Paleologus, Sophia, 566, 568
Palestine (păl'ĕs·tīn), in 20th century, 921–922
Palmerston (päm'ẽr·stŭn), Henry John Temple, Viscount, 795
Pan-American Union, 893
Pan-Slav Movement, 841–842
Panama (păn'à·mä'), Canal, 891, 972
Papacy, during the Renaissance, 362–363; and the Reformation, 403–405, 416–418; and Counter-Reformation, 433–436, 438–442, 560, 638, 658, 726, 735, 740–743, 809–810,

816, 914. See also Church, Catholic Church, Papal States, Schism
Papal curia, 434
Papal States, during Babylonian Captivity, 416–417, 434; in 15th century, 421, 422, 434–435; in 16th century, 472, 508, 512
Paris (păr'ĭs), 559, 560, 642, 724; Commune of (1871), 801
Paris, treaty of (1763), 580, 594; (1783) 598; (1856), 731, 773
Parlement of Paris, 528–529, 621
Parliament Act, British (1911), 797–798
Parliament, British, in 16th century, 417–418, 430, 490; in 17th century, 494–500, 695–696, 700, 702, 795, 797–798, 917. See also Commons, House of; Lords, House of
Parma (pär'mä). See Italy
Partition Treaties, 574, 582
Pascal (pàs'kàl'), Blaise, 535
Pasteur (päs'tûr'), Louis, 743, 784, 785
Paul I, Czar, 655
Paul II, Pope, 362
Paul III, Pope, 434, 437–438, 442
Paul IV, Pope, 442
Pavia, battle of (1525), 421
Peace Societies, 836
Pearl Harbor, attacked by Japanese (1941), 976
Peasants, in 17th century, 522; in 18th century, 614, 635, 637, 693; in 19th century, 726, 756. See also Serfdom
Peasants' War, Germany, 411, 423
Pekin (pē'kĭn'), 395
Perry, Commodore Matthew Calbraith, 875
Pershing, General John Joseph, 852
Persia (pûr'zhà), in 17th century, 590
Peru (pĕ·rōō), South America, in 16th century, 585, 588; in 17th century, 590
Pétain (pā'tăɴ'), Marshal Henri Philippe, 965
Peter III, of Aragon, 362–363
Peter I (the Great), of Russia, 568–570
Peter III, of Russia, 570, 580
Peter V, of Portugal, 772
Petition of Rights (1628), 495
Petrach (pē'trärk), Francesco, 364, 366
Philip II, of Spain, 422, 428, 444, 448, 454, 455, 458–459, 477, 558, 590
Philip III, of Spain, 558
Philip IV, of Spain, 538
Philip V, of Spain, 540–541, 559
Philip the Handsome, 389, 393
Philip, Landgrave of Hesse, 427
Philippines (fĭl'ĭ·pēns), in Middle Ages, 588; controlled by U.S., 891; liberated (1944), 978
Philosophes the, 617
Philosophy, in 17th century, 604–605; 18th century, 582, 619
Physics, in 17th century, 603–604; in 18th century, 610; Russia, 568; in 19th century, 782

Physiocrats (fĭz'ĭ·ō·krătz), 619
Pico della Mirandola (pē'kŏ dĕl'lä mĕ·rän'dŏ·lä), Giovanni, 366
Piedmont (pēd'mŏnt), 664. See also Sardinia, Kingdom of
Pietism, 686
Pilgrimages, 410
Pirates, 427
Pisa (pē'zà), 360
Pisano (pē·zä'nŏ), Niccolo, 371
Pitt, William, Earl of Chatham, 593
Pitt, William, the younger, 666, 668
Pius (pī'ŭs) II, Pope, 362
Pius IV, Pope, 438–440
Pius V, Pope, 442
Pius VI, Pope, 621
Pius VII, Pope, 659, 686, 740
Pius IX, Pope, 720, 721, 726, 735, 736, 739, 740, 742, 914
Pius XI, Pope, 914
Pizarro (pĭ·zär'ō), Francisco, 398, 590
Plato (plā'tō), 366, 610
Platonic Academy, in Florence, 366
Plehve (plā'vĕ), Venceslas de, 762
Pléiade, 486–487
Pobiedonostev (pŭ·byĕ·dŭ·nôs'tsĕf'), Constantine, 762, 763
Poggio Bracciolini (pôd'jŏ brät'chŏ-lē'nĕ), 366
Poincaré (pwăɴ'kà'rā'), Raymond, 842, 925, 927–928
Poland (pō'lănd), in 17th century, 506, 513, 519–520, 556, 560, 566, 568, 572, 573, 578, 580; in 18th century, 572–574, 582; in 19th century, 668, 677, 679, 708, 758; in 20th century, 857, 899, 930, 931, 944, 959, 962–965, 983
Polish Succession, War of (1733–1736), 578
Poliziano (pō'lēt·syä'nŏ), Angelo, 367
Polo (pō'lŏ), Marco, 395–396
Polo, Matteo, 395
Polo, Nicolo, 395
Poltawa (pŏl·tä'vä), battle of (1709), 569
Pombal (pōɴm·bäl'), Marquis of, 621
Pomerania (pŏm'ẽr·ā'nĭ·à), 509; annexed by Sweden, 575; taken by Prussia, 576
Pompadour (pôɴ'pà'dōōr'), Marquise de, 579
Poor Law, English (1834), 704
Popish Plot (1678), 544
Population, in modern times, 596, 693, 765–772, 785–786; Austria, 553; England, 525; Europe, 525; France, 630, 928; Norway, 525, 768; Russia, 902; Sweden, 519, 766; Thirteen American Colonies, 596; United States, 883
Port Arthur, 878
Portugal (pōr'tụ̆·găl), in 15th century, 384–386, 396–400; in 16th century, 447, 464, 472; in 17th century, 509; role in Middle Ages explorations, 588, 590; in 17th century, 514, 520, 575; in 18th century, 559, 592, 620–621, 669; in 19th century, 679, 772; in 20th century, 772, 974; colonies, 590, 771–772

GENERAL INDEX

Poussin (pōō'săɴ'), Nicolas, 535
Prague (präg), peace of (1635), 507; treaty of (1866), 749, 750, 751
Précieux, the, 487
Presbyterianism, 548; in Scotland, 456; in England, 499. *See* Calvinism
Pressburg (prĕs'bŏŏrκ), treaty of (1805), 666, 670
Printing, 381, 486; in 18th century, 568
Proletariat, origins, 474–475; after Industrial Revolution, 699–700, 788
Propaganda, in World War I, 854
Protectorate, England, 499–500
Protestantism, divergence of creeds, 411–412; and counter-Reformation, 433–434, 440; in England, **454–458** in France, **450–454**; in Germany, 412, 426–427; in Netherlands, 448–450; in Scotland, 455–459; in 18th century, 573; in 19th century, 686–687. *See* Lutheran, Calvinism, Anglican, Presbyterian, Anabaptist.
Proudhon (prōō'dôn'), Pierre Joseph, 722, 759–760
Provençal literature, 364
Provence, Count of (Louis XVIII of France), 632
Prussia (prŭsh'à), in 17th century, 519, 553, 576; in 18th century, 562, 563, 570, 574, **575–583**, 593, 644; in 19th century, 666–668, 679, 681, 687, 696, 717, 806, 808, 827. *See also* Germany
Prussian System, the, 747–748
Ptolemaeus (tŏl'ē·mē'ŭs), Claudius, 395, 602
Pultawa (pŏl'tä·vä), battle of (1709), 569
Puritans, in England, 492–500; in New England, 415, 542, 543
Pym (pĭm), John, 496
Pyrenees (pĭr'ē·nēz), peace of the (1659), 484, 510, 513, 520, 538

Quadrilateral, the (Italian fortresses), 739
Quadruple Alliance. *See* Concert of Europe
Quebec (kwĕ·bĕk'), 593; Act (1774), 596, 598, 812
Quesnay (kĕ'nā'), François, 619

Rabelais (rȧ'b'·lĕ'), François, 486
Racine (rȧ'sēn'), Jean, 534, 583
Radetsky (rä·dĕts'kē), Joseph Wenzel, Count, 720, 736
Radewyn, Florentius, 380
Radicalism, France, 707
Rambouillet (räɴ'bōō'yĕ'), Marquise de, 407
Ramillies (rȧ/mē'yē\ battle of (1706), 540
Rapallo (rä·päl'lŏ), treaty of (1920), 861
Raphael (răf'ȧ·ĕl), Sanzio, 370
Rasputin (rŭs·pōō'tyĭn), Grigori Efimovich, 896
Rationalism, rise of, 608–610; reaction against, 685–687

Ravenna (rȧ·vĕn'ȧ), battle of (1512), 392
Realism, in literature, 724
Reform Bill, British (1832), 704, 706, 710, (1867), 797; (1884), 797; (1918), 798
Reformation, Catholic, **433–436**. *See* Counter-Reformation
Reformation, Protestant causes, **403–405**; in England, **416–418**, 454–455; in France, 428–430, **450–452**; in Germany, **404–412**; in Scotland, **455–456**; in Switzerland, **412–416**. *See* Protestantism, etc.
Reformed Church (Calvinist), 413; in Switzerland, 413–416; in France, 452. *See also* Presbyterian
Regency, Council of (1512), 424
Regensburg (rā'gĕns·bŏŏrκ), colloquy of (1541), 434
Reichstag (rīκs'täκ'), German, 749, 806, 934, 938–940
"Reign of Terror," French (1793–94), 648
Reinsurance Treaty (1887), 828–829
Religion, in 17th century, 487–488, 568, 591; in 19th century, 686–687
Religious toleration, in 17th century, 535, 548; in 18th century, 610–611
Renaissance, in Italy, 353–371; in Northern Europe, **380–383**, 486
Reparations, German, 859, 926–927, 935
Republican Party (United States), 952
Republicans, French, in 19th century, 720
Requesens (rā'kȧ·sāns'), Don Luis, 449
Restitution, Edict of (1629), 506
Reuchlin (roiκ'lĭn), John, 382
Revolution, French (1789–99), 563, 570, 629–639
Revolution of 1688–89 (English), 547–548
Revolution of 1848–49, 711–722
Rhodes (rōdz), Cecil, 815
Ribbentrop (rĭb'ĕn·trŏp), Joachim von, 962
Ricardo (rĭ·kär'dō), David, 700
Richard, Duke of York, 387
Richard III, of England, 387
Richelieu (rē'shĕ·lyû'), Armand de, Cardinal, 476, **482–484, 506–508**, 514, 526, 528, 537, 613
Risorgimento (rē·sôr'jĕ·mĕn'tŏ), the, 734
Rivera (rĕ·vā'rä), Primo de, 772
Roads, in 17th century, 522. *See also* Transportation
Robespierre (rô'bês·pyâr'), Maximilien, 643, 646, 648–649
Rochefoucauld (rôsh'fōō'kō'), François, Duc de la, 534
Rochelle, La (là·rŏ'shĕl'), 483
Roman Republic (1849), 736
Romantic Movement, 684–689
Rome (rōm), in age of Renaissance, 362, 421, 565; and Revolution of 1848–49, 721; united to Italian kingdom, 742; liberated (1944), 975
Ronsard, de (dĕ rôɴ'sàr'), Pierre, 487

Roosevelt (rō'zĕ·vĕlt), Franklin D., 890, 960, 965, 982, 986
Roses, Wars of the, 387–388
Rosny (rō'nē'), Marquis of. *See* Sully
Rossbach (rŏs'bäk), battle of (1757), 580
Roundheads, 497
Rousseau (rōōs'sō'), Jean-Jacques, 612, **624–625**, 635, 656, 687
Roussillon (rōō'sē'yôɴ'), 480, 510
Royal administration, in England, 430; in France, **477–479, 483–484**
Royalists, and civil war in England, 497–499; French, in 19th century, 802
Rudolf II, Holy Roman Emperor, 480, 502–503
Rumania (rōō·mā'nĭ·à), autonomous, 729; in 19th century, 773–774, 785, 828; in 20th century, 959; in World War I, 686; in Little Entente, 930; in World War II, 967–968; after 1945, 983
Rupert (rōō'pĕrt), Prince, 497
Russia (rŭsh'à), in 17th and 18th centuries, 506, 519, 562, 563, **565–574**, 580, 593, 653; 19th century, 655,666, 668, **670–671**, 672–673, 679, 681, **690–692**, 696, 708, 728–729; 773–774, 775, 795, 824–825, 827–828; in 20th century, 830–831, 833, 841–842, 844, 846, 850, 878, **896–906**, 912, 949, 950, 967–968; after World War I, 950, 954–956, 958; in World War II, 960–962, 963–978; foreign policy, 903–905, 949–951, 956, 978, 986; Five Year Plans, 954–956
Russian novel, 692
Russian Revolution (1917), 896–898
Russo-Finnish War (1939–40), 967
Russo-German Pact (1939), 962
Russo-Japanese accord (1941), 967
Russo-Japanese War (1904–05), 825, 830, 878, 892
Russo-Turkish War (1877), 774
Rye House Plot (1683), 546
Ryswick, Peace of (1697), 540

Saar (zär) Valley, 944
Sacraments, 404, 410, 413
Sadowa (sä'dŏ·vä), battle of. *See* Königgrätz
Saint Bartholomew's Day, Massacre of, 453–454
Saint Gothard (gŏth'àrd), battle of (1663), 576
Saint Petersburg (pē'tĕrz·bûrg), founding of, 569–570
Saint-Simon (săɴ'sē'môɴ'), Henri de, 712
Saint-Simon, Louis de Rouvroy, Duc de, 534
Sainte-Beuve (săɴt'bûv'), Charles Augustin, 724
Saints, veneration of, 404, 410, 413
Salmeron, Alfonso, 436, 440
San Martin (sän' mär·tēn'), José de, 893
San Stefano (sän stä'fȧ·nō), treaty of (1878), 774, 775
Sardinia (sär·dĭn'ĭ·à), Kingdom of;

385, 395, 420; in 17th century, 556; in 18th century, 560, 650, 652; in 19th century, 679, 681, 696, 734, 735. *See also* Italy, Piedmont, Savoy
Savonarola (săv′ŏ·nȧ·rō′lȧ), Girolomo, 357
Savoy (sȧ·voi′), in 17th century, 560; ceded to France (1860), 738
Saxony (săk′sŏ·nĭ), Electorate of, 506–507, 569, 578, 580; Kingdom of, 679, 808
Scandinavia. *See also* Denmark, Finland, Sweden, Vikings
Scheer (shār), Admiral Reinhard, 848
Scheldt (skĕlt), river, 541
Schiller (shĭl′ēr), Johann Friedrich, 687
Schleswig (shlăs′vĭk), annexed to Prussia (1866), 749
Schleswig-Holstein (shlăs′vĭk·hŏl′shtīn), 766
Schlieffen (shlē′fĕn) Plan, 843
Schmalkalden (shmäl′käl′dĕn), League of, 426–427
Schmalkaldic War, 427
Schönbrunn (shûn′broōn), treaty of (1809), 600–605, 608–611, 670
Schwarzenberg (shvär′tsĕn·bĕrĸ), von, 744
Science, in 17th century, 552; modern, 600–607, **779–787**
Scientific academies, 605
Scotland, in 16th century, **455–456**; in 17th century, 491, 496, 497, 500, 548
Scott, Sir Walter, 687
Sculpture, in Renaissance, 371; modern, 535, 618, 768
Sea Beggars, 449
Sea power. *See* Armaments
Sebastopol (sĕ·băs′tŏ·pŏl), siege of (1854–55), 729
Second Empire, French, 715, 724–731
Second Estate. *See* Nobles
Second Republic, French, 715
Sedan (sĕ·dăn′), battle of (1870), 752
Selassie (sĭl·lä′syĕ), Emperor Haile (hī′lĕ), 957
Sepoy (sē′poi) Mutiny (1857), 598, 812, 868
September Massacres (1792), 642
Serbia (sûr′bĭ·ȧ), in 19th century, 773–775, 828; in 20th century, 959; and Austria-Hungary, 841–842, 844. *See also* Yugoslavia
Serfdom, in France, 615–616; in Russia, 756. *See also* Peasants
Settlement, Act of (1701), 548–549
Seven Weeks' War (1866), 748, 749, 750
Seven Years' War (1756–63), 570, 579–580, 593, 594, 596
Sévigné (sā′vē′nyā′), Marie de Rabutin-Chantal, Marquise de, 534
Sforza (sfôr′tsä) family, 360, 363, 421
Sforza, Francesco, Duke of Milan, 360–361
Sforza, Ludovico (Il More), 391–392
Sforza, Maxmilian, Duke of Milan, 392
Shakespeare, William, 491, 583

Shaw, George Bernard, 799
Shelley, Percy Bysshe, 687
Shimonoseki (shē′mŏ·nō·sā′kĕ), treaty of (1895), 825
Shipping. *See* Transportation
Siam (sī·ăm′) (Thailand), 976
Sicily (sĭs′ĭ·lĭ̄), in age of Renaissance, 362–363, 385, 395, 420; ceded to Duke of Savoy, 542; in 18th century, 560; in 19th century, 739; in 20th century, 975
Sickingen (zĭk′ĭng·ĕn), Franz von, 424
Siena (syĕ′nä), republic of, 359, 360
Sieyés (syā′yâs′), Emmanuel Joseph, 653
Silesia (sĭ·lē′shĭ·ȧ), acquired by Prussia, 578, 580, 582, 593
Singapore (sĭng′gȧ·pōr′), 917, 976
Sino-Japanese War (1894–95), 824, 875; after 1937, 822
Sistine (sĭs′tēn) Chapel, 370
Six Acts, England, 695
"Six Points" of Chartism. *See* Chartist movement
Sixtus (sĭks′tŭs) IV, Pope, 362, 386
Sixtus V, Pope, 442
Slave trade, 541, 592, 704
Slavophiles (släv′ŏ·fīlz), Russia, 758
Slavs (slävs), characteristics of, 566; in Austro-Hungarian Empire, 717, 749
Smith, Adam, 599, 700
Sobieski (sŏ·byĕs′kĕ), John, King of Poland, 519, 554, 556, 573
Social Democratic Party. *See* Socialist Party, German
Social insurance, English, 916; German, 810
Social legislation, in 16th century, 474; British, 799
Socialist Party, French, **711–714**, 803, 804–806; German, 809–810; Italian, 907–908; Russian, 762, 938–940
Society, in Italian Renaissance, **353–356**; English, in 16th century, **490–491**; French, in 17th century, 487. *See* Feudalism, Cities
Society of Jesus, founding and organization, **434–438**, 443; and the Counter-Reformation, 487, 501, 621, 809
Sophia of Hanover, 548
South Africa, 814
South African War. *See* Boer War
South German States, 668, 751
Soviets (sō′vĭ·ĕts′), 898. *See* Russia after World War I
Spain (spān), in Middle Ages, **384–386**, 393–395, **398–400**, 419–420, **421–424**, 433, 438, **444–447**, 464, 472, 588, 590–594; in 17th and 18th centuries, 494, 500, 503–504, 508, 509–510, 514, 520, 553, **556–559**, 575, 578, 591, 598, 620–621, 696; in 19th century, 769–771; in 20th century, 958, 972; revolution (1931), 772, 958; and American War of Independence, 598; and French Revolution, 650; and Napoleon, 668; and

Spanish American War (1898), 771, 825; Colonial empire, 590, 695, 771
Spanish-American War (1898), 891
"Spanish Fury" (1576), 449
Spanish Guelderland, ceded to Prussia, 541
Spanish Succession, War of (1701–13), 548, 556, 560, 569, 578, 591
Spencer, Herbert, 784
Spenser (spĕn′sēr), Edmund, 491
Spinning, machines for, 699
Spires, Diet of (1526), 426; (1529), 412
Stalin (stä′lyĭn), Joseph, 899, 950, 982, 986
Stalingrad (stä′lĕn·grät′), battle of (1942–43), 968
Stanislaus Leszczynski (stăn′ĭs·lȧs) (lĕsh·chĭn′y′·skĕ), of Poland, 569
Stanley, Henry Morton, 822
Star Chamber Court, 388, 496
States General, in France, in Later Middle Ages, 375, 388–389; in 18th century, 630–632; in Netherlands, 449. *See also* National Assembly, French
States of the Church. *See* Papal States
States, system of territorial, 514–521
Statute of Westminster (1931), 922
Steam engine, 699
Stein (shtīn), Heinrich Friedrich Karl, Baron vom, 671
Stettinius, Edward R., Jr., 982
Stolypin (stŭ·lĭ′pyĭn), Peter, 763
Storthing (stōr′tĭng) (Norwegian Parliament), 766
Strafford (străf′ērd), Thomas Wentworth, Earl of, 496
Strasbourg (strȧz′boor′), 413, 509, 538
Streltzi (strĕl′tsĭ), revolt of the, 568
Stresemann (shtrā′zĕ·män), Gustav, 937
Strindberg (strĭn′băr′y′), August, 768
Strozzi (strôt′tsē), Palla, 356
Struensee (shtroō′ĕn·zā′), Johann Friedrich, Count, 621
Stuarts, restoration of, 542, 548
Styria (stĭr′ĭ·ȧ), duchy of, 395, 554. *See also* Austria
Submarine boats, in World War I, 847–848
Succession, Act of, 550
Suez (soō·ĕz′) Canal, 727, 814, 847, 965, 972
Suffrage, extension of, in Great Britain, 702–704
Sulerman (sü·lä·män′) I, the Magnificent, Sultan, 426
Sully (sü′lē′), Duke of, 477–479
Sumatra, 590
Sun Yat-sen (soōn′ yät′sĕn′), 874
Supernatural, in medieval thought, 604–605
Supremacy, Act of (1559), 455
Sweden (swē′dĕn), in 17th and 18th centuries, **506–509**, 513, 519, 538, 560, 566, 568, 569, 573, 575, 621; in 19th century, 679, 765–766; in 20th century, 767, 974, 983
Swift, Jonathan, 552
Swiss Confederation, 392, 412–413

GENERAL INDEX

Switzerland (swĭt′zẽr·lănd′), and Reformation, 412–416; in 17th century, 509, 514, 655, 663, 769, 974
Sybel (zē′bĕl), Heinrich von, 746
Syndicate (săn′dē·ᴋà′), French, 803–804
Syria (sĭr′ĭ·à), in 20th century, 972

Taille. See Taxation in France
Talleyrand-Périgord (tà/lā/rän·pā′-rē/gôr′), Charles Maurice de, 672, 675–677
Tangiers (tăn·jẽrs′), 543
Tannenberg (tän′ĕn·bĕrᴋ), battle of (1914), 844
Tartar (tä′tẽr), Empire, 395
Tauler (tou′lẽr), John, 380
Taxation, in England, 430–431, 495–496; in France, 375, 391, 479–480, 483; in Netherlands, 424, 448–449; in Spain, 423, **447**; on colonies in 18th century, 596; Stamp Tax (1765), 596; Townshend Acts, (1767), 596; in 18th century France, 616–617; in 19th century France, 656
Tennis Court Oath (1789), 632–633, 638
Tennyson, Alfred, Lord, 795
Territorial states, rise of, **375–377**; and the Reformation, 405, 411; economic policy, **470–474**
Terrorists, Russian, 760
Test Act, English (1673), 546–547
Theative order, 434
Theology, in 18th century, 608, 610
Thiers (tyâr), Louis Adolphe, 711–712, 754, 802
Third Estate, French, in 17th century, 528–529; in 18th century, 615–616, 630. *See also* States General, Bourgeoisie
Third Republic, French, 746, 802
"Third Section," Russia, 692, 756
Thirty-Nine Articles of Religion, 455
Thirty Years' War, **501–510**, 511, 513, 576, 600
Thorwaldsen (tōōr′vàl′s'n), Albert Bertel, 768
Tilly (tĭl′ĭ), Johann Tserklaes, Count, 504–507
Tilsit (tĭl′zĭt), Peace of (1807), 668, 670
Tolerance, growth of, 608
Toleration Act, English (1689), 547, 549
Tolstoi (tŭl·stoi′), Aleksei Konstantinovich, 692
Tolstoy (tŭl·stoi′), Count Leo, 759
Tories (English political party), 544, 546, 695, 702. *See also* Conservatives, Whigs
Toul (tōōl), annexed by Louis XIV, 509, 538
Toulouse, University of, 428
Tours (tōōr), battle of, 520
Townshend Acts (1767), 596
Trade. *See* Commerce
Trade Boards Act (1909) (British), 799–800
Trade routes, in 20th century, 970. *See* Exploration

Trade Union Act (1871) (British), 799
Trade unions, 788
Trade Wars (1652–1674), 591
Trafalgar (trăf′àl·gär′), battle of (1805), 666
Trajan (trā′jăn), Roman Emperor, 110
Transportation, in 17th century, 518, 522; in 19th century, 780; in 20th century, 969–974
Transylvania (trăn′sĭl·vā′nĭ·à), 556
Treaty of Portsmouth (1905), 878
Trent (trĕnt), Council of (1545–63), 436–440
Triple Alliance, 827, 829–830
Triple *Entente*, 829–831
Troppau (trŏp′ou), Congress of (1820), 679
Troppau Protocol (1820), 681, 692, 696
Trotsky (trŏts′kŭ·ĭ), Leon, 899, 950
Truman, Harry S., 982, 988
Tudor (tū′dẽr) family, 387–388, 430
Tunis (tū′nĭs), French occupation of, 816
Turenne (tü′rĕn′), Henri de la Tour d'Auvergne, Vicomte de, 508, 532, 538
Turgener (tōōr·gyā′nyĕf), Aleksandr Ivanovich, 692
Turgot (tür′gō′), Anne Robert Jacques, 621, 624
Turin (tū′rĭn), treaty of (1860), 739
Turkestan (tûr′kĕ·stăn′), 729
Turkey (tûr′kĭ), in 17th century, 519–520, 554–556, 560, 563, 566, 569, 620; in 18th century, 569, 573, 574, 697, 728; in 19th century, 772–774, 833; in 20th century, 835, 842–843, 846, 852, 861–862, 974, 988
Turks. *See* Turkey
Turner, J. M. W., 687
Tuscany (tŭs′kà·nĭ), in 17th century, 559
Tyrol (tĭr′ŏl), county of, 395, 554

Ukraine (ū′krān), 556
Ulm (ōōlm), battle of (1805), 666
Ulster (ŭl′stẽr). *See* Ireland
Ultramontanism (ŭl′trà·mŏn′tà-nĭz′m), 686
Ultra-royalists, France, 693
Uniformity, Act of (1662), 518, 543
Union, Act of (1707), 548
Union of South Africa. *See* South Africa
Union of Soviet Socialist Republics. *See* Russia after World War I
Unitarians, 547
United Nations, The, 981–986
United Provinces. *See* Netherlands, Dutch
United States, 579, 795; established, 598; growth, 883–895; resources, 973–974; foreign policy, 696, 891, 948–949, 988; population, 883; in World War I, 847–854; after World War I, 883–895; in 20th century, 952; defense forces, 891–892, 973; in World War II, 970–980; after 1945, 987–988

Universities, Renaissance, 381
Uruguay (ū′rōō·gwā), 893
U.S.S.R., *see* Russia, in 20th century
Usury. *See* Money lending
Utilitarians, 702
Utrecht (ū′trĕkt), Union of (1579), 449–450; Peace of (1713–14), **540–541**, 550, 556, 559, 591, 592

Valla (väl′lä), Lorenzo, 367
Valmy (vàl′mē′), battle of (1792), 644
Valois (và/lwà′), Margaret de, 453
Vassals. *See* Feudalism
Vatican library, 362; Council (1869–70), 742–743
Vauban (vō′bäɴ′), Sébastien le Prestre de, 532
Vendée (vän′dā′), insurrection in, 646
Venice (vĕn′ĭs), **360–362**, 392, 421, 520, 559–560, 652, 677. *See also* Italy
Verdun (vĕr′dûɴ′), 538, 844
Verona (vĕ·rō′nà), Congress of (1822), 221, 681
Versailles (vẽr′sä′y′), palace of, 532, 534, 632, 637, 754
Versailles, treaty of (1919), 857–861, 907, 926, 930, 938, 950, 958
Vervins (vẽr′văɴ′), treaty of (1598), 477
Vicar, office, 376
Victor Amadeus II, of Savoy, 560
Victor Emmanuel I, of Sardinia, 696
Victor Emmanuel II, of Sardinia and, after 1860, of Italy, 736, 737, 738, 739
Victor Emmanuel III, of Italy, 908
Vikings, 565. *See also* Denmark, Finland, Scandinavia, Sweden
Vienna (vĕ·ĕn′à), 519; siege of (1683), 556, 573, 670; treaty of (1864), 748
Vienna, Congress of. *See* Congress of Vienna
Villafranca (vēl′lä·fräng′kä), truce of (1859), 738
Vinci (dä vēn′chē), Leonardo da, 370
Virgil (vûr′jĭl), 610
Visconti (vĕs·kōn′tē) family, 360
Visconti, Filippo Maria, Duke of Milan, 360
Visconti, Gian Galeazzo, Duke of Milan, 359–360, 391
Visconti, Giovanni Maria, Duke of Milan, 360
Visconti, Matteo, Vicar of Milan, 359
Visconti, Valentina, Duchess of Orléans, 360, 391
Vittorino da Feltre (vēt′tŏ·rē′nŏ dä fĕl′trä), 356
Vladivostok (vlà/dĭ·vŏs·tôk′), 873, 906
Voltaire (vŏl·târ′) (François Marie Arouet), 569, 572, 582, 593, 617–619, 686, 687
Vulgate, 440

Wages and Hours Law (1938), 890
Wagner (väg′nẽr), Richard, 688
Wallace, Alfred Russel, 784
Wallenstein (wŏl′ĕn·stīn), Prince, 504–507
War debts, 927

GENERAL INDEX

War of Devolution, 538
War of Liberation, against Napoleon, 672
War of the Austrian Succession, 578, 593
War of the Polish Succession, 578
War of the Spanish Succession, 540–541
Wars of Religion, in France, **450–459**
Wartburg (värt'bōŏrk) 410; Festival (1817), 690
Washington Conference (1922–23), 880, 892, 917, 956
Waterloo (wô'tẽr·lōō), battle of (1815), 672
Watt, James, 699
Wealth, as Cause of Renaissance, 353, 356. *See* Capital, Money economy
Webb, Sidney and Beatrice, 799
Weimar (vī'mär) Assembly (1919), 859–861, 934
Weimar Constitution, Germany, 940, 954
Wellington, Arthur Wellesley, Duke of, 669, 672, 677, 704
Wells, Herbert George, 799
Wenceslas (wĕn'sĕs·lôs), Holy Roman Emperor, 360
Wesley, Charles, 686
Wesley, John, 686
West Indies, 594
Westminster, Convention of (1756), 579
Westphalia (wĕst·fā'lĭ·à), Kingdom of, 668

Westphalia, peace of (1648), **508–509**, 513, 519, 575–576
Whigs (English political party), 540, 544, 546, 549, 702, 704. *See also* Liberals
White Sea, discovery of, 456
Whitney, Eli, 699
William I, of Prussia, German Emperor after 1871, **746, 748**, 749, 752, 754, 806, 809–810, 827
William I, of United Netherlands, 679, 708, 768
William II, German Emperor, 810, 830–831, 852, 856
William of Nassau, Prince of Orange, 448–450
William of Orange, King of England as William III, 538, 540, 546, 547, 548, 550, 591, 624
William IV, of England, 704
Wilson, Woodrow, and the World War, 848–865, 928
Witt, John de, 538
Witte (vĭt'ĕ), Sergei de, 762
Wittenberg (vĭt'ĕn·bẽrk), 407, 410
Wittenberg, University of, 407
Wolfe, James, General, 593
Wolsey (wŏŏl'zĭ), Cardinal, 417
Woman Suffrage, in Great Britain, 798
Wordsworth, William, 687
Working class. *See* Proletariat, Socialist party
Workingmen's Compensation Act, British (1906), 799
World Court, 866

World War I, 836–838, **841–854**
World War II, causes of, 945–962, 963–980; aftermath, 981–989
Worms, Diet of (1521), 408–410, 421, 424
Worms, Edict of (1521), 426
Wren, Christopher, 552
Württemberg (vür'tĕm·bẽrk), in 19th century, 664–666, 749, 808

Xavier (zā'vĭ·ẽr), Francis, Saint, 436, 875
Ximenes (zĭ·mē'nēz), Francesco, Cardinal, 433

Yalta (yäl'tä) Conference (1945), 986
"Young Italy," 735. *See also* Mazzini, Joseph
Yorkist family, 387
Young, Owen D., 927
Young Plan (1929), 927
Ypres (ē'pr'), 844
Yugoslavia (yōō'gȯ·slä'vĭ·à), in 20th century, 861, 930, 972, 983

Zeeland (zē'lănd), 449
Zemstvos (zĕmst'vōs), 756–758
Zola (zô'là'), Émile, 802
Zollverein (tsōl'fīr·rīn'), 717, 746, 749
Zorndorf (tsŏn'dôrf), battle of (1758), 580
Zurich (zōōr'ĭk), 412–413
Zwingli (tsvĭng'lĭ), Huldreich, 412–413

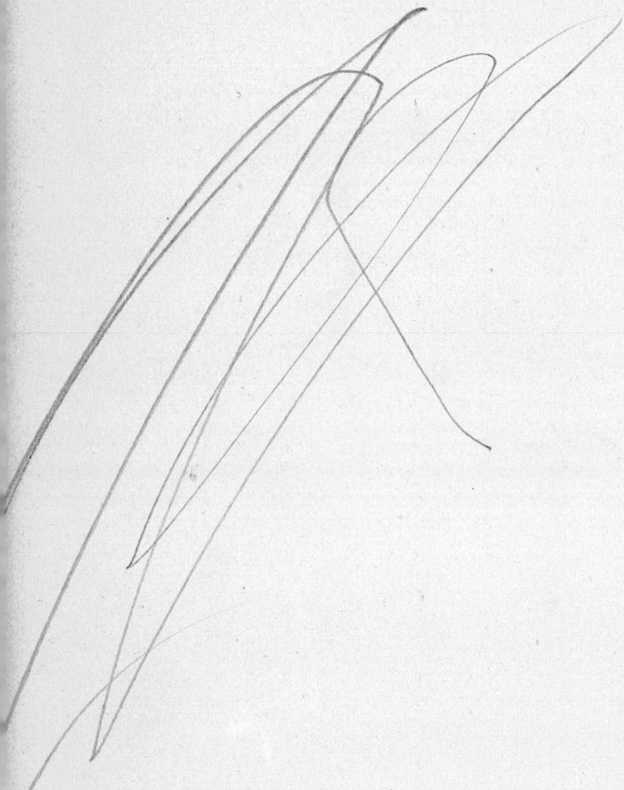